Praise for George Omu[illegible] from Sybex

"Omura's explanations are concise, his gra[illegible] practical."

CADalyst

Definitely a must-have . . . Omura explains the depth and breadth of AutoCAD better than anyone else."

John Lynch, Former Vice President,
Advanced Products Group, Autodesk

I am a recent owner of your terrific AutoCAD book. I am new to AutoCAD, and your book is an excellent resource, which provides a very clear step-by-step approach to learning the product.

Neil Silver
Alberta, Canada

Your book is a bible to AutoCAD.

P. Roy Choudhury
Calcutta, India

The most comprehensive tutorial I have read. Mr. Omura has done an excellent job bringing AutoCAD 14 to a level just about anyone can comprehend and master.

Don Panzer
Philadelphia, Pennsylvania

MASTERING™ 3D STUDIO VIZ® 3

George Omura

San Francisco • Paris • Düsseldorf • Soest • London

Associate Publisher: Cheryl Applewood
Contracts and Licensing Manager: Kristine O'Callaghan
Acquisitions and Developmental Editor: Cheryl Applewood
Editor: Rob Siedenburg, Publication Services
Production Editor: Al Davis, Publication Services
Technical Editor: Scott Onstott
Book Designer: Franz Baumhackl
Graphic Illustrator: (for line art) Don Waller, Publication Services
Electronic Publishing Specialist: Jason Brown, Publication Services
Proofreaders: Phil Hamer, Jenny Putman, Jim Rogers, Eric Hamrin
Indexer: Matthew Spence
CD Technicians: Keith McNeil, Siobhan Dowling
CD Coordinator: Kara Eve Schwartz
Cover Designer: Design Site
Cover Illustrator/Photographer: Jack D. Myers

Library of Congress Card Number: 00-106427

ISBN: 0-7821-2775-4

Manufactured in the United States of America
10 9 8 7 6 5 4 3 2 1

Software License Agreement: Terms and Conditions

The media and/or any online materials accompanying this book that are available now or in the future contain programs and/or text files (the "Software") to be used in connection with the book. SYBEX hereby grants to you a license to use the Software, subject to the terms that follow. Your purchase, acceptance, or use of the Software will constitute your acceptance of such terms.

The Software compilation is the property of SYBEX unless otherwise indicated and is protected by copyright to SYBEX or other copyright owner(s) as indicated in the media files (the "Owner(s)"). You are hereby granted a single-user license to use the Software for your personal, noncommercial use only. You may not reproduce, sell, distribute, publish, circulate, or commercially exploit the Software, or any portion thereof, without the written consent of SYBEX and the specific copyright owner(s) of any component software included on this media.

In the event that the Software or components include specific license requirements or end-user agreements, statements of condition, disclaimers, limitations, or warranties ("End-User License"), those End-User Licenses supersede the terms and conditions herein as to that particular Software component. Your purchase, acceptance, or use of the Software will constitute your acceptance of such End-User Licenses.

By purchase, use, or acceptance of the Software you further agree to comply with all export laws and regulations of the United States as such laws and regulations may exist from time to time.

Software Support

Components of the supplemental Software and any offers associated with them may be supported by the specific Owner(s) of that material but they are not supported by SYBEX. Information regarding any available support may be obtained from the Owner(s) using the information provided in the appropriate read.me files or listed elsewhere on the media.

Should the manufacturer(s) or other Owner(s) cease to offer support or decline to honor any offer, SYBEX bears no responsibility. This notice concerning support for the Software is provided for your information only. SYBEX is not the agent or principal of the Owner(s), and SYBEX is in no way responsible for providing any support for the Software, nor is it liable or responsible for any support provided, or not provided, by the Owner(s).

Warranty

SYBEX warrants the enclosed media to be free of physical defects for a period of ninety (90) days after purchase. The Software is not available from SYBEX in any other form or media than that enclosed herein or posted to *www.sybex.com*. If you discover a defect in the media during this warranty period, you may obtain a replacement of identical format at no charge by sending the defective media, postage prepaid, with proof of purchase to:

SYBEX Inc.
Customer Service Department
1151 Marina Village Parkway
Alameda, CA 94501
(510) 523-8233
Fax: (510) 523-2373
e-mail: info@sybex.com
WEB: HTTP://WWW.SYBEX.COM

After the 90-day period, you can obtain replacement media of identical format by sending us the defective disk, proof of purchase, and a check or money order for $10, payable to SYBEX.

Disclaimer

SYBEX makes no warranty or representation, either expressed or implied, with respect to the Software or its contents, quality, performance, merchantability, or fitness for a particular purpose. In no event will SYBEX, its distributors, or dealers be liable to you or any other party for direct, indirect, special, incidental, consequential, or other damages arising out of the use of or inability to use the Software or its contents even if advised of the possibility of such damage. In the event that the Software includes an online update feature, SYBEX further disclaims any obligation to provide this feature for any specific duration other than the initial posting.

The exclusion of implied warranties is not permitted by some states. Therefore, the above exclusion may not apply to you. This warranty provides you with specific legal rights; there may be other rights that you may have that vary from state to state. The pricing of the book with the Software by SYBEX reflects the allocation of risk and limitations on liability contained in this agreement of Terms and Conditions.

Shareware Distribution

This Software may contain various programs that are distributed as shareware. Copyright laws apply to both shareware and ordinary commercial software, and the copyright Owner(s) retains all rights. If you try a shareware program and continue using it, you are expected to register it. Individual programs differ on details of trial periods, registration, and payment. Please observe the requirements stated in appropriate files.

Copy Protection

The Software in whole or in part may or may not be copy-protected or encrypted. However, in all cases, reselling or redistributing these files without authorization is expressly forbidden except as specifically provided for by the Owner(s) therein.

To Mom

Acknowledgments

The talents of many people have gone into the creation of this book, and I'd like to express my gratitude to everyone who has worked so hard to make it possible. With gratitude, I'd like to thank Melanie Spiller, who originally helped launch this project, and Cheryl Applewood at Sybex for her patience and understanding all through the writing process. My gratitude also goes to Colleen Strand, to Dan Mummert, for obtaining permissions, and to Rodda Leage for work in securing the software for the companion CD.

At Publication Services, I'd like to thank Jan Fisher, Customer Service Representative; Jason Brown, Coordinator; and Rob Siedenburg, Editor, along with the rest of the staff for their patience and efforts in the editing and production of this book. A big thanks also goes to Scott Onstott, Technical Editor, who gave many excellent comments and suggestions and kept me on the right track.

I'd like to thank the many members of ELS Architecture and Planning with whom I've had the great pleasure to work: Clarence Mamuyac, Ed Noland, Jamie Rusin, Bruce Bullman, and David Petta all contributed samples from their projects for reproduction in this book. The 3D modeling work of Jeff Zieba, Chris Jung, Sudthida Chunkarndee, Ally Watts, and William Gordon appear in a number of the ELS renderings as well. I would also like to give a special thanks to Deanna Niebuhr and Janette Gross at ELS for their efforts in securing the all-important permissions to reprint the ELS images, and to David Fawcett for including me in so many great 3D projects.

At Autodesk, a special thanks to Noah Kennedy for his positive encouragement in the early stages of this book and to Denis Cadu for his help in obtaining software.

And finally, as always, a big thanks to my family—Cynthia, Arthur, and Charles—for their constant support and understanding throughout this project.

Contents at a Glance

Contents

Introduction

Much of your work as a designer involves sketches and drawings throughout the design process. Such graphic representations of designs not only help convey your ideas to others, they also help you see problems with a design and help you refine your ideas. 3D computer modeling and animation take design visualization way beyond hand-drawn sketches by allowing you to create a complete replica of your design and look at it from virtually any point of view.

With 3D Studio VIZ 3, you can apply color, texture, and lighting to see how variations of these elements affect your design. You get a realistic view of your design so that you can make better decisions as you progress through the design process.

Mastering 3D Studio VIZ 3 is intended to help architects and designers visualize and present their designs through images, 3D models, and animations. This book focuses on the use of 3D Studio VIZ 3 as a modeling and presentation tool. Since *Mastering 3D Studio VIZ 3* is focused on design issues, you won't find an in-depth study of character animation or animated special effects, nor will you find a book that describes every single tool and function available.

You *will* find step-by-step tutorials covering the major functions that you'll need as a designer. These tutorials are based on years of experience using 3D Studio VIZ and its precursor, 3D Studio Max, on real projects with real deadlines and requirements. You'll learn how to construct complex geometric forms and how to apply lighting and materials to study a design. You'll also learn how to create effects to emphasize parts of your design for presentations.

How to Use This Book

The goal of this book is to give you the appropriate skills to produce professional-level presentations of your ideas from conceptual designs to finished renderings and animated walk-throughs. Once you've mastered those skills, you'll be equiped to confidently explore on your own 3D Studio VIZ 3 and its rich set of tools and options.

To get the most from this book, you'll want to read the chapters sequentially from front to back, doing the tutorial exercises as you go along. Each chapter builds on the skills you learned from the previous chapter, so you can think of this book as your personal, self-paced course on 3D Studio VIZ 3.

The first three chapters are intended to help you become familiar with the way 3D Studio VIZ 3 works and how it is organized. If you are already familiar with VIZ, you may want to skim through these chapters to become familiar with some of the new features. Chapters 4 and 5 show you how to build a fairly complex building, using a variety of tools. These chapters introduce you to some of the more common methods of construction in VIZ. Chapters 6 through 10 show you how to use lighting and materials. Chapters 11 through 13 cover animation, and Chapters 14 through 16 delve into some of the finer points of modeling and rendering.

At the back of the book, you'll find a set of appendixes that offer general reference information on some of the more commonly used tools in VIZ. Once you've worked through the first half of the book, you can use the appendixes as an aid in your own exploration of VIZ. In fact, you may find it useful to skim over the appendixes once you've completed the first three or four chapters so you'll have some understanding of their content. You can then refer to the appendixes as you work through the rest of the book.

Finally, before you get started with the tutorials, make sure you've installed the sample files from the companion CD. You'll need those files to complete many of the exercises. (See Appendix A for details on installing the sample files.)

NOTE **It is important that you set up VIZ to recognize the location of the sample files from the companion CD. Make sure you perform the instructions given in the section entitled "Adding a Map Path to Help VIZ Find Bitmaps" in Chapter 8. If you like, you can set up VIZ as described in that section, right after you've installed the samples.**

What You'll Find

To give you a better idea of what you'll find in this book, here is a summary of the chapters and their contents.

In Chapter 1, you'll get an introduction to the VIZ interface, and you'll get your first look at VIZ objects and how they are created. You'll also learn how to perform some basic editing operations such as moving, scaling, and copying objects. Toward the end of Chapter 1, you'll be introduced to the different ways you can view your designs in VIZ.

Chapter 2 delves deeper into the workings of VIZ objects. You'll learn about the different types of objects available in VIZ and how you can use them to create the shapes you want. You'll learn how to manipulate VIZ's core set of shapes, called primitives, into more complex shapes. You'll also learn about the different ways you can duplicate shapes, and why these different duplication methods can help you quickly build your design.

Chapter 3 looks at how you can create complex forms from simple lines. Here you'll learn how to manipulate a basic type of object called a spline shape, and turn it into a wall or a wineglass. You'll look at other wall creation options as well.

In Chapter 4, you are introduced to object and editing methods that are common to architectural projects. In this chapter, you begin to model a well-known building, using a hand-drawn sketch as a background. You also focus on drawing objects that have unusual shapes.

In Chapter 5, you continue working on the building you started in Chapter 4 by exploring ways to organize part of the design. In this chapter, you learn how to use object names and layers to help identify parts of the design. You also continue your exploration of modeling complex forms by building a complex roof form.

Chapter 6 uses another well-known building as a vehicle for introducing you to cameras, lighting, and animation. Here you learn how to place cameras to obtain the view you want. You also learn about the different types of lighting and how to use them. Toward the end of the chapter, you are introduced to animation when you create a short flyby of a building.

In Chapter 7, you build on the work you will have done in Chapter 6 while exploring materials. You are introduced to the many different properties of materials, such as color and bump map textures. You also learn how to align a texture to a surface.

Chapter 8 continues with lighting and background control. You learn how to control shadows and background to affect the mood of your renderings. You are also introduced to methods for adding props such as trees and foliage to a design.

Chapter 9 offers a look at the finer points of lighting, materials, and shadows. You learn how you can create a more realistic effect in your renderings by placing lights in strategic locations. You also learn how to add a material to a single surface of an object.

Chapter 10 shows you different ways of using VIZ files. You learn how to combine files efficiently to allow distribution of work among other members of a design team. You also discover ways to share data between files. The later part of the chapter shows you how you can view and store different versions of a rendered view.

Chapter 11 introduces you to animation. You learn how to create and control the animation of a camera to produce an animated flyby of the building you worked on in earlier chapters. You are also shown how you can edit an animated object's motion, preview your animation, and control lights over time.

Chapter 12 continues your look at animation by exploring the options for file animation output, backgrounds and props, and other walkthrough animation tools.

Chapter 13 covers some of the more technical issues you'll face when you're ready to distribute your animations. You'll learn about the different video storage options that are available and how they work. You'll also learn methods for getting the best quality from your animations.

Chapter 14 explains how you can make use of Photoshop and other image-editing programs to enhance your use of VIZ. You'll learn how to quickly convert your own scanned image into custom-made props such as trees or foliage for your VIZ design. You'll also learn how bitmap images can be used to create geometric forms in VIZ.

Chapter 15 continues your look at Photoshop and VIZ by showing you how you can convert a scanned image of a car into a 3D model of a car. Here you learn methods for editing meshes to shape them into smooth forms. In the second half of the chapter, you learn how to match a design to a background image to create a montage.

Finally, Chapter 16 shows you how you can use AutoCAD files with VIZ. You'll learn the different ways that you can combine both 2D and 3D AutoCAD data with VIZ design files. You'll lean the best ways to prepare an AutoCAD drawing for import into VIZ, and you'll learn how you can use a single AutoCAD file as a shared data source for both AutoCAD and VIZ designs. Toward the end of this chapter, you'll be shown how to create stairs and import truss models from AutoCAD.

System Requirements

This book assumes that you already have 3D Studio VIZ 3 and a Pentium-based PC on which to run the software. In addition, you should perform a full installation of 3D Studio VIZ, including the optional tutorials and plug-ins. (See Appendix A for more on the installation of VIZ for this book.) The following list shows you the minimum system requirements for VIZ:

Pentium II or III CPU at 300MHz or better

128MB RAM

3GB free disk space before VIZ software installation

1024 × 768 × 16-bit color display

CD-ROM drive

Windows NT 4 or 2000

Windows 98 will work, but VIZ performs much better on Windows NT 4 or Windows 2000.

WARNING **If you are running VIZ on Windows 98, make sure you have downloaded and installed the `core.dll` software patch from the Autodesk Web site. See Appendix A for details.**

The 3GB of free disk space includes space for sample files and general work space for your projects. For later chapters, you may want to have a copy of AutoCAD version 14, 2000, or 2000i and Photoshop 5.5. You can obtain a trial version of Photoshop from the Adobe Web site. As of this writing, you can order a trial version of AutoCAD 2000i from Autodesk's Web site. It is not essential to have these other programs, but you may find them useful companions to VIZ.

What's on the Companion CD

As mentioned earlier, you will want to make sure that you've installed the sample files from the companion CD included with this book. They are needed for many of the exercises that you'll encounter. You'll find installation instructions for the sample files in Appendix A. You'll also find a variety of other sample files and applications on the companion CD that will help you in your work with VIZ.

chapter 1

Getting to Know VIZ

FEATURING

- *Getting Started*
- *Touring the Interface*
- *Working with Objects*
- *Getting the View You Want*

Getting to Know VIZ

Welcome to Mastering 3D Studio VIZ. The Kinetix product, 3D Studio VIZ, is a 3D modeling and rendering program geared toward the design professional. It is based on the very popular 3D Studio Max program, but with a few omissions and additions. As architects and industrial designers are not particularly interested in character animation, many of the features related to character animation in 3D Studio Max have been left out of VIZ. But you shouldn't feel that you've gotten some cut-rate 3D software. VIZ includes many tools designed to help you visualize your ideas. You can think of 3D Studio VIZ as a version of 3D Studio Max that has been customized for the design professional.

3D Studio has been around for quite a while, starting out as a DOS-based program. Among some of its earliest users were many AutoCAD users looking for a good rendering tool. 3D Studio later became popular with game developers and in the film and broadcast industries. Its earliest DOS-based version was unique in being one of two serious 3D animation programs that ran on a desktop computer. When Windows became the dominant operating system, 3D Studio was reborn as 3D Studio Max, a completely rewritten version of the original 3D Studio. Today, 3D Studio Max competes with other high-end animation products such as SoftImage and Lightwave. Although Max has much to offer designers, it is increasingly being developed with a specific focus on the entertainment industry. VIZ was created to address the specific needs of architects and industrial designers using 3D Studio.

3D Studio VIZ offers most of the same powerful features as 3D Studio Max at about half the cost. It is unique in its goal of offering high-level rendering and animation tools for the design professional. In fact, there are many features that directly address the needs of users of the most popular 2D design program, AutoCAD. Among the new features in 3D Studio VIZ 3, you'll find enhanced linking with AutoCAD, which eases the flow of design data between the two programs. VIZ 3 now offers a layer tool and ray traced objects that let you simulate realistic refractions and reflections from materials such as glass and water. If you are a Lightscape user, you can include advanced radiosity rendering in your work, which offers unparalleled, real-life rendering of lighting effects.

NOTE Radiosity rendering is a method of rendering whereby the interaction of light and materials is accurately simulated in the computer. This means that a light source's intensity, color, and direction can be reproduced within the framework of a 3D computer model. If a surface has a color, the light from a source reflects that color as it bounces around in a space. The net result is an image that in many cases cannot be distinguished from an actual photograph. Lightscape is a product from Discreet, a division of Autodesk.

FIGURE 1.1

A sample of a 3D model using raytraced objects.

3D Studio VIZ is also designed to take advantage of the Internet. With its Asset Browser and an Internet connection, you can quickly acquire 3D models and props that are available on the Web. File sharing across the Internet is also integrated into VIZ through its file system and file sharing capabilities.

Getting Started

In this chapter, you'll be introduced to the 3D Studio VIZ interface. Many of VIZ's components are typical for a Windows program, but quite a few are unique, so let's get started with our tour.

After installing 3D Studio VIZ 3, start by doing one of the following:

Double-click the 3D studio icon on the desktop.

Choose Start ➢ Programs ➢ Autodesk 3D Studio VIZ ➢ 3D Studio VIZ R3

You'll see a variety of components in the 3D studio window (see Figure 1.2), some that are familiar and others that are not.

FIGURE 1.2

The standard 3D Studio VIZ window.

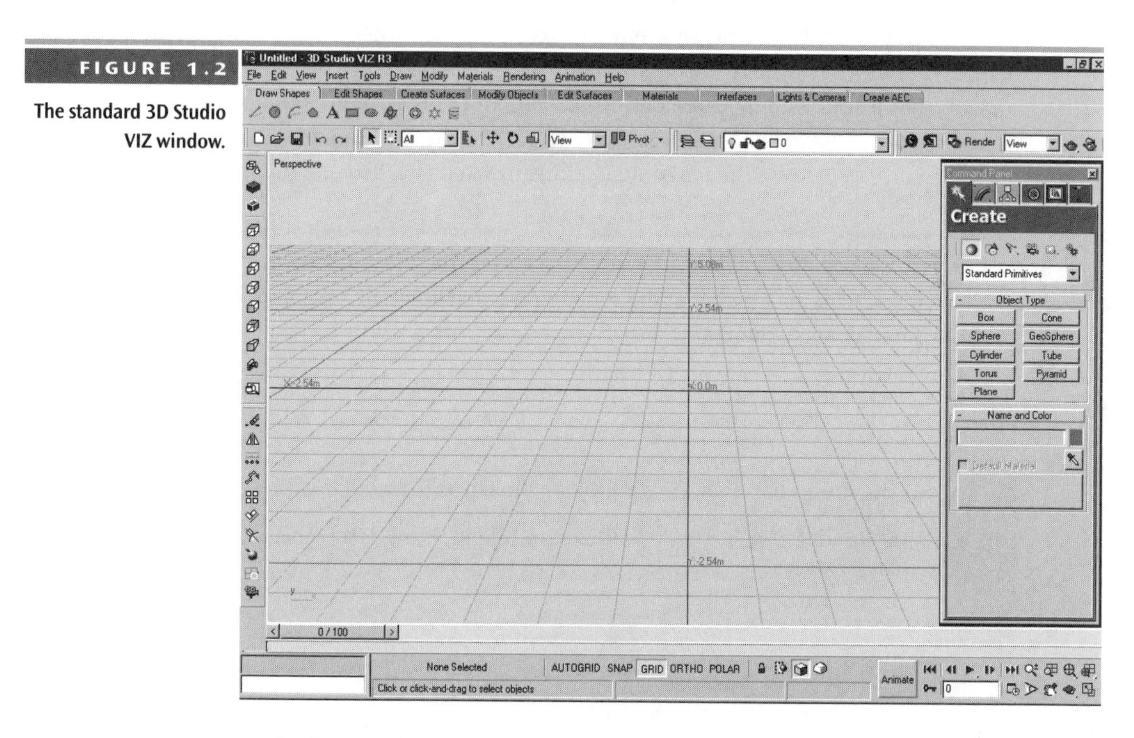

At the top, you see a typical menu bar and standard toolbar. Sandwiched between them is something called a tab panel, which offers custom tools and macros geared toward specific tasks. In the center, you see the viewport area, which currently shows a perspective view. At the bottom of the screen, you see the viewport navigation tools for adjusting your views in the main viewport. You also see the time controls for creating animations, the prompt line and status bar, and something called the MaxScript Listener (for creating macros). On the right-hand side, you see the command panel that contains nearly all of the tools you'll use to create and edit objects in VIZ. Let's take a closer look at each of these components.

Touring the Interface

VIZ has a wealth of tools available to you, and their sheer number can be overwhelming. To get a basic understanding of the VIZ window, let's look at each of the window components individually, starting with the menu bar.

The Standard Menu Bar

At the top of the screen is the main menu bar. Here you find the typical Windows commands for file maintenance, as well as commands specifically for 3D Studio VIZ.

The options in the menu bar are organized like most other Windows applications. Clicking an option issues a command, and you are expected to take some action. An option that is followed by three periods, called an ellipsis, opens a dialog box, usually to allow you to make changes to settings related to the option name. An option with a right-pointing arrow displays more options in what is called a *cascading menu*.

NOTE If you are familiar with AutoCAD, you see that the menu bar contains many of the same options. Be aware that the commands found under these options act differently from those found in AutoCAD.

File Edit View Insert Tools Draw Modify Materials Rendering Animation Help

Try out the menu bar by taking a look at the Units Setup dialog box.

1. Choose Tools ➢ Drafting Settings ➢ Units Setup… The Units Setup dialog box displays.

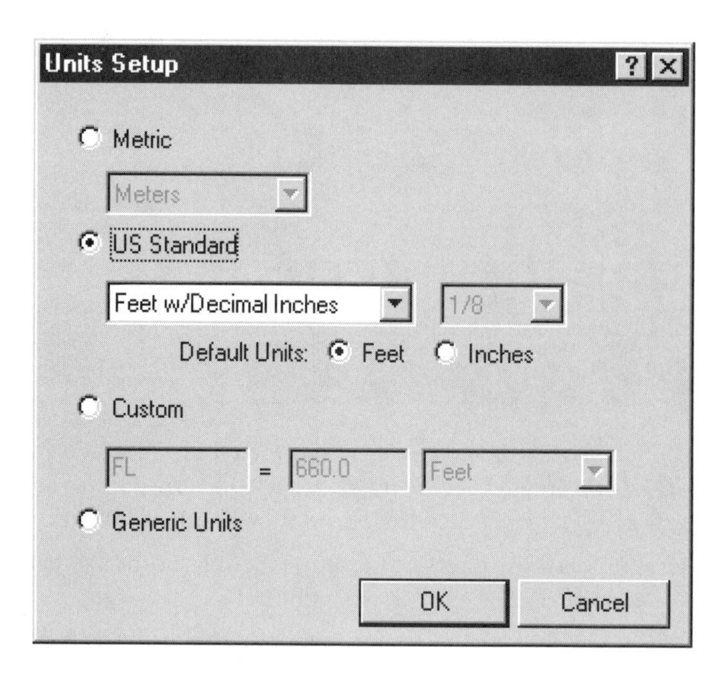

2. Make sure the US Standard radio button is selected and the Decimal Inches radio button is selected under Default Units.
3. Click OK to close the Units Setup dialog box.

Here you see a typical cascading menu and that the ellipsis indicates an option with a dialog box. By checking the Units Setup dialog box, you also ensure that, in future exercises, you're working with the same units that are discussed in this book. Now let's continue with a look at the Tab panel.

The Tab Panel

Below the menu bar is the Tab panel. This is a new feature in VIZ 3 that offers a quick way to get access to commonly used tools and macros. Some of the tabs contain options that duplicate the standard 3D Studio VIZ tools, and other tabs offer custom macros for building architectural or mechanical components. As you click a tab, a set of tools related to the tab displays in the space just below the tabs, much like the tabs of a typical Windows dialog box. For example, if you click the Draw Shapes tab, you see a set of tools. As you might guess, clicking the icon for one of these tools lets you draw the object indicated by the tool icon.

If you place the cursor on a Tab panel tool icon for a second, you see a tool tip appear. Tool tips give you a quick reminder of what the tool is used for.

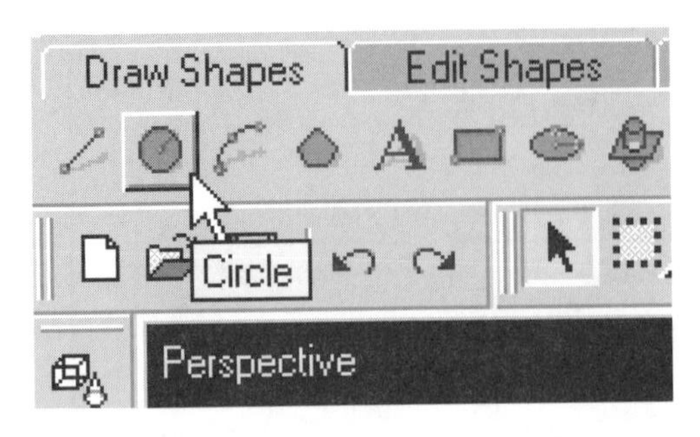

The Tab panel also offers a way to organize your VIZ window when you have a lot of toolbars up on the screen. Any toolbar can be turned into a tab on the Tab panel for easy access. Here's a little exercise to show you how it works.

1. Right-click the Interface tab at the far right of the Tab panel. You see a pop-up menu displaying a list of tab options.
2. Click the Convert to Toolbar option in the menu. The Interface tab becomes a toolbar.

3. Right click the Interface toolbar. A different pop-up menu displays. Notice that you have a Dock option at the top. This allows you to dock the toolbar at the VIZ window border.
4. Click the Move to Tab Panel option on the menu. The Interfaces toolbar returns to its location on the Tab panel.

As you see, the Tab panel offers a nice organization tool for multiple toolbars.

Changing the Look of VIZ

3D Studio VIZ is something of a chameleon. It can change its appearance, depending on the focus of your modeling needs. If your 3D Studio VIZ window doesn't look the way it does in the figures in this book, click the Interfaces tab, then click the icon to the far left, just below the tabs. Its tool tip label reads *Load default VIZ interface*. This sets up your VIZ windows to the interface you see in this book.

The Standard Toolbar

Just below the Tab panel are the standard toolbars. The standard toolbar tools also offer tool tips to help you remember their purpose.

To the far left of the toolbar are the typical Windows file options.

Next to the Windows options is a set of tools for selecting objects. These selection tools let you select objects by clicking them or by selecting them by name. You can also set the method for selecting objects by using a selection window, which provides a way of indicating a selection by placing a rectangle, circle, or other border around the objects.

To the right of the selection tools are the transformation tools. This next set of tools lets you move, rotate, or scale objects. You can also set the center of the transform using the Pivot options.

To the right of the transformation tools are the layer tools. These tools allow you to organize your drawing by separating objects into layers. If you are an AutoCAD user, these tools are already familiar to you.

The next group of tools to the right of the layer tools are the materials and rendering tools. The materials tools give you control over the appearance of objects. With the materials tools you can create color, texture, opacity, and other material characteristics, and then apply these characteristics to objects in your model.

The rendering tools give you control over the output of your 3D Studio VIZ model. Unlike output from most applications, output from 3D Studio VIZ is most likely to be image or multimedia files. The rendering tools let you set the type and size of output, from single, large format stills to video-ready animations.

TIP If you're working with a screen resolution of 1024 × 768 or less, you may want to move the Render toolbar to the Tab Panel to have access to all of its tools. Right-click the Render toolbar, and then select Move to Tab Panel in the pop-up menu.

To the far left of the screen are two toolbars stacked vertically. The top toolbar is the Shade/View toolbar that offers options for controlling the display of your model. Here you can set the way 3D Studio VIZ displays your model. You can also select from a set of predefined views such as isometric, perspective, and the standard orthographic projections of top, front, and right side views. Again, if you're an AutoCAD user, you see some familiar tools in this toolbar. (I've shown the Shade/View toolbar horizontally to conserve space.)

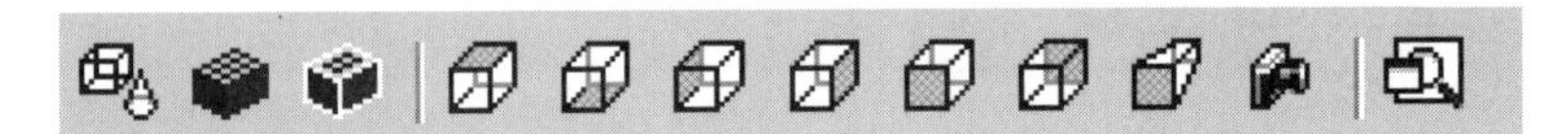

Below the Shade/View toolbar is the Modify toolbar, which contains options for editing your model. This toolbar represents only a fraction of the editing functions, but it does offer some of the more frequently used editing tools such as Delete, Mirror, and Array.

Toolbar Flyouts

You may have noticed that some of the tools in the standard toolbar show a small arrow in the lower right corner of the tool icon.

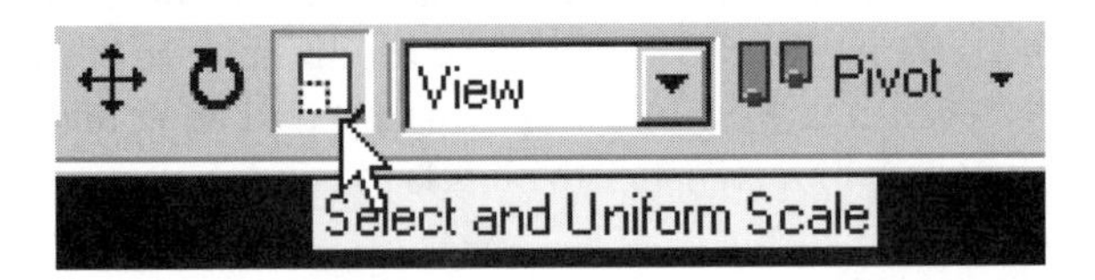

That arrow indicates that the tool is one of several offered in a *flyout*. A flyout is like a graphical version of options in a menu bar. If you click and hold a tool that is part of a flyout, you see a set of other tools appear. For example, if you click and hold the Select and Uniform Scale tool, two other tools appear.

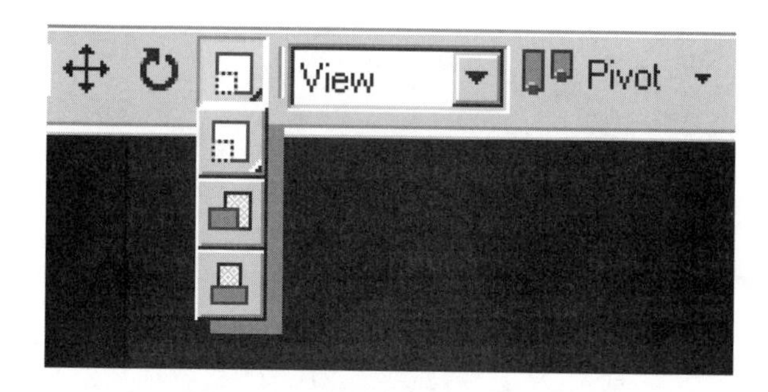

Once you select an option from a flyout, it becomes the default button that you see in the toolbar.

The Viewport

At the center of the window is the *Viewport* (see Figure 1.3). This is where you'll be doing most of your modeling work. In a blank file, the viewport shows a grid that you can use as a reference for orientation and size. The grid is labeled with distances in the current, default unit setting. The labels also indicate the X and Y axes. If you look in the lower left corner of the viewport, you see the world axis that indicates the orientation of the X, Y, and Z axes. The world axis helps you get your bearings when looking at other types of views.

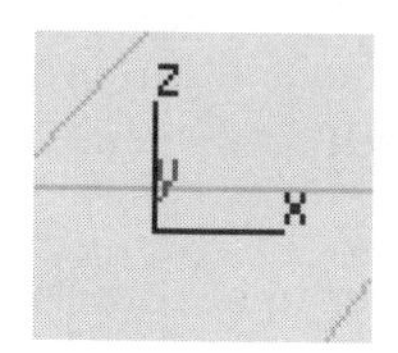

Right now, the viewport shows the perspective view as indicated in the label in the upper left corner. You can also tell that it is a perspective view by the way the grid converges in the distance. As you'll see toward the end of this chapter, you can configure and view your model in a variety of ways, depending on your needs.

Tools for Working with the Viewport

At the bottom of the window, there are several other options that are divided into four sections: the status bar, the prompt line, the time controls, and the viewport navigation tools (see Figure 1.4). Most of these tools affect the viewport, either by modifying the display of the viewport directly, or by affecting the way you interact with objects within the viewport.

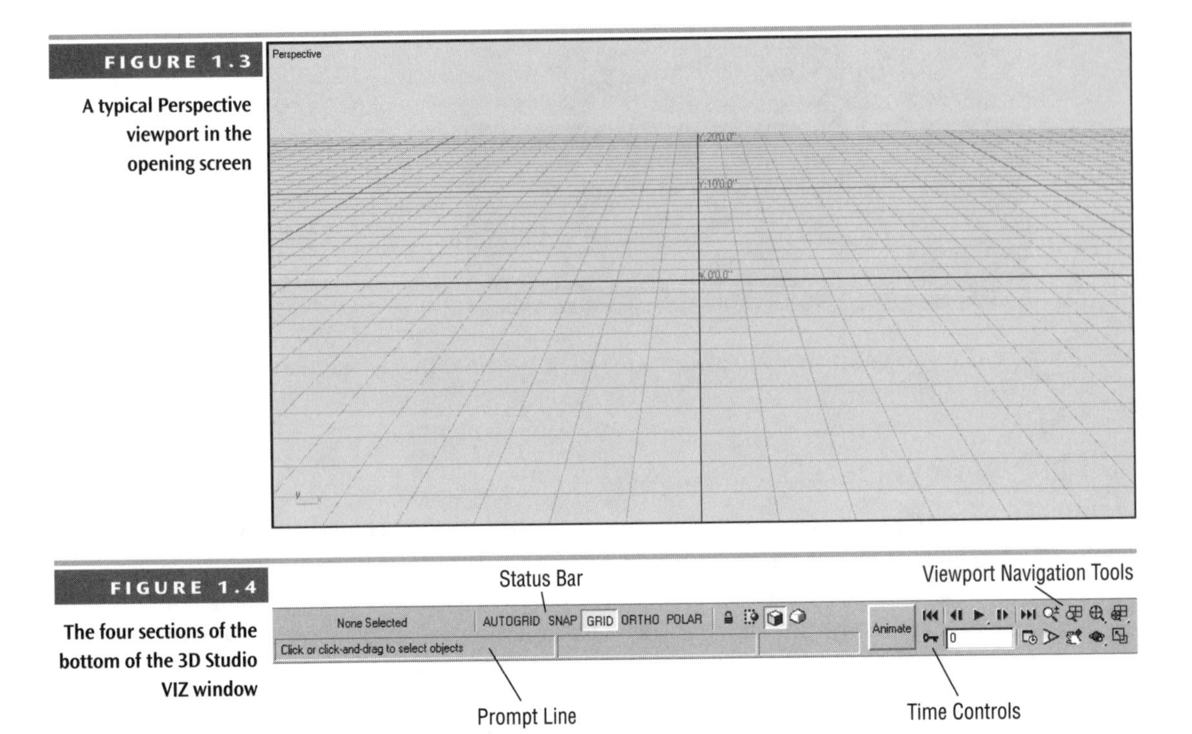

FIGURE 1.3

A typical Perspective viewport in the opening screen

FIGURE 1.4

The four sections of the bottom of the 3D Studio VIZ window

The viewport navigation tools give you control over the main graphic display in the center of the window. With these tools, you can zoom and pan over the display, or alter the viewpoint of your model. You can also switch between multiple views and a single view. Try the following:

1. Click the Min/Max toggle button in the far lower-right corner of the window. This is a tool you'll be using often.

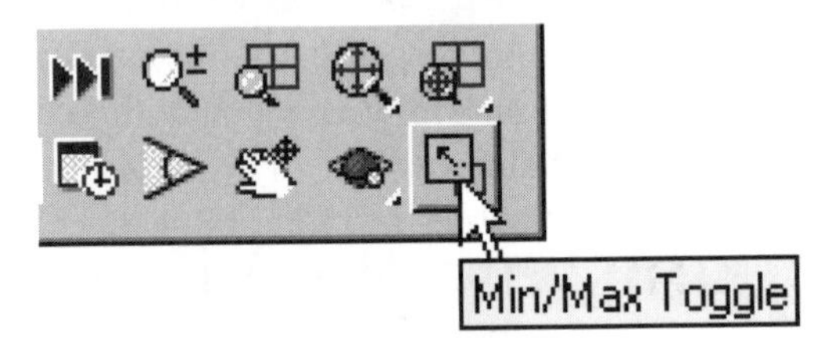

The graphic display changes to display four separate viewports. Each viewport shows a different type of view as shown in Figure 1.5. Notice that the viewports are labeled in their upper left corners.

2. Click the upper left viewport labeled Top. Notice that the border of the Top viewport becomes highlighted.

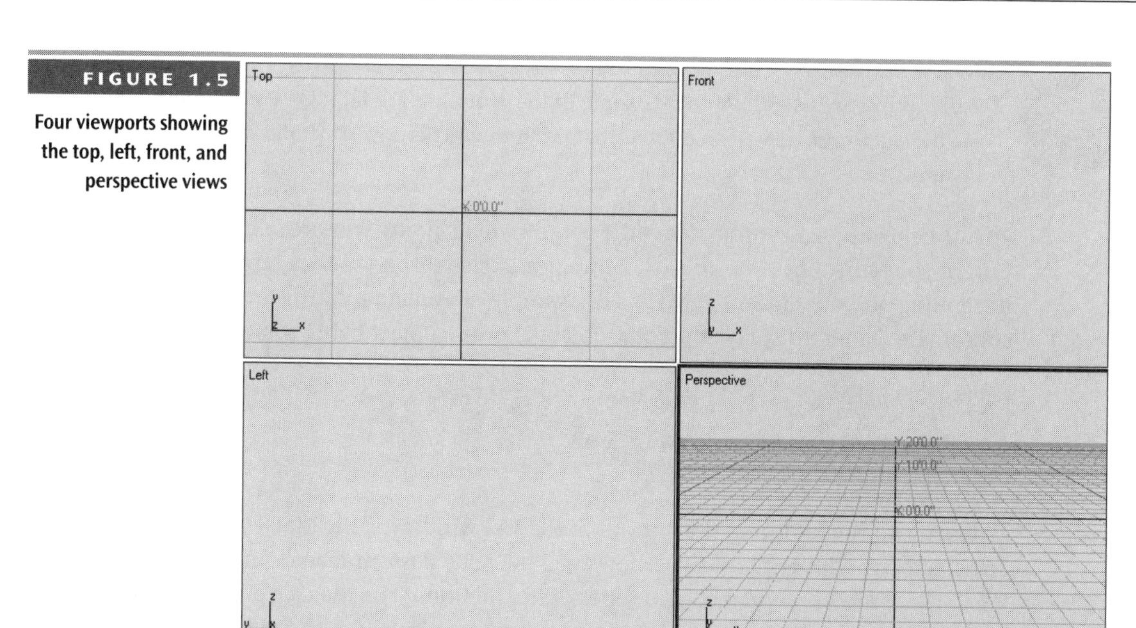

FIGURE 1.5

Four viewports showing the top, left, front, and perspective views

3. Click the Min/Max toggle tool again. Now the Top viewport fills the graphic area. Notice how you can quickly expand the view of a viewport to see more detail.
4. Click the Min/Max toggle again, then click in the Perspective viewport.
5. Click the Min/Max toggle to restore your original window setup.

You've just seen how you can expand the graphic area into multiple viewports showing the top, front, left, and perspective views. There are several other views and viewport arrangements available, as you'll see later in this chapter.

To the left of the viewport navigation tools are time control tools. These tools give you control over the animation functions of VIZ. Here, you can set your creations in motion by selecting the length of time for your animation, as well as the precise location of objects within that time frame.

To the left of the time control tools is the prompt line. Here you find tools to aid you in general drafting and model construction. For example, the Grid tool turns the display of the grid on or off.

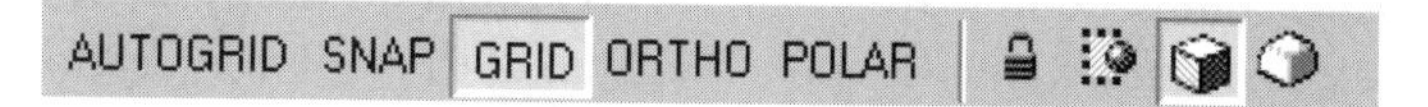

TIP If you are used to AutoCAD, some of these options are familiar. For example, you see the snap, grid, and ortho options that perform functions in 3D Studio similar to those in AutoCAD.

Just below these drafting aids is the coordinate readout. This area displays the location of your cursor in X, Y, and Z coordinates. It also displays other types of data, depending on your current activity. For example, if you are rotating an object, the coordinate readout displays the rotation angle of the object being rotated.

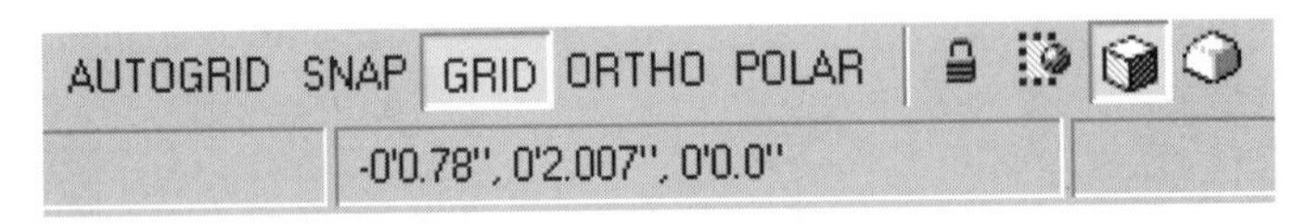

Finally, to the far left at the bottom of the VIZ window is the MaxScript Mini Listener. MaxScript is a tool that allows you to create custom macros in 3D Studio VIZ. Macros are like a prerecorded series of instructions. The MaxScript Mini Listener serves two functions: the pink area displays your activity when the MaxScript MacroRecord function is turned on. The white area provides a space where you can enter commands through the keyboard.

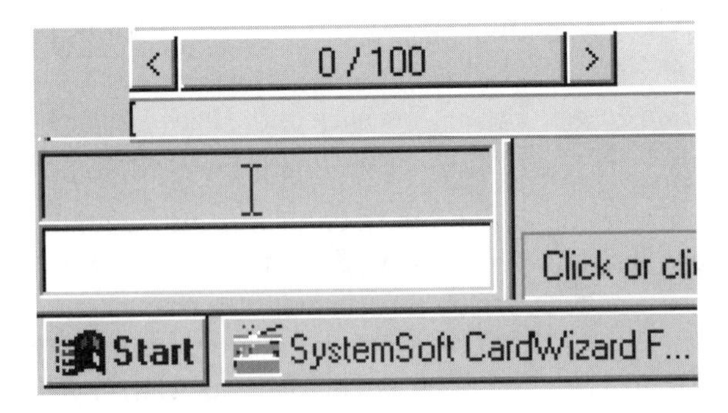

Getting to Know the Command Panel

You'll be using the Command Panel for most of your work in VIZ. If you're an experienced AutoCAD user, you might think of the Command Panel as the equivalent to the AutoCAD command line; it is a single entry point for nearly all of the program's functions. The Command Panel offers nearly all of the tools for creating and editing in VIZ. You'll be spending a lot of time in this panel, so it is worth your while to become familiar with it at this early stage.

First, let's look at how the Command Panel is organized. Across the top, you see a set of six tabs, each displaying an icon.

From left to right, the tabs are Create, Modify, Hierarchy, Motion, Display, and Utilities. As you click a tab, you see the tab's name appear just below the tab icon. Also, when you click a tab, the functions relating to the tab appear in the rest of the Command Panel. Here's a brief rundown of what each tab offers:

Create allows you to create two-dimensional and three-dimensional objects. You can also create light sources, cameras, and helper objects that are used to determine distance and relationships between objects. Light sources, cameras, and helpers are objects that do not appear when your view is rendered.

Modify gives you control over the dimension and shape of your objects. You find tools to extrude, twist, and bend your objects. You can also control methods for applying material definitions to objects in this tab.

Hierarchy offers a set of tools aimed primarily at animation. The options under this tab let you build relationships between objects to simulate joint movement or to constrain motion of one object in relation to another. It also offers a way to control the location of an object's pivot point, and you can reposition an object's pivot point with this tab.

Motion is another tab that gives you control over animation. Here you can control the actual motion of objects over time and view the paths of objects.

Display lets you hide or unhide objects in your model. There are times when you may not want a particular object visible while you render your model or while you're editing a complex model full of objects. Display lets you temporarily hide objects from view.

Utilities is a kind of catch-all tab that provides access to special features and plug-ins. This is where you find the Camera Match utility that lets you match your model view to a photograph. You can also get access to the MaxScript customization features under this tab.

TIP **You may notice that the Command Panel is *floating* over the graphic display, hiding a portion of it. You can dock the Command Panel by double-clicking its title bar. You may also right-click the Command Panel's title bar and then select Dock. This brings the entire graphic display into view. In addition, you may close the Command Panel entirely**

by clicking the close button (the one with the X in the upper right corner of the window). To bring the Command Panel back, right-click the blank area of any toolbar, then select Command Panel from the pop-up menu. (You can also right-click the Command Panel's title bar to dock the panel on the left side of the screen.)

Understanding VIZ's Tools

There are a few ways of working in VIZ that are a bit unusual for a Windows program. In this section, you'll explore the Create tab of the Command Panel as a way to understanding some of VIZ's quirks. There aren't many, but understanding them now will make it easier for you to learn the program.

Getting to Know Scrolling Panels and Rollouts

3D Studio VIZ has a rich set of creation and editing tools; so many in fact that VIZ's programmers had to come up with a way to get to them easily without making the program too arcane. There are two tools that VIZ incorporates to help you navigate its interface; the *scrolling panel* and the *rollout*. A scrolling panel is an area that can be scrolled up or down using a hand cursor. A rollout is a set of tools that can be opened or closed, much like a drawer in a dresser. Let's start by looking at how a scrolling panel works.

1. Click the Create tab of the Command Panel. You notice a row of icons just below the title of the tab. These icons are buttons, or tools, that offer different types of objects.

2. Place the cursor over the tool that looks like a movie camera. Notice that a tool tip displays, offering the name of the tool.
3. Go ahead and click the Camera tool. You see the options change below the tools.

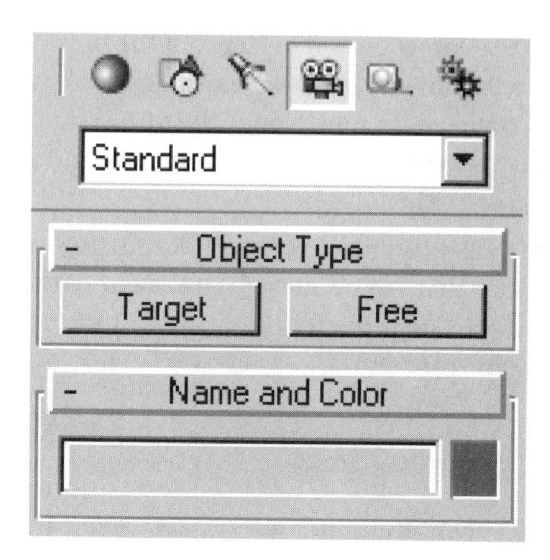

4. Click the button labeled Target. A set of additional options appears. Although it may not be obvious, these options extend beyond the bottom of the Command Panel.

5. Move your cursor down to a blank spot in the Command Panel. The cursor changes to a hand.

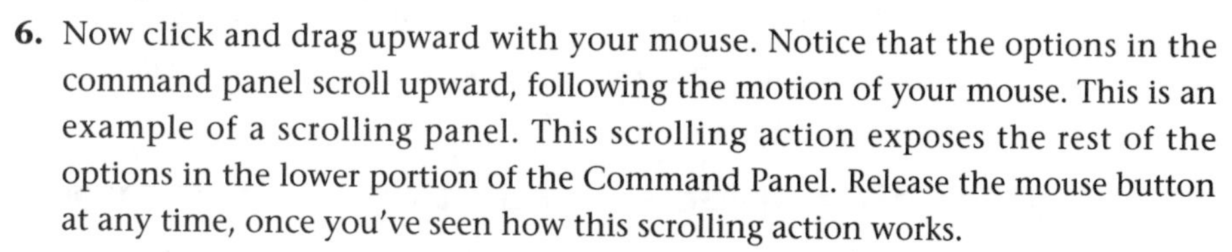

6. Now click and drag upward with your mouse. Notice that the options in the command panel scroll upward, following the motion of your mouse. This is an example of a scrolling panel. This scrolling action exposes the rest of the options in the lower portion of the Command Panel. Release the mouse button at any time, once you've seen how this scrolling action works.

7. Place the cursor on a blank area again, so that the hand cursor displays. Then click and drag downward to view the Target and Free buttons under the Object Type bar.

In this exercise, you see that the entire set of options can be changed by clicking a single tool. You can also see that the set of tools can extend beyond the bottom of the Command Panel. The hand cursor can be used to scroll the options upward or downward. This allows VIZ to offer a wide variety of options within the limited space of your display.

The standard toolbar also acts like a scrolling panel whenever a portion of the toolbar extends beyond the screen area. For example, if your screen resolution is 1024 × 768, a portion of the Render toolbar is not visible to the right of the screen. If you place the cursor on a blank area of the Render toolbar, it turns into a hand cursor. You can then click and drag to the left to display the additional tools.

When you clicked on the Target button in step 4 of the previous exercise, a set of options appeared under a button labeled Parameters. There are two other buttons, labeled Object Type and Name and Color. Notice the Minus sign to the far left of the button. These buttons are called *rollouts*. They let you open and close a set of options to get them out of the way. Try the following:

1. Click the rollout labeled Parameters. The options below the Parameters rollout disappear. Also notice that the minus sign to the left of the rollout changes to a plus sign. This indicates that the rollout is in its closed state and that you can open it by clicking the rollout.

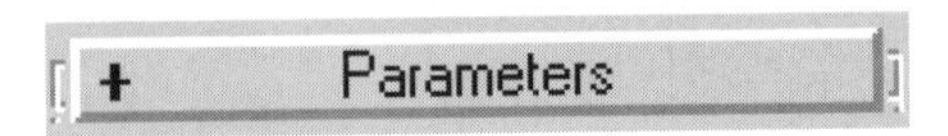

2. Click the rollout labeled Name and Color. It too closes and displays a plus sign to the left.

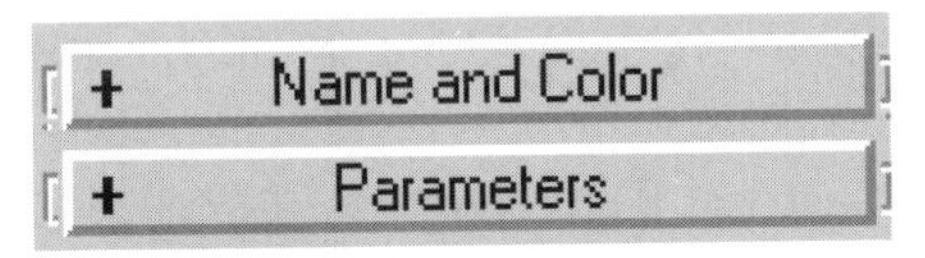

3. Click the Parameters and Name and Color rollouts again to display the options.

In this and later chapters, you'll explore the rollouts that appear in the Command Panel and throughout the program.

Creating Objects and Setting Their Parameters

By now, you've seen most of VIZ's interface and how it functions. There are a few more tools and methods that you will want to know about before you really delve into using VIZ. In the following exercises, you'll get a chance to create a simple object, and in the process, you'll be introduced to a few new tools.

1. In the Create tab of the Command Panel, click the Geometry tool at the top of the panel.

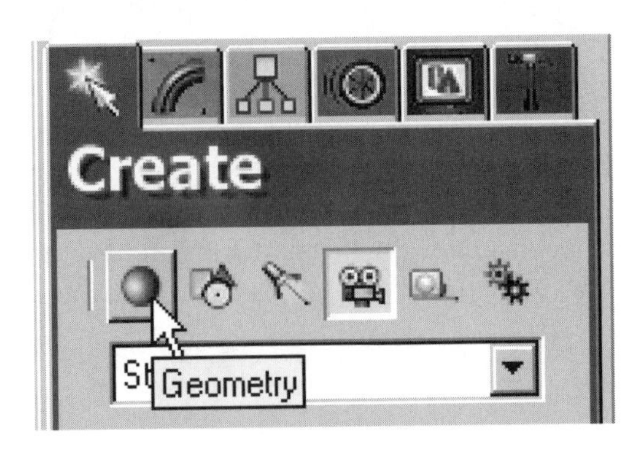

You see the Object Type rollout with a set of object types.

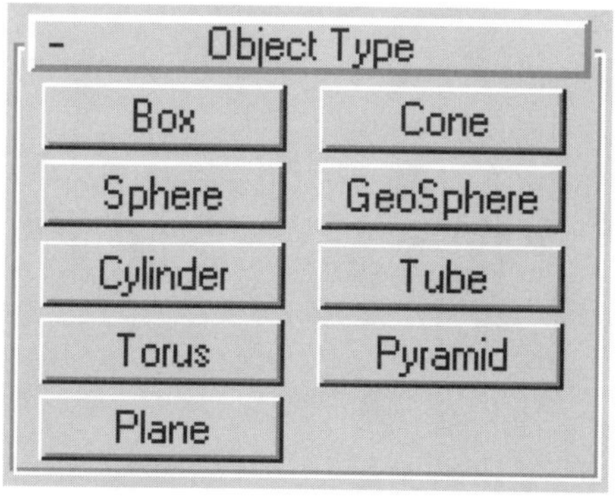

2. Click the Box button. Additional rollouts appear in the Command Panel. These include Creation Method, Keyboard Entry, and Parameters. Notice that a message displays in the Prompt line that says, "Click and drag to begin creation process." Also, the cursor in the graphic area displays as a cross, telling you that you're in object creation mode.
3. Place the cursor at the center of the graphic area at coordinate 0,0 and click and drag diagonally to the upper right corner of the screen—don't let go of the mouse button just yet. As you move the mouse, a rectangle follows your cursor. Notice that the values in the Length and Width input boxes in the Parameters rollout change as you move the mouse.
4. Place the cursor so the rectangle looks similar to the one shown in Figure 1.6, then release the mouse button. You don't have to match the rectangle in the figure exactly.

   Now as you move the cursor, the rectangle changes in height. Notice that the Height parameter in the Parameters rollout also follows the change in height.
5. Adjust the height so that the Height parameter shows about 20 and click your mouse. The box is now fixed at the height you selected. It should look similar to Figure 1.7.

FIGURE 1.6

The rectangle so far

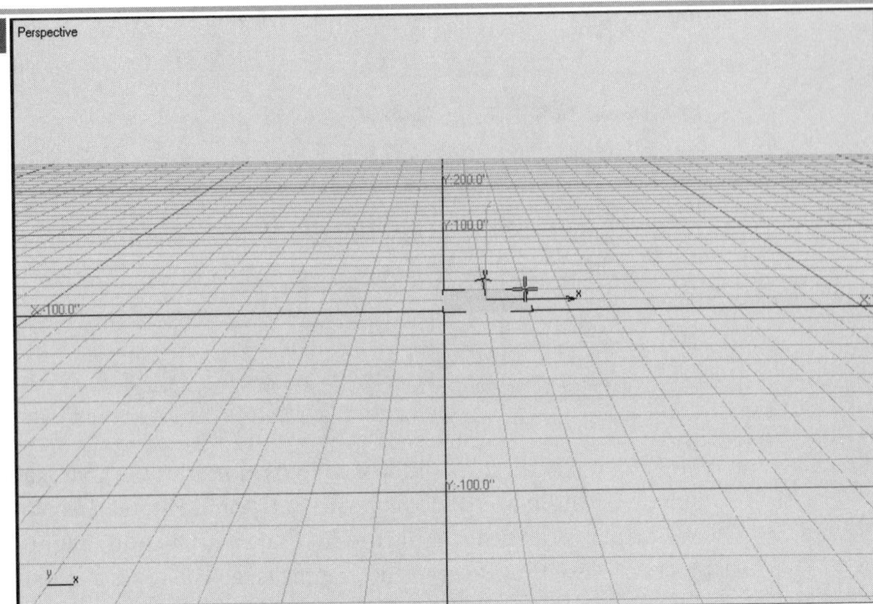

FIGURE 1.7

The finished box

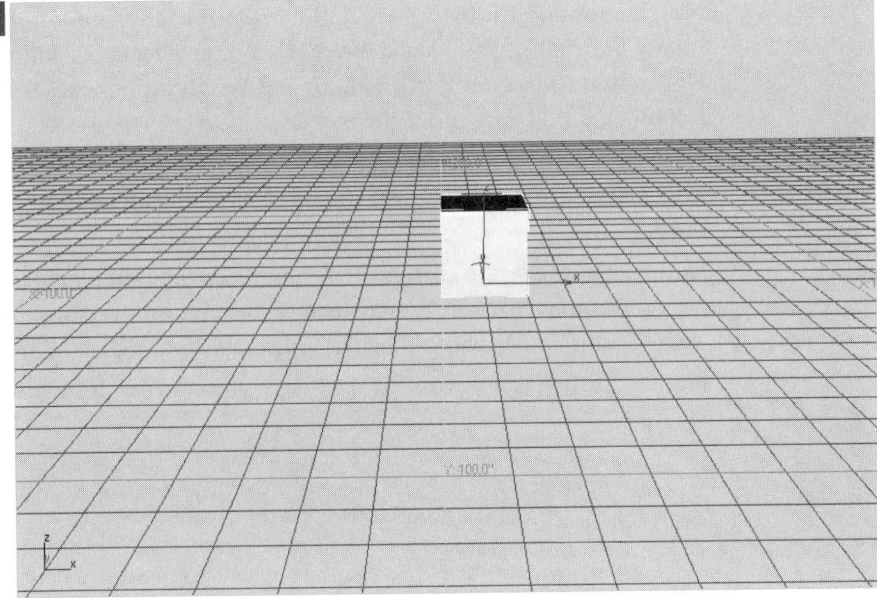

You've just created your first object in VIZ, and in the process you have seen how the dimensions of an object are reflected in the Parameters rollout. Once you've created an object, you can continue to modify the object's parameters, as the following exercise demonstrates.

1. In the Parameters rollout, locate the Width input box, and click the upward pointing arrow to the right of the box several times. These arrows are called *spinners,* and they allow you to graphically adjust the value of the input box they are associated with. Notice that the box in the perspective view begins to widen as the value in Width input box increases.

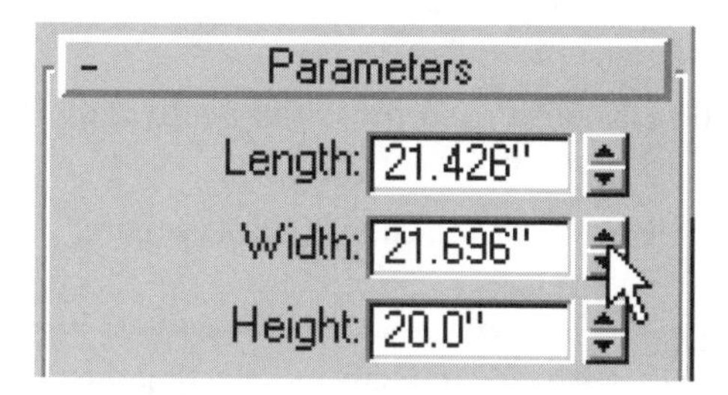

2. Momentarily click and hold down the left mouse button while pointing to the upward arrow of the Width spinner. Notice that the box continues to grow in width as you hold the mouse button down.
3. Right-click the spinner arrow. The box shrinks in width to 0. Right-clicking the spinner changes the spinner value to its default, which in this case is 0.
4. Click and drag the mouse upward from the Width spinner. The box gradually grows in width. Click and drag downward, and the width shrinks back down.
5. Click and drag the Width Spinner upward until the cursor reaches the top of the screen; then continue moving the mouse upward. Notice that the cursor reappears at the bottom of the screen. This *circular* action of the spinner lets you scroll continuously without being limited by the screen area.

TIP **While adjusting a spinner, you can immediately undo any changes you make by right-clicking the mouse while still holding the left mouse button. This allows you to quickly experiment with spinner settings while you work.**

You've just seen how you can change the parameters of an object by using the spinner. Now let's take a look at the old fashioned way of entering values into input boxes.

1. Click the Length input box in the Parameters rollout, and type **20↵**. Notice how the box's length changes.
2. Press the Tab key. Notice that the Width value is now highlighted.

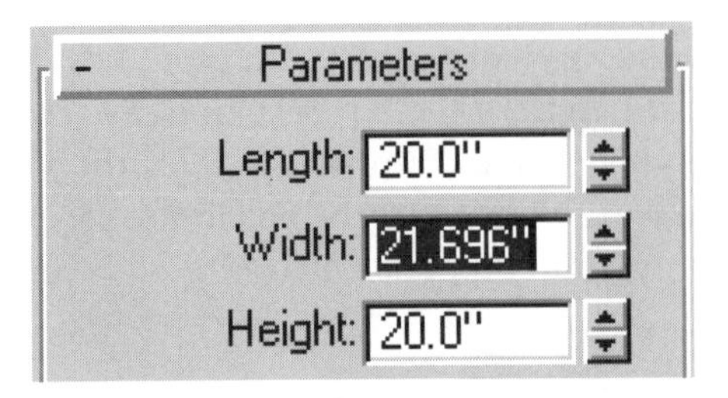

3. Type **20↵** for the width and then press Tab again. The Height value is highlighted.
4. Enter **20↵** again. The box is now a cube 20 units square.

NOTE **You can also create a cube directly by selecting the Cube check box in the Creation Method rollout.**

If there is a series of related input boxes, such as the Length, Width, and Height boxes in the previous exercise, the Tab key lets you advance from one value to the next. You'll find that numeric input boxes and spinners are quite common throughout 3D Studio VIZ.

TIP **If you hold the Ctrl key while you move a spinner, the rate of change in the spinner value increases. The Alt key has the opposite affect, decreasing the rate of change. The higher the numeric value in the spinner, the faster the rate of change, and vice-versa.**

Working with Objects

Now that you've seen the main elements of the VIZ interface, let's take a look at how you interact with objects in the viewport. You'll start by looking at a way to move the cube you've just created. Then, you'll take a look at how you can view your cube from different angles.

Selecting and Moving

VIZ's basic editing tools are simple and straightforward, although it may take a little explaining to grasp the finer points. As with most graphics programs, you use a selection tool to select objects. This tool is typically shown on the toolbar as an upward-pointing arrow that looks like the standard Windows cursor.

1. Click the Select Object tool in the standard toolbar.

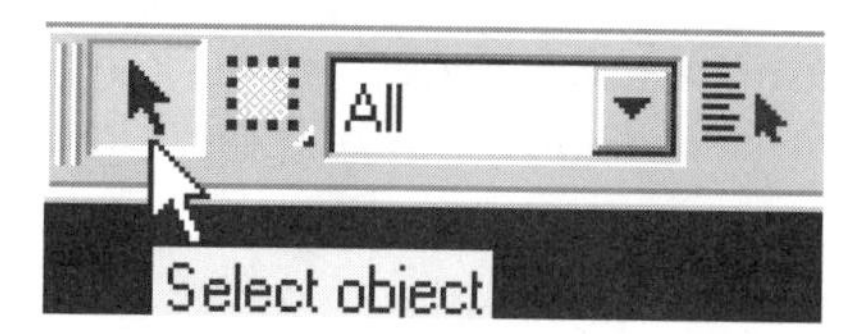

2. Click in a blank area of the viewport. This clears any selections that may currently be active.
3. Move the cursor over the cube. Notice that the cursor turns into a plus sign. This tells you that the cursor has found a selectable object.
4. Click the cube. A graphic displays, showing the X, Y, and Z orientation of the cube in relation to the viewport. Also notice that something like 3D *corner marks* appears at the corners of the cube. These are called *selection brackets,* and they are indicators that show you graphically the objects that are selected.

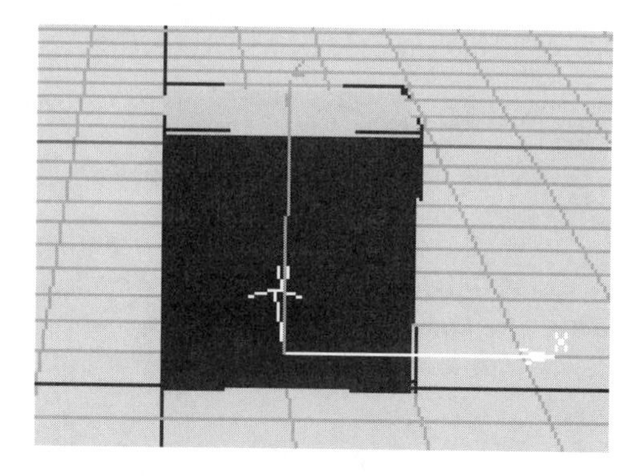

With the cube selected, you can go to the Modify tab of the Command Panel and edit its properties. Or you can use any number of other editing tools to affect the cube.

Let's continue by looking at one of the more basic editing tools you'll use—the Select and Move tool.

1. Click the Select and Move tool. Notice that the graphics indicating the box selection change and new ones appear.

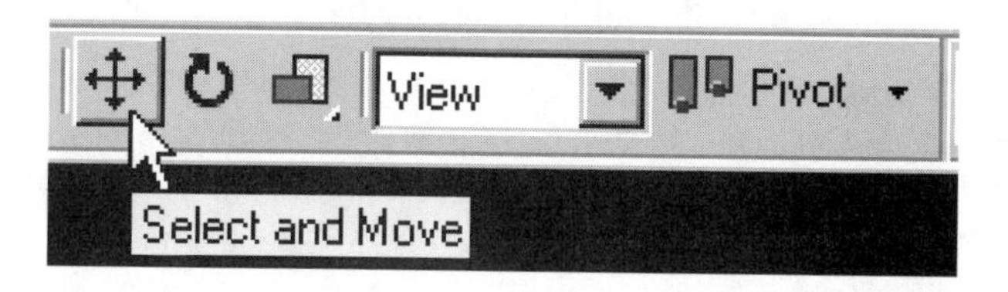

2. Place the cursor on the cube. It changes into the Select and Move icon.
3. Place the cursor on the red arrow representing the X axis and move the cursor to the blue, upward-pointing arrow representing the Z axis. Alternate the placement between these two arrows and notice how the X and Z labels change when you do this.
4. Click and drag the red X coordinate arrow to the right. The cube now moves in the X axis. When you click and drag the X arrow, movement is constrained along the X axis.
5. Click and drag the blue Z coordinate arrow upward. Now movement is constrained in the Z axis. As you may guess, clicking and dragging the green Y coordinate arrow constrains movement in the Y axis.
6. Now click and drag the cube slowly in a circular motion, taking care not to click a coordinate arrow. (You still have to have the cursor over the cube.) If you click an object in a location other than the coordinate arrows, but still on the object, you can freely move the object in the X-Y plane. Notice that the coordinate location of the object is displayed in the status line just below the drafting tools.

Constraining Motion the Old-fashioned Way

If you're an experienced 3D Studio user, and you're wondering where the old X, Y, Z constraint buttons are, you can find them by right-clicking any blank area of a toolbar, and then selecting Constraints. The Constraints toolbar displays. You can also right click a selected object, then select Transform from the pop-up menu. You can then select from a list of constraint options.

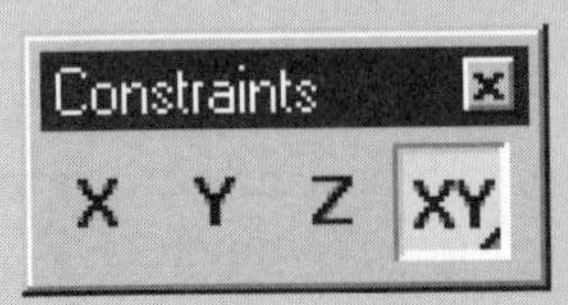

The tools in the Constraints toolbar constrain the motion of an object on the X, Y, or Z axis. For example, to constrain motion in the X axis, click the Select and Move tool, then click the X tool in the Constraints toolbar. The selected object's motion is constrained to the X axis. Prior to 3D Studio VIZ 3, this was the only method available to constrain motion.

Another important function that the Constraints toolbar offers is the selection of the default *free motion* plane. In step 6 of the previous exercise, you were able to move the cube freely in the X-Y plane, but you were constrained to that plane. The Constraints toolbar lets you select the default plane to which you are constrained. The tool to the

Continued on the next page

far right is a flyout offering three options: XY, YZ, and ZX. You can select the plane in which you want to constrain motion by selecting one of these three options. The XY option is fine for nearly all of your work, but every now and then, you'll want to use one of the other options, so it's good to be aware of this tool.

Finally, a tool that is related to the Transform tool is the Lock Selection tool.

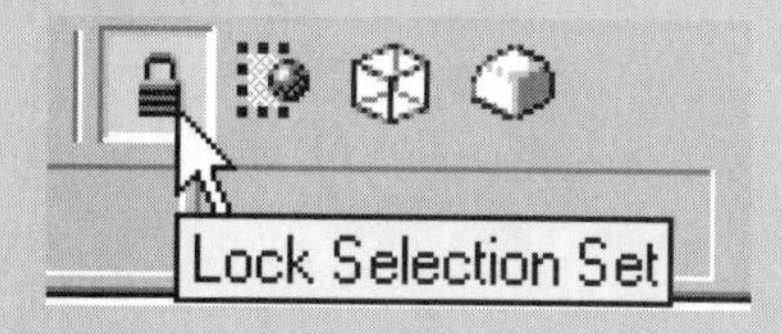

This tool helps to prevent the accidental loss of a selection from clicking the mouse. It also allows you to use the transform tools without actually placing the cursor on the selected objects.

As you see, moving an object in VIZ is fairly straightforward. But what if you want to move an object a specific distance or to a known position? The following exercise demonstrates how this is done.

1. With the cube still selected, right-click the Select and Move tool in the standard toolbar.

   The Move Transform Type-In dialog box displays.

   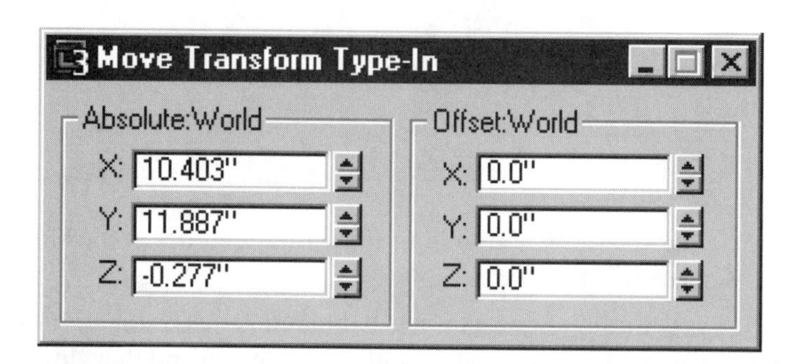

   You see two groups in this dialog box, the Absolute: World group and the Offset: World group. The Absolute: World group lets you enter the specific coordinate where you want to move your object. The Offset: World group lets you enter a relative distance from the object's current location.

2. Move the dialog box so that you see the cube clearly, then in the Offset: World group, click in the X input box and type **10**↵. The box moves 10 units to the right.
3. In the Offset: World group, click and drag the Z spinner upward. The box moves vertically.

4. In the Absolute: World group click on the Z input box and enter **1**↵. The box moves so that its base is exactly at 1 for the Z coordinate.
5. In the Absolute: World group, right-click the X value spinner. Remember that right-clicking a spinner converts the value associated with the spinner to its default, which in this case is 0. Notice that the box moves to 0 for the X coordinate.
6. Right-click the spinners for the Y and Z coordinates in the Absolute: World group. The cube moves to the center of the screen at the origin (coordinates 0,0,0).

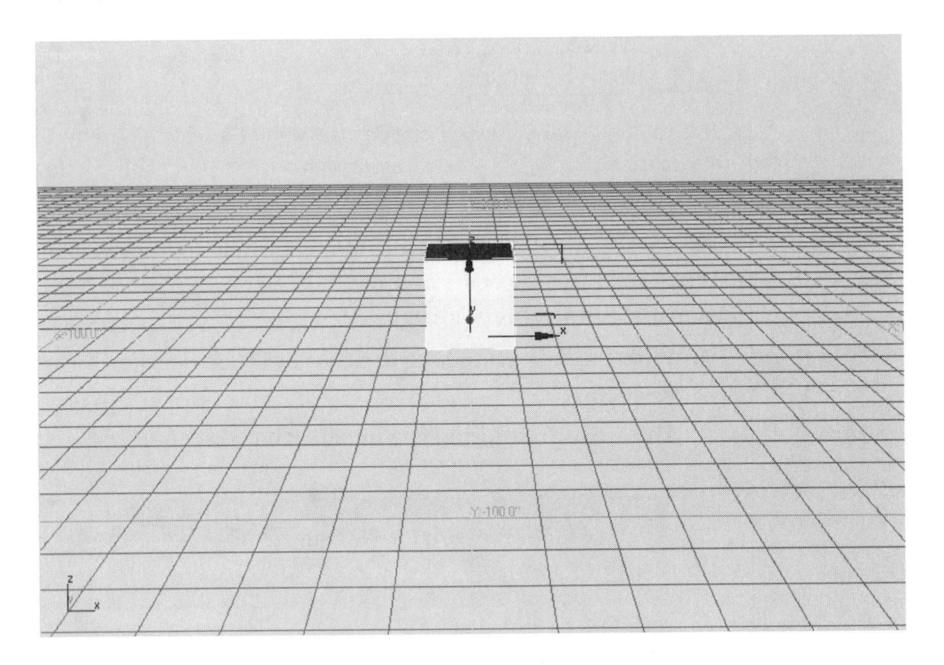

7. Click the Close button in the upper right corner of the Move Transform Type-In dialog box to close it.

Just as with the spinners in the Command Panel, the spinners in the Move Transform dialog box let you set values by clicking and dragging. You can also set return-to-default values by right-clicking the spinners.

Rotating and Scaling Objects

Besides moving objects, the Transform tools also include the Rotate and Scale tools. These tools work in a way similar to the Move tool. Try the following set of exercises to see exactly how they work.

TIP The Move, Rotate, and Copy tools can also be activated by right-clicking an object and selecting Move, Rotate, or Uniform Scale from the pop-up menu.

1. Click the Select and Rotate tool.

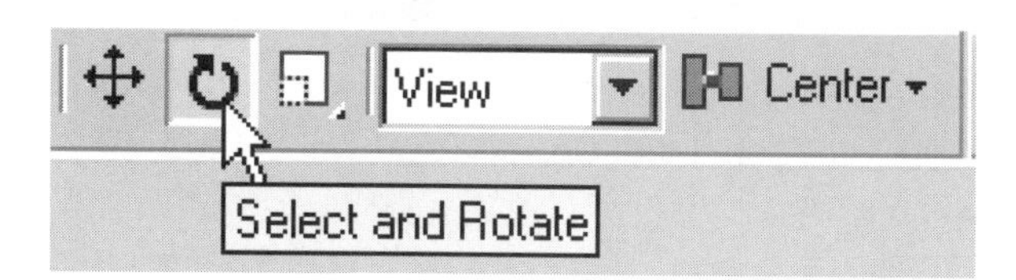

2. Click and drag the X axis arrow upward. The box rotates about the X axis.
3. Right-click the Select and Rotate tool. The Rotation Transform Type-In dialog box displays.

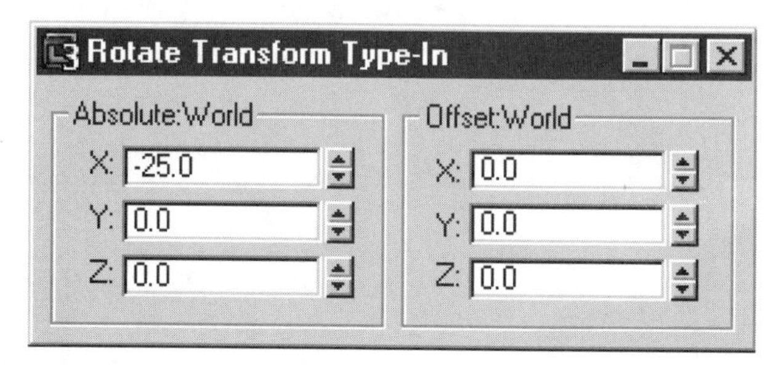

Notice that the X value in the Absolute: World group is not zero, because you rotated it in step 2.

4. Move the Rotate Transform Type-In dialog box to the lower left corner of the viewport so you can see the box clearly.
5. Right-click the X spinner under Absolute: World group to set the X value rotation back to zero. Notice that the box snaps back to its original orientation.
6. Close the Rotate Transform Type-In dialog box.

The Select and Rotate tool's methods are the same as those for the Select and Move tool. You can rotate an object graphically by clicking and dragging the object, or, with an object selected, you can right-click the Select and Rotate tool to enter an exact rotation value. The Absolute: World group of the Rotate Transform Type-In dialog box controls the orientation in relation to the object's original orientation when it was created. The Offset: World group controls the orientation relative to the object's current orientation.

Now try out the Scale tool.

1. With the box selected, click the Select and Uniform Scale tool in the standard toolbar.

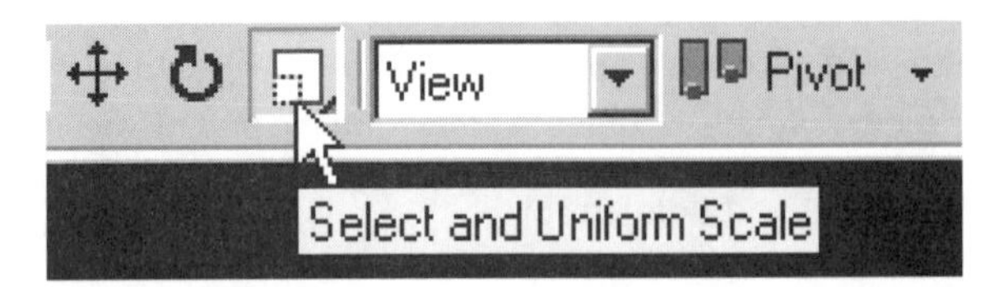

2. Click and drag the box upward. The box grows uniformly in size.
3. Right-click the Select and Uniform Scale tool. The Scale Transform Type-In dialog box displays.

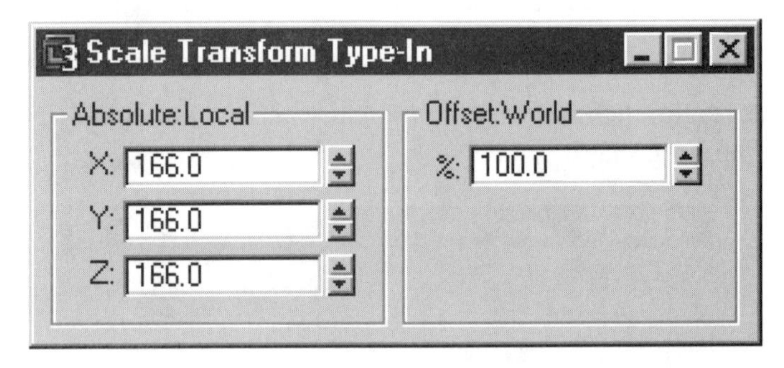

The values in this dialog box are percentages. The Absolute: Local values are percentages of the original size of the object. The Offset: World value is the scale in relation to the current size.

1. Click and Drag the Z spinner upward in the Absolute: Local group. Notice that the box grows in the Z axis.
2. Right-click the Y axis spinner. The box distorts to a 0 value in the Y axis.
3. Click in the X value input box and enter **100↵**. The box's X value is restored to its original size.
4. Press the Tab key to move on to the Y value input box and enter **100↵**.
5. Press the Tab key again to move to the Z input box. Then enter **100↵**.
6. Close the Scale Transform Type-In dialog box.

The box is now restored to its original size. The Select and Scale tool works in a slightly different way from the other two transform tools. For one thing, a zero value in the Scale Transform Type-In dialog box does not return the selected object to its original shape. This is because the values in the dialog box represent percentages.

Also, clicking and dragging the X, Y, or Z transform gizmo on the object does not affect the scale of the object in the individual axes. The object is uniformly scaled in all directions. You can, however, scale the object independently in each axis, using the Scale Transform Type-In dialog box. The Select and Uniform Scale tool in the standard toolbar is also one of three tools in a flyout. The other two tools, Select and Nonuniform Scale, and Select and Squash, let you alter the scale nonuniformly by dragging.

Copying an Object

You've covered just about all the ways of moving, rotating, and scaling an object in the perspective viewport. If you want to copy an object, you use the same methods you would use to move, rotate, or scale objects—with the addition of holding down the shift key. Try the following to see how copying, or cloning as it's called in VIZ, works. (Copying is one of the forms of a more general function called cloning.)

1. Make sure the Select and Move tool is active and make sure the cube is selected.
2. While holding down the shift key, move the cube to the right by dragging. A second cube displays.
3. Release the mouse button. The Clone Options dialog box displays. This dialog box lets you control the type of copy you are making as well as the name of the new object.

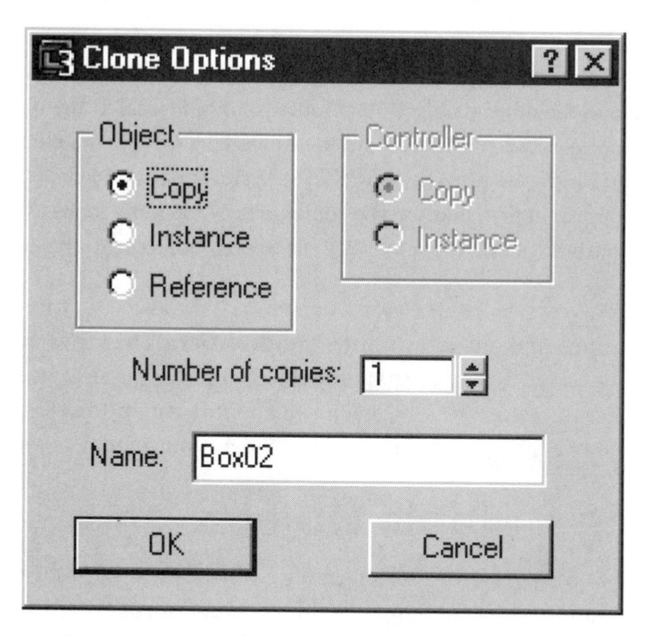

4. In the Object group of the Clone Options dialog box, make sure Copy is selected.

5. Click OK. The new box is now added to your model.

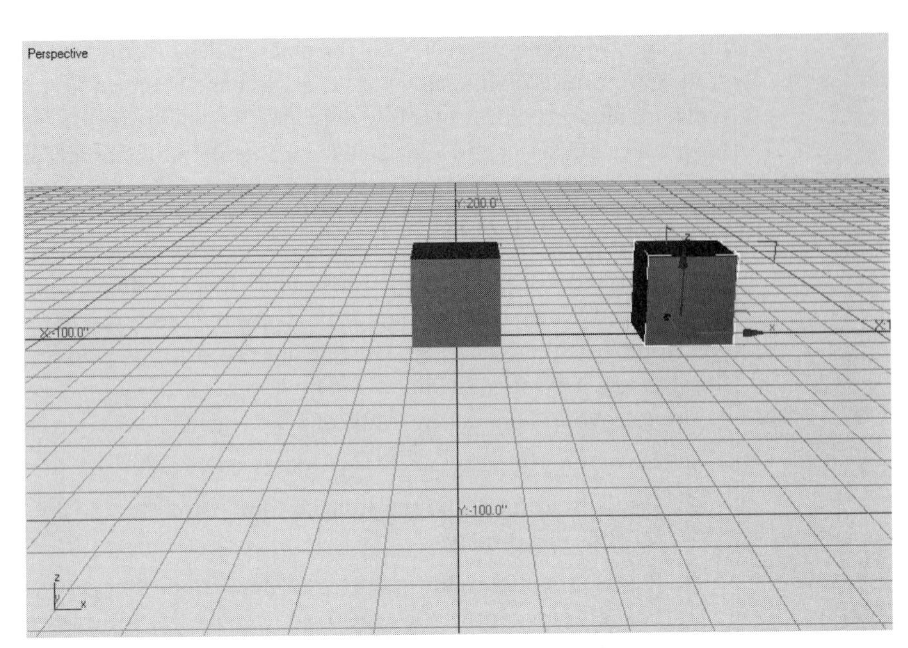

TIP There may be times when you want to make a copy of an object in the exact same location as the original object. To accomplish this, first select the object you wish to copy and then select Edit ➢ Clone from the menu bar. You see the Clone Options dialog box that you saw in the previous exercise. Set your options and click OK. Note that no new copies appear at first, because the copies occupy the same space as the original. (You can accomplish the same thing by shift-clicking an object with the Select and Move tool.)

In step 4, you selected the Copy option in the Clone Options dialog box. This option creates a distinct copy of the original object. The other two options, Instance and Reference, create copies that are linked to the original so that changes in one object affect the other. You'll learn more about these options later in Chapter 2. For now, let's move on to learn about ways to view your model.

Selecting Multiple Objects

You've now learned how to select, move, and copy a single object, but what do you do if you want to move or copy several objects at once? You can select multiple objects, or *selection sets* as they are called in VIZ, using two methods. The first is actually one employed in other graphics programs.

1. Click the Select Object tool on the standard toolbar.
2. Click on a blank area of the viewport to clear any selections you may already have.
3. Click and hold your mouse at a point below and to the left of the original cube, then drag to the right and upward. Notice that a dotted rectangle follows your cursor, as shown in Figure 1.8.
4. Continue to drag the cursor up and to the right until it encloses both cubes. Then release the mouse button. Both cubes are selected.

FIGURE 1.8

Placing the selection rectangle around the cubes

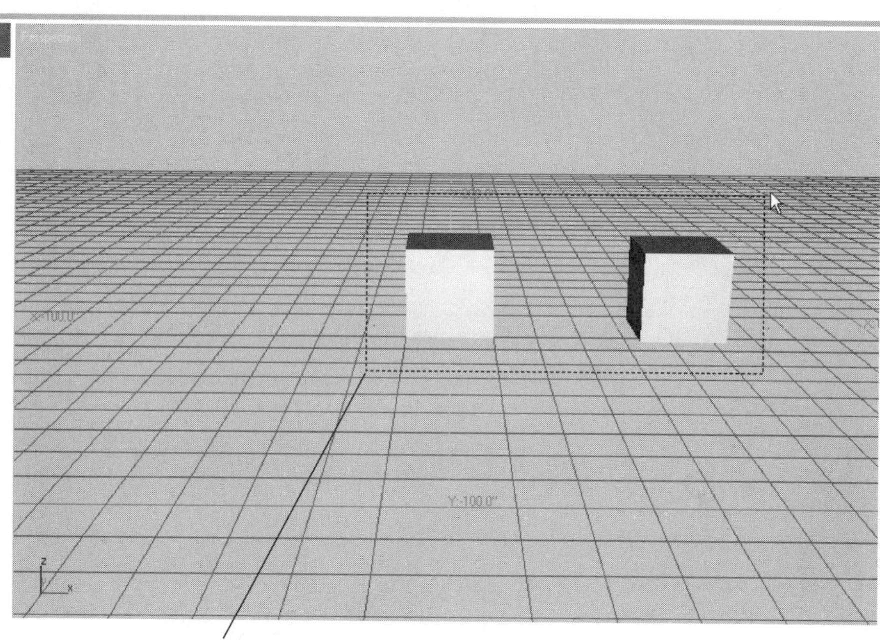
Click and drag from here.

Notice that both cubes show their bounding boxes, and a transform gizmo displays between the two cubes, showing you that the two objects are selected. There are a couple of other ways you can select objects, which you'll learn about in a moment, but first, let's use the current selection to make a few more copies of the cube.

1. Click the Select and Move tool in the standard toolbar.
2. Shift-click and drag the Y axis arrow downward so that copies of the two cubes appear in the location shown in Figure 1.9. You don't have to be exact about the placement of the copies.

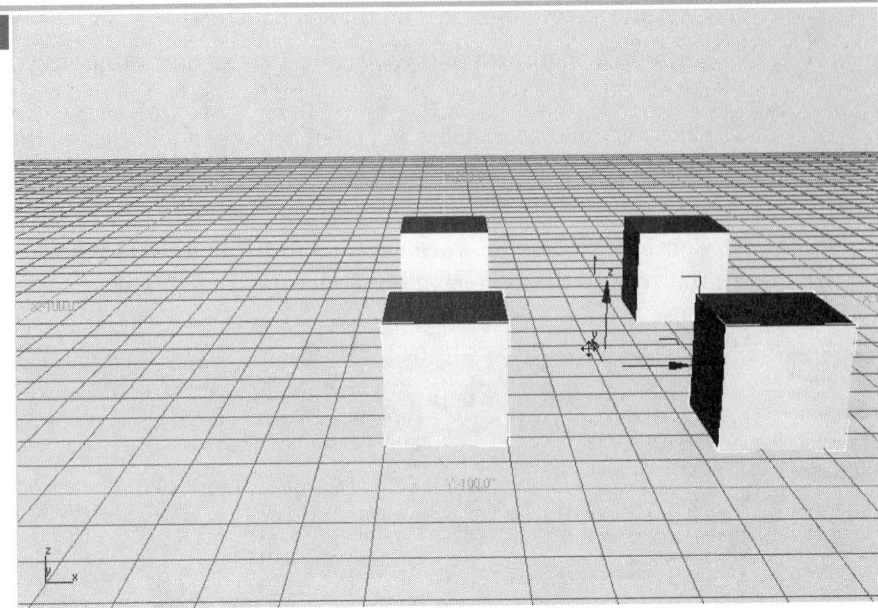

FIGURE 1.9

Place the copies just below the middle of the cube in the center foreground

3. When you've got the copies in place, release the mouse button.
4. In the Clone Options dialog box, make sure Copy is selected in the Object group and click OK.

The four cubes help demonstrate some of the other selection methods available to you. First, let's look at another property of the selection window.

1. Click the Select Object tool.

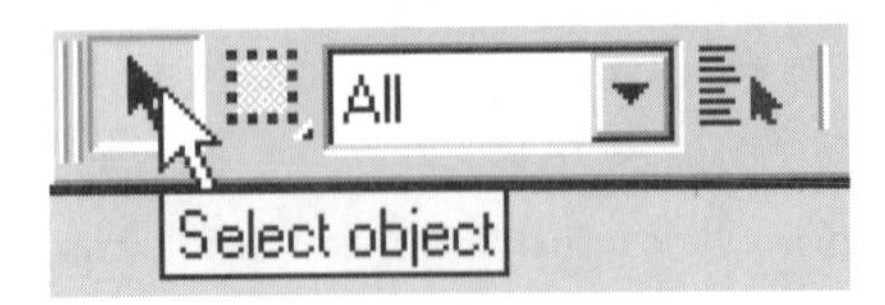

2. Click on a blank spot in the viewport to clear your selection set.
3. Now click and drag the cursor from the point indicated in Figure 1.9.
4. Drag the rectangle up and to the right so that it just crosses over the cube in the back right corner, as shown in Figure 1.10, and release the mouse button. Three of the four cubes are selected.

FIGURE 1.10

Selecting points for a crossing window

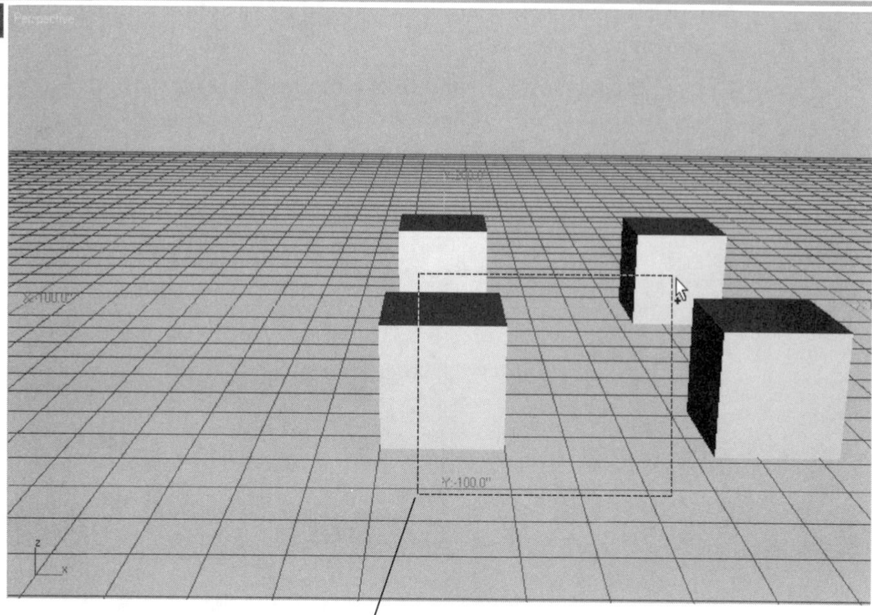

Click and drag from here.

Notice that you didn't have to enclose the cubes to select them. In the current selection mode, you only need to have the selection window cross over the desired objects. This is known as a crossing window. If you're an AutoCAD user, this type of window should be familiar to you.

You can change the way the selection window works using the Crossing/Window selection tool. The following exercise demonstrates how it works.

1. Click a blank area in the drawing to clear your selection set.
2. Click the Crossing Selection tool at the bottom of the window.

   Notice that the icon changes to one showing a sphere completely within a dotted rectangle.

   This tells you that you are now in Windows Selection mode.

3. Click a point below and to the right of the cube in the center foreground, as shown in Figure 1.11.
4. Drag the rectangle up and to the right until it partially includes the cube in the back right corner, as shown in Figure 1.11, then release the mouse button. Notice that the only objects selected are the two cubes on the left.

FIGURE 1.11

Placing a selection window

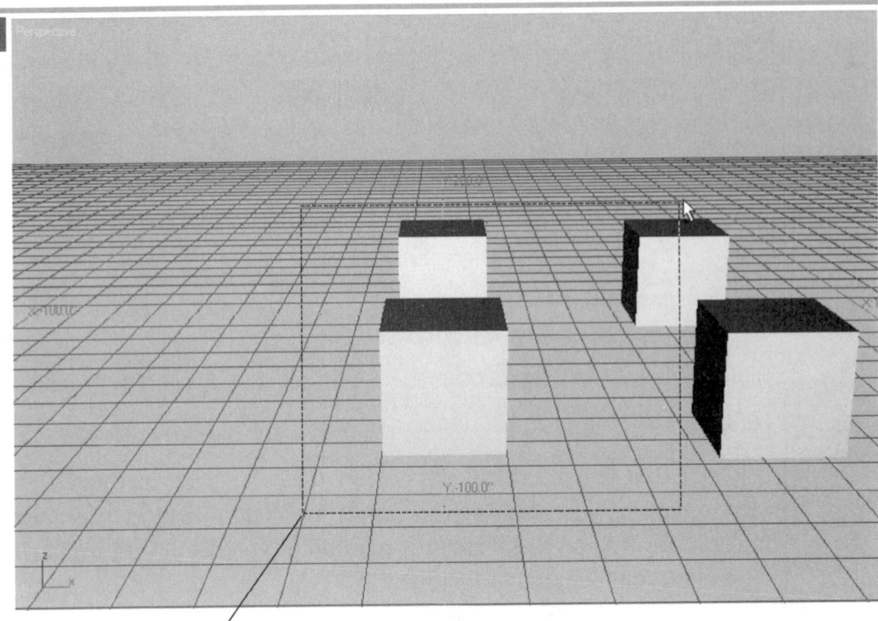
Click here to start the selection window.

When you use the Window Selection mode, only objects that are completely within the selected window are selected. Unlike the crossing window, objects that are partially inside the selected window are left out of the selection.

If the need arises, you can use the Ctrl key in conjunction with a window or crossing selection to continue to add more objects to your selection set.

1. Ctrl-click a point above and to the left of the cube in the upper right of the viewport, as shown in Figure 1.12.
2. Drag the window down and to the right so that it completely encloses the two cubes to the right and release the mouse button. Now all four cubes are selected. You can also remove objects from your selection set by using the Ctrl key with a window or crossing selection.
3. Hold down the Ctrl key and then place a window around the cube in the upper right of the screen, as shown in Figure 1.13.

FIGURE 1.12

Adding objects to your selection set using the Ctrl key and a window

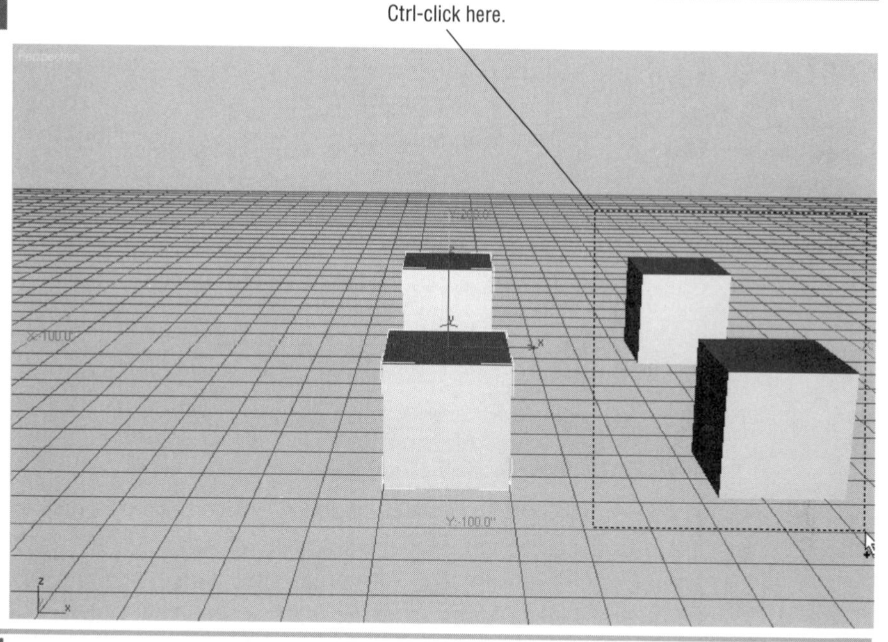
Ctrl-click here.

FIGURE 1.13

Removing an object using the Ctrl key and a window

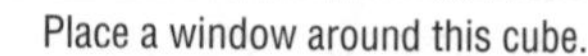
Place a window around this cube.

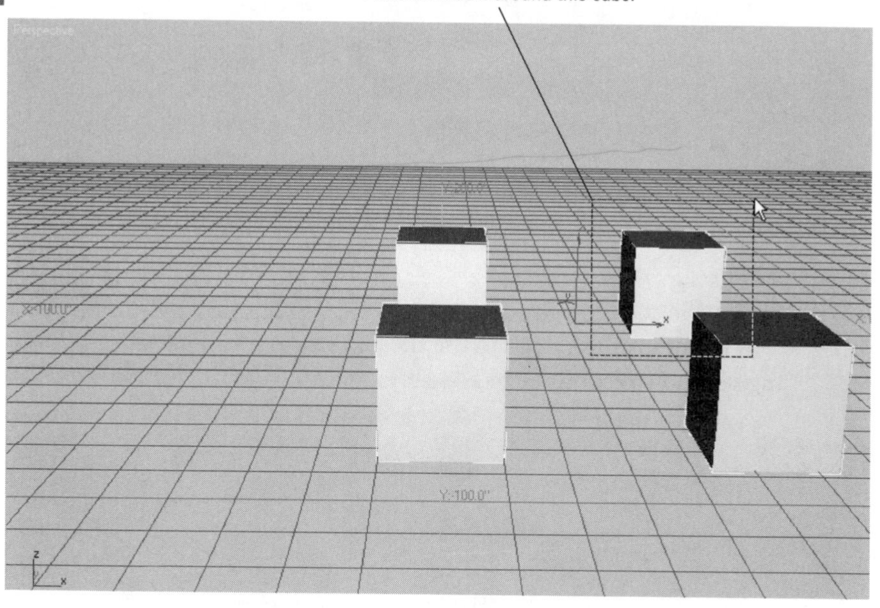

TIP When you've got several objects in close proximity to each other, and you only want to select certain objects within the group, you can Ctrl-click single objects to add or remove them from a selection set.

Right now, you've only got a few objects in your model, but as your model develops, you'll find that selecting objects in a crowded model becomes more of a challenge. Knowing about the different selection modes you've just used will go a long way toward making your work easier.

There is one more selection method you'll want to know about that is an invaluable tool as your model becomes more complex. You can select objects by their names, using the Select Objects dialog box. The following is a quick exercise that will introduce you to this important tool.

1. Click the Select by Name tool in the standard toolbar.

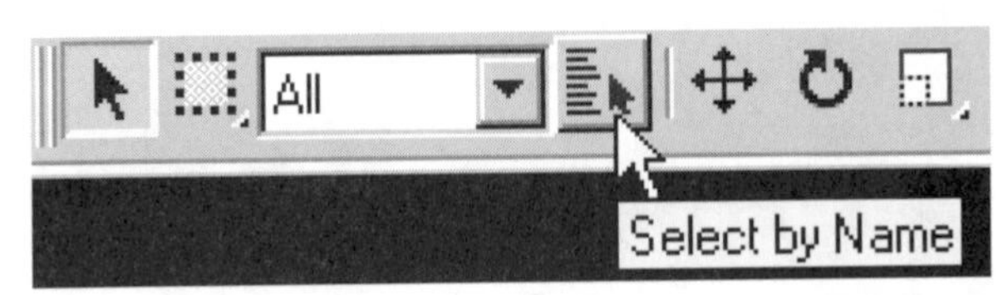

The Select Objects dialog box displays. Notice that a list displays, showing the names of the objects in your drawing. Right now, the list shows the default names given to the objects by VIZ. You can always change the name of an object in the Command Panel. (You can rename an object on every tab except Utilities.)

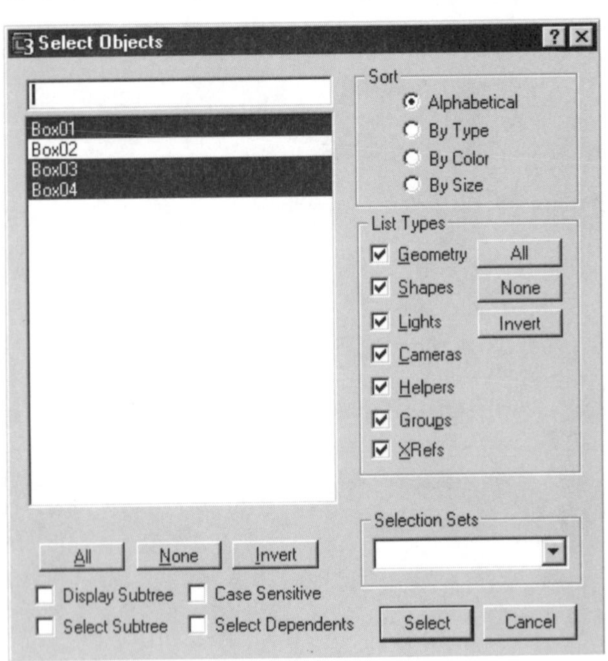

2. Click the None button at the bottom of the dialog box. This clears the selection set.
3. Click Box02 and then Ctrl-click the Box04 listing in the list of object names. The listing lets you select multiple names as you would in a typical Windows list

box. You can shift-click to select a group of adjacent names, or Ctrl-click to select a group of individual names.

4. Click the Select button. The two boxes are selected.

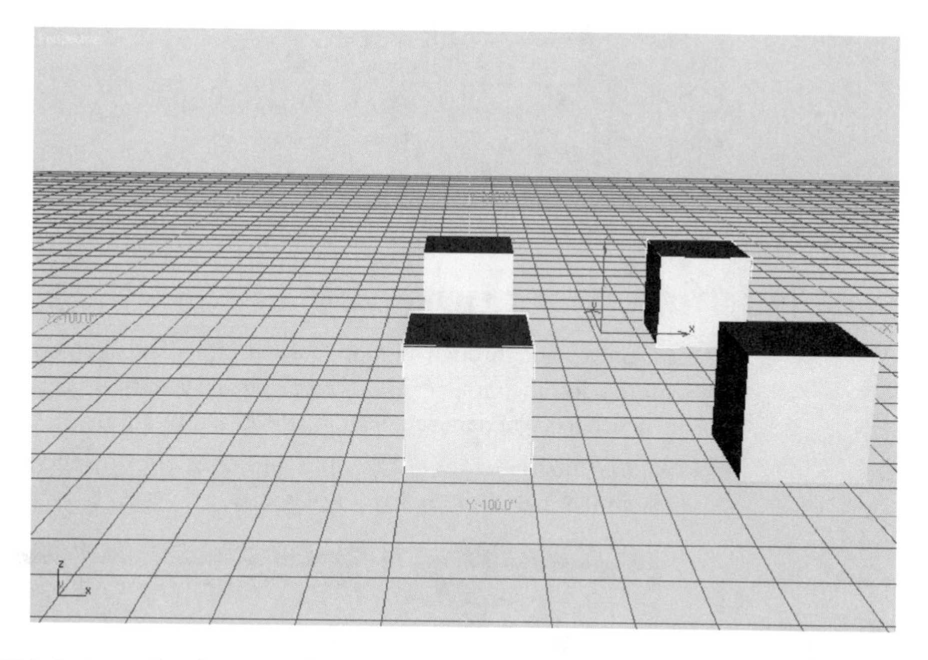

This last exercise shows you how to select objects based on their names, but it also indirectly shows you the importance of the names of objects. Giving objects meaningful names helps you locate and select them more easily, especially in a crowded model. You have several opportunities for naming objects. If you don't give an object a meaningful name at first, it's easy enough to change it later on. You can see here that 3D Studio is a parametric object-oriented program (unlike AutoCAD), because every object has its own name. Each object has its own parameters that can be accessed from the Modify panel.

Whenever you create an object in 3D Studio VIZ, you have the opportunity to give the new object a name. If you don't indicate a new name, VIZ gives the new object a name for you. If the new object is a copy of an existing one, the new name that VIZ provides is the name of the original object, with a number appended to its name. You can easily change the name of an object by selecting the object and then entering a new name in the object name input box at the top of the tab. (Objects can be named and renamed in every panel except for Utilities.)

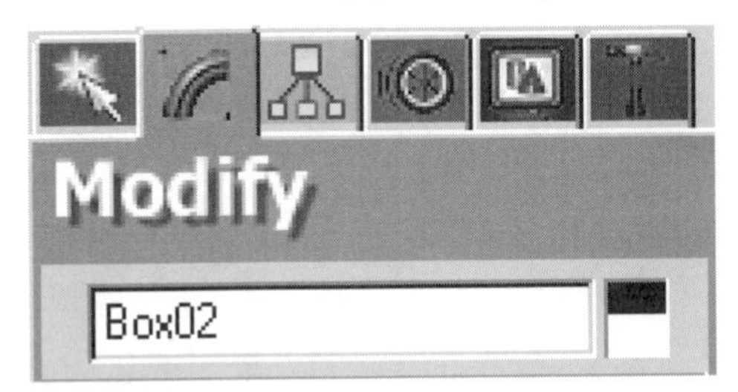

Naming Selection Sets

Suppose you've gone through a lot of effort selecting a set of objects, and you know you will want to select the same set of objects again at a later time. VIZ offers the Selection toolbar, which lets you name a selection set for later recall. Here's how it works.

1. Right-click the standard toolbar and then click Selection from the pop-up menu. The Selection toolbar displays.

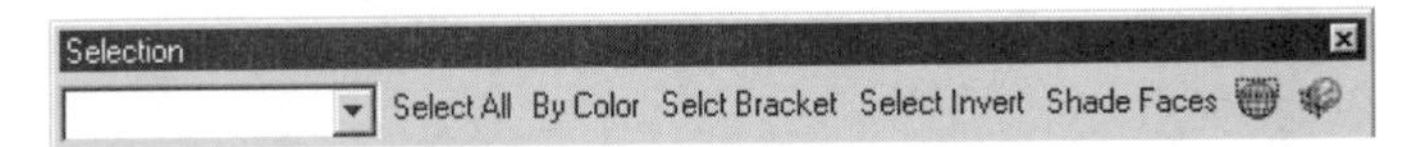

2. Make sure two of the cubes are selected. It doesn't really matter which two, because you're just practicing using the Selection toolbar.
3. Click inside the Selection input box to the far left of the Selection toolbar.
4. Type the name **Sample**↵. You've just given the current selection set a name. (By the way, the name you enter for selection sets is limited to 15 characters.)
5. Click in a blank area of the viewport to clear the current selection set.
6. In the Selection toolbar, Click on the downward-pointing arrow to the right of the Selection input box. Select Sample. The two boxes you selected earlier are now the current selection set.

In these early stages of learning VIZ, the concept of named selection sets may seem simple, but it's one tool you'll likely be using quite a bit as you expand your skills.

Editing Named Selection Sets

Named selection sets are not fixed in stone. You can add to or subtract from them, or you can delete them entirely through the Edit Named Selections dialog box.

1. Open the Edit Named Selections dialog box by choosing Tools ➢ Edit Named Selection.

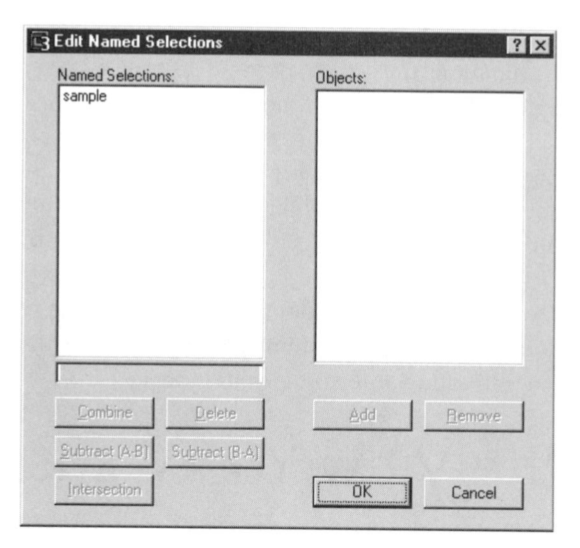

2. Click the name Sample in the Named Selections list on the left side of the dialog box. In the Objects list box to the right, you see a list of objects included in the Sample selection set.
3. Click the Add button. The Add to Named Selection dialog box displays.

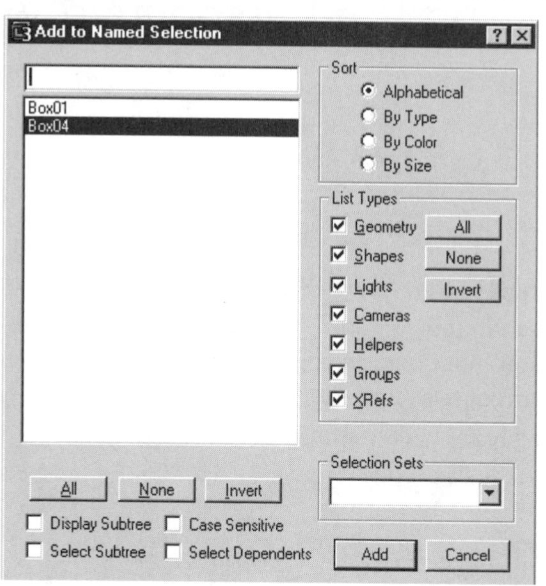

4. Select one of the names in the list and click Add. The name you selected now appears in the Objects list in the Edit Named Selections dialog box.
5. Click OK to close the dialog box. Select Sample from the Selection toolbar drop-down list to refresh the selection. Now you see that three of the cubes are selected.

The dialog box you saw in step 3 is identical to the Select Objects dialog box you saw earlier, and it functions the same way. You select the name of the object you wish to add to the named selection set from the list on the left. Notice that the list contains only the names of objects that are not currently a part of the named selection set.

You've now seen most of the selection tools you'll need to get started with VIZ. There are a few other selection tools you'll learn about as you work with VIZ, plus you'll get a chance to apply the tools you've learned so far as you start to build and edit 3D models in later chapters.

In the next section, you'll learn about the tools that enable you to view your model from different angles, and most importantly, you'll learn how these different views can aid you in creating and editing your model.

Getting the View You Want

So far in this chapter, you've done all of your work without making any modifications to the point of view of your model. Now let's take a look at ways you can control your view. Understanding the viewport controls is essential for manipulating objects in your model, so take some time to become familiar with all of the tools in this section.

Understanding the Perspective Viewing Tools

If you look at the viewport tools in the lower right corner of the VIZ window, you'll see some tools that are common among most graphics programs. These include the magnifying glass and the hand. Other tools in this area may be a bit more mysterious. In this section, you'll learn how these tools let you get around in your model.

Panning and Zooming Your View

Let's start by looking at the tool with the hand icon, known as the Pan tool. Like similar tools in other programs, the Pan tool displaces your view up or down, or to the left or right. But in VIZ's perspective viewport, you are also changing your point of view. Do the following to see what this means.

1. Click the Pan tool.

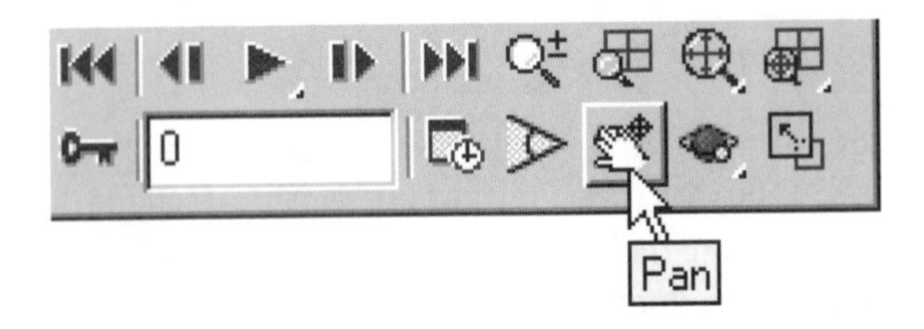

2. Click and drag the viewport to the left and upward until the cubes are roughly centered in the viewport.

3. Click and drag the viewport in a circular fashion. Notice that your view of the model appears to change as if you were moving sideways while looking at the cubes.

Next, try the Zoom tool.

1. Click the Zoom tool.

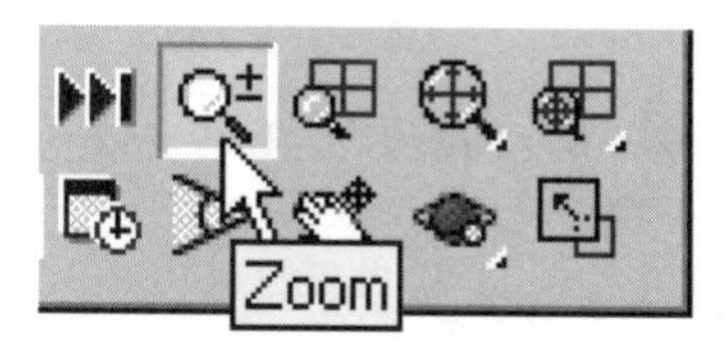

2. Click and drag the Zoom tool upward from the center of the viewport. Notice how you appear to get closer to the cubes.
3. Click and drag the cursor downward in the viewport. Now you appear to be moving away from the cubes.
4. Continue to click and drag downward until your view looks similar to the one shown in Figure 1.14.

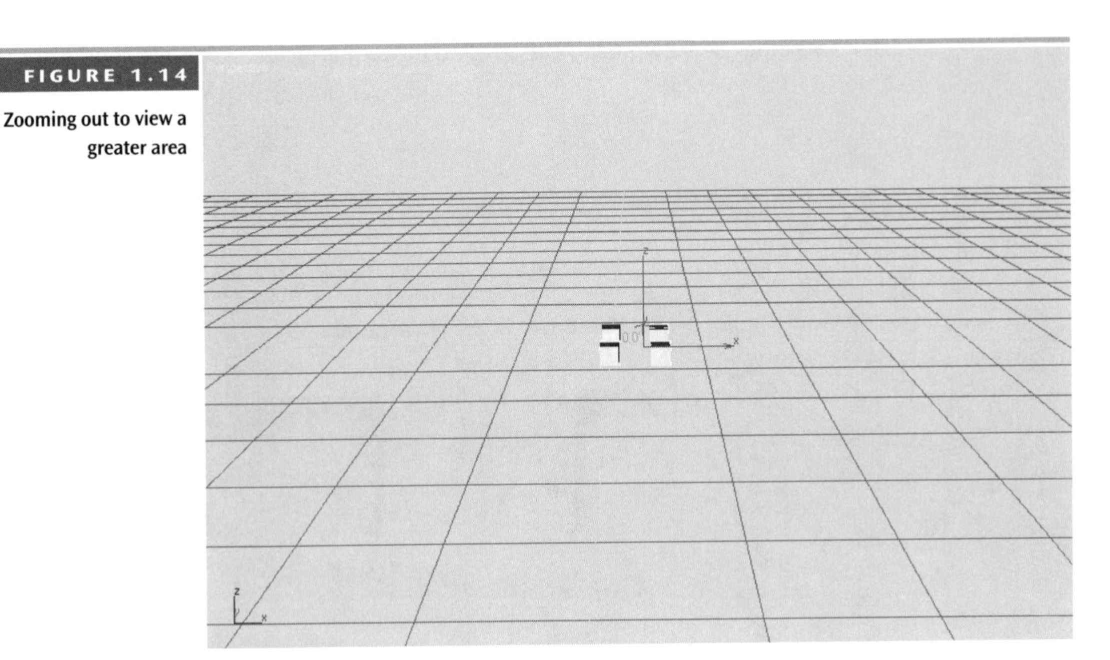

FIGURE 1.14

Zooming out to view a greater area

Again, as with other graphics programs, the Zoom tool enlarges or reduces your view. In VIZ's perspective viewport, the Zoom tool has the effect of moving you closer to or farther away from the objects in your model.

You may have also noticed that, as you moved farther away, the grid became denser. Then at a certain point, the grid changed to a wider interval. VIZ does this so that the grid doesn't overwhelm the view when it becomes too dense.

Now suppose you don't like the last view change you made and you want to go back to the previous view. Try the following to return to the previous view.

1. Choose View ➢ Undo View Zoom. You return to the previous view. (You may also press Shift-Z.)
2. Choose View ➢ Undo View Zoom or press Shift-Z again. Your view returns to the view prior to the last view.
3. Choose View ➢ Undo Pan. You return to the view you had before you panned your view.

The View ➢ Undo View command lets you step back to a previous view in case the last view change you made is one you don't like. View ➢ Undo undoes any view change, regardless of which viewport tool you used last.

WARNING View Undo should not be confused with the Edit ➢ Undo command. Edit ➢ Undo undoes creation and editing operations but not view changes.

Saving a View You Like

If you happen to get a view that you know you want to go back to later, you can save a view with the View ➢ Save Active command from the menu bar. Use it next to save a view that you'll return to later in this chapter. And, as you'll see in Chapter 6, you can also create a camera object and align it to a view.

1. Click the Zoom Extents tool to set up your view for the next exercise. Zoom Extents causes the viewport to display the entire model.

2. Now save this view by choosing View ➢ Save Active Perspective View.

The Zoom Extents tool repositions your view so that the entire model just fits within the viewport, filling the viewport as much as possible. If you're an AutoCAD user, you are familiar with this tool, because its counterpart in AutoCAD performs the same function.

WARNING You can restore the default perspective view (the one you see when you open a new file) in a blank file by clicking the Zoom Extents tool or by choosing File ➢ Reset to reset the design.

Changing Your Viewing Angle

There are two other tools that are specifically designed for viewing 3D objects. The Field-of-View tool changes your field of view. It appears to do the same thing as the Zoom tool, but as you'll see in the following exercise, there is a significant difference between the Zoom and Field-of-View tools. You can think of the Field-of-View tool as a zoom lens on a camera, but the Zoom tool is like physically moving closer or farther away from an object. The Field-of-View tool has the potential of distorting your view just as a super-wide-angle fisheye lens or super telephoto lens tends to distort a photograph. Then there is the Arc Rotate Selected tool, which lets you rotate your view around a selected object. First, let's start with the Field-of-View tool.

1. Save the current view by choosing View ➢ Save Active Perspective View. This lets us return to the current view later on.
2. Click the Field-of-View tool.

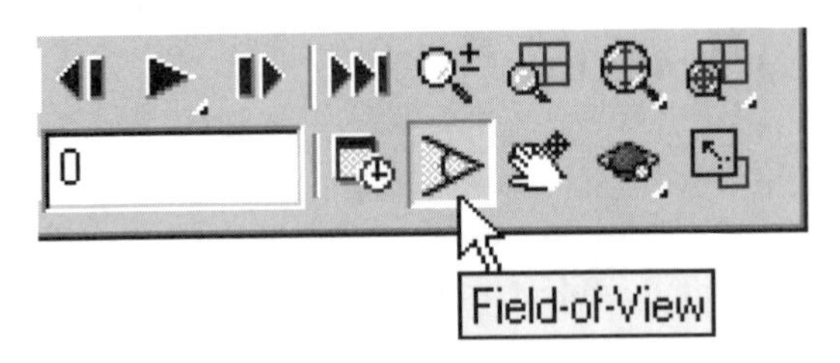

3. Place the cursor in the viewport and click and drag downward until your view looks similar to Figure 1.15.

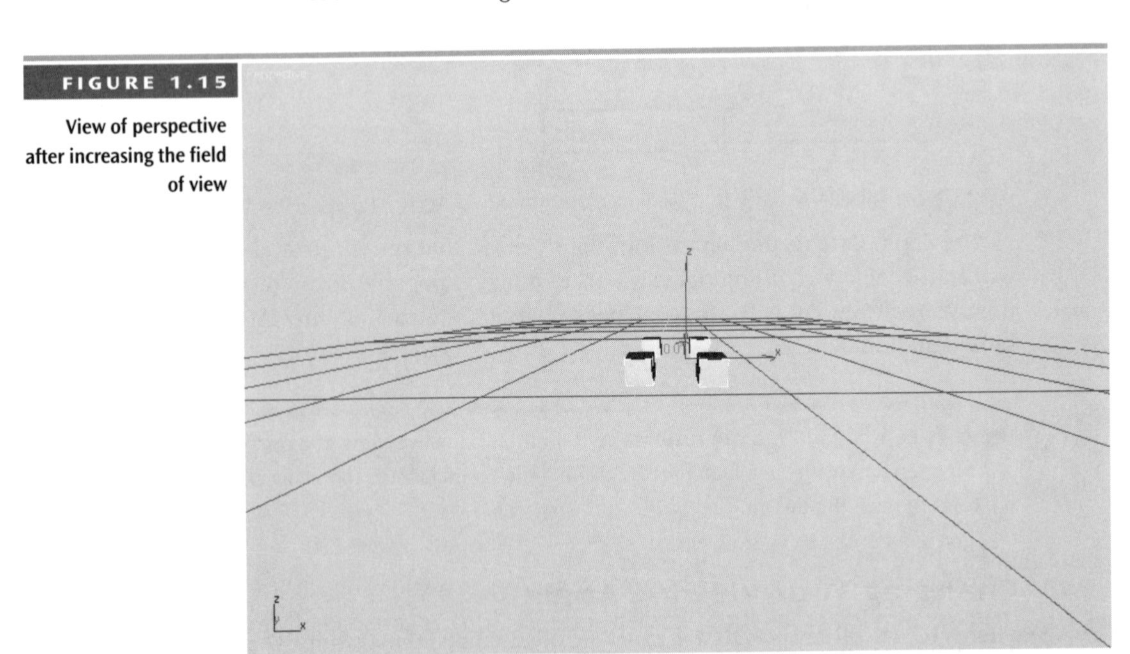

FIGURE 1.15

View of perspective after increasing the field of view

In one sense, it appears as though you've zoomed out from the cubes, but if you compare this view to the zoomed-out view in the previous exercise, you notice a difference.

When you use the Zoom tool in the perspective viewport, your view changes as though you were physically moving closer or farther away from the cubes. As the name implies, the Field-of-View tool widens or narrows your field of view, much as a zoom lens on a camera does. You're not actually changing the distance from the object, but instead you're changing the area your viewport displays. Until you find yourself in a situation where you really need to change the field of view, you may want to refrain from using the Field-of-View tool.

Now let's take a look at the Arc Rotate tool.

1. First, return to the view you had before you used the Field-of-View tool by selecting View ➢ Undo View Field-of-View.
2. Click the Select Object tool. Click in a blank space in the viewport to clear any selections that may be active. In the next exercise, you'll see why this is significant.
3. Click the Arc Rotate tool.

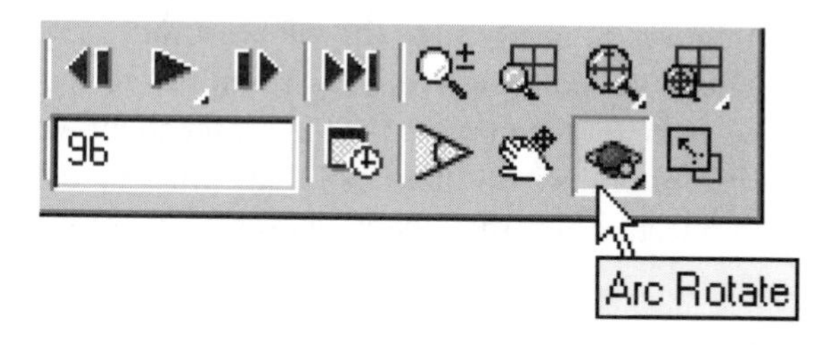

You see a green circle with squares at each of the four cardinal points on the circle. If you place the cursor inside the circle, the cursor looks like two ellipses overlapping each other.

4. Place the cursor on the square at the far left of the circle. Notice that the cursor changes shape to what looks like a horizontal ellipse.
5. With the cursor on the square, slowly click and drag the cursor to the right. Notice how the view rotates.
6. Place the cursor on the square at the top of the circle. Now the cursor changes to a vertically oriented ellipse.
7. With the cursor on the square, click and drag the cursor downward. The view now rotates in that direction.

The squares on the green circle are like handles that you can grab and turn to change your view orientation. The left and right squares constrain the rotation to the horizontal plane, and the top and bottom squares constrain the rotation to the vertical plane. If you prefer, you can adjust the view freely without constraint in the vertical or horizontal direction by clicking and dragging the cursor anywhere within the circle. You can also rotate the view by clicking and dragging anywhere outside the circle. The following exercise demonstrates these features. Pay attention to the shape of the cursor in each step.

1. Place the cursor anywhere within the circle; then slowly click and drag in a small, circular motion. Notice how the view changes as if your point of view were rotating around the group of cubes.
2. Place the cursor anywhere outside the circle; then slowly click and drag in an up-and-down motion. Now the view rotates around the circle as if you were tilting your head from side to side.

You may have noticed that the cursor changes, depending on whether you're inside or outside the circle. This gives you further cues regarding the way the Arc Rotate tool affects your view.

You've been introduced to nearly all of the viewport tools. There's one more feature of the Arc Rotate tools you'll want to know about before you move on. The Arc Rotate tool uses the center of the viewport as the center about which it rotates. VIZ offers two other versions of the Arc Rotate tool that allow you to select the center of rotation based on a selection. Try the following exercise to see how these variations work.

1. Choose View ➢ Restore Active Perspective View to restore the view you saved earlier.

2. Click the Select Object tool from the standard toolbar.
3. Click the cube in the left side in the back row.

4. Click and hold the Arc Rotate tool to open the flyout, then select the tool in the middle of the flyout. This is the Arc Rotate Selected tool.
5. Slowly click and drag the cursor within the circle. Notice how the view appears to be fixed at the center of the selected cube.
6. Slowly click and drag the cursor in a vertical motion outside the circle. The view appears to rotate around the selected cube.
7. Return to the saved view by choosing View ➢ Restore Active Perspective View.

NOTE The third tool at the bottom of the Arc Rotate flyout is the Arc Rotate SubObject tool. This tool rotates a view about a subobject level selection. You'll learn about subobject level editing in chapter 4.

By being able to select an object or set of objects as the center of rotation for your view, you are better able to set up your views for rendering or editing. The combination of Zoom, Pan, and the Arc Rotate tools allows you to obtain just about any view you may need as you work within VIZ's perspective viewport. But you aren't limited to a perspective view of your model. In fact, there are many situations where the perspective view is not ideal, especially when editing your model. In the next section, you'll look at other viewport types that give you greater flexibility in creating and editing objects in your model.

Using Multiple Viewports

So far, you've done all of your work in the Perspective viewport, but this isn't the only view you have available. You saw earlier how you can divide the VIZ window so that it displays four equal viewports, each representing a different view. Let's go back to that viewport arrangement to explore the uses of some of VIZ's display tools. The first item you'll look at is the way that the Field of View tool changes when your active viewport changes.

1. Click the Min/Max Toggle tool in the set of Viewport navigation controls. VIZ's window changes to display four viewports.

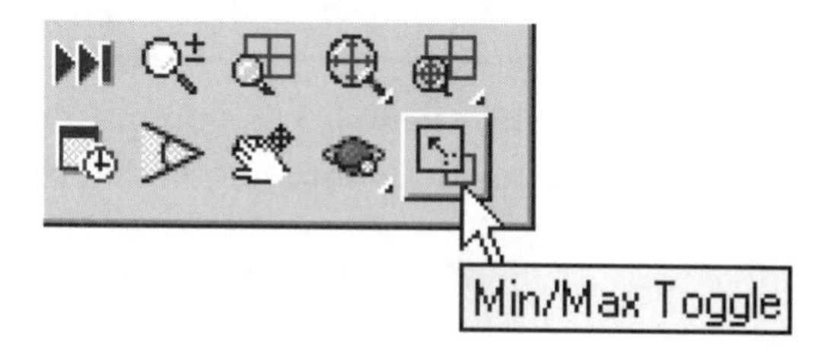

2. Click anywhere in the viewport labeled Top in the upper left corner of the display. Notice that the Field-of-View tool changes to a magnifying glass with a rectangle. This is the Region Zoom tool.

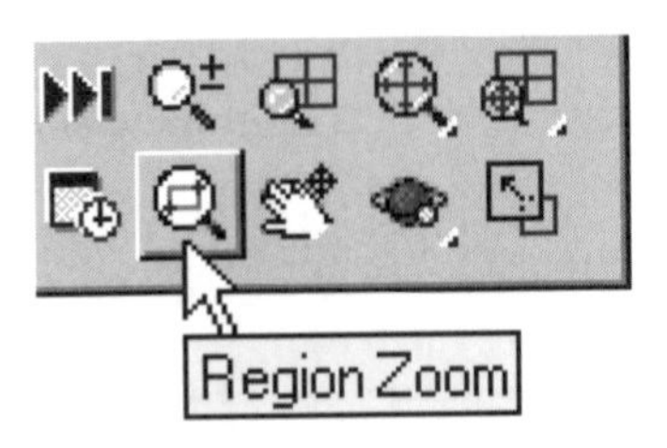

Also notice that the Top viewport now shows a thick border around it, indicating that it is the current active viewport.

3. Click the Region Zoom tool.
4. Click and drag on a point below and to the left of the cubes as shown in Figure 1.16. As you drag the cursor, you see a rectangle appear. Don't let go of the cursor just yet.
5. Position the rectangle above and to the right of the bottom row of cubes as shown in Figure 1.16 and then release the mouse button. The view enlarges to the region you just indicated with the Region Zoom tool.

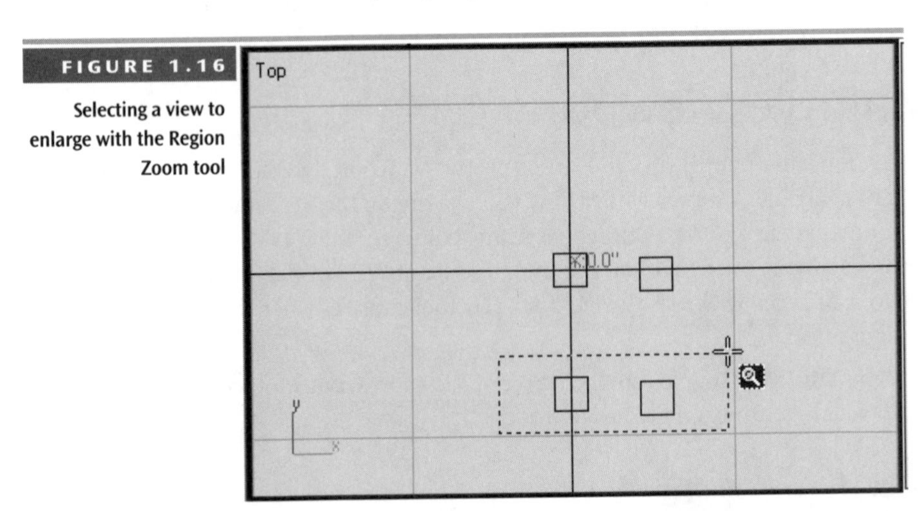

FIGURE 1.16 Selecting a view to enlarge with the Region Zoom tool

The Region Zoom tool acts like the magnifying tools in many other graphics programs. Also, the Zoom and Pan tools perform the same functions in orthogonal views in VIZ as they do in other programs, allowing you to zoom in and pan over the view.

You may have noticed two other tools in the Viewport navigation controls that haven't been discussed yet. They are the Zoom All and Zoom Extents All tools. Now that you have multiple viewports displayed, you can try out these two tools.

1. Click the Zoom All tool.

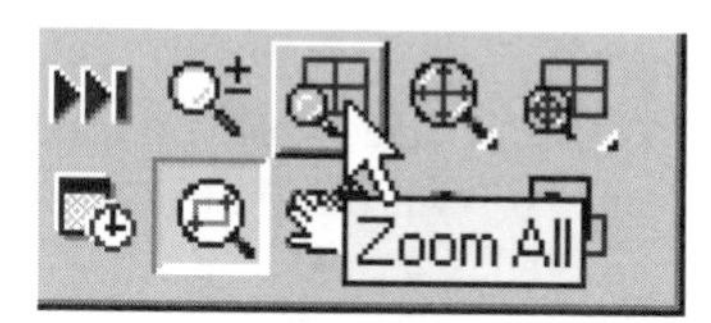

2. In any viewport, click and drag the cursor upward. Notice that the view in all of the viewports is enlarged to take in as much of the four cubes as can be displayed.
3. Click and drag the cursor downward and the views expand to show more of the model area.
4. Click the Zoom Extents All tool.

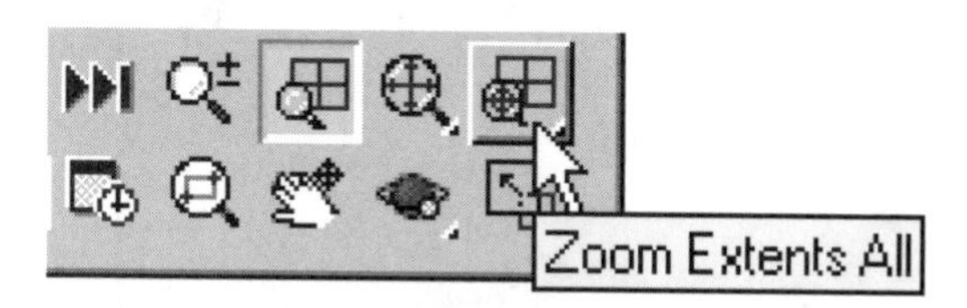

All of the viewports change to show enlarged views of the cubes.

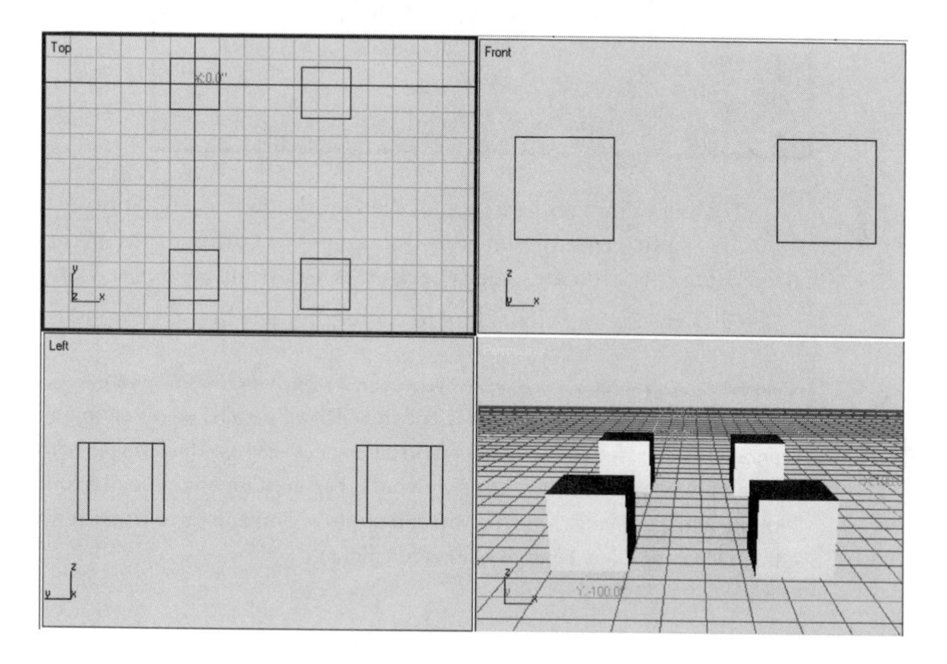

Although not as frequently used as the other viewport navigation tools, the Zoom All tool and Zoom Extents All tool can be helpful when you need to adjust the overall view of your model in multiple viewports.

You should be aware that the Arc Rotate Selected tool you used in the Perspective viewport also works in the other viewports. Try it out on the Top viewport in the next exercise.

1. Click the Arc Rotate Selected tool.
2. Click and drag from the center of the Top viewport upward and to the right so it shows a view similar to Figure 1.17.

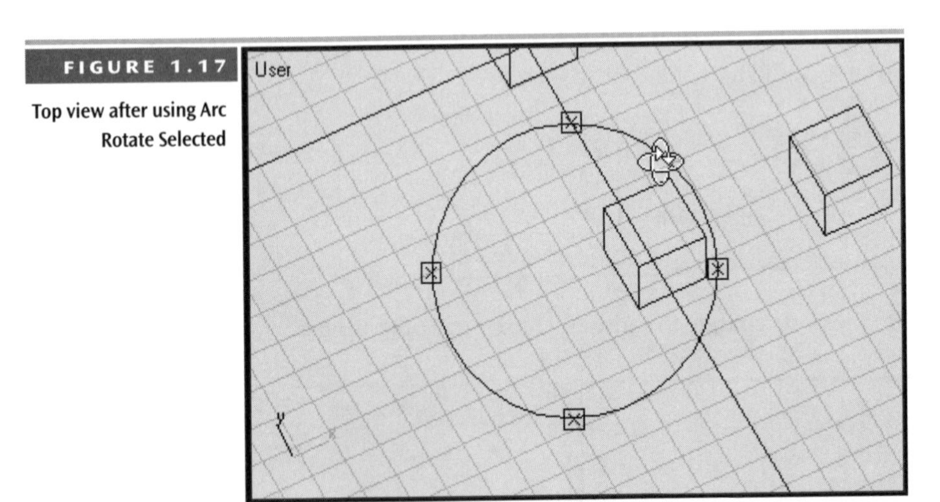

FIGURE 1.17

Top view after using Arc Rotate Selected

The view changes to a type of 3D view known as an axonometric projection. Also notice that the label in the upper left corner of the viewport now reads User. This indicates that the view is a custom view based on your changes.

3. Click the Zoom Extents tool to center the view in the viewport.

NOTE An axonometric view is one in which all parallel edges of an object are shown parallel as opposed to convergent as in a perspective view. The familiar isometric view is a type of axonometric view. User viewports can contain any type of axonometric view. Unlike Perspective viewports, you can apply region zooms to User viewports, making them ideal for many types of editing functions.

The 3D view in the upper left corner of the display differs in many ways from the perspective view you've been working with. But, as you'll see in the next section, it's different only because a few of the settings for that viewport are different from those of the perspective viewport.

Changing the Viewport Display and Configuration

If you compare the User viewport with the Perspective viewport, you notice two things that are different. First, as mentioned in the previous exercise, the User viewport shows a 3D orthographic projection. The second difference is that the User viewport is not shaded. The cubes are displayed as simple line outlines called a wireframe view. These display characteristics can be modified for each viewport.

In the following exercise, you'll see how you can alter viewport settings to obtain specific view characteristics such as shading and perspective.

1. Right click the User label in the upper right corner of the User viewport. A pop-up menu displays.

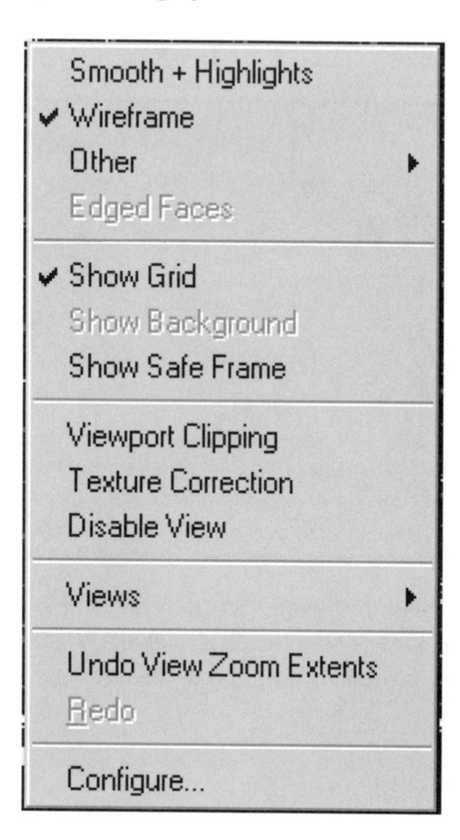

2. Select Smooth + Highlights from the menu. The cubes now appear shaded, just as they do in the Perspective viewport.

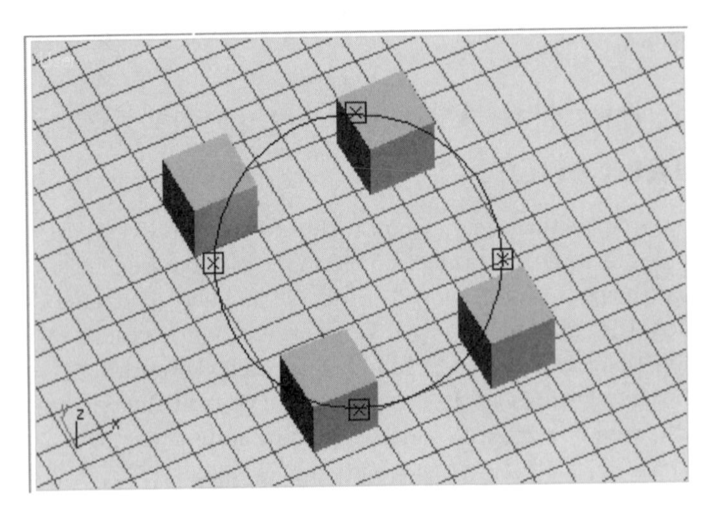

3. Right-click the Perspective viewport label. Then select Wireframe from the pop-up menu. The perspective view changes to a wireframe representation.

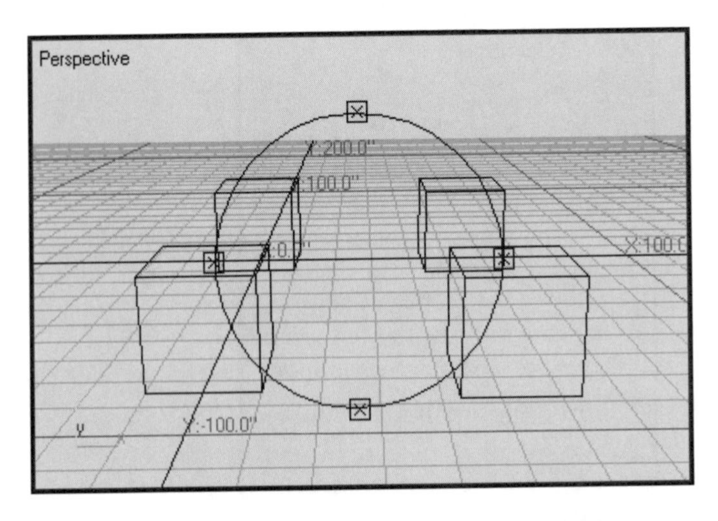

Notice that the pop-up menu is the same for both the User and Perspective viewports. This menu gives you control over the display characteristics of the viewport. Try out a few other options in the Viewport pop-up menu.

1. Right-click the User label and then select View ➢ Perspective. The user view changes to a perspective view. Notice that the label changes to read Perspective, so that you now have two Perspective viewports.

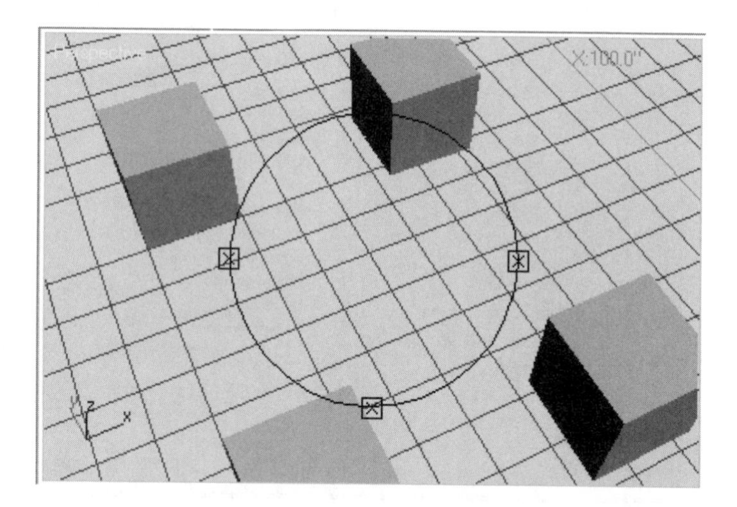

2. Right-click the Perspective label of the upper left viewport, then select View ➢ Top. The view now changes back to the original top view. Notice that the cubes are still shaded.
3. Right-click the Top label and select Wireframe. The view returns to its original state.

Now all of the viewports show wireframe views of the cubes. Wireframe views are often better for many types of editing operations. Wireframes also redraw faster when your model is very large and full of complex geometry. Another type of view called Bounding Box is even faster than Wireframe views, but Bounding Box views reduce the representation of objects to rectangular boxes.

Besides changing the way the viewport displays your model, Wireframe also gives you control over the layout of the viewports themselves. The following exercise shows you the variety of layouts you can create in VIZ.

1. Choose View ➢ configure... The Viewport Configuration dialog box displays.

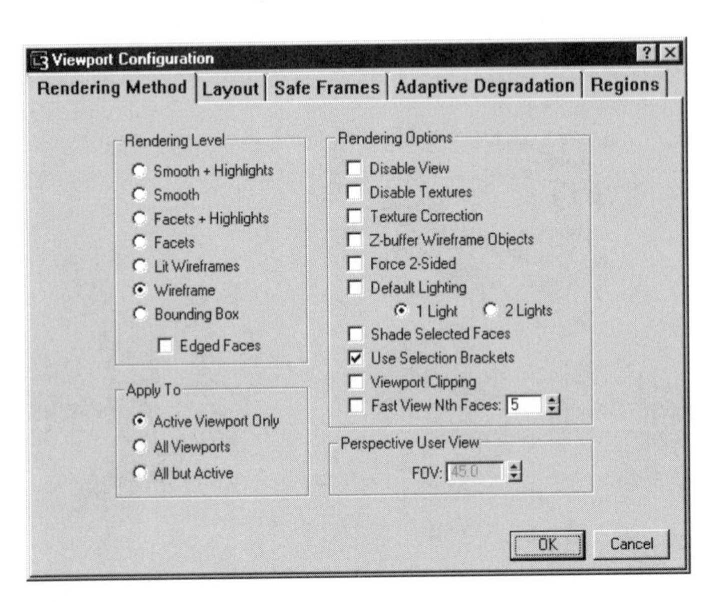

2. Click the Layout tab. You see the current viewport layout along with a set of predefined layouts above.

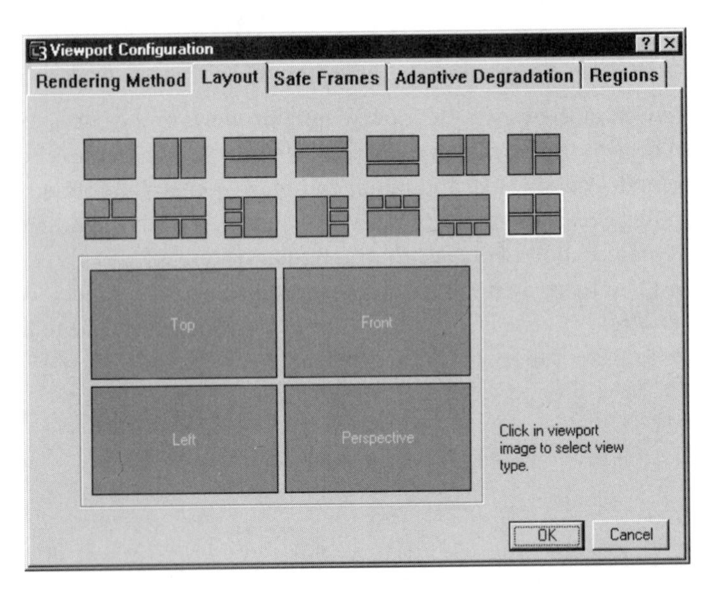

3. Click the layout that looks like three small rectangles stacked on the left side with one large rectangle on the right.

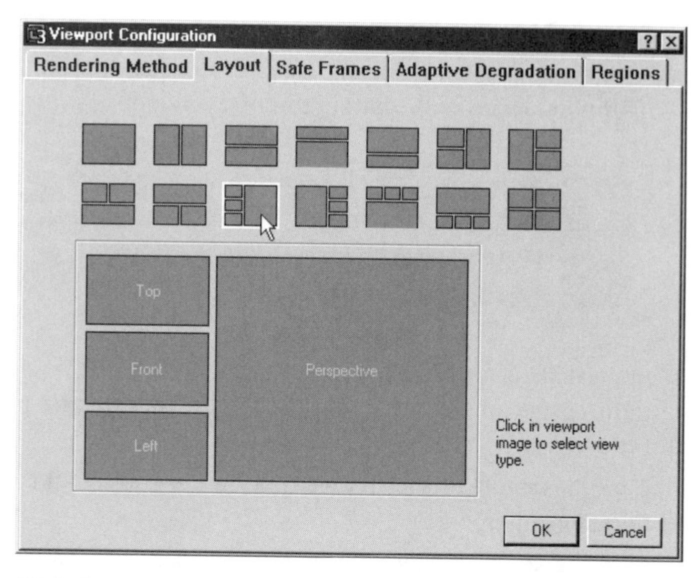

4. Click OK. The viewports change to the selected layout.

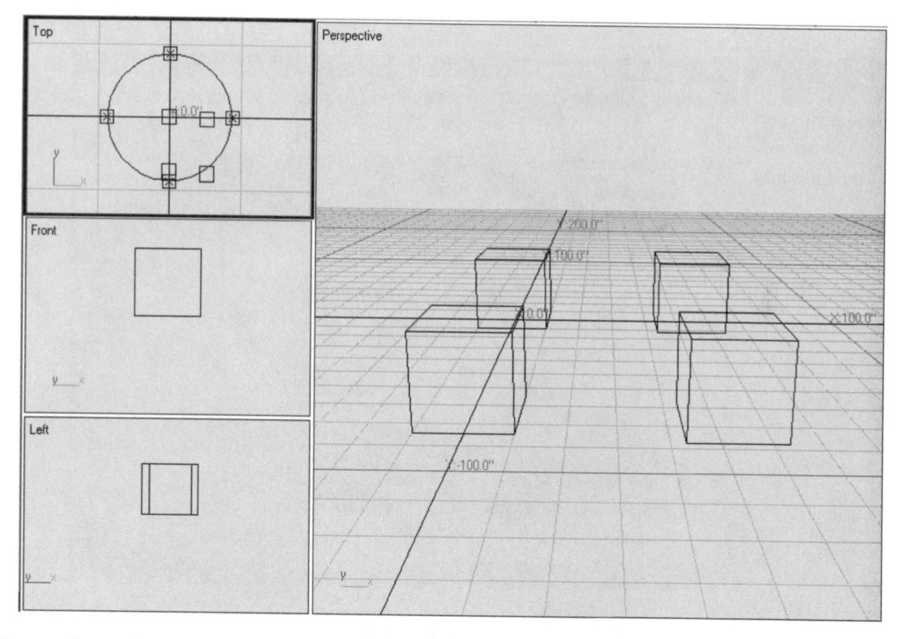

Users of previous versions of VIZ may find this layout more comfortable than before. It has been the default layout for a few of the 3D Studio Max and VIZ versions.

You aren't limited to the *canned* layouts either. You may decide that you want the layout to reflect a more traditional mechanical drawing layout with a top, front, and right side view. Here's how you can set up such a viewport arrangement.

1. Choose View ➢ Configure...
2. With the Layout tab selected, click the four equal viewports layout, which is the rightmost layout in the bottom row of layout options.

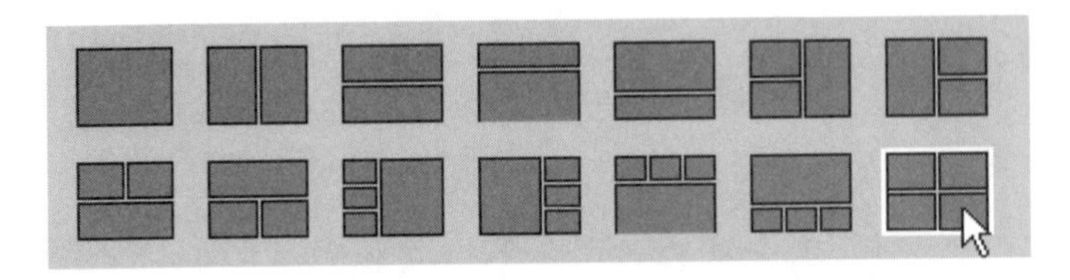

3. In the main layout graphic, click the sample viewport labeled Front in the upper right corner of the large sample layout; then in the pop-up menu, select Perspective.
4. Click the sample Perspective viewport in the lower right corner and select Right from the pop-up menu.
5. Click the sample left viewport in the lower left corner and select Front from the pop-up menu. The sample layout should look like Figure 1.18.

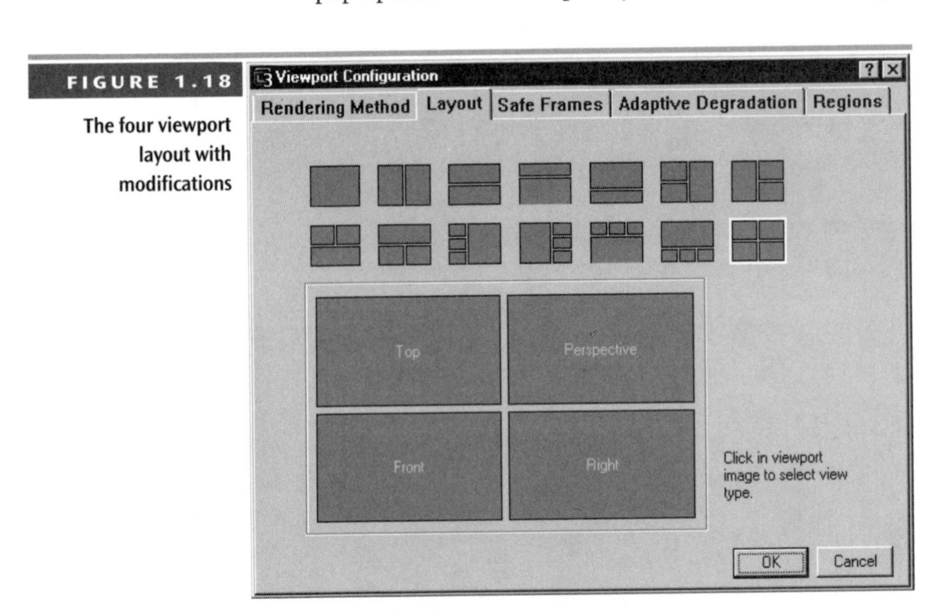

FIGURE 1.18

The four viewport layout with modifications

6. Click OK. Now you have a layout that shows the top, front, and right-side views, plus a perspective view arranged in a more traditional manner.

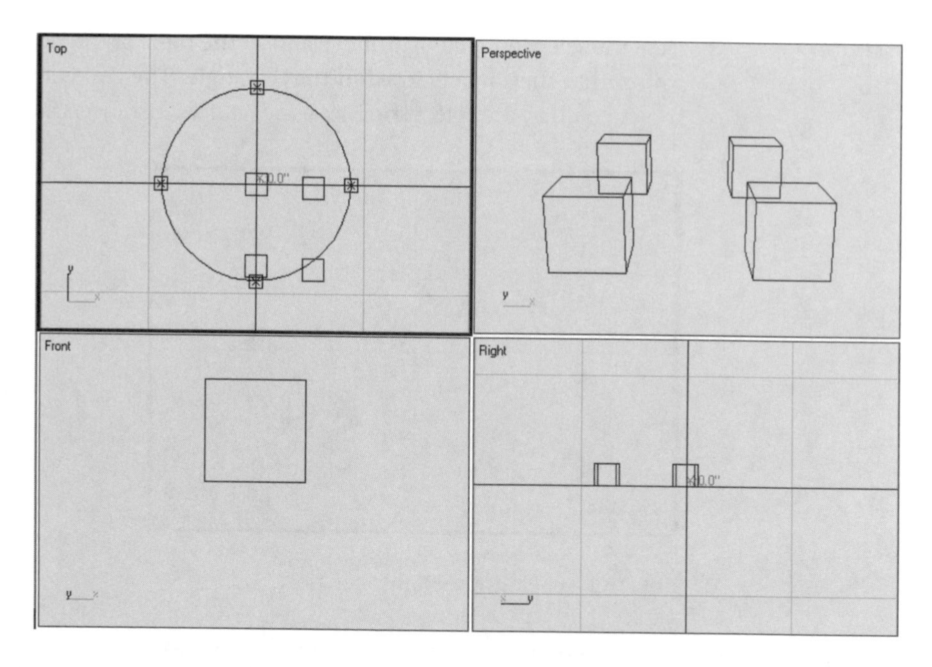

As you can see from what you've learned so far, 3D Studio VIZ has a wide array of display options, but most of the time you will stick to one viewport layout that you are comfortable with. For the purposes of this book, you'll use the default layout that shows the four equal size viewports.

Before you conclude your tour of VIZ interface, let's see how the Move tool acts in the non-perspective viewports. The following exercise will give you a feel for the ways that you can use multiple viewports to your advantage.

1. Click the Select and Move tool.
2. In the Top viewport, click and drag from a point below and to the left of the bottom row of cubes.

3. Drag the selection rectangle above and to the right of the two cubes in the lower row so that they are enclosed in the rectangle. The two cubes are selected. This shows you that the Select and Move tool can select objects as well as move them.

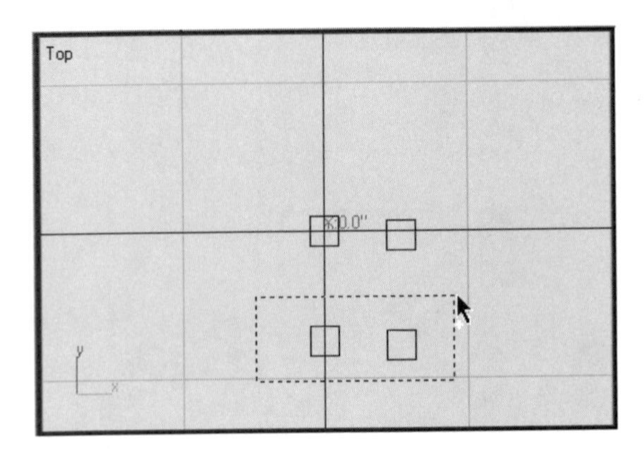

4. Now right-click in the Right viewport.

TIP By right-clicking in a viewport, you can make it active without disrupting any selections you may have active at the time.

5. In the Right viewport, click and drag the green Y arrow upward. Notice how the cubes move in the front and perspective views as you do this.
6. Position the cubes so they are about half the height of a cube higher than their original position.
7. Click and drag the red X axis of the cubes to the right of the screen so they merge with the cube to the right, as shown here.

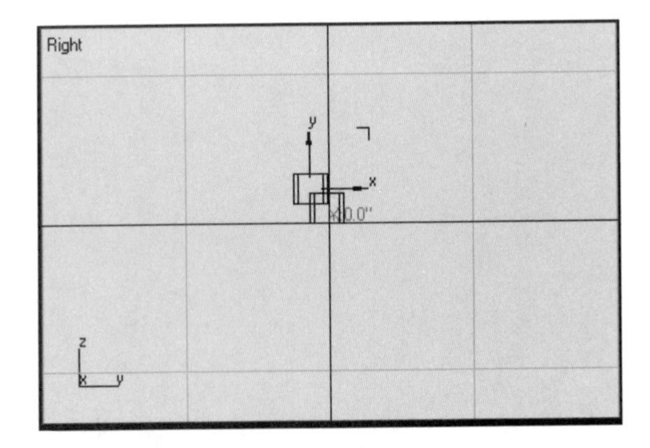

8. You can save this file or discard it. You won't need it any more.

In this exercise, you've seen a number of methods in action. First, the Select and Move tool can be used to select objects as well as move them. This can help you quickly move objects by reducing the number of clicks. You'll want to be a bit careful, however, as you can easily select and move the wrong object when you're in a hurry.

You also saw how you can right-click in a viewport to make it active. Had you simply clicked in the Right viewport in step 4, you would have lost the selection set you created in step 3.

Finally, you saw how objects in VIZ do not conform to one of the basic rules of physics: In the physical world, two objects *cannot* occupy the same space at the same time. In VIZ more than one object *can* occupy the same space at the same time. This characteristic can be useful in a number of ways as you build models in 3D Studio VIZ.

Summary

In this introduction to 3D Studio VIZ, you've learned how to use the many different tools available in VIZ. You saw how some work in familiar ways, while others, like the spinners and rollouts, are a slight departure from other typical Windows programs. You were also introduced to some of the basic object creation and editing methods in VIZ. These basic methods are the foundation on which you will build your skills in this program.

You've covered a lot of ground in this first chapter. Don't worry if you can't remember everything. You'll be exposed to many of these tools frequently as you work through the following chapters. In the next chapter, you'll take a closer look at how objects are created and edited.

chapter 2

Introducing VIZ Objects

FEATURING

- *Understanding Standard Primitives*
- *Molding Standard Primitives with Modifiers*
- *Making Clones that Share Properties*
- *Looking at Extended Primitives*

Introducing VIZ Objects

If you've never used a 3D modeling program before, you may find the behavior of objects in VIZ to be rather unusual. Objects in VIZ are very dynamic and malleable, and they can be fairly complex. 3D Studio, in particular, has an unusual way of allowing you to edit shapes. In this chapter, you'll get an introduction to the ways that you can create and form objects, and in the process, you'll see that you can get just about any shape from just a handful of basic object types.

Most 3D modeling programs typically offer basic building blocks called *primitives*. Primitives are basic shapes on which you can build to form your model. VIZ offers two types of primitives from which you can start to build forms: Standard Primitives and Splines. Let's start off by looking at Standard Primitives. We'll get to Splines in Chapter 3.

Understanding Standard Primitives

In Chapter 1, you used the Create tab of the Command Panel to create a cube. Take another look at the command panel to see what else it has to offer.

1. Start 3D Studio VIZ.
2. Click the Create tab in the Command Panel.

3. Click the Geometry button just under the Create tab label.

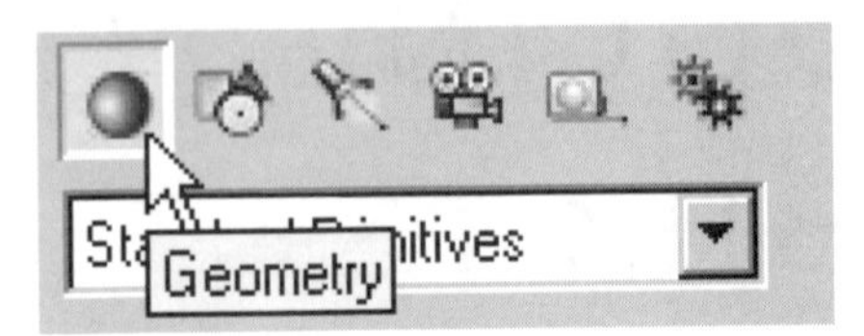

NOTE **Notice that there is a list box that displays the name Standard Primitives just below the Create tools. There are other types of objects that you can use by selecting them from the list box. For now, you'll concentrate on the Standard Primitives.**

You see a rollout called Object Type that contains the Standard Primitives. You've already used the primitive type box in Chapter 1.

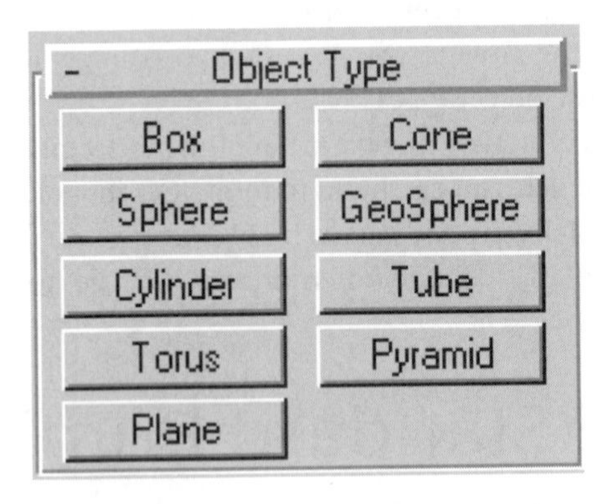

There are eight other object types, shown in Figure 2.1. To create any of these primitives, you use a method that is similar to the one you used to create the cube in Chapter 1.

FIGURE 2.1

A view showing all of the Standard Primitives

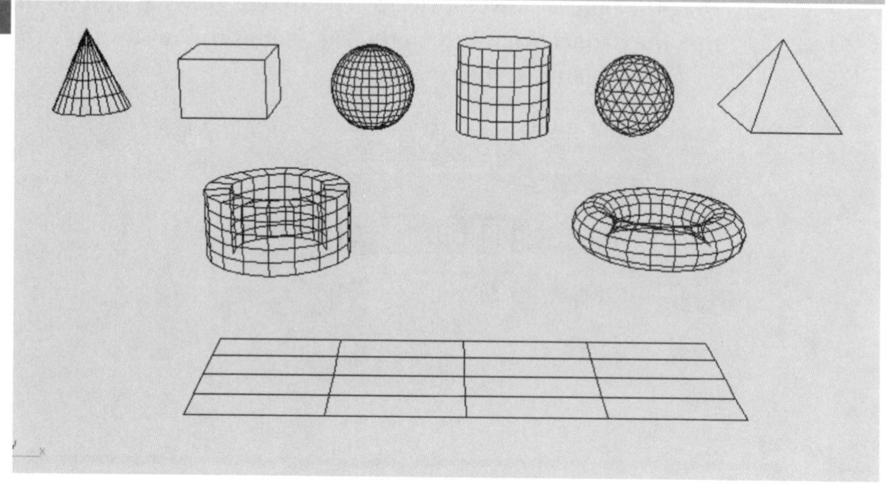

To create a box, you first click and hold inside the viewport to establish one corner of the base of the box, then drag and release the mouse button to select the other corner of the base. You then adjust the height of the box by moving the mouse. When you've found the height you want, you click the mouse again. In short, you clicked and dragged to determine the base dimension, then clicked to establish the height. To create a sphere, you click and hold to set the center point of the sphere, then drag and release to set the radius. Try it out in this exercise.

1. In the Object Type rollout, click the Sphere tool.

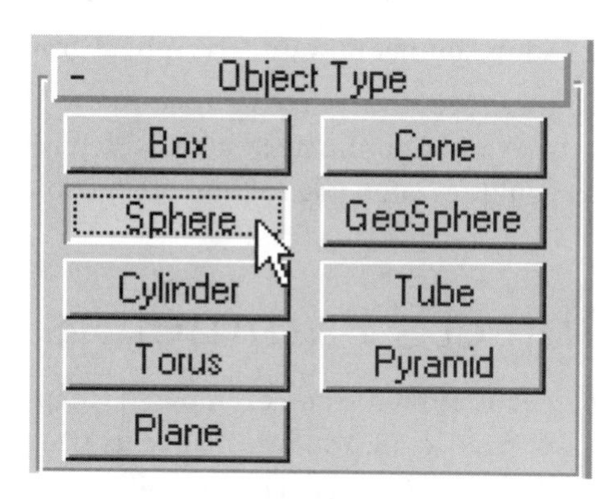

2. Click and hold in the viewport near the origin.

3. Drag the mouse slowly forward. The sphere grows as you do this. Also notice that the Radius input box in the Parameters rollout displays the radius of the sphere as you move your mouse.

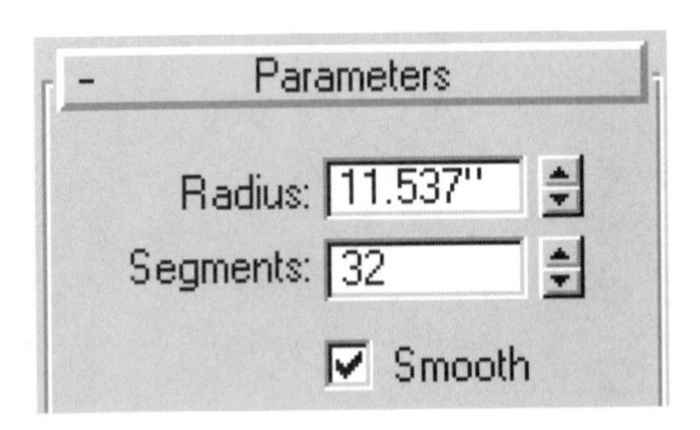

NOTE **If the parameters rollout does not display dimensions in feet and inches, then set the Units Setup dialog box for US Standards with Decimal Inches as the Default Units. See the section *The Standard Menu Bar* in Chapter 1 if you're unsure about how to do this.**

4. Release the mouse to complete the sphere.

You may recall that you were able to adjust the parameters of the cube after you created it. You can do the same with the sphere.

1. Click the Radius input box in the Parameters rollout.
2. Type **6**(cr). The cube now has a 6-inch radius.
3. Click and drag the Radius spinner upward. The sphere grows in size.

Notice that, by default, VIZ places the sphere's center on the plane defined by the grid. The grid shows you the World Coordinate System, which is the main coordinate system for your model. As you'll see later, you can use other coordinate systems as you need them.

Adjusting an Object's Parameters

You can see from the sphere (and from the box example in Chapter 1) that the shape of a standard primitive is not fixed at all. You can change its size and other properties using the tools available in the Command Panel. This ability to adjust the parameters of an object is referred to as *parametric modeling*. In a real sense, you don't actually have to be too accurate in your initial placement and creation of a primitive object, because you can refine its shape later by entering values in the parameters rollout.

Try modifying the sphere's other parameters to see the variety of shapes you can generate from just one type of object.

1. In the Parameters rollout, click the Radius input box, then enter **2'**(cr). This changes the radius of the sphere to 2 feet. You have to use the apostrophe in this case to represent feet, since in Chapter 1 you set the default units to be decimal inches.
2. Scroll down the panel until you see the Hemisphere input box. Remember, to scroll down a panel, you place the cursor on a blank area of the panel until you see the hand cursor; then you click and drag the panel up or down.

TIP If you look carefully at the command panel, you'll see a thin black and gray bar on the right side of the scrolling portion of the panel. You can click and drag the gray portion of this panel to scroll the panel up or down.

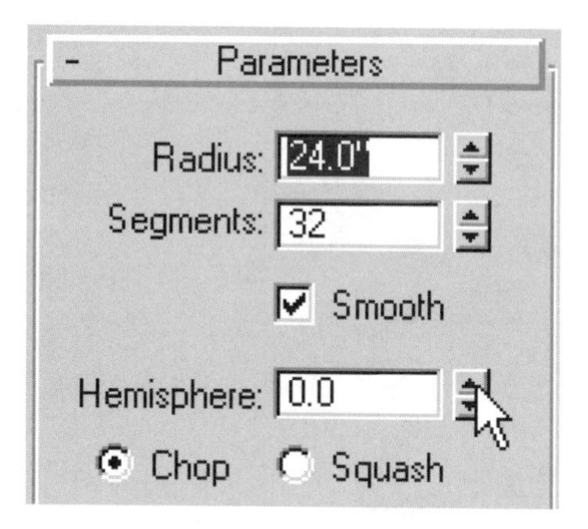

3. Click and drag the Hemisphere spinner upward and watch the sphere. It starts to collapse into a dome from the bottom up.
4. Highlight the entire value in the Hemisphere input box, then enter **0.5**(cr). This gives you an exact hemisphere.

NOTE For the sake of clarity on the printed page, there will be leading zeros before a decimal measurement. For the most part, you won't need to type these.

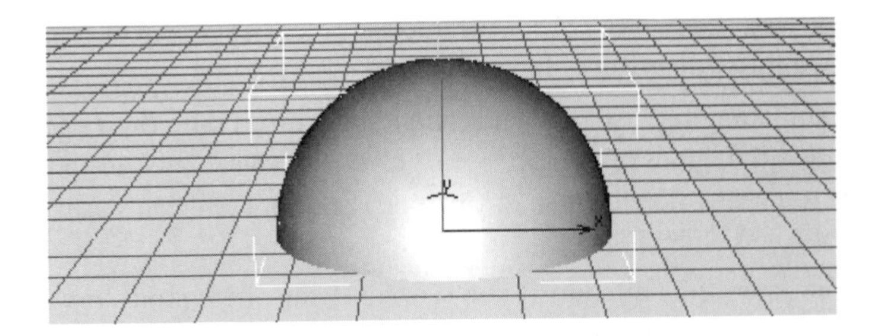

You can further adjust the shape of the sphere by removing a section. The Slice From and Slice To input boxes allow you to do this.

1. Locate the Slice From input box below the Hemisphere input box, click the Slice On check box, and then click and drag its spinner upward until it reads 135. This value is the angle in degrees from the Y axis to the beginning of the slice.

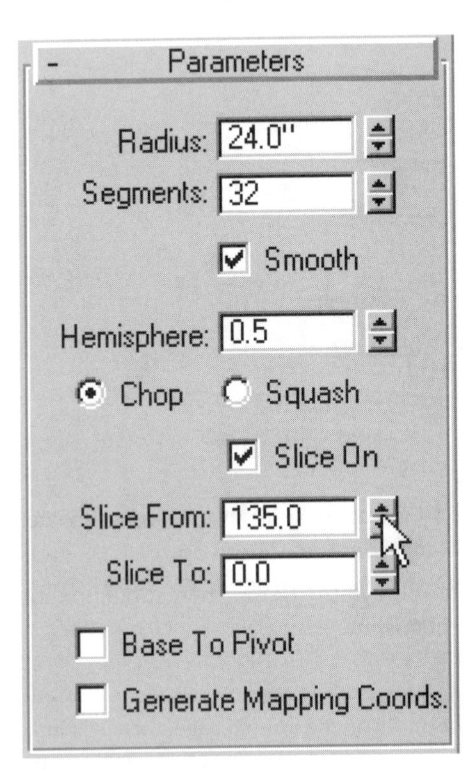

2. Click and drag the Slice To spinner downward until it reads –135 (minus 135). Your hemisphere now looks as if it had a segment removed.

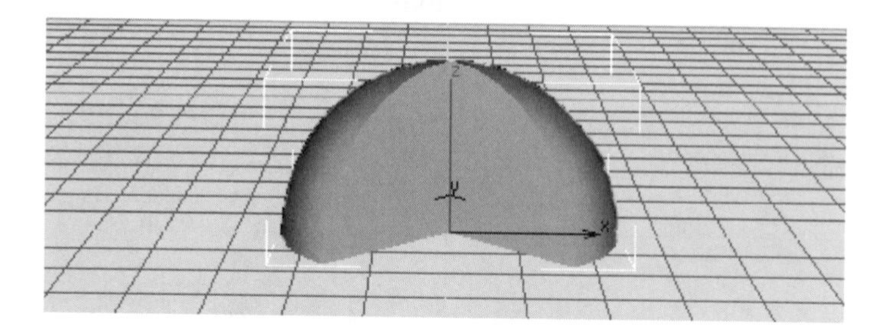

As you can see, there are a variety of parameters that you can use to modify the shape of an object, and each object has a different set of parameters that are appropriate to that object. For example, the Cylinder offers parameters for radius and height as well as Slice From and Slice To. The Slice From and Slice To parameters for the Cylinder let you create a segment of a cylinder in a manner similar to the sphere example.

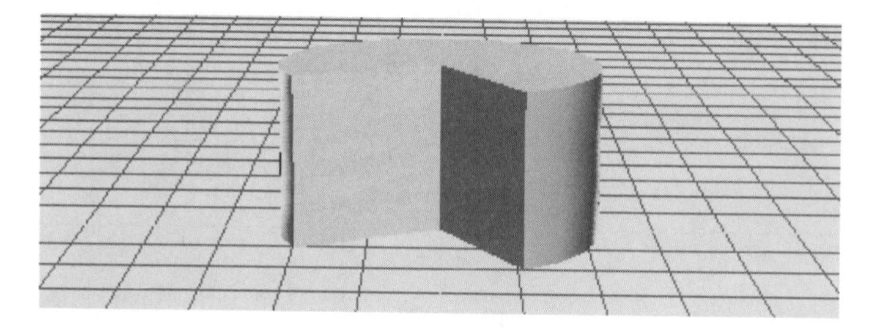

In the Parameters rollout for the sphere, there are a couple of other parameters that appear, which you will want to know a little more about. The Smooth parameter is a check box that turns smoothing on and off. Smoothing is a feature of VIZ found in most 3D modeling programs. It removes the hard edge between the facets that make up the object. Try the following to see firsthand how this works.

1. Click the Slice On check box to remove the check mark from this setting. The Hemisphere returns to its full shape.
2. Make sure the sphere is selected.

3. Click the Smooth check box to remove the check mark. (The Smooth check box is just below the Radius and Segments input box in the Parameters Rollout.) Notice that the sphere now looks faceted. You're seeing the facets that make up the sphere.

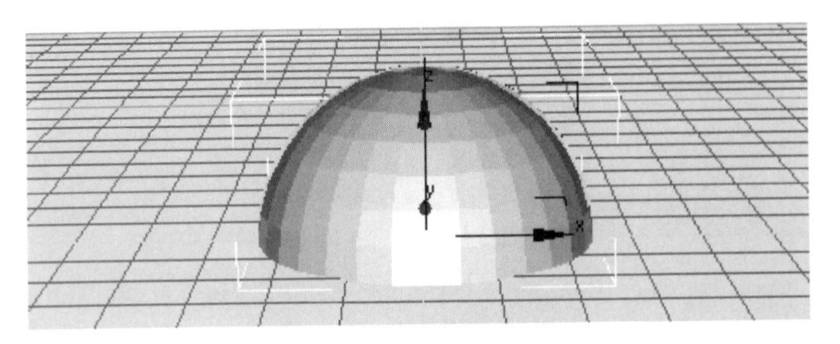

4. To see the construction of the sphere more clearly, right-click the Perspective viewport label in the upper left corner of the viewport, then select Wireframe. You see the facets of the sphere more clearly in the wireframe.

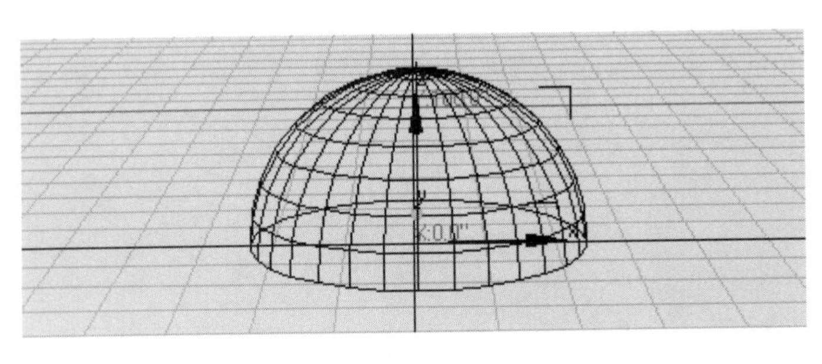

Here you see that, with smoothing turned off, the sphere looks as if it had a rough surface. In fact, all objects are faceted regardless of whether they are supposed to be smooth or not. The Smooth parameter is present for all of the curved primitives, namely the Cone, Sphere, GeoSphere, Cylinder, Tube, and the Torus (donut shape).

Now let's look at another parameter that is somewhat related to the Smooth parameter. The Segment parameter gives you control over the number of facets that make up an object. Try the following to see how the Segment parameter affects the sphere.

1. Click and drag the Segments parameter downward until the Segment's value is 12.

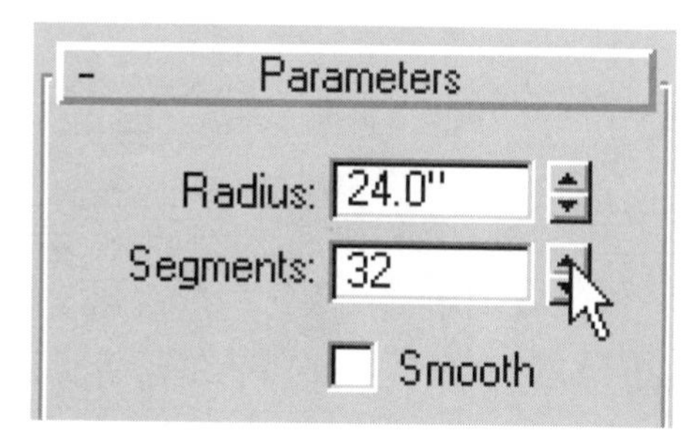

Note what happens to the sphere. Its surface segments become fewer.

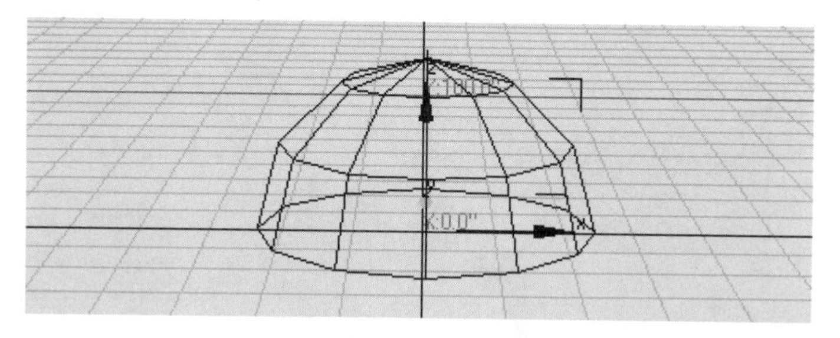

2. Right-click the Perspective label in the upper left corner of the viewport, then select Smooth + Highlight from the menu. The faceting is clearly shown.

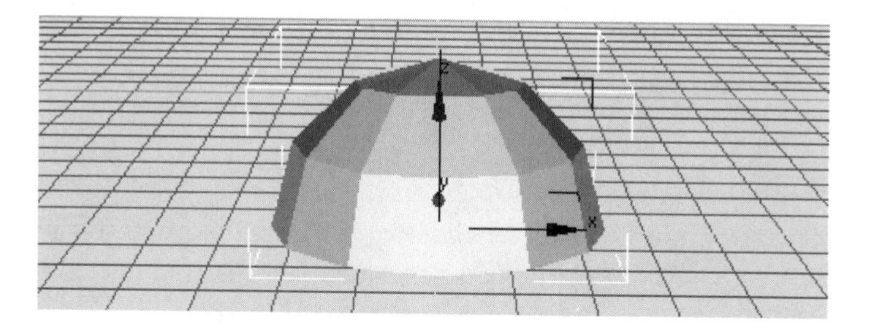

3. Now click the Smooth check box to turn on smoothing. You see the sphere's surface appear smoother, although you can detect the faceting.

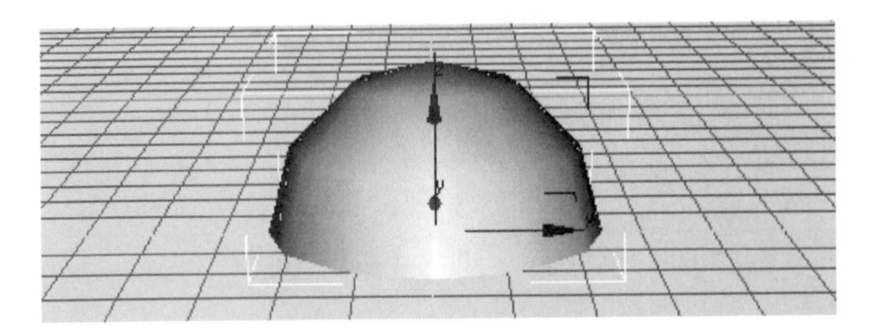

4. Click and drag the Segments spinner downward so that the Segment's value reads 4. The Sphere becomes a pyramid shape with the edges rounded.

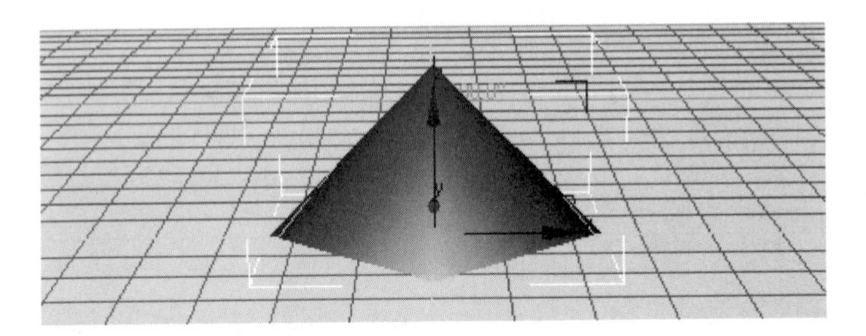

5. Click the Smooth check box again to turn off smoothing. The sphere now looks like a pyramid with flat surfaces.

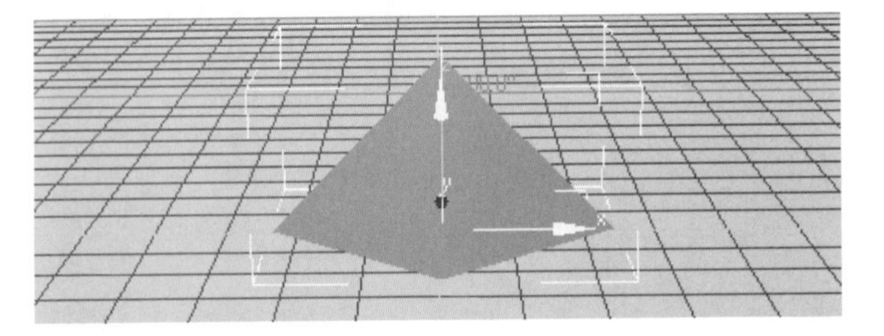

Smoothing provides the illusion of a gradual curve, hiding the facets that are required to construct objects. In the extreme case where a sphere is reduced to four sides, smoothing still provides the illusion of a smooth edge, but does not hide the sharp corners along the profile of the sphere.

In situations where you need to show a smooth curved surface, the smoothing parameter is essential. All objects can have a smoothing parameter applied to them, even if they do not have a smoothing parameter by default. You'll learn about when and how to apply smoothing to objects in later chapters. For now, let's move on to learn about other parameter features and other primitives.

Accessing Parameters

You can set an object's parameters in the Create tab of the Command Panel immediately after creating the object. But if you create several objects and then decide you want to modify the parameters of an object you created earlier, you'll need to use the Modify Panel.

1. Click in a blank area of the viewport to clear your selection set. When you create an object, it is automatically the current selection, so you click to clear the previous selection of the sphere.

2. Click the Select object tool, then click the sphere. Notice that the sphere's parameters do not appear in the Create tab of the Command Panel.

3. Click the Modify tab of the Command Panel. You'll see the parameters for the sphere. You can now make adjustments to the sphere from the Parameters rollout.

The modify tab displays the parameters of any object you select. Your selection must, however, be a single object. The Modify tab is the doorway to editing all objects in your model, as you'll see a little later in this chapter.

Looking at the Other Primitives

You've now used the Box and Sphere tool to create objects. You won't be trying out every standard primitive in this chapter, but to give you a sense of how they work, here is a rundown of the other Standard Primitives. The method of creation for all of these objects is quite similar to the Box and Sphere, so you shouldn't have any trouble if you want to experiment with them.

The Plane primitive is perhaps the simplest of all. Click and hold to establish one corner of the plane, then drag to locate the other corner. Once you are happy with the size of the plane, release the mouse. See Figure 2.2.

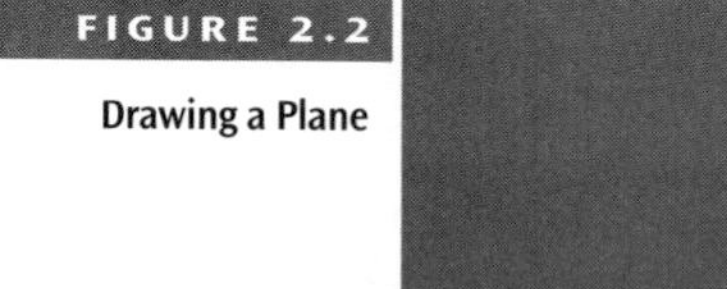

FIGURE 2.2

Drawing a Plane

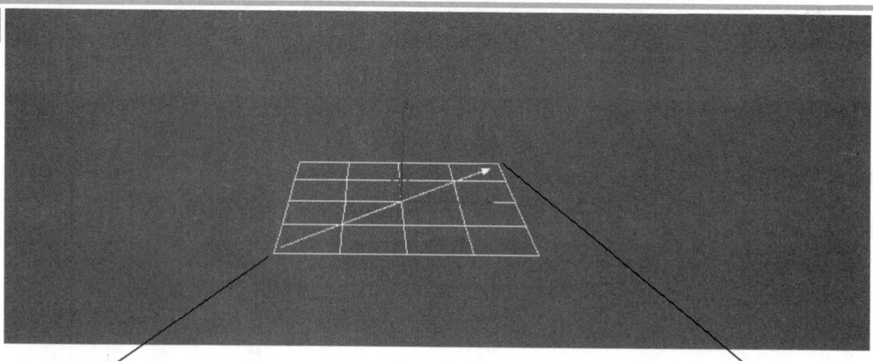
Click to place corner...
Drag to opposite corner.

The Box, Cylinder, and Pyramid all work in a similar way. First, click and hold to set one corner of the box or pyramid, or as in the case of the cylinder, the center point. Drag to locate the other corner of the box or pyramid, or the circumference of the cylinder. Release the mouse when you are satisfied with the size of the base. Next, move the mouse forward or backward to establish a height. Click when you want to fix the height. See Figure 2.3.

FIGURE 2.3

Drawing a Box, Cylinder, or Pyramid

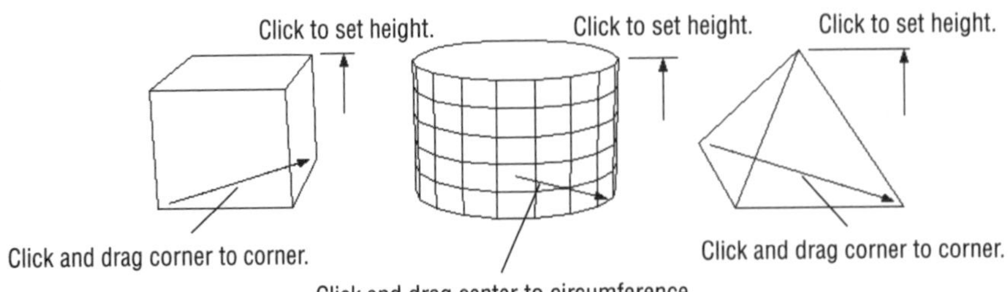
Click to set height.
Click to set height.
Click to set height.
Click and drag corner to corner.
Click and drag corner to corner.
Click and drag center to circumference.

The Sphere and Geosphere are created in the same way. Click and hold to establish the center point, then drag to locate the radius. When you're satisfied with the radius, release the mouse button. See Figure 2.4.

FIGURE 2.4

Drawing a sphere or geosphere

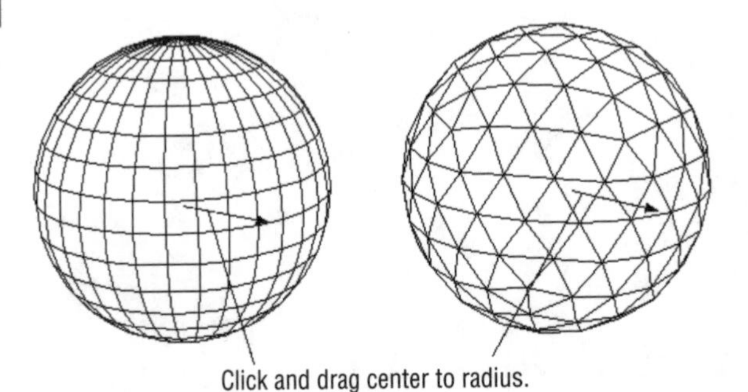
Click and drag center to radius.

What's the difference between Sphere and Geosphere?

You may notice that, on a superficial level, both the Sphere and Geosphere create the same thing, a sphere. But if you look at the wireframe view of each of these objects, you'll see that there is a structural difference. The sphere is created with horizontal and vertical segments, much like the longitude and latitude lines on a globe. The Geosphere is constructed like a geodesic dome, with triangles.

Continued on the next page

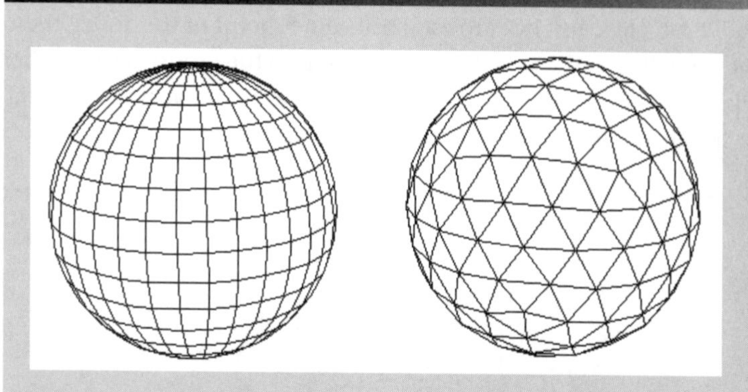

The sphere's construction lets you convert it into a dome of varying configurations, but the geosphere can only be an exact hemisphere. The advantage of the geosphere is its modeling *plasticity*. As its shape is derived from a less regular construction, it can be molded more easily into other shapes. Also, it requires fewer facets to simulate a smooth surface, something that is important when creating a very complex model that contains a lot of objects.

The Cone, Torus, and Tube are a bit more complicated in the construction method, although these three objects are similar in the number of steps needed in their creation.

The Cone starts with a click and drag to establish its center and base, just like the cylinder. And as with the Cylinder, the next step is to establish the height by positioning the mouse, then clicking to set the height. But unlike the Cylinder, the Cone requires an additional step to establish the radius of the top of the Cone as shown in Figure 2.5.

FIGURE 2.5

Drawing a Cone

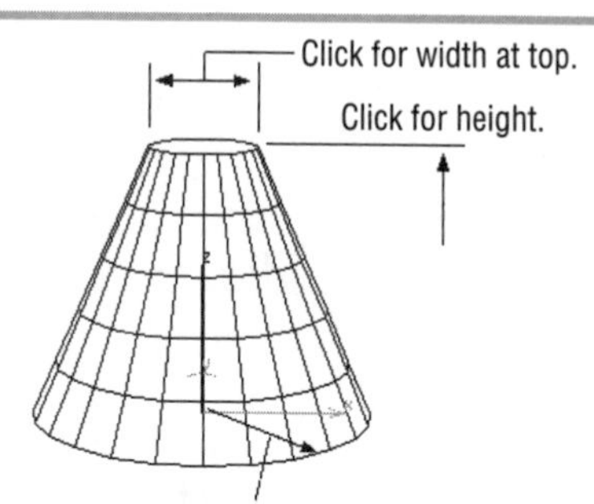
Click for width at top.
Click for height.
Click and drag from center to circumference.

The Torus is the most unusual of the Standard Primitives in its construction method. First, click and hold to establish center point of the Torus, then drag to locate the overall radius as shown in Figure 2.6. Release the mouse button when you are satisfied with the radius. Next, move the mouse forward or backward to establish the diameter of the Torus *body*. Click the mouse when you're satisfied with the diameter.

FIGURE 2.6

Drawing a torus

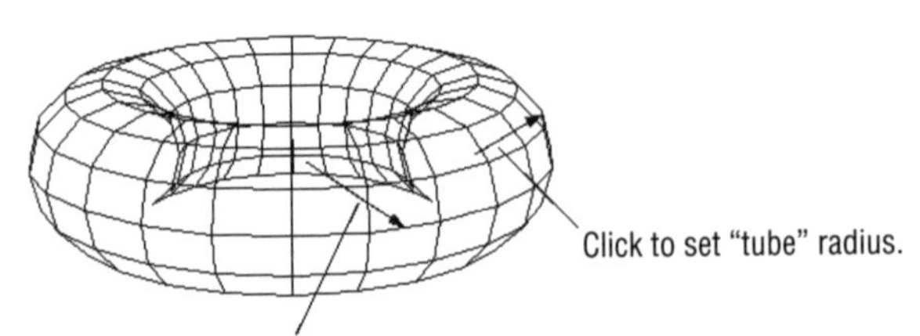
Click to set "tube" radius.
Click and drag center to overall radius.

Finally, the method for creating a Tube is similar to the method for creating the Cylinder, but with a slight twist. Click and hold to select the center of the Cylinder, then drag to establish the inside diameter. Release the mouse to fix the inside diameter in place. Move and click the mouse to establish the outside diameter, as shown in Figure 2.7. Finally, move and click the mouse to establish the height.

FIGURE 2.7

Drawing a tube

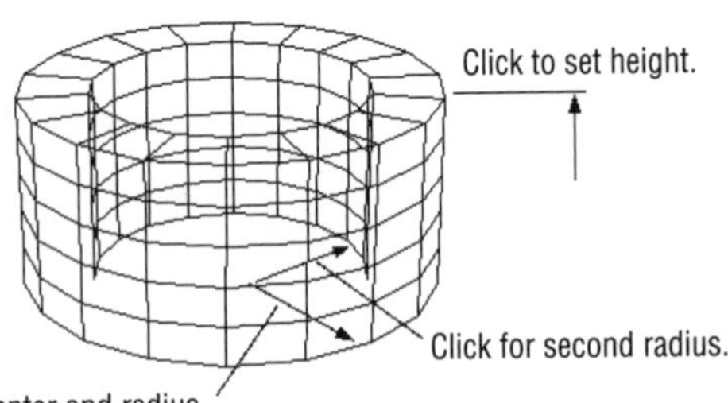
Click to set height.
Click for second radius.
Click and drag for center and radius.

Remember that you can make adjustments to the dimensions of the primitives after their creation. In fact, you may find it easier to just quickly place a primitive in your model, without much care in determining its size, and then adjust the dimension of the primitive in the Parameters rollout to *fine tune* the shape of the primitive.

Molding Standard Primitives with Modifiers

You've seen how Standard Primitives have basic parameters that can be modified any time after the creation of the primitive. There are also tools called Modifiers that can further act on a primitive to change its shape. You might think of modifiers as invisible attachments that add functions to a primitive, in much the same way that a software plug-in adds functions to your Internet browser or other program.

Adding a Modifier

In this section, you'll explore a few of the Modifiers offered in the Modify tab of the Command Panel. There are quite a few modifiers, so you won't be able to try out all of them now, but you'll get to use a few of the more commonly used ones. Think of this section as a general introduction to modifiers. You'll get to explore the use of other modifiers in other chapters.

You'll start your exploration of Modifiers by creating a box. You'll use the box to try out the modifiers.

1. Choose File ➢ New to start a new file. You'll see a message asking you whether you want to save changes to the current design. Click No. Next, you'll see another dialog box with three options.

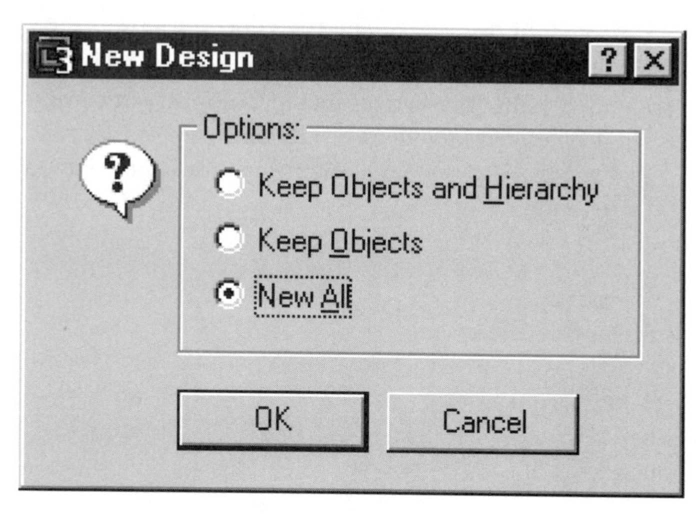

2. Click the New All radio button, then click OK.

3. Click the Zoom Extents tool to display the default view for a new file.
4. Click the Create tab in the Command Panel and then click the Box button.

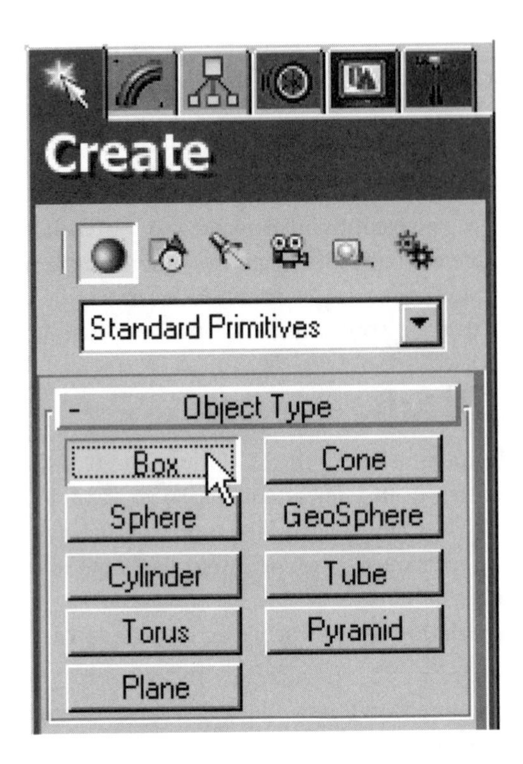

5. In the Creation Method rollout, click the Cube radio button.
6. Click a point near the origin, then drag the base of the box so that the length and width parameters show a value of approximately 48 inches.
7. Right-click the Perspective label in the upper left corner of the viewport, then select Wireframe. You'll use a wireframe view so that you can better see changes that you make to the box's parameters. You should have a view that looks similar to Figure 2.8.

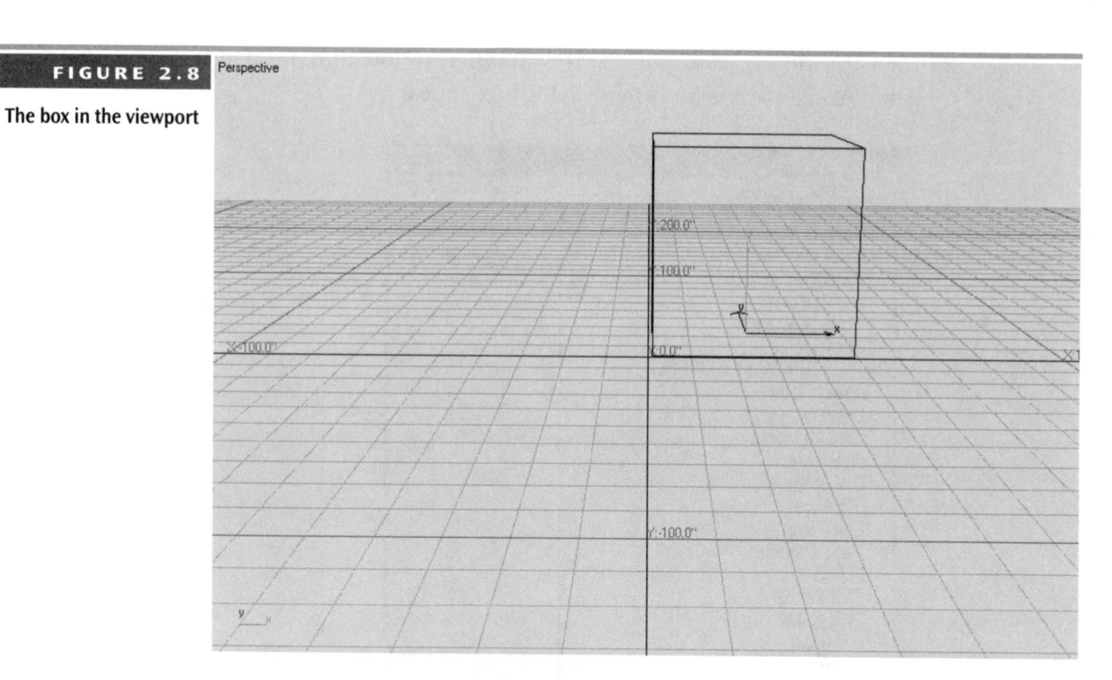

FIGURE 2.8

The box in the viewport

Now let's add a modifier to change the shape of the box to a curved box.

1. Make sure the box is selected. Click the Modify tab in the Command panel.

Make note of the parameters rollout. You'll see the standard Length, Width, and Height options as well as the Length Segs, Width Segs, and Height Segs, options below. In a moment you'll see what these Segs options do.

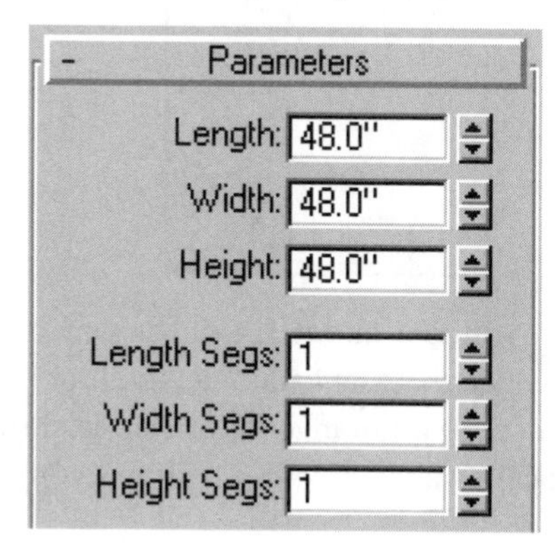

2. Click the More... button under the Modifiers rollout at the top of the command panel. You'll see the Modifiers dialog box appear.

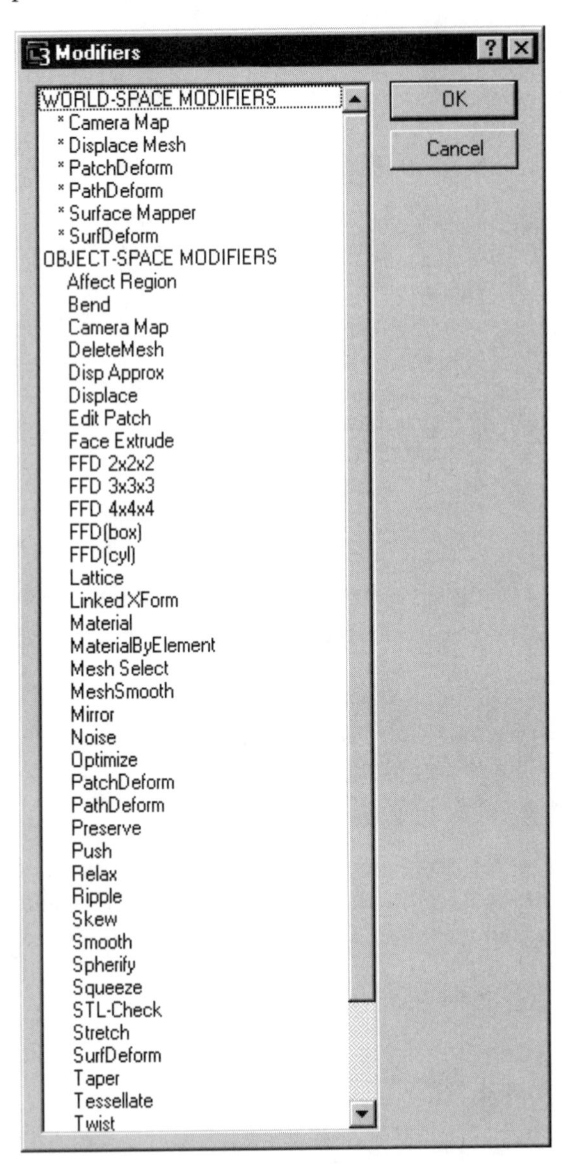

3. Click the Bend modifier, which is about 1/4 of the way down from the top of the list, then click OK. Notice that the Parameters rollout changes to show a set of Bend options. You'll also see an orange outline appear, superimposed on the box. This orange box is called a Gizmo, and it shows you the general effect of the Modifier.

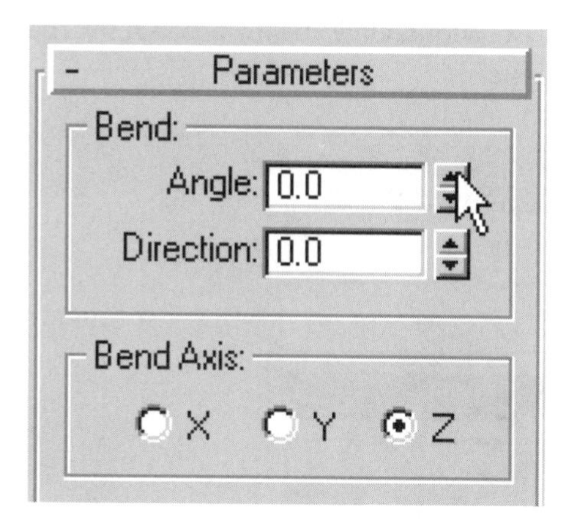

4. In the Bend group of the Parameters rollout, click and drag the Angle spinner upward and watch what happens to the box. It bends to the right.

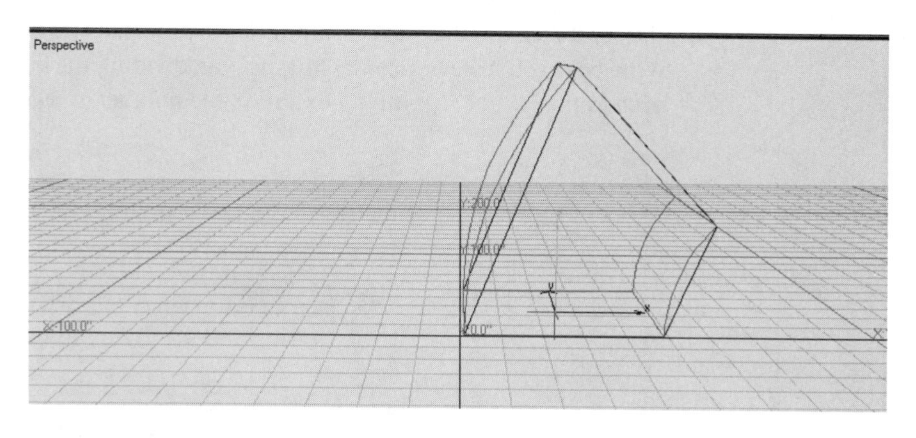

5. Adjust the Angle spinner so that its value reads 60. Alternately, you can highlight the angle value and then enter **60↵**.

The bend modifier has its own set of parameters that can alter the shape of an object. This is typical for any modifier you might use on an object. Adding a modifier doesn't mean, however, that you cannot return to the original parameters of the object to make changes there.

Accessing Modifier Parameters

You've just applied the bend modifier to the box, but the result may not be exactly what you expected. The box now looks like a trapezoid. To get the box to appear curved, you'll need to make use of the Segs parameters you saw earlier as part of the box's original set of parameters.

1. In the Modifier Stack rollout, click the drop-down list that shows Bend. You'll see Bend and Box appear.

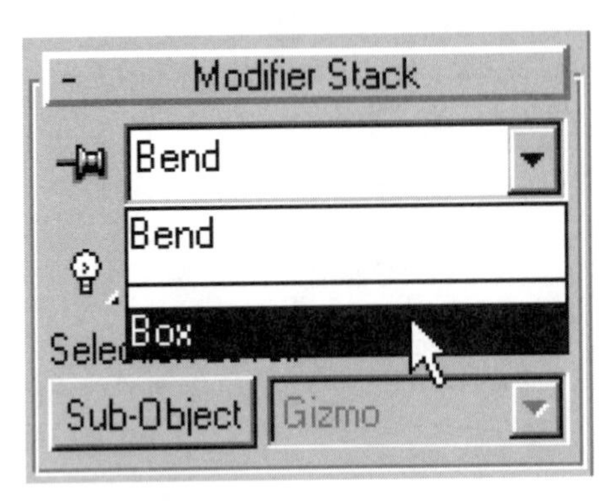

2. Click Box from the list. Notice that the Original Box parameters appear under the Parameters rollout.
3. Click and drag the Height Segs spinner slowly upward and notice what happens to the box. You'll see horizontal lines appear, dividing the box horizontally. The value in the Height Segs input box shows the number of segments.

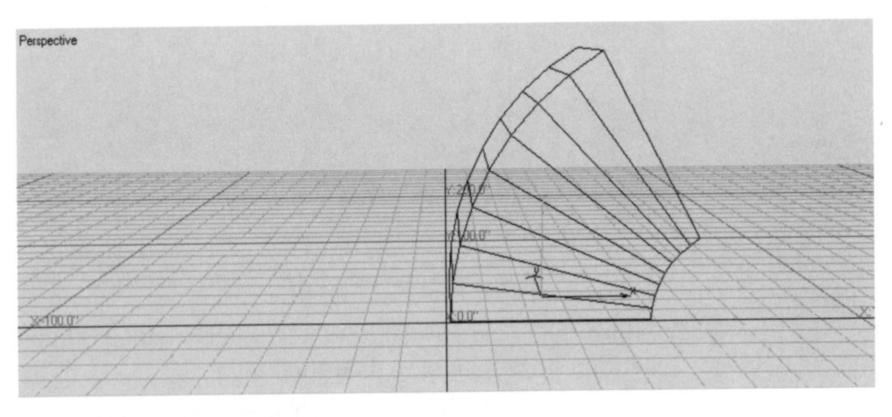

Also note that the box now appears to be curved.

4. Set the Height Segs value to 8.

In this exercise, you saw how you can increase the number of segments in the box, which in turn allows the Bend modifier to give the box a curved appearance. You also saw how the Modifier Stack offers access to the box's original parameters through the drop-down list in the Modifier Stack rollout. The Modifier Stack plays a key role in your ability to edit objects in VIZ, as you'll see in the rest of this and other chapters.

Now let's try making another adjustment to the Bend parameters.

1. Click the Drop-down list in the Modifier Stack rollout again.
2. This time, click the Bend option from the list. (The Bend options appear in the Parameters rollout.)
3. Click the Direction spinner in the Parameters rollout and drag it upward. Notice how the box rolls around as it changes the direction of the bend.
4. Adjust the Direction value to **180**. This causes the bend to point in a direction that is at an angle of 180 degrees from its original direction.

Once again, you moved from one set of parameters to another. This time you switched from the box's basic parameters to the Bend Modifier parameters. As you adjusted the Direction spinner in step 3, you saw how the box appeared to roll around as it changed the direction of the bend.

NOTE You may have noticed an orange shape superimposed over the box the first time you applied the Bend tool. This shape is known as a *gizmo*—in fact, you'll see the word gizmo in the modifier stack rollout whenever the Bend modifier is selected. The gizmo lets you see how the modifier is being applied to an object. You can apply any of the Transform tools to the gizmo to further change the way a modifier affects an object. You'll get a chance to edit the gizmo of other modifiers in later chapters.

Coordinates in VIZ

One feature that stands out in VIZ's perspective viewport is the grid. The grid offers some orientation in an otherwise empty space, and it also shows you the coordinates of the space. You may remember from high school geometry that the X and Y axes form the basis of a standard 2D Grid, with the X axis defining the horizontal or width dimension and the Y axis forming the length dimension. You also have the additional Z axis that forms the height dimension. The grid you see in a new file shows you the *World Coordinate System*, which is the basis of your model's coordinates. The World Coordinate System is fixed and cannot be moved. You can, however, adjust the spacing of the grid and the type of units you wish to use. Later, you'll learn about *User Grids*, which allow you to create *local* coordinates that can be placed anywhere.

In a new file, you can see the origin of the world coordinate system at the center of the view. The origin is where the X, Y, and Z zero coordinates intersect. The origin is frequently used as a reference point for your model. It is also used as a common reference point between separate model files that need to be combined later. If you're an AutoCAD user, you'll know how the World Coordinate System's origin can be used to keep external reference drawings aligned. In VIZ, you can use the origin to align different models in a similar way.

Continued on the next page

VIZ also uses another coordinate system based on what is called *object space*. Object space is the coordinate system of individual objects. You see evidence of this object space in the form of an X, Y, Z coordinate gizmo that is displayed within an object when it is first created or when it is selected. All modifiers act on objects within their object space. The center of the object space is represented by the origin of the object's XYZ coordinate gizmo. See Figure 2.8.

FIGURE 2.8

The grid in the Perspective viewport with a model showing the X, Y, and Z axes

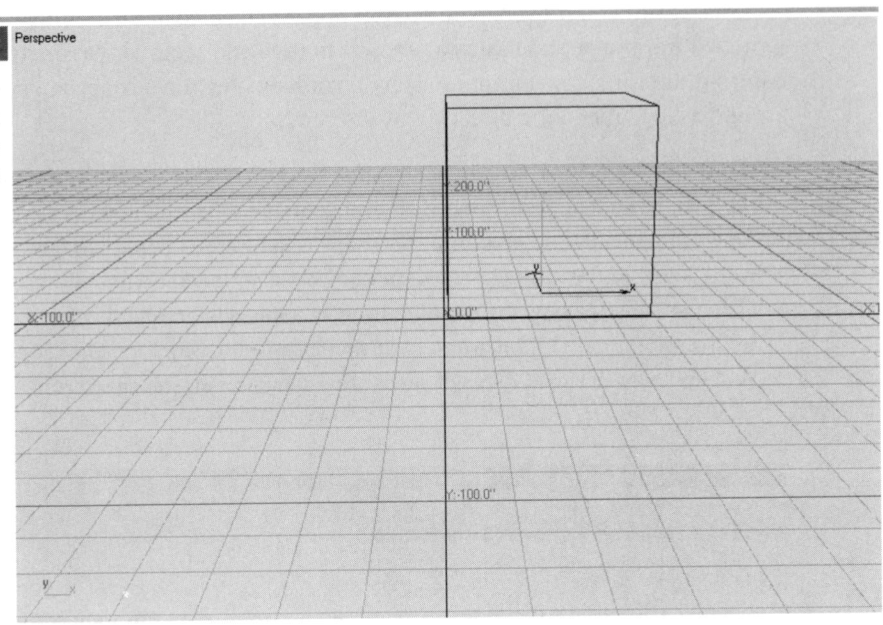

Now let's try another modifier. The Taper modifier does just what you might guess: it tapers an object.

1. Start by changing the view to one that will show more of the box. Choose View ➢ Views ➢ SW from the menu bar.

2. Click the Zoom Extents tool in the Viewport Navigation Controls.
3. In the Modifiers rollout, click More…

4. In the Modifiers dialog box, click Taper (near the bottom of the list), then click OK. Now the Parameters rollout shows a different set of options.

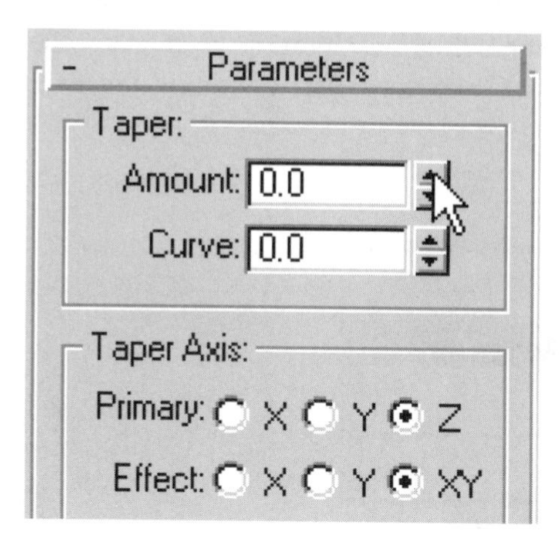

5. Click and drag the Amount spinner downward in the Parameters rollout. The box tapers vertically. You also see the orange gizmo change shape as you adjust the Amount spinner.
6. Click and drag the Curve spinner upward until it reads –0.3 (minus point three). The box now has a slight bulge.

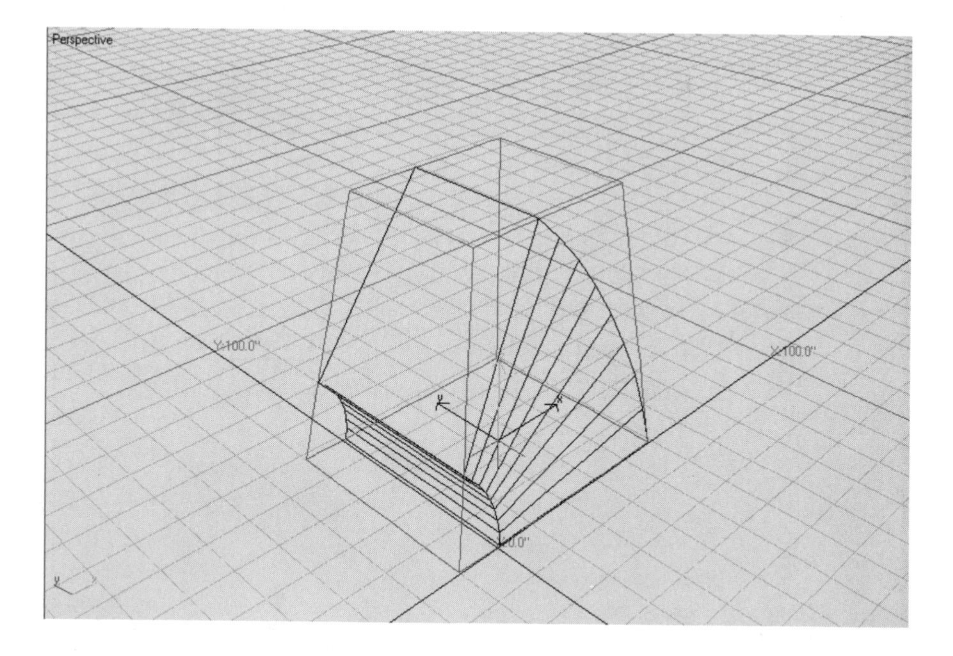

Although this is an interesting shape, you may have expected the box to taper along its curved length instead of straight up. You can change the effect of the Taper modifier by changing its position on what is called the *modifier stack*. The modifier stack is like a collection of modifiers, each one stacked on another one, just as they appear in the Modifier Stack drop-down list. Right now, the list looks like Figure 2.9.

FIGURE 2.9

Modifier Stack drop-down list

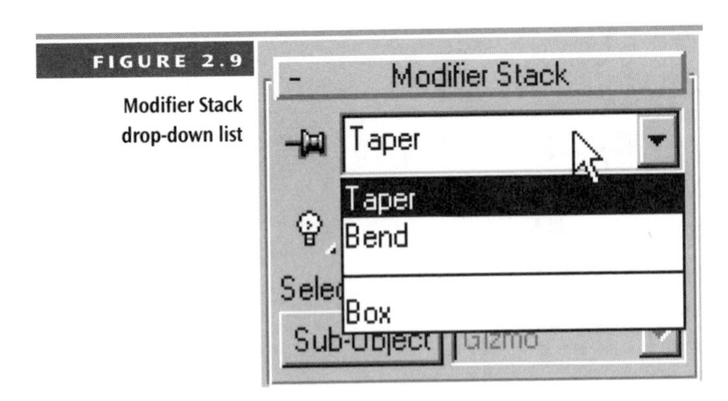

Taper is at the top, as it is the last modifier you added to the Box. Below Taper is Bend, and below Bend is the box itself. You can change the order of the modifiers in the stack to obtain a slightly different effect on the box. Try the following to see how this works:

1. Click the Edit Stack tool in the Modifier Stack Rollout.

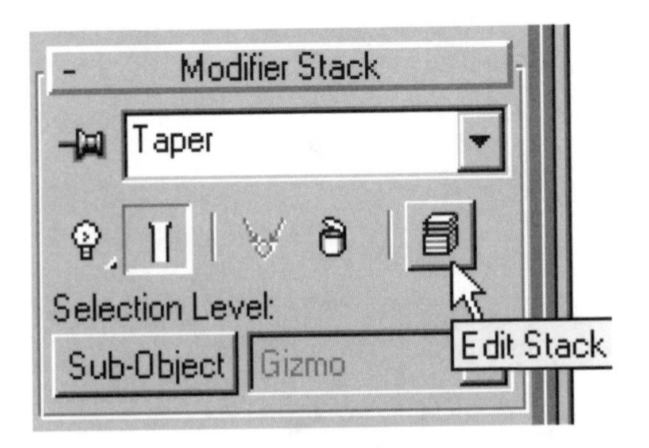

The Edit Modifier Stack dialog box displays.

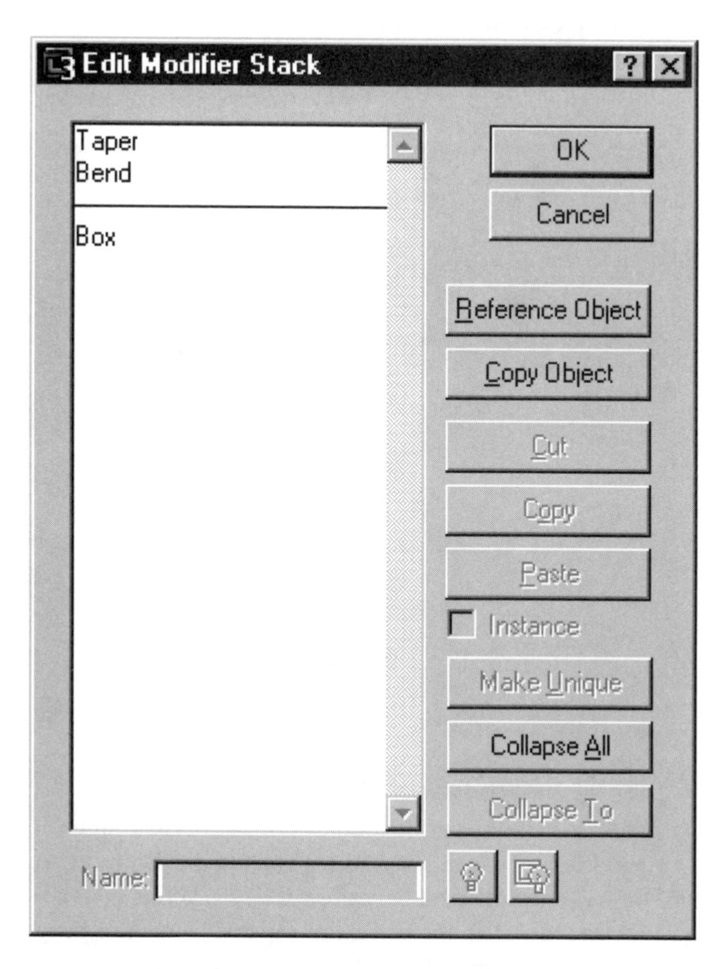

2. Click the Taper option in the list, then click the button labeled Cut. The Taper option disappears. Note that the Box now returns to its previous form (the form it had before you applied the Taper modifier).

3. Click the horizontal bar just above the Box option in the list, then click the button labeled Paste. The Taper option appears just above the line, effectively changing the order of modifiers in the modifier stack. Also note the change in the shape of the box. It now tapers along the length of its bend.

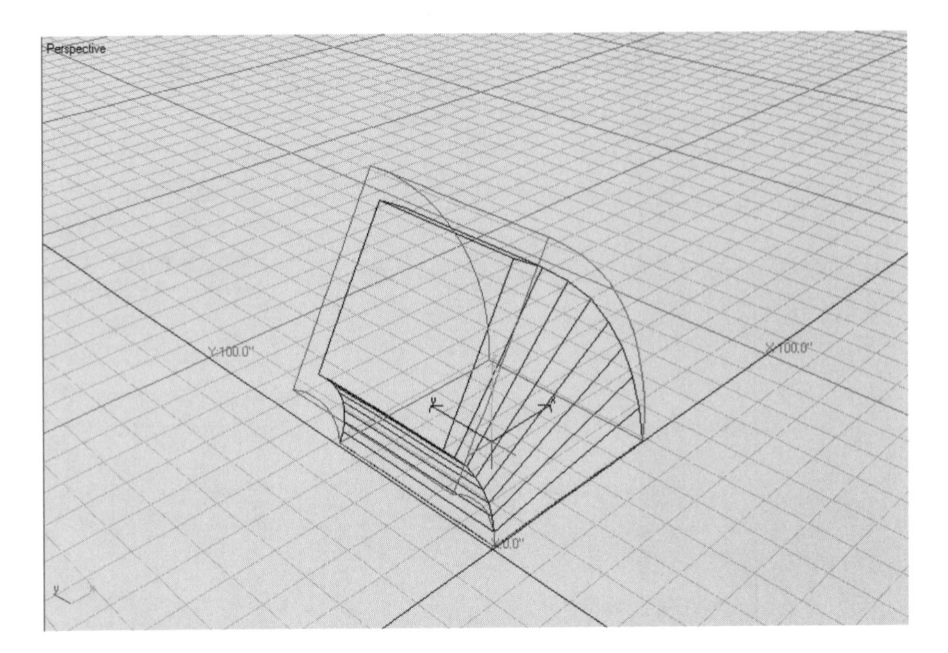

4. Click OK to close the Edit Modifier Stack dialog box.

This exercise demonstrates a couple of things. First, you see how to change the order of modifiers in the modifier stack. You also see how a change in the order affects the way multiple modifiers affect the box. When you move the taper modifier below the bend modifier, the box is first tapered before it is bent, giving the modified box a completely different shape. This is an important point to remember (the order of the modifiers in the stack affects the way the modifiers work).

Inserting Modifiers Where You Want Them

Another point to be aware of is that when you add a modifier it will be inserted into the stack just above the modifier that is current in the modifier stack drop-down list. For example, if you had opened the modifier Stack drop-down list and selected Box *before* adding the Taper modifier, then the taper modifier would have been placed between the Bend and Box listing in the Modifier stack, just as they appear at the end of the last exercise. Instead, you added the Taper modifier with the Bend modifier displayed in the drop-down list, which placed the Taper modifier above the Bend modifier. You then had to use the Edit Modifier Stack dialog box to move it between the Box parameters and Bend modifier.

What Can You Do With Primitives and Modifiers?

Some examples of objects that are built with the help of modifiers are the binoculars and drawer pulls shown in Figure 2.10. Several objects were used for the binoculars, including cylinders and a few objects called splines. A taper modifier was used to taper the large end of the binoculars, and a combination of taper and skew modifiers was used in the main body. The drawer pulls are just cylinders with a Squeeze modifier applied. The Squeeze modifier gives the cylinder a slight bulge at the top while tapering the sides down.

FIGURE 2.10

Samples of objects created from primitives with modfiers applied to them

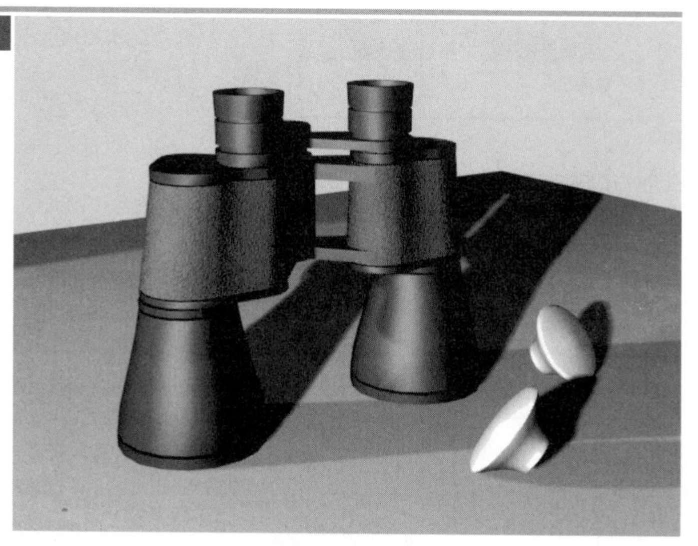

Understanding the Modifier Stack Tools

You've seen how the Edit Stack tool can be used to view and edit the Modifier Stack. There are a few other tools alongside the Edit Stack tool that you've probably noticed.

These other tools offer ways to manage the modifier stack. The following set of exercises will let you see firsthand what they do.

TIP **The Edit ➢ Temporary Buffer command performs the same function as AutoCAD's Mark option under the Undo command. You can save your drawing in its current condition in case you want to return to this condition later. It lets you try out various *what if* scenarios without fear of losing your work up to a certain point.**

1. First choose Edit ➢ Temporary Buffer ➢ Save from the menu bar. This command acts like a place marker to which you can return if you want to experiment.
2. In the Command Panel, select Bend from the Modifier Stack drop-down list.

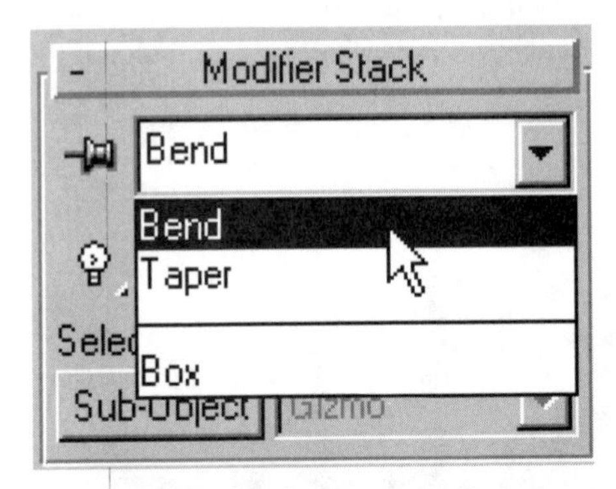

3. Click the lightbulb icon with the Active/Inactive modifier toggle tool tip toward the left of the row of Modifier Stack tools.

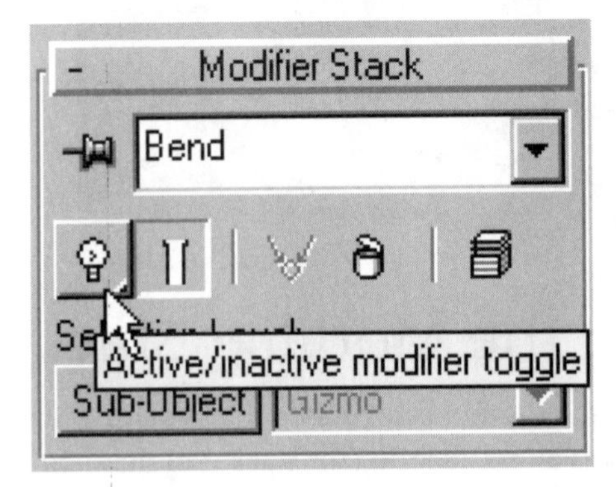

This tool turns off the current modifier listed in the Modifier stack input box. Notice that the box reverts to the shape you would have without the Bend modifier.

4. Click the Active/Inactive modifier toggle again to turn Bend back on.
5. Select Taper from the Modifier Stack drop-down list.

6. Click the Active/Inactive modifier toggle again. Notice how this time the box reverts to the shape it had before Taper was added.
7. Now choose Edit ➢ Temporary Buffer ➢ Restore. You see a message box asking if it's OK to restore. Go ahead and click OK. Your box returns to its original state (as it was before step 1).

The Active/Inactive modifier lets you turn a modifier on or off so you can quickly view the effects of removing a modifier from the stack without actually having to remove it.

A somewhat similar tool is the Show End Result On/Off tool. This tool doesn't actually affect the end result of the object's shape the way the Active/Inactive modifier does. The Show End Result tool simply shows you the shape of the object at the currently selected Modifier Stack level. The following sample demonstrates this.

1. Select Taper from the Modifier Stack drop-down list.

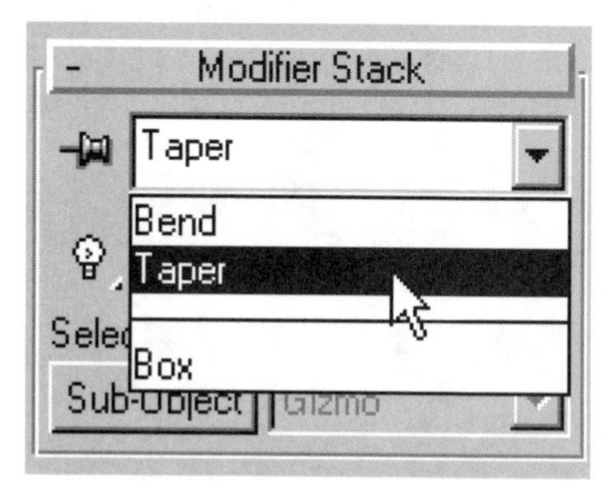

2. Click the Show End Result On/Off tool. The viewport shows the box in its form before the Bend modifier is applied.

3. To see that this doesn't actually affect the end result of the box, click the Select object tool and then click a blank area of the model to clear the selection. The box returns to its original form complete with all the modifiers active.

4. Click the box to select it again, then choose Taper from the Modifier Stack drop-down list. The box again returns to the form it had before the Bend modifier was applied.
5. Click the Show End Result On/Off tool again. The viewport again displays the box in its final form.

You may have noticed that the Show End Result icon changed when you clicked on it in step 2.

This helps you remember whether the Show End Result tool is on or off.

Now suppose you want to simply delete a modifier from the stack. You can do so by using the Remove Modifier From the Stack tool.

1. Select the Taper tool from the Modifier Stack drop-down list.
2. Click the Remove Modifier From the Stack tool. Its trash can icon says it all. Now the Taper modifier is permanently removed from the modifier stack, and the box reverts to the form it had before you added the Taper modifier.

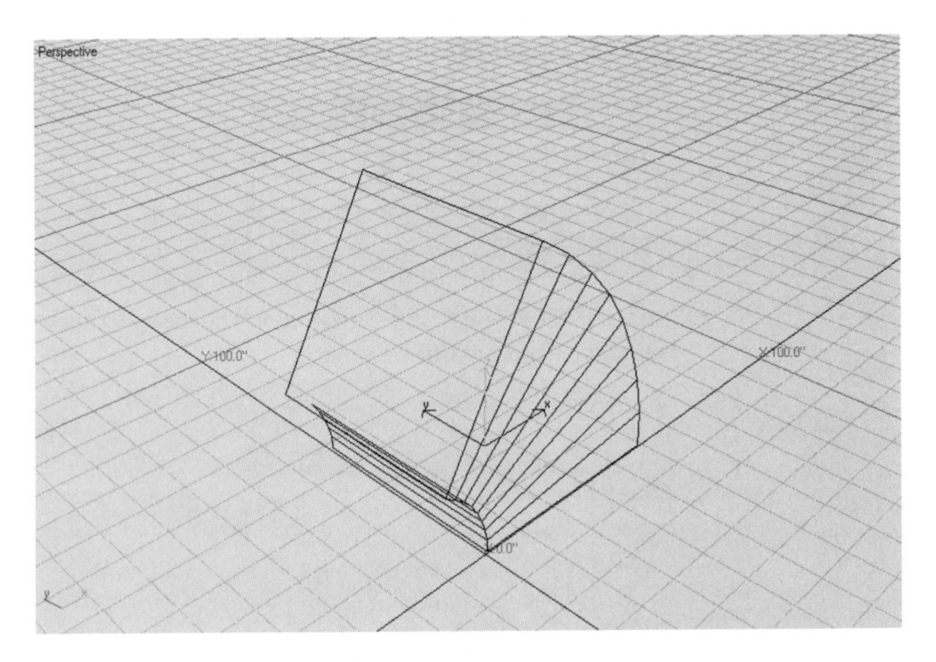

3. Choose Edit ➢ Temporary Buffer ➢ Restore to restore the Taper modifier.

The Remove Modifier From the Stack tool is a quick way to remove a modifier. You can accomplish the same thing by clicking the Edit Stack tool to open the Edit Modifier Stack dialog box, selecting the modifier you want to remove, and clicking the Cut button.

Another button you haven't tried yet is the Make Unique button. This button is relevant only when you have special types of clones called *instances* or *references*. You may recall that in Chapter 1 you had a choice of the type of clone you made while using the Select and Move tool. In the next section, you'll learn more about these other types of clones.

How VIZ Sees Objects

Let's take a break from the tutorial for a moment to look at a concept called *object data flow*. When you create and edit an object in VIZ, you are creating data that VIZ evaluates to display your model. The order in which that data is evaluated is known as the object data flow. VIZ *sees* objects as a stream or flow of data in a particular order. The order in which this data is evaluated affects the outcome of the data, or in more concrete terms, the order affects the behavior and appearance of the object in your model.

You already saw an example of object data flow when you looked at the order of modifiers in the Modifier Stack. There you saw that the order in which modifiers appear in the stack affects the shape of a box. VIZ also applies this data flow to the overall object by evaluating all modifications made to an object in a specific order.

The first piece of data VIZ looks at is the Master Object. This is the object as you first create it, including a set of parameters, its position, and its orientation.

The next item is the modifier or set of modifiers you apply to an object. These are evaluated in their order in the Modifier Stack, as you've already seen. Of course, if there are no modifiers, VIZ skips to the next piece of data.

The third item in the data flow is the transformations applied to the object. Remember that transformations are the movement, scaling, or rotation of an object. Even though you may have moved the object *after* having applied modifiers, VIZ will evaluate the object's move transformation before it evaluates its modifiers. Transformations include cloning, since clones are an option of the Move transform tool. The one exception to this occurs when you use the Xform (transform) modifier that places transform operations within the bounds of the Modifier Stack.

VIZ evaluates the properties of an object last. Properties are the object's name, color, layer assignment, display, and rendering properties, to name a few. Object properties also include shadow casting and receiving, and motion blur. This means that even though an object acquires a default color and name as soon as it is created, VIZ evaluates the name and color last.

So to summarize object data flow, VIZ looks at object data in the following order:

1. Master Object
2. Modifiers
3. Transforms
4. Properties.

The ramifications of object data flow are not obvious at first, but keep the concept in the back of your mind as you work with VIZ. It will help you understand the behavior of the program and ultimately give you better control over your models.

Making Clones that Share Properties

The Modifier Stack plays a major role in allowing you to mold objects to a desired shape, but you can go a step farther and have modifiers act across several objects instead of across just one. In Chapter 1, you may have noticed two clone options: Instances and References. Instances and References are more than just clones of objects; they share modifiers so as to make the changes you make to one clone affect all the other clones. This can be a great editing aid when you have multiples of the same object, such as columns in a building or lighting fixtures. By making Instance clones, for example, you can place the objects in your model before you've actually finalized the particular parameters of the objects.

Creating an Instance Clone

The Instance and Reference clones are quite similar, though with a subtle but powerful difference. You'll start by examining the simpler of the two types of clones, the Instance.

1. Make sure the Box is selected, then click the Select and Move tool.
2. Shift-click and drag the red X coordinate arrow to the right. Then move the copy of the box along the X axis toward the upper-right corner of the viewport so that its bottom corner is at about the 110-inch X axis mark. You can use the grid to see the distance of your copy.

3. Release the mouse button. The Clone Options dialog box displays.

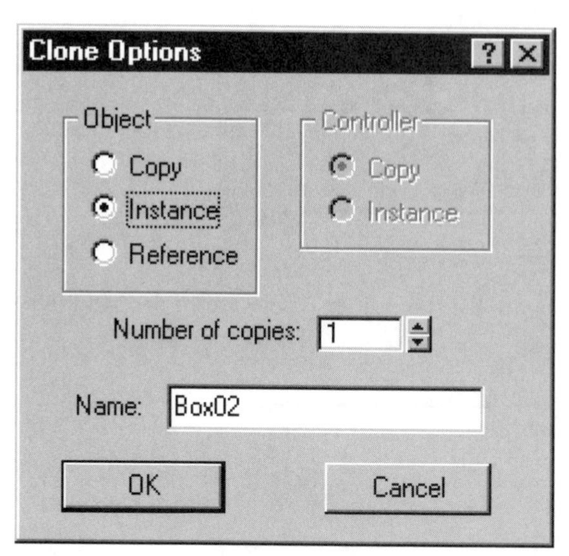

4. Click the Instance radio button in the Object group, then click OK. You now have an Instance clone of the original box.

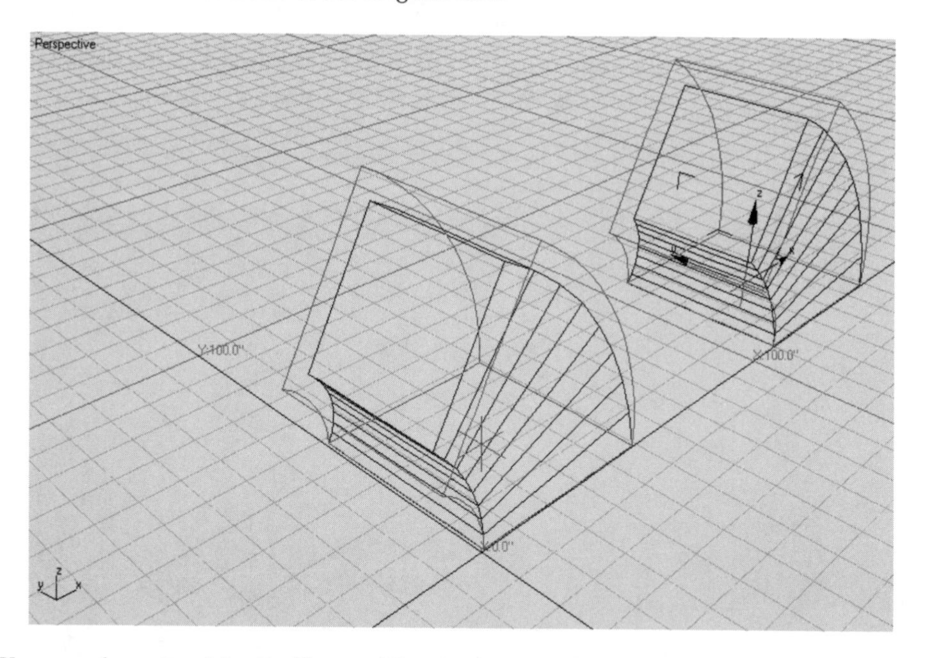

You now have two identical boxes. The similarities of the two boxes go beyond appearances, as the following exercise demonstrates.

1. With the box to the right selected, make sure the Modify tab in the Command Panel is selected.

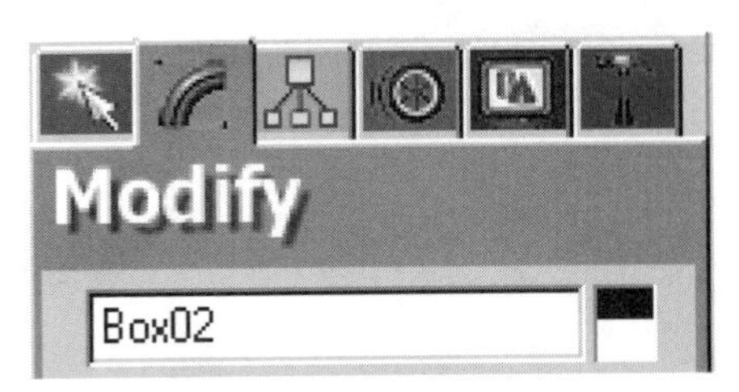

2. Make sure the Bend modifier is selected in the Modifier Stack drop-down list.

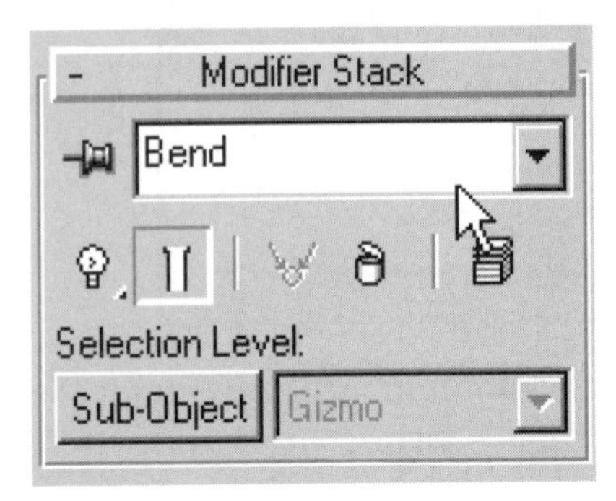

3. Click and drag the Angle spinner upward in the Parameters rollout until its value reads 90. Notice that both boxes change shape simultaneously.

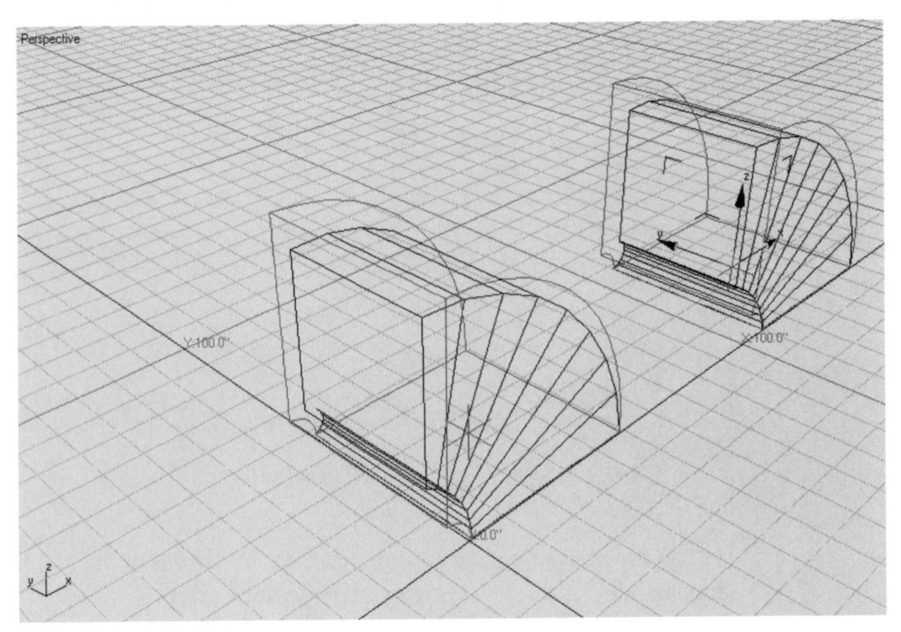

Any parameter change you make to either of the boxes will be reflected in its instanced clone. Furthermore, if you add other modifiers to either of the clones, each will have the modifier applied to its modifier stack. This is true because Instance clones share modifiers in their respective modifier stacks. This sharing of the modifiers is what distinguishes an Instance clone from an ordinary copy.

Understanding the Reference Clone

Another Clone option is Reference. A Reference clone also shares modifiers in its modifier stack, but in addition it can allow you to include modifiers that are not shared.

1. Select the box in the foreground. Then with the Select and Move tool, shift-click and drag its green Y axis arrow to the left to a location similar to the one shown in Figure 2.11.

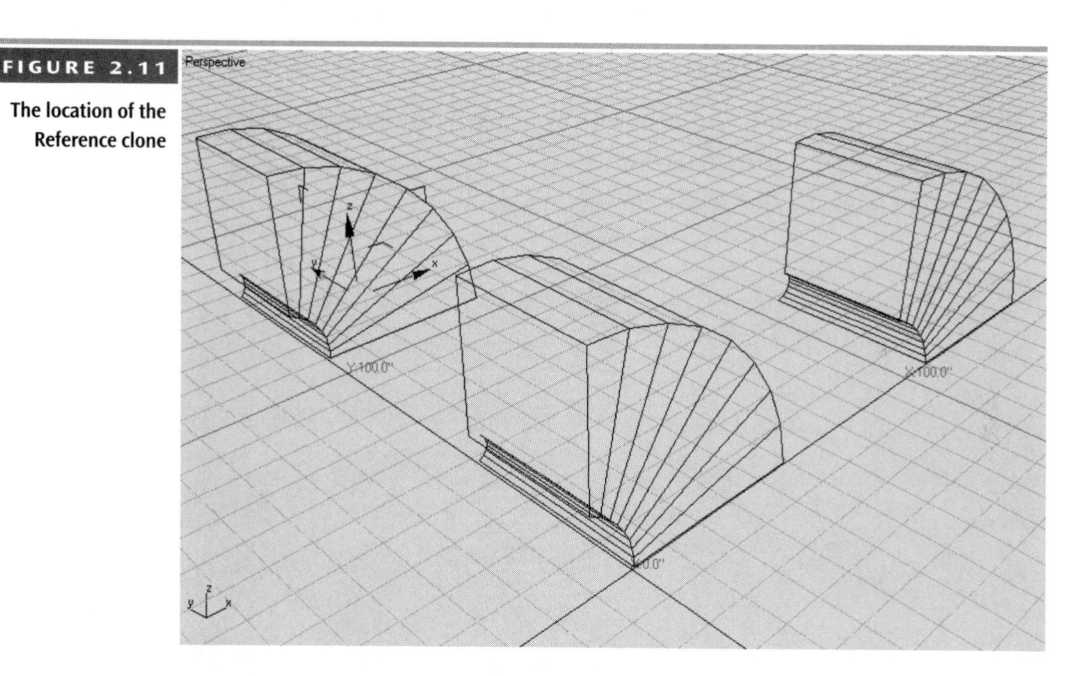

FIGURE 2.11 The location of the Reference clone

2. In the Clone Options dialog box, click the Reference radio button, then click OK.
3. Click the Clone farthest to the right to select it.
4. Change the Bend Angle parameter back to 60. Now all three of the clones change shape.

5. Click the newest clone to the far left to select it and look at the Modifier Stack. No parameters are offered and the Modifier Stack drop-down list shows a line.

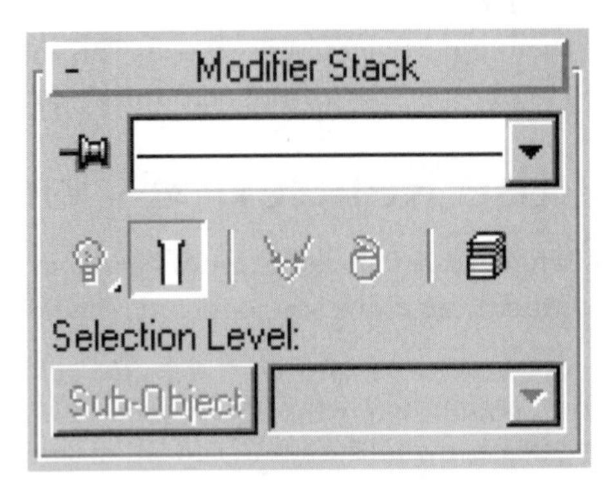

Although it may appear that no parameters are available, a little further investigation reveals that the shared modifiers of all the clones are also accessible through the instance.

1. With the Instance clone selected, click the Modifier Stack drop-down list.
2. Select Taper from the list.
3. In the Parameters rollout, adjust the Amount spinner downward to read –85. All of the clones change shape.

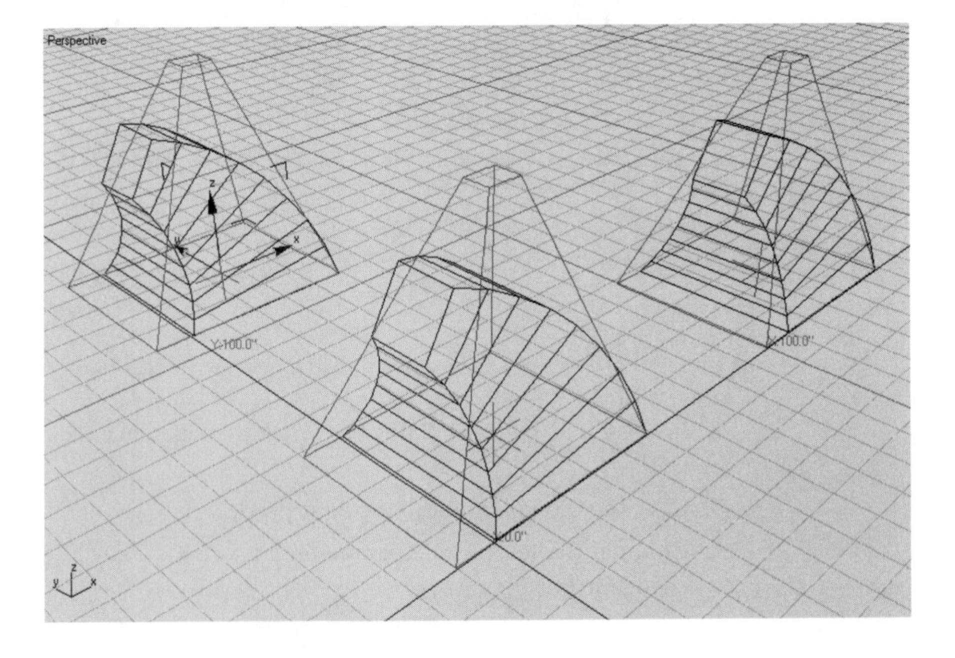

Here you can see that the Reference clone is really just like the Instance clone, but with one major difference. The Reference clone's modifier stack contains a line at the top. This line divides the shared modifiers from potential unshared modifiers. Try the following exercise to see how that line affects the sharing of modifiers.

1. With the box to the left selected, click the modifier stack drop-down list and select the line at the top of the list.
2. Click the More button in the Modifiers rollout, select Twist, then click OK. The Twist modifier is now added to the top of the modifier stack of the selected box.
3. In the Parameters rollout, click and drag the Angle spinner upward so that its value reads 70. Notice that the box changes shape independently of the other boxes.

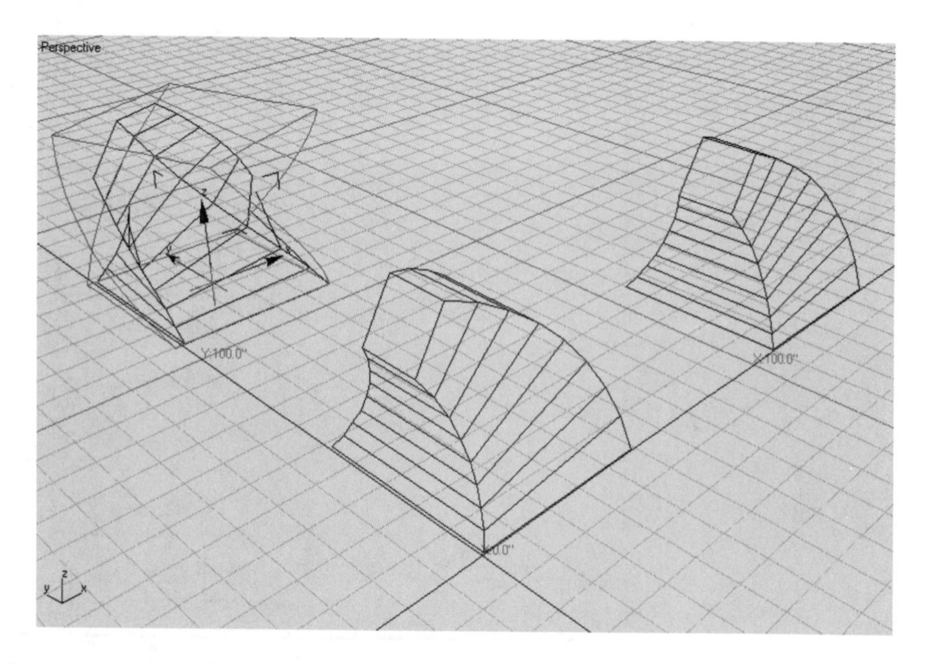

Here you see that the line in the modifier stack allows you to apply a modifier independent of the other shared modifiers. Try testing this by moving the Twist modifier below the line.

1. Click the Edit Stack tool in the Modifier Stack rollout.
2. In the Edit Modifier Stack dialog box, select Twist at the top of the list, then click the Cut button. Twist is removed from the list.

3. Click the Bend option to select it, then click the Paste button to paste the Twist modifier above the bend option. You'll see the Twist option appear above Bend but below the line.

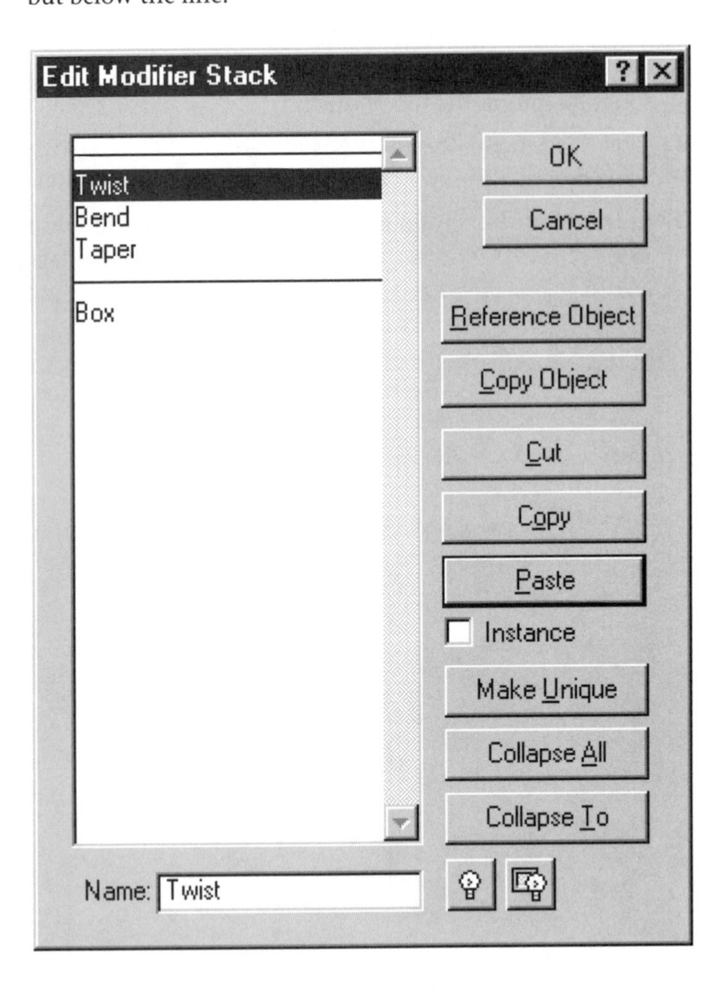

Move the Edit Modifier Stack dialog box so you can see the boxes in the viewport. Now all three boxes share the twist modifier.

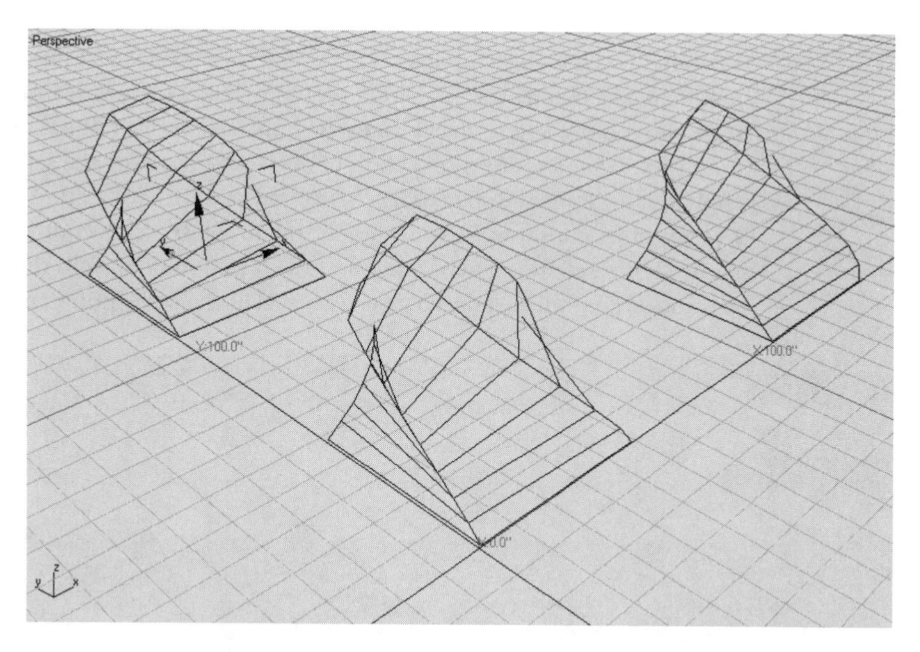

4. Select the twist modifier and click Cut to remove it, then click OK.

The Reference Clone's modifier stack shows you that the stack can be manipulated in quite a number of ways to achieve an effect across multiple objects. Next, you'll see another way that the stack can be used in conjunction with a modifier to apply the transform tools to multiple objects.

TIP If you're an AutoCAD user, you might think of Instance and Reference clones as being similar to Blocks in AutoCAD. But as you can see from these exercises, they are far more flexible in VIZ, as they can share some parameters and at the same time include parameters that are independent of the original object.

Scaling and Rotating Objects with Transform Tools

Now that you have a set of objects in your model, lets take a break from our look at modifiers to examine the Transform tools. In Chapter 1, you learned how you can scale and rotate a single object using the transform tools in the standard toolbar. You can also scale and rotate a collection of objects by selecting the set of objects and applying the Scale or Rotate tools. When you do this, by default, VIZ affects all of the selected objects uniformly. For example, if you rotate a collection of objects, they all rotate about a common axis. If you scale a collection of objects, they all change their scale, including the distance between objects in the collection (see Figure 1.12).

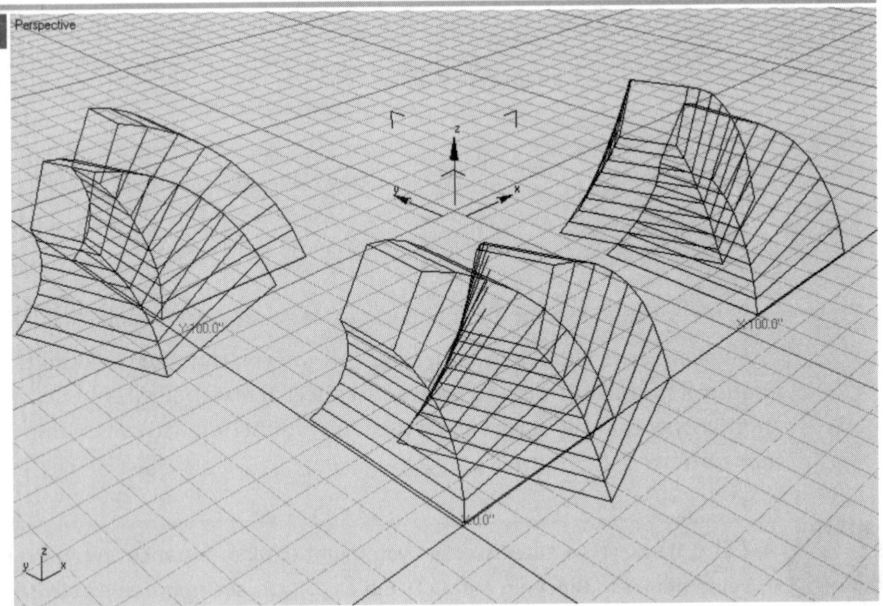

FIGURE 1.12A

Scaling and rotating objects in a selection set

FIGURE 1.12B

Scaling and rotating objects in a selection set

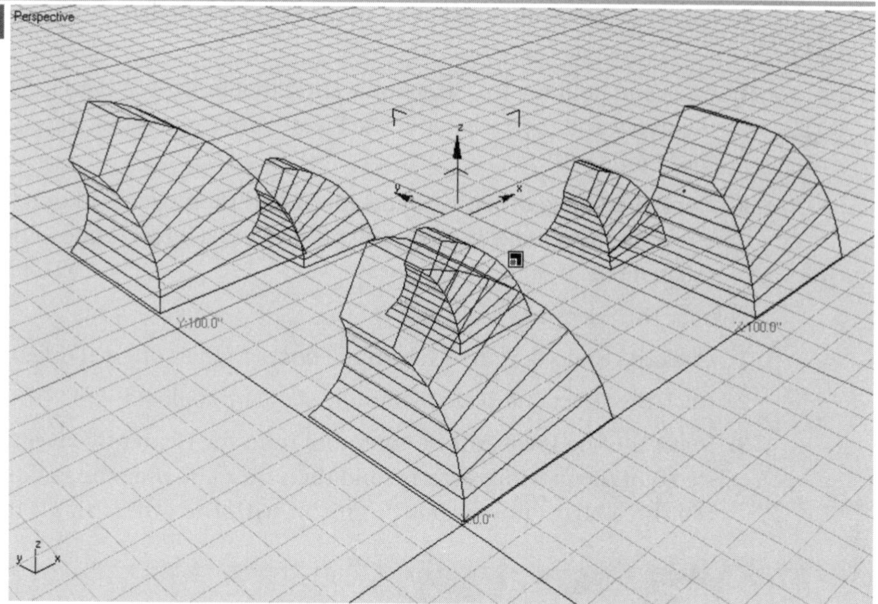

VIZ offers a few options that alter the way objects are affected by the transform tools. In this section, you'll learn firsthand how these Transform Center options give you a higher degree of control over the transform tools.

First try rotating one of the clones by itself.

NOTE **Though the exercise involves a set of cloned objects, the transform tools in the standard toolbar do not care whether the selected objects are clones of each other or simply a set of dissimilar objects.**

1. Click the Select and Rotate tool in the standard toolbar.
2. Click the box in the middle of the viewport in the foreground.
3. Click and drag the red X coordinate axis upward. The box rotates independently of the others.

4. Click the Undo button to return the box to its original orientation.

Here you see that the Rotate tool only affects the currently selected clone. You also see that you can use the axis gizmo to control the orientation of the rotation. Let's take a look at how the Rotate tool affects a group of objects.

1. Click the Select Object tool, then select all four objects. You can either click and drag a region enclosing all of the objects or Ctrl-click on each individual object.

2. Click the Select and Rotate tool in the standard toolbar.

3. Click and hold the Use Selection Center tool in the standard toolbar to open the flyout and then select the Use Pivot Point Center tool. This is the tool with the Pivot label.
4. Click the Use Pivot Point Center tool and then click and drag the red X axis arrow on the middle box. Now all of the cloned boxes rotate in unison with the original box.

Next try the Select and Scale tool.

1. Click the Undo button to return the boxes to their original orientation.
2. Click the Select and Scale tool in the standard toolbar.
3. Select the Use Pivot Point Center tool from the Center flyout just as you did in step 3 of the previous exercise and then click and drag the middle box. Each of the three boxes now scales in unison with the others about its own center.

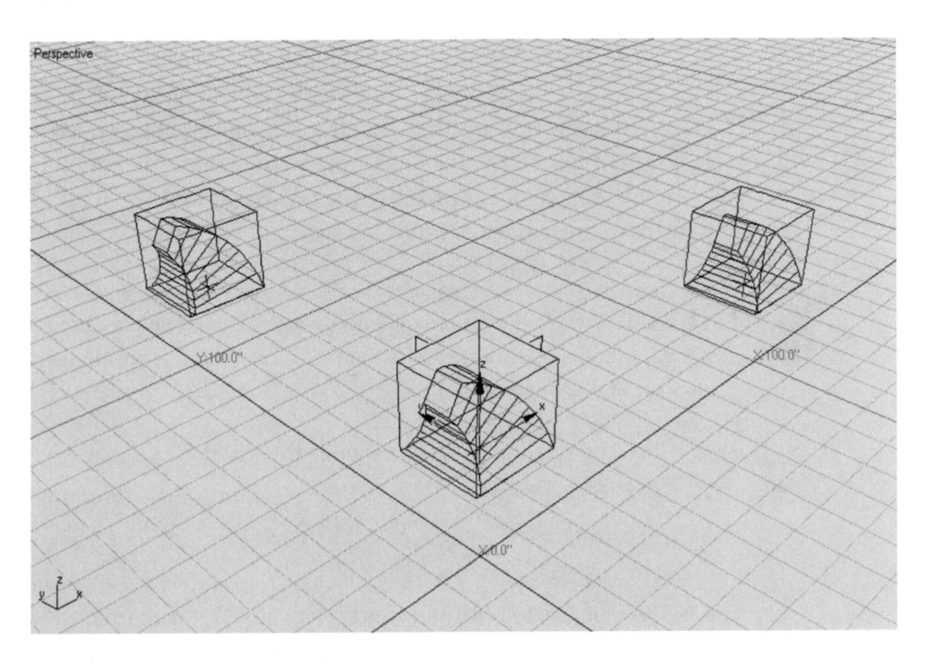

4. Click the Undo tool to return the boxes to their original size.

You've seen how the Use Pivot Point Center tool affects the Rotate and Scale transform tools. Next try the Use Transform Coordinate Center tool to see its effect on the Scale tool.

1. Click and hold the Use Pivot Point Center tool and then select the Use Transform Coordinate Center tool from the flyout. (This is the tool with the Xform label.)

   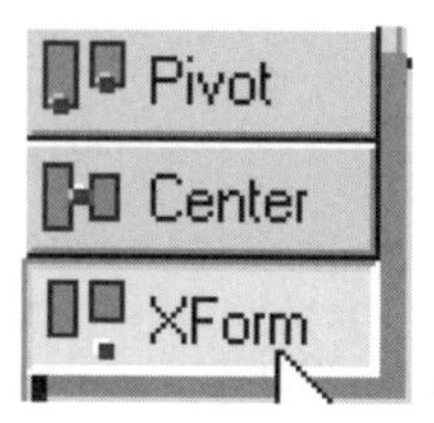

   Notice that the axis gizmo now appears at the origin of the world coordinate system on the grid.

2. Click and drag any of the selected objects. Notice that they change in scale about the origin of the model.

3. Click the Undo button twice to return all of the clones to their original orientation.

TIP **You can use the Undo tool to undo as many as 20 steps back. You may also set the number of steps VIZ will allow for Undo. To set the number of steps, choose Tools ➢ Options. Choose the General tab at the Options dialog box and then set the Undo Levels spinner to the value you want.**

As you can see from the previous exercise, the Transform Center options allow you to select the center location of the currently active transform tool. They are a simple set of tools that enhance your ability to control the transform tools. You haven't had a chance to try all of the options with all of the transform tools, so here's a summary of the Transform Center tool functions.

Use Pivot Point Center places the center of the transformation at the center of the selected object. If multiple objects are selected, each object is transformed about its own object space.

Use Selection Center places the center of the transformation at the center of the set of selected objects. This differs from User Pivot Point Center in that all objects move, scale, or rotate about a common, single point rather than about their individual object space center points.

Use Transform Coordinate Center is the default setting in new files, and it places the center of transformation at the origin of the world coordinate. Or if you are using a User grid, the center of transformation will be at the origin of the User grid. This option, in conjunction with a user grid, is useful for moving, scaling, or rotating an object or set of objects in relation to a specific point in a model.

NOTE Since this section is mainly concerned with Modifiers, I should mention the Xform Modifier here. The Xform modifier lets you scale and rotate objects from the modifier stack. This has the advantage of allowing you to apply transform tools to cloned objects without having to individually select the objects. It also has the effect of applying the transform tools to a specific position in the object data flow. Normally, transforms are evaluated after the modifiers, but you can *insert* transforms within the modifier stack using the Xform modifier.

Making a Clone Unique

At some point, you may decide that you want to turn a clone into a unique object so that it no longer reacts in unison with other clones. This can be done easily with the Make Unique tool.

1. Click the Select object tool, then select the clone to the far left.
2. Make sure the modify tab is selected in the Command Panel, then open the Modifier Stack drop-down list and select the horizontal line just above the Box listing.

3. Click the Make Unique tool just below the drop-down list. The selected box is now an independent object that is no longer connected to the other two clones.

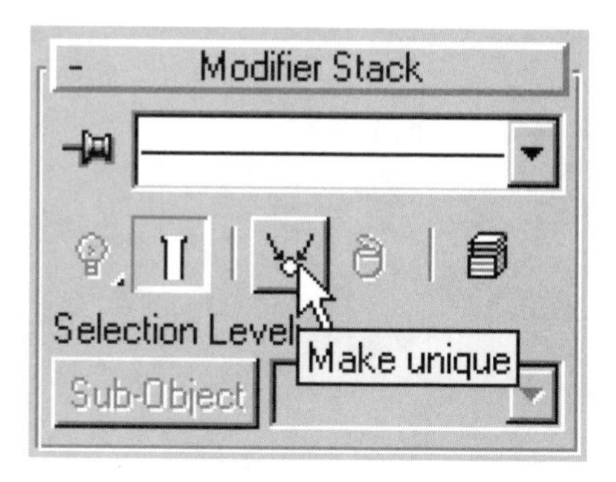

The horizontal line in the modifier stack separates the basic object type from the modifiers listed above it, but here you see another use for the line. It allows you to make a cloned object unique. Note that in the Reference clone to the far left, the horizontal line appears again at the top of the list. If you add more modifiers to that clone, those additional modifiers will only affect that clone and not the others. You can think of the line as a Uniqueness modifier.

Cloning a Modifier

You've learned the many ways that you can clone an object and edit those clones together. You've also seen most of the major methods used to create objects from primitives. Before you finish this chapter, there is one more feature you'll want to know about. At times you may want to clone just one modifier instead of an entire object. This allows you to have an object maintain a degree of uniqueness and still have at least one modifier *cloned* so that it acts on a set of objects. The following exercise will demonstrate the principle.

First make a copy of one of the clones.

1. Click the Select and Move tool.
2. Shift-click and drag the red Y coordinate arrow of the box to the far right.

3. Drag the copy to a location behind the box in the foreground so the set of boxes forms a square.

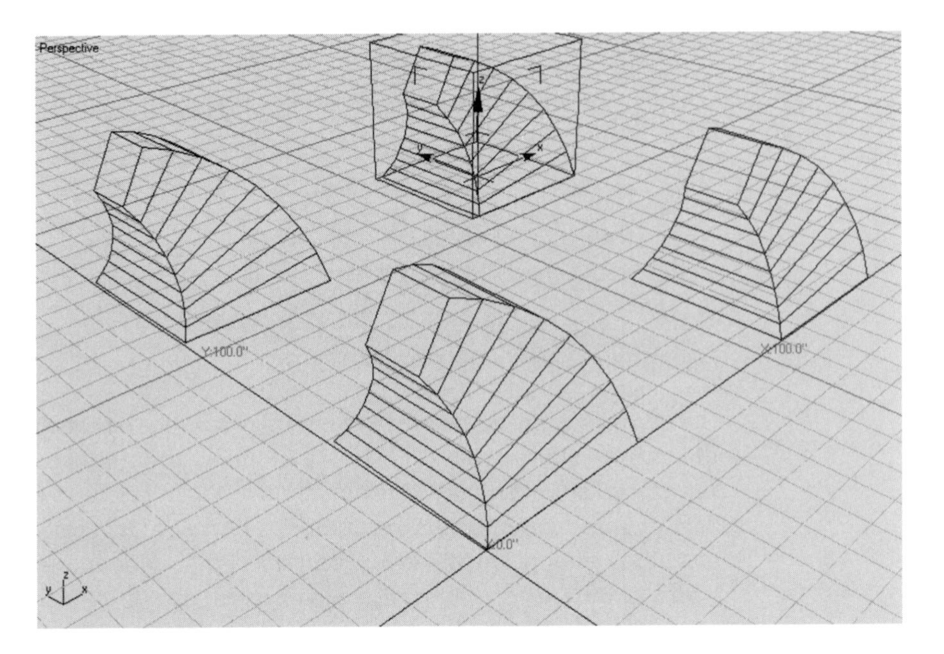

4. In the Clone Options dialog box, click the Copy radio button, then click OK.
5. Click the Select object tool and select the box in the middle foreground.

6. Click the Modify tab of the Command Panel. You'll see the modifier gizmo for the clones. Notice that the copy you just made does not show its gizmo, indicating that it is not a clone.

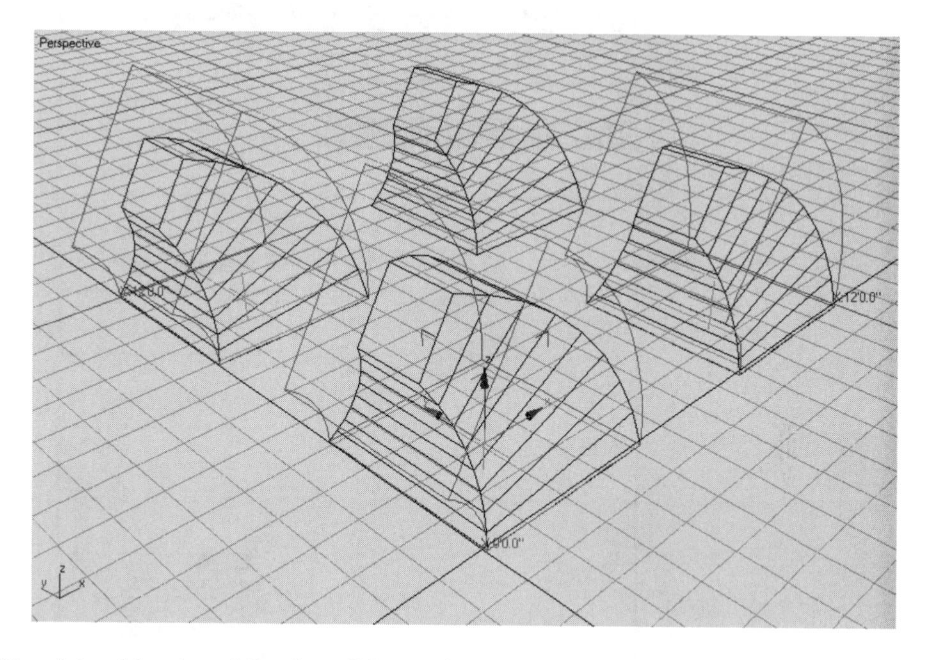

Now lets add a cloned Bend modifier to the new copy. Start by copying the modifier to the clipboard.

1. With the box in the foreground selected, click the Edit Stack tool.
2. In the Edit Modifier Stack dialog box, click the Bend modifier in the list.
3. Click the Copy button, then click OK to close the dialog box.

For the final step, add the copied modifier to the new object.

1. Click the new box you created in the last exercise.
2. Click the Edit Stack tool. Then in the Edit Modifier Stack dialog box, click the Bend option. Place the new Bend modifier above the old one and then delete the old Bend modifier.

3. Click the Instance check box. This is important. (Otherwise the pasted modifier you add will not act in unison with the other copies.)

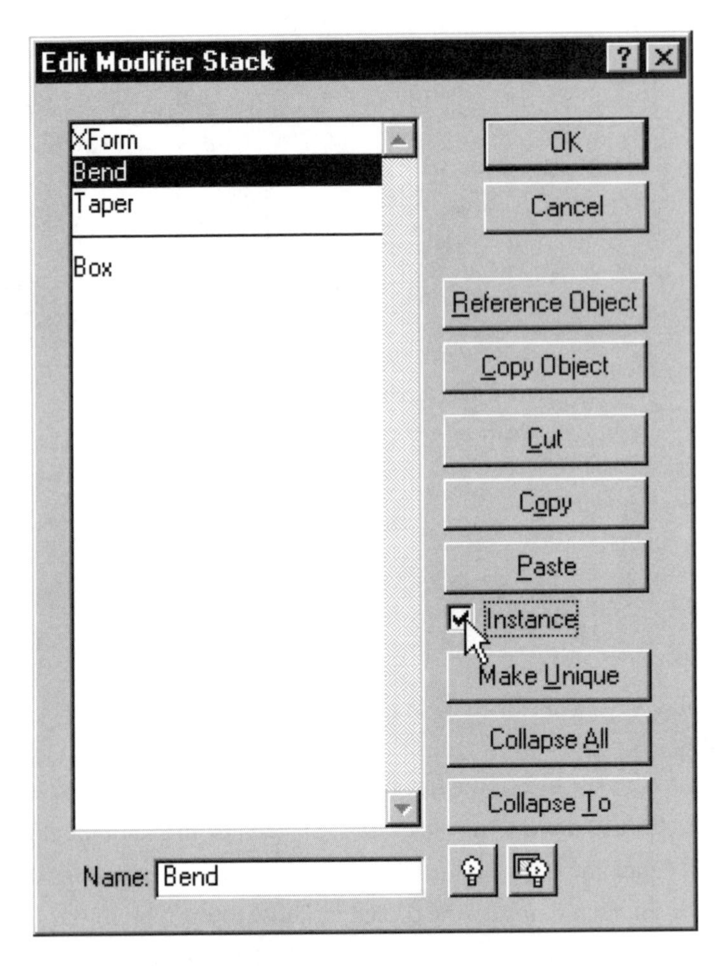

4. Click Paste. A second Bend modifier appears in the list.
5. Click the Bend modifier just above the Taper modifier and then click Cut. You don't need two bend modifiers on top of each other.
6. Click OK.

You've just created an instance clone of the Bend modifier. Now let's see the results.

1. Click the box in the foreground.
2. Click the Modifier Stack drop-down list, then select Taper. Notice that the Taper gizmo appears for two of the boxes. The gizmo does *not* appear for the copy you just created, nor does it appear for the box that you made unique.

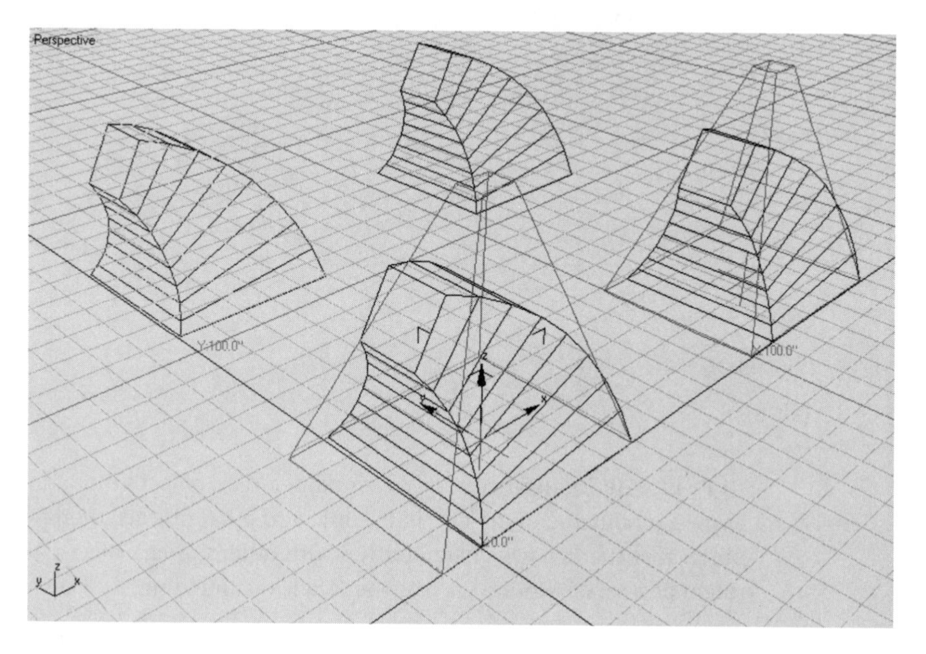

3. Try adjusting the Amount spinner in the Parameters rollout. The instance and reference clones move in unison with the original box, but the newest copy does not.
4. Click the Modifier Stack drop-down list again, then select Bend. Notice how three of the boxes show the bend gizmo.

5. Change the Angle spinner to 90. Three of the objects change their shape.

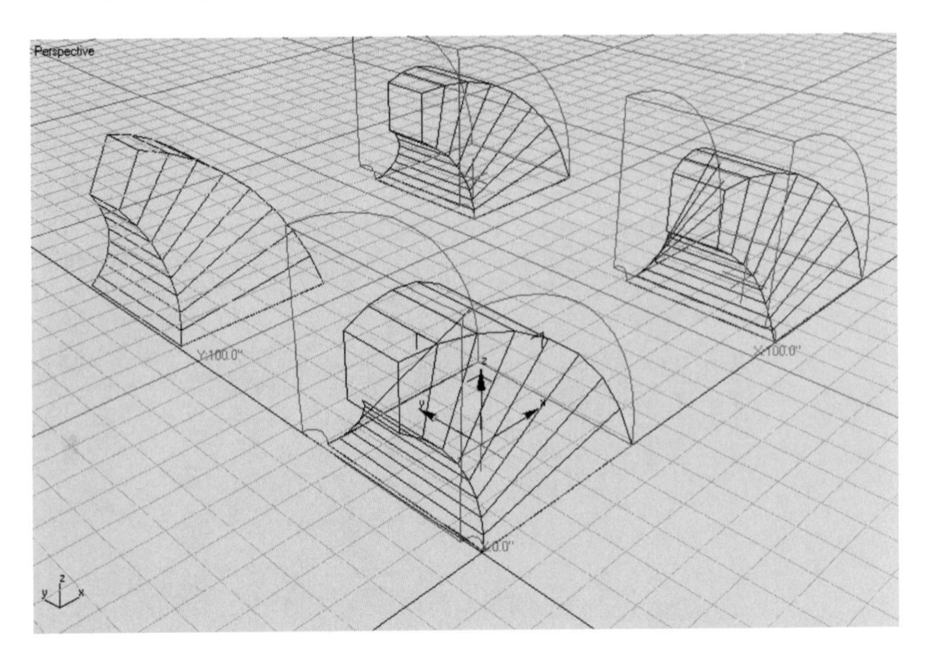

By placing an instance copy of a modifier in an object's modifier stack, you can apply a modifier to an object that is linked to other objects, thereby allowing a unique object that shares a few characteristics with other similar objects. An example of this might be a set of windows across the façade of a building, as shown in Figure 2.13.

FIGURE 2.13

A façade of a building using cloned references for windows

Most of the windows are identical, with the exception of one or two. The window design can be modified for one window, and all the windows are affected. Some of the windows may need to share only a few (but not all) of the parameters of the rest of the windows.

Looking at Extended Primitives

Before moving on to the next chapter, you may want to be aware of the Extended Primitives. These are a set of primitives that offer a few more parameters than the Standard Primitives. In most cases, the extended primitives offer shapes with smoothing applied to their corners. Some of the other Extended Primitives are complex shapes such as the Hedra and Gengon. Figure 2.14 shows the extended Primitives and some of the parameters that control their shape. You can get to the Extended Primitives by clicking the Geometry tool in the Create tab of the Command Panel, then selecting Extended Primitives from the drop-down list that appears just below the Create tools.

FIGURE 2.14

Extended Primitives

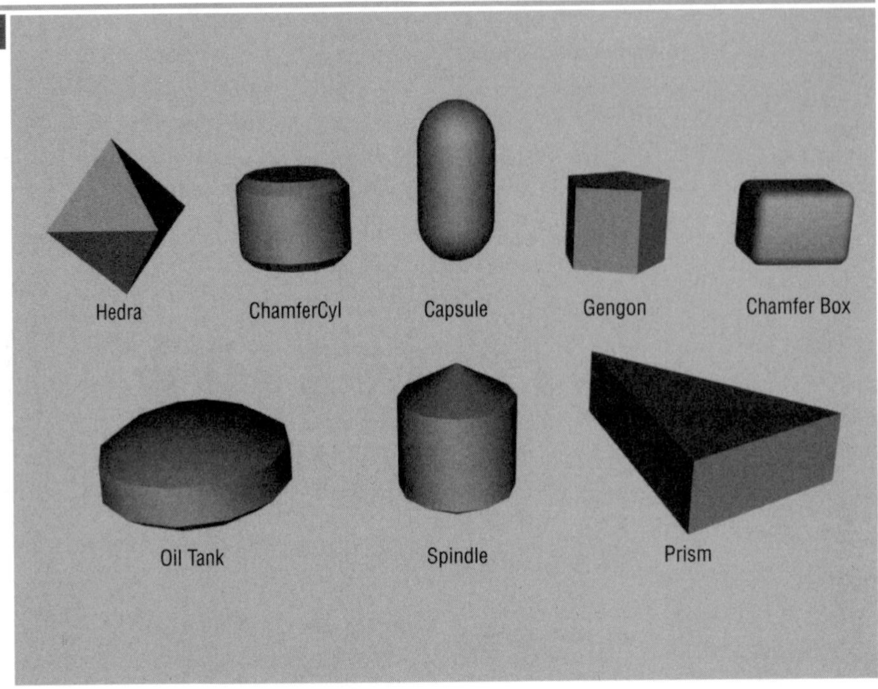

In several of the Extended Primitives, you'll see a Fillet parameter. This controls the radius of the corners. For example, the ChamferCyl primitive has a Fillet parameter that works in conjunction with a Fillet Segment parameter to control the rounding of its top and bottom edges. The Oiltank and Spindle primitives use a Blend parameter to round their corners.

Modeling a Couch

Up until now, you've just been creating random forms using the Primitives. In this last set of exercises, you'll get a chance to create a small couch to try out some of the tools you've learned so far.

Start by setting up a new file.

1. Save your sample drawing as **My sample.max**, then choose File ➢ New.
2. In the New Design dialog box, choose New All, then click OK.

3. Click the Min/Max tool in the Viewport Navigation controls to view all four viewports.

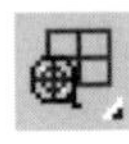

3. Click the Zoom Extents All tool in the Viewport toolbar to set all of the viewports to their default views.

You'll start your model by creating the base frame. For this you'll use one of the extended primitives discussed earlier.

1. Click the Create tab of the command panel.
2. Click the Geometry tool, then select Extended Primitives from the drop-down list.

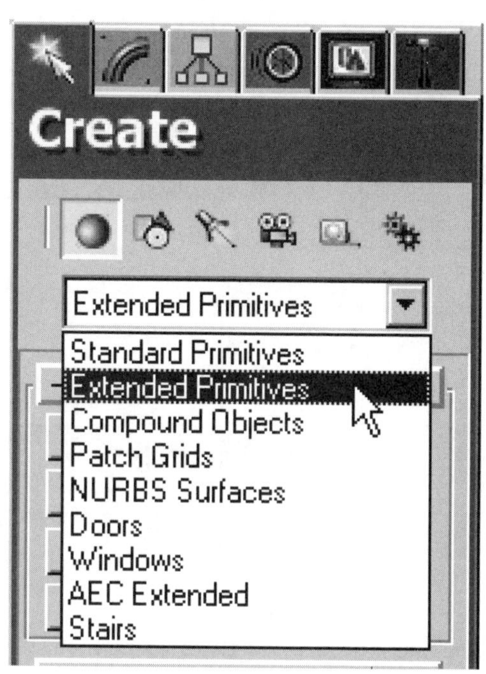

3. Click the Chamfer Box tool, then click the Keyboard Entry rollout.

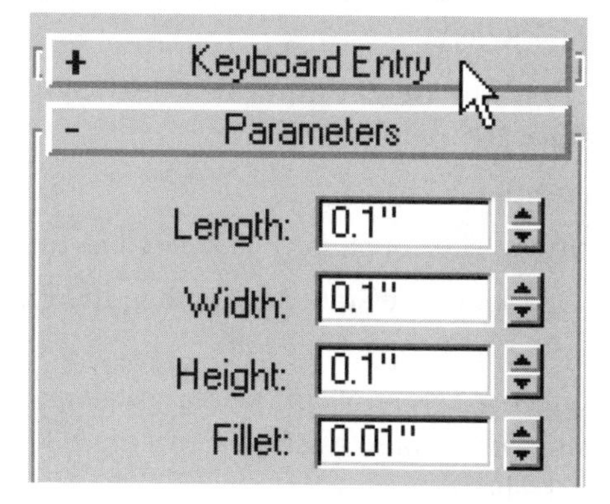

4. Click the Length input box in the Keyboard Entry rollout and enter **20"**(cr).
5. Press Tab to advance to the Width input box and enter **44"**(cr).
6. Press Tab again to advance to the Height input box and enter **9"**(cr).

7. Press Tab and enter **1″**(cr) for the Fillet value.
8. Click Create. The base is created.
9. Click Zoom Extents All to get an enlarged view of the base.

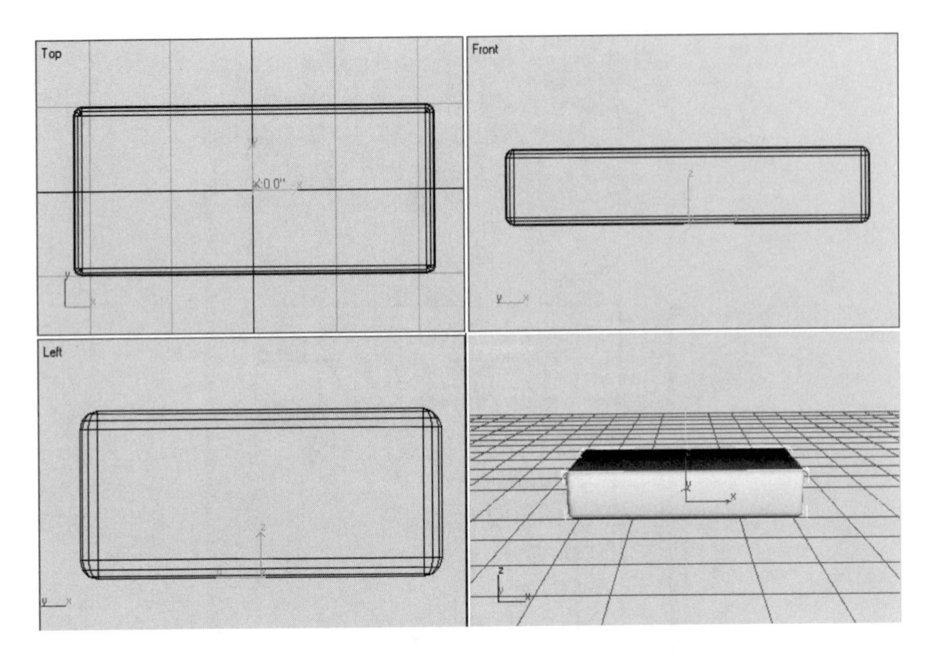

In this exercise, you created the base strictly by using the keyboard Entry rollout. Now create the back of the couch.

1. Click the Length input box of the Keyboard Entry rollout to select the entire value there, then enter **8″**(cr).
2. Press Tab twice to go to the Height input box, leaving the Width input box unchanged. Then enter **26″**.
3. Press Tab again, then enter **2″**(cr).
4. Click the Create button. The couch back is created in the middle of the base.
5. Click the Select Move tool in the Standard Toolbar, then right-click in the Top viewport to make it active.
6. Click and drag the green Y axis arrow of the seat back upward to move the seat back to the back side of the base as shown in Figure 2.15. Click the Zoom Extents All tool to get a better view.

FIGURE 2.15

Moving the seat back into position

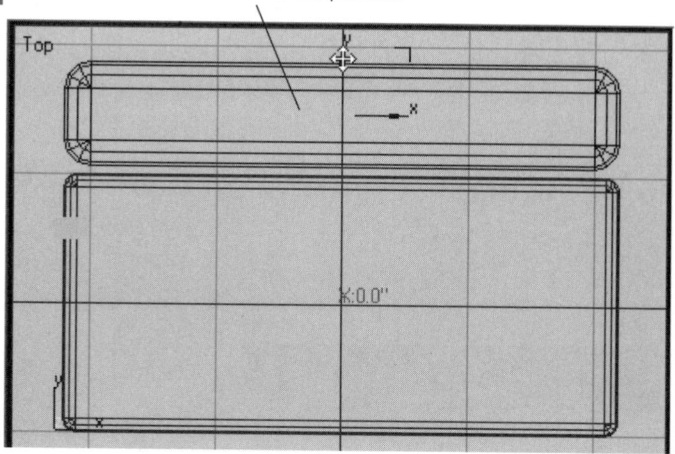
Move the seat back to this position.
Top

Let's also rotate the seat back so it is angled slightly backward.

1. Click the Select and Rotate tool in the Standard Toolbar.
2. Click and drag the red X axis arrow upward and watch the coordinate readout at the bottom of the window. When the readout shows –8 (minus eight) degrees, release the mouse button.

Now apply a Squeeze modifier to the back to add an arch to its shape.

1. Click the Modify tab in the command panel, then click the More button in the Modifiers rollout.
2. Select Squeeze from the Modifiers dialog box, then click OK.
3. Go to the Axial Bulge group in the Parameters group and click and drag the Amount spinner upward until its value reads .14.
4. Press Tab and set the Curve value to 3.

Notice that the seat back shows a gizmo bending upward, but the back itself does not bend. This is because the back is only made up of a single segment in the horizontal direction.

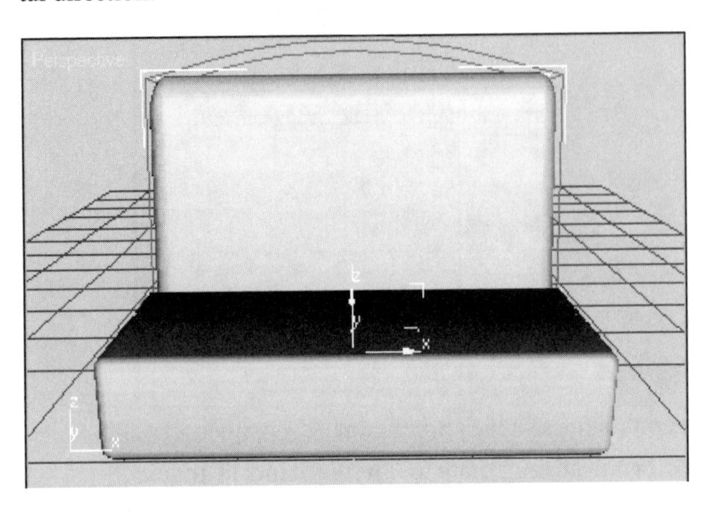

To allow the Squeeze option to take affect, you need to increase the number of horizontal segments in the seat back.

1. Click the drop-down list in the Modifier stack and select Chamfer Box.
2. Scroll the command panel up until you see the Width Segs input box under the Parameters rollout.

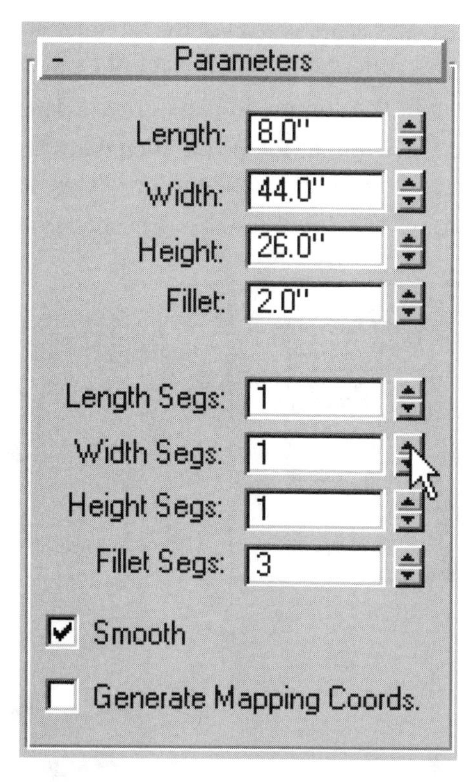

3. Click the Width Segs input box and enter **20**(cr). The back divides into 20 segments, and a curve appears at the top of the back.
4. Click the Zoom Extents All tool in the Viewports toolbar to get a better look at your work so far.

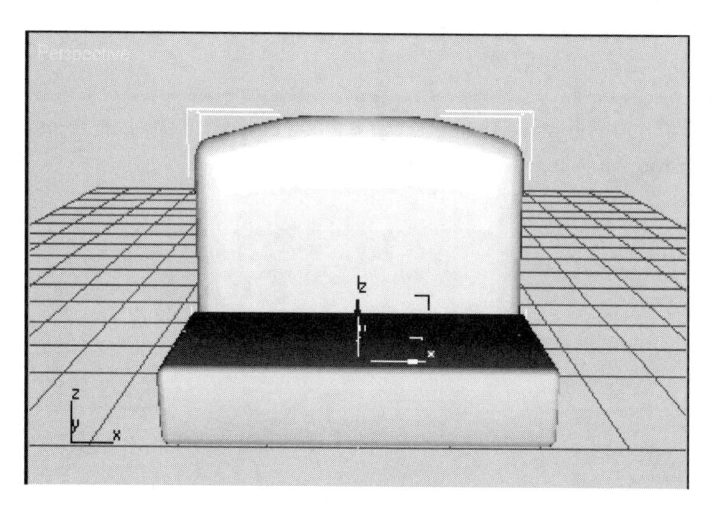

Now let's add the arms. Once again, you'll use the Chamfer Box extended primitive, but this time you'll use a different modifier to adjust its shape.

1. Click the Create tab in the command panel, then click Chamfer Box again.
2. Click the Keyboard Entry rollout to open it, then enter **28″** for the Length, **7″** for the width, **22″** for the height, and **2″** for the fillet value.
3. Click the Create button. The arm appears in the center of the base.

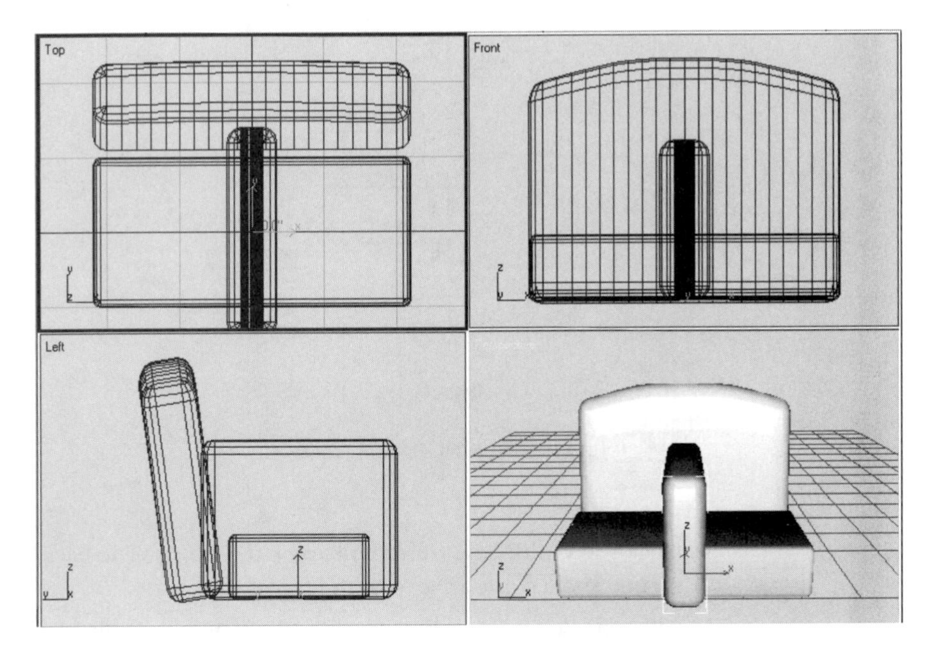

4. Click the Select and Move tool, then, in the Top viewport, click and drag the arm into the position shown in Figure 2.16.

TIP **If you place the Select and Move cursor on the corner mark of the Transform gizmo, you can move the arm freely in the XY plane.**

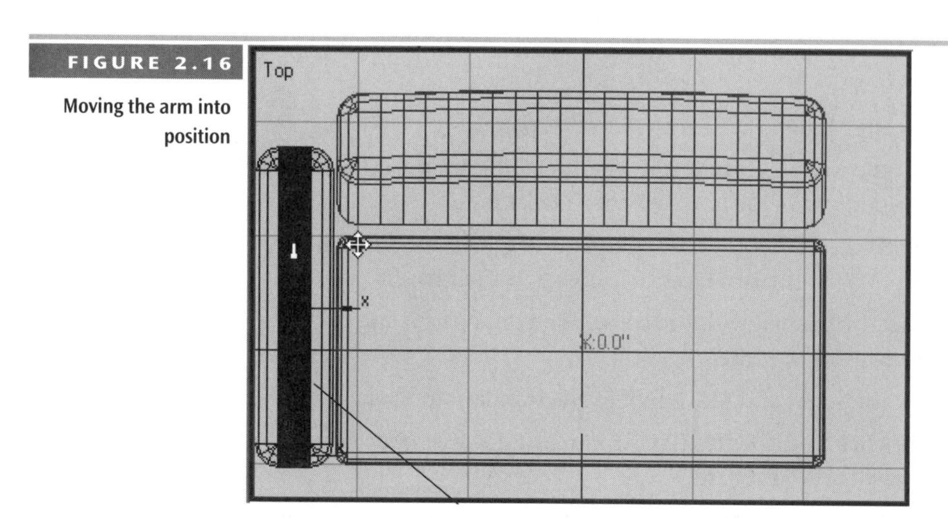

FIGURE 2.16
Moving the arm into position

5. Shift-click and drag the red X axis arrow of the arm to the right until you see a copy of the arm in the position shown in Figure 2.17.

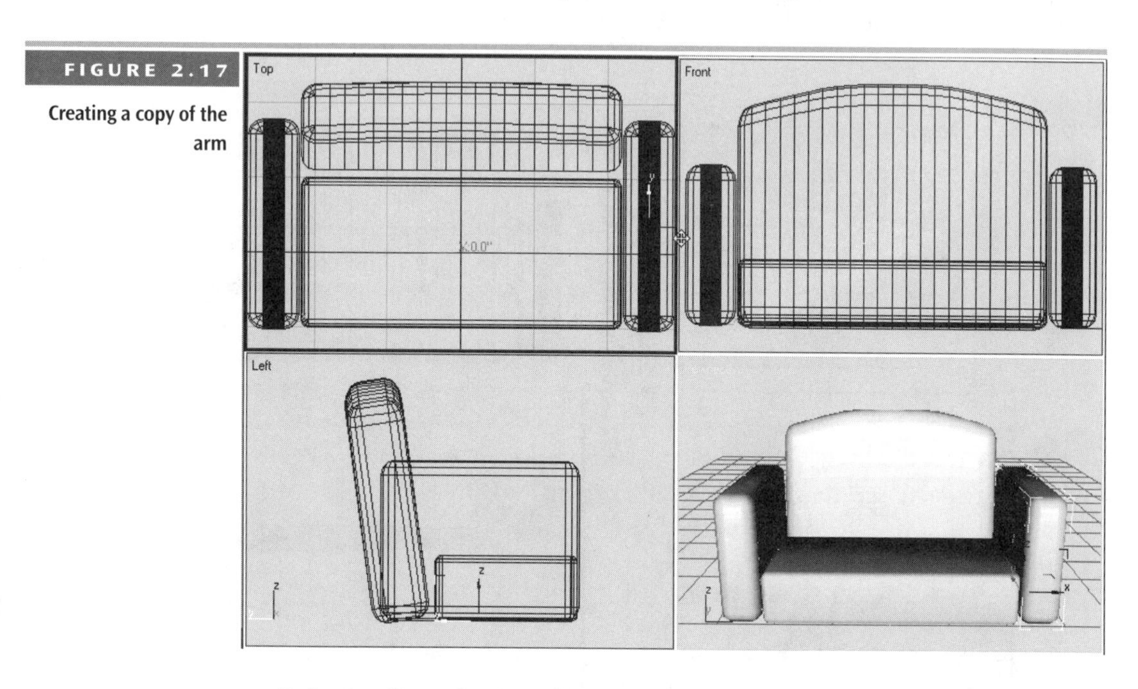

FIGURE 2.17
Creating a copy of the arm

6. In the Clone Options dialog box, click instance, then click OK.

You made an instance copy because in the next step you want to taper both arms simultaneously.

1. Click the Modify tab of the command panel.
2. Click the More button in the Modifiers rollout, select Taper near the bottom of the Modifiers dialog box, and then click OK.
3. In the Parameters rollout, click and drag the Amount spinner until its value reads 0.17. Both arms taper, narrowing at their bases.

You're nearly finished with the couch. The final part is the seat cushions. For that, you'll use a copy of the base.

1. Click the Select and Move tool in the standard toolbar.
2. Right-click in the Left viewport to make it active. This viewport offers the clearest view of the seat base.
3. Click the seat base to select it, then shift-click and drag the green Y axis arrow upward until you have a copy of the seat base as shown in Figure 2.18.
4. In the Clone Options dialog box, click the Copy radio button. Then click OK. You don't want this copy to be linked to the base.

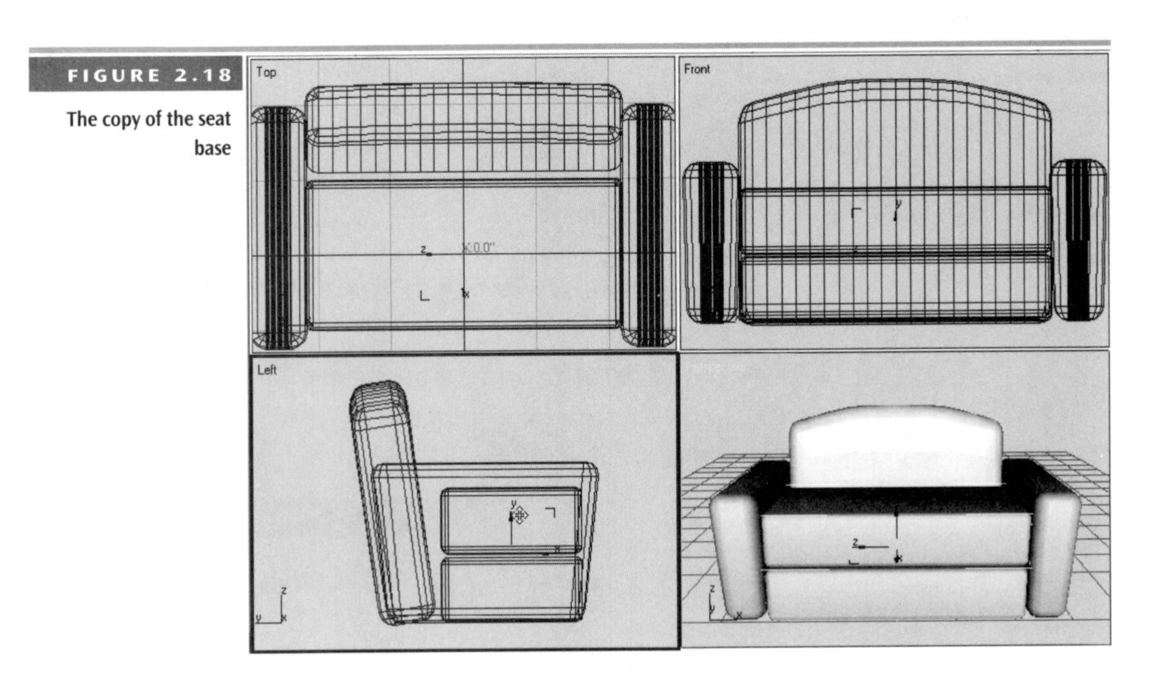

FIGURE 2.18

The copy of the seat base

You need to change a few parameters for the cushion. It's a bit too thick, and you'll want two cushions to fit in the seat, so you'll have to reduce the width of the cushion.

1. Click the Modify tab of the command panel.
2. Change the Length and Width values in the Parameters rollout to **22″**.
3. Press Tab and change the Height value to **7″**.
4. With the Select and Move tool selected, right-click in the Top viewport, then click and drag the red X axis arrow of the cushion to the left to place the cushion as shown in Figure 2.19.

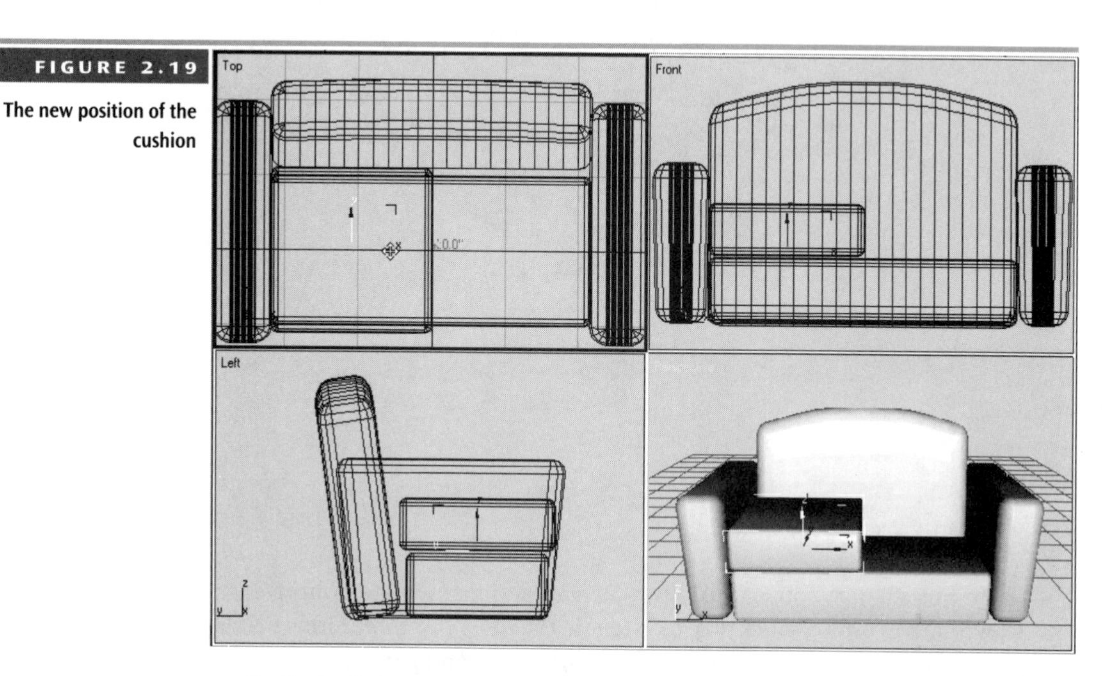

FIGURE 2.19

The new position of the cushion

5. Shift-click and drag the red X axis arrow to the right to make a copy of the cushion on the right side of the couch.
6. In the Clone Options dialog box, click Instance, then click OK.

The couch is complete. To get a better view do the following:

1. Right-click the Perspective view to make it active.
2. Choose View ➢ Views ➢ SW.
3. Click the Zoom Extents All tool in the Viewport toolbar.
4. Click the Min/Max Toggle in the Viewport toolbar. Your view will look like Figure 2.20.

FIGURE 2.20

The completed couch

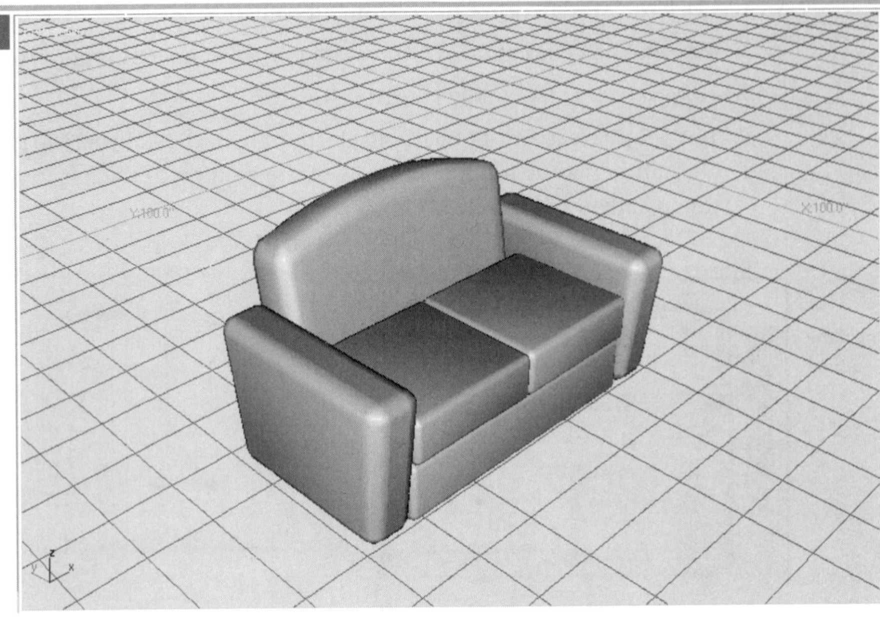

5. Save the file as MyCouch.max.

Summary

In this chapter, you learned how to create and manipulate primitive objects. Primitives offer a quick way to generate the most common forms you'll be working with in your modeling. You saw how the Command panel plays a key role in object creation and editing. In particular, you examined the role of the Modifier Stack in modeling objects. You'll come back to the Modifier stack frequently throughout this book, but this introduction will serve as the foundation on which you'll build other skills.

While there is still a lot to cover, you've now learned the basic tools you'll need to explore 3D Studio VIZ with confidence. In the next chapter, you'll learn about another type of primitive called a *Spline*. The spline offers a way to quickly create complex shapes. You can manipulate splines using the same tools you learned about in this chapter, plus you have the added advantage of being able to control the basic outline of the shape.

chapter 3

Creating Shapes with Splines

FEATURING

- *Drawing with Splines*
- *Modifying a Shape Using Sub-Object Levels*
- *Drawing Walls with Splines*
- *Using Canned Shapes to Add Walls*
- *Joining Closed Splines with Boolean Tools*
- *Creating a Solid Shape with Splines*
- *Splines as Tubes*
- *Using the AEC Walls and Doors*

Creating Shapes with Splines

In the last chapter, you learned about VIZ's standard primitives and how they can be shaped by parameters and modifiers into an infinite variety of forms. In this chapter, you'll continue your look at primitives with an exploration of *splines*. Splines are a type of primitive that are in a way even more *primitive* than the ones you looked at in Chapter 2. You can create more varied forms with splines than you can with the Standard Primitives, but they require a bit more work to use.

In general, you can think of splines as objects composed of straight or curved line segments. Splines do not enclose any volume and are basically two-dimensional, with the exception of the Helix, which is a 3D spiral.

Strictly speaking, a spline is a 2D line whose shape is controlled by its vertices. *Bézier* splines are a type of spline that includes features for controlling its curvature. VIZ stretches this definition of spline a bit by allowing you to move a spline's vertex to any location in 3D space. Still, splines are initially created as two-dimensional objects, with the exception of the Helix. Like the standard primitives in VIZ, most splines are parametric, that is, they can be modified at any time using parameters like the width and length parameters of the Box standard primitive.

The beauty of splines is that with them you can create an outline of virtually any 2D shape, then extrude the outline into the third dimension. You can also use splines as paths for a variety of purposes such as camera motion for animated sequences, or the path for a *loft,* which is a type of extruded form along a path.

In this chapter, you'll learn how to use splines to create complex forms. You'll see how you can apply modifiers to enhance splines, just as you did with standard primitives. You'll also begin to explore methods for editing objects on what is called the *sub-object* level. This is a level of editing at which you can manipulate the components that make up an object.

Drawing with Splines

I mentioned that *most* VIZ shapes are parametric, that is, they offer a set of parameters that let you modify the shape at will. One type of spline, called the *Line,* is the exception. The Line spline does not offer parametric editing. Once you've created a Line, you cannot use parameters to modify its shape. Lines behave more like the common splines used in other computer design and drafting programs.

As you'll see in this and later chapters, the ability to edit the location and characteristics of an object's vertices is an essential part of creating and editing forms in VIZ. In this chapter, you'll begin work with splines and their associated vertices to gain a better understanding of how you can manipulate objects in general. You'll start with the most primitive of the primitive objects, the Line. With the Line spline tool, you can draw line segments, curves, squares, or just about any 2D shape you want. Such shapes can then be extruded in a manner similar to the standard primitives you saw in the last chapter. So let's get started by drawing a simple rectangle using a Line spline.

1. Start 3D Studio VIZ, then click the Min/Max toggle tool to reveal the Top, Left, and Front viewports.
2. Click the Top viewport, then click the Min/Max toggle tool again to enlarge the viewport.
3. If it isn't selected already, click the Create tab in the Command Panel.

4. Click the Shapes tool. Note that the drop-down list shows splines.

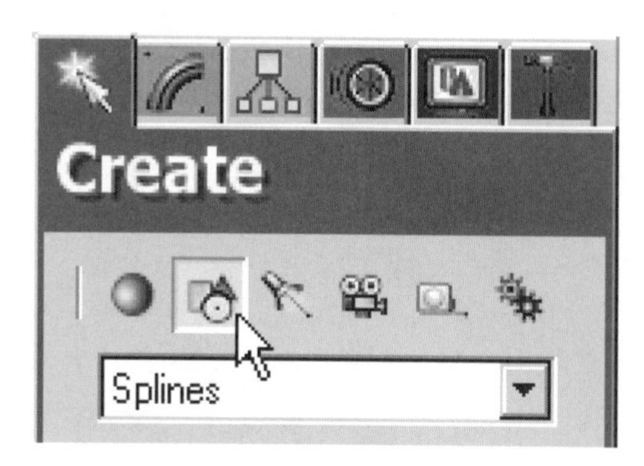

5. Click the Line button in the Object Type rollout. (You may instead select Line from the Draw Shapes tab of the Tab Panel.) Notice that a set of new rollouts appears in the bottom half of the Command Panel.

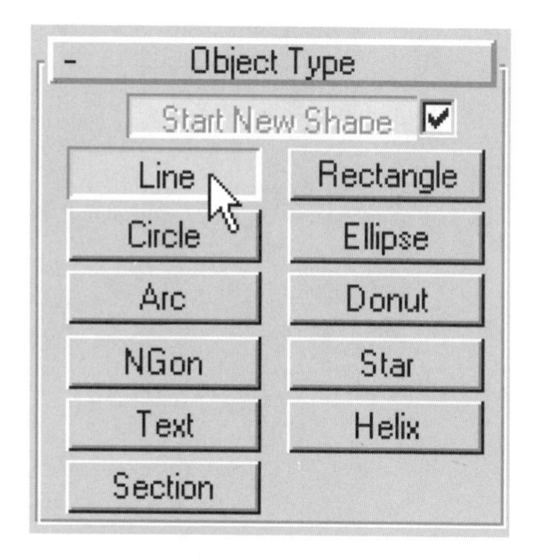

The Line options that appear in the Command Panel offer a variety of ways to construct a spline from line segments.

Drawing Straight-Line Segments

Now you're ready to draw a spline made of line segments. Use Figure 3.1 to help you select points as you draw the spline in the next exercise. You don't have to be too exact, because you're just practicing right now.

1. Click a point near coordinate 0.0",10'0.0",0.0" just above the 0,0 origin in the viewport. You can use the coordinate readout at the bottom of the VIZ window to locate the point. Now as you move the cursor, a rubber-banding line follows from the point you just clicked.

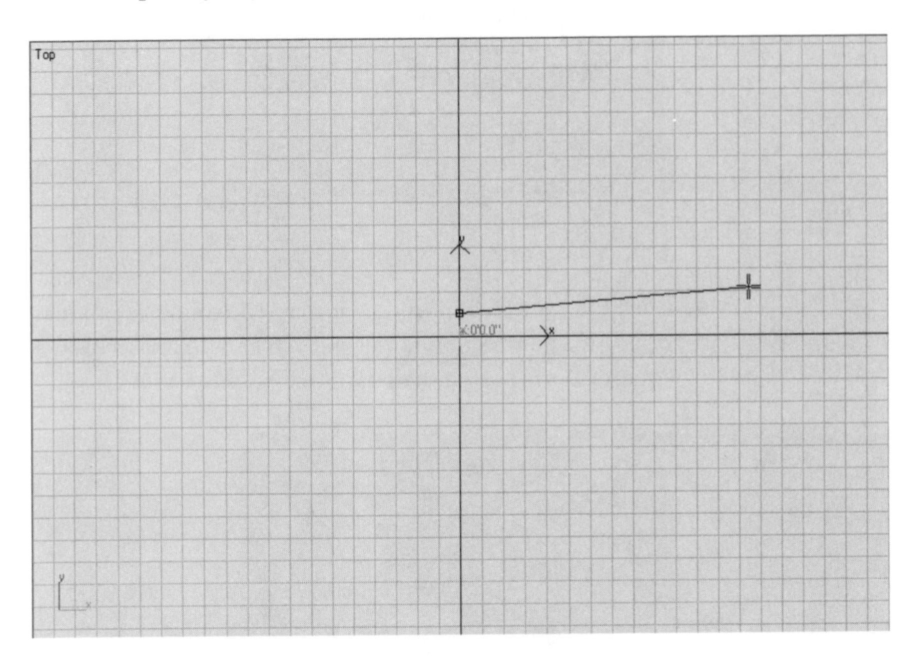

2. Place the cursor near the 15′ X coordinate directly to the right of the first point, then click. You can use the coordinate readout again to locate a relative coordinate near 15′0.0″,0.0″,0.0″. A line segment is fixed between the two points you selected. (Don't worry if your line segment is not exactly straight.)

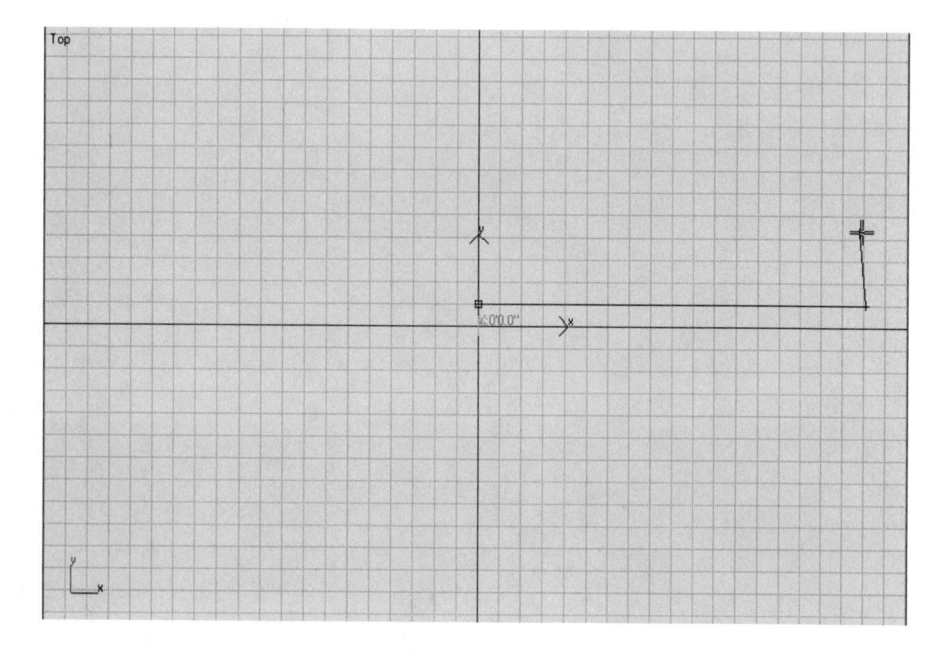

3. Click a point about 10′ in the Y direction, then click again as shown in Figure 3.1.

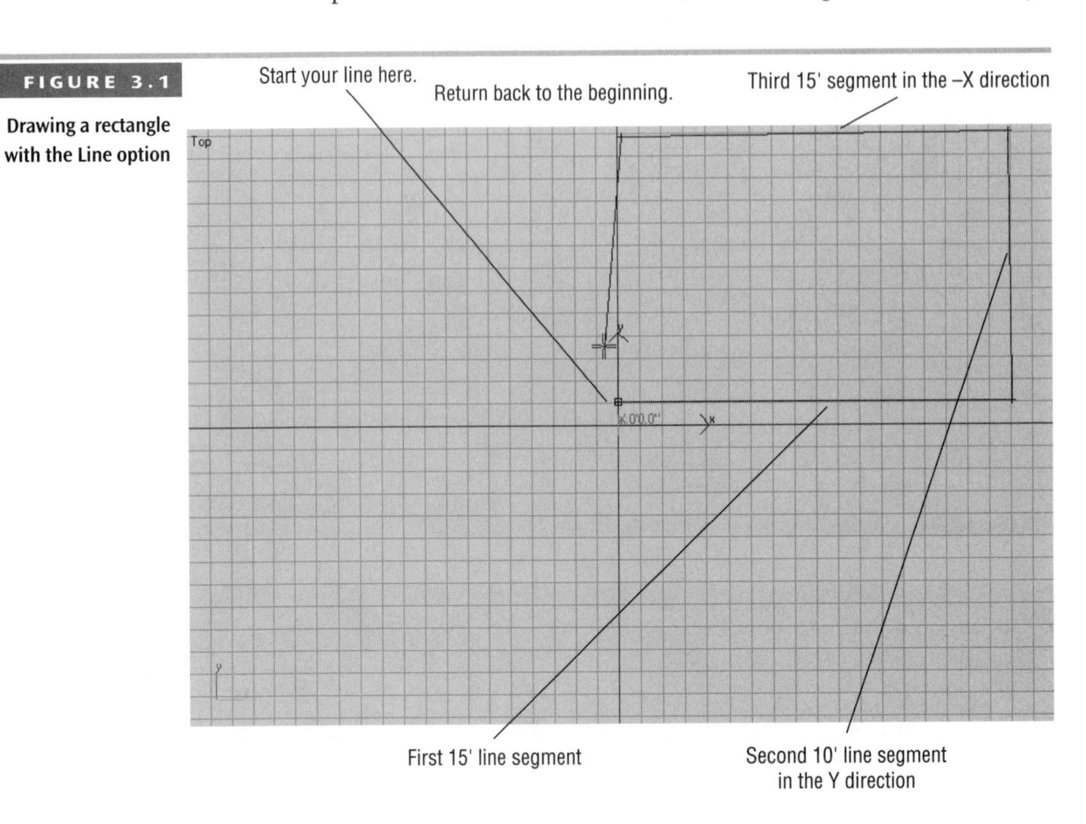

FIGURE 3.1

Drawing a rectangle with the Line option

4. Finally, click the beginning of the line segment at coordinate 0,0. You'll see a dialog box asking you whether you want to close the spline tool.

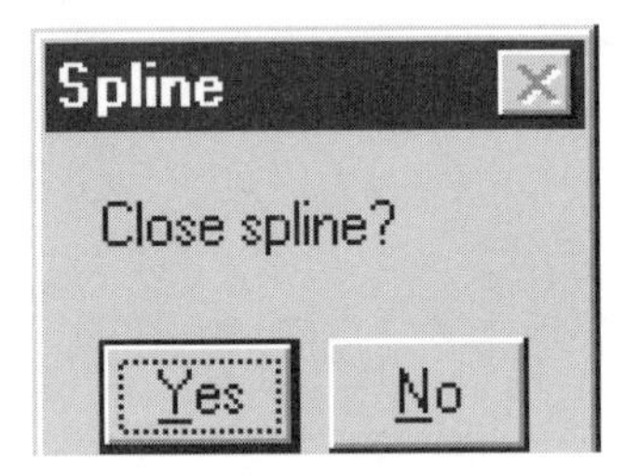

8. Click Yes. The rectangle is complete, and VIZ awaits your next point selection to draw another spline.

You've just drawn a rectangle. It's not necessarily straight, but now you know that you can draw a rectangle by clicking on points in the drawing area. You also saw that you can close the set of line segments by clicking on the beginning point.

The Spline dialog box appears, offering you the option to either close the set of line segments or leave it open. When you select Close, the beginning and end points of the spline are connected exactly end to end.

Constraining Lines Vertically and Horizontally with Ortho

Some of the lines you drew may not have been drawn so as to be perfectly horizontal or vertical. VIZ offers a tool that constrains your lines to perfectly horizontal and vertical lines, much like a T-square and triangle constrain your lines when you draft on a drafting board. Draw another rectangle using the Ortho mode.

1. Make sure the line button is still active—it should be green in color and should appear to be in a down position.
2. Click a point about 10" directly below the 0,0 coordinate, as shown in Figure 3.2. Once again, you see a rubber-banding line.
3. Press the F8 key. You see an orange compass appear at the point you selected and the line is constrained to horizontal and vertical directions. Also notice that the Ortho Button at the Bottom of the VIZ window is active.

4. Point the cursor downward and notice that a red number shows the direction of your line in degrees (see Figure 3.2).

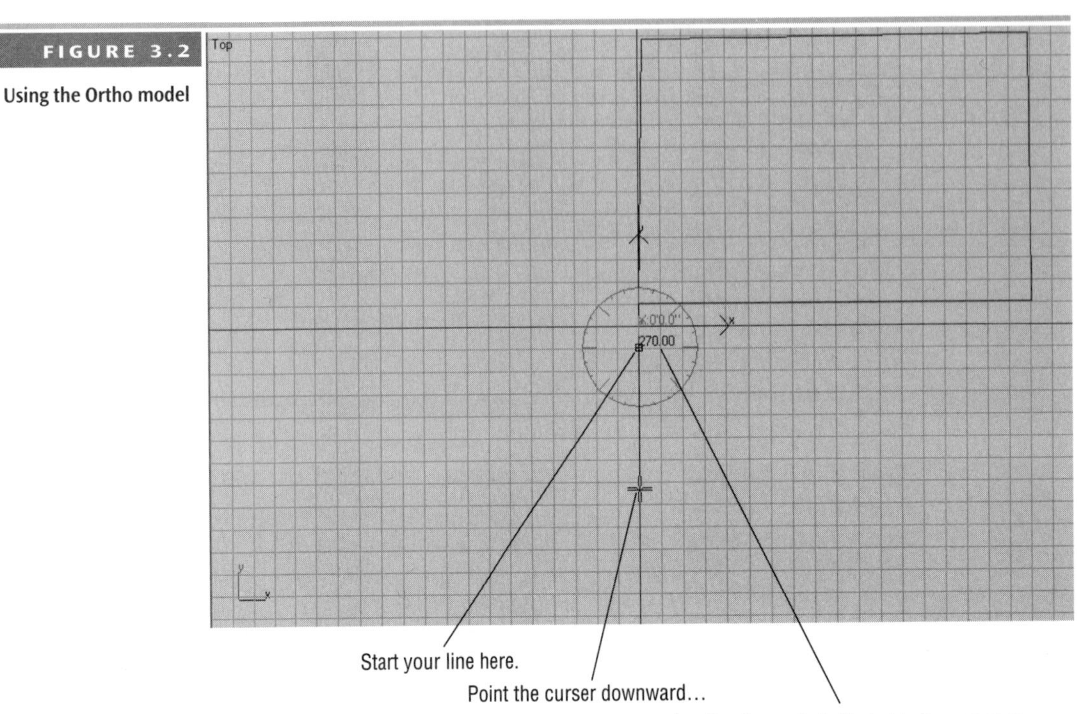
Top
270.00
Start your line here.
Point the curser downward...
and notice the angle indicated in the compass.

FIGURE 3.2

Using the Ortho model

5. Press F8 again, then move your cursor around the orange compass graphic. Now the number at the center of the graphic changes for every 5 degrees of angle from the horizontal or vertical at which your line displays. Also notice that your line *jumps* every 5 degrees. Now the Polar button at the bottom of the VIZ window is active.
6. Press F8 again. The orange compass disappears, and the rubber-banding line moves freely again.
7. Press F8, then click a point roughly 15′ to the right.
8. Point the cursor downward and click a point 5′ below the last point.
9. Point the cursor to a point 15′ to the left and click. Notice that as you select points, the orange compass moves to the last-selected point.
10. Press F8 twice to exit the Ortho and Polar modes, then right-click with your mouse to exit the line tool.

As you might guess, you can activate the Ortho or Polar mode by clicking either the Ortho or Polar button at the bottom of the VIZ window. You cannot click these buttons while you are in the middle of drawing a spline or line segment. The F8 key lets you access these modes while in the middle of drawing a spline.

Drawing Curves

The Spline tool also allows you to draw curves, as the next exercise demonstrates.

1. With the Line button still selected, click and drag from a point near coordinate –14′0.0″,9′0.0″,0.0″ to the right, as shown in Figure 3.3.

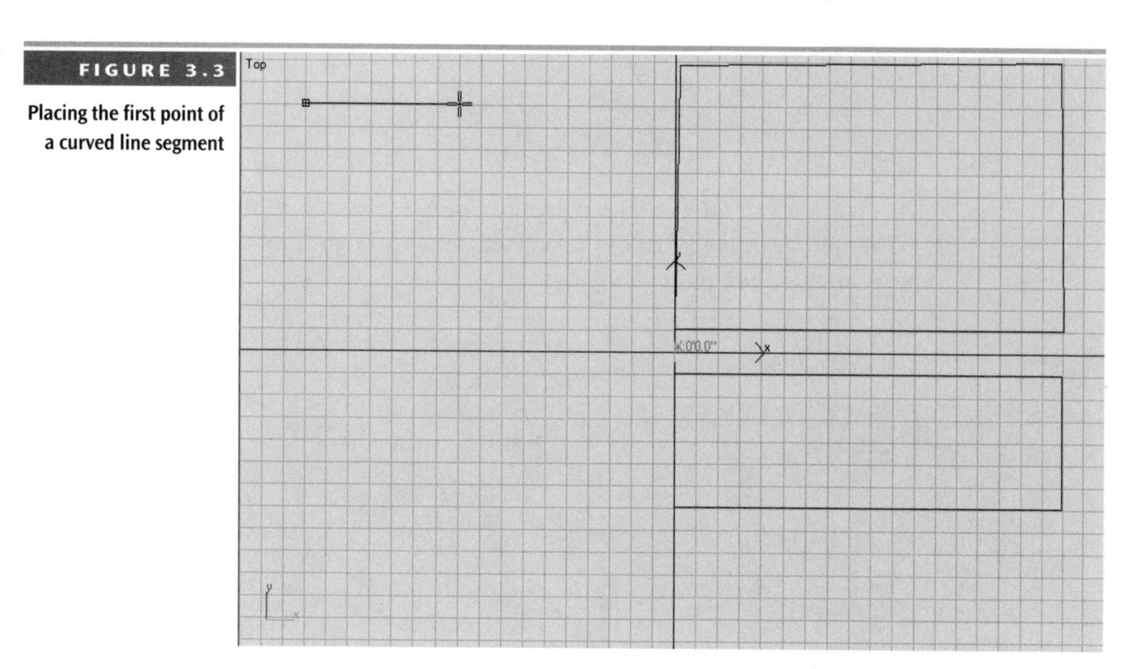

FIGURE 3.3

Placing the first point of a curved line segment

2. Continue to drag the mouse approximately 5 feet to the right, then release the mouse button. You can use the coordinate readout to estimate your distance. Now as you move the mouse, the line becomes a curve emerging from the starting point in the general direction indicated by the first two points you selected.

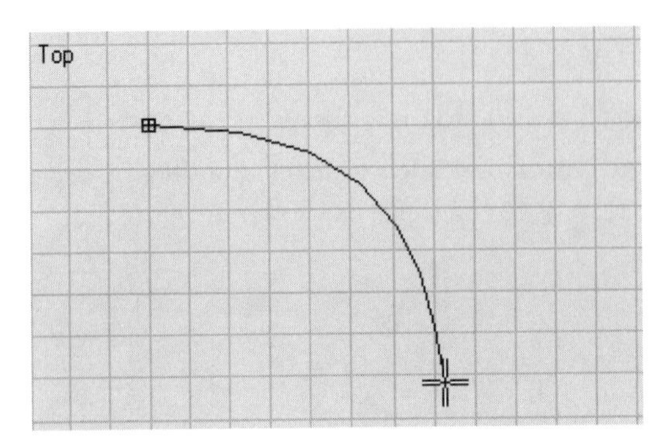

3. Click a point about 6 feet to the right and 6 feet downward, as shown in Figure 3.4. The spline's curved shape is now fixed, and a straight rubber-banding line appears from the last point you picked.

FIGURE 3.4

Drawing a curved spline

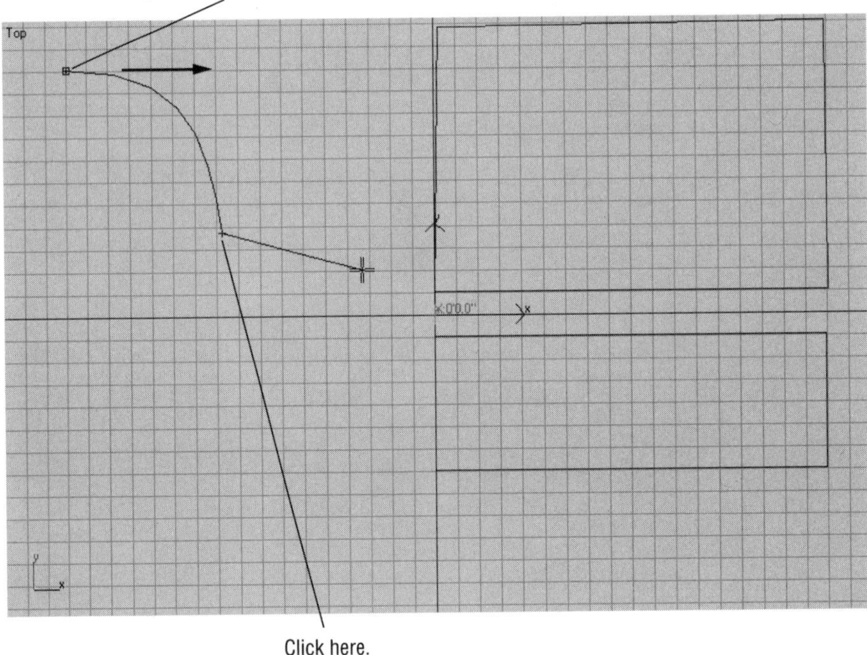

4. Click another point near the origin of the drawing at coordinate 0,0. A straight line segment is added.
5. Press the right mouse button to end your line input.

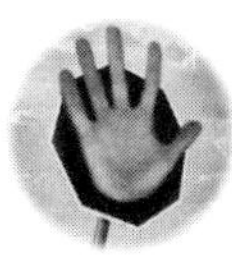

WARNING **It is fairly easy, especially when you're in a hurry, to accidentally click and drag a point, in which case you'll get a curve in your line segment. If you just want a straight line segment, take care not to accidentally drag your mouse while clicking. You can also set the Drag Type to Corner in the Creation Method rollout of the Line button.**

Here you see that by clicking and dragging a point, you can add a curve to the spline. A single click gives you a straight *corner* point. Once you've drawn a spline, you can later edit a curve in a spline, add more vertices, remove existing ones, or even convert a corner vertex into a curved one for rounded corners.

Lathing a Spline

Next you'll create a wineglass using a spline. This will give you a chance to see how you can edit a spline to achieve a desired affect.

1. Click each spline you just drew and press the Delete key to erase each one. You won't be needing them anymore.
2. Click the Min/Max tool in the Viewport navigation controls to view all of the viewports. Then click the Front viewport to activate it.

3. If it isn't active already, click the Line button in the Create tab of the Command Panel. (You may instead select Line from the Draw Shapes tab of the Tab Panel)

4. Draw the profile of the wine glass shown in Figure 3.5. You can use the coordinate readout and Figure 3.5 to locate the point indicated in the figure. Don't click and drag any of the points and don't worry if your placement is not exact. You'll want to get the general outline. Then later you'll learn how to apply a curve to a spline.

TIP If you click a point accidentally, you can go back to the previous vertex by pressing the Backspace key.

FIGURE 3.5

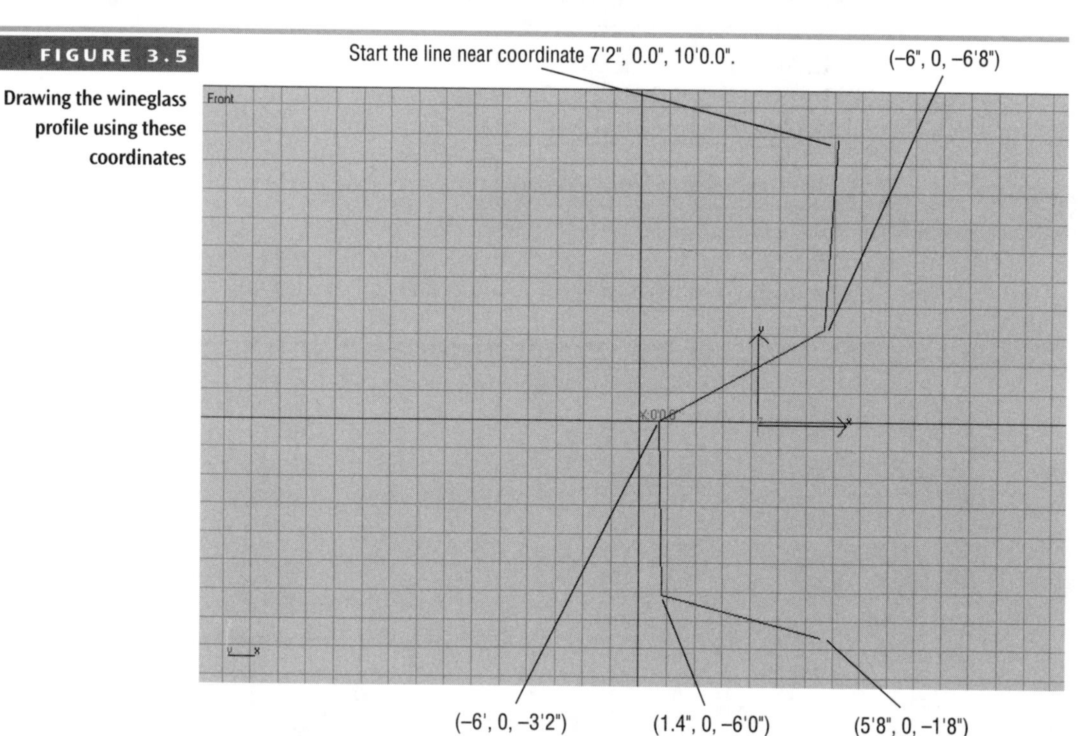

Drawing the wineglass profile using these coordinates

The dimensions of the glass are exaggerated to fit the Front viewport. To save some effort, you're just drawing the profile in the space provided without rescaling the view. You can always scale the glass down to a normal size later.

The next step is to turn the profile into a 3D wineglass.

1. With the spline profile selected, click the Modify tab in the Command panel.

2. Click the Lathe button in the Modifiers rollout.

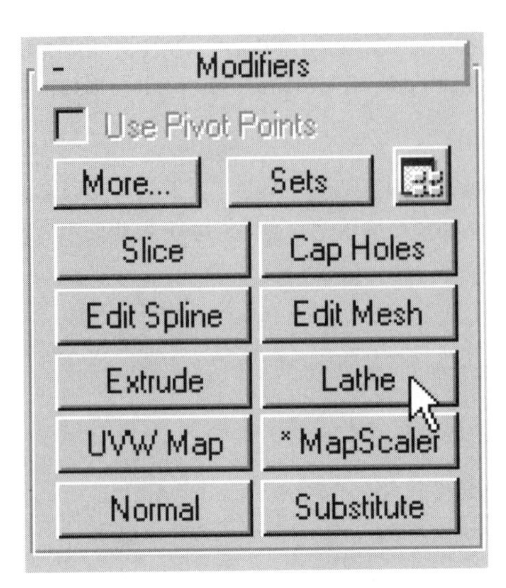

The cylinder is revolved with the profile of the spline.

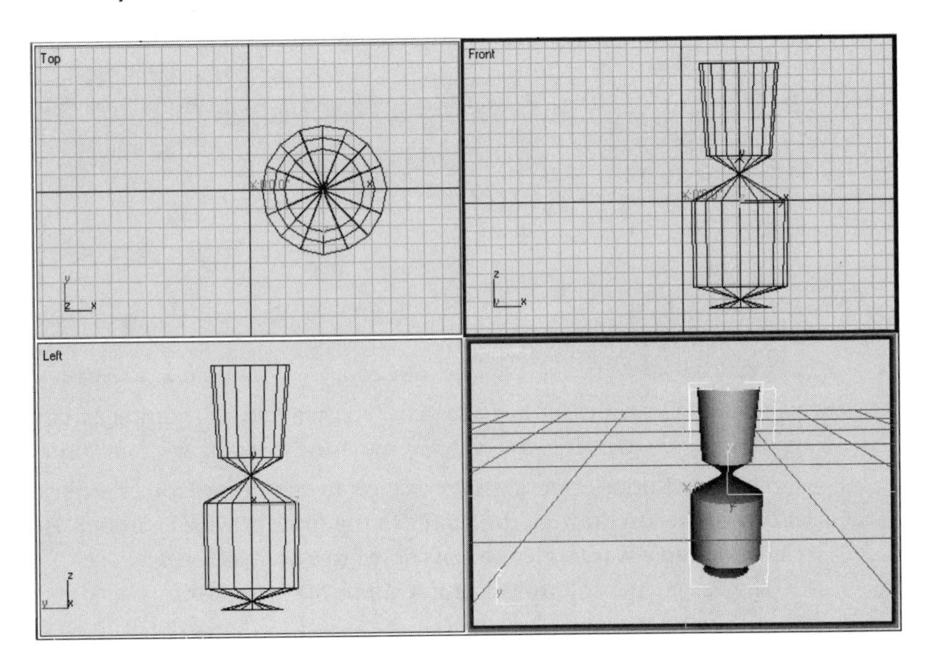

The shape isn't quite what you would expect. The Lathe tool extruded the spline profile about the profile's center, which is not necessarily where you want the extrusion to occur. You can make some simple adjustments to a spline on a *Sub-Object level* to get the exact shape you want.

Modifying a Shape Using Sub-Object Levels

Objects in VIZ are fairly complex entities that offer *built-in* parameters for controlling their shape. As you saw in Chapter 2, you can add even more control by using modifiers. But parameters and modifiers are limiting when it comes to some of the more minute and detailed changes you might want to perform on objects. For example, parameters allow you to adjust the overall height and width of a box, and modifiers allow you to taper the overall shape, but what do you do when you want to add a bulge to one surface or remove one side of a box? To affect these types of changes, you need to gain access to objects on a more fundamental level than parameters and modifiers provide.

VIZ offers that access through sub-object level editing. In this section, you'll explore sub-object level editing by making changes to the wineglass spline. Sub-objects in a spline are the lines or curve segments of the spline and the vertices at each line segment intersection. When you enter into the sub-object level of an object, you gain access to these sub-objects. Each sub-object can be edited and its characteristics can be altered to fine-tune the object's shape.

Modifiers can also be edited on a sub-object level, though you are usually limited to editing the Transform gizmo. Still, by gaining control over the Transform gizmo, you can make adjustments to the way modifiers affect the object. You'll start your exploration of sub-object editing by adjusting the Lathe modifier's Transform gizmo.

Adjusting the Transform Gizmo

The wineglass profile you created in the last exercise isn't quite where it should be in relation to the center of the Lathe axis. You can move the center axis of the Lathe modifier to the location you want by moving the modifier's Transform gizmo.

1. Make sure Lathe appears in the Modifier Stack drop-down list, then click the Sub-Object button in the Modifier Stack rollout.

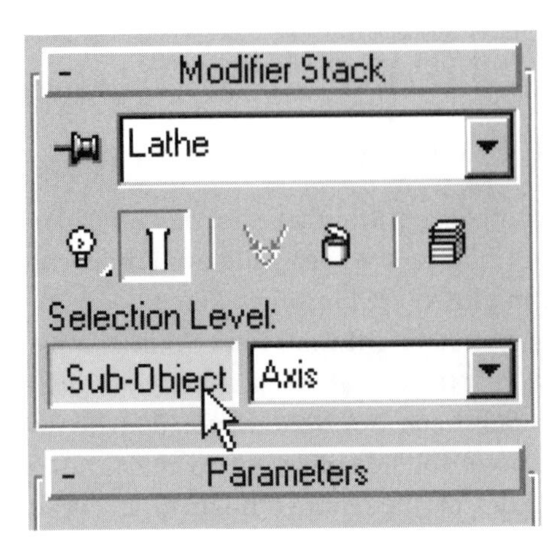

The word Axis in the Sub-Object drop-down list is no longer grayed out. Also, the Transform gizmo changes in appearance, indicating that it is now available for editing.

2. Click the Select and Move tool. Then, in the Front viewport, click and drag in the red X axis arrow of the Transform gizmo to the left until it looks like Figure 3.6: now the extruded spline looks more like a wineglass.

FIGURE 3.6

Moving the Transform gizmo

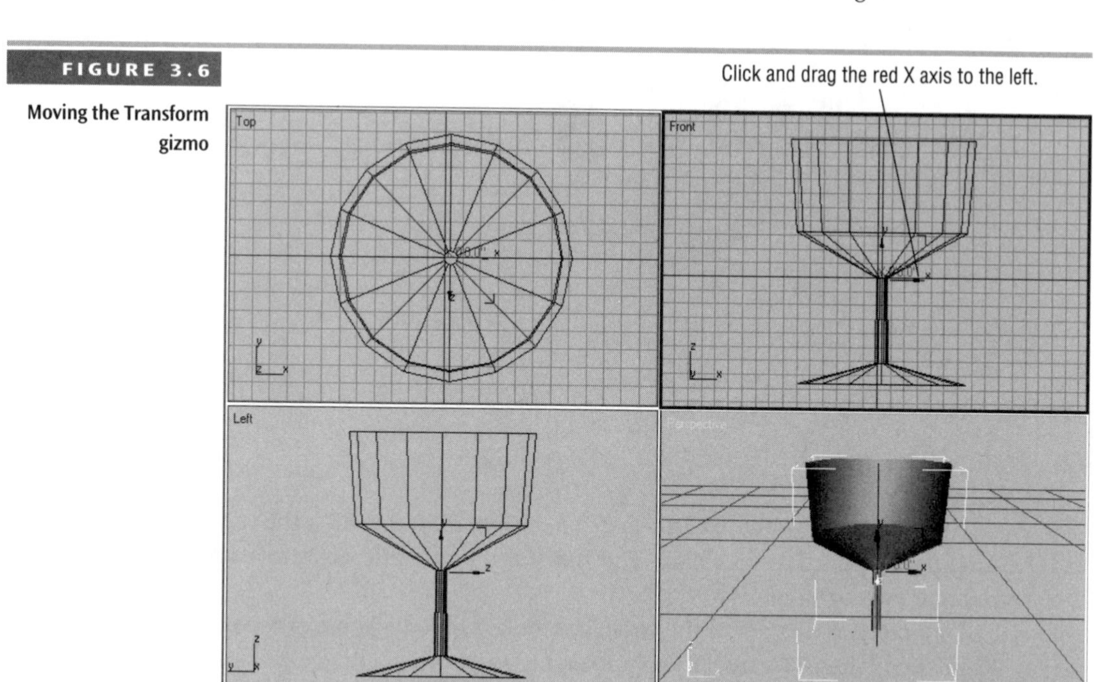
Click and drag the red X axis to the left.
Top
Front
Left

3. Click the Zoom Extents All tool to get a better view. Your perspective view should look similar to that of Figure 3.7.

FIGURE 3.7

The wineglass so far

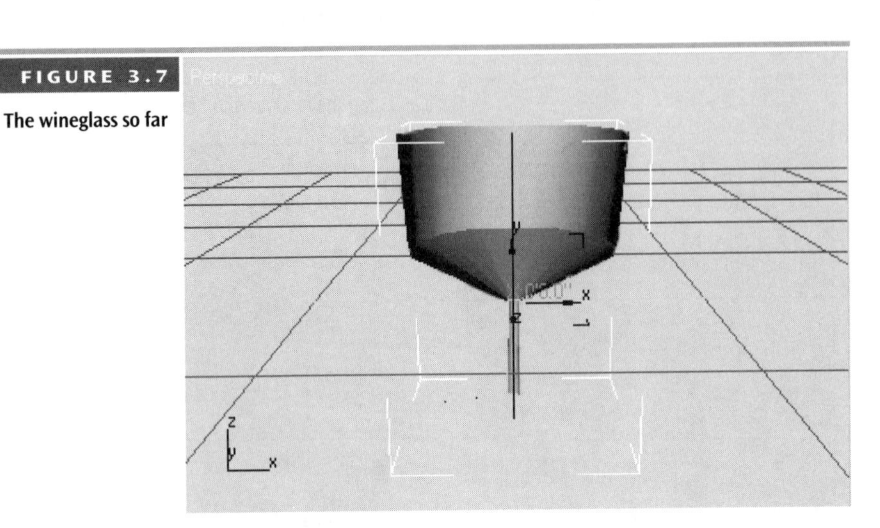

Here you see how the Transform gizmo can be moved to alter the way the Lathe modifier is applied to the spline. The Transform gizmo offers control over the way modifiers act on an object.

Your perspective view of the wineglass looks a bit odd. Some of the parts seem to be missing. This is because of the way surfaces in 3D modeling programs are generated. To make a long story short, 3D surfaces are only visible on one side. Like a one-way mirror, they appear solid from one direction and transparent from the other. You can find a more detailed description of this phenomenon in the sidebar entitled "Why Surfaces Disappear" later in this chapter. In a later exercise you'll also see how you can correct a surface model with disappearing surfaces. For now, let's continue our look at splines.

Smoothing Out Spline Corners

You now have a wineglass that looks a bit crude. Next, you'll smooth out some of the rough spots by returning to the spline and editing it.

1. Click the drop-down list in the Modifier Stack and select Line. Your view of the wineglass returns to the spline you drew earlier. Notice that the options below the Modifier Stack rollout change to a set of options related to the spline.

2. Click the Sub-Object button in the Modifier Stack. The Vertex option is highlighted.

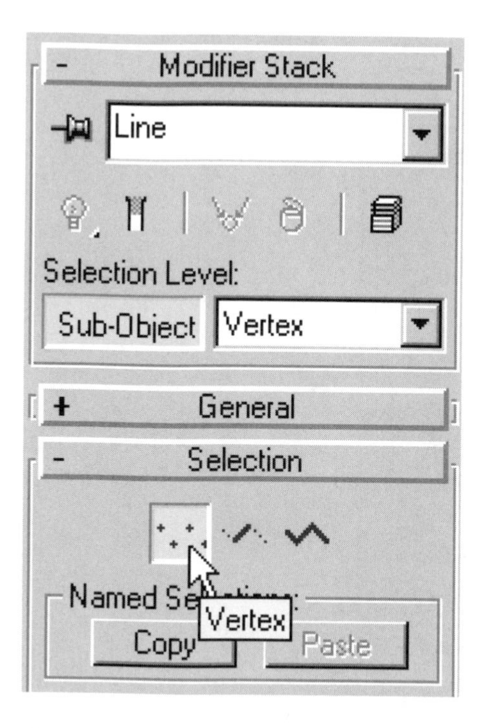

3. Click the second vertex of the spline, as shown in Figure 3.8, to select it.
4. Right-click the second vertex. A list of options appears in a pop-up menu.

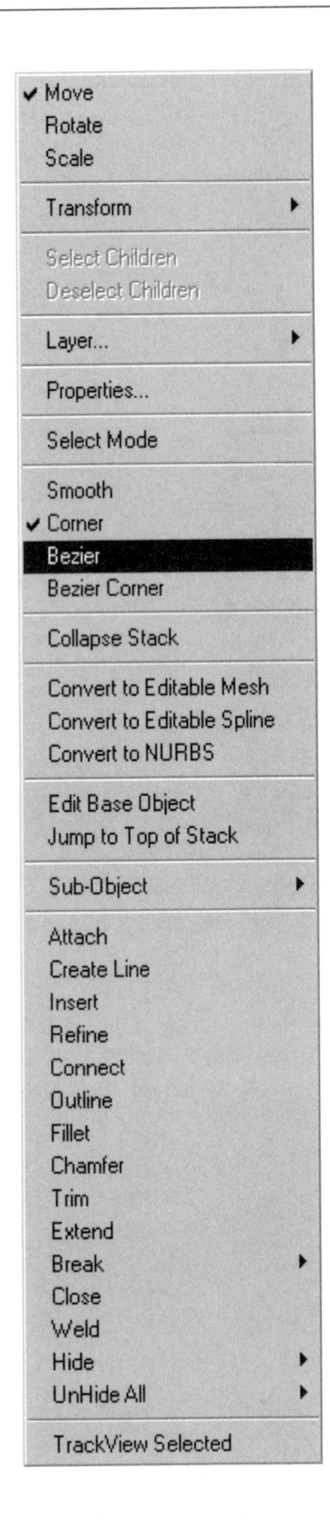
Move
Rotate
Scale
Transform
Select Children
Deselect Children
Layer...
Properties...
Select Mode
Smooth
Corner
Bezier
Bezier Corner
Collapse Stack
Convert to Editable Mesh
Convert to Editable Spline
Convert to NURBS
Edit Base Object
Jump to Top of Stack
Sub-Object
Attach
Create Line
Insert
Refine
Connect
Outline
Fillet
Chamfer
Trim
Extend
Break
Close
Weld
Hide
UnHide All
TrackView Selected

5. Click the Bézier option. The line curves and two handles appear emerging from the vertex.

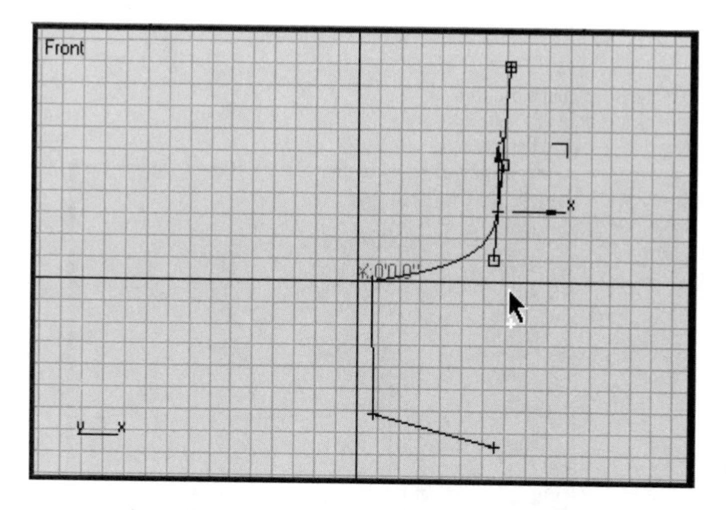

The Bézier option turns a vertex into a control point for a Bézier curve. You can then manipulate the curve by adjusting the handles that appear.

1. With the Select and Move tool active, click and drag one of the Bézier handles to deform the spline to the shape shown in Figure 3.8. Notice that as you move the handle, the opposite handle moves in the opposite direction in a mirrored fashion.

FIGURE 3.8

Click and drag the handle of the vertex.

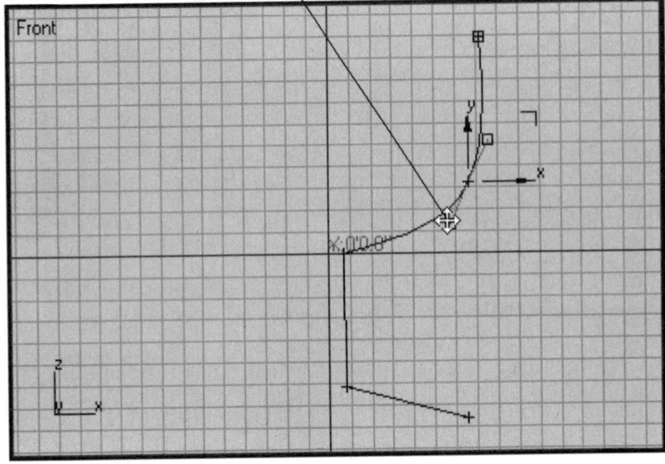
Use the Select and Move tool to click and drag this handle to adjust the curve of the glass.
Front

2. Click the next vertex toward the stem of the wineglass as shown in Figure 3.9.

FIGURE 3.9

Click the next vertex to select it.

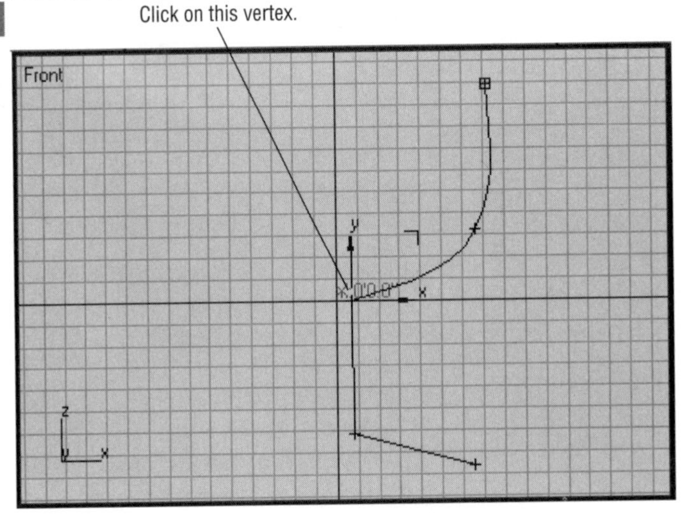
Click on this vertex.
Front

3. Right-click the vertex you just selected, then select Bézier corner from the pop-up menu. Now you see two handles from this vertex, but this time the handles are not opposite each other. Instead, they point in different directions.

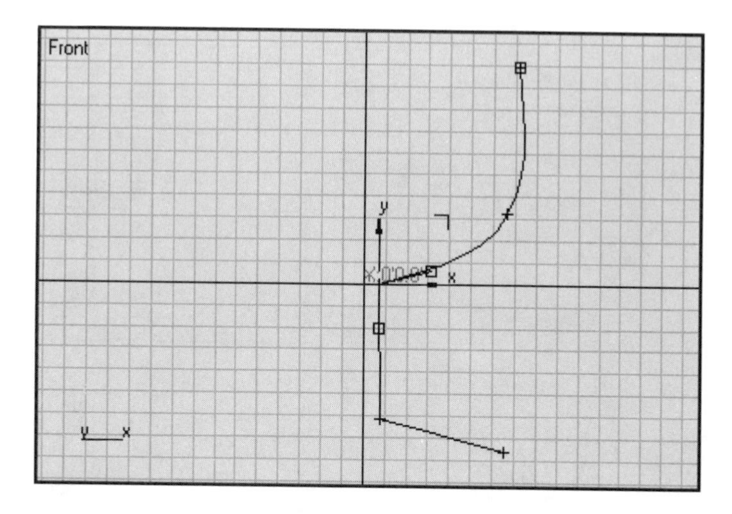
Front

4. Click and drag each of the Bézier handles to a position similar to the ones shown in Figure 3.10. Notice that the Bézier Corner option lets you control the curve from the vertex in both directions.

FIGURE 3.10

The new location for the Bézier corner handles

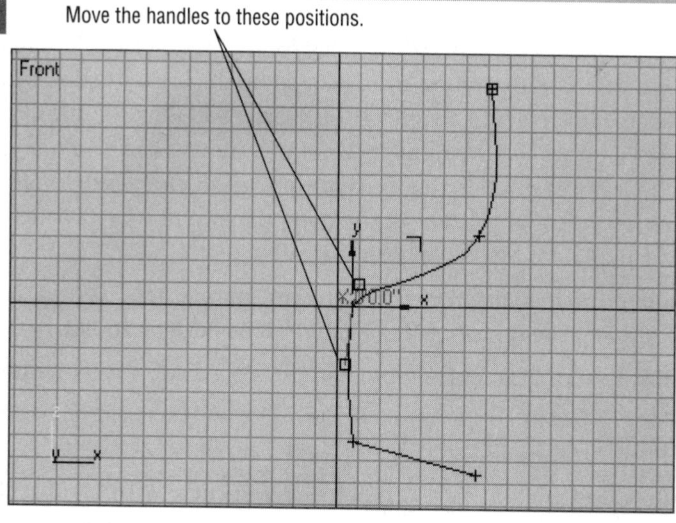
Move the handles to these positions.
Front

5. Click the Modifier Stack drop-down list and select Lathe. You now see how your changes to the spline translate to the form of the wineglass as shown in Figure 3.11.

FIGURE 3.11

The view of the wineglass so far

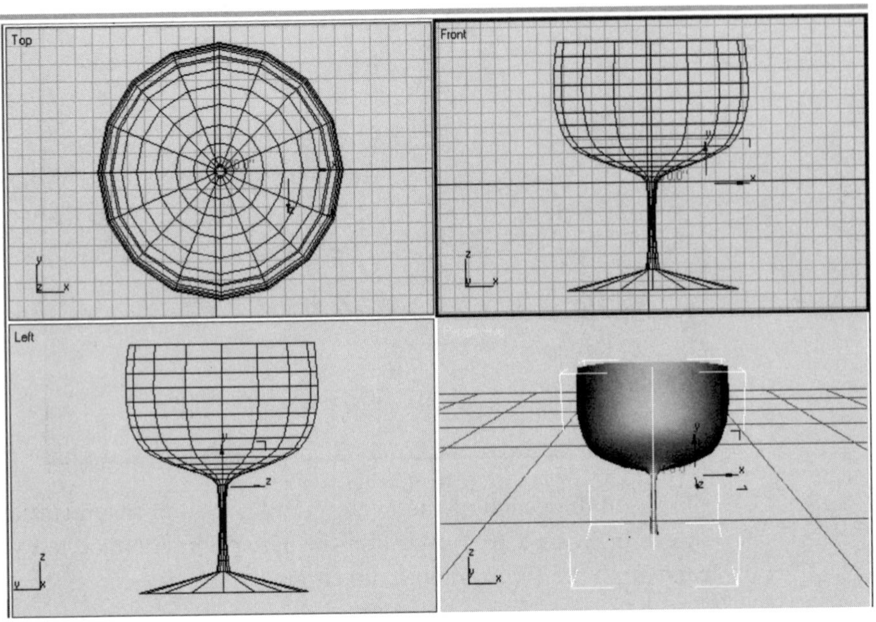

In the last few exercises, you have begun to see that splines are really made up of components, or *sub-objects*, as they are called in the Modifier Stack rollout. You used the Transform gizmo to reposition the axis used by the Lathe modifier. You also changed the characteristics of a vertex by using the Sub-Object option to access other editing tools. For example, the right-click menu options allow you to change the shape of an object just by changing the type of vertex being used. Here's a listing of all the vertex options that you saw in the pop-up menu in step 3 of the last exercise along with an explanation of what they do.

Smooth turns a sharp corner into a rounded one. This has an effect similar to that of the Bézier option without offering the Bézier handles.

Corner turns a Bézier or smooth corner into a sharp corner with no curve.

Bézier converts a corner into a Bézier curve with symmetric handles that allow you to adjust the *pull* and direction of the curve.

Bézier Corner converts a corner to a Bézier curve with handles that allow you to adjust the *pull* and direction of the curve. Unlike the regular Bézier option, Bézier Corner allows you to control the handles independently in both directions from the vertex.

Remember that to use the corner options, you need to have the Sub-Object option selected in the Modifier Stack rollout, and you need to have the Vertex option selected.

Understanding the Spline Right-Click menu

In the wineglass exercise, you used a right-click menu that appeared when you right-clicked the vertex of a selected spline. Many of the options in that menu are actually duplicates of options in the Modifier tab of the Command Panel and the standard toolbar. These options provide a quick way to get to options that relate specifically to the object you're editing. You don't have to sort through a set of buttons in the Command Panel, many of which are grayed out. Be aware, however, that the options in the right-click menu are often abbreviated versions of those found in the Command Panel, and frequently don't offer keyboard input. If you want to edit an object visually, the right-click options work just fine, but if you need to enter exact dimensions, you will want to go to the Modify tab of the Command Panel and use the tools and options there.

Creating Thickness with a Spline

The wineglass is currently an object with no thickness. To make this glass really appear more realistic, you'll want to give it some thickness. Here's how it's done.

1. Click the Modifier Stack drop-down list and select Line.
2. Make sure the Sub-Object button is active. It should appear yellow.

3. In the drop-down list next to the Sub-Object button, select Spline. (You can instead select the Spline button in the Selection rollout.)

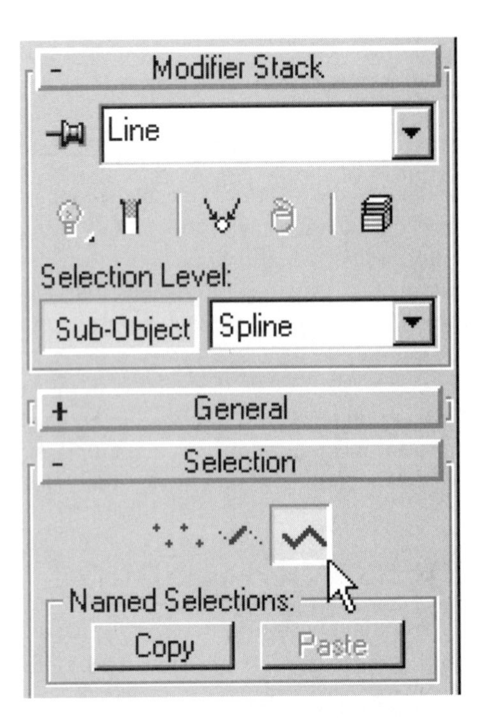

4. Click the spline. Notice that now the entire spline turns red, indicating that it is selected.

5. Scroll down the Modify panel until you see the Outline button.

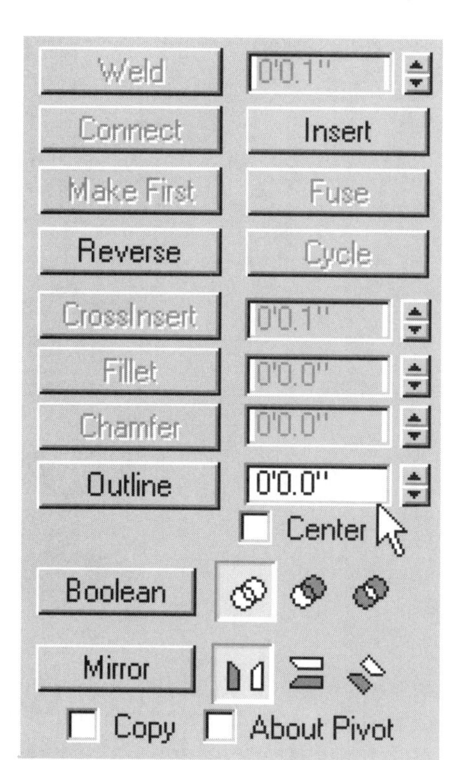

6. Click the input box to the right of the Outline button and change its value from 0'0.0" to 2". The spline is converted to an outline.
7. Scroll back up to the Modifier Stack drop-down list, click it, then select Lathe. You now see the entire glass, including those portions of the glass that did not appear, because of the arrangement of the normals.

TIP A normal is a mathematical concept indicating a vector pointing perpendicularly away from a plane. The positive direction of a surface's normal indicates which side appears solid.

8. Choose file ➢ Save and save your wineglass model.

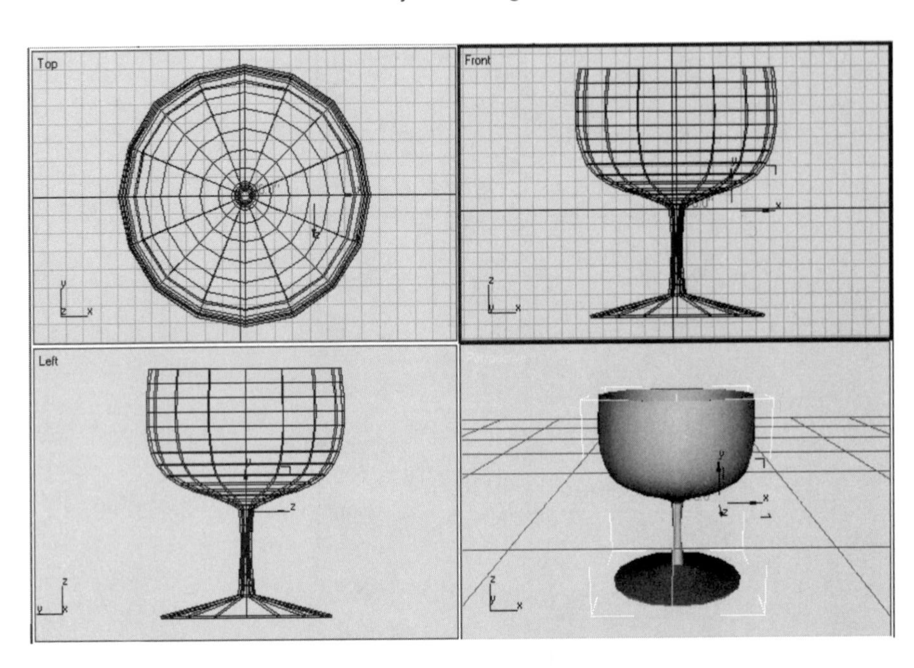

In step 6, when you entered a value for the Outline, VIZ outlined the single-line spline into an outline using the spline, thereby creating a double-lined spline. In this context, entering this value has the effect of creating a cross section with thickness.

The Outline option generates an outline using the existing spline as one side of the outline. To determine the side on which the outline appears, check the direction in which the original spline was created. For example, if a spline is drawn from left to right, the outline will appear on the top side, as shown in Figure 3.12.

TIP The Center check box just below the Outline input box causes the outline to be centered on the original spline instead of creating the outline on either side of the spline.

FIGURE 3.12

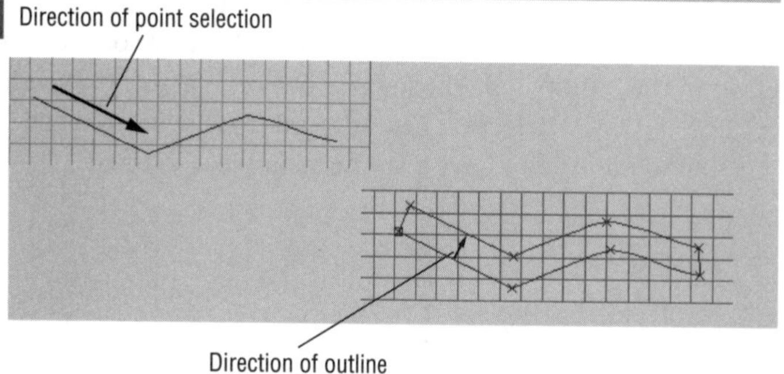

How to determine the side of the outline

If you're not sure of the order in which a spline was drawn, you can click the Show Vertex Numbers check box in the Selection rollout of the Modify tab.

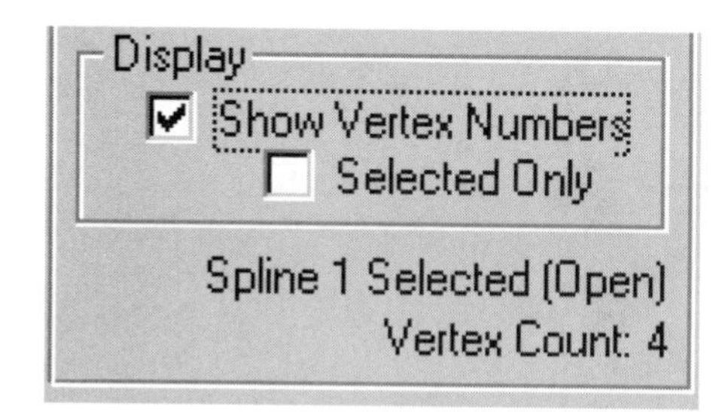

You'll need to have the object in question selected and also the Sub-Object button selected. With the Show Vertex Numbers check box selected, you'll see each vertex numbered with a small blue number, indicating the order in which the vertices were created.

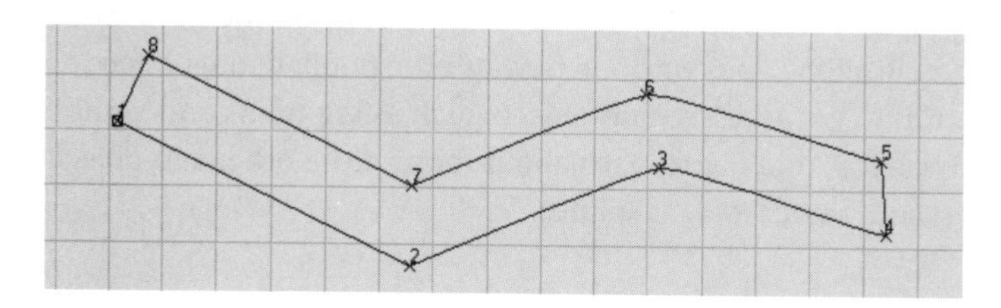

If you want the outline to appear on the opposite side, you can either enter a negative value for the offset distance, or you can reverse the order of the vertices using the Reverse button in the Modify tab. The Reverse button is active only when you select Spline from the Sub-Object Selection Level drop-down list or from the button in the Selection rollout. You must also have a Spline sub-object selected.

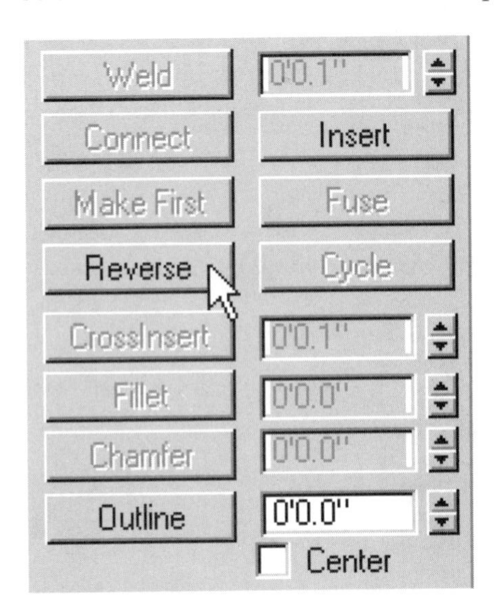

So far, you've used the sub-object options and parameters to adjust the spline curve to a shape that really gives the impression of a wineglass. The steps you took while editing the spline are really very similar to what you would do for other types of objects. As you've seen in some of the rollouts, there is a bewildering array of options you can apply to a sub-object, but you've really covered the main points regarding sub-object editing. As you continue through the book, you will need to select the Sub-Object button to get access to sub-objects such as segments and vertices. As you work through this book, you'll also learn about most of the other sub-object options. For now, let's continue our look at splines.

Why Surfaces Disappear

At times as you model objects in 3D Studio, you may find that surfaces disappear. You know the surfaces are there, because you can see them in wireframe mode. Where do these surfaces go?

To understand why surfaces disappear, you need to know one basic fact about 3D computer models: a surface has only one visible side. The other side of a surface is invisible. This may sound crazy, but it's true for nearly all 3D computer rendering programs.

Surfaces are visible or invisible, depending on the direction of their *normals*. A *normal* is a mathematical concept indicating a vector pointing perpendicularly away from a plane (as defined by at least 3 points); the direction of the normal is determined by the order and direction in which these points are created. Figure 3.13 shows a typical object face and its normal. All objects in VIZ are made up of triangular surfaces like the one shown in Figure 3.13.

In most situations, you'll be creating *volumes* in 3D Studio VIZ. When you create a volume such as a box or the lathed outline of a wineglass, VIZ will automatically align the normals of the surfaces so that they all point outward, away from the interior of the volume. In fact, this is what happened when you used the Outline option on the spline for the wineglass. Instead of creating a surface using a single layer of surfaces, the Outline option created a closed volume with a distinct interior and exterior. If you looked between the lathed outline splines, you would see that from the inside out, the wineglass is invisible!

In most situations, VIZ takes care of the normals in objects, but if you import objects from AutoCAD, sometimes surfaces disappear. There are a number of methods you can use to fix these disappearing surfaces from AutoCAD. You'll learn about those methods as you begin to work with materials later in this book.

FIGURE 3.13

A diagram showing the relationship of the creation of a surface to the normal of a surface

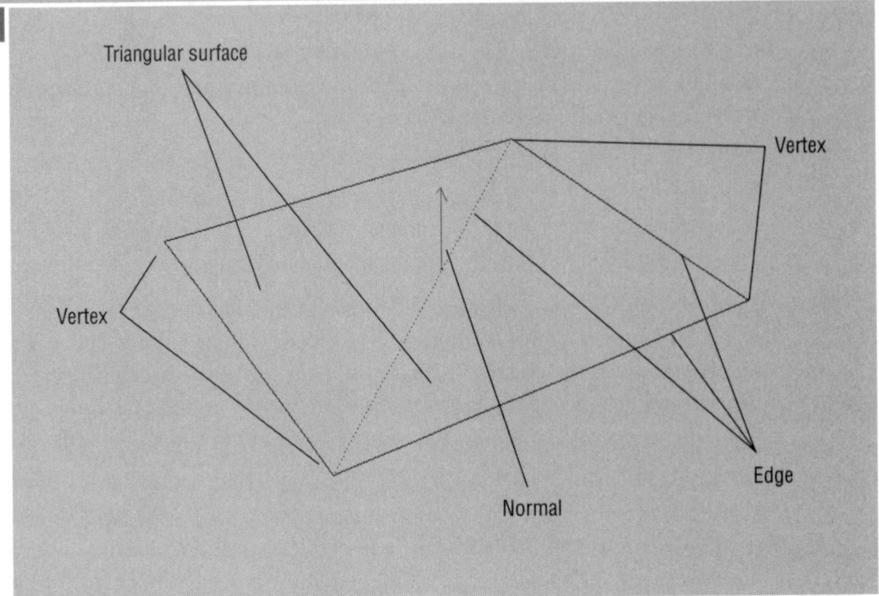

Rendering the Glass

Let's take a break from modeling and take a preview look at materials and rendering. To get a better idea of what the wineglass actually looks like, try the following exercise to add material and render the glass.

1. First make sure the glass is selected, then click the Material Editor tool on the left of the rendering toolbar.

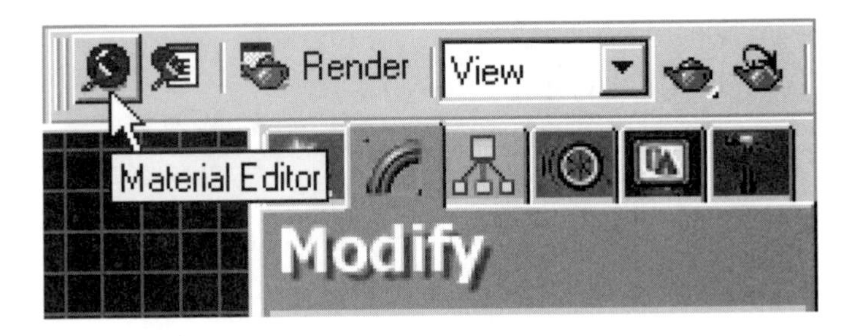

The Material Editor dialog box appears.

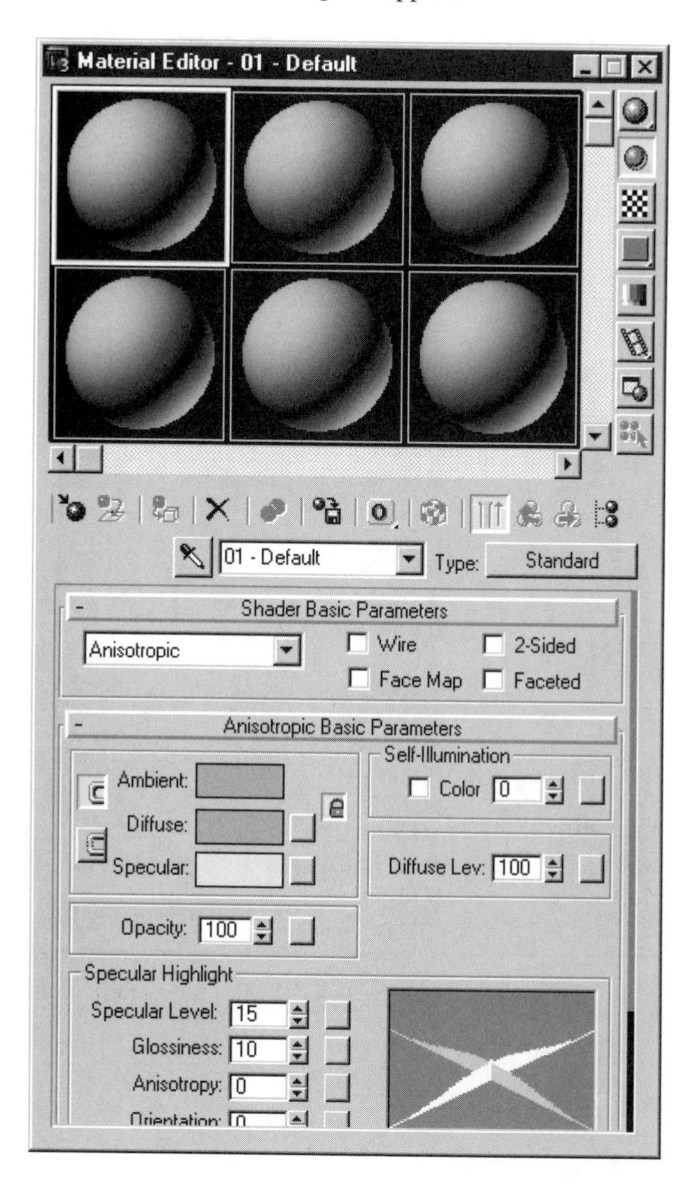

2. In the Material Editor dialog box, click the Get Material tool.

The Material Map Browser dialog box displays.

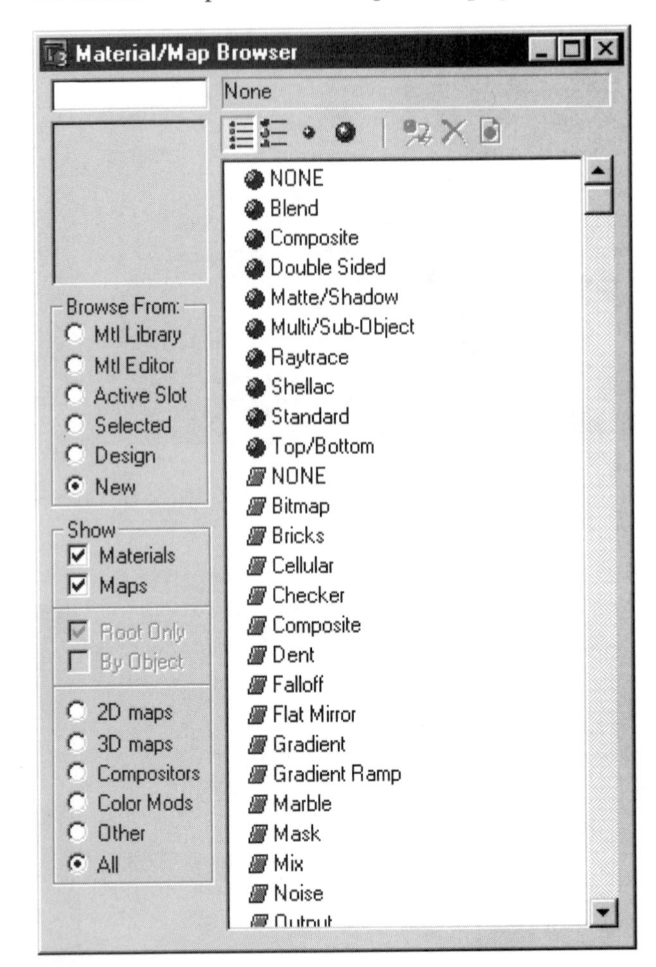

3. In the Browse From group, click the Mtl Library radio button.

4. Scroll down the list to the right until you find Glass-Clear, then double-click it.

5. Close the Material/Map Browser dialog box, then in the Material Editor dialog box, click the Assign Material to Selection tool.

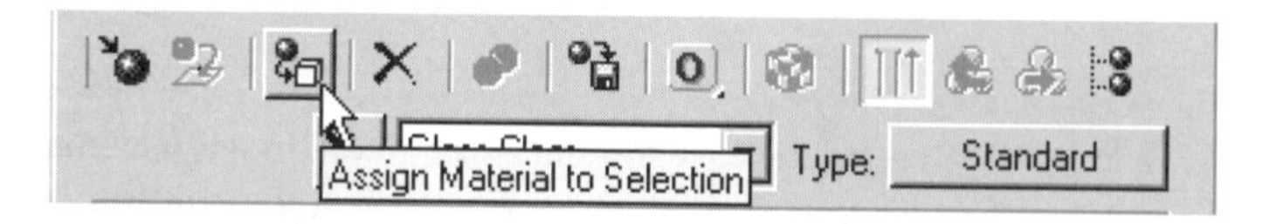

6. Close the Material Editor dialog box.
7. Click the Perspective viewport to make it active. Then click the Quick Render tool in the standard toobar.

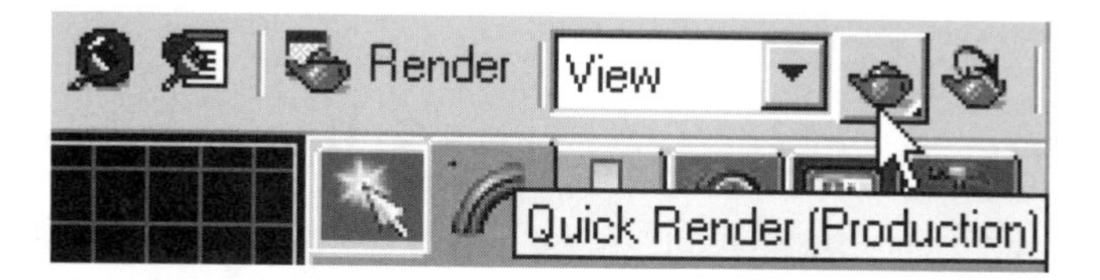

The glass is rendered in the render window.

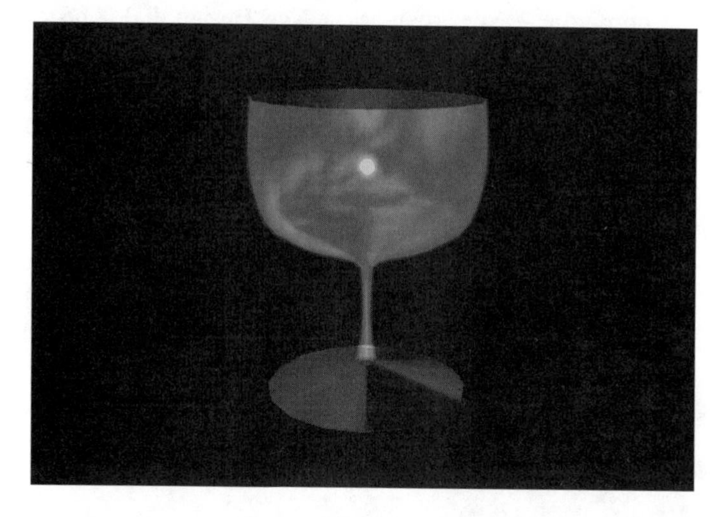

You've very quickly assigned a material to your model and rendered it to get a taste for what is in store. Later in this book, you'll learn more about the materials and rendering feature of VIZ. For now, let's continue with a look at drawing walls with splines.

Drawing Walls with Splines

You've just seen how you can create a wineglass using a spline and the Lathe modifier. Now let's look at a type of object that is simpler in many ways, but that requires quite a different approach to using splines. Walls are usually drawn with straight-line segments, and they require a fairly high degree of accuracy. In the following exercise, you'll learn how to draw a spline using exact coordinates.

NOTE VIZ offers a set of AEC tools in which a wall tool is included. *AEC* is an acronym for *architecture, engineering, and construction.* The AEC tools offer specialized functions geared toward the creation of building components such as walls and stairs. VIZ's AEC wall tool works in a way that is slightly different from the splines described here, and it offers some time-saving features for inserting doors and windows. You'll learn about the AEC tools at the end of this chapter. For now, you'll use the wall example to explore some of the ways you can use splines.

Drawing Accurate Line Splines

You'll start by setting up a top view in a new file that will include the area in which you'll draw the walls. The walls will cover a 20' square area, so you'll want to include an area that covers about 20' square.

1. Choose file ➢ New, then at the New Design dialog box, choose New All and click OK.
2. Choose Tools ➢ Drafting Settings ➢Unit Setup… Then in the Units Setup dialog box, click the US Standard drop-down list, select Feet w/Decimal Inches, click the inches radio button, and click OK.

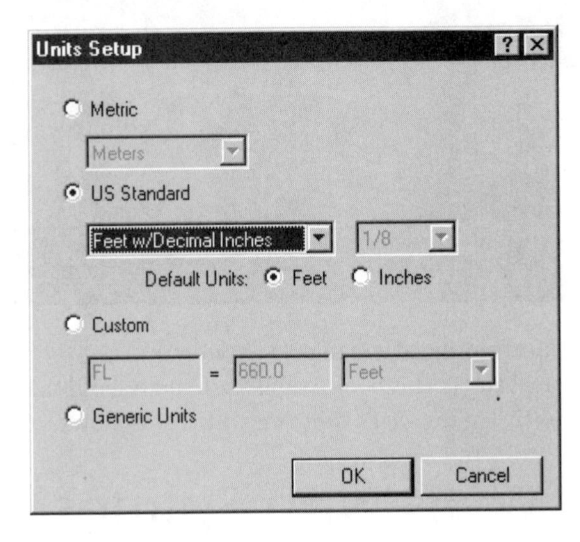

3. Click the Zoom Extents All tool to restore the views to their default orientation.

4. Click the Top viewport, then click the Min/Max toggle tool to enlarge it.
5. Click the Zoom tool and zoom out until you see the 12'0.0" grid appear in the viewport, as shown here.

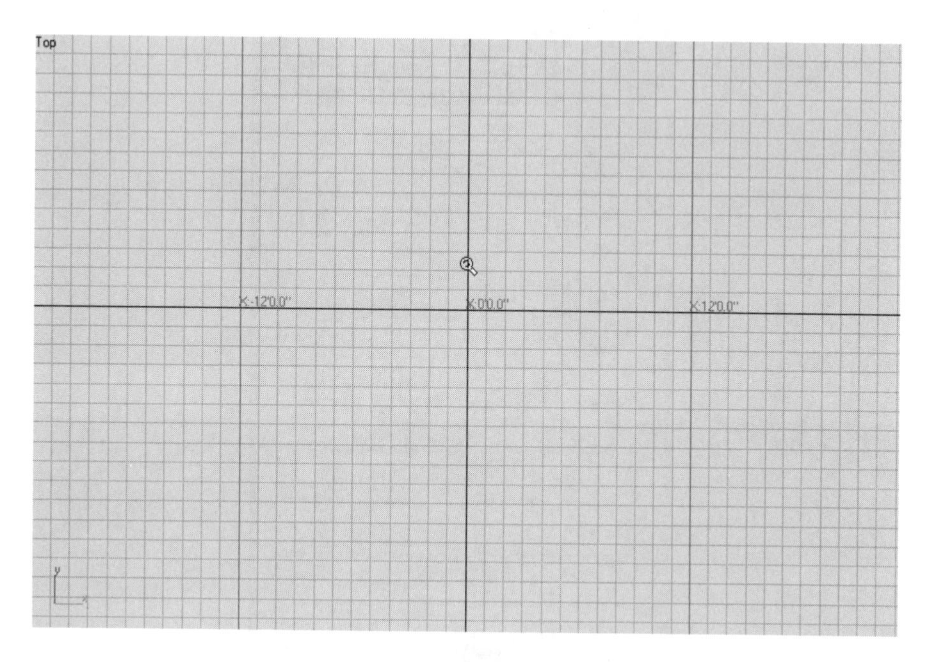

6. Click the Pan tool and pan the view downward and to the left so that the 0,0 coordinate is in the lower left corner of the viewport, as shown here.

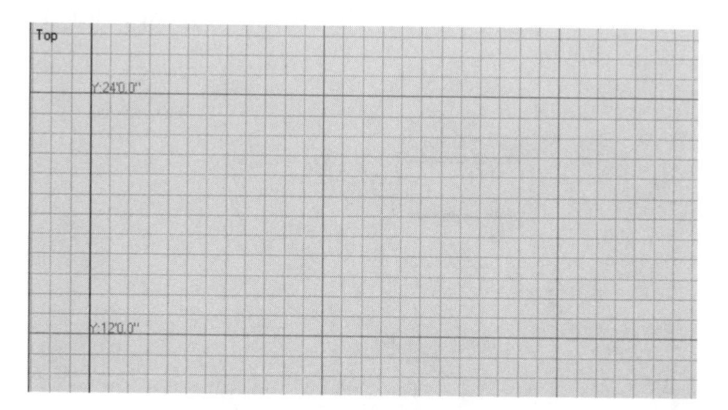

Now you're ready to start drawing. You'll draw an L-shaped room that is 20' by 20' with each leg 10' long.

1. If it isn't already selected, click the Create tab of the Command Panel.

2. Make sure the Shapes tool and Splines from the pop-up list are selected. Then click the Line button.

3. Use the Hand cursor to scroll the Create panel upward until you see the Keyboard Entry rollout, and click it. The Keyboard Entry rollout is at the bottom of the panel.

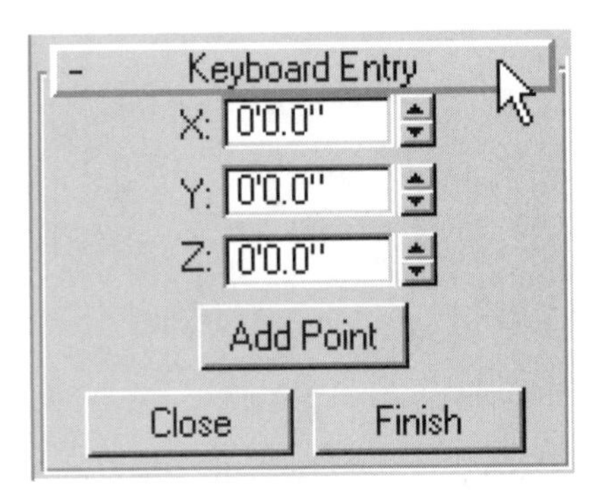

You will see three coordinate input boxes and three buttons labeled Add Point, Close, and Finish. These are the tools you'll use to accurately place the wall.

1. Click the Add Point button. This starts the wall by inserting the start point at the coordinates shown in the coordinate input boxes. Because the input boxes show the coordinates 0,0,0 for the X, Y, and Z coordinates, the line starts at 0,0,0.
2. Click the X input box, then enter **20'**↵.

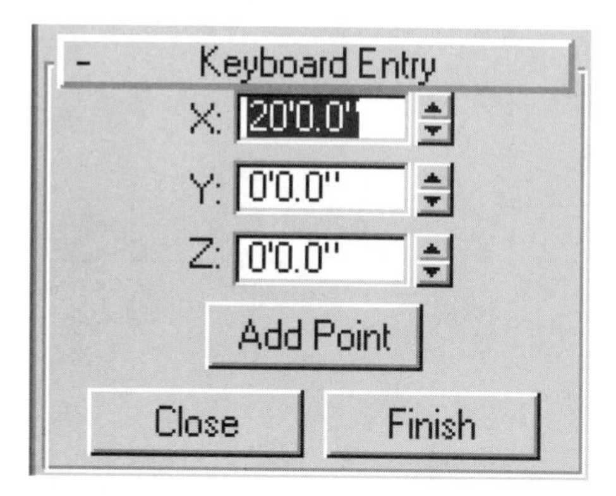

3. Click the Add Point button again. It isn't obvious, but you've just added a line segment from coordinate 0,0,0 to 20',0,0.
4. Click the Y coordinate, enter **10'**↵, then click the Add Point button. Another line segment is added.
5. Click the X coordinate input box, enter **10'**↵, and click the Add Point button.
6. Click the Y coordinate input box, enter **20'**↵, and click Add Point.
7. Click the X coordinate input box, enter **0**↵, and click Add point.
8. Click the Close button.

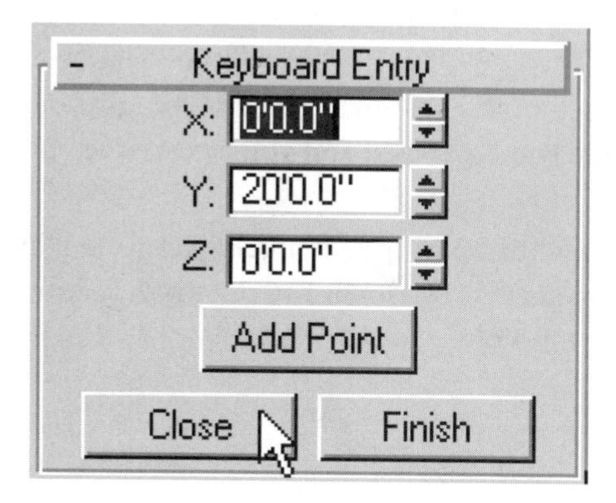

You've just drawn the basis for the walls.

9. Click the Zoom Extents tool to get an overall view of your walls.

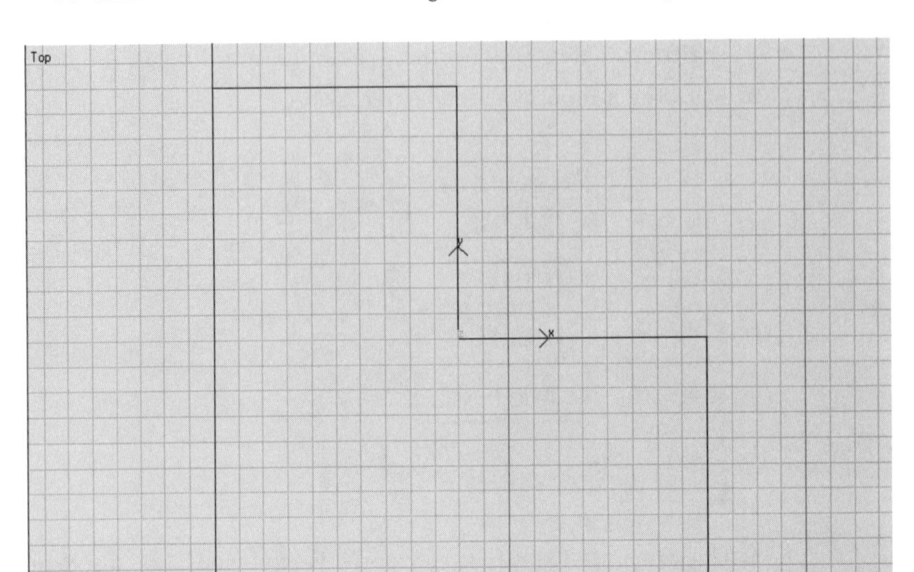

As you can see from this exercise, you can enter coordinate values to place the corners of the walls accurately. Because you started at the world coordinate origin 0,0,0, it is fairly easy to determine the coordinate location of your walls.

Giving Walls Thickness

Right now, you've got only a single line representation. To give the walls thickness, you can use the Outline tool you used in the wineglass exercise.

1. Click the Modify tab of the Command Panel. Because you just created the wall outline, the outline is still selected and you can see the options for the spline in the Modify tab.
2. Click the Sub-Object button in the Modifier Stack rollout and then select Spline from the Selection Level drop-down list. Alternately, you can click the Spline tool in the Selection rollout.

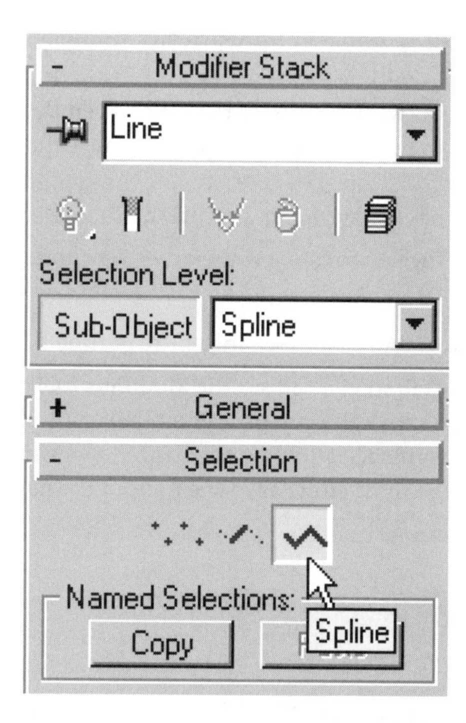

3. Scroll down the panel so you can see the Outline button.

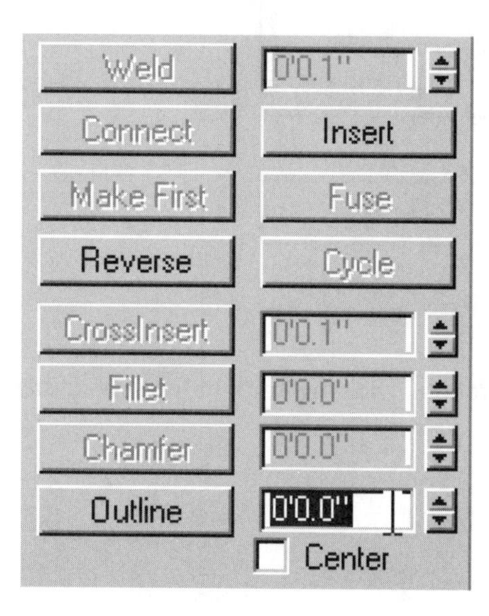

4. Click the input box next to the outline button, then enter **5"**↵. Notice that a new spline outline appears inside the original outline. This is the inside face of the wall.

When you used the Outline option in the wineglass example, VIZ turned the single line into a single continuous outline of the wineglass section. In this wall example, you actually have two splines with one inside the other. Even though there are two splines, VIZ considers this to be one object. This is so because the new spline was created while you were in the Sub-Object level of the line. As you'll see in the next exercise, concentric closed splines behave in an unusual manner.

1. Click the Min/Max Toggle tool to view the other viewports.

2. Click the Zoom Extents All tool to see the entire outline in all the viewports.
3. Scroll up the Modify tab so you can see the Modifiers rollout. Remember that to scroll the panel, you move the cursor over a blank spot in the panel until you see the hand icon, then click and drag the hand downward to move to the top of the panel or use the thin scroll bar to the right of the panel.
4. Click the Extrude button.

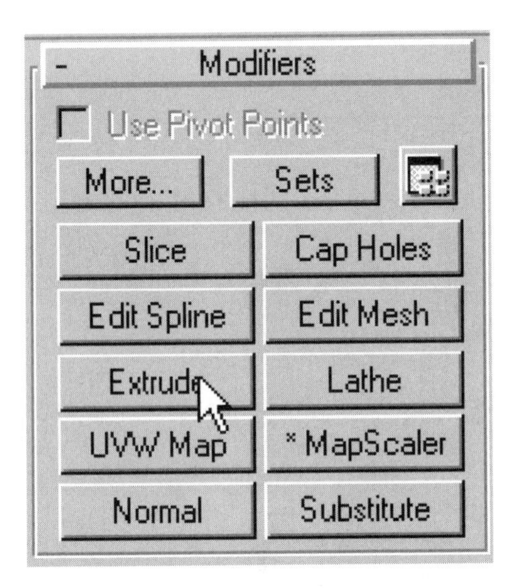

5. In the Parameters rollout, click the Amount input box, then enter **8'**↵.

6. Make sure the Segments input box shows a value of 1. As walls are usually vertical planes, you don't need the extra segments in the wall's vertical plane. You now have a wall that is 8′ tall.

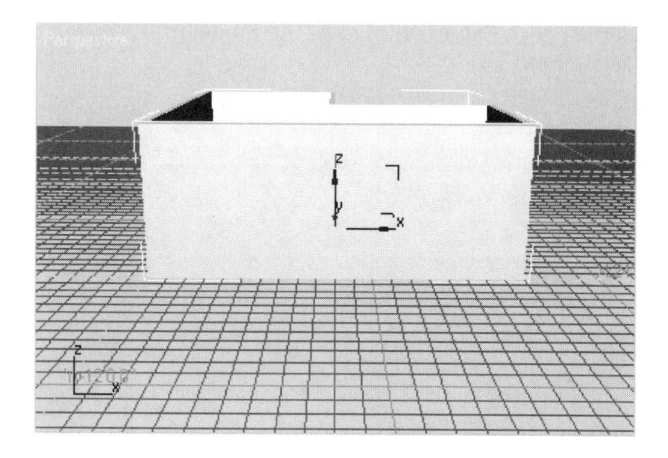

TIP **AutoCAD users will find it easier to import 2D floor plans into VIZ and then to extrude the walls of the floor plan in VIZ. You'll learn how to import 2D objects in Chapter 5.**

If you're an AutoCAD user, you may find drawing walls with accurate dimensions a bit more difficult. It can be done, but as you've just seen, you need to translate the wall dimensions into coordinates. You can use a tool called the *User Grid* as an aid to drawing accurately.

Using Grids and Snaps to Align Objects Accurately

You've seen how you can enter coordinate data for splines using the Keyboard Entry rollout. The example you experimented with was simple enough, but entering coordinates can become quite cumbersome and tedious for any wall configuration that is even slightly more complex. There are several tools that can help make drawing walls easier: user grids and snaps. User grids are non-printable grids that you can align to any orientation or object geometry you want. You can use them to set up a *local* coordinate system in which to add other objects. Snaps are a set of options that let you accurately select specific geometry on existing objects such as endpoints of line segments, midpoints of lines, and intersections. Snaps also let you select grid points.

In the next exercise, you'll use grid objects and snaps to add some additional walls to the existing set of walls. Start by setting up a view that will allow you to see your work.

1. Click the Top viewport, then click the Min/Max Toggle tool in the viewport toolbar.
2. Choose view ➢ Views ➢ NE to get a northeast isometric view of your model.
3. Click the Zoom Extents tool to fit the model in the view.

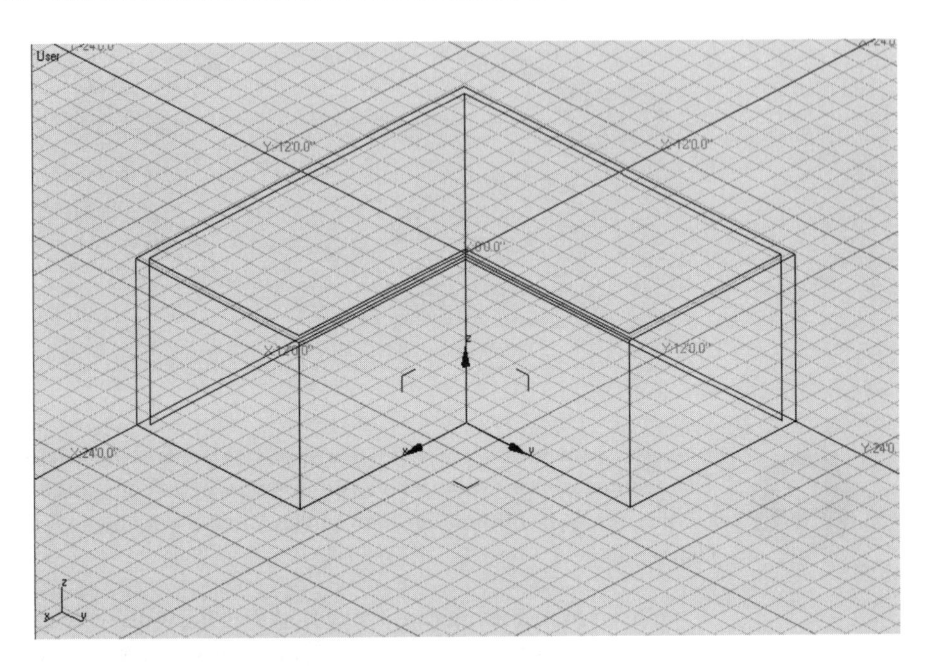

Now you're ready to add a user grid. First, you'll place it randomly in the drawing, then you'll move it into a position that allows you to add a new wall through the keyboard.

1. If it isn't selected already, click the Create tab of the Command Panel.
2. Click the Helpers tool.

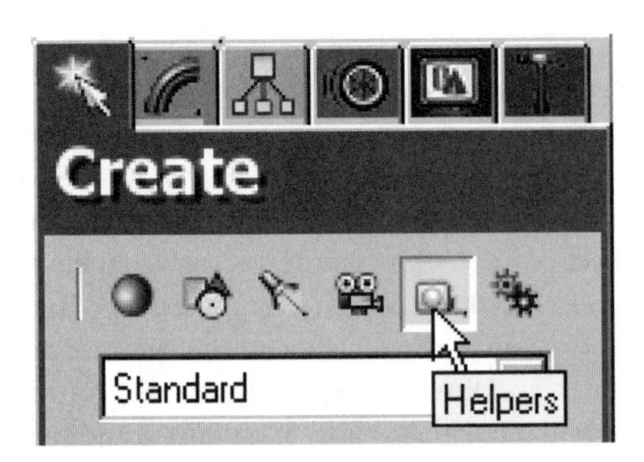

3. Click the Grid button in the set of buttons under the Object Type rollout.

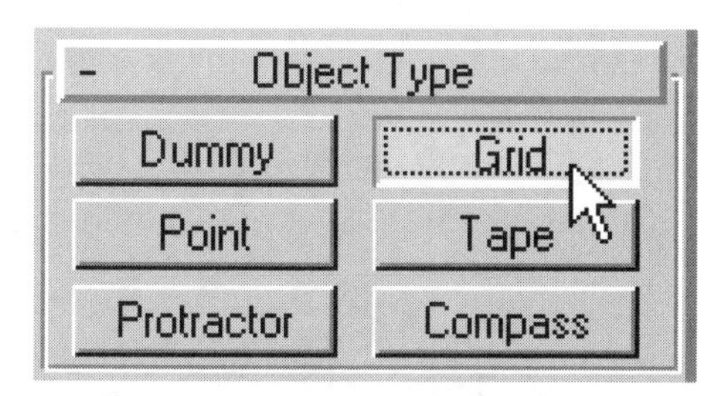

4. Click and drag downward from a point in the upper right corner of the view as shown in Figure 3.14. Just approximate the location—it doesn't have to be exact.

FIGURE 3.14

Adding a user grid

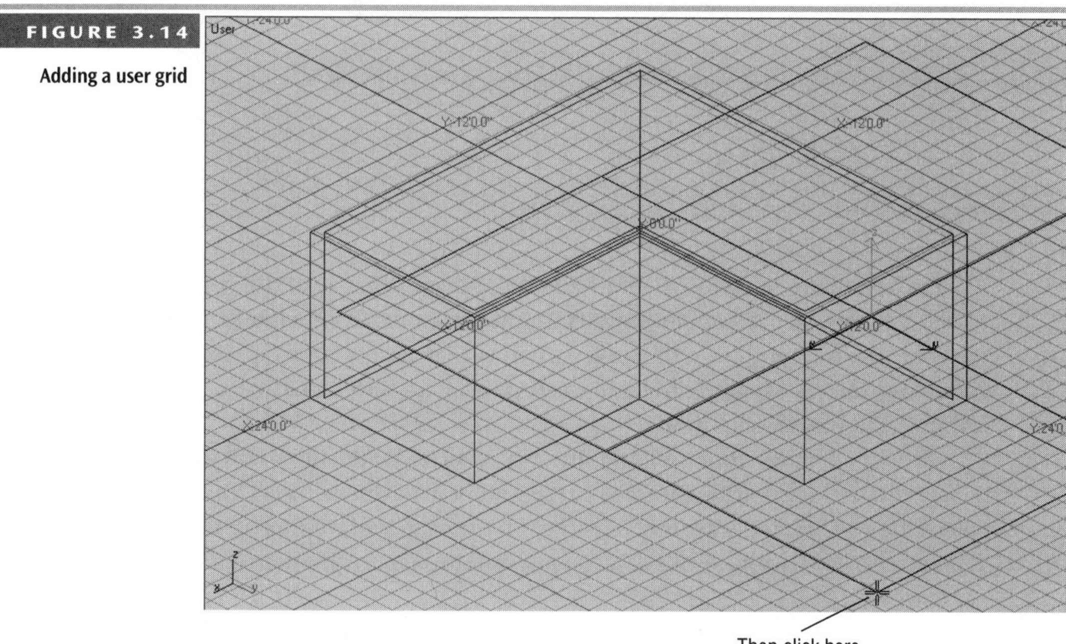

5. Release the mouse button near the location shown in Figure 3.14. You will see a grid display that is similar to the one in Figure 3.15.

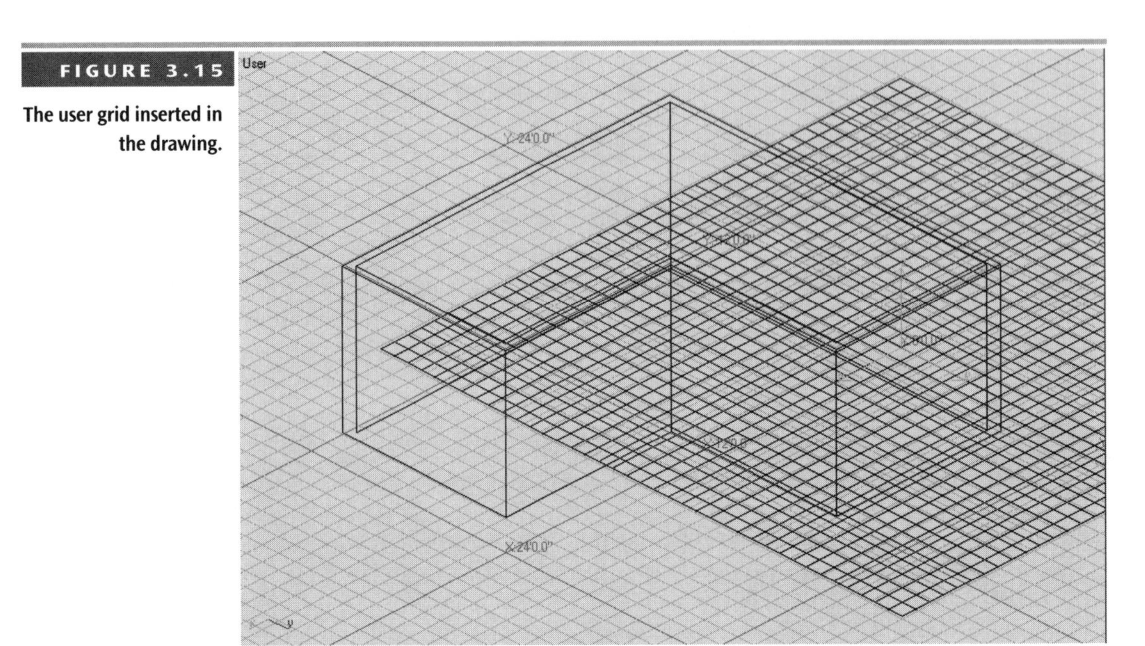

FIGURE 3.15

The user grid inserted in the drawing.

You don't have to be too accurate about the shape and size of the grid. As with all other VIZ objects, you can *fine-tune* its parameters in the Command Panel after it is created. You can set the width and length as well as the grid spacing. In this set of exercises, you're only using the grid to create a local coordinate system from which you can draw additional walls.

Next, you'll move your user grid into a position that will allow you to enter coordinates relative to an existing feature of the walls you've drawn so far. To accurately place the grid, use the snap tool. First, set up the snap tool to connect to the geometry you plan to work with. In this case, you'll want to snap to grid points and endpoints of objects.

1. Right-click the Snap tool button in the toolbar at the bottom of the VIZ window. The Grid and Snap Settings dialog box displays.

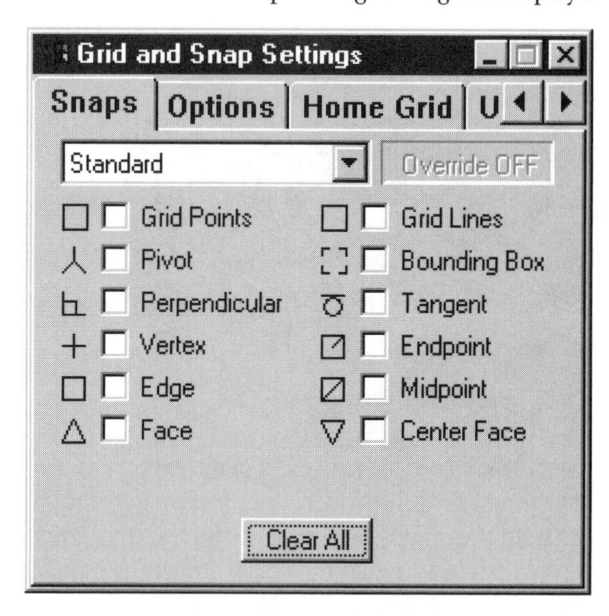

2. If it isn't already selected, click the Snaps tab, then click the Grid Points check box and Endpoint check box.
3. Go ahead and close the Grid and Snap Settings dialog box.
4. Click the Snap tool to make it active. You'll know it's active if the button looks like it is *down*.

Now you're ready to move the grid using the Snap settings to guide your movements.

1. Click the Select and Move tool in the standard toolbar.

   Now, as you move the cursor over the viewport, you'll see a blue snap marker appear on the grid.

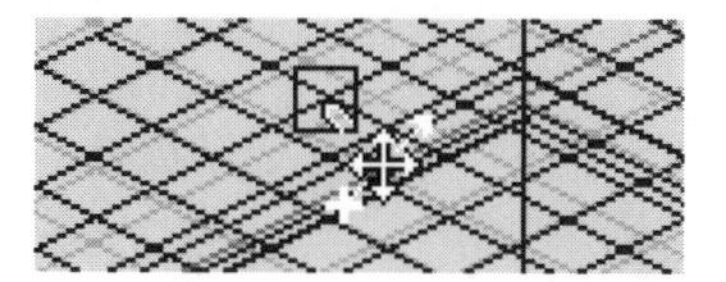

   The cursor jumps to grid points on the user grid. You may also notice that it jumps to the endpoints of the walls you've drawn so far.

2. Place the cursor so that it is on the 0,0 origin of the user grid. You can spot the origin by locating the Transform gizmo.

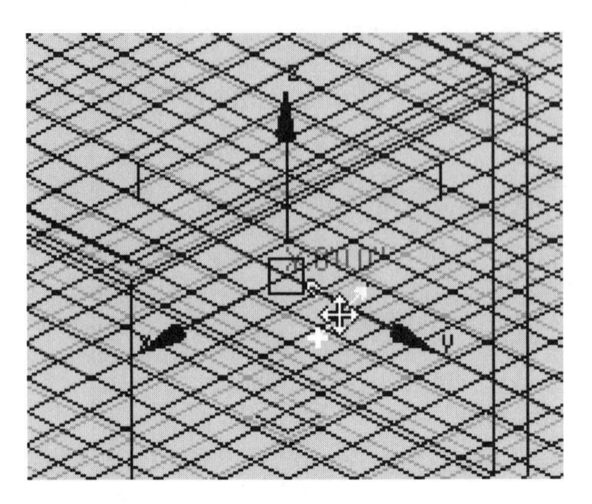

3. Click and hold the origin, then drag the grid to the corner of the wall, as shown in Figure 3.16. Make sure that the cursor shows the endpoint graphic before you release the mouse button.

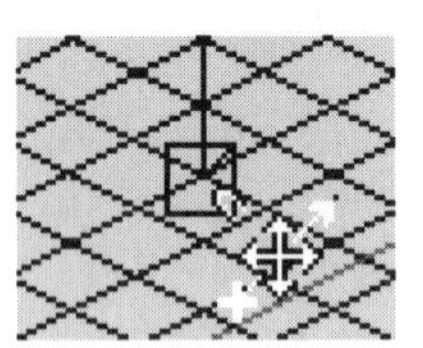

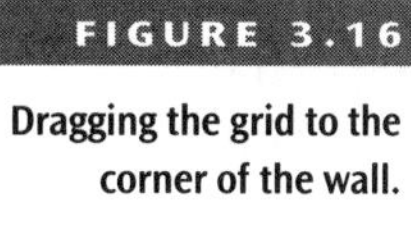
FIGURE 3.16

Dragging the grid to the corner of the wall.

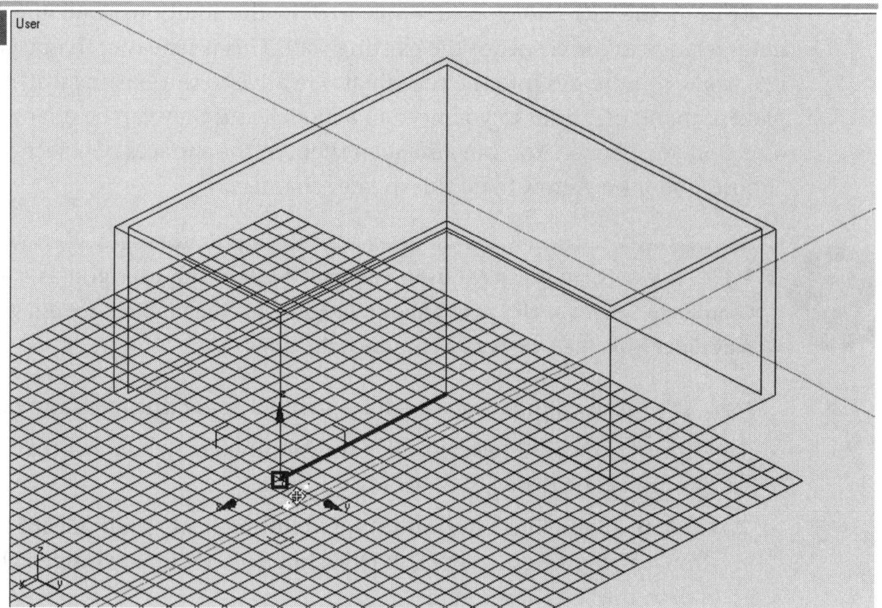

Now you're ready to start drawing the wall addition.

1. Click the Shapes tool in the Create tab of the Command panel.

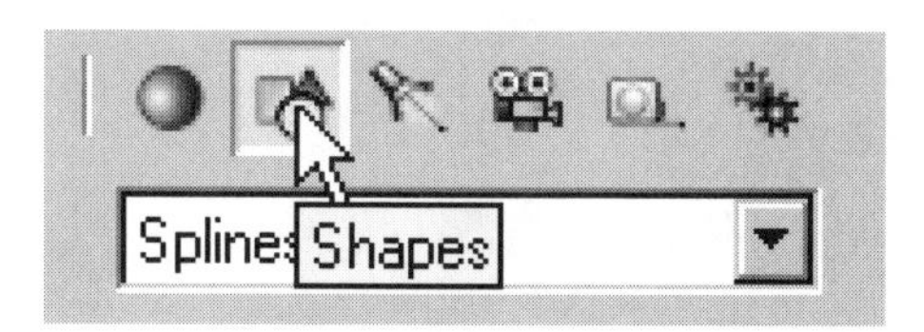

2. Click the Line button in the Object Type rollout.
3. Scroll the Command Panel up until you see the Keyboard Entry rollout, then click it to open it.
4. With the X, Y, and Z values set to **0** in the Keyboard Entry rollout, click the Add point button. This starts the new line at the 0,0 coordinate of the user grid.
5. Click the X value, enter **12'**↵, and click the Add Point button.
6. Click the Y value, enter **10'**↵, and click the Add point button.
7. Click the X value again, enter **–10'**↵, then click the Add point button.
8. Click the Finish button to exit the line tool.

By using the user grid, you were able to draw the additional wall line using coordinates relative to the corner of the existing wall. This is far easier than trying to translate world coordinates into the coordinates relative to the existing walls. You can place as many user grids as you need in a model, and they can be oriented in any direction you choose. You can also align them to the surfaces of objects if you so choose. You'll learn how to do this in later chapters.

TIP **If you're an AutoCAD user, you can think of the user grid as a kind of User Coordinate System or UCS as it is known in AutoCAD. The methods for using the user grid may differ from the UCS, but its purpose is the same.**

Now let's finish the additional wall by giving it some thickness and height.

1. With the new wall selected, click the Modify tab. Remember that, since the wall has just been created, it is already selected.
2. Click the Sub-Object button in the Modifier Stack, then select Spline from the drop-down list next to the Sub-Object button. (You may instead click the Spline tool in the Selection rollout.)

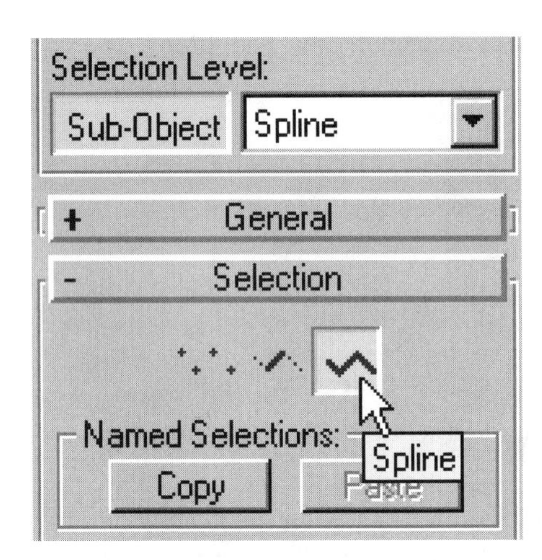

3. Select the spline. Scroll down the Command Panel until you see the Outline button and enter **5″↵** in the input box next to the Outline button. Once you press ↵, the wall will be given a thickness of 5″.

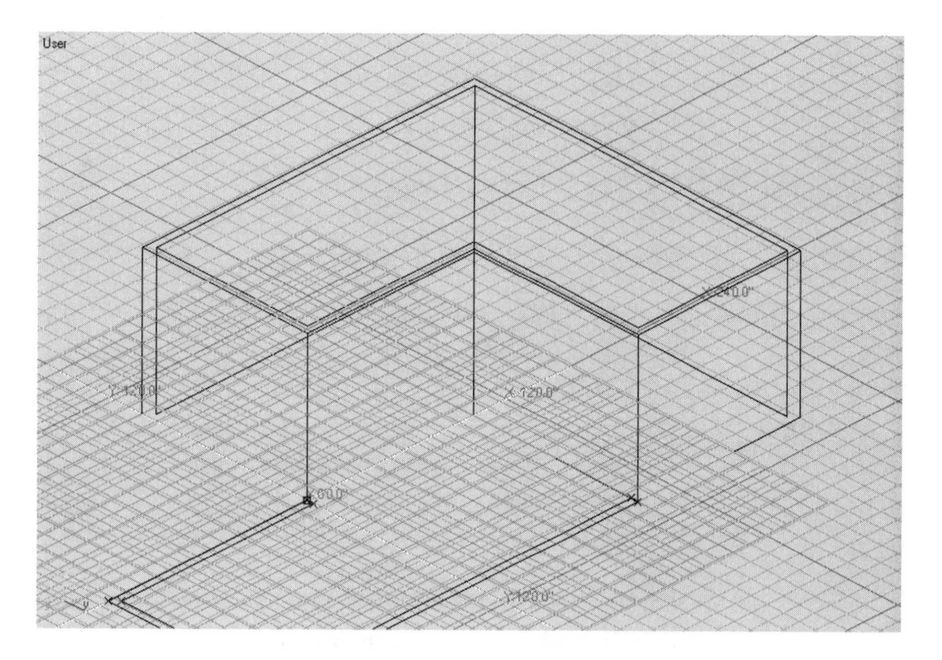

4. Scroll back up to the top of the Command Panel so you can see the Modifiers rollout and click the Extrude button. Make sure that the Amount value in the Parameters rollout is set to **8′**. Your additional wall now appears in place.

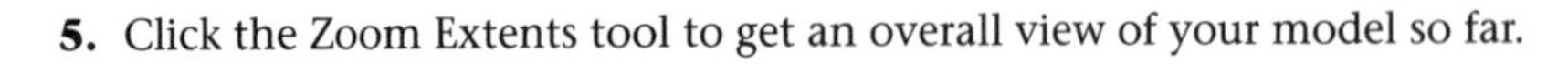

5. Click the Zoom Extents tool to get an overall view of your model so far.

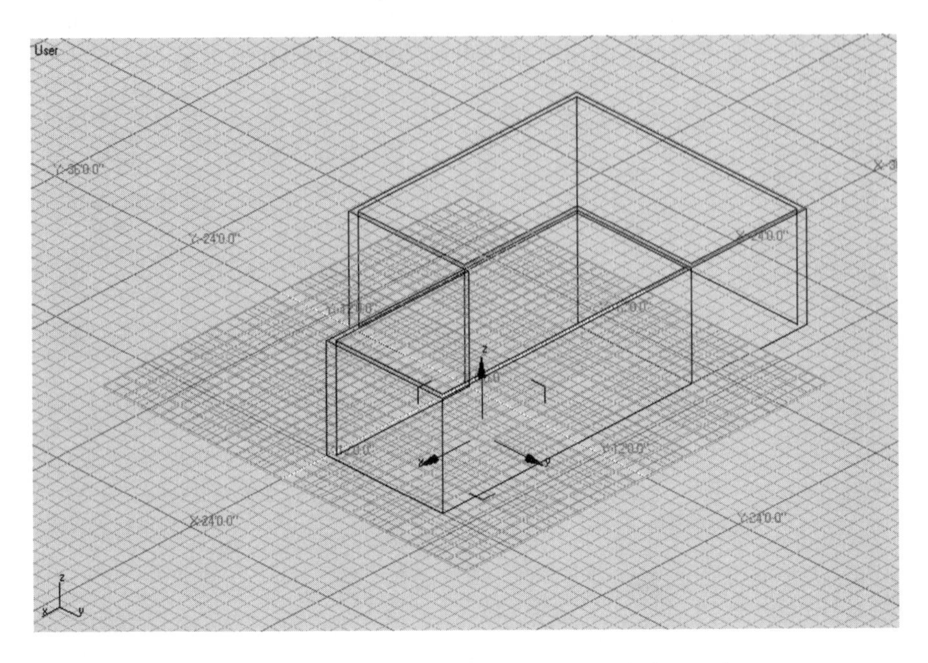

Once again, you used the outline option to convert a single line spline into an outline, giving the wall a thickness. Unlike other parameters, an outline cannot be changed by simply changing a parameter once it is in place. This is true for most sub-object functions. You can make changes at sub-object levels, such as changes to the vertices or line segments.

TIP **Another way to draw line segments is to set the Snap setting to Grid Points, then set the grid spacing to the smallest value you need to work with. Then, as you select points for the line, you can read the coordinates readout at the bottom of the VIZ window. You'll see that the coordinates show your current position relative to the last point you selected in the X, Y, and Z coordinate format. You can adjust the grid spacing in the Grid and Snap Settings dialog box under User Grids or Home Grids.**

Understanding the Snap Settings

While you were working to add the new wall, you got a glimpse of the Grid and Snap Settings dialog box, and you activated two of the Snap options from that dialog box. Take a moment to look at that dialog box again. You can see quite a few snap options, of which you only used two. You won't be using all of those options in this book, so here's a listing that describes the other snap options.

Grid Points Snap to intersection of grid lines

Pivot Snap to an object's pivot point as represented by Transform gizmo

Perpendicular Snap to perpendicular to line segments and edges

Vertex Snap to vertices

Edge Snap to edges

Face Snap to faces

Grid Lines Snap to the intersection of grid lines

Bounding Box Snap to bounding box corner

Tangent Snap to tangent of curves and circles

Endpoint Snap to endpoints

Midpoint Snap to midpoints of line segments and edges

Center Face Snap to the center of face

Clear All Button Clear all snap settings

Standard/NURBS Drop-down list reveals a different set of snaps for NURBS objects

You may have noticed a graphic next to each of the Snap options in the Grid and Snap Settings dialog box. When a snap setting is selected, the cursor will display the graphic associated with the snap setting whenever the cursor approaches a geometry that matches the snap setting. For example, if you select the Endpoint snap setting, when Snap is turned on and the cursor approaches and touches an endpoint, the cursor will display the graphic associated with the Endpoint Snap.

Adjusting a Wall Location

The wall you just added isn't quite aligned properly with the first set of walls. If you look at a top view of the walls, you'll see that the new wall is offset by the width of the wall where the new wall meets one of the corners of the old wall (see Figure 3.17).

To move the new wall section into place, you'll need to work with the vertices of the wall. Once again, this means working with the wall on a sub-object level. The following exercise will give you some first-hand experience with some simple vertex transformations. Start by returning to the top view of the walls.

1. Right-click the User viewport label in the upper left corner of the viewport.
2. Select View ➢ Top. Your view changes back to the top view.
3. Click the Select object tool, click the User Grid, then press the Delete key. You don't need the user grid any more.
4. Click the Zoom Extents tool to get an overall view of the model. Your view will look similar to Figure 3.17.

FIGURE 3.17

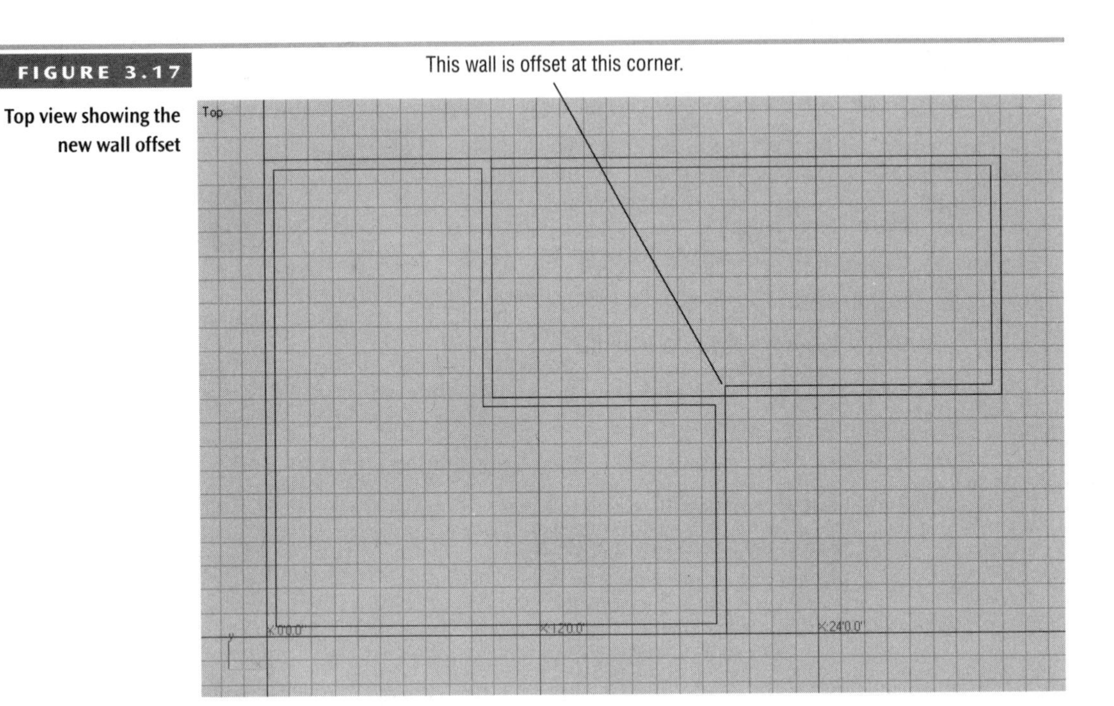
This wall is offset at this corner.
Top

Top view showing the new wall offset

Now you can see the offset more clearly. Let's go on to the work of moving the wall into alignment with the existing wall. First, set up the Snap for endpoints. You don't want to accidentally snap to a grid point.

1. Right-click the Snap button at the bottom of the VIZ window.
2. In the Grid and Snap Settings dialog box, make sure that Grid Points is not checked and Endpoint is checked, then close the dialog box.

Next you'll move the wall section.

1. Click the Select object tool, then click the new wall.
2. Click the Modify tab of the Command Panel.
3. Select Line from the Modifier Stack drop-down list.

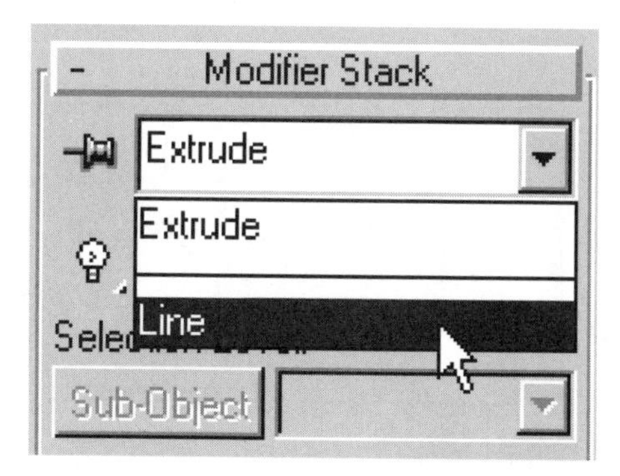

4. Make sure the Sub-Object button is selected, then select the Vertex from the Selection Level drop-down list. (You may instead click the Vertex tool in the Selection rollout.)

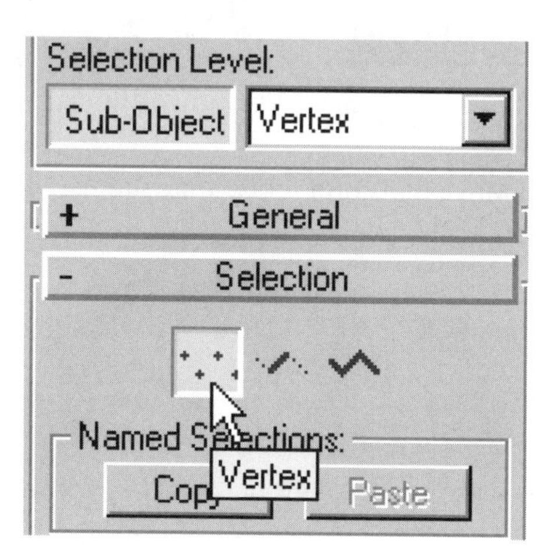

5. With the Select Object tool active, place a window around the vertices you want to move. Do this by clicking and dragging a window, as shown in Figure 3.18. You'll see the selected vertices turn red, with arrows showing the coordinate directions.

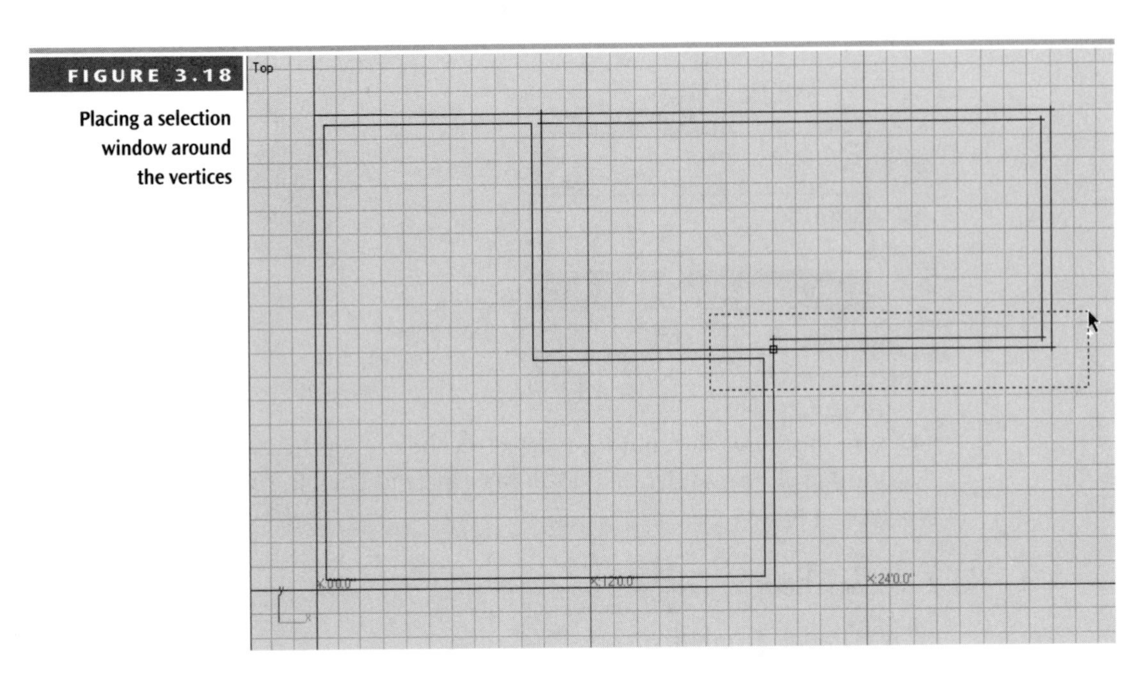

FIGURE 3.18

Placing a selection window around the vertices

6. Click the Select and Move transform tool on the standard toolbar.

7. Place the cursor on the wall vertex as shown in Figure 3.19. When you see the endpoint snap marker, click and drag the vertex downward to the location of the vertex just below it, as shown in Figure 3.20.

FIGURE 3.19

Selecting the vertex to move

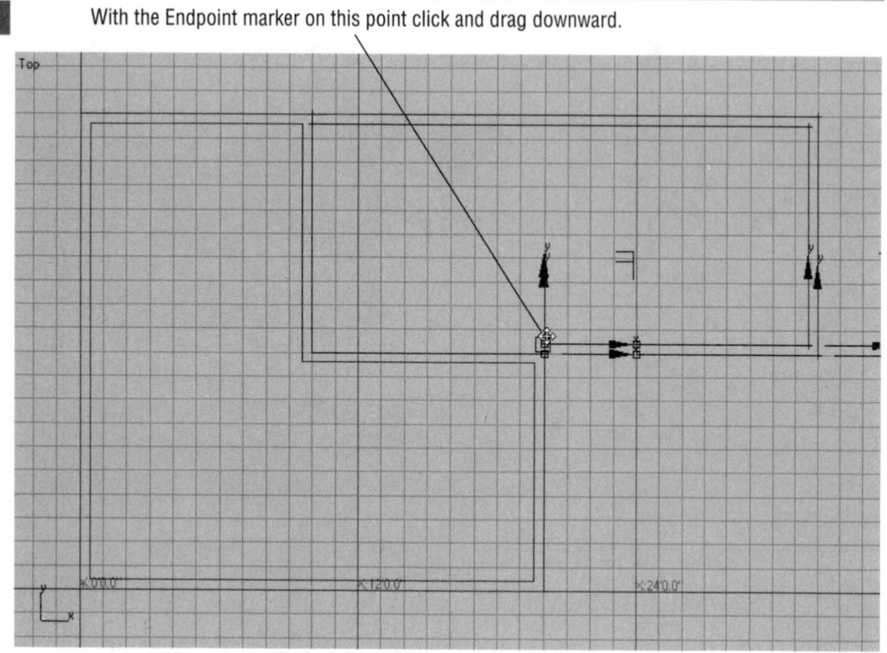
With the Endpoint marker on this point click and drag downward.
Top

FIGURE 3.20

When the cursor snaps to this endpoint release the mouse button.

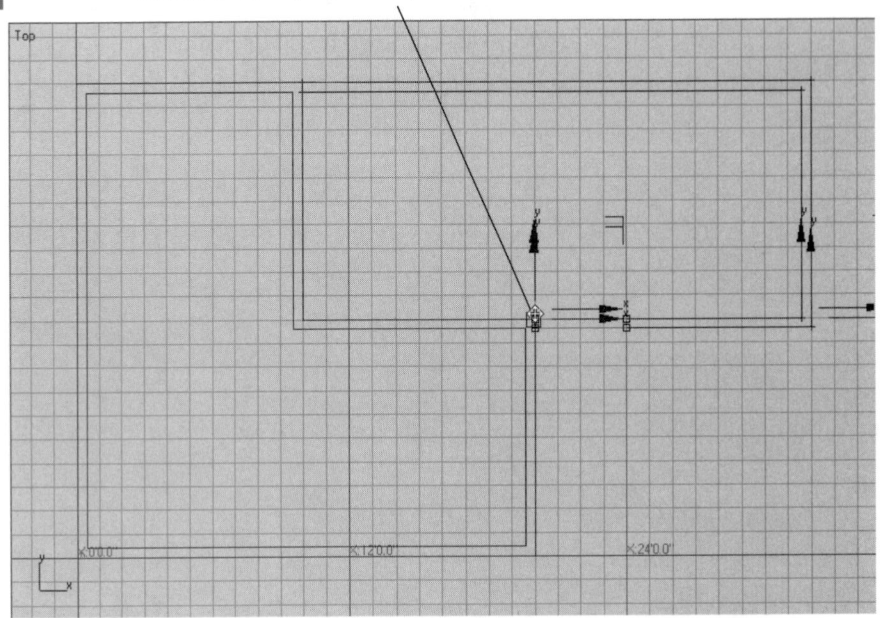

Selecting the new location of the vertex

You've moved the selected vertices into place. Now let's take a look at the results.

1. Click the Min/Max toggle tool to view all of the viewports.
2. Click the Zoom Extents All tool to show all of the model in all viewports. Notice that the new walls no longer appear as walls. Because you are editing the lines in the modifier stack, VIZ displays the wall as a spline.
3. Click the Sub-Object button in the Modifier Stack to turn it off.
4. Click the drop-down list in the Modifier Stack rollout and select Extrude. The wall reappears at its full height.

You've just seen how you can move a set of vertices, thereby stretching a wall into a new location. As you can see, you need to enter the Sub-object level of editing before you can make changes to vertices, but once you do, you have a good deal of freedom to edit parts of an object.

If you're working with architectural models, you'll find that you use this operation frequently to *fine-tune* parts of a model. You'll get a chance to edit the vertices of objects in a number of ways as you work through this book.

TIP If you find that you cannot select another object while editing your model, it may be because you currently are editing an object on a sub-object level. Check to see if the Sub-Object button is selected. If it is, turn it off, then select the next object to be edited. By doing so, you are going from the sub-object level to the object level.

Using *Canned* Shapes to Add Walls

You've learned how you can create walls with simple lines. Lines are perhaps the most basic type of object you can draw with, and you'll use them often when creating your models. But for walls of a floor plan, you can use another object type that can simplify your work.

VIZ offers a number of 2D shapes that can help make quick work of your modeling efforts, as long as you know how to apply them. In this section, you'll use the Rectangle spline to add a room to your current plan.

1. Click the top viewport, then click the Min/Max Toggle tool to enlarge it.
2. Click the Zoom tool, then click and drag downward on the Top viewport so that you get a view of a larger area.

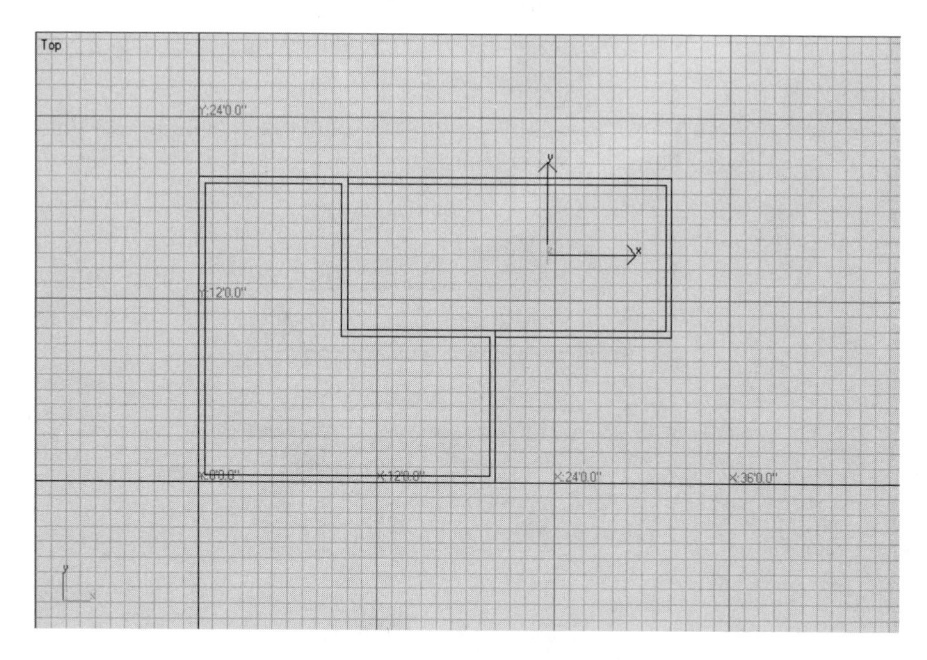

3. Click the Create tab of the Command Panel and click the Rectangle tool.

4. Right-click the Snap button to open the Grid and Snap Settings dialog box, click the Grid Points option, and close the dialog box. You'll use the grid snap to help you create the next set of walls.
5. Make sure the Snap tool is turned on, click and drag from coordinate 26',0,0, then drag out a rectangle that is 14' wide by 15' deep. You can use the coordinate readout at the bottom of the screen to read the dimensions of your rectangle as you move the mouse.

Just as in the previous exercise, you start out with a single line representation of the wall. In this case, it's a rectangle that is 14' by 15'. You were able to use the grid and snap together in this exercise to place the rectangle and determine its size.

The next step in adding the wall is to combine it with the existing walls. The rectangle needs to have a portion of its upper left corner removed. To make the plan a little more interesting, you'll also add a curve to the lower right corner.

Combining and Editing Splines

With the Outline tool, you learned that spline objects can be composed of multiple splines, accessible on the spline sub-object level. In this section, you'll see how to combine two spline objects into one, and you'll learn how, once joined, you can edit the new object to form new shapes.

1. Click the Select object tool in the standard toolbar and click the wall that intersects the rectangle you just drew, as shown in Figure 3.21.
2. Click the Modify tab in the Command Panel, then, in the Modifier Stack drop-down list, select Line.

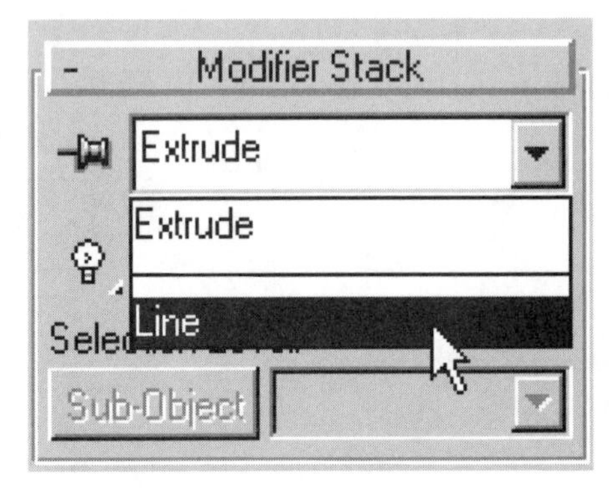

3. Scroll down the Command Panel to the Geometry rollout, and click the Attach button.

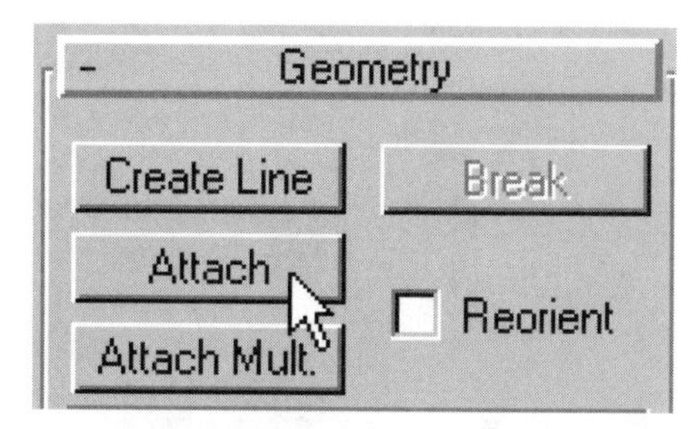

4. Move the cursor on top of the rectangle you added in the last exercise. You'll see the Attach cursor appear when the cursor finds an available object to attach.

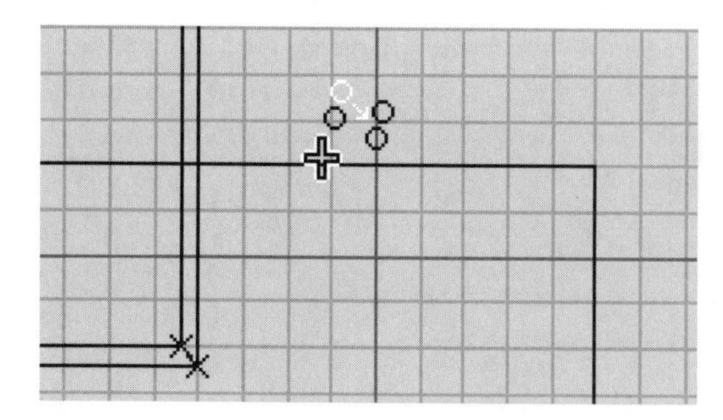

5. Click the rectangle.

FIGURE 3.21

Click the wall you created in the last exercise, then click it again to select its spline component.

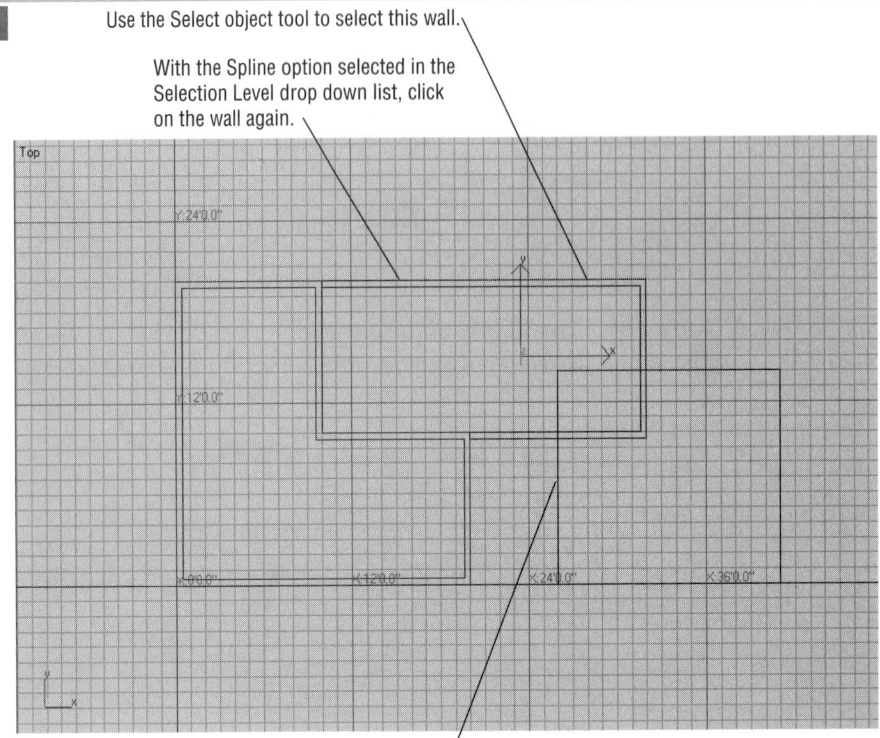
Use the Select object tool to select this wall.
With the Spline option selected in the Selection Level drop down list, click on the wall again.
Top
With the Attach option selected, click on the rectangle.

6. Click the Attach button again to deactivate it.

You've just attached the rectangle to the wall object you selected at the beginning of this exercise. Earlier you saw how the Outline option created two concentric rectangles to form a rectangular wall. That was a clue that objects can contain multiple splines. The outer and inner walls of that rectangular wall are separate splines contained within the same object. In this last exercise, you added the rectangle you just created to the wall of the previous exercise.

Next, you'll see how you can trim the parts of the rectangle that you don't need.

1. Click the Region Zoom tool.

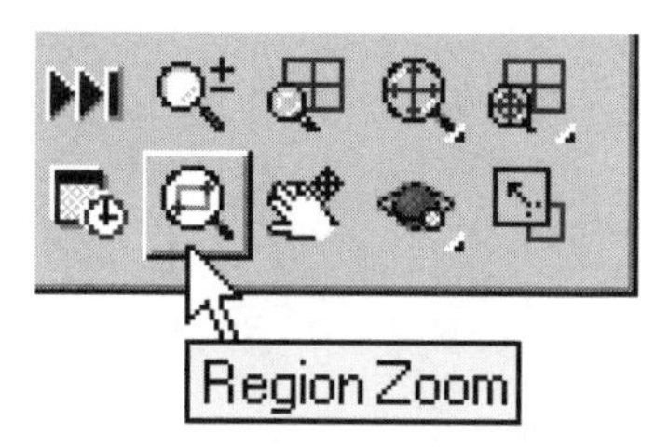

2. Then place a zoom window around the area shown in Figure 3.21 to enlarge that area.

FIGURE 3.22

Placing a Region Zoom window around the rectangle corner

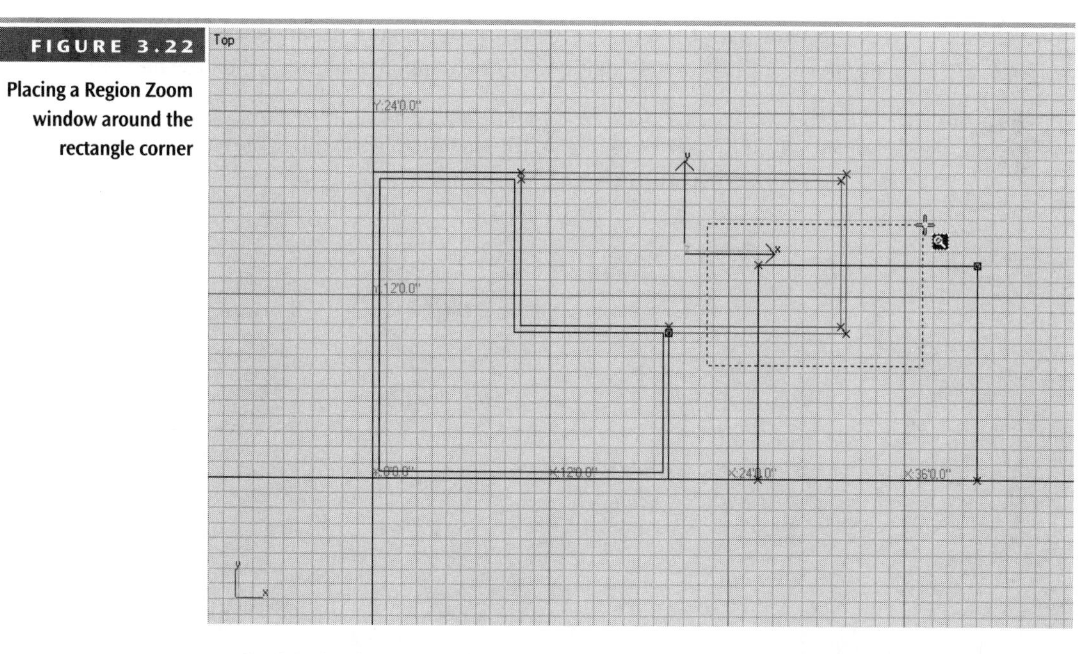

3. With the wall selected, click the Sub-Object button and select Spline from the Selection Level drop down list. You may also click the Spline button in the Selection rollout.

4. Locate the Trim button in the Command Panel and click it.

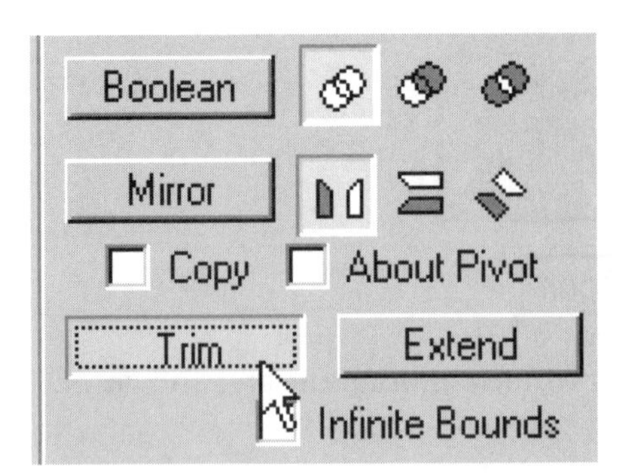

5. Click the Trim tool, then place the cursor on the upper-left corner of the rectangle. Notice how the cursor changes to a graphic that indicates the trim operation.
6. Go ahead and click the rectangle in the location shown in Figure 3.23. The corner of the rectangle is trimmed back to the wall.

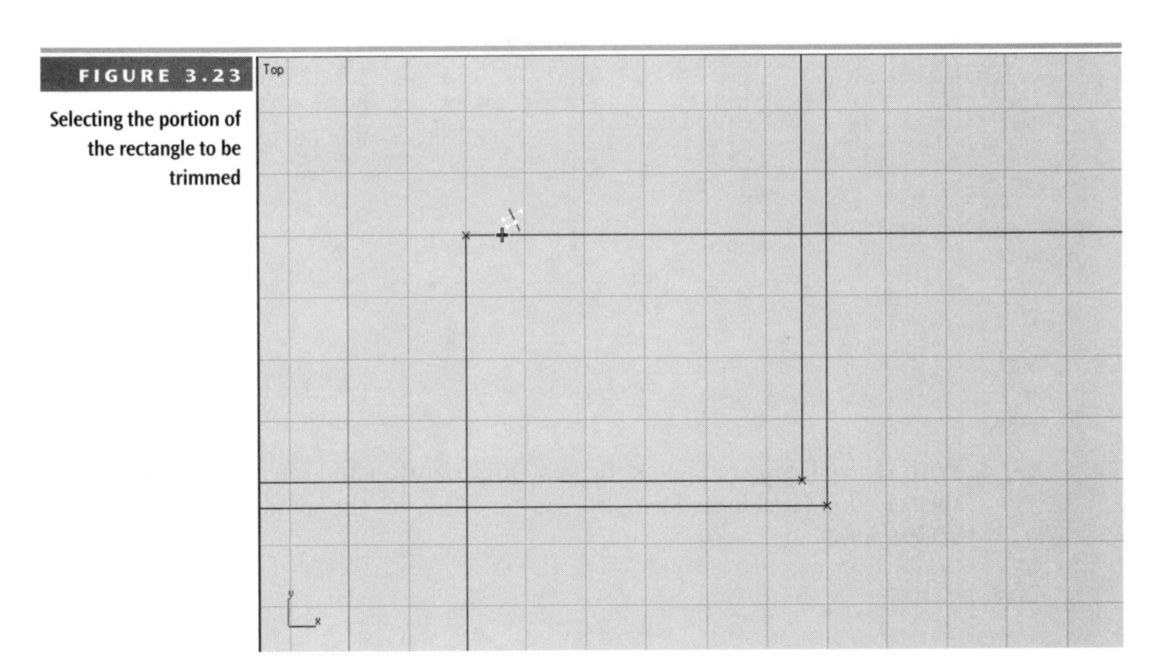

FIGURE 3.23

Selecting the portion of the rectangle to be trimmed

7. Click the Trim tool to deactivate it.
8. Click the Zoom Extents tool to get an overall view of the walls.

The Trim tool will trim a spline to the nearest spline that is a part of the same object. Trim ignores any splines that are not included in the current object. This is why you had to attach the rectangle before you used the Trim tool.

You can continue to trim a spline by clicking on the side you wish to trim. The spline will then trim back to the nearest spline that is part of the currently selected object. Figure 3.24 shows an example of what the rectangle would look like if you continue to click the remaining endpoints of the rectangle with Trim.

FIGURE 3.24

Click the endpoints of the rectangle to trim it back to the outside of the wall.

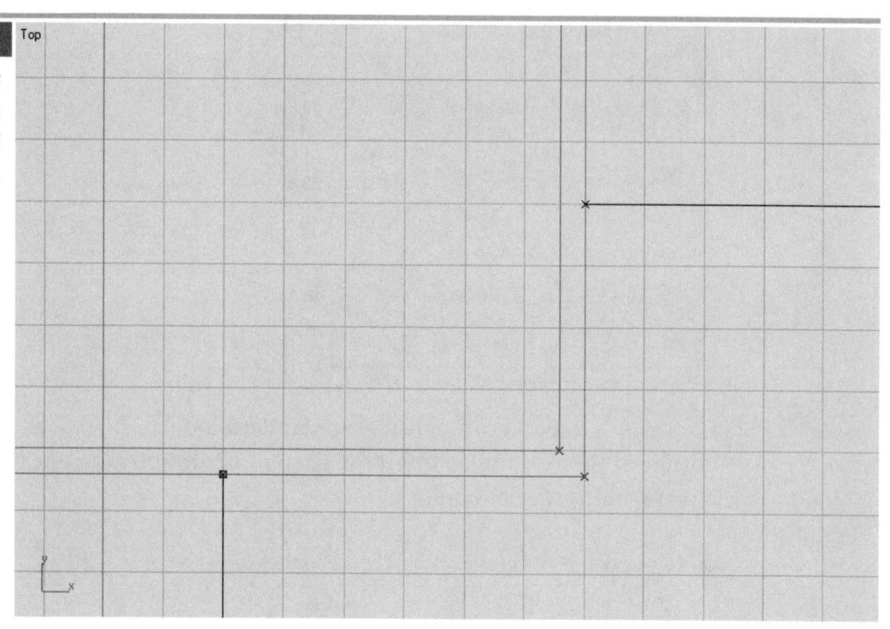

You won't be trimming the rectangle any farther than you have in step 6. Instead, in a later exercise in this chapter, you'll use the rectangle in its current configuration to learn how you can merge two sets of lines using the Boolean spline tool.

NOTE **Later in Chapter 4 you'll learn about the Boolean Compound Object, which creates new objects by combining existing ones through Boolean operations. Boolean Compound Objects are different from those created through the Boolean options in the Spline's sub-object level.**

Now let's see how you go about adding a rounded corner to a spline using the Fillet tool.

NOTE AutoCAD Users will find that the Fillet tool is similar in effect to the AutoCAD Fillet tool, although it works in a very different way.

1. Scroll to the top of the Command Panel, then click the Vertex tool. (You may instead select Vertex from the Selection Level drop-down list.)

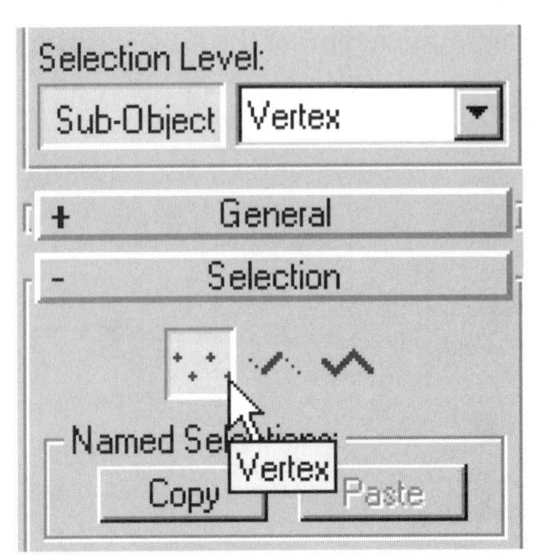

2. Click the Select object tool from the standard toolbar, then click the lower right corner of the rectangle. You'll see the Transform gizmo appear at the corner along with the Bézier handles.

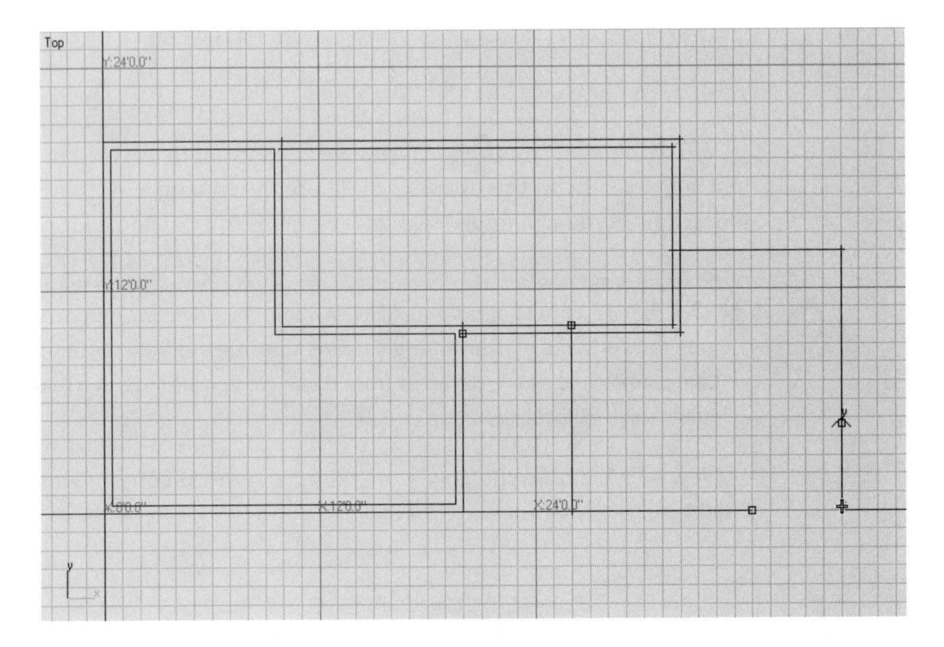

3. Scroll down the Command Panel until you see the Fillet button.
4. Click and drag the fillet input box spinner upward and notice what happens to the corner. Don't release the mouse button just yet. As you move the spinner, the corner turns into a radius.

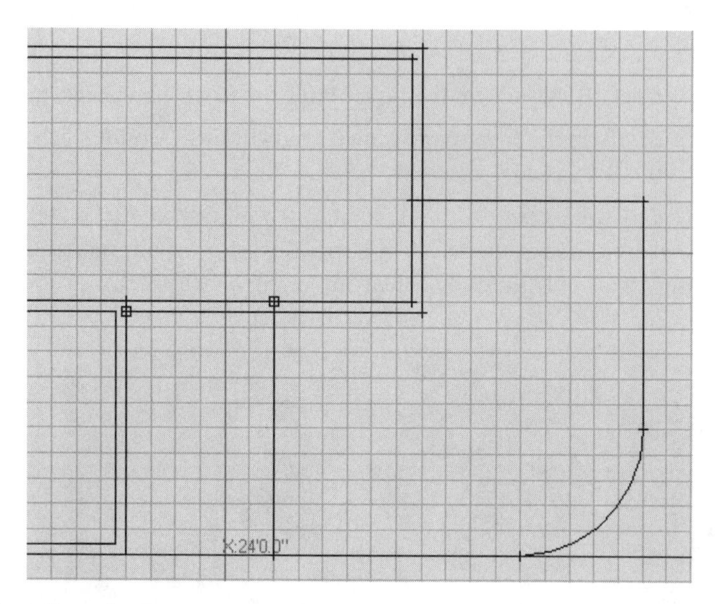

5. Adjust the Spinner until the Fillet value reads 5', then release the mouse button. If you happen to release the mouse button before you get to 5', click the undo button and repeat steps 4 and 5.

The Fillet tool is an option of the Vertex sub-object, so you need to be in the Vertex Sub-object editing mode before you can use it. Now to finish off the new wall, use the outline tool once again.

1. Scroll up to the Selection rollout and click the Spline tool.

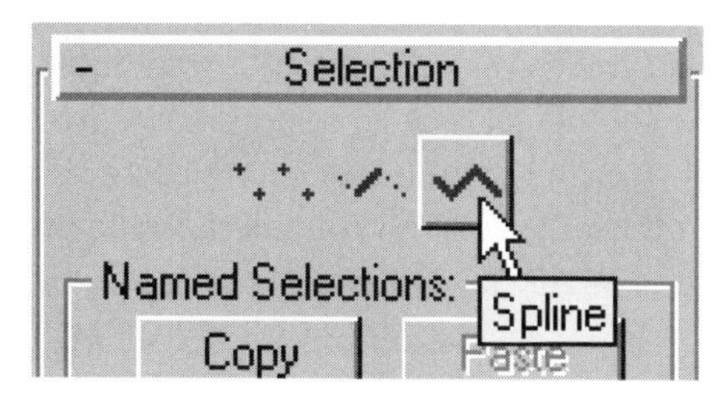

2. If it isn't already selected, click the Select object tool, then click the filleted rectangle. It turns red when it is selected.

3. Scroll down the Command Panel to get to the Outline tool.

4. Enter **5"↵** in the Outline tool's input box. The rectangle is outlined.

Take a look at the final results.

1. Click the Min/Max Toggle tool to view all of the viewports.
2. Scroll up the Command Panel, then click the Modifier Stack drop-down list and select Extrude.

Because the rectangle is attached to the wall spline you created earlier, it is also affected by the Extrude modifier. Figure 3.25 shows your model up to this point, from an angle that shows off all of the components.

FIGURE 3.25

The perspective view of the walls

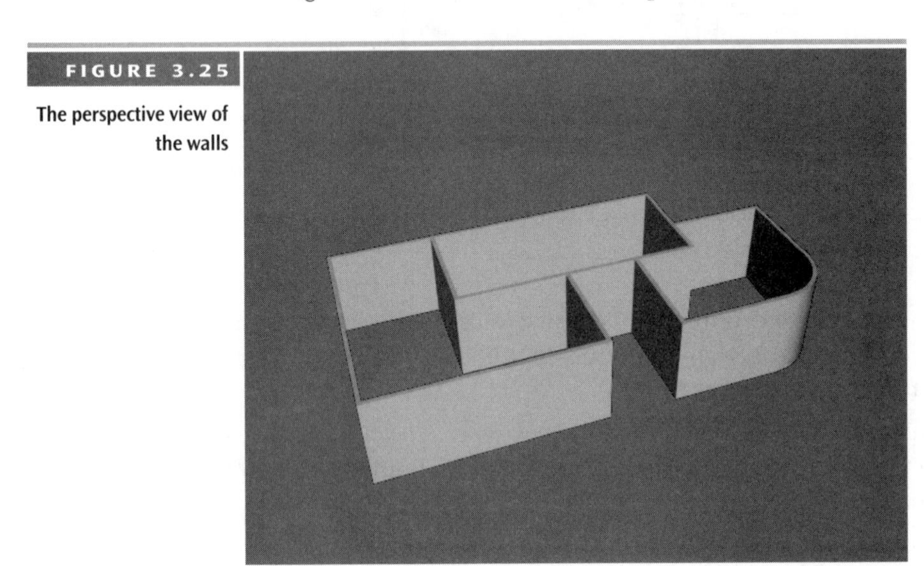

As you work with splines, you'll see that the type of tool options you can use to edit a spline depend on the sub-object type you select in the Selection rollout or the Selection Level drop-down list. Fillets and Bézier curves can be edited when the Vertex sub-object is selected. Trim is available when you select Spline in sub-object option levels. The Attach option is available in object mode as well as in all sub-object levels.

Joining Closed Splines with Boolean Tools

In the last exercise, you combined the rectangle with a wall to form a wall object that is made up of two splines. The added rectangle protrudes into the wall that it is joined with as shown in an enlarged view of the walls in Figure 3.26.

FIGURE 3.26

The walls joined at a corner

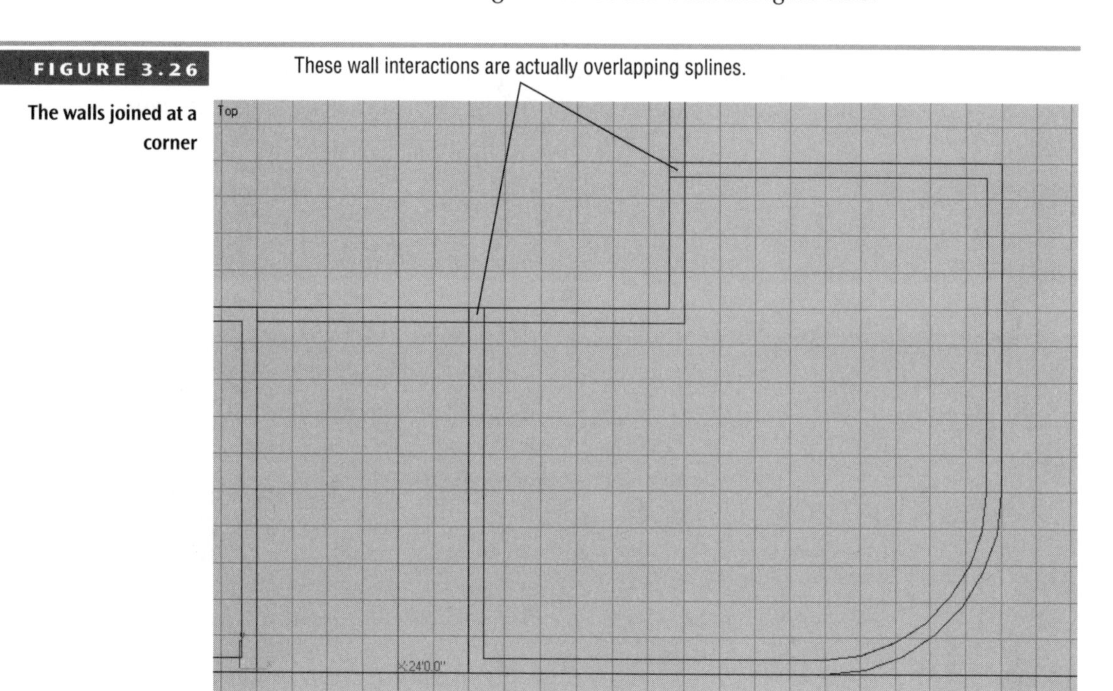
These wall interactions are actually overlapping splines.
Top
24'0.0"

Although these wall intersections do not adversely affect your ability to work with the model, you may eventually want to merge the wall intersections into a clean joint. You can do this by using the Boolean option.

1. Make sure the Top viewport is active, then click the Min/Max tool to enlarge the Top viewport.
2. Select Line from the Modifier Stack drop-down list. The newest addition to your drawing appears in red because it is selected.

3. Make sure that Spline is selected in the Selection Level drop-down list, then scroll down the Command Panel until you see the Boolean tool.

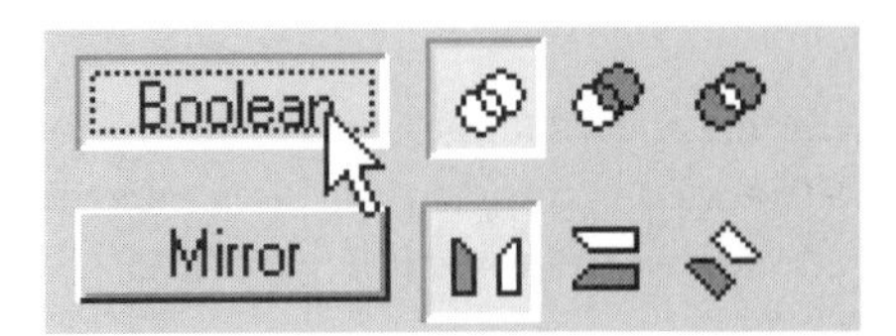

4. Click the Boolean tool, then, in the top viewport, move your cursor to the other wall that is connected with the currently selected wall, as shown in Figure 3.27.

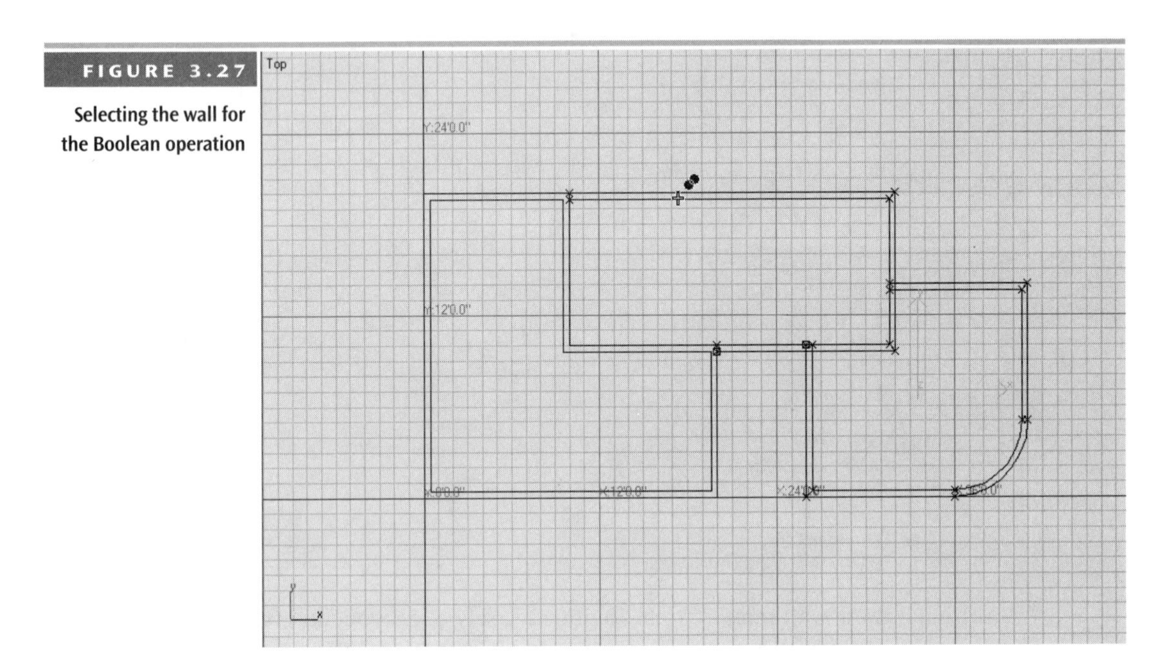

FIGURE 3.27

Selecting the wall for the Boolean operation

5. Notice that the cursor shows an icon, indicating that it has found a candidate for the Boolean operation.
6. Go ahead and click the wall. The wall intersects for a neat connection.

7. Scroll up the Command Panel and click the Sub-Object button to deactivate it. You can now see the corners more clearly as shown in Figure 3.28.

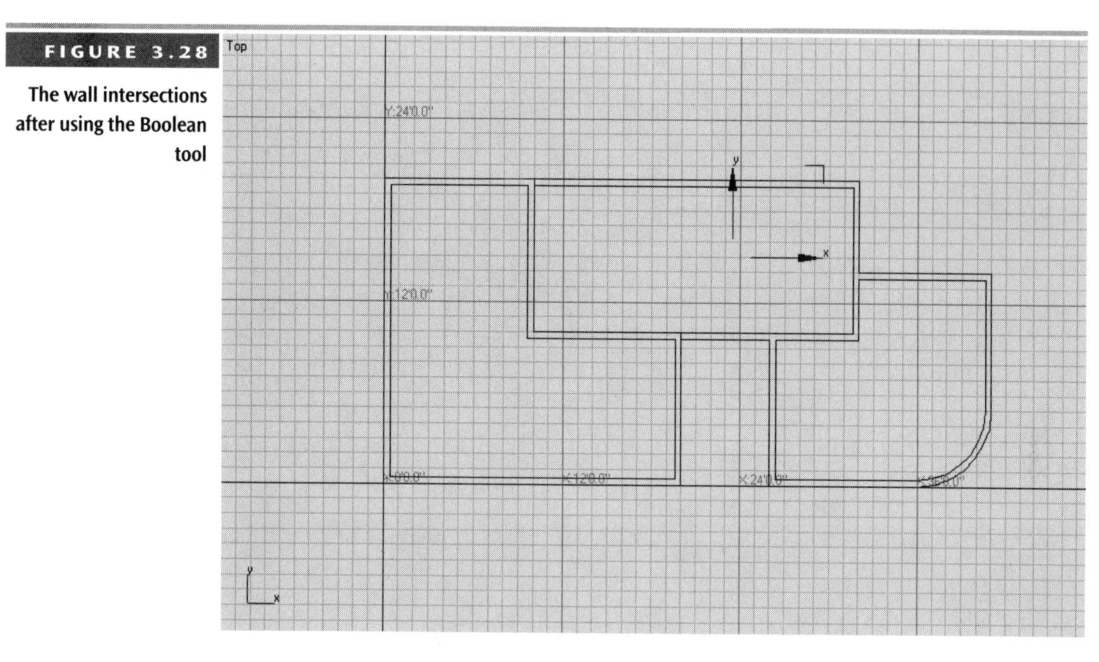

FIGURE 3.28

The wall intersections after using the Boolean tool

8. Select Extrude from the Modifier Stack drop-down list to restore the wall height.

You can use the Boolean tool to join any closed splines such as those that form the two walls from the last exercise. Figure 3.29 shows you some examples of other splines that are joined using this tool. Besides joining spline outlines, you can subtract outlines or obtain the intersection of two outlines.

FIGURE 3.29

Examples of Boolean operations on closed splines

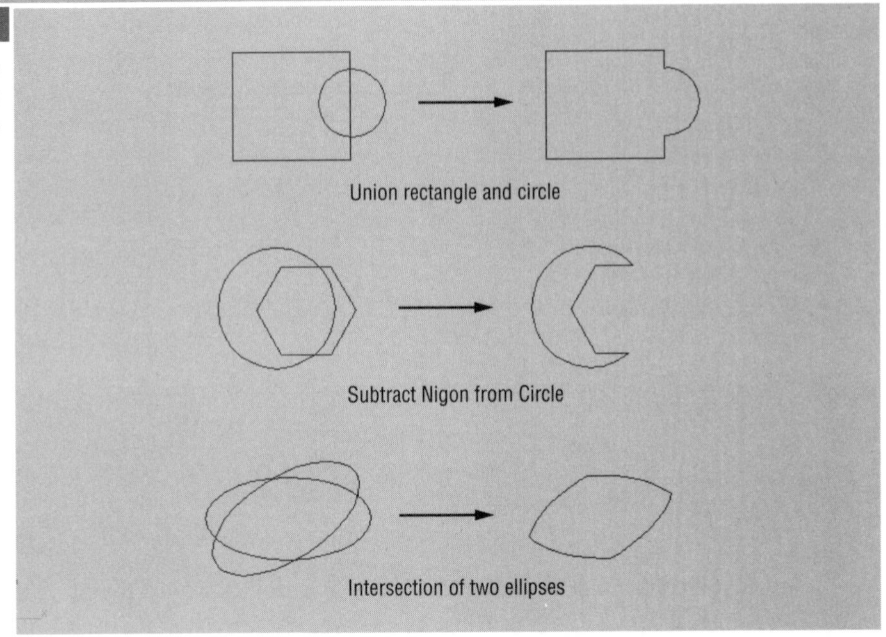

To perform these other types of Boolean operations, follow the same steps you used to join the wall intersections in the last exercise. The only difference is, just before you select the object to be joined, click the appropriate Boolean option from the buttons to the left of the Boolean tool, as shown in Figure 3.30.

FIGURE 3.30

The Boolean options

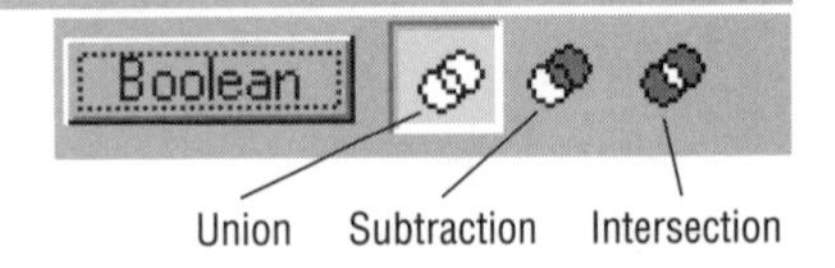

TIP Remember that to perform Boolean operations on splines, the splines need to be attached and they need to be closed. You also need to be at the Spline Sub-Object level to use the Spline Boolean operations.

Creating a Solid Shape with Splines

You've been using splines to create outline shapes such as the profile of the wineglass and the walls of a floor plan. You can also create solid forms like those of the primitive objects you saw in the last chapter. Splines let you go beyond the primitive shapes of circles, rectangles, and squares to form just about any shape you need.

In the following exercise, you'll use a spline to create a ceiling for the walls that you've created so far. This involves creating an outline of the walls, then using the Extrude modifier to give the outline some thickness.

Start by setting up a view that will make it easier to add the ceiling.

1. Choose View ➢ Views ➢ SW, then click the Zoom Extents tool. You will see an isometric view of your walls.

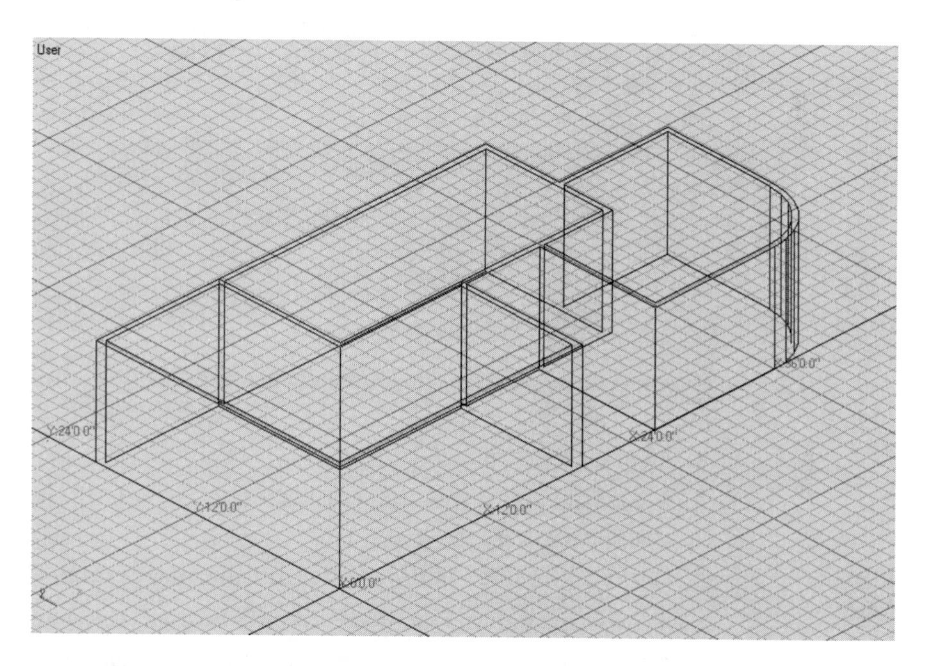

2. Click the Arc Rotated Selected tool.

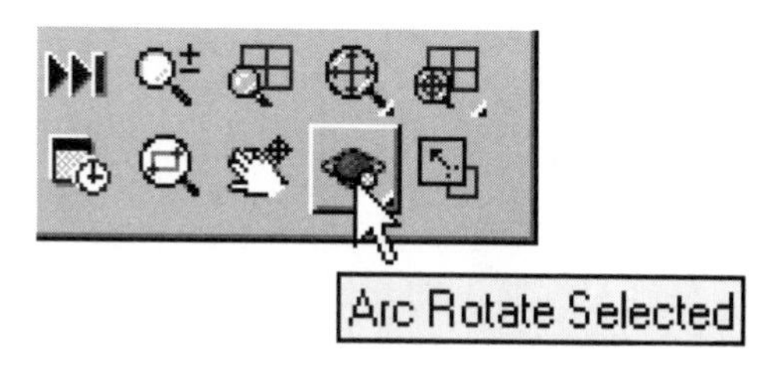

3. Click the top-most square on the green circle and drag downward until you get a view similar to Figure 3.31. This will give you a clear view of all of the walls' outside corners.

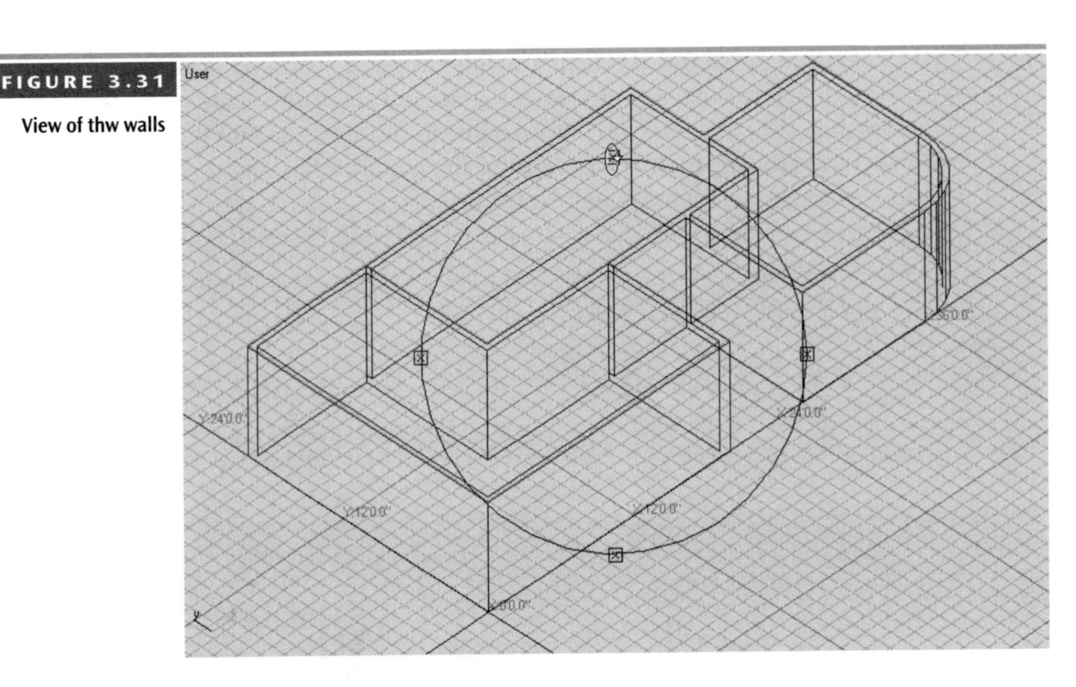

FIGURE 3.31

View of thw walls

Next set up the snap tools to accurately place the spline at the perimeter of the walls.

1. Right-click the Snap tool.
2. In the Grid and Snap Settings dialog box, click Clear All, and click the Endpoint check box.
3. Click the Minimize button of the Grid and Snap Settings dialog box to close it.

Now you're ready to add the spline that will become the ceiling.

1. Click the Create tab of the Command Panel, then click the Shapes tool if it isn't already selected.
2. Click the Line tool.

3. Click the outside corners of the walls as shown in Figure 3.32. When you get to the rounded corner, click the point indicated in the figure. You'll move and reshape that corner later.

FIGURE 3.32

Selecting the vertex

Select this endpoint at the top at the wall for the rounded corner.

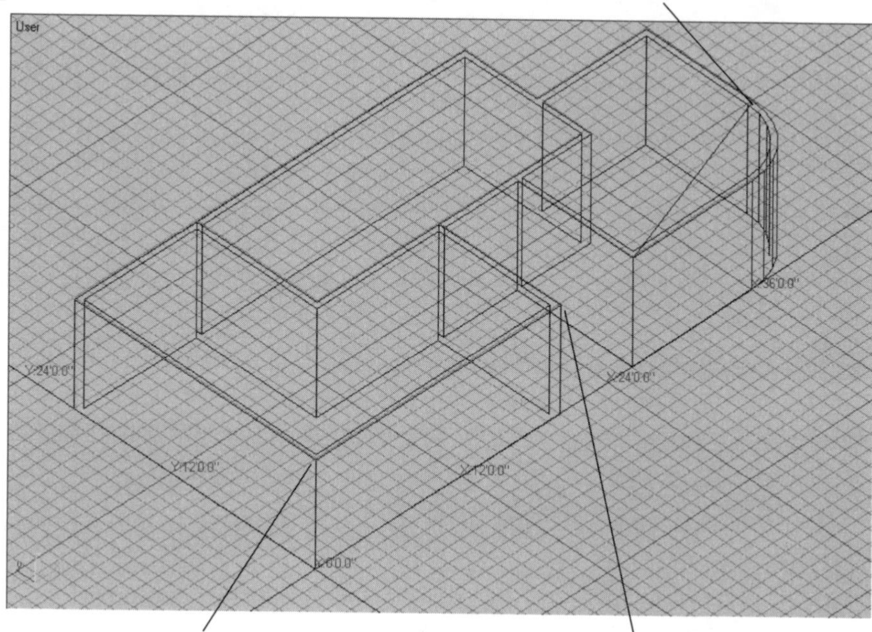

Start the line at this corner.

Continue to select the corners indicated by the squares.

4. When you return to the starting corner, click it, and in the Close spline dialog box, click Yes.

You've got the roof plane outlined with a spline. Now you need to make an adjustment to the corner where the walls are rounded.

1. With the ceiling spline selected, click the Modify tab in the Command panel.
2. Click the Vertex tool in the Selection rollout, then click the Select and Move tool in the standard toolbar.

3. Click the vertex at the corner where the wall is rounded, as shown in Figure 3.33.

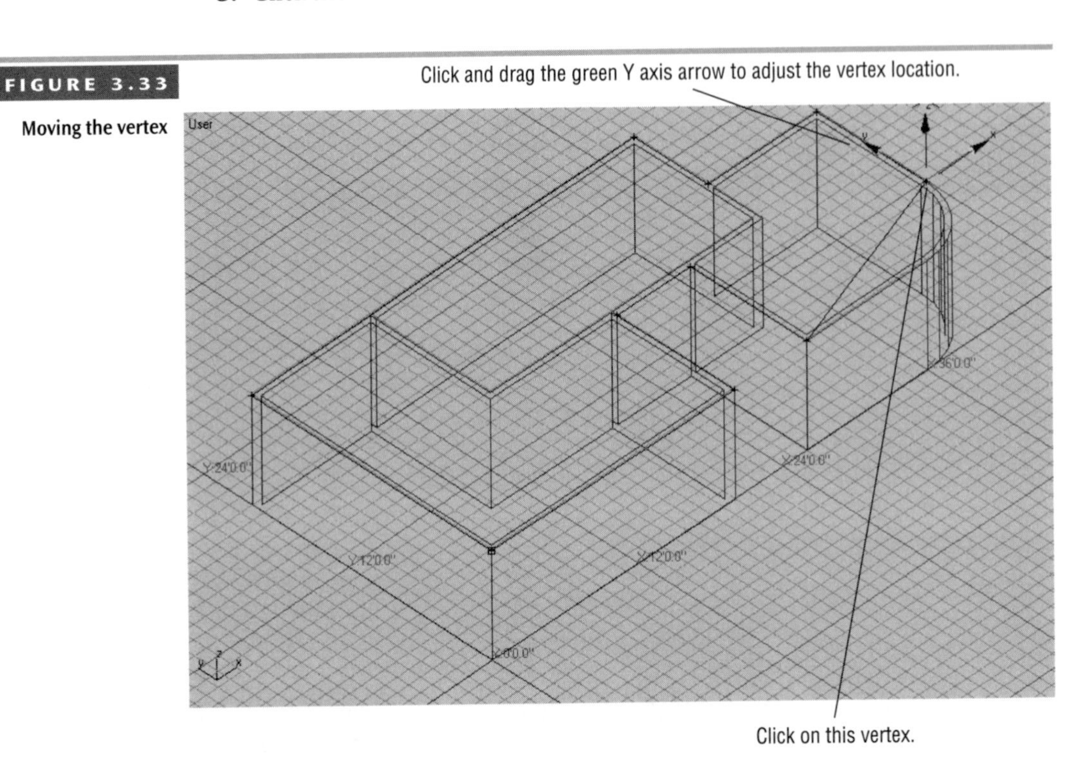
Click and drag the green Y axis arrow to adjust the vertex location.
User
Click on this vertex.

FIGURE 3.33

Moving the vertex

4. Click and drag the green Y coordinate arrow toward the right and align the wall as shown in Figure 3.34.
5. Scroll down the Command Panel until you see the Fillet tool.

6. Click the Fillet tool input box so that the entire value is highlighted, then enter **5'↵**. The corner is filleted to match the wall as shown in Figure 3.34.

FIGURE 3.34A

The spline after filleting

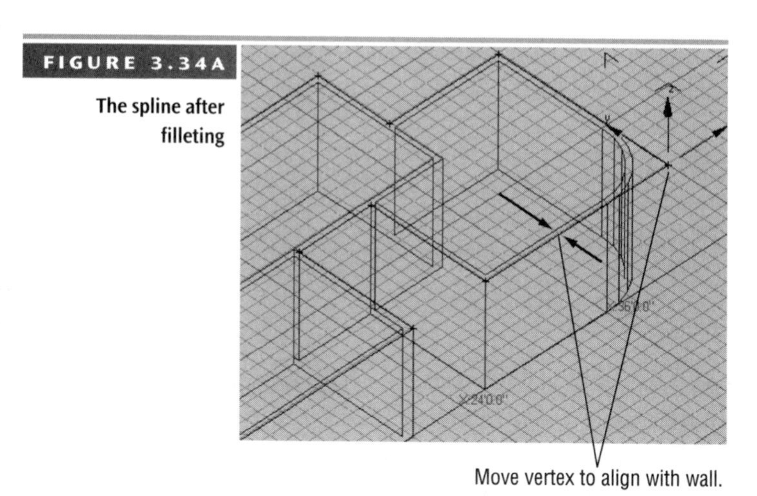
Move vertex to align with wall.

FIGURE 3.34B

The spline after filleting

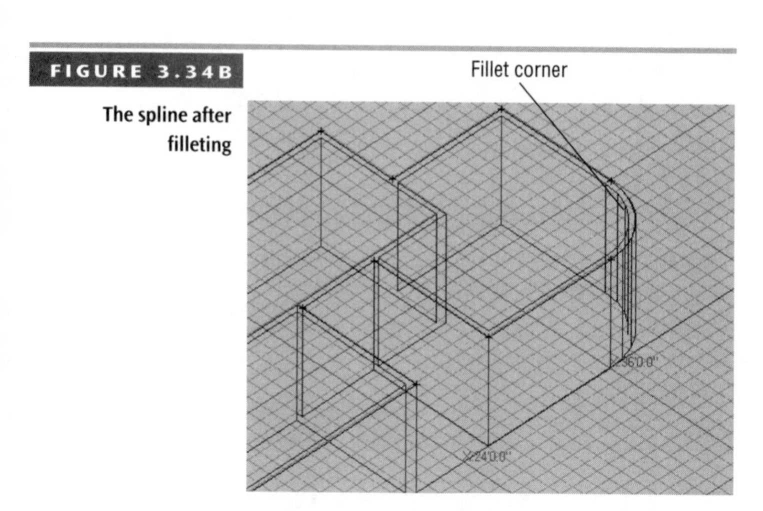
Fillet corner

For the final operation, you'll need to give the new spline a thickness. Typically, you would make a floor around 10 to 12 inches thick. Use the Extrude modifier to extrude the spline to a thickness of 12".

1. Scroll up the Command Panel to the Modifier rollout.
2. Click the Extrude modifier.

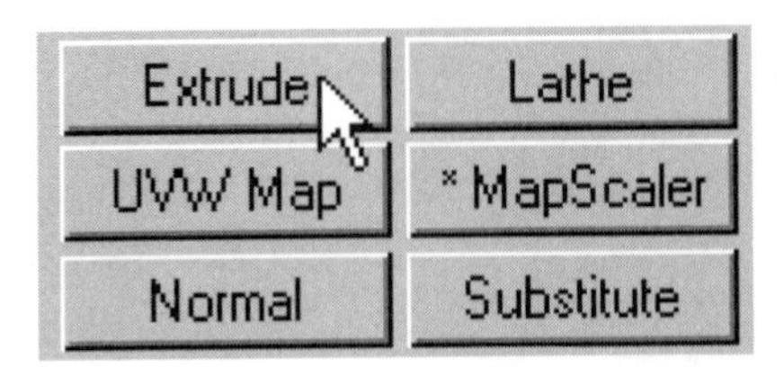

3. Go to the Parameters rollout, click the Amount input box, and enter **12"↵**. The spline extrudes into a thick slab-like object in the shape of the wall outline as shown in Figure 3.35.
4. Click the Min/Max tool to see all the viewports of the walls.

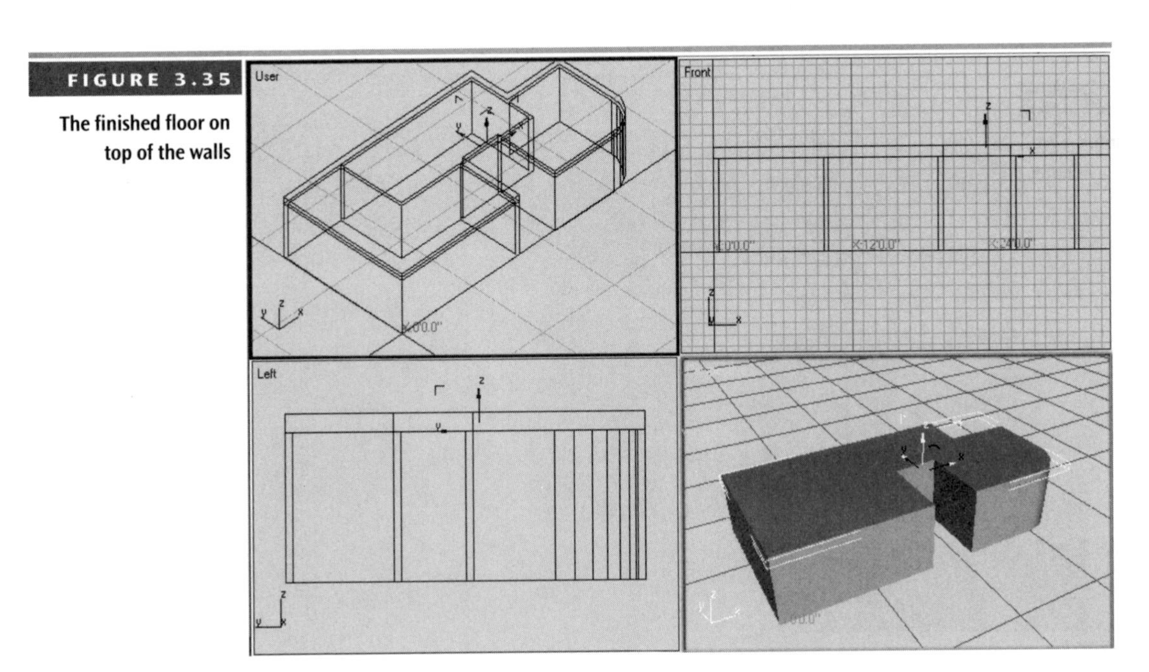

FIGURE 3.35

The finished floor on top of the walls

You only extruded the wall outline 12" but it could easily have been extruded several feet. You could also copy the spline vertically and use the outline tool to form the exterior walls of a second floor.

You've seen a few examples of using splines to create walls and a floor. There are many ways to create walls, and you aren't at all limited to the methods shown here. Later chapters will discuss even more ways that walls can be created. For now, let's move on to a look at other spline types.

Understanding the Different Spline Types

You've already used the line spline and the rectangle spline, and you've gotten a taste for methods used to edit them. Before you continue, you'll want to know a little about the other spline types. Table 3.1 shows the different spline options, how they are created, and some of the editing characteristics of each object.

You may want to experiment by creating them in a separate file. Remember that you can extrude most of them into the third dimension using the Extrude modifier and the Loft creation tool, which extrudes a shape along a spline path (that you'll learn about in Chapter 5). The Helix cannot be extruded, but it can be used as a path for animated motion or for lofts.

Table 3.1 Creation methods for splines *(Continued on next page)*

Items separated by / denote radio button options. Italics denote button group names.

Spline Name and Function	Creation Method	Creation Options	Parameters
Line Draws splines	Click points to place line segments. Click and drag adds smoothing when Smooth is selected for Initial or Drag type group	*Initial Type:* Corner/Smooth *Drag Type:* Corner/ Smooth/ Bézier	*Interpolation:* Steps, Optimize, Adaptive *Rendering:* Renderable (as tube), Thickness, General Mapping Coords.
Circle Draws circles	Click center and drag radius [Center] Or click twopoints to locate points on circumference edge [Edge]	Edge/Center	Radius
Arc Draws arcs	Click start point and drag to place end point, then adjust and click for radius [End-End-Middle]. Or click center, drag to radius and first end, click second end [Center-End-End]	End-End-Middle/Center-End-End	Radius, From, To, Pie Slice (creates Pie-slice shape), Reverse
Ngon Draws regular polygons	Click center then drag to place radius [Center] Or click to place one edge then drag for other edge [Edge]	Edge/Center	Radius, Inscribe/Circumscribe, [number of] Sides, Corner Radius, Circular
Text Draws text	Click to place text Text	Input box for entering text	Font, Size, Kerning, Leading, Text, Manual Update
Section Draws a section plane and creates a 2D outline of intersecting objects	Click to place section center point, drag to place corner. Create Shape button creates spline outline of object intersecting Section shape.	*Update:* When section moves/ When section selected/ Manually *Selection Extent:* Infinite/ Section Boundary/Off	Length, Width
Rectangle Draws rectangles	Click first corner, drag for other corner [Edge] Or Click center and drag for corner [Center]	Center/Edge	Length, Width, Corner Radius
Ellipse Draws ellipses	Click first tangent edge and drag for other edge [Edge] Or Click center then drag for edge [Center]	Edge/Center	Length, Width
Donut Draws two concentric circles	Click center then drag for first radius, click for second radius [Center] Or click first point on circumference then drag for second point on circumference, click for second radius [Edge]	Edge/Center	Radius 1, Radius 2

Table 3.1 Creation methods for splines

Items separated by / denote radio button options. Italics denote button group names.

Spline Name and Function	Creation Method	Creation Options	Parameters
Star Draws star shapes	Click center then drag for inner vertices, click again for outer vertices.		Radius 1, Radius 2, [number of] Points [of star], distortion [twist], Fillet Radius 1, Fillet Radius 2
Helix Draws a 3D helix [spiral]	Click center, drag first radius, click height, click second radius [Center] Or Click first circumference point, drag second circumference point, click height click second radius [Edge]	Edge/Center	Radius 1, Radius 2, Height, Turns, Bias CW [clockwise]/ CCW [counter-clockwise]

You've seen how you can edit the rectangle and line through the Modify tab of the Command Panel. In most cases, you need to select the Edit Spline modifier to gain access to the sub-object levels of a spline. The exception to this is the Line spline, which will display its sub-object level options as soon as you select the Modify tab.

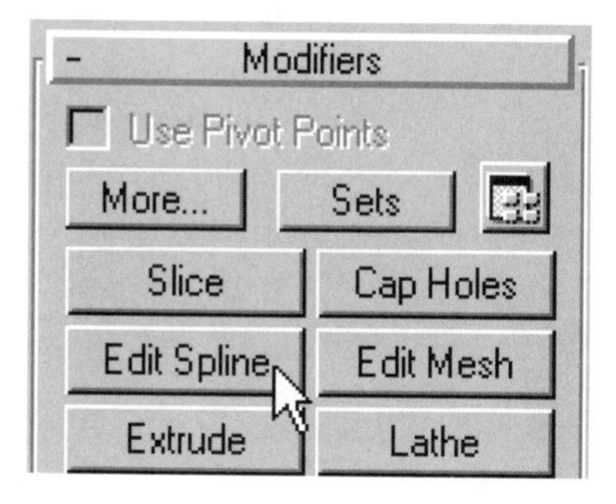

Once you've selected Edit Spline, you can make changes to the vertices, line segments, or whole spline using the Sub-Object button and the Selection Level drop-down list. You can even attach or detach components of a spline to create new forms, as you'll see in the next chapter.

Reducing Parametric Splines to Editable Splines

Another way to gain access to a splines sub-object level is to click the Edit Stack button, then select Editable Spline from the pop-up menu. This exposes the sub-object level of the selected spline in a way similar to the Edit Spline modifier but it does so by reducing the spline to an editable spline. The spline then looses its parametric functions. If you know you won't need to parametrically modify a spline, however, this can be a good way to simplify your model.

Reducing a spline to an editable spline also helps to reduce the memory requirements of your model. VIZ must reserve additional memory from your system in order to maintain the parameters of objects. By converting a spline into an editable spline, VIZ no longer needs to reserve that additional memory for the spline. And as your model becomes larger, these memory issues become more pressing.

Splines as Tubes

Before you move on to the next chapter, you'll want to know about one feature of splines that makes them very useful for architectural applications. So far, you've used splines as a basis for other shapes, but splines can also be used just by themselves to create tubular shapes such as handrails or structural elements. The following exercise will demonstrate this.

1. Save the walls you've drawn as a file called Mywalls.max.
2. Choose File ➢ New. In the New Design dialog box select New All and click OK.
3. If it isn't already enlarged, click the Perspective viewport, then click the Min/Max Toggle tool to enlarge the viewport to fill the screen.
4. Click the Zoom Extents tool to bring the view into its *home* position.
5. Click the Create tab in the Command panel, and select Line.

6. Draw the spline shown in Figure 3.36, following the instructions shown in the figure. You don't have to be exact about the point locations, as this is just a demonstration of a rendering feature of splines.

FIGURE 3.36

Drawing a spline with both straight and curved elements

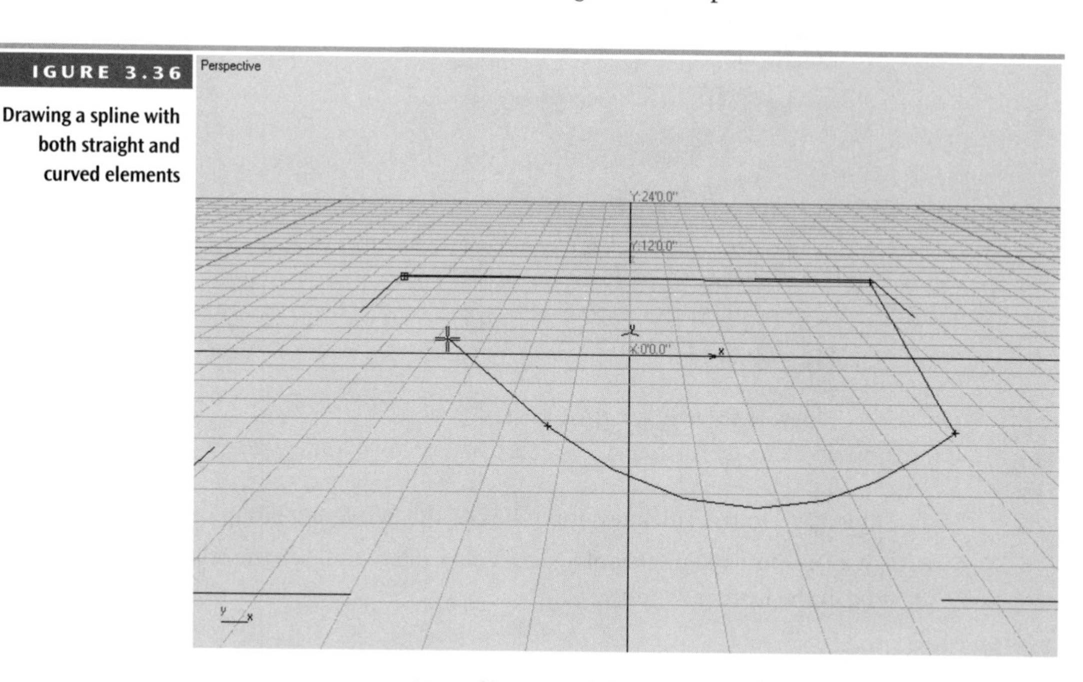

The spline you just drew has no depth or width—it's just a line. If you were to render it, the spline would be invisible, because it has no surface to render. You can change a parameter for the spline, however, that will allow you to render a spline as if it were a tube. Try the following to see what this means.

1. Click the Quick Render button in the Render toolbar to see how the spline renders.

   The Render window appears and the spline is rendered, but nothing appears in the Render window.

2. Click the Minimize button in the upper right corner of the render window to temporarily hide it.
3. Click the Modify tab of the Command Panel.
4. Click the General rollout to open it.

5. Click the Renderable check box in the Rendering group.

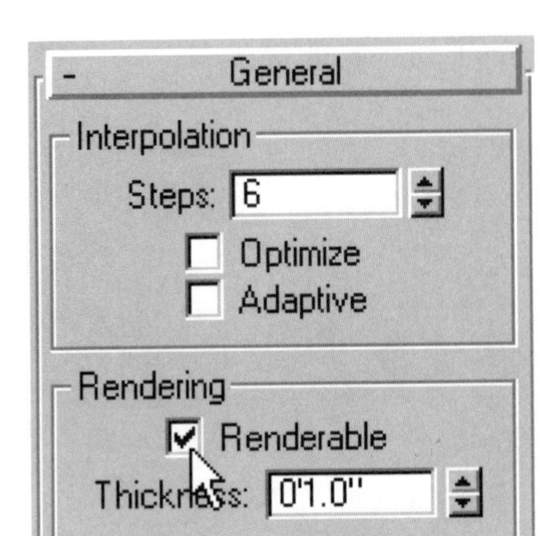

7. Enter **12"↵** in the Thickness input box of the Rendering group.
8. Click the Quick Render tool again. This time, you'll see the spline as a round tube in the Render window.

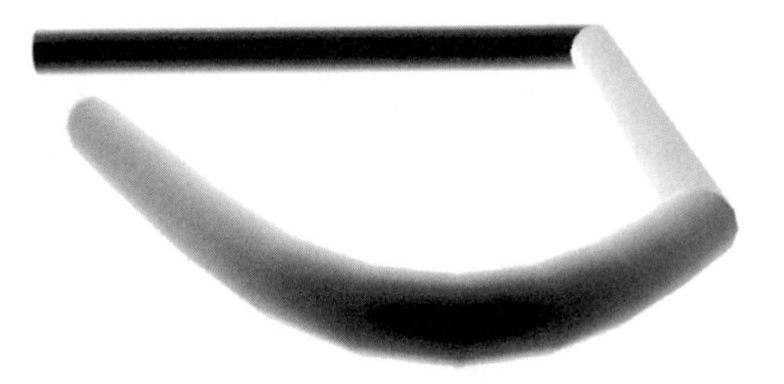

As you can see, even though your spline appears as a single line in the viewports, it is transformed into a tube in the rendered view. This feature can save you time and memory if all you need is a tube shape. In a later chapter, you'll see how this feature can be used to generate trusses, guardrails, and other architectural features.

You also got a chance to see an object rendered. In later chapters, you'll see how you can use the Render tools to create image files and animations.

Using the AEC Walls and Doors

I've shown you how to create walls using the spline tool. By doing this, you were able to learn about many of the spline's characteristics, and you were introduced to the concept of sub-objects. VIZ also offers another tool that is tailored to drawing walls: the AEC Wall. The AEC Wall tool works in a way similar to the spline, but you don't have to extrude or offset the wall to get a thickness and height.

Try drawing some walls and adding some doors in the next exercise.

1. Choose File ➢ New and create an all new file. You don't need to save the spline from the last exercise.
2. Click the Min/Max Toggle tool, then click the Zoom Extents All tool to set up the default views.
3. If the upper left viewport's label shows User, right-click the label and select Views ➢ Top from the pop-up menu.
4. Click the Create AEC tab in the Tab Panel and click the Wall tool. Alternately, you may select the Create tab from the Command Panel, click the Geometry button, select AEC Extended from the Geometry drop-down list, then select Wall from the Object Type rollout.

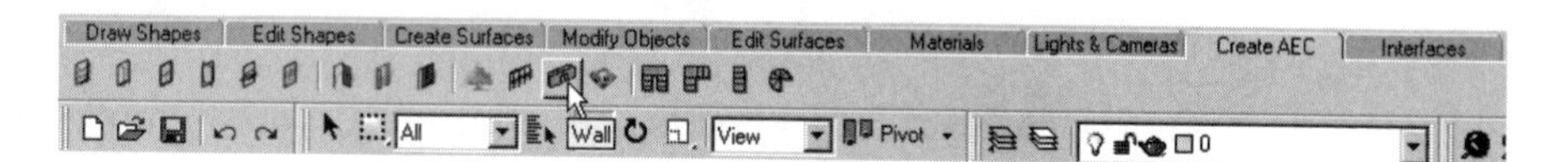

Notice that the Command Panel shows the Parameters of the wall in the Width and Height parameters.

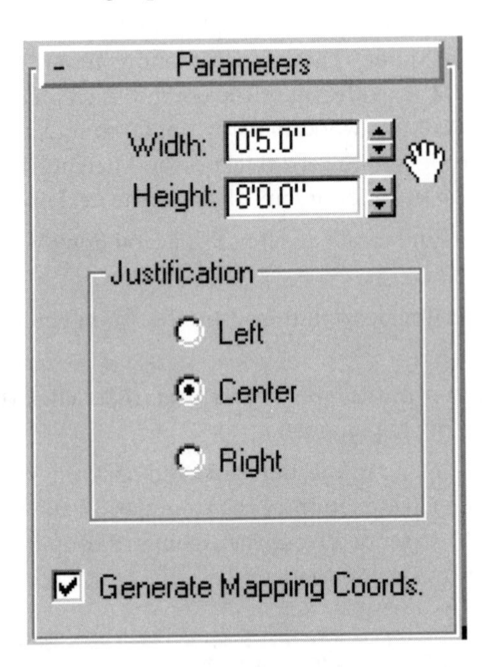

You also see a set of Justification options that allow you to determine how the walls are drawn in relation to the points you select.

5. In the Top viewport, click the origin to start your wall. As you move the cursor, you see a rubber-banding wall display in the viewports.

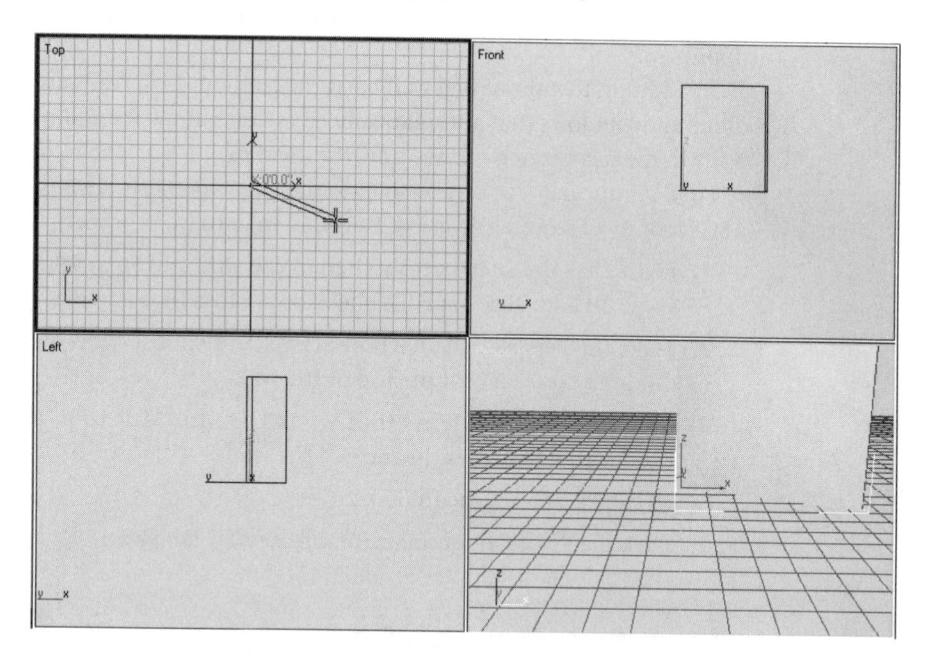

6. Click a point to the right, as shown in Figure 3.37, then click another point above that first point so that you create an L-shaped wall configuration.

FIGURE 3.37

Drawing the AEC wall

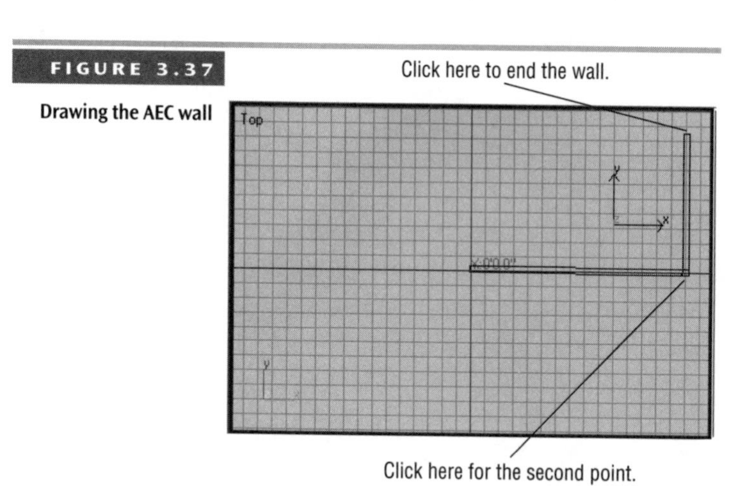

7. Right-click to finish drawing wall segments.
8. Click the Zoom Extents All tool to get a better view of your wall.

Placing the points for a wall works the same way as placing points for straight-line segments. You can use the Keyboard Entry rollout to input coordinates just as you did earlier with the spline walls. The AEC Walls tool offers a quick way to lay out a basic floor plan.

In addition to a simplified wall creation method, AEC Walls also allows you to add doors and windows that automatically create openings. Try adding a door to your walls in the next exercise to see how they work.

First, set up Snap in order to snap to the edge of objects. This is important, as the AEC Door tools require the use of the Edge snap to work properly with walls.

1. Right-click the Snap button, then in the Grid and Snap Settings dialog box, click Clear All and click the Edge check box. Close the Snap dialog box.
2. Make the Perspective viewport active, and choose View ➢ Views ➢ SW so you can get a clear view of the top of the wall.
3. Click the Zoom Extents tool, click the Min/Max tool, and click the Zoom Extents tool to center the view of the wall.

Now you're ready to place a door.

1. Click the Pivot Door tool in the Create AEC tab panel.

2. Place the cursor on the top edge of the wall as shown in Figure 3.38, then click and drag along the top edge to establish the width of the door opening. You can watch the Width parameter in the Create tab of the Command Panel to get a readout of the door width. You can also edit the width parameter later.

FIGURE 3.38

Starting the door placement

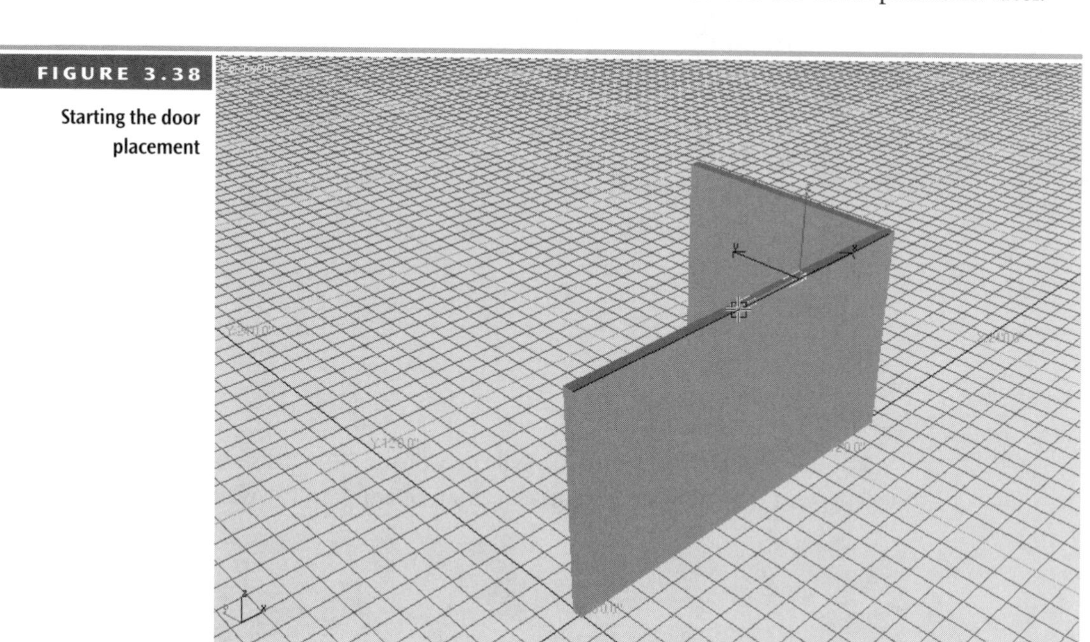

3. Move the cursor to the opposite side of the wall so you see the edge snap marker, then click that location. This sets the depth of the door.
4. Move the cursor down the wall to its base, then click the bottom edge of the wall. This sets the height of the door.
5. Right-click to end the Pivot Door placement.

To finish off this exercise, make some final adjustments to the door you just created.

1. Click the Modify tab in the Command Panel.
2. In the Parameters rollout, change the door height to 6'7" and the width to 3'.

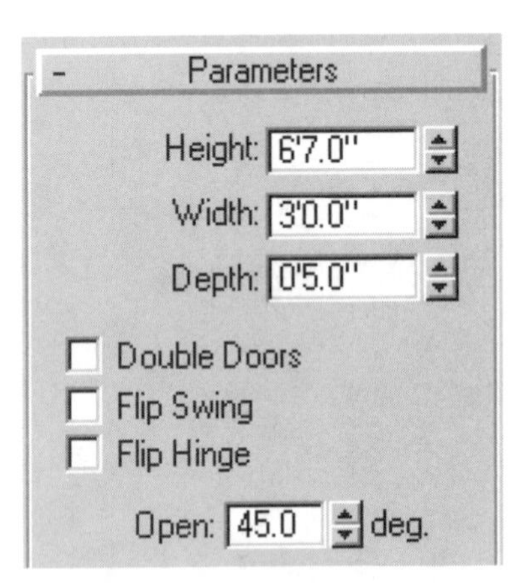

3. Click and drag the Open spinner to set the value to 45. This sets the door swing to 45 degrees. The door opens and reveals an opening in the wall.

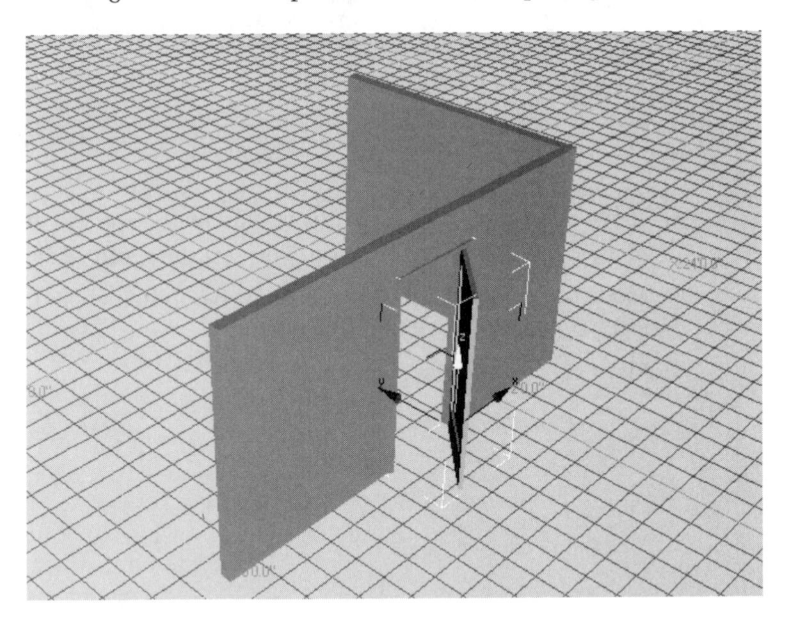

Here you see a unique feature of the AEC door tool. It automatically places an opening in the AEC wall. AEC doors will not do this for walls you create using splines. It only works with AEC walls. Another feature of AEC doors is that you can move the door, and the opening will move with it.

If you look at the parameters for the Pivot Door you created in the last exercise, you'll see that you can set quite a few parameters that you can adjust. You can set the door frame size and the dimensions of the door leaf. You can even get down to details like adding glass or beveled panels.

Summary

You've seen how splines can be created and edited, and you've also had a brief introduction to the concept of sub-objects. You've really just scratched the surface of what splines can do.

In the next chapter, you'll use an architectural project as a basis for exploring a number of VIZ's features. You'll get a chance to see how you can trace over a scanned image and you'll continue to look at splines with a focus on sub-object editing. You'll also learn how you can sculpt objects by subtracting one shape from another or by adding shapes together.

chapter 4

Editing Meshes for Complex Objects

FEATURING

- *Creating an Opening in a Wall with Boolean Operations*
- *Tracing over a Sketch*
- *Editing Meshes*
- *Using Instance Clones to Create Symmetric Forms*

Chapter 4: Editing Meshes for Complex Objects

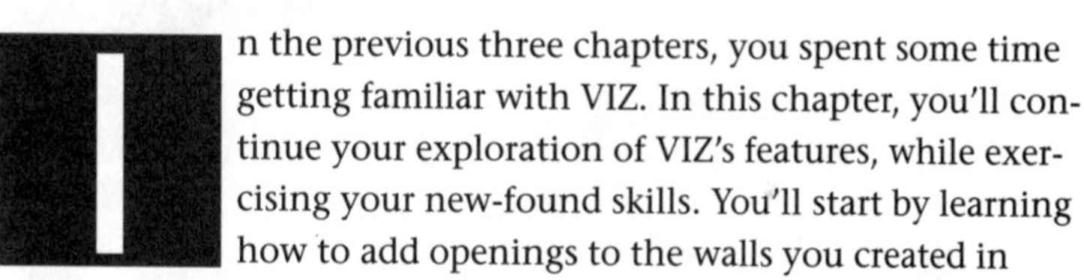

In the previous three chapters, you spent some time getting familiar with VIZ. In this chapter, you'll continue your exploration of VIZ's features, while exercising your new-found skills. You'll start by learning how to add openings to the walls you created in Chapter 3. Then you'll learn how you can import scanned images that you can use to trace over. In the process of tracing over a floor plan, you'll further explore methods for creating and editing forms using splines. You'll also be introduced to ways you can edit extruded shapes.

Creating an Opening in a Wall with Boolean Operations

In the last chapter, you created a set of walls that completely enclosed a space. You'll need to add wall openings between the enclosed spaces of your model. To do this you'll use *Boolean* operations to remove portions of a wall.

Boolean operations are methods you can use to join two objects together, subtract the shape of one object from another, or obtain a shape that is the intersection of two objects. Figure 4.1 illustrates the effect of Boolean operations on some sample shapes.

FIGURE 4.1

Examples of Boolean operations

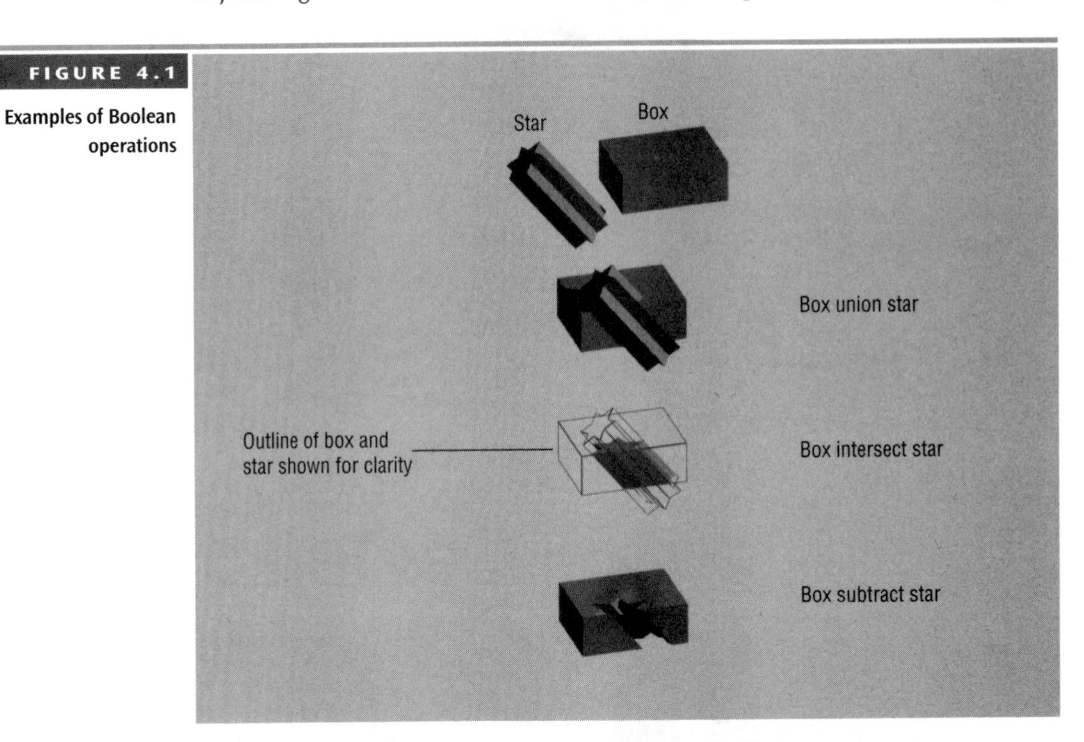

VIZ allows you to use two objects to form new shapes using Boolean operations. Those shapes are referred to as the *Operands* of the Boolean operations. In the following exercise, you'll use a simple box to form the opening in your walls. The existing wall is one operand, and the box that forms the opening is the other operand.

Hiding Shapes That Get in the Way

Start by setting up your wall model and creating an object you'll use to subtract from the walls.

1. Open the Mywalls.max model you created in the last chapter.
2. If your VIZ window only shows a single viewport, click the Min/Max Toggle to view the four viewports.

You'll need to hide the ceiling of your model in order to more easily work on the model. Here's a quick way to temporarily hide objects if they're in your way.

1. Use the Select object tool to select the ceiling.
2. Click the Display tab of the Command Panel, then, in the name input box just below the Display label, change the name to Ceiling. This will help you find the ceiling later.

3. Look for the On/Off rollout in the Command Panel and click the Selected Off button. The Ceiling displays.

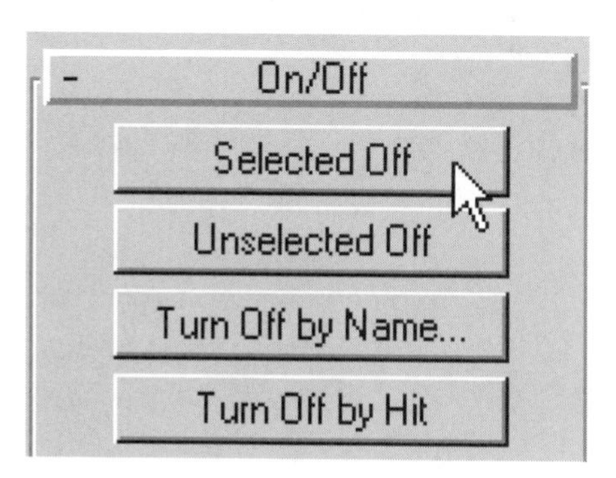

4. The ceiling hasn't really gone anywhere. You've just turned it off. Just so you know where to look when you do need to turn it back on, click the Turn On by Name… button in the On/Off rollout.

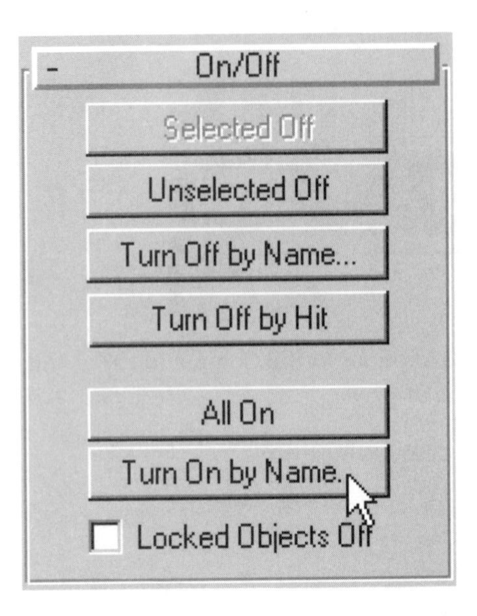

The Turn On by Name dialog box displays.

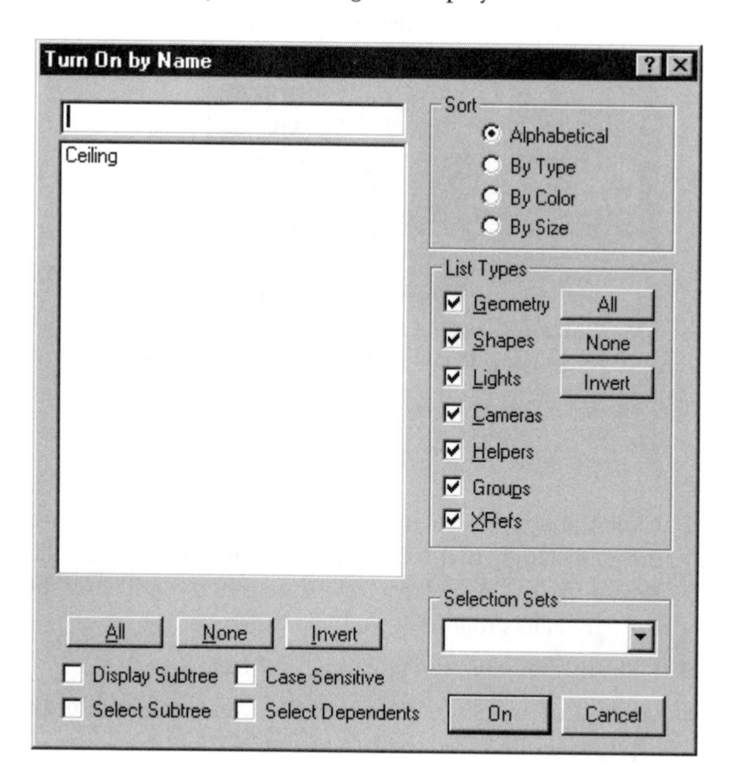

5. You can see that the Ceiling is listed in the box. To turn it back on, you would click the name in the list, then click On. You want to keep it off for now, so click Cancel.

Creating the Shape of the Opening

Now you're ready to get to work on the walls. Your first step is to create the shape of the opening. You can think of this shape as the negative space of the opening or as the shape that is to be removed from the wall.

1. Click the User viewport to make it active. Then right-click the User label in the upper left corner of the viewport and select Top. You can also enter **T**↵ to change the viewport to a Top view.
2. Click the Zoom Extents tool so you can see the entire plan in the viewport.

3. Click the Geometry tool in the Create tab of the Command Panel and make sure Standard Primitives is selected in the drop-down list.

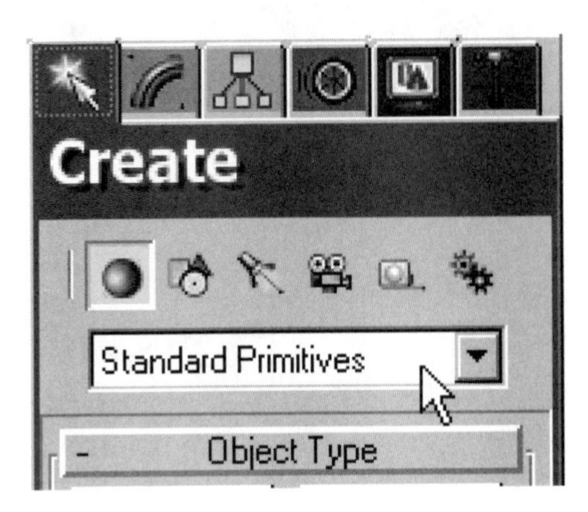

4. Click the Box in the Object Type rollout. Then in the top viewport, click and drag a rectangle that is roughly 3 feet by 3 feet square to the location shown in Figure 4.2. You don't have to be exact since you'll enter the exact dimensions in the Parameters rollout.
5. Make the height of the box roughly 7 feet.
6. Go to the Parameters rollout of the Create tab and set the Length and Width input boxes to **3'** and the Height to **6'8"**.

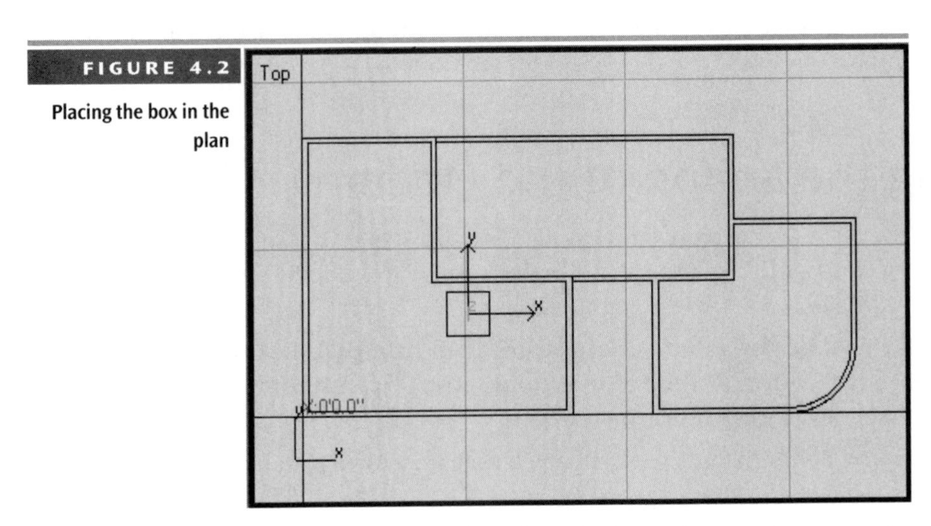

FIGURE 4.2

Placing the box in the plan

You've now got a box that will be used to create an opening. The next step is to place the box in the location for the opening.

1. Click the Select and Move tool in the standard toolbar and move the box to the location shown in Figure 4.3. Remember that you need to place the cursor on the selected object. Then, when you see the Move cursor, click and drag the object into position.
2. Shift-click and drag the box to make a copy of the box in the location shown in Figure 4.3.
3. At the Clone Options dialog box, click Copy, then click OK.

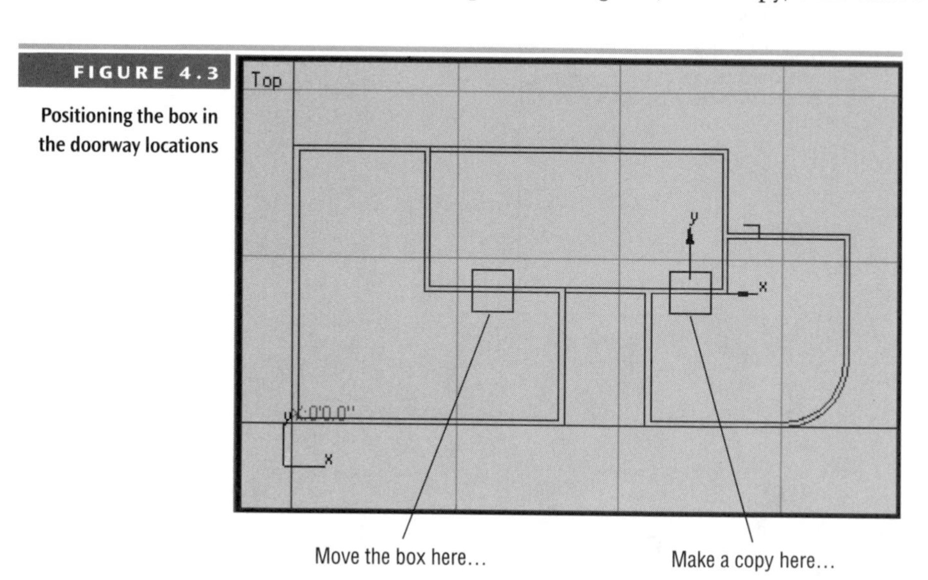

FIGURE 4.3

Positioning the box in the doorway locations

Subtracting the Opening from the Wall

Now select the wall that will have the opening and locate the Boolean tool in the Command Panel.

1. Click the Select object tool, then click the first wall you created (shown in Figure 4.4). First select the object from which you want to subtract the opening.

2. Click the Geometry tool in the Create tab and select Compound Objects from the drop-down list just below the row of tools.

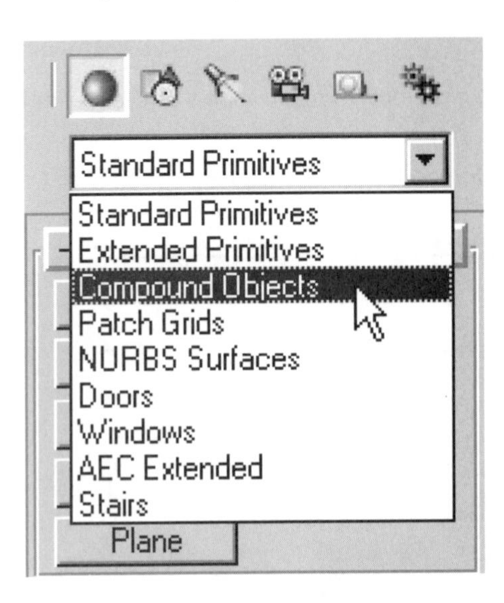

3. Click the Boolean button. The Boolean options appear in the Command Panel.

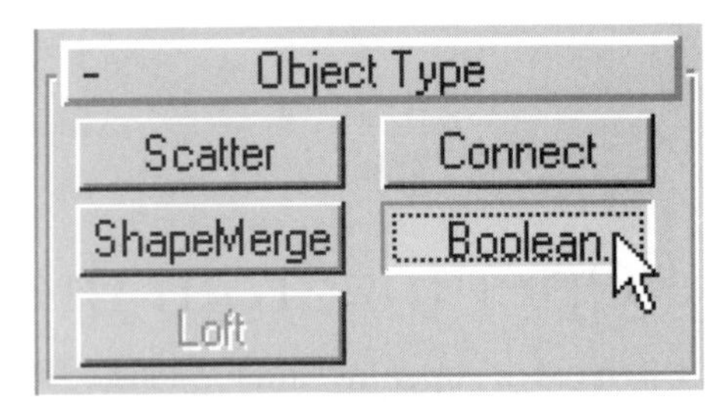

4. Click the Pick Operand B button in the Pick Boolean rollout.

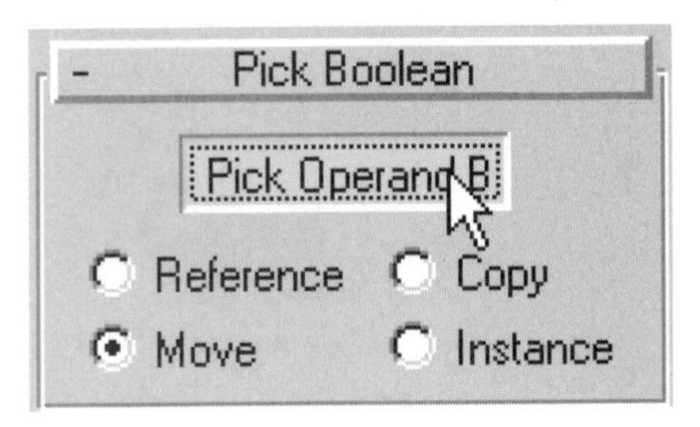

5. Click the box that intersects the wall as shown in Figure 4.4.

FIGURE 4.4

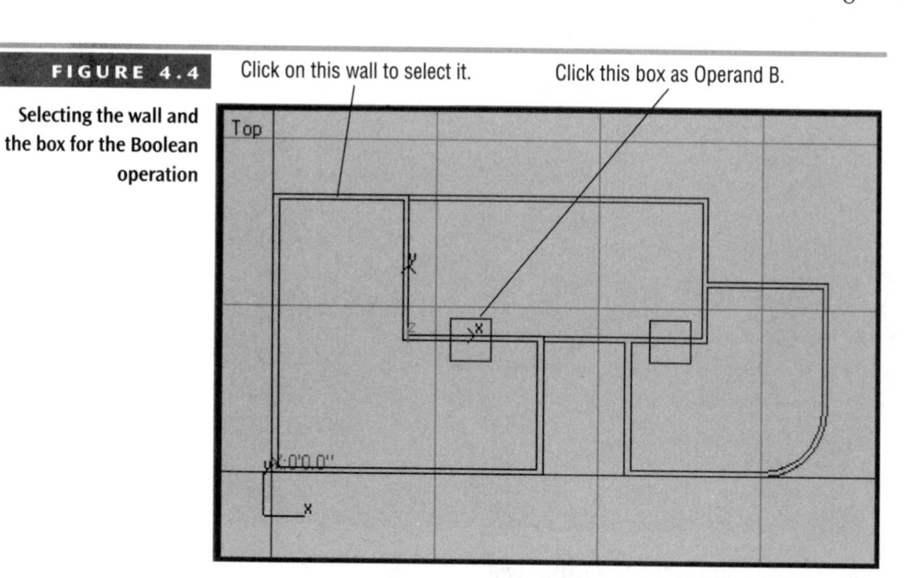

Selecting the wall and the box for the Boolean operation

6. Scroll down the Command Panel to the Parameters rollout and make sure that the Subtraction (A-B) radio button is selected.

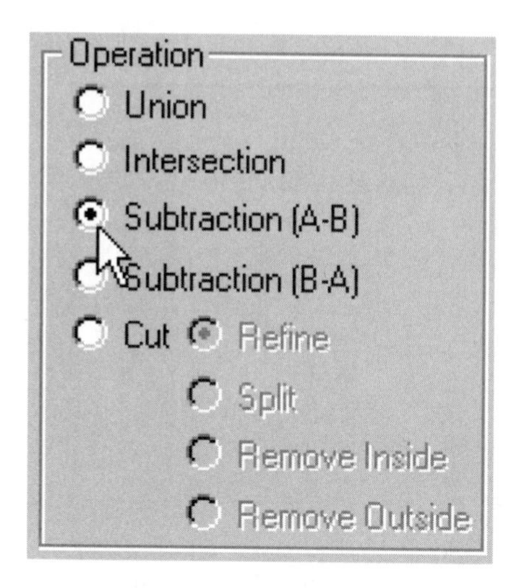

If you look in the Perspective viewport, you'll see that an opening appears in the wall where you located the box (see Figure 4.5).

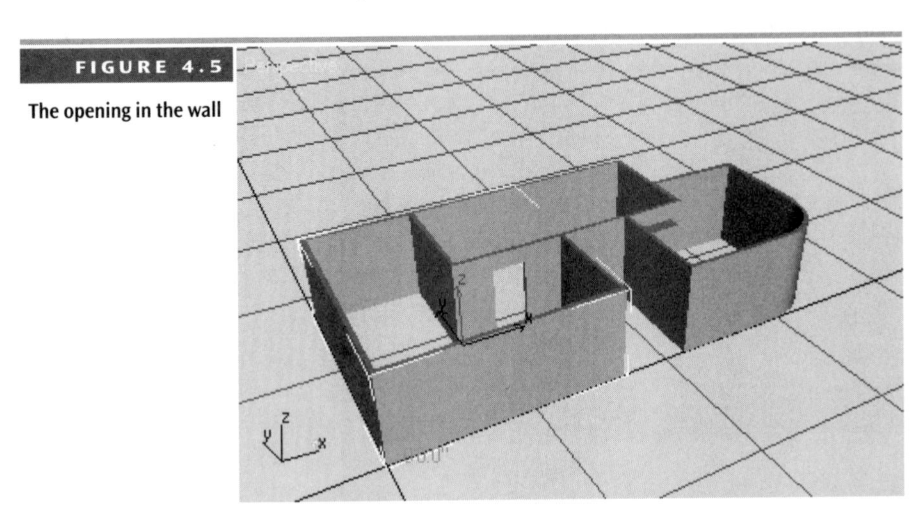

FIGURE 4.5

The opening in the wall

Now repeat the operation for the other wall.

1. Click the Select object tool, then click the second wall, as shown in Figure 4.6.

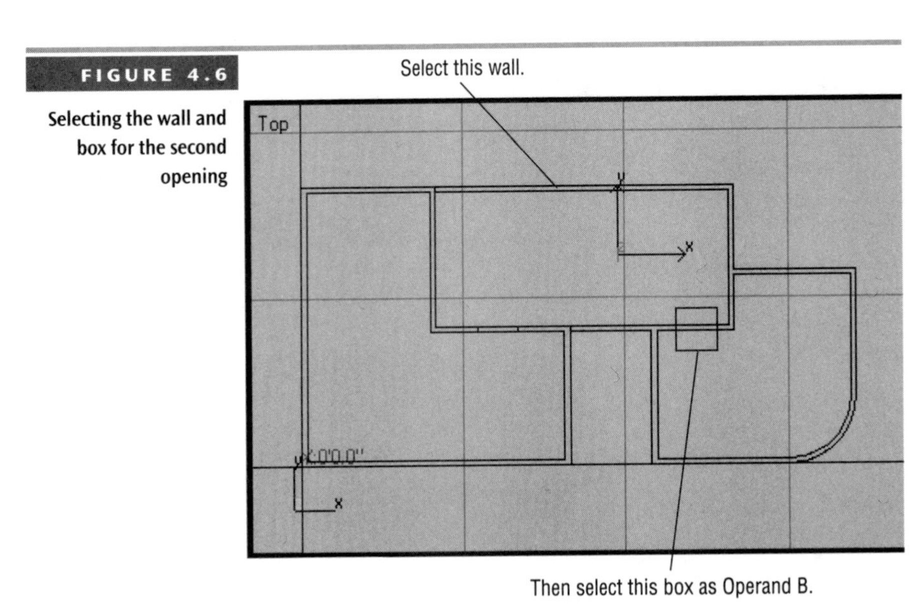
Select this wall.
Top
Then select this box as Operand B.

FIGURE 4.6

Selecting the wall and box for the second opening

2. Click the Boolean button in the Object Type rollout of the Command Panel.

3. Click the Pick Operand B button, then select the box shown in Figure 4.7. The second opening appears as shown in Figure 4.7.

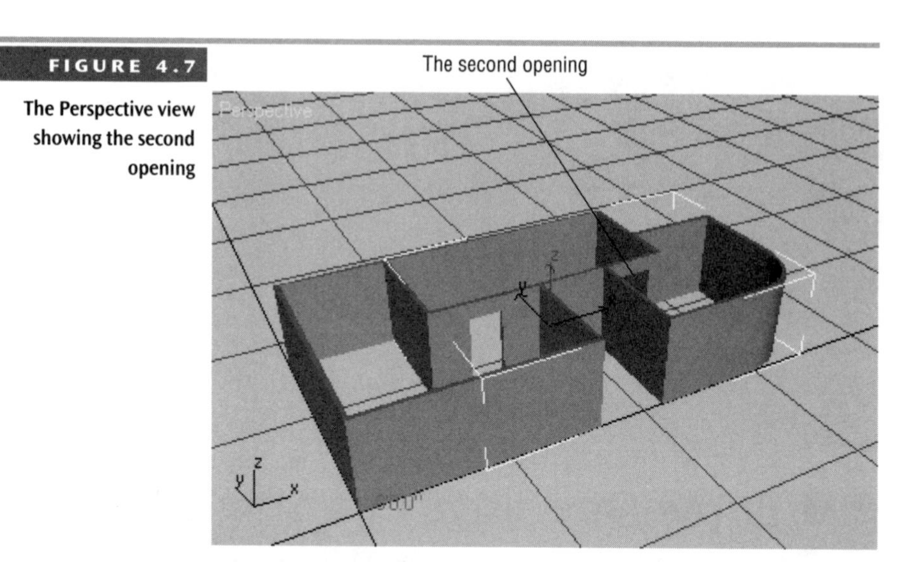

FIGURE 4.7

The Perspective view showing the second opening

In this example, you created a simple rectangular opening in the wall. The shape of the opening can really be anything you want it to be. You just need to create the geometry, using primitives or extruded splines. In addition, the object that you are subtracting from doesn't have to be a thin plane such as the wall in this example. It can be any geometry you want, and the subtracted shape will leave its impression. Figure 4.8 shows some examples of other Boolean subtractions to give you an idea of other possibilities.

Some samples of Boolean subtractions

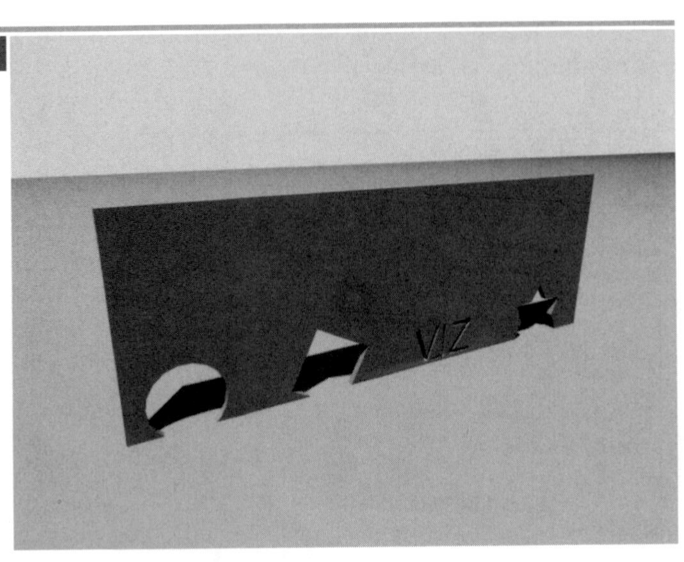

Creating Multiple Openings in a Single Wall

You can only perform one Boolean operation on an object. If you need to do multiple Boolean operations you have two options. For example, suppose you want to create several openings in one wall. To do this you can create the opening shapes, convert them to editable meshes, then use the editable mesh Attach option in the modify toolbar to join several meshes together into one object. You can then subtract that object from the wall. You can also attach several boxes together into a single object. You can then subtract all of the boxes from the wall at once.

Another method is to perform the Boolean operation to create one opening as described in the previous exercise, then convert the resulting wall and opening into an editable mesh as described later in this chapter. You can then perform another Boolean subtraction on the same wall. For the next opening, convert the wall into an editable mesh again, then perform the next Boolean subtraction. The drawback to this method is that you cannot edit the openings by going back and changing the size of the boxes. You can, however, edit openings in the mesh at sub-object levels.

Making Changes to the Opening

Now suppose that you decide to increase the size of one of the openings. You can go back and modify the box so that it is wider. This, in turn, will increase the opening size.

1. Click the Select tool in the Standard toolbar, then click the first wall as shown in Figure 4.9.

2. Click the Modify tab in the Command Panel and scroll down the panel to the Display/Update rollout. Click the Display /Update rollout label to open the rollout.

3. Click the Operands radio button. The box reappears in the viewports.
4. Scroll back up to the Modifier Stack rollout and click the B: Box 01 listing under the Operands group of the Parameters rollout.

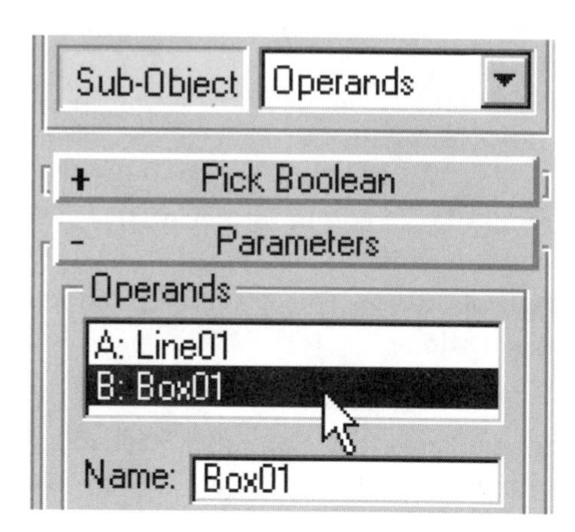

Open the Modifier Stack drop-down list and select Box. The Command Panel options change to show the parameters for the box.

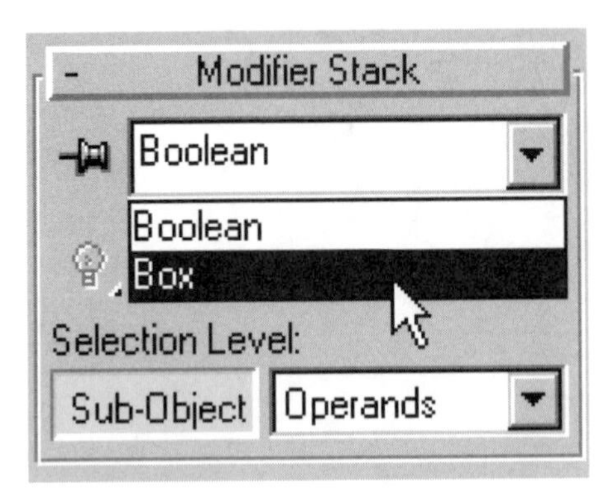

5. In the Parameters rollout, change the Width input box value to **6'**. The box changes in width. Notice how the box changes in the viewports as you edit the Width parameter.
6. Go back to the drop-down list in the Modifier Stack rollout and select Boolean.
7. Scroll back down the Command Panel to the Display/Update rollout and click the Result radio button.

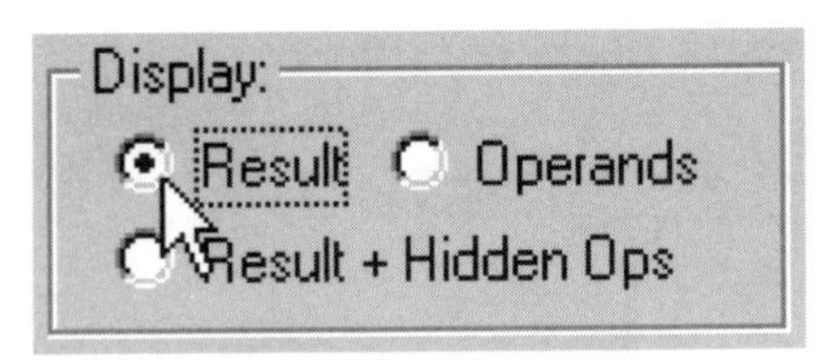

Now you can see the result of your edit in the perspective viewport. The opening is now 6 feet wide instead of 3 feet wide.

Besides altering the shape of the box, you can also reposition it to change the location of the wall. Here's how it's done.

1. Click the Operands radio button again to view the box.
2. Scroll up the Command Panel to the Modifier Stack rollout and make sure that the Sub-Object button is active. It should be yellow in color.

3. Click the Select and Move tool in the Standard toolbar. Then click and drag the box to the left so that it intersects the corner of the wall as shown in Figure 4.9.

FIGURE 4.9

Moving the box to change the location of the wall opening

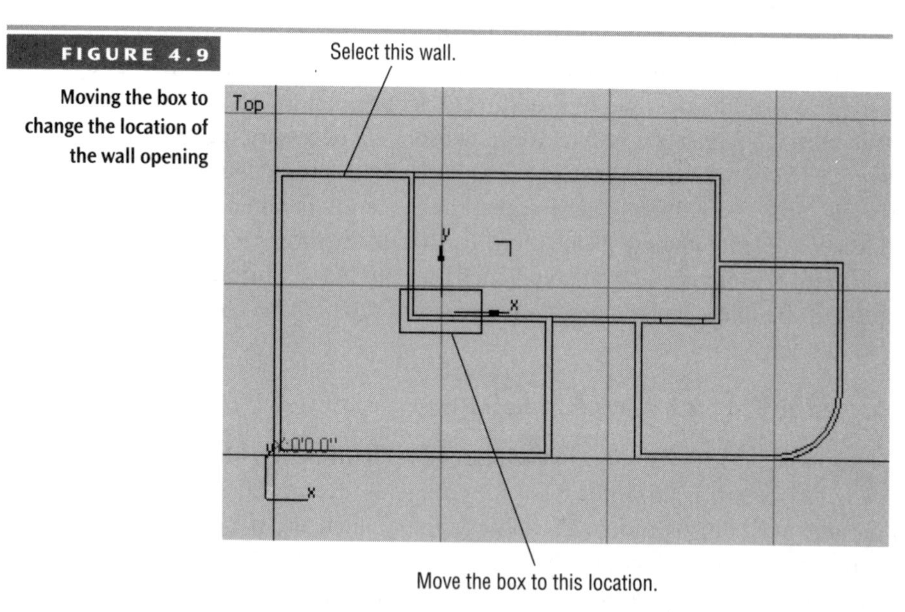
Select this wall.
Top
Move the box to this location.

4. Click the Sub-Object button to turn it off, scroll back down the Command Panel to the Display/Update rollout, and click the Result radio button. The new wall opening configuration appears in the Perspective viewport, as shown in Figure 4.10.

FIGURE 4.10

The result of moving the box operand

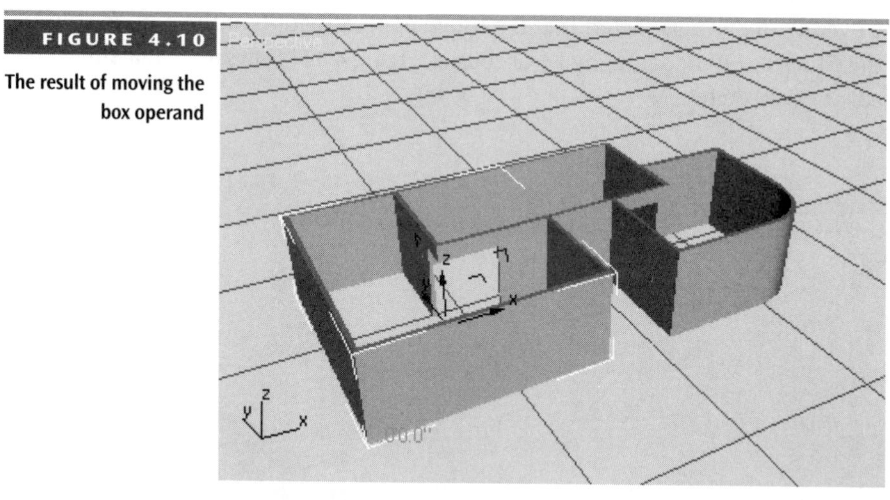

5. Save the Mywalls.max file.

The tricky part of moving the Operand B in this last exercise is making sure that the Sub-Object option is active and that Operand B is selected in the Operands list in the Boolean Parameters rollout.

These exercises demonstrate that you can alter the shape of the opening by modifying the parameters of the object you used to create the opening. The trick here is to know how to get to the box operand in order to edit its parameters. It's a good idea to first make the subtracted operand visible. It's not absolutely necessary, but it helps to see the operand as you make changes. Use the Modifier Stack drop-down list to gain access to the operand. Once there, you can open the operand's parameters and make changes to its geometry or change its location. To change the location of either of the operands within the Compound Object, you click the Sub-Object button and select the operand. The operands are considered sub-objects of the Boolean construction.

Tracing over a Sketch

You can't always predict when or where you'll have a brilliant design idea. Frequently, ideas arise when we're sitting around a table sketching out ideas in a brainstorming session or perhaps even during lunch. The basic tools of pencil and paper offer the spontaneity needed to express ideas freely.

Once you've created an inspired sketch, VIZ can offer a way to allow you to quickly transfer your inspiration into a 3D model. Among its view options, VIZ supplies a tool that displays a scanned image in a viewport for a variety of purposes, including the tracing of design sketches.

In this section, you'll continue your exploration of splines by importing a sketch and tracing over it. You'll use a sketch that is a rough approximation of the building known as the Chapel of Ronchamp, by Le Corbusier. Figure 4.11 shows a 3D-massing model based on this sketch.

FIGURE 4.11

3D model of Ronchamp

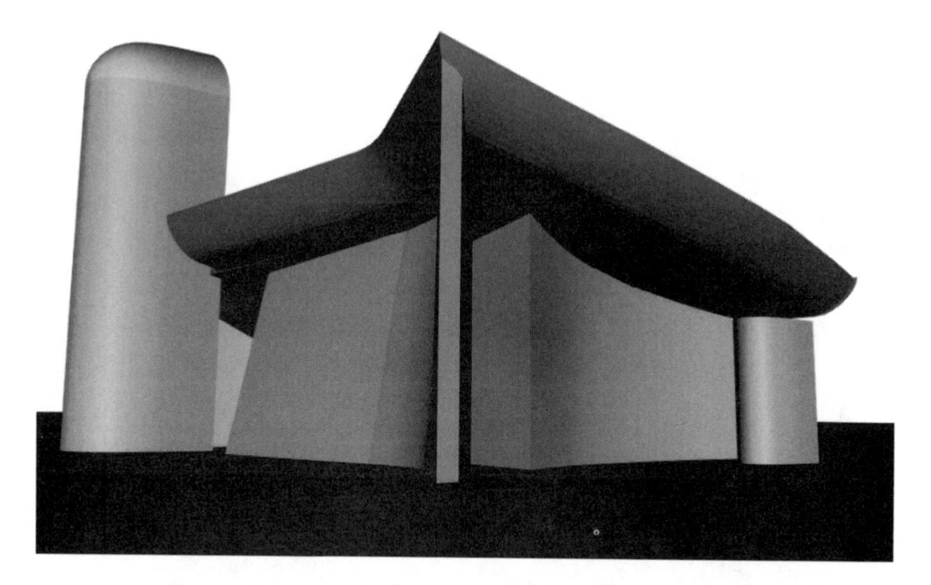

This building offers the opportunity to examine how you might use splines to create shapes other than simple straight walls such as those you created in the last chapter. You'll also be introduced to other methods for forming shapes by combining splines and primitives. (My apologies to Le Corbusier for creating a less than perfect representation of one of his most admired buildings!)

Importing a Bitmap Image

Importing a bitmapped image is fairly simple, but there are a few settings you have to watch out for. In the following exercise, you'll import from the companion CD an image that is a sketch of the Ronchamp floor plan. The sketch shows a grid that is spaced at approximately 4.5 meters (see Figure 4.12).

FIGURE 4.12

The bitmap image of the Ronchamp floor plan

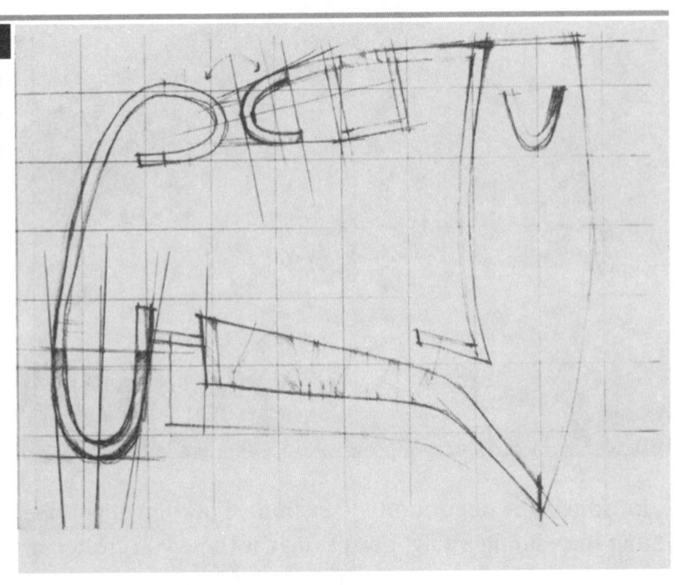

You'll import this image into the Top viewport, so first set up VIZ so you can see only the Top viewport enlarged.

WARNING **You'll need a file from the companion CD, so make sure you've installed the sample files before you start.**

1. Open a new file in VIZ.
2. Click the Top viewport, then click the Min/Max toggle tool to enlarge the Top viewport.
3. Click Zoom Extents tool to set up the Top viewport to its default view with the origin at the center of the view.

Now you're ready to import and set up your scanned floor plan.

1. Click View ➢ Viewport Image ➢ Select… The Viewport Image dialog box displays.

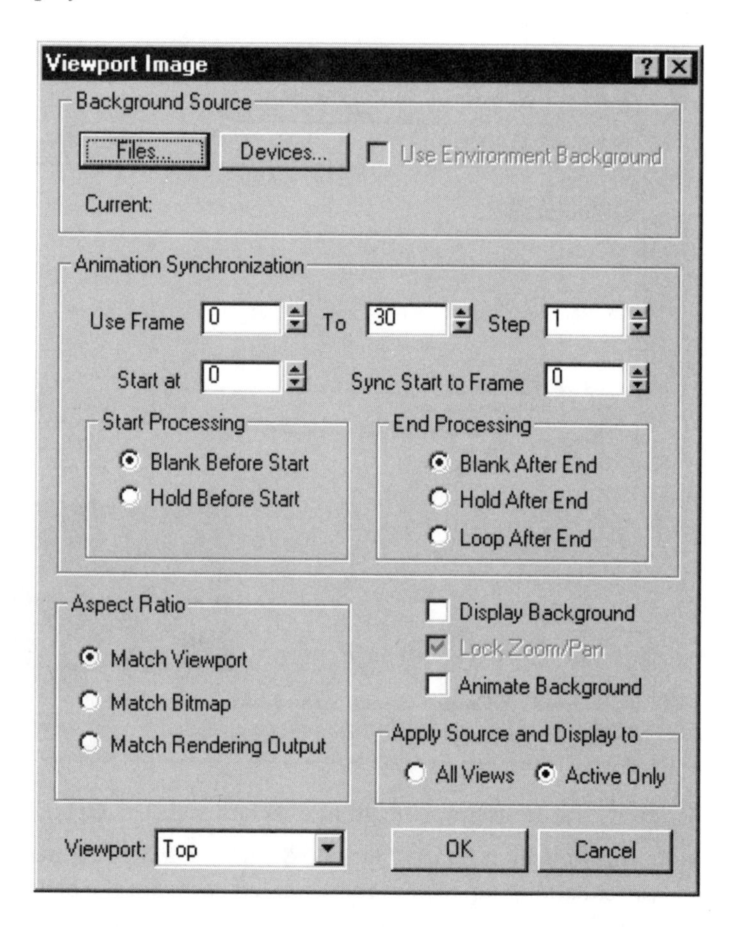

2. Click the Files button at the top of the dialog box. The Select Background Image dialog box displays.

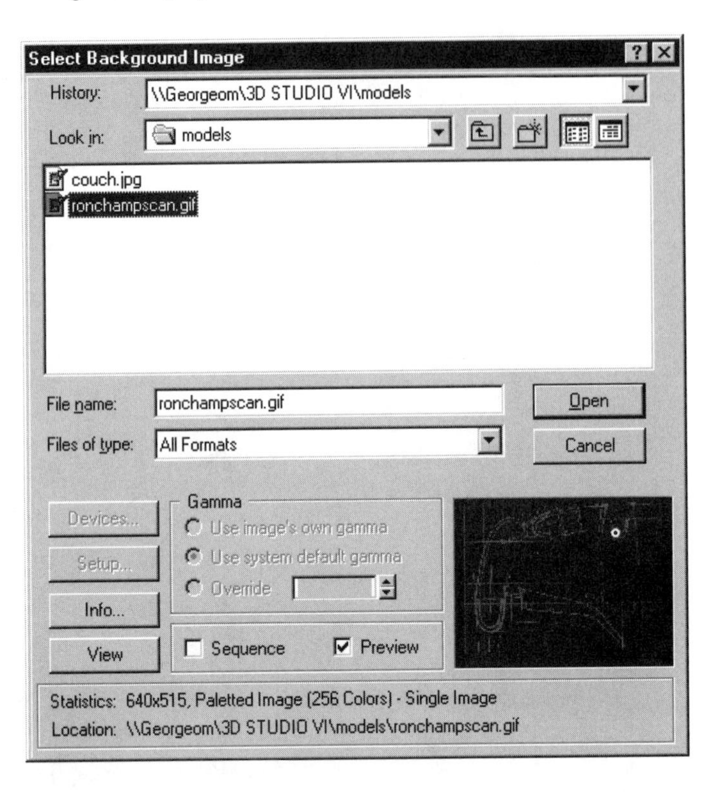

3. Locate the Ronchampscan.gif file, click it, and click Open.
4. In the Viewpoint Image dialog box, click the Match Bitmap radio button in the Aspect Ratio group toward the lower left corner of the dialog box.
5. To the right of the Aspect Ratio group, click the Lock Zoom/Pan check box. This is important, as it will lock the image to the viewport. Any pans or zooms you perform will act on the imported bitmap image as well.

6. Click OK. The image appears in the Top Viewport.

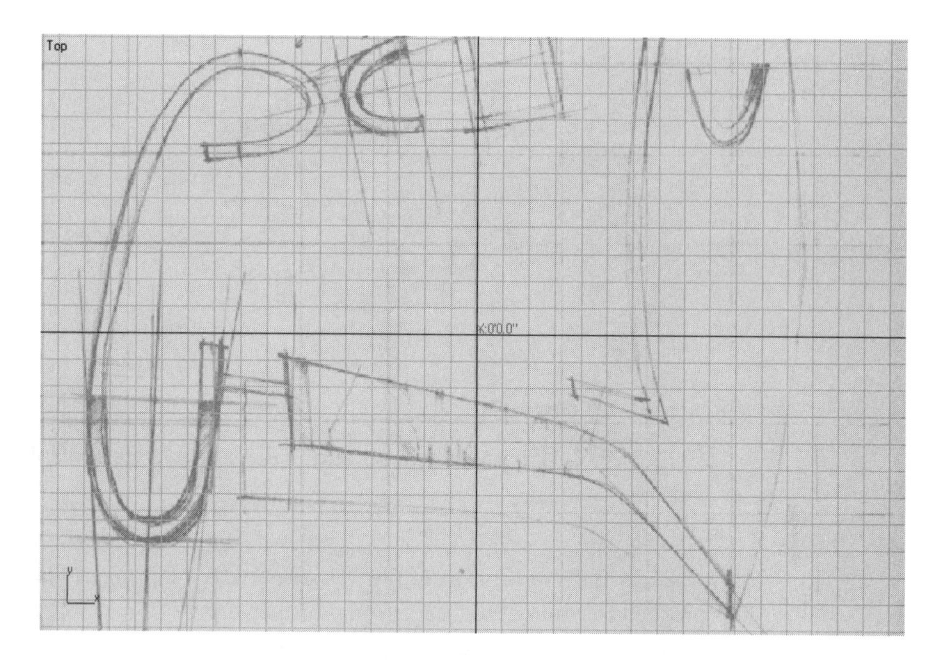

Scaling the Image to the Model's Space

The image is placed in the viewport in a somewhat arbitrary fashion, regarding its size. It would be most desirable to size the image so that it is to scale—that is, the distances represented by the image are the same as those in the VIZ model. You can approximate the correct scale, although you won't be able to get it exact. Here's how it's done.

Start by setting up the units you'll be working with.

1. Choose Tools ➢ Drafting Settings ➢ Units Setup… The Units Setup dialog box displays.

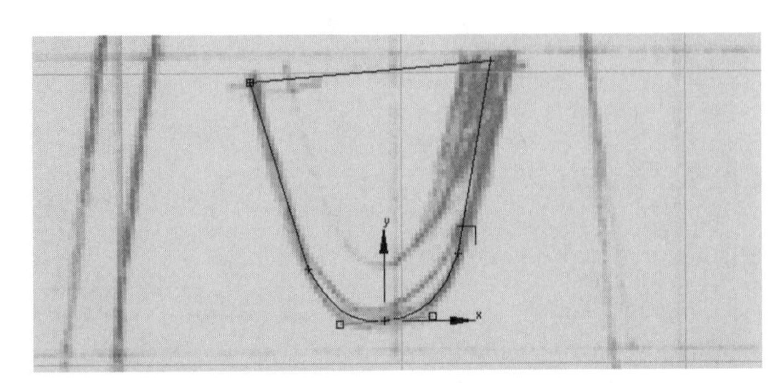

2. Click the Metric radio button and make sure Meters is displayed in the Metric drop-down list.
3. Click OK.

You'll use meters in this example, because this is a European building project. Now let's proceed to scaling the image to the proper size.

If you look at the scanned image carefully, you'll see a grid whose spacing is about 4.5 meters. You see 10 grid spaces in the horizontal direction. The image was carefully cropped to be as close as possible to a width of 10 grid units. VIZ imports an image so that its width will just fit in the viewport, so if you set the width of the viewport to match the width of the image, you've got a fairly close scale relationship between the sketch and the dimensions in VIZ.

To begin adjusting the image scale, set the width of the viewport to match the width of the bitmap image. The simplest way to do this is to first set up a grid that matches the grid in the sketch.

1. Right-click the Grid button at the bottom of the VIZ window. The Grid and Snap settings dialog box displays with the Home Grid tab selected.

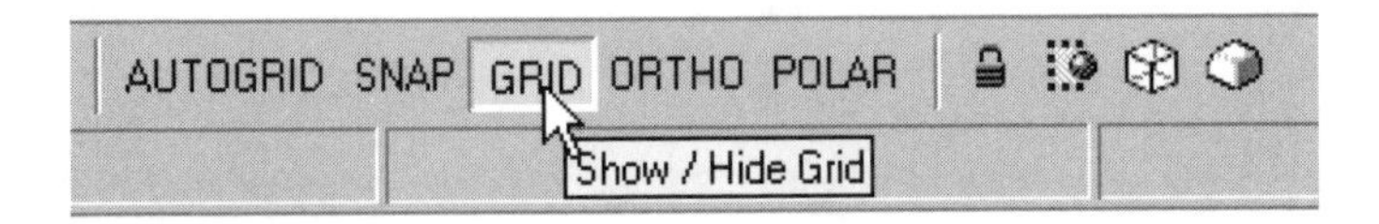

2. At the Grid and Snap Settings dialog box, set the Grid spacing to 4.5m and make sure the Major Lines every Nth input box shows 10.

3. Close the dialog box, and click the Zoom tool.

4. Click and drag the zoom cursor from the center portion of the viewport downward until you see 10-grid spacing just fit in the viewport, as shown in Figure 4.13. When you click and drag from the center, the view will stay centered as you zoom out. If you need to, use the Pan tool to adjust the horizontal position so that the 0 Y axis is at the center of the viewport.

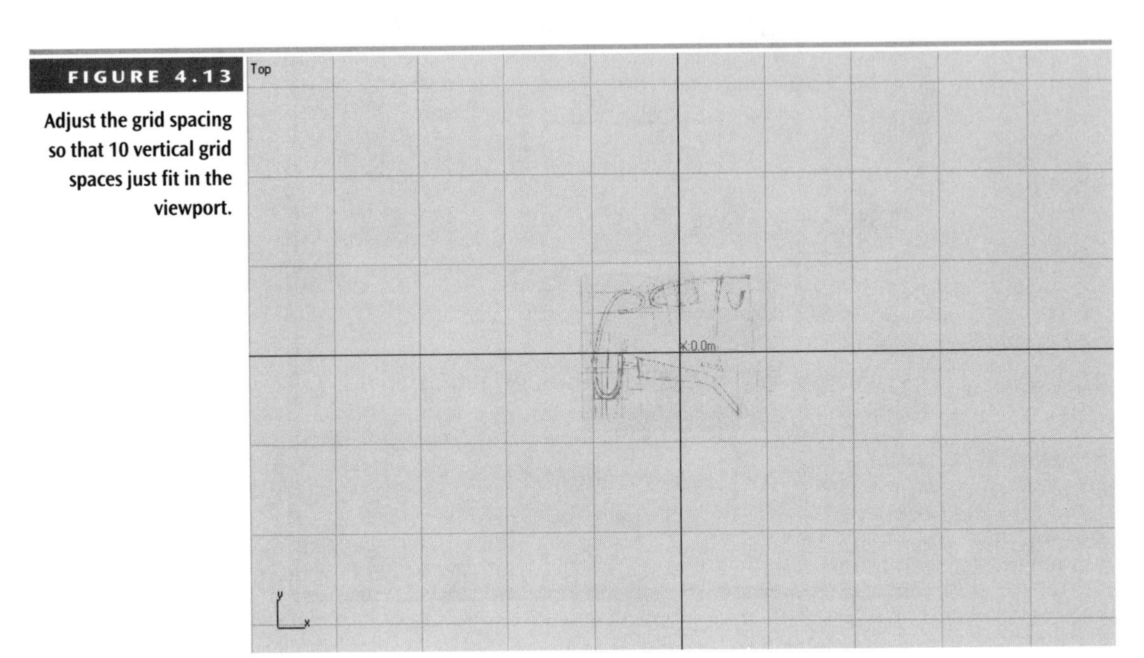

FIGURE 4.13

Adjust the grid spacing so that 10 vertical grid spaces just fit in the viewport.

5. Choose View ➢ Viewport Image ➢ Reset Transform. The image will fill the entire viewport. Note that the vertical grid lines of the image are fairly close to the vertical grid lines of the viewport, as shown in Figure 4.14.

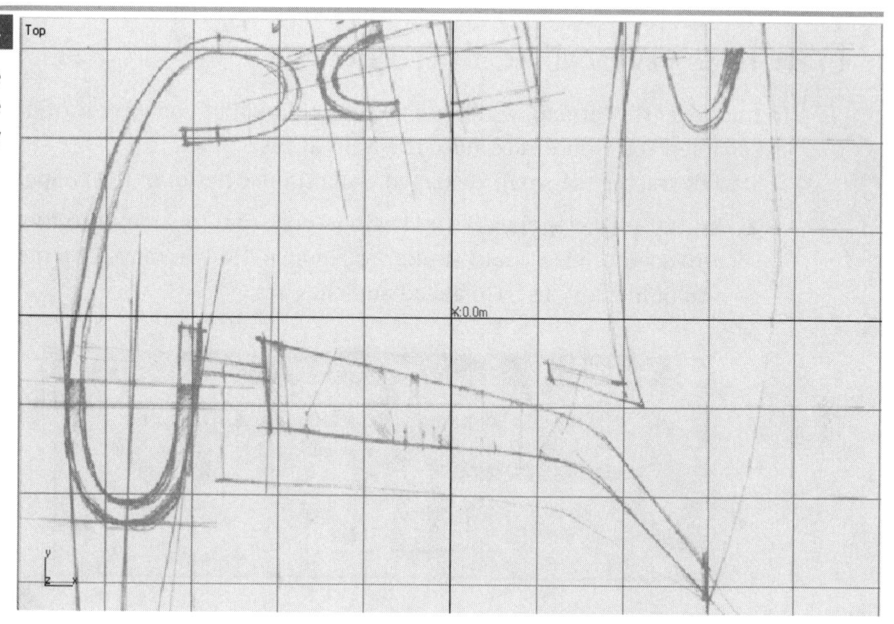

FIGURE 4.14

The viewport with the image adjusted to the new viewport display

If you need to, you can also adjust the vertical location of the grid. This will require the use of a low-tech device: a sticky-back note.

1. Take a sticky-back note and place it so its top edge is aligned with one of the horizontal grid lines of the scanned image.
2. Click the Pan tool and carefully pan the view downward until one of the horizontal viewport grid lines is aligned with the top edge of the sticky-back note.
3. Choose View ➢ Viewport Image ➢ Reset Transform. The grid will align vertically with the grid in the image.
4. Once you've got the viewport grid as closely aligned to the image's grid as possible, choose View ➢ Save Active Top View. By saving this view, you can quickly reset the image to the viewport in the event that you inadvertently loose the image.

The grids may not align perfectly, but for this sketch you should have the alignment close enough. You now have a fairly close match to the scale of the actual building. You can see through this exercise that there is some preparation of the image involved. First of all, a grid should be placed on the sketch so that you have some scale reference. Secondly, the width of the image needs to be cropped to a whole grid unit so that you can use the image width to match the viewport.

Now that you have the image to a size that makes some sense scalewise, you can get on with the real work of building the model.

Tracing over the Image

To trace over the bitmap, you'll use the line spline that you were introduced to in the last chapter. You won't trace all of the walls at first.

Start by tracing the small U-shaped wall on the exterior of the chapel.

1. In the Top viewport, use the Region Zoom tool to zoom into the U-shaped wall area so your view looks similar to Figure 4.15. You may get a message warning you of memory use. Go ahead and click Yes.

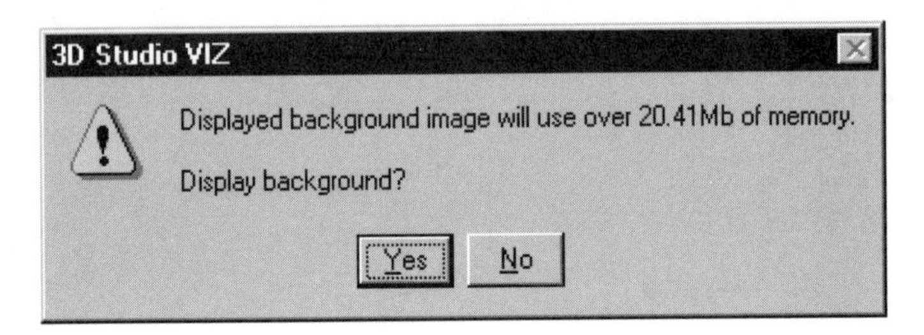

2. Click the Create tab of the Command Panel, and click Shapes.

3. Click the Line button in the Command Panel, and trace over the outside of the wall, using single clicks to select the points shown in Figure 4.15.
4. For the last point, click the beginning of the spline. In the dialog box, go ahead and close the spline.

FIGURE 4.15

Tracing the wall

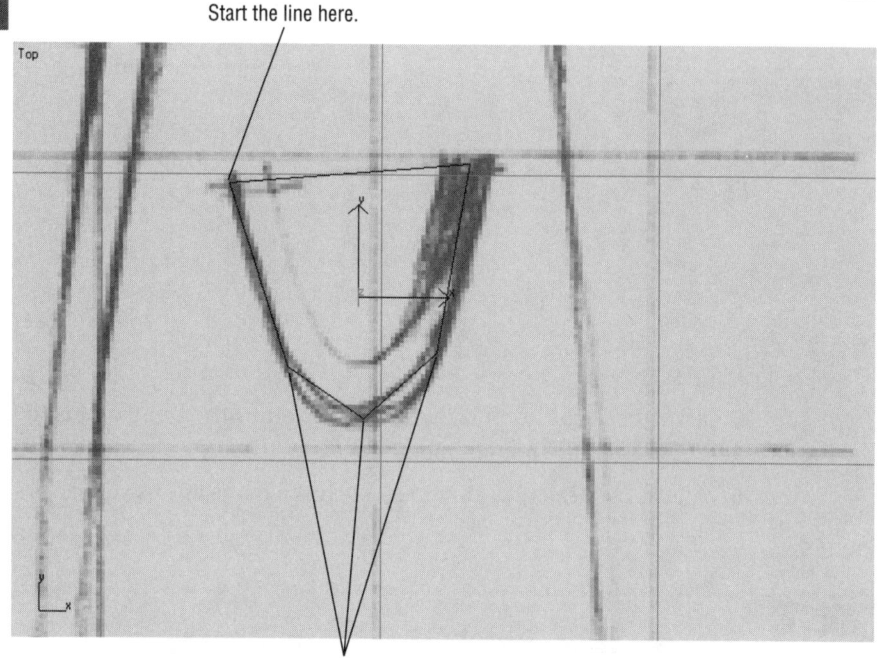
Start the line here.
Top
Continue selecting points in a counter-clockwise direction as shown here.

The line needs to be curved, so use the Bézier Vertex option to form the curve of the wall.

1. Click the Modify tab of the Command Panel, and click the vertex tool in the Select rollout.

2. With the Select object, right-click the middle vertex of the wall, as shown in Figure 4.16.
3. Select Bézier from the list of options in the Pop-up menu.
4. Click the Select and Move tool in the Standard toolbar, then click and drag the Bézier handles to a position similar to the one shown in Figure 4.16. You'll want to smooth the bottom curve to match the bitmap image.

FIGURE 4.16

Editing the middle vertex

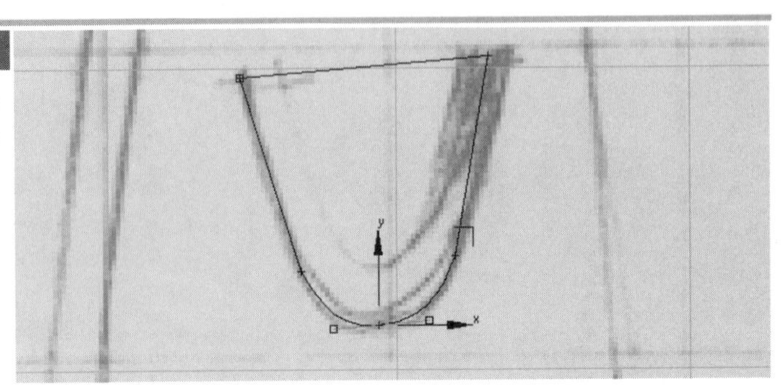

5. Right-click the second vertex to the left of the one you just edited and select Bézier from the pop-up menu.
6. Adjust the Bézier handles to smooth the curve at this vertex, as shown in Figure 4.17:

FIGURE 4.17

Editing the second vertex to the left of the middle vertex

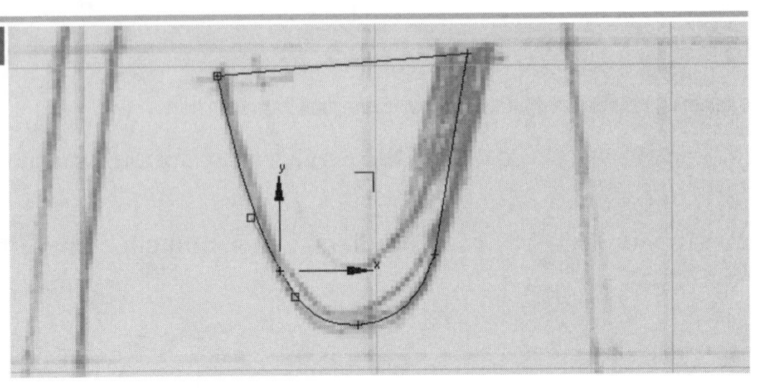

7. Right-click the other vertex to the right, select Bézier from the pop-up menu, and adjust the Bézier handle so that the wall looks symmetrical (see Figure 4.18).

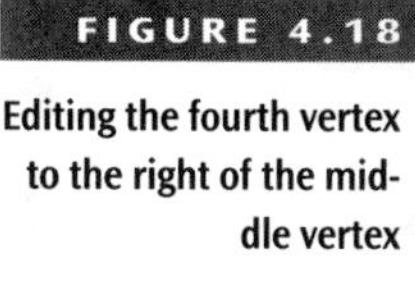
FIGURE 4.18

Editing the fourth vertex to the right of the middle vertex

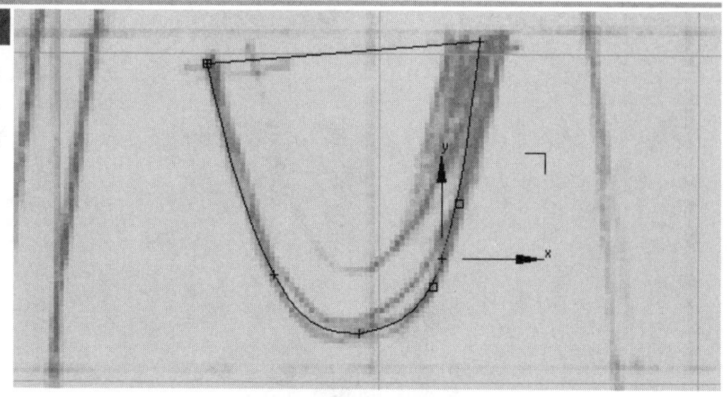

Now you've got the general outline of the wall. You could extrude the spline now to get the general shape of the wall, but the design calls for a bit more elaboration.

Building Objects from Traced Lines

The shape of the wall starts at its base as a solid form, and as you move up the height of the wall, it becomes a shell. In the transition area, you have a sloped roof that covers the enclosed portion of this piece of the chapel (see Figure 4.19).

FIGURE 4.19

Looking at the form of the U-shaped wall

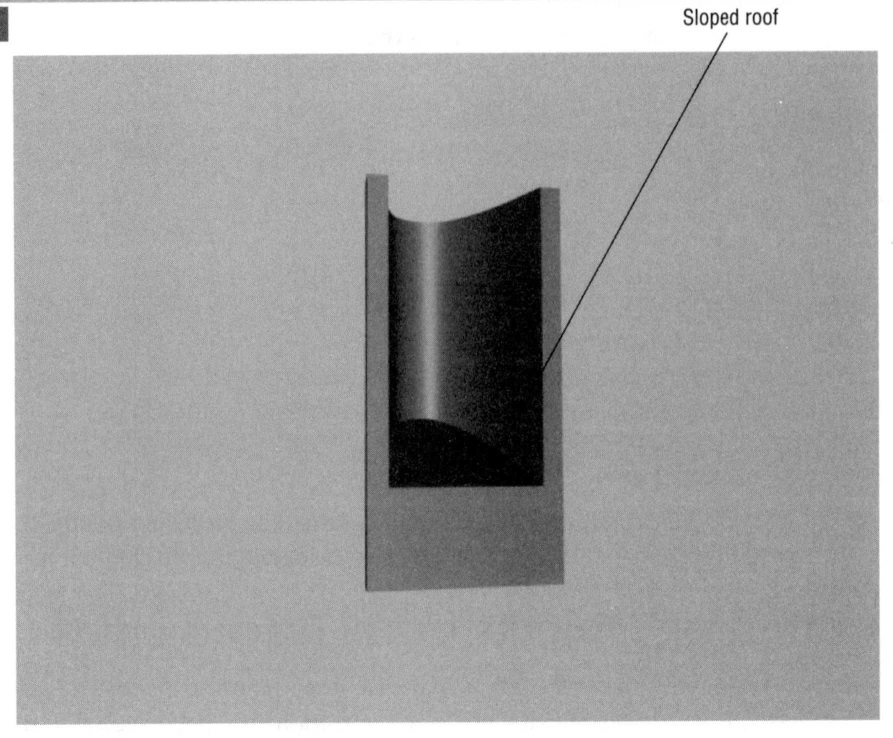

To obtain this form, you'll make a copy of the wall you've just drawn, then form it to create an object matching the void of the upper part of the piece. Once you have the void object, you can subtract it from the main outer part of the wall, using the Boolean operation you learned about earlier in this chapter.

Create the Void Outline

To create the void object, you'll get a chance to explore some new spline editing tools. First, you'll make a copy of the existing wall outline, then you'll edit the copy to get the outline of the void object.

1. Click the Sub-Object button in the Command Panel to deactivate it.

2. With the Select and Move tool selected, shift-click and drag the wall you just created to the right so you have a copy as shown in Figure 4.20.

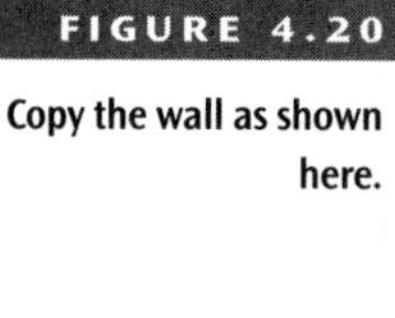

FIGURE 4.20

Copy the wall as shown here.

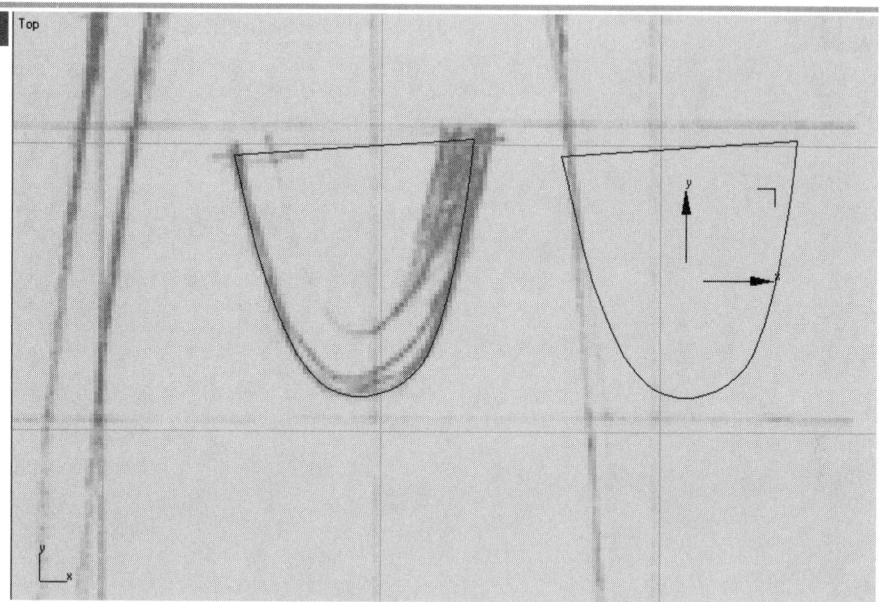

3. In the Clone Options dialog box, click Copy and then click OK. You don't need an instance or reference copy for this part.

Next you'll work on the copy to form the void outline.

1. With the copy of the wall selected, click the Spline tool in the Selection rollout of the Command Panel.
2. Scroll down the Command Panel to the Outline input box, click the input box and enter **0.4**↵. This creates an outline that is 0.4 meters thick.
3. Scroll back up to the top of the Command Panel, and click the Segment tool under the Selection rollout. You can also select Segment from the Selection Level drop-down list.

4. Click the straight line segment at the top of the interior wall outline, as shown in Figure 4.21, then press the Delete key to delete the line.

FIGURE 4.21

Delete the straight line segment.

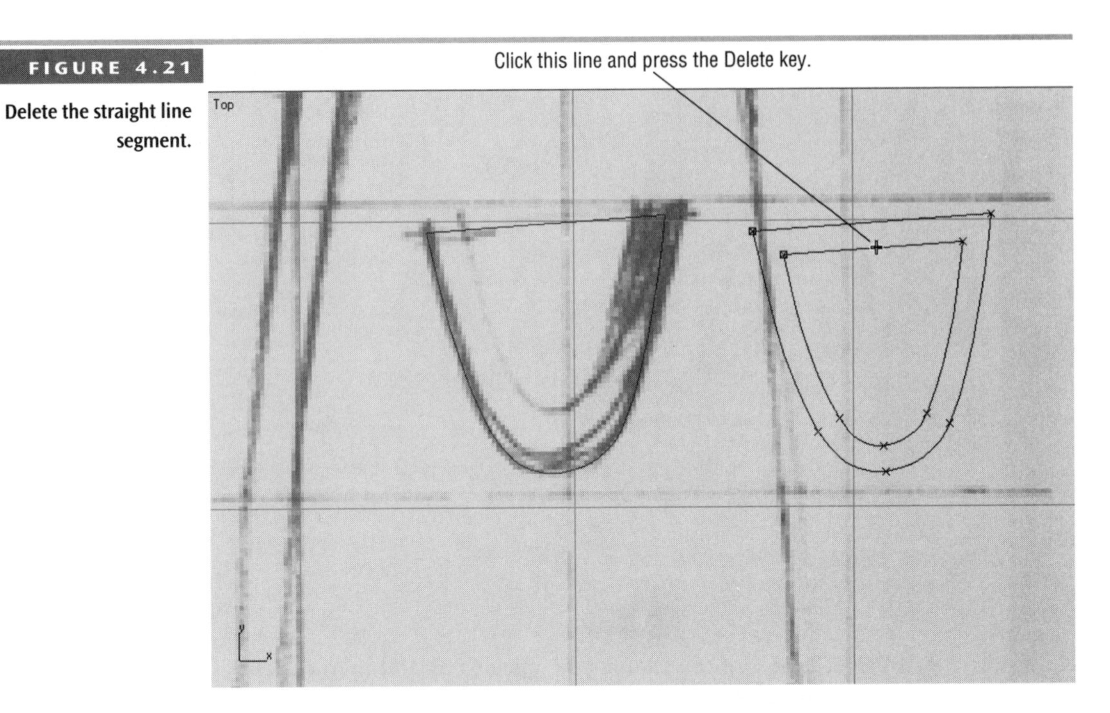
Click this line and press the Delete key.
Top

With the straight segment deleted, you can extend the remaining portion of the line to the outside edge of the wall.

1. Click the Spline tool under the Selection rollout again, and click the remaining portion of the interior wall outline so that it turns red.
2. Scroll down the Command Panel and click the Extend button. Alternately, you can right-click and select Extend from the pop-up menu.

3. Place the cursor on the left endpoint of the inside wall so that the Extend cursor displays, as shown in Figure 4.22, and click the line. It extends to the outside line.

FIGURE 4.22

Extending the inside wall to the straight line segment of the outside wall outline.

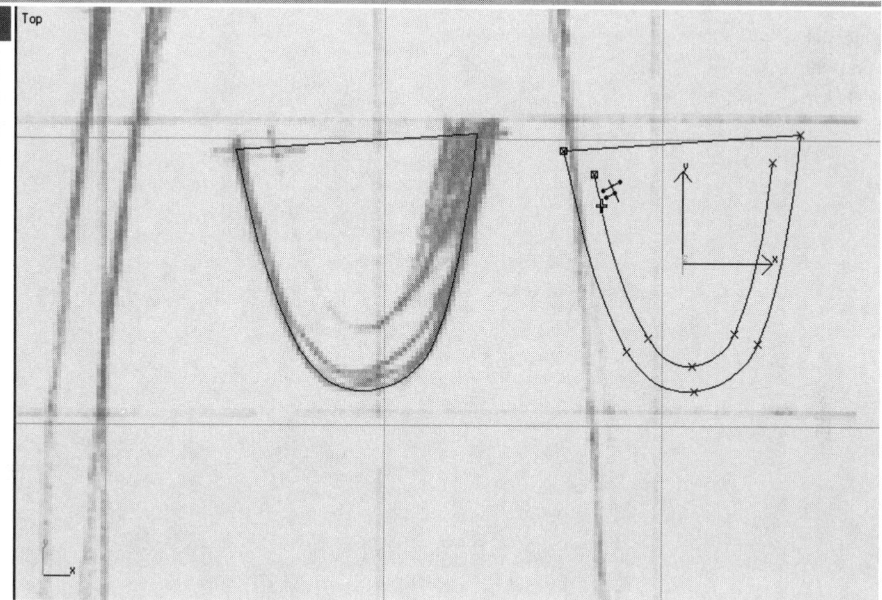

4. Click the other end of the inside wall so that it too extends to the straight line segment of the outside line.
5. Click the Extend button in the Command Panel to deactivate it, and click the Close button in the Command Panel. You can also right-click and select Close from the pop-up menu.

6. Click the Select Object tool, click the outside wall outline, as shown in Figure 4.23, and press the Delete key to delete it.

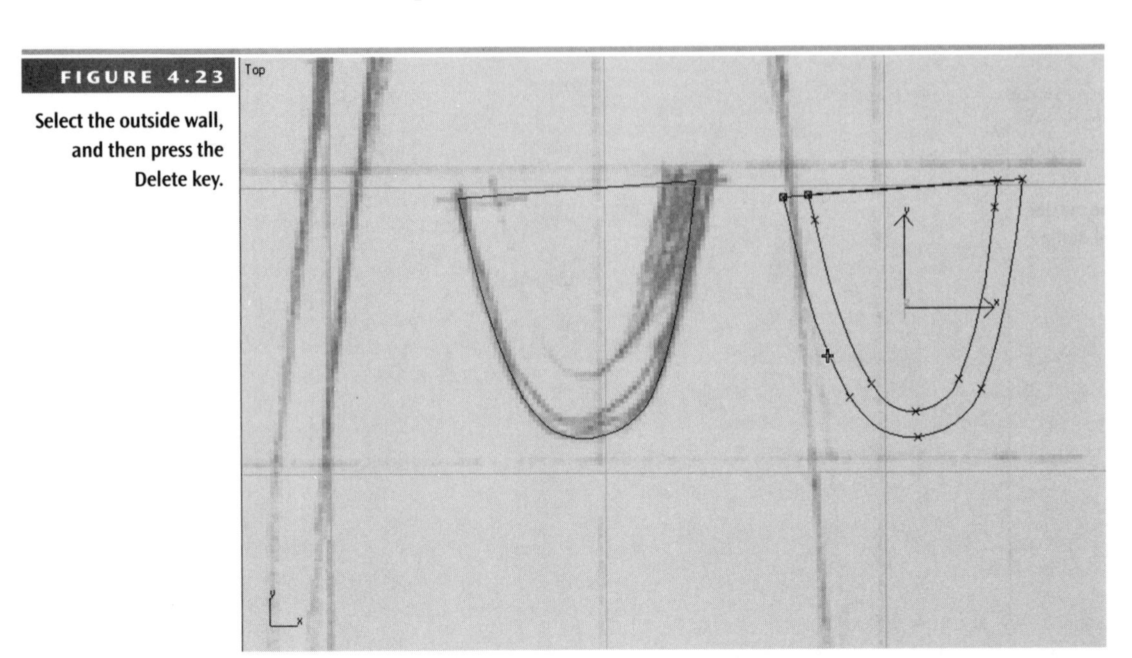

FIGURE 4.23

Select the outside wall, and then press the Delete key.

7. Scroll back up to the top of the Command Panel and click the Sub-Object button to deactivate it.

You've got the outline of the shape you want to subtract from the wall. Now move it into position.

1. Right-click the Snap tool at the bottom of the window.
2. In the Grid and Snap Settings dialog box, click the Clear All button, then click Midpoint and close the Grid and Snap Settings dialog box.
3. If it isn't already active, click the Snap button to make the snap tool active.

4. With the Select and Move tool selected, place the cursor on the midpoint of the straight line segment of the wall copy, as shown in Figure 4.24. Then when you see the Midpoint cursor appear on the line, click and drag the wall outline to the straight segment of the original wall, as shown in Figure 4.24.

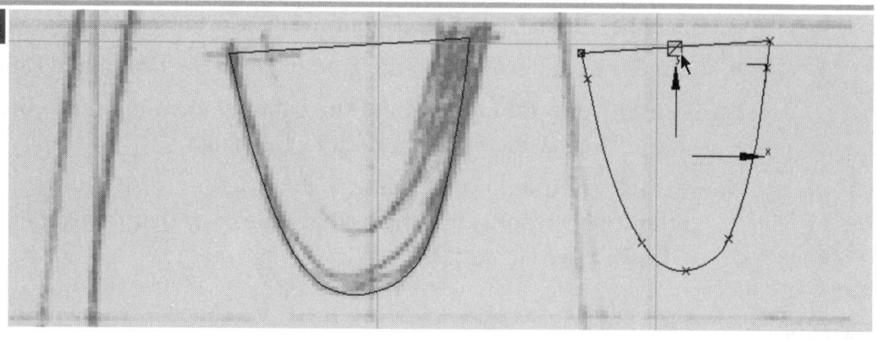

FIGURE 4.24A

Selecting and moving the wall copy using the Midpoint snap

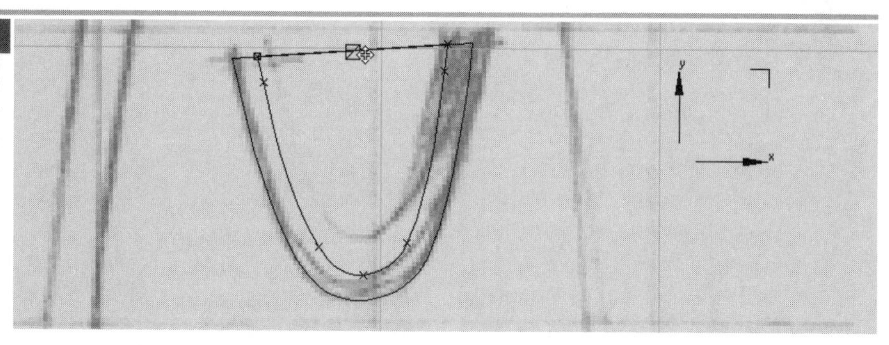

FIGURE 4.24B

Selecting and moving the wall copy using the Midpoint snap

Forming the Wall Void

Now you're ready to extrude both the wall and the wall void. First move the void object to the elevation where the void begins.

1. Click the Min/Max Toggle tool in the Viewport toolbar to see all four viewports.
2. Click the Perspective viewport, and click the Zoom Extents tool.
3. With the inside wall outline selected, right-click the Select and Move tool. The Move and Transform Type-In dialog box displays.
4. Click the Z input box of the Absolute: World group, then enter **2.5**↵ for 2.5 meters.
5. Close the Move and Transform type-In dialog box and click Zoom Extents again to see both wall outlines. The inside wall outline now appears to be somewhat above the outside wall outline.

Now it's time to extrude the two outlines. This piece of the chapel is about 7.5 meters high, so you can extrude both pieces to this height. The height of the void is somewhat arbitrary, as it is to be subtracted from the main, outside form of the wall.

1. Click the Snap tool to turn it off. It may be a distraction during the next few operations.
2. Click the original, outside wall outline to select it.
3. Click the Extrude button in the Modify tab of the Command Panel.
4. Click the Amount input box of the Parameters rollout and enter **7.5**↵ for 7.5 meters. The outside wall appears at its full height.

Now extrude the interior void shape.

1. In the Top viewport, click the wall outline copy that forms the interior outline of the wall (see Figure 4.25).

FIGURE 4.25

Select the form of the interior outline.

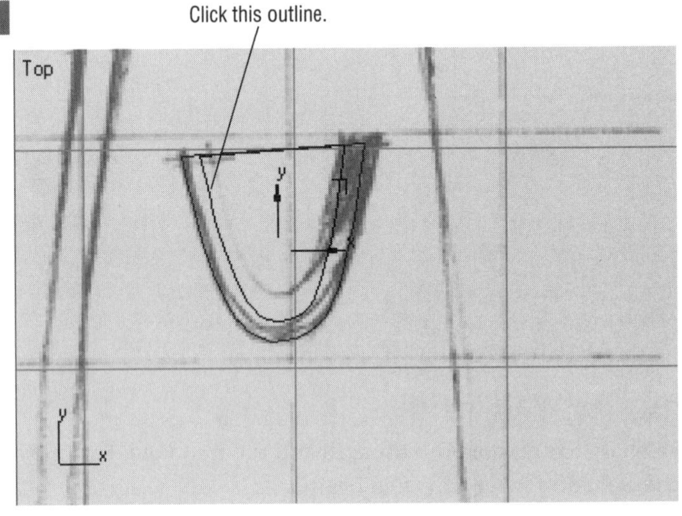
Click this outline.
Top
y
x

2. Click the Extrude button in the Modify tab of the Command Panel. The object extrudes to the same height as the other wall. VIZ applies to the current extrusion the last value you entered for the first extrusion.
3. Click the Perspective viewport and click the Zoom Extents tool to get a better look at the two extrusions.

Adding a Taper to the Void

You're almost ready to subtract the interior void object from the outer wall object. You need to apply the taper modifier to the void object to get the sloping roof that you see in Figure 4.19.

1. With the Perspective viewport selected, click the Min/Max toggle tool to enlarge the view.
2. Click the Arc Rotate Selected tool in the Viewport Toolbar. The green Arc Rotate circle appears in the viewport
3. Click and drag the left-hand square on the circle to the right so that you get a view similar to Figure 4.26.

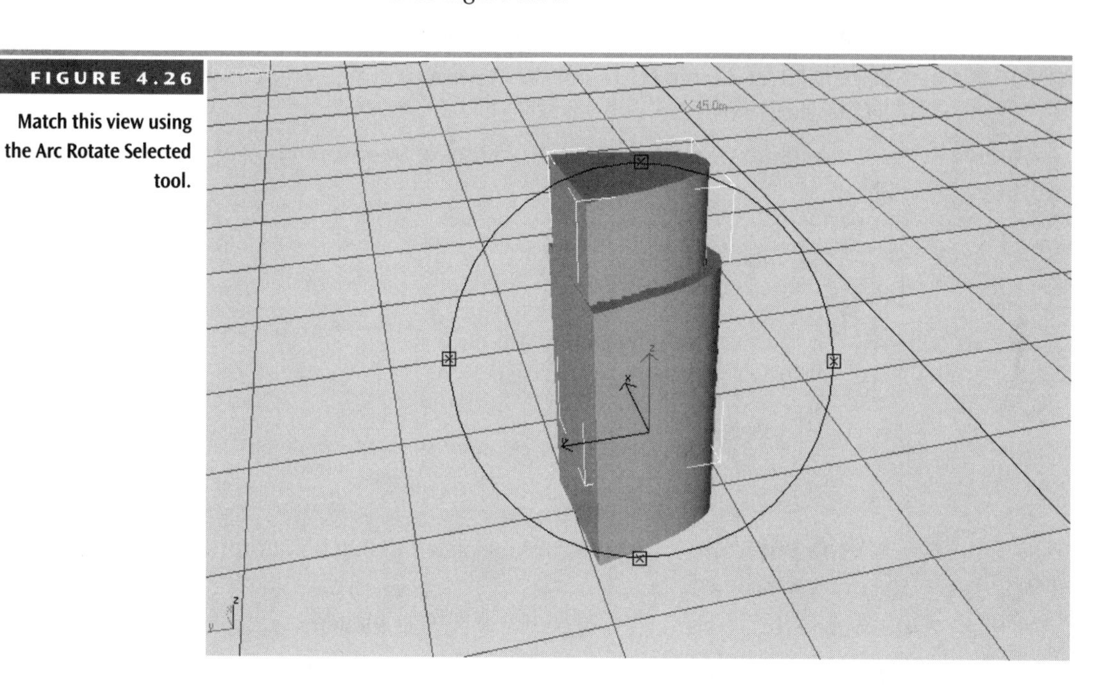

FIGURE 4.26

Match this view using the Arc Rotate Selected tool.

4. Click the Select Object tool, then click the void object.
5. Ctrl-right-click the inside wall shape and select Isolate Tool from the pop-up menu. The viewport changes to show only the interior wall shape and the Isolated dialog box displays.

By using the Isolate tool, you can more easily view and edit an object that may be partially hidden by other objects in your model. Now you can apply the Taper tool to the selected object and see its effects more clearly.

1. Click the More... button in the Modify tab of the Command Panel.
2. Select Taper from the Modifiers dialog box and click OK.
3. Click the Primary Y radio button under the Taper Axis group of the Parameters rollout. This causes the taper to occur in the Y axis.
4. Click the Effect Z radio button of the Taper Axis group. This constrains the taper effect to the Z axis.
5. Set the Amount of the taper to **0.38** in the Amount input box of the Parameters rollout.

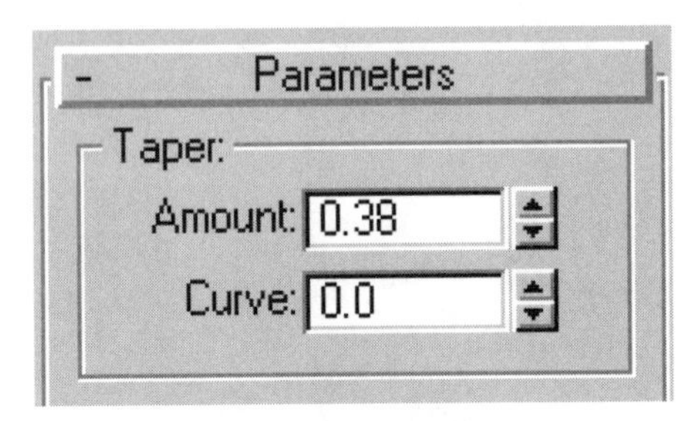

6. Click the Exit Isolation button in the Isolated dialog box to restore the view of the other wall object.
7. Click the Min/Max Toggle tool on the Viewport toolbar.
8. Right-click in the Top viewport to make it active. Then click the Min/Max Toggle tool again to enlarge it. When you see a display warning message, click Yes. If you click No, you'll loose the orientation of the bitmap image to the top viewport.

You're just about ready to subtract the inside wall shape from the outside shape, but there's one little detail you will want to take care of.

Aligning the Taper Modifier to the Object

The Taper modifier acts on the shape in a direction that is aligned with the world coordinate system. You really want the Taper modifier to be aligned with the void object, which is slightly skewed in relation to the world coordinate system. You may recall that you can adjust the orientation of a modifier by adjusting its gizmo. In the next exercise, you'll rotate the Taper gizmo to align it with the inside wall shape.

1. With the Taper modifier still active in the Modifier Stack, click the Sub-Object button in the Modify Tab of the Command Panel. You should see the word Gizmo in the Selection Level drop-down list.
2. Click the Select and Rotate tool in the Standard toolbar.
3. Carefully click and drag the Blue Z axis of the coordinate arrow downward until the rectangular gizmo is aligned with the top edge of the wall, as shown in Figure 4.27.

FIGURE 4.27

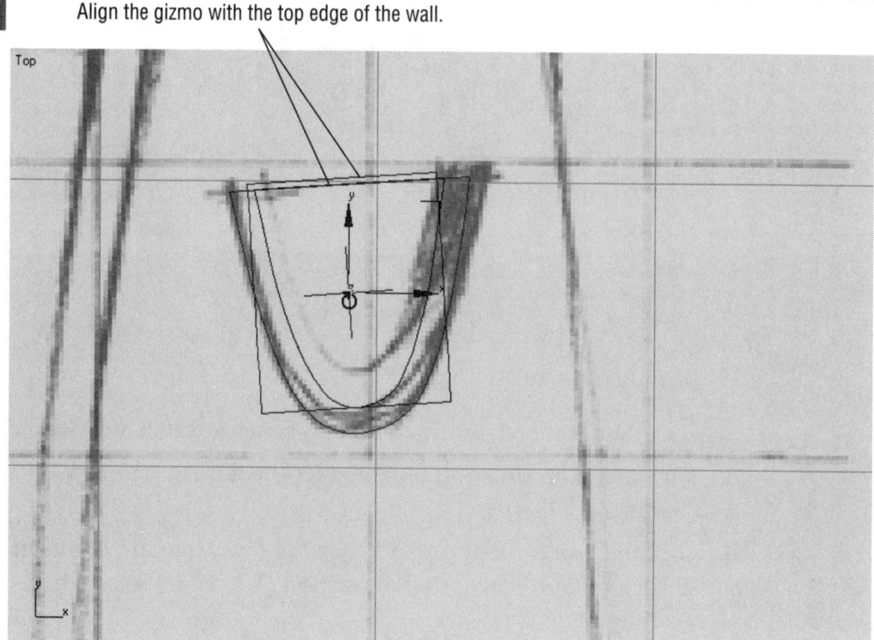
Align the gizmo with the top edge of the wall.
Top

Click and drag the Z axis to rotate the Taper gizmo.

4. Adjust the gizmo so that its top edge is aligned with the straight segment of the void object, and release the mouse button.
5. Next, click the Select and Move tool and move the gizmo "upward" along the Z axis so that the gizmo is in the middle of the void object. This places the taper at the bottom of the void where it is needed to form the sloped roof.
6. When you're done, click the Sub-Object button to deactivate it.

You're now ready to subtract the void object from the outer wall object.

1. Click the Min/Max Toggle tool to get a view of all of the viewports.
2. Click the Select Object Tool from the Standard toolbar. Then, in the Top viewport, select the outer wall object, as shown in Figure 4.28.

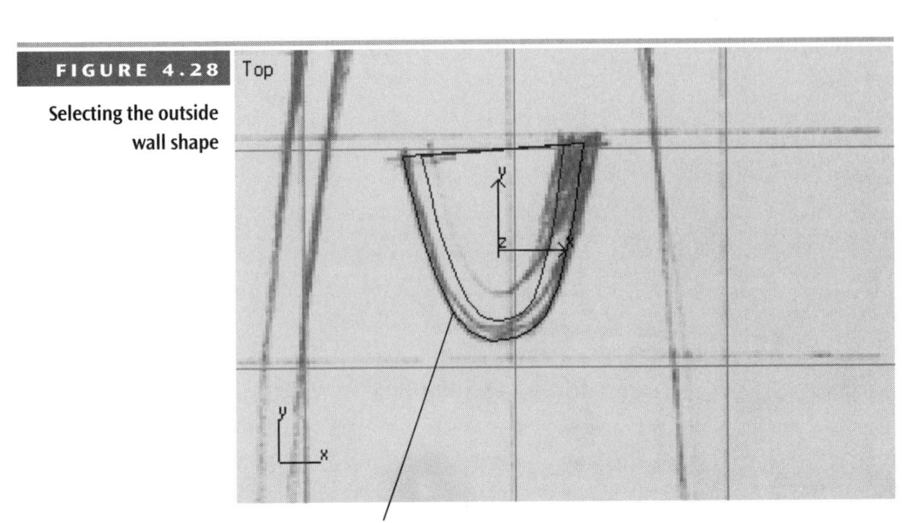
Top
Click this wall shape.

FIGURE 4.28

Selecting the outside wall shape

3. Click the Create tab in the command panel and click the Geometry tool.
4. Click the drop-down list just below the Create category buttons and select Compound Objects.
5. Click the Boolean button and click the Pick Operand B button under the Pick Boolean rollout. Make sure Subtraction (A-B) is still selected.

6. Click the void shape. It is subtracted from the outer wall object to form the final shape of the wall. You can see the result in the Perspective viewport.

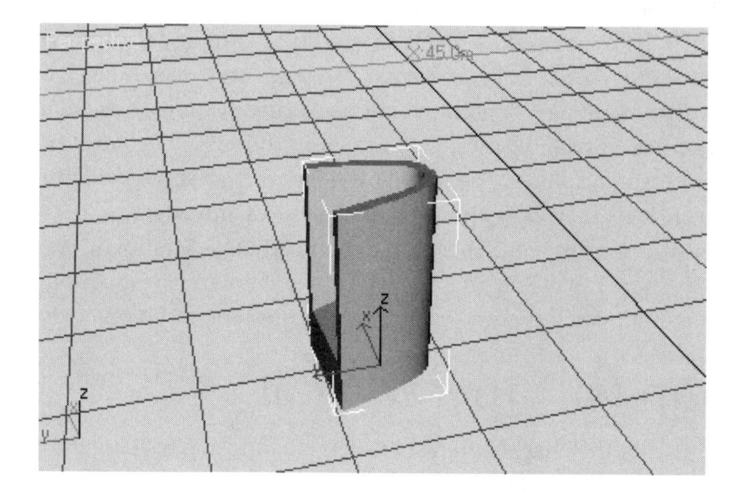

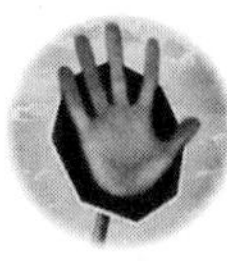

WARNING **If for some reason you don't get the results shown here, it may be because the Subtraction option is not selected under the Operation group of the Parameters rollout. Scroll down the Command Panel and check to make sure that Subtraction (A-B) is selected.**

You've just created part of the Ronchamp building using a number of spline editing techniques. The method shown here is just one of a number of ways you could have used to create the wall. Through this method, you were able to try out some spline editing tools, and you also got a chance to practice using some other methods you learned in previous chapters.

Now let's move on to another part of the building to examine another way of editing objects.

Editing Meshes

You've been introduced to VIZ objects in the form of the Standard Primitives, Splines, and AEC walls. It also helps to think about VIZ objects in terms of Parametric and Non-parametric objects. This can be a bit confusing, since virtually all objects in VIZ start out as parametric objects. But, as you'll see, a lot of your work with objects will depart from the parametric level of editing as soon as you begin editing objects in earnest. In fact, you've already seen this with the spline examples in this and previous chapters.

In your introduction to VIZ objects, you created simple forms and adjusted them through the use of the object's parameters. Parameters are great for establishing the initial dimensions and characteristics of an object. They can also serve as a convenient way to make adjustments to objects as you progress through the design process. But eventually, you'll begin to make changes on a deeper level, bypassing the parameters altogether. At this point, you'll be editing 3D objects as *Editable Meshes*. Editing 3D objects as editable meshes is similar to the sub-object level editing you've already performed on splines. The main difference is that you have some additional sub-object levels to work with in the form of faces and edges.

In this section, you'll begin to explore Editable Meshes by creating the South wall of the chapel. You'll learn how you can convert an extruded spline into an editable mesh, then you'll proceed to modify the mesh on a sub-object level.

Creating a Tapered Wall

The part of the chapel you just created was unusual because it was a curved wall. Ronchamp contains many curved walls, but they shouldn't pose a problem to you now, since you've had some experience drawing such shapes and extruding them. One wall of the chapel is quite unusual, however. The south wall tapers in two directions, plus it has a curve in it. In the following set of exercises, you'll look at a way to create such a wall in VIZ, and in the process you'll be introduced to some additional methods for editing sub-objects.

You'll start, as usual, by outlining the plan of the wall. Once again, you'll trace over the imported bitmap sketch using a line. First, set up your view to prepare for tracing.

1. Click the Top viewport to make it active, then click the Min/Max Toggle tool to enlarge it. Click Yes at the Display background warning.

2. Choose View ➢ Zoom ➢ Out. Click the Pan view and pan the view so the south wall is centered in the view. The View ➢ Zoom ➢ Out command makes it easy to view a greater area of your imported image, because the standard Zoom tool reacts slowly and is unpredictable in the viewport with the imported bitmap.

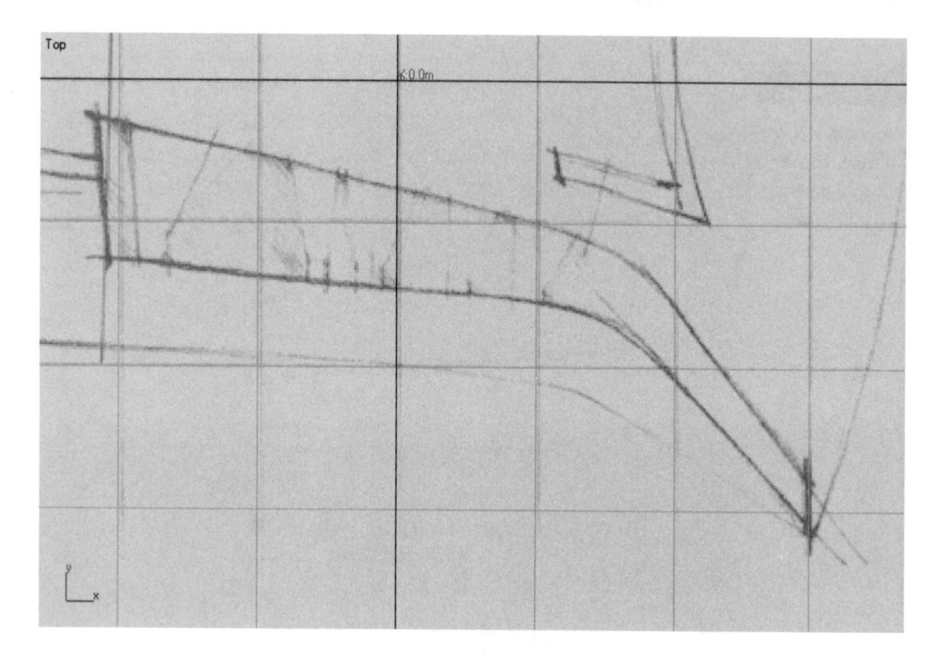

Now you're ready to trace the wall.

1. If it isn't already selected, click the Create tab of the Command Panel and click the Shapes tool.
2. Click Line, then draw the line, as shown in Figure 4.29.

FIGURE 4.29

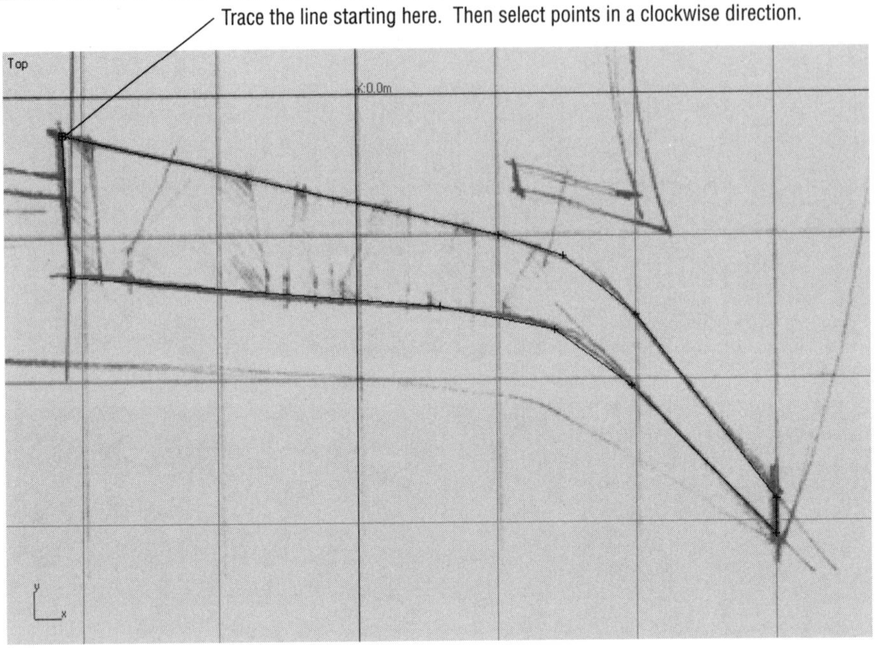

Trace the south wall as shown here. The vertices are shown here for clarity.

Trace the line starting here. Then select points in a clockwise direction.

3. At the last point, click the beginning of the line and go ahead and close it.
4. Click the Modify tab of the Command Panel, and click the Vertex tool in the Selection rollout.
5. Click the Select and Move tool in the Standard Toolbar, right-click the vertex shown in Figure 4.30, and select Bézier from the Pop-up menu.

6. Using the Bézier handles, adjust the curve of the wall so that it looks similar to Figure 4.30. You'll want the curve of the wall to join the straight portions of the wall in a tangent.

FIGURE 4.30

Selecting and editing the vertex

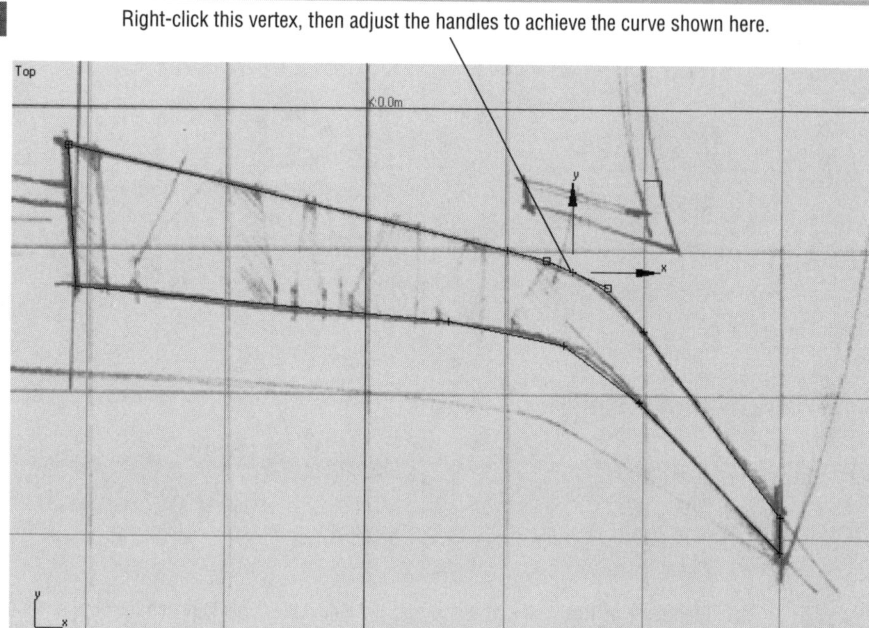
Right-click this vertex, then adjust the handles to achieve the curve shown here.
Top
X:0.0m

7. Click the vertex across the wall from the one you just edited, then select Bézier.
8. Adjust the curve of this vertex so it looks similar to Figure 4.31.

FIGURE 4.31

Editing the second vertex

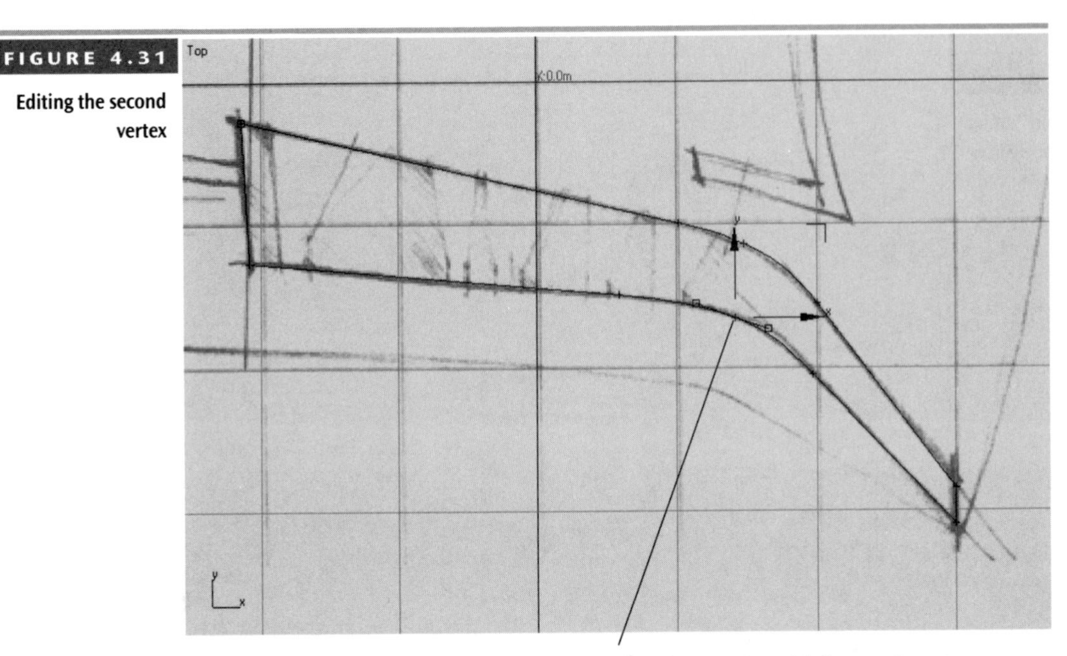

Right-click on this vertex, select Bézier, and adjust the curve to match the one shown here.

Now it's time to extrude the wall. The wall forms a peak at its eastern-most end, and that peak is approximately 14 meters high. You'll want the wall to be at least 14 meters high so you have enough material to work with.

1. You're already in the Modify tab of the Command Panel, so click the Extrude button under the Modifiers rollout. If you're continuing from the last section, the wall will extrude to the last height you entered.
2. Change the value in the Parameter rollouts Amount input box to **14**, for 14 meters. Also make sure that the Segments value is set to **1**.
3. Click the Min/Max Toggle tool.
4. Click the Perspective viewport and then click the Zoom Extents tool to get a better look at the south wall so far.

5. Click the Arc Rotate Selected tool, then click and drag the right-most square of the Arc Rotate circle to the left until your view looks similar to Figure 4.32.

FIGURE 4.32

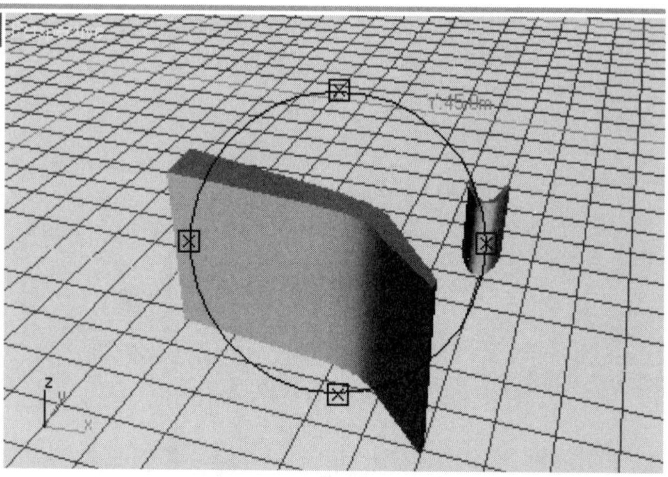

The Perspective view after rotating with the Arc Rotate Selected tool

6. Click the Min/Max tool to enlarge the perspective view.

You now have the basic form of the wall, but it tapers vertically. Not only that, but the taper is not uniform across the entire wall. It tapers more at its west end, and it doesn't taper at all at its east end. To accomplish this non-uniform taper, you won't be able to use the Taper modifier. Instead, you'll edit the mesh directly by rotating some of the edges.

Converting the Spline to a Mesh

To edit the south wall, you'll need to convert the extruded spline to an editable mesh to take advantage of the special features of mesh objects. You can then make the appropriate changes at the sub-object level of the mesh to get the volume you want. Start by setting up the view to aid in your editing.

1. Right-click the Perspective label in the upper left corner of the perspective viewport and select Wireframe.

2. Click the Arc Rotate Selected tool in the Viewport toolbar, then click and drag the square at the top of the Arc Rotate circle downward so your view looks similar to Figure 4.33. You'll want to get a good view of the top of the wall.

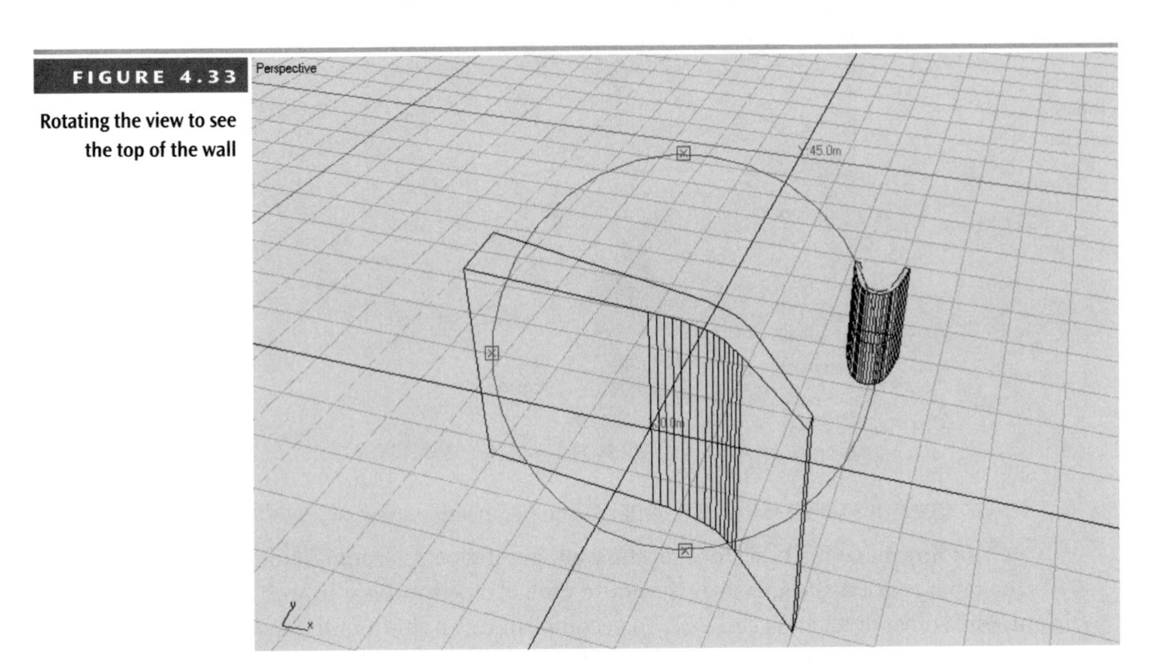

FIGURE 4.33

Rotating the view to see the top of the wall

3. Click the Zoom tool and click and drag upward in the viewport to enlarge the view of the wall. It should look similar to Figure 4.34.

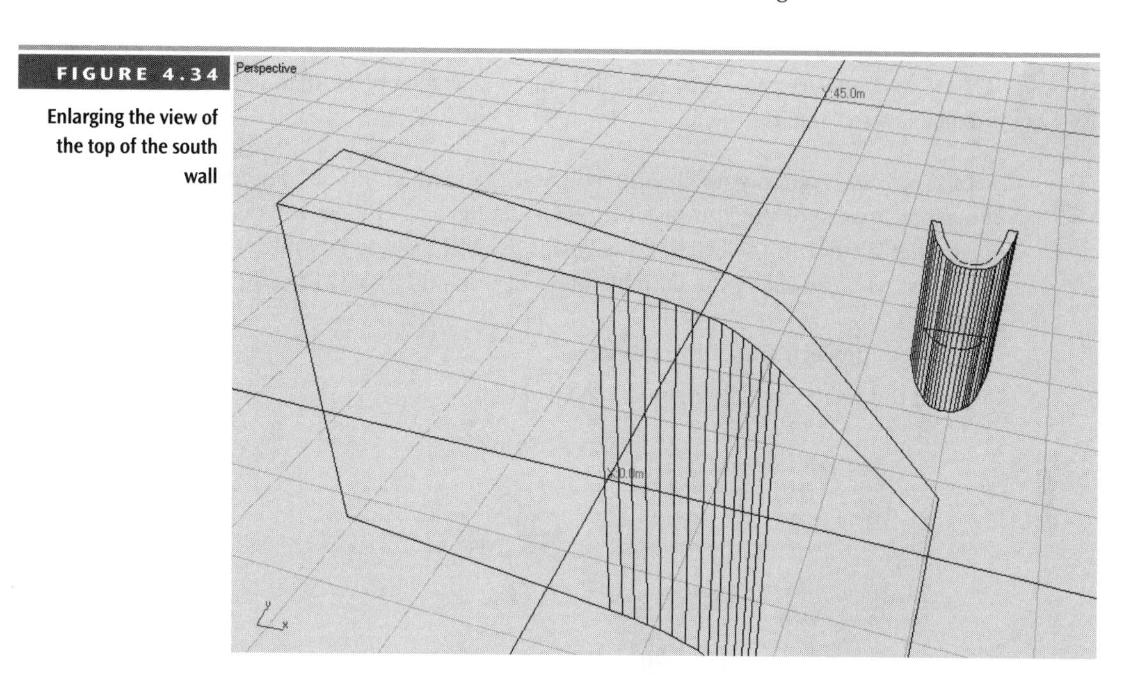

FIGURE 4.34

Enlarging the view of the top of the south wall

Editing the Edge of a Mesh

Now you're ready to start editing the wall. You'll use the Edit Mesh modifier to gain access to the Sub-Object tools, and then you'll learn how to use a new selection tool, the Fence Selection Region, to select an edge of the wall for editing.

1. First make sure that the south wall is selected. Then click the Edit Stack button in the Modify tab of the Command Panel.

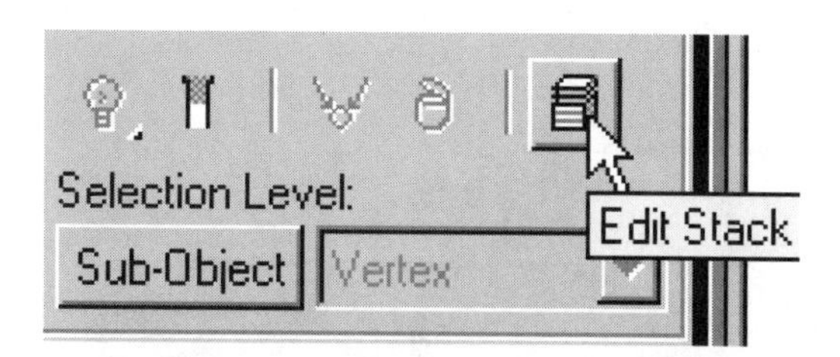

2. In the Edit Modifier Stack dialog box, click Collapse All, then click OK. You'll see a Warning message telling you that "This will remove everything in the stack of all selected objects."

3. Go ahead and click Yes at the warning message. You've just converted your extruded spline into an editable mesh.

TIP **As a shortcut, you may right-click on the selected object, then select Convert to Editable Mesh from the menu.**

In some cases, when you click the Edit Stack button, you'll be presented with a list of options instead of the Edit Modifier Stack dialog box. The list will depend on the object that is currently selected. Usually this list will include Editable Mesh. If you see such a list, you can select the Editable Mesh option and bypass the Edit Modifier Stack dialog box.

Now let's proceed with editing the wall.

1. In the Selection rollout, click the Edge tool.

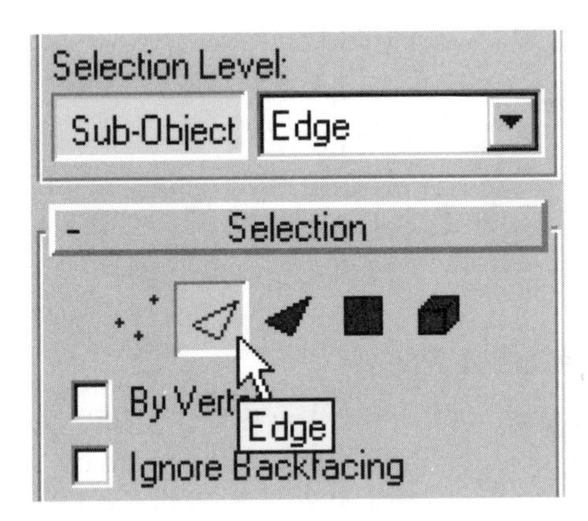

2. In the Standard toolbar, click and hold the Rectangular Selection Region tool until its flyout displays, then drag the mouse down to the bottom option, the Fence Selection Region.

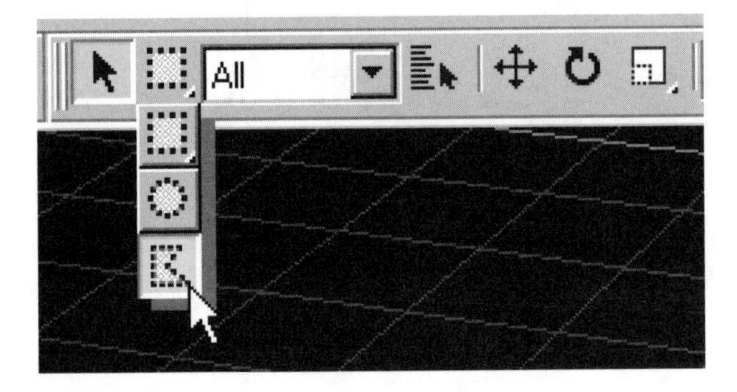

You are going to select the top edge of the wall that is closest to you, so you'll need a selection tool that can let you select a free-form area.

3. Click the Select Object tool and click and drag a short distance just to the left of the wall, as shown in Figure 4.35. This starts the Fence Selection.

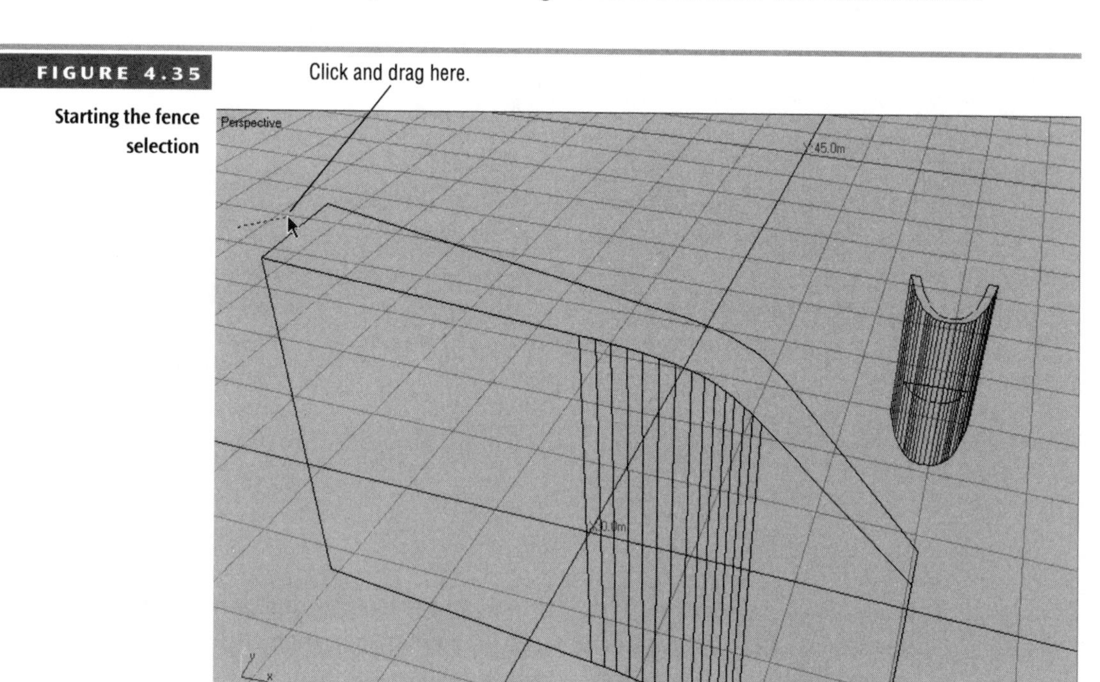

FIGURE 4.35

Starting the fence selection

4. Continue to click points so that the front-top edge of the wall is completely enclosed by the selection, as shown in Figure 4.36.

FIGURE 4.36

Enclosing the front-top edge of the wall

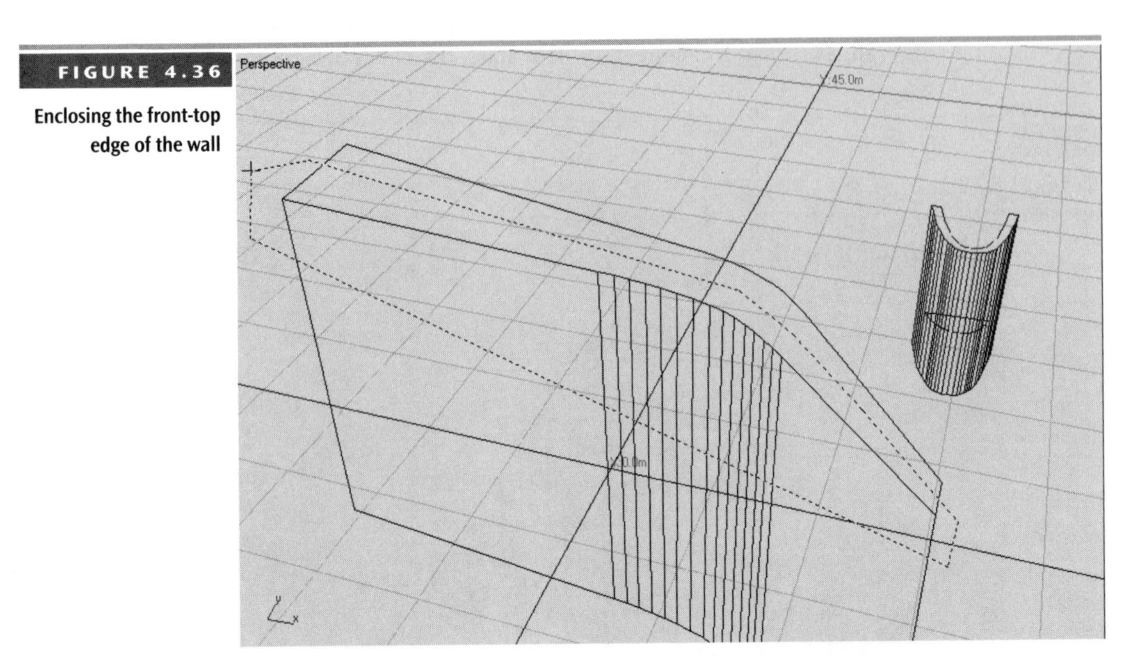

5. To finish your selection, bring the cursor to the beginning point of the fence selection region until the cursor turns into a plus sign, then click. The edge you enclosed will turn red, indicating that it has been selected.

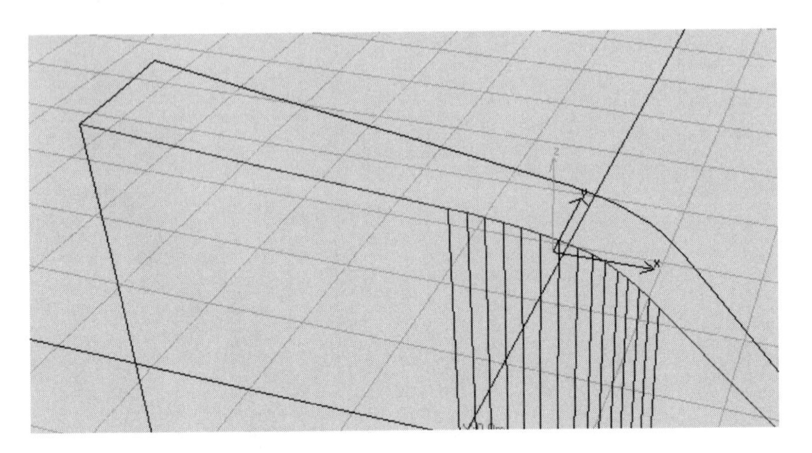

Now that you have the edge selected, you will want to rotate it. The best view for this operation is the top view, so the first thing to do is to go to the top view.

1. Click the Min/Max Toggle to view all of the viewports, right-click the Top viewport, then click the Min/Max Toggle again to enlarge the top viewport.

2. Click the Select and Rotate tool in the Standard Toolbar.
3. Place the cursor on the Z axis of the Xform gizmo, and then click and drag upward until the edge is rotated in such a way that it appears to be parallel to the other edge of the wall. You can look at the coordinate readout and set the angle to −7 (minus seven) degrees.

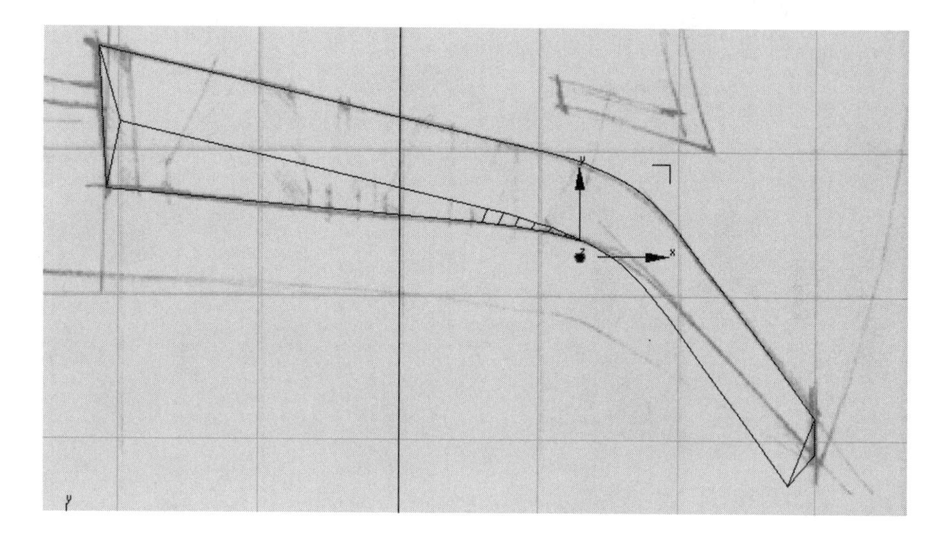

4. Click the Select and Move tool, then click and drag the edge upward so that the top edges are closer together (see Figure 4.37).

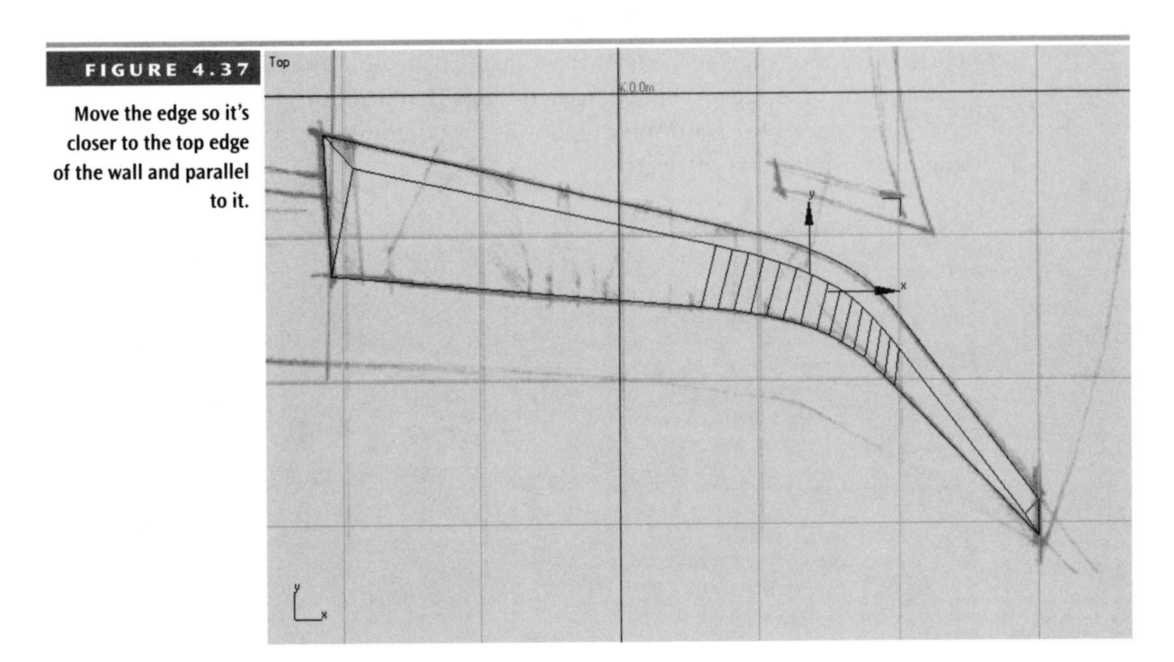

FIGURE 4.37

Move the edge so it's closer to the top edge of the wall and parallel to it.

Moving a Single Vertex

You've managed to taper the outer wall of the south wall. The right end of the wall is a vertical surface that does not taper, so you need to realign the upper corner to its original location. You can do this by moving the vertex and using the endpoint snaps.

1. Click the Vertex tool in the Selection rollout of the Command Panel.
2. Click the vertex shown in Figure 4.38 to select it.

FIGURE 4.38

Select the corner of the top of the wall.

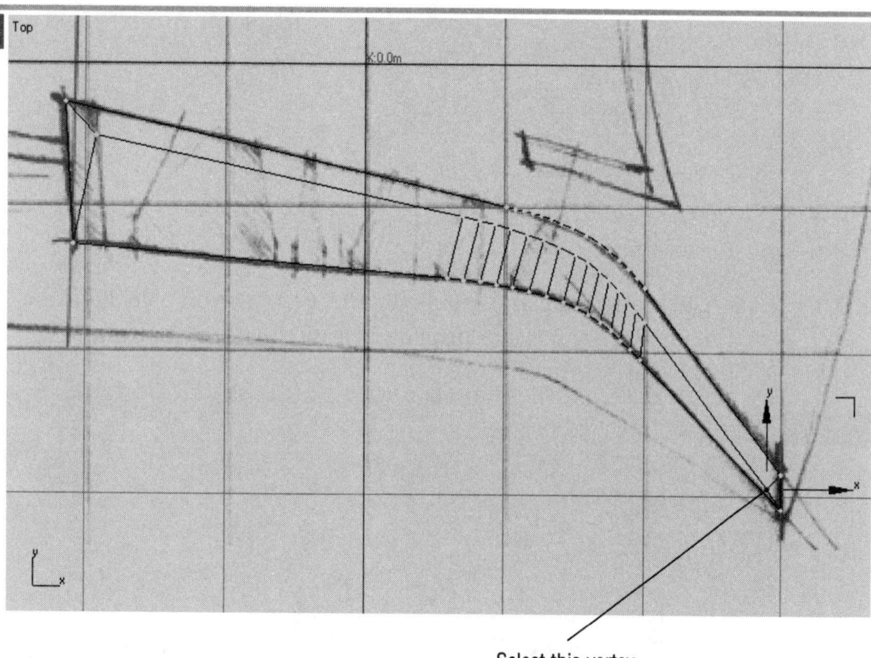

You've got the vertex selected and are ready to move it into position. Before you do, you'll want to adjust a few settings to make sure you get the results you want.

Now you're ready to move the vertex. To get a perfect alignment, use the Snaps.

1. Right-click the Snap tool at the bottom of the VIZ window.
2. In the Grid and Snap Settings dialog box, click the Clear All button, then click Endpoint.
3. Close the Grid and Snap Settings dialog box and make sure the Snap tool is on.

4. Click the Select and Move tool. Then place the cursor on the selected vertex so that the Endpoint Snap cursor displays.

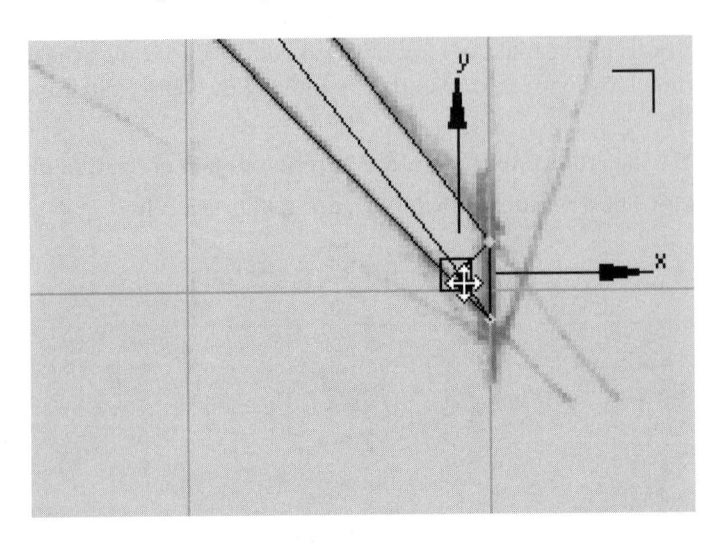

5. Click and drag the cursor to the vertex shown in Figure 4.39. When the Endpoint Snap cursor displays, release the mouse button.

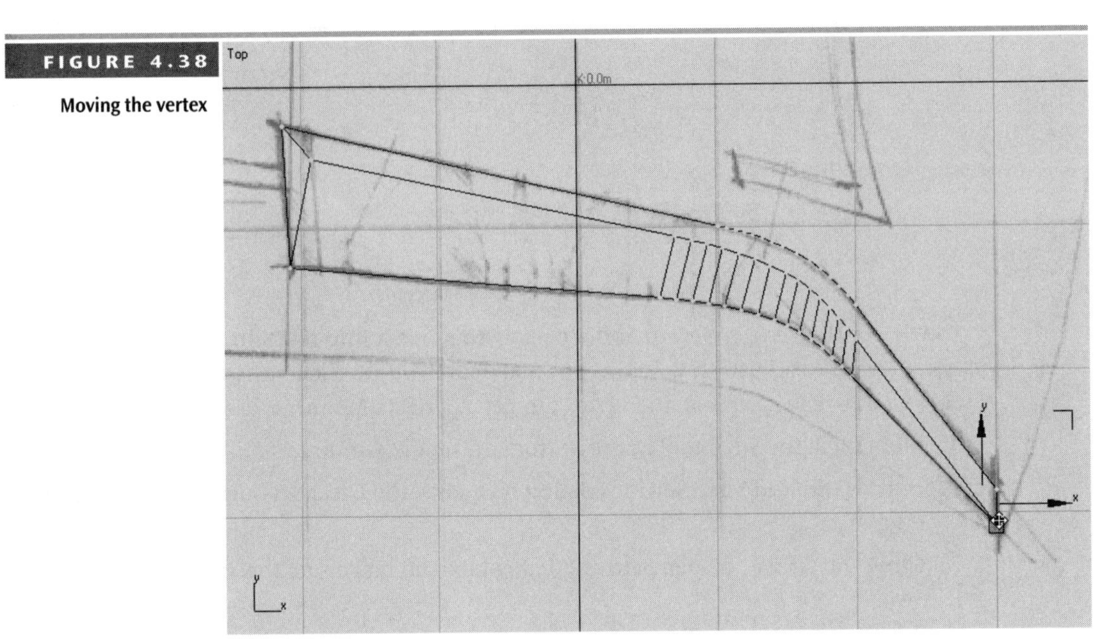

FIGURE 4.38

Moving the vertex

6. Click the Min/Max Toggle tool to get a look at the results in the Perspective viewport.

Now you've got the east end of the wall back to its original configuration. You can move on to editing the interior side of the wall.

Using Constraints

In the last exercise, you were able to move a vertex to a point exactly above another vertex by using the Endpoint Snap. You might have thought the two vertices would merge into one point. Instead, the vertex you moved was constrained to its Z axis location, and it remained above the vertex you snapped to.

VIZ automatically constrains the movement of objects to the plane of the current view. In the case of the last exercise, you were moving the vertex in the top viewport so the vertex's movement was restrained to the plane of the top view. Had you been in the Left or Front view, the movement of the vertex would have been restrained in the plane defined by those views.

You may find that you need to temporarily free yourself from the constraints of a viewport and use some other criteria to constrain the movement of an object. You can do so by using the Constraints toolbar. You can open the Constraints toolbar by right-clicking the blank portion of any toolbar and then selecting the Constraints option from the pop-up menu. Another option is to right-click during the transform operation and select Transform to get a constraint option from a cascading menu.

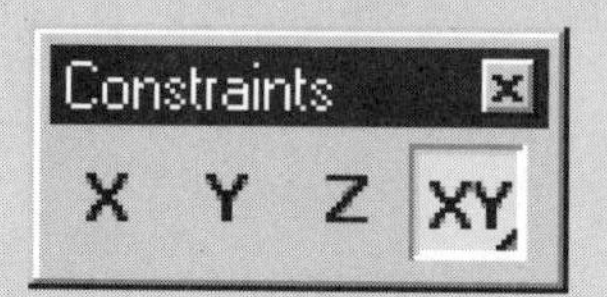

By selecting the options in the Constraints toolbar, you can limit motion to the X, Y, or Z axis, or you can use the XY flyout to restrain motion in one of three planes: the XY, YZ, or ZX planes.

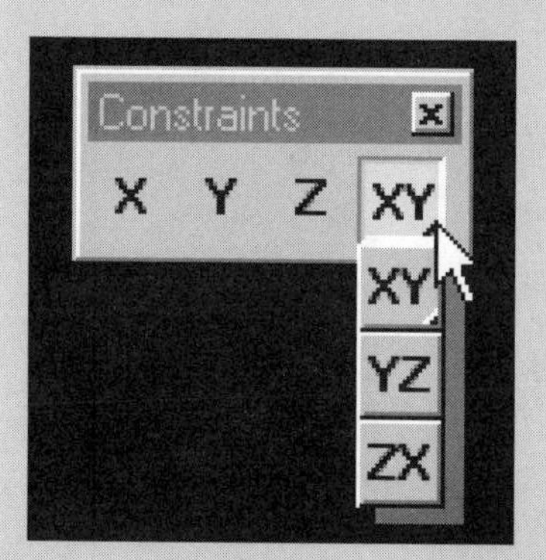

These constraint tools are particularly useful if you're editing in the Perspective viewport or in a User viewport that shows an isometric view.

Flattening a Surface

The interior side of the wall also tapers inward toward the top, but that taper only occurs along the straight portion of the wall, starting from the curve and progressing to the left. In this situation, you need to move only the vertex at the end of the wall corner.

1. Click in the Left viewport, then click the Zoom Extents tool. You'll use this view to help adjust the taper of the wall.
2. Right-click in the Perspective view, then use the Select object tool to select the two vertices on the top left corner of the wall, as shown in Figure 4.40. You can use the Rectangular Selection Region setting to select the vertices with a rectangular window.

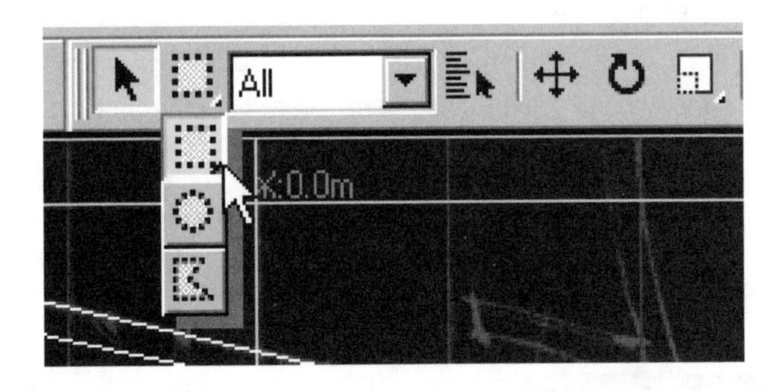

FIGURE 4.40

Select these verticies with a rectangular selection.

Selecting the corner vertex

3. Right-click the Left viewport, turn off Snap, and then with the Select and Move tool selected, click and drag the green X axis to the right. Adjust the wall so that is looks similar to Figure 4.41.

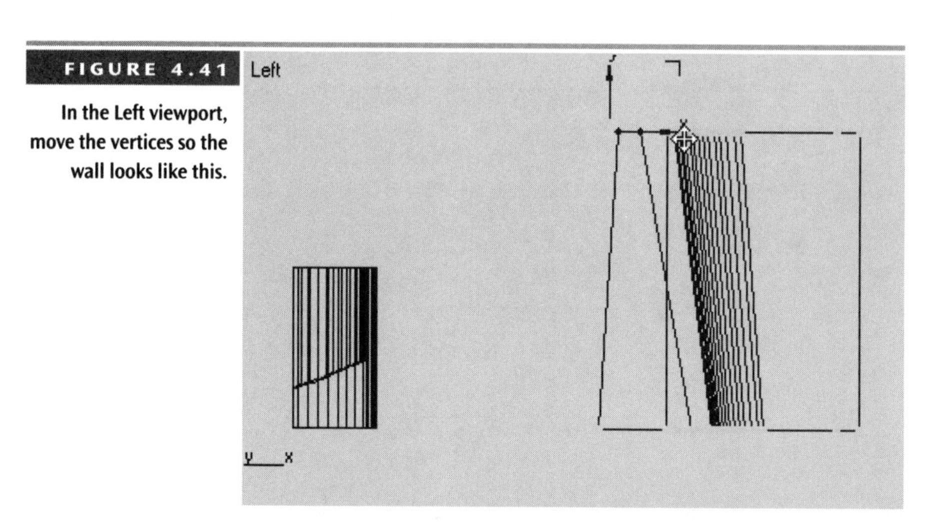

FIGURE 4.41

In the Left viewport, move the vertices so the wall looks like this.

Now you've got both sides of the wall tapering inward. There's one problem with the wall now. The west end to the left of the wall is twisted and not flat, because of all of the changes you've made to the vertices. You can quickly flatten that end of the wall using the View Align button.

1. Click the Select object tool, then, in the top viewport, click and drag a selection region so that all of the vertices of the left end of the wall are selected, as shown in Figure 4.42.

FIGURE 4.42

Selecting the vertices of the left side of the wall

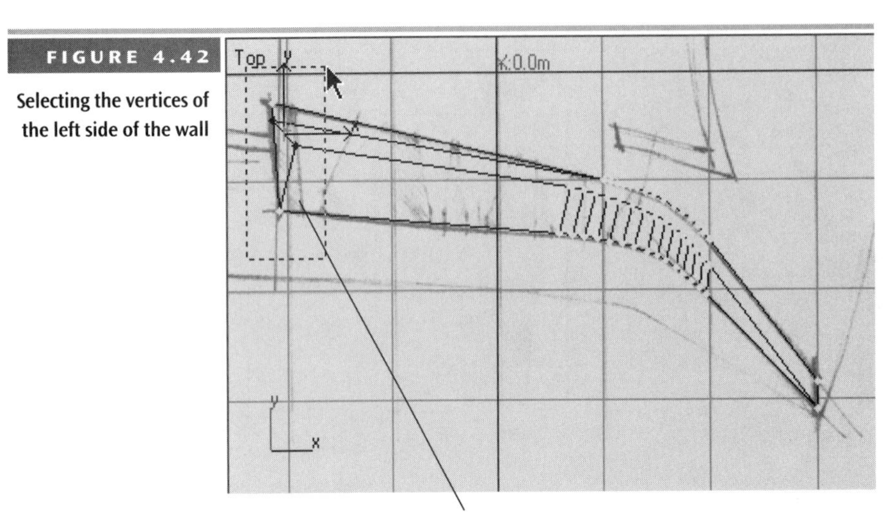

2. Right-click in the Left viewport to make it active.
3. Scroll down the Command Panel until you see the View Align button, and click it.

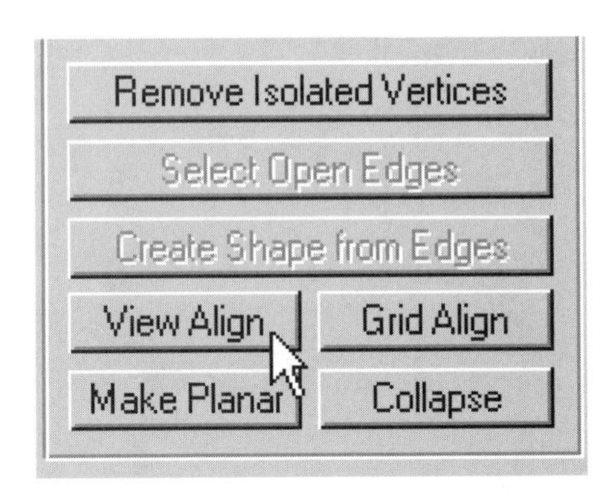

The selected vertices are aligned to the left viewport, forming a flat plane.

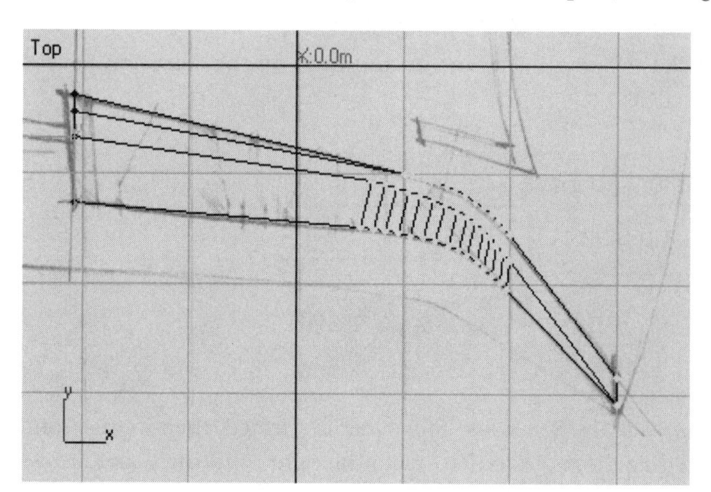

The align tool *flattened* the left side of the wall so that it became a plane parallel to the active viewport, which in this case was the Left view.

You might have noticed a few other buttons in the group with the View Align button. Grid Align will align the points to the current active user grid or to the nearest grid line in the World Grid. Make Planar will cause all of the selected points to be coplanar, taking the average location of all of the points to determine the plane. Collapse will cause all the selected points to converge into a single point.

Tapering the Top of the Wall

To finish off the wall, you'll need to slope the top of the wall downward from right to left. This will be a uniform slope so you can use the Taper modifier for this operation.

1. Right-click the Front viewport, then click the Zoom Extents tool to get a better view of the wall.
2. Click the Sub-Object button to deactivate it. Then click the More button in the Modify tab of the Command Panel.
2. Click Taper in the Modifiers dialog box, then click OK.
3. In the Parameters rollout, set the Amount input box value to **0.09**. This is roughly equivalent to 8 degrees.
4. In the Taper Axis group of the Parameters rollout, click the X Primary radio button and the Z Effect radio button. This causes the taper to occur only in the X axis.

The Taper occurs from roughly the midpoint of the wall, which causes the left side to drop and the right side to rise like a balance scale. But you want to maintain the height of the wall at its highest point instead of having it rise. You can adjust the center of the taper by moving the Xform gizmo.

1. Click the Sub-Object button, and then, in the Selection Level drop-down list, select Center.

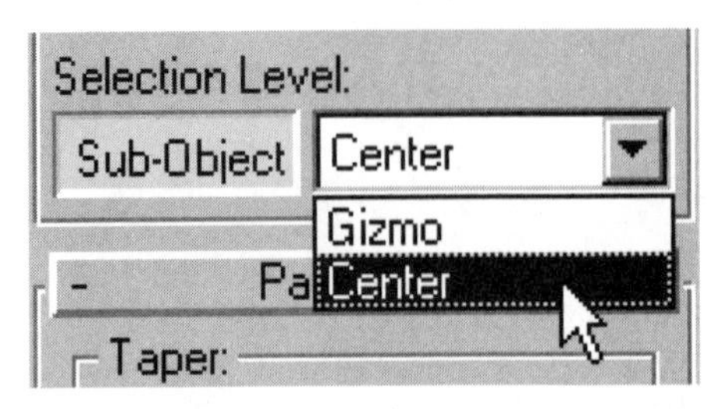

2. Make sure the Select and Move tool is selected, then in the Front viewport, click and drag the red X axis arrow to the right until the Y axis arrow is aligned with the right edge of the wall.

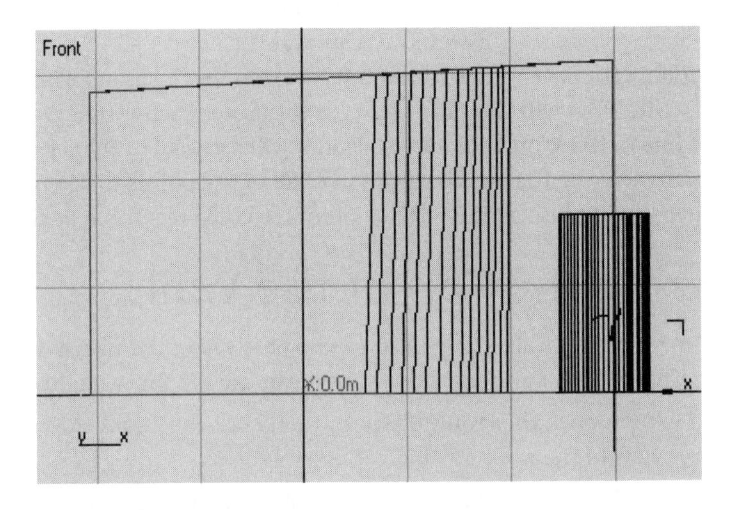

Notice that the wall drops down in height. If you play with the Amount parameter spinner, you'll see that the top of the wall now changes its taper angle in relation to the right end of the wall. Make sure that you set the Amount value back to **0.09**.

The wall is also tapered to the north, so you'll want to apply the Taper Modifier again.

1. Click the More button in the Modify tab of the Command Panel, click the Taper option in the Modifier dialog box again, and click OK.
2. In the Parameters rollout, set the Taper Amount input box value to **−0.1** (minus **zero** point one). This is equivalent to roughly 10 degrees.

3. In the Taper Axis group of the Parameters rollout, click the Y Primary radio button and the Z Effect radio button. This causes the taper to occur only in the Y axis.

You now have an editable mesh to which you've applied two Taper modifiers. You could convert the wall to an editable mesh again, thereby combining the effects of the Taper modifiers into a single editable mesh. But later you'll need to make further adjustments to the taper of the wall to fit the roof, so for now, you'll keep the modifiers in place.

Now you've completed the main shape of the south wall. Next to the roof, the south wall is the most complex part of the building, so it took quite a bit of effort to construct. In the next set of exercises, you'll create the towers of the chapel. These towers are a bit easier to build, but they are also a bit tricky.

Using the Edit Mesh Modifier

In the beginning of this section, you converted an extruded spline into an editable mesh. You could have used the Edit Mesh modifier to gain access to the same mesh sub-object level you used to edit the south wall. The advantage to using the modifier is that you can return to the spline level in the Modifier Stack to make changes at that level. The disadvantage is that your model uses more memory to store the Edit Mesh modifier. The Edit Mesh modifier also inserts more complexity into the object data flow, which can cause unpredictable results as your model becomes more complex.

The Edit Mesh modifier is a great option while you're in the process of creating an object and you aren't quite sure you want to commit to a particular set of changes. It allows you to return to other levels of the Modifier Stack and experiment. It also helps to maintain the parametric characteristics of objects so that you have more flexibility in shaping an object. But once you've created an object you are happy with, it's a good idea to convert objects to editable meshes for the sake of data flow simplicity and efficient memory use.

Using Instance Clones to Create Symmetric Forms

The towers of Ronchamp actually enclose smaller *mini* altars apart from the main altar at the east end of the building. The towers' forms reflect the shape of a nun's hat. To create the towers, you'll create half of the tower plan, then mirror that half to complete the rest of the plan. This will ensure that the walls are symmetrical, and it will also give you the parts you need to construct the top of the tower.

Adding a User Grid to Aid Tracing

First, set up the top view to trace the plan of the tower. As the tower is slightly skewed from the axis of the main floor, adding a user grid will help in creating it.

1. Click the Top viewport to make it active, then click the Min/Max toggle to enlarge it.
2. Click the Pan tool in the Viewport toolbar and pan the view so that the large tower plan is centered in the viewport, as shown in Figure 4.43.
3. Click the Zoom Region tool and place the Zoom Region window around the tower plan, as shown in Figure 4.43.

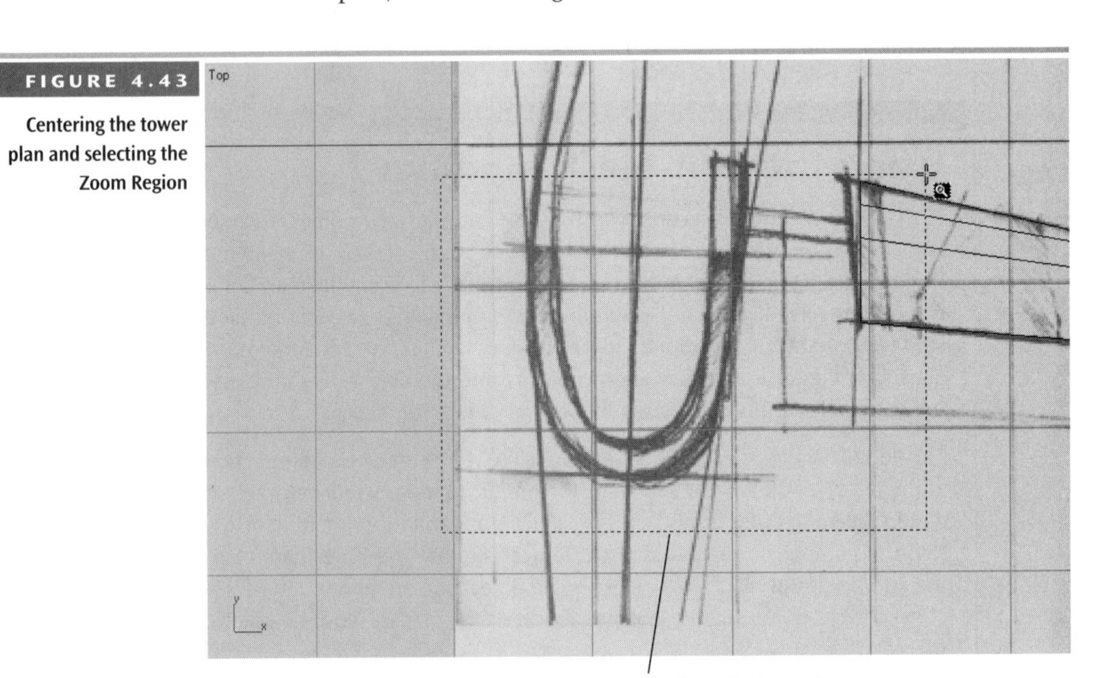

FIGURE 4.43 Centering the tower plan and selecting the Zoom Region

4. Click the Create tab in the Command Panel, and click the Helpers button.

5. Click Grid, then click and drag a grid across the viewport, as shown in Figure 4.44. As you're aligning the grid, place its vertical centerline at the center of the plan, as indicated in Figure 4.44.

FIGURE 4.44

Adding a grid to the viewport

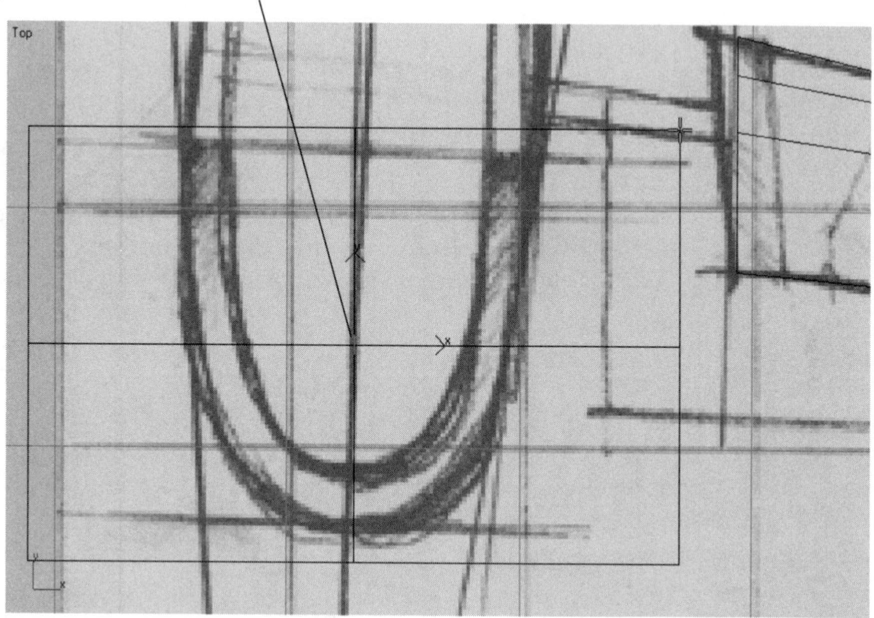
Place the grid so it is centered on this point.
Top

6. The grid is a bit too dense. To adjust its spacing, go to the Spacing group in the Parameters rollout and change its value to **2**, representing 2 meters.

7. To align the grid with the tower, click the select and rotate tool in the standard toolbar and then carefully click and drag the Z axis arrow upward so that it is aligned with the lines indicating the top edge of the tower (see Figure 4.45). As the angle is very slight, you just need to rotate the grid slightly.

FIGURE 4.45

Aligning the grid with the tower plan

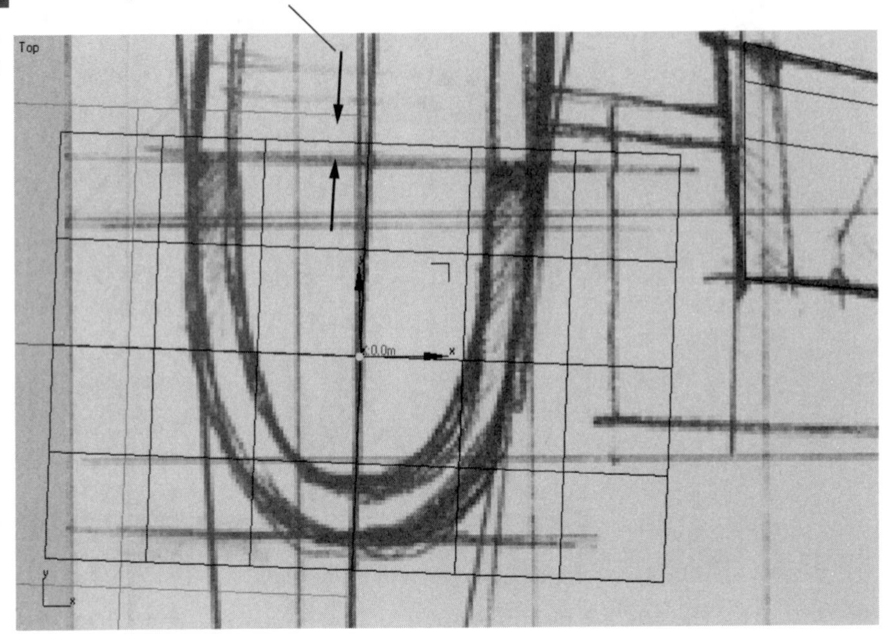
Rotate the grid so that it is aligned with this line in the sketch.
Top

Building the Tower Walls

Now you're ready to lay out the tower. Start by tracing the left side of the tower plan.

1. Click the Shapes button in the Create tab of the Command Panel.
2. Click the Line tool in the Object Type rollout.

3. Draw the lines shown in Figure 4.46, starting from the upper left corner of the plan. Finish the line at the centerline of the grid. Right-click the mouse when you're finished drawing the lines.

FIGURE 4.46

Drawing the left half of the tower plan. The vertices are shown for clarity.

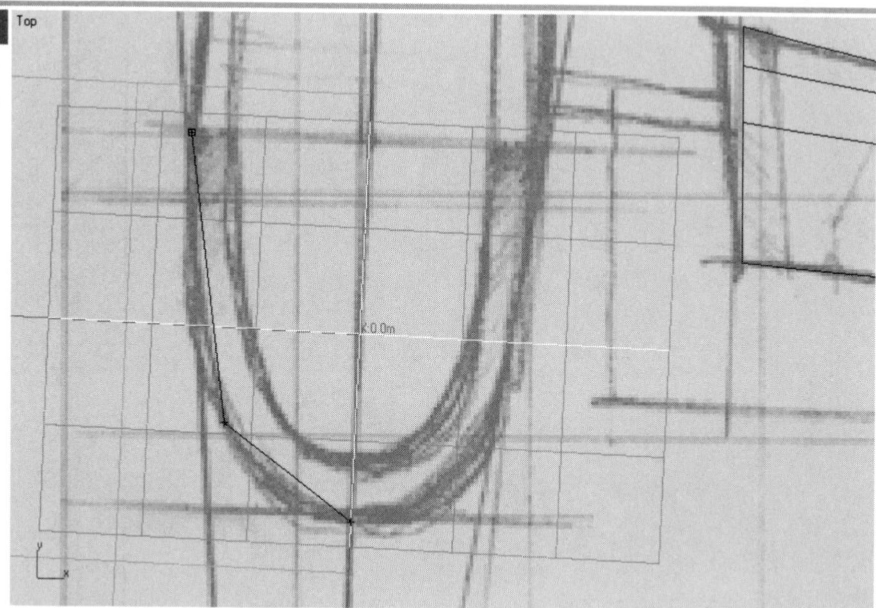

4. Click the Modify tab in the Command Panel and click the Vertex tool.

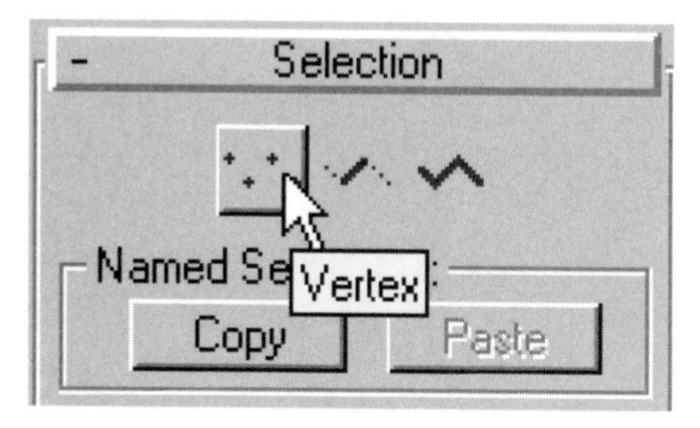

5. Right-click the last vertex in the lower half of the viewport and select Bézier from the pop-up list.

6. Click the Select and Move tool and adjust the Bézier handle of the selected vertex to the location shown in Figure 4.47.

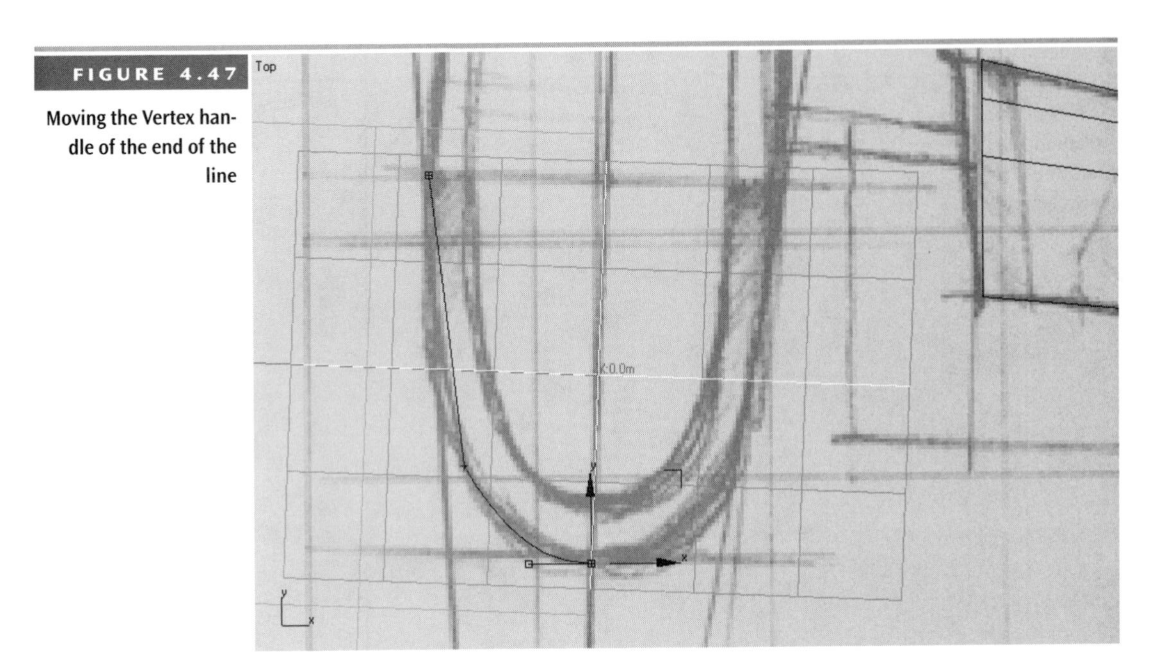

FIGURE 4.47

Moving the Vertex handle of the end of the line

7. Right-click the middle vertex, choose Bézier from the list, and adjust the handles so that the line looks similar to Figure 4.48.

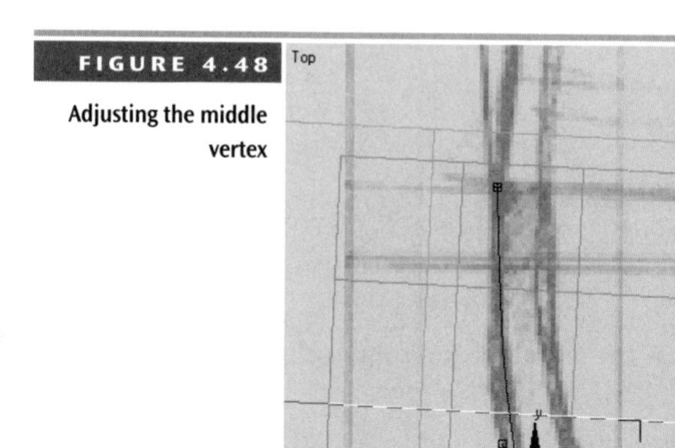

FIGURE 4.48

Adjusting the middle vertex

8. To add thickness to the wall, click the Spline tool in the Selection rollout and scroll down the Command Panel to find the Outline button.

9. Click the Outline input box and enter **0.5**↵. The line becomes a wall with a thickness of 0.5 meters.

The next step is to mirror the wall you just created. You'll want to use the Y axis of the user grid you set up earlier as the mirror axis. You do this by selecting Grid from the Reference Coordinate System drop-down list on the Standard toolbar.

1. Scroll back up to the Modifier Stack rollout in the Command Panel and click the Sub-Object button to deactivate it.

2. Click the Reference Coordinate System drop-down list to view its options.

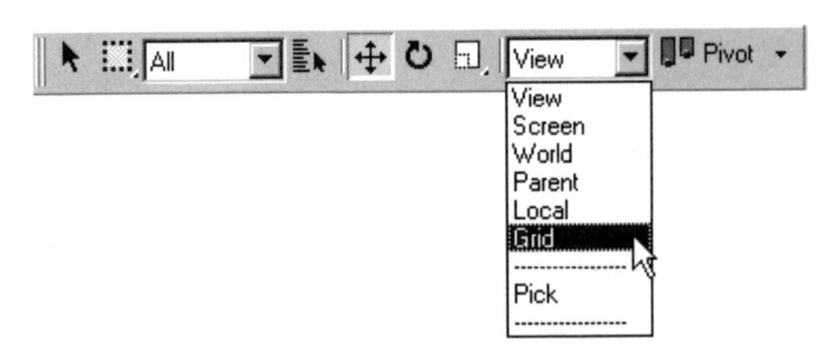

3. Select Grid from the list. Notice that the Xform gizmo rotates slightly to match the user grid orientation.
4. Click the Mirror tool in the Modify toolbar.

5. In the Mirror: Grid Coordinates dialog box, click the Y radio button in the Mirror Axis group.

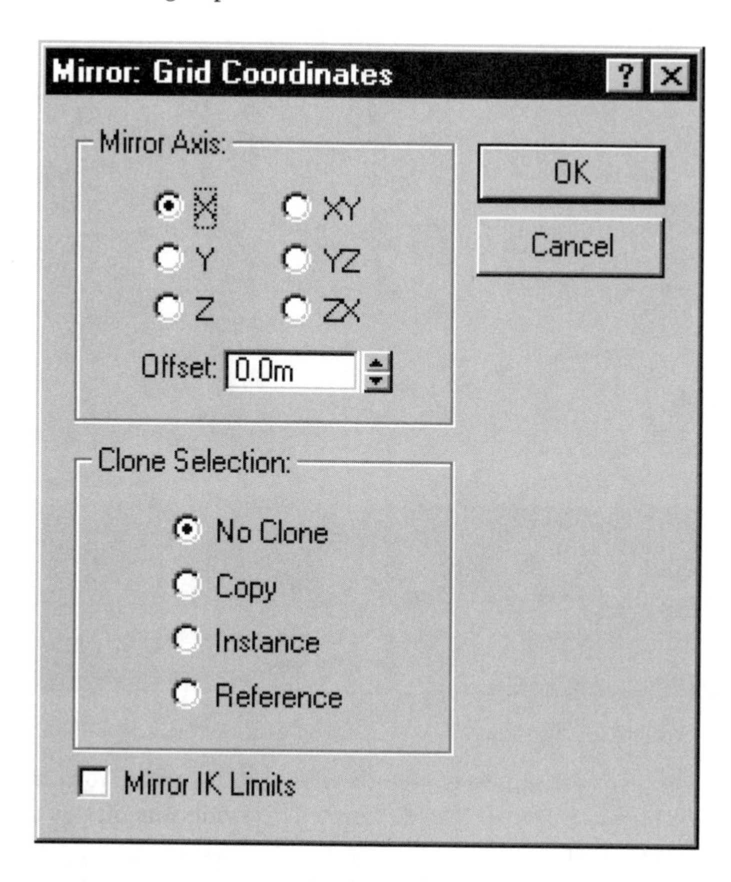

6. Click the Reference radio button in the Clone Selection group and click OK. You see a mirrored copy of the wall you just drew.
7. Click the Select and Move tool and click the Snap button at the bottom of the VIZ window. Remember that the last time you set the Snap settings, you set them to endpoint.

8. Using the Endpoint snap, click and drag the bottom endpoint of the wall half you just created to the bottom endpoint of the original wall so that they meet end to end, as shown in Figure 4.49.

FIGURE 4.49

Moving the second half of the wall into place

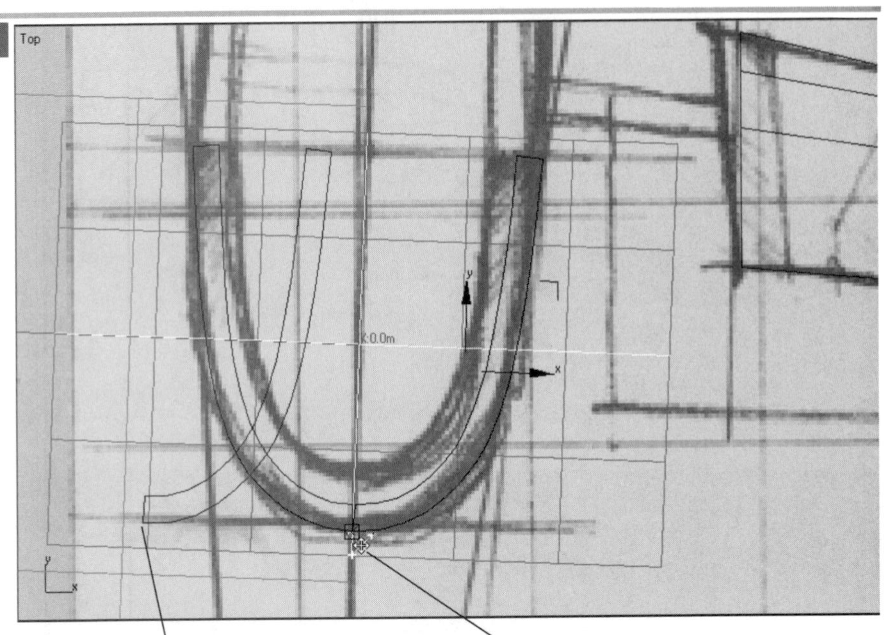
Top
Move the copy from here...
Move the copy from here...

The plan of the tower is a bit too wide at the opening. You can adjust one side of the plan, and as the two halves are references, adjustments you make to one side will affect the other side.

1. Turn off Snap. Then select the left half of the tower plan.

2. Click Vertex in the Selection rollout of the Command Panel. Then use a Rectangular Selection Region and select the two wall corner vertices at the top of wall, as shown in Figure 4.50.

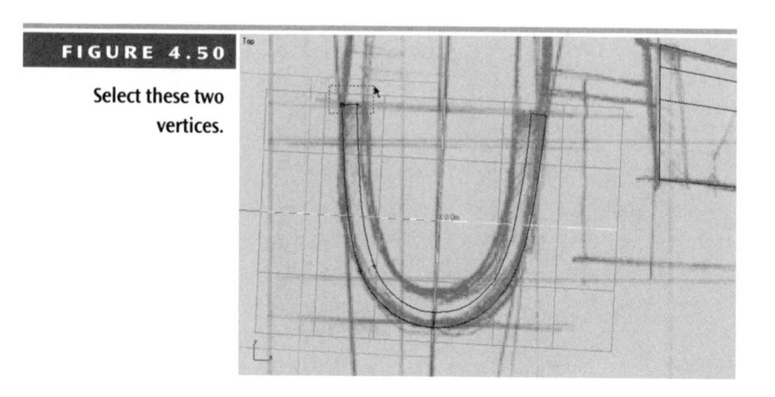

FIGURE 4.50

Select these two vertices.

3. Select Grid from the Reference Coordinate System drop-down list.

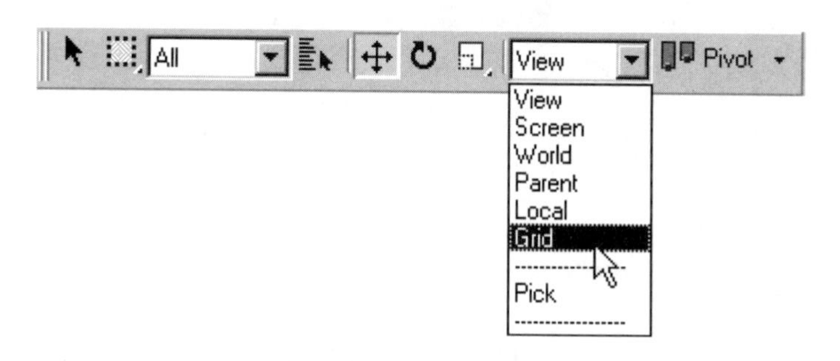

4. Click and drag the red X axis arrow to the left a slight amount so that the walls look similar to Figure 4.51.

FIGURE 4.51

Moving the ends of the tower wall inward

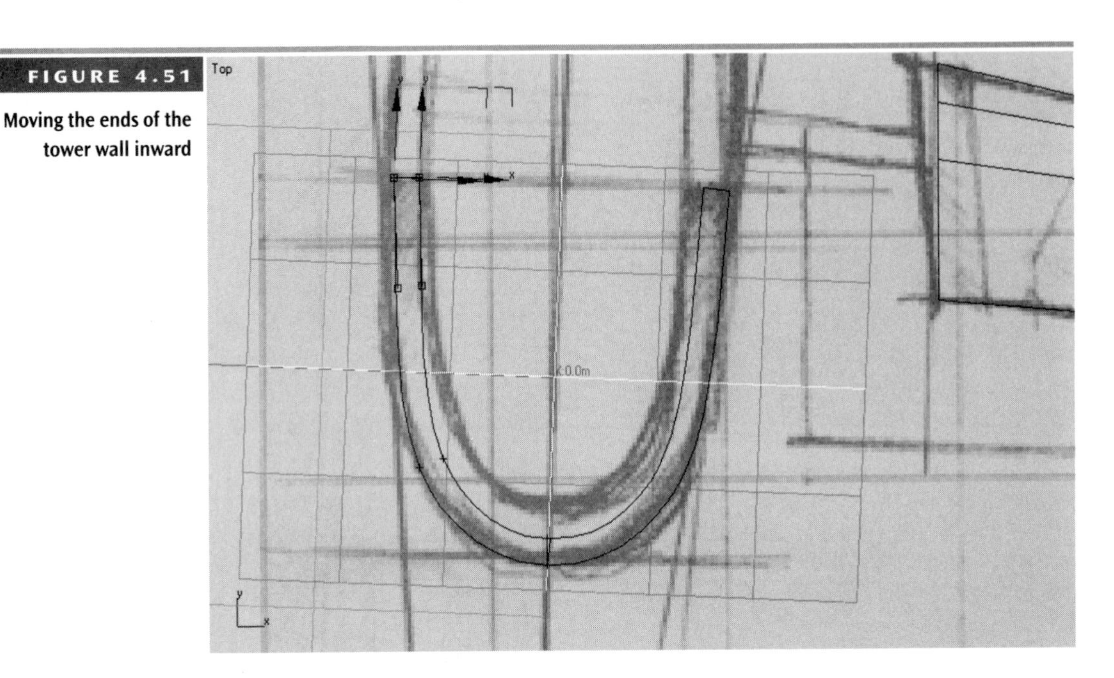

Because they are reference clones, both ends of the wall move in unison toward the centerline of the tower plan.

Adding the Vaulted Ceiling

You'll need another copy of the wall half to use later to cap the tower. This copy will be extruded using the Lathe modifier to form the vaulted ceiling of the tower.

1. Click the Sub-Object button to deactivate it. Then, using the Select and Move tool, Shift-click and drag the right half of the tower plan to the right.
2. In the Clone Options dialog box, click Copy. Then enter the name "Vault" into the Name input box and click OK.

Now you're ready to extrude the plan into a tower. The overall height of the tower is 22 meters. Subtract 2 meters for the vaulted ceiling for a height of 20 meters for the straight portion of the tower.

1. Click the Min/Max Toggle tool in the Viewport toolbar.
2. Click the Select Object tool in the Standard toolbar, and click the left half of the tower plan.

3. Click Extrude in the Modifiers rollout of the Command Panel.
4. In the Amount input box of the Parameters rollout, change the value to **20m**.
5. Click the Perspective viewport and click the Zoom Extents tool to get a better view of your model.

To finish off the basic shape of the tower, you need the vaulted ceiling.

1. In the Top viewport, select the right-most copy of the tower plan outline.
2. Click Lathe in the Modifier rollout of the Command Panel.
3. Change the Degrees value in the Parameters rollout to **180**. The ceiling won't look quite right, but in the next step, you'll fix things.
4. Click the Sub-Object button in the Modifier Stack and then use the Select and Move tool to click and drag the red X axis arrow to the left until the shape of the vault appears to be about the same width as the extruded tower plan (see Figure 4.52).

FIGURE 4.52

Using Lathe to form the ceiling

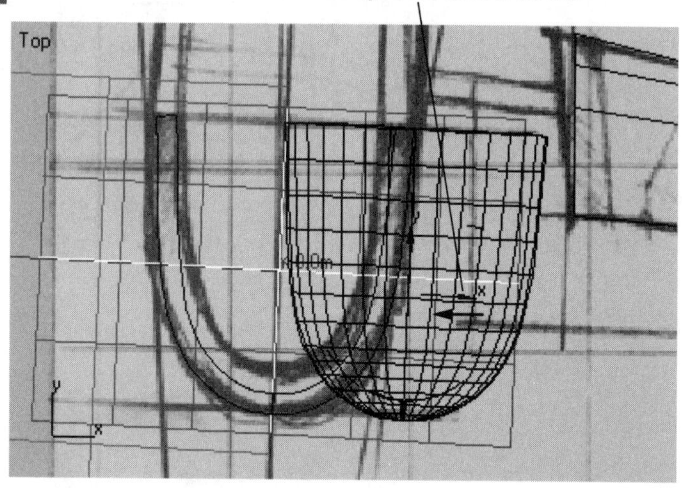
Click and drag the red arrow to the left.
Top

Next you'll move the vaulted ceiling into position and adjust its width to fit exactly over the vertical walls of the tower.

1. Click the Sub-Object button to deactivate it. You don't want the next operation to operate on a sub-object level so turn off this option.
2. Right-click the Select and Move tool to open the Move Transform Type-In dialog box.
3. In the Absolute: World group, change the Z input box to **20** to raise the vault to 20 meters, then close the dialog box.

The Vaulted ceiling is in its proper Z axis location. Now you need to place the ceiling exactly over the vertical wall.

1. Right-click the Top Viewport and click the Min/Max Toggle to enlarge it. This will help you move the ceiling more accurately.
2. Click the Snap tool to activate it, then place the cursor on the upper right-most corner of the vaulted ceiling, as shown in Figure 4.53.
3. When you see the endpoint cursor, click and drag the mouse to the upper right corner of the wall, as shown in Figure 4.53.

FIGURE 4.53

Moving the vaulted ceiling into place above the vertical wall

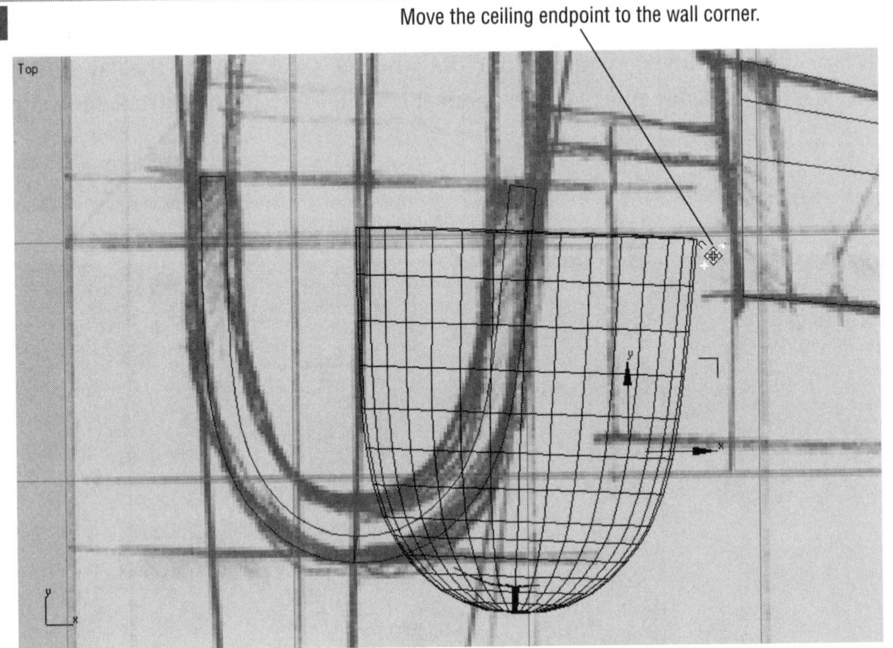
Move the ceiling endpoint to the wall corner.
Top

Now adjust the ceiling width so that it fits precisely over the vertical wall.

1. Turn off Snap.
2. Click the Sub-Object button in the Command Panel, then click and drag the red X axis arrow to adjust the width of the vault so that it fits exactly over the wall on the left side of the vault (see Figure 4.54).

FIGURE 4.54

Adjusting the width of the vaulted ceiling to fit the wall

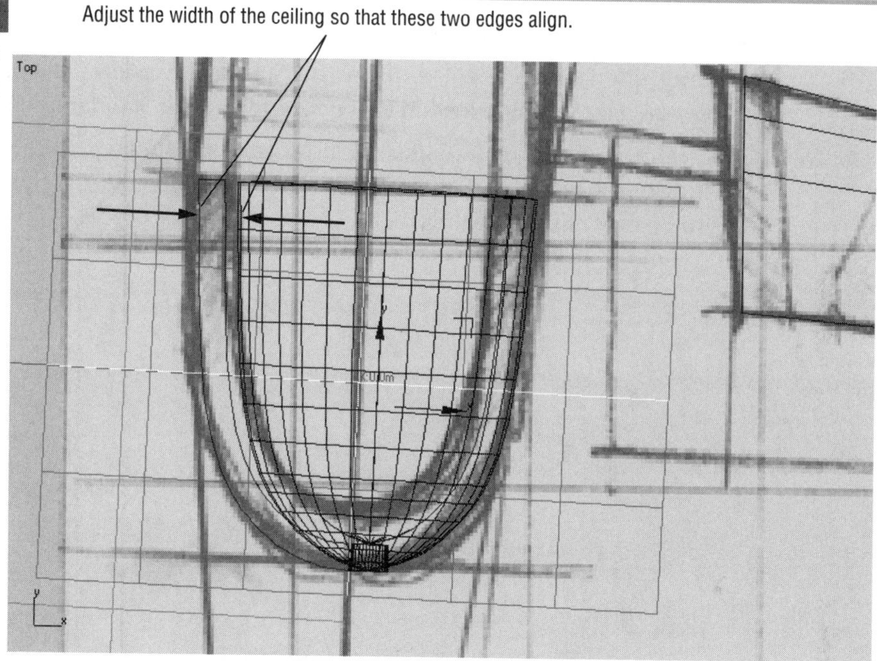
Adjust the width of the ceiling so that these two edges align.
Top

3. Click the Min/Max Toggle to view the other viewports.
4. Delete the User Grid you created earlier. You won't be needing it anymore.

Creating the Smaller Towers

You've got one tower completed. There are two smaller towers of a similar configuration. You can make a copy of the large tower you just created and then edit the copy to create the smaller tower. First, copy the tower and move the copy into its new location at the north side of the building.

1. Click the Top viewport and click the Min/Max tool to enlarge it.
2. Click the Zoom Extents tool to get an overall view of the plan so far.
3. Click the Select Object tool on the Standard toolbar, and make sure the Rectangular Selection Region tool is selected on the Standard toolbar.
4. Click and drag a rectangular window around the tower you just created, as shown in Figure 4.55. This will select all three components of the tower: the two wall halves and the ceiling.

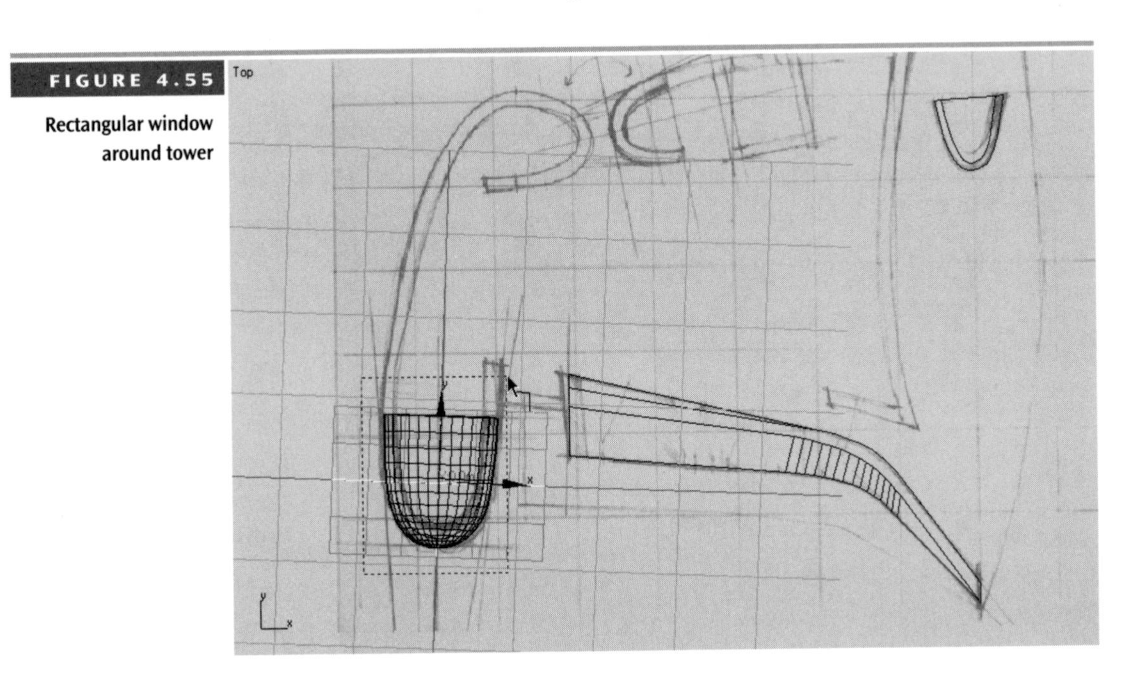

FIGURE 4.55

Rectangular window around tower

5. Click the Select and Move tool, then shift-click and drag the tower to the location of the smaller tower, as shown in Figure 4.56.

FIGURE 4.56

Moving the tower copy to a new location

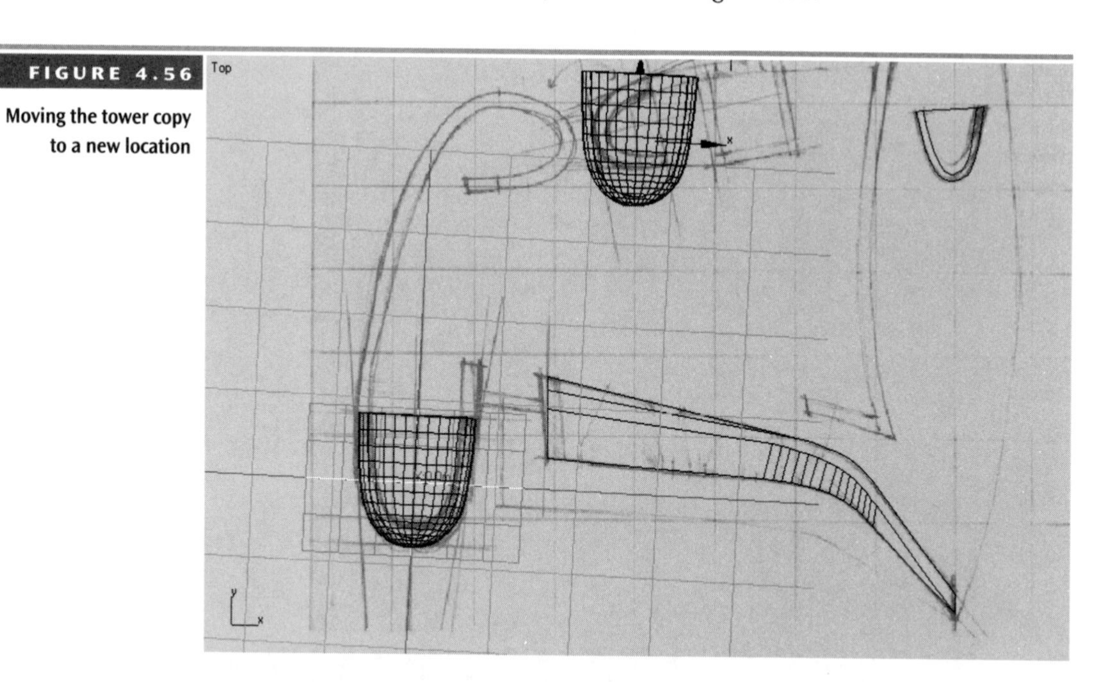

6. At the Clone Options dialog box, click Copy and click OK.

The copy is a bit too large and it is oriented in the wrong direction. You'll need to rotate the tower copy, then scale it down.

1. Pan the view so that the tower copy is centered in the viewport, and use the Region Zoom tool to enlarge the view of the tower as shown in Figure 4.57.

FIGURE 4.57

Centering the tower copy in the viewport and selecting a region to enlarge

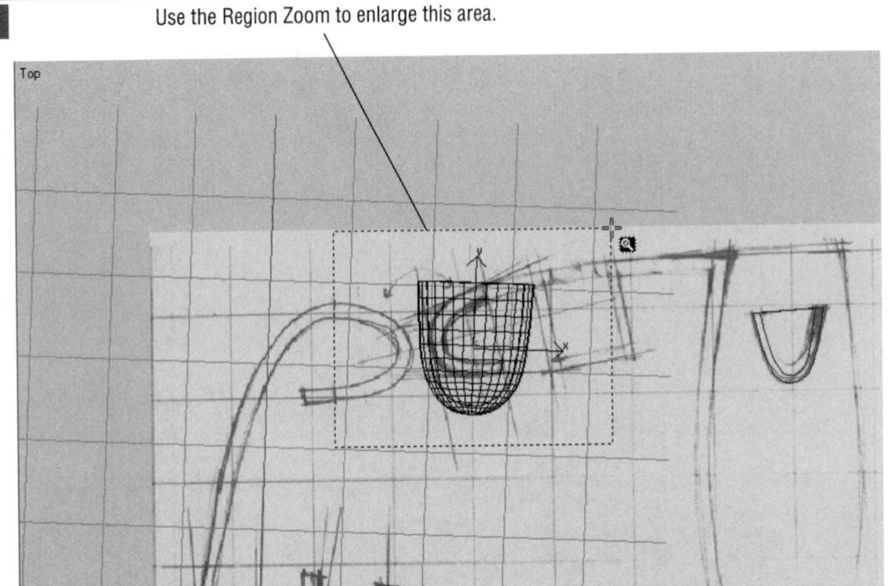

2. Click the Rotate tool, and then click and drag the blue Z axis upward until the tower is aligned with the image of the smaller tower in the imported bitmap sketch. You can use the centerline in the sketch to help you align the tower.
3. Use the Select and Move tool to center the tower over the sketch.
4. Click the Scale tool and click and drag the tower downward until it is about the same width as the sketch of the smaller tower (see Figure 4.58).

5. Recenter the tower using the Select and Move tool. Use the Select and Scale tool to refine the size of the tower until it fits over the sketch in a way similar to Figure 4.58.

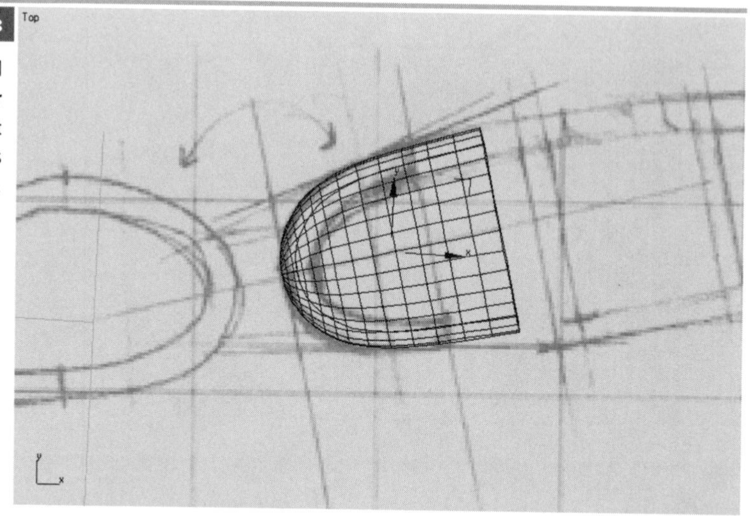

FIGURE 4.58

Fine-tune the size and location of the tower over the sketch so that it looks similar to this figure.

You may also need to play with the rotation of the tower to get the tower in the correct orientation. You don't need to be too fussy about the tower, however. Just use this as an opportunity to get used to the Move, Scale, and Rotate features of VIZ.

When you scaled the copy of the tower, VIZ scaled it down in all directions. This causes the tower copy to be *floating* in space. It needs to be brought back down to the ground level.

1. Click the Min/Max tool, then click the Front Viewport.
2. Make sure the entire tower copy is selected, then use the Select and Move tool to move the tower downward so that its base rests on the plane of the world coordinate system, as shown in Figure 4.59.

FIGURE 4.59

Move the tower down to ground level.

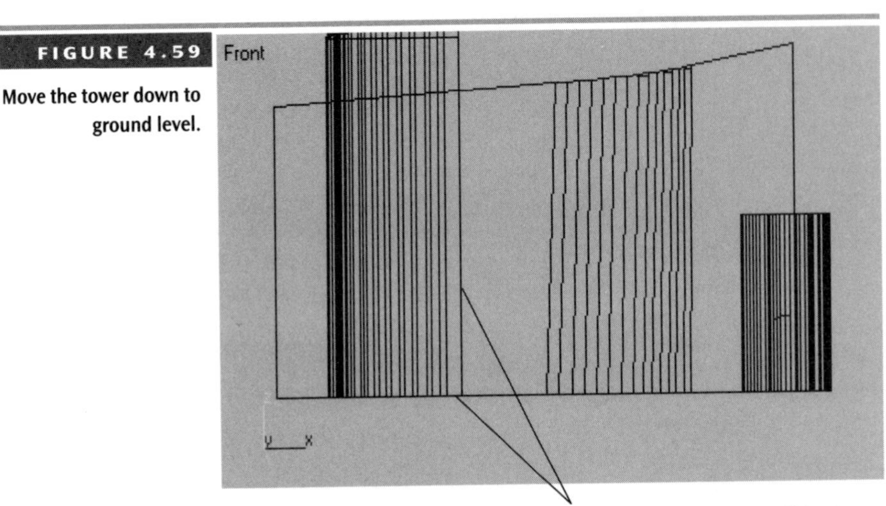
Front
y
x
Move the tower downward so its base rests on the "ground" level.

Editing the Tower Walls

You've gotten the tower in the location and orientation you like. Now you'll need to adjust the wall thickness. Because you scaled the tower down in size, the thickness of the walls was also scaled down. You'll need to set them to the same thickness as the other walls. Here's where VIZ's ability to edit at sub-object levels really helps.

1. Right-click the Top viewport and click the Min/Max Toggle tool to enlarge the Top viewport.
2. Click the Object Select tool, and click the tower ceiling. You'll be able to tell if you've selected the ceiling by the name Vault01 just below the Modify tab label.
3. Click the Display tab of the Command Panel. Then click Selected Off. You'll want to temporarily turn off the ceiling so you can see the walls more clearly.

4. Click the tower wall half, as shown in Figure 4.60.

FIGURE 4.60

Select the tower wall.

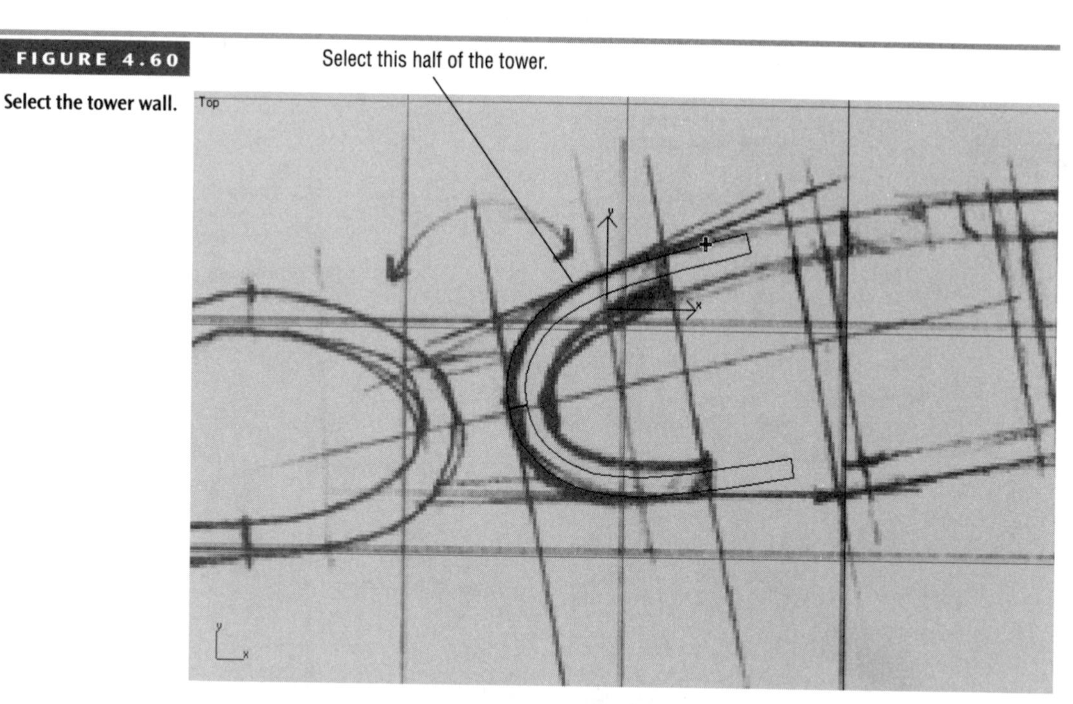

5. In the Modify Tab of the Command Panel, click the Modifier Stack drop-down list and select Line.
6. In the Selection rollout, click the Segment tool.

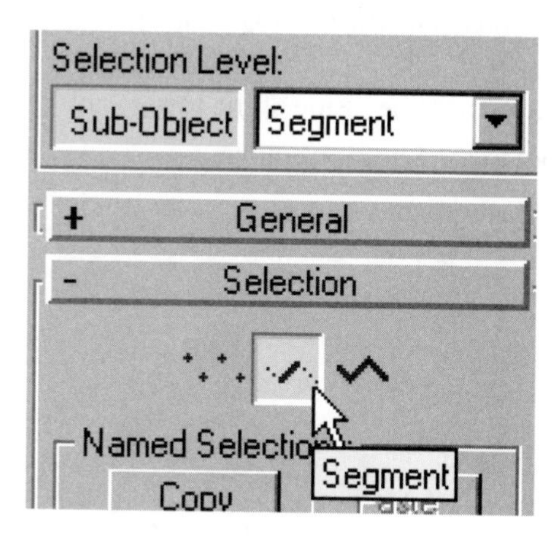

7. Click the line segment of the wall shown in Figure 4.61 and press the Delete key.
8. Continue to delete the other three segments, as shown in Figure 4.61. Do not delete any of the segments that represent the outside edge of the wall.

FIGURE 4.61

Deleting the line segments of the tower wall

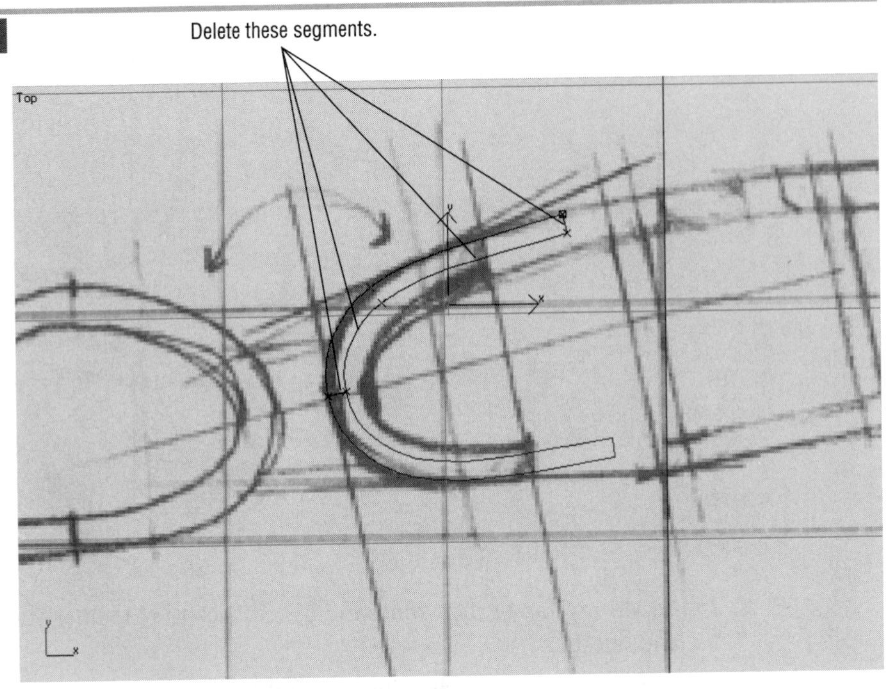
Delete these segments.
Top

You may notice that as you delete the line segments, they are also deleted in the cloned half of the wall.

Now you'll need to reconstruct the inside of the tower wall.

1. Click the Spline tool in the Selection rollout.

2. Click the remaining outline of the wall, as shown in Figure 4.62.

FIGURE 4.62

Selecting the remaining outline of the wall

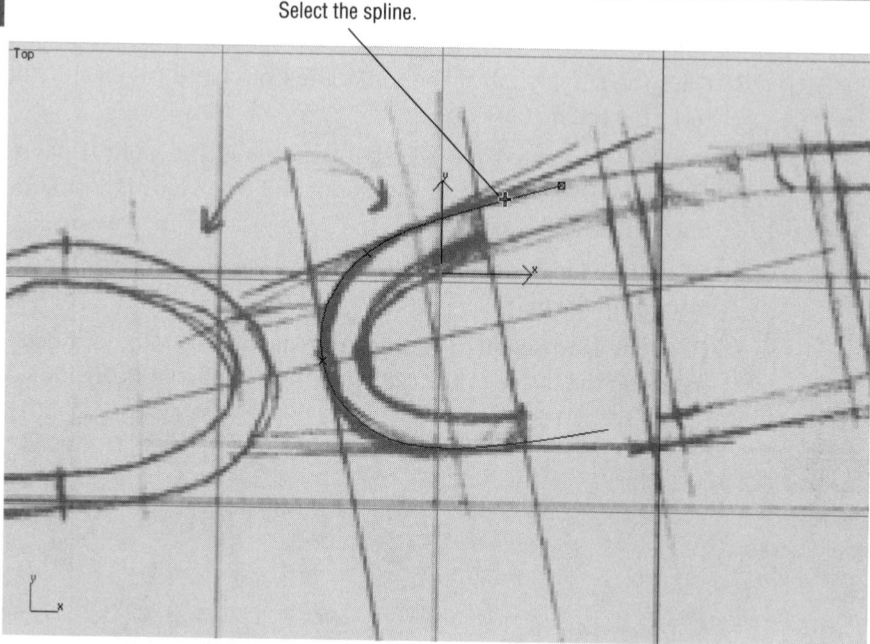

3. Scroll down the Command Panel to the Outline button, then enter **0.66↵** in the Outline Input box. The outline of the wall appears in both halves of the tower wall.

Although you only edited one half of the tower wall, the changes are reflected in the other half and in the vaulted ceiling. This shows one of the big advantages of careful use of the instance and reference clones. The cloning occurred at the spline level, so changes to the spline affect the instanced clone.

You also saw that you can edit the spline without affecting the Extrude modifier that had been applied to the spline. Here is an example that shows when it is appropriate not to immediately convert an object into an editable mesh as you did with the south wall. You are able to make changes to the tower wall thickness while still maintaining the overall shape of the tower. Later, when you're satisfied with the tower's general shape, you can convert it to an editable mesh.

The walls are now at the appropriate thickness. You need to change the ceiling in the same way. You'll use the same method to modify the ceiling as you did for the walls.

1. Scroll up the Command Panel and select Extrude from the Modifier Stack drop-down list.
2. Click the Display tab at the top of the Command Panel, and click All On. This turns the ceiling back on.
3. Use the Select object tool to select the ceiling. The Vault01 name should appear under the Display label of the Command Panel letting you know that the ceiling is indeed selected.
4. Click the Modify tab in the Command Panel, and click Line in the Modifier Stack drop-down list.
5. Click the Line Segment tool in the Selection rollout, and delete the line segments on the inside of the ceiling outline, as shown in Figure 4.63.

FIGURE 4.63

Deleting the inside lines of the ceiling

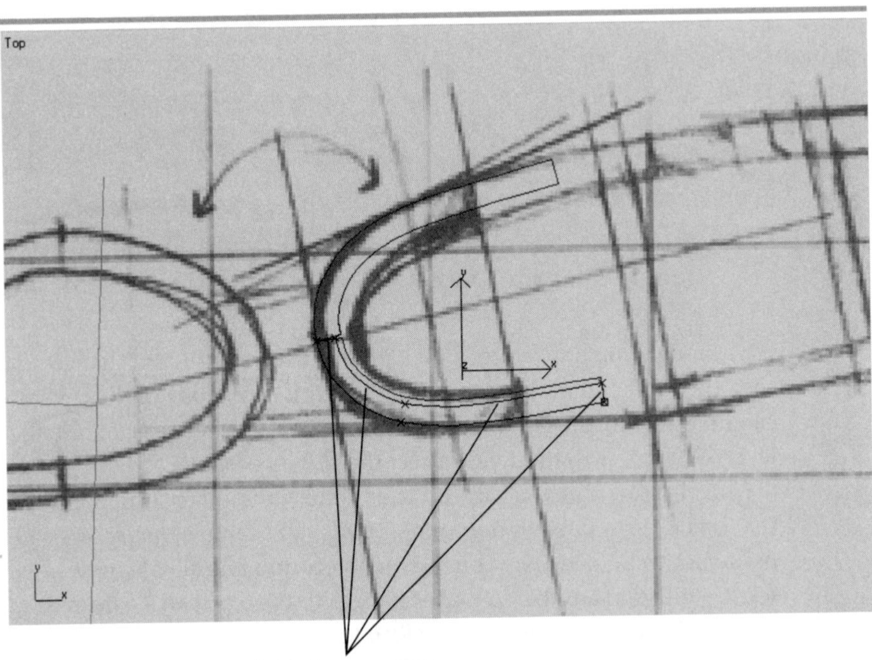
Top
Delete these segments.

6. Click the Spline tool in the Selection rollout. Then scroll down the Command Panel to the Outline button.

7. Set the Outline value to **0.66** to match the walls. You may recall that the original tower walls were 0.5 meters thick. You have to set the scaled down cloned walls to 0.66 meters because of the way VIZ works with parametric objects (see "Object Data Flow and Scaled Parametric Objects" later in this chapter).
8. Scroll back to the top of the Command Panel and select Lathe from the Modifier Stack drop-down list. The lathe portion of the ceiling is restored. Now the second tower is complete.

Once again, you were able to edit a spline without affecting the modifier that is applied to the spline.

You've got one more tower to create. This one will be easy as it is a mirror of the smaller tower you just created.

1. Use the Object Select tool and the Rectangular Selection Region to select all of the tower you just created.
2. Click the Mirror tool in the Modify toolbar.

3. At the Mirror: Screen Coordinates dialog box, make sure the X radio button is selected in the Mirror Axis group and the Instance option is selected in the Clone Selection group. Then click OK.
4. Click the Select and Move tool and move the tower copy to the left to the location of the second smaller tower, as shown in Figure 4.64.

FIGURE 4.64

Moving the second smaller tower into place

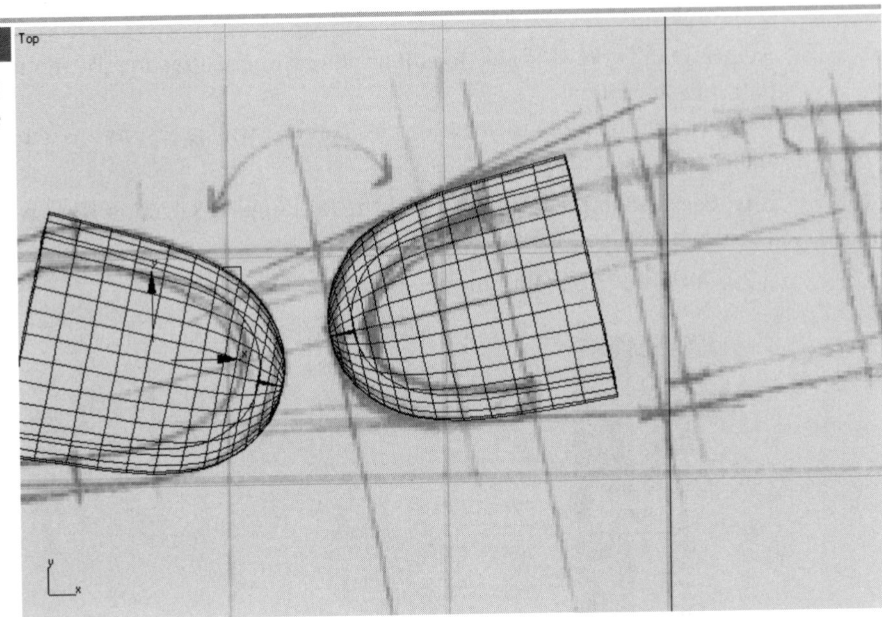

5. Click the Pan tool and pan your view to the right so that the second tower appears in the center of the screen, as shown in Figure 4.65.
6. Use the Select and Rotate tool to rotate the new tower so that it is oriented in a way similar to that shown in Figure 4.65.

FIGURE 4.65

The final location of the second smaller tower

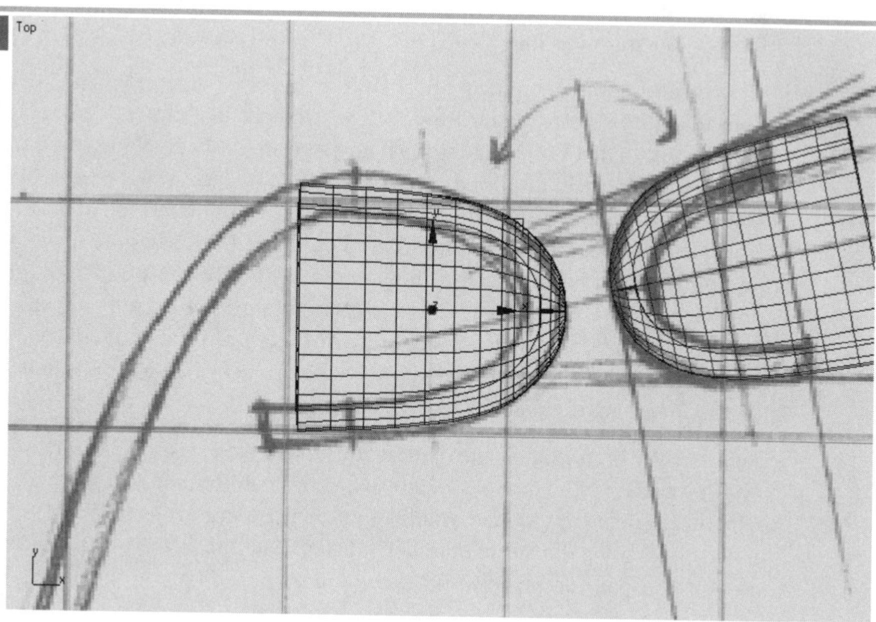

7. To see your results so far, click the Min/Max toggle.

The smaller towers could use a little more work to refine their forms, but for now, you've got the general form of towers in place.

Object Data Flow, Scaled Parametric Objects, and Editable Meshes

You may have noticed that when you edited the wall thickness for the cloned tower, you had to use an outline value that was greater than the actual thickness of the typical walls of the chapel. The original tower wall had a thickness of 0.5 meters, yet, on a sub-object level, you had to make the new tower walls 0.66 meters to make them the same width as the other walls. This is because when you scale an object, the dimensional parameters of the original spline from which the walls were extruded are not affected.

Continued on the next page

When you cloned the tower, then scaled the clone down, the width of the cloned walls remained at their original 0.5 meters at a sub-object level, even though the walls are thinner than before relative to the rest of the model. To see this more clearly, try creating a 24-inch cube. Scale the cube down to about half its size, then check it parameters in the Modify tab. You'll see that the parameters still show that it is a 24-inch cube, even though you know it is half its original size. This can cause a good deal of confusion.

The reason for this seemingly odd behavior becomes clearer when you consider the object data flow discussed in "How VIZ Sees Objects" in Chapter 2. You may recall from that discussion that VIZ evaluates the data associated with an object in a particular order before the object is displayed. The order of that data evaluation is Master Object, Modifiers, Transforms, and Properties. The object's parameters fall under Master Object, which is the first item in the object data flow while transforms are third in the evaluation order. The transforms affect the way the Master Object is displayed, but they have no affect on the Master Object's internal parameters or other data at its sub-object level. The net result of this is that when parametric objects are scaled up or down in size, their parameters remain at their original values before being scaled even though the object itself appears larger or smaller than its original size.

Another way of saying all this is that the object really exists in its own space, called object-space (space means a 3D Cartesian coordinate system with an origin and a grid). Objects are defined, sculpted, modified in object-space. Objects can be transformed in object space using the Xform modifier. Moving, Rotating, and Scaling (AKA Transforming) an object actually occurs in world-space and is applied later in the object data flow.

Continued below

TIP **Objects can be transformed in world-space to align with object-space by using the Local Reference Coordinate System.**

Another way to look at it is to consider the Master Object as having internal data that include their own unit of measure and coordinate system, called object-space. These internal data are unaffected by modifiers, transforms, and properties. The modifiers, transforms, and properties you apply to an object really only affect the object's appearance in the VIZ viewport.

This all changes when you convert an object to an editable mesh. In terms of VIZ data, an editable mesh is a more fundamental way of representing the object on a mathematical level, even though its appearance is identical to that of the original object from which it was derived. Once you convert an object to an editable mesh, the editable mesh becomes the Master Object in the data flow. This new Master Object then inherits the properties and structure of the original object while the modifiers are collapsed into the original Master Object. You can then apply more modifiers and transforms to this new Master Object and the process goes on.

Drawing the Remaining Walls

There are still a few other walls that need to be added as well as the roof. As a review of some of the earlier skills you've learned, go ahead and add the other walls, starting with the west wall on the left side of the floor plan.

1. Click the Min/Max Toggle tool to enlarge the top view again. Then click the Zoom Extents tool to view the entire Top view.
2. Use the Region Zoom tool to zoom into the area shown in Figure 4.66.
3. In the Create tab of the Command Panel, click the Shapes button if it isn't already selected, then draw the line shown in Figure 4.66.

FIGURE 4.66

Drawing the west wall, as shown here. The vertices are marked for clarity.

4. Click the Modify tab, then click the Vertex button in the selection rollout.
5. Convert all of the points on the line to Bézier curves. Adjust the Bézier handles to match as closely as possible the curve shown in Figure 4.67.

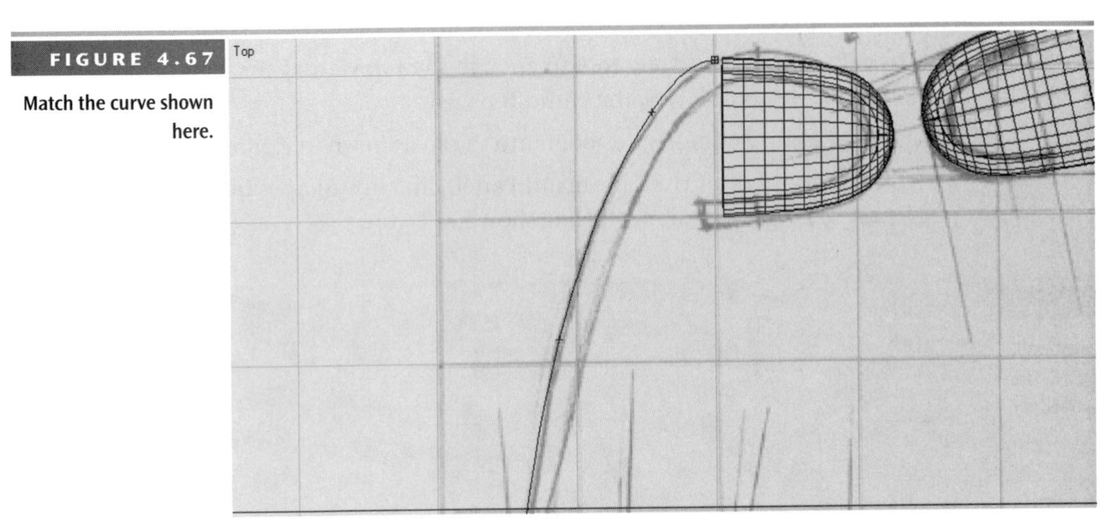

FIGURE 4.67 Match the curve shown here.

6. In the Modify Tab of the Command Panel, click the Spline tool in the Selection rollout, scroll down the panel, and then, in the Outline input box, enter **0.5**↵. The west wall will convert to a thick wall.
7. Scroll back up to the top of the Command Panel and select the Extrude button.
8. In the Amount input box of the Parameters rollout, enter **9.5**↵.

The west wall will need some editing later. For now, continue with the addition of the north wall.

1. Choose View ➢ Undo View Zoom, then zoom into the area shown in Figure 4.68.
2. Draw the line shown in Figure 4.68 and convert the vertices indicated in the figure to Bézier curves. Adjust the Bézier handles so the line follows the curve of the sketch. By now, this should be a familiar process.

FIGURE 4.68

Drawing the north wall

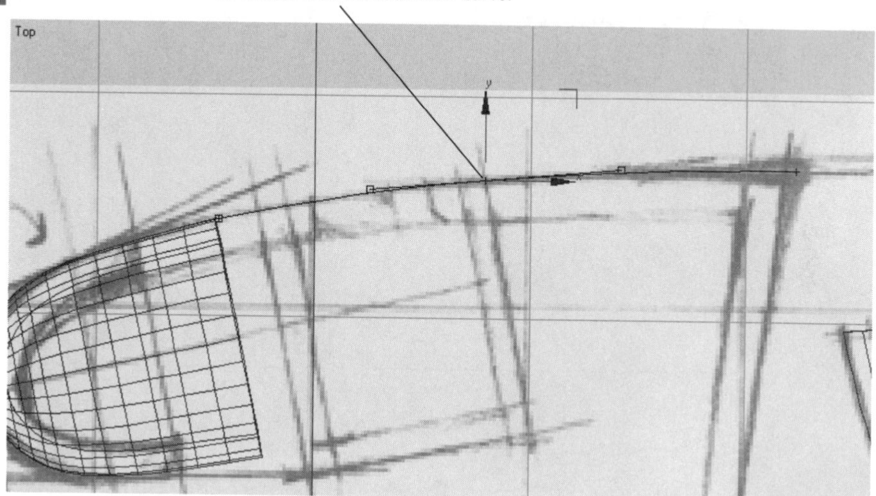
Turn the middle vertex into a Bézier curve.
Top

3. Click the Spline tool in the Selection rollout and scroll down to the Outline button to set the wall outline to **0.5** meters. If your wall outline appears on the wrong side of the line, click the Undo tool and reenter the outline value as **−0.5** (minus zero point five). (Or you can click the Reverse button and reenter the 0.5 Outline value.)
4. Scroll back up to the top of the Command Panel and click the Extrude button. VIZ uses the last value you entered for the extrude amount, so the wall automatically extrudes to 9.5 meters.

Finally, add the east wall to the model.

1. Choose View ➢ Undo View Zoom to return to the overall view of the plan, then zoom into the area shown in Figure 4.69.
2. Draw the line shown in Figure 4.69.

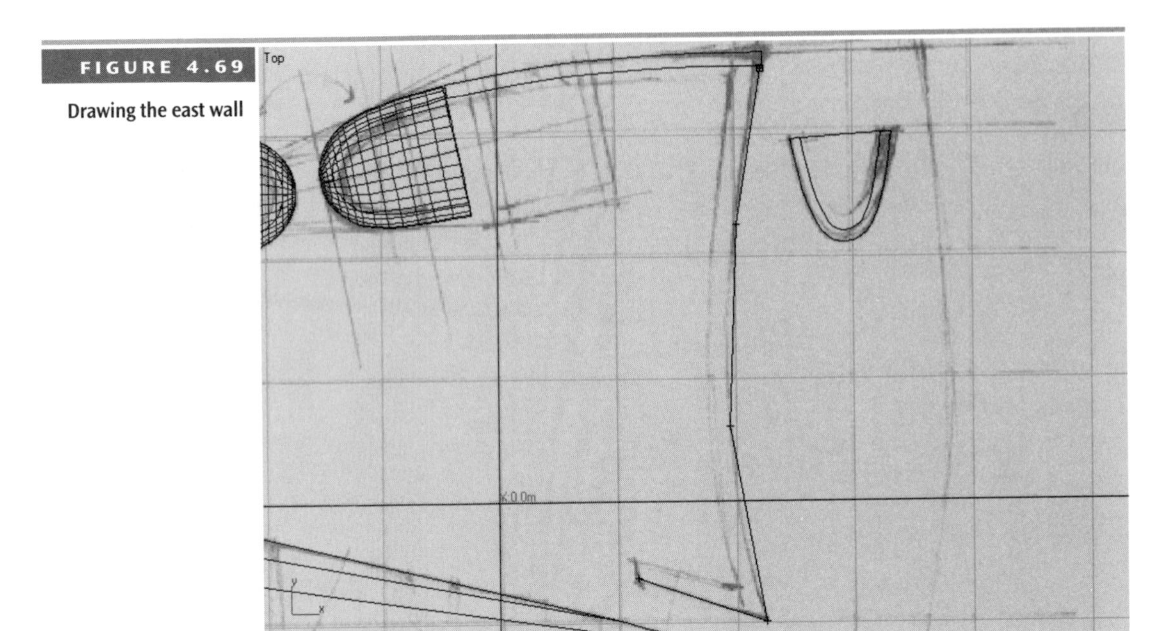

FIGURE 4.69

Drawing the east wall

3. Convert the vertices shown in Figure 4.70 into Bézier curves and adjust the Bézier handles to match the curve of the sketch.

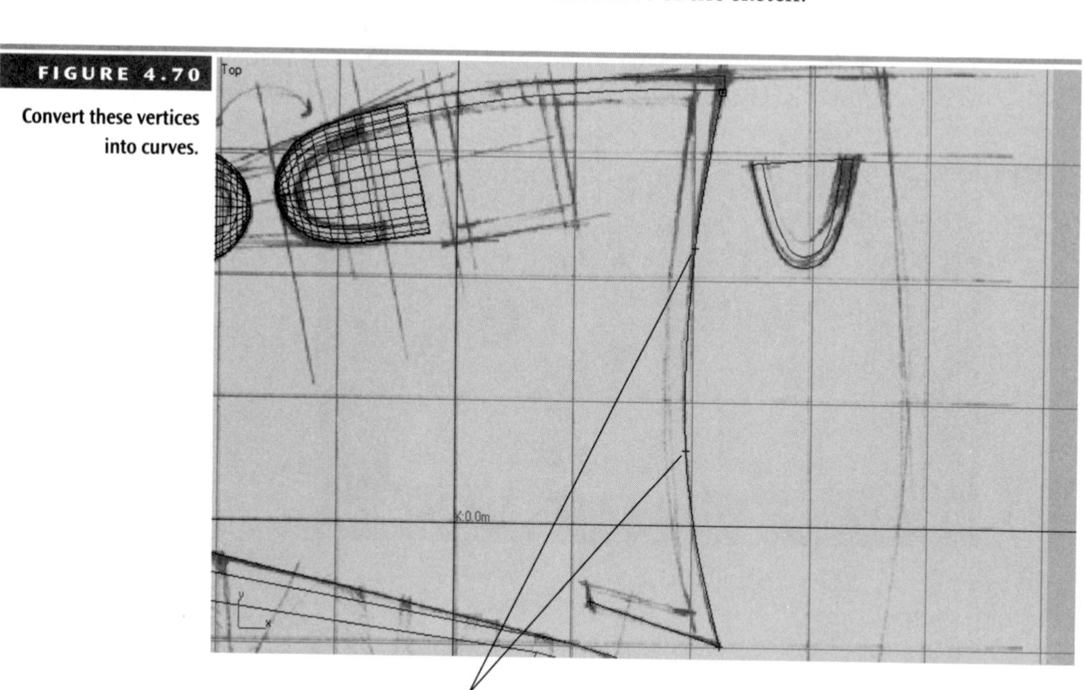

FIGURE 4.70

Convert these vertices into curves.

Bézier curves.

4. Use the Outline option to create an outline that is 0.5 meters wide.
5. Extrude the east wall to a height of 11 meters.
6. Click the Min/Max Toggle to view all of the viewports.

You've created most of the major structure of the chapel. If you're familiar with the Chapel at Ronchamp, you'll see that there are a few areas where the model doesn't quite match the real building, but in general, you do get the overall flavor of the design. Refining the details will come later. There's also the roof to be created, which you'll work on in the next chapter. For a view of the chapel so far, see Insert Figure 4.71.

FIGURE 4.70

View of the chapel so far

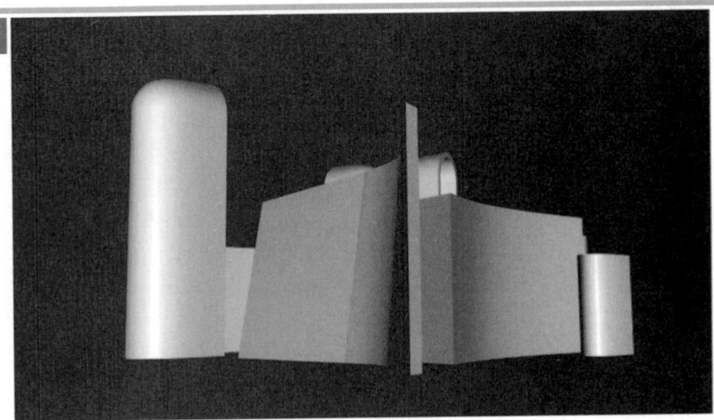

Summary

In this chapter, you learned how to get into the Sub-Object level of an object and make adjustments. You've also seen how you can use Instance clones to your advantage when you created the towers. You'll find that no matter how your model is generated, you'll go to the Sub-Object level to edit vertices and edges frequently.

Along the way, you were introduced to methods that help you isolate parts of your model for easier editing. In an early part of the chapel exercises, the Isolate tool let you see a part of your model without the surrounding parts interfering with your viewing. The Display tab of the Command Panel let you hide the ceiling of the tower to allow access to the walls.

In the next chapter, you'll continue the chapel by creating the roof. There you'll be introduced to the concept of extruding splines along a path. You'll also learn about layers and how they can be used to help organize your model.

chapter 5

Organizing and Editing Objects

FEATURING

- *Naming Objects*
- *Organizing Objects by Layers*
- *Adding the Roof*
- *Adding the Remaining Parts of the Roof*

Organizing and Editing Objects

VIZ allows you to create fairly complex models in a very short time. In the last chapter, you built the beginnings of a fairly complex building. To continue working on that building, you'll need to employ some organizing tools, just to be able to see your work clearly.

In this chapter, you'll continue work on the Chapel at Ronchamp model. You'll be introduced to the loft compound object that allows you to extrude a shape along a path to form complex shapes. You'll also learn more ways to create and edit extruded spline shapes. Along the way, you'll learn how to organize your work through the use of object names and layers.

Naming Objects

Perhaps one of the simplest things you can do to help keep your model organized is to give objects in your model meaningful names. You were introduced to this concept in Chapter 2. Let's go ahead and name all of the parts of the Chapel project in preparation for creating the roof.

1. Open the Chapel model in VIZ. You may also use the Ch05a.max file from the companion CD.
2. If only one viewport is visible, click the Min/Max Toggle tool.
3. Click the Zoom Extents All button to get a view of all of the parts of your model.
4. In the Top viewport, use the Objects selection tool to select the South wall as shown in Figure 5.1.
5. In the Name and Color rollout of the Create tab, change the existing name to South wall. If you're in the Modify tab, change the name that appears just below the Modify label at the top of the tab. You can change the name of an object in either place. [You can change the name of an object in any tab except for Utilities.]
6. Click the wall to the west as shown in Figure 5.1 and change its name to West wall.
7. Repeat this process for the north and east walls and the freestanding exterior wall in the upper right of the plan.
8. Finally, name the tower ceiling objects as shown in Figure 5.1.

FIGURE 5.1

Selecting walls in the Top viewport

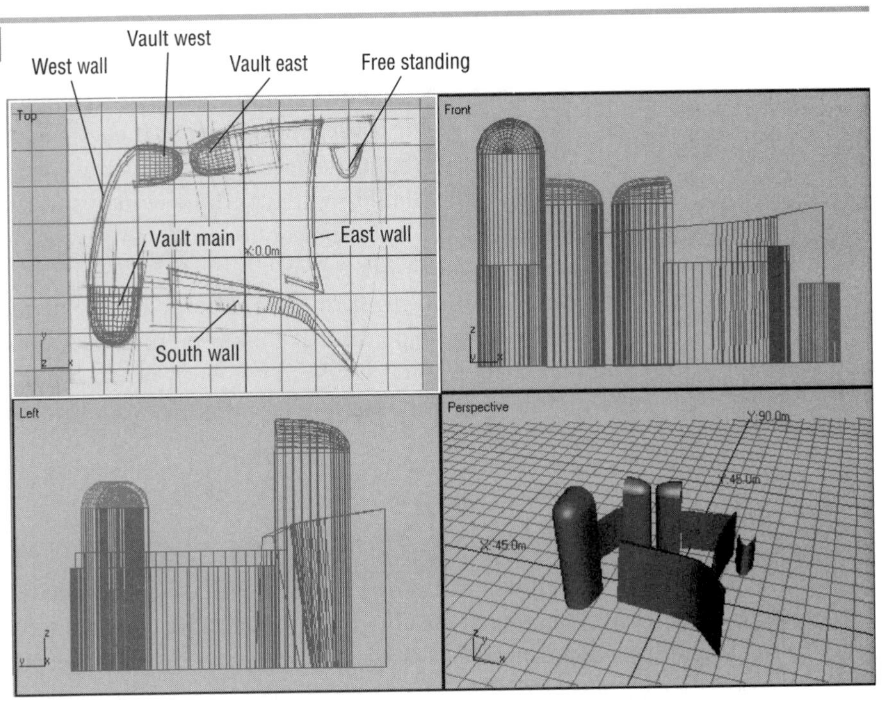

You've gotten just about all of the walls named except for the tower walls. Right now, it's difficult to gain access to the tower walls because the ceiling vaults are in the way in the plan view, and their arrangement in the other views is overlapping. The easiest way to get to the tower walls is to temporarily turn the ceiling vaults off. Go ahead and do that in the next exercise.

1. Click the Select by Name tool on the standard toolbar.

The Select Objects dialog box appears.

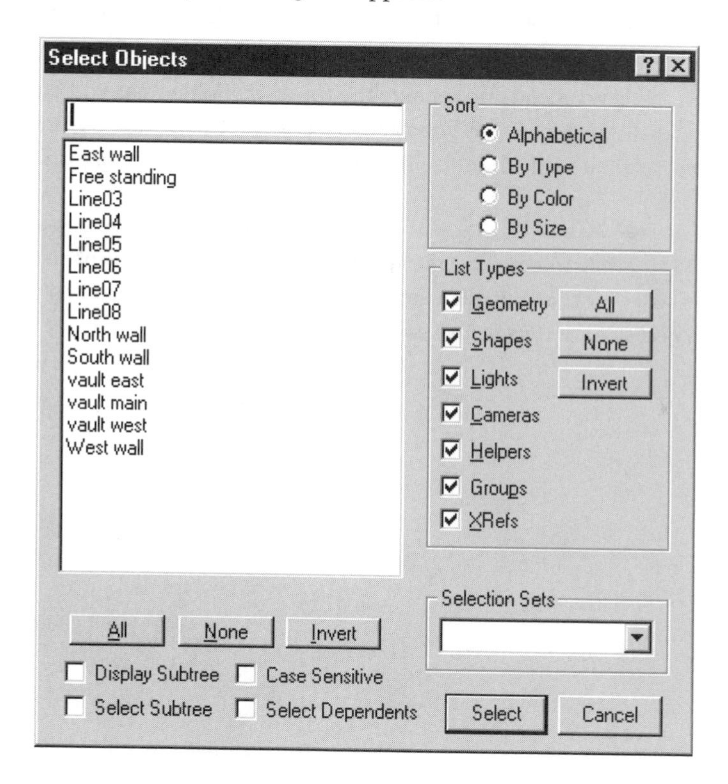

2. Ctrl-click the Vault objects to select them from the list, then click Select. The objects are selected.
3. Click the Display tab in the Command Panel.

4. Click the Selected Off button in the On/Off rollout of the Command Panel. The ceiling vault objects disappear as shown in Figure 5.2.
5. Now go ahead and rename the tower wall objects as you did with the other walls using Figure 5.2 as your guide. Click the Create tab, use the Select object tool to select a wall, then use the Name and Color input box to enter the new name.

TIP **While you may use the Modify tab to change the name of an object, the Create tab Is faster for changing the name of multiple objects since you don't have to wait for the object's parameters to load each time you make a selection.**

FIGURE 5.2

Naming the tower walls

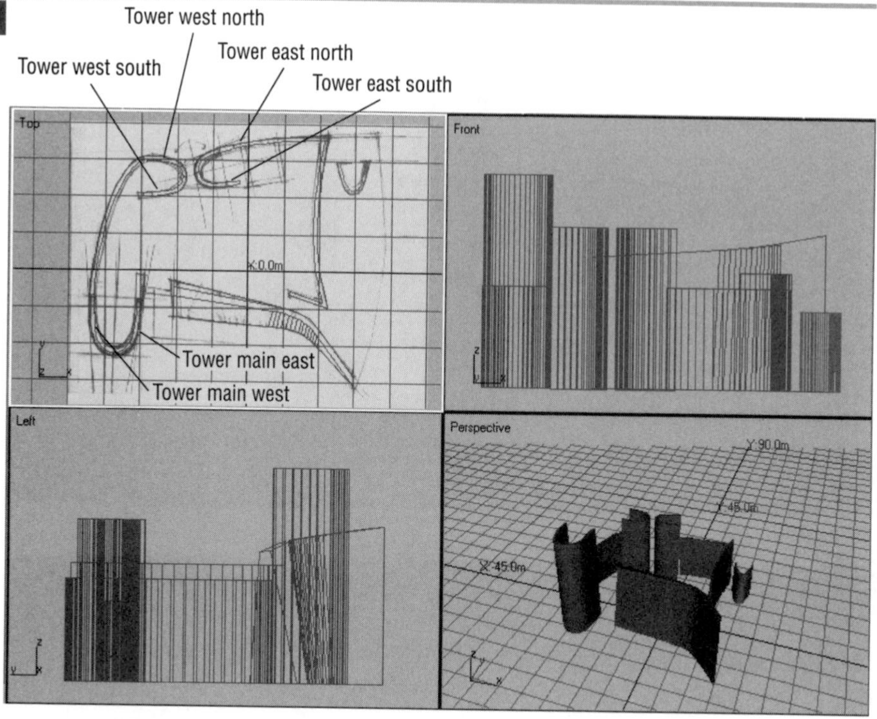

To finish the process, turn the ceiling vaults back on.

1. Click the Display tab in the Command Panel.

2. Click the Turn On by Name… button.

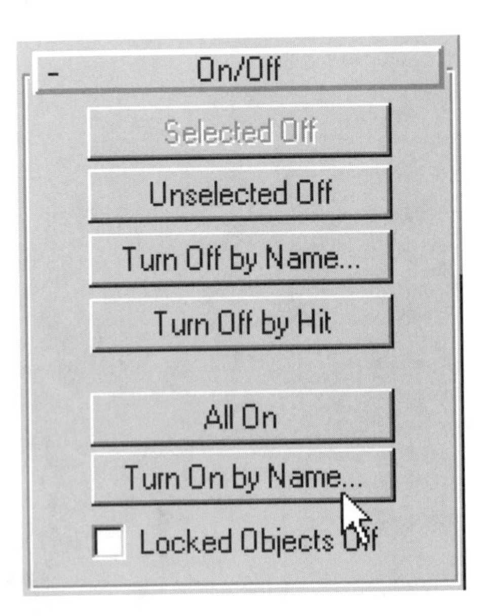

The Turn On by Name… dialog box displays.

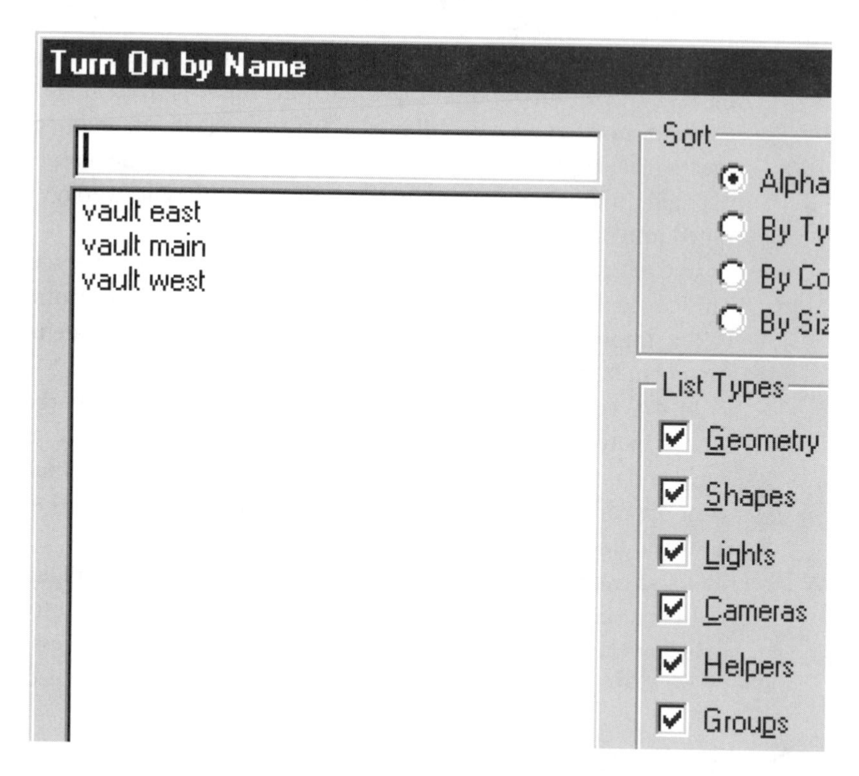

3. Click the All button on the lower left hand side of the dialog box, then click On. The ceiling vault objects appear again.

If you know that you simply want to turn back on all objects that were turned off, you can click the All On button in the On/Off rollout. Here you used the Turn On by Name dialog box just so you know that, if you need to, you can selectively turn objects on by name. This points out the usefulness of meaningful names for objects. If the object names are not descriptive, you will have a difficult time determining which object in the list is the one you want to turn on.

Another point to consider when naming objects is their alphabetical listing. In the Sort group of the Select Objects and Turn On by Name dialog boxes, you have the option to sort the names of the objects in a variety of ways. By default, names are sorted alphabetically. To further help keep track of an object, you might consider how its name will appear in the alphabetical listing. For example, you were asked to name the Tower objects in a way that would keep them grouped together in the listing. The name Tower appears first, then the location (Main, East or West), then the component that the object represents such as east or west. This hierarchical naming scheme helps keep objects grouped together in a listing.

Organizing Objects by Layers

Another way to keep your model organized is through the use of Layers. The idea of Layers comes from pin drafting where different disciplines literally drew their parts of a design on different layers of media. For example, in an architectural drawing, the mechanical engineer would draw ductwork and piping on a separate sheet that was overlaid on the floor plan of the drawing. The different overlays were eventually combined into one sheet through reprographic techniques.

In CAD, layers are used to help keep drawings organized and easier to manage. This concept is taken a step further by organizing types of graphics into walls, doors, ceiling information, etc. In addition, notes and dimensions are usually separated into their own layers as well.

In VIZ, you can use layers in a similar way by organizing part of your model by the type of material you'll be applying to each object. For example, the walls that will be stucco might be placed in a layer called Stucco. If the ceiling vaults are to be given the same appearance as the walls, you might combine them into the Stucco layer as well. Roof and floor components will be given their own layers too. You might even go farther and create layers for window glass, mullions, wood detail, and so on.

In this section, you'll begin to explore layers by using them to organize objects in the Chapel model by their material assignments. You'll use these different layer/material assignments in later chapters to apply materials to objects.

Setting up Layers

Start by setting up a few layers in your Chapel model that you'll use for objects.

1. Click the Layer Properties tool on the standard toolbar.

The Layer Properties dialog box displays.

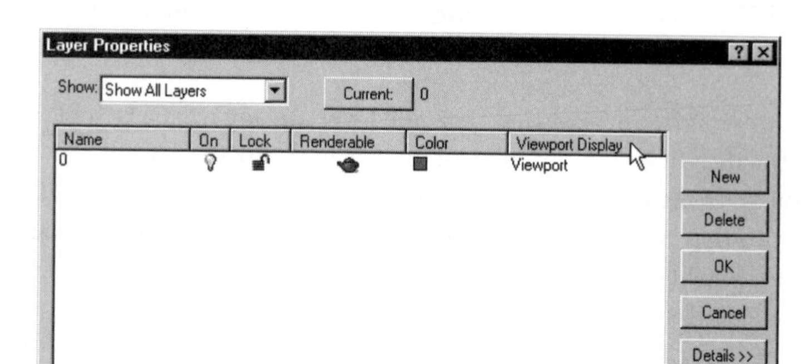

2. Click the New button. A listing called **Layer1** displays. The new listing name is highlighted so you can change the name just by typing.
3. Type the name **Stucco**. It appears in place of the **Layer1** name.
4. Click New again, then type **Concrete roof**. You've just created another layer called Concrete roof.
5. Click New again and type **Floor**.
6. Click New again and type **Tower walls**.
7. Click New again and type **Vault**.
8. Click OK to close the layer Properties dialog box.

TIP **If you're an AutoCAD user, you'll notice that most of the methods for creating and using layers are identical to those for AutoCAD.**

You might have noticed that one layer already exists. Layer 0 is always present and is the default layer on which all objects in a new file are created. All of the objects you've created in the Chapel model, for example, reside on layer 0. You may even notice that the color column in the Layer Properties dialog box shows an off-white color for the 0 layer. This is the same color that you see on objects when you see the Shaded view in the Perspective viewport.

Assigning Objects to Layers

Now that you've got some new layers, go ahead and assign some of the walls to the Stucco layer. This is fairly easy to do: you select the object then use the Layer drop-down list on the standard toolbar to select a layer for the object.

1. Click the Select by Name tool on the standard toolbar.

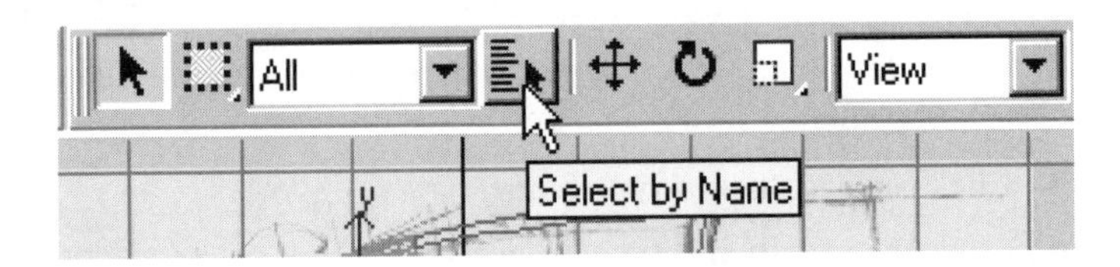

The Select Object dialog box appears.

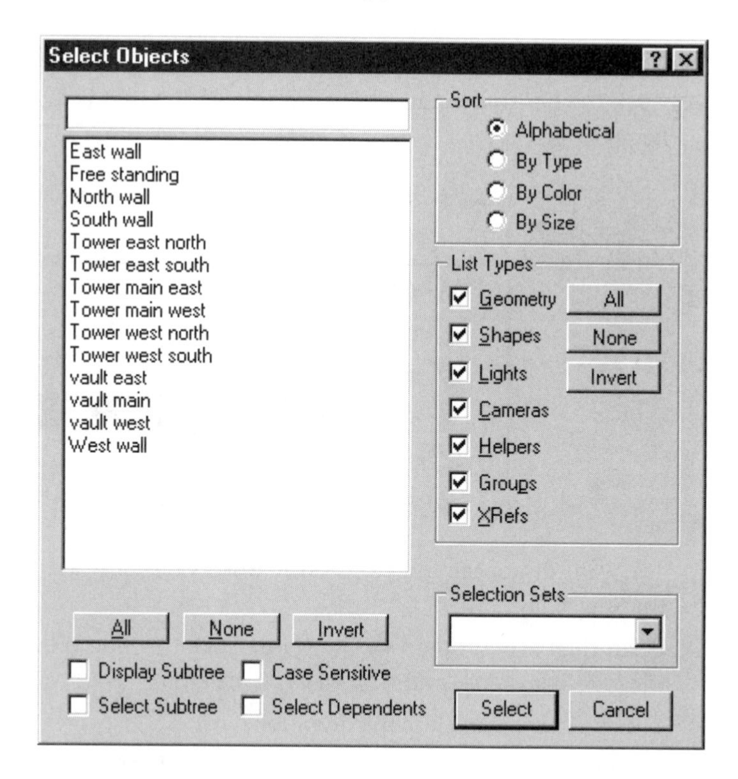

2. Ctrl-click the East wall, North wall, South wall, West wall, and free-standing wall, then click Select.
3. Click the Layer drop-down list, then select Stucco. The walls you selected in step 2 are now on the Stucco layer.
4. Open the Select Objects dialog box again. This time, select the tower walls.
5. Open the Layer drop-down list and select all of the objects whose names begin with Tower.
6. Select Tower walls from the Layer drop-down list.
7. Open the Select Objects dialog box a third time and select the three objects whose names begin with Vault.
8. Select Vault from the Layer drop-down list.

Now try a little experiment to make sure that the ceiling objects are really on the Vault layer.

1. Click the Layer drop-down list again.
2. Click the lightbulb icon in the drop-down list that is to the left of the Stucco name.

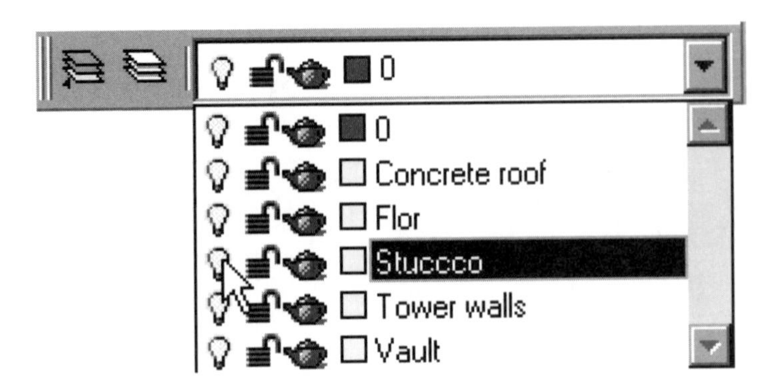

The walls disappear and you see the towers standing alone. You've just turned the Stucco layer off.

3. Open the Layer drop-down list again. Click the Stucco lightbulb again to turn the Stucco layer back on. The walls reappear.
4. Click a viewport to close the drop-down list.

Earlier you used the display tab of the Command Panel to turn off individual objects. You can see from this exercise that you can also turn off an object through its layer assignment by turning off a layer. In this exercise, you used the lightbulb icon in the layer drop-down list to turn the stucco layer on and off. You can use the lightbulb icon in the Layer Properties dialog box to do the same thing.

Assigning Color to Layers

Another way to help you keep track of objects and their layers is to assign a unique color to layers. This helps you to visually keep track of layer assignments and can help in your everyday editing tasks by *toning down* the appearance of objects that you are not currently editing. Layer colors also give you a visual reference for object groupings.

1. Click the Layer Properties tool to open the Layer Properties dialog box.
2. In the layer listing, click the color swatch associated with the Stucco layer as shown in Figure 5.3.

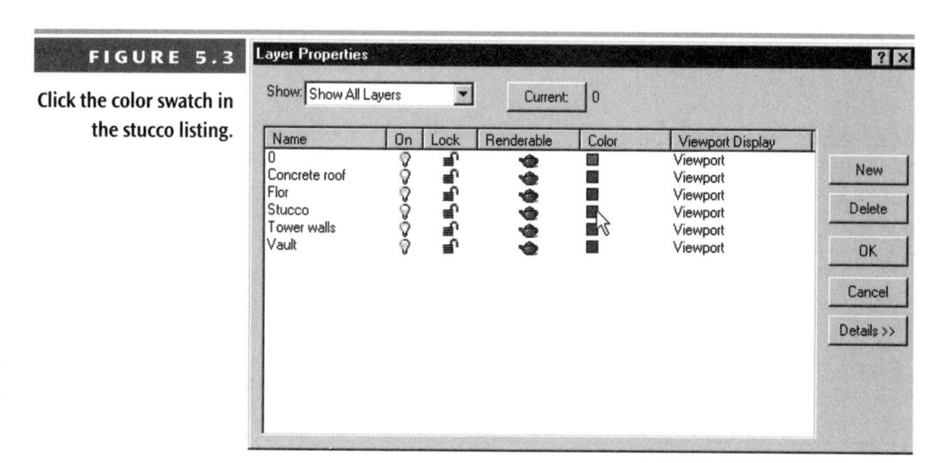

FIGURE 5.3

Click the color swatch in the stucco listing.

The Object Color dialog box displays as shown in Figure 5.4.

3. Click the dark brown color swatch as shown in Figure 5.4, then click OK. Now you see the color you selected in the color swatch for the Stucco layer in the Layer Properties dialog box.

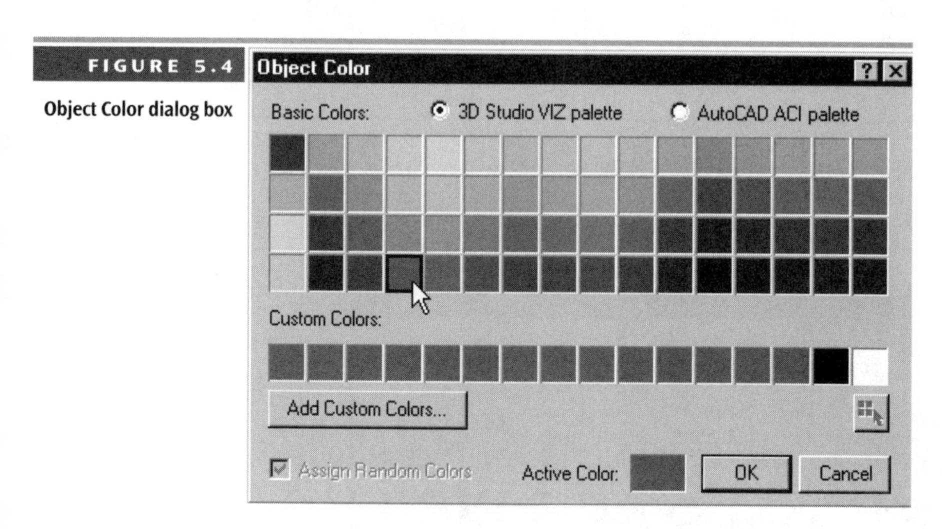

FIGURE 5.4

Object Color dialog box

4. Click OK. The objects assigned to the Stucco layer are now the color you selected in step 3 as shown in Figure 5.5.

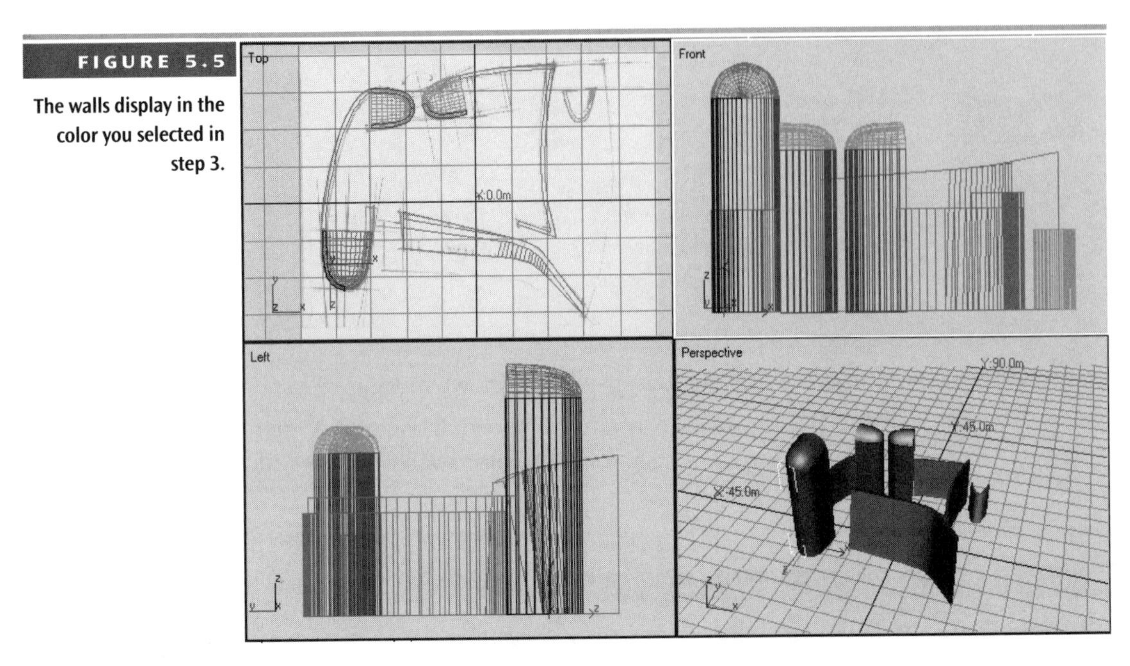

FIGURE 5.5

The walls display in the color you selected in step 3.

5. Go ahead and set the color for the rest of the new layers. Use Figure 5.6 as a guide.

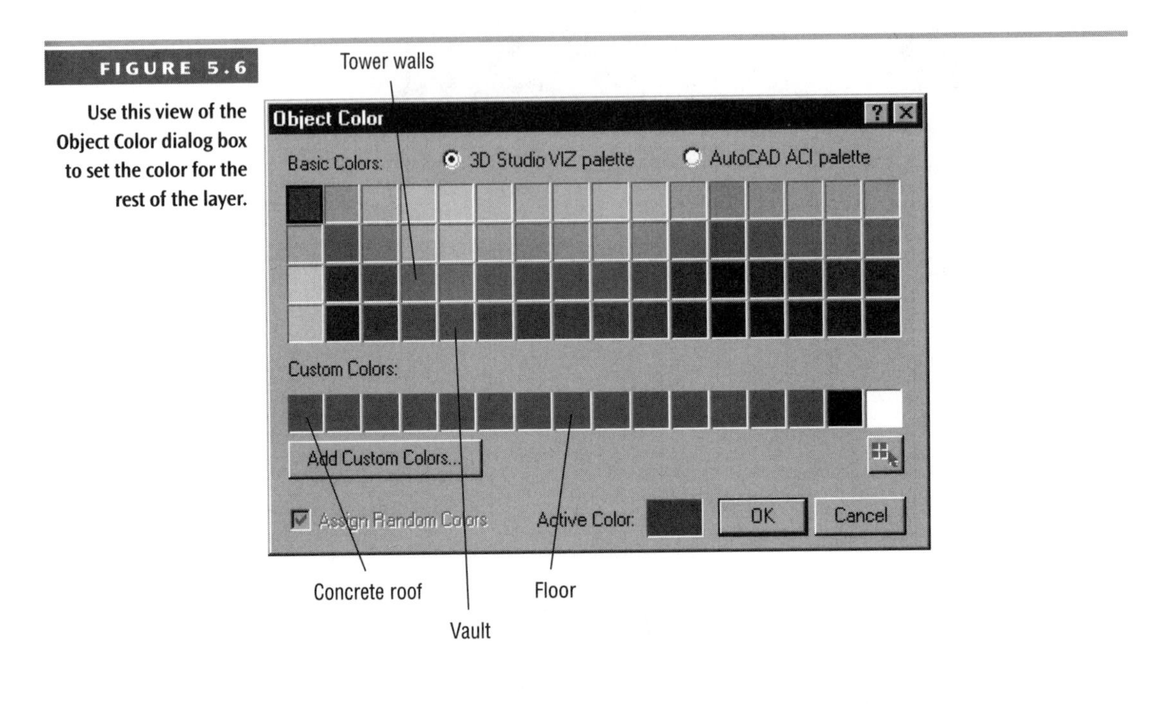

FIGURE 5.6

Use this view of the Object Color dialog box to set the color for the rest of the layer.

TIP You can use a layer as a selection criterion. To do this, select all the objects assigned to a specific layer by choosing Edit ➢ Select by ➢ Layer... You can then choose from a list of layers presented in a dialog box.

The layer color or object color property you've been working with so far only defines the color of the objects as you work with them in wireframe views. These colors also appear in shaded views until you assign materials to the objects. At that point, the shaded views of objects will show a facsimile of the materials assigned to objects rather than the object's color property.

Setting the Current Layer

New objects you create are automatically assigned to the current layer. When you created your first box in Chapter 1, it was assigned to layer 0, the only layer in existence at the time.

As you saw in previous exercises, selecting a layer from the drop-down list while an object is selected causes the selected object to be assigned to the selected layer, but it doesn't make that layer current. If you want to make a layer current, first make sure that no objects are selected before you select a layer from the Layer drop-down list. You may also use the Layer Properties dialog box. Open the Layer Properties dialog box, select the layer name from the list, and click Current.

What if an Object Doesn't Change to Its Layer Color?

If you find that an object retains its original color even after it has been assigned to a layer of another color, then the object has its Display Properties setting set to By Object. The By Object setting forces objects to maintain their properties, including color, regardless of their layer settings. One quick way to tell whether an object's color is assigned By Object or By Layer is to look at the color swatch next to the object's name in the Create or Modify tab of the Command Panel.

If the color swatch shows black and white, its color assignment is By Layer. If it shows a single color, it's By Object, which means that its color property is not affected by its layer assignment.

Continued on the next page

You can change an object's property setting from By Object to By Layer. This change causes the object to inherit its display properties from its assigned layer. To make this change, use the Select Object tool to select an object, then right-click the object and select Properties from the Pop-up menu. The Object Properties dialog box displays.

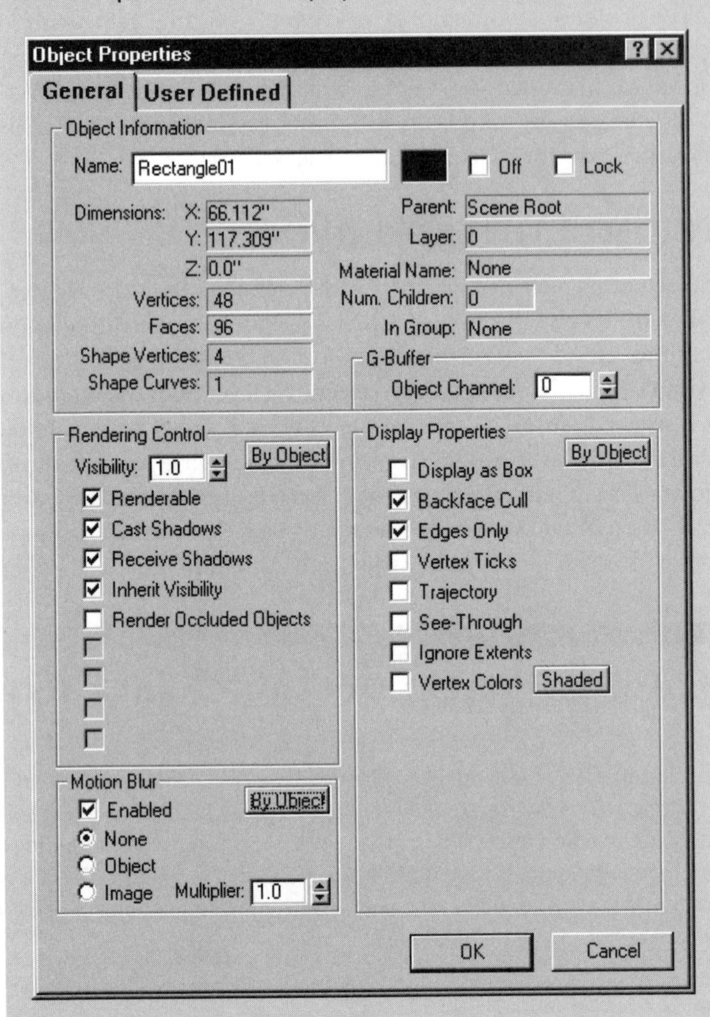

Click the By Object button in the Display Properties group. This will cause the Display Properties check boxes to gray out. The By Object button changes to read By Layer.

You will also see that the By Layer button is available for the Rendering Control and Motion Blur groups of the Object Properties dialog box. Just as with Display Properties, the By Layer button lets you determine whether the Rendering Control and Motion Blur properties are controlled by the individual object or by the layer to which the object is assigned. You'll learn more about Rendering controls and Motion Blur in later chapters.

Adding the Roof

Now that you've gotten your model a bit more organized, you're ready to add the roof. In this section, you'll look at how you can use splines to extrude shapes into unique forms. The roof exercises will also offer an opportunity to explore the uses of layers and object names to help keep the clutter down and aid in the modeling process.

Setting up the Shapes to Form the Roof Edge

The roof of the Chapel at Ronchamp has a unique shape. Its east and south edges form a prominent feature in the design. The shape of the roof edge looks somewhat like the hull of a boat (see Figure 5.7).

FIGURE 5.7

A view of the Chapel showing the roof feature at the southeast corner. This shape may pose a challenge to most modeling programs, but VIZ can easily handle the creation of this shape. It will take a bit of careful planning.

To begin the process, you'll draw two splines. One spline will represent the cross section shape of the roof edge, and the other spline will define the shape of the roof's edge along the length of the south and east sides. The cross section shape and the shape of the roof's edge will be combined through a process called Lofting to form the 3D roof edge.

Lofting is a process whereby a cross section shape is extruded along a path. The result of this lofting is called a loft object. Loft objects are a bit like Boolean objects in that they are the result of the combination of multiple objects, namely the cross section shape and the path. The term lofting comes from shipbuilding, and it refers to the method of laying out the contours of a ship's hull. Like a ship's hull, the cross sectional shape of a loft can vary along the path. As you'll see later, you can adjust the shape of the loft along the path by adjusting the profile at various points along the path.

Let's start the lofting process by turning off part of the model so you can see your work more clearly. You'll be able to use the bitmap sketch background for some of your work, and the East wall will aid in placing the height of the roof, so turn off all of the model except for the East wall.

1. Use the Select object tool to select the East wall. Or, if you prefer, you might practice using the Select by Name dialog box to do this.
2. Click the Display tab of the Command Panel. Then click the Unselected Off button in the On/Off rollout.

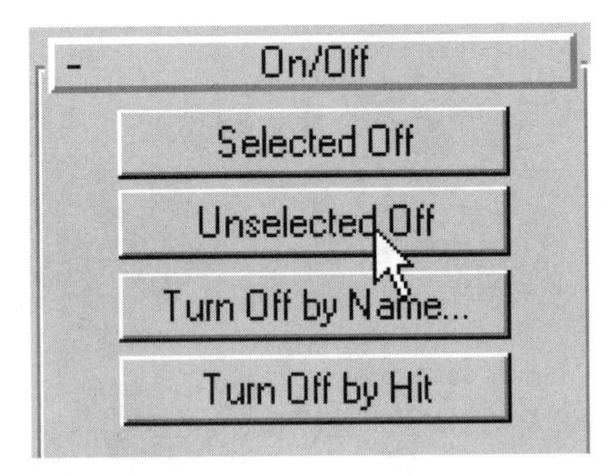

All of the walls disappear except for the East wall. Now draw the profile for the extruded roof edge.

1. Use the Region Zoom tool to zoom into the portion of the Front viewport shown in Figure 5.8.

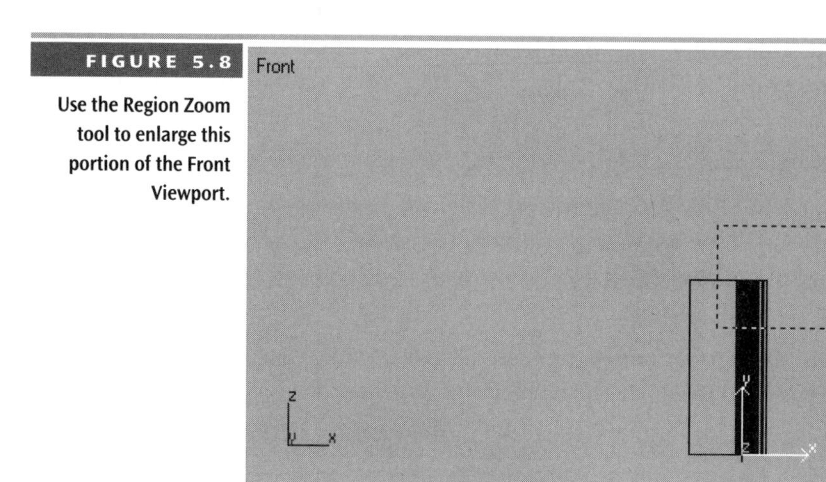

FIGURE 5.8

Use the Region Zoom tool to enlarge this portion of the Front Viewport.

2. Click the Create tab of the Command Panel. Then click the Shapes button and also click Rectangle.
3. In the Front viewport, click and drag a rectangle from the top right corner of the East wall as shown in Figure 5.9. You don't need to be exact about the placement or size of the rectangle.

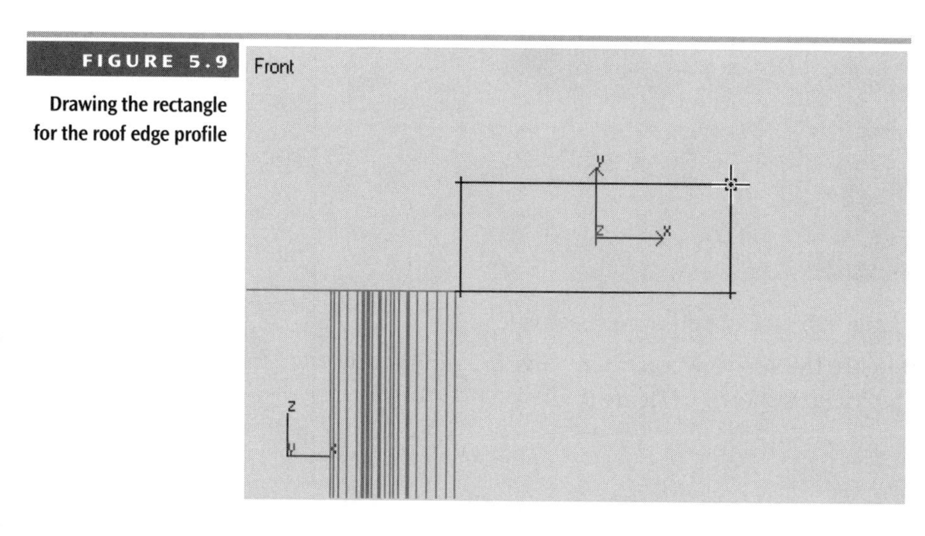

FIGURE 5.9

Drawing the rectangle for the roof edge profile

4. In the Parameters rollout of the Command Panel, change the Length value to **1.8** and the Width value to **4**.

You've got the basic outline of the profile drawn, but it needs a curve in the lower right corner of the rectangle, so add that next.

1. Click the Modify tab in the Command Panel, then click the Edit Stack button and select Editable Spline. You won't be needing the parametric features of the rectangle and you'll save memory by converting the rectangle to an editable spline.
2. Click the Vertex tool in the Selection rollout of the Command Panel.
3. Use the Select and Move tool to right-click the vertex at the lower right corner of the rectangle. Then select Bézier Corner from the list.
4. Right-click the Select and Move tool on the standard toolbar to open the Move Transform Type-In dialog box.
5. Enter **–2.5**↵ in the X input box of the Offset: Screen group. Then close the Move Transform Type-In dialog box. The rectangle changes shape.
6. Use the Select and Move tool to adjust the Bézier handles so they look like the ones in Figure 5.10.

FIGURE 5.10

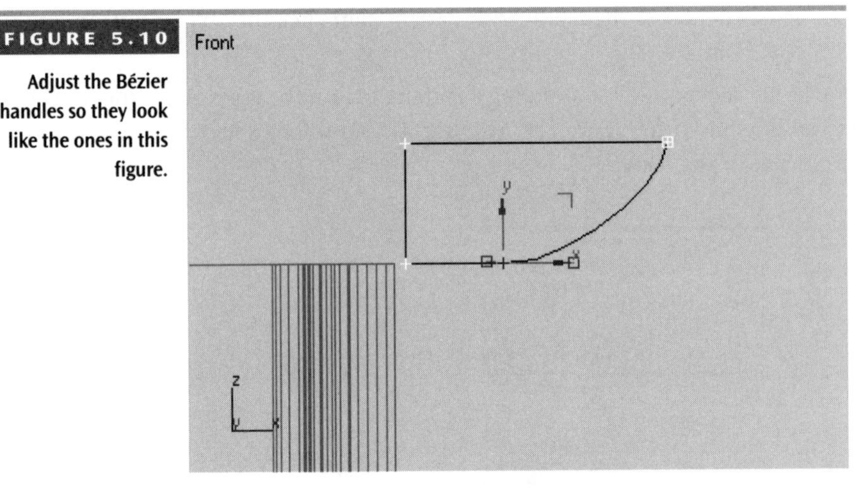

Adjust the Bézier handles so they look like the ones in this figure.

7. Click the Sub-Object button to deactivate it.
8. Right-click the Top viewport, then move the profile upward to the north edge of the building as shown in Figure 5.11.

FIGURE 5.11

Move the profile to this location.

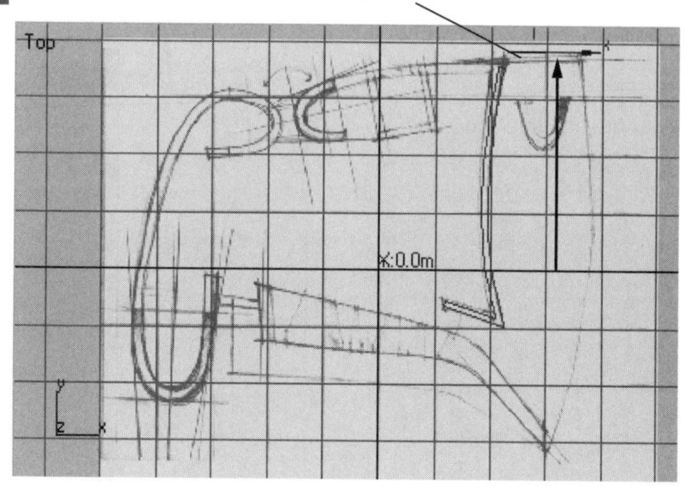
Top
X:0.0m

Move the profile to the north edge of the building.

NOTE You may notice that VIZ placed the profile on the X axis as you see it in the Top view. By default, VIZ places objects on the plane defined by the X, Y, and Z axes of world space. When you draw objects in the Top or Perspective viewports, they are placed on the plane defined by the XY axes of the world coordinate system. For the Front and Back viewports, objects are placed on the plane defined by the XZ axes, and for the Left and Right viewports objects are placed on the plane defined by the YZ axes.

You've got the profile ready. Now it's time to create the path over which the profile will be extruded. This time you'll trace over the bitmap sketch to obtain the profile of the roof edge.

1. Right-click the Top viewport to make it active. Then click the Min/Max Toggle tool to enlarge the Top viewport.

TIP You may also press the W key to enlarge a viewport.

2. Click the Create tab in the Command Panel. Click the Shape tool if it isn't already active. Then click Line.
3. Draw the line shown in Figure 5.12, starting from the west end of the South wall.

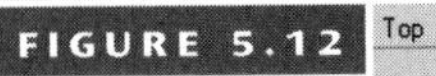

FIGURE 5.12

Draw this line starting at the square shown at the lower left end of the line.

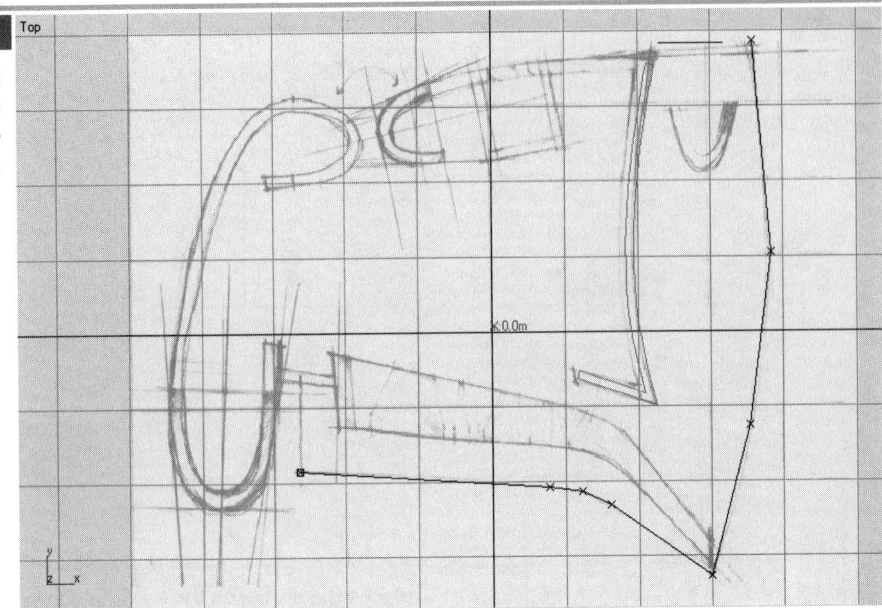

4. Click the Modify tab. Then click the Vertex tool in the Selection rollout.
5. Convert the vertices shown in Figure 5.13 into Bézier curves by right-clicking them and selecting Bézier from the pop-up menu.

FIGURE 5.13

Convert these vertices into Bézier curves to duplicate the shape shown here.

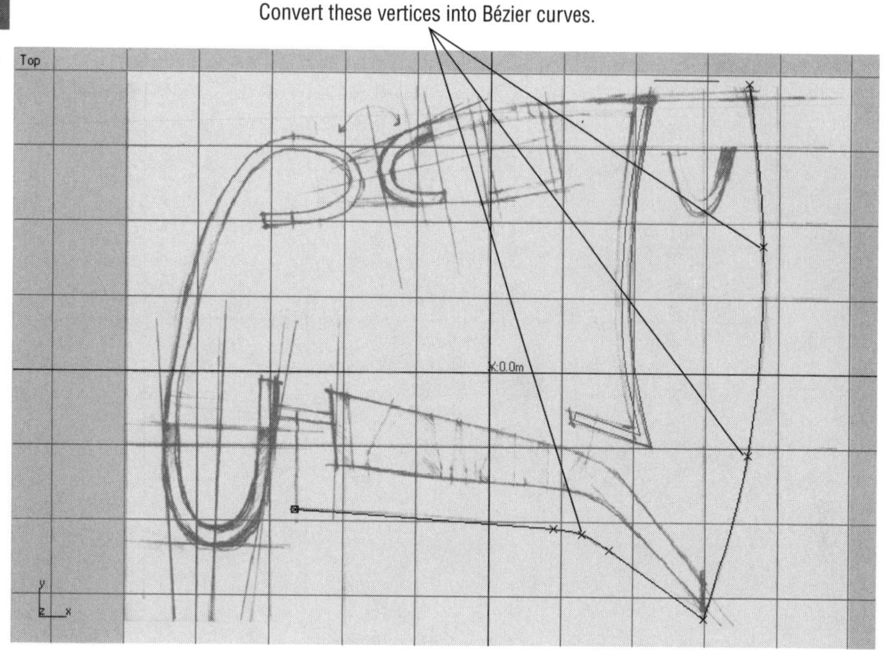
Convert these vertices into Bézier curves.
Top
X:0.0m

You may want to zoom in temporarily to adjust the Bézier curve of the South wall. Use the View ➢ Undo Region Zoom to return to the overall view of the plan. The Shift-Z keystroke combination performs the same function as View ➢ Undo Region Zoom.

You've now got the path you want for the loft, but you need to take one more step before you use the path. The path now defines the outside edge of the loft, but you want the shape to follow the inside edge of the path. I'll explain why after you've created the loft. It will be easier to see the reason then.

To create a path that forms the inside edge of the extrusion, you'll use the Outline tool, then you'll delete the line segments that you don't need.

1. With the Modify tab selected, click the Spline tool in the Selection rollout of the Command Panel.
2. In the Outline input box near the bottom of the panel, enter **4**↵ to create an outline 4 meters wide. This is the same width as the roof edge profile you created earlier.
3. Scroll back up to the Selection rollout, then select Segment.
4. Ctrl-click the segments shown in Figure 5.14, then press the Delete key to delete them.

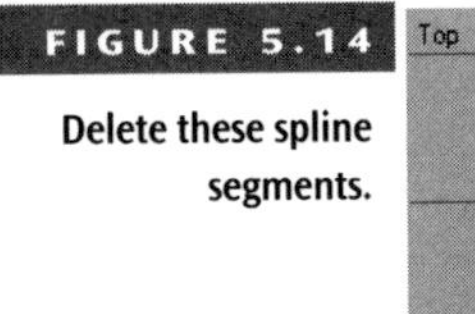

FIGURE 5.14

Delete these spline segments.

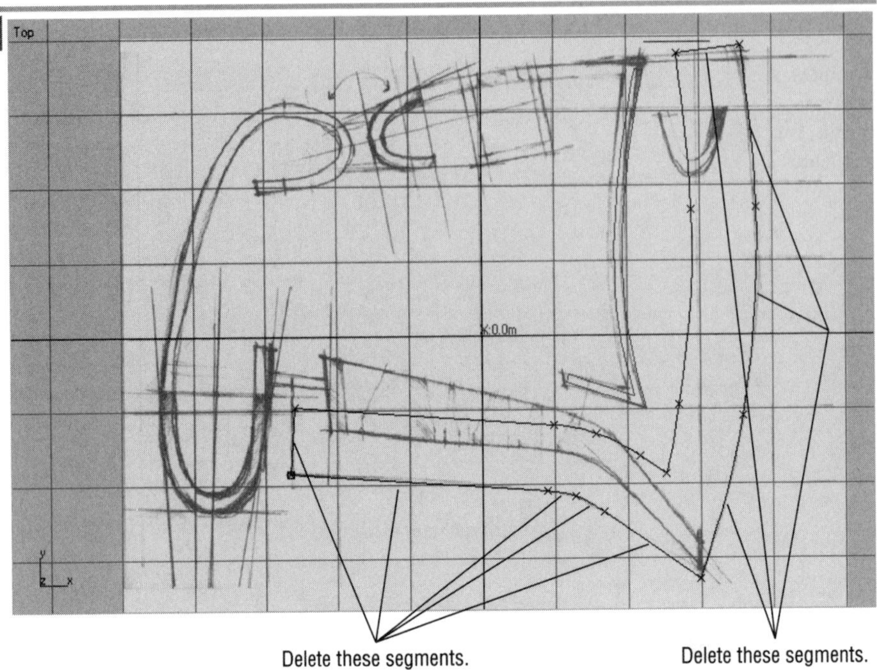
Top
Delete these segments.
Delete these segments.

Now you've got a path that defines the inside edge of the loft. You're just about ready to perform the actual loft, but before you do that, move the path out of the floor plan area. This will allow you to make adjustments to the path later.

1. Click the Sub-Object button to deactivate it. Then, if it isn't already selected, click the Select and Move tool.
2. Move the spline path to the location shown in Figure 5.15.

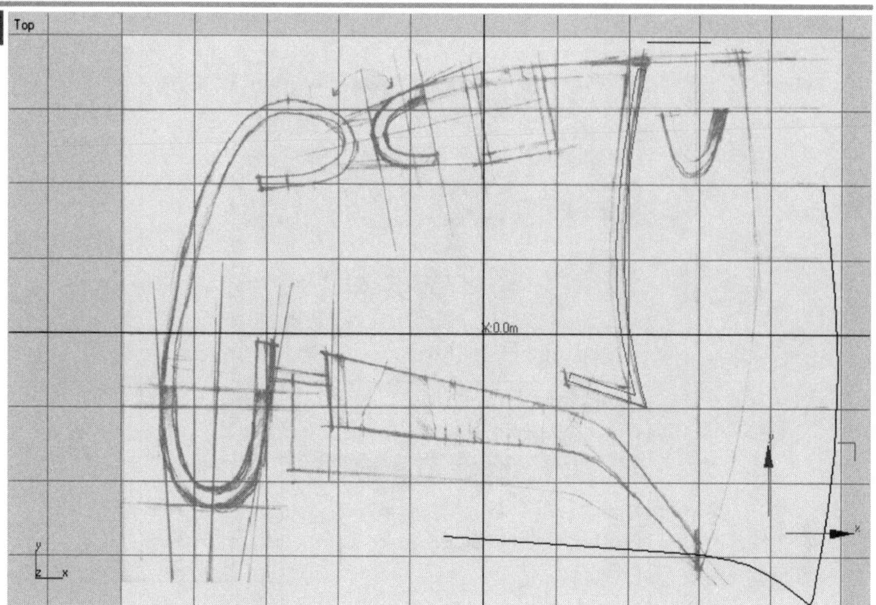

FIGURE 5.15

Move the spline path to the location shown here.

Lofting an Object

Now you are ready to loft the shape you created earlier. You'll use the Loft modifier in the Modify tab to perform this maneuver.

1. Click the profile rectangle shape you created earlier to select it.
2. Click the Create tab in the Command Panel. Then click the Geometry tool.

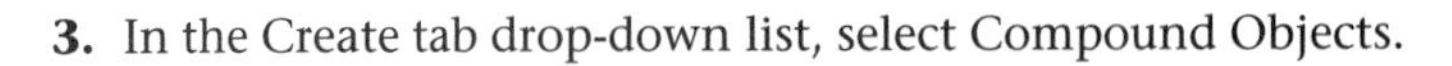

3. In the Create tab drop-down list, select Compound Objects.

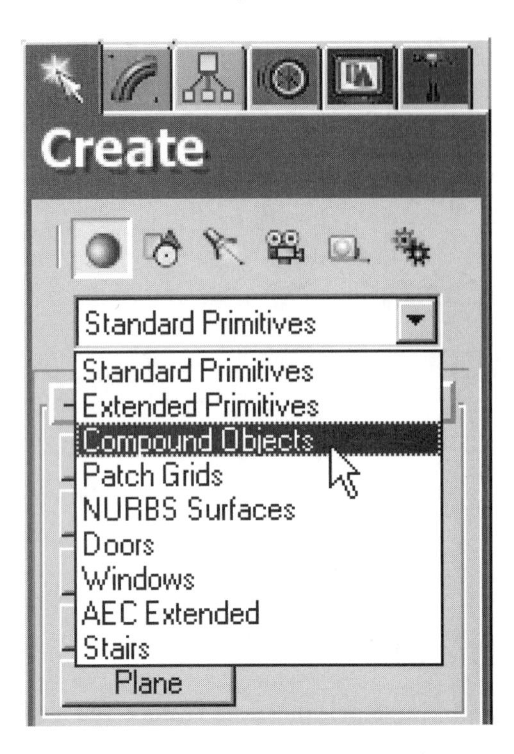

4. Click the Loft button in the Object Type rollout.

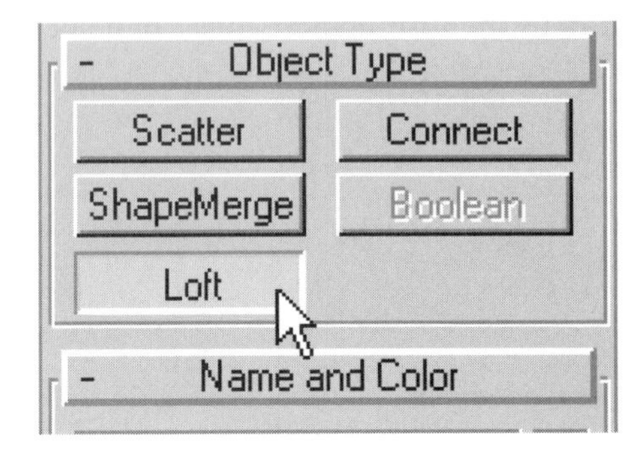

5. Click the Get Path button in the Creation Method rollout and make sure the Instance radio button is selected.

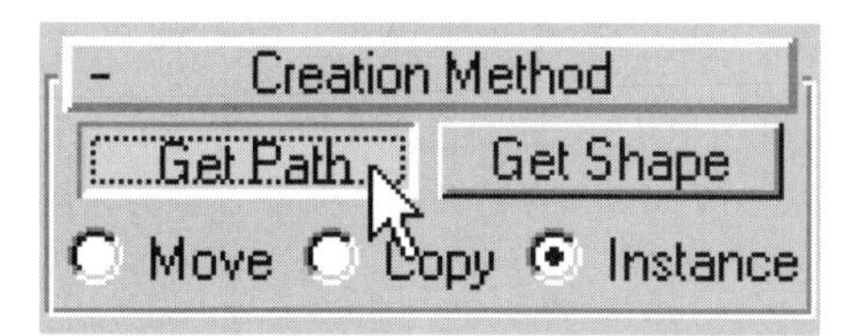

6. Move the cursor over the spline you created in the last exercise. Notice that the cursor shows an ellipse marker. This tells you that the cursor has found an object that can be used as a path for the loft. Click the spline path you created in the last exercise. The profile extrudes along the shape of the path as shown in Figure 5.16.

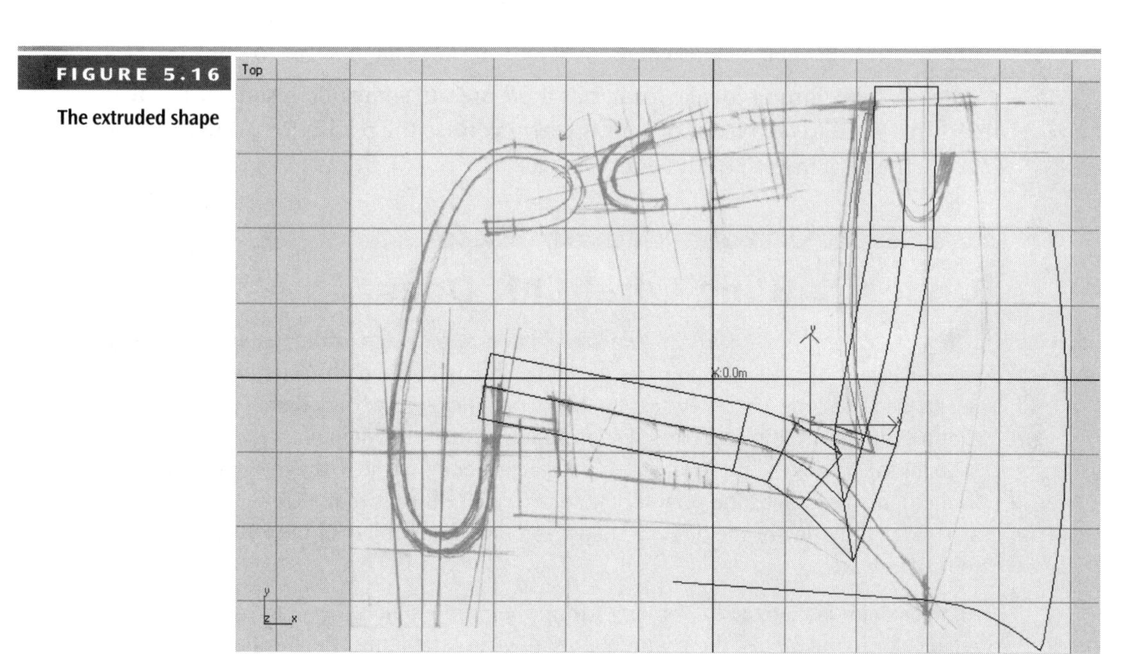

FIGURE 5.16

The extruded shape

The shape is a bit crude looking. Just as with other lofted objects, you can set the number of segments used along the path. To get a smoother looking extrusion, increase the number of segments along the path. Here's how it's done.

1. Scroll down the Command Panel to the Skin Parameters rollout label and click it.

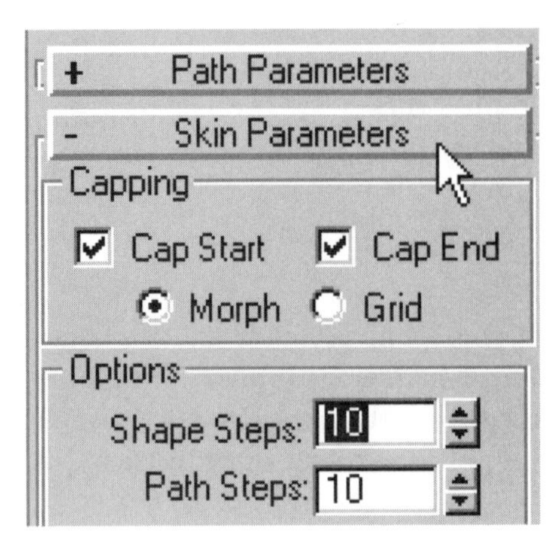

2. Change the Shape Steps value to **10** and the Path Steps value to **10**.

The loft is beginning to take form, but there are still some odd results from the loft object that need to be fixed. And this is where you see the reason for using the inside edge for the path instead of the outside edge.

Understanding What Loft Does

When you create a Loft, you are given the option to have the loft make an instance or reference copy of the shape to place at the beginning of the path. The default is to create an instance copy. This allows you to make modifications to the original profile object that will in turn modify the cross section shape of the loft. When you create the Loft, a clone of the original shape is placed at the starting point of the path. The clone is placed in the same location as the original shape, so it isn't obvious that a clone has been created. Also, the clone of the original shape becomes a sub-object of the loft, as you'll see in this next exercise.

Another point is that the loft emerges from the profile object as if the path were perpendicular to the face of the profile shape. You can later adjust the location of the loft, using the transform tools.

If you prefer, you can select the path first, then use the Get Shape button in the Creation Method rollout to select the profile object. If you create a loft in this way, then the path will define the location of the loft object instead of the profile.

Adjusting the Loft Profile in Relation to the Loft Path

In the sharp corner of the loft you see overlap, caused by the loft bending over itself as it turns the sharp corner. Figure 5.17 shows this overlap.

FIGURE 5.17

Overlap of corner

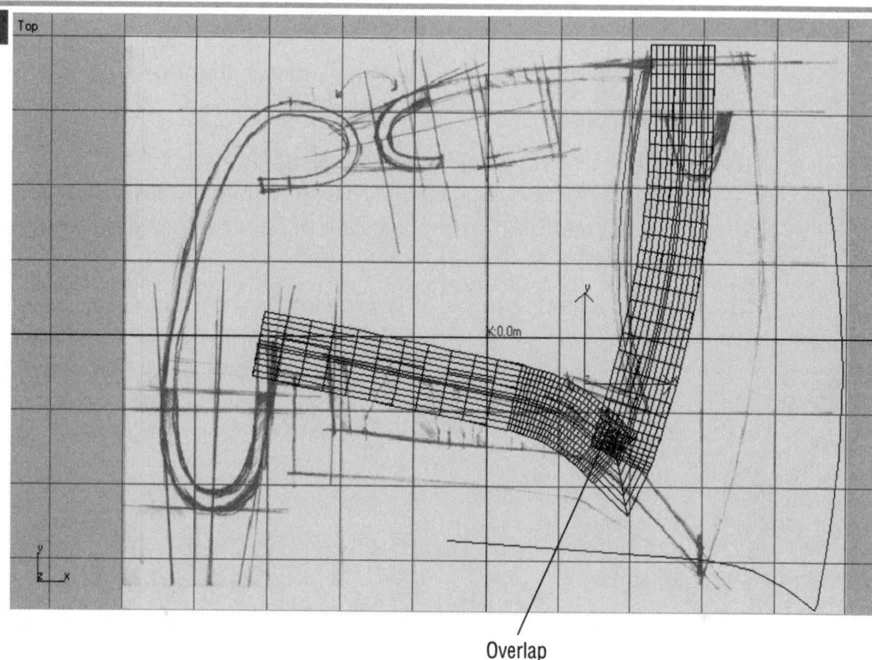

This overlap can cause some undesirable results in your model later on when you apply materials and render the model. To remove the overlap, you need to adjust the location of the path in relation to the profile. Before you do that, it may help you to understand what VIZ does when you create a loft in the first place.

By default, when the Loft is created, it aligns the loft path at the center of the shape (see Figure 5.18). This causes the bending that you see in Figure 5.17. You want to move the loft path to the left of the shape so that instead of the loft bending over itself, it pivots around the sharp corner. The following exercise will show you how this is accomplished.

First, set up a view so you can see the relationship of the loft shape and the path more clearly.

1. Click the Min/Max Toggle tool, then right-click the Front viewport.
2. Click the Arc Rotate Selected tool and adjust the view so it looks similar to Figure 5.18. You need to be able to see the beginning of the loft shape and the corner clearly.
3. Click the Min/Max toggle tool to enlarge the view.

Now you are ready to adjust the shape and loft alignment.

1. Click the Modify tab in the Command Panel.
2. With the loft object selected, click the Sub-Object button in the Command Panel. A new rollout called Shape Commands displays. Remember that the Loft modifier creates an instance clone of the original shape and uses it as a sub-object of the lofted shape.
3. Click the top edge at the end of the loft as shown in Figure 5.18.

FIGURE 5.18

The view of the lofted object including the path and the shape

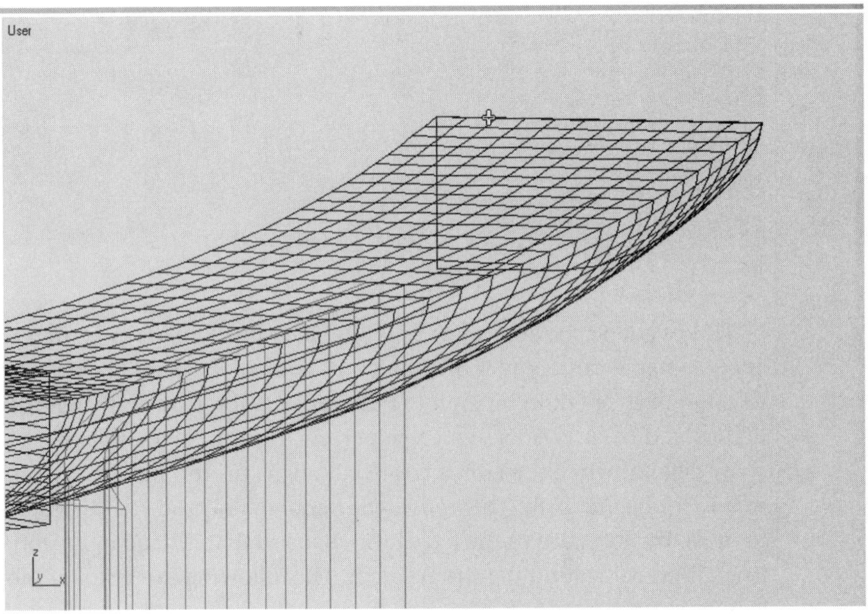

User

You'll see a partial red outline of the shape you used as the profile for the loft. The options under the Shape Commands also become active and are therefore no longer grayed out.

4. Click the Left button in the Align group.

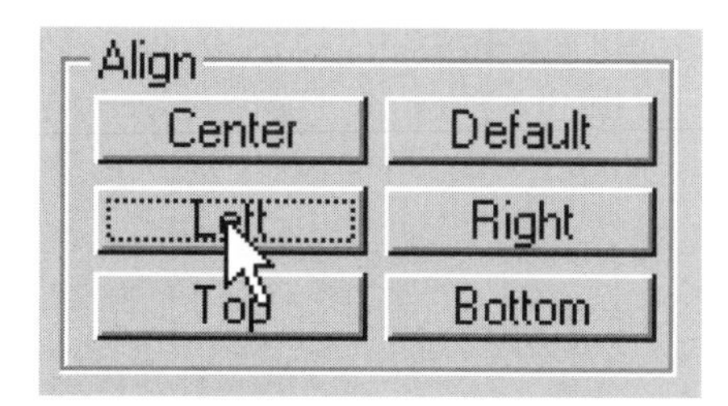

The lofted shape now moves so that the path forms the inside edge of the lofted shape instead of the centerline as shown in Figure 5.19.

FIGURE 5.19

The lofted shape after aligning the path with the left side of the rectangle profile

5. Click the Min/Max Toggle tool to get a look at the Top view. Now the overlap at the corner disappears and you have a clean looking corner.

Note the new relationship of the loft path to the shape in Figure 5.19. You can also see the original rectangle shape you created earlier, now that the alignment of the shape has shifted to the left side.

The Left button moved the path to the far left edge of the rectangle profile shape. Other buttons in the Align group cause the path to be aligned with different parts of the profile shape as indicated by the button name.

The Top and Bottom buttons align the path with either the top or bottom edge of the shape without affecting the current left-to-right alignment. This means that if the path is currently aligned with the left of the shape, then clicking the Top or Bottom button will align the path with the top left or top bottom of the shape. If the path is aligned with the center of the shape, then clicking the Top or Bottom button will align the path with the center-top or center-bottom of the shape.

Fine-Tuning a Loft Object

You now have a pretty good replica of the Chapel's roof edge, but suppose that you wanted to make some refinements to the shape. Suppose, for example, that you want to make some slight adjustment in the relationship of the path to the shape, or perhaps you just want to make adjustments to the curve of the path.

In this section, you'll explore some of the ways a loft object can be fine-tuned. The changes you make to your model in this section will be for experimentation purposes only, so you'll use the temporary buffer to store your work in its current state so you can return to it later.

In the last exercise, you saw how you can use a set of buttons to align the loft path with the loft shape. Now let's see how you can use the Select and Move tool to *manually* align the path with the shape.

1. To save the model in its current state, choose Edit ➢ Temporary Buffer ➢ Save.

2. Click the Compare button in the Shape Commands rollout. The Compare window appears. As you'll see next, this window allows you to view the relationship of the path to the shape.

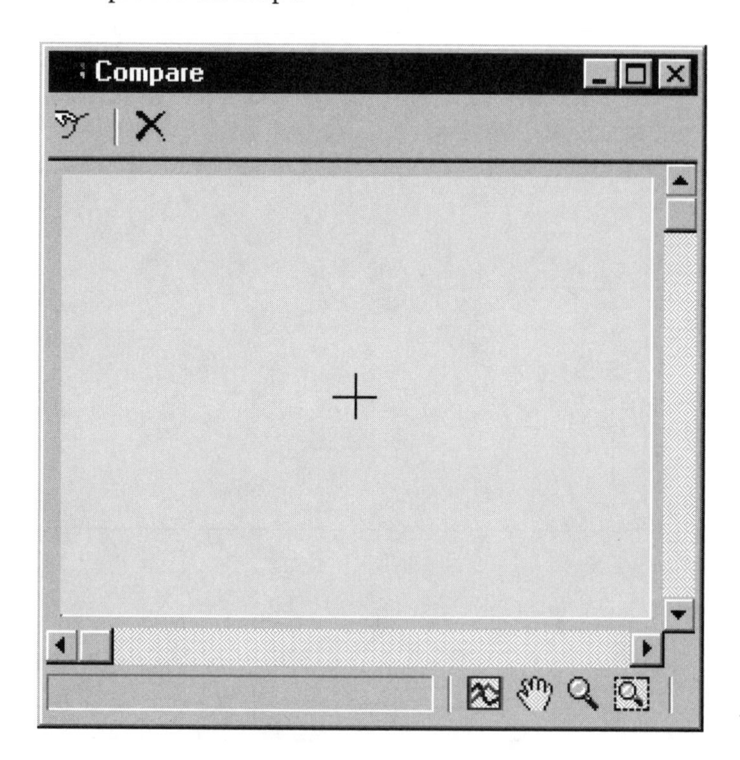

3. Click the Pick Shape tool in the Compare dialog box, then click the sub-object shape outlined in red in the User viewport.

   The shape appears in the Compare dialog box.

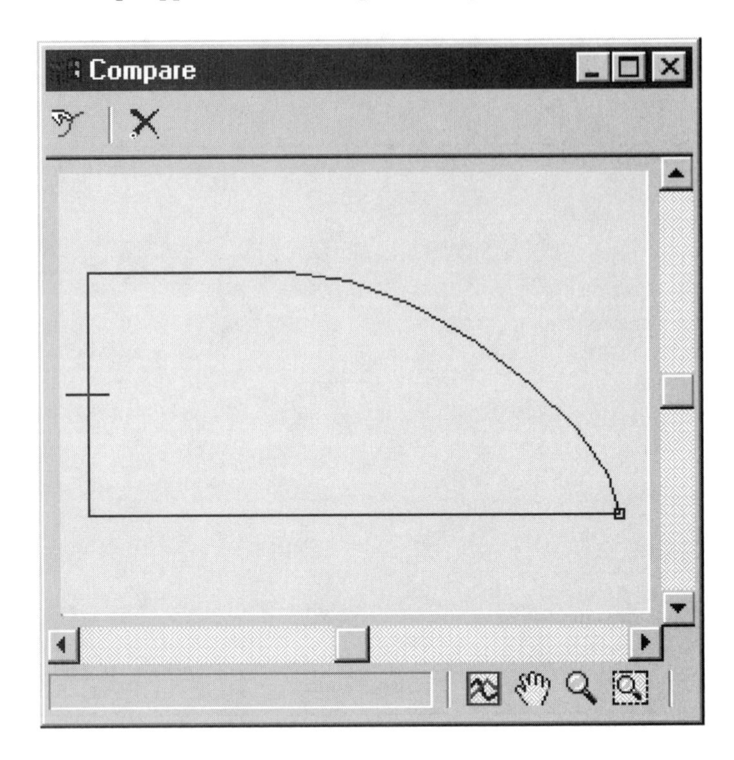

4. With the Sub-Object button still active and the shape selected, click the Select and Move tool and drag the red X axis arrow of the profile to the right as shown in Figure 5.20. As you do this, the loft shape temporarily disappears, and you can more easily see the relationship of the shape to the path. You also see the shape move in the Compare window. The plus sign in the left half of the Compare dialog box indicates the location of the loft path.

FIGURE 5.20

Drag the X axis arrow to the right and watch the effect on the loft shape.

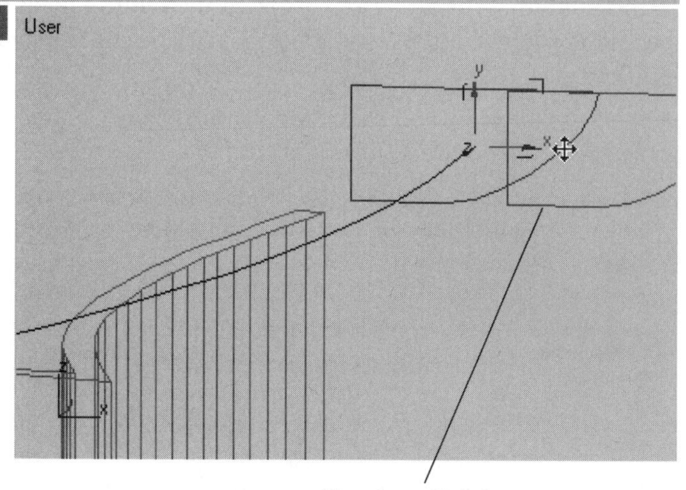

5. Click the mouse button to place the profile shape. The profile is now fixed in its new position in relation to the path.
6. You don't really want to keep this last change you made, so click the Undo button to return the profile to its original location before you started this exercise.

Here you see that by using the sub-object level, you can adjust the relationship of the loft shape to the loft path by moving the loft shape. You don't actually move the original shape profile. Instead, you move the instance clone of the shape that the Loft has placed at the beginning of the path. The Compare dialog box also gives you a view that helps you align the path with the shape.

Using Different Shapes Along the Loft Path

The loft object is basically a uniform shape along its length. Suppose you want the form of the loft to change along the path. You can do this by introducing additional shapes along the path. Here you'll begin to see the similarities between VIZ's loft and the lofting used in shipbuilding.

In the roof edge example, the chapel roof flattens slightly as it bends outward to the east. You can add this flattening by including a larger version of the original shape profile at the point where the flattening occurs. Try the following exercise to see how this works.

1. Click the Sub-Object button in the Command Panel to deactivate it.
2. Use the Select and Move tool to select the original rectangle shape you created for the profile of the loft (see Figure 5.21).

3. Shift-click and drag the red X axis arrow to the right to make a clone of the shape. In the Clone Options dialog box, make sure the Copy radio button is selected and click OK.
4. Click the Sub-Object button in the Modify tab of the Command Panel, then click the Vertex tool in the Selection rollout.
5. Click the Select and Move tool on the standard toolbar and select the three vertices shown in Figure 5.21. You can either use a selection window or Ctrl-click each vertex.

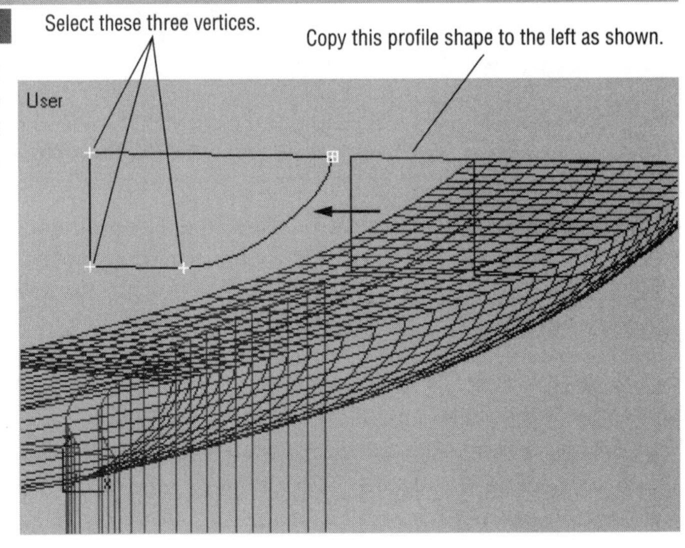
Select these three vertices.
Copy this profile shape to the left as shown.
User

FIGURE 5.21

Create a clone of the original rectangle shape, then select its vertex.

6. Click and drag to the right any of the red X axis of the shape so that the shape looks like Figure 5.22.

FIGURE 5.22

Move the vertex shown here to a new location to the left.

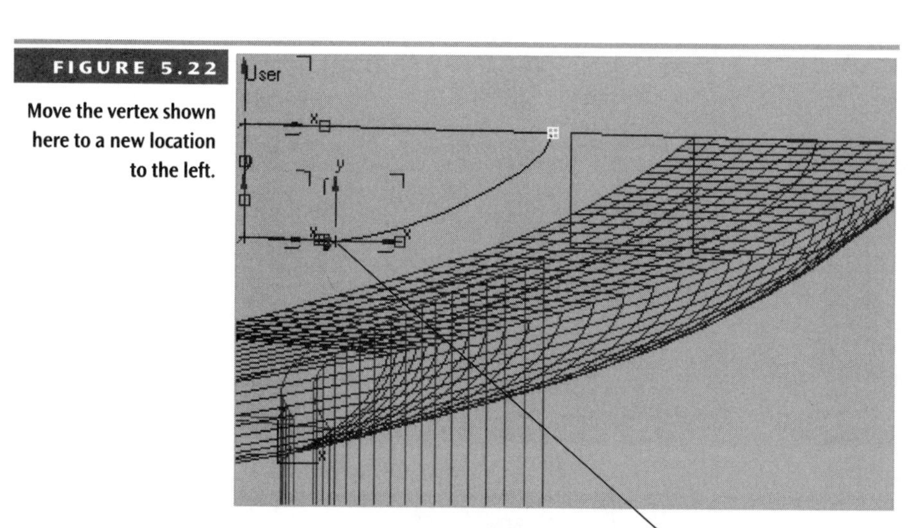

You've created a modified version of the loft profile that you'll use to *flatten* the loft profile at its eastern-most point.

1. Click the Sub-Object button to deactivate it.
2. Click the Loft shape to select it. You should see the name Loft01 at the top of the Modify tab of the Command Panel.
3. Scroll down the Command Panel to the Path Parameters rollout and click to open it. Path parameters lets you select a location along the path where you can get a new shape.

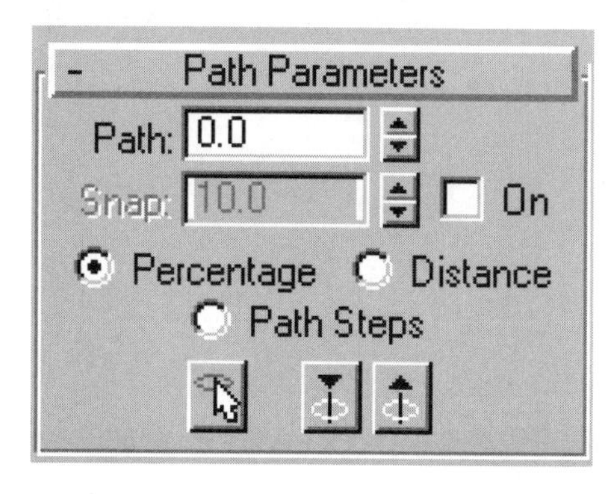

4. Click and drag the Path spinner upward. As you do this, the loft object temporarily disappears and you see a small yellow X marker move along the loft path as shown in Figure 5.23.

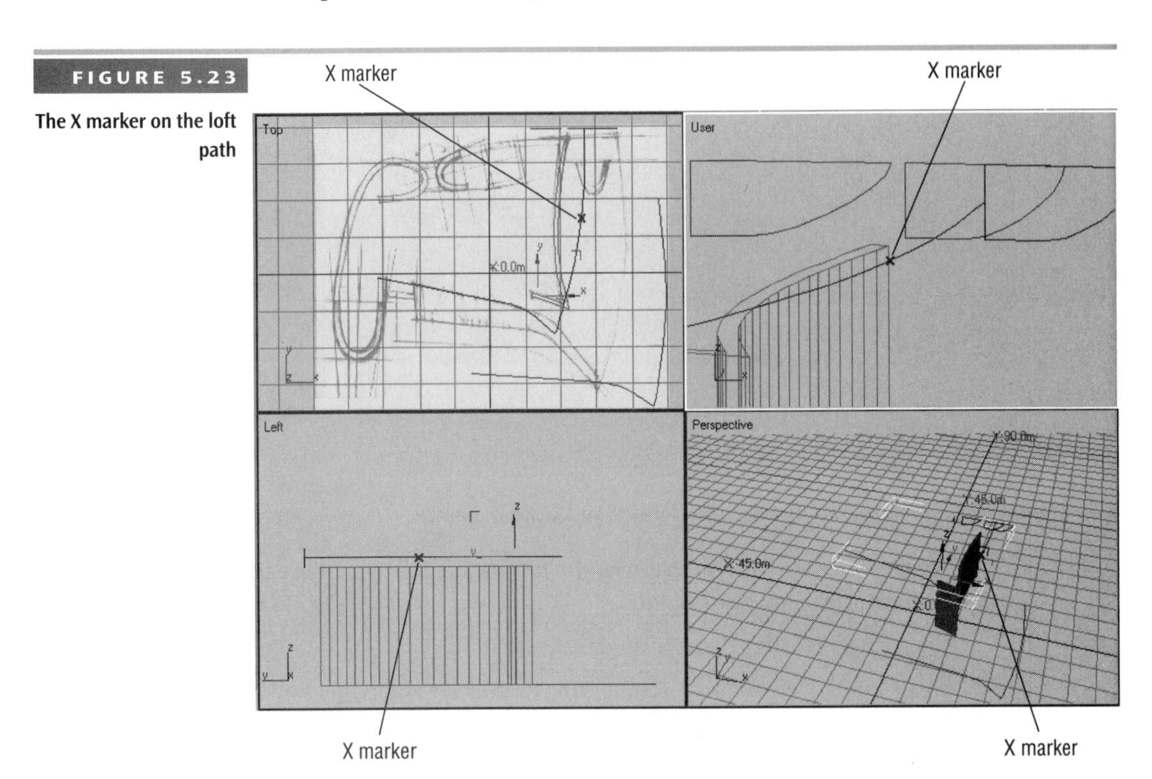

FIGURE 5.23

The X marker on the loft path

5. Adjust the spinner so that the path value is 22.5. This places the X marker at a point that is 22.5 percent of the way along the length of the entire path.
6. Scroll up the Command Panel to the Creation Method rollout and click Get Shape.

7. Place the cursor on the new, modified rectangle shape and click it. The loft object changes to include the new shape as shown in Figure 5.24.

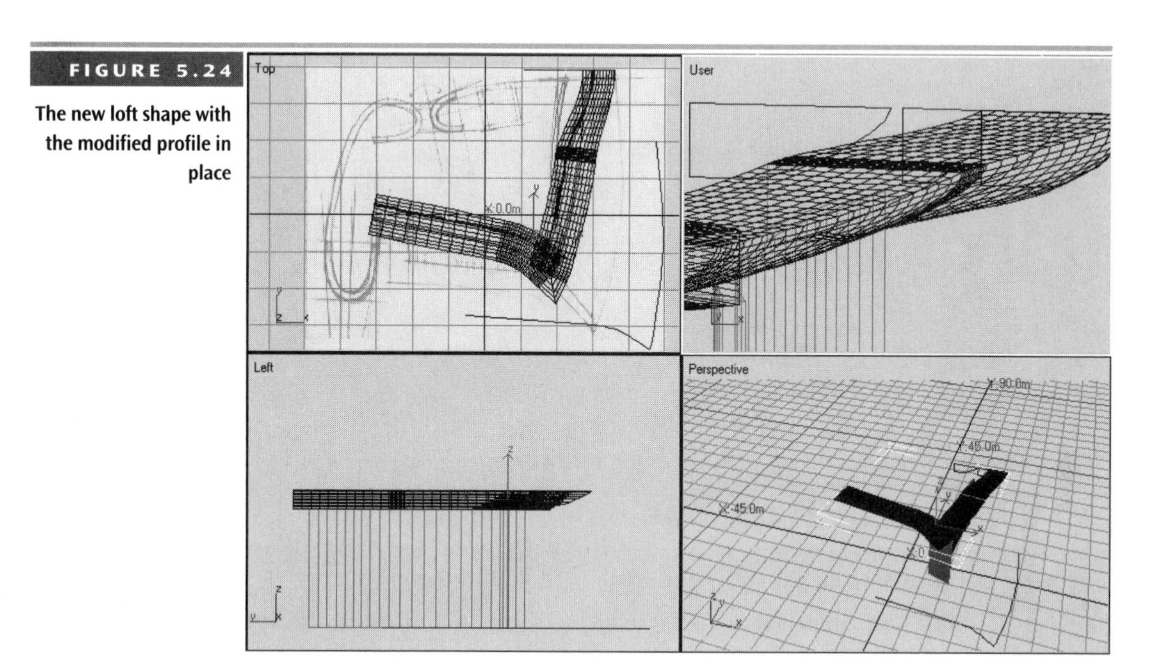

FIGURE 5.24 The new loft shape with the modified profile in place

The result of the new loft isn't quite right. To get a smoother shape, you'll need to align the new shape with the original profile shape. Here's how it's done.

1. Click the Sub-Object button. VIZ returns to the original selected shape at the beginning of the loft.
2. With the Select and Move tool selected, move the cursor to the location of the new shape along the path as shown in Figure 5.25. The cursor changes to a plus sign when it has located the shape (it may be difficult to actually see the shape in the path).

3. Click the new shape.

FIGURE 5.25

Click the loft as shown here.

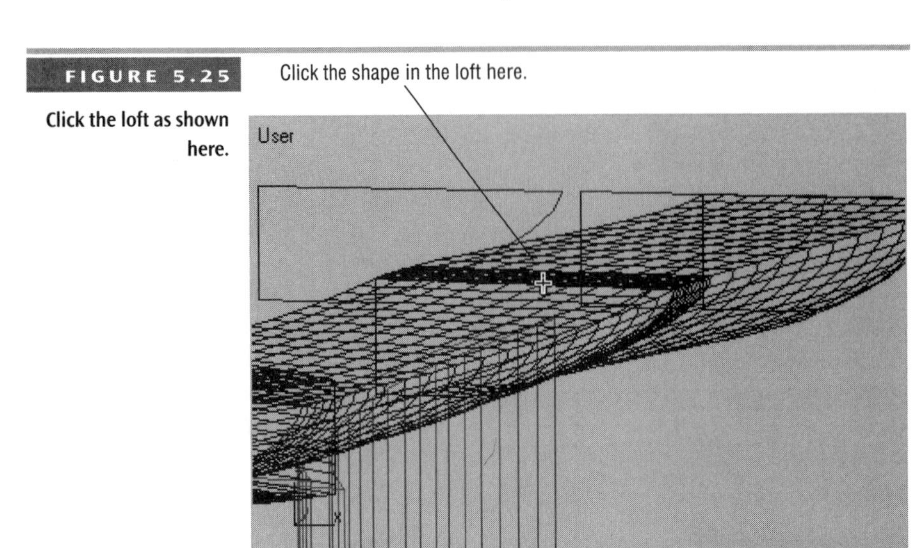

The new shape is now outlined in red within the loft shape.

4. To help align the shapes, click the Compare button in the Shape commands rollout.
5. Click the Pick Shape tool on the Compare menu bar.

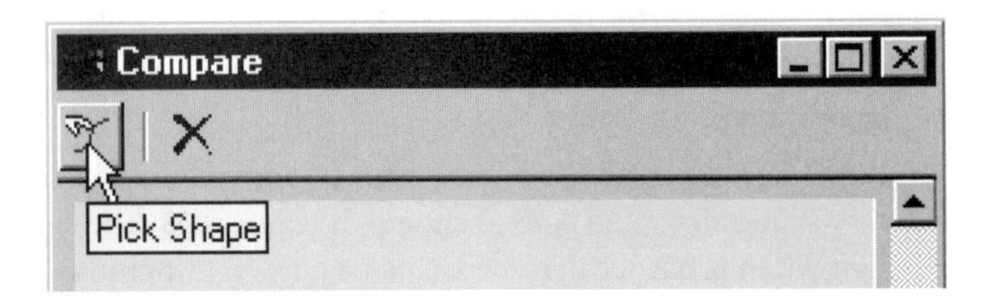

6. Click the same new shape you selected in step 3. The shape appears along with the original shape in the Compare window.

7. Click the Zoom Extents tool in the lower left corner of the Compare dialog box to get a better view of the shapes.

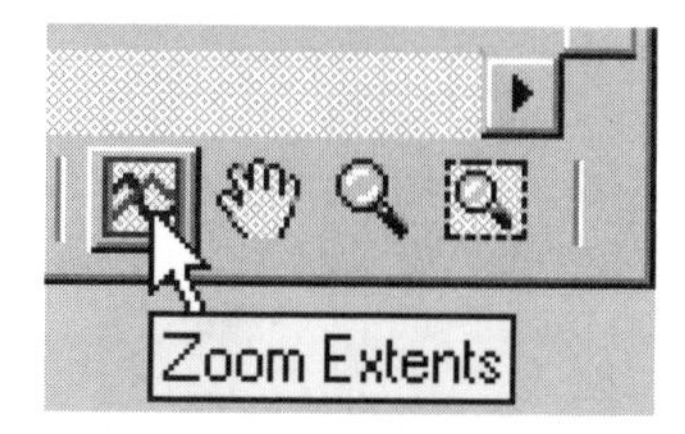

The Compare window aids in aligning the new shape to the path.

8. In the User viewport, use the Select and Move tool to move the X axis of the new shape to the right. As you move the shape, watch the Compare dialog box and align the two shapes as shown in Figure 5.26.

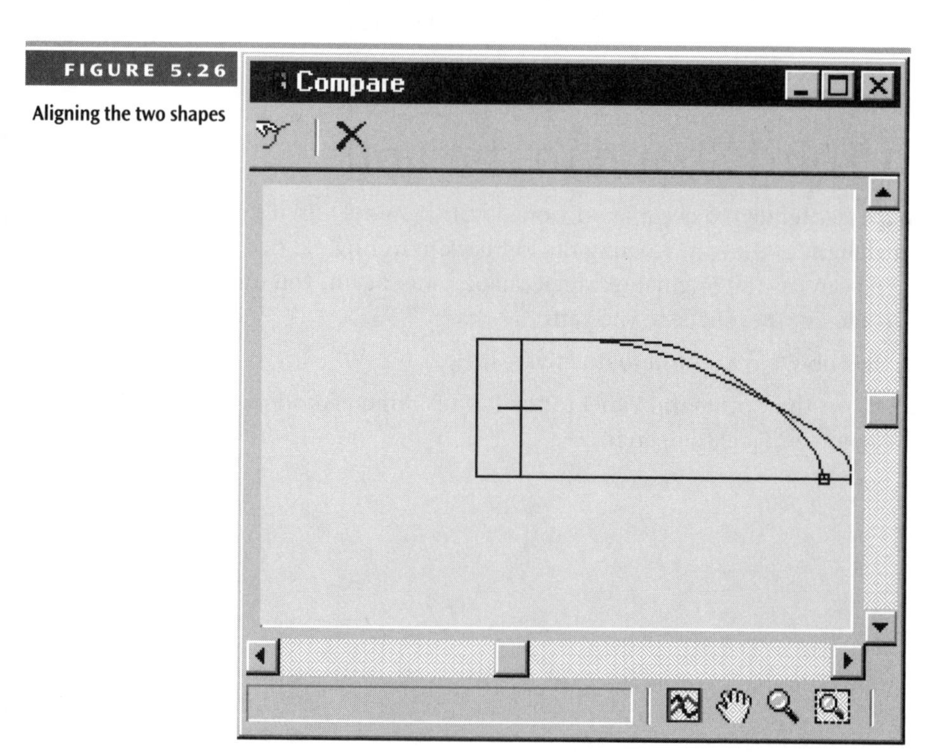

FIGURE 5.26

Aligning the two shapes

With the alignment shown in Figure 5.26, the new shape is aligned to the left side and along the top edge of the loft shape.

9. Close the Compare dialog box to get a better view of all of the viewports.

If you look at the Top viewport, you'll see that the new loft shape now uses the new shape as the profile for the rest of the loft (see Figure 5.27).

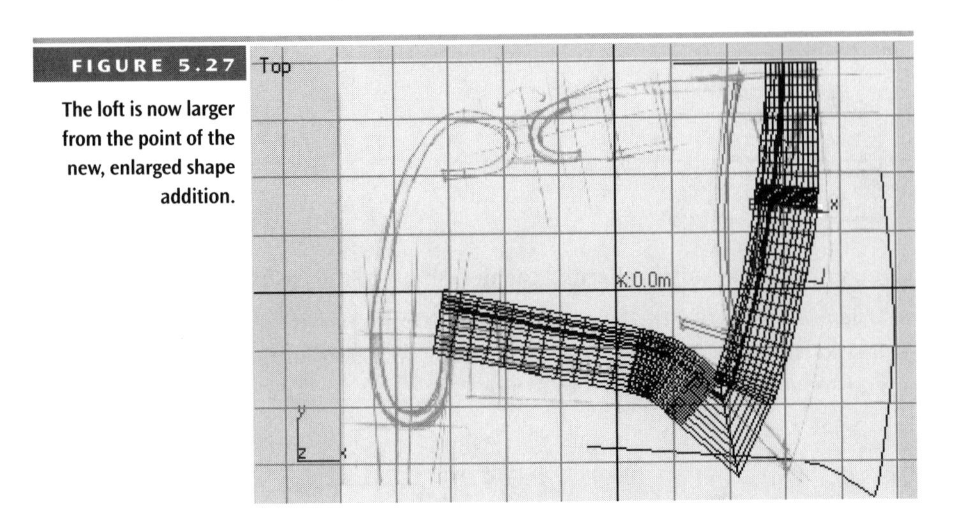

FIGURE 5.27 The loft is now larger from the point of the new, enlarged shape addition.

Adding a Third Shape to the Loft

The new shape is intended to occur at only one location in the loft; it's not the shape for the entire length of the loft. To bring the loft back to its original size past the flattened area, you can use the original rectangle shape. Once again, you use the Get Shape tool to add another shape to the path.

1. Click the Sub-Object button to deactivate it.
2. Scroll down the Command Panel to the Path Parameters rollout and click the Path Parameters label to open it.

3. Click and drag the Path spinner upward so the yellow X marker moves to the location shown in the Top viewport in Figure 5.28.

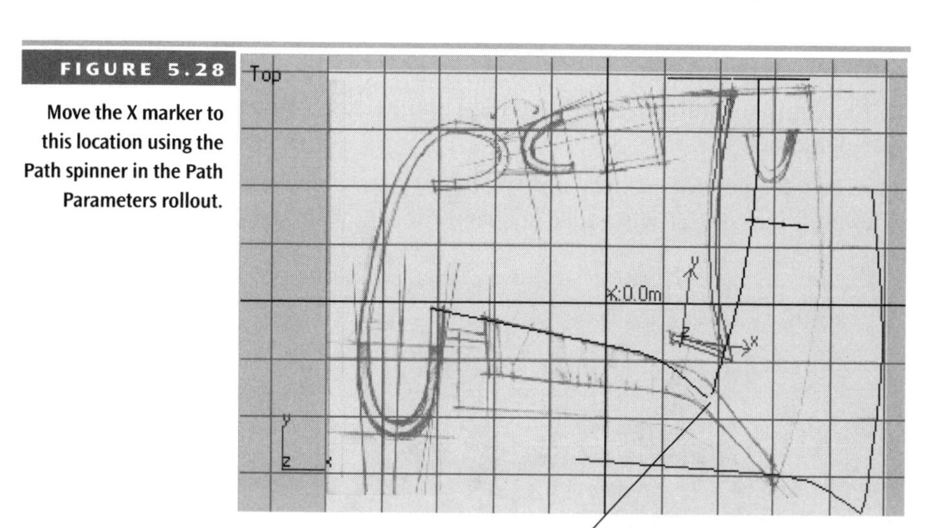
Top
X:0.0m
Move the marker to this location.

FIGURE 5.28

Move the X marker to this location using the Path spinner in the Path Parameters rollout.

4. Go to the Creation Method rollout and click the Get Shape button.
5. In the User viewport, click the original rectangle shape as shown in Figure 5.29. The loft changes to include the original shape at its new location.

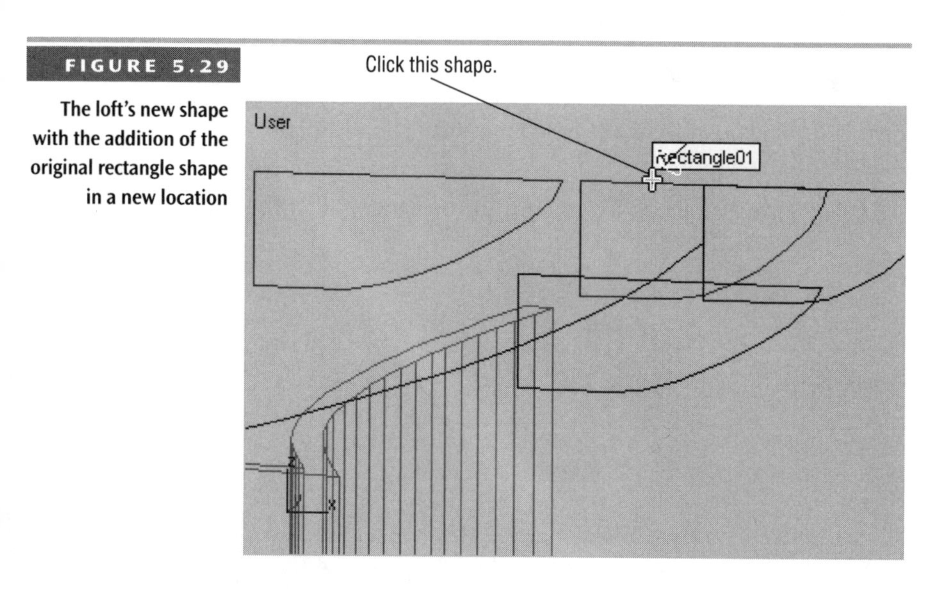
Click this shape.
User
rectangle01

FIGURE 5.29

The loft's new shape with the addition of the original rectangle shape in a new location

Just as with the enlarged shape, you need to align the new shape addition.

1. Scroll up the Command Panel to the Sub-Object button and click it.
2. In the User viewport, click the location of the new shape addition as shown in Figure 5.30.
3. Click the Compare button in the Shape Commands rollout to open the Compare window.
4. Click the Pick Shape tool on the Compare dialog box toolbar and then, in the User viewport, click the newly added shape in the loft as shown in Figure 5.30.

FIGURE 5.30

Click here to select the new shape addition.

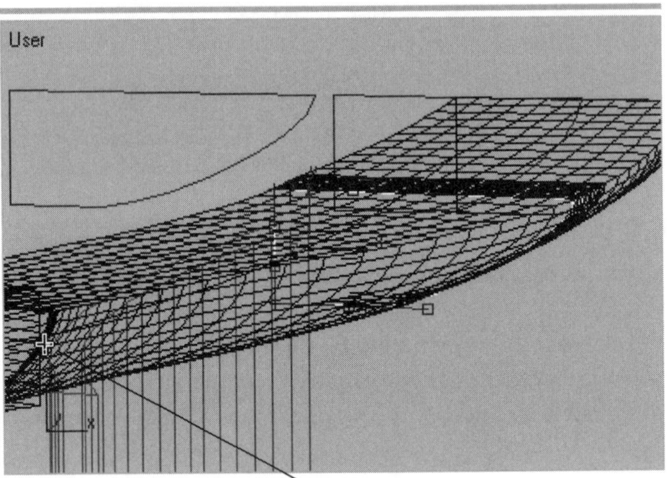

User

Click the shape in the loft at this location.

5. Click the Zoom Extents tool at the bottom of the Compare dialog box to enlarge the view of the three profiles.
6. Move the Compare dialog box to the right so you can see all of the Top viewport.

7. In the Top viewport, use the Select and Move tool to move the shape sub-object to the right along its red X axis. Use the Compare window to align the new shape with the original loft shape as shown in Figure 5.31.

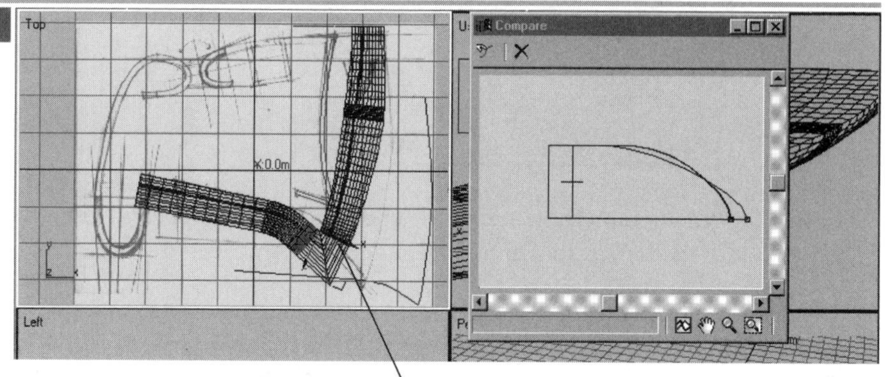
Top
Compare
X:0.0m
Left
Use the Select and Move tool to move the red X axis to the right.

FIGURE 5.31 Align the new shape with the other two shapes.

8. Close the Compare dialog box to see all of the viewports.

You can adjust the alignment of the shapes that comprise a loft at any time using the Sub-Object button. You can also adjust the location of a shape along the path by changing the Path Level value in the Shape Commands rollout. Try the following to adjust the location of the bulge.

1. With the Sub-Object button still active, click the enlarged shape in the loft as shown in Figure 5.32.

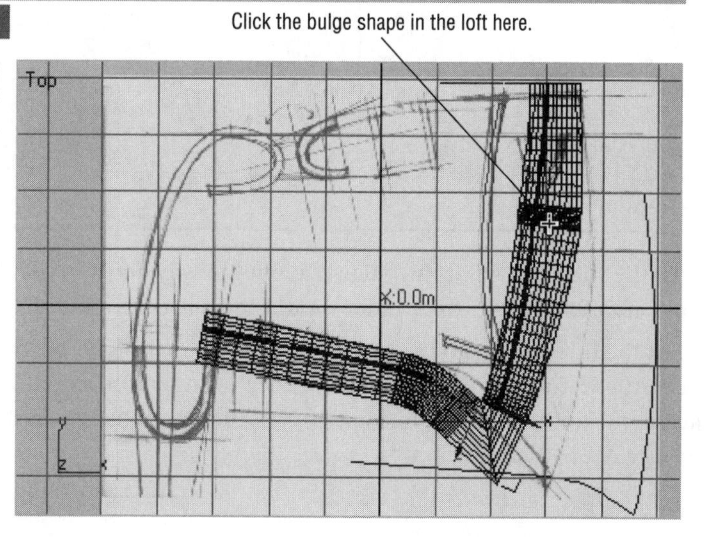
Click the bulge shape in the loft here.
Top
X:0.0m

FIGURE 5.32 Click the shape sub-object that defines the bulge of the loft.

2. In the Shape Commands rollout, click and drag the Path Level spinner downward. Notice that the bulge shape moves toward the beginning of the loft path.

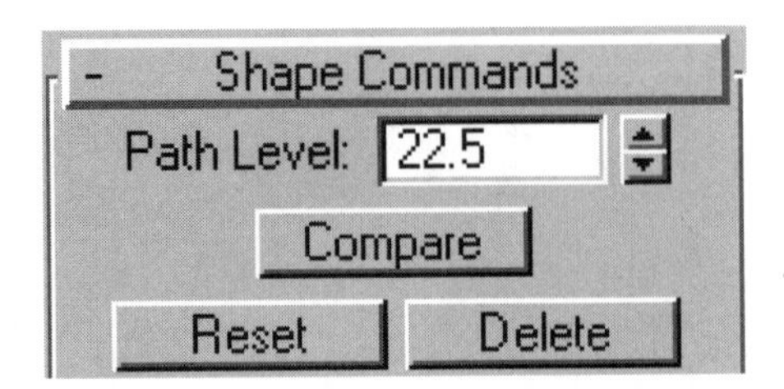

When you release the mouse button, the bulge appears closer to the beginning of the loft, as shown in in Figure 5.33.

FIGURE 5.33

Top viewport showing bulge

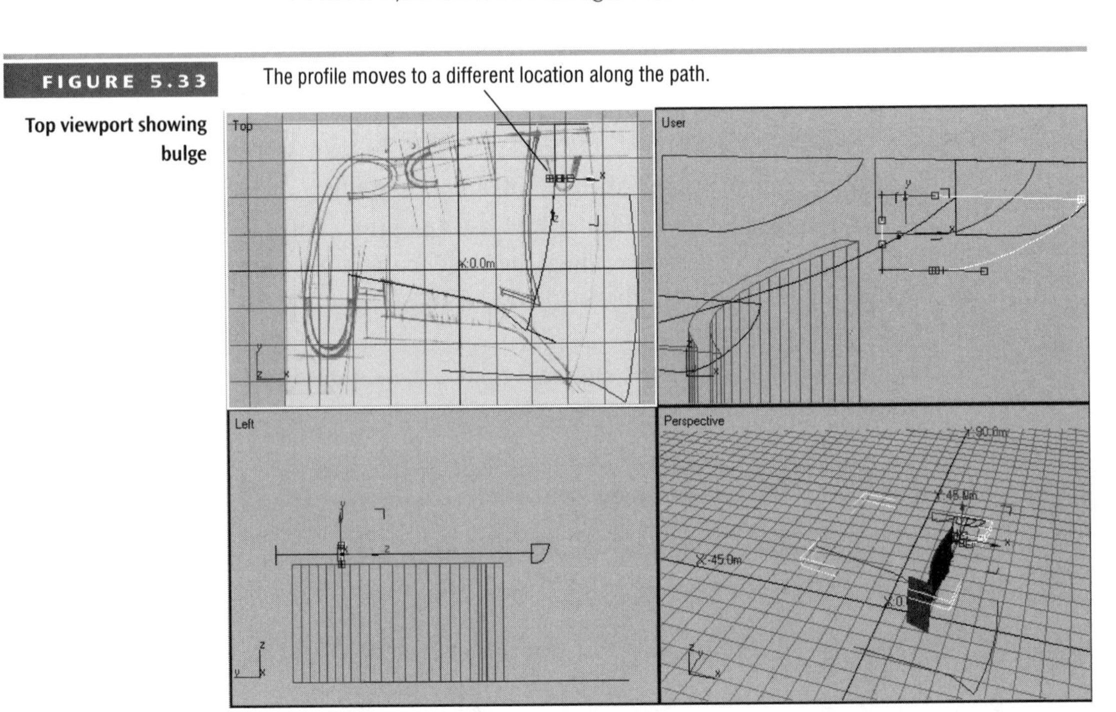

3. Adjust the spinner so that the bulge is about halfway between the first and third shapes along the path. The spinner should show a value around 25.5.

With all of the fine-tuning you've been doing, the overall shape of the roof edge has gotten a little distorted, especially near the beginning of the loft path. You can make adjustments to the loft path to compensate for minor changes in the loft by editing the original path object.

Using the Path Clone to Edit the Loft Path

Remember that earlier in this chapter you were asked to move the original loft path to the right of the model. This was done so you could have a clear view of the path in order to edit it. In the next exercise, you'll make changes to the loft by editing the original line you used to define its path.

First, rotate the loft so that it is aligned with the sketch bitmap.

1. Click in the Top viewport. Then click the Min/Max Toggle tool to enlarge the viewport.
2. Click the Sub-Object button in the Command Panel to deactivate it. Click the Select and Rotate tool, then click the loft object.
3. Click the Reference Coordinate system drop-down list on the Standard Toolbar and select View.

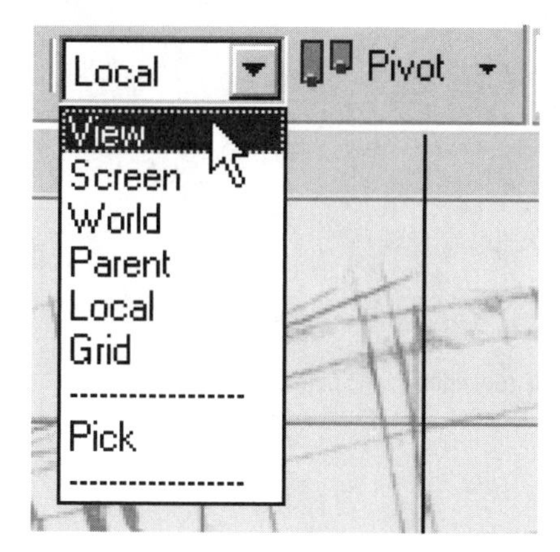

4. Click and drag the Z coordinate axis of the loft object downward so that the bottom edge of the loft object aligns with the edge of the roof in the sketch as shown in Figure 5.34.

FIGURE 5.34

Align the roof with the sketch along the bottom edge.

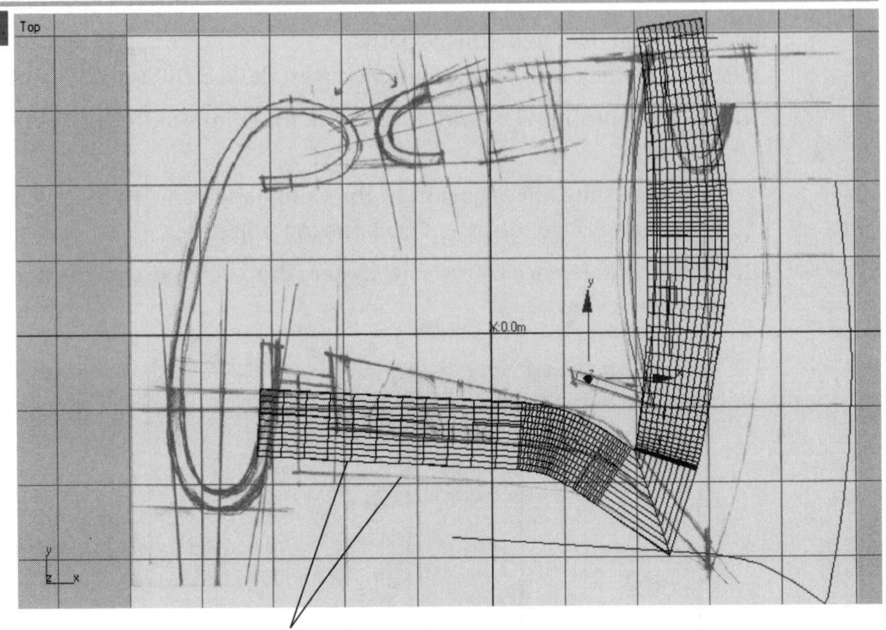
Top
Align this edge of the roof with the roof edge on the bitmap.

5. Click the Select and Move tool and move the roof so that its corner is aligned with the corner of the bitmap sketch as shown in Figure 5.35.

FIGURE 5.35

Align the roof corner with the corner in the sketch.

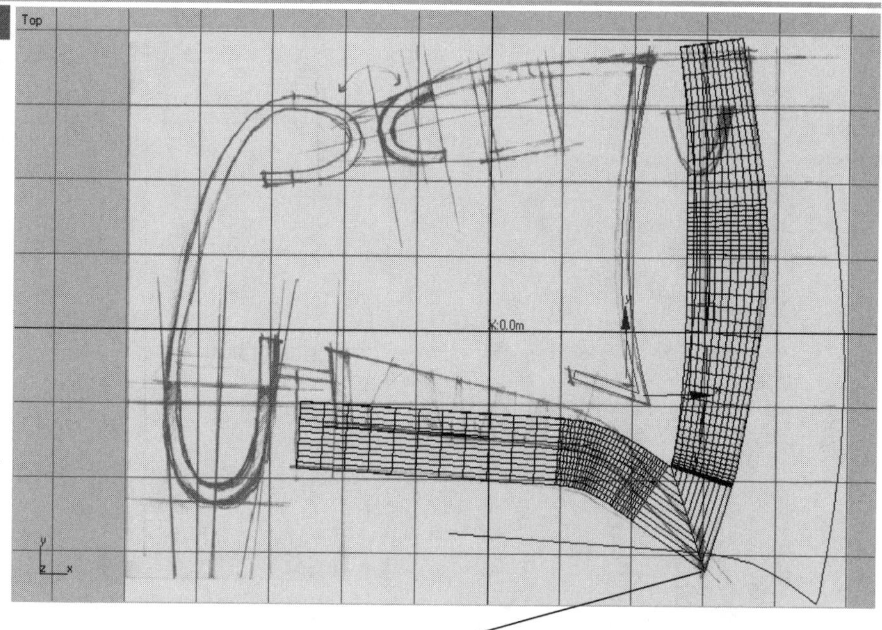

Move the roof so that its corner aligns with the roof corner on the bitmap image.

Now you can use the bitmap sketch as a guide to adjusting the curve of the loft. The south edge doesn't need to be edited in any way, as it is fairly well aligned with the sketch. The east edge of the roof needs to be *tweaked* a bit to conform to the outline in the sketch.

Start by adjusting the curve of the roof from the northern-most end.

1. Click the curve you created to define the path of the loft as shown in Figure 5.36, then click the Vertex tool in the Modify tab of the Command Panel.

2. Click the beginning vertex at the top of the curve as shown in Figure 5.36.

FIGURE 5.36

Select the curve, select Vertex from the Selection rollout, then click the beginning vertex as shown here.

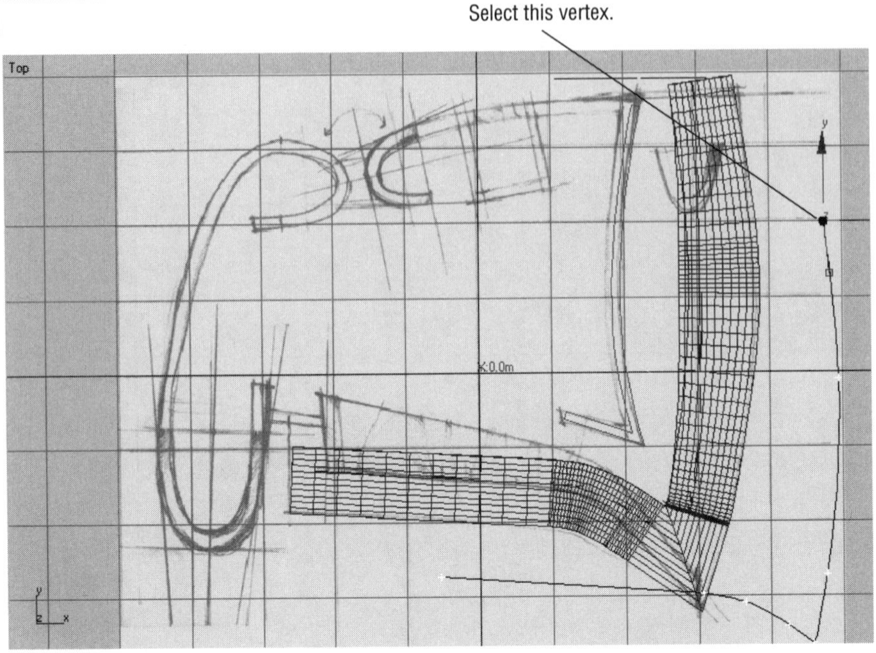

Select this vertex.

3. Make sure the View option is selected in the Reference Coordinate System drop-down list. Then click the Select and Rotate tool and rotate the vertex counter-clockwise so that the curve looks similar to the one shown in Figure 5.37. As you drag the Select and Rotate tool, you'll notice that the view of the loft disappears revealing the path and shapes that make up the loft. You only need to rotate the curve a little. If you rotate the curve too much, you can click the Undo tool and start over.
4. Click the Select and Move tool and move the vertex farther upward so the north edge of the roof extends slightly beyond the north wall.
5. Click the Sub-Object button to deactivate it.

FIGURE 3.37

Rotating the vertex

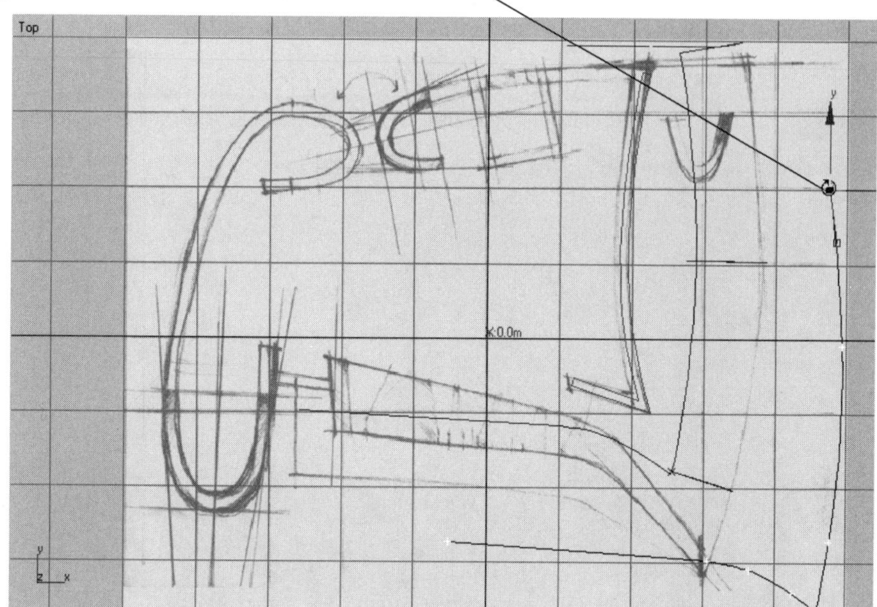
Click and drag downward to rotate this vertex counter clockwise.
Top

The roof edge is now aligned with the roof sketch and you've completed the south and east edges of the roof. You can see how editing the original path affects the loft object. The loft modifier created an instance clone of the original path object and incorporated the clone into the loft. This allowed you to make changes to the original and have those changes affect the loft.

You may want to save the original loft shapes in case you want to edit the loft later, but you may not want them appearing in your model as they can contribute to the visual clutter of the viewports. Instead of deleting them, you can place them on their own layer for safe keeping, then turn that layer off.

1. Click the Layer Properties tool, then click New in the Layer Properties dialog box.
2. Type **Layout** for the new layer name and click OK. This is the layer in which you'll store your shapes and path.

3. Click the Select object tool on the standard toolbar. Then Ctrl-click the two loft shapes you used to create the loft (see Figure 5.38). Leave the Loft Path visible for now.

FIGURE 5.38

Selecting the loft shapes and path

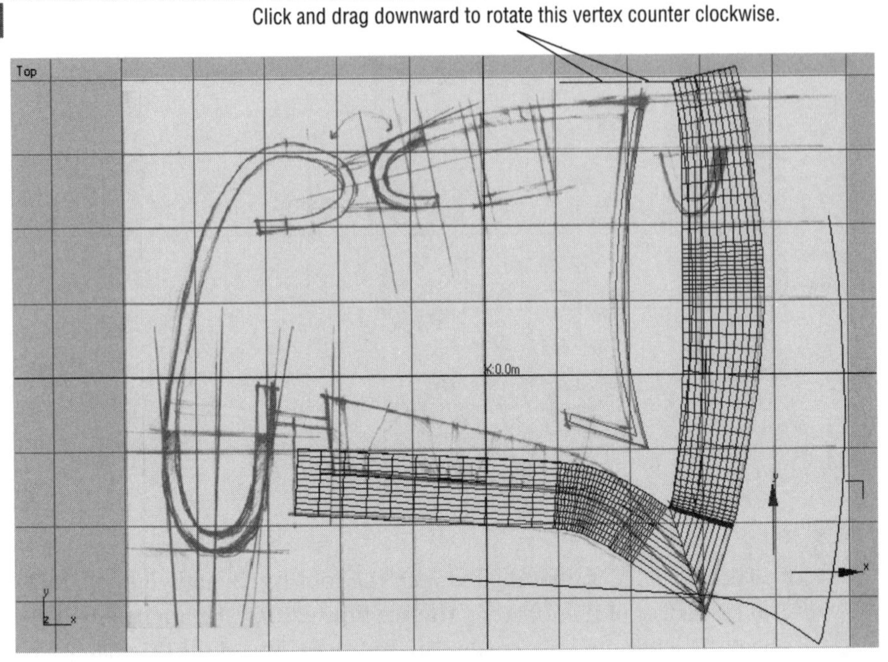

4. Click the Layer drop-down list on the standard toolbar and select Layout.
5. Open the Layer drop-down list again and click the lightbulb icon associated with the Layout name. The shapes disappear.

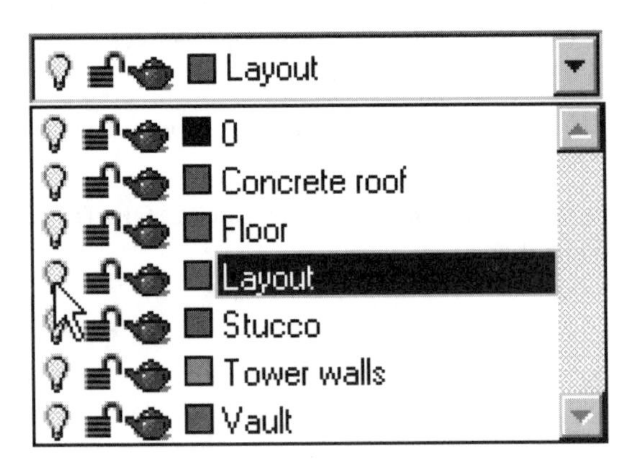

Adding the Remaining Parts of the Roof

There's still a good portion of the roof that needs to be built. It would be simple to just fill in the remaining portion with a flat, extruded shape, but the design calls for a *trough* through the center of the roof. This trough starts out at the west end of the roof and gradually flattens to meet the east end of the roof that you just created (see Figure 5.39).

FIGURE 5.39

The remaining portion of the roof

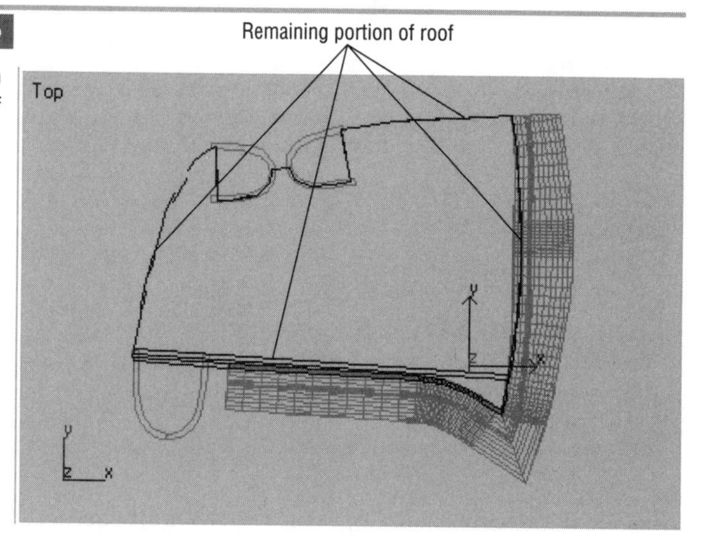

There are a number of challenges in adding this part of the roof. You need to create a shape that transitions from a fairly steep curve to a shallow one at the east end of the roof. You also need to merge this roof addition to the roof edge you just created.

The simplest way to create the remaining part of the roof is to use the original path object to define the east and south sides of the roof addition. Since the path already constitutes the form of the portion of the roof you lofted, it will make it easier to fill in the odd volumes. The north and west sides will have to be added.

Adding Segments to an Existing Spline

Start by making a copy of the original path object. You'll use the copy as two sides of a closed shape that will become the rest of the roof.

1. Click the Select and Move tool, then Shift-click and drag the path object to the location shown in Figure 5.40. You want to align the path to the inside edge of the existing roof, but you don't have to be absolutely exact at this point.

FIGURE 5.40

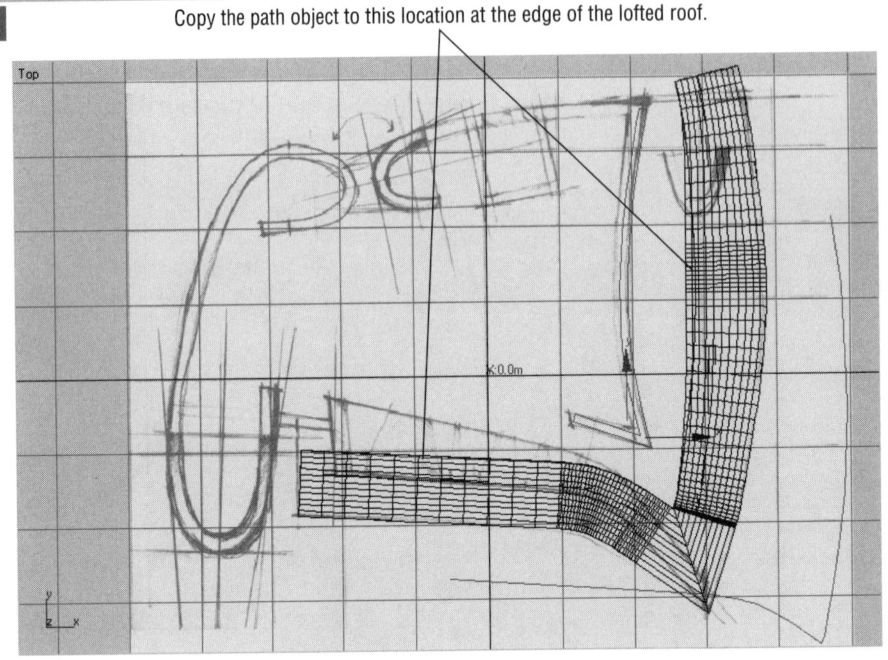
Copy the path object to this location at the edge of the lofted roof.
Top

Copying the path object and aligning it with the roof. The path thickness is exaggerated here for clarity.

2. In the Clone dialog box, click Copy, then click OK. If you need to, adjust the rotation of the newly copied line so that it lines up with the lofted roof as shown in Figure 5.40.

TIP **While adjusting the rotation, you can right-click the Select and Rotate tool and fine-tune the rotation angle of the object by adjusting the Z axis spinner.**

3. Click the lofted roof you created in the previous exercise, then click the Layer drop-down list on the standard toolbar.
4. Select Concrete Roof.
5. Open the list again and click the lightbulb associated with the Concrete roof layer to turn that layer off.

You'll want to turn off the roof for now so it doesn't interfere with your view of your current work. You'll use the bitmap sketch and the West wall to make the additional north and west sides of the outline. You'll need to first turn on the West wall.

1. Click the Display tab in the Command Panel.
2. Click the Turn On by Name... button.
3. In the Turn On by Name dialog box, click West wall from the list, then click On. The West wall appears in the drawing.

Now you're ready to add. This time, you'll try something new. Instead of creating a new object, you'll add line segments to an existing one.

1. Select the new spline you just created and click the Modify tab.
2. Click the Spline tool in the Selection rollout.
3. Scroll down the Command Panel to the Geometry rollout and click the Create Line button.

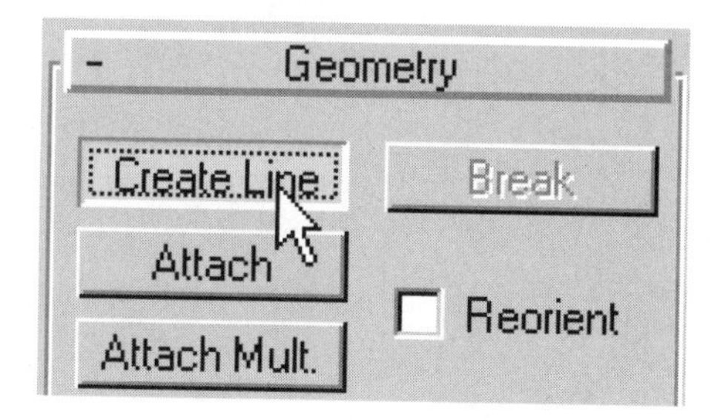

4. Place the cursor on the endpoint shown in Figure 5.40. Notice that a graphic marker appears by the cursor.

   This tells you that if you click this endpoint, the resulting line will be joined automatically to the spline at that point.

5. Click the endpoint. A rubber-banding line emerges from the endpoint.

6. Draw the rest of the line as shown in Figure 5.41. Try to keep the line within the West wall. When you get to the end, right click to exit.

FIGURE 5.41

Adding the line segments

Start the new line segment here.

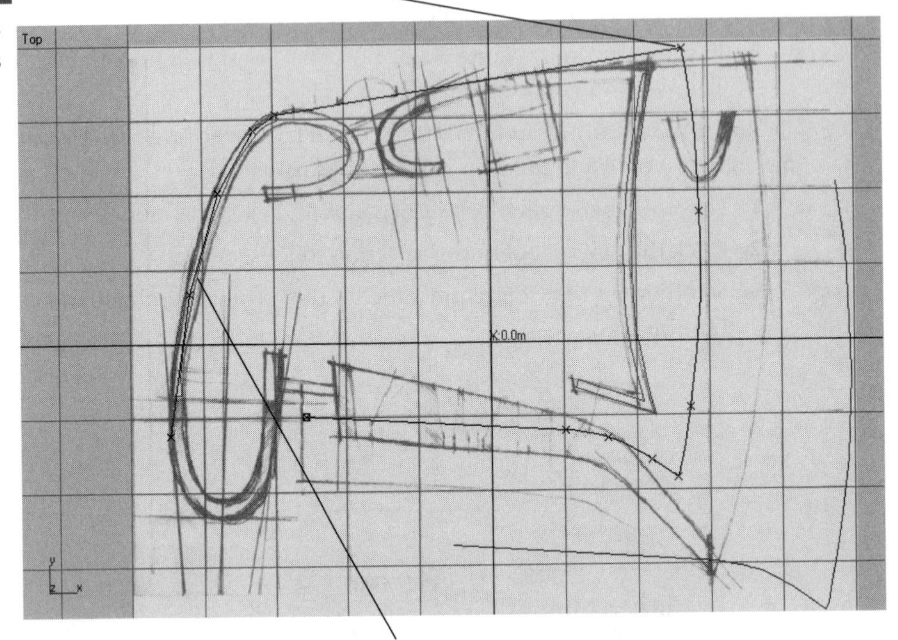
Top
0.0m
Draw the line inside the West wall.

Here you saw that you can add segments to the end of an existing spline. This allows you to preserve the shape of the line while adding additional segments.

You may wonder why you didn't close the line in the last exercise. You want to preserve the shape of the east and south edges as much as possible. You also want to extend the south edge to the west edge to maintain the south edge's orientation. In Chapter 3, you used the Extend tool to extend line segments. Use it again here to help close the roof outline.

1. Click the Create Line button to deactivate it. Then scroll down the Command Panel to the Extend button and click it.
2. Click near the endpoint shown in Figure 5.41. The line you clicked extends to the new line segment.
3. Click the Extend button to deactivate it.
4. Scroll up to the Selection rollout in the Command Panel and click the Vertex tool.

5. Click and drag the endpoint shown in Figure 5.42 to the endpoint of the segment you just extended.

FIGURE 4.42

Move one endpoint to meet the other endpoint.

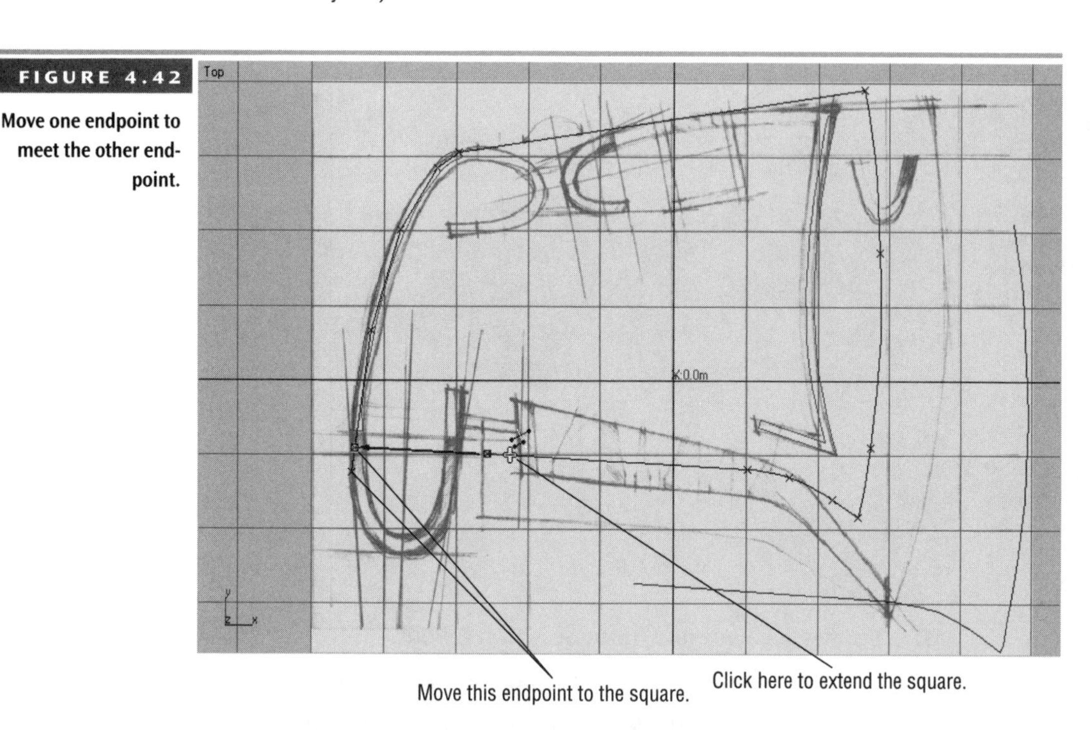

6. At the Weld coincident endpoints message, click Yes.

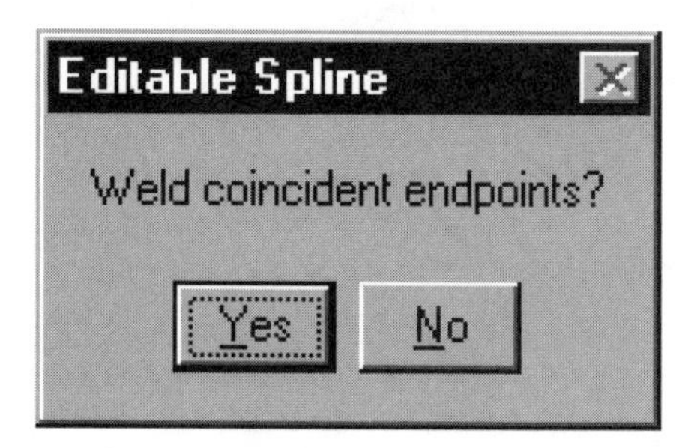

Now that you have the outline to complete the roof, there are still a few more things you need to do before moving on to extruding and editing the roof shape. Later, you will be adding the *trough* to the roof. This will require some additional vertices along the east and west sides of the roof in order to facilitate a smooth trough shape (see Figure 5.43). The additional vertices allow VIZ to create additional facets like folds in a sheet of paper.

You'll also want to divide the outline into two sections: one section will isolate the trough from the curved corner at the south side of the roof. The curve will introduce some unwanted faces into the shape, causing the trough to appear less uniform.

FIGURE 5.43

You will want to isolate the trough of the roof corner so that the corner does not introduce any undesirable effects.

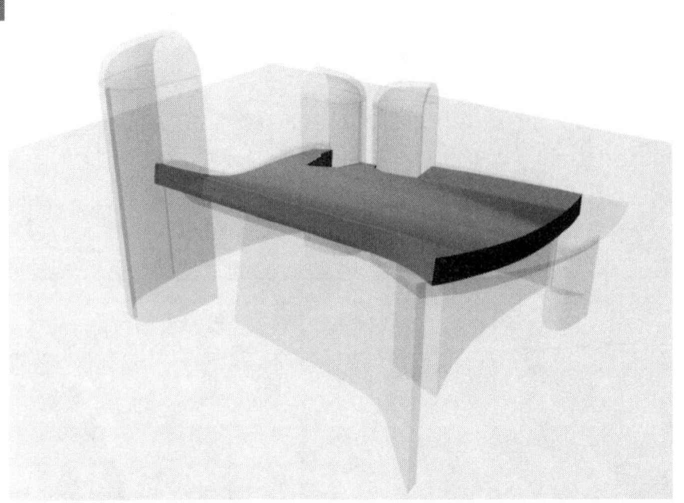

1. Click the Segment tool in the Selection rollout.
2. Scroll down to the Geometry rollout and click the Break button.
3. Place the cursor on the outline but don't click it just yet. Notice that the cursor shows an icon telling you that you have found a breakable object.

4. Click the points on the outline as indicated in Figure 5.44. The line segment breaks at the points you click. The square indicating the beginning of the segment moves to the new location.

FIGURE 5.44

Breaking the outline at two points

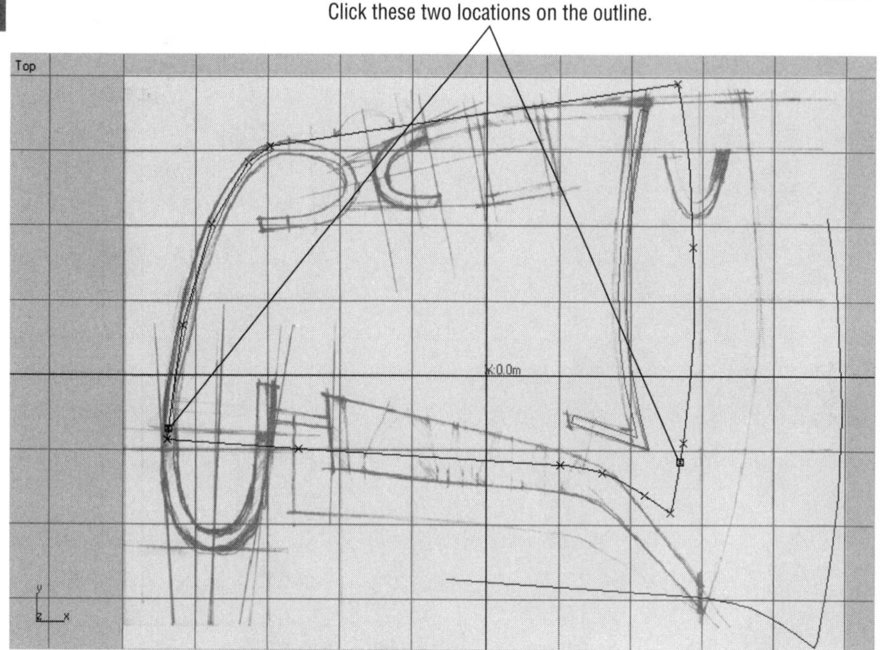
Click these two locations on the outline.
Top

5. Click the Break button to deactivate it.

You now have two separate splines. The lower spline separates the corner of the roof edge from the rest of the roof. You'll need to close both splines so that when they are extruded, they will form a solid shape rather than a simple extruded line.

1. Scroll up to the top of the Command Panel and click the Spline tool in the Selection rollout.
2. Right-click the lower spline to select it, then select Close from the pop-up menu.
3. Right-click the other spline and select Close from the pop-up menu. You now have two closed splines as part of the roof addition.

4. One or both of the new line segments may be curved as shown in Figure 5.45. To straighten the segment, do the following.

FIGURE 5.45

Straightening the curved line segment

Right click on these segments.
Top

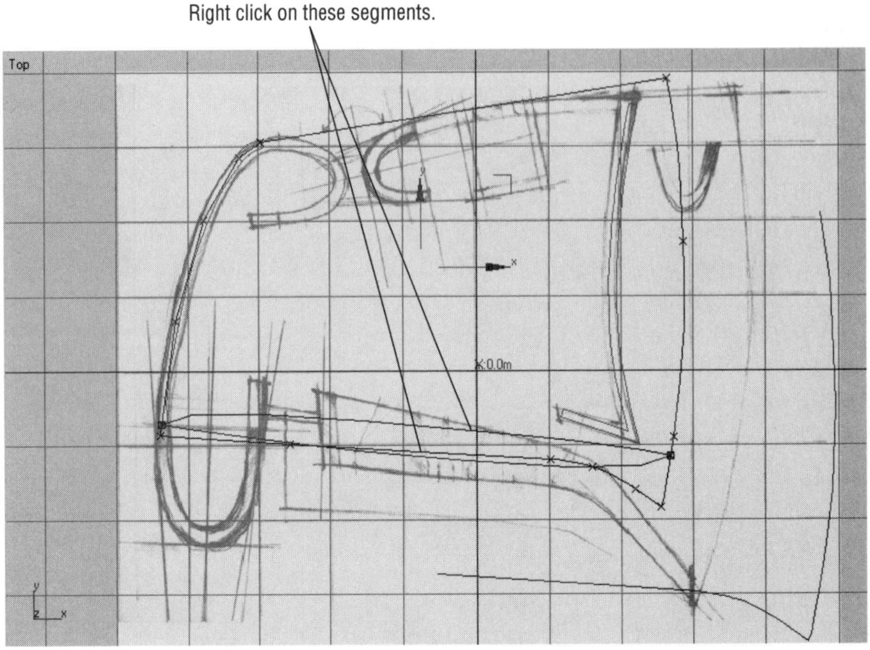

1. Click the Segment tool in the Selection rollout.
2. Right-click one of the curved segments, then select Line from the pop-up menu. The line straightens.
3. Repeat step 2 for the other curved line segment. Your line should now look similar to the one in Figure 5.46.
4. Finally, you'll need to remove the extra vertex on the added segments. Click the Vertex tool in the Selection rollout. Then click the vertex shown in Figure 5.46 and press the delete key.

The next step is to generate some vertices in the larger of the two roof outlines that you can use to *mold* the shape of the roof. You can divide a segment into smaller, equally spaced segments by using the Divide button in the Geometry rollout. By dividing a line segment, you add vertices as well.

1. With the Segment tool selected in the Selection rollout, scroll down the Command Panel to the Divide button.

2. Ctrl-click the line segments on the left side of the outline as shown in Figure 5.46.

FIGURE 5.46

With Spline selected, right-click these segments and select Line from the pop-up menu.

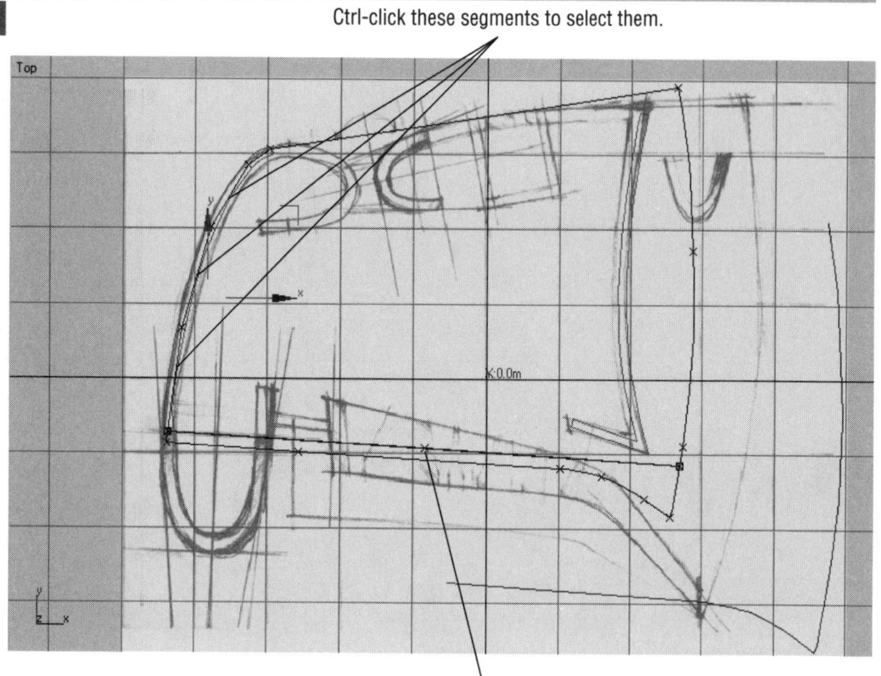
Ctrl-click these segments to select them.
Top
Delete this vertex.

3. In the Divide input box, enter **7**↵, then click the Divide button. The selected segment is divided into 7 segments as shown in Figure 5.47.

FIGURE 5.47

The segment divided

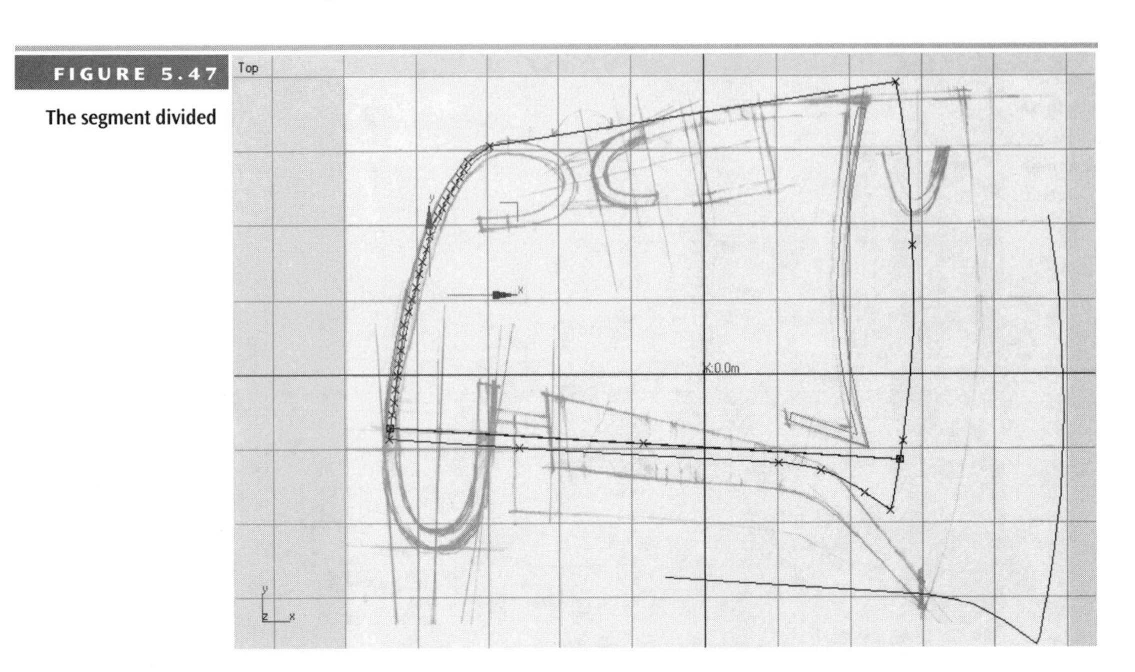

Each segment is divided into 7 segments for a total of 21 segments. You need to divide the other side of the roof outline as well in order to give VIZ enough vertices to generate a smooth shape. The right side is already divided into 3 segments, so you'll want to divide each of those segments so that, overall, the right side has a number of segments similar to what the left has.

1. Click the longest of the three segments on the right side of the outline as shown in Figure 5.48.
2. Change the Divide input box value to **12**. Then click the Divide button.

3. Click the next segment as shown in Figure 5.48, then divide it into 9 segments.

FIGURE 5.48

Divide the segments on the right side of the outline into 12 and 9 divisions, respectively, as shown here.

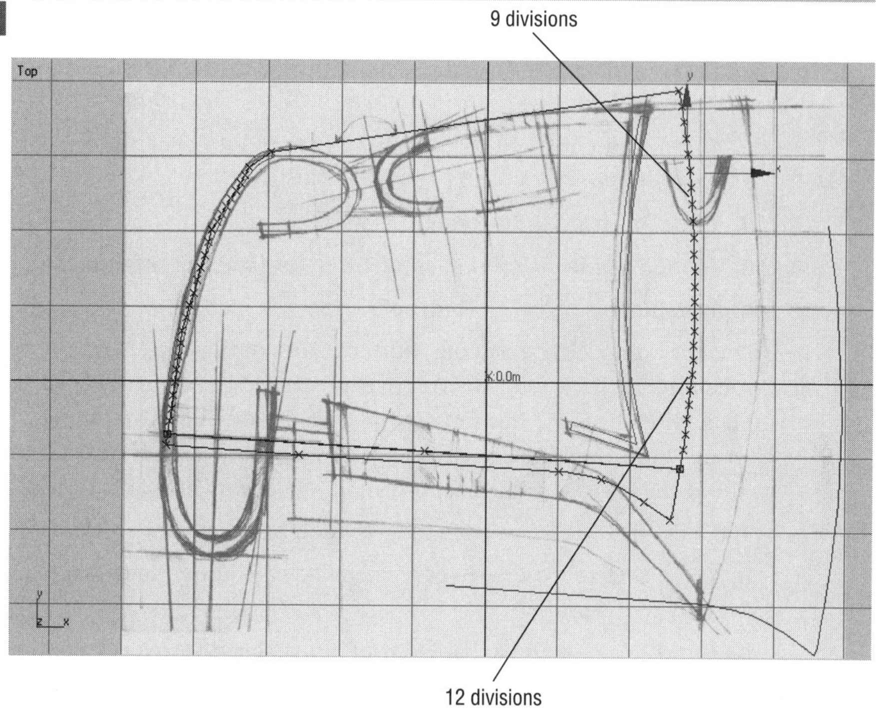

With the divisions in place, you are ready to extrude the new portion of the roof.

Unequal Divisions

In some situations, you may find that the Divide tool creates unequal divisions. This is usually due to having Bézier vertices at the endpoints of the line segment you are dividing. To obtain even divisions, use the Vertex option in the Selection rollout, right-click the vertex at the end of the line segment you are working on, then select Corner from the pop-up menu. Do this for each endpoint of the line segment. Once this is done, the Divide tool will divide the segment into equal divisions.

Using Soft Selections to Pull Vertices

You're ready to extrude the shape into a mesh that will form the rest of the roof. Once the extrusion is done, you can then take steps to form the *trough*. Here you'll learn how to use Soft Selection to *pull* a set of vertices a non-uniform distance. Start by extruding the shape.

1. Scroll to the top of the Command Panel, then click the Sub-Object button to deactivate it.
2. Click the Extrude button in the Modifiers rollout.
3. In the Parameters rollout, enter **1.8** in the Amount input box.
4. Rename this object to **Flat roof**.

Though it may not be obvious, both outlines of the object you've been working on extrude into a solid form. Now you're ready to add the trough. For this operation, you'll employ the Soft Selection option. This option allows you to select and edit a set of vertices with varying degrees of force. It's a concept that is difficult to explain, but the following exercise will reveal in a more direct way how Soft Selection works.

1. Click the Min/Max toggle tool to view the other viewports.
2. Right-click the User viewport, then click the Zoom Extents tool to get an overall view of the roof.
3. Right-click on the extruded roof, then select Convert to Editable Mesh. You won't need the parametric feature of the extruded shape and converting the roof to an editable mesh will save memory.
4. Click the Vertex tool in the Selection rollout of the Modify tab.
5. Right-click the Top viewport. Then use the Select object tool and a rectangular selection region to select the vertex shown in Figure 5.49.

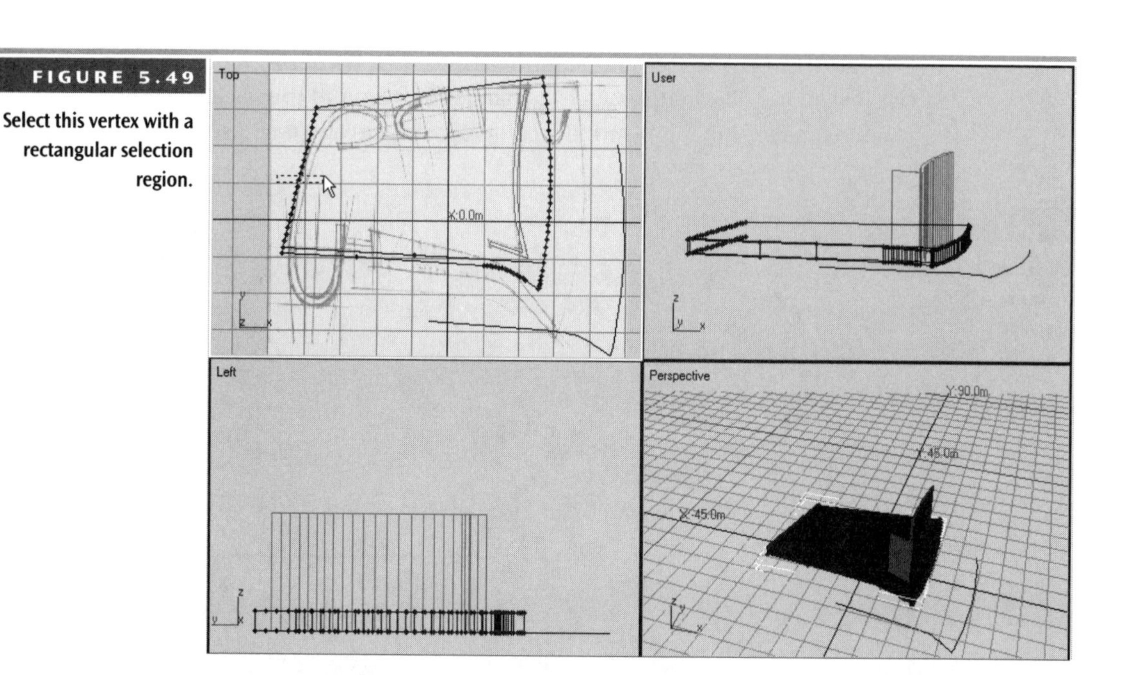

FIGURE 5.49

Select this vertex with a rectangular selection region.

By using the rectangular selection region in the Top viewport, you select both the top and bottom vertex at this location.

You want to move a set of vertices downward in the Z axis to create a dip in the surface at the west end of the roof. If you move the vertices you selected so far, you'd get a very sharp dip, which is not what you want.

1. Scroll down the Command Panel and click the Soft Selection rollout button to open it. Then click the Use Soft Selection check box.

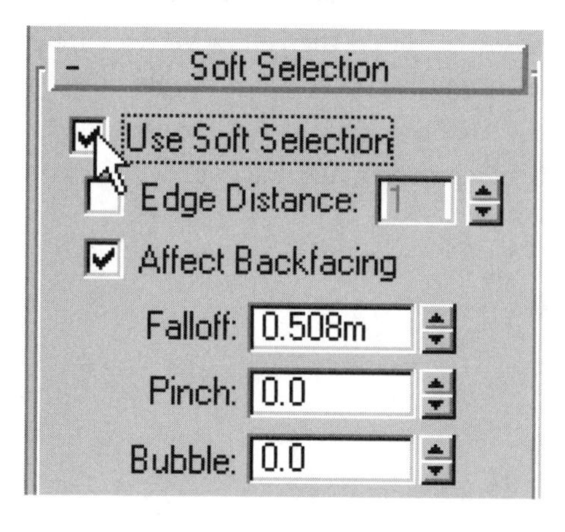

2. Click and drag the Falloff spinner upward and, as you do this, watch the Top and User viewports. The vertices start to change color around the selected vertices. As you move the spinner upward, the colors spread outward (see Figure 5.50).

FIGURE 5.50

As the Falloff value increases, the vertices change color.

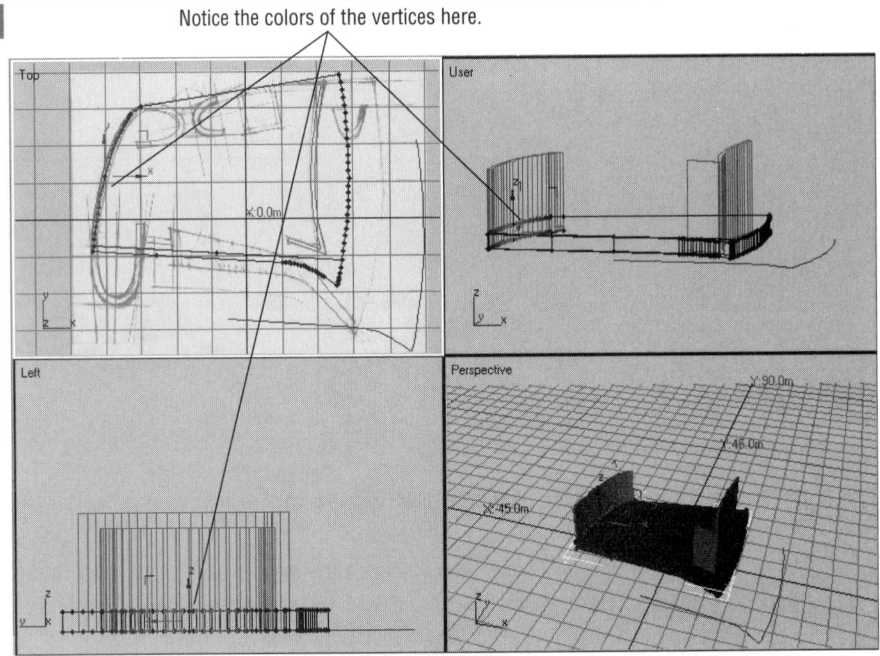
Notice the colors of the vertices here.
Top
User
Left
Perspective

The changing color indicates the strength of the selection of those vertices. Red is the strongest selection, while yellow is the weakest.

3. Adjust the Falloff spinner so that the yellow vertices are close to the corners of the roof but not touching the corners. This should be a value of about **10** in the Falloff input box.
4. Right-click the Left viewport to make it active.

5. Click the Select and Move tool if it isn't already selected, then, in the Left viewport, click and drag the Z axis downward until the view looks similar to Figure 5.51.

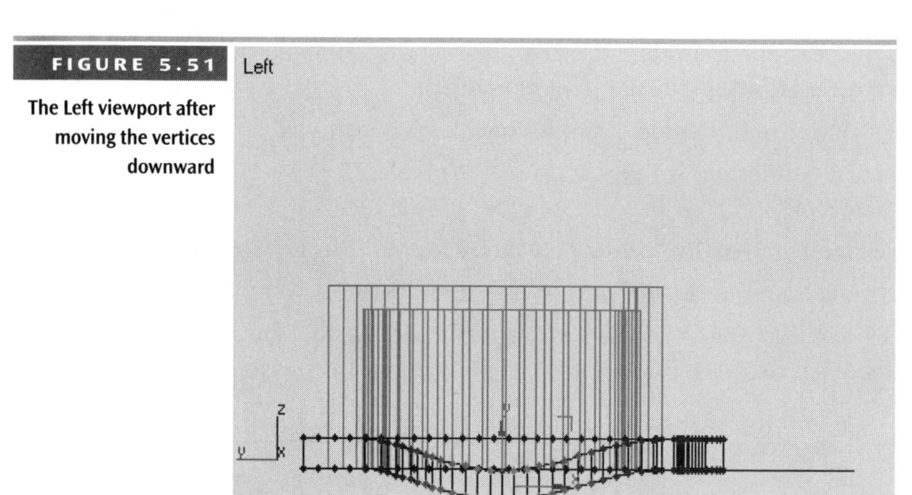

FIGURE 5.51 The Left viewport after moving the vertices downward

6. When you've finished moving the vertices, click the Sub-Object button in the Command Panel to deactivate it.

You see that the *force* of the downward motion tapers off as you move away from the originally selected vertices. This causes the selected vertices to form a curve. It's a bit like the way a piece of foam rubber reacts when you press on it with your finger.

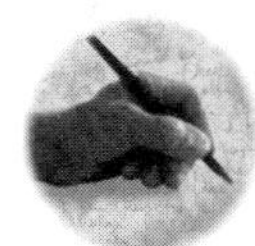

NOTE **You can adjust the way that the soft selection options affect the vertices by making changes to the Pinch and Bubble settings just below the Falloff setting. Pinch causes the selection to create a spiked form when a set of vertices is selected and moved, while Bubble causes the selection to create a wave-like form. The Graphic below these settings displays a sample of their effect.**

The roof is nearly complete. You need to merge the new portion of the roof with the lofted edge. The entire roof, including the lofted portion, is slightly bent along the east-west axis, so you'll apply a Bend modifier to the entire roof. After that is done, the roof needs to be rotated in both north-south and east-west axes. The final step will be to trim off the excess portions of the roof that overhang the North and West walls.

1. Click the Layer drop-down list on the standard toolbar and click the lightbulb icon associated with the Concrete roof layer to turn that layer on.

2. In the Left viewport, use the Select and Move tool to move the new roof section to the same level as the lofted roof edge, as shown in Figure 5.52. You may want to maximize the view to align the two roof parts.
3. With the new roof section still selected, click the Layer drop-down list and select Concrete roof to assign the new roof to that layer.

The next step is to bend the roof slightly along the east-west axis.

1. Select Edit ➢ Select by ➢ Layer… Then at the Select By Layer dialog box, click Concrete roof.
2. In the Modify tab of the Command Panel, click More in the Modifiers rollout.
3. Select Bend from the Modifiers dialog box, then click OK.
4. In the Parameters rollout, set the Bend Angle value to **12,** the Direction to **90,** and the Bend Axis to **Y.** The roof will bend slightly upward as shown in Figure 5.52.

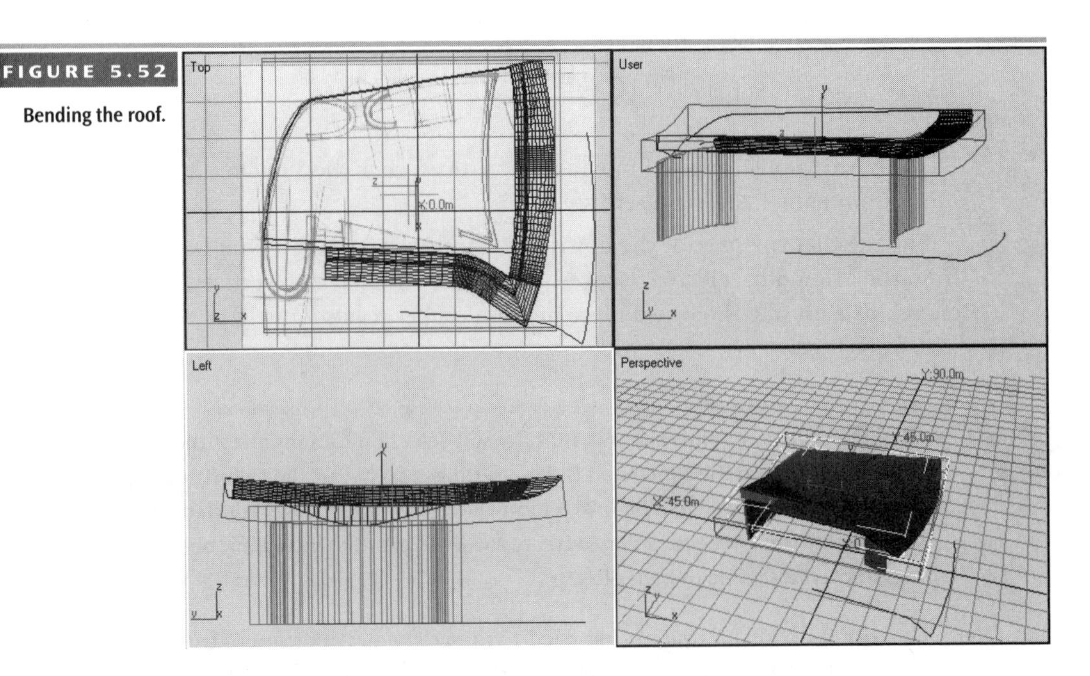

FIGURE 5.52

Bending the roof.

For the next operation, you want the rest of the model visible so you can align parts of the roof to existing walls.

1. Click the Display tab in the Command Panel, then click the All On button in the On/Off rollout.
2. Click the Select and Rotate tool, then right-click in the Left viewport.
3. Click and drag the Z axis arrow downward so that the angle readout in the status line shows 10 degrees.

4. Use the Select and Move tool to adjust the vertical and horizontal position of the roof in the Left viewport so it looks similar to Figure 5.53.

FIGURE 5.53

Adjust the roof's vertical location so it looks similar to this view.

You'll also need to rotate the roof slightly about the north-south axis.

1. Right-click the User viewport, then right-click the User label in the upper left corner of the viewport and select Views ➢ Front or type **F**↵.
2. Click the Zoom Extents tool to get an overall view.
3. Click the Select and Rotate tool, then click and drag downward on the Z axis arrow so the readout in the status line shows 2 degrees.

The roof is pretty well situated now, so you can *trim* the excess roof area on the north edges of the roof.

1. Click the Top viewport and then click the Min/Max toggle tool to enlarge it.
2. Choose Edit ➢ Select By ➢ Layer, then at the dialog box, click Vault. Then click OK.
3. In the Display tab of the Command Panel, click Selected Off to turn off the Tower vault layer so you can see the walls clearly.
4. Click the Create tab in the Command Panel, Click the Shapes tool, and then click the Line button.

5. Draw the outline indicated in Figure 5.54. This will be the shape that you'll use to subtract from the roof. When drawing the outline, try to follow the inside surface of the north wall.

FIGURE 5.54

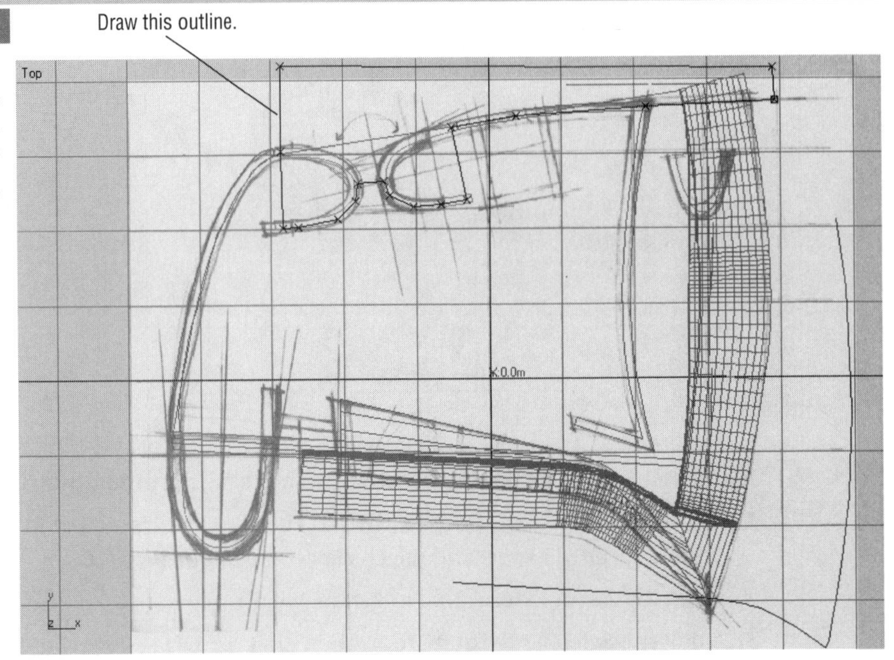

Draw the outline shown here. You'll use this outline in a Boolean operation to *trim* the roof edge to the wall.

5. Click the Sub-Object button to deactivate it and then click Extrude in the Modifier rollout.
6. Change the Amount input box value in the Parameters rollout to **20'** for 20 meters. The height is somewhat arbitrary as it only needs to be high enough to engage the roof.

Now you're ready to subtract the form you just created from the roof. Since the roof is in two parts, you'll have to do this twice.

1. Click the Layer drop-down list and click the lightbulb icon associated with the Concrete roof layer to turn it on.
2. Select the Flat roof object.
3. Click the Create tab. Then click the Geometry button and select Compound Objects from the drop-down list.
4. Click Boolean, then scroll down the Command Panel and make sure that Subtraction A-B in the Operation group is selected.
5. Click the Pick Operand B button, then click the Copy radio button just below it.

6. Click the shape you created in the last exercise. The roof is trimmed back to the wall.

You also need to trim the end of the lofted roof edge. Since you used the Copy option when you selected the Operand in the last exercise, the original shape you created earlier remains in the model. You can use it to subtract the end of the lofted shape.

1. Use the Select object tool to select the Loft01 object of the roof.
2. Click Boolean, then click the Pick Operand B button.
3. Click the Move radio button just below the Pick Operand B button. Then click the shape you created in the previous exercise.
4. Click the Min/Max tool to view all four viewports.

The roof is now complete, and you're nearly finished with the massing model of the Chapel. The West wall now needs some attention.

The South wall follows the contour of the roof to form a gentle curve at the top. To form the top of the West wall, you'll use the Soft selection options again.

1. Click the Perspective viewport, then click the Min/Max tool to enlarge it.
2. Click the Arc Rotate Selected tool and use it to adjust your view to look similar to the one shown in Figure 5.55.

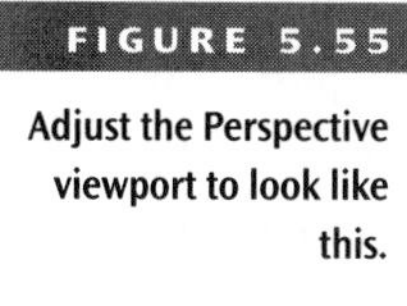

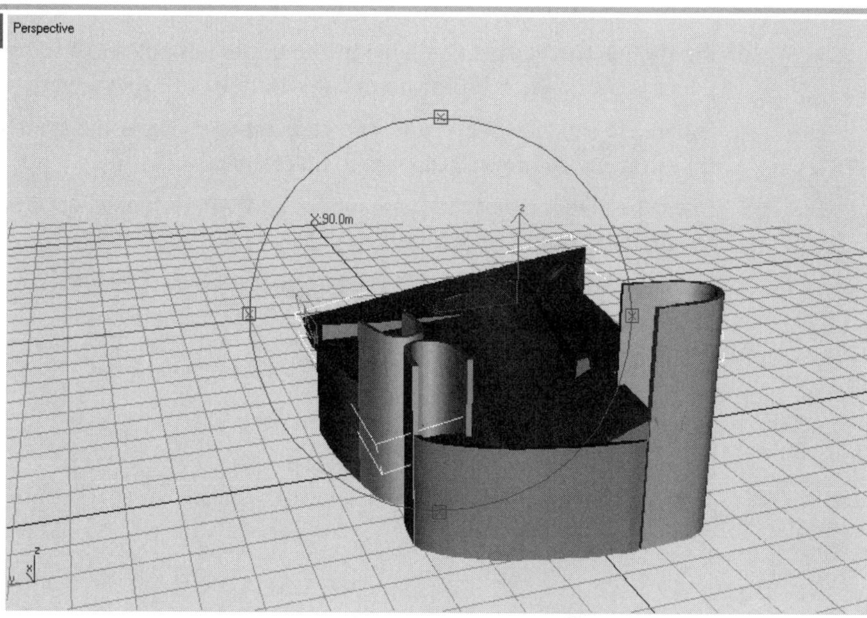

Adjust the Perspective viewport to look like this.

3. Use the Zoom and Pan tools to enlarge the perspective view as shown in Figure 5.56.

FIGURE 5.56

Enlarge the view of the West wall.

4. Right-click the Perspective label in the upper left corner of the viewport, then select Wireframe. A Wireframe view will help you locate vertices for editing.

   You've got the view set so now you can edit the wall. You'll start by moving the right-top end of the wall upward to meet the roof.

5. Click the Select Object tool and click the West wall to select it, then click the Modify tab in the Command Panel.

6. Click the Edit Mesh button in the Modifier rollout, then click the Vertex tool in the Selection rollout.

7. Use the Fence Selection Region tool to select the vertices at the top end of the wall as shown in Figure 5.57.

FIGURE 5.57

Select these vertices.

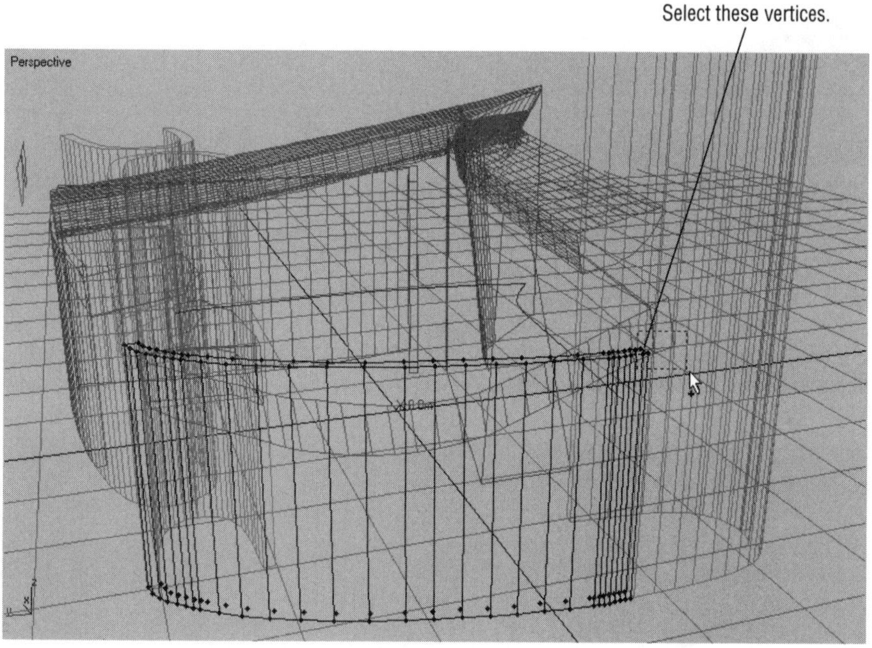

Select these vertices.

Perspective

1. Click the Soft Select rollout to open it.
2. Click the Use Soft Selection check box.

3. Click and drag the Falloff spinner upward to set its value to about **8.5**. You'll see the yellow vertices extend to about the middle of the trough on the roof as shown in Figure 5.58.

FIGURE 5.58

The soft selected vertices extend to about the middle of the roof.

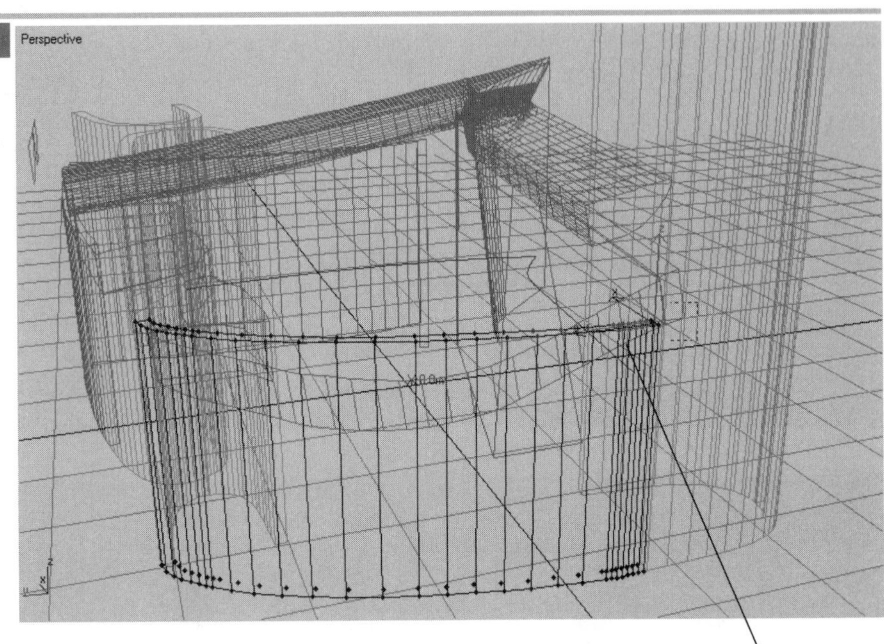

4. Click the Select and Move tool, then select World from the Reference Coordinate System drop-down list. This ensures that you move the vertices in relation to the world coordinate system while in the Perspective viewport.

5. Click and drag the Z coordinate arrow upward until the top of the wall matches the height of the top surface of the roof as shown in Figure 5.59.

FIGURE 5.59

Move the top of the wall to match the height of the roof.

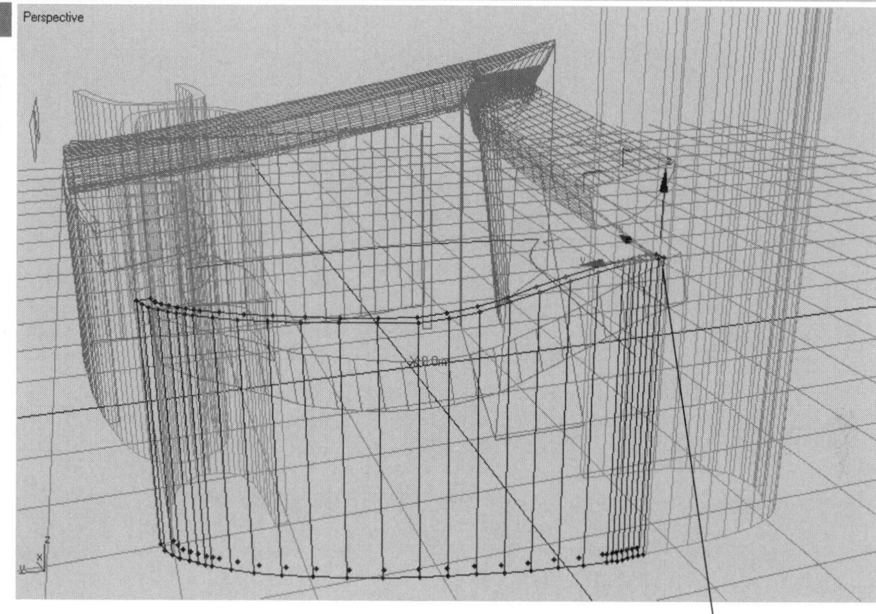
Perspective
Move the vertices to this location.

6. Select the two vertices at the dip of the wall as shown in Figure 5.59, then click and drag the Z coordinate arrow downward to create the low portion of the wall.
7. Scroll up to the top of the Command Panel and click the Sub-Object button to deactivate it.

8. Click Zoom Extents to get a better look at your model so far.

FIGURE 5.60

The model thus far

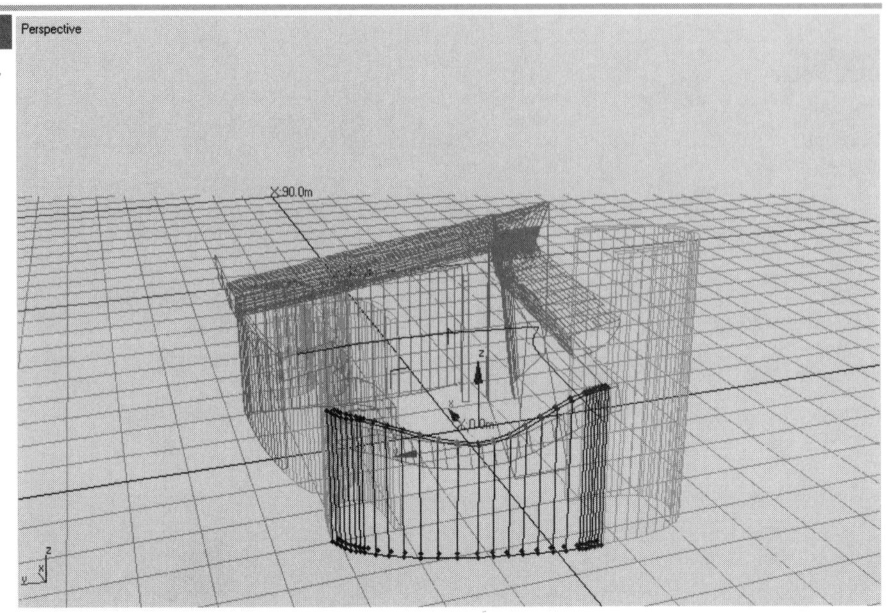

At this point, you should have a pretty good facsimile of the Chapel at Ronchamp. There are a few more adjustments you'll need to make to the East and South walls so that they will be better aligned with the roof.

1. Click the Min/Max Toggle tool to view all of the viewports.
2. Click the Select by Name tool, then select East wall at the Select Objects dialog box and click Select.
3. In the Modify tab of the Command Panel, click More, then select Taper from the Modifiers dialog box.
4. In the Taper Axis group, click the Y Primary radio button and the Z Effect radio button.
5. Adjust the Amount value to –0.3. This will tilt the top of the East wall so it is aligned with the roof.

The South wall also needs a little adjustment so it doesn't poke through the top of the roof.

1. Click the Select by Name tool. Then at the Select Objects dialog box, click South wall and click Select.
2. In the Command Panel, make sure the Taper modifier is shown in the Modifier Stack drop-down list, then adjust the Taper Amount value in the Parameters

rollout so that the top of the South wall aligns with the roof as seen from the Left viewport (see Figure 5.61).

FIGURE 5.61

Adjust the top of the South wall so it is aligned with the roof.

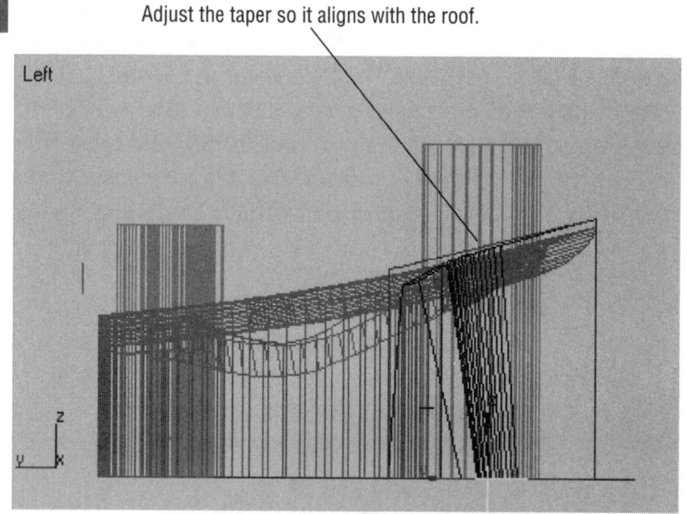
Adjust the taper so it aligns with the roof.
Left
z
y
x

3. Click the Sub-Object button and then select Center from the Selection Level drop-down list.
4. In the Left viewport, click and drag the Y coordinate axis arrow to the right to adjust the height of the South wall as shown in Figure 5.62.

FIGURE 5.62

Adjust the Center gizmo to change the height of the wall taper.

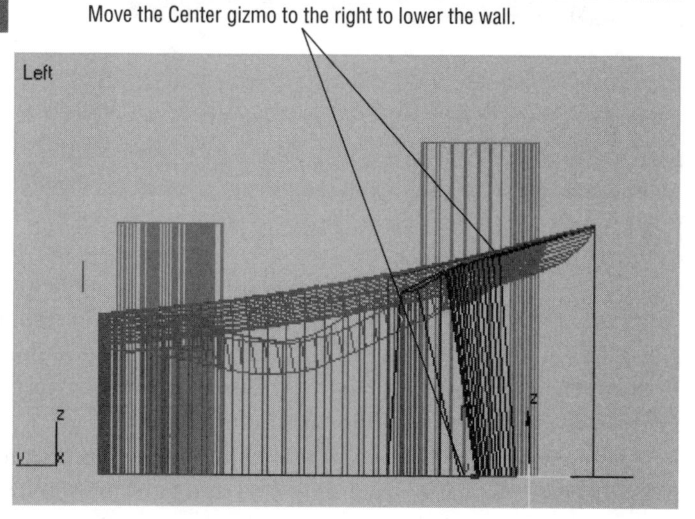
Move the Center gizmo to the right to lower the wall.
Left
z
y
x
z

5. Click the Display tab of the Command Panel and click All On in the On/Off rollout.

If you like, you can go back and make adjustments to the various parts of the model to make them fit together a bit better, but this has really been an exercise to help you become familiar with VIZ through the use of a fairly complex model.

There is still much to do to this model to *flesh out* the details. The window openings in the North and South walls need to be added. For that, you can create the shape of the openings, then use the Boolean tools to subtract those shapes from the walls. Meanwhile, you can enjoy the fruits of your labor by examining the model in the Perspective viewport and doing some quick study renderings (see Figure 5.63).

FIGURE 5.63

A sample rendering of the Chapel so far

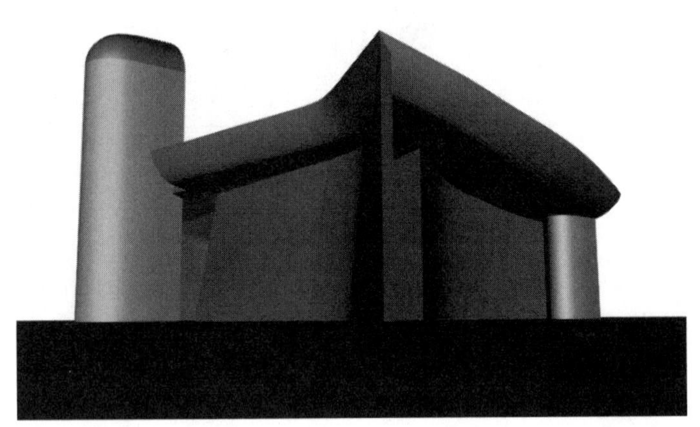

Summary

The Chapel at Ronchamp is a fairly complex building full of unusual forms. In Chapter 4 and in this chapter, the Chapel model has given you the opportunity to explore many of the modeling features of VIZ without being constrained by rectangular boxes. In fact, VIZ has the potential to free the designer from at least a few of the limitations that have restrained the design process in the past.

This concludes your use of the Chapel at Ronchamp design. In Chapter 6, you'll use another Le Corbusier design to explore cameras and lighting. You'll use the Villa Savoye design to set up a scene including lighting and camera motion.

chapter 6

Adding Cameras and Lights

FEATURING

- *Importing an AutoCAD Drawing*
- *Understanding the VIZ Camera*
- *Lighting Your Model*
- *Rendering a View*
- *Adding Ambient Light*
- *Creating a Quick Study Animation*

ADDING CAMERAS AND LIGHTS

Up until now, you've been concentrating on methods of constructing forms in VIZ. In this chapter, you'll get a chance to learn some of the ways you can control the appearance of the objects you build. You'll also get a chance to see how you can import AutoCAD files directly into VIZ.

There are really three main elements that affect the look of your model: materials, cameras, and lighting. In this chapter, you'll be introduced to cameras and lighting. In VIZ you use Cameras in much the same way as you would a real camera. You have control over where the camera is pointed, the camera's location, and the focal length of the camera lens. The camera in this case is both a still and a motion camera, as you'll see later in this chapter.

Lighting is one of the more interesting subjects in VIZ. You can use lighting to create effects, emphasize parts of your model, or simply set up a daytime scene. Through lighting, you can control shadows, manipulate reflective color, and simulate lighting fixtures, based on specifications from a lighting manufacturer. It is best to think of lighting in VIZ as a kind of paint tool to add emphasis, color, or a sense of realism to your model.

Importing an AutoCAD Drawing

In this chapter, you'll use a 3D model that was created in AutoCAD. The model is of Villa Savoye, another building designed by Le Corbusier.

TIP **If you're an AutoCAD user and would like to find out how the Villa Savoye model was created in AutoCAD, you can find a full tutorial in *Mastering AutoCAD 2000,* Premium Edition.**

1. Start VIZ, then in the default Untitled file, choose Insert ➢AutoCAD DWG… A standard file dialog box displays.
2. Use the File dialog box to locate and open Savoye6.dwg. This is a file from the companion CD, so look for this file in the drive and folder where you installed the sample files.

   When you open the file, you see the DWG Import dialog box.

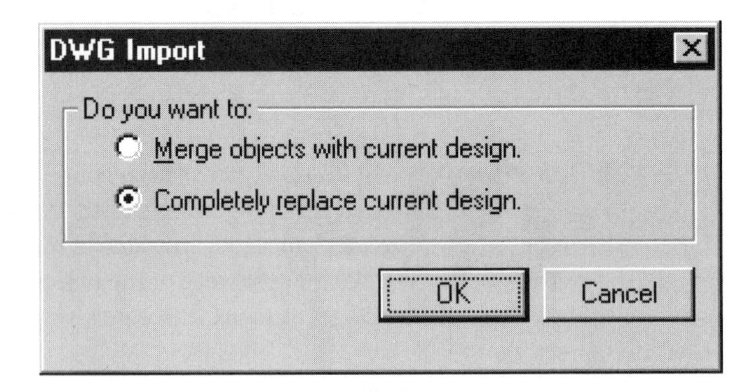

3. Click the Completely Replace current design check box, then click OK. You then see the Import AutoCAD DWG file.

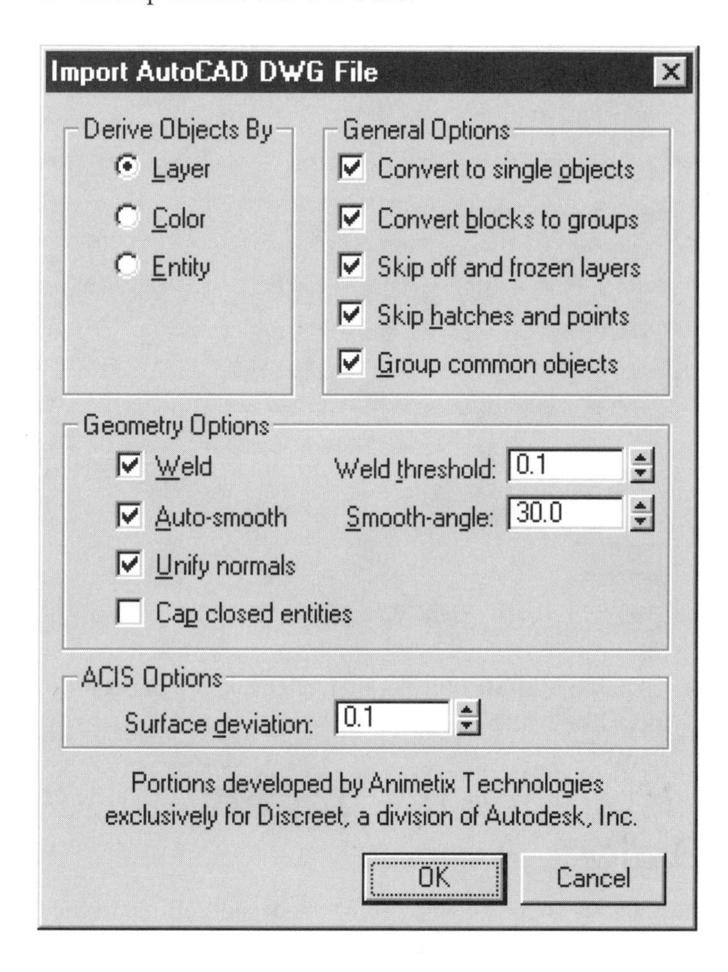

4. Accept the default settings by clicking OK. VIZ takes a moment to reconstruct the model, which then displays in the Perspective viewport.

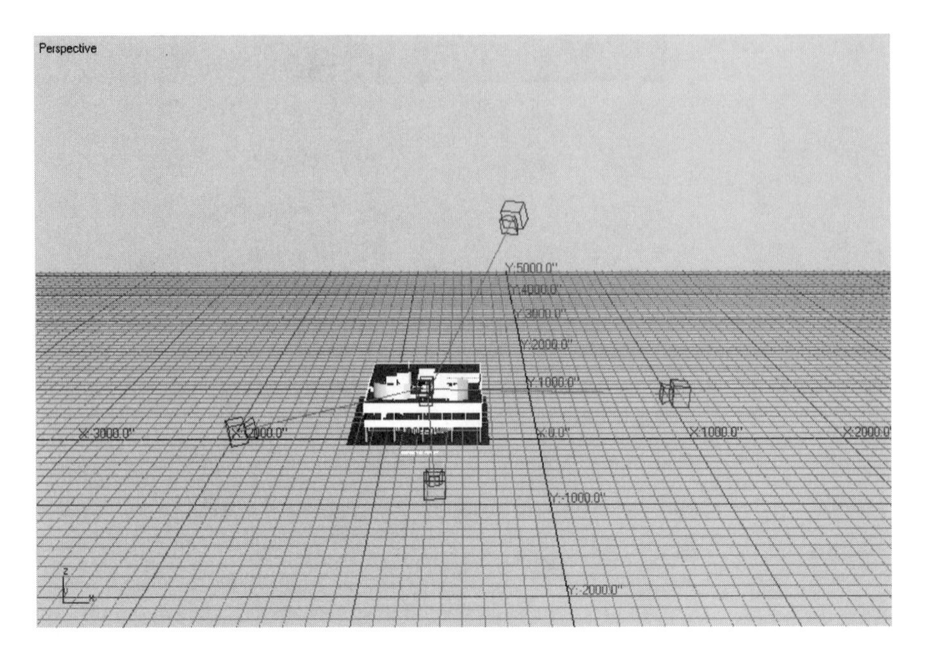

5. Click the Min/Max toggle, then click Zoom Extents All to see what the model looks like in all four viewports.

Understanding the Import AutoCAD DWG File Dialog

In the previous exercise, you accepted the default settings in the Import AutoCAD DWG file dialog box. This dialog box offers a wide range of settings that give you control over the conversion process. If you use AutoCAD to construct your 3D models, you may want to take a closer look at this dialog. Here's a rundown of its options.

Derive Objects By

This option lets you determine whether VIZ creates objects based on AutoCAD layers, colors, or by individual entity. The setting you select affects the General Options. In general, it is a good idea not to select the Entity option unless the file is very small or you have a specific need to have each AutoCAD entity converted to a VIZ object.

General Options

These options determine how objects are organized. For example, if you choose Layers in the Derive Objects By group, then select Convert to Single Objects in the General Options group, VIZ will convert all of the objects on a layer into a single VIZ object. VIZ may further divide objects on a common layer into VIZ objects, depending on the type of source object. For example, all 3D Solids on the same layer will be combined into one object.

Convert Blocks to Groups does just what it says. It converts AutoCAD Blocks into VIZ groups. Groups provide a way to organize a collection of VIZ objects into a single selection (similar to AutoCAD Groups).

The Skip Off and Frozen Layers and **Skip Hatches and Points** options also do just what they say. They cause VIZ to ignore objects on AutoCAD layers that have been turned off or are frozen, and Hatch and Point objects.

Group Common Objects causes VIZ to group objects of similar type into VIZ groups. For example, objects on a single layer would be combined into a group.

Geometry Options

These options let you determine how converted AutoCAD objects are combined to form VIZ objects. The Weld option causes objects' surfaces that share an edge to be joined into one object. This in turn affects how normals are unified (pointing in the same direction) and how smoothing is applied.

Weld Threshold determines the distance between objects before they are welded.

Auto-smooth assigns smoothing to the surfaces of objects.

Smooth Angle lets you control the angle at which smoothing takes place.

Unify Normals causes VIZ to attempt to set normals so they point away from the center of an object, thereby making all surfaces visible. This option works best on closed AutoCAD splines that have a thickness or on AutoCAD 3D Solids.

Cap Closed Entities converts closed lines and polylines into VIZ splines, then applies an Extrude modifier. The Extrude modifier then has the Cap Start and Cap End options turned on.

ACIS Options

AutoCAD's ACIS objects are converted into VIZ Mesh objects. The ACIS options give you control over the accuracy of conversion from AutoCAD to VIZ. The Surface Deviation control lets you control the accuracy of ACIS surfaces. A lower number creates more accurate objects while a larger number creates less accurate objects.

NOTE The Insert ➢ AutoCAD .DXF option in the Menu bar offers similar options to the Insert ➢ AutoCAD .DWG options.

What Do AutoCAD Objects Become in VIZ?

If you work with both VIZ and AutoCAD, it helps to know what VIZ does to AutoCAD objects in the conversion process. Table 6.1 shows you two columns indicating AutoCAD objects and their corresponding converted VIZ objects. Take a moment to look at this table to get a feel for the way the two programs compare. Remember that in some cases, converted VIZ splines will have the Extrude modifier applied if the corresponding AutoCAD object has thickness.

Table 6.1: COMPARING AUTOCAD OBJECTS TO THEIR IMPORTED VIZ EQUIVALENTS

AutoCAD Object	Imported VIZ Object
Line, 2D and 3D Polyline, Spline, Mline, Region, 2D Solid, Trace	Spline shape. AutoCAD Solids and Traces become closed spline shapes.
Arc, Circle, Ellipse, Polyline Donut, Text (using TrueType or PostScript fonts)	Arc shape, Circle shape, Ellipse shape, Donut shape, Text shape
3D Face, Polyline and Polyface Mesh, ACIS Object (3D Solids, ACIS curves)	Mesh objects
Blocks	Object or group, depending on option selected in import dialog box
UCS Grid helper	Point helper
Perspective Views	Target camera with AutoCAD View name
Point Light	Omni light
Spotlight	Target spot
Distance Light	Directional light

There are numerous ways in which you can use AutoCAD and VIZ together. Besides importing AutoCAD 3D files, you can also import AutoCAD 2D files to be used as a basis for building your 3D model in VIZ.

Next, you'll continue your look at VIZ's cameras and lights by looking at a view from an existing camera and adding a new camera in your imported model.

Understanding the VIZ Camera

Besides the building, you see several blue lines with odd shapes at their endpoints. These are VIZ cameras. They are the VIZ equivalent to the AutoCAD Views. The AutoCAD View names are translated directly into VIZ camera names, so each camera in the Savoye4 model corresponds to the AutoCAD View name. This next exercise shows you how you can bring up a VIZ camera view.

1. Right-click the Perspective viewport.
2. Press the C key. The Select Camera dialog box displays.

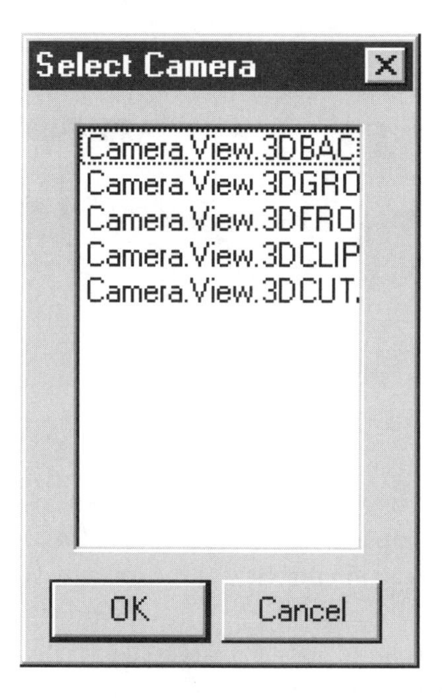

Click Camera.View.3Dground from the list, then click OK. The lower right view changes to the selected camera view (see Figure 6.1).

FIGURE 6.1

The 3Dground camera view

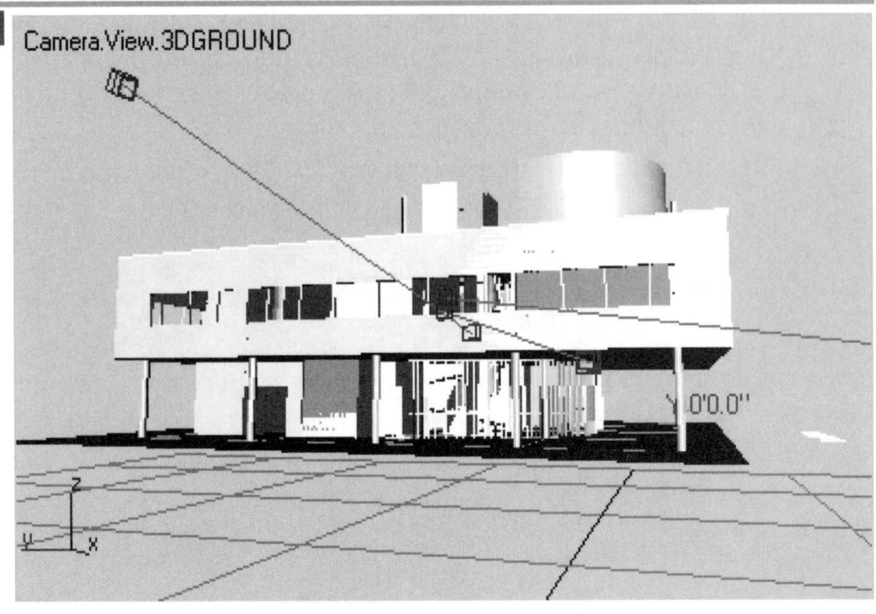

Adding a Camera

You've seen how Views are imported from AutoCAD. In the next exercise, you'll add a new camera in VIZ. All of the imported cameras are external views of the model. You'll add a camera that shows an interior view of the courtyard on the second floor of the model.

1. Right-click the Top viewport to make it active, then use the Zoom Region tool to enlarge the view so that it looks similar to Figure 6.2.

2. Click the Cameras tool in the Create tab of the Command Panel.

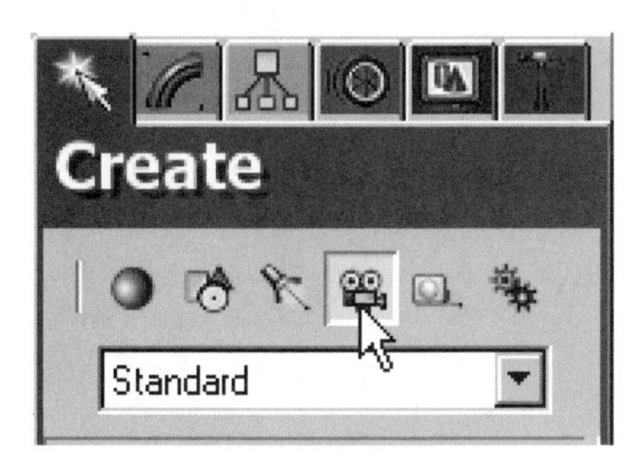

3. Click the Target button in the Object Type rollout.

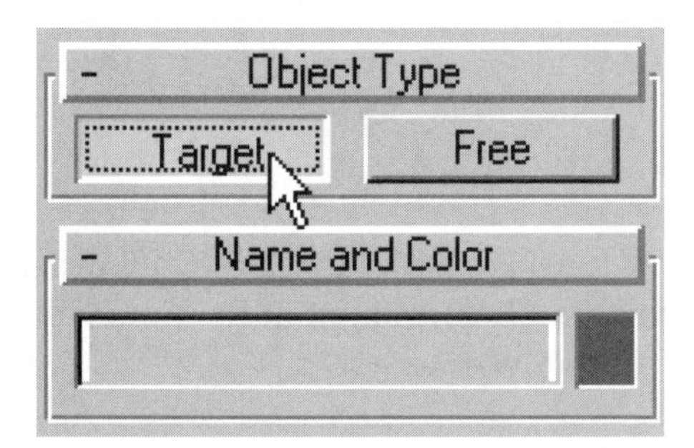

4. In the Top viewport, click and drag the point shown in Figure 6.2.

FIGURE 6.2

Click and drag this point to place the camera.

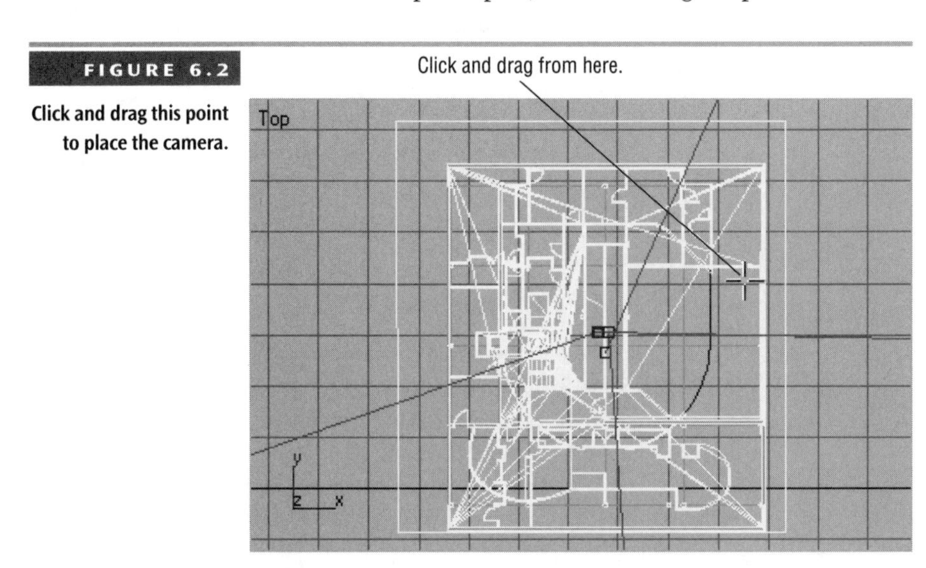

5. Move the cursor toward the lower left of the viewport. As you do, you see a rubber-banding line from the point you selected in step 2. Click the point shown in Figure 6.3.

FIGURE 6.3

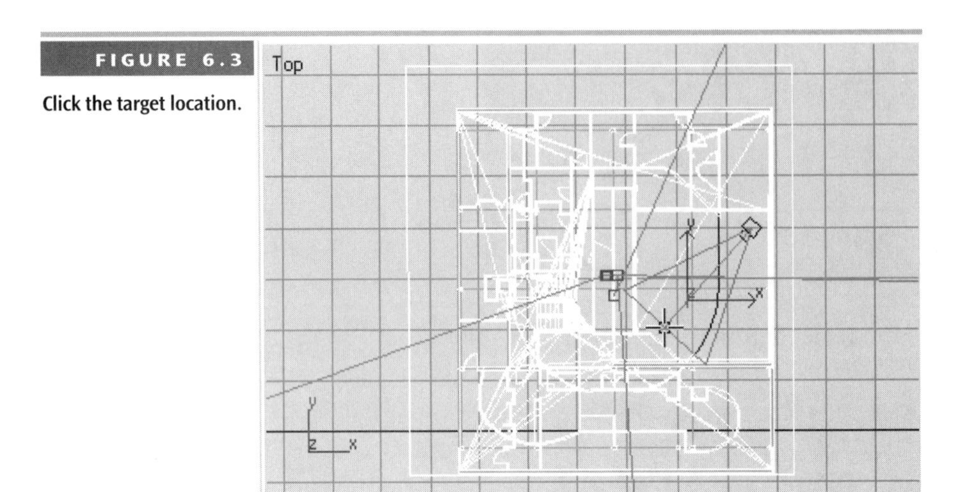

Click the target location.

6. You've just created a camera as shown in Figure 6.4. Now give your new camera a name. In the Name and Color rollout in the Command Panel, change the name from Camera01 to **Mycamera.**

FIGURE 6.4

The new camera

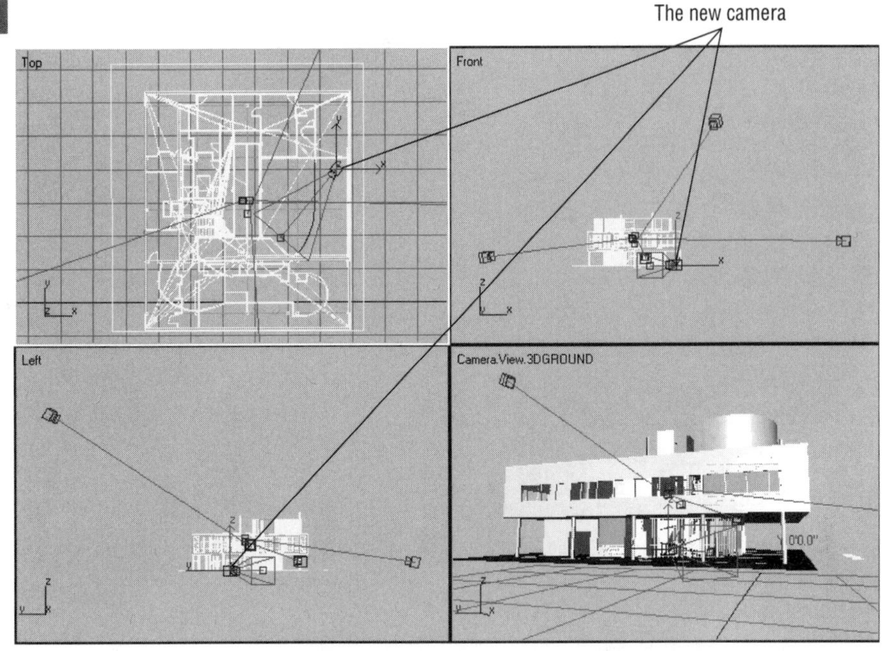

7. Click the Camera View.3DGROUND viewport, then type C.
8. Click Mycamera from the list. The viewport changes to show the view from your new camera.

NOTE **VIZ automatically assigns the name Camera01 to the first camera created in a design. Additional cameras are called Camera02, Camera03, etc. To help associate a camera with a view, you might consider naming your cameras with meaningful view names, just as you would name geometry in your model.**

Your new camera displays as a simplified camera shape while the camera target simply displays as a square handle. The camera's field of view is also shown as a cyan triangle. Notice that the camera displays on the ground plane defined by the XY coordinates. As with all newly created objects, the camera and target originate by default on the XY plane of world space. The camera's current location will not give you a view of the courtyard, which is on the second floor. You can later move the camera into position to get a courtyard view. But first take a moment to study the Camera parameters in the Command Panel.

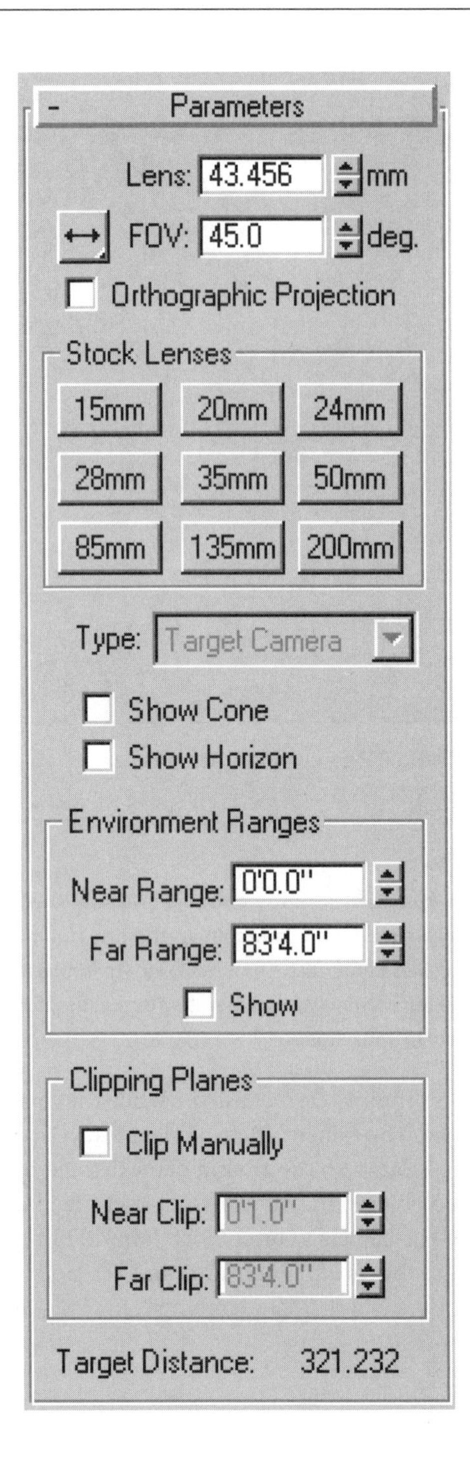
Parameters
Lens: 43.456 mm
FOV: 45.0 deg.
Orthographic Projection
Stock Lenses
15mm
20mm
24mm
28mm
35mm
50mm
85mm
135mm
200mm
Type: Target Camera
Show Cone
Show Horizon
Environment Ranges
Near Range: 0'0.0"
Far Range: 83'4.0"
Show
Clipping Planes
Clip Manually
Near Clip: 0'1.0"
Far Clip: 83'4.0"
Target Distance: 321.232

You have the option to define a variety of camera settings. At the top of the Parameters rollout, you see the Lens setting that adjusts the camera's focal length. A camera's focal length determines its field of view. In fact, just below the Lens setting is the FOV setting (that stands for field of view). If you prefer, you can enter the field of view in degrees instead of the focal length. When you change one setting, the other setting also changes in an inverse relationship. VIZ offers a default focal length of 43, or an FOV of 45, which is close to the typical focal length found in most cameras. (A setting of 43 simulates the human eye.) Below the Lens and FOV settings, you can select from a set of predefined focal lengths or "Stock Lenses."

You might also notice a check box labeled Orthographic Projection. As you might guess, this check box lets you change the view from a perspective to an orthographic projection. With this setting checked, your camera view will appear as a flat projection instead of a perspective view. The Orthographic Projection check box is handy for creating rendered elevations of building models.

Adjusting the Camera Location

As with any other VIZ object, cameras can be moved or rotated using the Transform tools (scale has no effect). Cameras and their targets are treated as separate objects when you apply the Move transform tool. Even though the Camera and Target are separate objects, they are linked together as you'll see a bit later. In the next exercise, you'll see how moving your camera affects its view.

1. Right-click the Left viewport. Then use the Zoom Region tool to enlarge the view of the building as shown in the lower left corner of Figure 6.5.
2. Click the Select by Name tool on the standard toolbar. Then in the Select Objects dialog box, Ctrl-click the Mycamera.Target listing and click Select. By doing this, you include both the Mycamera camera and Mycamera.Target in the selection.
3. Click the Select and Move tool and then in the Left viewport click and drag the green Y coordinate arrow upward. Watch the Mycamera viewport. The view looks as though you were riding an elevator up to the second floor.

4. Set the vertical camera location so that the Mycamera viewport looks similar to the Mycamera view in Figure 6.5.

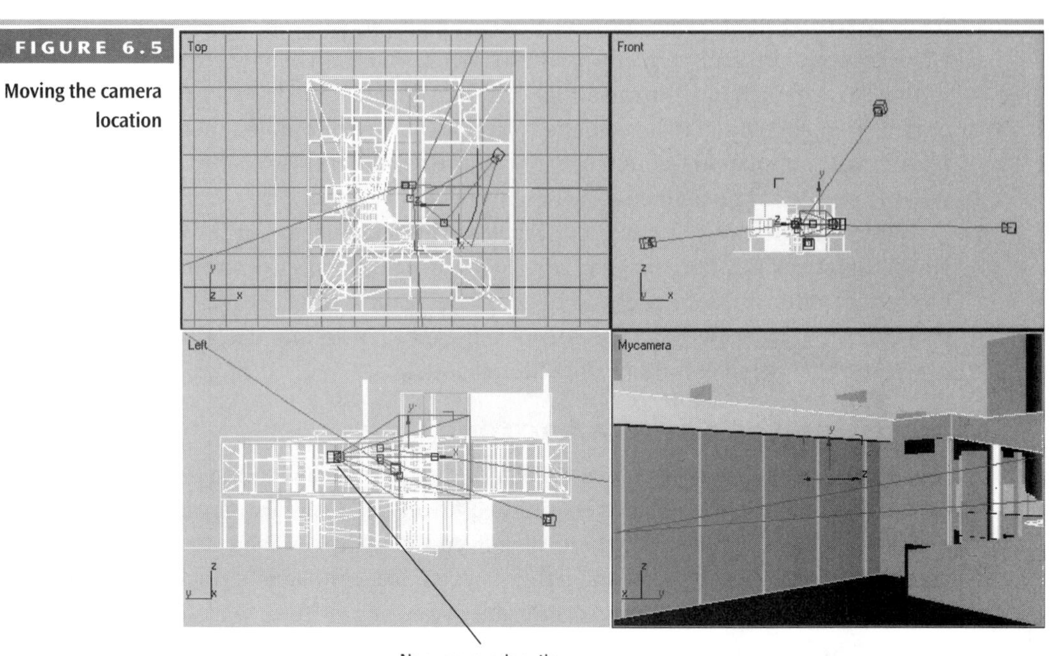

FIGURE 6.5
Moving the camera location

While you are moving the camera location, you get immediate visual feedback by watching the camera viewport. In this exercise, you moved both the camera and target together to adjust the view. Next, you'll fine-tune the camera view by just moving the target.

TIP If you want to match a camera to an existing viewport view, you can do so by taking the following steps: Select a camera and then make sure the viewport view you want to match is currently active. Click View ➢ Extra ➢ Match Camera to View.

Adjusting the Target

The Mycamera camera is at an elevation that roughly approximates the height of a person. Both the camera and target are at the same elevation. You'll want to drop the target location down a bit to center the view of the courtyard.

1. Click the Select by Name tool on the standard toolbar.

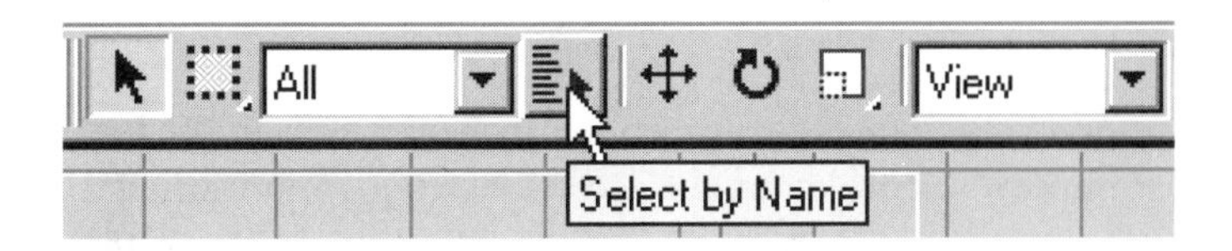

2. In the Select Objects dialog box, locate and click Mycamera.Target. Then click Select.
3. In the Left viewport, click and Drag the Y coordinate arrow upward until the Mycamera viewport looks similar to Figure 6.6.

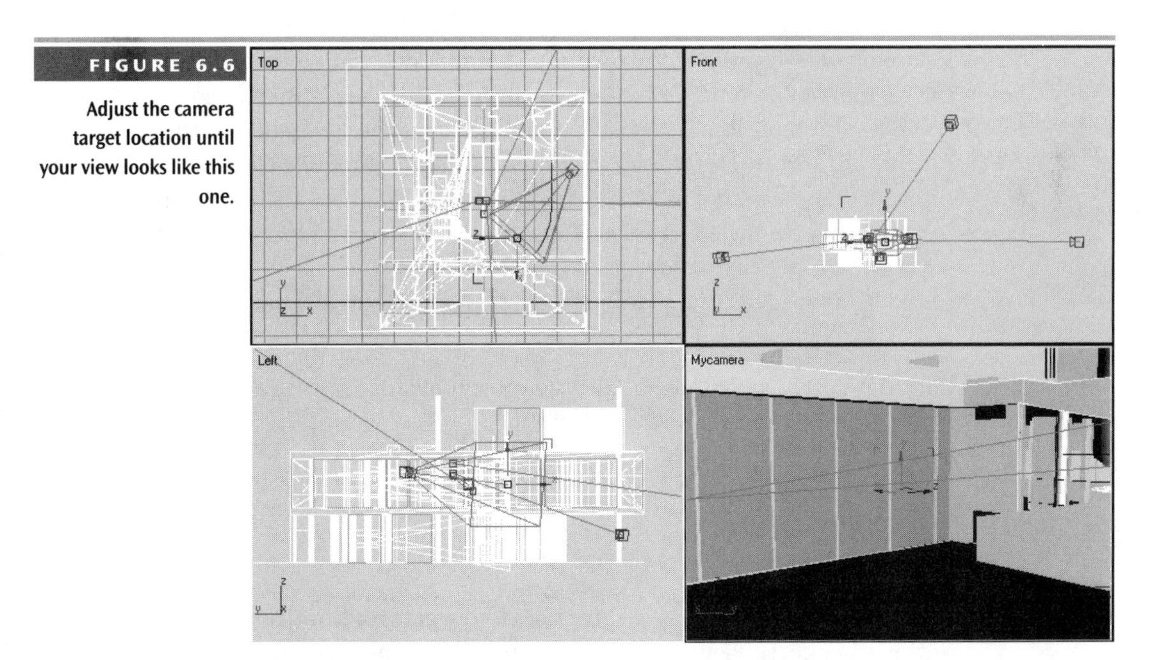

FIGURE 6.6

Adjust the camera target location until your view looks like this one.

In this exercise, you used the Select Objects dialog box because it would have been difficult to select the camera target in the middle of the model. The Select Objects dialog box simplifies the selection process when the object you need to select is too close to other objects to select.

Editing the Camera Location with the Viewport Tools

In the previous chapters, you used the Viewport tools in the lower right corner of the VIZ window to control your Perspective viewport. You learned that in a Perspective view, the tools offered on the Viewport toolbar changed to offer tools more appropriate to the Perspective view. Similarly, when you have a camera view assigned to a viewport, the Viewport toolbar offers a set of tools uniquely suited to the camera. These camera viewport tools serve not only to alter the view in the Camera viewport, but also to edit the camera location and orientation.

Using the Dolly Camera and Field of View Tools

To get a close-up view of a particular portion of your model, you typically use the Zoom Region tool or Zoom tool. In a Camera viewport there really isn't an equivalent to the Zoom Region tool. You do have two tools that have the same effect as the Zoom and Field of View tools for the Perspective viewport. The Dolly Camera tool acts exactly like the Zoom tool in a Perspective viewport. You have the added advantage of being able to see the effect of the Zoom tool on the camera location. Try the following exercise to see firsthand what Zoom does.

1. Select the Mycamera camera and then right-click the Mycamera viewport to make sure it is active.
2. Click the Dolly Camera tool on the Viewport toolbar.

3. Click and drag upward in the Mycamera viewport and notice what happens in the other three viewports. The Mycamera viewport enlarges and you can see the camera move closer to the target in the other viewports. Notice that only the camera moves; the target remains stationary.
4. Click the Undo tool to return the camera to its original location (where it was before you used the Dolly tool).
5. Click the Field of View tool, then click and drag upward in the Mycamera viewport. Notice what happens to the camera in the other three viewports.
6. Click the Modify Tab and watch the camera parameters as you adjust the Field of View tool. Notice that the Lens and FOV settings change with the adjustments of Field of View tool.

7. Adjust the view so that the Lens parameter shows around 35 mm.

The Field of View tool alters the camera field of view just as it does for the noncamera Perspective viewport. The only difference is that now you can see its effect by watching the camera. As you click and drag the Field of View tool, you see the cyan-colored Field of View gizmo change in the Top, Left, and Front viewports (see Figure 6.7).

FIGURE 6.7

The field of view of a camera changes when you click and drag the field of view tool.

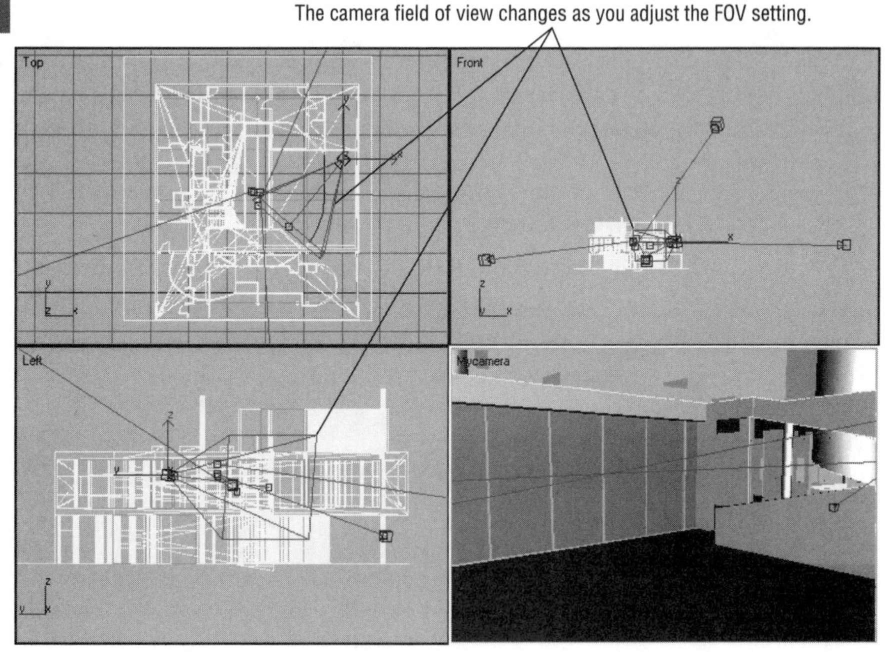
The camera field of view changes as you adjust the FOV setting.
Top
Front
Left

A tool that performs a function similar to that of the Field of View tool is the Perspective tool.

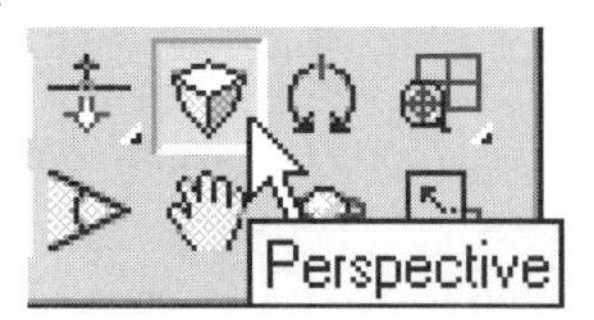

The Perspective tool also changes the camera's field of view, but it simultaneously moves the camera closer to or farther away from the model. This has the effect of keeping the size of the image the same in the Camera viewport while the field of view changes.

Panning your Camera View

Like the Dolly Camera and Field of View tools, the Truck Camera tool moves the camera as it alters the camera view. You can see exactly how the Truck Camera tool works by the way that it moves the camera and target.

1. Click the Truck Camera tool in the Viewport tools.

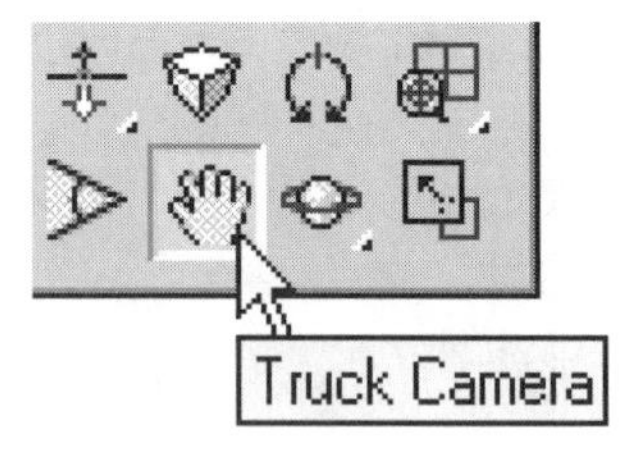

2. In the Mycamera viewport, click and drag the Truck Camera tool and watch what the camera does in the Top, Left, and Front viewports.
3. Click the Undo tool to return the camera and target to their previous locations.

The camera and target move together in a path perpendicular to the direction that the camera is pointing.

Rotating the Camera

You've used the Arc Rotate tool to move your point of view in the Perspective viewport. When you are working with a camera viewport, the function of the Arc Rotate tool is divide into two tools: the Orbit Camera tool and the Roll Camera tool.

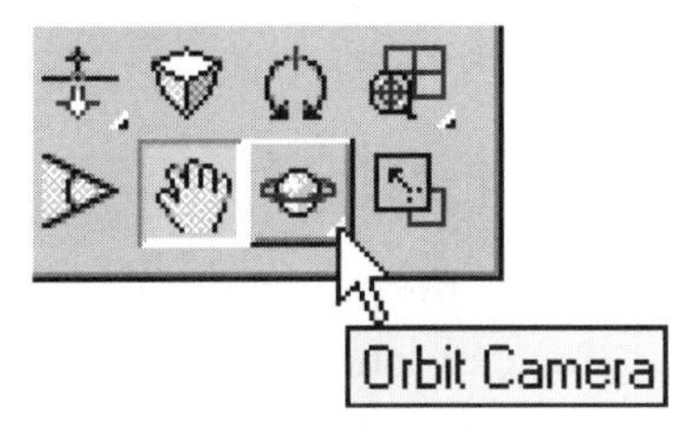

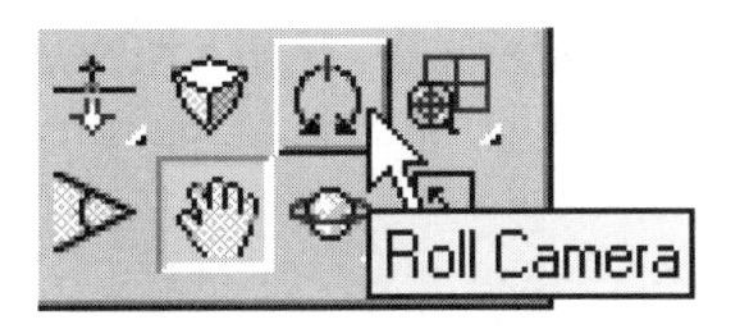

The Orbit Camera tool performs the same function as clicking in the center of the green circle of the Arc Rotate tool. Your camera location rotates about the camera target location, remaining at a fixed distance from the target. You won't see the green circle that you see with the Arc Rotate tool. If you want to limit the camera motion to horizontal or vertical, you can hold the shift key down as you click and drag the mouse.

The Roll tool performs the same function as clicking and dragging the outside of the green circle of the Arc Rotate tool. The camera view rotates.

A third option can be found as a flyout option under the Orbit Camera tool. You can Click and hold the Orbit Camera tool to reveal the Pan Camera tool.

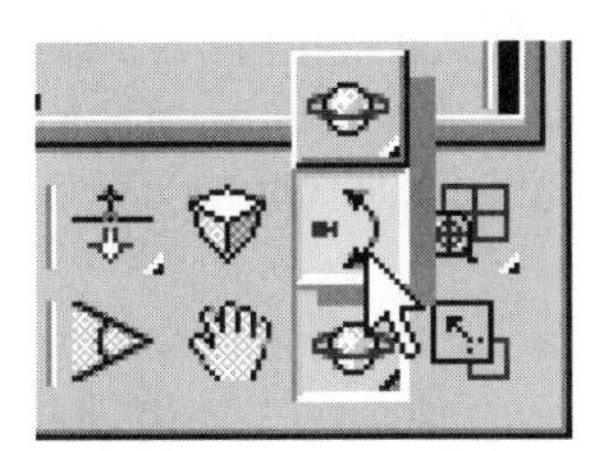

The Pan Camera tool lets you change the direction in which the camera is pointing as if it were on a fixed tripod. Holding down the Shift key while using the Pan Camera tool constrains the motion to either a vertical or horizontal plane.

Lighting Your Model

As I mentioned earlier, lighting is one of the most important tools at your disposal. A successful rendering of your model will depend largely on your ability to control and manipulate lighting in your model. There's a lot to cover in this topic, so you'll start with an overview of the different types of lights available in VIZ.

Understanding the Types of Lights

So far, you've been depending on the default lighting in VIZ. In a Perspective viewport with Smooth + Highlights turned on, the light source is from the viewer location. In a Camera viewport, the default light source is in the same location as the camera.

VIZ offers five standard light types and two Lightscape lights. The standard lights are Target Spot, Target Direct, Free Spot, Free Direct, and Omni. These types of lights can be divided into two categories. The lights that have Target in their name are lights that use a target point similar to that of the Camera and Camera Target you were introduced to earlier in this chapter. The target point can be moved separately from the light source, and it directs the orientation of the light.

Lights that have Free in their name are light sources that do not require the placement of a target point. Free lights can be freely rotated and moved without having to edit a target location. The drawback to the Free lights is that they're a bit more difficult to aim. The advantage is that they're a bit easier to manipulate. Here's a brief rundown of what these different types of lights are.

Target Spot is like a spotlight in a theater. It projects a focused beam of light that can be aimed in a specific direction. The Target Spot is perhaps one of the most versatile light sources offered in VIZ.

Target Direct, otherwise known as Directional lighting, is a source whose light rays are parallel. The main difference is that a spotlight is a concentrated source, like a flashlight, while a directional light acts more like the sun. It is like a single, very distant light source.

Free Spot is similar to the Target Spot, except that it has no target point. With a Target Spot, you must move the target location to rotate the light. A Free Spot can be freely rotated in any direction using the Transform tools.

Free Direct is the same as the Target Direct light, except that it does not use a target point. Like the Free Spot, Free Direct can be rotated freely without involving a target point.

Omni acts like a lightbulb radiating light in all directions. Like the Target Spot, Omni is a versatile light source that you'll use frequently.

Lightscape lights are light sources that are modeled after real light sources. In general, you would use these light sources if you intend to export your model to the Lightscape software to create truly accurate lighting models. Once in Lightscape, these lights offer the ability to truly model the way light works in the real world. Lightscape lights can be set to simulate the light intensity, color, temperature, and light distribution of commercially available light fixtures. If you intend to export your model to Lightscape, and you want the ultimate in realism in your renderings, you'll use these light sources. Be aware, however, that within VIZ, these Lightscape lights do not offer the same level of realism as they do in Lightscape.

There are two Lightscape lights: Target Point and Free Point. Both types of light offer the same parameters. The main difference between the Free and Target point light sources is that, just as with the standard lights, Target Point offers a specific target location while Free Point does not.

Lightscape lights are organized in a slightly different way from the standard lights. Both Target Point and Free Point offer three basic types of light sources: isotropic, spotlight, and web distributed. Here is a brief description of these light types.

Isotropic light source is basically like a lightbulb that sends light out in all directions.

Spotlight is just as the name implies: it's a light source that can be pointed in a specific direction like a spotlight.

Web Distribution lets you control the light intensity produced by the luminaire in any given direction according to specific photometric data based on real-world measurements.

Another lighting feature you'll want to know about is Ambient lighting. Ambient lighting can best be described as the secondary, indirect light that is not from a particular source. You can think of ambient light as the light you get on an overcast day when the light source seems to be from all directions. Ambient light is also an important light source to understand. You can use it to bring out hidden detail or, conversely, to suppress detail.

Unlike the other light sources, ambient lighting is set in the Environment dialog box that can be opened by choosing Rendering ➢ Environment...

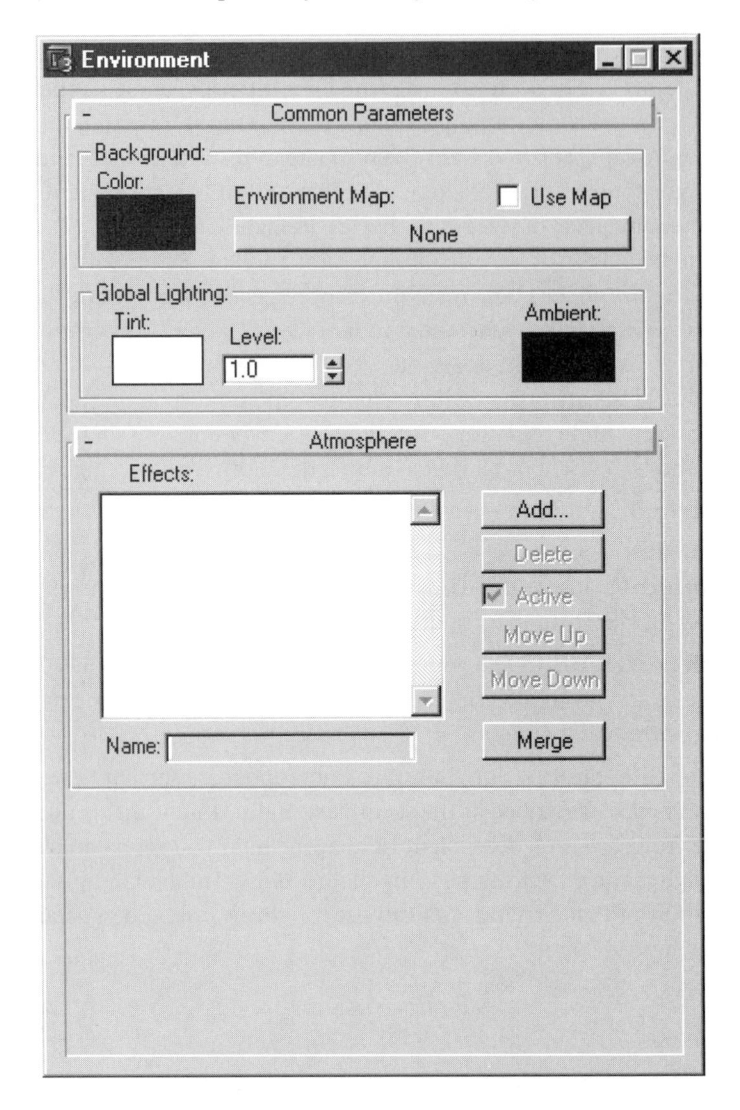

NOTE Lightscape is a product by Discreet, which is itself owned by Autodesk. It is a product designed to generate highly accurate, photo-realistic renderings of a space by simulating the actual physical characteristics of light, using a rendering process called *radiosity.* The Lightscape lights are plug-ins from the Lightscape product to allow VIZ users to prepare designs for export into Lightscape. You can then use Lightscape to create highly accurate lighting simulations.

Adding a Spotlight to Simulate the Sun

VIZ offers a way to accurately simulate the sun, including the correct sun angle, depending on the time of day and the location of the illuminated object on the earth. You'll see how the Sun option works later on in the sidebar entitled Placing a Sun Accurately. To get a feel for how lighting works in general, you'll use a spotlight to simulate the sun.

NOTE **While a spotlight may not be the best type of light to simulate the sun, it is a type of light that you'll use often, so it makes a good introduction to lighting.**

VIZ lets you control the intensity as well as the *spread* of the spotlight. You can focus the light down to a very narrow beam like the headlights of a car, or you can spread the light out in a wide angle like the light from a desk lamp. To simulate the sun with a spotlight, you can place a Standard Target Spotlight in your model at the relatively large distance from the model of about 250 feet. Like the Target Spot camera you created earlier, the Target Spotlight requires the placement of both the light source and the target of the light.

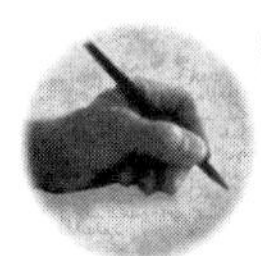

NOTE **The process for adding an Omni or Free light is nearly identical to that for adding a Spotlight. The main difference is that an Omni or Free light doesn't require a target point.**

To see the overall effects of the light you're about to add, change the camera view back to the 3DGROUND view.

1. In the Mycamera viewport, right-click the Mycamera viewport label in the upper left corner of the viewport.
2. Select Views ➢ Camera.View.3DGROUND.
3. Now add a light source. This procedure is similar to adding a Target camera.

4. Click the Create tab of the Command Panel, then click the Lights tool.

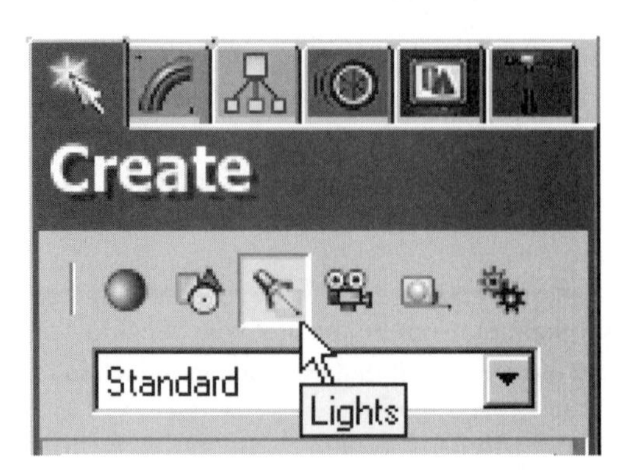

5. Click the Target Spot button to activate it.
6. Right-click the Top viewport. Then click and hold at a point in the lower left corner of the viewport as shown in Figure 6.8.

   As you move the cursor, you see the camera appear at the point where you clicked, and the spotlight target follows your cursor. A rubber-banding line joins the camera and target.
7. Move the cursor to a point in the center of the model plan as shown in Figure 6.8. Then release the mouse button.

FIGURE 6.8

Placing the Target Spotlight.

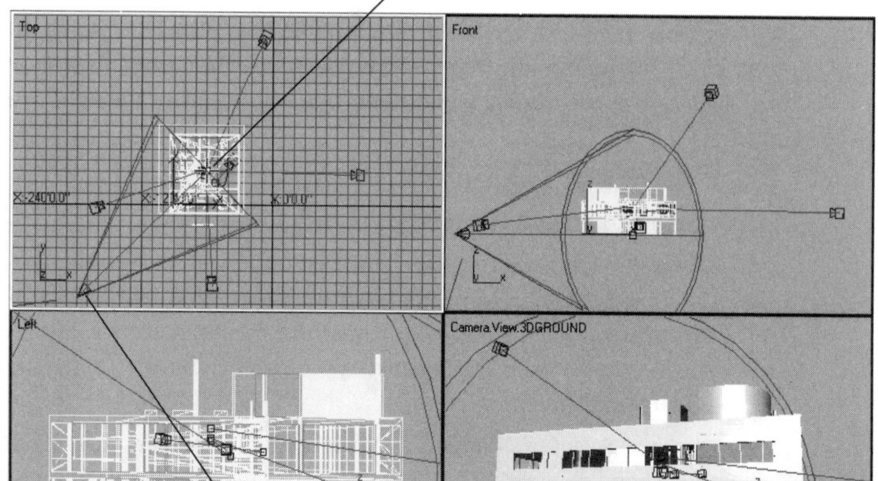
Click here to place the light target.
Top
Front
Left
Camera.View.3DGROUND
Click and drag here to place the light source.

Once the Target Spotlight is placed, it takes over as the light source in the model. Your Mycamera viewport changes in appearance to show the new lighting conditions.

8. Type **SUN** in the Name and Color rollout input box so you can identify this new light source.

As you can see from the options in the Command Panel, you have quite a few alternatives available for controlling the characteristics of a spotlight. You can always go back and make changes to a spotlight so, for now, you've accepted the default light settings.

Moving a Light

Notice that in the Front viewport the Spotlight displays horizontally. VIZ places the light and light target points flat along the XY plane. You must then move it into position, just as with the camera you created earlier. Let's move the light to a point high in the sky.

1. Click the Front viewport to make it active.
2. Use the Zoom and Pan tools to adjust the Front view so that it looks similar to Figure 6.9.
3. Click the Select and Move tool on the standard toolbar. Then click and drag the Y axis arrow of the SUN light into the position shown in Figure 6.9. Once you've moved the light source, you see a change in the lighting of the Mycamera viewport.
4. Click the Select by Name tool on the standard toolbar. Then click SUN.Target in the list and click Select.
5. With the Select and Move tool active, click and drag the light's target location upward as shown in Figure 6.9.

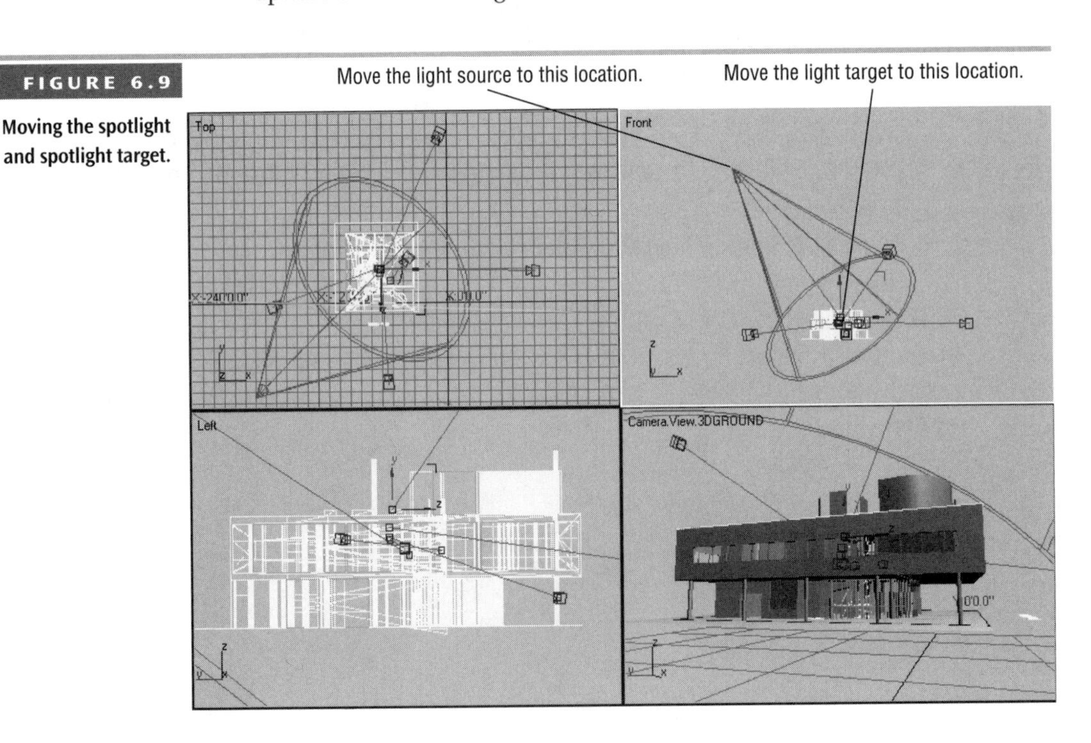
Move the light source to this location.
Move the light target to this location.
Top
Front
Left
Camera.View.3DGROUND

FIGURE 6.9

Moving the spotlight and spotlight target.

As you see from this exercise, moving the spotlight is similar to moving a camera. The light source and its target move independently. You also see that the Mycamera viewport gives you immediate feedback regarding the light's effect on your model.

Placing the Sun Accurately

VIZ offers a tool that will accurately place a sunlight source in your model. This feature can be useful for shadow studies where they may be required. You can use the SunLight System to place a Free Directional light source representing the sun at a particular time of day and for an object at a specific location on earth. You also need to set a North Direction parameter to accurately orient your model in the north-south direction.

To use the SunLight System tool, you'll need to know the location of your building or site and the date and time you wish to use for the sun's position. Once you've established these criteria, you can take the following steps:

1. Click the Create tab in the Command Panel.
2. Click the Systems tool in the Create Tab.

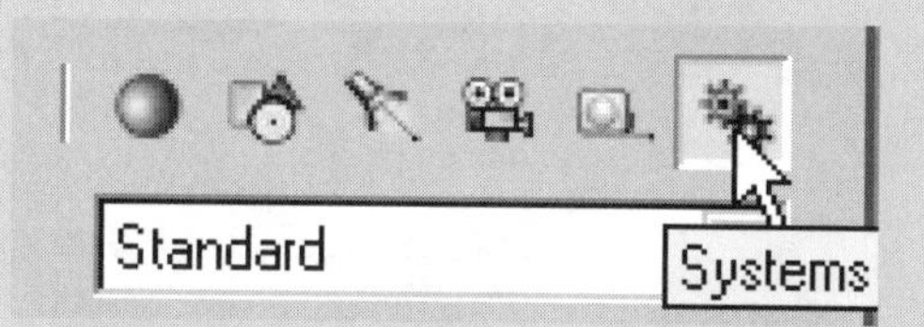

3. Click Sunlight in the Object Type rollout.

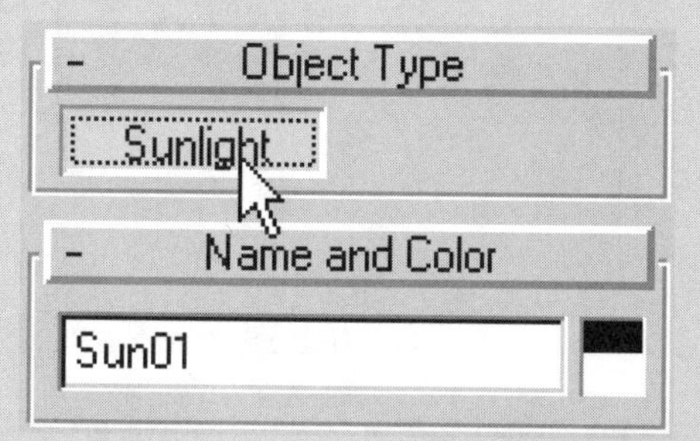

You'll see the parameters appear for the SunLight System.

Continued on the next page

4. Enter the time and date for the sun's location in the Time group.

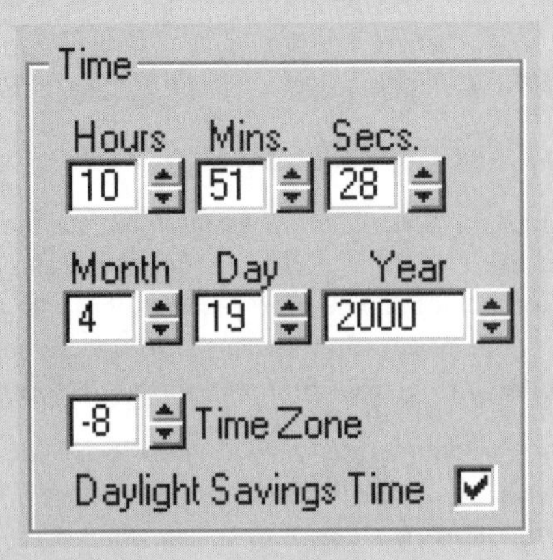

5. Click the Get Location button in the Location group. The Geographic Location dialog box displays.

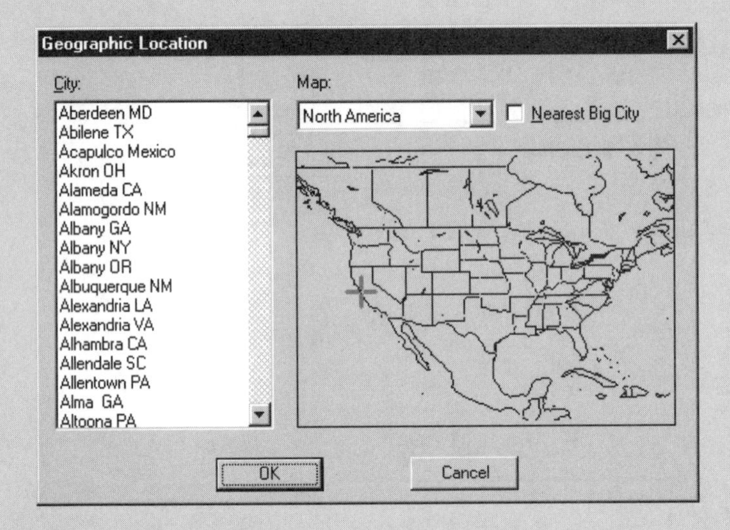

6. Select a world location map from the drop-down list, then select the city from the City list.
7. Click OK. You'll see the latitude and longitude of the selected location display in the Location group. If the Geographic Location dialog box does not offer a location near your site, you can enter the latitude and longitude directly in the appropriate input boxes of the Location group. You also want to set the North Direction parameter. This

Continued on the next page

tells VIZ where true, polar north is in relation to your model. Zero degrees is a positive Y direction in your Top viewport, whereas 90 degrees is a positive X direction.

8. Once you've entered all of the data for your site location, click and drag near the center of the building in the Top viewport of your model to place the compass portion of the SunLight System.

9. Let go of the left mouse button and drag to set the target distance from the compass to the sun. The distance isn't crucial, because the intensity of the simulated sun does not vary with distance. Once you've selected a distance, VIZ places a Free Directional Light in the model that simulates the sun.

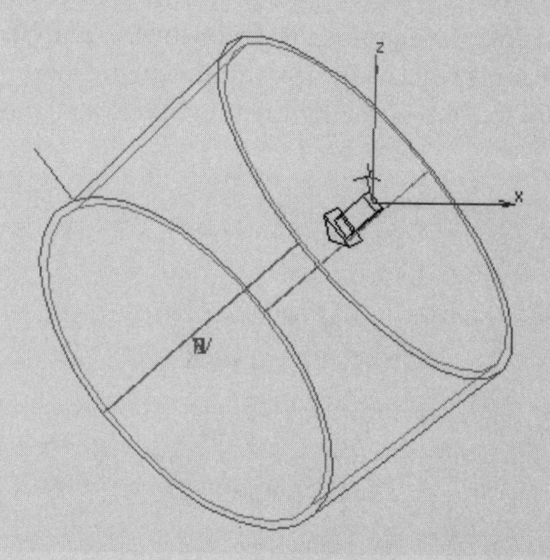

This light will be pointing in the appropriate direction for the time, date, and location that you entered for the Sunlight Control Parameters in the previous steps.

Once you've placed the sun, you can use the Motion tab in the Command Panel to alter the date and time for the sun. You can also adjust the North Direction, Latitude, and Longitude from the Motion tab. The Modify tab will let you adjust the standard settings for the Free Directional light, such as intensity, color, etc. In fact, you may need to adjust the falloff parameter of the Sunlight to cover your model completely. If you need to, you can move the light to a convenient location and, as long as you don't change the orientation of the light, it will provide an accurate representation of the sun's angle. The light is already set up to use what are called Ray Trace (or raytraced) shadows, an option that produces an accurate but time-consuming representation of shadows. You'll learn more about Ray Trace shadows in Chapter 8.

Editing a Spotlight

There are many settings available for your new spotlight. You can set the intensity, color, and even the shape of the light, just to mention a few of the settings. But the two settings you'll be using the most are the light intensity and the light cone. The light intensity is set in the General Parameters rollout, and the light cone is set in the Spotlight Parameters rollout.

Let's start by looking at the Hotspot and Falloff settings.

1. First, use the Select object tool to select the SUN Spotlight object.
2. Click the Modify tab in the Command Panel, then scroll down and click the Spotlight Parameters rollout button to open the Spotlight Parameters rollout.
3. Click and drag the Falloff spinner downward until its value reaches 12. Notice that the light is reduced in size, shining on only a very small part of the model. Also notice that when you reduce the Falloff value the Hotspot value also drops.

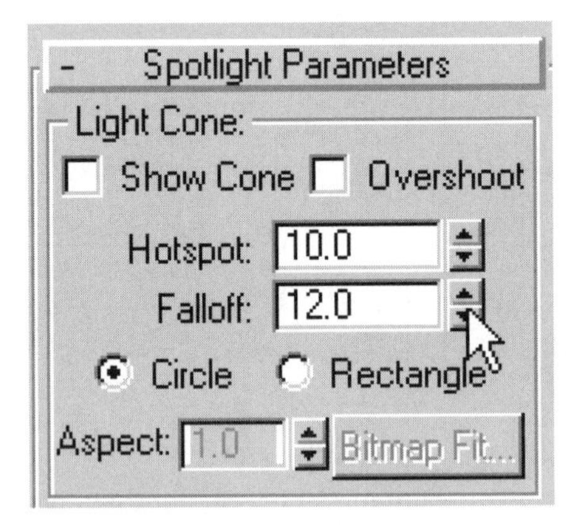

4. Click and drag the Hotspot spinner upward until it reaches a value of about 50. The light spreads out to cover a larger area. Notice that the Falloff value increases.
5. Now click and drag the Hotspot spinner downward to about 20. This time the Falloff value remains where it was last set while the Hotspot value drops.
6. Set the Hotspot value to about 34 and the Falloff value to about 36.

The Hotspot and Falloff spinners control the *spread* of the Target Spotlight. The Hotspot value controls the area covered by the most intense portion of the light, while the Falloff value controls where the light falls off to zero intensity. There is a continuous gradient between the maximum intensity of the light within the hotspot and zero intensity at the edge of the falloff cone. This is difficult to see in the

Mycamera viewport, but it will be more obvious in a rendered view. You'll learn about the differences between the Hotspot and Falloff of a spotlight in the next chapter.

Now try setting the light intensity. This is done through the Multiplier.

1. Click and drag the Multiplier spinner downward in the General Parameters rollout.

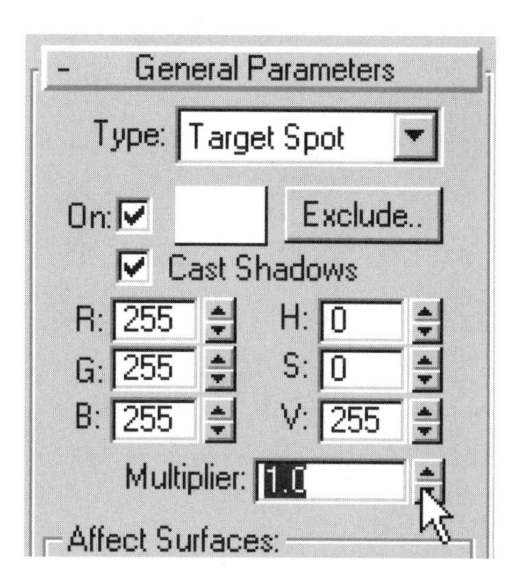

   As you reduce the Multiplier value, the view in the Mycamera viewport dims.

2. Click the Undo tool on the standard toolbar to return the Multiplier value to 1.

The Multiplier spinner controls the overall intensity of the light source. You can also change the color of the light source using RGB or HSV values. You can select a color using the Color Selector shown in Figure 6.10. To open the Color Selector dialog box, click the color swatch in the General Parameters rollout.

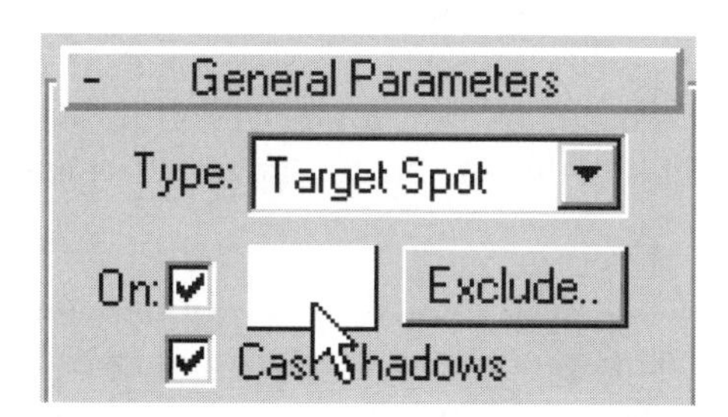

FIGURE 6.10

Color Selector dialog box

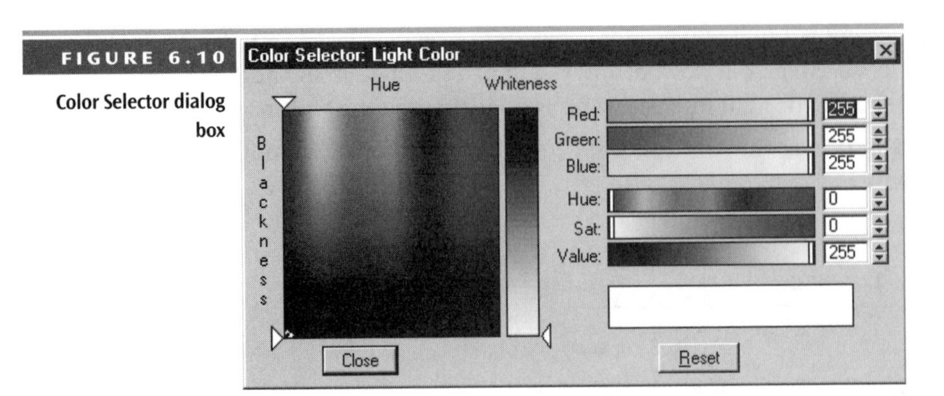

The Color Selector dialog box lets you see the color as a sample in the lower right corner of the dialog box.

Finally, if you decide that the light you selected originally is not appropriate for the task at hand, you can use the Type drop-down list to change the type of light used.

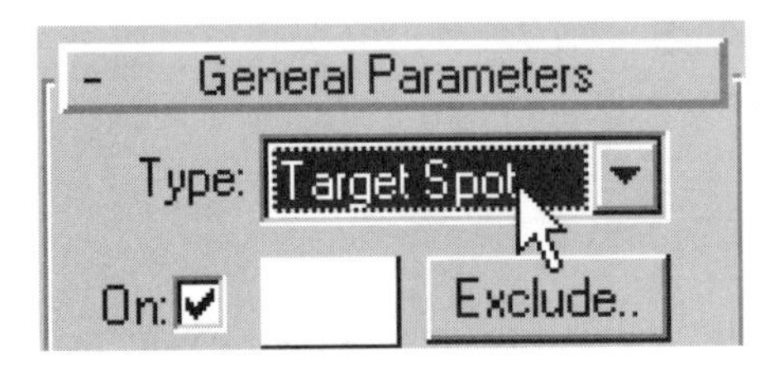

This tool offers a convenient way to change a light type without having to erase the light and create another one.

Changing the Light Type

Once you've placed a light in your model, you're not stuck with your choice of light type. You can change the light type in the Modify tab of the command panel.

You were asked to create a sunlight source using a Target Spotlight. There isn't anything wrong with using such a light for the sun, but the Target Direct is actually a more appropriate light source for the sun.

NOTE The light rays from a VIZ Target Direct or Free Direct light are parallel just as the rays from the real sun are parallel in relation to the earth. The rays from the sun are parallel due to the relative sizes of the sun and the earth and the vast distance between the sun and earth. Even though the sun appears to be a point light source, its diameter is about 109 times greater than that of the earth. We are also about 93 million miles from the sun, so from our perspective, the rays of light from the sun are parallel.

Here's how you can change from Target Spot to Target Direct.

1. Click the Type drop-down list in the General Parameters rollout, then select Target Direct.

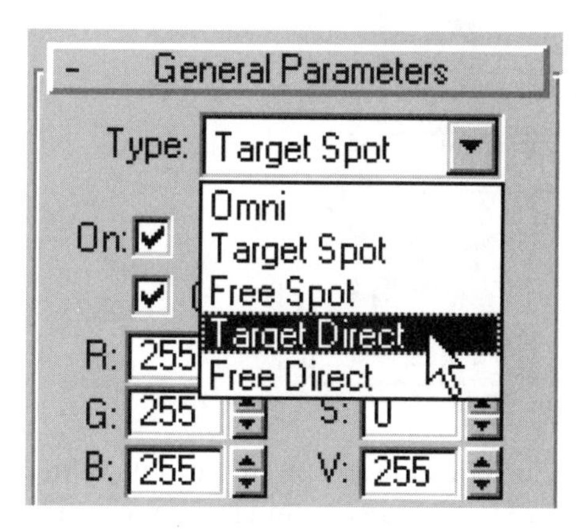

Notice that the light changes its icon in the viewports to indicate a Target Direct light object. You might also notice that, instead of showing a cone, the light shows a narrow cylinder to indicate the direction and parallel spread of the light rays. This cylinder can be seen most clearly in the Left viewport.

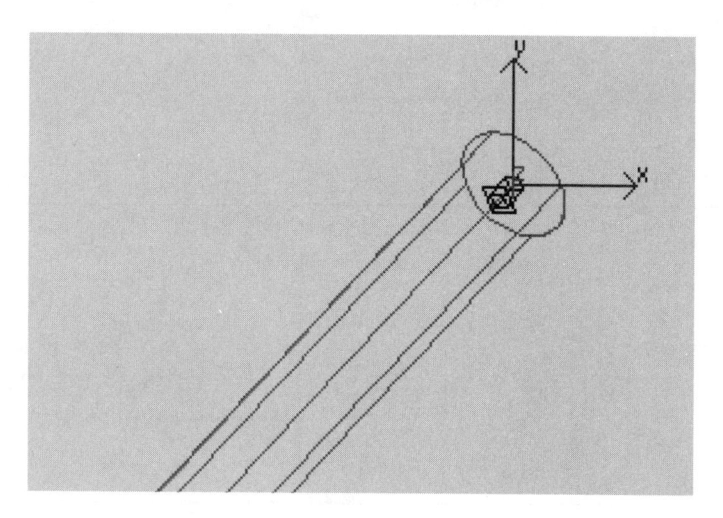

2. Scroll down the Command Panel and click the Directional Parameters rollout.

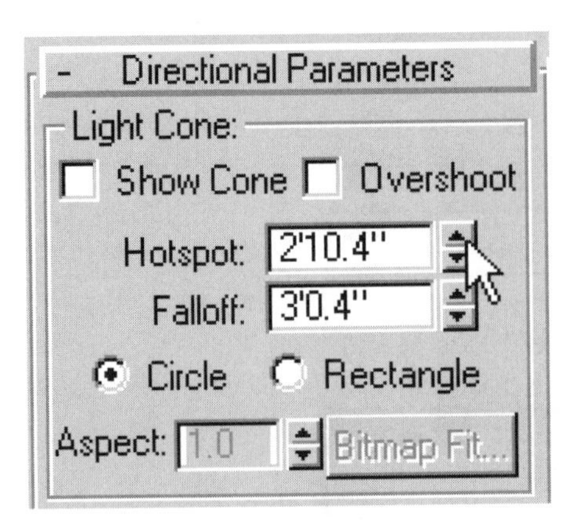

3. Click and drag the Hotspot spinner upward until its value reads around 56. You see the light enlarge to form a large cylinder as shown in Figure 6.11.

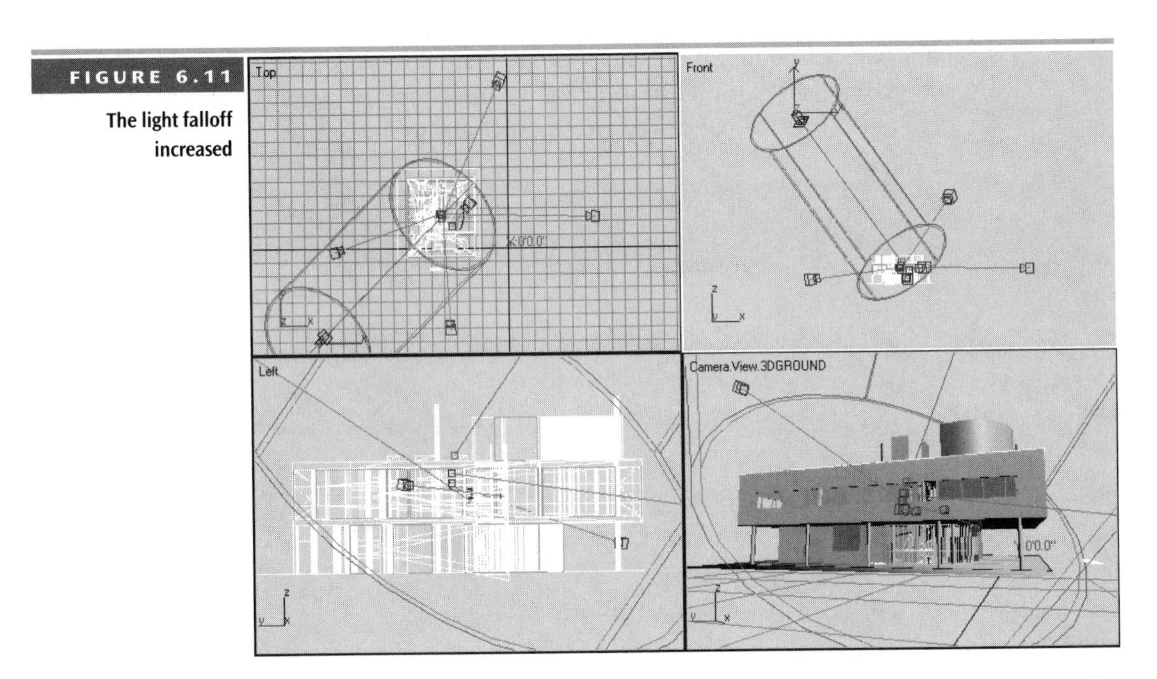

FIGURE 6.11

The light falloff increased

As described earlier, the Target Direct light source produces a light whose rays are parallel, so the light appears as a cylinder. The light rays from a Target spotlight diverge so the light forms a cone. Both light sources offer a Falloff option to soften the edge of the light.

There are many other parameters associated with the light objects, and you'll get to use a few more in later chapters. For now, lets move on to see how lighting and camera locations affect your rendering.

Rendering a View

One of the main reasons for using VIZ in the first place is to get an idea of how your design will look before it is actually built. While you can get a fairly decent idea of how it looks in the Perspective and Camera viewports, you need to render your model to get a finished looking image.

The Rendering facility that VIZ offers lets you create a wide range of images from quick study renderings to photo-realistic images. You can also generate animated walk-throughs or virtual reality environments.

NOTE With the help of additional equipment or software, you can also create video clips and QuickTime VR files.

All of these types of output are produced through the Render Design dialog box and the Quick Render tool. You were been introduced to the Quick Render tool in Chapter 2. In this section, you'll get a closer look at some of the ways you can control your rendered output.

Try the following exercise to get a good look at the rendering options you have available.

1. Make sure the Mycamera viewport is active, then click the Render Design tool on the Render toolbar.

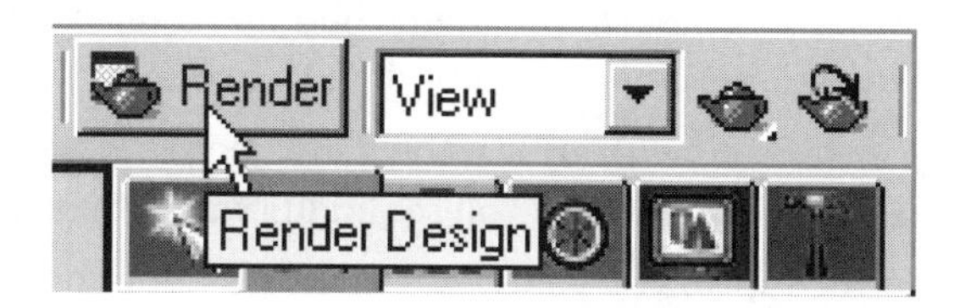

The Render Design dialog box displays.

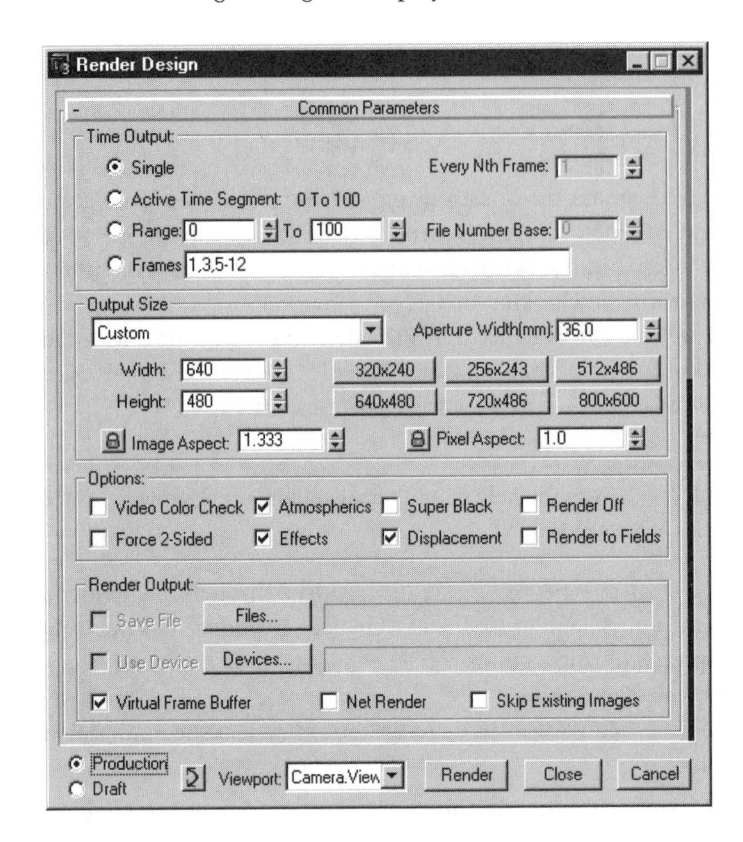

Like the Command Panel, the Render Design dialog box offers a vertical scrolling panel with rollouts. The main rollout is called Common Parameters, and it offers the more common settings you'll encounter in your work.

2. Place the cursor over a blank area in the dialog box until you see the hand cursor. Then click and drag upward. You see additional rollouts with more settings.
3. Scroll back to the top so you can view the entire Common Parameters rollout.

Let's take a moment to examine the Common Parameters rollout. At the top you see a group labeled Time Output. These settings offer control over animation output, though its use isn't necessarily limited to animation work. You'll see later how these settings can be used for automating the rendering of several views of a model such as the elevations of a building.

The next group, Output Size, offers control over the size of the image file that Render generates. You can control the width and height in pixels, or select from a set of predefined, standard image sizes.

The Options group offers control over special effects and rendering tools. Some of these options are concerned with animation files destined for video, while others control more general effects of the renderer.

Finally, the Render Output group lets you determine the type of file output to be generated.

Let's create an image file.

1. Click the Files... button in the Render Output group of the Render Design dialog box. The Render Output File dialog box displays.

WARNING **The files you see in your list box will differ from what you see here.**

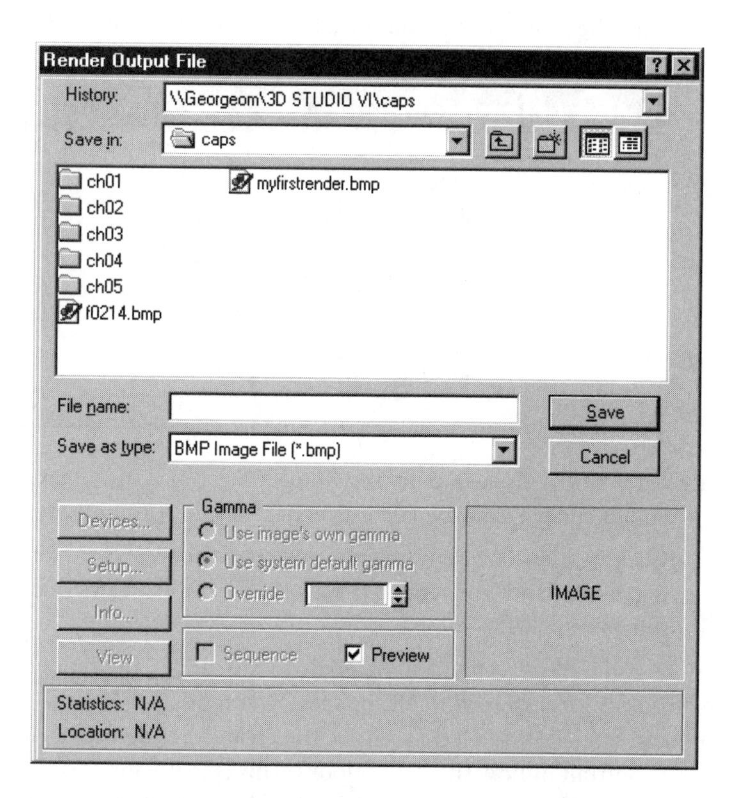

With the exception of a set of options in the lower half of the dialog box, the Render Output File dialog box is a typical File dialog box.

2. Enter **Myfirstrender** in the File name input box. Notice that the Save as Type drop-down list shows BMP as the file type. This is the standard default image file type. You can choose from a wide range of other file types by selecting one from the Save as Type drop-down list.

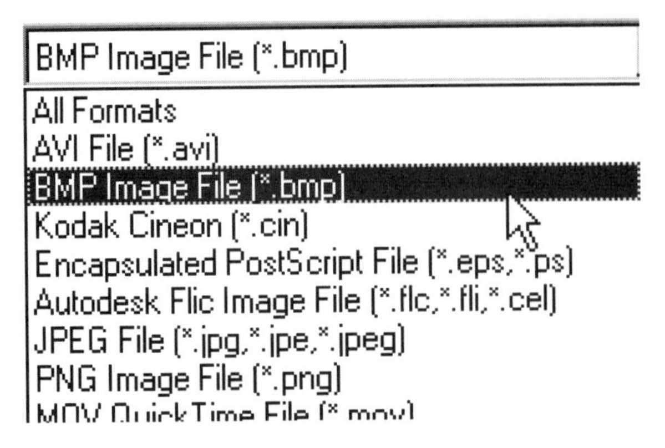

3. Click the Save button. You'll see the BMP Configuration dialog box.

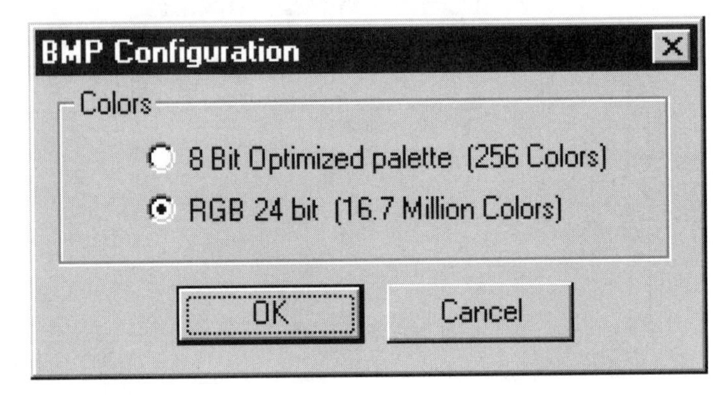

4. Click OK. You return to the Render Design dialog box. The file name you entered displays in the File listing next to the Files button.
5. Click Render. The Render window opens and shows the progress of the rendering. Notice that the rendered view shows the shadows that are cast by the light source.

Since you haven't yet added materials to the model, the rendering displays with the default colors assigned to all surfaces. Your rendering has the appearance of a cardboard model. While it may not be the greatest rendering, it does offer a fairly accurate portrait of how the design looks. This is really just a start. The process of creating a finished rendering or animation involves a repeated cycle of rendering, adjusting, and rendering again (and again) until you've reached a look you are pleased with.

As you progress through the chapters in this part of the book, you'll learn this process firsthand. We'll explain the method for adding materials and for further enhancing the rendered image in the next chapter. But for now, let's continue with our tour of rendering with a quick peek at animation.

NOTE If you're familiar with the Villa Savoye design, you may notice that some parts of the building are missing. All of the parts are there, but their normals are not aligned properly, so they disappear when the model is rendered. You'll learn how you can set up VIZ to render both sides of a surface, regardless of the direction of the normals.

Adding Ambient Light

The rendering shows a picture with lots of contrast. The lighted areas are bright enough, so you cannot see any detail in the shadows. This is because there is no ambient light in the model. In the real world, there is usually some ambient light that is bounced off the objects. Indoor ambient light comes from light that is bounced off walls, floors, and ceilings, while outdoor ambient light comes from clouds and the general sky glow.

If you add ambient light to your scene, you'll begin to see more of the objects in the shadows, and you'll give your rendering a little friendlier appearance. Here's how you add ambient light.

1. Close the Rendered view and the Render Design dialog box to make room on the screen.
2. Choose Rendering ➢ Environment from the menu bar. The Environment dialog box displays.
3. Click the Ambient color swatch in the Global Lighting group.

The Color Selector displays (see Figure 6.12).

4. Click and drag the triangular slider in the Whiteness column downward as shown in Figure 6.12. This adjusts the general brightness of the ambient light.

FIGURE 6.12

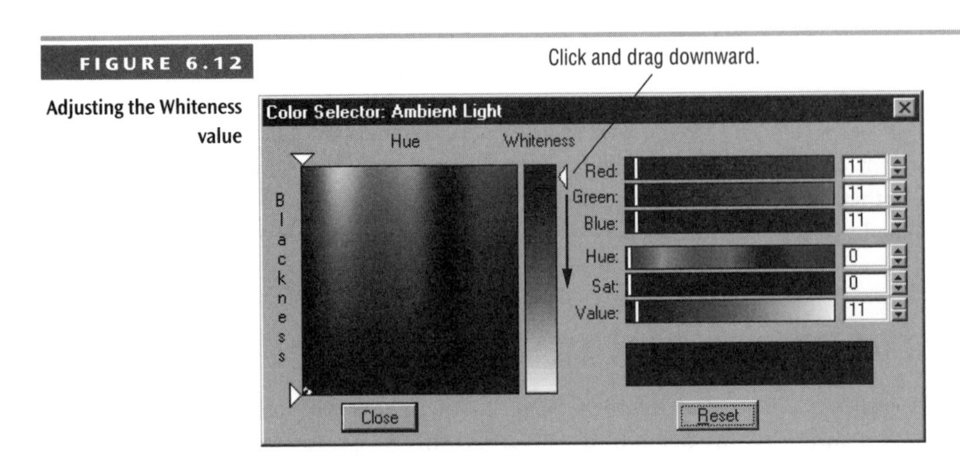

Adjusting the Whiteness value

5. As you move the triangular slider, notice that the Value spinner changes. Adjust the Value setting to 100, then click Close.
6. Close the Environment dialog box.

You've increased the ambient light so that objects in shadow will be more visible. To see the results, you'll have to render the model. This time, you'll make a few changes to the settings in the Render Design dialog box.

You can also force VIZ to render both sides of surfaces. Remember that normally VIZ only renders the side of a surface that has its normal pointing toward the viewer. But in the translation from the AutoCAD DWG file, the normals are often not translated correctly.

1. Click the Render Design tool.
2. This time you don't want to save a rendered view to a file, so click the Save File check box in the Render Output group to turn this option off.

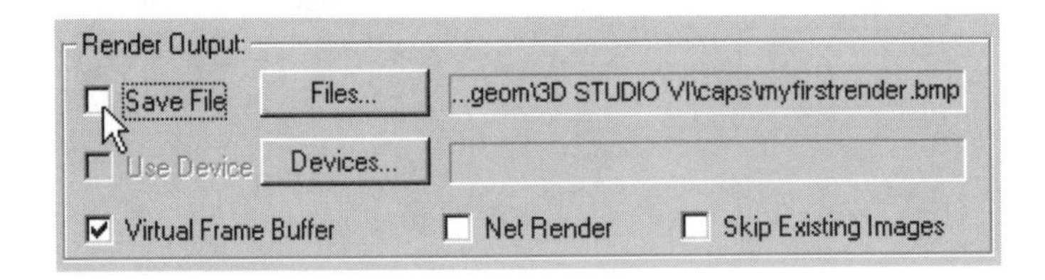

3. In the Options group, click the Force 2-Sided check box to turn this option on.

Options:
Video Color Check | Atmospherics | Super Black | Render Off
Force 2-Sided | Effects | Displacement | Render to Fields

4. Click Render. Now you can see more of the detail in the shadows as shown in Figure 6.13. You can also see the surfaces that had disappeared in the previous rendering.

FIGURE 6.13

The model with ambient lighting increased

In this exercise, you just increased the amount of ambient light in your model. As you can see from the Color Selector dialog box, you can also tint the ambient light with color if you so choose. This can be useful for interior views of rooms that have a predominant color, or for sunset exterior views.

TIP **Since artificial lighting usually has a slight orange cast, as a general rule, adding an orange cast to interior scenes helps give interior scenes a more natural appearance. Likewise, outdoor scenes can be improved by adding a bit of blue to the light source.**

You also saw that you can force VIZ to render both sides of the surfaces of a model. This caused the rendering time to increase. Another option is to select the objects that are not rendering properly and reverse the direction of the normals for those objects. This is feasible for small models but, for larger models, the time required to revise the normals can make such an effort impractical. Forcing two-sided rendering is often the best way to resolve problems with normals, even if it means increasing rendering time.

NOTE Reversed normals are frequently a problem with models imported from AutoCAD. They aren't usually a problem with models created entirely within VIZ.

Creating a Quick Study Animation

A single image such as a rendering can show a lot of detail, but an animated view of a design can offer a better sense of form and space. If an animated view is properly done, you can also get a better sense of the scale of a design.

When you create an animation, you are literally rendering several hundred still images that are later combined to form the frames of an animated movie. Since you are generating so many mini-renderings, animations take quite a bit longer to produce than still images. To see firsthand how the animation process works, try the following exercise.

Animation in VIZ begins by getting into animation mode. You get into animation mode by simply clicking the Animate button on the Time Controls toolbar.

1. Click the Animate button on the Time Controls toolbar in the lower right corner of the VIZ window.

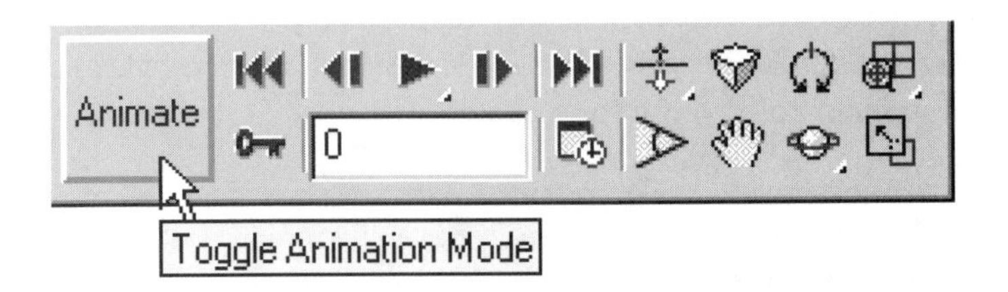

The button turns red to let you know that you are in Animate mode.

2. Click and drag the Time slider to the far right. The Time slider sits just below the viewports.

When you start to animate your model, you can think of your animation as a self-contained slice of time. That time is divided into 30 divisions per second. Each of those divisions is called a frame, and each frame is a single, still image.

The Time slider shows two numbers. The first number is the current frame, and the second number is the total number of frames in your slice of time. The default slice of time VIZ offers is 100 frames, or a little over three seconds of animation. You can increase that number by using the Time Configuration dialog box, which you will see a bit later in this chapter. For this presentation, you'll stick with the 100 frames, which is equivalent to about three seconds of animation time. When you move the slider to the far right, you change your position in your slice of time to the last frame, or frame 100.

This may seem a bit confusing right now, but the next exercise will give you a first-hand impression of how time works in VIZ.

Adding Camera Motion

VIZ starts out by giving you 100 frames of time. The slider bar you just used lets you move through the frames quickly. To get a better picture of how this works, lets add some motion to the model.

1. Right-click the Camera.View.3DGROUND viewport label in the upper left corner, then select Views ➢ Camera.View.3DFRONT. You'll use this view in the animation example.
2. Click the Top viewport to make it active.

3. Click the Select and Move tool, then click the 3DFRONT camera object. This is the camera at the very bottom of the Top viewport as shown in Figure 6.14.

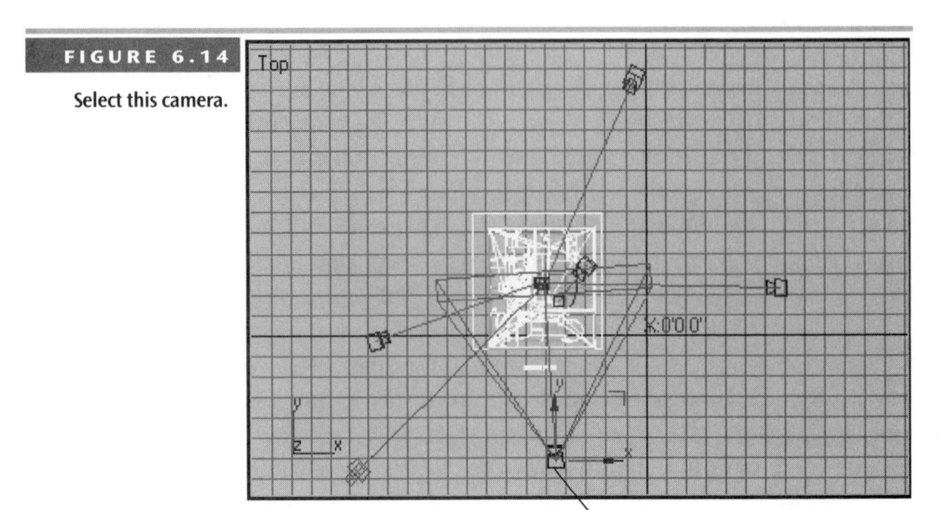

FIGURE 6.14

Select this camera.

Select this camera.

4. Move the Mycamera camera to the location shown in Figure 6.15.

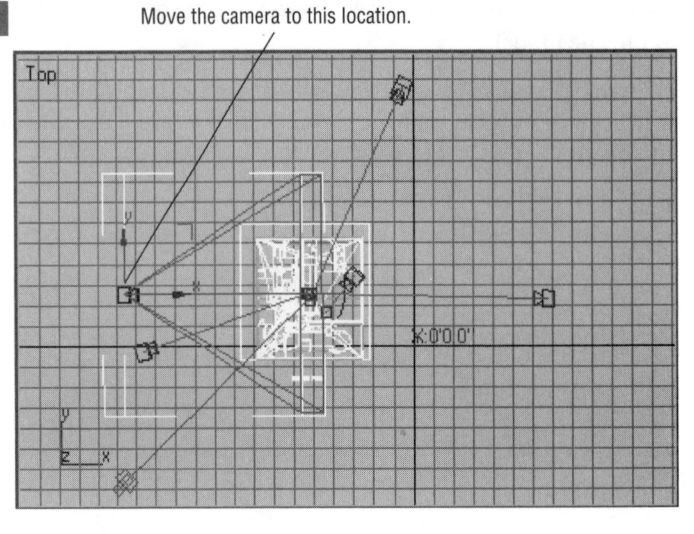

FIGURE 6.15

Move the 3DFRONT camera to this location.

5. Now click and drag the Time slider slowly from its position at the far right to the far left. Notice what happens to the 3DFRONT viewport.

The view changes dynamically as you move the bar. Also notice that the camera in the upper left viewport moves, showing you its location at each frame.

You have just created a camera motion by simply selecting a frame using the slider bar (which you also did in the exercise prior to the last one), then positioning the camera in the new location for that frame. Moving objects while in Animate mode changes their location in time as well as within the space of the model. Had you moved the camera with the Animate mode turned off, you would have simply moved the camera with no resulting motion over time.

Setting Adaptive Degradation

You might notice that, as you move the Time slider, the image in the `Camera.View.3DFRONT` viewport is reduced to wireframe boxes. This reduction of quality is a feature called Adaptive Degradation, and it lets you get a sense of the motion without taxing your video hardware and slowing down the real-time preview. You can control how Adaptive Degradation affects your viewport display through the Adaptive Degradation tab of the Viewport Configuration dialog box. To get to this dialog box, choose View ➢ Configure…, or you can right-click the viewport label and select Configure from the pop-up menu. The Viewport Configuration dialog box displays.

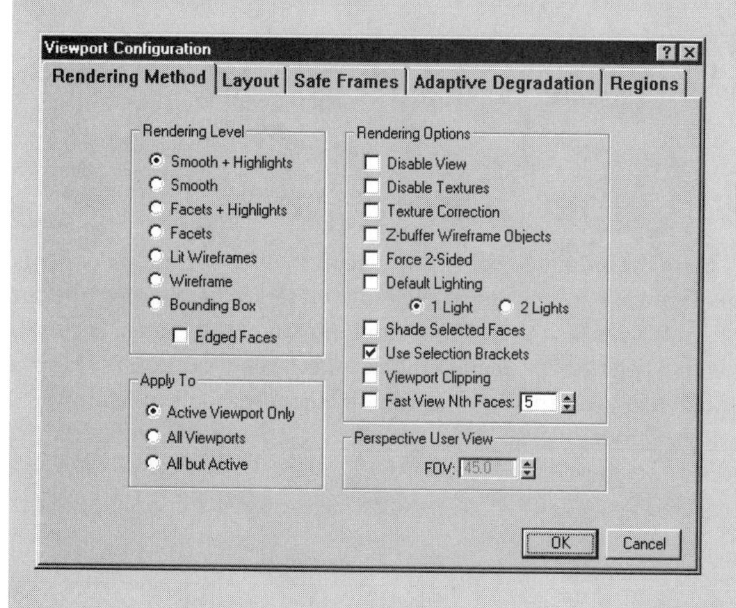

Continued on the next page

This dialog box lets you control the way objects are displayed in a viewport. The Render Method tab offers general settings for the way VIZ displays objects in the viewport.

If you click the Adaptive Degradation tab, you see the options that control the way VIZ displays objects as you move the Time slider.

The General Degradation group controls the viewports that are not active, whereas the Active Degradation group controls the viewport that is affected by the Time slider's motion.

Adjusting the Camera Path

If you study the animated perspective view as you move the slider bar back and forth, you may notice that you alternately move closer to the building and then farther away from it. This is so because the motion path of the camera is a straight line between the beginning camera location and the end location as shown in Figure 6.16. As the camera moves through its path, or *trajectory* as it is called in VIZ, it also moves closer to the model.

FIGURE 6.16

The camera trajectory

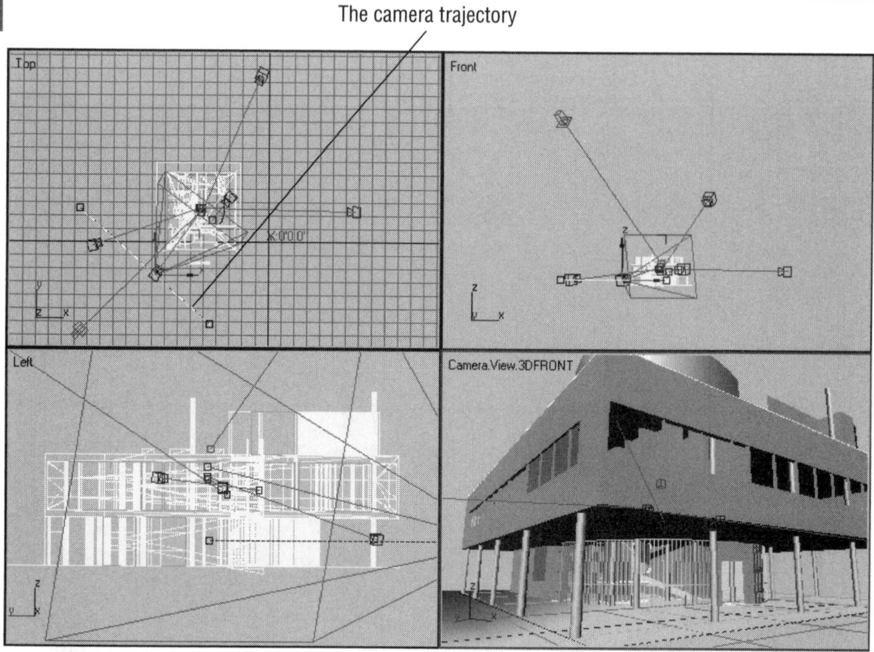

Let's assume you don't want that effect, and that you want the camera to stay as consistent a distance from the model as possible. To achieve that effect, you can move the Time slider to position the camera at its closest position to the model, then move the camera farther away at that point in time with Animate on.

1. Move the Time slider to the middle of the slider position so that the slider shows 50/100. This places your camera at frame 50.

You can also enter **50**➢ in the Time Control input box.

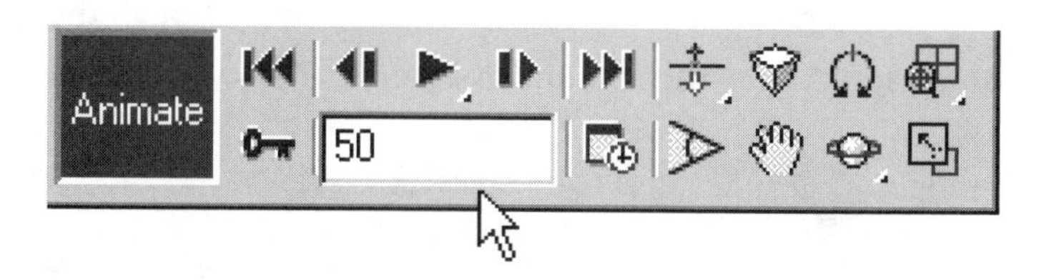

2. Use the Select and Move tool to move the camera away from the model to a location similar to the one shown in Figure 6.17.

FIGURE 6.17

The new location of the camera at frame 50

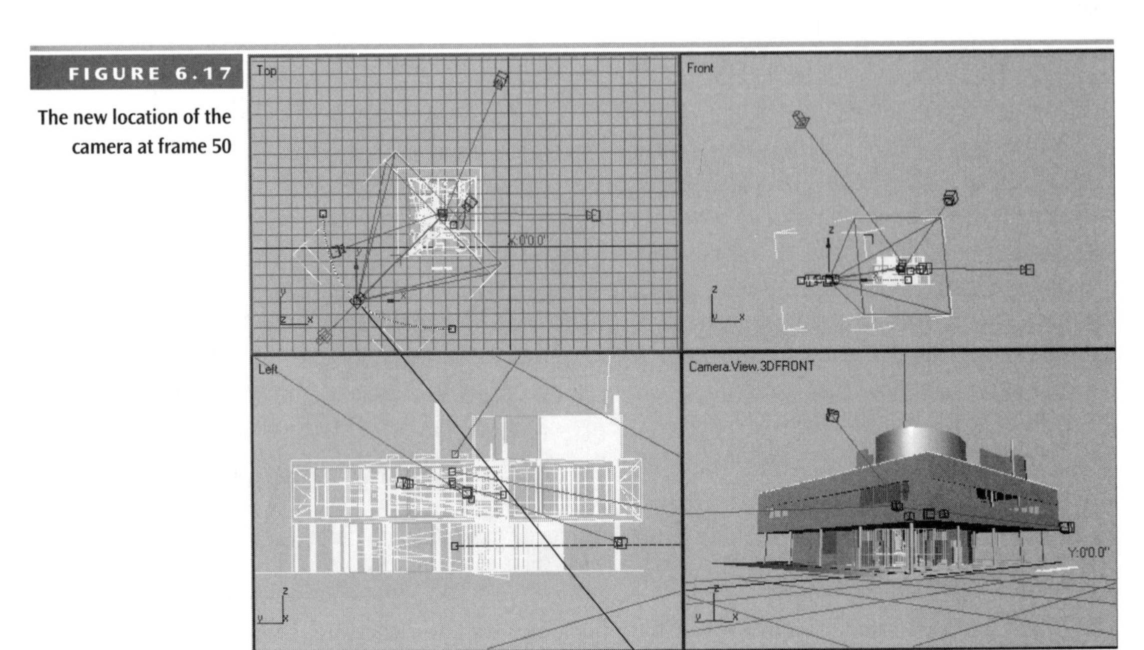

3. Right-click the Camera.View.3DFRONT viewport, then click the Play button in the Time controls.

The viewport displays the effect of the camera through the frames.

4. To stop the playback of the camera animation, click the Stop button.

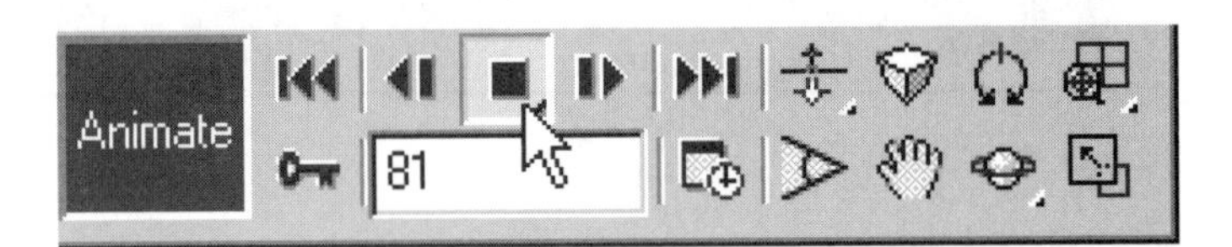

5. Right-click the Top viewport, then click Play again. Notice that this time you see the camera motion in the top viewport.
6. Click the Stop button to stop the playback.

Here you see how moving the camera at a particular frame in the Time slider affects the camera motion. When you altered the camera location in this last exercise, you were actually adding what is called a *keyframe* to the camera path. A keyframe is a point along the camera path that directs its motion. You can think of the camera path as a spline and the keyframe as a control point or vertex on that spline.

There is evidence of this keyframe in the space just below the Time slider. Look at the middle of the Time slider, and you'll see a gray dot at the 50/100 location as shown in Figure 6.18. This dot tells you that a keyframe exists at that point in time. A careful examination of the slider reveals that there are also two other gray dots, one on either end of the slider. (The dots at either end are only partially visible, but they are there.)

FIGURE 6.18

The dots below the Time slider indicate the location of a keyframe.

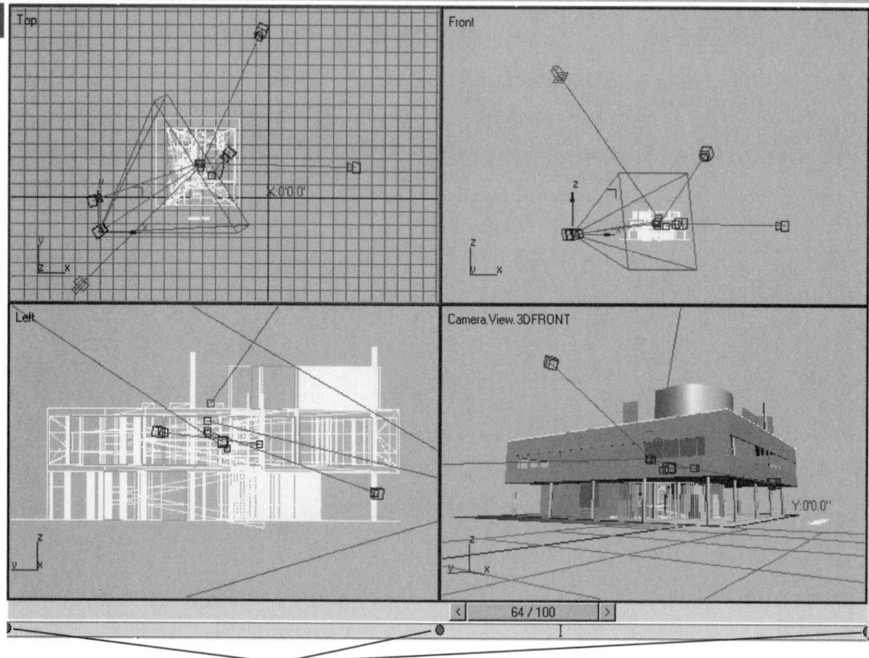

The keyframe dots below the Time slider appear only when an object that is animated is selected. Since the camera is selected, you can see the keyframe dots.

1. Right-click the keyframe dot in the middle of the Time slider.
2. Select Goto Time from the pop-up menu.

The Time slider moves to the keyframe location, and the view from that location is displayed in the Mycamera viewport. The Goto Time option offers a quick way to move the camera to a keyframe location.

Viewing the Camera Trajectory

When you're working on an animation sequence, it helps to see the animation path or trajectory of an object. For example, if you could see the path of the camera in the last exercise, it would make it easier to determine the distance between the camera and the model throughout the animation. There are a number of tools that VIZ offers to display the camera path as well as the location of the keyframes along the path. The following exercise will show you some of those tools.

1. First make sure that the Camera.View.3DFRONT camera is still selected, then click the Motion tab in the Command Panel.
2. Click the Trajectories button in the Motion tab of the Command Panel.

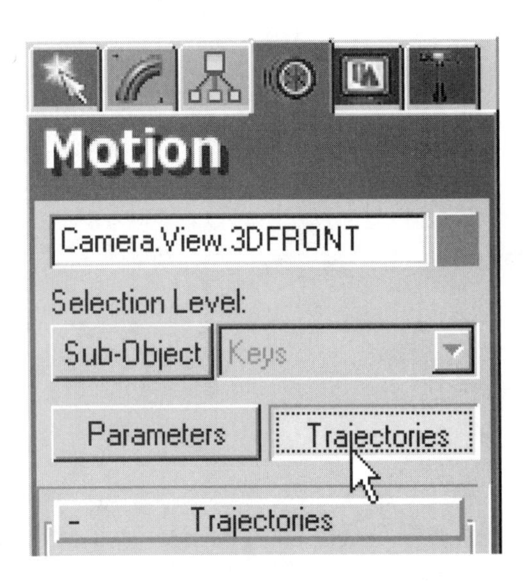

Now you can see the path of the camera as a dotted line in the Top, Left, and Front viewports as shown in Figure 6.19.

FIGURE 6.19

The viewports showing the camera path

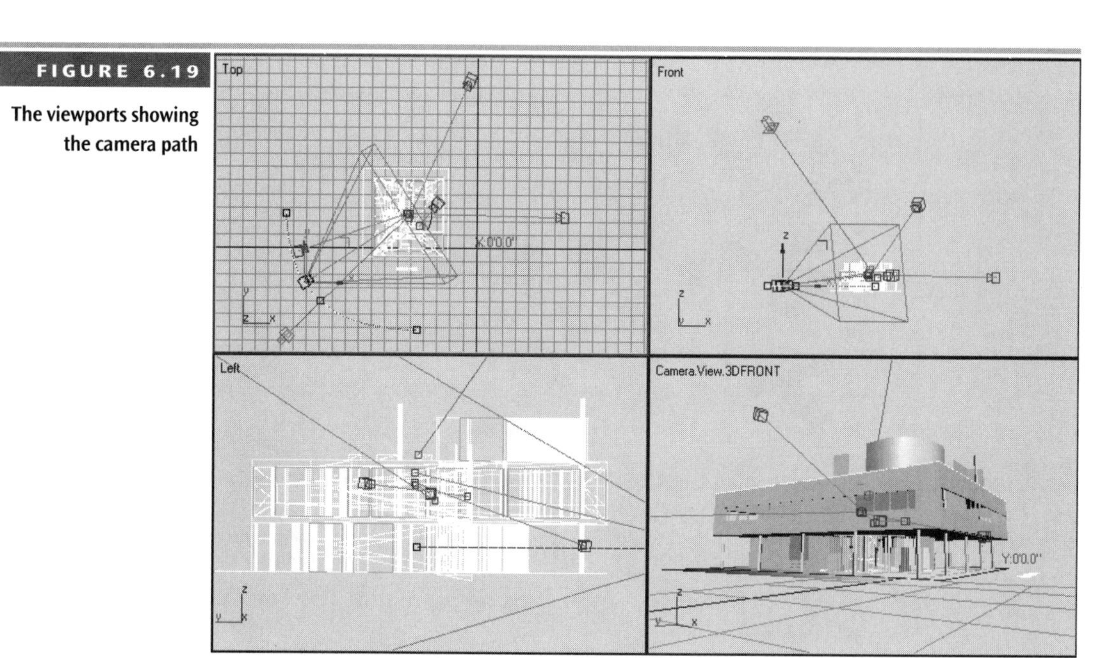

3. Right-click the Top viewport and click the Min/Max tool to enlarge it.
4. Move the Time slider to the 75/100 position to get a better view of the keyframes.

   You can see the keyframes as small squares in the path. The dots in the path represent the individual frames of the animation.
5. Use the Select and Move tool to move the camera slightly to the right.
6. Move the Time slider to the 25/100 position.

By moving the camera in step 5, you added another keyframe to the path. You can add a keyframe without having to move the camera by using the Parameters button in the Motion tab of the Command Panel.

1. Click the Parameters button in the Motion tab of the Command Panel.
2. With the Time slider at the 25/100 position, click the Position button in the Create Key group of the Look At Parameters rollout. You've just added another keyframe at frame 25.

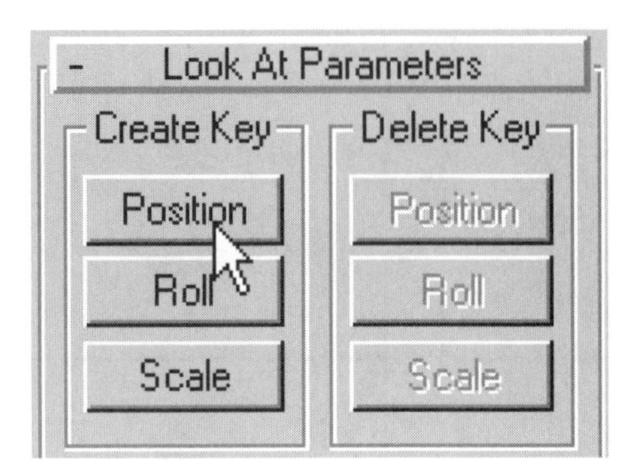

The Position button in the Create Key group lets you add a keyframe without changing the position of the camera.

1. Click the Keyframe dot at the 75/100 position, then right-click it.
2. Select Delete selected keys from the pop-up menu. The keyframe is removed from the camera trajectory.

Just as with objects in your model, you can select multiple keyframe dots that appear below the Time slider. You can then right-click a keyframe dot and select an option from the pop-up menu to edit the selected keyframes. In this last, brief exercise, you deleted a single keyframe using the right-click pop-up menu.

Controlling the Camera Trajectory Visibility

When you clicked the Parameters button in a previous exercise, the camera trajectory disappeared. This is because the path is typically only visible when the Trajectory button is selected. You can permanently turn on the path visibility through the Objects Properties dialog box.

1. Right-click the Camera.View.3DFRONT camera. Then click Properties… in the pop-up menu. The Object Properties dialog box displays.

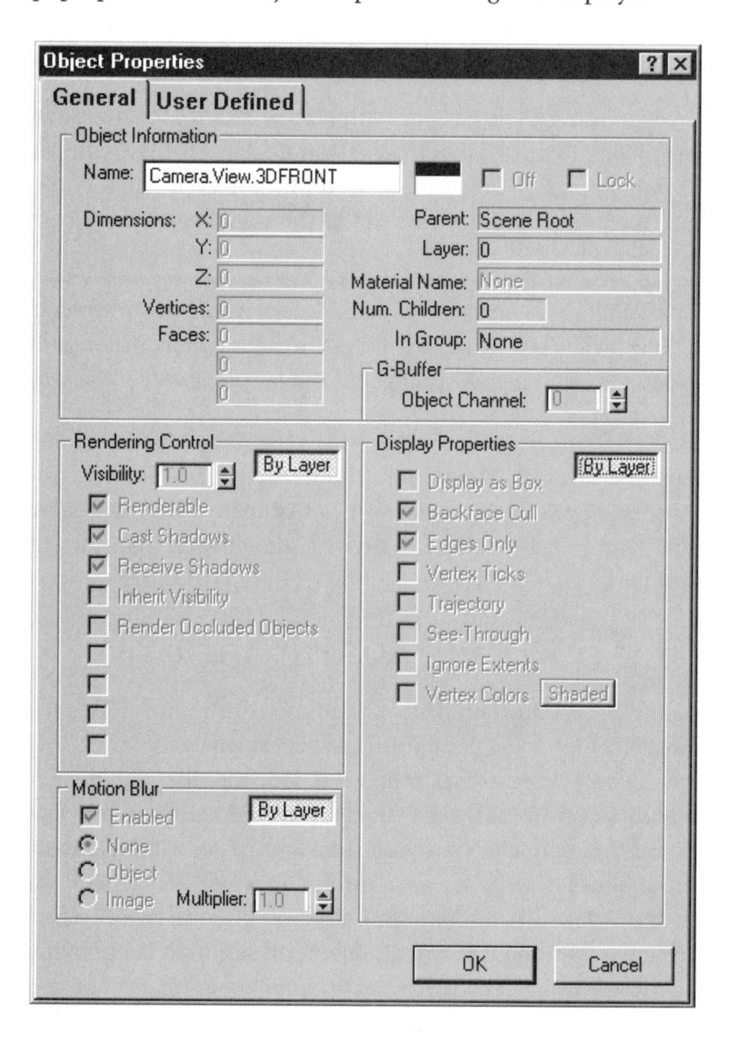

2. Make sure that the Button in the upper right corner of the Display Properties group shows *By Object*. If it shows *By Layer*, click it to change it to *By Object*.
3. Click the Trajectory check box. This turns on the path trajectory display.
4. Click OK to close the dialog box.

Now you can see the camera path and keyframes for the Camera.View.3DFRONT camera object. By turning on the path trajectory display, you can more easily edit the camera path. You'll want to turn it off, however, when you're editing the model, because the path trajectory can add to the visual clutter of a complex model.

TIP **Another way to control the trajectory visibility is to select the animated object, click the Display tab, then place a check in the Trajectory option in the Display Properties rollout. Note that this will change the display properties of the selected object from By Layer to By Object.**

Once you've established the keyframes of your animation (the beginning and end frames are also keyframes), you can edit them to further refine your camera motion. You'll see how that's done in a later chapter. For now, lets get a preview of this animation.

Creating a Preview Animation

Rendering even a short animation is a time-consuming affair, so you'll want to make sure that the motion in your animation is exactly what you want before you commit to actually producing a final animation. One tool that will help you determine what your animation will look like is the Preview animation. A preview animation is really a very crude facsimile of how your final animation will look. It should only be used to get a rough idea of whether your animation works in a general way. Still, it can reveal many of the flaws in your animation that might otherwise go unnoticed, such as a jerky camera motion or a camera-object collision that isn't obvious.

Try the following exercise to create a preview animation of your work so far.

1. Click the Min/Max toggle tool to get a view of all of the viewports. Then click the Camera.View.3DFRONT viewport.
2. Choose Rendering ➢ Make Preview. The Make Preview dialog box displays.

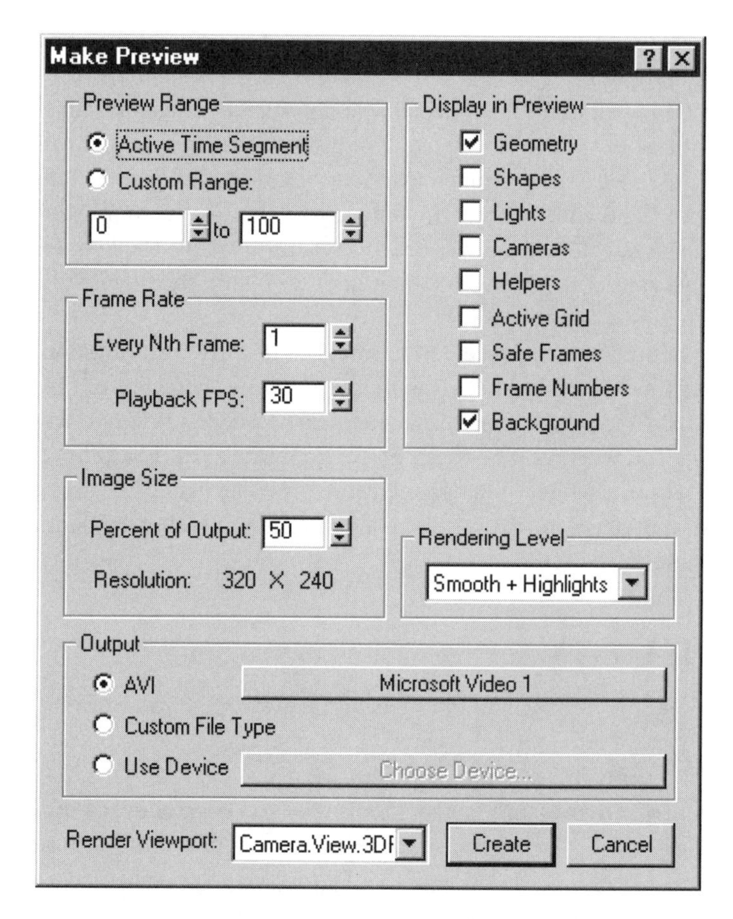

3. Click the Create button. You'll see a small version of the model in the viewport area, as the preview is created. Then the Windows Media Player opens and plays back the preview.
4. Click the Animate button to deactivate it. If you're not actually working on animation motion, it's a good idea to keep it turned off.

If you have another application designated to play back AVI files, then you will see that application instead of the Windows Media Player.

The preview is crude, but it does give you a good feel for the camera motion through the model. The model itself is not rendered, and the lighting effects are not rendered accurately.

If you look at the Make Preview dialog box, you see that you have several options that control the preview animation. You can have the animation display the frame number, grid, or light locations, for example, by clicking the check box next to each of these items. Or you can control the size of the animation using the Percent of Output input box (100 percent is equal to a 640 × 480 image).

If you want to limit the preview to a particular range of frames, you can specify that range in the Preview Range group. The Rendering Level drop-down list lets you determine whether the preview renders a shaded view, a wireframe view, or a bounding box view, which shows the objects of the model as simple boxes. The Output group gives you control over the AVI settings. Finally, the Render viewport drop-down list lets you select a viewport to render. By default, the preview animation is that of the currently active viewport.

When VIZ creates a preview animation, it saves the animation as a file called _design.avi (the name begins with an underline character) in the Previews folder of the main VIZ folder. Every time you create a preview, VIZ overwrites this file without asking you whether it's OK or not. If you create a preview animation that you want to save, choose Render ➢ Rename Preview. The File dialog box that displays lets you save the last preview animation under a different name, thereby permanently saving the preview.

Summary

Cameras provide the ability to create the exact view you want by giving you control over camera and target placement. You've also seen how you can control camera motion through VIZ's animation features.

Along with cameras, lighting tools give you control over a design's appearance. With lighting, you can add shadows that enhance a scene with realism and depth. Ambient light lets you bring out detail in the darker regions of a scene. It takes some practice and experience to use these tools with confidence, but with the knowledge you've gained in this chapter, you'll be off to a good start in using them.

In the next chapter, you'll begin to explore another major tool in building your designs: the Material Editor. With the Material Editor you can add texture and lifelike detail to your model. Materials can provide a quick way to enliven your design and provide a sense of realism. You'll see firsthand how you can quickly add interest to a design by adding materials to the Villa Savoye model.

3D STUDIO VIZ GALLERY

In a night scene of the Avery Aquatic Center, Target Spot lights were used to both illuminate the sign and reflect light from the sign surface. The diving platform in the background is illuminated internally with Omni lights. The background is a bitmap image. A very low ambient light was used to help illuminate the trees.

The daytime rendering of the Avery Aquatic Center uses people and trees from a third-party plug-in from Archsoft called Realpeople.

Avery Aquatic Center, Stanford University

ELS Architecture and Urban Design

An early rendition of the dive tower for the Avery Aquatic Center uses a Noise Bump map to create ripples in the water.

Avery Aquatic Center, Stanford University

ELS Architecture and Urban Design

The 3D model of the Church Street Plaza project was used to generate standard exterior elevations using the technique described in Chapter 12.

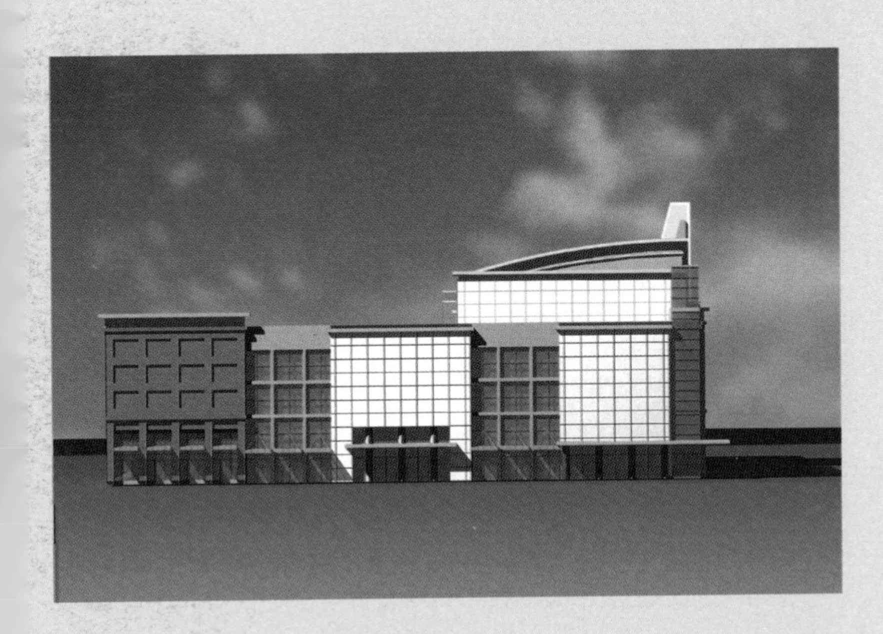

Church Street Plaza, Evanston, Illinois

ELS Architecture and Urban Design

This perspective view of the Church Street Plaza project was originally created in AutoCAD, then rendered in VIZ. Omni lights are used inside the building for illumination.

In contrast to the night scenes on the next page, the daylight view of the Denver Pavilions project shows off the structure of the sign.

Church Street Plaza, Evanston, Illinois (top) and Denver Pavilions (bottom)
ELS Architecture and Urban Design

The same model from the previous page was used for the night scene, but this time it was lit using a single directed light and ambient light. Night renderings of the Denver Pavilions project enabled designers to visualize the effects of lighting on the perforated metal screen behind the sign. Colored Target Spot lights are projected onto the screen to produce a multicolor pattern.

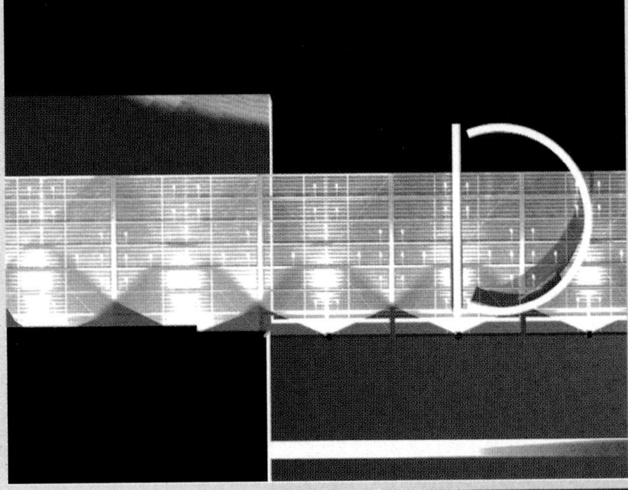

Denver Pavilions, three views

ELS Architecture and Urban Design

These interior views of a shopping mall are lit using only ambient light. This mimics a diffused light scattered by bright walls. The storefronts are bitmap montages mapped to a wall surface just behind the glass. These bitmaps are photographs of actual storefronts from an existing mall.

An exterior view of a proposed mall shop was rendered in VIZ, and then a watercolor effect was applied in Photoshop to give the image a hand-painted look. The trees and people are from Archsoft's Realpeople plug-in to VIZ. Notice how the trees in the foreground frame the view.

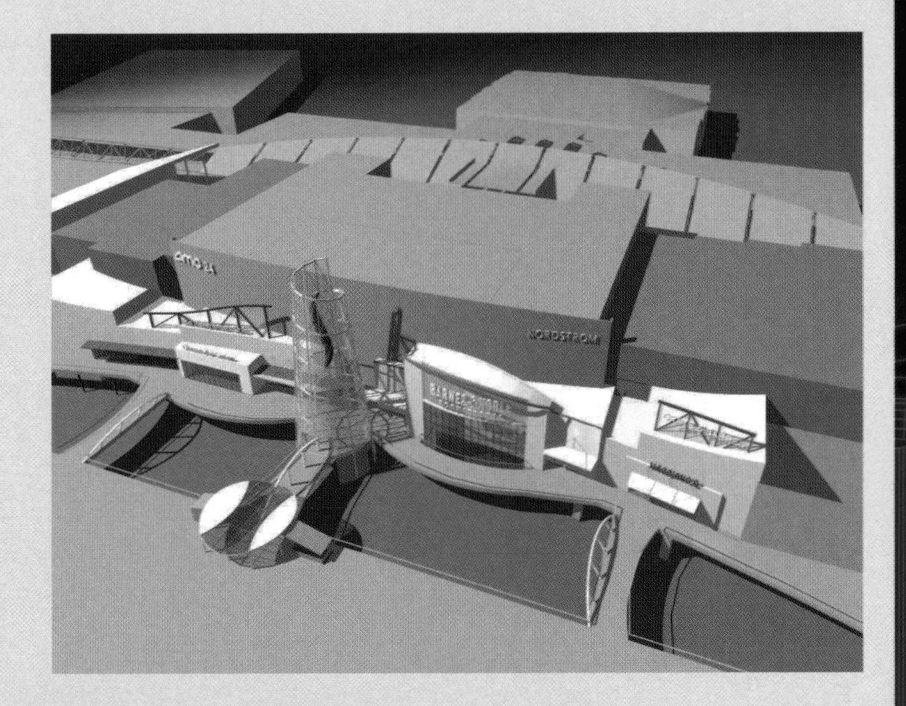

A bird's-eye view of a mall was used to help show the layout of the building and the location of the anchor stores. Once the model is built, views like this are easily created using a camera object.

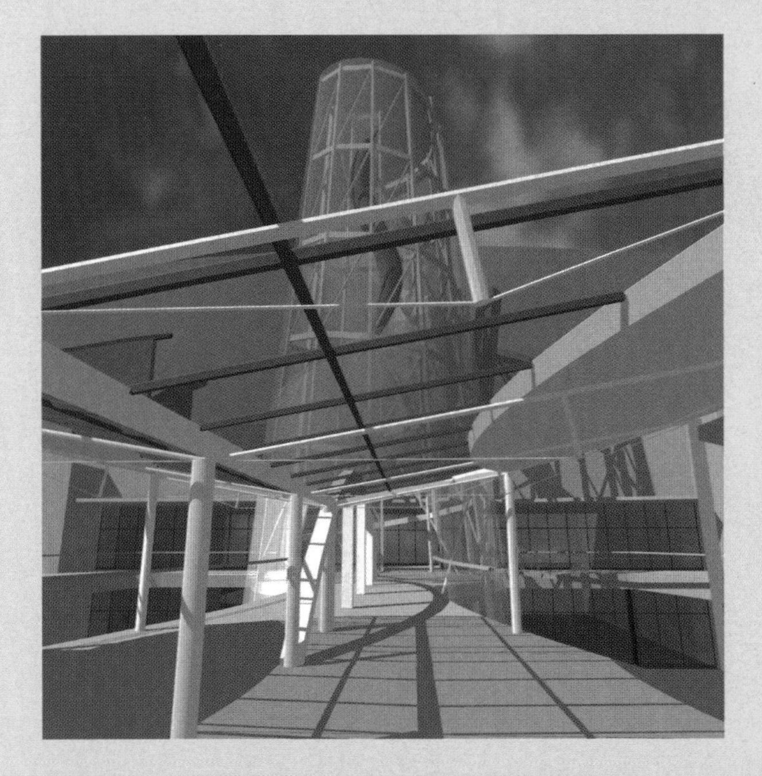

A series of renderings of a mall's entrance from the parking structure shows how the entrance tower will appear. The tower is a steel structure with a screen mesh. The mesh was simulated using a semi-transparent material map. A Raytrace shadow was used to enhance the detail of the view.

Various Studies

ELS Architecture and Urban Design

Various Studies

ELS Architecture and Urban Design

From start to finish, the Vincent Park Boat House renderings were created in 18 hours, spread over four days.

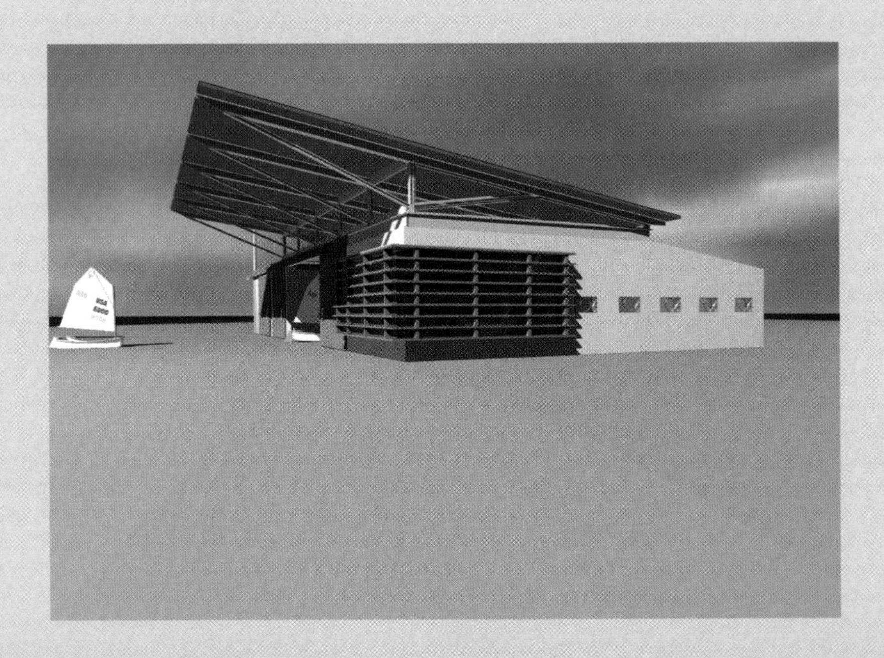

Vincent Park Boat House, Richmond, California

ELS Architecture and Urban Design

The doors were animated so that they could be shown both open and closed for various still views. The boats were also animated to add or remove them, depending on the view angle.

Vincent Park Boat House, Richmond, California

ELS Architecture and Urban Design

A single model of Pioneer Place was used to generate all of the elevation and perspective views for presentations. The buildings behind the main structure were added in Photoshop, and their contrast was reduced to fade them into the background. The sky was also added in Photoshop.

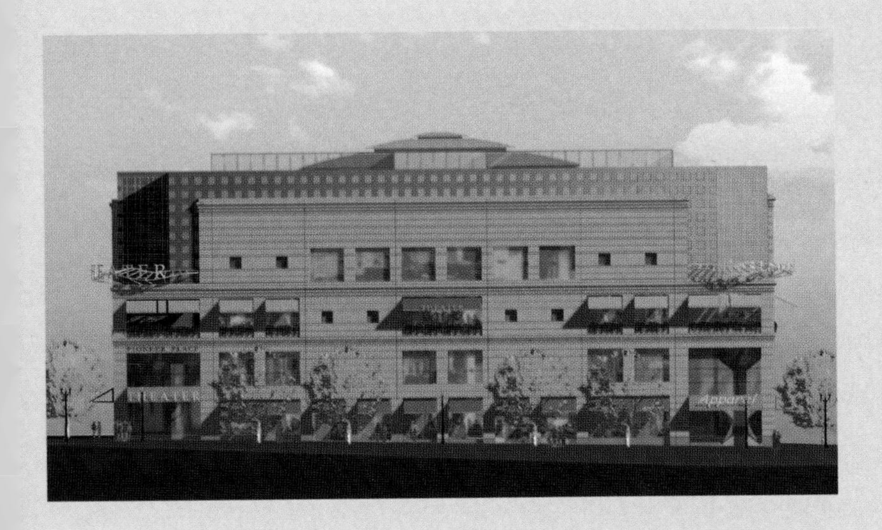

In these elevations of one of the buildings in the Pioneer Place project, trees and people were added in Photoshop. The trees were made transparent to show off the storefront at the street level. The storefronts were created by placing a wall just behind the glass and applying an image map of store interiors to the wall.

Pioneer Place, Portland, Oregon

Developer: The Rouse Company
ELS Architecture and Urban Design

The Pioneer Place project encompassed several blocks. This axonometric bird's-eye view of the project helped to show the building in the context of the downtown area. The main buildings were rendered with custom materials, while the white buildings used a simple default material. Notice that some of the buildings in the foreground use a translucent material in order to allow a better view of the buildings in the project.

Pioneer Place, Portland, Oregon

Developer: The Rouse Company
ELS Architecture and Urban Design

Pioneer Place, Portland, Oregon

Developer: The Rouse Company
ELS Architecture and Urban Design

chapter 7

Enhancing Models with Materials

FEATURING

- *Understanding Bitmap Texture Maps*
- *Adding Materials to Objects*
- *Understanding Mapping Coordinates*
- *Editing Materials*
- *Selectively Rendering Parts of Your Model*
- *Adding a Material to the Walls*
- *Mapping Materials to All the Faces of an Object*

Enhancing Models With Materials

The materials feature of VIZ lets you simulate surface color, texture, transparency, and even reflectance and roughness or bumpiness. The Material Editor in VIZ lets you create and modify materials that you can then apply to objects to achieve a realistic effect.

In this chapter, you'll be introduced to the Material Editor and how it can be used to add color and realism to your model. You'll also take a closer look at the rendering process and learn ways to improve the speed of your rendering. You'll see how materials and rendering affect each other, and you'll be introduced to the different rendering options available in VIZ.

Understanding Bitmap Texture Maps

To simulate a surface material, VIZ offers the Surface Materials Library. This is a library of simulated materials you can assign to objects. Each material contains properties such as color, reflectance, transparency, and roughness. Many materials also make use of image maps or *bitmaps* to simulate the look of complex surfaces such as marble, wood, or brick. Other materials use *procedural* maps.

A bitmap is an image file that shows a graphic sample of the material. One common bitmap image is marble, another is brick. You might think of a material that uses bitmaps as a kind of decal or sticker that is placed on a surface. There are several ways to use bitmaps in the properties of a material: texture maps, bump maps, and opacity maps, specular maps, shininess maps, self-illumination maps, and reflection maps, to name a few. Diffuse maps are the most common use of bitmaps and are the easiest to understand.

Procedural maps use mathematical formulas instead of bitmap images to simulate a texture. Unlike bitmaps, procedural maps often have parameters that can be set to control their visual effects, and they have a more uniform appearance when applied to objects that have unusual shapes or that are sliced or cut open in some way. For example, you can use the wood procedural map to create an elaborate carved wood sculpture, and the wood grain appears more realistic than if you applied a wood bitmap to the sculpture. Objects such as smoke, that might normally be difficult to simulate, can also be simulated using a procedural map.

In this introduction to materials, you'll be focusing on bitmap texture maps.

Diffuse Color Maps

One of the many predefined materials that VIZ offers is brick. Brick is an example of a texture map. Whenever you assign the brick material to an object, VIZ *pastes* a bitmap image of a brick wall to the object when it is rendered, so that the object looks like a brick surface (see Figure 7.1).

FIGURE 7.1

An example of a bitmap image (left) used as a texture map to simulate a brick wall

Ambient/Diffuse Maps

VIZ calls texture maps such as this brick example *Ambient/Diffuse* color maps because the bitmap is reflected in ambient and diffuse light. You can use a different bitmap for ambient and diffuse, but generally these two are tied together. To get a better idea of the different types of light an object reflects, look at Figure 7.2. It shows a sphere indicating the different ways that light is reflected off an object.

FIGURE 7.2

A sample sphere showing different types of reflected light

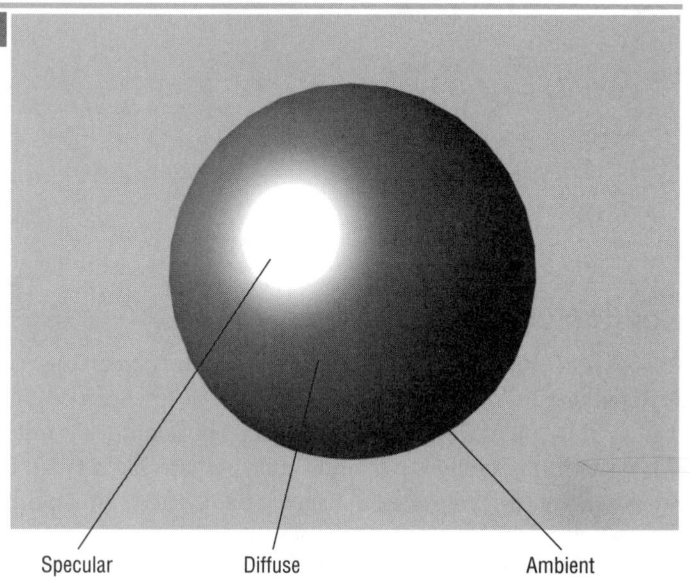

When the ambient light in a model is increased, you begin to see the dim portions of an object or those parts that are in shadow. The Ambient map appears in this area. The Diffuse map appears in the brighter portions of a model which can be lit by any type of light besides ambient light. The ambient and diffuse maps blend together so that, as the ambient light increases, the ambient maps seamlessly merge with the diffuse maps.

Specular Maps

Specular maps that are full-color image bitmaps only appear in specular highlights of a surface. On a shiny object, the specular portion of the object would normally appear white, as shown in Figure 7.3. You can have the specular region of an object display a surface feature by using specular maps as shown in Figure 7.3.

FIGURE 7.3

A sphere with a specular map displaying a shiny pattern

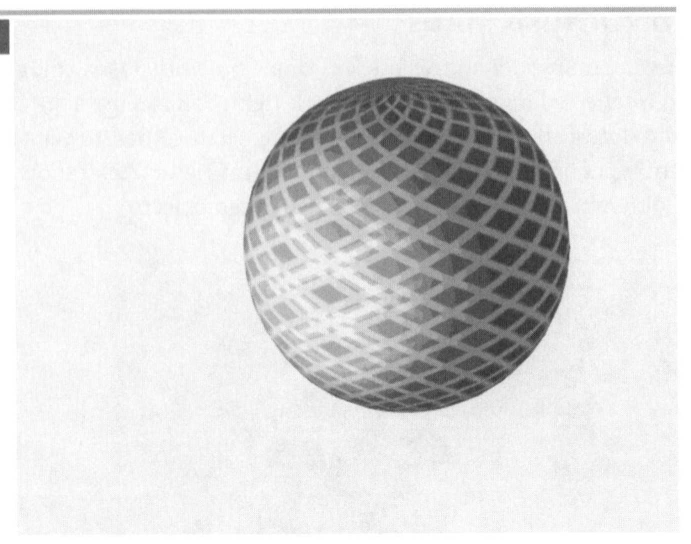

Glossiness Map

Glossiness maps also affect the specular region of a shiny object, but instead of displaying a colored texture, a glossiness map controls the level of glossiness on a surface. You would use a glossiness map on an object whose surface is not uniformly glossy, but is instead alternately rough and shiny, perhaps like a faded painted surface of a car where some places have been polished, while others remain dull.

Self-illumination Maps

Using the self-illumination feature, you can create materials that appear to glow. A self-illumination map is a gray scale bitmap image that determines the *glow* of a surface based on the bitmap's gray scale intensity. White is the brightest glow, while black is no glow at all.

Opacity Maps

Opacity maps make use of black and white bitmap images to control opacity and transparency. For example, you can turn a solid surface into an intricate filigree using an opacity map as shown in Figure 7.4.

FIGURE 7.4

A single, blank surface can be made to appear quite intricate by using opacity maps. The bitmap image to the left was used to turn a simple rectangular object into an intricate screen.

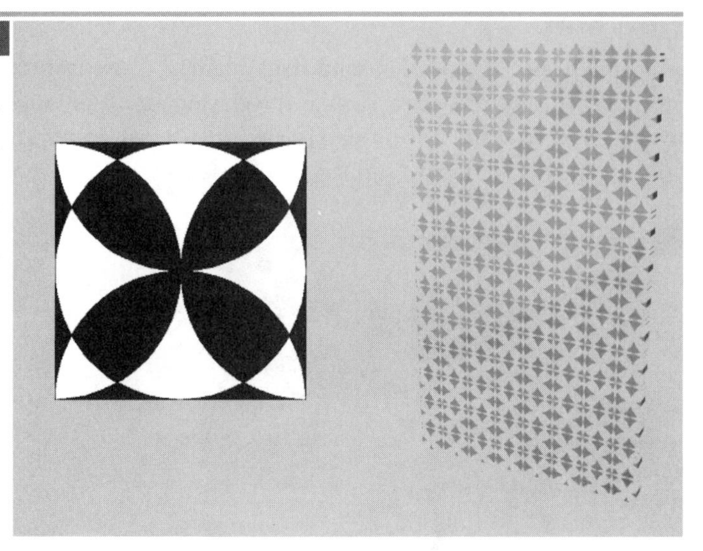

Bump Maps

You can also simulate a bumpy texture using gray scale bitmap images. Figure 7.5 shows a 2D bitmap image and objects rendered with a material that uses the bitmap to simulate a bumpy surface. VIZ converts the different intensities of light and dark tones of the gray scale bitmap into high and low points on the bumpy surface. Color bitmaps can also be used for bump maps, though the color information in the bitmap is not used. Just as with gray scale images, the intensity of the color determines the bumpy texture.

FIGURE 7.5

A bumpy surface can be simulated, using a gray scale bitmap shown at left. The light portions of the bitmap translate to high points in the bumpy surface while the darker portions of the bitmap translate to low points.

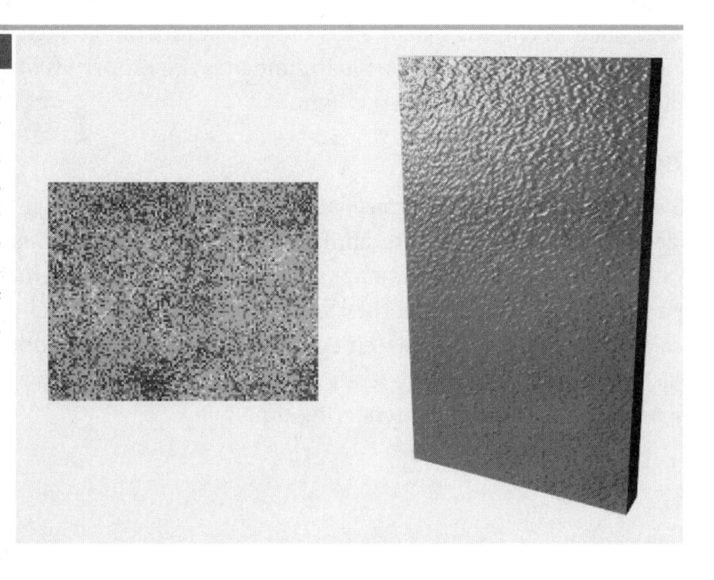

Reflection Map

A reflection map is a special type of bitmap assignment. It is used where you want a material that appears to be reflective, such as the glass in an office building or a lake or pond. In an animated scene, the bitmap image you use will *move* just as reflections move when you pass by a reflective surface. See Figure 7.6.

FIGURE 7.6

Reflection maps give the impression of a reflective surface such as the glass and floor in this rendering.

Refraction Map

A refraction map is similar to a Reflection map, but instead of giving the appearance of a reflection, such as chrome ball, it gives the appearance of a refracted image such as looking at a crystal ball. A refraction map simulates the properties of glass, water, or of other transparent material that bends light.

Displacement Map

A bump map simulates a bumpy surface, but it doesn't actually change the geometry of the model. Displacement maps are similar to bump maps in that they alter the shape of a surface, but displacement maps go one step further and actually modify the geometry of the object to which they are applied. You can, for example, turn a flat surface into a dome by using a displacement map. You need to be cautious when you use a displacement map, as it can generate a large number of faces on an object, thereby increasing the file size and rendering time.

Surface Properties

There are some materials that rely solely on the properties of color, reflectance, and opacity and do not use maps of any kind. Metal-Cherry Red, from the standard VIZ material library, for example, is a material that doesn't use a bitmap. Instead, it uses color and specular levels to simulate the appearance of a metallic substance. Unlike Brick, Metal-Cherry Red doesn't require an image or pattern to simulate the appearance of metal (see Figure 7.7).

FIGURE 7.7

Examples of surface materials that do not require bitmaps

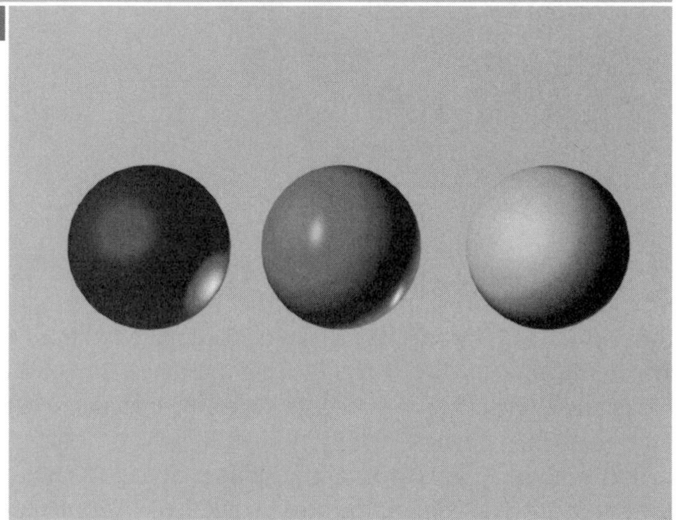

Most materials are a mixture of texture, bump, or opacity maps and color, specular levels, or transparency. Bitmaps and material properties are combined to simulate detail you would otherwise find impossible to recreate through surface or solid modeling alone (see Figure 7.8).

FIGURE 7.8

A simple sphere object with a single surface material that makes use of many of the different types of maps and properties available in VIZ

Adding Materials to Objects

For our tutorial, you'll start by selecting a few standard materials from a list and applying them to the model. Then, after checking the appearance of the material with another rendering, you'll look at ways to adjust the material to better suit your model.

The glass in the model appears as an opaque blue material. The blue color is inherited from the AutoCAD layer color of the original DWG file. VIZ offers a glass material that is both transparent and shiny, and it includes a bitmap reflection that simulates the reflection of a partially cloudy sky. In the next exercise, you'll add the glass material to the model.

1. Open the Ch07a.max file from the sample files on the Companion CD, or you may use the file you created in Chapter 6.
2. Click the Material Editor tool on the Material toolbar.

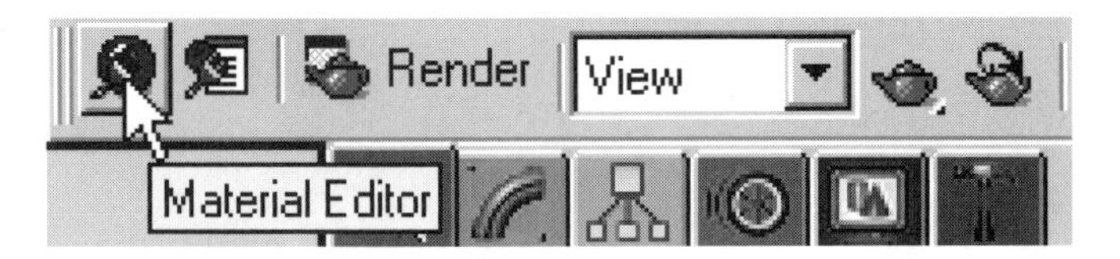

The Material Editor dialog box appears.

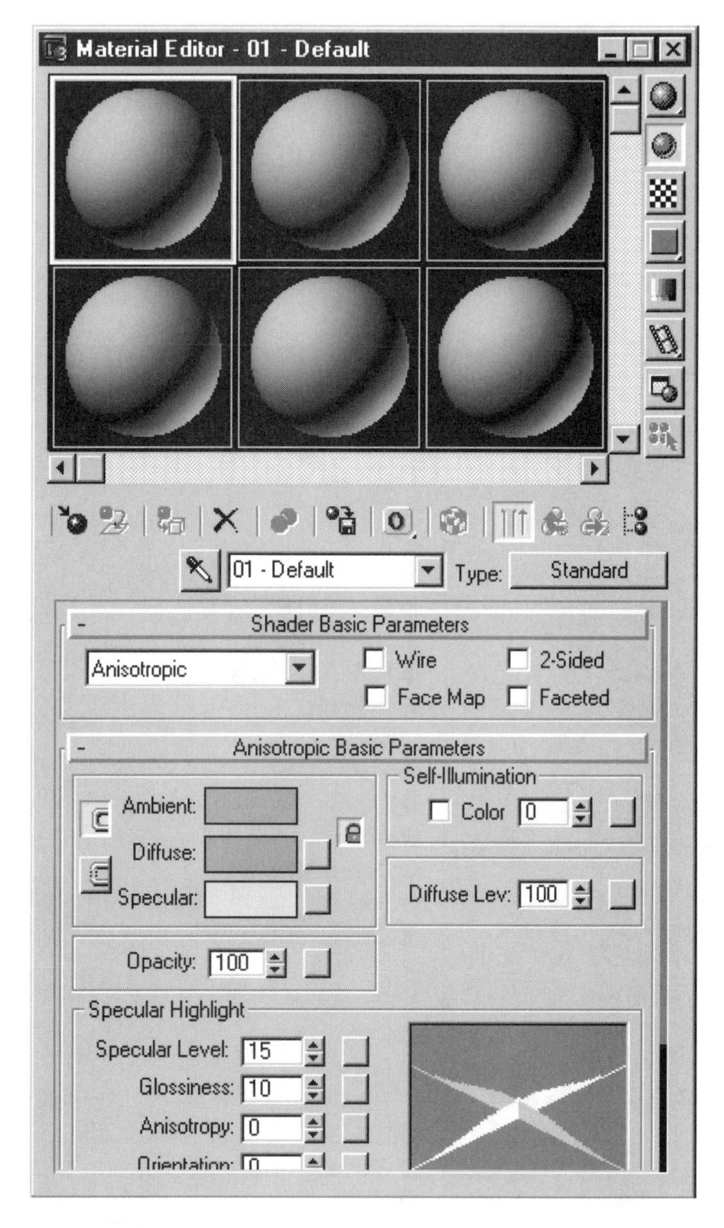

At the top you see a set of sample slots which are preview images of materials. Right now, there are no materials in the Material Editor so the slots all show the same blank sphere. Also notice that the top left slot is outlined with a thick white border. This tells you that it is currently the active slot.

3. Click the Get Material button on the toolbar just below the sample images of spheres.

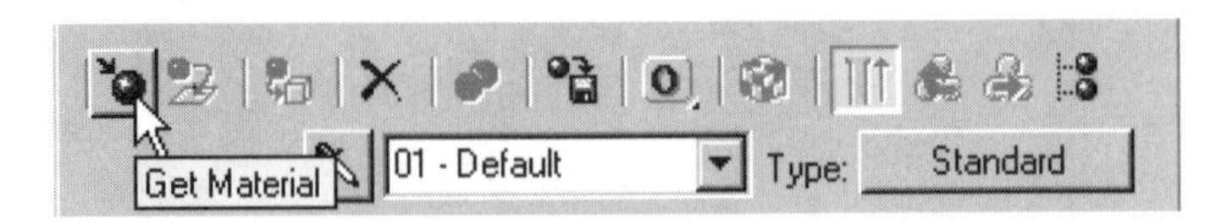

The Material/Map Browser appears.

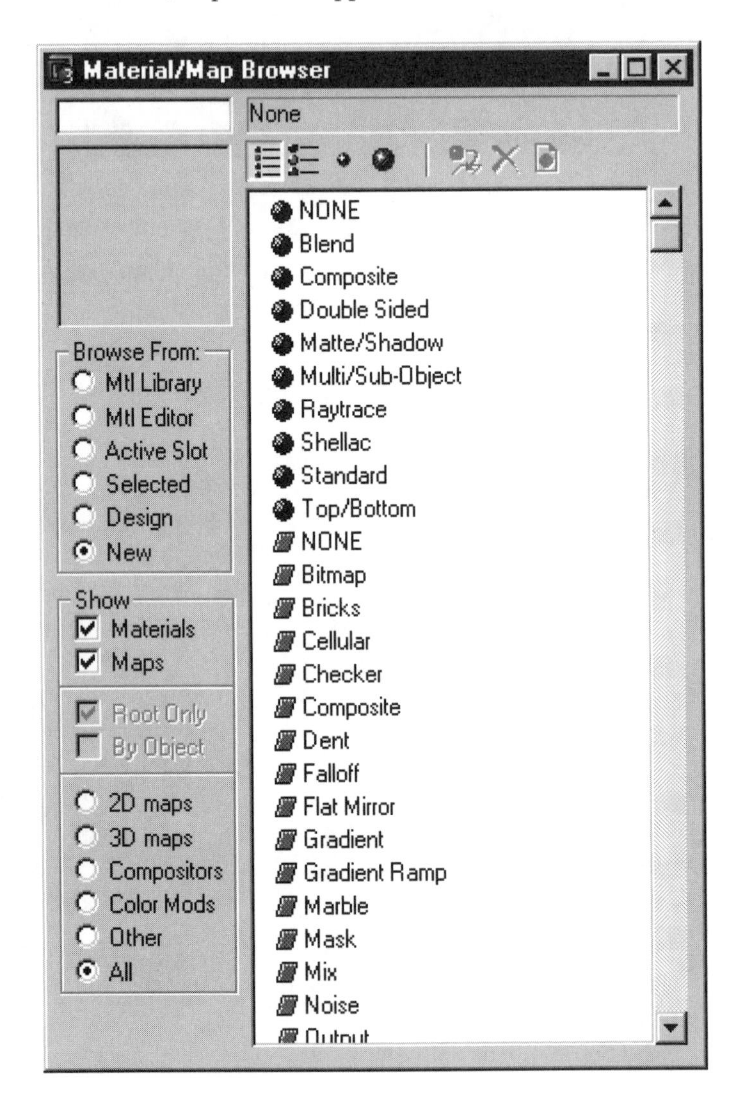

4. In the Browse From radio button group, click Mtl Library. This opens the standard VIZ Material Library and displays the materials stored there. The list box to the right will change to display a set of materials.
5. Scroll down the list and click Glass-Clear (Standard). The list is in alphabetical order, so you need to scroll about one third of the way down the list. Once your choice has been selected, you see a sample of the material in the sample viewer in the upper left corner of the dialog box.
6. Double-click Glass-Clear. The Glass-Clear material appears in the Material Editor in the upper left sample slot. Also notice that the name Glass-Clear appears in the drop-down list just below the row of tools.
7. Close the Material/Map Browser.

You've just loaded a material from the standard VIZ material library into the Material Editor. This is the first step in assigning a material to an object. Now go ahead and assign the Glass-Clear material to the glass in your model.

1. Click the Select by Name tool on the standard toolbar. You may need to move the Material Editor dialog box to get to the Select by Name tool.
2. Click the [Glass.03] item in the list, then click Select. The brackets denote groups in VIZ.
3. Go back to the Material Editor dialog box and click the Assign Material to Selection tool.

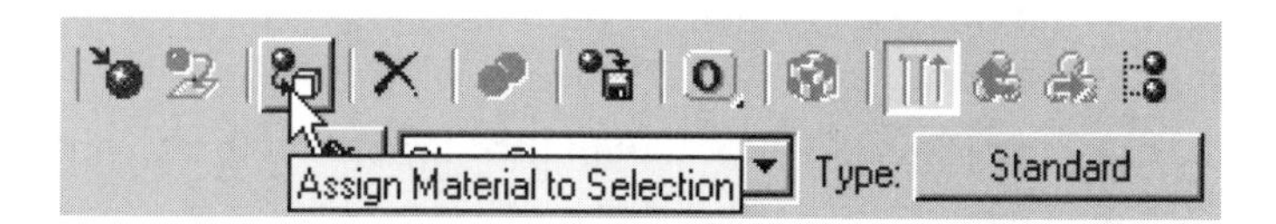

The glass will appear in the viewports as a dotted pattern.

It may not be obvious that the glass is present in your model, so let's take a quick look at a rendered view to see the results of adding the glass.

1. Close the Material Editor and right-click the Camera.View.3DFRONT viewport to make it active. Then click the Render Design tool on the standard Render toolbar.

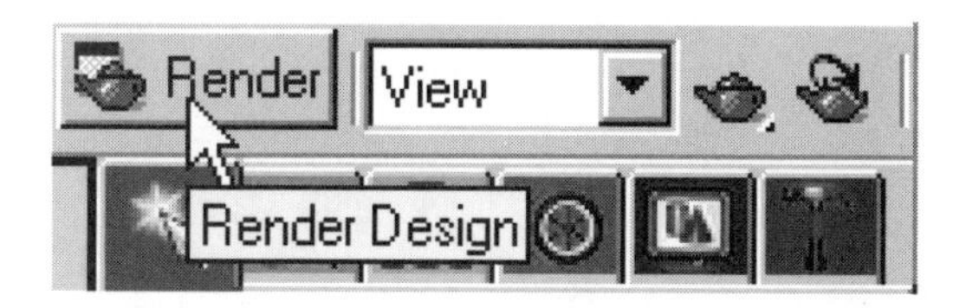

2. In the Render Design dialog box, make sure the Save File check box is turned off. You don't need to save the rendering to a file.
3. Click the Render button. You see a rendered view of the building with the glass appearing as a transparent material as shown in Figure 7.9.

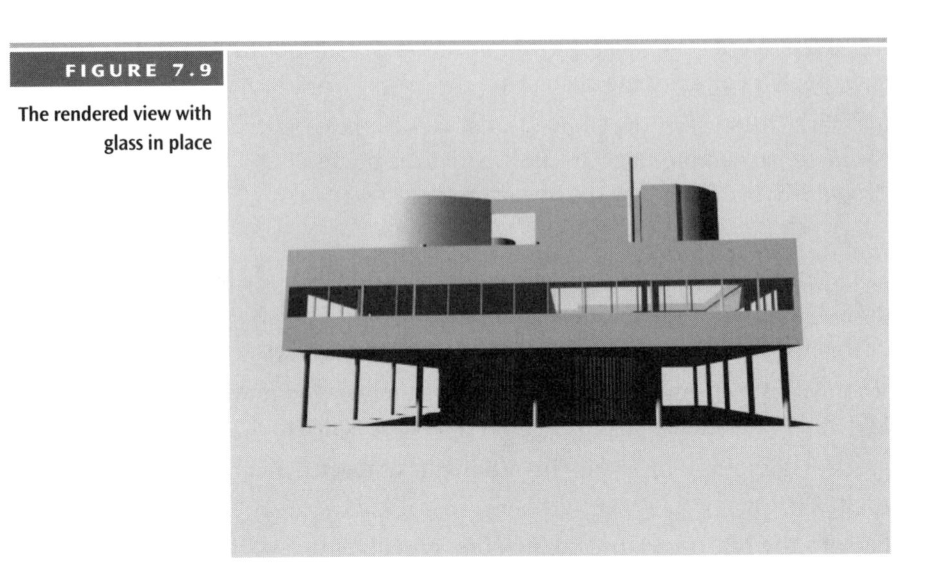

FIGURE 7.9

The rendered view with glass in place

It's difficult to tell whether the glass is really there. Next, you'll modify the parameters of the glass material to give it a bit more substance so it is easier to see in the rendering.

1. Click the Material Editor tool in the Material toolbar to open the Material Editor dialog box.

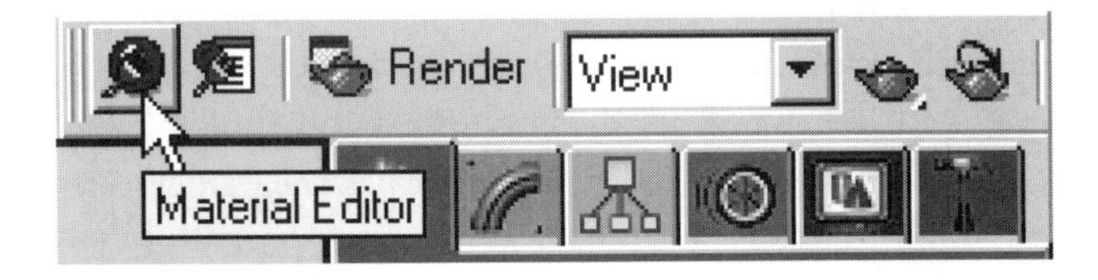

2. Notice that the Glass-Clear material is still selected and is the current material in the dialog box.

3. Change the Opacity setting in the Phong Basic Parameters rollout to **50**. Notice that the sample slot showing the glass darkens. The glass also darkens in the Viewports.
4. Click the Quick Render tool. This time the glass is more apparent in the rendering.

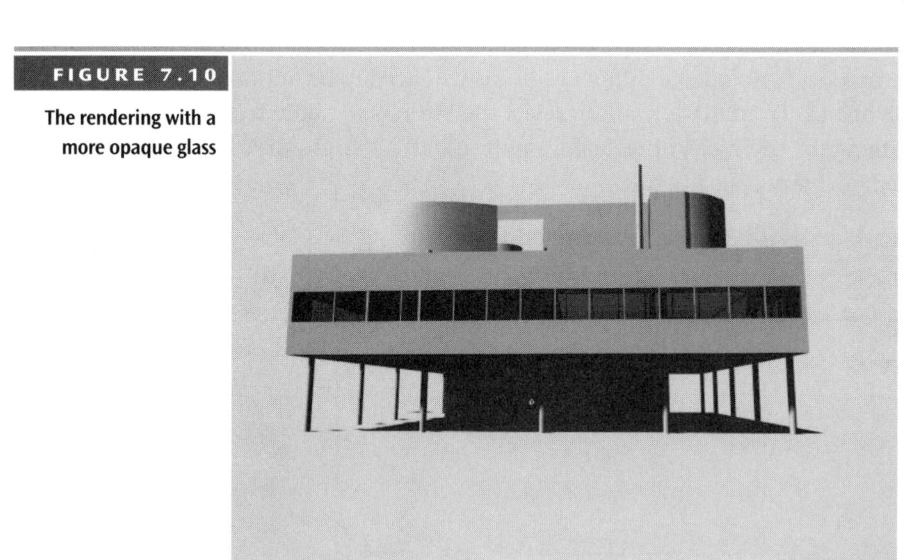

FIGURE 7.10

The rendering with a more opaque glass

You've just added a material to an object and then modified the material. Through the method just shown, you can add materials based on the object's name, as in the Glass.03 object. Be aware that, although you changed the glass opacity parameter in the model, the change did not affect the Glass-Clear material in the Viz Material Library. The parameter change only affected the material within the model. You can save changes back to the VIZ material library using the Put to Library tool on the Material Editor toolbar. This copies the current material to the library from which it came.

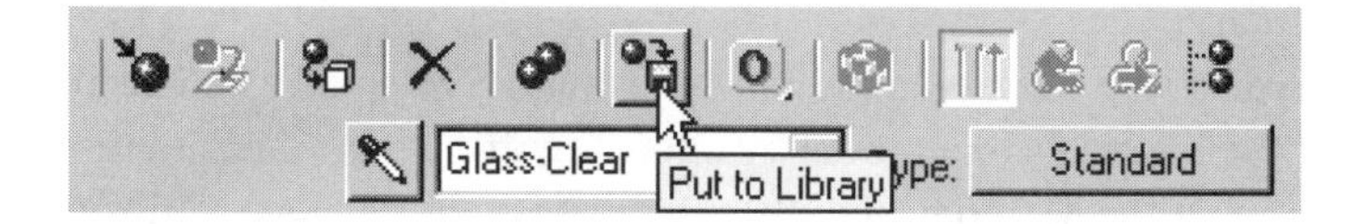

Understanding Material Libraries

You imported the Glass-Clear material from the VIZ Material Library. This library is actually a file called 3dviz.mat, and it can be found in the matlibs sub-folder of the 3dviz3 folder. You aren't limited to this one material library. You can create your own library from materials you create in the Material Editor, or you can use libraries from third-party producers. To open a different library, you need to be in the Material/Map Browser dialog box. From there, you can select the Mtl Library radio button in the Browse From group, then select the Open… button in the File group. You then see the Open Material Library dialog box.

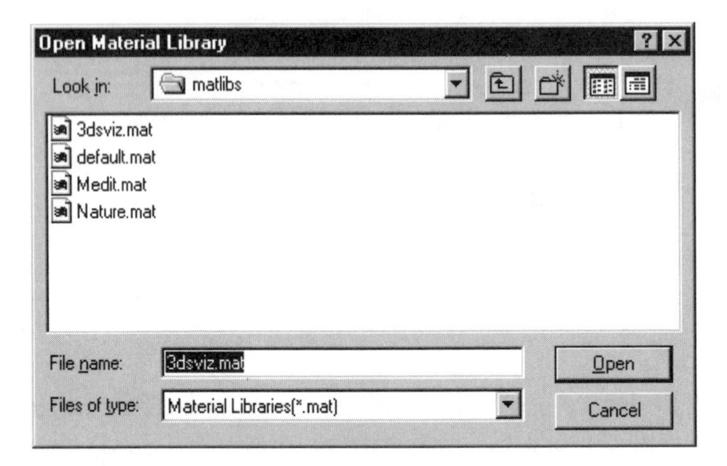

You can select a library from the listing in this dialog box.

To create a new library, click the Mtl Editor option in the Browse From group, then click Save As… in the File group. You see the Save Material Library dialog box, which is a typical file dialog box. You can then enter a name for your library and click Save. The materials in the Sample Slots of the material Editor will be saved in your new material library.

You can also save selected materials by using the Selected radio button, or you can save all of the materials in a model by choosing the Design radio button. Both of these options in the Material/Map Browser expose the Save As… button in the File group, allowing you to save or create a material library.

Adding Material Mapping Coordinates

If you just want to manipulate the color, transparency, and shininess of an object, you can usually create or use a material that doesn't use bitmaps to simulate a texture. Once you start to add a texture using bitmaps, you will need to specify how that texture is applied to the object. You'll want to tell VIZ the size of the texture in relation to the object as well as its orientation on the object. For example, you wouldn't want brick to appear with its courses running vertically as in the example shown in Figure 7.11, nor would you want the brick pattern to be quite so large.

FIGURE 7.11

A brick wall with the brick course running vertically and at a large scale

To control how materials are applied to objects, you will want to know how to use the *UVW Map* modifier. The UVW map modifier lets you precisely control the way a material is placed on an object. In the next exercise, you will create a ground object and add a grass surface. The material you will use, Ground-Grass, uses a bitmap image to give the appearance of grass (see Figure 7.12). As part of the exercise, you will use the UVW Map modifier to establish the orientation and size of the Ground-Grass material in relation to the object.

What Does UVW Mean?

The UVW in the name UVW Map refers to the coordinates of a material map. They indicate the direction of a map in a way similar to the XYZ Cartesian coordinates that you're already familiar with. The letters UVW are used to differentiate map coordinates from the standard XYZ coordinate designation and were chosen simply because they precede XYZ in the alphabet.

UVW map coordinates need to be differentiated from XYZ coordinates because, while they indicate direction in a way similar to XYZ coordinates, they do not treat measured distances in the same way. In a Cartesian coordinate system, distances are measured at

Continued on the next page

specific intervals of feet, or meters, or whatever measurement system you're using. UVW map coordinates, on the other hand, are measured as a percentage of width and height of a surface. Instead of feet or meters, UVW maps use real values from zero to one. The value used represents a percentage of the overall width of the surface being mapped, with 1 being equal to 100 percent of the surface width.

Since the coordinate values in a UVW map are based on a percentage, a U value of 0.5 can represent a different measured distance from a V value of 0.5. For example, imagine a rectangular surface with a U and V coordinate system whose origin is the lower left corner of the rectangle. The upper right corner of the rectangle would then be the coordinate 1,1, even though the length and width of the rectangle are not equal to each other. This may seem a bit odd at first, but if you consider that material maps are used to match an image to a surface, you begin to see the reason behind the UVW map system. The relationship between a map and a surface is more important that their actual dimensions. You can think in terms of "what percentage of the surface does the map cover?" rather than how many square inches does the map cover.

First, you need to create an object to represent the ground. Use a simple box for this purpose.

1. Click the top viewport, then use the Zoom tool and zoom out so that your view looks similar to Figure 7.12. Use the Pan tool to center the building in the viewport.

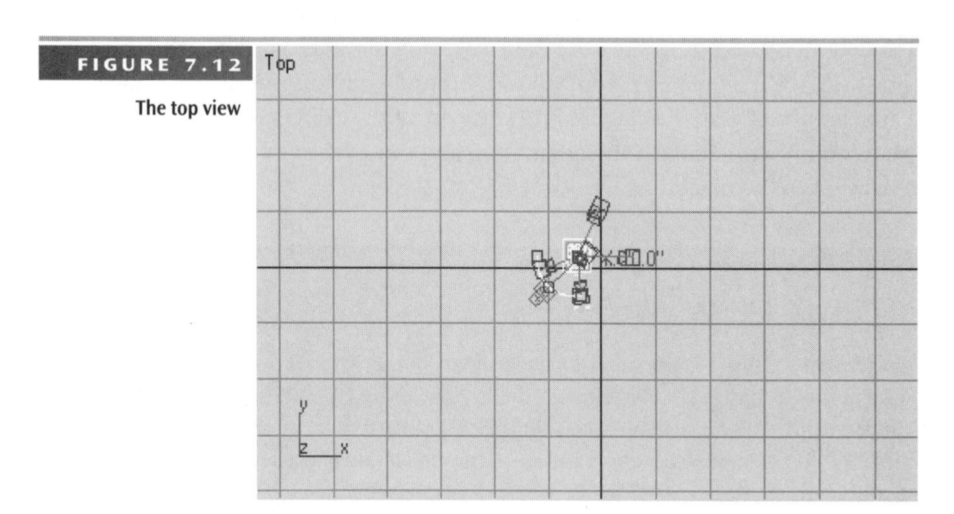

FIGURE 7.12

The top view

You want to zoom out so you can create a large enough box to fill the scene without showing any obvious edges in your camera views.

2. Click the Create tab of the Command Panel, click the Geometry tool, and then click Box.
3. Place the box shown in Figure 7.13 in the top viewport.

FIGURE 7.13

Placing the box in the top viewport

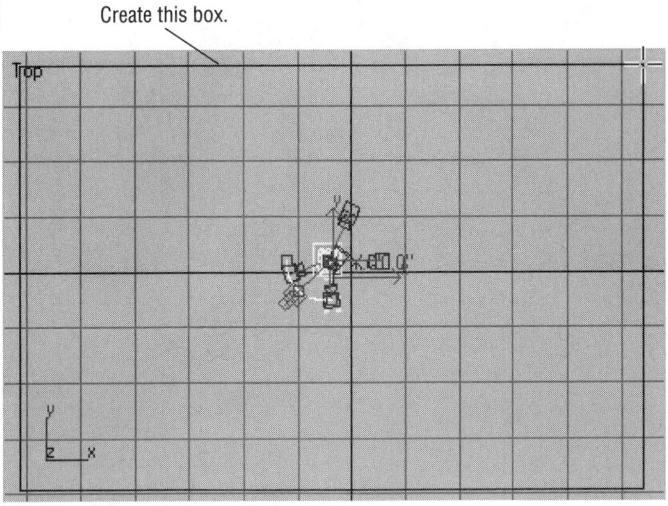

Create this box.

4. Specify a height that is about –5 feet (minus five feet).
5. Give the new box the name **Ground** in the Name and Color rollout input box.

Now you're ready to apply a material to the ground object. Just as with the glass, you'll use the Material Editor and Material/Map Browser to select a material from VIZ's standard material library.

1. Click the Material Editor tool on the Rendering toolbar. Then in the Material Editor dialog box, click the sample image in the middle of the top row of samples.

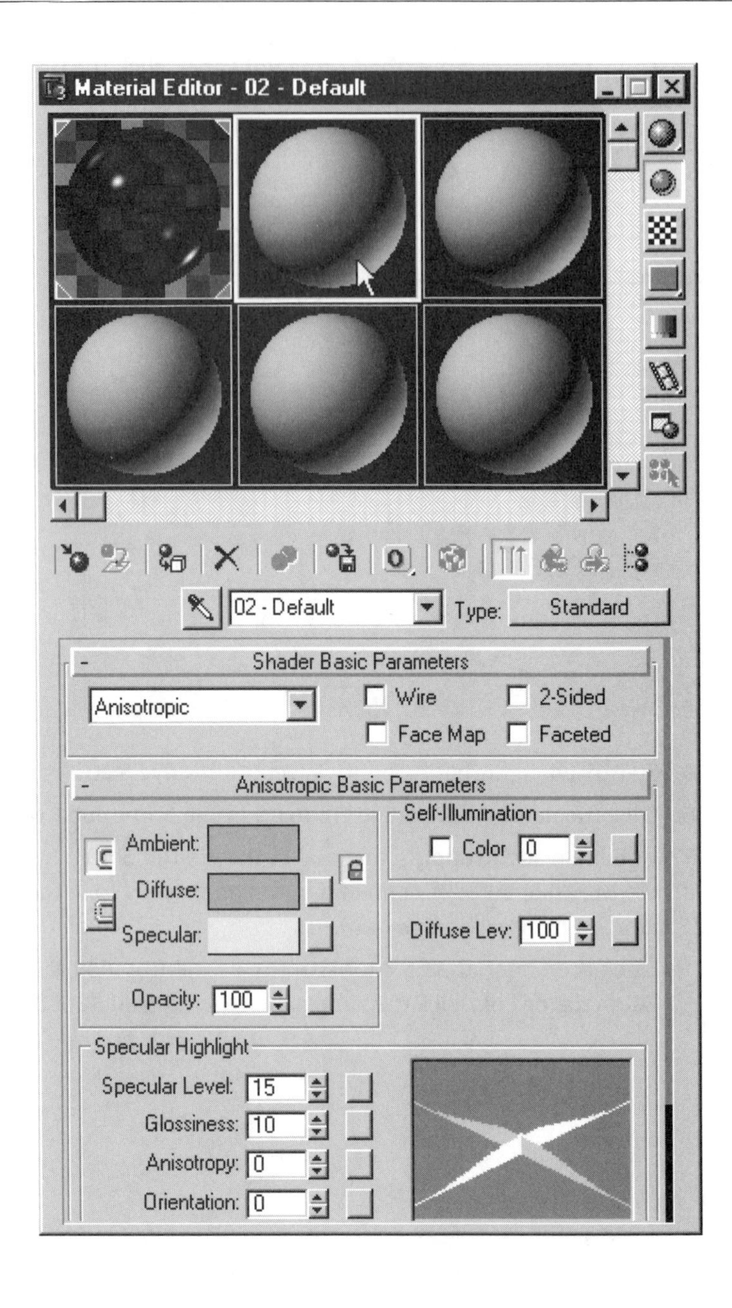
Material Editor - 02 - Default
02 - Default
Type:
Standard
Shader Basic Parameters
Anisotropic
Wire
2-Sided
Face Map
Faceted
Anisotropic Basic Parameters
Self-Illumination
Ambient:
Color
0
Diffuse:
Specular:
Diffuse Lev:
100
Opacity:
100
Specular Highlight
Specular Level:
15
Glossiness:
10
Anisotropy:
0
Orientation:
0

2. Click the Get Material tool just below the samples.

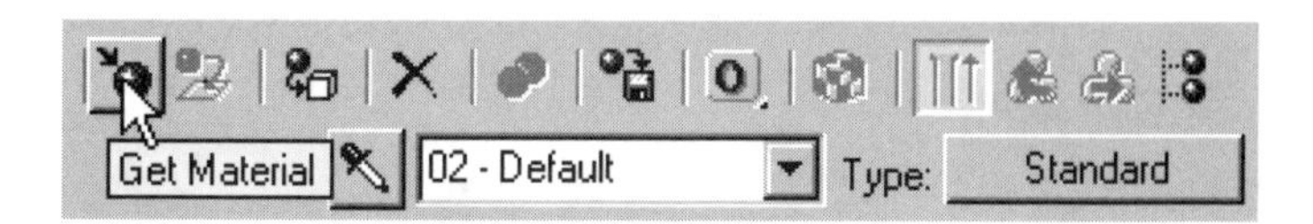

3. In the Material Map Browser dialog box, click the Mtl Library radio button in the Browse From group.
4. Scroll down the list to locate the Ground-Grass listing, then double-click it. You'll see the Sample slot in the Material Editor change to show the Ground-Grass material.
5. Close the Material/Map Browser.
6. Make sure that the Ground object is selected in your model, then click the Assign Material to Selection button in the Material Editor dialog box.

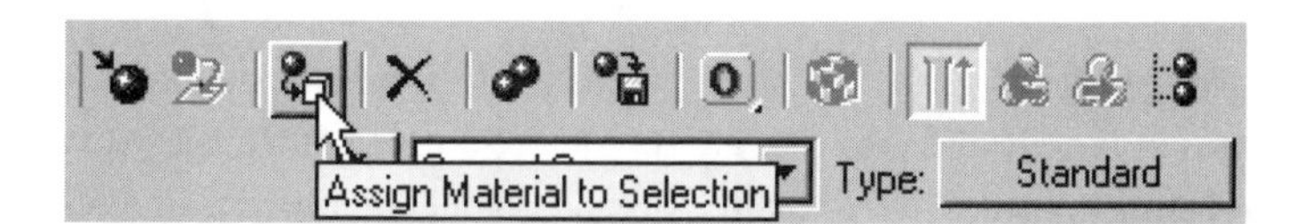

7. To see the result of the new ground object and its material, right-click the Camera viewport, then click the Quick Render tool on the Render toolbar.

FIGURE 7.14

The rendered view with the ground object added

Although the ground is there, it may not be what you expected. Instead of a ground plane that looks like grass, you see a green surface that varies in color but with no distinct pattern. The reason for this is that the bitmap image is stretched to fill the entire ground object as shown in Figure 7.14. The camera view sees the grass as if it were a very near close-up view.

You'll want to scale the Ground-Grass material to a size that is more in line with the ground object's size. This is done with the UVW Map modifier.

1. Close the Rendered view and make sure the ground object is selected.
2. Click the Modify tab in the Command Panel.
3. Click the UVW Map button in the Modifiers rollout.

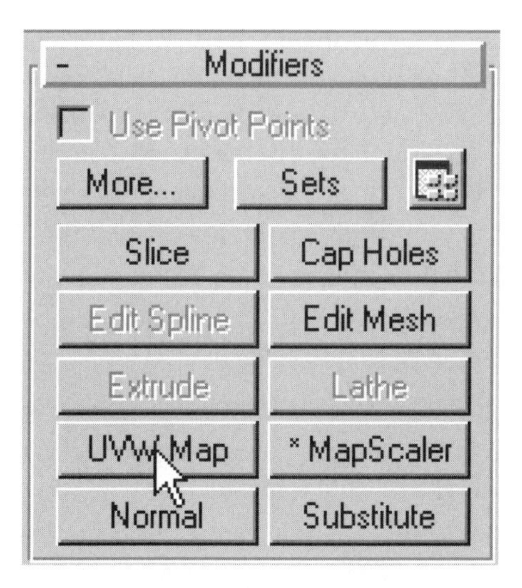

The outline of the ground object changes color. What you are seeing is the UVW Map gizmo outlining the ground object.

4. Click the Sub-Object button. The UVW Map gizmo changes color to indicate its orientation. You see a green edge on the right side of the gizmo.

Let's take a moment to study the UVW Mapping gizmo. It has one green edge and has a point on one side (see Figure 7.15).

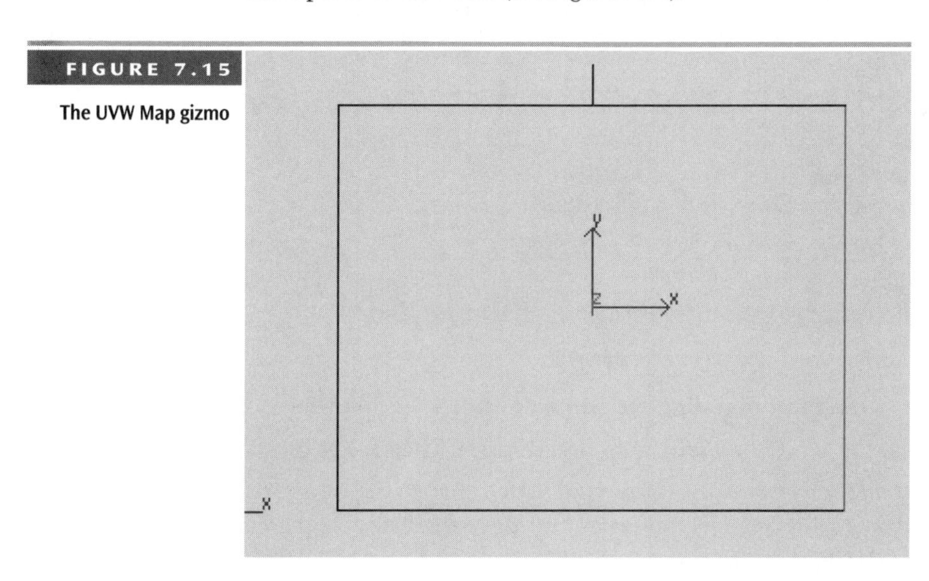

FIGURE 7.15

The UVW Map gizmo

The color and the point help you orient the UVW Map Gizmo on an object by showing you which way is "up" and which ways are "left" and "right." You'll get a more detailed look at the UVW Map Gizmo after the current exercise. Let's continue by adjusting the Gizmo to reduce the size of the material on the ground object.

The UVW Map gizmo is now selected. To change the scale of the Ground-Grass material in relation to the ground object, you need to scale down the Gizmo.

1. Click, then right-click the Select and Scale tool on the standard toolbar.
2. At the Scale Transform Type-In dialog box, enter **1**↵ in the Offset: Screen spinner input box and then close the dialog box.
3. Close the Scale Transform Type-In dialog box.

The gizmo is now very small compared to the viewport, and it is lost in the building at the center of the viewport. You'll want to move it so you can see it again.

1. Click the Select and Move tool and click and drag the axis gizmo to the right until you can see the UVW Map Gizmo. It will look like a very small square as shown in Figure 7.16.

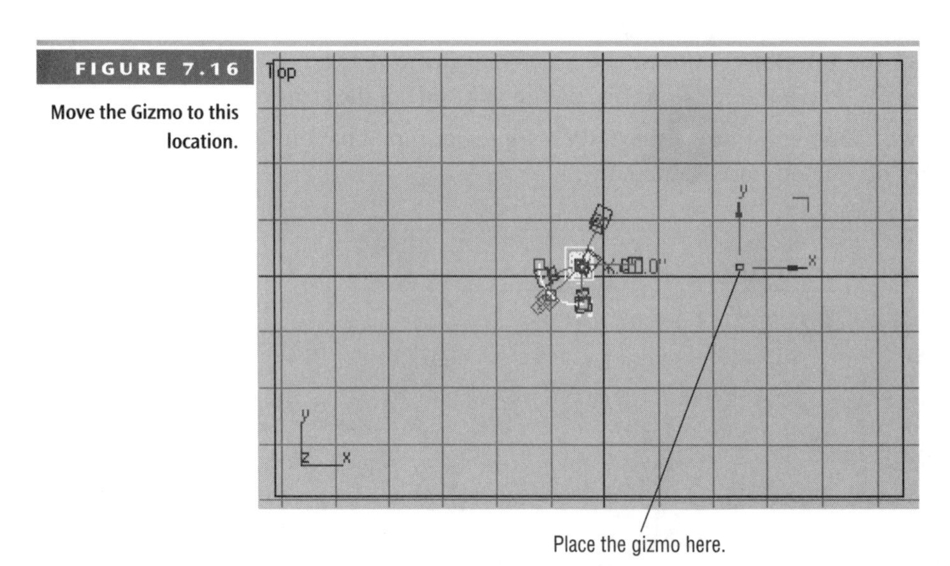

FIGURE 7.16

Move the Gizmo to this location.

To see the effect of scaling the gizmo down, do the following.

2. Click the Sub-Object button to deactivate it. Then select the SUN light source.
3. In the Modify tab of the Command Panel, change the Hotspot parameter in the Directional Parameters rollout to **120 degrees**. This will increase the area that the SUN light source covers.
4. Right-click the camera viewport and then click the Quick Render tool.

Now you can see the grass patterns emerging. When a texture map is smaller than the object it is assigned to, VIZ *tiles* the map to fill the object. This means that the map is repeated in a row and column array to fill the object's surface (see Figure 7.17).

FIGURE 7.17

The rendered view of the villa with the Ground-Grass UVW Map altered

Since the material is repeated or *tiled* over the ground object, a pattern emerges giving the ground the appearance of a manicured baseball field.

Understanding Mapping Coordinates

The UVW Map Modifier you added in the last exercise told VIZ the size, location, and orientation of the material on the object it is assigned to. At render time, the image is usually applied to the object in a repeated or *tiled* fashion. You can also set a material to apply the bitmap just once, for example, a label on a wine bottle. In this section, you'll take a closer look at the UVW Map modifier.

What Happens When You Add the Mapping Coordinates

The UVW Map gizmo you saw in step 5 is a visual representation of the mapping coordinates. Its shape and color are aids in helping you see the bitmap's orientation more clearly. As mentioned earlier, the point at the top of the icon represents the top of the bitmap, while the green shows the right side. These indicators can tell you at a glance whether the bitmap image of the material you are using is upside down, mirrored, or backward in relation to the object to which the coordinates are being applied as shown in Figure 7.18.

FIGURE 7.18

The UVW Map gizmo in relation to a material bitmap

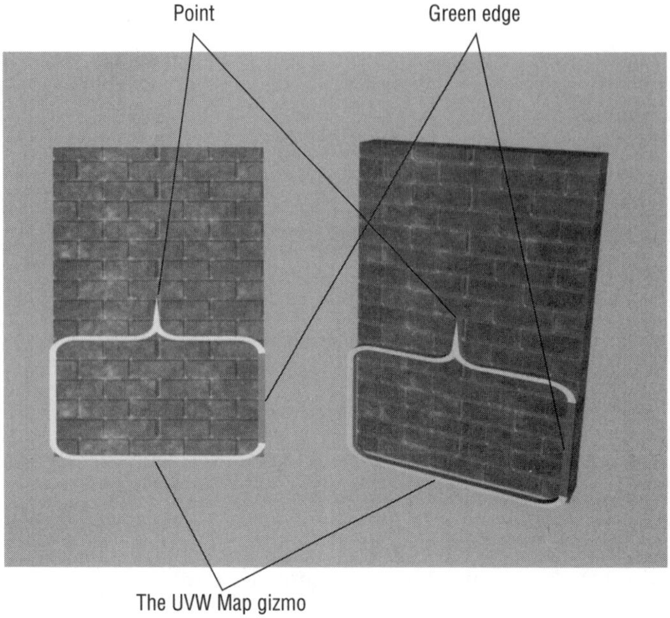

The orientation of the bitmap in this exercise is really not that important, but it can be important for texture maps that do have a specific orientation such as a brick pattern, or a single image such as a wine label or a road sign.

Figure 7.19 shows the UVW Map gizmo in relation to the ground object as it appears in step 1 of the previous exercise. The gizmo represents the outline of the bitmap image associated with the Ground-Grass material. Figure 7.19 shows the relationship of the gizmo to the bitmap image, as well as the resulting rendered ground object as seen from the top view.

FIGURE 7.19

A comparison of the UVW Map gizmo and the actual bitmap image as it is applied to the ground object

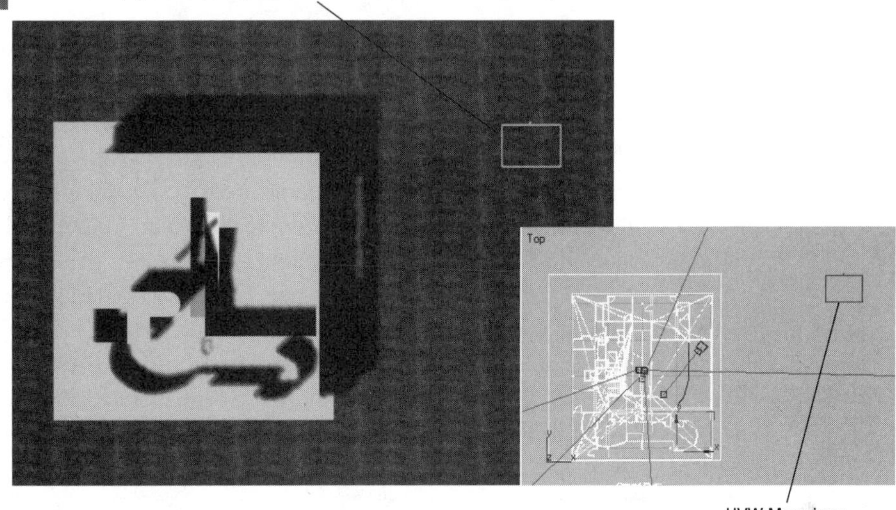

Notice that the gizmo shows the approximate size of the bitmap in relation to the object to which it is being applied. When the model is rendered, multiple copies of the image are applied over the entire surface of the object like tiles on a kitchen counter.

Figure 7.20 shows another way that the gizmo affects the appearance of a material. You see a brick wall with the gizmo rotated. The bricks are angled and aligned with the UVW Map gizmo.

FIGURE 7.20

A sample brick wall with the UVW Map gizmo rotated 30 degrees

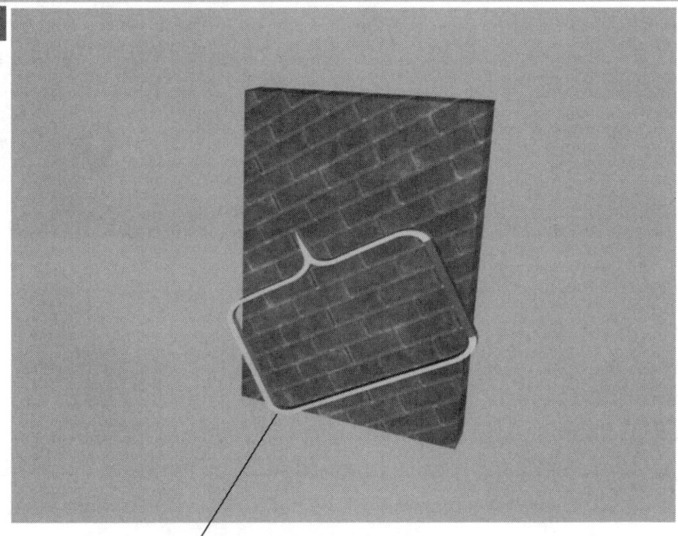

Adjusting the UVW Map gizmo

You have a number of options for controlling the size, shape, and orientation of the UVW Map gizmo. These will be crucial to your ability to accurately place materials on an object or face. Here are descriptions of the Alignment group options as they appear in the command panel.

Region Fit lets you fit the UVW Map gizmo to a specific rectangular area. This is useful for situations where you want a texture map to fit exactly over a specific region of an object. When you choose this option, you can select two points to define the two diagonal corners of the UVW Map gizmo. The process is similar to selecting a zoom region or creating a rectangle. Since this option lets you select any two points, it will stretch and distort the UVW Map gizmo in either the X or Y axis. To orient the UVW Map gizmo right side up, pick two points over the region starting with the lower left corner (see Figure 7.21).

FIGURE 7.21

To the left, a Region Fit UVW Map is placed on a wall in the Front viewport. To the right, a rendered view with the UVW Map is superimposed on the view.

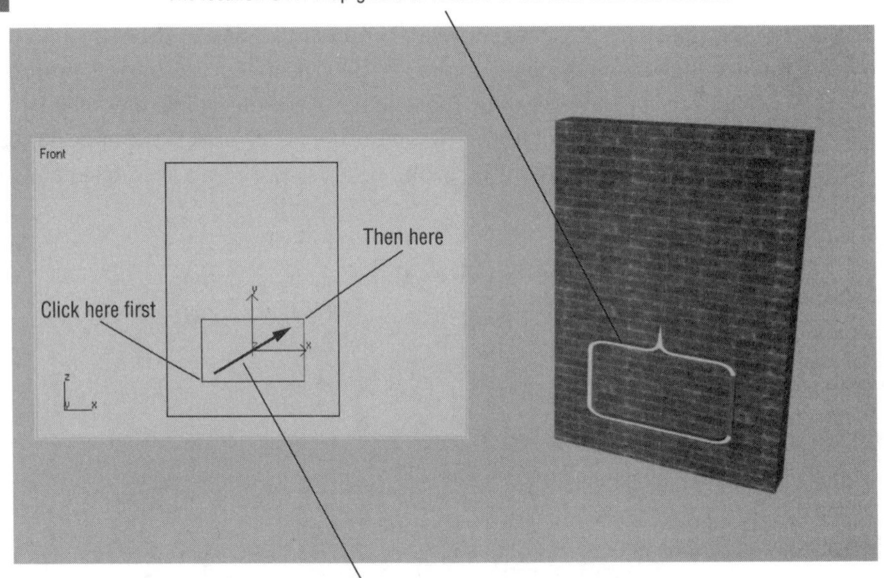
The location UVW Map gizmo in relation to the final rendered surface.
Front
Then here
Click here first
Drag to form region.

Bitmap Fit adjusts the UVW Map gizmo's proportion to fit the shape of a particular bitmap image. This option uses the current UVW Map size and alters the proportions to fit the bitmap proportions. The option is helpful if you want the bitmap to be displayed accurately in its original form. It also helps if you want a better idea of the bitmap's shape as you assign the mapping coordinates to objects.

View Align aligns the UVW Map gizmo to a viewport. This option can help you locate a UVW Map or quickly align it to a viewport.

Center centers the UVW Map gizmo on an object's surface.

Fit stretches the UVW Map gizmo over the surface of an object to make it fit exactly.

Normal Align aligns the UVW Map gizmo to the normal of a surface of the object to which the mapping is attached.

Acquire sets the UVW Map gizmo to match the mapping coordinates of an object that already has mapping coordinates assigned to it.

Reset resets the UVW Map gizmo to the VIZ default size and orientation.

Controlling the Tiling Effect

When you added the Ground-Grass material to the ground object and reduced the size of the UVW Map, the grass appeared at a smaller scale and was repeated over the entire surface of the ground in a rectangular array. This repetition of the map is called tiling. If you've ever played with the Windows desktop, you may already be familiar with the idea of tiling.

Tiling is on by default, but you can turn it off for situations when you want only a single image to appear over the surface. Figure 7.22 portrays the same brick wall shown in Figure 7.21, but this time the tiling is turned off. The brick pattern only appears in the region defined by the UVW Map gizmo. The rest of the wall surface is rendered, based on the Basic Parameters of Ambient, Diffuse, and Specular color.

FIGURE 7.22

The brick wall rendered with the Tile setting turned off

The tile settings are located in the Material Editor dialog box. Here's how to locate the Tiling parameters.

1. Open the Material Editor.
2. Scroll down the list of rollouts to the Maps rollout and open the Maps rollout if it is not already open.
3. Locate the map you want to adjust, then click its button. For example, for the Ground-Grass material, click the Diffuse Color Map button labeled Tex #9(GRASS.jpg). The parameters for that particular map display in the Material Editor.
4. In the Coordinates rollout, locate the Tile check boxes.

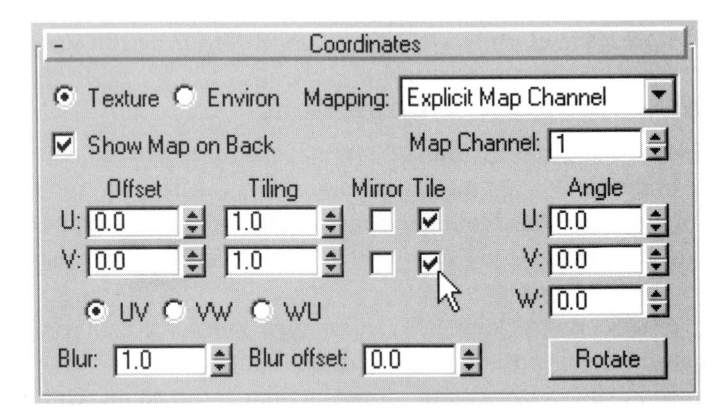

5. Once you open the Coordinates rollout, you can click the U and V Tile check boxes to remove the check boxes. Don't change this setting for your villa model, however. You want to keep the Tile setting turned on.

Understanding the Different Types of Mapping

When you first apply a material to an object, VIZ uses its default *Planar* map. As you might guess from its name, this type maps the bitmap image to a plane or flat surface as shown in Figure 7.22. This option projects a flat image onto a surface. The orientation of the UVW Map gizmo in relation to the object affects the appearance of the material. Figure 7.23 shows how the same texture map can be projected onto a box with different effects.

FIGURE 7.23

A box with mapping coordinates oriented in different ways. The texture map is identical in each example.

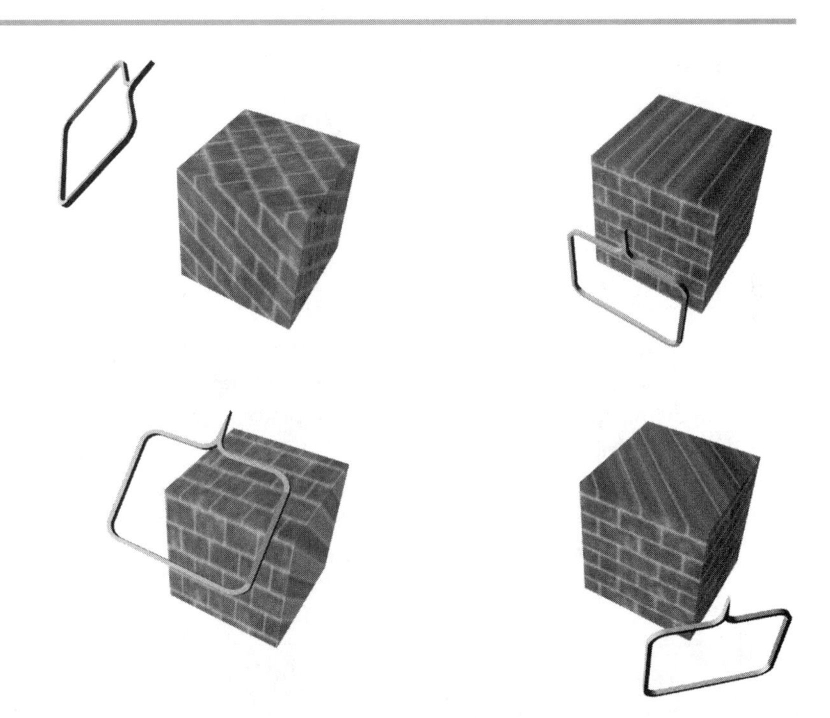

As you can see from Figure 7.23, you aren't limited to using a planar map parallel to the surface you are mapping to. You can create some interesting effects by reorienting the UVW Map Gizmo.

But what do you do if you want to map an image to a cylindrical or spherical object? VIZ offers several other map types to facilitate mapping to non-planar surfaces.

If you look at the Parameters rollout for the UVW Map modifier, you see the radio button options shown in Figure 7.24.

FIGURE 7.24

Mapping options

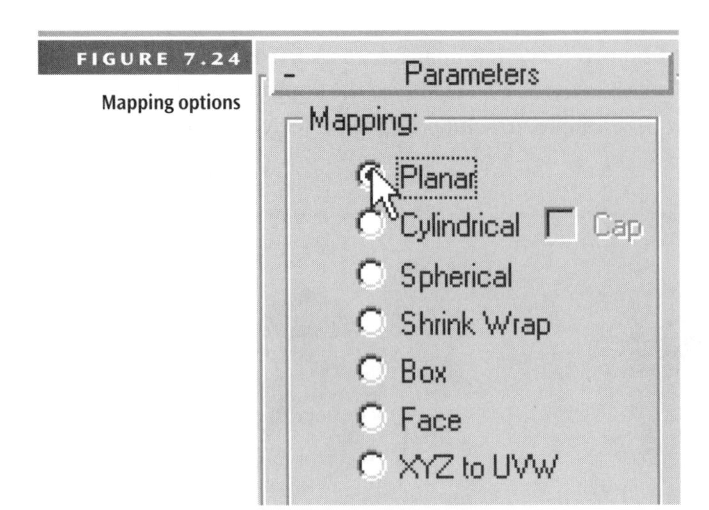

The *cylindrical* map curves the bitmap into a cylindrical shape, then projects the map outward from the center of the cylinder. Naturally, you would use this type of mapping on cylindrical objects. You will want to place such a map in the center of the object.

When you choose this map, the UVW Map gizmo changes to a Cylindrical one as shown in Figure 7.25. You would then place this map in the center of a cylindrical object, and assign it to the object. You can also distort the map by moving the UVW Map gizmo closer to one side or the other or rotating the map so it isn't aligned with the object.

FIGURE 7.25

A view of the UVW Map gizmo when using the cylindrical mapping type, along with a sample of an object that uses this mapping type

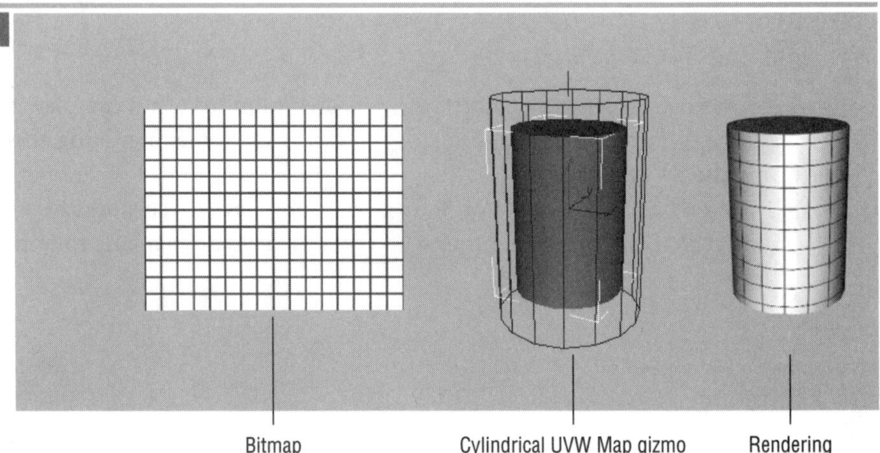

The *Spherical* map curves the bitmap into a spherical shape. To understand how it works, imagine taking the rectangular bitmap image and curling it around a spherical shape; then squeeze the top and bottom ends of the bitmap like a candy wrapper (see Figure 7.26). One use of this mapping type is to portray a model of the earth. You could use the spherical mapping type to place a flat map of the earth on a sphere.

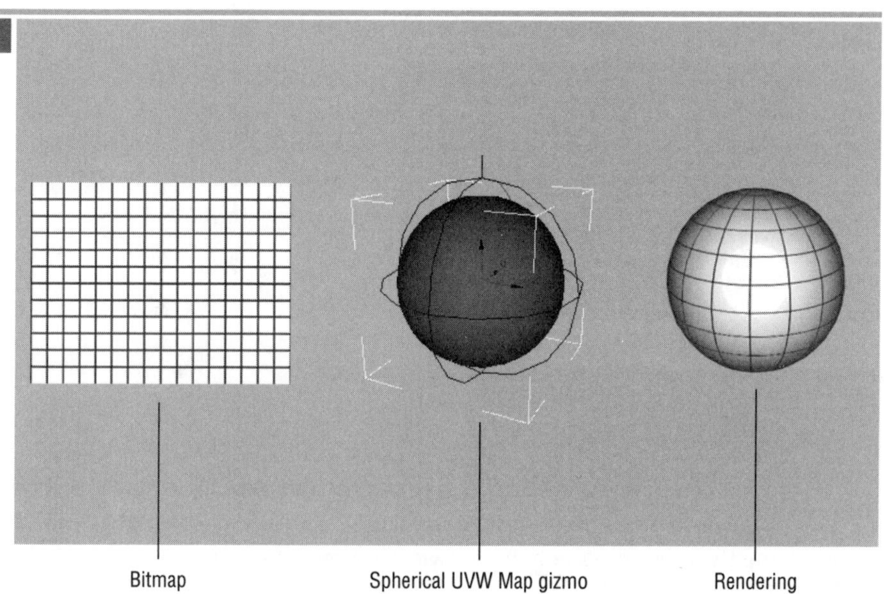

FIGURE 7.26

The Spherical map wraps the bitmap around a sphere.

As with the cylindrical mapping type, the UVW Map gizmo changes to a different shape when the spherical mapping type is chosen, as shown in Figure 7.26. You would place this Map in the center of the spherical shape that requires mapping.

Shrink Wrap is similar to spherical, but instead of wrapping the image around a sphere as shown in Figure 7.27, imagine wrapping a sphere in plastic wrap with the bitmap image tied at one end. Figure 7.27 shows a rendering using the same sphere and UVW Map gizmo shown in Figure 7.26. The only difference is that the sphere in Figure 7.27 uses Shrink Wrap mapping instead of the Spherical mapping of Figure 7.26.

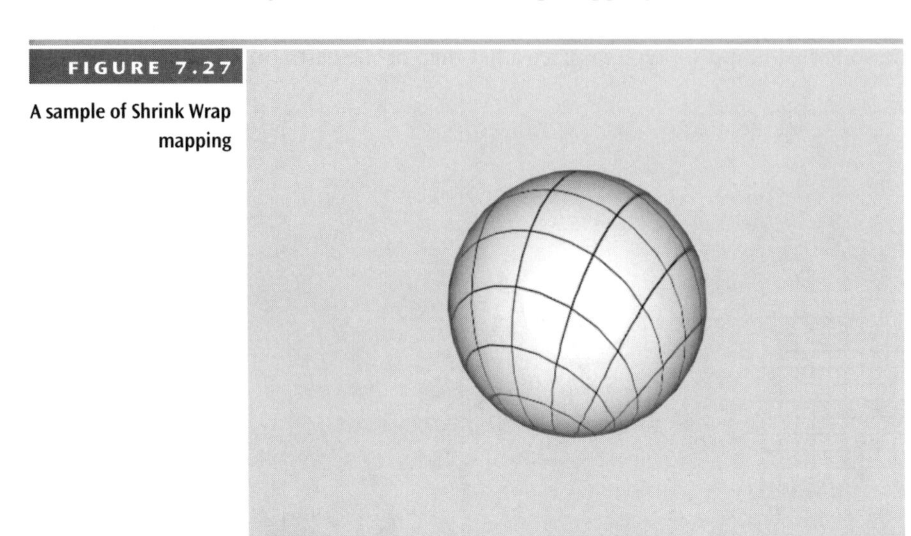

FIGURE 7.27

A sample of Shrink Wrap mapping

Box mapping is similar to Planar, but instead of a single plane, Box projects the image onto four sides as shown in Figure 7.28. You may find that you use Box mapping the most, especially if your work involves buildings.

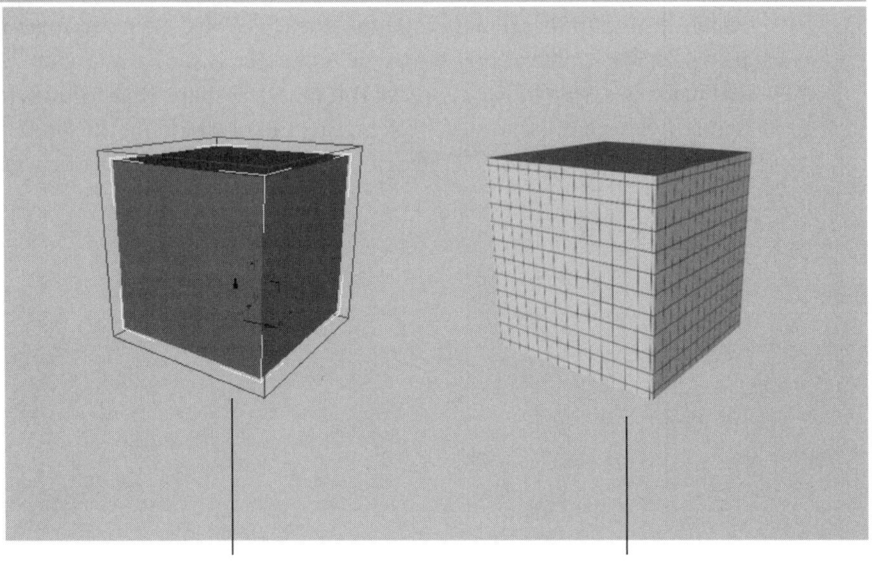

FIGURE 7.28

Example of Box mapping

Face mapping is similar to box, but instead of projecting the image onto the sides of a box, Face projects the image onto each individual face of an object. This is easiest to see in a faceted object such as the 12-sided sphere shown in Figure 7.29.

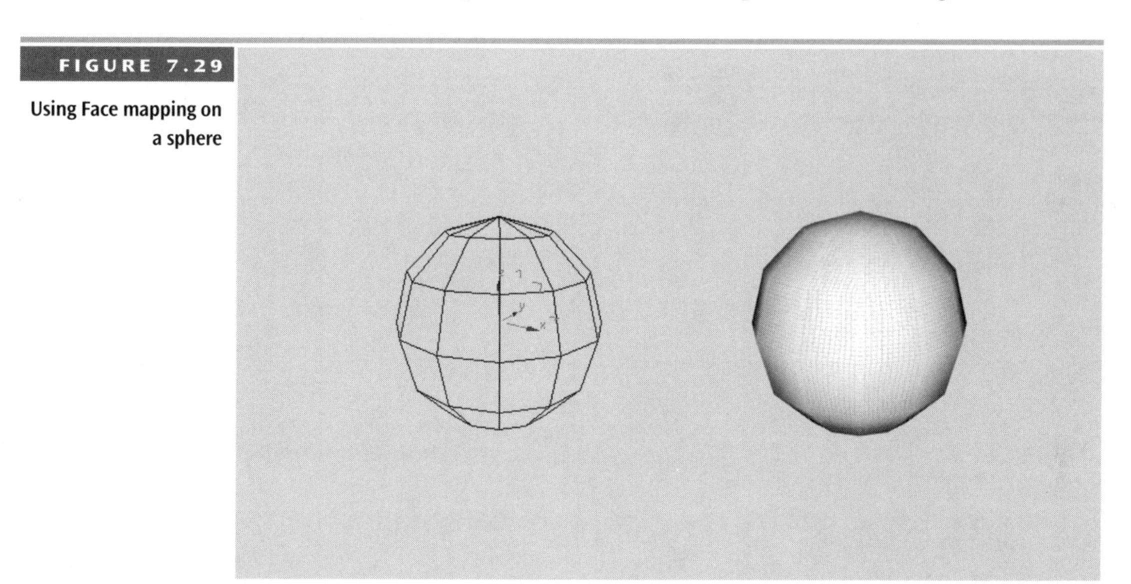

FIGURE 7.29
Using Face mapping on a sphere

Even if smoothing is used to smooth out the surface of the sphere, Face mapping will project the image onto the individual faces of the object.

XYZ to UVW is mainly used for Procedural Maps. A procedural map is a map that relies on a mathematical formula rather than a bitmap image. The XYZ to UVW Map aligns a procedural map to the local coordinates of the object to which it is assigned. This has the effect of *sticking* the map to the object so that if the object is stretched non-uniformly, the map will stretch with the object as if the map were a rubber sheet stretched over the object.

While we've suggested that you use each map type with its corresponding object shape, you can achieve some unusual effects by mixing map types with different surfaces. For example, if you use a planar map on a cylinder, the image is stretched as it is projected toward the edge of cylinder as shown in Figure 7.30.

FIGURE 7.30

A sample of a planar map used on a cylindrical surface

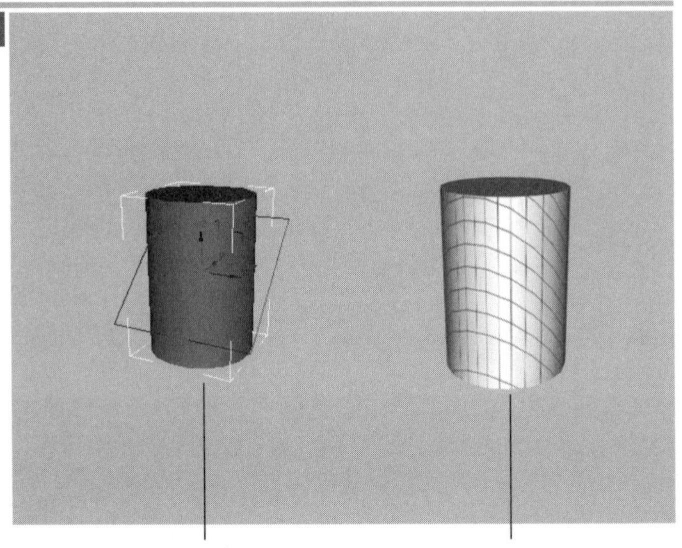

Just below the Mapping Radio buttons are the Length, Width, and Height input boxes. As you might guess, these options let you enter a numeric value for the length, width, and height of the UVW Map gizmo. Their spinners also let you graphically adjust the size of the gizmo.

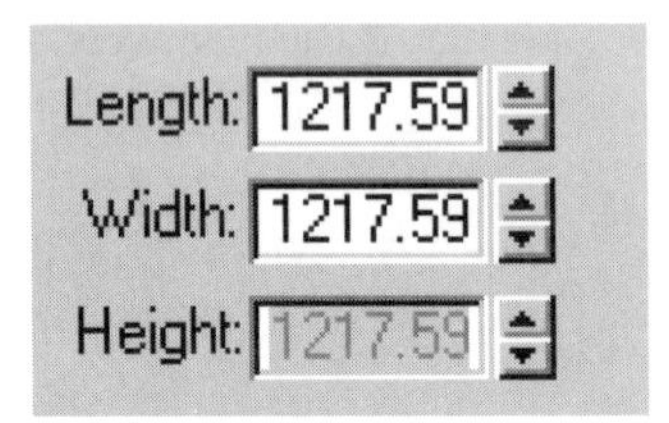

Finally, if you want to increase the tiling of the bitmap image within the area defined by the UVW Map gizmo, you can do so using the U Tile, V Tile, and W Tile input boxes at the bottom of the Parameters rollout.

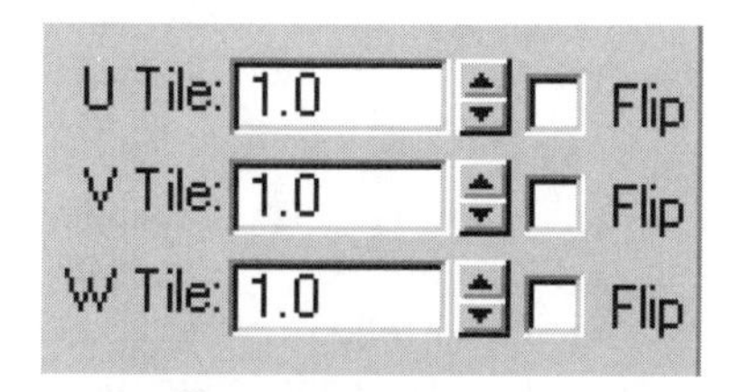

These options are set by default to 1, causing a single image to appear within the area of the UVW Gizmo. You can produce multiple images within the UVW Map gizmo area by increasing the values in these input boxes. This offers a quick way of increasing the density of the tiled image without having to enter the Material Editor dialog box. Figure 7.31 shows the same brick wall displayed in Figure 7.21, but this time the U and V tile settings have been changed to 2.

FIGURE 7.31

The Brick wall sample shown with the U and V Tile parameters set to 2

The mapping coordinate tools we've been discussing give you a high degree of control over the way your material assignments affect your model. As is the case with many VIZ tools, your skill in using them will develop over time. As with any craft, practice makes perfect.

The Generate Mapping Coordinates Option

Many of the VIZ objects you encounter will have a check box labeled Generate Map Coords. as one of their parameters. This offers another method for applying mapping coordinates.

The Generate Mapping Coordinates option applies a sort of custom mapping coordinate to standard primitives. For example, if you create a Box standard primitive and select Generate Mapping Coordinates in the Box's parameter rollout, materials mapped to the box will behave as if the Box UVW Mapping modifier were applied to the box. A Sphere primitive with the Generate Mapping Coordinates option selected will behave as if a spherical mapping were applied. As an added benefit, the mapping will conform to any changes applied to the shape of the object. If a box's width is increased, the mapping coordinates will automatically follow the width change (though this may actually be undesirable for some types of material such as brick or tile).

You have less control over the mapping coordinates with the Generate Mapping Coordinates option, because objects that use it do not have an adjustable map gizmo. However, you can still control the UVW tiling to adjust the density of the map over the object. This can be done using the Material Editor dialog in the Coordinates rollout for the material map you are working with.

In the case of a lofted object, the Generate Mapping Coordinates option is the only way to apply a material that will conform to a loft's unusual shape. If you apply a UVW Mapping modifier, the modifier will take control over the mapping coordinates.

Note that imported objects, such as those found in AutoCAD models, do not have a Generate Mapping Coordinate option. They require a UVW Mapping modifier whenever bitmap materials are applied.

Editing Materials

The last time you rendered your Villa Savoye model, the glass was virtually invisible, and the ground color and texture looked too strong and unnatural. In this section, you'll learn how to use the Materials Editor to adjust both the Glass and Green Vines materials to improve your image.

Adjusting Bitmap Strength

We'll start our exploration of the Materials Editor by making a few changes to the Ground-Grass material. In the last rendering, the ground looked unnatural. You can see the grass pattern repeated regularly so that it looks almost like a manicured baseball field. Also, the ground surface is quite flat. Let's adjust the material so that it looks a bit more like a natural grass surface.

1. Click the Material Editor tool in the Render toolbar to open the Material Editor dialog box. The sample of the Ground-Grass material is shown on a sphere, but the surface you are applying the material to is flat. You can get a preview image on a cube instead of on a sphere to get a sample view that is more in line with the object you are mapping to.
2. Click and hold the Sample Type tool in the set of tools to the left of the dialog box. You see a flyout containing two additional sample types.

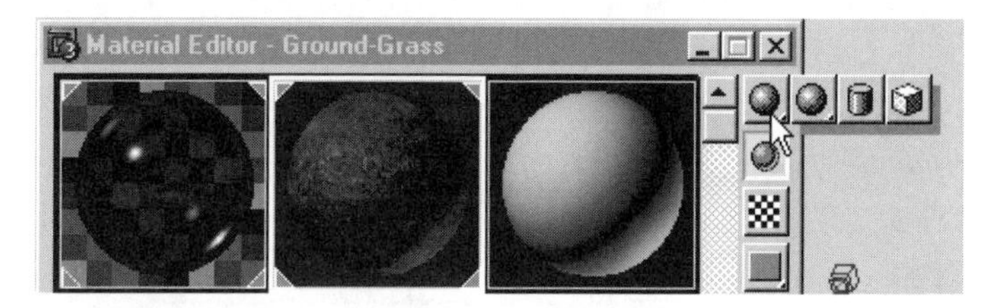

3. Drag the mouse over to the cube. Release the mouse. The sample changes to a cube shape.

Now the sample gives us a better idea of what the Ground-Grass material looks like, and it certainly looks similar to the sample in our model. In the rendering of the model, the Ground-Grass material is a bit too strong, so you need to tone it down for our ground object. Here's how we do it.

1. Click and drag the sample Ground-Grass slot from the middle of the top row to the next box to the right. You see a copy of the material in the upper right box. This gives us a copy of the material settings that we can play with without affecting the original settings. It also lets us compare two settings side by side. As you can see from all the slots available, you can make many copies and variations.
2. Click the original Ground-Grass slot in the middle of the top row to make it active.
3. Scroll down the Material Editor panel until you see the Maps rollout and then click the Maps rollout bar to open it. You see the map options as a list with

check boxes you can use to turn a map feature on or off. There is also an amount spinner to set the strength of the map, and there are map buttons to select the type of map (see Figure 7.32).

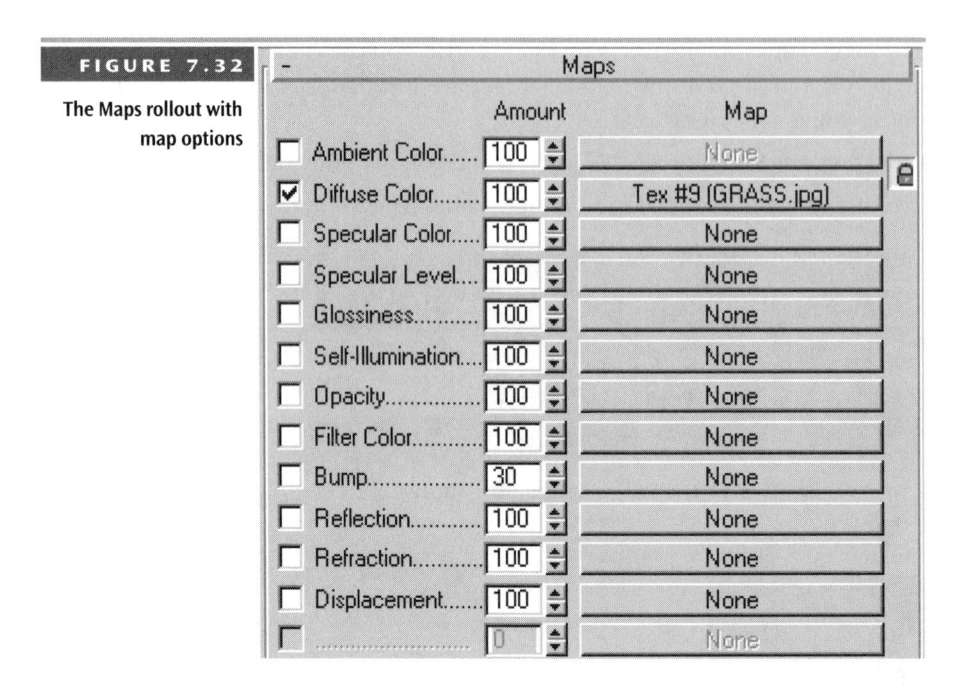

FIGURE 7.32

The Maps rollout with map options

4. Adjust the Amount spinner in the Diffuse Color row to read 30. This decreases the strength of the `Grass.jpg` texture bitmap to 30 percent.
5. Click the Quick Render tool. The pattern on the ground of the rendered view is less apparent.

   The sample slot now shows that the grass pattern isn't so strong. The grass is greener and the regular pattern of the bitmap tiling isn't quite so obvious.

When you reduced the strength of the texture map in step 4, you reduced the strength of the bitmap image. This caused the colors in the Phong Basic Parameters rollout to have a stronger effect.

Before we go on, look over the other options in the Maps rollout (see Figure 7.33). You've just seen how the Amount spinner affects the strength of a map. The buttons in the Map column to the far right let you select a map type, which can be a bitmap or a procedural map. If you click a button that is labeled None, you will open the Material/Map Browser, which offers the selection of maps as shown in Figure 7.33.

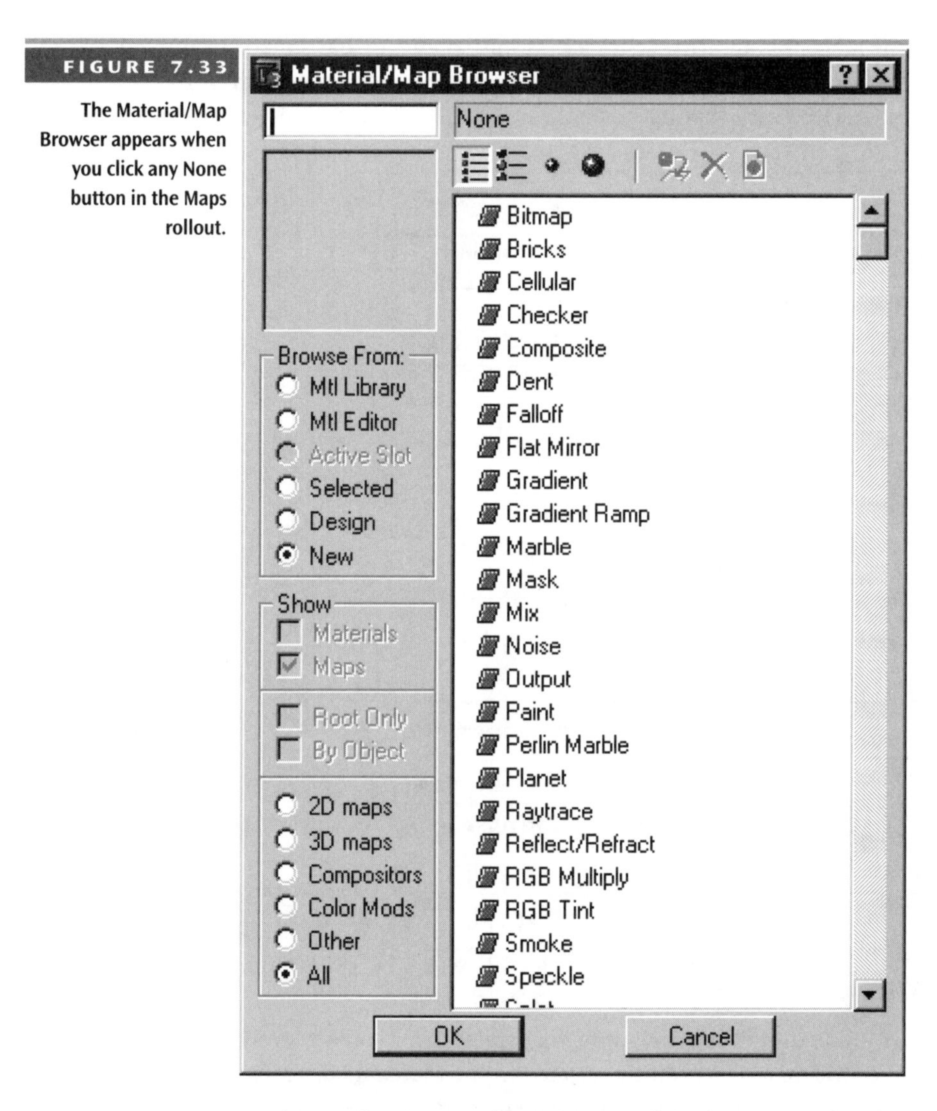

FIGURE 7.33 The Material/Map Browser appears when you click any None button in the Maps rollout.

If you select Bitmap from the top of the list, you will then have the opportunity to select a bitmap image file. The other options are procedural maps.

Back in the Maps rollout, if you click a button that already has a map assigned to it, such as the Tex #9(Grass.jpg) button, the Material Editor changes to show the parameters associated with that map (see Figure 7.34).

FIGURE 7.34

A view of the options for the Text#9(Grass.jpg) button

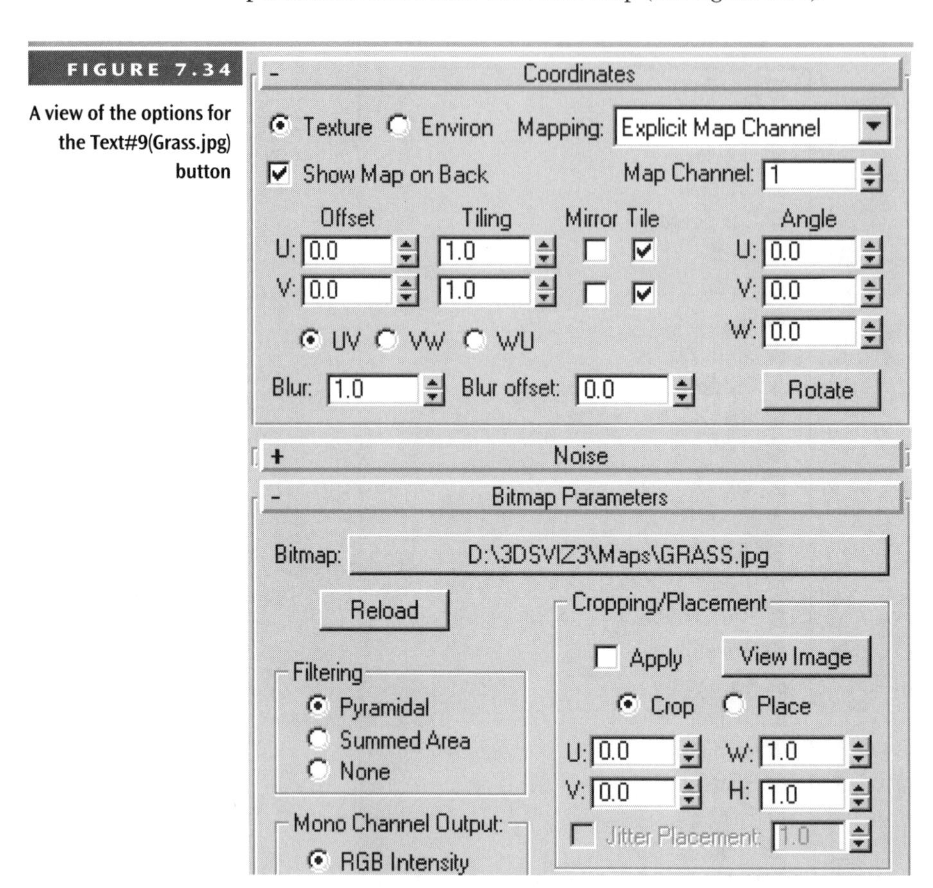

You might think of these options as being similar to Sub-object levels. They are components of the material currently selected in the Material Editor. From here, you click the Go to Parent button on the Material Editor toolbar to return to the Maps rollout.

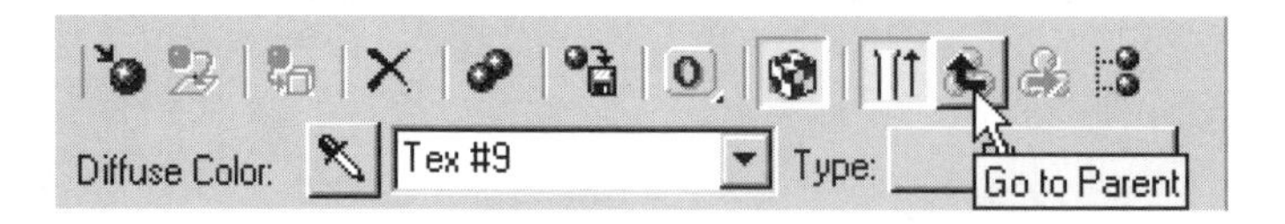

You'll get a chance to work with these settings a bit more in the next chapter. For now, let's continue by looking at how you can adjust the color of a material.

Adjusting the Material Color

With the strength of the Texture map diminished, you can begin to make some color adjustments using the Phong Basic Parameters rollout. *Phong,* by the way, is the name given to a method of shading that all 3D Rendering programs use.

1. In the Material Editor, scroll back up to the Phong Basic Parameters rollout.
2. Click the green color swatch labeled Ambient. You'll see the Color Selector dialog box appear.
3. Click and drag the Sat spinner all the way up so that its value is 255. This is the Saturation spinner, and it controls the intensity of the color.
4. Click and drag the Value spinner up until its value shows 70. This controls the lightness of the color.

You may notice that, as you adjust these color settings, the large color swatch at the bottom left corner of the dialog box changes (see Figure 7.35). This sample swatch is divided into two halves. The left half is the color as it is set when you first open the dialog box. The right half shows the color under your new settings. This swatch gives you the ability to compare your new color with the old one.

FIGURE 7.35

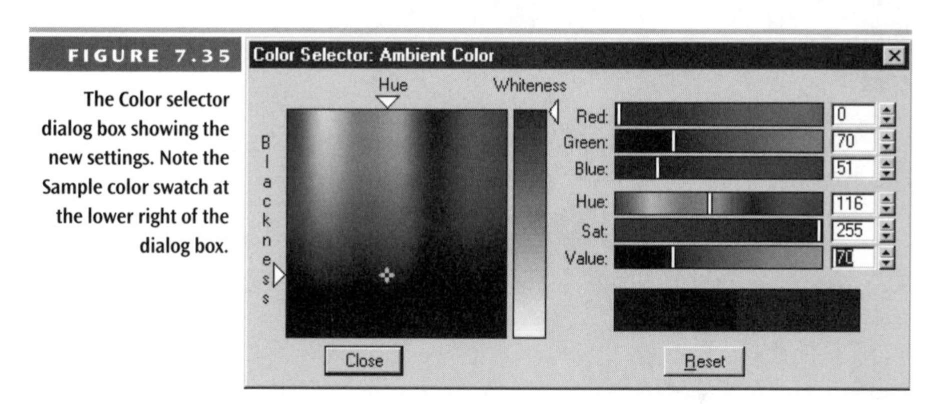

The Color selector dialog box showing the new settings. Note the Sample color swatch at the lower right of the dialog box.

Right now, you see a slightly brighter, "greener" green on the right side of the color swatch. If for some reason you decide that the changes you've just made are not what you want, you can click the Reset button at the bottom of the swatch to return the settings back to where they were before you made any changes. The Reset button allows you to experiment with colors while the Color Selector dialog box is open.

Let's see the results of your color modification.

1. Click the Close button in the Color Selector.
2. Click the Quick Render tool in the Render toolbar and watch carefully as the renderer renders the ground object

The color difference is subtle, but the ground is definitely greener with the increase in the saturation of the Material Editor's ambient setting.

You've seen how you can adjust color in the Color Selector dialog box by making changes to the Sat and Value spinners. The Hue spinner lets you select the color or hue from a slider or spinner.

If you prefer, you can also control color using the R, G, and B (red, green, and blue) sliders and spinners. You may notice that these settings automatically change as you adjust the Hue, Sat, and Value settings.

Copying Color Settings

The Phong Basic Parameters rollout offers three color settings: Ambient, Diffuse, and Specular. The Ambient color you just experimented with is the color of an object in a shadow or in very low lighting conditions. The Diffuse color is the color of an object under normal or good lighting conditions, and the Specular color is the color of an object with a very bright light shining on it (see Figure 7.36).

FIGURE 7.36

The basic areas defined by the Ambient, Diffuse, and Specular settings

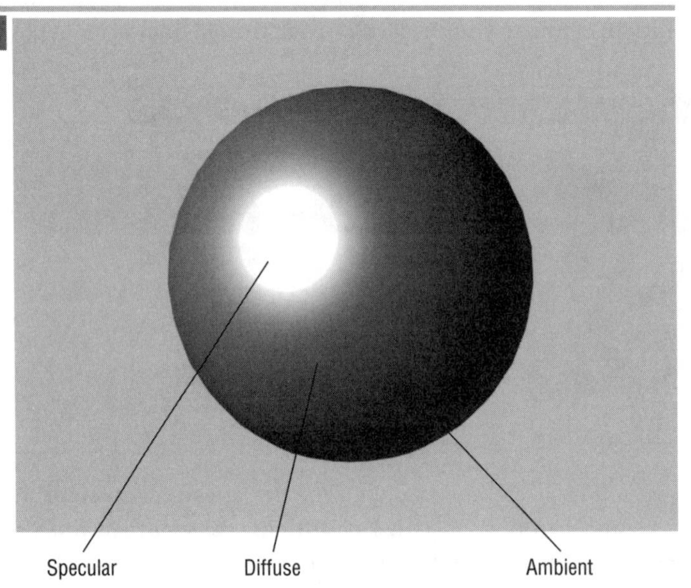

VIZ offers you the ability to adjust the color of an object under these three basic lighting conditions so that you can make subtle variations in the appearance of an object. Each of these three color types can be set just as you set the ambient color in the last exercise. You can also copy or swap colors between these settings just by clicking and dragging the color swatch. Try the following exercise to copy the ambient color to the diffuse color setting.

1. Click and hold the color bar next to the Ambient button.
2. Drag the cursor away from the bar. Notice that a rectangle appears and moves with the cursor.
3. Place your cursor on the bar next to the Diffuse button, then release the mouse button. You see the Copy or Swap Colors dialog box.

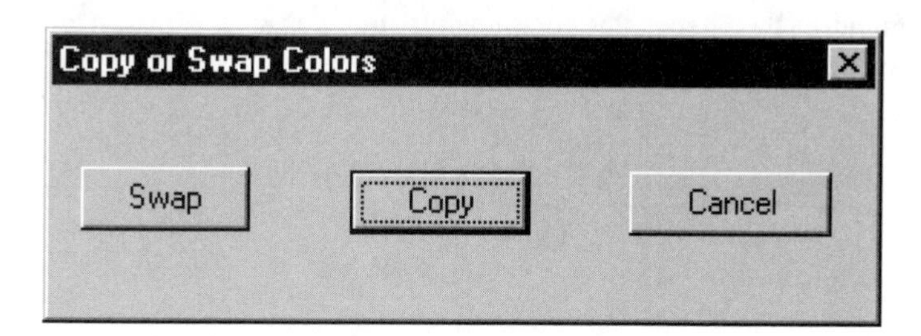

4. Click Copy. The Ambient color now appears in the Diffuse color swatch.

If you had selected the Swap option in the Copy or Swap Colors dialog box, you would see the two ambient and diffuse colors exchange places. By clicking and dragging color swatches you can quickly match a color. In many situations, you may want to tone down an object's appearance. Making the ambient and diffuse colors the same can easily do this.

TIP **In general, it is a good idea to have the hue and saturation of the ambient color match those of the Diffuse color. You can lower the value setting of the Ambient color to determine the darkness of areas in shadow.**

Understanding Shaders

As you work with the Materials Editor, you'll notice that you have a set of options under the Shader Basic Parameters rollout. You can think of Shaders as different rendering methods applied to objects when they are rendered. The primary Shader options are found in the Shader Basic Parameters drop-down list. This list offers seven shaders: Anisotropic, Blinn, Metal, Multi-Layer, Oren-Nayar-Blinn, Phong, and Strauss.

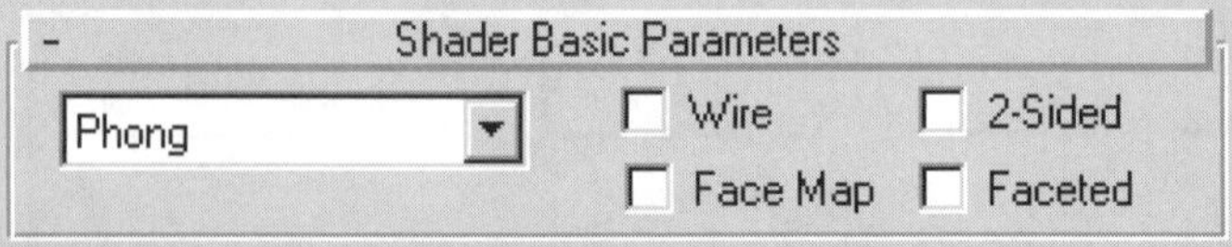

Shader Basic Parameters
Phong
Wire
2-Sided
Face Map
Faceted

Don't let these strange sounding names scare you off. They are just different methods VIZ uses to render highlights and diffuse and ambient lighting on objects. You choose a shader depending on the type of material you are assigning the material to. For example, the Oren-Nayar-Blinn shader is best used for non-shiny materials such as fabric or wood. The Metal shader is useful for metallic objects. The default shader for new objects is the Anisotropic shader, which is good for shiny objects. Here's a rundown of the shaders and their specialties.

Anisotropic measures the difference of shininess from different angles and renders highlights accordingly. This shader is best used for very shiny objects.

Blinn offers a softer highlight than Phong, particularly for objects with which you want to show highlights from lights bouncing off at low angles.

Metal, as the name suggests, is a shader designed for metallic objects. It is specifically designed to simulate the characteristics of light bouncing off a metallic surface.

Multi-layer is similar to Anisotropic, but it offers more control. It is especially useful in controlling highlight effects, which makes it highly appropriate for shiny objects.

Oren-Nayar-Blinn offers a high degree of control over the effects of diffuse lighting on an object. It is especially useful for matte or rough objects.

Phong offers a general shader for smooth, uniform surfaces and can be used as an all-purpose shader.

Strauss is similar to the Metal shader with simpler controls.

When you select one of these shaders from the Shader Basic Parameters drop-down list, the Basic Parameters rollout will change to offer options specifically geared toward that shader. You may want to stick with one or two of these shaders to start out, then experiment with others as you become more familiar with VIZ. By offering these shaders, VIZ gives you more control over the way objects look and also makes its own rendering faster.

Continued on the next page

In addition, there are four check boxes that control how a material is rendered.

Wire renders a material in wireframe mode.

2-Sided forces a material to be 2 sided so the appearance of a surface is not dependent on its normal.

Face Map causes a mapped bitmap to appear on the faces of an object in a way similar to the Face Map parameter for the UVW Map gizmo.

Faceted forces smoothed objects to be rendered as faceted.

Selectively Rendering Parts of Your Model

Rendering in VIZ is a cyclical process of rendering, adjusting, then rendering again. By allowing you to render a portion of your model, you can save time by reducing the time you spend in these revision cycles. Try re-rendering your model with the changes in the Diffuse color but this time, just render the ground object.

1. In the camera viewport, click the ground object to select it.
2. Click the Render Type drop-down list on the Render toolbar, then click Selected from the list.

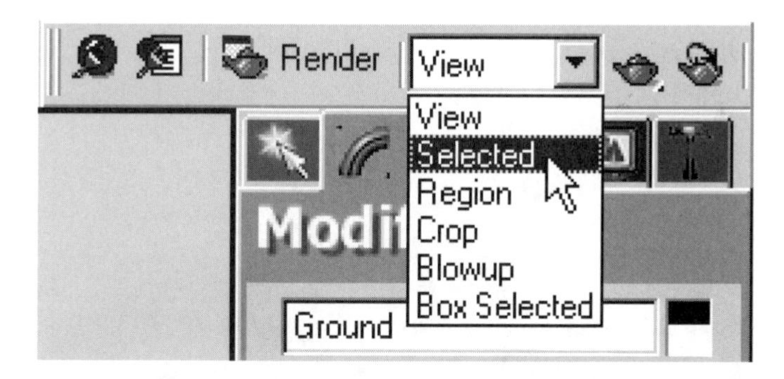

3. Click the Quick render tool. Your camera view is rendered with just the ground object re-rendered.

In this instance, the rendering process was much faster. By rendering a selected object or set of objects, you can save some time if you're just rendering to see the results of some changes you've made to your model. There are other options in the Render Type drop-down list that you'll want to know about. Here's a rundown of those options and what they do.

View is the option you've used for most of the exercises so far; it renders the current viewport in its entirety.

Selected renders just the objects selected.

Region renders a selected region of the viewport. When you choose this option, you are asked to select a region in the currently active viewport. An adjustable marquee that displays in the viewport allows you to select a rectangular area of the viewport (see Figure 7.37). Once an area is selected, VIZ will render only the selected portion of the viewport and nothing else. If you've previously rendered the full viewport, the region you select will be overlaid onto the last rendered view in the render window. This can save lots of time if you need to re-render only a part of a view.

Crop lets you crop an area for rendering. It works just like Region, but instead of leaving any previous rendering in the render window, it crops the rendering to the area you selected.

Blowup works like the Region and Crop options, but instead of keeping the view size the same as the overall viewport, Blowup enlarges the selected region to fill the rendering window.

Box Selected calculates the width and height of the current selection's bounding box, then offers a dialog box that lets you specify the width and height of the rendered image size. The default size VIZ offers is based on the bounding box.

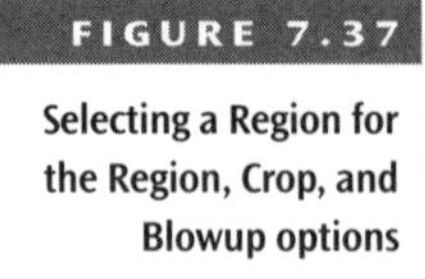

FIGURE 7.37

Selecting a Region for the Region, Crop, and Blowup options

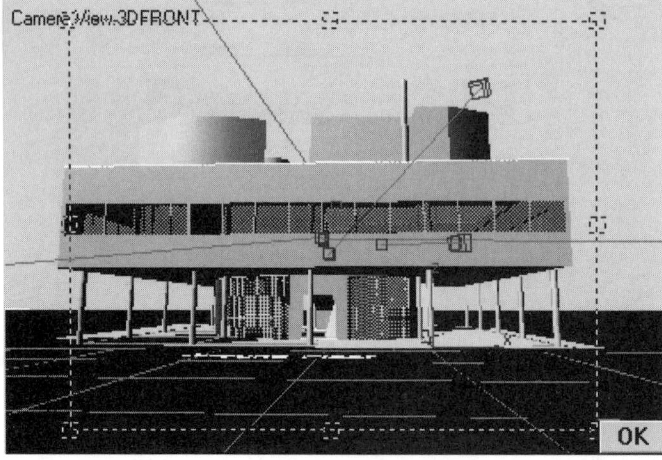

Of all the options listed, View, Selected, and Region are the ones you'll use the most. Region, in particular, can be especially useful if you want to change part of a rendering that takes a lot of time to process.

Adding a Material to the Walls

You've added a glass material and a ground material to your model, and in each case you've made a few modifications. In this section, you'll apply a material to the walls of the Villa, but instead of using a pre-existing material, you'll create an entirely new one. The material you create will be fairly simple, but the exercises here will give you a chance to play with some of the settings you haven't tried yet.

Selecting a Shader

Shaders are a set of methods VIZ uses to render materials (see the Understanding Shaders sidebar). When you create a new material, one of the main items you need to determine is which shader to use. Walls are usually matte surfaces, so the wall material should use a shader that is best suited to such a surface. If you look at the discussion of shaders in the Understanding Shaders sidebar, you'll see that the Oren-Nayar-Blinn shader is best suited to matte surfaces, so you'll start by selecting that shader for your new wall material.

1. Open the Material Editor, then click the lower left sample slot. You'll use this slot for your new wall material.
2. In the Material name drop-down list, change the name to **wall**.

3. In the Shader Basic Parameters rollout, click the drop-down list and select Oren-Nayar-Blinn from the list.

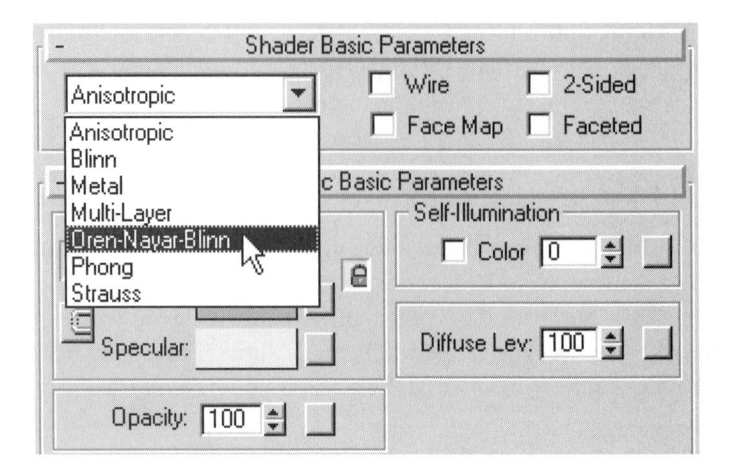

4. Click the 2-Sided check box to force this material to render 2-sided. If some of the surface materials seem to disappear, this will force them to appear correctly in the rendering.

NOTE **The 2-Sided option is frequently needed in models that have been imported from AutoCAD. It is not usually as critical for models built entirely within VIZ.**

Notice how the Wall sample slot changes. It looks like a sphere with a dull surface. The options in the Basic Parameters rollout also change. In fact, the name of the rollout changes from Anisotropic Basic Parameters to Oren-Nayar-Blinn Basic Parameters, and you see the additional Roughness parameter. You can increase the matte appearance of the material by increasing the Roughness value.

Next, apply the new material to the walls and render the model.

1. Close the Material Editor dialog box, then click the Select by Name tool on the standard toolbar.

2. In the Select Objects dialog box, Ctrl-click all the items that have WALL in their name, such as INT-WALLS and WALL-JAMB. Then click Select.

3. Open the Material Editor again. With the Wall sample selected, click the Assign Material to Selection tool.

4. Click the Quick Render tool on the Render toolbar. The building is rendered in a darker color.

Here you see that, by changing the type of shader you use, you actually change the value of the material. In this case, the material gets darker. This is because the Oren-Nayar-Blinn shader puts emphasis on the Ambient and Diffuse range of color parameters.

Fine-tuning Color

The building is too dark, so you'll want to brighten the color of the wall material.

1. Close the Rendered view window and go to the Material Editor dialog box.
2. Click the Diffuse color swatch in the Oren-Nayar-Blinn Basic Parameters rollout. The Color Selector dialog box displays.
3. Change the Value setting to **255**, the highest possible setting.

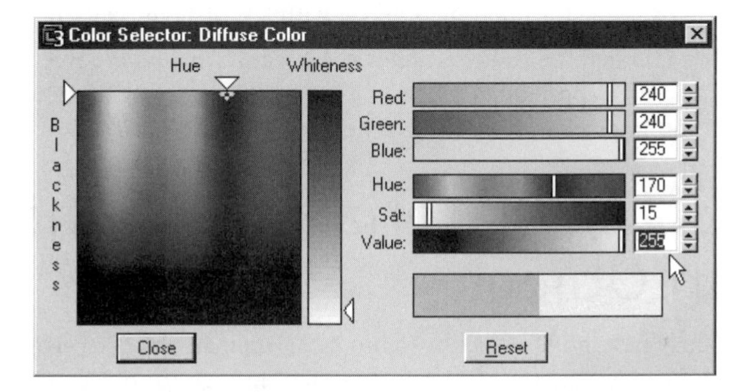

Both the Ambient and Diffuse color swatches now appear to be completely white. In the Oren-Nayar-Blinn shader, Ambient and Diffuse are linked together, so changes in one color are mimicked by the other colors.

4. Close the Color Selector dialog box, then click the Quick Render tool again to see the results.

The building now renders in a lighter color, but there is a blue cast to the color. You really want the surface to be a more neutral or grayer color. Although the color swatch in step 3 appears white, the color's Hue setting still affects the color of the surface. Try the following to see the effects of the Hue setting on a material whose value is set to 255.

1. Minimize the Rendered window, then go to the Material Editor and click the Diffuse color swatch again.

2. In the Color Selector dialog box, change the Hue setting to **35**. This moves the Hue range into the yellows and away from blue.

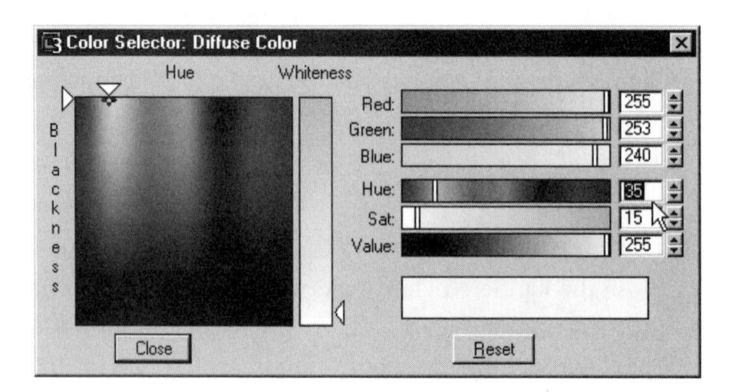

3. Close the Color Selector dialog box and then click the Quick Render tool again. This time the building is grayer with less of a blue color in the walls.

Even though the value setting is as high as it can get, the Hue setting still affects the material's appearance, albeit in a very subtle way. Often, these subtle changes are the most important as well as the most elusive.

Mapping Materials to All the Faces of an Object

You may have noticed that in Figure 7.23, when an object receives a Planar mapping coordinate system, the texture is projected through the object. Faces that are perpendicular to the mapping coordinate face show streaks instead of the texture map. In many situations, and especially in architectural applications, you will want the map to appear on all the different faces of the object. If you find you need to map a material to an object that has multiple sides, such as the walls of a building, you will want to use the Box option of the UVW Map. The Box Map projects a map in the six coordinate directions giving each surface its own map. If the form you are working with is not rectilinear, you may want to use the Face map (see Figure 7.38).

FIGURE 7.38

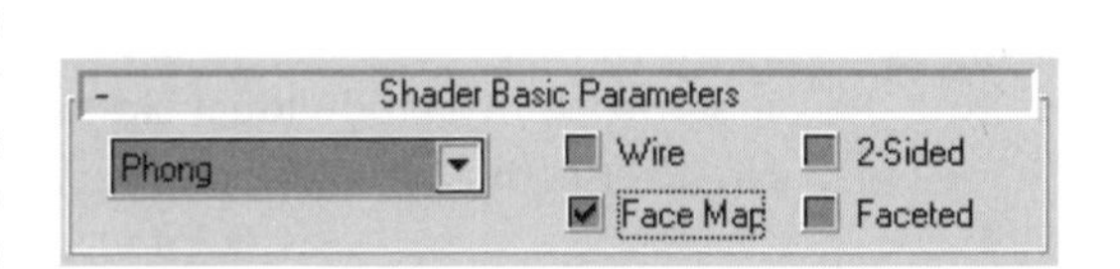

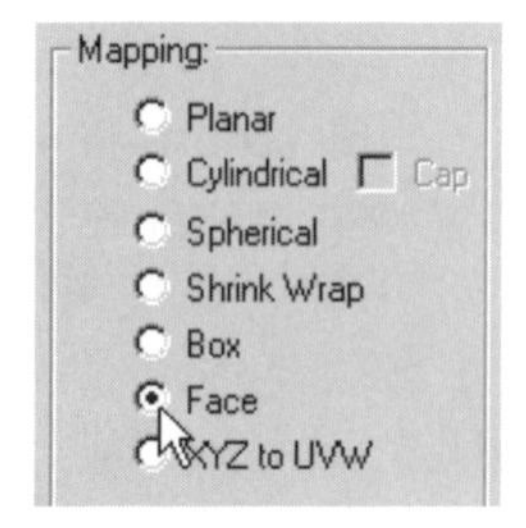

You can find the Face Map option in the Material Editor under the Shader Basic Parameters rollout or in the Modify tab of the Command Panel in the Sub-Object level of a UVW Mapping modifer.

When the face map option is selected, the material is projected onto each face of the object as shown in Figure 7.39. The Face Map option in the Material Editor takes precedence over the UVW Map setting.

The Face Map option ignores any mapping coordinates you may have applied to the object, so it is more difficult to control the orientation of the material. In situations where you need absolute control of the orientation of the material, you may need to detach the faces of the object and assign mapping coordinates and materials to each face individually. See "Adding the Front to the Car" in Chapter 15.

FIGURE 7.39

A sample rendering using the Brick material with the Face Map option turned on

If the image orientation isn't a problem, but the scaling is, you do have the option of changing the scaling of the material when using the Face Map option. You can do this by adjusting the U, V, and W Tile input boxes in the Mapping parameters of the UVW Map modifier as shown in Figure 7.40.

These options let you set the scale of the bitmap image in relation to the surface it is being assigned to. In Figure 7.40, the U and V scales are set to 2, which causes the bitmap to be reduced to one quarter of its normal size. Figure 7.41 shows the result of this setting on the same object shown in Figure 7.39. By adjusting the UVW Map tile settings, you are only affecting the tile setting for the individual faces of an object. Even so, the effects of the Face map can be effective for many non-rectilinear forms.

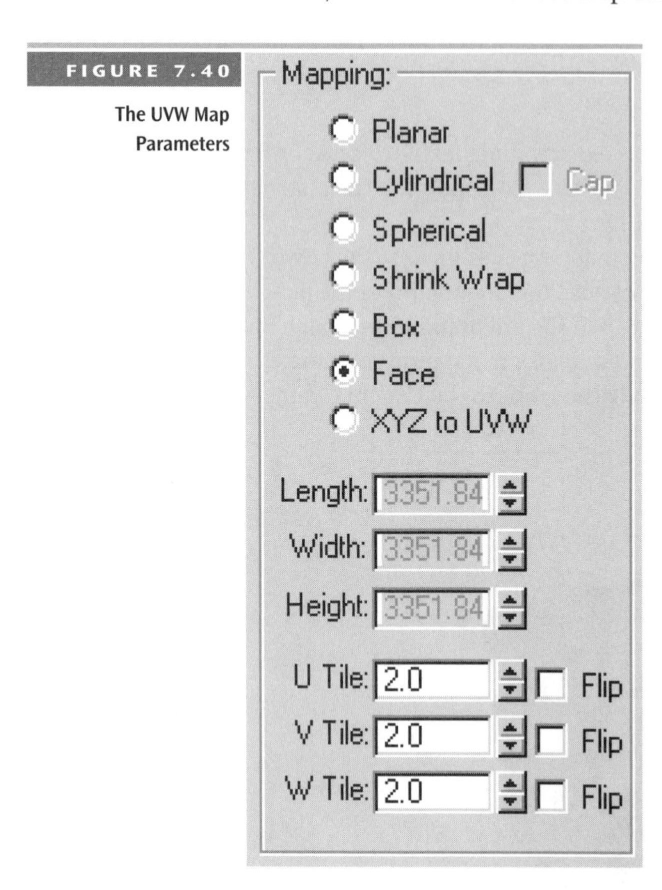

FIGURE 7.40

The UVW Map Parameters

FIGURE 7.41

The object rendered with the Brick material Mapping Parameters U and V scale setting set to 2

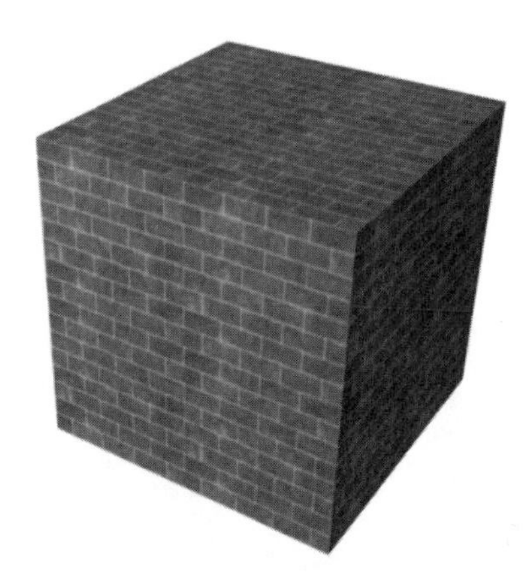

The brick sample shows how orientation is affected by the Face Map option. Other materials such as square tiles or sand and stucco textures would not pose the problem of improper orientation.

TIP **If you want the map coordinates to conform closely to the shape of an object, you may want to consider using the Generate Mapping Coordinates option for standard primitives. See *The Generate Mapping Coordinate Option* sidebar earlier in this chapter.**

Summary

You haven't quite finished your rendering, but you've gotten a good start. In this chapter, we've introduced to you the different ways you can edit your model. You've also seen that, by making changes to materials, you can greatly alter the appearance of your rendering. The materials editor is a powerful tool, so you will want to get as familiar as possible with it.

Chapter 8 delves deeper into the Material Editor's features. In addition to a continued look at materials, you'll also learn more about lighting and how to add a backdrop to your design.

chapter 8

Controlling Lights and Materials

FEATURING

- *Adding a Background*
- *Adding Effects with Light and Shadow*
- *Adding a Highlight with an Omni Light*
- *Adding Props*
- *Using Bump Maps*

Controlling Lights and Materials

In the last two chapters, you learned the basic operations of the Material Editor. You also learned how to do a simple animated flyby. In this chapter, you'll concentrate on the Material Editor. You'll also start to play with lighting to achieve the effects you want. Once you've mastered the use of effects, there won't be anything you can't render.

You'll start by making some adjustments to the model by adding a background scene and adjusting some lights. Next, you'll focus on creating some props and further editing some existing materials. By the end of this chapter, you'll have the basic tools you need to start doing some real work on your own.

Adding a Background

In the movie industry, artists are employed to produce background images (called mats) to simulate special environments, such as mountainous terrain, a canyon, or the interior of a space station. You can employ a similar technique using VIZ's background option.

The following exercise will show you how to quickly add a sky by adding a bitmap image for a background.

1. Start VIZ and open Savoye8.max from the sample files of the companion CD.
2. Choose Rendering ➢ Environment… The Environment dialog box displays.

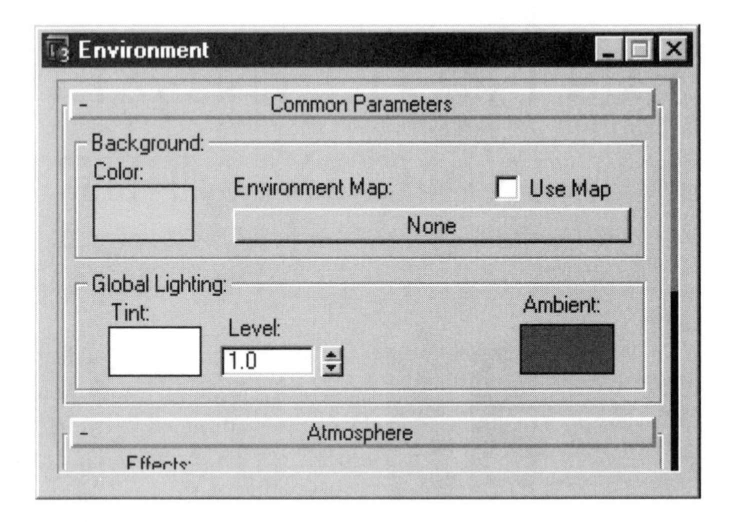

3. Click the Use Map check box, then click the Environment Map button labeled None just below the Use Map check box. The Material/Map browser displays.

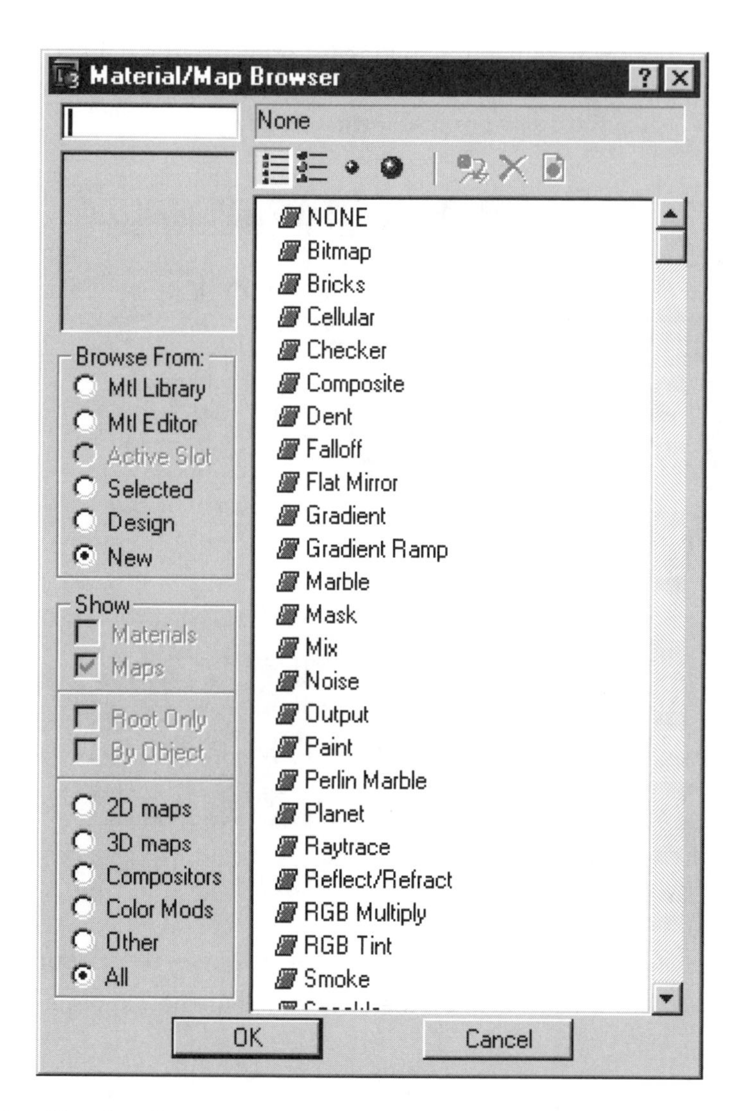

4. Click the Bitmap option in the list of maps, then click OK. The Select Bitmap Image File dialog box displays.

5. Use the scrollbar to scroll the list of files to the right. Then locate and select Sunset.jpg. You'll see a sample image of the selected file in the lower right corner of the dialog box, as shown in Figure 8.1.

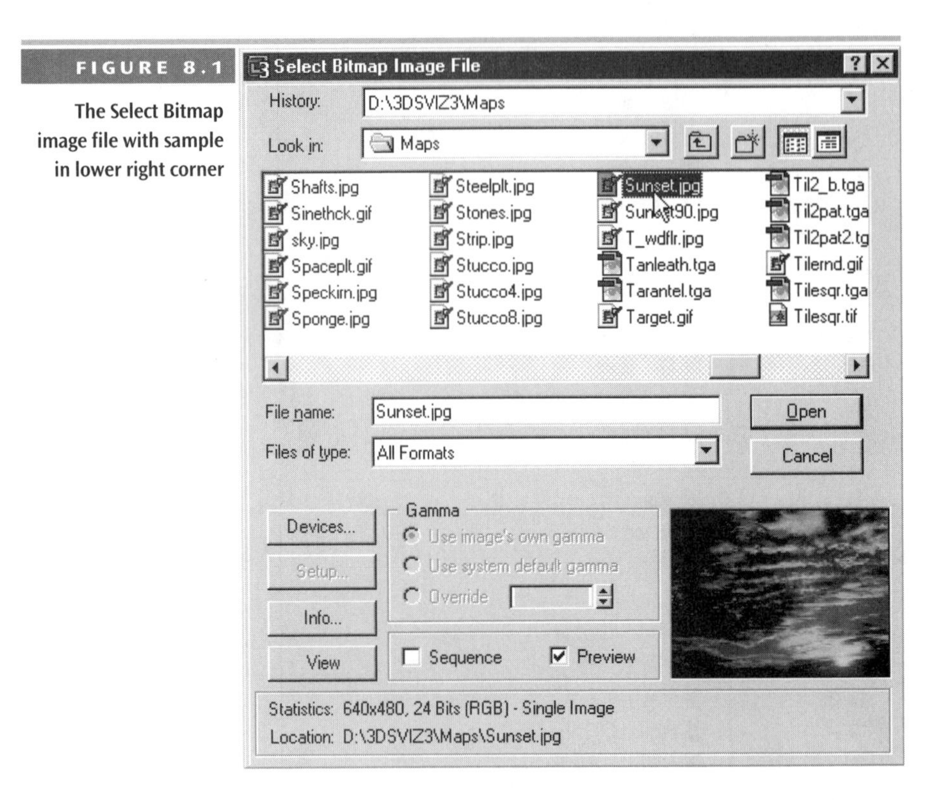

FIGURE 8.1

The Select Bitmap image file with sample in lower right corner

At the bottom of the dialog box, you'll also see the statistics of the file.

6. Click Open. Note that the name of the file now appears on the Environment Map button.

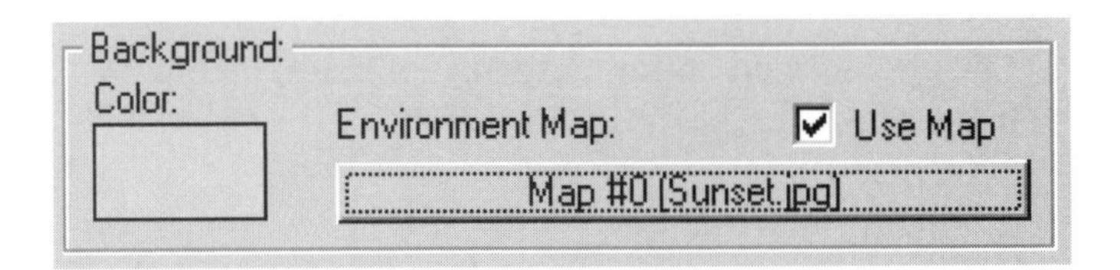

7. Close the Environment dialog box. Make sure that the Camera.View.3DFRONT viewport is currently active and then click the Quick Render button to see the result of your background addition. The model is rendered with a sky in the background as shown in Figure 8.2

FIGURE 8.2

The sky in the rendering

You see the background in the rendered view, but it doesn't appear in the camera viewport. If you prefer, you can set up VIZ to display the same background you use in your rendered view in the camera viewport.

1. Choose View ➢ Viewport Image ➢ Select… The Viewport Image dialog box appears.

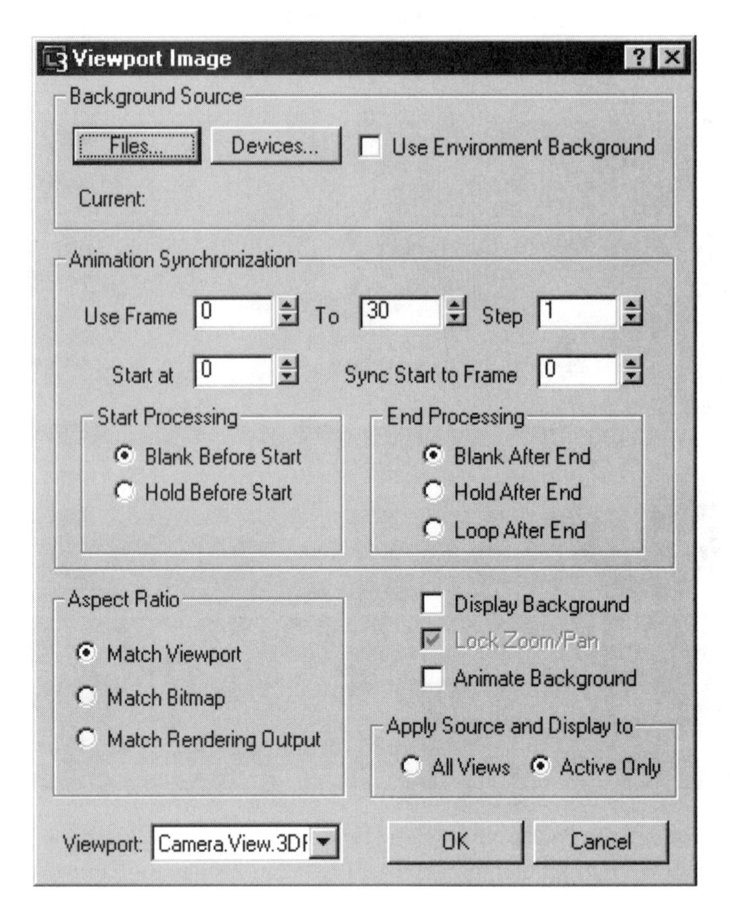

2. At the top of the dialog box, click the Use Environment Background check box to place a check there.

3. Toward the lower right portion of the dialog box, click the Display Background check box to place a check there. Then click OK. The background appears in the Camera viewport as shown in Figure 8.3

FIGURE 8.3

The 3DFRONT Camera viewport with the background added

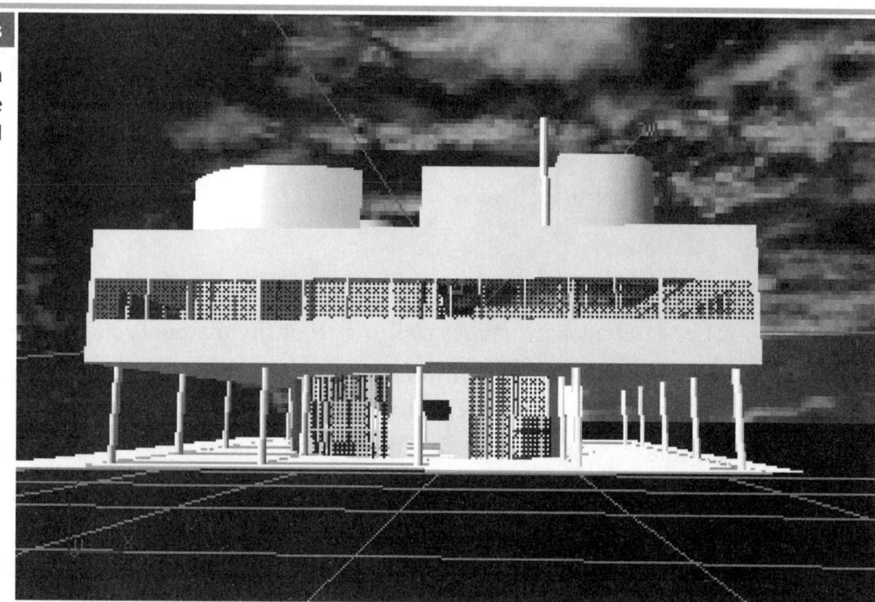

Making Adjustments to the Background

In many cases, the background image will need to be adjusted to fit the scene. The background image may not fit the rendering correctly, or it may be too dark or light. You might notice that the sunset background has a dark band along the right edge and it is a bit dark. In this section, you'll learn how to use the Material Editor to make adjustments to the background.

1. Click the Material Editor tool in the Render toolbar.
2. At the Material Editor dialog box, click the sample slot in the middle of the bottom row. Then click the Get Material tool.

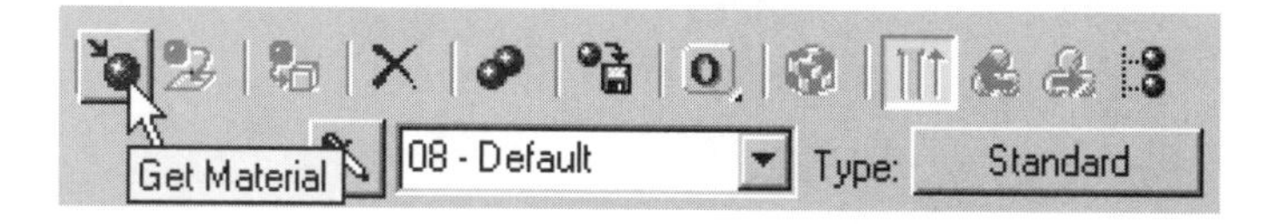

3. In the Material/Map Browser dialog box, click the Design radio button in the Browse From group.

The Materials list changes to show all of the materials currently in the model.

4. Select the listing that shows (Sunset.jpg) in its title. You see a sample of the material in the preview window in the upper left corner of the dialog box.
5. Double click the (Sunset.jpg) listing. The Sunset image displays in the selected sample in the Material Editor. Options for the background also display in the lower half of the Material Editor.

Once you've got the background image in the Material Editor, you have access to parameters that control its appearance. Next you'll use the Output rollout to crop out the black band that appears on the right side of the image in the rendered view.

1. Go to the Bitmap Parameters rollout and click the View Image button in the Cropping/Placement group.

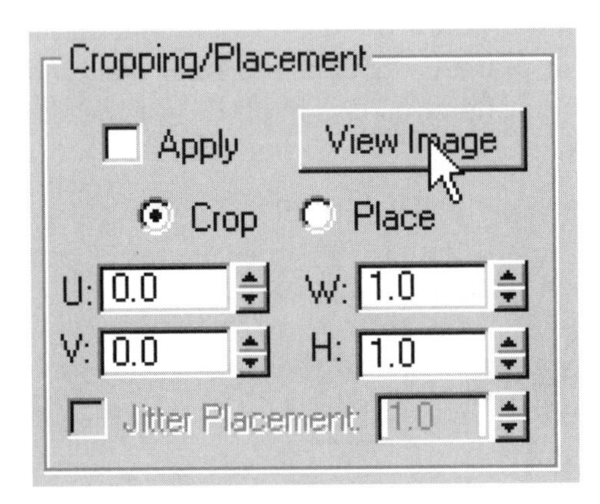

The Specify Cropping/Placement dialog box displays as shown in Figure 8.4.

FIGURE 8.4

Selecting the area used in the rendered background

2. Click and drag the marquee handle on the far right side of the image to the left as shown in Figure 8.4. As you move it, notice that the W spinner at the top of the dialog box changes to show you the percentage of change you are applying to the image width.
3. Adjust the marquee handle on the right side until the W spinner reads 0.98.
4. Next, click and drag the top marquee handle downward until the V spinner shows 0.015, then close the Specify Cropping/Placement dialog box.
5. Click the Apply check box in the Cropping/Placement group of the Material Editor dialog box. Notice that the background in the camera viewport changes to fill out the background area.
6. Go ahead and close the Material Editor, then click the Quick Render tool. The view is rendered with the background filling the edges of the image.

The Cropping/Placement group gives you a lot of control over the placement of the image in the background. Now let's take a look at how to adjust the brightness of the background image.

1. Open the Material Editor again.
2. Scroll down the Material Editor to the Output rollout, then click the Output button to open the rollout at the very bottom. You see a graph and a set of check boxes and spinners.

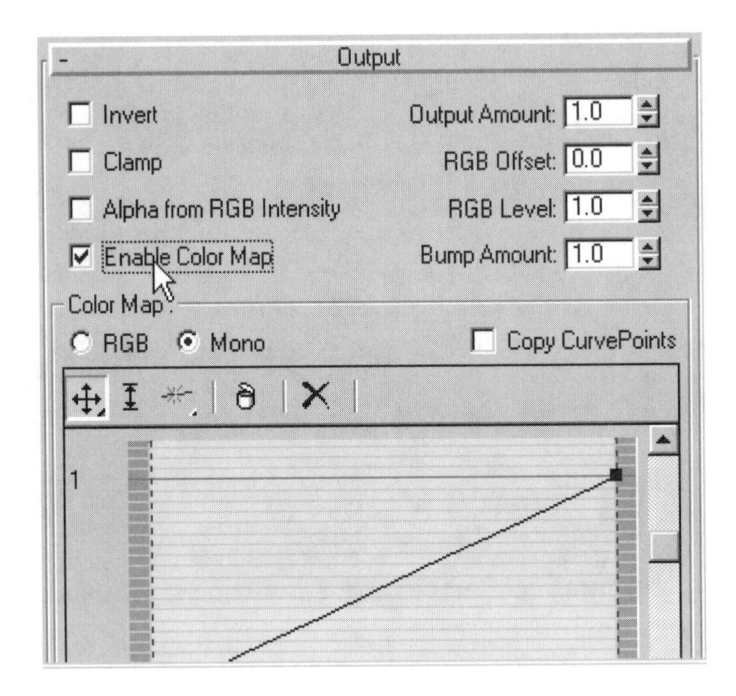

3. Click the Enable Color Map check box in the Output rollout. The graph is highlighted so that you are able to adjust its settings.

If you're an Adobe Photoshop user, then the Color Map graph should be somewhat familiar to you. It lets you adjust the tonal range of an image by manipulating the line in the graph. Right now, the line is straight from 0,0 in the lower left corner to 1,1 in the upper right. You can adjust brightness, contrast, and tonal range of an image by adding control points to the line and then moving the control points. The next exercise will show you some of the Color Map functions.

1. Scroll the Output rollout upward so you can see all of the Color Map and then click the Add Point tool on the Curve toolbar.

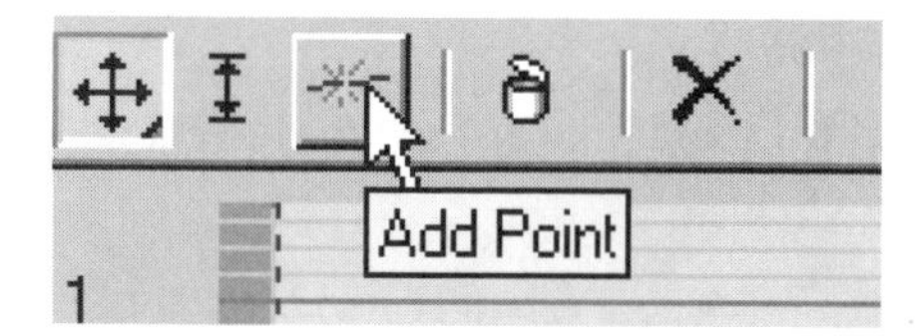

2. Click the color map graph line at its midpoint as shown in Figure 8.5. A square handle displays on the line.

FIGURE 8.5

Click the midpoint of the line.

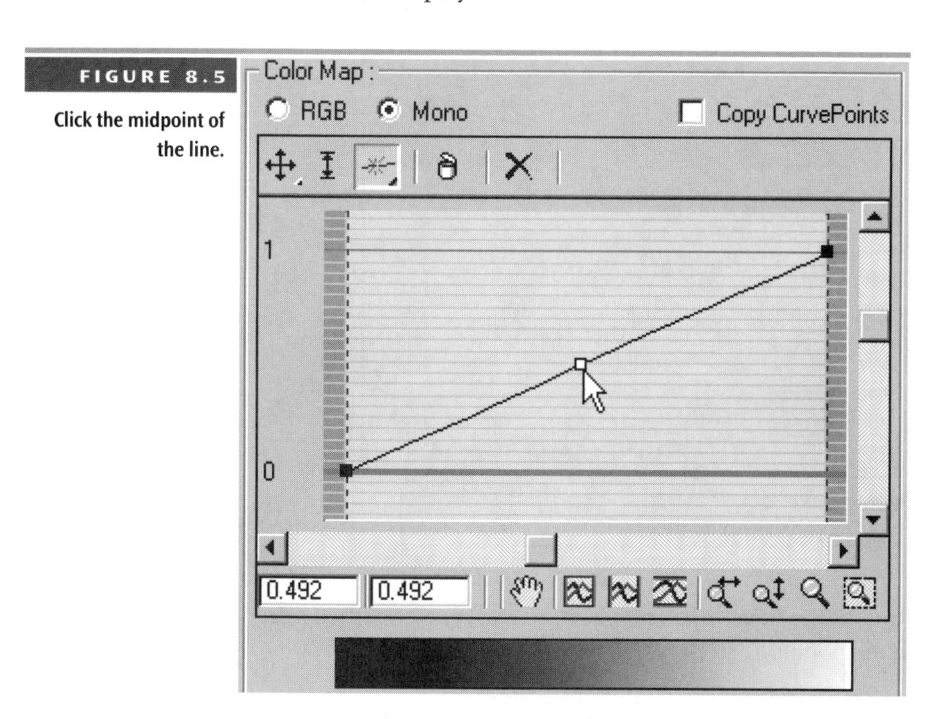

3. Click the Move tool on the Curve toolbar.

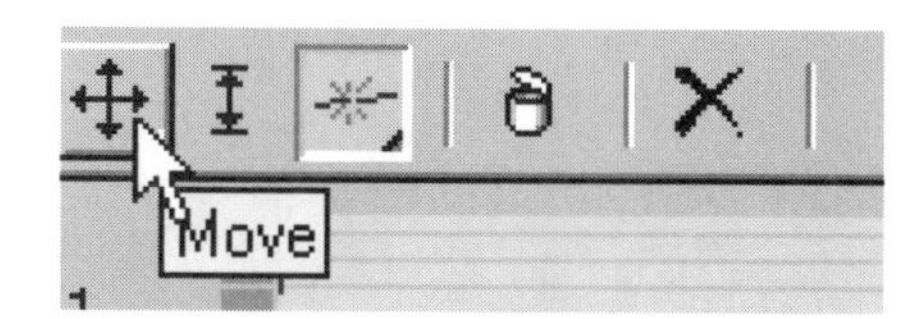

4. Click and drag the handle you just created upward and notice what happens to the sample slot image in the Material Editor. It gets brighter.

By adjusting the line upward at its midpoint, you've increased the amount of the brighter tones in the image. Let's see what other options you have to edit the curve. You can get direct feedback on the effect of your changes by viewing the sample bar at the bottom of the Output rollout.

1. Scroll the Material Editor panel upward so you have a good view of the sample bar as shown in Figure 8.6.

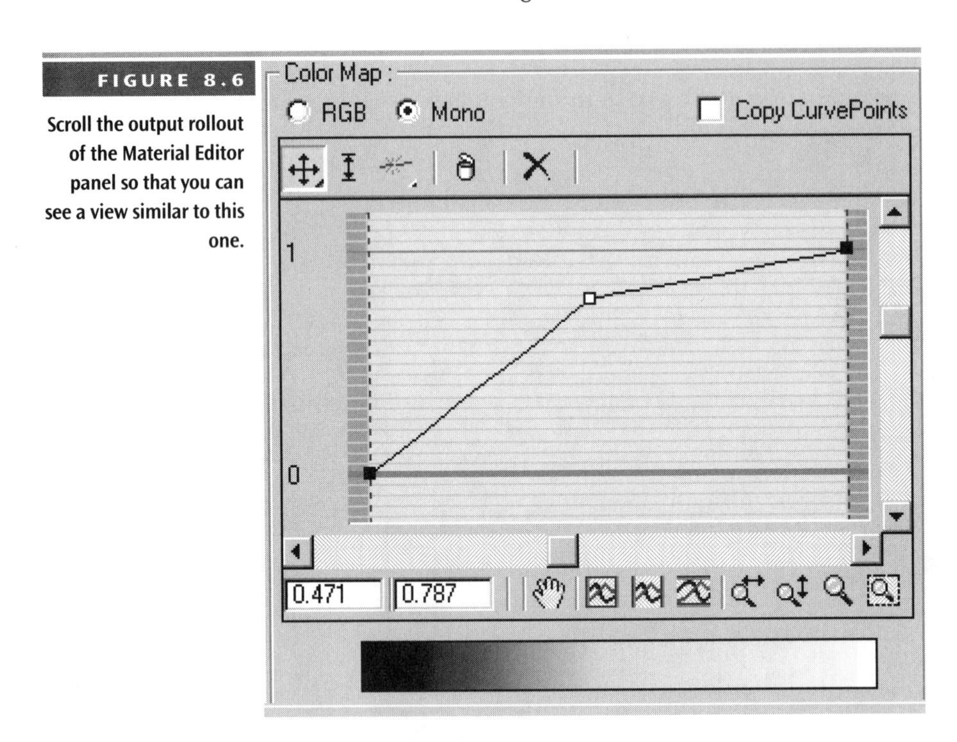

FIGURE 8.6

Scroll the output rollout of the Material Editor panel so that you can see a view similar to this one.

2. Right-click the handle you moved in the last exercise, then select Bézier Smooth from the pop-up list.

3. Move the handle back to its midpoint position, then adjust the Bézier handles so they look like those in Figure 8.7. The sample image fades in contrast, and the gray area of the sample tonal range at the bottom of the graph widens.

FIGURE 8.7

The Bézier handles in a new orientation

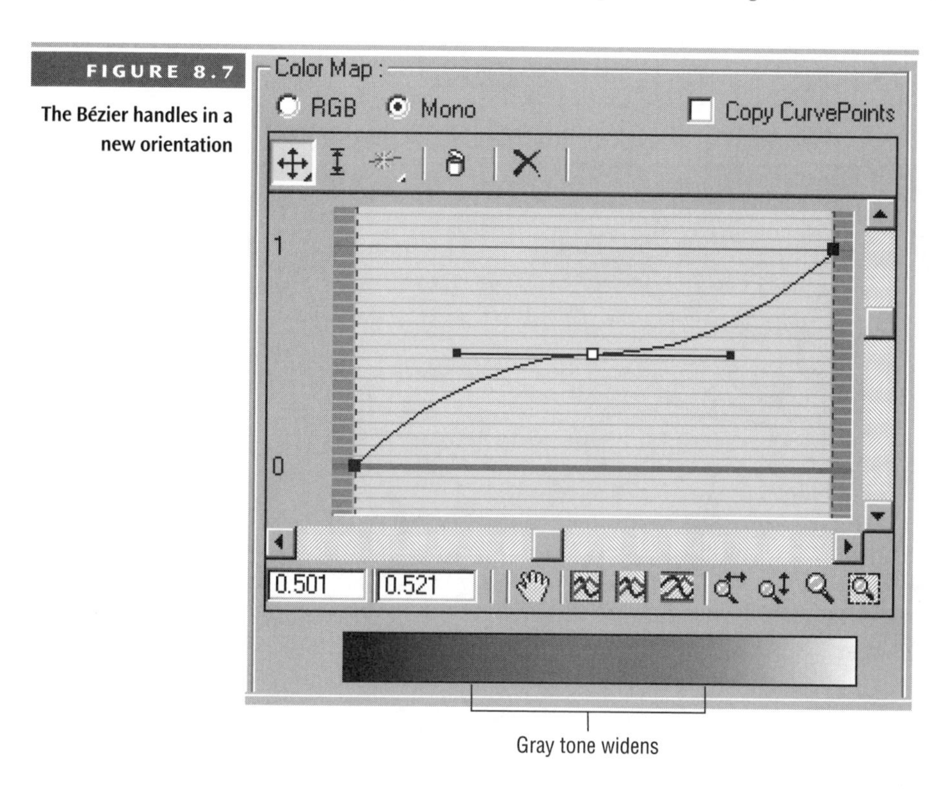

4. Now adjust the handles to look like Figure 8.8. The sample image increases in contrast, and the gray area in the tonal range sample shrinks.

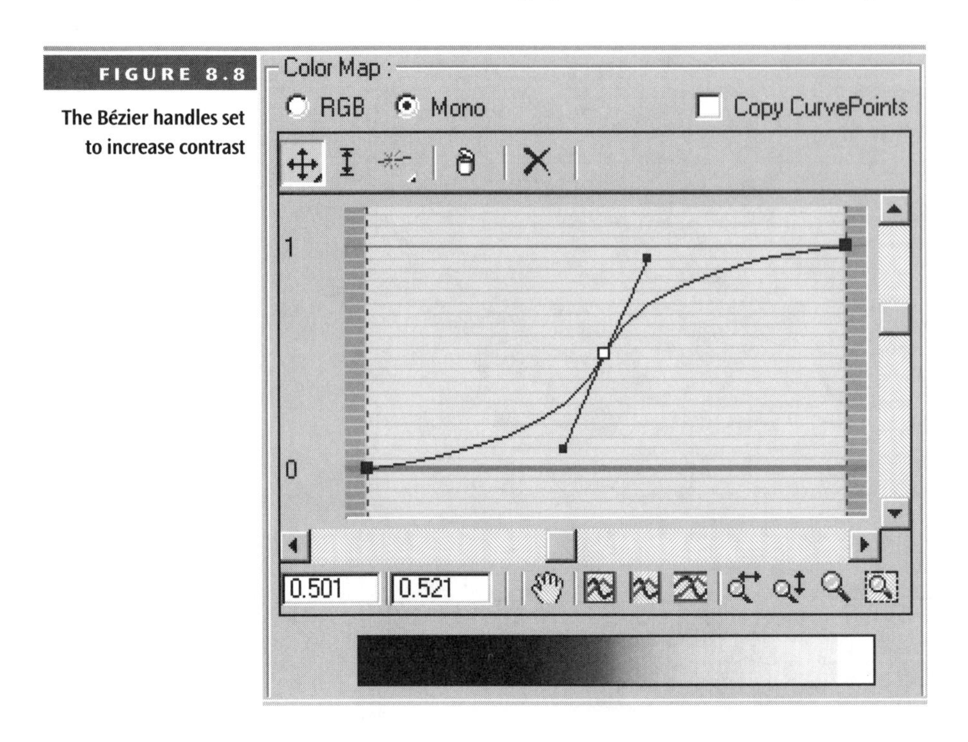

FIGURE 8.8

The Bézier handles set to increase contrast

5. Finally, reposition the curve handle to the left so it looks like Figure 8.9. Notice that the white area of the tonal range sample expands, whereas the black area contracts as if it were following the handle. Also notice that the sample image brightens.

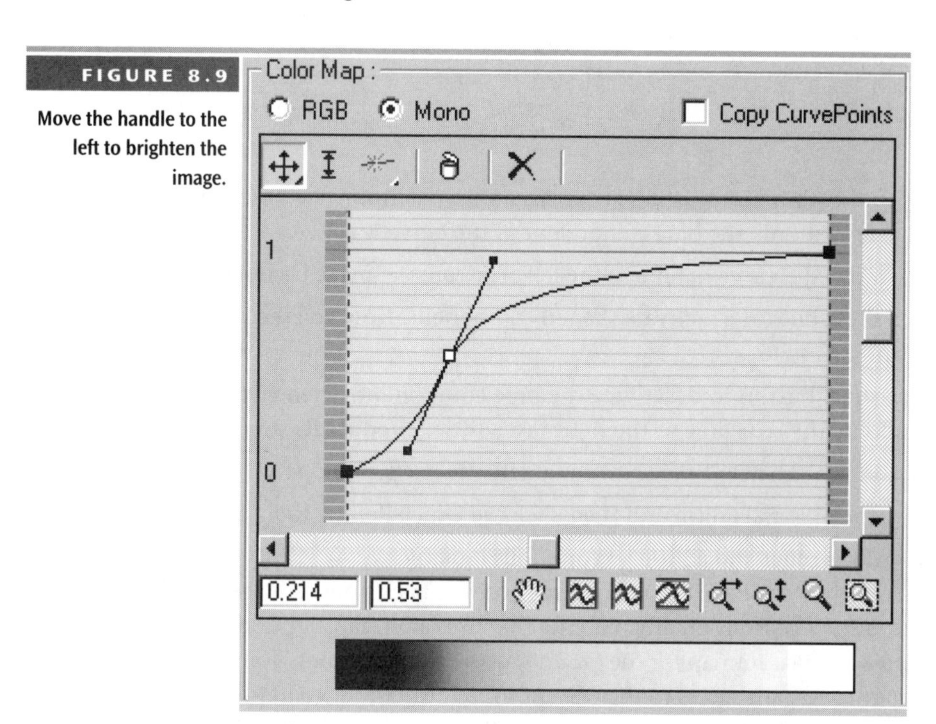

FIGURE 8.9

Move the handle to the left to brighten the image.

6. To apply the image changes to your model, click in the Camera.View.3DFRONT viewport. The background in the 3DFRONT viewport changes to match the sample in the Material Editor.

Besides the overall tone of the image, you can also manipulate the curves for each of the red, green, and blue color components. For example, suppose you want to increase the blue and downplay the red in the background. You can use the R, G, and B tools to isolate each color.

1. Click the Copy CurvePoints check box and then click the RGB radio button at the top of the Color Map group. Copy CurvePoints forces the RGB settings to use the current curve settings.

2. Click the R and G tools on the Output toolbar to deactivate them.

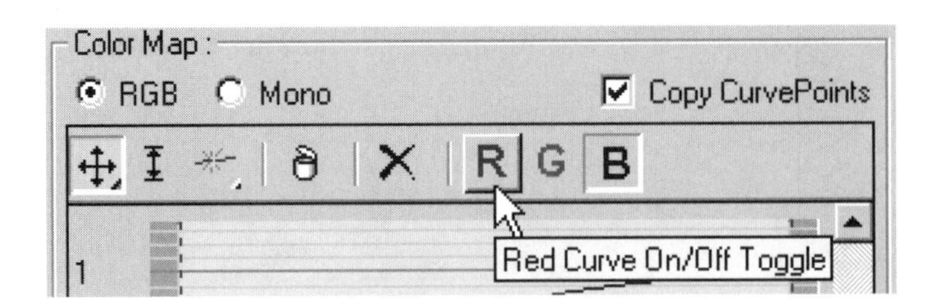

The tools should look as if they are in an up position. The line is now blue to indicate that only the blue component of the curve is active.

3. Now move the curve handle to the left. The sample image becomes bluer.
4. Click the R button to activate the red component. Now you see two curves, one red and one blue.
5. Click the B button to deactivate the blue component. Then click and drag the handle on the red curve to the right just a little to reduce its strength.
6. Click in the 3DFRONT viewport to update the background in your model.
7. Close the Material Editor and then click the Quick Render tool.

Now the sky is bluer and a little less ominous looking.

You've seen that you have a lot of control over the background image. In fact, you can use the Output options on any material that uses a bitmap. For example, you can edit the Ground-Grass bitmap for the ground, using the same tools you just used on the background. To gain access to the Output rollout for Maps, go to the Maps rollout and click the button for the map you want to edit. For example, you can click the GRASS.jpg Diffuse map for the Ground-Grass material. You'll find the Output rollout at the bottom of the Map parameters that appear in the Material Editor.

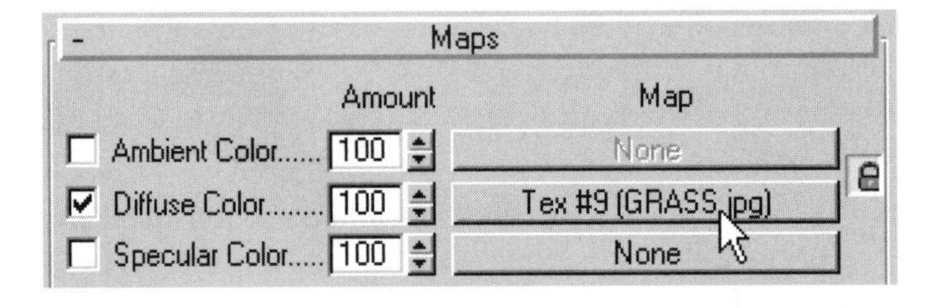

Adding Effects with Light and Shadow

You've seen how a single direct light can be used to simulate the sun. You can also use lighting to add emphasis or to provide a sense of drama. Shadows can be controlled to provide a seemingly sharp, strong light source or a softer, more diffuse interior light. In this section, you'll take a look at some of the more commonly used lighting options, starting with shadows.

By default, the shadow option for lights is turned on so that when you render your model, you see shadows cast. If you look carefully at your last rendering, you'll see that there are indeed shadows from the columns and the rest of the building. The shadows are not exactly right, however. There are parts of the model that show light *bleeding* through the shadows as shown in figure 8.10

FIGURE 8.10

With the current shadow settings, the shadow is not completely correct, as shown in this picture.

Column shadows don't touch columns.
Light "leaks" through in some places.

You might also notice that the shadows from the columns don't quite start at the column bases.

There are a few options you can use to correct these problems. Let's start with the Shadow Map Parameters of the Target Direct light object you're using to simulate the sun.

1. Click the Target Direct light object named SUN. This is the light in the lower corner of the building in the top viewport.

2. Click the Modify tab in the Command Panel to view the parameters for the Sun.
3. Scroll down the panel tot he Shadow Map Params rollout and click it to open. You see the Bias, Size, and Sample Range settings.

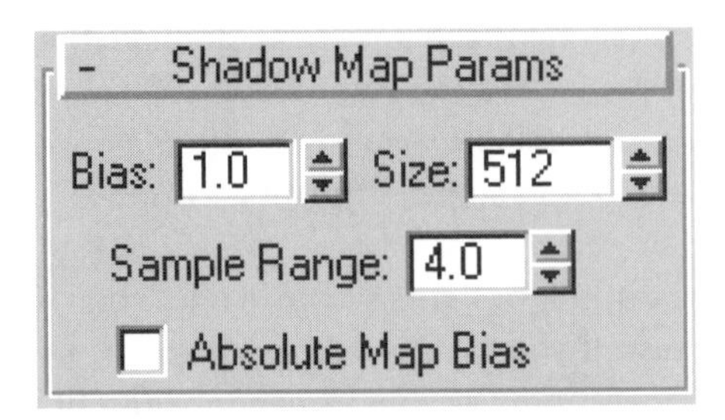

4. Click the Bias setting and enter **0.2**↵ to change its value from 1 to 0.2. By reducing this number, you bring the shadow closer to the object that is casting the shadow.
5. Right-click the 3DFRONT viewport and then click the Quick Render tool in the Render toolbar. This time the shadow is rendered more accurately, filling in those portions it missed in the previous rendering (see Figure 8.11).

FIGURE 8.11

The new rendering with the shadows filled in

Softening Shadow Edges

Another option that lets you control the softness of the shadow edge is Sample Range. In some situations, you may want the edge of the shadow softer for partially cloudy outdoor scenes or for interior views with combined diffuse and direct lighting. The following exercise shows the effect of Sample Range.

1. Set the Sample Range to 10.
2. Click the Quick Render tool to see the effects of the new Sample Range setting as shown in Figure 8.12.

FIGURE 8.12

The shadow edges are softened with a greater Sample Range setting.

You can see the effects of a softer shadow by looking at the shadows of the columns. Also notice that the shadows of the columns disappear on the ground below the building. The Sample Range setting is high enough to obliterate the thin column shadows.

A soft shadow edge lends realism to objects in indoor settings and in closeup views of outdoor objects, but in some situations, a sharp, crisp shadow edge is more desirable. There are two ways to achieve a sharp shadow edge. You can manipulate shadow settings in VIZ to obtain a high degree of accuracy in the shadow representation, or you can go with an entirely different shadow rendering method offered by VIZ, called

Ray Trace Shadows. This method models the actual path of light to generate shadows. Ray Trace shadows are more accurate, but they can add a lot of time to the rendering process. They also produce a sharp shadow edge, so in situations where a soft shadow is desired, you will have to use the default Shadow Map type of shadow or some combination of both Ray Trace shadows and Shadow Map shadows.

In the next section, you'll look at how you can set up Shadow Map to create a sharper shadow edge.

Understanding Shadow Maps

So far, you've been using the default *Shadow Map* method for casting shadows. A shadow map is a temporary bitmap image of the shadows cast by objects in the model. You never actually see this bitmap. VIZ uses it to determine the shape and location of the shadow in a model. Since the shadow map is really a bitmap image, a shadow's sharpness is dependant on the resolution of the shadow map. If the shadow map has a small size setting, it creates a shadow that is rough around the edges, like a low resolution rendering. Figure 8.13 shows a sample model with a very low-resolution shadow map that clearly displays the shadow map pixels around the shadow edge.

FIGURE 8.13

This image shows a shadow with a low Shadow Map size setting coupled with a low Sample Range setting of 0.1.

You can increase the Shadow Map Size setting to reduce the stairstepping effect of the shadow edge. Figure 8.14 shows the sample image again with the Size setting doubled from the previous figure.

FIGURE 8.14

Increase the map size setting to even out the shadow edge.

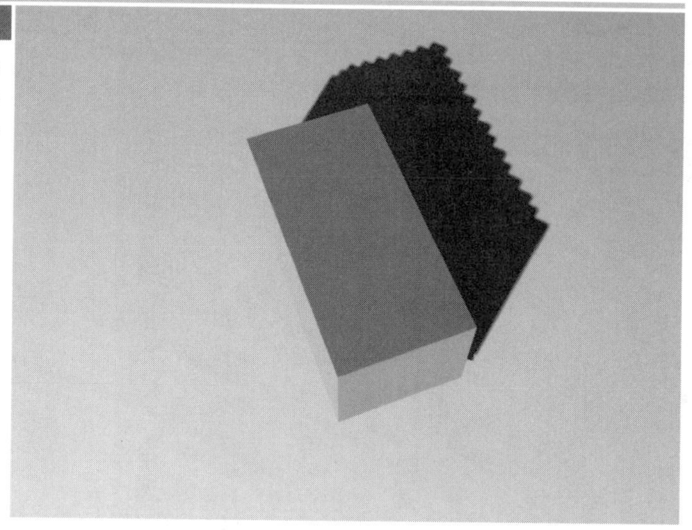

A larger shadow map makes for a more even shadow edge. If the shadow map size is too great, however, it will consume greater amounts of memory and increase rendering time.

Another setting that is directly related to shadow map size is the spread of the light source. The shadow map is directly related to the area that is lit by the light source casting the shadow. If the area or spread of the light is decreased, the shadow map must also include a smaller area. If the shadow map size is reduced relative to the object casting the shadow, then more of the shadow map area can be devoted to the shadow outline. This has the effect of reducing the jagged edge of the shadow. Figure 8.15 shows the same model and light source as shown in Figure 8.14, but the hotspot has been reduced in size so the light is focused on a smaller area. Notice that the edges of the shadow appear less jagged.

FIGURE 8.15

The box and light with a decreased hotspot and falloff area

You can control the jagged edge of the shadow to some degree by using the Sample Range setting. In the last exercise, you saw how the map sample range controls the softness of the edge of the shadow. A smaller map sample value makes for a sharper shadow but also reveals more of the shadow map's bitmap edge. If the Sample Range setting is too low, you begin to see the stairstep edges of the pixels of the shadow map, as shown in Figure 8.13.

The sample range value is actually the number of pixels in the rendered image that are blended to soften the edge of the shadow. This has the effect of hiding the pixelated shadow edges as shown in Figure 8.16. Here you see the same image as shown in Figure 8.15 but with an increased sample range.

FIGURE 8.16

The same image as in Figure 8.15, but with a sample range of 6

If you look carefully, you can still detect the stairstep edge of the pixelated shadow map, particularly along the vertical edge shadows. But if you aren't looking for it, you may not notice it. You can also further increase the softness of the shadow edge by increasing the difference between the Hotspot and Falloff settings. As the Sample Range setting decreases, however, the hotspot/falloff difference has less effect.

Taking all of this into account, you need to increase the shadow map size and reduce the sample range to sharpen the shadow edge. You also need to keep the lighted area as narrow as possible while still keeping all of the objects in your scene lighted. So to get the sharpest shadow from a Shadow Map shadow, you need find a balance between the map size, sample range, light spread, and to some degree the hotspot/falloff difference. Figure 8.17 shows the sample box and light with a sample range of 1, a map size of 2048, and a Falloff setting as close to the hotspot setting as possible.

FIGURE 8.17

A fairly sharp shadow achieved with a high size setting and a low sample range

TIP To see firsthand the effects of these settings, try sharpening the shadows on the villa model.

1. First, choose Edit ➢ Temporary Buffer ➢ Save to save the model in its current state.
2. In the Shadow Map Params rollout, change the Size value to 3000.
3. Change the sample range to 1.
4. Click the Render tool on the Render toolbar to open the Render Design dialog box.
5. Click the 800 × 600 button in the Output Size group. This will give you a better look at the result of the rendering.

6. Click the Render button. Notice how the shadow appears to be sharper. You may also notice that the shadow is indeed more jagged around the edges in some locations (See Figure 8.18).

FIGURE 8.18

The villa rendered with a sharper shadow

Using Ray Trace Shadows

You may feel that using the Shadow Map settings in the last exercise requires too many compromises to achieve the sharpest shadows. If you want the sharpest, most accurate shadows possible, you'll want to use Ray Trace shadows.

As mentioned earlier, Ray Trace shadows derive the shadow's form by modeling the path of light from the light source to the shadow surface. The benefits are a very accurate shadow with no stairstep edges. You do pay a penalty in increased rendering time, but in many cases, the increase in time is well worth it. Figure 8.19 shows two images of a fairly complex model. The model contains translucent elements as well as some detailed elements. The top image is the model rendered with a shadow map, whereas the second is rendered using Ray Trace shadows. The Ray Trace shadows show much more detail.

FIGURE 8.19A

A comparison of Shadow Map shadows to Ray Trace shadows

FIGURE 8.19B

A comparison of Shadow Map shadows to Ray Trace shadows

With Ray Trace shadows, you don't have to be concerned with map sizes and sample ranges. Try the following exercise to see how Ray Trace shadows affect the villa model.

1. In the Modify tab of the Command Panel, scroll down to the Shadow Parameters rollout and click to open the Shadow Parameters.
2. Click the Shadow Map drop-down menu in the Object Shadows group and select Ray Trace Shadows.

3. Click the Quick Render tool on the Render toolbar. The villa is rendered with smoother looking shadows, as seen in Figure 8.20.

FIGURE 8.20

The villa rendered using Ray Trace Shadows.

While the differences are not as dramatic as those shown in Figure 8.19. the Ray Trace Shadow rendering of the Villa does show smoother shadows, particularly on the lower right side of the image. You also see more detail in the shadow behind the window at the right side of the image. You can increase the spread of the light source now without affecting the sharpness of the shadows.

Adding a Highlight with an Omni Light

Next you'll learn how to add a highlight to the glass. By adding a highlight, you will be able to see that there is indeed glass in the windows, and it adds a bit of interest to the rendering. You'll also get a chance to see some of the unique features of Omni light.

1. Go to the Create tab in the Command Panel, then click the Lights tool.

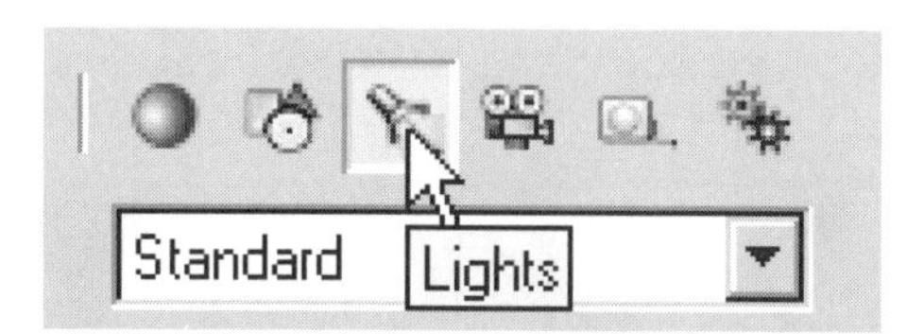

2. Right-click the Top viewport, then use the Region Zoom tool to enlarge the Top view so it looks similar to Figure 8.21.
3. Click the Omni button; then, in the Top viewport, click the location shown in Figure 8.21. You don't need to be exact about the location, because the Highlight tool you'll use later will place the light accurately for you.

FIGURE 8.21

Place the Omni light in this location.

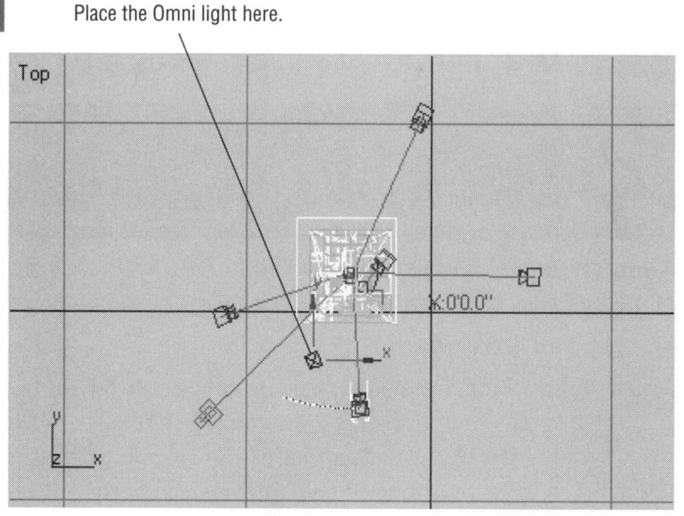

You might notice that the shaded 3DFRONT camera view lightens due to the addition of a new light source.

4. With the Omni light selected, choose Modify ➢ Place Highlight. The cursor changes to the Place Highlight icon.
5. Go to the 3DFRONT viewport and click the location shown in Figure 8.22.

FIGURE 8.22

Click here to place the highlight on the glass.

You'll see the Omni light change its location.

6. Click the Quick Render tool on the Render toolbar. The view is rendered with a bright highlight on the glass.

The Place Highlight command places the currently selected light in a location that produces a highlight reflection at the location you selected in step 4. But the Omni light also shines on the rest of the building, washing out some detail. Fortunately, you can set VIZ's lights to shine on the selected object instead of the entire model.

1. With the Omni light selected, click the Modify tab of the Command Panel.
2. In the General Parameters of the Omni light, click the Exclude... button.

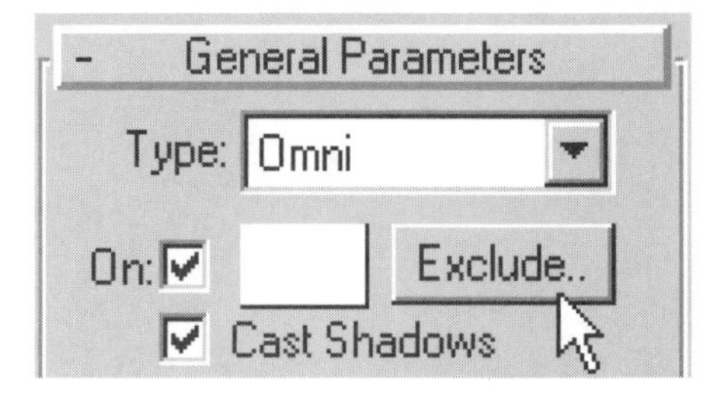

3. In the Exclude/Include dialog box, click the Include radio button in the upper right corner of the dialog box.
4. In the Scene Objects list, click Glass.03 to select it, then click the transfer button that points left as shown in Figure 8.23. Glass.03 moves from the list on the left to the list on the right.

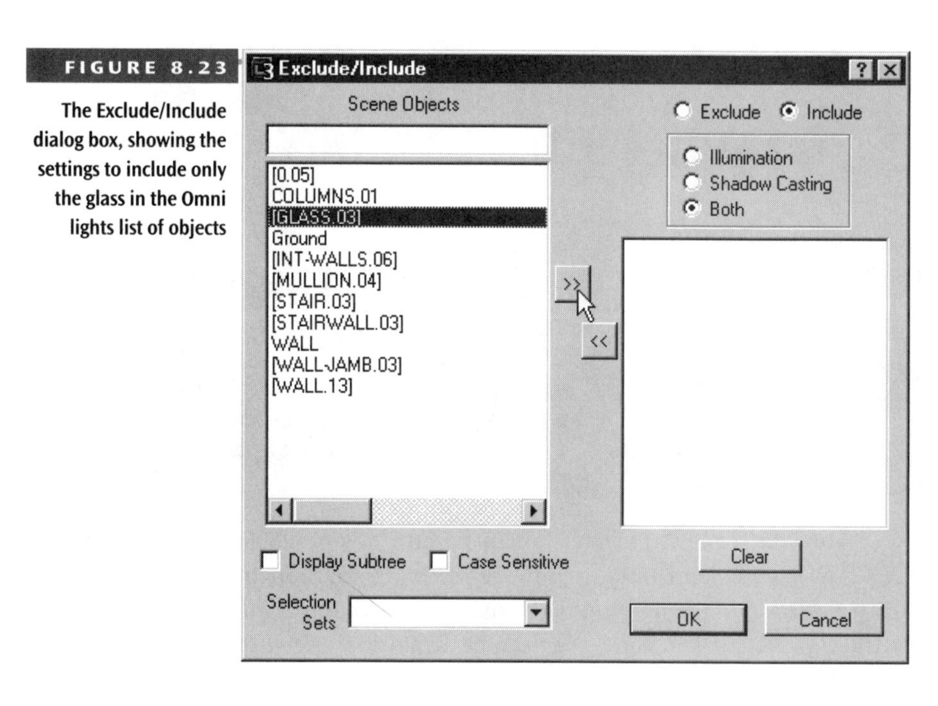

FIGURE 8.23

The Exclude/Include dialog box, showing the settings to include only the glass in the Omni lights list of objects

5. Click OK to close the Exclude/Include dialog box, then click the Quick Render tool. Now the highlight is limited to the glass, as shown in Figure 8.24.

FIGURE 8.24

The villa rendered with a highlight on the glass

At times, you may be requested to stretch reality a bit when producing renderings. The highlighted glass adds some interest to the rendering, even though it isn't necessarily a realistic portrayal of the lighting in the model. The highlight effect is not exclusive to the Omni light. The same effect can be achieved using virtually any type of light you choose.

The ability to select the objects that individual lights affect also gives you some freedom to play with a scene, adding emphasis to some areas while downplaying others.

Now suppose you are asked to increase the size of the highlight on the glass so that it covers more area. You might think that you'll need to adjust the lighting in some way, and normally you would edit some of the Omni light's properties. But in the case of glass, you need to edit the glass itself. To spread the highlight of the glass over a wider area, you set the *glossiness* of the glass.

1. Click the Material Editor tool.
2. In the Material Editor dialog box, click the Glass sample.
3. In the Phong Basic Parameters rollout, go to the Specular Highlights group and change the Glossiness value to 40. Notice how this change affects the glass sam-

ple slot and the graph to the right of the Specular Highlight group. The highlight in the sample is enlarged, and the graph shows a wider bell curve.

4. Close the Material Editor, then click the Quick Render tool. Now the highlight on the glass is spread over a greater area, as seen in Figure 8.25

FIGURE 8.25

The rendering with a decrease in glossiness of the glass

Looking at Omni Light Options

Since you're working with an Omni light, let's take a look at some of the other Omni light parameters that control its functions. You've seen how you can select the objects that the Omni light affects. The Include/Exclude dialog box is a feature common to all lights. And, just as with all other lights, you can control shadows in the manner described in previous exercises. You can also control the Attenuation of the Omni light. The Attenuation settings let you control the distance of the light's reach. By default, Attenuation is turned off. Try the following exercise to see how you can control an Omni light.

1. First, save the Villa model as Myvilla.max.
2. Open the 08omni.max file. This is the file shown in Figure 8.26, and it is one of the files you can install from the companion CD.
3. Click the Quick Render tool to get a rendered view of the model. You see a rendering that looks like Figure 8.26

FIGURE 8.26

An omni light used to light a simple scene

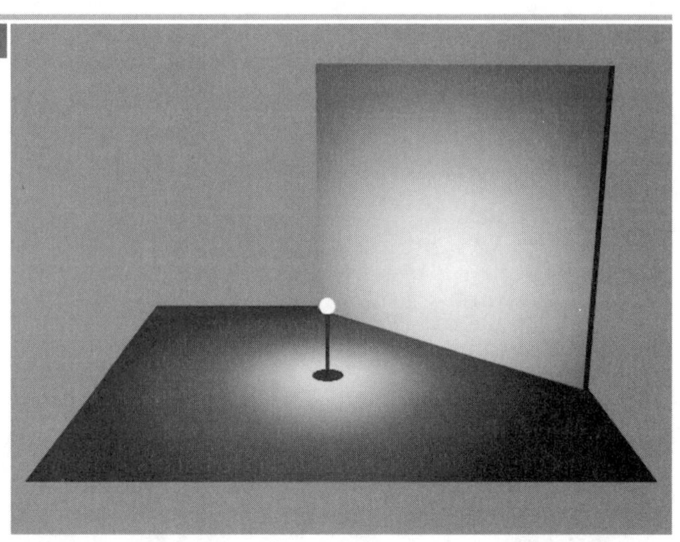

The 08omni.max model is a simple scene of a light pole, a ground plane, and a wall. The light pole has an Omni light at the center of its globe. The globe itself has been excluded from the effects of the Omni light so that the light is unrestrained beyond the globe. The Omni light in this rendering has been inserted into the scene with its default settings unchanged.

The light from the Omni light casts a shadow from the pole, but is otherwise unrestrained. You can adjust the attenuation, however, to limit the range of the light. Try the following exercise to get a feel for the attenuation settings.

1. Click the Select Objects tool, then in the Select Objects dialog box, click Omni01 from the list and click Select.
2. Click the Modify tab of the Command Panel, then scroll down the panel to the Attenuation Parameters and click to open the panel.
3. Click the Use check box in the Far Attenuation group. A pair of sphere gizmos displays around the omni light, as shown in Figure 8.27

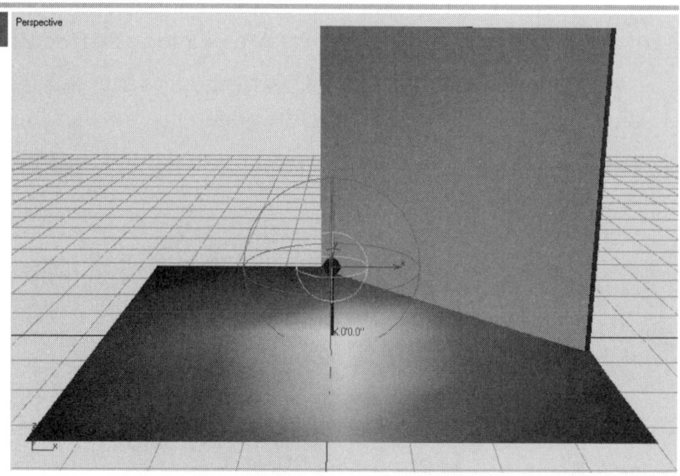

FIGURE 8.27

The perspective viewport showing the Far Attenuation spheres

4. Click and drag the Far Attenuation End spinner upward so that its value reads 37 feet.
5. Click the Quick Render tool. You now see the light attenuated to a distance of 37 feet. It casts a dim light against the wall.

FIGURE 8.28

The rendering with Attenuation turned on and the End distance set to 37 feet

The End distance setting controls the farthest reach of the light. You can also set the distance of maximum brightness, using Far Attenuation's Start setting.

1. Click and drag the Far Attenuation Start setting spinner upward so that its value reads 22 feet. Notice that the center white gizmo just touches the wall.
2. Click the Quick Render tool. Now the light on the wall is much brighter.

FIGURE 8.29

The rendering with the Far Attenuation Start setting at 28 feet

The Start and Far Attenuation settings act a bit like the Hotspot and Falloff settings in direct lights and spotlights.

You've probably noticed that Attenuation Parameters also offers a Near Attenuation group. The settings in this group give you control where the Omni light begins to take effect (not possible in the real world), as demonstrated in the following exercise.

1. Click the Use check box in the Near Attenuation group. Blue attenuation gizmos display in the viewport.

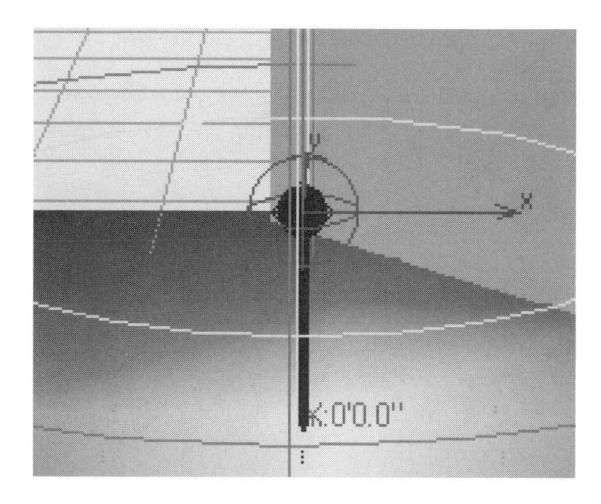

2. Set the Near Attenuation Start value to 15 feet and the Near Attenuation End value to 17 feet.
3. Click the Quick Render tool. Notice that the shadow of the pole appears to expand and soften, as shown in Figure 8.30.

FIGURE 8.30

The scene rendered using the Near Attenuation parameters

This time the Near Attenuation settings are limiting the near distance that the light affects. In this scene, it creates the effect of a larger, softer shadow being cast by the pole, though the dark area is actually the result of the Near Attenuation setting limiting the near range of the light cast by the Omni light.

NOTE While VIZ offers this ability to control the Near Attenuation of an Omni light, this kind of near attenuation is not possible in real life.

Adding Props

In the last chapter, you learned how to use the Material Editor to make adjustments to materials. In this section, you'll look at ways to create materials from scratch. We'll focus on creating trees that we'll add to the building model.

You can approach building trees in two ways: you can model them leaf for leaf, or you can project an image of a tree onto a flat surface. If you are creating a model you intend to animate with camera locations that are close to the trees and foliage, you may want to consider modeling trees with more detail, at least for trees that are close to the camera. VIZ comes with several detailed trees that you can use right away.

On the other hand, if you are creating a model for a still image, or if the camera motion of your animation doesn't get too close to the trees, you can usually get by with flat projections. The advantage of a flat projection tree is that it takes much less time to render. Another advantage is that you can include a specific type of tree in your scene. For example, you may be asked to show trees that are native to the location of a site, or are of a type that the client has specifically requested.

There are a few programs available that will generate natural 3D foliage for you, if you need that kind of detail. Onyx Tree by Onyx Computing (`www.onyxtree.com`) and Digimation's Tree Factory (`www.digimation.com`) are two such products. A third company called ArchVision offers a unique type of tree that renders faster than fully modeled foliage, yet offers a realistic appearance from any direction of view.

The following exercise shows you how to use bitmap images of trees to create a projected, flat tree. Among other things, you'll learn how to use Opacity maps to create a complex shape from a plain rectangle.

Adding a Map Path to Help VIZ Find Bitmaps

VIZ needs to know where different types of files are kept for its use. VIZ stores its bitmaps in a folder called Maps under the main VIZ folder. When you start to create your own materials, it may be a good idea to keep your own bitmap files in folders that are separate from the standard VIZ Map folder. For example, you might create a folder under the VIZ folder called Custom Maps to store your own bitmap files.

In this section, you'll use a bitmap file from the companion CD. The first step is to let VIZ know where to look for the files from the CD.

1. Choose Tools ➢ Configure Paths… The Configure Paths dialog box appears.

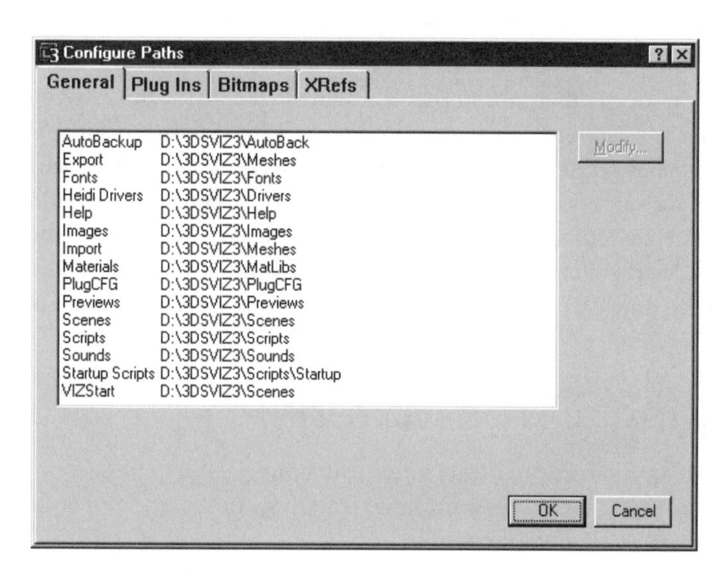

2. Click the Bitmaps tab. You see a list showing the current path where VIZ searches for bitmap files.

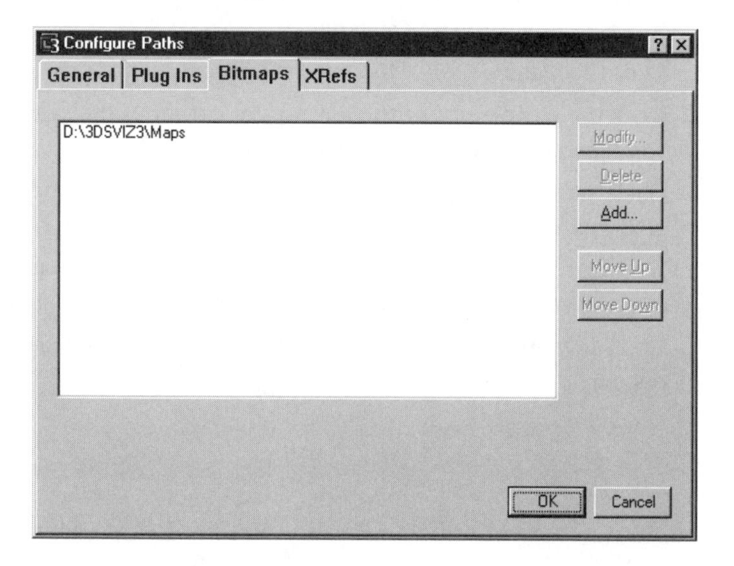

3. Click the Add button to the far right. The Choose New Bitmap Path dialog box appears. This is a typical file dialog box that lets you search for and select a folder.
4. Locate and select the folder that contains the bitmaps from the companion CD, then click Use Path.
5. Click OK in the Configure Paths dialog box.

Now you're ready to start using the bitmap files from the companion CD. You may have noticed other tabs in the Configure Paths dialog box. As you might guess, these other tabs let you indicate additional places to search: *General, Plug Ins*, and *Xrefs*, as the names of the tabs indicate. The General tab lets you determine where VIZ should look for various components of the program. PlugIns lets you add additional paths for PlugIns to VIZ. Xrefs lets you indicate where VIZ should look when searching for Xref files. Xrefs are model files that have been externally referenced into a file. Xrefs do not become part of the file into which they are imported, but remain separate files. In a later chapter you'll get a change to learn more about Xrefs.

Creating a Tree Material

Now you are ready to create a tree using image bitmap files from the companion CD. In this section you will learn how to apply a combination of texture maps and opacity maps to simulate a tree.

1. Close the 08omni.max file, then open to the Myvilla.max file you saved previously. If you didn't create Myvilla.max, you can use Savoye8b.max from the companion CD. In this exercise, you'll want to create the material in the file that will receive the tree material.
2. Click the Material Editor tool on the Render toolbar.
3. Click the sample slot in the lower right corner of the samples. This is the slot you'll use to construct the tree material.
4. Click the name drop-down list just below the toolbar and enter **Magnolia** to give your new tree material a name.

You've just created a new material. It doesn't have any distinguishing characteristics yet. Now let's add some parameters to this material to make it unique.

1. Scroll down to the bottom of the Material Editor to the Maps rollout and click to open it.

2. Click the Diffuse Map button labeled None.

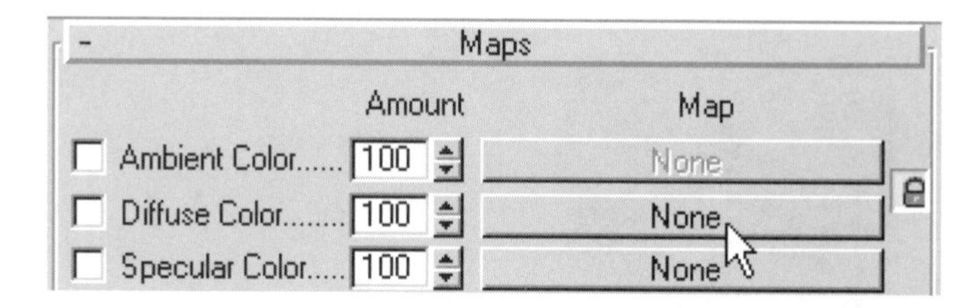

The Material/Map Browser displays.

3. Make sure the New radio button is selected in the Browser From group, then double-click the Bitmap option at the top of the list to the right. The Select Bitmap Image File dialog box appears.
4. Go to the Maps folder of the Companion CD folder.

   The History drop-down list at the top of the dialog box shows the folders that are listed in the Bitmaps tab of the Configure Paths dialog box. You can use this list to go quickly to your folder.
5. Click the MagnoliaIM.jpg file. You see a sample image in the lower right corner.
6. Click Open. Now you see the image wrapped around the sample sphere in the sample slot.

You've just added the bitmap for the Diffuse and Ambient maps. To get a better idea of what your Magnolia material looks like, you'll want to change a few settings for the sample slot you're using for the Magnolia material.

1. Click and hold the Sample Type tool in the column of tools to the right of the sample slots.

   A flyout with three tools displays.

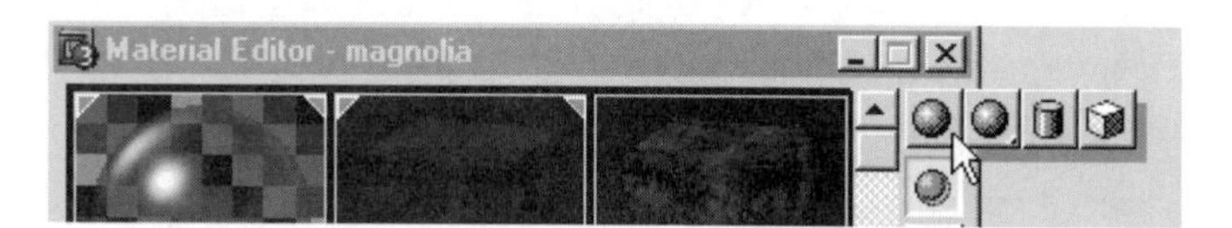

2. Select the tool that looks like a cube. The Magnolia sample slot changes to a cube.

You can add a background to check for transparency or opacity.

3. Click the Background tool in the column of sample slot tools.

A checkerboard background displays in the Magnolia slot.

Since your Magnolia material consists of only an Ambient/Diffuse bitmap, you see a tree on a black background applied to the cube. This is exactly how the bitmap looks. You need to set up the material so that the black background of the bitmap image is totally invisible. This is done by using an opacity map.

Hiding Unwanted Surfaces with Opacity Maps

An opacity map is a gray scale bitmap image that tells VIZ which part of the surface is opaque and which part is transparent. The black portions of an opacity map become completely transparent, whereas white is completely opaque. Shades of gray create varying degrees of opacity.

To see how this works, look at Figure 8.31. To the left you see an opacity map. The middle figure shows a simple rectangle in VIZ without a material assigned to it. The figure to the far right shows the same rectangle that is assigned a material using the opacity map at left. Notice that the portions of the opacity map that are black appear invisible in the rectangle.

FIGURE 8.31

A sample of an opacity map and an object to which it is assigned

You can also use shades of gray to simulate a semitransparent material or to gradually change the transparency of a surface. Color images can be used for opacity maps as well, though it's easier to visualize how gray scale images are translated into opaque surfaces.

Now that you have an understanding of what opacity maps are, lets add one to our tree material.

1. Click the Go to Parent tool on the Material Editor toolbar.

A Bitmap is considered a "child" of the material. When you added the bitmap file to the Magnolia material, you entered a type of sub-level for the material. The Go to Parent tool brings you back up to the "main" level of the material's parameters.

2. Click the Map button for the Opacity listing in the Maps rollout.

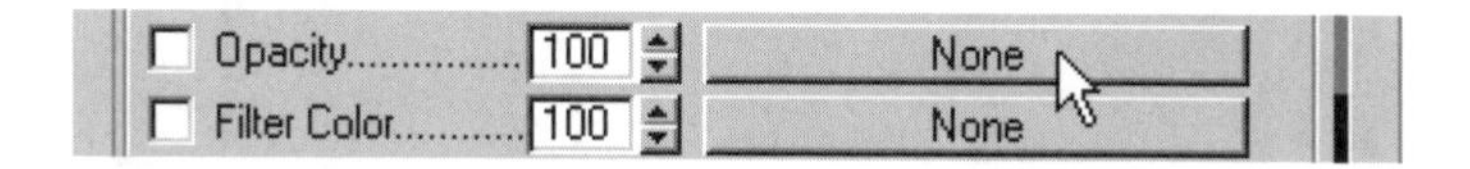

Once again, you see the Material/Map Browser dialog box.

3. With the New radio button selected in the Browse From group, double-click the Bitmap listing in the right-hand column.
4. In the Select Bitmap Image file, select MagnoliaOP.jpg. You see the sample image of the MagnoliaOP.jpg file in the lower right corner.

   This file is the same image as the MagnoliaIM.jpg file, but it has been reduced to black and white. The tree is white and everything else is black.

5. Click Open. Notice what happens to the sample image. Now you see the tree without the black background.

You've just created a material that, when applied to an object, will appear as a tree. At this point, you can apply your material to an object, but before you do that, let's look at a few of the tools on the Material Editor toolbar that can help you work with and understand materials.

1. Click the Material/Map Navigator tool on the Material Editor toolbar.

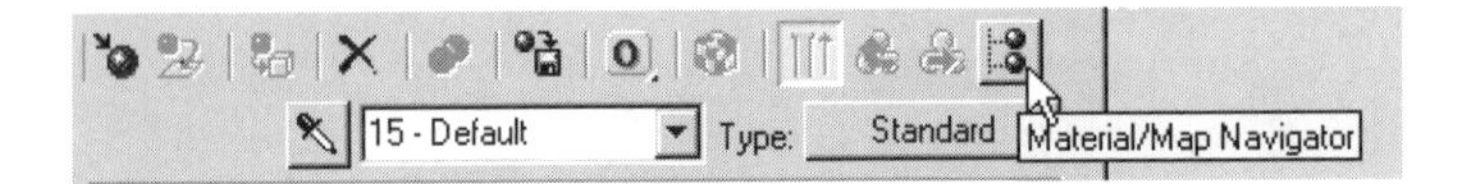

The Material/Map Navigator dialog box displays.

This dialog box gives you a clear picture of the way your new material is organized. You see the name at the top with two branches under it. Each branch is a map that you've added to your material.

2. Click the Diffuse Color listing in the Material/Map Navigator. The parameters in the Material Editor change to those for the selected map.
3. Click the View List + Icons tool in the Material/Map Navigator.

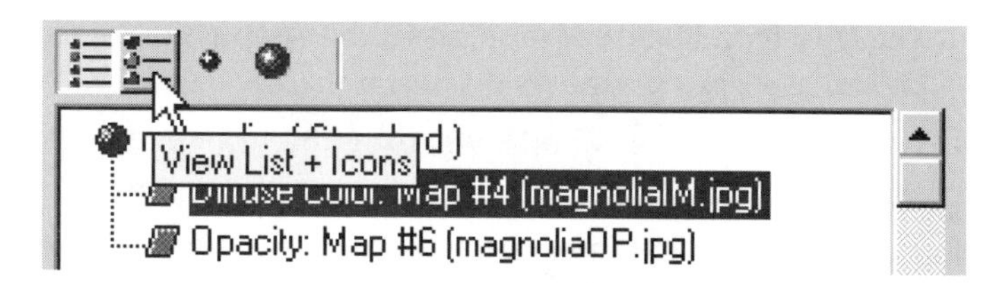

Now you see the actual images used for the maps, plus the resulting material at the top of the list. The arrangement of images shows you the material hierarchy.

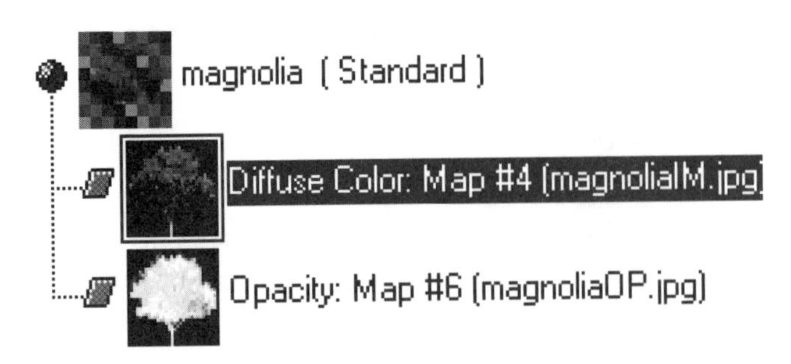

4. Click the Go Forward to Sibling button in the Material Editor dialog box. This moves you to the next material or map at the same level in the material hierarchy.

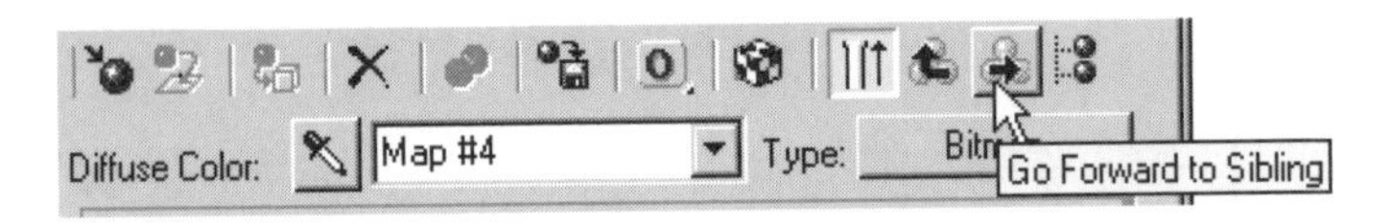

The parameters in the Material Editor dialog box change to the Opacity map parameters, and the Opacity map parameter listing in the Material/Map Navigator is highlighted. The Go Forward to Sibling button lets you advance through the different *child* levels.

5. Click the Show End Result tool on the Material Editor toolbar.

The Opacity map bitmap appears in the sample slot for the Magnolia material. This tool lets you see the results of any change you make to the child parameters.

6. Close the Material/Map Navigator and click the Go to Parent tool on the Material Editor toolbar to go up to the main parameter level.

Now let's add a tree to the model. First, you'll need to create an object for the Magnolia material. This will be a simple, flat, vertical rectangle.

1. Close the Material Editor to get a clear view of your viewports.
2. Click the Top viewport and click the Min/Max toggle tool to enlarge it.
3. Click the Create tab in the Command Panel, then click the Geometry tool.

4. Click Box, then create the box shown in Figure 8.32. Use the Length, Width, and Height parameters options to set the length to 0.1 inch, the Width to 24 feet, and the height to 24 feet. You want the box to be as thin as possible so its edge does not appear in any view.

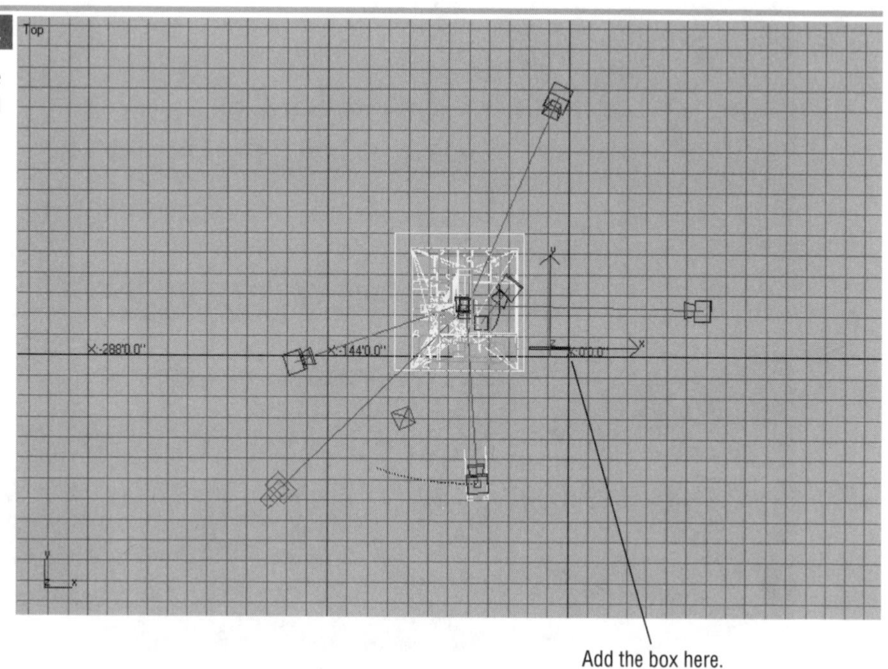

FIGURE 8.32

Placing the box for the tree material

5. Give the box the name **Tree01.**
6. Click the Min/max toggle tool to view all of the viewports.

In step 4, you may also create a Plane object in the Front viewport. To do this, you would select the Geometry button in the Create tab and select Plane, then place the plane in the Front viewport. Since a plane is basically a single face, you need to make sure that its normal is pointing toward the camera; otherwise, the plane object will be invisible. When the normal of a plane object is pointing toward the camera, the plane will appear as a solid surface. The Smooth+Highlight viewport option must also be turned on to see the solid surface. If you use a very thin box as described in the exercise, you can have either side of the box facing the camera. Now you've got an object to which you can apply the Magnolia material.

1. Open the Material Editor dialog box.
2. With the Magnolia material selected, click the Assign Material to Selection tool. The Magnolia material is now assigned to the box you just created.

3. Right click the 3DFRONT camera viewport, then click the Quick Render tool in the Render toolbar. The model is rendered with a tree in the background as shown in Figure 8.33.

FIGURE 8.33

The Villa with the tree added

The scene still looks a bit bare, so go ahead and make a few copies of the tree to give the impression that the building is surrounded by a grove of trees.

1. In the Top viewport, select the tree you just created and make the clones shown in Figure 8.34.

FIGURE 8.34

Making clones of the tree

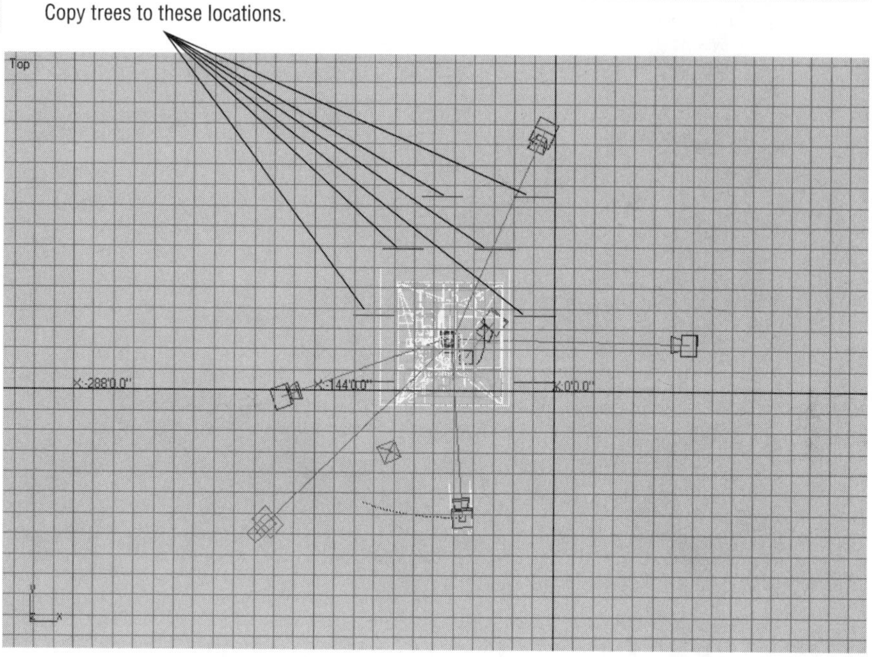

Copy trees to these locations.

2. Render the 3DFRONT camera view again.
3. Save the file to disk.

FIGURE 8.35

The rendered view with more trees

WARNING Objects with Opacity maps, such as the trees you just created, will cast a shadow that matches the Opacity map when you use a Ray Trace shadow. If you use a Shadow Map shadow, objects with Opacity maps will cast a shadow in the shape of the object to which the material is mapped. In the case of the trees, the use of Shadow maps will give you a rectangular shadow instead of a shadow in the shape of the tree. You'll get a closer look at the issue of shadows and trees in Chapter 9.

The trees really help give the rendering a realistic appearance (see Fig. 8.35). You can further enhance the rendering by varying the size of the trees and mirroring them so some of the trees appear as mirror images. This ads a bit more variety and makes it a little less obvious that the trees are identical. Of course, you can create different types of trees in the Material Editor and add them to the scene.

Adding VIZ's Plants

VIZ offers a set of fairly detailed trees and shrubs that can easily be added to any model. To access them, click the Create AEC tab in the Tab Panel, then click the Foliage tool. You may also click the Geometry button in the Create tab of the Command panel. From there select AEC Extended from the drop-down list. You'll see the Foliage button in the Object Type rollout.

You'll see the different types of foliage appear in the Create tab of the Command Panel. You can click the plant you want in the command panel and then click in the viewport to place it. Once the plant has been placed, you can use the transform tools in the standard toolbar to move, rotate or scale the plant. You can also use the Modify tab to alter other foliage parameters such as leaf density, plant height or even the shape of the plant.

NOTE In the previous exercise where you created the tree material in the Material Editor, you used two existing bitmap images for the Texture map and Opacity map. Chapter 14 describes how you can use Adobe PhotoShop to create your own bitmap images for Texture maps and Opacity maps. You can even use PhotoShop to create other textures such as granite, stucco, or marble.

The method we've shown you here for creating and adding trees also works for adding people. Or you can use this method to quickly add text or signage to a model where the proper fonts are not available in Windows. Adobe PhotoShop or another similar program can aid you in creating the texture and opacity maps for people. If you don't want to create your own, there are many third party sources for texture maps and models. Here is a partial list of companies that provide texture maps and models for VIZ.

ArchVision, `www.archsoft.com`

Acuris 3-D Models, `www.acuris.com`

Cyberprops, `www.3dsite.com/3dsite/store/index_cyber.html`

Ketiv Software, `www.ketiv.com`

Viewpoint DataLabs Int'l, `www.viewpoint.com`

In addition to texture maps, these companies also offer prebuilt 3D objects such as furniture, cars, appliances, cabinetry, and animals. If you are in a hurry to build scenes quickly, check out the library of objects offered by these and other companies.

Adjusting an Object to a Bitmap Shape

Sometimes you may find it necessary to match the object's shape to a bitmap's shape. For example, you may create a material that uses bitmap images of people standing. To avoid distorting the shape of the people, you would want to match the object as closely as possible to the bitmap (see Figure 8.36).

FIGURE 8.36

Two renderings with people used as bitmaps. The image to the left has distorted the people.

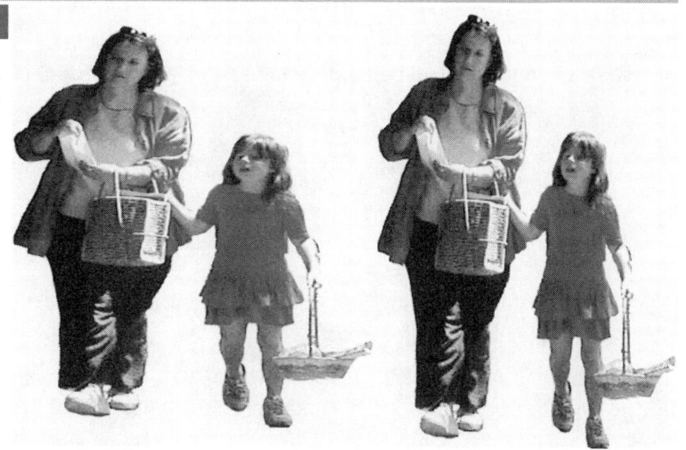

To do this, choose the Bitmap Fit Alignment option under the Parameters rollout of the UVW Mapping Modifier. You'll see a file dialog box similar to the one shown in Figure 8.1.

Locate the bitmap file associated with the material that uses the bitmap. Once the file has been selected, return to the VIZ screen, and the map gizmo will be adjusted to fit the aspect ratio of the selected bitmap.

Once you have the new map gizmo, you can adjust your object to fit as closely as possible to the map gizmo proportions. You may not be able to get an absolutely accurate match, but you can get close. Then, once you've gotten the object to the right proportions, use the UVW Mapping Fit option described in Chapter 7 to align the map exactly to the object.

Removing or Changing a Map

At some point, you may decide that you want to remove or change a map in a material definition. You can remove a map by following these simple steps.

1. Open the Material Editor.
2. In the Maps rollout, click the map button corresponding to the map you want remove.
3. Click the Type button (typically labeled Bitmap) on the Material Editor toolbar.

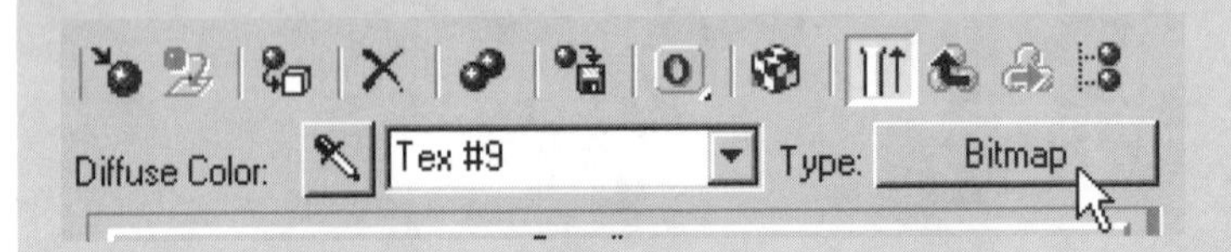

4. In the Material/Map Browser dialog box, click None, and then click OK to close the dialog box.

The map assignment will be removed for the selected map and the map button will show None. The Type button in step 3 can also be used to change a map from one type to another.

Using Bump Maps

Before we move on to the next section, let's take a quick look at bump maps. In Chapter 7, you saw a sample of a bump map in Figure 7.5. It showed how a gray scale image creates the impression of a bumpy surface. Bump maps can also generate other types of surface textures.

In the following exercise, you'll modify the ground material to make the ground appear more like a rolling surface than a flat one.

1. Click the Material Editor tool on the standard toolbar to open the Material Editor.
2. In the Material Editor, click the Ground-Grass sample slot in the middle of the top row.
3. Scroll down the Material parameters to the Maps rollout and open it.
4. Click the Bump Map button.

5. In the Material/Map Browser, make sure that the New radio button is selected in the Browse From group and then click Noise from the list. You'll see a sample of Noise in the upper left corner of the dialog box.

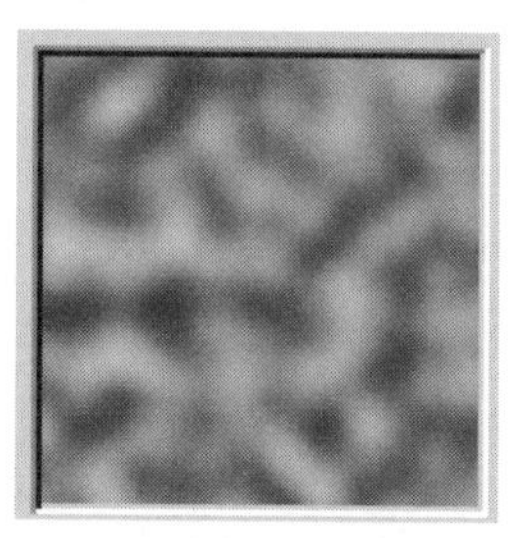

6. With Noise selected, click OK. The parameters for Noise appear in the Material Editor.

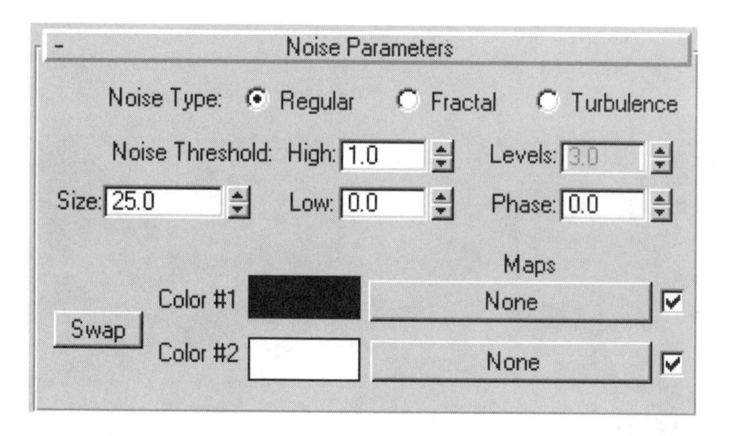

You may recall that a bump map uses varying shades of gray to determine the highs and lows of the bumps on a surface. The Noise material is a procedural map that generates a random pattern of gray tones. As a bump map, Noise will produce a random bumpy surface.

With the Noise map added, let's take a look at the ground as it is rendered.

1. Click the Select Object tool and then click the Ground object.
2. Choose Selected from the Render Type drop-down list on the Render toolbar.

3. Right-click the Camera.View.3DFRONT viewport, then click the Quick Render tool. You see the ground rendered in the Render Viewport.

The ground renders in a bumpy texture that looks more like the sandy surface of a beach. You'll want to spread the bumps over a greater surface to give the impression of a rolling, grassy surface.

1. Open the Material Editor dialog box.
2. In the Noise Parameters rollout, change the Size value to 150. This spreads the noise over a greater area of the surface to which it is applied.
3. Click the Quick Render tool again. This time the ground appears smoother.

Now try another Noise option to give the ground a more random appearance.

4. Go back to the Material Editor, then click the Fractal Noise Type radio button.
5. Open the Render Type drop-down list and choose View to render the entire view.
6. Click the Quick Render tool. You see the entire scene rendered with the ground appearing as an uneven, grassy surface, as shown in Figure 8.37.

FIGURE 8.37

The building rendered with a new texture map and bump map setting

The ground has a more natural appearance, and the Noise bump map reduces the regular tiled appearance of the Grass.jpg bitmap.

Summary

By now you've seen nearly all of VIZ's main set of tools, and with a little experimentation you can start to create some renderings on your own. You've seen how lighting can be controlled in both intensity and shadow and how you can limit the distance or reach of a light source. You've also explored a few of the many material options, such as ambient, bump, and opacity maps—and you have used a bitmap image in a number of ways, from creating a new material to setting a background scene. These are the primary tools you'll be using to create most of your renderings.

In the following chapters, you'll start to look at the ways you can use lighting and materials to achieve the effects you want and to show off your model in the best light.

chapter 9

Staging Your Design

FEATURING

- *Setting Up a New Scheme*
- *Assigning Materials to Parts of an Object*
- *Adding Reflected Light*
- *Setting Up an Interior View*
- *Playing with Light and Shadow*

Chapter 9: Staging Your Design

If you've ever taken a presentation drawing class, then you've probably been shown the importance of carefully observing the subject of your drawing. It's important to be aware of the details of a scene or landscape that might otherwise go unnoticed. By recording those details in your sketches and drawings, you create a sense of depth and realism.

When you create a scene in VIZ, it helps to recall those lessons in observation, even though you aren't creating a scene from real life. If you're creating a rendering of a building with lots of glass, it helps to go out and take a look at buildings and carefully study how glass reflects the surrounding landscape. If you're doing an interior rendering, you may find it helpful to find a room that is similar to the one you are rendering and carefully examine how the light is reflected throughout the room from various sources. By understanding the behavior of materials and light in the real world, you are better equipped to create realistic scenes in VIZ.

In this chapter, you'll take a look at what I call *staging*. Staging is the process of setting up lights and shadows to simulate the real world. While VIZ offers many tools to create lights, it doesn't necessarily simulate light accurately. Staging is a method of manipulating VIZ lights and shadows to recreate the way lights and shadows appear in the real world. One way to approach staging is to think of VIZ as an artist's palette, but instead of creating a painting with oil paints or water color, you are using lighting, shadows, and materials.

As part of your exploration of staging, you'll also look at methods for adding multiple materials to a single VIZ object. So far, you've been assigning materials to entire objects, but you can apply different materials to individual surfaces of an object. This is especially useful when you are using imported AutoCAD models that have not been set up for VIZ.

Setting Up a New Scene

We've been focusing on an exterior view of the model. Now it's time to see how we can create a more intimate view of the building. In this first section, you'll set up a camera and light to get a view of the second floor courtyard and interior room. In the process you'll have a chance to see how lighting can be used to add a sense of realism to a scene. Start by arranging a camera to view the interior space of the Villa model you've been working on.

1. Open the `Savoye9.max` file from the companion CD.
2. In the Camera.View.3DFRONT viewport, right-click the label and select View ➢ Mycamera. The courtyard view displays.
3. Right-click the Top viewport, then use the region zoom tool to enlarge the courtyard area so it looks similar to Figure 9.1.
4. Click the Select and move tool and click the camera in the upper right corner of the courtyard (see Figure 9.1). This is the Mycamera camera you created in an earlier chapter.

FIGURE 9.1

Top view of the courtyard

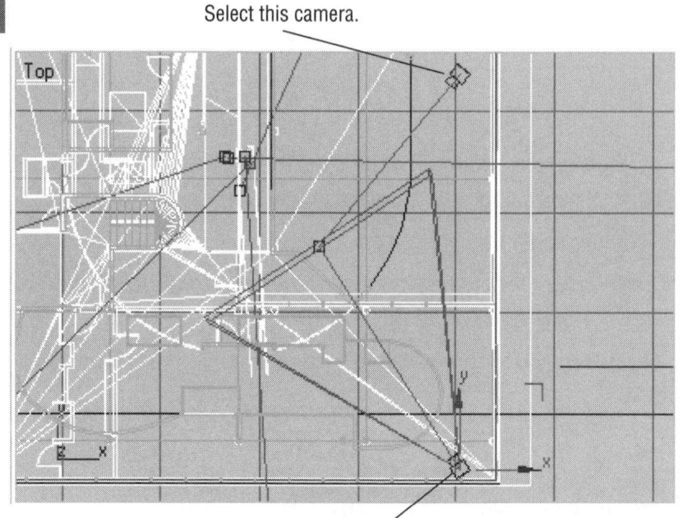
Select this camera.
Top
Move it to this location.

5. Move the camera to the location shown in Figure 9.1 in the interior of the villa. The Mycamera viewport will change to show the new camera view as shown in Figure 9.2.

FIGURE 9.2

The Mycamera viewport view after moving the camera

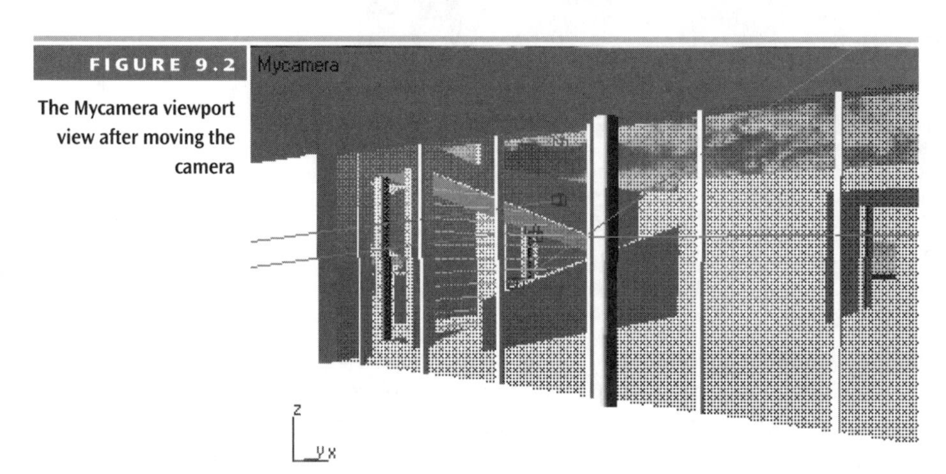
Mycamera

6. In the Parameters rollout of the Modify tab, adjust the Lens setting to 30 mm. This changes the field of view of the camera to include a bit more of the scene.

NOTE The lens setting and the FOV settings are inversely proportional.

You've got the camera situated in the interior of the building looking out toward the courtyard. Let's take a look at how this view renders.

1. Right-click with in the Mycamera viewport to make it active.
2. Click the Render tool, then in the Render Design dialog box, make sure the Save File is not checked in the Render Output group.
3. Click Render. The viewport will render and you'll see a scene similar to Figure 9.3.

FIGURE 9.3

The view from the interior rendered

The image is a bit cartoon-like. You can't really see any detail in the interior, and the courtyard itself is washed out and lifeless. To give the space a little more definition, you can add a material to the floor. The floor is actually part of an object that defines the floors, walls, and ceilings of the building. If you were to apply a material to the object that includes the floor, the entire building would appear as that material.

Assigning Materials to Parts of an Object

As you work with imported AutoCAD files in VIZ, you'll almost certainly find yourself faced with the situation where you want to add a material to a single surface of an object. This is the situation with the second floor of the villa. You could enter the sub-object level of the second floor of the villa to detach the floor surface, then treat the floor as a separate object. This works fine for some situations, but once the floor is detached from the rest of the second floor, any transformations you perform to the second floor mesh will not be synchronized with the floor pattern.

To maintain the connection of the second floor surface with the rest of the second floor object and add a separate material to the floor surface, you'll need to use another method of applying materials. A type of material called a Multi/Sub-Object material allows you to apply multiple materials to a single object. In the Villa example, you can use a Multi/Sub-Object material to apply a floor material to the second floor surface without affecting the walls and ceilings to which the floor is attached.

Opening a Group

When VIZ imports an AutoCAD file, it combines objects on AutoCAD layers into what are called *Groups*. A group is like a collection of objects that have been bound together to act like a single object. When you select a group, all of the objects in the group act like one object. You can temporally open a group to edit individual objects, or you can permanently break up the group.

NOTE **Groups are just like AutoCAD's concept of Groups and are a little like blocks.**

Before you can start to work on the second floor object to add a material, you'll need to gain access by opening the group to which the second floor object belongs. The following exercise will step you through the process.

1. Click the Select Objects tool on the standard toolbar.
2. In the Select Objects dialog box, click [INT-WALLS.06] and then click Select. The items in the dialog box that are shown in brackets are actually groups of objects.
3. Choose Modify ➢ Group ➢ Open.

NOTE To close a group, select a member of the group, then choose Modify ➢ Group ➢ Close.

With the group open, you now have access to the individual objects within the group. The next step is to select the second floor object so you can start to work with its material assignment.

1. Right-click within the Left viewport, then use the Region Zoom tool and zoom into the area shown in Figure 9.4. You want to see as much of the building as possible.
2. Click the Min/Max viewport toggle to enlarge the Left viewport. Your view should look similar to Figure 9.4.
3. Click the Select object tool, then select the building at the second floor level at the point shown in Figure 9.4.

Click here to select the building.

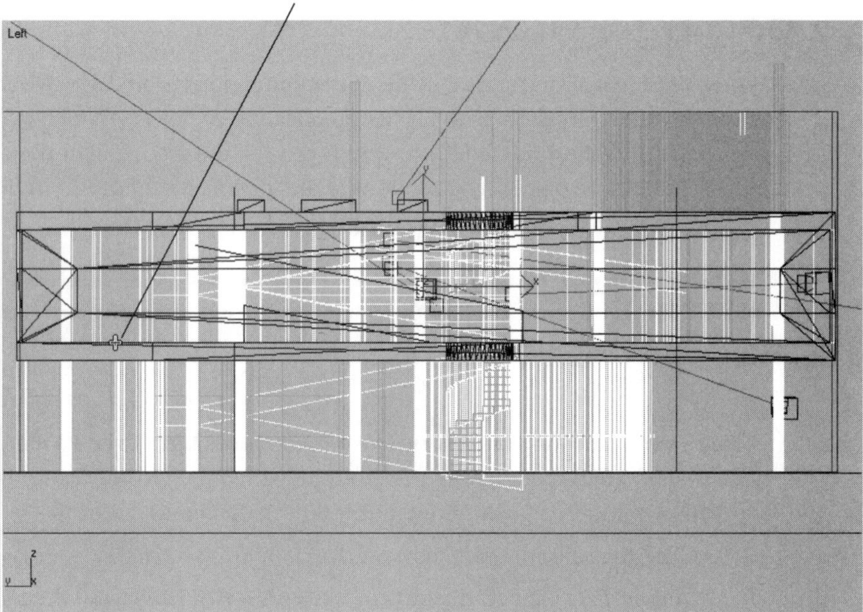
Left

FIGURE 9.4

Select the building by clicking at the point shown here.

You should see the name INT-WALLS.05 for the object name in the command panel. If you don't see this object selected then use the select by name tool and select INT-WALLS.05. Now you're ready to start working with Multi/Sub-Object materials.

Creating a Multi/Sub-Object Material

A Multi/Sub-Object material is like a group of materials collected under one material definition. Each material in this group is assigned a number to identify it within the collection of materials. It's easiest to understand when you've worked with it first hand, so let's get started.

You'll start by acquiring the material that is assigned to the INT-WALLS.05 object.

1. Click the Material Editor tool on the standard toolbar to open the Material Editor dialog box.
2. Use the scroll bar to the right of the sample slots to scroll down to a row of free slots below the ones that are currently occupied.
3. Click a slot containing an unused, default material.
4. Click the Get Material button on the Material Editor toolbar.

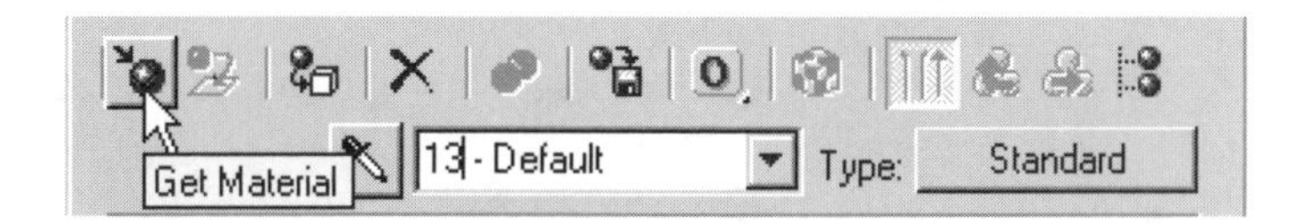

5. In the Material/Map browser, click the Selected radio button in the Browse From group. You'll see the material that is assigned to the INT-WALLS.05 object in the list box.
6. Double-click the material in the list box, then close the Material/Map Browser.

The Wall material now appears in the selected sample slot. This is the material you assigned to the walls of the villa earlier in the book. For this exercise, you'll create a new Multiple/Sub-Object material using the existing Wall material as a starting point.

The next step is to change the material from a standard one to a Multi/Sub-Object type material.

1. Enter the name **Wall Second Floor** in the material name input box. This assigns a new name to the material in the active slot.

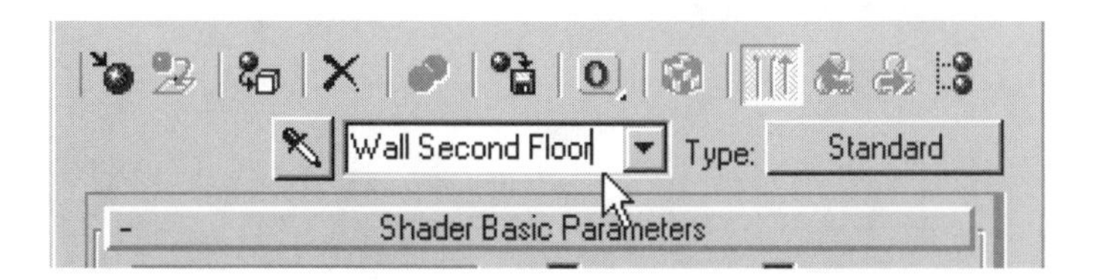

2. Click the Type button labeled Standard.

3. At the Material/Map browser, make sure that the New radio button in the Browse From group is selected, then select Multi/Sub-Object from the list box and click OK.

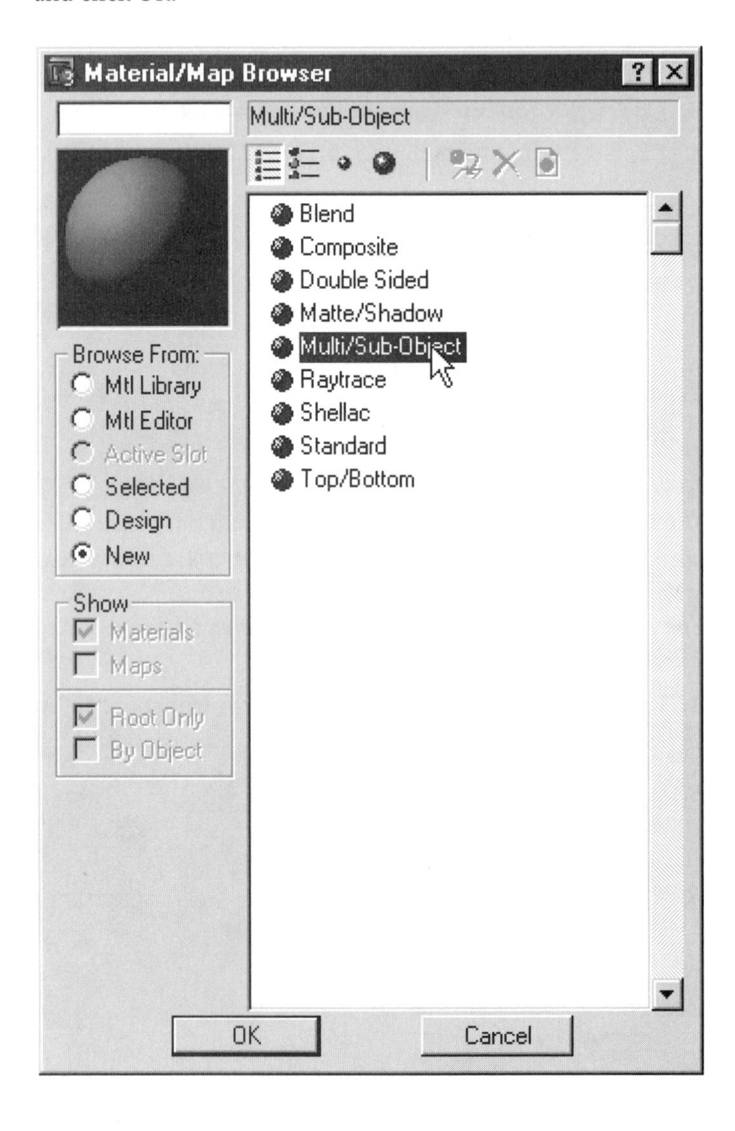

4. You see the Replace Material warning appear.

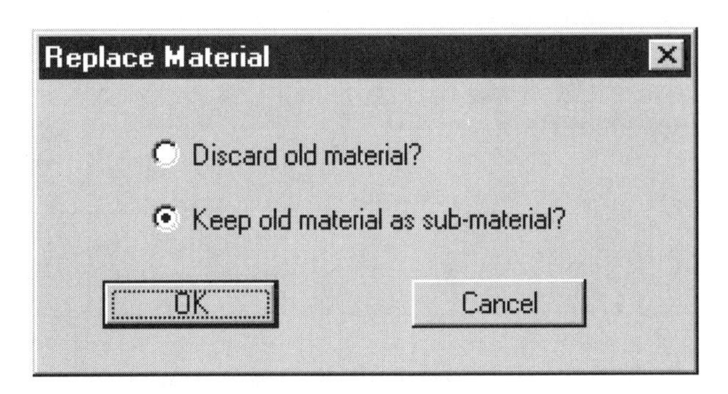

5. Make sure the Keep old material as sub-material? option is selected, then click OK. You return to the Material Editor with the Multi/Sub-Object Basic Parameters rollout.

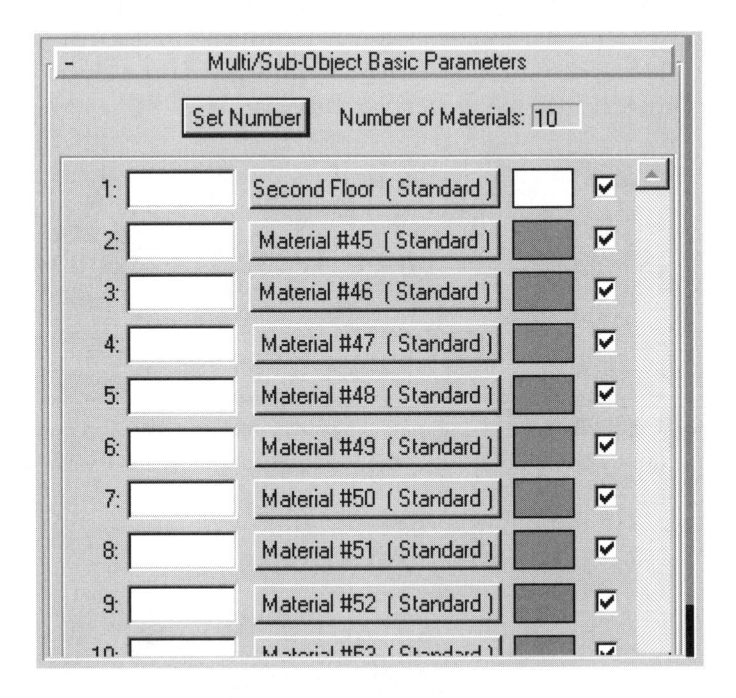

As you can see from the Material Editor, the Multi/Sub-Object material offers several listings for additional materials. Each material is a sub-material of the main, parent material. In this exercise you only need two sub-materials, so go ahead and reduce the number of available listings to 2.

1. Click the Set Number button in the Multi/Sub-Object Basic Parameters.
2. In the Set Number of Materials dialog box, enter **2** and click OK.

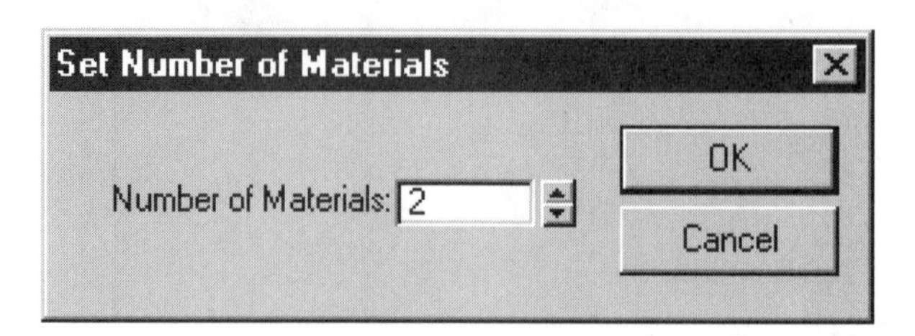

When you return to the Material Editor, you see only two sub-material listings. The existing wall material is number 1 and a yet undefined material is number 2. Now let's add the material that will become the floor surface of the second floor.

1. Click Material button in the number 2 position in the Multi/Sub-Object Basic Parameters rollout. The Material Editor dialog changes to show the parameters for a standard material. It may be difficult to tell that you're working with a Multi/Sub-Object material from the looks of the dialog box, but one clue is the Go to Parent tool that is on the toolbar.

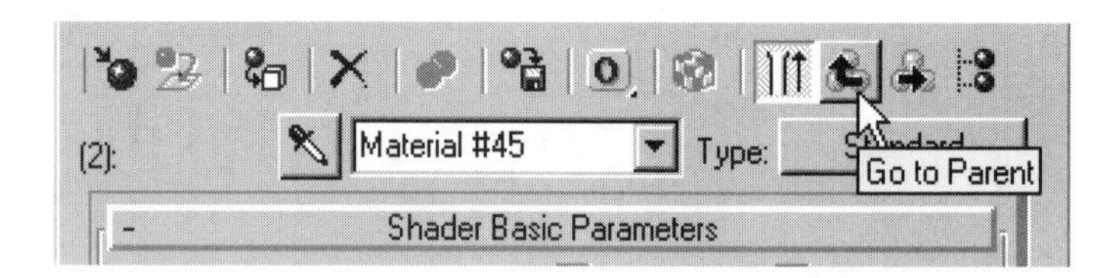

NOTE **While the rest of the dialog may look like a standard material, the presence of the GO to Parent tool tells you that you are really in a child level of a multilevel material definition.**

2. Click the Type button that's labeled Standard.

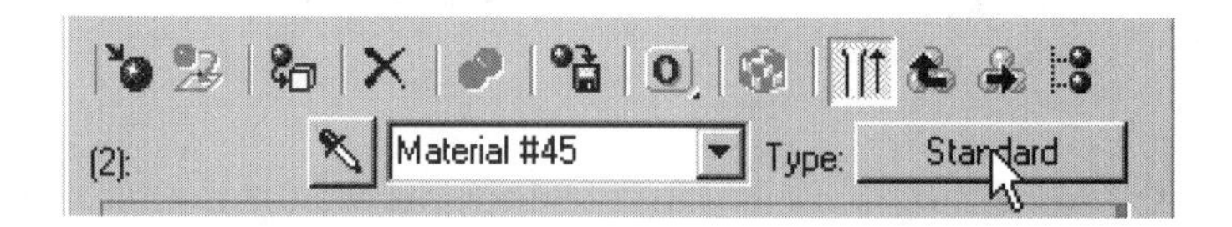

3. In the Material/Map Browser, click the Mtl Library radio button in the Browse From group, then scroll down the list. Select Stone-Granite Tiles (Standard).

4. Click OK to return to the Material Editor.
5. Back in the Material Editor dialog box, click the Go to Parent tool on the toolbar.
6. Click the Assign Material to Selection tool to assign the new Multi/Sub-Object material to the second floor object.

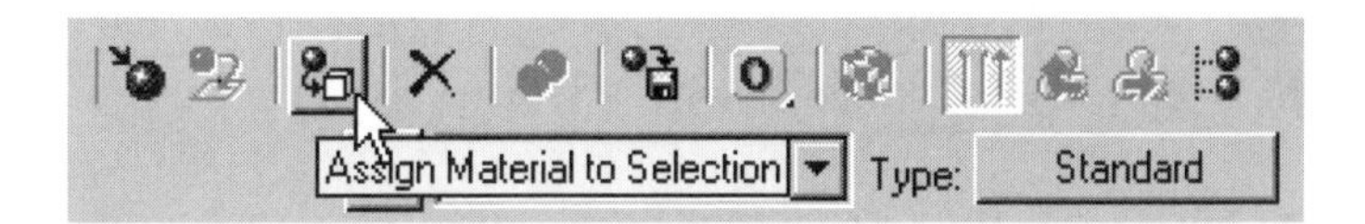

The new material is now applied to the second floor object, though nothing appears to have changed. Since the Wall sub-material is the same as the old Wall material originally assigned to the second floor, the villa hasn't really changed. You need to take a few more steps before the Stone-Granite Tiles sub-material will appear on the floor of the villa.

Applying a Sub-Material to an Object's Surface

When you import objects from AutoCAD, 3D Solids are converted into editable meshes. The second floor object of the villa, named INT-WALLS.05, was created from 3D Solids in AutoCAD, so in VIZ it is an editable mesh. To apply a sub-material to the face of an editable mesh, you'll need to isolate the faces to which the sub-material is to be applied.

1. Click the Modify tab on the Command Panel.
2. Click the Polygon tool in the Selection rollout.

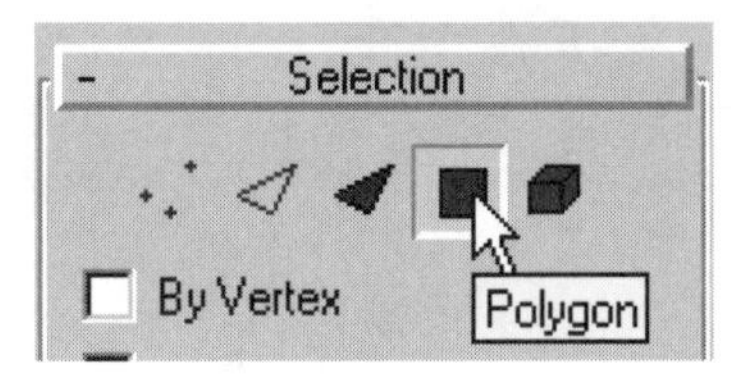

3. Click the Crossing Selection tool at the bottom of the VIZ window so that it changes to the Window Selection tool. You only want to select faces that are completely within a selection window.

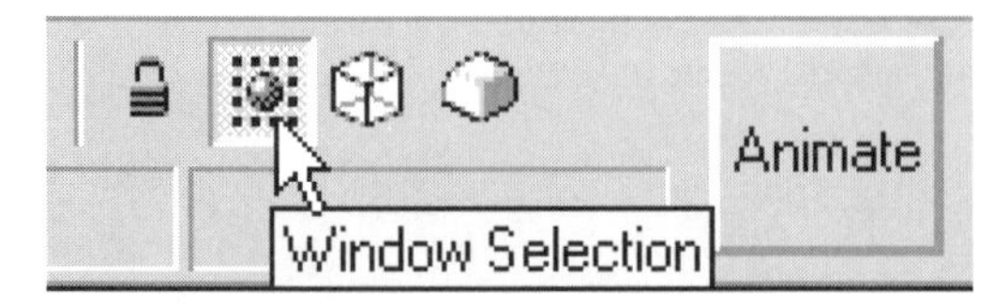

4. Click the Select object tool on the standard toolbar, then carefully place a rectangular region around the top surface of the second floor as shown in Figure 9.5.

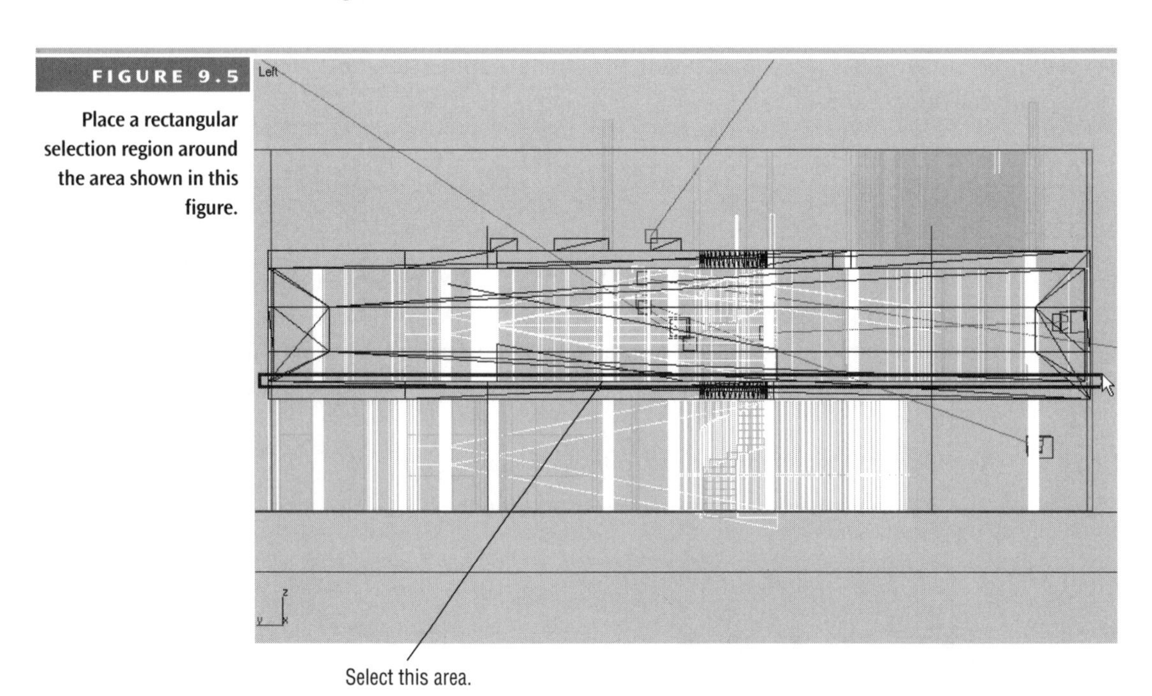

FIGURE 9.5

Place a rectangular selection region around the area shown in this figure.

You now have the floor surface of the second floor object selected. The next step is to assign the number 2 sub-material to this selected surface.

1. Scroll down the Modify tab to the Surface Properties rollout.
2. In the Material group, change the ID value to 2. Remember that the Granite Tile sub-material is the number 2 material in the Multi/Sub-Object Basic Parameters rollout, so by entering **2** for the Material ID, you are assigning the Granite Tile sub-material to the selected surface.

NOTE **An alternate method for assigning a sub-material to an object is to use the Material Modifier. This modifier offers a single parameter which is the Material ID number.**

There are a few more steps you need to take to complete the floor material assignment. Since the Granite Tile sub-material uses maps, you'll need to apply a UVW Map modifier to the second floor object.

1. Scroll up to the top of the Command Panel, then click the Sub-Object button to turn it off and return to the object level.
2. In the Modify tab of the Command Panel, click the UVW Map button.

By default, a planar UVW map is applied to the second floor object, and it is adjusted to fit the outline of the object. Since the outline is not an exact square, you'll want to adjust the UVW map proportions to a square so that the Granite Tile material map won't be distorted.

1. Scroll down the Modify tab to the UVW Mapping Parameters rollout.
2. Change the Length and Width Parameters to 60 feet each. This will place a single instance of the tile pattern on a 60-foot square area. Since the Granite Tile map is a 4 by 4 tile pattern, this will place a single 4 by 4 tile array on the entire floor area of the villa. If you render the Mycamera viewport now, you'll see that the floor contains a very large tile.

Since a single 4 by 4 array of tiles is currently spread over a 60-foot by 60-foot area, you can calculate that a single tile is exactly 15 square feet (60 feet divided by four).

To get the tiles down to a reasonable size, you can adjust the U Tile and V Tile settings in the UVW Mapping Parameters to a value that increases the number of tiles within the 60-foot square area. If you want the tiles to be 1 foot square, for example, you would set the U Tile and V Tile settings to 15.

1. Go ahead and change the U and V Tile settings in the UVW Mapping Parameters rollout to **15.**
2. Click the Min/Max viewport toggle tool to view all four viewports.
3. Right-click the Mycamera viewport, then click the Quick Render tool on the Render toolbar. Your rendering will look similar to Figure 9.6

FIGURE 9.6

The interior view thus far

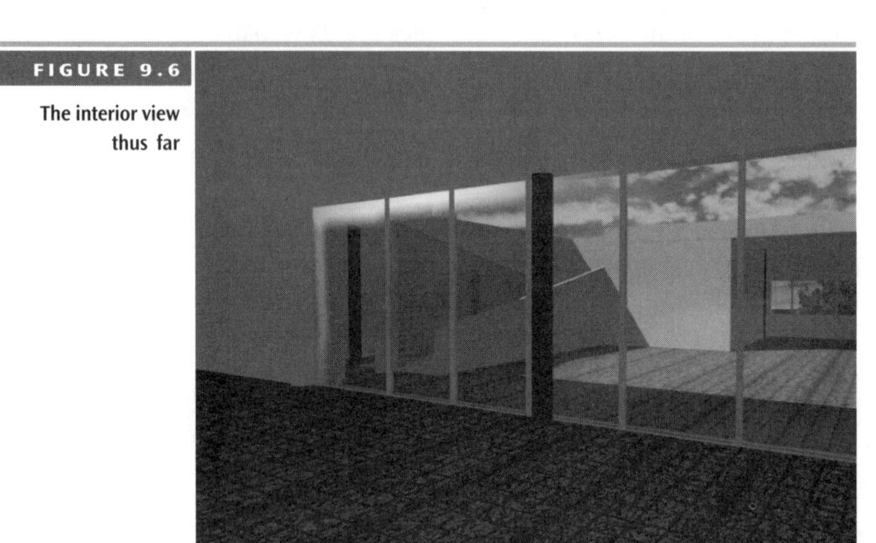

In these last few exercises, you can see how you can control the exact size of the granite tiles through the use of the UVW Map parameters. This is an important feature of VIZ so let's take a moment to review what happened. First, you applied the UVW Mapping to the second floor object. You then set the mapping to an exact value of 60 square feet. Once the exact dimension of the map is established, you can determine the size of the individual tiles of the granite tile by correlating the U and V Tile setting to the size of the UVW Mapping dimension. The default value of 1 for the U and V Tile setting means that one copy of the map is placed within the UVW Mapping Area. By changing the U and V Tile values to 15, you've created a 15 by 15 array of the Granite Tile map.

Using Multiple UVW Maps on a Single Object

If you're able to apply multiple materials to a single object, then you may begin to wonder if you can apply multiple UVW Maps to an object as well. After all, different surfaces may require different UVW Mapping settings. You can indeed apply multiple UVW Mapping modifiers to a single object. You can then correlate the different UVW Mapping modifiers to individual sub-materials through Map Channels. You can think of a Map Channel as a number that links a sub-material to a UVW Map modifier. The concept is simple, but the execution is a bit obscure. Here are the steps that you take to link a sub-material to a UVW Map.

The following list of steps is not part of the main exercise of this book and is here only to explain the process for linking multiple UVW Maps to multiple material maps.

1. Open the Material Editor, then select the Multi/Sub-Object material you want to work with. For this example, let's assume you are using the Wall Second Floor material.
2. Click the sub-material button from the listing in the Multi/Sub-Object Basic Parameters. For the Wall Second Floor material, click the Granite Tiles button.
3. Go to the Maps rollout and click the Map button for any active map.
4. In the Coordinates rollout, set the Map Channel to 2.

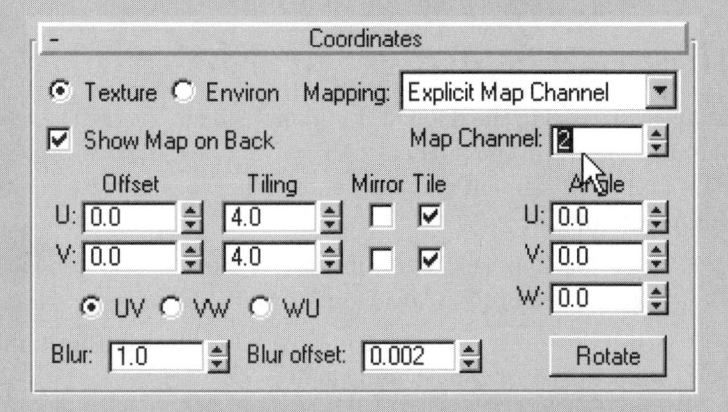

5. Click the GO to Parent tool in the Material Editor toolbar, then repeat steps 3 and 4 for the next active map button.
6. Set the Map Channel value for each map in the material.

Once you've assigned a map channel to the maps in a material, you can then assign a UVW Mapping modifier to the channel you assigned to the material.

Continued on the next page

1. Select the object to which the sub-material has been assigned. In our Villa example, you would select the INT-WALLS.05 object.
2. Add the UVW Mapping modifier, then scroll down the UVW Mapping Parameters to the Channel group.
3. Enter 2 in the Map Channel input box.

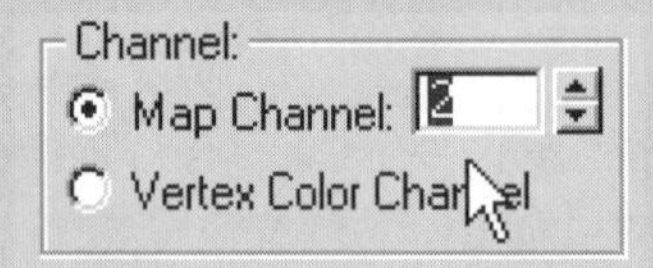

Map Channel 2 then links the current UVW Mapping modifier to the Granite Tile maps that have been assigned to Map Channel 2.

4. Adjust the other UVW Mapping Parameters according to your needs.

You can have as many as 99 map channels in a design, though chances are you will probably use only two or three in a project. You may have also guessed that you can use a different channel for each different map of a material. In the example given here, the same map channel is applied to all of the maps of the material. You can, however, apply a different UVW Mapping to the bump map or the diffuse map, thereby creating a different surface effect.

Editing the Granite Tile Material

Adding a material to the floor adds a bit more life to the scene. Now suppose you want to make the floor material look more like a red tile instead of granite. You can make a quick adjustment in the Materials Editor to gain some color and downplay the granite pattern a bit.

1. Open the Materials Editor; then, with the Wall Second Floor material selected, click the Granite Tiles listing in the Multi/Sub-Object Basic Parameters.
2. Scroll down the Material Editor panel to the Maps rollout, then change the Diffuse Color Amount setting to **50**.
3. Scroll back up to the top of the Material Editor and click the Diffuse color swatch in the Phong Basic Parameters.
4. In the Color Selector dialog box, change the Hue value to **16**, the Saturation (Sat) value to **210**, and the Value to **170**.
5. Back in the Material Editor, click and drag the Diffuse color swatch into the Ambient color swatch, then in the Copy or Swap Colors dialog box, click Copy.

Notice that the Color Selector dialog box now shows the color for the Ambient Color setting.

6. In the Color Selector, change the Value setting to **70**.
7. Go ahead and close the Color Selector.
8. Click the Go to Parent tool on the Material Editor toolbar to return to the Parent level of the Wall Second Floor material.

While you're in the Material Editor, let's make an adjustment to the glass material. In an earlier chapter, you set the glass to have a transparency value of 30. Since you are looking through the glass into the courtyard in this scene, you'll want the glass to be a bit more transparent.

1. In the Material Editor, scroll up to the top of the sample slots, then select the Glass-Clear-Dark material in the upper-left corner of the dialog box.
2. Set the Opacity value in the Phong Basic Parameters to **15**.
3. Click the Quick Render tool on the Render toolbar to see the effects of your material changes. The floor now appears redder with a bit less of a granite pattern (see Figure 9.7).

FIGURE 9.7

A rendered view with changes to the Stone Granite tile material and the glass

While the actual Villa Savoye did not use a red tile on the second floor, you'll use a red tile here to demonstrate some of the ways you can use Omni lights to simulate reflected light.

Adding Reflected Light

The floor pattern helps to define the floor and enhances the appearance of the model. But the courtyard still looks flat and cartoon-like. In real life, the light reflected from the floor would bounce off of the courtyard walls. While VIZ doesn't simulate light this way, you can add some lighting of your own to aid in the simulation.

In the next exercise, you'll add some Omni lights and adjust their color setting to create your own bounced light from the courtyard floor. First turn off the original Omni light you created for the highlight in the glass in Chapter 8.

1. Click the Select by Name tool.
2. In the Select Object dialog box, click Omni01, then click Select.
3. In the Modify Tab, click the On check box in the General Parameters rollout to remove the check and turn off the light.

Now you're ready to add some new lights.

1. Mimimize all of the dialog boxes that may be hiding the VIZ viewports.
2. Right-click the Top viewport to make it active.
3. Click the Min/Max viewport tool to enlarge the Top viewport.
4. Click the Create tab in the Command Panel, then click the Lights tool.
5. Click the Omni button, then click the location shown in Figure 9.8 to place an Omni light in the courtyard.
6. Give this new Omni light the name "Omni-court".

FIGURE 9.8

Placing an Omni light in the courtyard

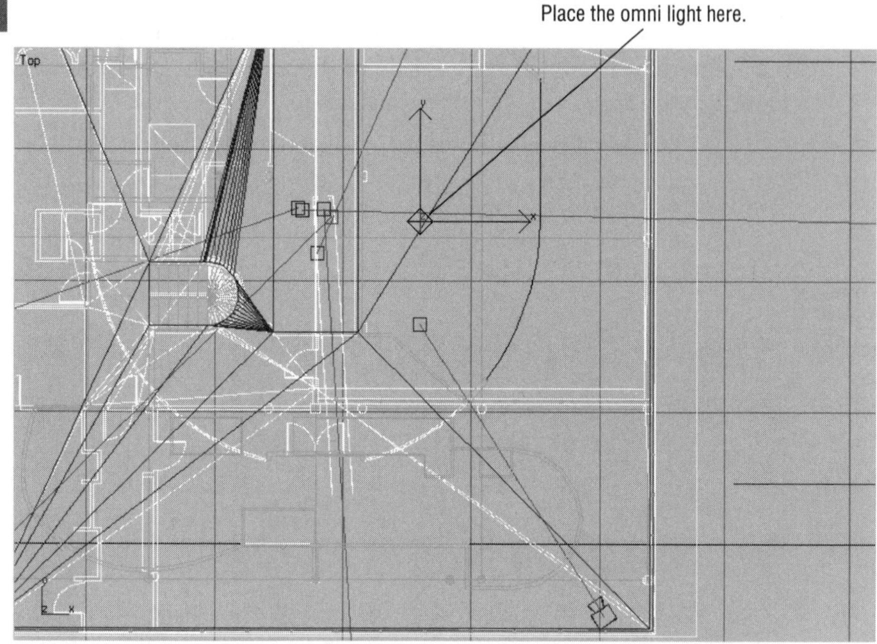
Place the omni light here.
Top

The Omni light is at 0 elevation. You'll want to raise it to a location that is just above the second floor surface in order to simulate the light bouncing off of that surface.

1. With the Omni-court light selected, click the Select and Move tool on the standard toolbar, then right-click the Select and Move tool.
2. In the Transform dialog box, change the Absolute: World Z value to 12 feet, 6 inches (or **12′6″**). This will raise the Omni light from the ground level to a level just above the floor of the courtyard.
3. Close the Transform dialog box.

Since the light bouncing off of the courtyard floor represents a broad area, in the real world it would throw off a very diffuse light. The Omni light, on the other hand, is a point source. You'll want to spread the bounced light source around a bit to give a more diffuse appearance. To do this, make a few clones of the Omni light.

1. With the Select and Move tool still active, shift-click the X axis of the Omni light's transform gizmo and make a clone just to the right of the current Omni light's position (see Figure 9.9).

FIGURE 9.9

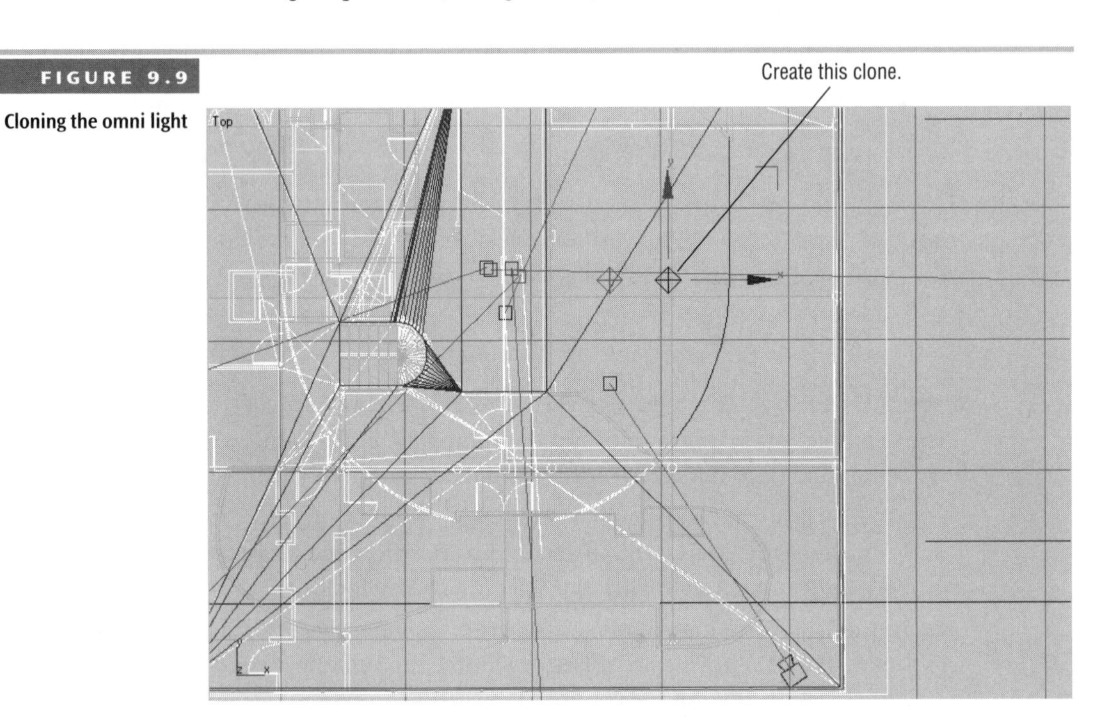

Cloning the omni light

2. In the Clone Options dialog box, click Instance. You'll see the importance of making the clone an Instance clone in the next few exercises.

3. Click OK to close the Clone Options dialog box.
4. Make two more Instance clones as shown in Figure 9.10.

FIGURE 9.10

Adding more Omni light clones

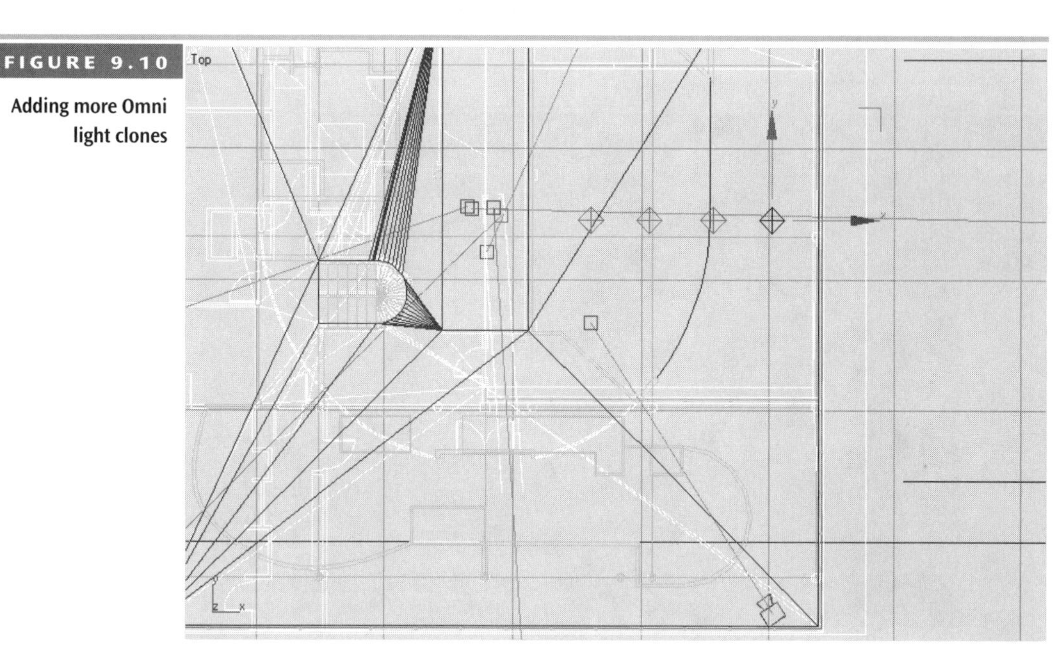

With the lights in place, you can make a few adjustments to them to simulate the bounced light from the floor. First of all, you'll want to reduce the intensity of the light. Right now, the Omni lights are at full intensity. You can adjust the intensity of all four of the lights simultaneously by adjusting any one of the clones. This is because you created Instance clones. Just as with primitive objects, lights can be instanced so that the edits made to one clone are simultaneously made to all the other clones.

1. Select one of the courtyard Omni lights, then click the Modify tab in the Command Panel.
2. Go to the General Parameters, then set the Multiplier spinner to **0.14**.
3. Click the color swatch in the General Parameters to open the Color Selector: Light Color dialog box.
4. Set the Hue to **20** and the Saturation to **60**, then close the dialog box. This will give the light a slight reddish cast, as if it were picking up the color of the floor.

5. Click the Min/Max Viewport toggle tool, then right-click the Mycamera viewport to make it active.
6. Click the Quick Render to get a view of your model so far. Your view will be similar to Figure 9.11.

FIGURE 9.11

A rendered view of the courtyard after adding the simulated bounced light

Now you begin to see more detail in the courtyard. The area around the ramps is better defined, and the alcove to the right shows more depth. You see the ceiling of the room in the foreground begining to appear. You also begin to see some shadows from the Omni lights, which are somewhat distracting. While the bounced light will cast some soft shadows, the ones that appear in the view are a bit too strong. The next step is to soften the shadows.

1. Select one of the courtyard Omni lights.
2. In the Modify tab of the Command Panel, scroll down to the Shadow Map Params rollout and click to open it.
3. Change the size setting to **256** and the Sample Range to **36**. Also set the Bias to **0.2**.

You may recall that reducing the Shadow Map Size setting reduces the amount of memory required when rendering the view, whereas the Sample Range setting softens the edges of a shadow. Since you have several lights casting shadows, you don't want them to use too much memory for shadow maps.

There is one more setting you need to make for the bounced light. You don't want the light to be affected by the glass in the foreground. Remember that when you use a shadow map, glass essentially becomes an opaque surface as far as the shadow is concerned. For this reason, you want the omni lights to ignore any glass in the model. Using the Exclude button in the General Parameters for the light in question, you can control the objects that are affected by a light source.

1. Make sure that a courtyard omni light is still selected, then in the Command Panel, click the Exclude button in the General Parameters rollout.
2. In the Exclude/Include dialog box, select GLASS.03.
3. Click the right-pointing arrow button between the two lists in the dialog box.

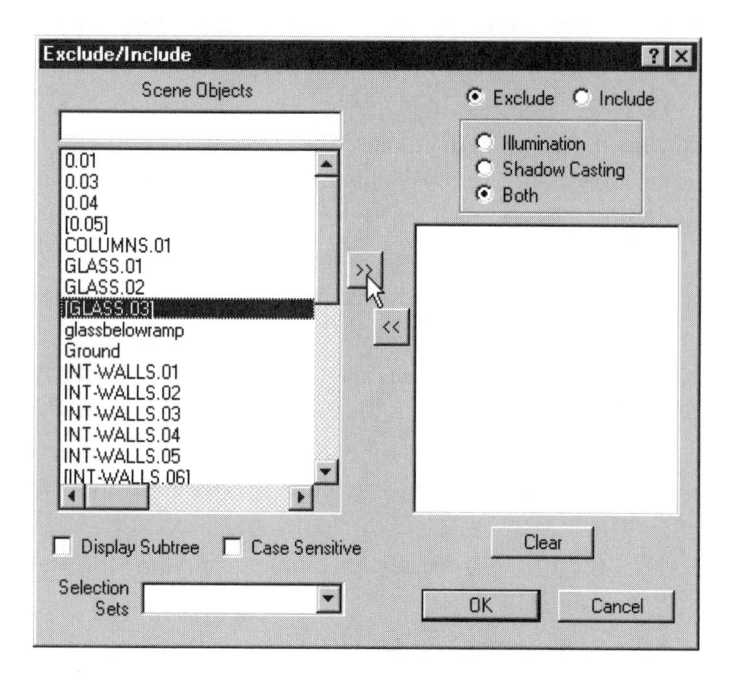

4. Click OK.
5. Click the Quick Render tool to get another look at your scene.

Now the ramp area shows the detail without the odd looking shadows. The walls show a hint of red from the bounced Omni lights. Here you see how you can use an Omni light with a low-resolution shadow map to help bring out some detail in the model.

Adding a Reflective Surface

Another courtyard element that can use some attention is the glass in the ramp area. Right now the glass appears totally transparent, but in real life the glass would reflect the scene around it. To produce such an effect on the glass, you can use what is called a Ray Traced map. A Ray Traced map is a procedural map that produces an accurate reflection based a on combination of the camera position and the reflective surface.

In the following exercise, you'll create a new glass material with a Ray Traced reflective map, then apply the new glass material to the ramp windows.

1. Open the Material Editor, then click the Sample slot next to the Stone-Granite Tiles slot.
2. Click the Get Material tool on the Material Editor toolbar, then click Design in the Browse From group. You'll use the glass material from the current design as a starting point for your new glass material.
3. In the list box, double-click Glass-Clear-Dark.
4. Back in the Material Editor, change the name of the glass material to Glass-Clear-Dark-Reflective.

Now you have a new material called Glass-Clear-Dark-Reflective that is a copy of the original glass material. You'll use this new material for the glass around the ramp.

1. Scroll down to the Maps rollout, then click the button labeled Tex #8(Sky.jpg). The panel jumps down a level in the material hiearchy to the settings for the bitmap.
2. Click the Type button labeled Bitmap just below the Material Editor toolbar.

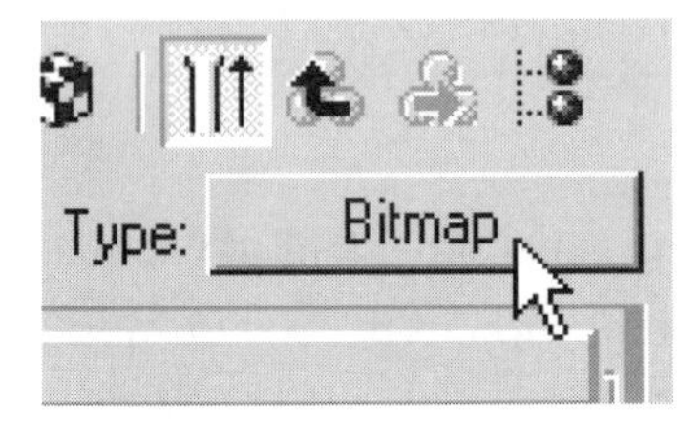

The Material/Map Browser displays.

3. Select Raytrace from the list, then click OK.
4. The Replace Map dialog box displays. Click the Discard old Map radio button, then click OK. The Ray Traced parameters replace those of the `Sky.jpg` bitmap parameters.
5. Go back up to the Material Maps level by clicking on the Go to Parent tool on the Material Editor toolbar.

6. Change the amount value of the Reflection map to **15**. This will reduce the strength of the reflection; otherwise the glass will look more like a mirror than a piece of glass.

You've now got a Ray Traced reflection map assigned to your new glass material. The next step is to add it to the glass.

1. Close the Material Editor and the Material Map Browser, then click the Select by Name tool.
2. In the Select Objects dialog box, select Rampglass and Glassbelowramp, then click the Select button.
3. Open the Material Editor again, and with the Glass-Clear-Dark-Reflect material selected, click the Assign Material to Selection button.
4. Close the Material Editor again, then click the Quick Render button. This time, as the view is rendered, you'll see a brief message just before the render scan line reaches the ramp glass telling you that the Ray Traced material is being set up. The finished rendering will show a reflection of the courtyard from the ramp glass as shown in Figure 9.12. You'll also notice that the rendering takes a bit longer to complete.

FIGURE 9.12

Rendered view with reflective map on glass

Now the courtyard is really beginning to look a bit more realistic. The simulated bounced light reveals some of the detail in the ramp and alcove areas, and the reflective glass adds to the sense of realism.

In the next section, you'll take a look at how the tools you've learned about so far can help improve the interior view of the villa.

Setting Up an Interior View

You've seen that you can dramatically influence the appearance of a scene by making a few adjustments to lighting and materials. In the beginning of this chapter, you went from a fairly flat, cartoon-like scene to one that is fairly realistic.

Now let's focus our attention on the interior space. In this section, you'll again add some bounced lighting to see how it influences the appearance of the interior. First, set up the camera to view more of the interior and less of the courtyard.

1. Right-click the Top viewport and click the Min/Max Viewport toggle to enlarge it.
2. Adjust the view so you can get a good look at the room toward the bottom of the viewport as shown in Figure 9.13.
3. Click the Select and Move tool; then click the Mycamera camera in the lower right corner of the building to select it (see Figure 9.13).
4. Shift-click and drag the camera to the location shown in Figure 9.13.

FIGURE 9.13

Moving the Mycamera camera

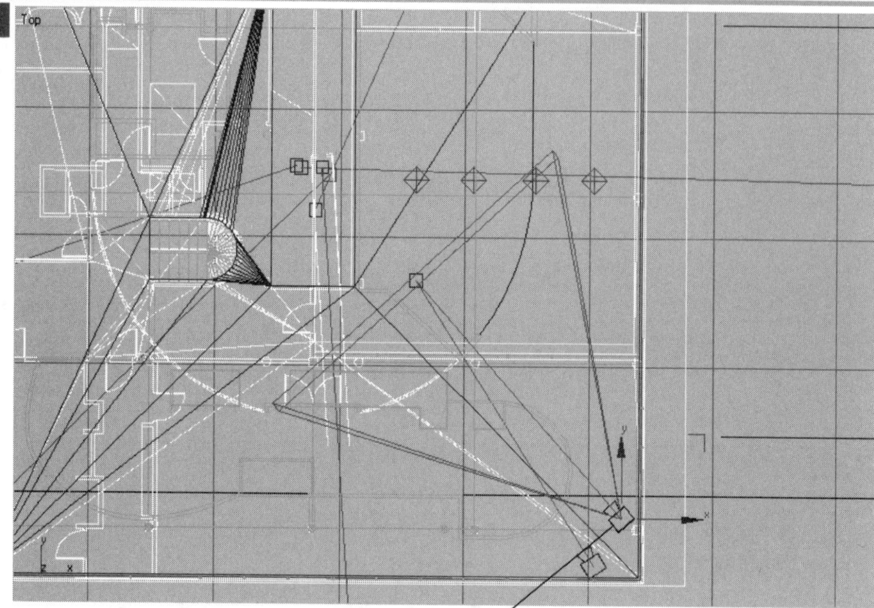

5. In the Clone Options dialog box, make sure the Copy radio button is selected, then click OK. Note that the name of the new camera is Mycamera01.

You've now got a new camera for your interior view. Next, rotate the camera so that you are looking down the room instead of out the window.

1. Click the Min/Max Viewport toggle to get a view of all four viewports.
2. Right-click the Mycamera label in the camera viewport, then select View ➢ Mycamera01.

3. Click and hold the Orbit Camera tool in the Viewport Navigation Control toolbar, then select Pan Camera from the flyout.

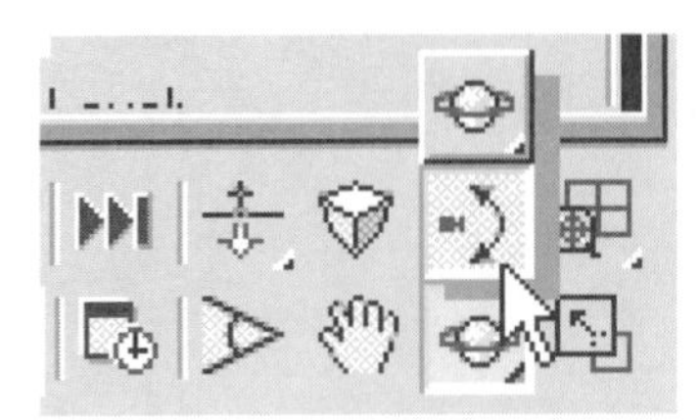

4. Shift-click and drag the cursor horizontally from right to left in the Mycamera01 viewport to adjust the view so that it looks like Figure 9.14.

FIGURE 9.14

The new Mycamera01 viewport

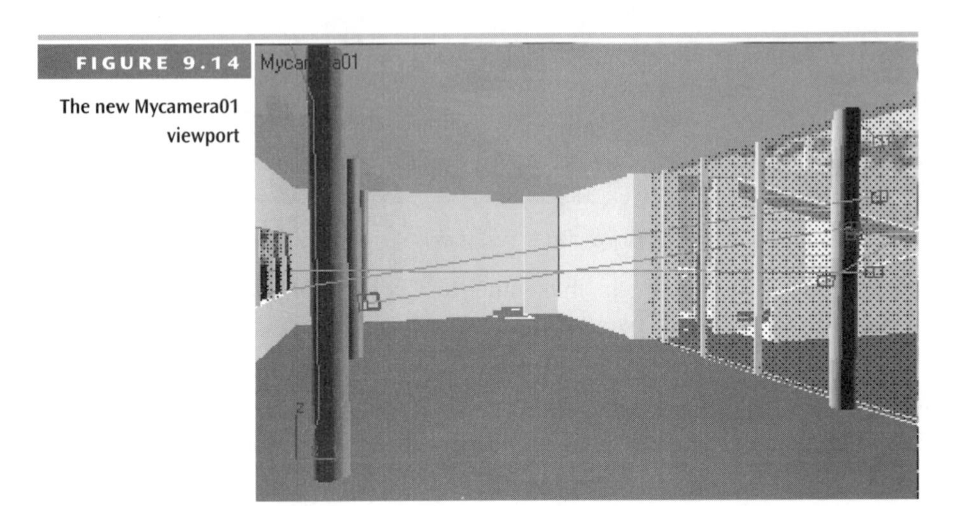

Hold the shift key while dragging the mouse; the Pan Camera tool is constrained to a horizontal motion.

NOTE In VIZ, the Shift key usually brings up the Clone Options dialog box, but in this context, the Shift key is being used as a constraint, as in many other software programs.

5. Click the Quick Render tool to get a look at the room. Your view should look similar to Figure 9.15.

FIGURE 9.15

A rendered view of the interior

Now you've got a view that shows you most of the interior of a room in the villa. You can also see some of the exterior courtyard. Just as the courtyard looked flat before you added the Omni lights, the interior has a flat appearance. It's also a bit dark. To add some depth to the room, you'll add some Omni lights again to simulate the light bouncing off of the floor near the windows on the left side of the room. This time you'll make use of the attenuation parameters to control the light's effect on the walls.

Start by copying one of the Omni lights that already exists in the courtyard. By cloning a light from the courtyard level, you save yourself the effort of moving the light into a vertical location above the second floor. Also, you won't have to set the color of the light, since it is reflecting off of the same surface material as the light of the courtyard is.

1. Use the Min/Max toggle tool to enlarge the Top viewport.
2. Right-click the Top viewport, then click the Select and Move tool in the standard toolbar.
3. Shift-click and drag the first Omni light to the left of the courtyard to the location shown in Figure 9.16. Place the light just below the row of columns and align it with the window mullion shown in Figure 9.16.

4. In the Clone Options dialog box, enter the name **Omni interior** in the Name input box.
5. Make sure the Copy radio button is selected, then change the name to **Omni interior01**. Click OK when you're done.

FIGURE 9.16

Copying an Omni light from the courtyard

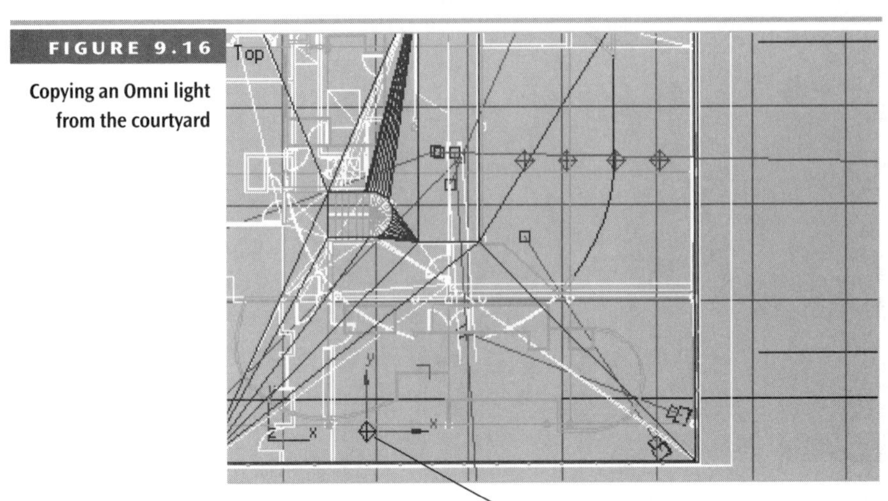
Top
Copy the Omni light to this location.

Next you'll make a row of 10 clones of the light you just copied. Each light will represent the reflected sunlight from each of the windows of the wall on the left. To simplify this operation, you'll use the Array tool. The Array tool lets you create a regular row of clones at a specific distance apart, as you'll see in the next exercise.

1. With the new Omni interior light selected, click the Array tool.

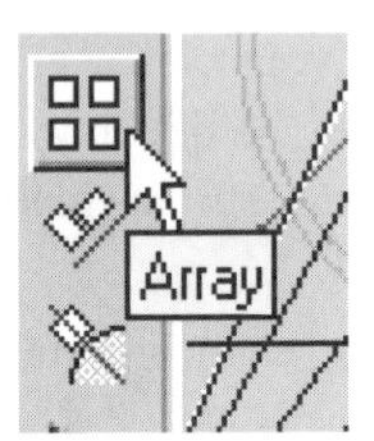
Array

2. In the Array dialog box, enter **4'2"**↵ in the X input box in the upper left corner of the dialog box in the Move row.

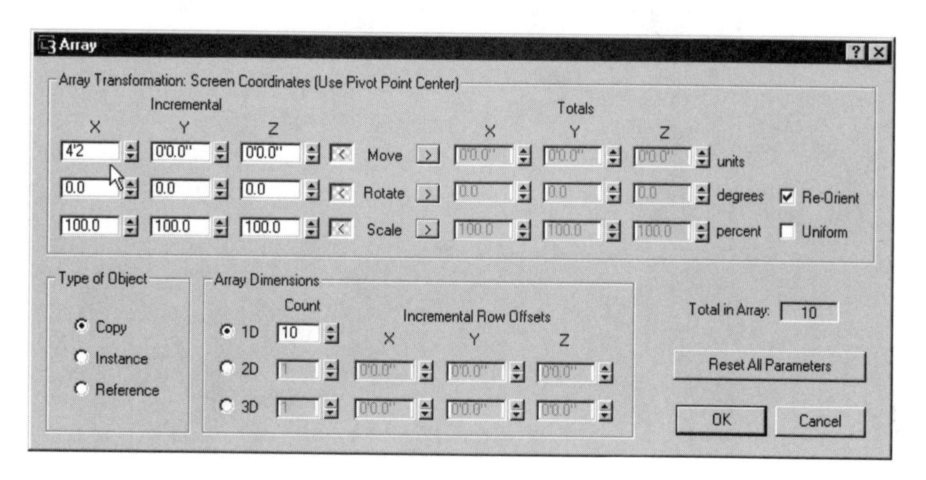

3. In the Type of Object group, click Instance.
4. In the Array Dimensions group, make sure the 1D radio button is selected, and that the Count is set to 10.
5. Finally, click OK. Ten clones appear in the Top viewport of the model.
6. Click the Min/Max Viewport toggle tool, Right-click the Mycamera01 viewport and then click the Quick Render tool on the Render toolbar.

Now you've got a set of lights that simulate the light bouncing off of the floor of the interior space. These lights can also serve to simulate the ambient light from the exterior of the building, as shown in Figure 9.17.

FIGURE 9.17

The interior with Omni lights added

Array Options

The Array tool can be a bit confusing to the first-time user, especially if you're an AutoCAD user. VIZ's Array tool works in a completely different way from AutoCAD's array. But after using it a few times, you can begin to see the logic behind it. For example, to create a regular 5 by 6 array of objects, take the following steps:

1. Select the object, then click the Array tool.
2. In the Array Transformation group, set the X Incremental value to the distance between objects on the X axis.
3. In the Array Dimensions group, click the 2D radio button, then set the Y Incremental Rows Offset to the distance between objects in the Y axis.
4. In the Count column of the Array Dimensions group, enter **5** in the 1D row, and **6** in the 2D row. This is where you tell VIZ the number of clones you want in the array.
5. Select the type of cloning you want to occur in the Type of Object group.
6. Click OK.

The radio buttons in the Array Dimensions group tell VIZ the type of array you want. If you select 1D, then only the settings in the Array Transformation: World Coordinates group are used for the array. If you select the 2D radio button, you then include the settings in the Incremental Row Offsets of the Array Dimensions group.

Continued on next page

If you want to include the Z axis in the array to create a 3D array do the following:

1. Repeat steps 1 through 4 of the previous set of steps.
2. Click the 3D radio button in the Array Dimensions group.
3. Enter the distance between objects in the Z column of the 3D row.
4. Enter the number of clones you want in the Z axis in the Count column of the 3D row.
5. Select the type of clone you want, then click OK.

As you can see from the Array dialog box, you can include rotation and scale tranformations with the cloned objects in the array. You can also include X, Y, and Z incremental values for offsets of the same dimension. You may want to get comfortable with using Array for creating simple, straight arrays before attempting these other options.

If you want to create a circular array, do the following:

1. Select the object; then select the Use Transform Coordinate Center from the Transform Center flyout on the standard toolbar. This establishes the origin of the design as the center of the array.
2. Click the Array tool.
3. Click the Reset All Parameters button.
4. Click the right-pointing arrow to the right of the Rotate label in the Array Transform: Screen Coordinates group.
5. In the Z column of the set of values under the Totals listing, enter **360**.
6. Click the 1D radio button in the Array Dimensions group and enter **12** for its Count value.
7. Click OK. The object will be cloned in a circular fashion.

As you can see from the rendering, the lights are a bit too bright (see Figure 9.17). They wash out the interior space as well as some of the courtyard surfaces, so you'll want to limit the reach of the lights. You can do this with the attenuation properties of the light. Also, since you made a copy of the courtyard Omni lights, the floor is excluded from the effects of the light. But in this case, you want the interior Omni lights to double as a source of outside ambient light, which would cast some ambient light on the floor besides the direct light from the sun.

Since these ten interior Omni lights are referenced clones, changing the settings for any one of the lights will change the settings for the other nine.

1. Close the Render window; then in the Top viewport make sure that the interior Omni light at the far right end of the row of lights is selected, as shown in Figure 9.18.

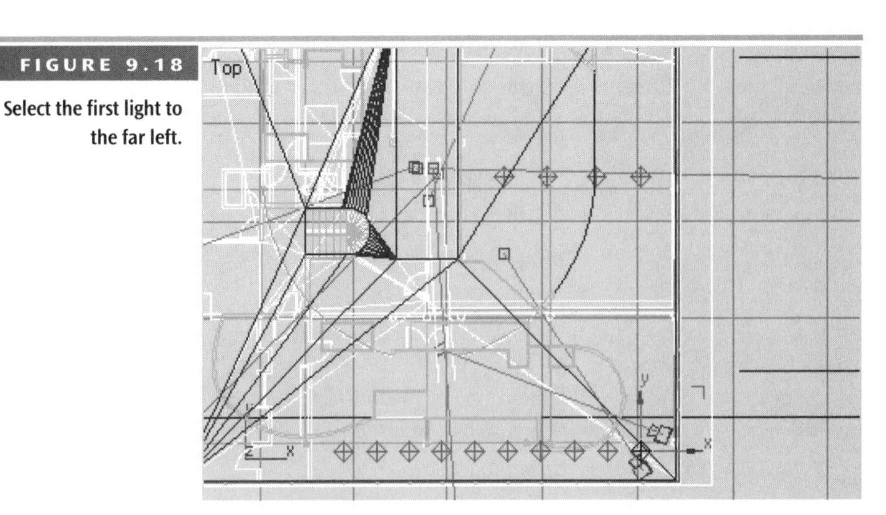

FIGURE 9.18

Select the first light to the far left.

2. In the General Parameters of the Modify tab, click the Exclude button in the General Parameters.
3. Click the Clear button at the bottom of the list to the right of the dialog box, then click OK. This removes the floor and glass from the Exclude list. The lights will now affect the glass and the floor of the interior space.
4. Scroll down the Command Panel, then click the Attenuation Parameters rollout to open it.
5. Click the Use check box in the Far Attenuation group; then set the Far Attenuation Start setting to **12'** and the End setting to **24'.**

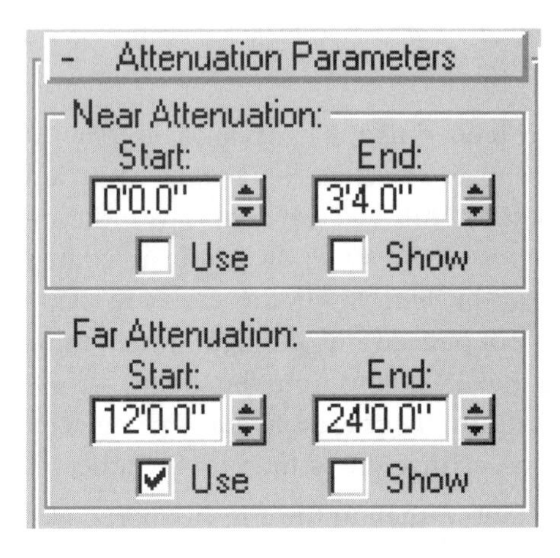

6. Click the Quick Render tool on the Render toolbar to see the results of your changes (see Figure 9.19).

FIGURE 9.19

The rendering after adjusting the Omni light settings

Now that you've gotten a bit more control over the interior lights, you see that the room begins to show a bit more depth. The lighting on the walls is varied, also adding a sense of depth. The columns and floor also receive light from the left, as if lit by the ambient light from the windows.

There's one more item that can use some improvement. The floor is a bit gray and lifeless. Even the reflected light from the windows on the left seems dull.

Since the floor is supposed to be of clay tiles in this example, you can make some adjustments to the color and highlights of the floor material to give it a bit more definition.

1. Open the Material Editor, then select the Stone-Granite Tiles sample slot.
2. In the Phong Basic Parameters, click and drag the Diffuse color swatch into the Ambient color swatch. This will intensify the color of the floor where it is in shadow.
3. In the Specular Highlights group, change the Specular Level setting to **50** and the Glossiness to **10**.
4. Click the Quick Render tool to see the results of the new floor material settings (see Figure 9.20).
5. Now save your current drawing as **Mysavoye.max**.

FIGURE 9.20

The room rendered with changes to the floor material

The room takes on a warmer feeling, and the change in the specular highlights brings out the floor pattern. You can even see that some of the shadows from the columns begin to emerge.

On some computers, the rendered image may appear too dark or too light. You can increase the overall light in a rendering by increasing the Ambient light setting.

1. Choose Rendering ➢ Environment. The Environment dialog box displays.

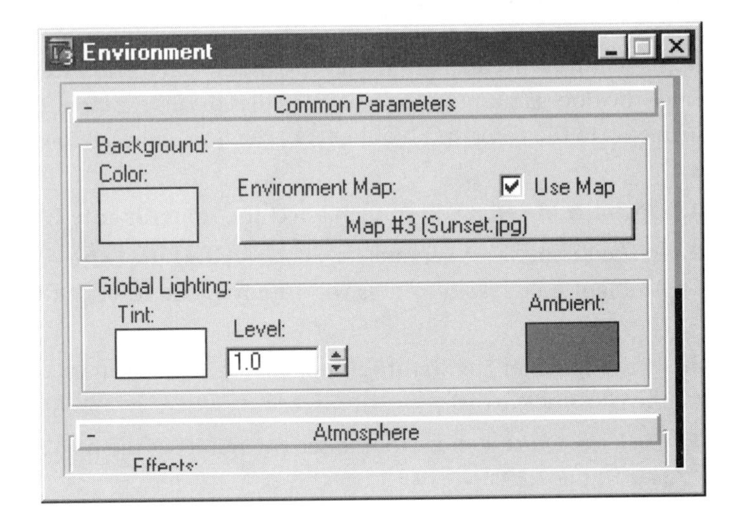

2. Click the Ambient color swatch to open the Color Selector.
3. Change the Value setting to **120**, then close the Color Selector and the Environment dialog box.
4. Render the view again. You see that the overall image brightness has increased at the expense of some contrast.

You've made a number of changes to the scene to simulate natural lighting conditions. With the addition of the Omni lights simulating the outside ambient light and with the reflected light from the floor, the room appears to have more depth than before. The 3D effect of the image is enhanced by the visual cues provided by the additional shadows and light.

Although you were given specific lighting settings to use in each exercise, in practice, you'd probably end up experimenting with the settings and locations of lights to arrive at something you like. The examples in these exercises show you some possibilities of how you can work with light to achieve an effect. Now you can apply what you've learned here to your own work.

Playing with Light and Shadow

You've seen how you can bring out the depth of a space by adding lights to simulate reflected light. In the Villa example you just looked at, you had a combination of direct light simulating the sun and a set of Omni lights to simulate reflected light. In this section you'll look at how you can play with shadows by using a combination of lights and objects.

In Chapter 8, I mentioned that, if you use a bitmap shadow, you can soften the edge of your shadows and that Ray Traced shadows bring out detail. Obtaining both effects in the same rendering can be a little tricky, but you may find that you need to do just that in some situations. The following series of exercises will show you how you can mix these two types of shadows to control the composition and appearance of a rendering.

Creating Two Suns

You'll use a model that was created for the Avery Aquatic Center on the Stanford Campus in Palo Alto, California. You'll be working on a view of the entrance to the center. The entrance is comprised of a tree-lined, paved walkway with a sign and a set of monuments. Let's take a look at the file and a first rendering.

1. Open the file named `Ch09aquatic.max`.
2. Make sure that the Camera02 viewport is selected, then click the Render tool.

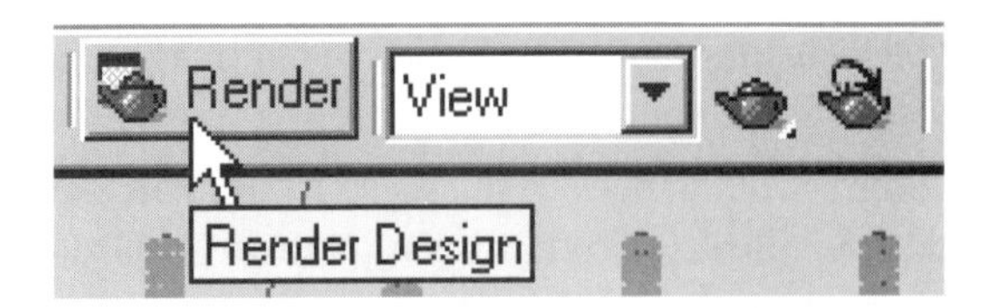

3. In the Render Design dialog box, click 640 x 480 and make sure the Save File check box is not checked, then go ahead and click Render. The rendered view is shown in Figure 9.21.

FIGURE 9.21

The Aquatic Center rendered

The trees in the rendering are simple, rectangular planes like the ones you created in Chapter 8. This time a set of different trees was added to simulate the appearance of the existing open space.

Notice the large, square shadow in the foreground. This is a shadow of the tree in the foreground. You can see part of this tree in the upper left corner of the rendering. All of the trees project a rectangular shadow, though it is less obvious in the trees toward the back. Also notice the odd shadows of the Avery Aquatic Center sign. The sawtooth pattern on the shadow is the result of the low resolution of the shadow map used by the direct light that simulates the sun. To give you a better idea of what the sign is supposed to look like, Figure 9.22 shows a diagram of the sign's design.

FIGURE 9.22

The design of the Avery Aquatic Center sign

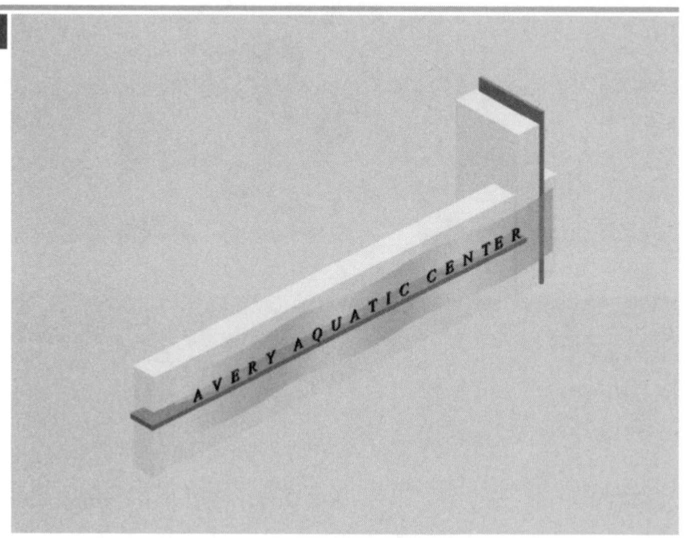

This sign poses an unusual problem in lighting, because it contains a wavy, perforated screen. At a distance, this screen looks like a translucent material, so it is given a material that is partially transparent. Even so, a Shadow Mask shadow doesn't work well with this design, nor does it work well with the trees.

You can improve the look of the sign by using a Ray Traced shadow for the sun, but the complexity of the model combined with a Ray Traced shadow will substantially increase the rendering time. You want to minimize the rendering time if you can, especially if you are working toward a deadline. Figure 9.23 shows the same rendering with the sun's shadow parameter changed to a Ray Traced shadow.

FIGURE 9.23

A second rendering with a Ray Traced shadow setting

With a Ray Traced shadow, the sign looks fine, but the tree shadow looks a bit odd because the trees in the scene are really just flat, vertical planes. In reality, the tree would cast a larger shadow. The tree shadow in the foreground would also have a softer edge.

To obtain a fast rendering speed and still maintain a crisp shadow on the sign, you can use two different light sources for the sun. One light will project a Ray Traced shadow specifically for the sign and trees, while the other will project a Shadow Map shadow for the rest of the model.

Adding a Second Sun

You saw in previous chapters that you can select objects for illumination and shadow casting for each light in your model. In the following exercise, you'll remove the sign and trees from the effects of the current sunlight; then you'll create a second sun that will only affect the trees and the sign. This second sun will be set to use a Ray Traced shadow.

1. Minimize the render window, then select the Directed light in the User viewport. This is the light used to simulate the sun.
2. In the Modify tab of the Command Panel, click the Exclude button in the General Parameters rollout. The Exclude/Include dialog box displays.

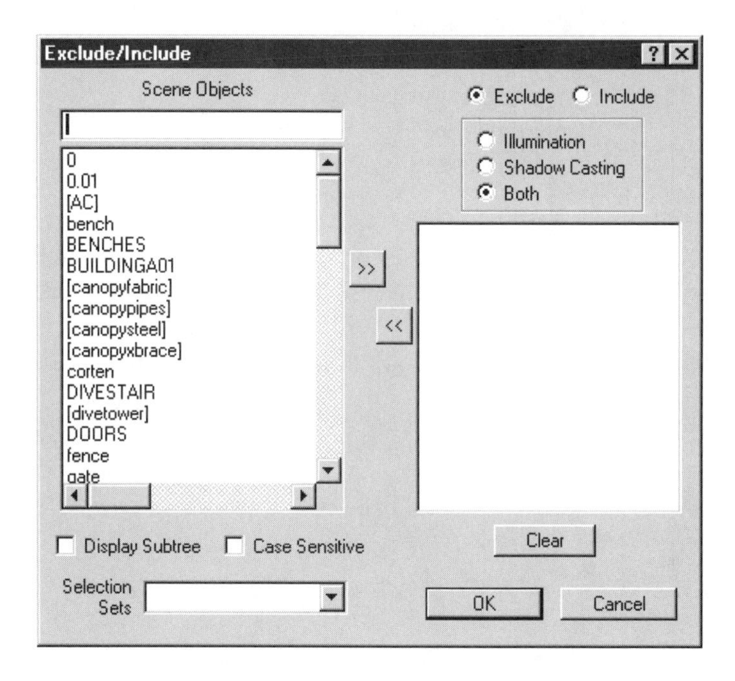

3. Scroll down the list box to the left and select each object whose name begins with SIGN: SIGNbody, SIGNmetal, SIGNmetal2, SIGNscreen, SIGNtext01, and SIGNtower.
4. Click the right-pointing arrow to move the selected items to the list box to the right.

5. Scroll farther down the list on the left and select each item whose name begins with Tree, except Treeshadow. These are Tree01 through Tree04 and the three Treecamphor items.
6. Click the right-pointing arrow again to include these trees in the list box on the right.
7. Click OK to exit the dialog box.

8. Right-click the Camera02 viewport and click the Quick Render tool. Now you see the rendering with the trees and sign appearing rather dark as shown in Figure 9.24.

FIGURE 9.24

The rendering with the trees and sign excluded from the sunlight object

You need to illuminate the sign and trees with a light. To do this, make a copy of the existing sun and change its shadow parameter to Ray Traced.

1. If it isn't selected already, select the SUN directed light in the User viewport.
2. Choose Edit ➢ Clone.
3. In the Clone Options dialog box, choose the Copy radio button and enter **SUNraytraced** for the name. Click OK to close the dialog box.
4. In the Modify tab, click the Exclude button in the General Parameters rollout. The Exclude/Include dialog box displays. Notice that the list on the right includes the same items you excluded from the original SUN light object.
5. Click the Include radio button in the top right of the dialog box. This causes the new light to include only the items listed in the list box to the right, instead of excluding those items.
6. Click OK to close the dialog box.

You've created a second sun that only illuminates the sign and the trees. The original SUN directed light illuminates everything else. Now you've got one more important step to take. You need to set the new sun to cast a Ray Traced shadow.

1. Scroll down the Command Panel to the Shadow Parameters rollout and open it if it isn't already open.
2. Click the Object Shadows drop-down list and select Ray Traced Shadows.

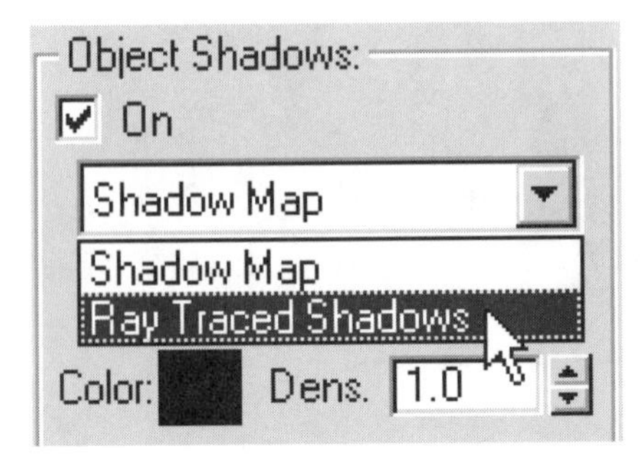

3. Make sure the Camera02 viewport is selected, then click the Quick Render tool. The rendering will take a bit more time when it gets to the sign. Once it's done, you'll see a view similar to Figure 9.25.

FIGURE 9.25

The design rendered with the Shadow Map and Ray Traced shadow light sources

While it took longer to render, it still rendered considerably faster than if you had used a Ray Traced shadow for the entire scene. But there is something missing. The sign and trees don't cast shadows. This is because the ground plane is not included in the set of objects affected by the SUNraytraced sun object. You could include the ground in the SUNraytraced light, but you'd increase the rendering time, and you'd have the same effect as you would if you simply changed the original sun to project a Ray Traced shadow.

To get around this problem, you can add some additional props that will cast shadows from the original SUN directed light that is casting a Shadow Map shadow.

Using Invisible Objects to Cast Shadows

The trees in this model produce a good deal of shade; considerably more than even the shadows created by the Ray Traced shadow version of the rendered Camera02 view you saw earlier. To simulate the shade from the trees, you can employ 2D shapes in the form of a tree shadow. These shapes can be used to cast shadows from the SUN directed light that uses a Shadow Map shadow. This combination will produce a softer shadow, which offers a somewhat more pleasing effect, especially for shadows in the foreground.

To save some time, these Shadow shapes have already been included in the Avery Aquatic model. In the next exercise, you'll turn these shadow objects on and render the view to see how they work.

1. Click the Display tab in the Command Panel.
2. Click All On in the ON/Off rollout. You'll see the 2D shadow object appear in the model as shown in Figure 9.26.

FIGURE 9.26

The 2D shadow objects appear in the model.

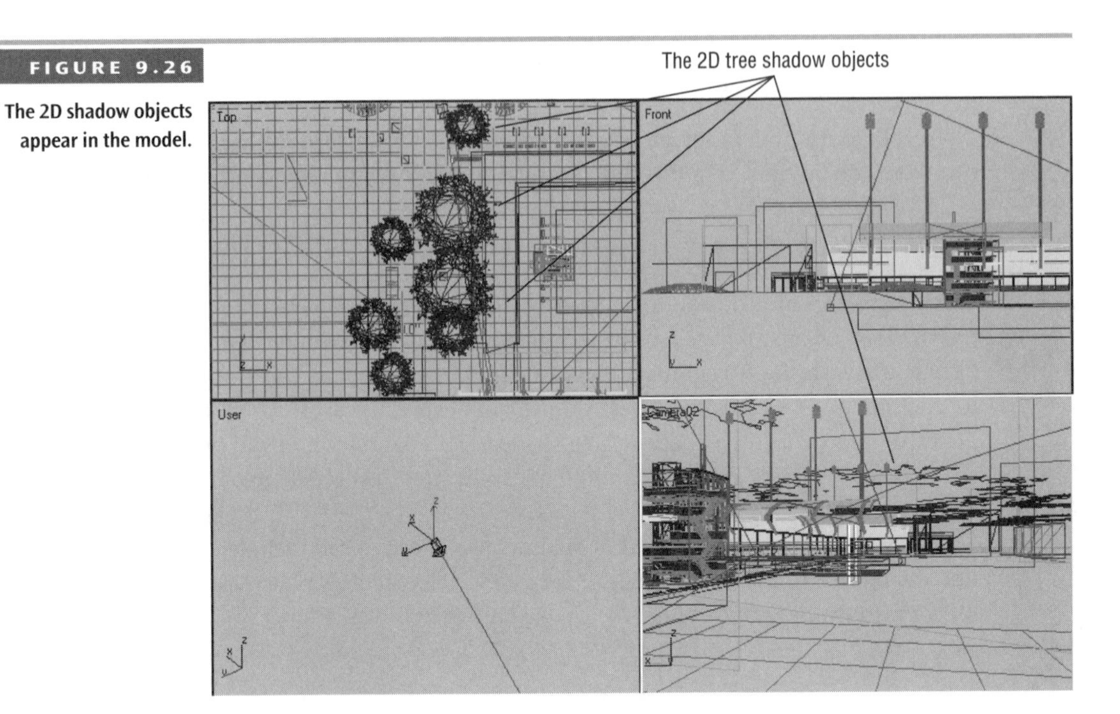

3. Click the Quick Render tool. The view is rendered with the additional shadows being cast by the 2D shadow objects, as shown in Figure 9.27.

FIGURE 9.27

The scene rendered with tree shadows

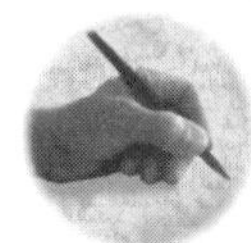

NOTE **Another technique for creating shadows is called a gobo light. In this technique, you assign a projector map (a bitmap usually) to a light, and the light will cast a shadow in the shape of the bitmap. A projector map can be added to a light through the Projector Map group of the Lights Parameters rollout. Projector maps can also be animated to simulate the shadows of trees being blown by the wind.**

The character of the rendering changes dramatically with the addition of shadows. The walkway has a more inviting appearance, instead of the somewhat harsh, sunlit open space. Also, the shadow in the foreground helps soften the composition by introducing a change in the ground plane.

Since you were spared the work of actually building and placing the shadow objects, you'll want to know some of the details of their construction. The shadow objects, named Treeshadow in the model, are 2D surfaces formed into the shape of a tree shadow. If you look in the Camera02 viewport, you'll see that they are placed at about the height of the bottom of the tree canopy (see Figure 9.28).

FIGURE 9.28

The Camera viewport with the Treeshadow objects at the level of the bottom of the tree canopy

This location offers a more accurate placement for the shadow on the ground plane.

If you look carefully at the Top viewport, you'll see that the Treeshadow objects are not centered on the trees for which they cast shadows. Instead, they are offset to the left and downward in the direction away from the light source. This simulates the way a tree shadow might be cast, given the sun angle in the design.

There's something else that is also quite unusual about the Treeshadow objects. While they cast shadows in the Camera02 rendering, they don't appear in the rendered view, even though they are plainly visible in the Camera02 viewport. You may recall that when you created a wineglass in an earlier chapter, parts of the glass disappeared when it was rendered. This was due to the alignment of the normals on a single surface. Remember that a surface really only has one visible side. The Treeshadow object takes advantage of this by orienting its normals toward the sky and away from the camera's point of view. The end result is that VIZ does not render the Treeshadow object, but the trees still cast shadows.

You can create a Treeshadow object by starting with a plane or a star spline shape, editing its vertices to form a shape like the shadow of a tree. You can also form one random shape, then make multiple copies and join the copies into one object.

Using a Clone to Cast Shadows

The Avery Aquatic rendering is just about finished. Unfortunately, the sign itself looks as if it were floating in the rendering, as if it were pasted in. It appears to be dislocated because it doesn't cast a shadow.

You want the sign to cast a shadow using the original SUN directed light that uses a Shadow Map shadow. To do this, you'll make a copy of the main sign components that cast shadows. Those copies will be included in the set of objects that cast shadows from the original SUN directed light.

1. Click the Select by Name tool on the standard toolbar.
2. In the Select Objects dialog box, select the SIGNbody and SIGNtower objects from the list, then click Select. These are the two main components of the sign.
3. Choose Edit ➢ Clone, then in the Clone Options dialog box, make sure that Copy is selected and click OK. VIZ creates copies of the objects you've selected, appending the number 01 to the name of each object.

You don't want these new objects to affect the rendered scene in any way other than to cast a shadow from the SUN directed light. To avoid any interference with other objects, you can reduce the size of these new objects so that they are smaller than the objects from which they were cloned.

1. Click the Select by Name tool again, then in the Select Objects dialog box, select SIGNbody01.
2. Click the Select and and Uniform Scale tool on the standard toolbar.
3. In the Transform flyout, select Center. This will cause the SIGNbody01 object to stay centered within the original SIGNbody object as it is scaled down, thereby keeping the SIGNbody01 object completely nested within the SIGNbody object (see Figure 9.29).

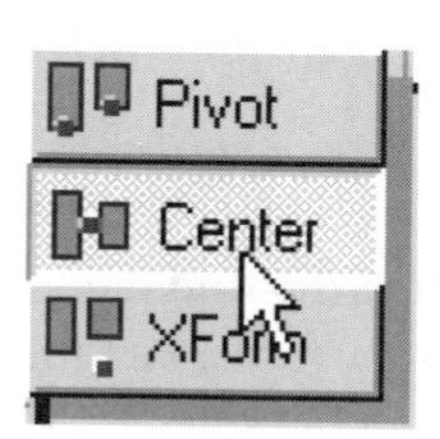

FIGURE 9.29

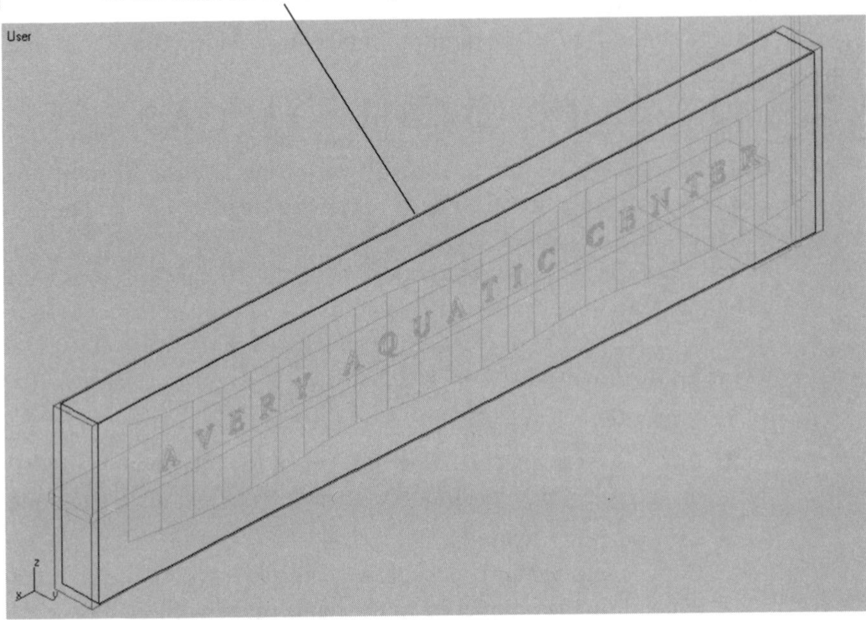
The dark outline shows the SIGNbody01 clone.
User
AVERY AQUATIC CENTER

The SIGNbody01 object is nested within the SIGNbody object.

4. Right-click the Select and Uniform Scale tool to open the Scale Transform dialog box.
5. Change the Offset:World spinner value to read **98%**.

You've now made the SIGNbody01 object smaller than the original object from which it was cloned. Repeat the process for the SIGNtower01 object.

1. Click the Select by Name tool again, then in the Select Objects dialog box, select SIGNtower01.
2. In the Scale Transform type-in dialog box, change the Offset:World spinner value to read **98%**. This time the Scale Transform dialog box was already open, so you didn't have to reopen it. VIZ also maintains the Use Selection Center Transform flyout option.
3. Click the Select by Name tool once again and select SIGNbody01 and SIGNtower01.
4. Now choose Draw ➢ Group ➢ Create.
5. In the Group dialog box, enter **Signshadow** and click OK. By grouping the newly created objects, you can keep them together and manage them more easily. From now on, you'll see the pair of objects listed as a single group called [Signshadow] in the Select Objects dialog box.

The new objects are automatically included to cast shadows from the original light source, and since you haven't explicitly included them with the objects lit by the SUNraytraced directed light, they aren't affected by that light.

Rendering Regions of a Scene to Save Time

To add the shadows from the sign, you could render the entire scene over again, but this can take time. Since most of the scene is fine, and you only need to re-render fairly localized portions of the view, you can use a render option that will render just the area of a viewport you need. The following exercise will demonstrate this feature.

1. Make sure that the Camera02 viewport is selected.
2. Click the Render Type drop-down list on the Render toolbar, then select Region.

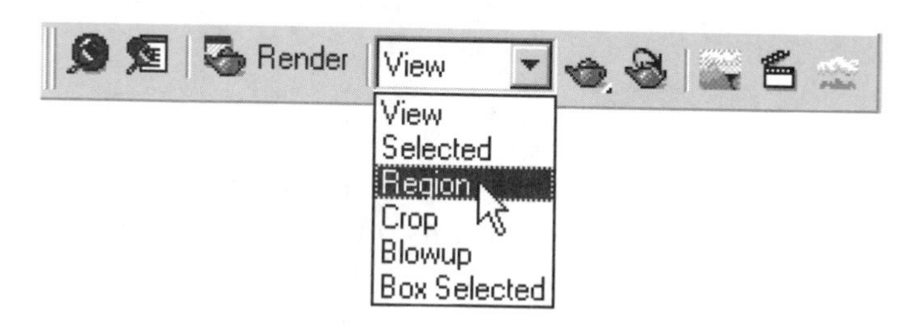

3. Click the Quick Render tool. You'll see a dotted outline appear in the Camera02 viewport along with an OK button in the lower right corner.
4. Click and drag inside the dotted outline and move it over the area where the sign shadow will appear as shown in Figure 9.30.
5. Click and drag the squares on the Render Region outline to adjust its width to encompass the entire area where the shadow will appear, as shown in Figure 9.30. Don't make it too large.

FIGURE 9.30

Moving the Render Region outline over the area to be rendered

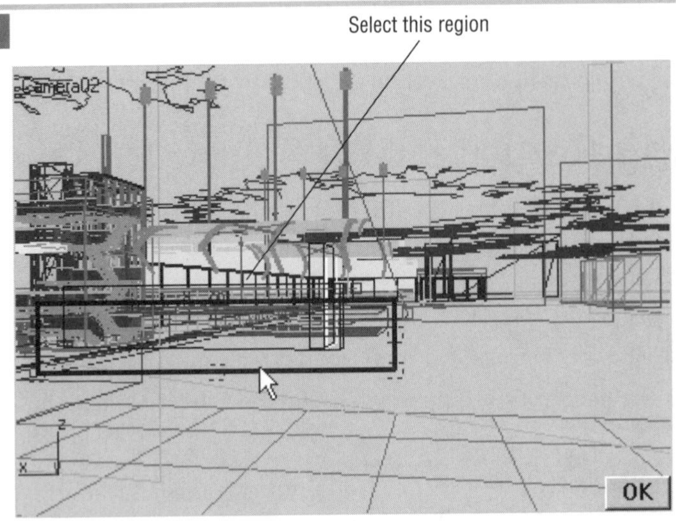

6. Click the OK button in the lower right corner of the viewport. VIZ will begin the rendering procedure, but this time, it will only render the area defined by the Render Region you created in step 5. The scene displays, complete with the shadow from the sign (see Figure 9.31).

FIGURE 9.31

The completed rendering of the Aquatic Center entrance

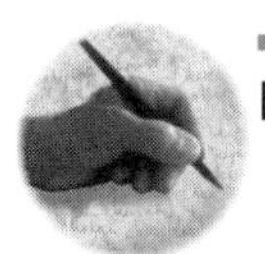

NOTE If you decide you don't want to continue with the rendering, you can press the Escape key instead of clicking OK in step 6.

The rendering you've created uses a lot of props and some behind-the-scene additions to create the illusion of a realistic scene.

Summary

There are a lot of ways that you can manipulate your designs to create the scene you want. You've seen just a few of those ways in this chapter. I hope that you'll come away from this chapter realizing that VIZ is really just a tool that can be manipulated in any number of ways to achieve that perfect rendering. After all, a traditional artist would not balk at the idea of exaggerating a color here or a shadow there to improve the composition of a hand-drawn rendering.

In the next chapter, you'll continue to work with the Villa design by adding furniture and other props. You'll also look at ways to create a night scene.

chapter 10

Working with Files

FEATURING

- *Adding Furniture*
- *Gaining Access to Materials and Objects from Other Files*
- *Arranging Furniture with Xrefs and the Asset Browser*
- *Replacing Objects with Objects from an External File*
- *Arranging Furniture with Xref Designs*
- *Using the Virtual Frame Buffer to Save, Compare, and Print Rendered Views*

Working with Files

The term *design* in VIZ refers to your model files. If you're a 3D Studio Max user, you may be more familiar with the term *scene* to describe your model. In this chapter, you'll look at ways that you can access and utilize your designs while developing your renderings and animations. VIZ offers a variety of ways that can help you improve your workflow. You can divide a file into smaller pieces and recombine them while keeping those pieces unique. This can help you manage large designs that require the work of several people. Other tools let you quickly update objects in your design, or perform what-if scenarios to try out different options.

You'll create some new pieces of furniture and bring in some additional furniture from the companion CD. In the process you'll lean about the different ways that you can combine and access your designs.

Adding Furniture

In Chapter 9, you added lighting to the interior of the Villa model to help define the interior space. At this point you can start to add furnishings to give the room a sense of scale and a lived-in look. You'll start by making some modifications to the couch you created in Chapter 2. By doing so, you'll get a chance to work with groups. After that, you'll begin to build a scene containing the new chair and couch and some additional furniture from the companion CD. Finally, you'll add the furniture to the Savoye model and render it.

Editing the Couch

Start by modifying the couch you created in Chapter 2 to turn it into an overstuffed chair.

1. Open the Couch you created in Chapter 2. You may also use `09couch.max` from the companion CD.
2. Enlarge the perspective view, then change the view to a wireframe.
3. Delete the seat cushion on the right side of the couch.
4. Select the base of the couch and change its width to 22 inches.
5. Select the back of the couch; then in the Modify tab of the Command Panel, select ChamferBox from the Modifier Stack drop-down list.
6. Change the seat back width to 26 inches. Your chair should look similar to the one shown in Figure 10.1.

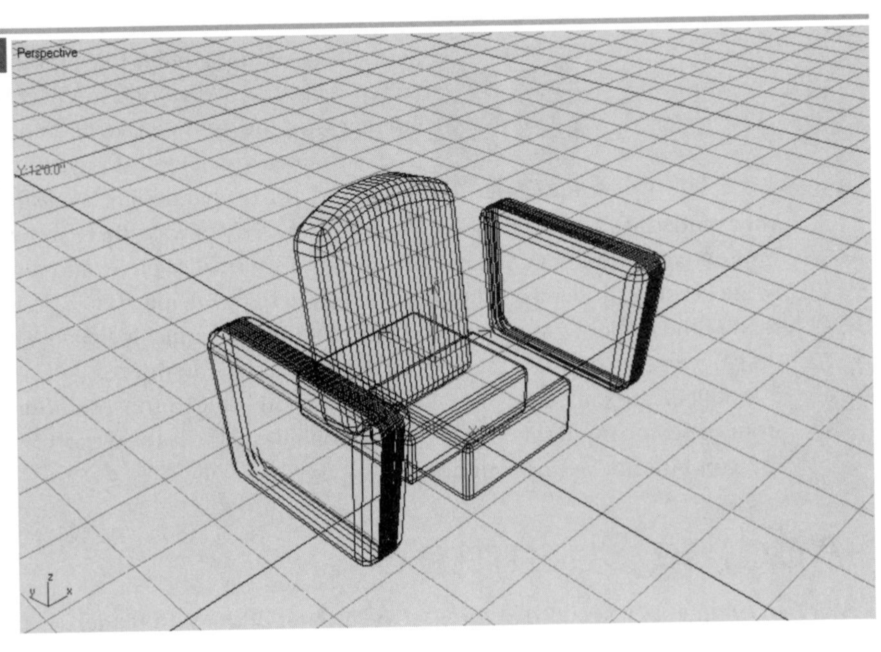

FIGURE 10.1

Adjusting the seat components to a size more in line with a single chair

Now you've got the components of the seat to a size more in line with a single chair. The next step is to move all of the components into position.

1. Click the Min/Max Viewport toggle to view all four viewports.
2. In the Front viewport, move the remaining seat cushion to be aligned with the back and base of the chair.
3. Move the arms of the chair next to the seat base so it looks similar to Figure 10.2.

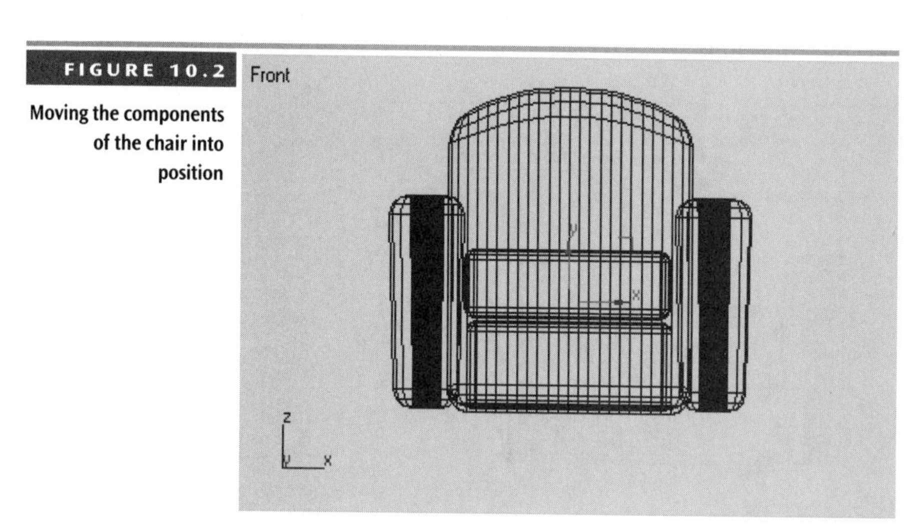

FIGURE 10.2

Moving the components of the chair into position

Grouping the Components of the Chair

The chair is made up of several objects. For convenience, you'll want this set of objects to act like one object when it is selected. To do this, you can use the VIZ group feature. You'll create a group a single object; then you'll add other objects to that group.

1. Select the chair back.
2. Select Draw ➢ Group ➢ Create. The Group dialog box displays.

3. Replace the default Group01 name with **Bigchair01**, then click OK.
4. Now select the base, cushion, and both arms; then choose Modify ➢ Group ➢ Attach.
5. Place the cursor on the chair back and notice that you have a selection cursor displaying as shown in Figure 10.3. This selection cursor will display when the cursor passes over a group. Click the chair back, which is now part of the Bigchair01 group. Now all of the components of the chair are contained in the Bigchair01 group.

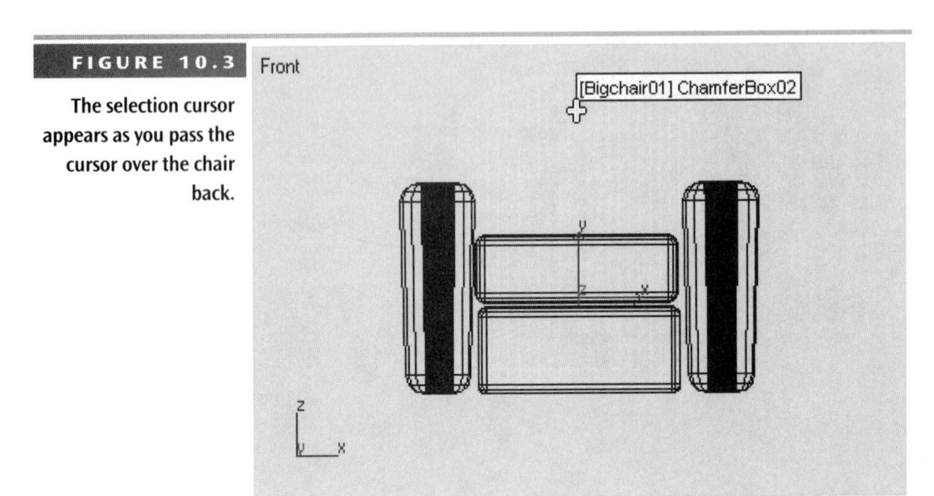

FIGURE 10.3 The selection cursor appears as you pass the cursor over the chair back.

6. Click the Select by Name tool on the standard toolbar. You'll see the name Bigchair in brackets indicting that Bigchair is a group. Click Cancel when you're done looking at the list.

While you could have created the Bigchair01 group all at once by selecting all the components of the chair in step 1, this exercise gave you the opportunity to see how you can add objects to a group that has already been created.

The chair will now act as a single object for selection and transform operations. You saw earlier how you can open a group to edit individual objects within a group by choosing Modify ➢ Group ➢ Open. You can close a group backup by first selecting a member of the group, then choosing Modify ➢ Group ➢ Close. To add other objects to the group, repeat steps 4 and 5 of the previous exercise. To detach an object from a group, first open the group, then select the object you want to detach and select Modify ➢ Group ➢ Detach.

Adding a Material to the Chair

For the final touch to the chair, you'll want to add a fabric material. In this exercise, you'll use a fabric from the VIZ standard material library and modify it a bit to fit the chair.

1. Select the chair.
2. Click the Material Editor tool on the standard toolbar.
3. In the Material Editor, click the Get Material tool.

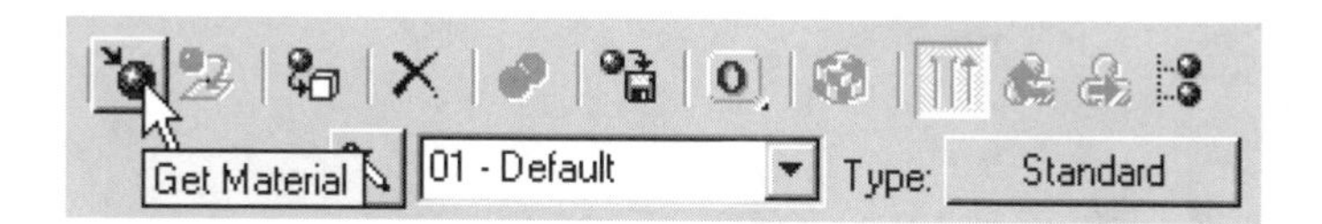

4. In the Material/Map browser dialog box, click Mtl Library from the Browse From group, then locate and double-click the Fabric-Blue Bumpy listing in the list box to the right.
5. Close the Material/Map browser; then in the Material Editor, click the Assign Material to Selection tool.

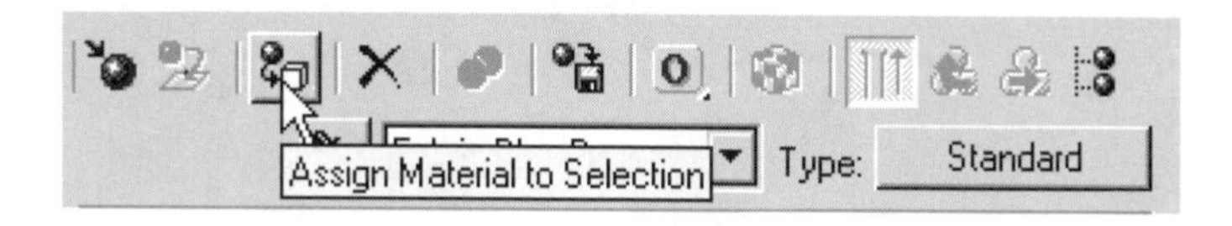

6. Close the Material Editor.

Since the material uses a map, it will require a UVW Map modifier applied to the chair.

1. With the chair still selected, click the Modify tab on the command panel.
2. Click the UVW Map modifier in the Modifier rollout.
3. Scroll down the command panel to the Parameters rollout and click Box in the Mapping group.
4. Click the Sub-Object button to access the UVW Mapping gizmo.
5. Click the Select and Scale tool on the standard toolbar; then in the Perspective viewport, click and drag downward. As you do this, watch the status bar and adjust the percentage to about 50 percent.

NOTE You may also adjust the U, V, and W Tile parameters for the UVW Map modifier to 0.5 to scale the size of the map in relation to the object.

6. Click the Sub-Object button to return to the Object level.
7. Do a quick rendering of the model so far. Your chair should look similar to Figure 10.4.

FIGURE 10.4

The chair rendered

The material is a bit shiny for chair fabric, and the color is a bit strong. For the final touches to the chair, you'll reduce the shininess and tone down the color.

1. Close the Render window. Then open the Material Editor.
2. Open the Maps rollout and reduce the amount of the Diffuse Color setting to 40 percent.
3. Reduce the Bump setting to 200.

4. Scroll up to Shader Basic Parameters, click the drop-down list to the left, and select Oren-Nayar-Blinn. You may recall that this shader is more appropriate to matte surfaces.

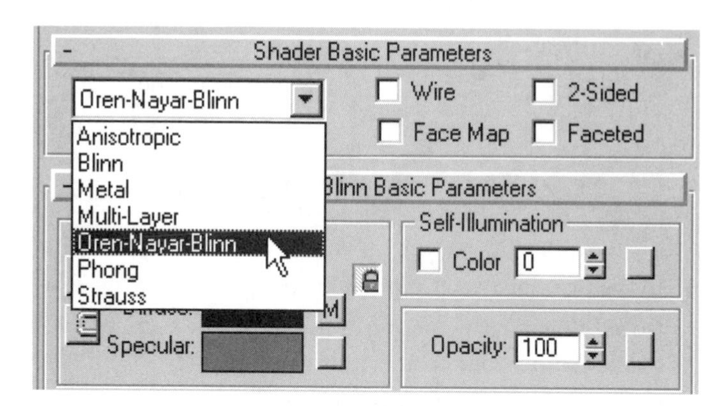

5. Click the Diffuse color swatch in the Oren-Nayar-Blinn Basic Parameters, then in the Color Selector set the Hue to 160, the Saturation to 20, and the Value to 200.

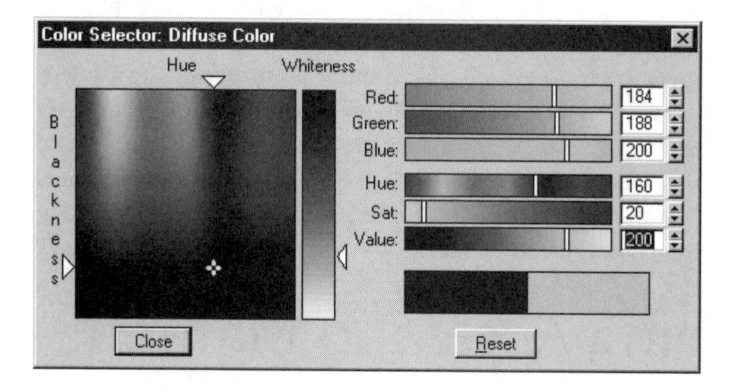

6. Close the Color Selector, then back in the Oren-Nayar-Blinn Basic Parameters, click and drag the Diffuse color swatch into the Specular color swatch.

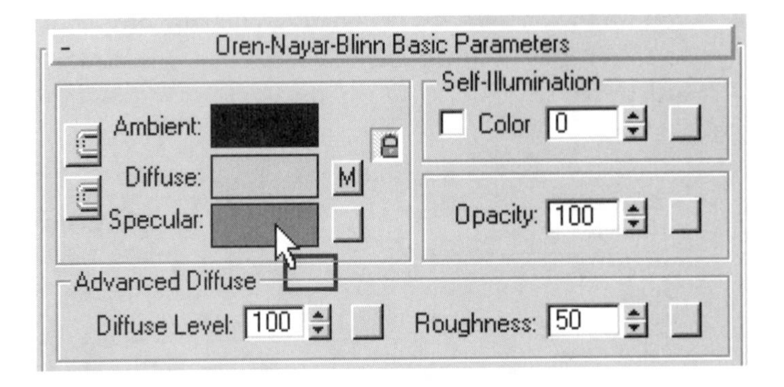

6. In the Copy or Swap Color dialog box, click Copy.
7. Do another quick rendering of the chair. The surface looks a bit more like that of a softer fabric. Your chair is now ready for use.
8. Save the chair as **Mybigchair.max**.

In this series of exercises, you got a chance to work with groups. You were able to add the same material to a group and you applied the UVW Mapping modifier to the group as well. If you open the group, check the UVW Mapping modifier for the individual objects; you find that each object shares the UVW Mapping modifier.

You also saw how you could quickly reuse an existing model to create a new, similar model. You were able to make use of the parameters of the objects that make up the chair to quickly modify their proportions and define a new chair.

Now let's go back to the original couch and finish it off. You'll want to group the parts of the original couch together, just as you did with the chair. You'll also want to give the couch the same material as the new chair and apply a UVW Map modifier.

Gaining Access to Materials and Objects from Other Files

In this section, you'll repeat the process you used to combine the parts of your original couch into a single group. You'll also use a new tool called an Xref to transfer the modified fabric material you created in the `Mybigchair.max` file to the `Couch.max` file.

Xrefs are a way to include other VIZ files in your designs without having to actually combine file data into a single file. For example, you may want to create a file that contains the furniture arrangement for an office, but you want to keep that furniture data separate from the actual office design file. You can Xref the office design into your furniture file so that you can accurately locate the furniture Then when you're done, you can remove the Xref of the office design in a single step. The furniture file then maintains its independence from the office design file. This avoids duplication of data and keeps your disk storage space requirements down. You can then Xref the furniture file into the office design file whenever you need to show furniture.

Xrefs can be used as an organizational tool to help reduce the complexity of large design models by segregating similar types of objects into separate files. Xrefs are also useful for dividing work between members of a design team. In an interiors project, for example, you can have one designer working on a floor layout, while another designer works on floor patterns or lighting.

VIZ offers two ways to use Xrefs. The Xref Design dialog box lets you combine whole design files into a single file. The Xref Design dialog box also allows you to divide portions of a design into separate files so that a design can be edited by several individuals. If you think you may need to edit objects brought in as Xrefs, you can use the Xref Object dialog box. You can apply transforms and modifiers to individual objects that have been imported using the Xref Objects dialog box, though such changes will not affect the source file.

As an introduction to Xrefs, you'll use the Xref Objects dialog box in the following exercise to import a material into the `Couch.max` file. Xrefs aren't necessarily the only way to import materials, but you'll use the Xref Objects dialog box in this way to see firsthand how this dialog box works.

NOTE **If you are an AutoCAD user, you will find that the VIZ Xref tools perform the same functions as the AutoCAD Xref tools, though VIZ uses a different set of dialog boxes.**

First, as a review, use the group command in VIZ to group the parts of the couch together.

1. Open the `09couch.max` file from the companion disk, or use the `Couch.max` file you created from Chapter 2.
2. Click the Select by Name tool in the standard toolbar.
3. In the Select Objects dialog box, click the All button at the bottom of the list box, then click Select. This selects all of the objects in the design.
4. Choose Draw ➢ Group ➢ Create; then at the Group dialog box, enter **Couch01** for the name and click OK.

Now you've got the objects collected into a group called Couch01. The next job is to add the material. You used the Fabric-Blue Bumpy material from the Standard Material library, but you modified it for the `Mybigchair.max` file. You could reconstruct the modifications you made to the material, but that would be time consuming. Instead, try using the Xref Objects command to import the material from the Mybigchair.max file.

1. Choose Insert ➢ Xref Objects… The Xref Objects dialog box displays.

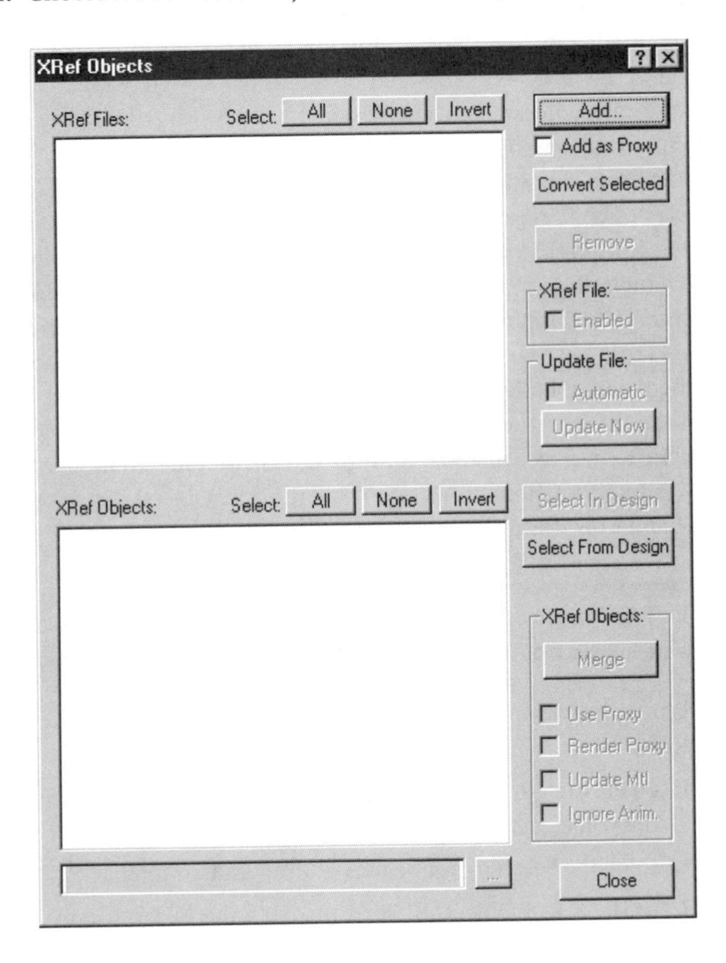

2. In the Xref Objects dialog box, click the Add button in the upper right corner.
3. In the Open File dialog box, locate and open the `Mybigchair.max` file. The Xref Merge-Mybigchair.max dialog box displays.

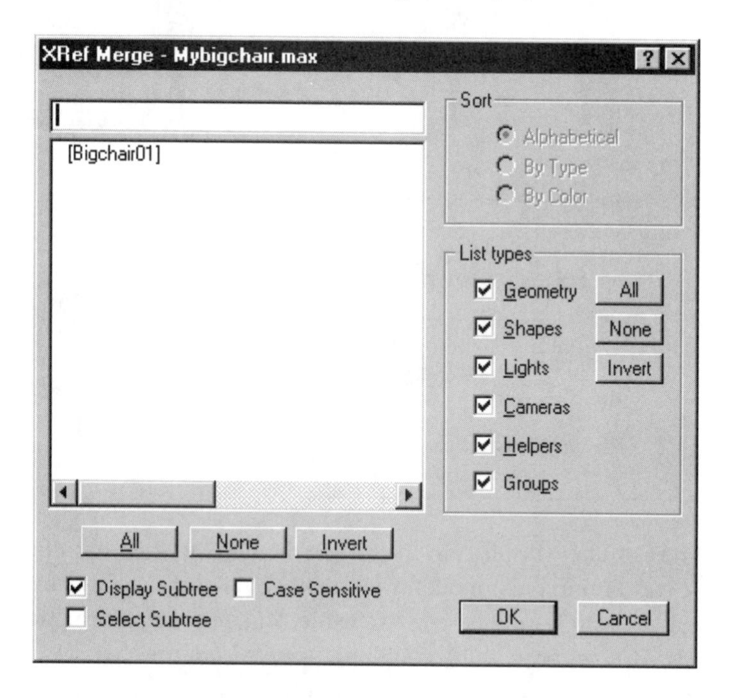

4. Notice that you have two list boxes; one shows the file you've used as an Xref, and the other shows the objects contained in the file. Click [Bigchair01] from the list, then click OK. The dialog box closes and the chair displays in the drawing.
5. Click Close in the Xref Objects dialog box. You see the chair enmeshed in the couch.

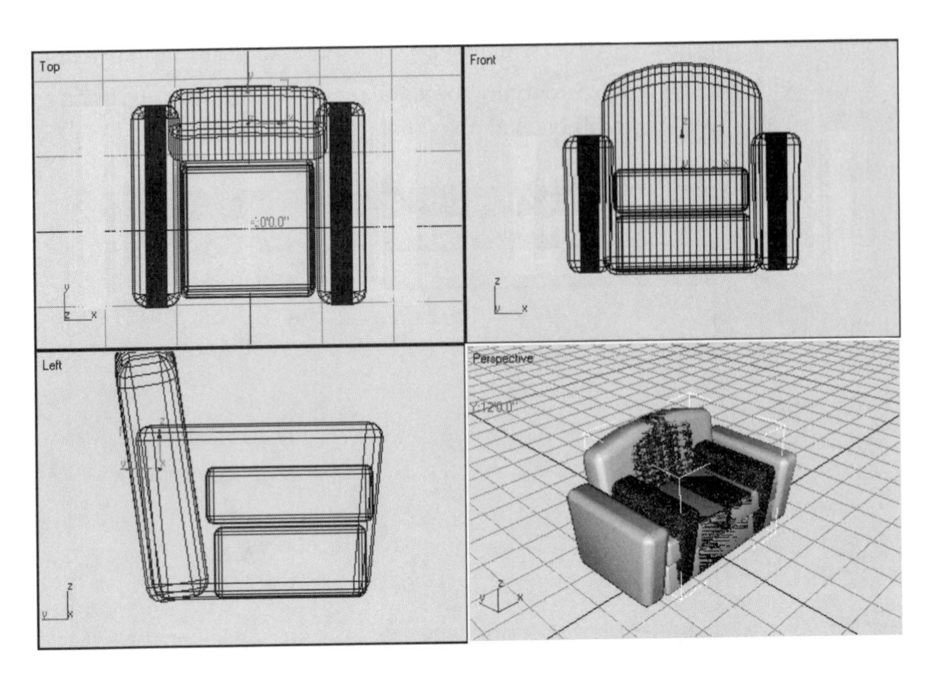

The chair now displays in the Couch model. The chair hasn't really become a complete part of the couch model. You might think of an Xref as a kind of *guest* that is visiting but doesn't really belong to the file. Still, you can use the transform tools on the "guest" Xref, or acquire materials and objects from the Xref.

1. Click the Material Editor tool in the Render toolbar.
2. In the Material Editor dialog box, click the Get Material tool.

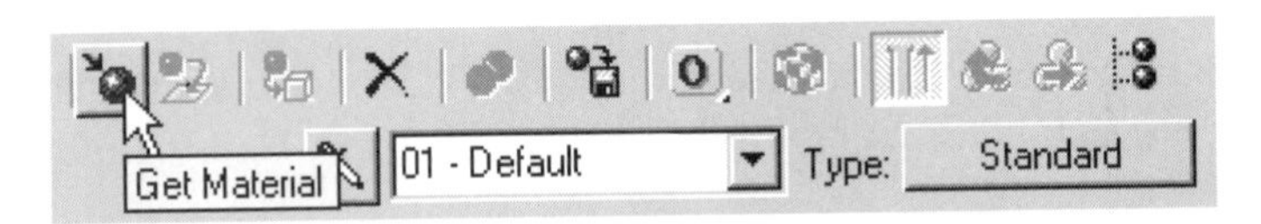

3. In the Material/Map browser, click the Design radio button in the Browser From group, then double-click the Fabric-Blue Bumpy listing.
4. Close all of the open dialog boxes.

You've just imported a material from the `Mybigchair.max` file. You don't need the chair in your couch file, so let's remove it:

1. Choose Insert ➢ Xref Objects...; then in the Xref Objects dialog box, click Mybigchair.max, listed in the top list box.
2. Click Remove. You see a warning message asking whether you really want to remove the selected Xrefs from the scene.

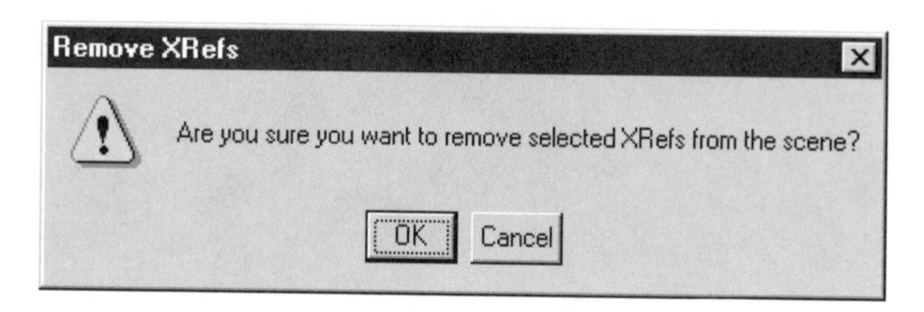

3. Click OK. Go ahead and close the Xref Objects dialog box.

The chair disappears, leaving your Couch file as it was before you imported the chair. Now you can apply the newly acquired material to the couch.

1. Select the couch.
2. Open the Material Editor dialog box.
3. With the Fabric-Blue Bumpy material selected, click the Assign Material to Selection tool.
4. Close the Material Editor dialog box.

For the final step, you'll need to make sure the couch has mapping coordinates. You'll use the same basic coordinates you used for the chair.

1. Click the Modify tab, then click UVW Map.
2. In the Parameters rollout, click Box.
3. Click the Sub-Object button to gain access to the UVW Mapping gizmo.
4. Click the Select and Scale Transform tool on the standard toolbar, then right-click the Select and Scale Transform tool again to open the Scale Transform type-in dialog box.
5. Enter **50** in the Offset: World input box, then close the dialog box.
6. Click the Sub-Object button in the Modify tab to return to the object level of the design.

6. Do a quick rendering of the couch.

Options for Importing Materials

You have several other options for importing materials from another file. First, you can go to the `Mybigchair.max` file and save the fabric to the standard Material library under a new name. To do this, click the Put to Library tool in the Material Editor dialog box. You can also set up a new Material library and place the fabric there. Here are the steps for creating a new Material library:

1. Click the Material/Map Browser tool in the Render toolbar.
2. In the Material/Map Browser dialog box, click the Mtl Editor radio button in the Browse From group.
3. Click the Save As... button in the File group.
4. Enter a name for your new Material library file.

You can then retrieve the fabric from the new library, using the Material/Map Browser. This method is helpful when you are working on a team that needs to have access to a common set of materials.

A third option is to use a max design file as if it were a Material library. Here are the steps to do this:

1. Click the Material Editor tool on the Render toolbar.
2. In the Material Editor dialog box, click the Get Material tool.

Continuued on the next page

3. In the Material/Map dialog box, select the Mtl Library radio button in the Browse From group.
4. Click the Open... button in the File group.
5. In the Open Material Library dialog box, select 3Dstudio VIZ (*.max) from the File of Type drop-down list.
6. Locate and open the `Mybigchair.max` file.
7. In the Material/Map Browser dialog box, double-click Fabric-Blue Bumpy in the list box. The imported material appears in the Material Editor dialog box sample slot.

This is perhaps the fastest method for obtaining a material from another file.

You were able to import a material from another file, using the Xref Object dialog box. As you might guess, materials are not the only things you can import. For example, if you wanted to import the seat back from `Mybigchair.max`, you could have done that by selecting the object from the bottom list of the Xref Objects dialog box and selecting Merge. Once an object is merged, it becomes part of the current file's database. Here is a listing of the options available in the Xref Objects dialog box, describing their function.

Add Opens a file dialog box, allowing you to select a file containing objects to Xref.

Add as Proxy Lets you use Xref objects as *stand-ins* for other Xref objects in the current file. This is useful for study renderings and animations because it allows you to temporarily substitute simplified geometry for complex geometry in a design.

Set Lets you select the file to become the Xref.

Convert Selected Converts a selected object in the current design into an Xref object. The selected object or objects are removed from the current design and saved as `.max` files; then they are reinserted into the current file as Xref objects.

Remove Removes all Xref objects from the current design.

Xref File Turns off selected objects.

Update File Controls how Xref objects are updated.

- *Automatic* updates Xref objects whenever the source file is saved.
- *Update Now* lets you manually update Xref objects. It updates objects from the current state of the source file.

Select in Design Lets you select objects in the viewports based on the objects selected in the Xref Object list box.

Select from Design Lets you highlight objects in the Xref Object list box based on selected objects in the viewports.

Xref Objects Gives you additional control over the Xref objects that are selected in the Xref Objects list box.

- *Merge* converts selected Xref Objects into actual objects in the current design.
- *Use Proxy* displays the proxy version of the selected object.
- *Render Proxy* renders proxy objects in place of the selected object.
- *Update Mtl.* updates the material assignment of the selected object from the source object whenever a file update occurs. With this option off, the objects geometry is updated by the material does not change. It is important to note that you can edit the material assigned to an Xref object, so if you turn the Update Mtl option on, you run the risk of reversing any material changes you've made to Xref Objects.
- *Ignore Anim.* causes VIZ to ignore animations applied to Xref objects.

Once you've imported an Xref object, you can use the Transform tools to edit it. You can also modify an Xref object using the Modify tab in the Command Panel. With an Xref object selected, the Modify tab gives you control over the way Xref proxy objects behave and are displayed. The options found in the Modify tab correspond to the Xref Objects area of the Xref Objects dialog box.

Arranging Furniture with Xrefs and the Asset Browser

Now that you've got a chair and a couch, you can begin to use them to create a setting for the interior of the Villa model. In this section you'll use the chair you created—plus some other furniture that is available on the companion CD—to create the interior setting.

In the process of arranging the furniture, you'll get a chance to explore another way of using Xrefs. This time you'll use the Xref Design option to temporarily combine the Villa model with a new furniture file to help lay out the furniture. You'll also look at how you can import geometry from one VIZ file to another through the Merge command and the Asset Browser. The Asset Browser is a tool to help you manage your projects by giving you a seamless way to access data from your own computer, your network, and the Web.

Let's start by taking a look at how the Merge command can be used to import VIZ file data.

1. Choose File ➢ Reset to create a new file and reset the new file to VIZ's default settings. You see the Reset warning message.

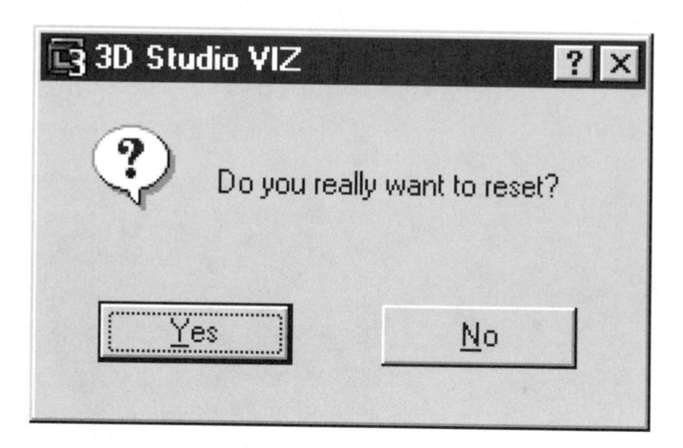

2. Choose File ➢ Merge… The Merge File dialog box displays. This is a typical file dialog box.
3. Locate and open the `Couch01.max` file you just created. The Merge dialog box appears.

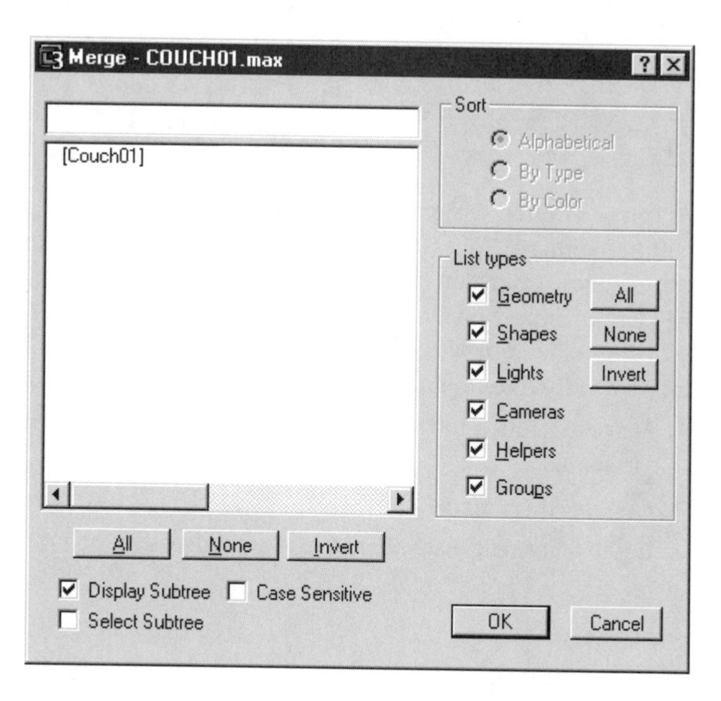

The Merge dialog box shows a listing of objects from the file you selected. Since the `Couch01.max` file contains a single group, you see the group name in the list. Had you not grouped the objects in the Couch01.max file, you would see the individual object names listed.

4. Select [Couch01] from the list, then click OK. The couch displays at the origin of the model.

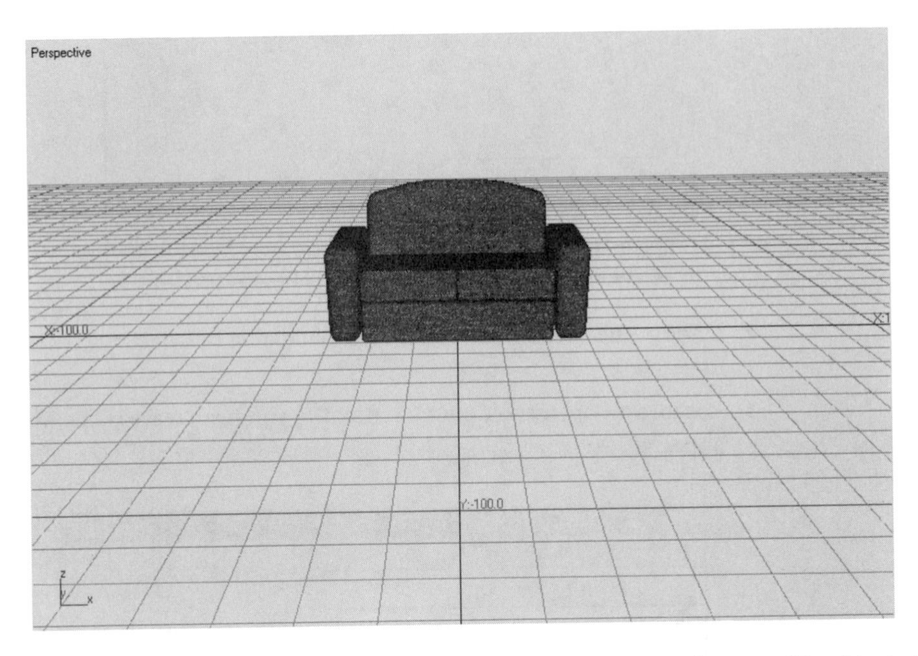

As you saw in step 4, Merge gives you the opportunity to select specific objects to import from other VIZ files, though in the case of the Couch, you really had only one object to choose from. You can also import cameras, or geometry from other models using Merge. Unlike Xref Objects, the objects you import using Merge become a part of the current files database and have no link to the source file.

Let's try the Merge command again by adding the chair you created earlier.

1. Move the couch to the right 62 inches so that it is at the far right side of the viewport.
2. Choose File ➢ Merge…
3. In the Merge File dialog box, locate and select `Mybigchair.max` and click Open.

4. In the Merge dialog box, click [Bigchair01] and click OK. This time you see a dialog box warning you that a duplicate material name exists in the current design.

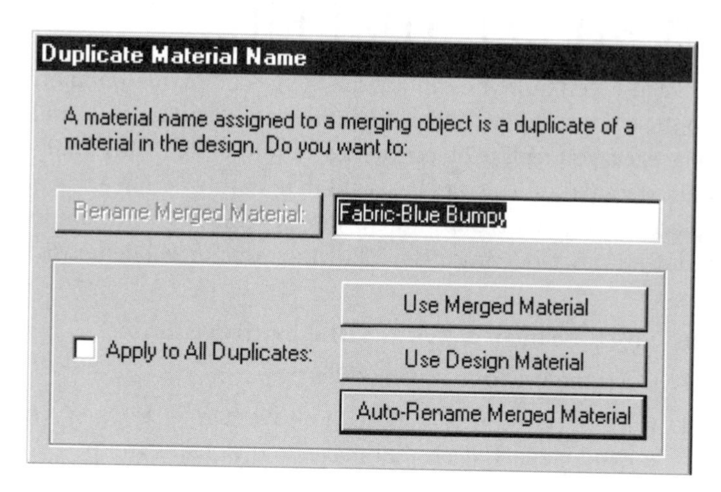

5. Go ahead and click Use Design Material. The chair displays at the origin of the file.
6. Click the Select and Move tool from the standard toolbar, then shift-click and drag the chair to the left 62 inches.
7. In the Clone Options dialog box, click the Instance option, then click OK.

In step 4, at the Duplicate Material Name dialog, you have four options:

- You can rename the imported duplicate material by entering a new name in the input box near the top of the dialog box. This will maintain both the merged material and the material in the current design as unique materials.
- You can click Use Merged Material to replace the material in the current file with the material of the merged file.
- You can click Use Design Material to maintain the current material and discard the duplicate in the merged file.
- Or you can click Auto-Rename Merged Material to have VIZ rename the merged material to maintain it as a unique material.

In step 5, you were instructed to select the Use Design Material option. This caused VIZ to use the Fabric-Blue Bumpy material currently in the file to be the material used in both the chair and the couch.

Replacing Objects with Objects from an External File

You've just seen how you can use the Merge command to import parts of a design into the current design. Another command called *Replace* is similar to Merge, but Replace lets you replace objects in the current design with similarly named objects from external files. This can be useful in updating design elements. You can also use Replace to temporarily substitute complex geometry with simple *stand-in* geometry for quick study renderings. The following exercise will demonstrate how Replace works.

1. Save the current design as **VillaFurniture.max**.
2. Open the `Mybigchair.max` file.
3. Click the chair, then choose Modify ➢ Group ➢ Open. This gives you access to the individual objects that make up the chair's group.
4. Click the chair back to select it, then click the Modify tab of the Command Panel.
5. Click the Modifier Stack drop-down list and select Chamfer Box.
6. Modify the width parameter so that it is 34 inches in width.
7. Choose Modify ➢ Group ➢ Close to close the group, then save the file.

You've made a slight modification to the chair. Now you can use Replace to see how you can update the chair in the `VillaFurniture.max` file to the new chair design.

Before you actually perform the Replace operation, you need to change the name of the object that forms the back of the couch. Remember that you created the `Bigchair01` file from the `Couch01` file, so both the couch and chair share objects of the same name, even though they may not all be the same shape. The Replace command works by replacing objects in one file with objects of the same name from another file. You don't want to replace the back of the couch, so you'll have to change the couch back object's name first.

1. Save the `Mybigchair.max` file; then open the `VillaFurniture.max` file.
2. Select Couch01, then choose Modify ➢ Group ➢ Open.
3. Click the Couch01 back. When you place the selection cursor on the back you should see the name [Couch01] ChamferBox02.
4. In the Modify tab of the Command Panel, change the name of the object, ChamferBox02, to **Couchback01**.
5. Choose Modify ➢ Group ➢ Close.

Now you're ready to replace the back of the chair with the one you modified earlier.

1. Choose File ➢ Replace.
2. In the Replace File dialog box, locate and select Mybigchair.max, then click Open. The Replace dialog box displays.

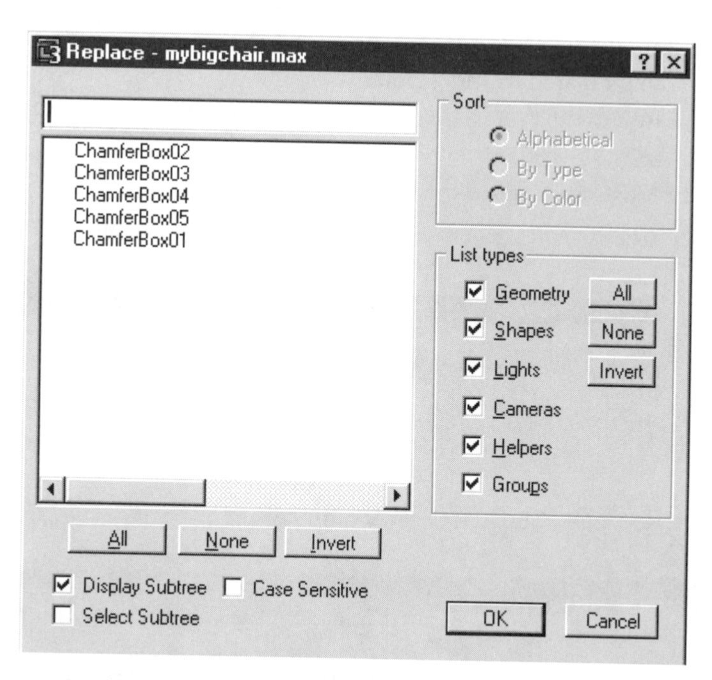

3. Select ChamferBox02, then click OK. You'll see a warning message.

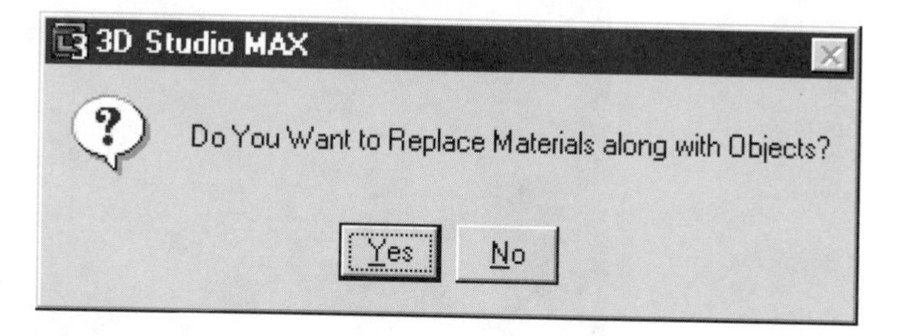

4. Click Yes. The chair back will be replaced with the new chair back you edited earlier.

Notice that the back was replaced in both the original chair and in the instance clone of the chair. Had you made a copy instead of an instance clone, only the original chair back with the same name, ChamferBox14, would have been replaced. This demonstrates that instance clones are replaced along with the original objects.

Importing Files from the Asset Browser

Like the Merge command, the Asset Browser lets you import a file into the current file. It doesn't let you pick and choose which parts of a file are imported, but it does perform other functions such as opening VIZ files in a second VIZ session or browsing the Web for materials and geometry.

As an introduction to the Asset Browser, try the following exercise. You'll use the Asset Browser to import another copy of the chair.

1. Move the chair to the back of the view.
2. Choose Tools ➢ Asset Browser. You see the following message:

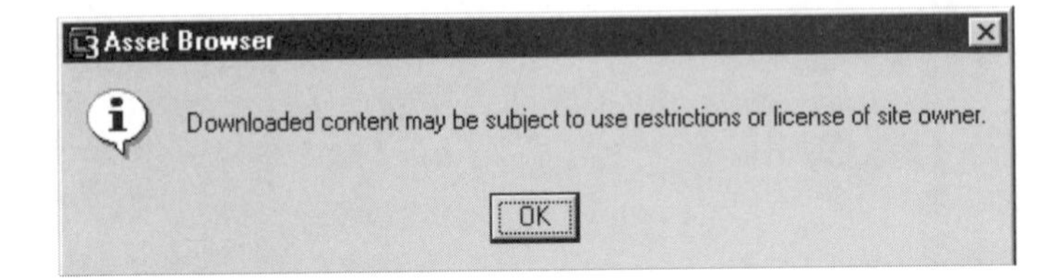

3. Click OK. The Asset Browser displays.

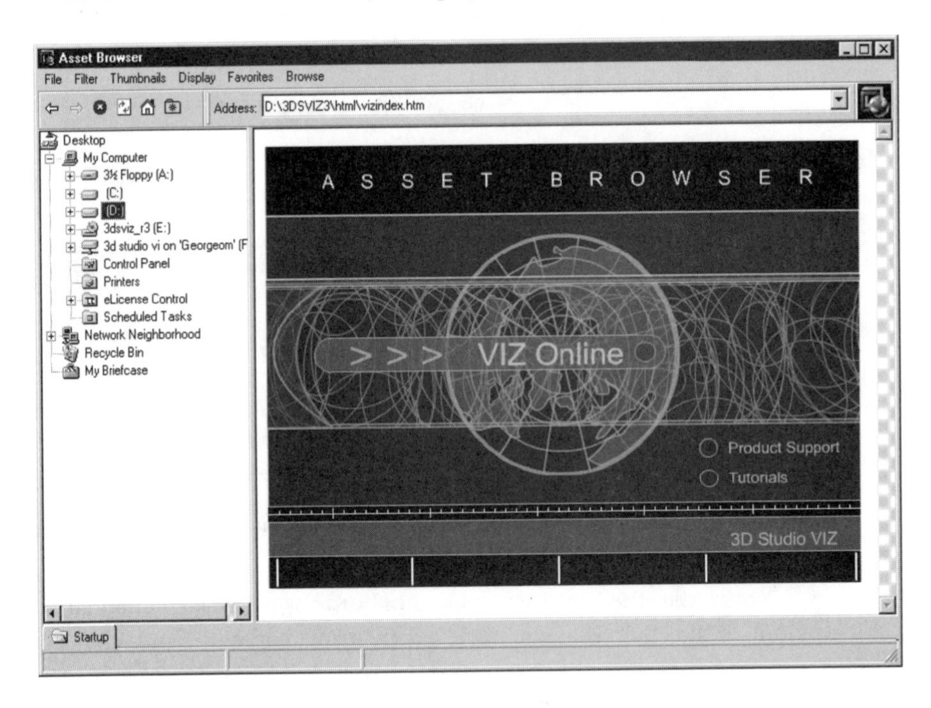

NOTE If you use a standard telephone modem to connect to the Internet, you see a message asking whether you want to log on to your Internet Service Provider. If you are using a cable modem, DSL, ISDN, or T1 line, or if you are connected to the Internet through your company's network, you see the Asset Browser immediately after clicking OK in step 3.

You can browse the contents of your computer and view thumbnail images of VIZ files and image files. You can then drag and drop files into VIZ, just as you would from the Windows Explorer. One special feature of the Asset Browser is its ability to let you drag and drop VIZ components from Web sites that contain what is called VIZable content. Geometry, textures, and lighting can be acquired directly from sites containing VIZable content. AutoCAD .DWG files, Max files, IGES, and STL files are all types of geometry files that can be dragged and dropped from VIZable Web sites.

Before you look at the Asset Browser's Internet capabilities, try the following exercise to see how it works within your own computer.

1. On the explorer bar to the left of the Asset Browser, locate the `\3dsviz3\Maps` folder and click it. The window to the right displays the image files contained in `\3dsviz3\Maps`.

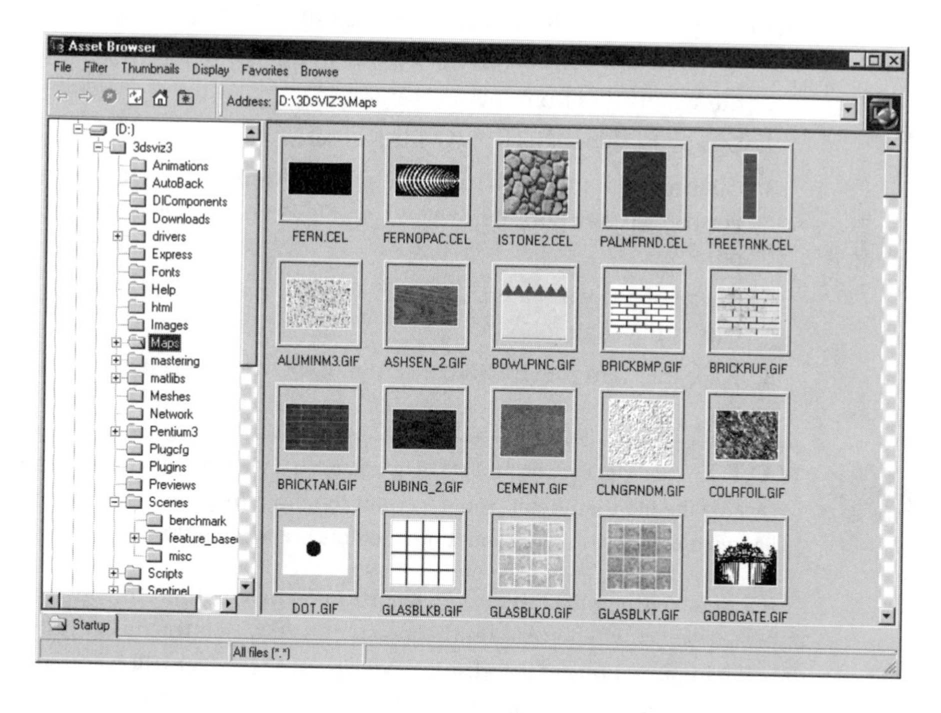

2. Choose Thumbnails ➢ Small (50 × 50). The images become smaller, allowing you to see more of them.
3. Scroll down the list on the left and expand the `\3dsviz3\Scenes` folder by clicking the plus sign to the left of the Scenes folder.
4. Click the `\3dsviz3\Scenes\misc` folder. Again, you see a set of thumbnail views of the files. Note that the Asset Browser shows you the content of the image files as well as of .MAX files.

NOTE **If all you see is a set of blank boxes, you can turn on the thumbnail views by choosing Thumbnails ➢ Create Thumbnails.**

You can drag and drop image files from the Asset Browser into a VIZ file. If you drag and drop an image into a viewport, it becomes a background. You get a message asking you whether you really want the image to be used as a background. If you drag and drop an image onto an object, the image will be mapped to the object.

You can also drag and drop image files into a Map slot in the Maps rollout of the Material Editor as an alternative way of importing image maps for materials. And as mentioned earlier, you can import VIZ (.MAX) files through the Asset Browser. Try importing your chair into the current scene using the Asset Browser.

1. In the Asset Browser, use the list box to the left to locate the folder containing the sample files from the companion CD.
2. Locate the `Mybigchair.viz` file and select it.
3. Click and drag the `Mybigchair.viz` file from the Asset Browser into the VIZ Perspective viewport. Once again, you'll see the Duplicate Material Name dialog box.
4. Click Use Design Material. The chair displays in the viewport. As you move the cursor, the chair follows.
5. Place the chair roughly in the center of the view and click.

NOTE **You can use the Asset Manager to open a VIZ file in a second session by double-clicking the file thumbnail. You may want to refrain from doing this if your system has limited memory. Also, you cannot run multiple instances of VIZ on Windows 98.**

If you have the four standard viewports open in VIZ, then the orientation of the imported object will depend on the viewport into which the object is dragged. If you drag the imported object into the Top viewport, the object will be oriented in the normal orientation. If you drag the object into the Left or Front viewport, the object will be oriented sideways with its Z axis pointing toward you from the viewport.

Let's try inserting a few more items, using the Asset Browser. This time try inserting a lamp from the companion CD into a Top viewport in VIZ.

1. In VIZ, click the Min/Max Viewport toggle to view all four viewports, then click the Top viewport and click the Min/Max Viewport toggle again to enlarge it.
2. Go to the Asset Browser and locate the file called `Torch1.max`. This is a file from the companion CD.
3. Click and drag the `Torch1.max` file into the VIZ Top viewport.
4. Adjust the location of the Torch1 lamp so that it displays in the left side of the viewport, as shown in Figure 10.5.
5. Go ahead and repeat steps 1 through 4 to insert the files named `Lamp01.max`, `Tablelarge.max`, `Tablesmall.max`, and `Bruer.max`. All of these files are from the companion CD. Use Figure 10.5 to locate the inserted objects.

FIGURE 10.5

Inserting objects from the Asset Browser

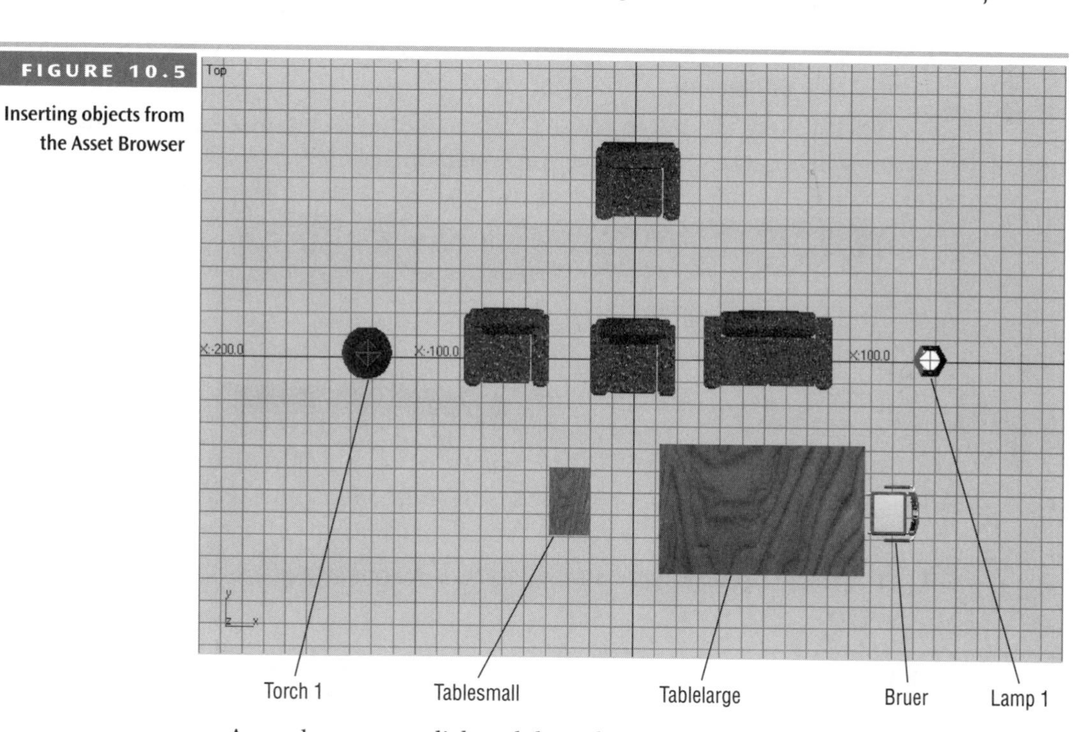

As a rule, you can click and drag objects easily from the Asset Browser to VIZ, using the Windows taskbar, as long as you insert the objects into a non-Perspective viewport. If you must insert an object into a Perspective viewport, you can do so under two conditions. You can click and drag into the VIZ button of the Windows taskbar if the Perspective viewport is expanded to fill the entire VIZ window. If several viewports are displayed, then you must click and drag directly from the Asset Browser to the Perspective viewport, bypassing the Windows taskbar. This requires that the Perspective viewport be at least partially visible with the Asset Browser window overlapping VIZ. You must follow this same procedure to click and drag bitmaps into the VIZ Material Editor.

Using VIZable Web Sites

You've seen how you have quite a few methods at your disposal for gaining access to files on your computer. The Asset Browser offers an additional capability of importing files from the Internet or from your company's Intranet.

The methods for doing this are similar to those for importing local files. The main difference is that, instead of using the list of file folders on the left side of the Asset Browser, you use the browser functions. To open a Web view and find the VIZ homepage in the right side pane of the Asset Browser, do the following:

1. In the Asset Browser, choose Display ➢ Web Pane. This changes the view in the right side window into a Web page view.
2. Click the 3D Studio VIZ Homepage button on the Asset Browser toolbar to make sure you're at the VIZ homepage on your local machine.

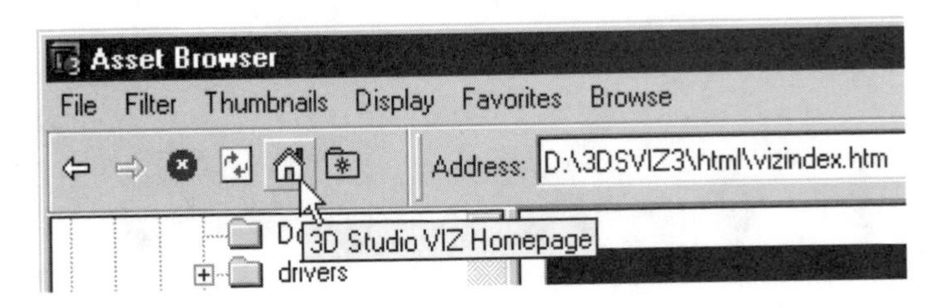

This page has three links. VIZ Online is the main link, which you'll explore next. You can also find product support information and online tutorials by clicking the links in the lower right corner of the page.

3. Click the VIZ Online link on the Asset Browser homepage. The VIZ Online page displays.

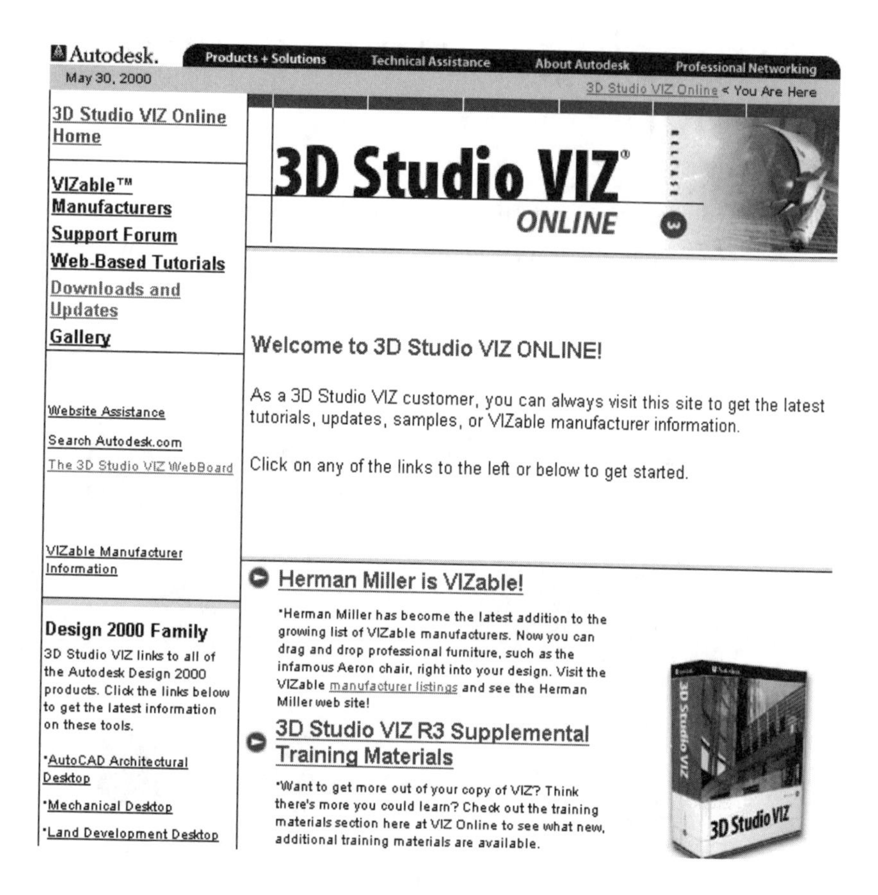

4. Click the VIZable Manufacturers link at the upper left corner of the page, then on the VIZable Manufacturers page, click the VIZable Product Manufacturers link in the middle of the page.

You can use the Asset Browser as you would other Web browsers to locate information on the Web. And as mentioned earlier, you can import materials, bitmap images, model geometry, and light objects from sites that offer such items. Or, if you prefer, you can use your Internet Explorer Web browser to perform the same functions.

Since Web pages change frequently, you won't be shown a tutorial on importing VIZable objects from the Web. It's really quite simple, though. Once you've located a VIZable object, click and drag it into your VIZ window, just as you did earlier with files from your own hard drive.

Arranging Furniture with Xref Designs

Now that you've got some furniture to work with, the next step is to lay out that furniture. Start by putting together a basic arrangement.

1. Go to the Top viewport and arrange the furniture in a way similar to that shown in Figure 10.6.

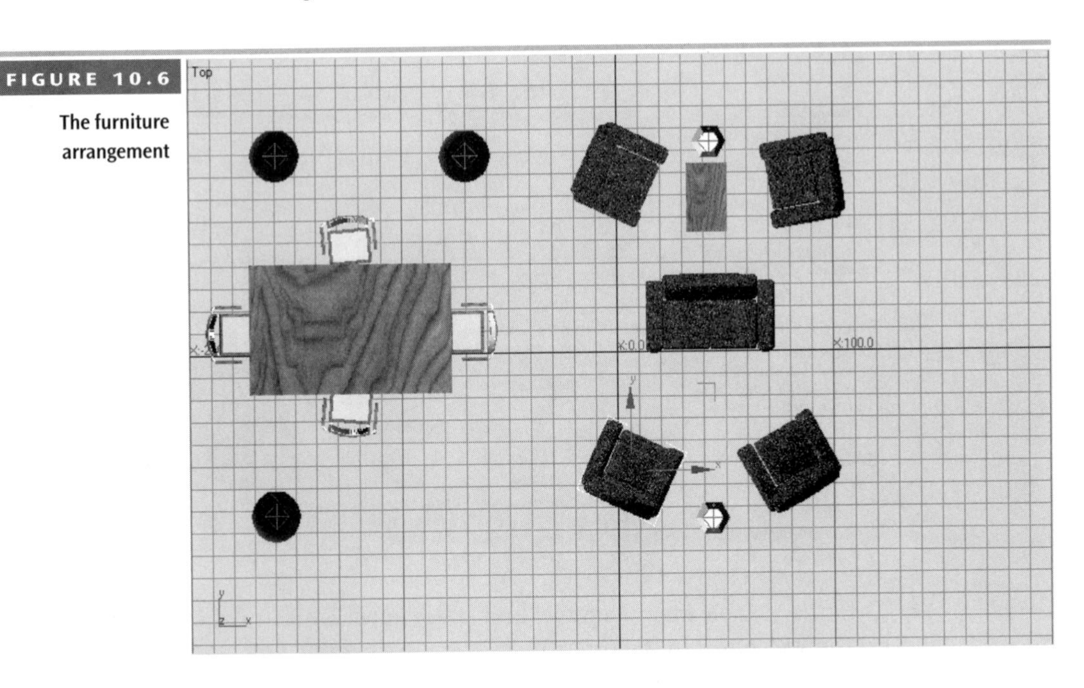

FIGURE 10.6 The furniture arrangement

2. Next, attach the Villa model as an Xref. This will give you a point of reference for the actual location of the furniture. Choose Insert ➢ Xref Designs… The Xref Designs dialog box displays.

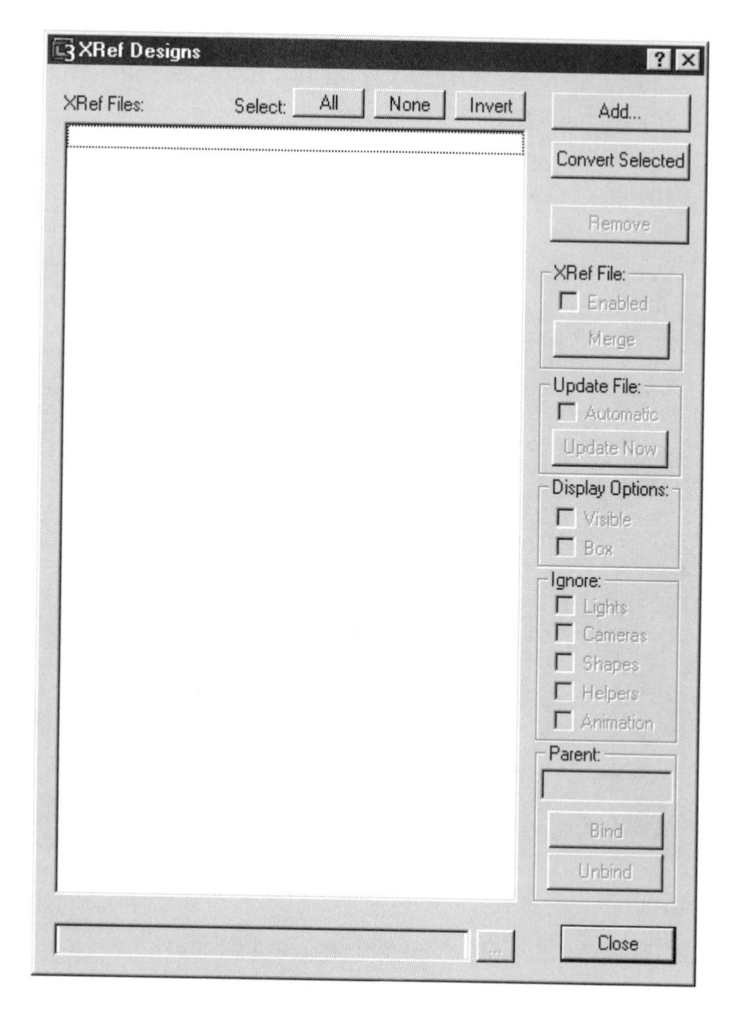

3. Click the Add button. The Open File dialog box displays. Locate and select the `Mysavoye.max` file, then click Open. You may also use `Mysavoye10.max` from the companion CD. The file name displays in the Xref Design dialog box as well as in the current design.
4. Click Close. You now see the Villa in the furniture layout.
5. Change to a wireframe view, then zoom out and adjust your view so it looks similar to Figure 10.7.

You see that the building is to the left of the furniture in the Top viewport. You want to move the furniture into the living room of the Xref Villa design.

1. Click the Select Object tool in the standard toolbar, then place a selection region around all of the furniture in the top viewport. You may notice that VIZ ignores the Xref design in the selection.
2. In the Top viewport, use the Select and Move tool to move the furniture into the living room area shown in Figure 10.7.

FIGURE 10.7

Move the furniture into the living room in the Top viewport

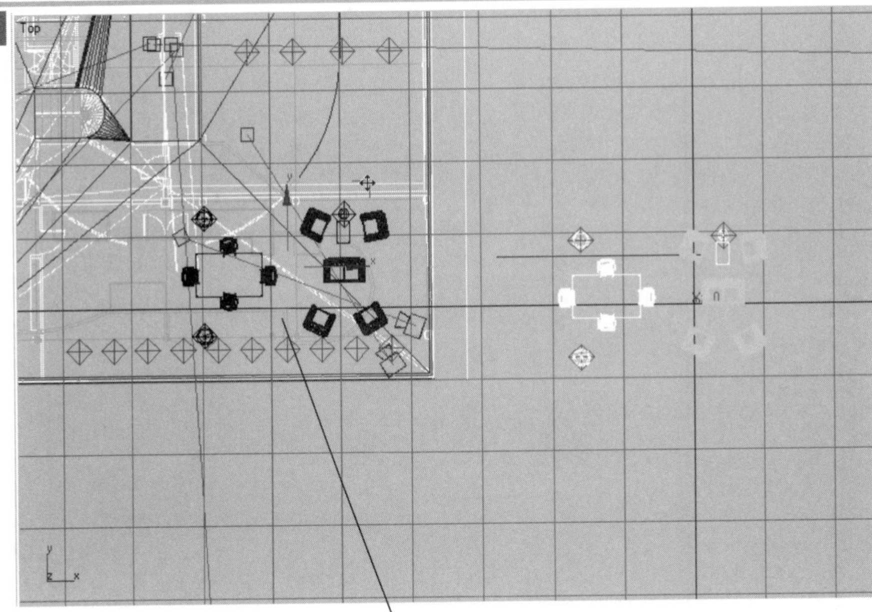
Top
Move the furniture to the interior of the villa.

3. Click the Min/Max Viewport toggle and adjust the Front viewport so that you can see the furniture and the second floor of the Villa as shown in Figure 10.8.

FIGURE 10.8

The Front viewport showing the furniture and the Villa's second floor

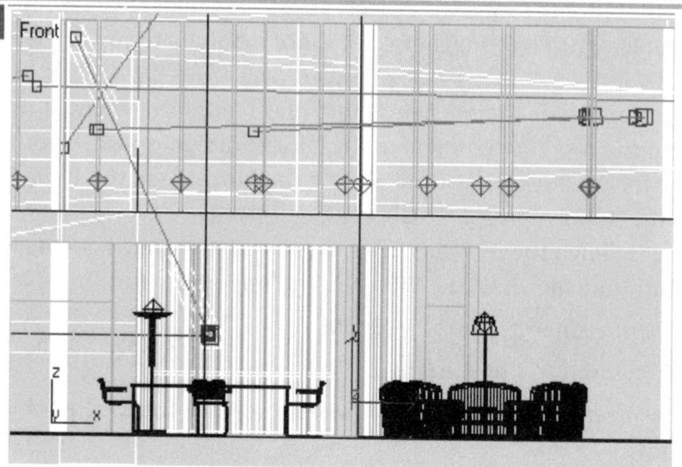

4. Move the furniture to the second floor. Do a rough placement in the Front viewport, then zoom in and make a finer adjustment to the vertical location of the furniture.

5. Go to the Top viewport and *fine tune* the furniture arrangement to fit the room, as shown in Figure 10.9.

FIGURE 10.9

Making final adjustments to the furniture placement

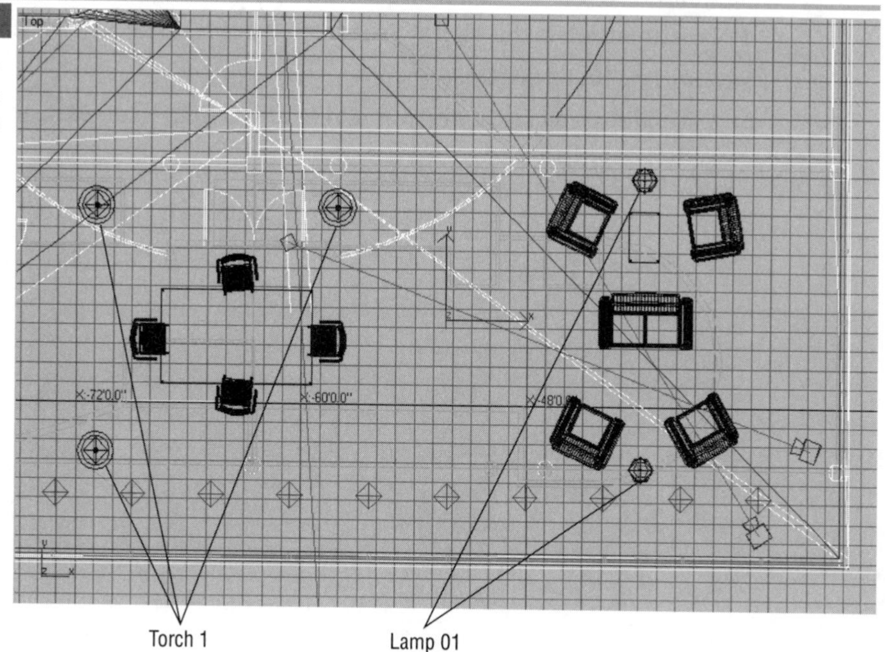

You might notice that the Xref objects are inaccessible. They are visible and will render, complete with lighting, but you cannot manipulate any of the objects in the Xref.

The important thing to note here is that the coordinate system of the Xref file is aligned with the coordinate system of the current design, so when you move the furniture to fit the Xref design, you are placing the furniture in the appropriate location relative to the Xref design coordinate system.

Next you'll switch the relationship of the two files you are working with. You'll close the Furniture file, open the Villa file, and import the furniture file as an Xref.

1. First remove the Xref of the Villa file.
2. Choose Insert ➢ Xref Designs…
3. In the Xref Designs dialog box, select the Villa file in the list box, then click Remove.
4. Click Close to exit the Xref Design dialog box.
5. Save the current file as **VillaFurniture.max**.

Now you're ready to place the furniture in your Villa design.

1. Open the Villa design file.
2. Choose Insert ➢ Xref Designs…
3. In the Xref Designs dialog box, click the Add button.
4. Locate and select the `VillaFurniture.max` file, then click Open.
5. Close the Xref Design dialog box.
6. Click the Mycamera01 viewport and render it. Your rendering should look similar to Figure 10.10.

FIGURE 10.10

A rendered view of the interior of the Villa living room with furniture

The lights that you brought into the `VillaFurniture.max` file contain omni light objects that illuminate the room. Try turning off the SUN light and bounced lighting effect in the Villa design to simulate a night rendering.

1. Click the Select by Name tool on the standard toolbar to open the Select Objects dialog box.
2. Select SUN, then in the Modify tab of the Command Panel, click the On check box to turn off the SUN directional light.

3. In the Top viewport, click the Omni-interior01 light in the interior of the room as shown in Figure 10.11.

FIGURE 10.11

Turn off the Omni-interior01 and Omni-court lights

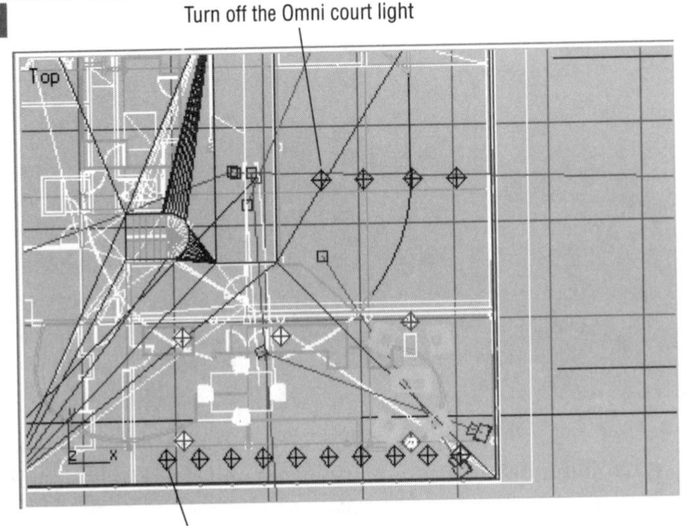
Turn off the Omni court light
Top
Turn off the Omni-interior01 light

4. Click the On check box in the General Parameters to turn off this light. Remember that since the other omni lights are instanced, they will also be turned off.
5. In the Top viewport, click the Omni-court light and turn it off as well.
6. Right-click the Mycamera01 viewport and click the Quick Render tool. You'll see the interior rendered using only the lights from the Xref file (see Figure 10.12).

NOTE You can darken the background using the Output rollout of the Material Editor to achieve a twilight effect, or replace the background entirely with a starry sky for a nighttime effect.

FIGURE 10.12

The interior rendered with lighting from the interior fixtures

Xrefs are useful, especially when your models become very complex. You can divide a model into several design files and Xref them together, for example, to help keep objects organized. This can also aid in situations where you must divide design tasks between several people. You can also nest Xref designs where an Xref contains other Xrefs. There are other settings offered by the Xref Scenes dialog box. Here is a listing of those options for your reference:

Add Lets you locate and select an Xref design.

Convert Selected Lets you convert objects in your current design into Xref designs. The selected objects are saved as .MAX files and are removed from the current design. They are then imported as Xref designs back into the current design.

Remove Completely removes a selected Xref design from the current design.

Xref File Gives you control over the way Xref designs are linked to the current design.

- *Enabled* lets you turn a selected Xref design on or off. This is useful if you want to temporarily remove an Xref design from the current design without completely removing the link to the Xref design. This option also removes the Xref design from memory, making more memory available for other operations.

- *Merge* merges an Xref design into the current design, thereby ending the Xref relationship.

Update File Controls how Xref designs are updated.

- *Automatic* updates Xref objects whenever the source file is edited and saved.
- *Update Now* lets you manually update Xref objects from the current state of the source file.

Display Options Controls the visibility of Xref designs in the viewports. They have no effect on how Xref designs are rendered.

- *Visible* turns the display of Xref designs on or off.
- *Box* converts the display of Xrefs into bounding boxes.

Ignore Lets you control the inclusion of specific types of objects from an Xref design. Note that items that are turned off will not be imported into the current design if Merge is used.

Parent Gives you control over the position and animation of an Xref design by associating, or *binding,* an Xref design to an object in the current design. *Bind* is the mechanism by which you make the association. First click Bind, then select the object that you want the selected Xref design to be bound to. The Xref design's origin will be aligned with the selected object's pivot point. You can use a dummy object as a Bind parent object.

You may then animate the bound object to animate the Xref design. *Unbind* will unbind the selected Xref design from the object to which it is bound. The Name field box at the top of the Parent group displays the name of the object to which a selected Xref design is bound.

Using the Virtual Frame Buffer to Save, Compare, and Print Rendered Views

While we're on the subject of file usage, you will want to know how you can save, compare, and print rendered views from the Virtual Frame Buffer. You learned from earlier chapters that you can set up VIZ to automatically save your renderings by using the Files button in the Render Design dialog box. In many cases, however, you may decide to set up the renderer to just render to the Virtual Frame Buffer, which displays the rendering result in a separate window on your screen. If you decide that you want to save the result from the Virtual Frame Buffer to a file, you can do so by clicking the Save Bitmap tool on the Virtual Frame Buffer window toolbar.

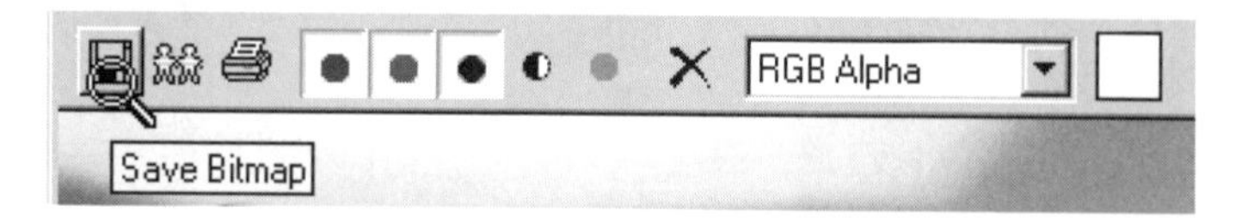

This tool opens the Browse Images for Output dialog box.

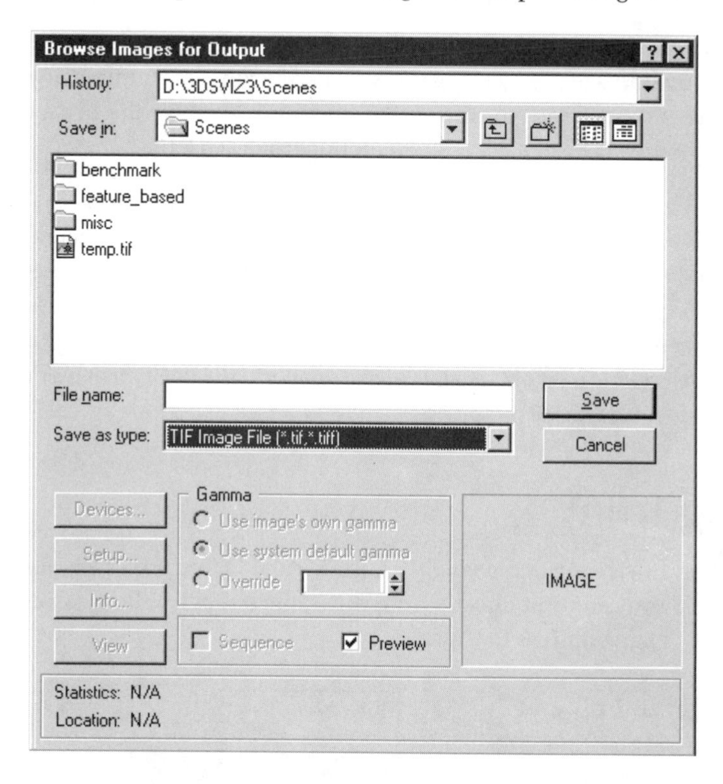

In this dialog box you can enter a file name, then select a file type for the image. You can choose from a fairly extensive list of bitmap image file types as listed here:

AVI .avi

BMP .bmp

Kodak Cineon .cin

Encapsulated PostScript .eps, .ps

Autodesk Flic .flc, .fli, .cel

JPEG .jpg, .jpe, .jpeg

PNG	.png
Quick Time	.mov; requires Apple Quick Time
SGI Image	.rgb
RLA	.rla
VIZ Rich Pixel File	.rpf
Targa	.tga, .vda, .icb, .vst
TIFF	.tif, .tiff

The Browse Images for Output dialog box also lets you set some of the parameters for the chosen image file by using the Setup… button. For example, if you select TIF Image File as the Save as type file option, the Setup button will open a dialog box that lets you choose between a color and a monochrome TIFF file.

NOTE The RPF file format offers support for arbitrary image channels beyond the standard RGB and Alpha channels. These additional channels can be used during post-production of animations for the inclusion of special effects. When you select the RPF file format at rendering time, VIZ will open the RPF Image File Format dialog box that allows you to select from a set of Optional Channels options. The RPF format is similar to the RLA format popular with SGI computers.

Printing Images

In addition to viewing and saving files, the Virtual Frame Buffer lets you print your renderings. You can print directly from the frame buffer by clicking the Print Bitmap tool on the Frame Buffer's toolbar.

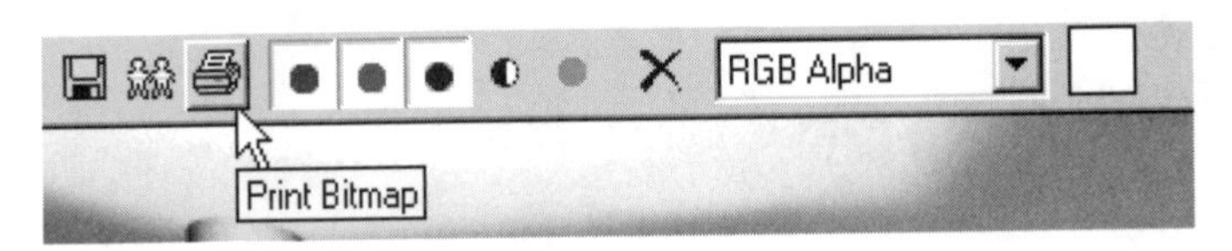

If you want to print an existing image file that you've saved to disk, you can do so from the Browse Image for Output dialog box. Click the Save Bitmap tool in the Virtual Frame Buffer window, then in the Browse Images for Output dialog box, locate and select an image file. If the Preview check box is checked, you'll see a thumbnail version of the file in the lower right corner of the dialog box. You can then click the View button in the lower left corner of the dialog box. VIZ opens another frame buffer window displaying the selected image. From this new frame buffer, you can click the Print Bitmap tool to print the image.

Opening multiple Frame Buffer Windows for Comparisons

The View button in the Browse Images for Output dialog box can be a handy tool if you want to compare a current rendering with a rendering that you have saved as a file. You can also open multiple frame buffer windows to view several versions of your design at once as you're rendering it. To do this, use the Clone Virtual Frame buffer tool.

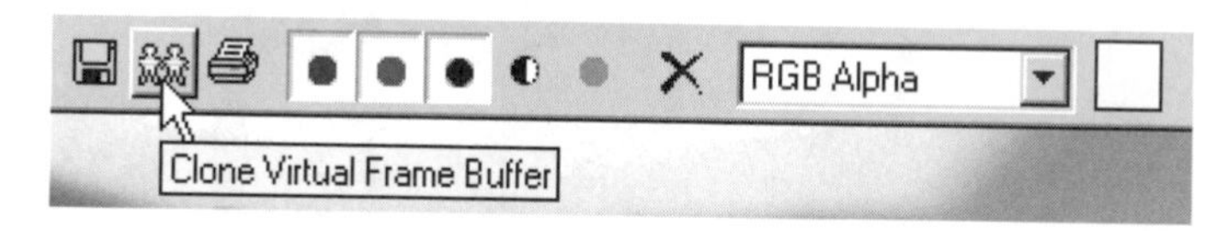

This tool will open a copy of the current fame buffer contents. You can then modify your design and render again. The cloned frame buffer will retain the original rendering, whereas the main frame buffer will display the revised design. You can make several Frame Buffer clones; one for each design variation you want to try. You can minimize the frame buffers while you are working and then maximize them later to view their contents.

Zooming, Panning, and controlling channels in the Virtual Frame Buffer Window

The Frame Buffer window also provides a set of functions that let you control various aspects of the Frame Buffer display. For example, you can enlarge an area of the frame buffer window to get a closer look at a detail in your rendering. To do this, hold the Ctrl key down while you click the mouse. When you press the Ctrl key, the cursor changes to a magnifying glass. Clicking the mouse zooms in on the view. Once zoomed in, you can pan by holding down the Shift key and clicking and dragging the mouse. Right-clicking while holding the Ctrl key zooms the view back out.

If you want to view the red, green, blue, or alpha channel of the virtual frame buffer, you can use the Enable Channel buttons on the frame buffer window toolbar as shown in Figure 10.13. Typically, all three of the Channel buttons are on. To view a single color, click the two channel buttons you do not want displayed. This turns them off. The Channel Display List is for RPF images. This drop-down list lets you display additional channels rendered when using the RPF file type that offers the special effects channels.

You can also view a monochrome version of the rendering by using the monochrome tool. Finally, you can clear the contents of the frame buffer by clicking the X tool.

FIGURE 10.13

The red, green, blue, and alpha channel tools

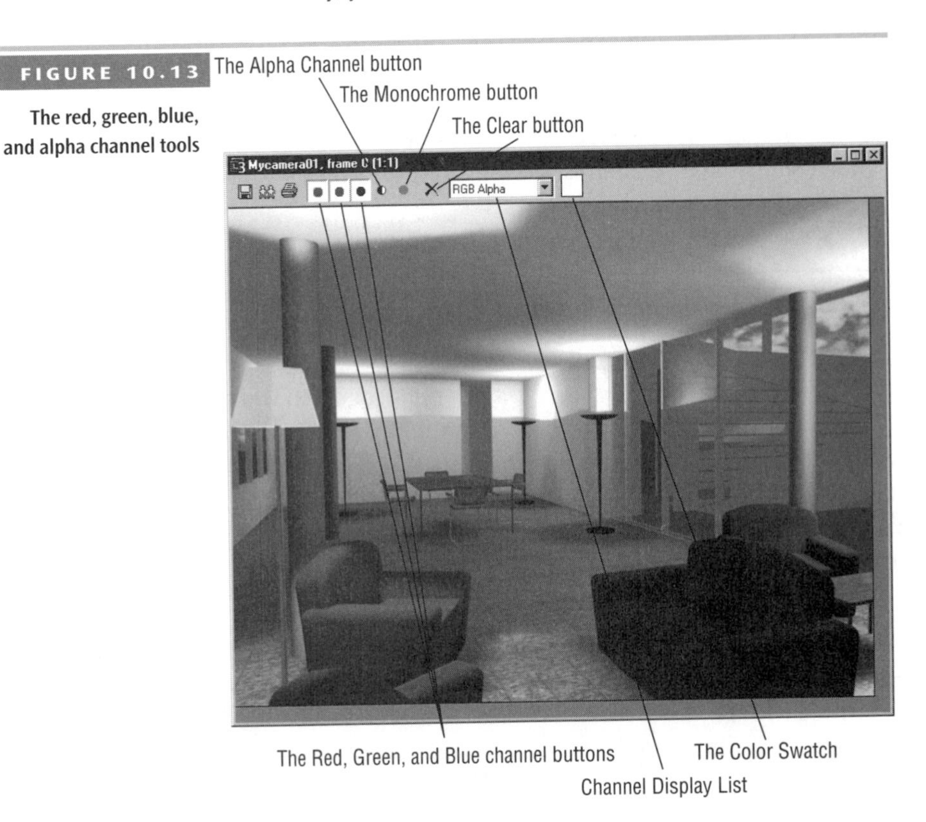

Obtaining Colors from External Bitmap Files

Perhaps one of the more interesting features of the Virtual Frame Buffer window is the seemingly innocuous color swatch. If you right-click in the Virtual Frame Buffer window, VIZ will record the color at the location of your cursor in the color swatch located to the far right of the Virtual Frame Buffer window toolbar. If you right-click and drag the cursor over the contents of the Virtual Frame Buffer window, you'll see a readout of the color over which the cursor passes.

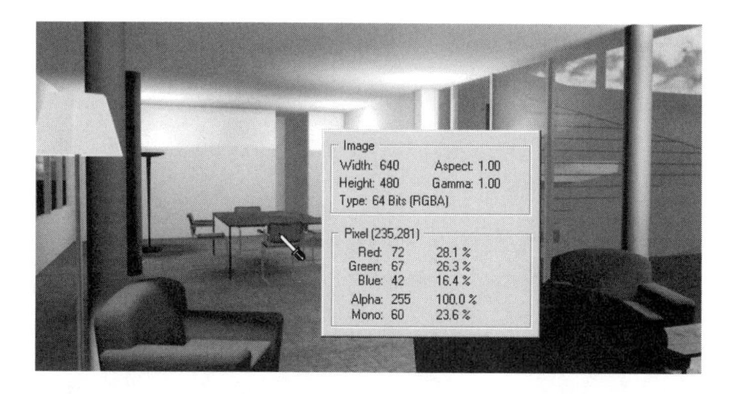

Once a color is selected and placed in the color swatch, you can then click and drag this color swatch to any other color swatch in VIZ.

This feature of the Virtual Frame Buffer color swatch is significant, because with it you can import colors from a saved bitmap image file. You may, for example, be asked to match a specific color from a color chip. You can scan the color chip and save it as a bitmap file. Then using the Virtual Frame Buffer window, you can open the scanned color chip file, right-click the color, then click and drag the color from the Virtual Frame Buffer color swatch to the Material Editor. You can then apply the material with the imported color to an object such as an interior wall.

NOTE **If you intend to use your scanner to match colors, make sure that your scanner and printer or other output device have been calibrated for accurate color reproduction.**

Summary

You've looked at the many different ways that you can use your VIZ files to construct and edit your designs. Some file options, such as saving and importing files, are fairly straightforward in their use. Others, such as Xref designs, are open to any number of uses. The Asset Browser offers you the ability to manage your files more easily, and doubles as a Web browser with which you can import items from the Web.

You also took a closer look at the Virtual Frame Buffer to see how rendered images can be stored, viewed, and printed. In the next chapter, you'll explore the animation process and learn about other ways of working with output files from VIZ, including ways of automating the creation of standard orthographic views.

chapter 11

Creating an Animation

FEATURING

- *Understanding the World of Video Time*
- *Creating Camera Motion*
- *Editing Keyframes*
- *Adding More Frames for Additional Camera Motion*
- *Adding Frames to the Beginning of a Segment*
- *Other Options for Previewing Your Motion*
- *Moving the Camera Target through Time*
- *Controlling Lights over Time*

Creating an Animation

Perhaps the most interesting and fun part of using VIZ is creating an animated presentation of your design. Animation can really bring your designs to life by adding motion over time.

Time is really the key ingredient to animation. This may sound a bit simplistic, but it will become clear as you work through the tutorials in this chapter that you need to pay close attention to the interaction of objects in your model through time. As you gather more experience animating your work, you'll start to develop an almost intuitive sense for what I call the *spacetime* of your model; the 10 to 20 seconds of each animated segment you create. You'll become intimately familiar with this spacetime as you move and adjust the elements of your model. So as you work through this chapter, be aware of how time is always the key component of animation.

Each camera move, light intensity change, and even object movement must be carefully choreographed to create a natural flow of your vision through time. I'll show you the basic tools needed to accomplish this. You will be working primarily by keyframing within VIZ. You'll use the building you've been working with from Chapter 3 to explore keyframing.

Understanding the World of Video Time

You may recall, from when you were a child, a special type of book called a "flipbook" that showed a crude animation of a cartoon character. Flipbooks are nothing more than a series of still pictures that, when "flipped through," give the impression of motion. Today, you can purchase software that will create flipbooks for you. You could probably even create a flipbook of your VIZ animation.

Flipbooks demonstrate, in a crude way, how television and film work. To give the impression of motion, your television is really flashing a series of still images at you. These still images appear so fast that your mind doesn't perceive them individually, but as a smooth stream of motion, just like the flipbooks. This process is called "flicker fusion", where the flickering images fuse in your perception to create the illusion of continuity through time.

In the US, we use what is called the National Television System Committee (NTSC) standard for television. This standard determines, among other things, the number of times per second these still images appear on your TV. The rate of images per second, or *frame rate* as it is more commonly called, is 29.97 frames per second (FPS). We usually round this up to 30 FPS for discussion purposes, but to be absolutely accurate, it is 29.97 FPS. This means that your TV displays one whole picture or *frame* each 1/29.97th of a second. So for 10 seconds, you will see 297.7 frames or complete pictures. (The European standards called PAL and SECAM use 24 frames per second.)

As you work in VIZ, you can think of each of these frames as a unit of time. For the sake of our discussion, we'll round this unit of time to 1/30th of a second. So 30 frames are equal to one second. This will become more apparent as you work through the tutorials.

Creating Camera Motion

In Chapter 6, you were shown a brief glimpse of the Animate tool. There, you created a short test animation that moved the camera around the building. In this section, you'll pick up from where you left off in Chapter 6 and start to refine the camera motion.

1. Open the `Mysavoye11.max` file. This is a file that is similar to the Villa file you completed in Chapter 9.
2. Right-click in the Mycamera01 viewport, then select Views ➢ Camera.View.3DFRONT. This changes the view to the camera you animated in Chapter 6.

3. Adjust the Top viewport so that you can see the building and the Camera.View.3DFRONT trajectory as shown in Figure 11.1.

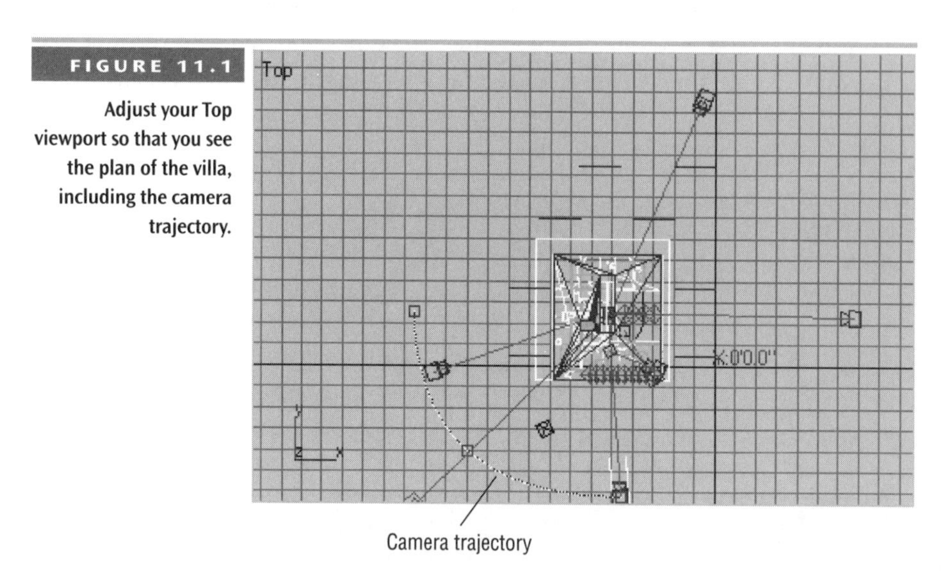

FIGURE 11.1

Adjust your Top viewport so that you see the plan of the villa, including the camera trajectory.

You may recall the Time slider at the bottom of the screen. This slider lets you find a specific point in time in your animation by sliding the button in the slider. Initially, you are given 100 frames, or about 3 seconds of time. Try the slider out. These 100 frames are indicated on the slider itself.

1. Click and drag the Time slider, moving it from side to side. Notice how the number in the slider changes. When you stop, the frame input box changes to show you your current frame number.

2. Move the slider to the far right. The number stops at 100. You aren't limited to 100 frames. You can increase the number of total frames through the Time Configuration dialog box. You'll see how this is done a bit later.
3. Click the Select by Name tool on the standard toolbar, then in the Select Objects dialog box, select Camera.View.3DFRONT and click Select. You'll see the keyframe dots appear below the Time slider.

If you did the exercises in Chapter 6, you saw how you can move a camera through time. To summarize that chapter's discussion on animation, the Time slider was set to

100, and then the camera was moved to a location that viewed the northeast part of the building. The original location of the camera remained, while a second location was created at frame 100. In the file you currently have open, you can see the camera location in the Top, Left, and Front views as you move the slider to frame 100. You can also see the camera trajectory, which is most clearly seen in the Top viewport (see Figure 11.2).

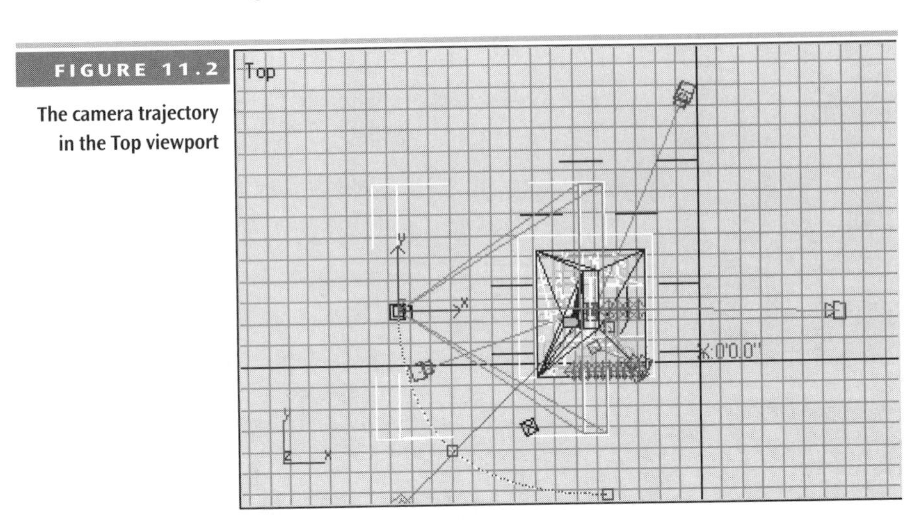

FIGURE 11.2

The camera trajectory in the Top viewport

Understanding Keyframes

The exercise in Chapter 6 further demonstrated that you can add what is called a *keyframe* to that trajectory. The keyframe displays as a small square on the camera trajectory. It is a point along the camera trajectory that can be manipulated in a number of ways to adjust your camera motion. In Chapter 6, a keyframe was created in the middle of the set of frames, frame 50, then it was moved so the camera path curved around the building.

The simplest adjustment to a keyframe is to move it. Notice that there are keyframes at the end and beginning of the camera path. These are automatically created as soon as you create motion for an object. Let's try changing the view of the last frame of this camera path by moving the end keyframe.

1. Click the Animate tool on the Time Controls toolbar. Remember that you need to have this tool active (showing red) when you are moving keyframes and adding animation to objects.

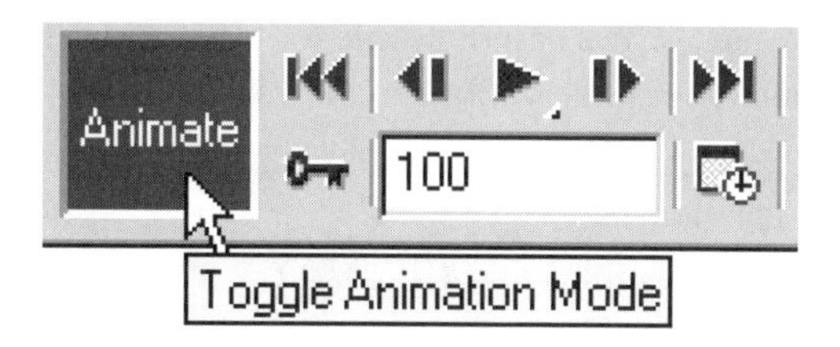

2. Click the Select and Move tool on the standard toolbar.
3. With the Time slider set to frame 100 (the far right), click the camera in the Top viewport.

Move the camera to the location shown in Figure 11.3. Notice what happens to the camera path.

FIGURE 11.3

Moving the camera keyframe for frame 100, the last frame

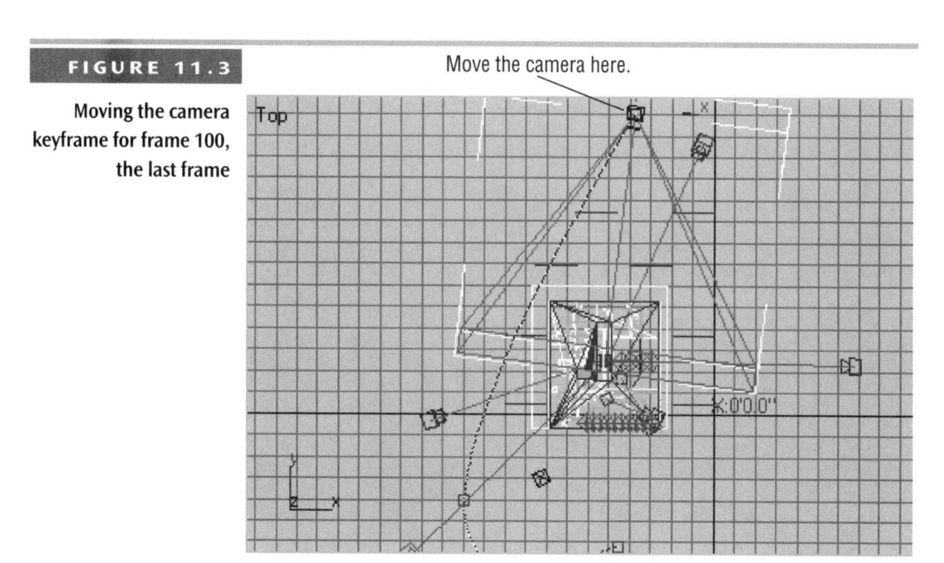

The tiny dots on the camera path show you graphically the location of the camera at each frame. They also indicate the change in speed of your camera over time.

Notice that after you move the last keyframe, the dots are spread apart between the middle keyframe at frame 50 and the last frame at frame 100. This tells you that the camera motion is faster between frames 50 and 100 than it is between frames 0 and 50. You know this because the distance between frames is greater from frame 50 to 100 than it is between frames 0 to 50. You can see a visual representation of this by creating a preview animation.

You might also notice that the camera path now crosses right through some trees. To smooth out the camera motion, and to avoid the trees, you will want to move the middle keyframe to frame 50. You can use some tools found in the Motion tab of the Command Panel to help you quickly move to keyframes.

1. With the Camera.View.3DFRONT cameras still selection, click the Motion tab of the Command Panel.
2. In the Key Info (Basic) rollout, click the left key selector arrow so that key number 2 is displayed in the box to the right.

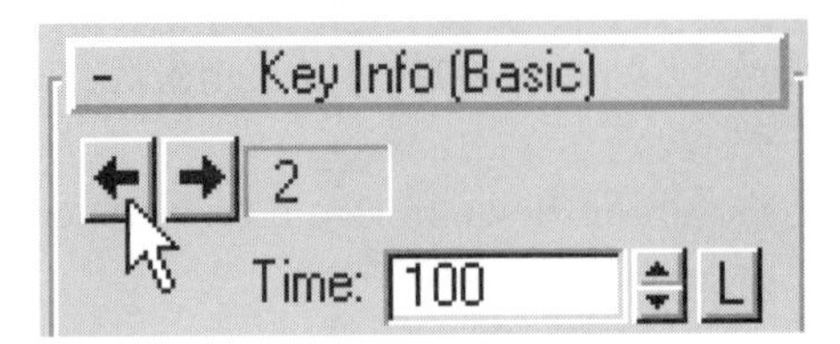

The camera moves to key 2 as does the Time slider. This shows you that the key selection arrows can quickly place your camera on the keyframe you want.

3. Click the Select and Move tool, then move the camera to the location shown in Figure 11.4.

FIGURE 11.4

Move the camera in the number 2 keyframe position to the location shown here.

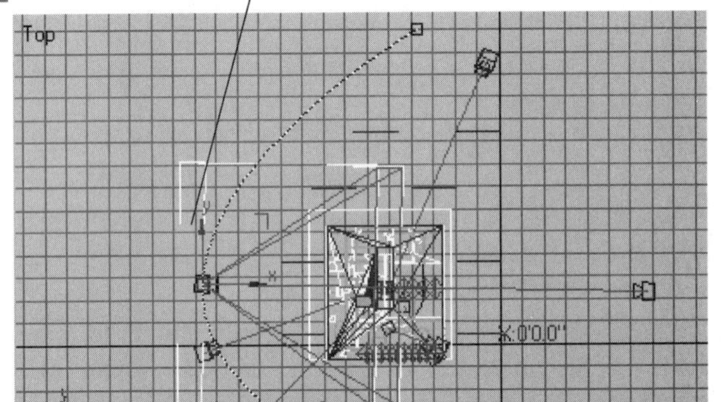

4. Right-click the Camera viewport, then choose Rendering ➢ Make Preview… The Make Preview dialog box displays.

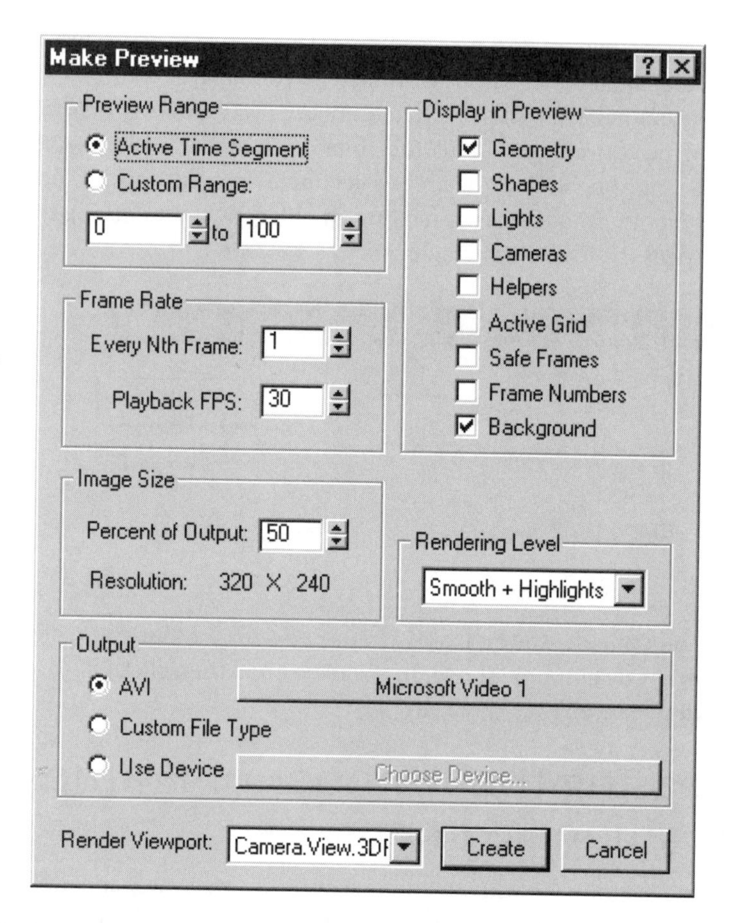

5. Click the Create button. You see each frame of the preview animation display on the screen. When VIZ has completed rendering the animation, the preview plays back in the Windows Media Player or whatever application you have set up to play back .AVI files.
6. Click the animation to stop the playback.

The preview shows that your camera motion is too fast. Also, the beginning and end are rather abrupt. Next you'll learn how to increase the overall number of frames in the current animation to slow the animation down.

Before we move on, however, I'd like to recap the steps involved in animating an object. You can create motion in VIZ by turning on the Animate button, selecting a point in time with the Time slider, and then moving the object to a new location. This creates a keyframe and an animation trajectory. Once a keyframe is created, you can move that keyframe by returning to that point in time, using the Time slider, then moving the object. If you select a frame that is not a keyframe, and then move the object, you create a new keyframe. This is easy to do, so be careful when moving cameras and objects with the Animate button active.

Keyframes can be deleted in a number of ways, the simplest of which is to right-click the keyframe dot under the Time slider, and select Delete Key. An animated object must be selected before the keyframe dots will appear. You can also add a key at any frame without actually moving an object by right-clicking the Time slider. Doing so opens the Create Key dialog box.

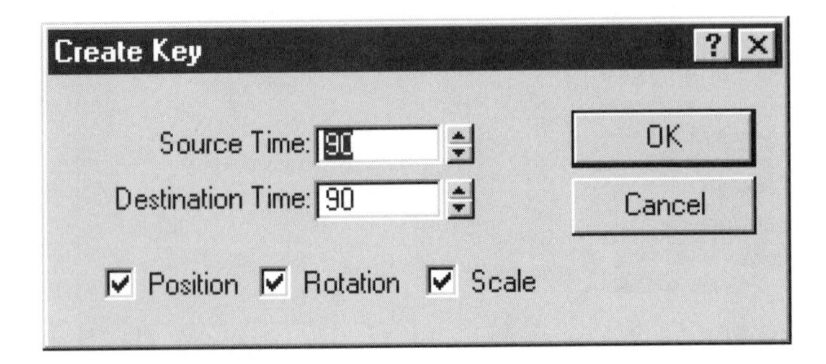

You can enter the type of keyframe as well as, a source and destination time other than the default time shown in the dialog box then click OK to accept the new keyframe settings.

Increasing the Number of Frames in an Animation Segment

In the beginning of this chapter, I mentioned that the standard frame rate for video is about 30 frames per second. So in order to lengthen the time in our building animation, we need to increase the number of frames over the camera path. Right now we have 100 frames, or about three seconds of animation. Let's see what we need to do to increase our current path to 300 frames.

1. Click the Time Configuration tool on the Time Controls toolbar.

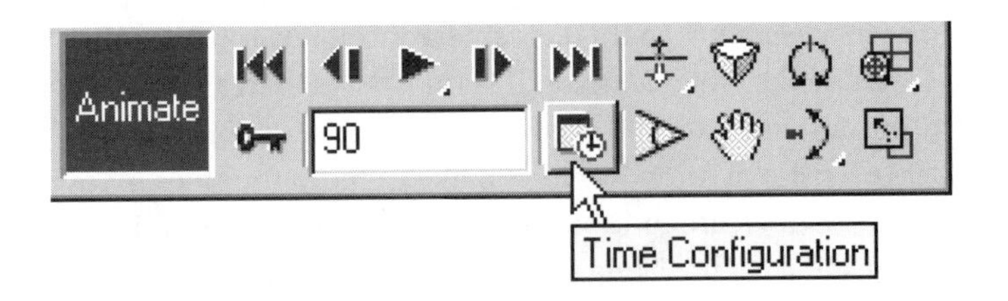

The Time Configuration dialog box displays.

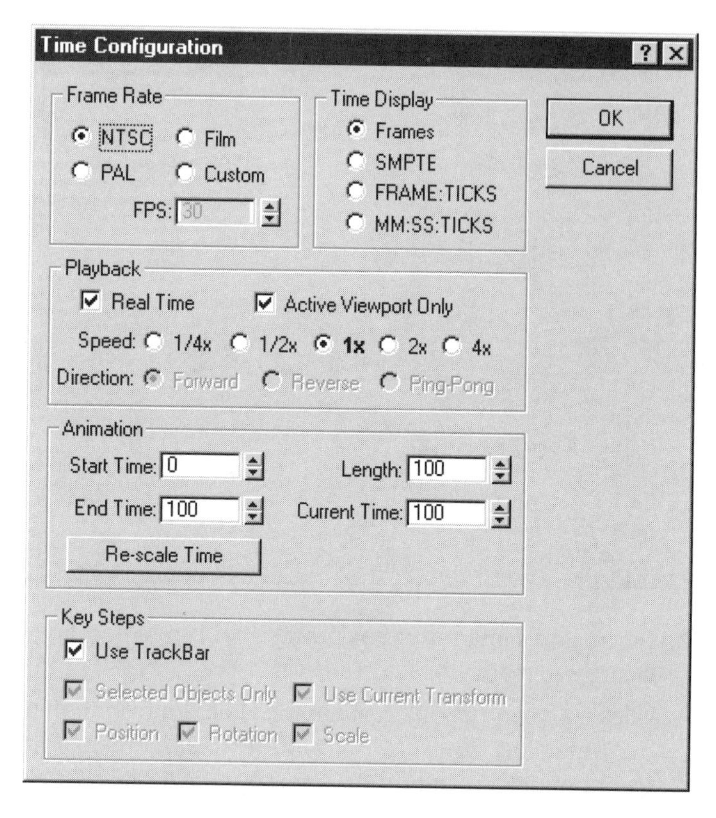

2. In the Animation group, click the Re-scale Time button. The Re-scale Time dialog box displays.

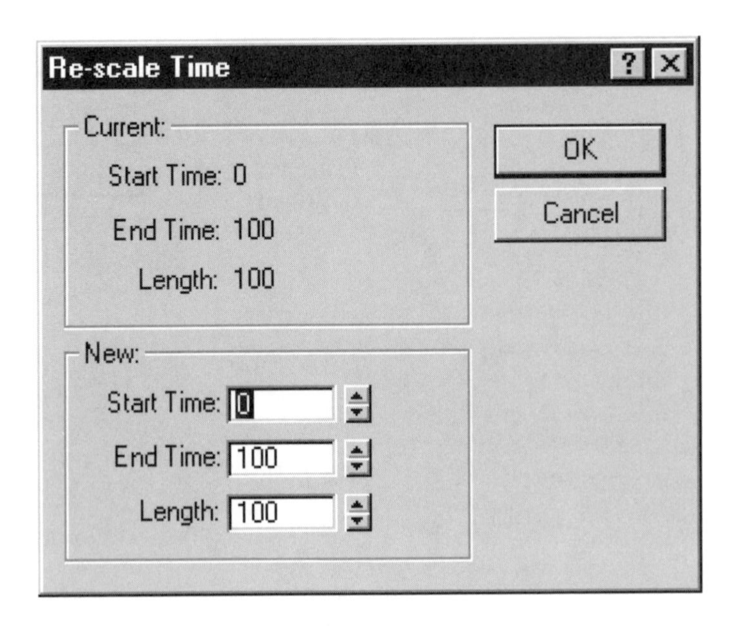

3. In the End Time input box, enter 300. When you press ↵ the Length value changes to match the End Time value.
4. Click OK, then click OK again in the Time Configuration dialog box. Notice that the Time slider now shows 300 for the total number of frames. You'll also see a greater number of dots in the Camera.View.3DFRONT trajectory.
5. Create another preview animation, making sure that you have selected the Camera.View.3DFRONT viewport as the render viewport. The animation is now slower.

In the Time Controls dialog box, you saw that you have an option to set the End Time as a separate value from the Length of the animation. VIZ lets you work with *active time segments*. An active time segment is a block of time within your animation with which you are working. Right now, that block of time includes the entire time of the animation, but you can set up VIZ to limit your active time segment to just a few frames of the overall time length. This feature is useful if you are working on a very large animation, yet want to isolate your work to a specific set of frames. You'll see how to work with active time segments in the next section. Right now, let's see how to smooth out the beginning and end of the camera path so it doesn't seem so abrupt.

Accelerating and Decelerating the Camera Motion Smoothly

Other Ways of Controlling Speed

If your animation is strictly for video or film, you have no alternative for controlling speed other than increasing or decreasing the number of frames in a segment. On the other hand, if you plan to have your animation shown exclusively on a computer monitor, you have other options.

Most video playback programs for computers allow you to vary the frame rate of your animation, though you probably would not want to go below 15 frames per second. Any slower and you will notice the jerkiness between frames.

There are many variables that affect the quality of computer playback of animations. Color depth, image size, and file types all affect how well an animation will appear on your computer screen. In general, an MPEG 1 file will play back nicely at 30 frames per second. MPEG 1 offers full color at a frame size of 352 by 240. If you want a larger size, you may need specialized display hardware to get a full 30 frames per second playback speed. There are a few video cards available that will perform hardware-assisted playback of MPEG 2 files that display a maximum frame size of 720 by 480. MPEG 2 is commonly used for satellite dish systems.

You don't want the camera just to suddenly start moving at its full rate, or your animation will seem jarring. You want the camera motion to start out slowly, then increase speed as if you were in a car starting out from a stoplight. The same is true for the end of the camera path. You want to slow down gradually and not stop instantly. You can control the acceleration and deceleration of the camera by setting the key tangent properties. These are available in the Key Info (Basic) rollout of the Motion tab.

1. With the Camera.View.3DFRONT camera selected, set the Time slider to the 0 frame position at the far left.
2. Select the Motion tab in the Command Panel, then scroll down to the Key Info (Basic) rollout.
3. Click and hold the Out button at the bottom of the rollout. You'll see a set of buttons. These are the tangent options for the keyframe.
4. Select the Slow tangent button. This is the button that looks like the top quarter of a bell curve.

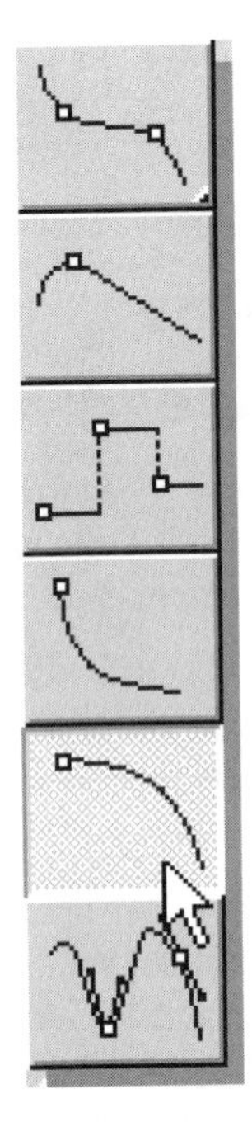

This button has the effect of slowing the camera motion as it approaches or leaves a keyframe. You may notice that now the dots on the camera trajectory are closer together as they approach the first keyframe. The shape of the trajectory also changes to one that is straighter than in frame 0.

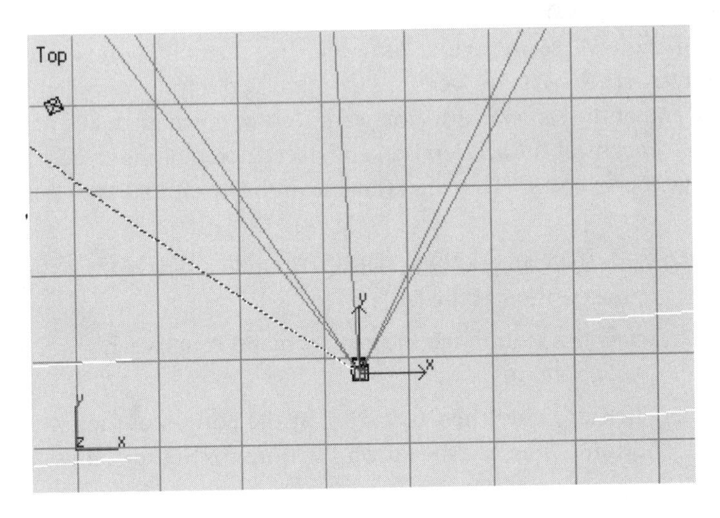

5. Create another preview animation of the camera.

You will notice that now the beginning of the animation starts out in a gradual acceleration from a stop. The *bunching up* of dots at the starting keyframe shows you that the frames at the beginning are closer together. As the frames move away from the starting keyframe they gradually spread apart, traversing a greater distance with each frame until a uniform frame-to-frame distance is reached. The net effect of all this is a smooth acceleration from the camera starting point.

Now adjust the ending keyframe to decelerate the camera motion gradually.

1. In the Key Info (Basic) rollout of the Motion tab, click the right key selection arrow until 3 is displayed in the key number box.

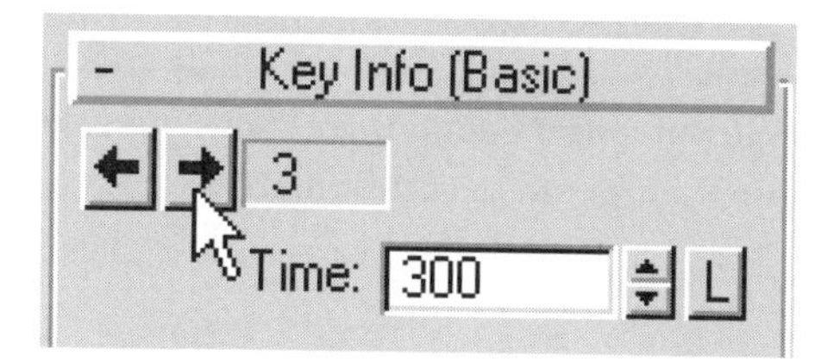

2. Click and drag the In button and select the Slow button. Since you want the camera to gradually decelerate the keyframe, you use the In button to make the setting. Just as with the first keyframe, you see the dots in the trajectory move closer together as they approach the last keyframe.

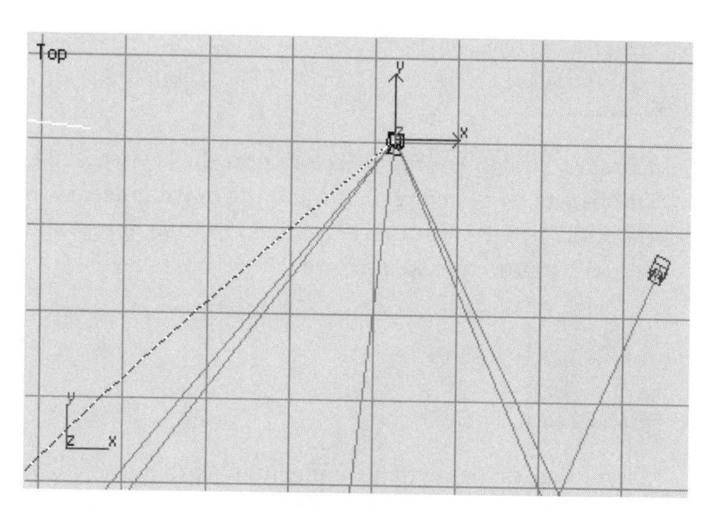

3. Create another preview to see the results.

In this second exercise, you adjusted the frame rate for the end of the camera path in a way similar to the beginning. As the frames approach the last keyframe, they gradually become closer together. The net effect is a deceleration of the camera motion.

This latest camera motion seems to move a bit faster than before. Since the frames have been moved closer to the beginning and end keyframes, they become more spread out over the rest of the trajectory, adding some speed to the camera motion. Remember that you are working with a finite number of frames, so as you move frames closer to the beginning and end, the rest of the trajectory has fewer frames, and fewer frames means faster motion.

Let's take a moment to get to know some of the other key tangent options. You already know what the Slow tangent option does. The default tangent option is called *Smooth*. As the name implies, the Smooth option offers a smooth transition through the keyframe. Here is a listing of all of the tangent options and what they are used for.

NOTE **The icons for the Out tangent options are shown here. The In icons for all but the Step tangent option are a mirror image of the out icons.**

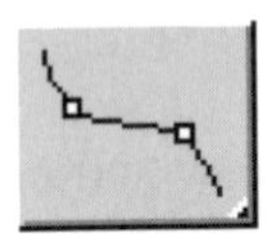

Smooth Creates a smooth transition through the keyframe.

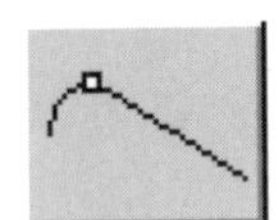

Linear Straightens the trajectory near the keyframe. If Linear is used for the Out parameter of one keyframe and the In parameter of the next, the resulting trajectory between the two keyframes is a straight line and the intervals between frames become uniform.

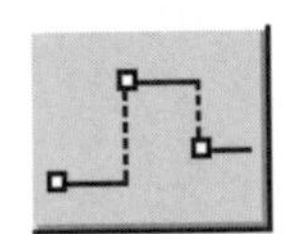

Step Causes the keyframe frame number to jump one frame to the next or prior keyframe, depending on whether Step is used for the Out or In keyframe parameter. For example, if Step is selected for the In parameter of the current keyframe, the prior keyframe's Out parameter will automatically be changed to a Step tangent and the prior keyframe's frame number will be one less than the current keyframe's frame number.

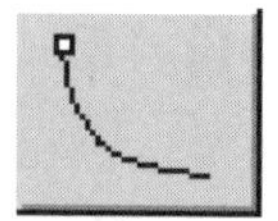

Fast Causes the rate of change to increase around a keyframe. For example, using Fast in keyframe 2 of the previous exercise will cause the camera to appear to speed up around the keyframe. The trajectory also becomes straighter near the keyframe.

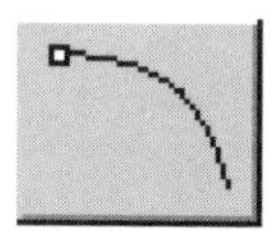

Slow Causes the rate of change to decrease around a keyframe. This has the opposite effect from that of the Fast tangent option.

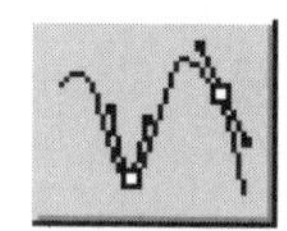

Custom Allows you to make fine adjustments to the rate of change through a keyframe. When Custom is selected, you can edit the rate of change through a keyframe in the Function Curves of the Track View dialog box.

You'll get a chance to use some of the other tangent options later in this chapter, including the Custom tangent option. Now let's continue with a look at some of the other ways a Keyframe can be edited.

Editing Keyframes

Keyframes are not set in stone, and its a good thing they aren't. A recurring theme in this part of the book is the cycle of editing, then testing, then editing again. This process applies to keyframes as much as it does to editing materials and lights.

In the following set of exercises, you will add more keyframes and then adjust them to further understand how they work. You'll focus on the Camera position keyframes, but as you will learn later, these changes can be applied to keyframes for other objects in your model such as the lights and geometry.

Moving a Keyframe's Location in Time

The camera path still comes a bit too close to the trees. This in turn blocks out the view of the building. Let's add another keyframe to the camera trajectory so we can pull the trajectory farther away from the trees without distorting it.

1. Move the Time slider to frame 210. The camera should appear at the location shown in Figure 11.5.

FIGURE 11.5

The location of the camera at frame 210

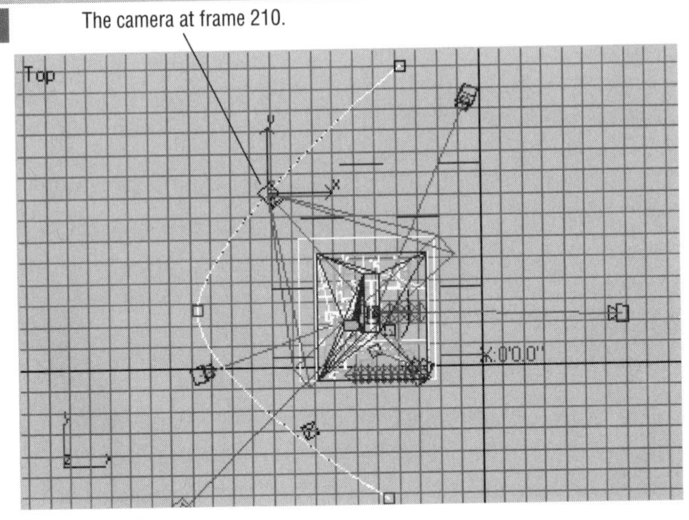

2. In the Look At Parameters rollout of the Motion tab, click Position under the Create Key group. You may also right-click the Time slider, then in the Create Key dialog box, make sure that just the Position option is checked and click OK.
3. Right-click the Top viewport, then click the Min/Max Viewport tool to get a better look at the camera trajectory.

When you add a new keyframe, VIZ automatically applies a Smooth tangent for the In and Out settings.

Now let's adjust the location of the second and third keyframes to make the trajectory a more symmetrical, curved path.

1. Move the current keyframe 3 to the location shown in Figure 11.6
2. Click the left key number arrow in the Key Info (Basic) rollout to go to keyframe 2, then move that keyframe to the location shown in Figure 11.6.

FIGURE 11.6

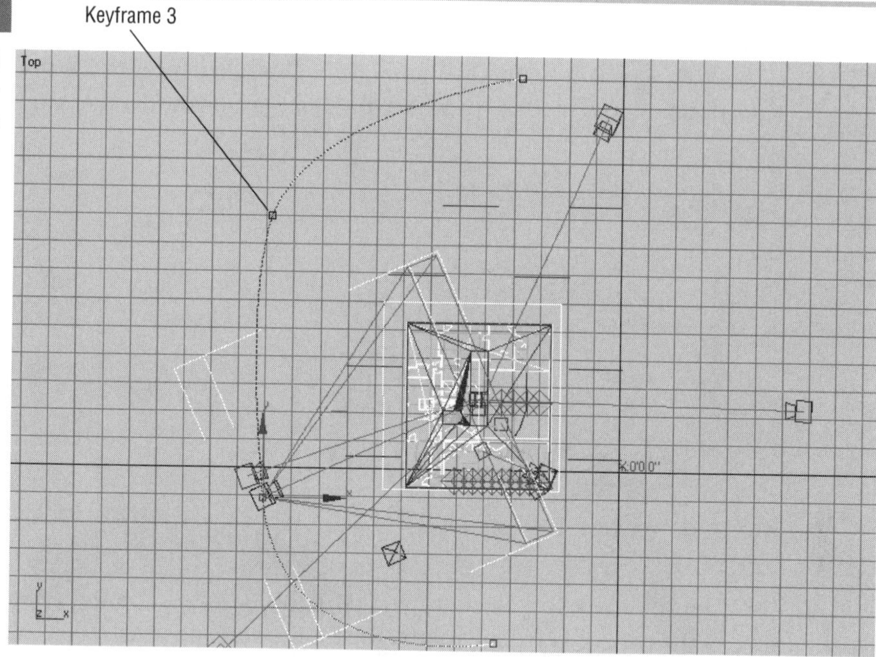

Moving keyframes 2 and 3 into their new locations

Take a moment to study the distribution of the dots along the camera trajectory. They are no longer evenly distributed over the path, but are crowded at the beginning of the trajectory and spaced out in the latter half. This will create an animation that will start out slowly, then suddenly speed up.

3. To adjust keyframe 2 so that it occurs a little earlier in the trajectory, change the Time value in the Key Info (Basic) rollout to **105**.

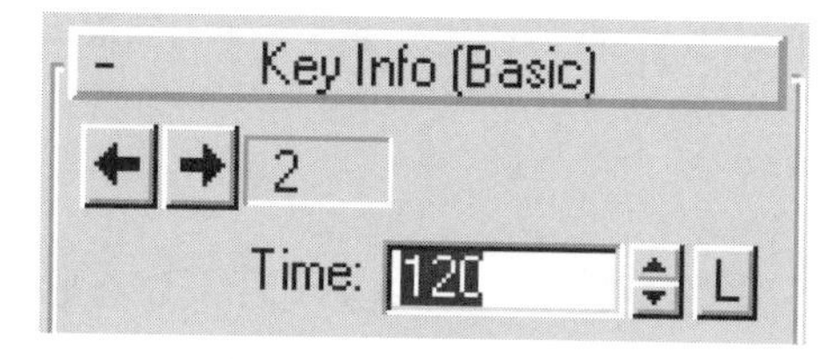

Notice how the trajectory changes in shape to accommodate the new setting.

4. Go to keyframe 3 and change its Time value to **200**.

Although the new frame numbers were provided to you in the previous exercise, you can use the Time spinner to adjust the time while watching the dots in the trajectory. As you adjust the Time spinner, the dots will change their location. When the dots appear more evenly spaced, then you know that the keyframe is in an appropriate location for a smoother camera motion.

Another way to even out the frames through a keyframe is to use the Normalize Time button in the Key Info (Advanced) rollout just below the Key Info (Basic) rollout.

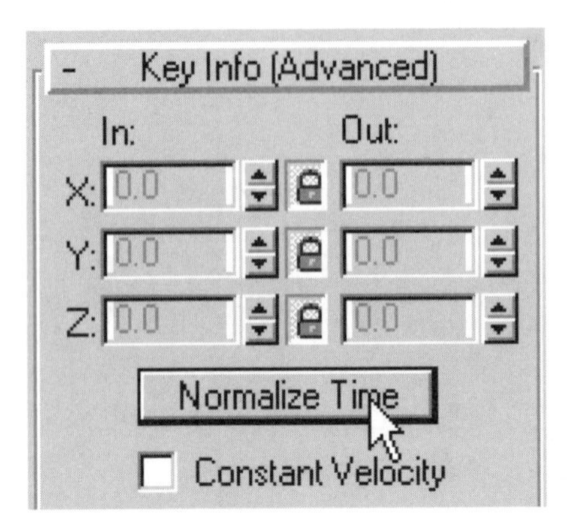

When you move to a keyframe and click this button, VIZ adjusts the location in time of the current keyframe so that the frames are more evenly spaced. The one drawback to using the Normalize Time button is that it makes the other keyframe parameters inaccessible.

Adding More Frames for Additional Camera Motion

Now let's suppose we want to add some additional camera motion to the current animation. It may seem as though you've used up all the available frames for the tour around the building. You can, however, add additional frames at the beginning or end of a segment of frames.

Adding Frames to the End of a Segment

Adding frames to the end of a segment is a fairly straightforward operation. Here's how it's done.

1. Click the Time Configuration tool on the Time Controls toolbar.
2. In the Time Configuration dialog box, enter **400** in the Length input box of the Animation group; then click OK.

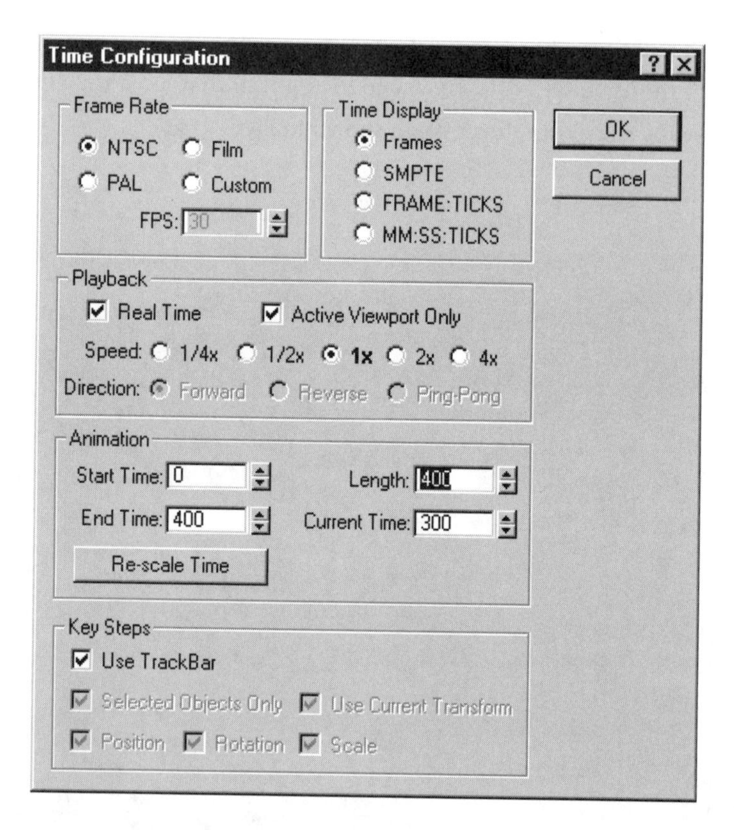

Notice what happens to the Time slider. Position 300 now appears at about three-quarters of the distance from the left side of the slider bar and the overall frame count now shows 400.

Although you added more frames to the animation, the additional frames had no effect on the existing frames. The number of frames in the camera path did not change. You simply added more frames to the end of the animation. Those additional frames are not yet being utilized.

Now let's make use of those extra frames.

1. Move the Time slider all the way to the right so that it reads 400/400.
2. Move the camera to the position shown in Figure 11.7.

FIGURE 11.7

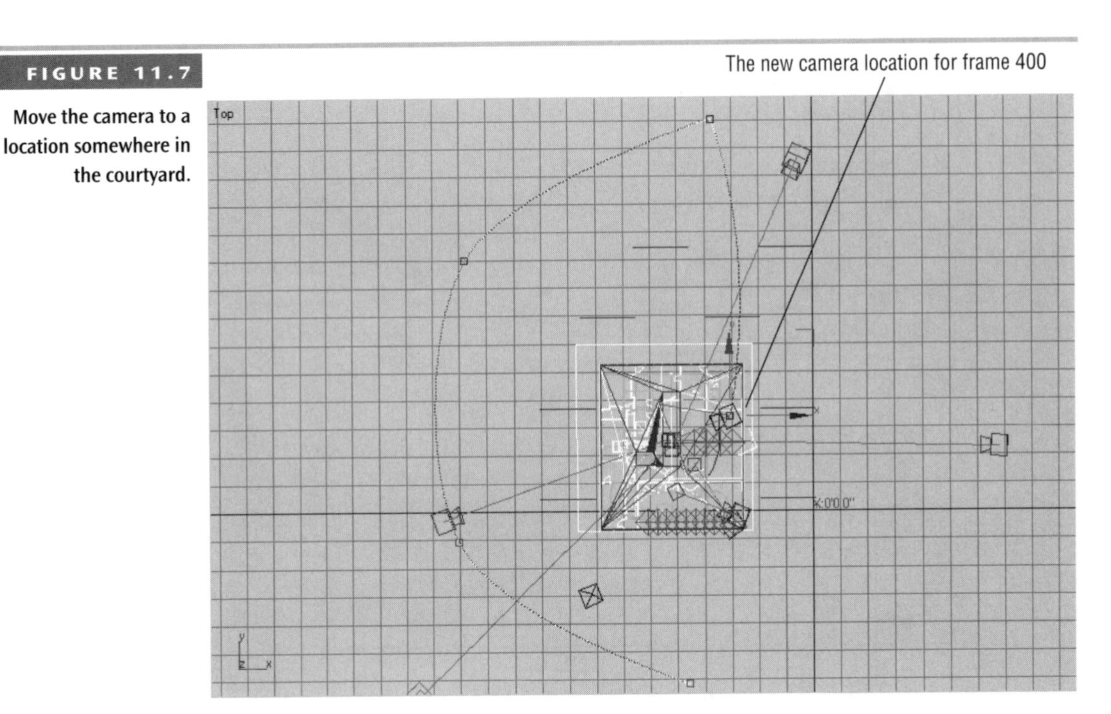

Move the camera to a location somewhere in the courtyard.

3. Click the Min/Max Viewport toggle to view all of the viewports.

Remember that one way to create a new keyframe is to select a new frame number, then move the camera or other VIZ object. In this case, you added more time, then set the Frame slider to the new end of the segment and moved the camera.

Your view at the end is too low. You'll want to move the end location of the camera to the courtyard level. This will create an animation that will give the impression of flying over the building.

1. With the camera still selected and the Select and Move tool still active, right-click the Select and Move tool.
2. In the Move Transform type-in dialog box, enter **16'** in the Z input box of the Absolute: World group. The camera will move to a vertical location similar to the one shown in Figure 11.8.

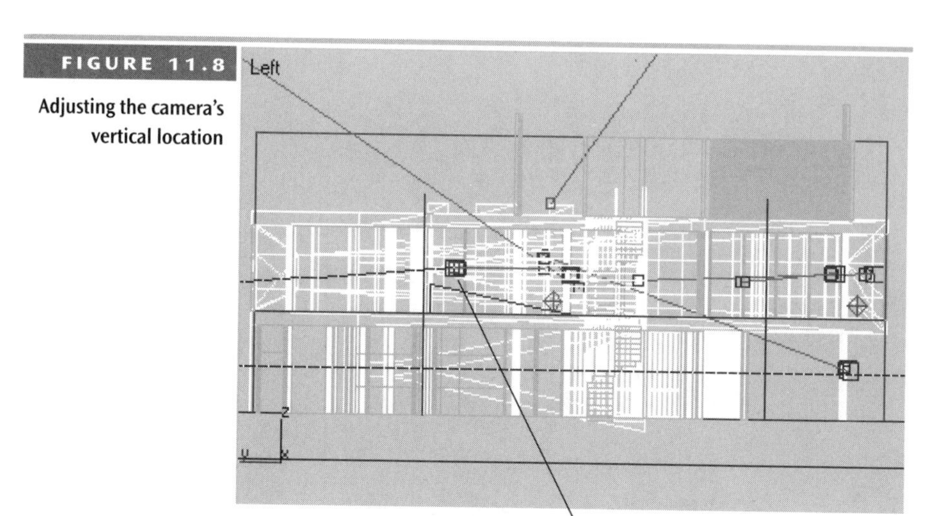

FIGURE 11.8 Adjusting the camera's vertical location

3. You'll want to have the camera slow down as it approaches this last keyframe, so in the Key Info (Basic) rollout of the Motion tab, set the keyframe to **5**, then select the Slow option for the In parameter.

Right now your camera trajectory moves the camera through the wall of the courtyard. You'll want to adjust the vertical location of the other keyframes so that the camera motion brings you above the building.

1. Use the Zoom and Pan tools to adjust the Left viewport view so that it looks similar to Figure 11.9. You want to be able to see all of the keyframes in the camera path.
2. Go to keyframe 4 and use the Select and Move tool to adjust the vertical height of the camera so that it looks similar to Figure 11.9. You can use the Move Transform type-in dialog box to set the camera height to 88 feet.
3. Adjust the vertical locations of keyframes 3 and 2 so that they look similar to Figure 11.9. Keyframe 3 is at a height of 44 feet and keyframe 2 is at a height of 12 feet.

FIGURE 11.9

Adjust the vertical position of the keyframes as shown here.

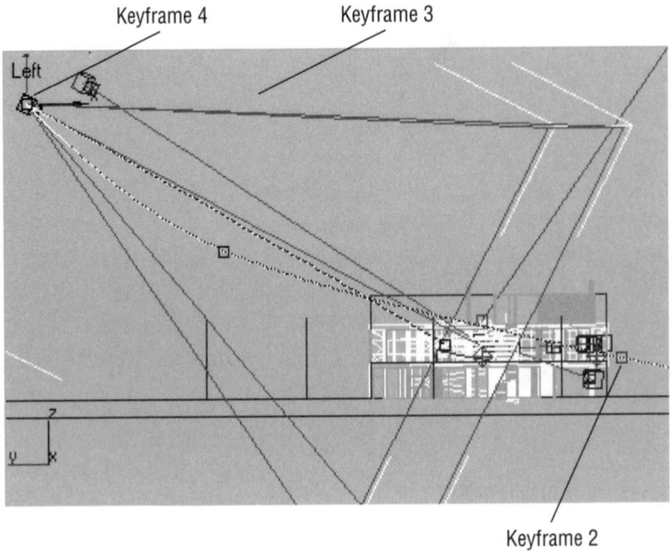

Keyframe 4
Keyframe 3
Left
Keyframe 2

4. Choose Render > Make Preview and make a preview animation of what you have so far.
5. In the Make Preview dialog box, make sure that the Preview Range setting shows 400 for the To value, then click Create to create the preview.

You may also move the Frame slider from far left to right. You get a sense of the motion while you watch the perspective view.

Adjusting the Camera Motion through a Keyframe

You'll want to refine the animation a bit more. Suppose you want to add a bit more time at keyframe 4 to pause at the bird's-eye view of the Villa. You'll also want to correct the part of the animation between keyframes 4 and 5 where the camera flies through the roof.

VIZ offers a variety of tools that let you *fine-tune* the motion of an object through a keyframe. The entry point to these tools is the *Track View*. The Track View gives you a graphic representation of an object's motion over time. In the following exercise, you'll be introduced to the Track View of the camera you've been working with.

1. With the Camera.View.3DFRONT camera selected, right-click the camera, then select Track View Selected. The Camera.View.3DFRONT Track View dialog box displays.

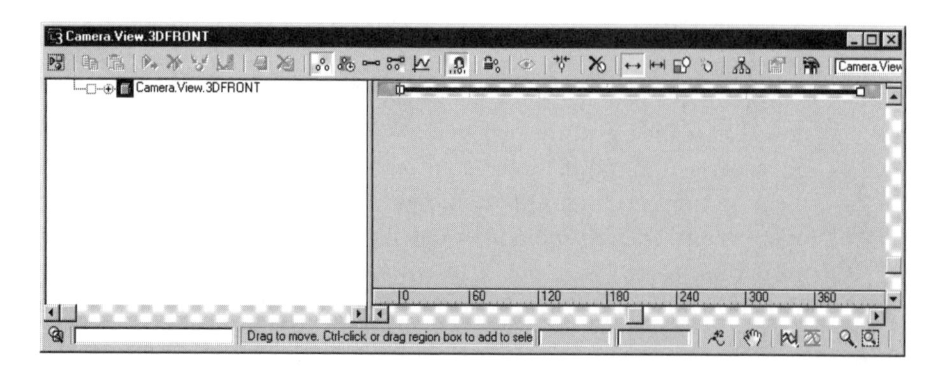

2. Click the Plus sign to the left of the Camera.View.3DFRONT listing in the left-hand panel. The list expands to show the hierarchy of the camera motion.
3. Click the Plus sign to the left of the Transform listing. More items appear in the list.

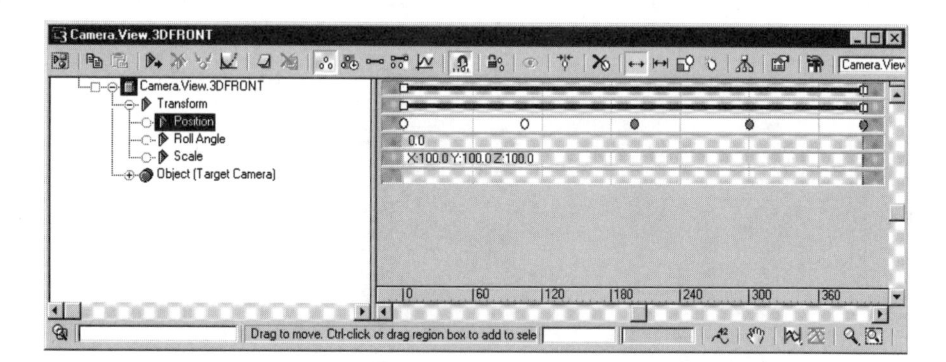

Take a moment to study the Track View dialog box. In the left panel, you see a hierarchical listing of the camera's motion. The camera name is at the top, followed by the Transform listing. Under Transform are three options labeled Position, Roll Angle, and Scale. These are the three types of transforms—move, rotate, and scale—that you can apply to any object, as you've learned from earlier chapters. In this case, they represent the transforms applied to an object over time, such as the Move transform you applied to the camera over time.

In the panel to the right you see a graph representing the camera's motion over time. The frame numbers are shown on the scale at the bottom of the panel. You see two black bars that correspond to the Camera and Transform listings in the left-hand panel. These are the range bars that indicate the range of time over which the items to the left are in motion. You also see the familiar keyframe dots that correspond to the Position listing in the left-hand panel. These dots represent the same dots that you see below the Time slider, and are referred to as *keys*. You'll also see a vertical line in the graph. That line indicates the current frame position of the camera.

You can think of the Track View dialog box as a mini version of the VIZ main window. Across the top of the dialog box, you see a set of tools that let you work on various aspects of the animation. You'll get a chance to work with some of these tools in the following exercises. At bottom right, a set of tools allows you to control the view of the graph. You can zoom in or out, pan, or view statistics of items in the graph, using these tools. Two input boxes toward the bottom middle of the dialog box display the current position and value of a selected key. To the left of the input boxes is a message box that provides messages for the current operation.

Compressing and Expanding Time

Now let's see how the Track View can be used to adjust the camera's transition through keyframe 4.

1. Move the Track View dialog box down so that you can get a clear view of the Top viewport.
2. Adjust the Top viewport so it looks similar to Figure 11.10.

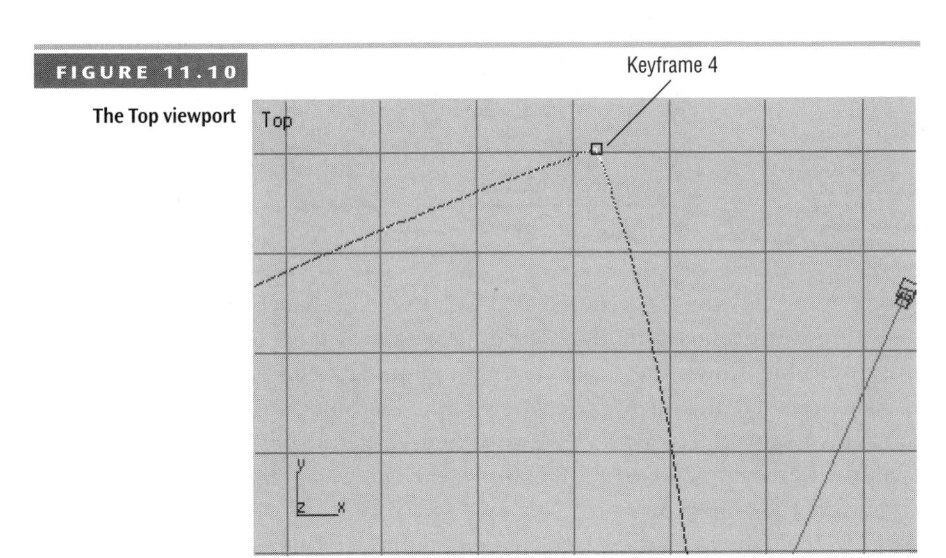

FIGURE 11.10

The Top viewport

3. In the Motion tab of the Command Panel, make sure that the Key Info (Basic) rollout shows key number 4. You should see the camera in the Top viewport at keyframe 4.
4. In the Track View dialog box, click the Position listing in the left-hand panel.

5. Click the Function Curves tool in the middle of the Track View toolbar.

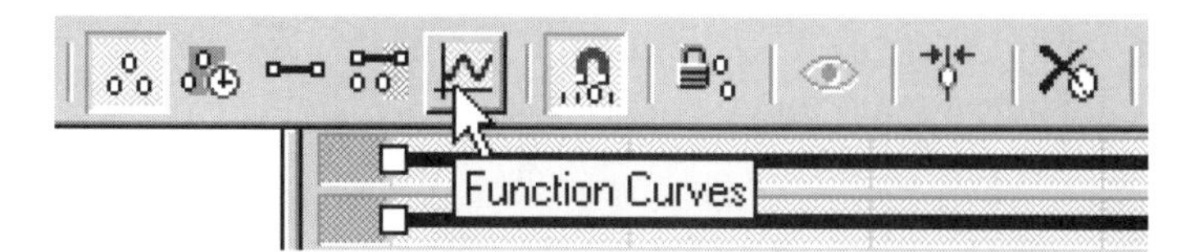

You'll see a set of curves replace the bars and keys in the right-hand panel. This is the Function Curves view of the keyframes. You'll learn more about these curves a bit later.

6. Click the Apply Ease Curve tool on the right side of the Track View tool bar.

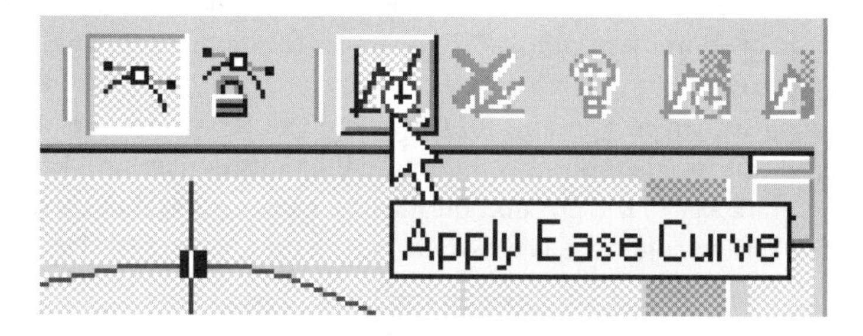

You see a plus sign appear to the left of the Position listing in the left-hand panel.

7. Click the plus sign to the left of the Position listing. The Ease Curve listing displays below the Position listing.
8. Click the Ease Curve listing in the left-hand panel. The Ease Curve function curve displays in the panel to the right.

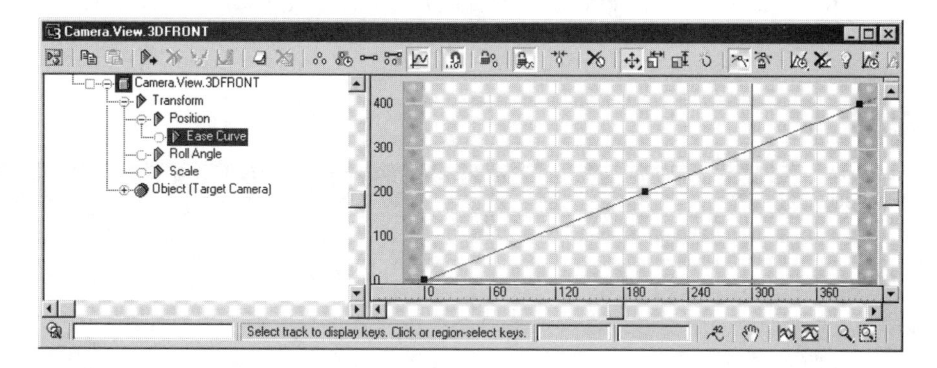

The Ease Curve graph displays a time scale in a straight line from 0 to 400. This is the current time you are using for the camera. You can adjust this curve to compress or expand time at various points along the camera trajectory. This may seem like a peculiar concept at first, but to help you understand the Ease Curve graph more clearly, consider how you used the In and Out keyframe parameters to select a tangent option. Selecting the Slow option for the first key had the effect of *compressing* or slowing time around that first keyframe.

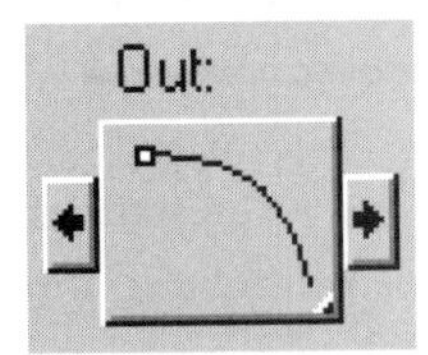

The result was a smooth transition from a stop. Likewise, you added the Slow tangent option to the In parameter of the last key to make the camera slow to a stop, instead of abruptly stopping. This is similar to compressing time before the last key.

The Ease Curve graph lets you compress or expand time in a way similar to the Slow or Fast tangent options for the In and Out key parameters. Let's try adjusting the In and Out speed around key 4 to make the transition around key 4 a bit smoother. First, add a key to the position on the Ease Curve graph that corresponds to keyframe 4. You'll then adjust the key to *compress* the time around the key.

1. Click the Add Keys tool on the Track View toolbar.

2. Click the graph at the point that corresponds to frame 300 as shown in Figure 11.11.

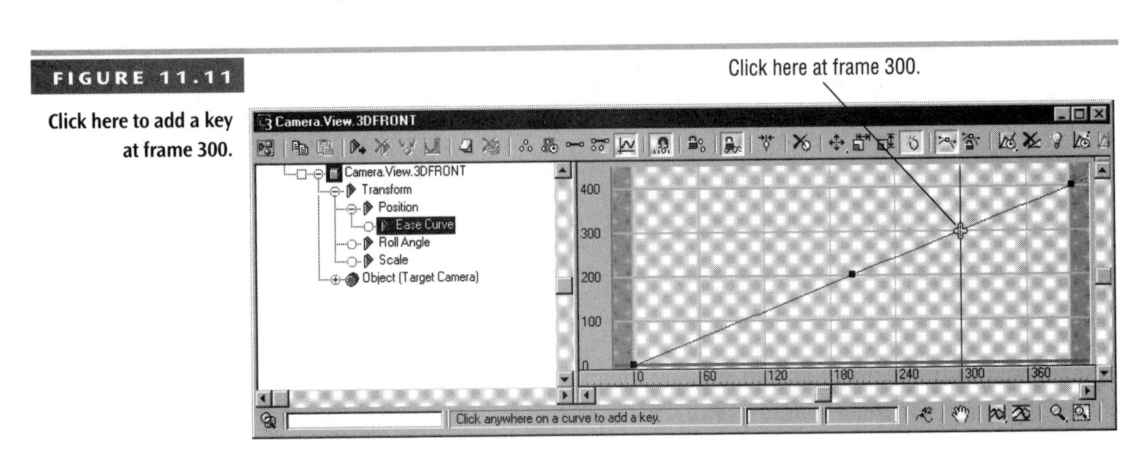

FIGURE 11.11

Click here to add a key at frame 300.

Notice that the two input boxes at the bottom of the Track View dialog box show the time coordinates of the key you just created.

NOTE The numbers you see may be different from the ones shown here.

3. You can fine-tune the location of the key by entering the exact coordinate values in these boxes. Click the box to the left and enter **300**, then press the Tab key and enter **300** again.
4. Right-click the key that you just added. The Camera.View.3DFRONT Ease Curve dialog box displays.

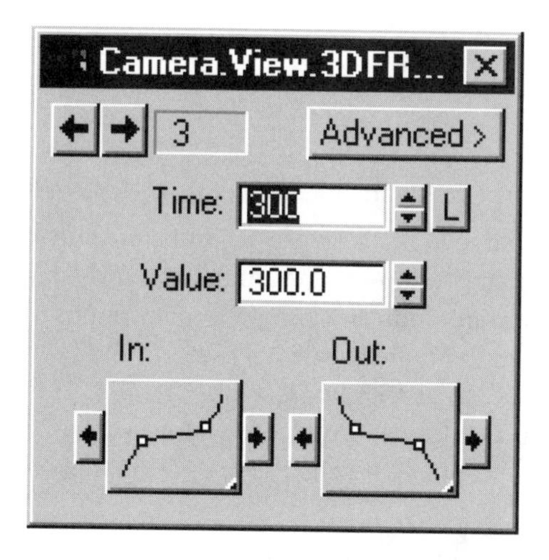

5. In the In parameters rollout, click the Select the Slow Tangent option from the flyout.

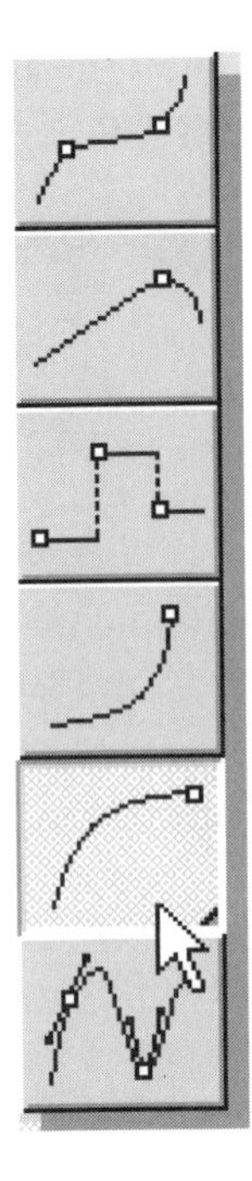

6. Do the same for the Out parameter, then close the dialog box.

Now notice how the curve looks. It levels off just before and after the new key. This leveling off indicates a compression in time around the key. A straight diagonal line as seen in the rest of the graph indicates a smooth, continuous flow of time.

Also notice that dots in the camera trajectory seen in the Top viewport are compressed a bit more than before as they approach keyframe 4. This tells you that the camera now slows down as it transitions into keyframe 4.

If you want even more control over the Ease Curve graph, you can use the Custom Tangent option.

1. Right-click the key at frame 300 on the Ease Curve graph.
2. In the Ease Curve dialog box, select the Custom Tangent option from the In fly-out, then close the dialog box.

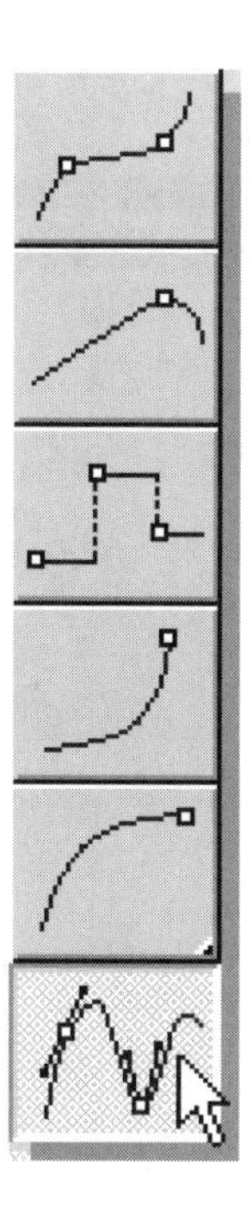

Notice that now you have a Bézier handle appearing at the key. You can adjust this handle vertically to control the shape of the curve through the key.

1. Click the Move Keys tool in the Track View toolbar

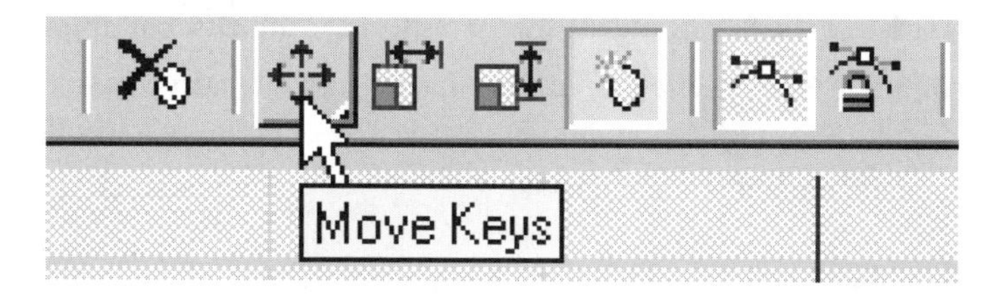

2. Click and drag the Bézier handle on the key upward. The curve follows the handle. Notice how the dots arrange themselves in the trajectory in the Top viewport. They start to compress, then expand again as they approach the keyframe.
3. You don't really want this configuration for the key, so click the Undo button on the VIZ standard toolbar to undo the change in the curve.
4. Now let's get rid of the key that's in the middle of the graph. Click the key in the middle of the graph to select it as shown in Figure 11.12.

Click the middle key.

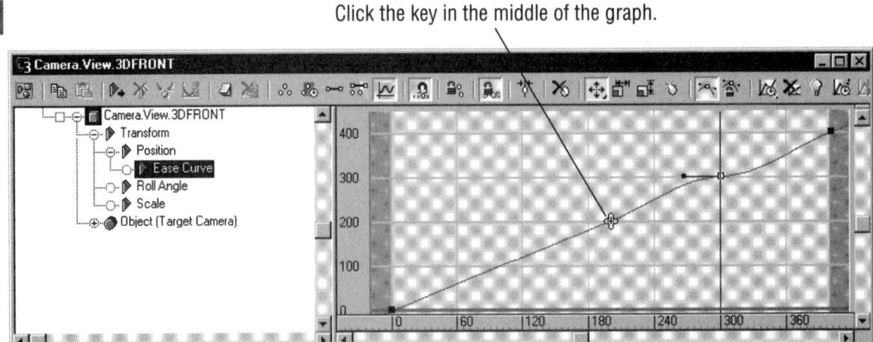

5. Click the Delete Keys tool on the Track View toolbar or just press the Delete key.

The key disappears. Notice how the curve changes. The transition into keyframe 4 is now more gradual.

Go ahead and make similar changes to the Ease Curve settings for the first and last key.

1. Right-click the first key to the far left of the curve. Then in the Curve dialog box, select the Slow tangent flyout option for the Out parameter.
2. Right-click the last key to the far right of the curve and select the Slow tangent flyout option for the In parameter. The curve now looks like a gentle slope with gradual transitions between keys.

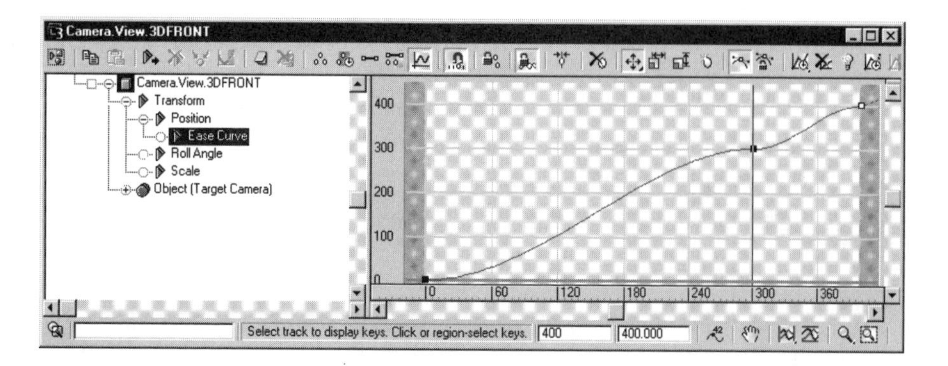

It is important to keep in mind that the Ease Curve tangent settings are really independent of the keyframe keys. You can compress and expand time anywhere along the timeline. For example, if you wanted to have the camera slow down between keyframes 1 and 2, you could create a key in the track view at frame 62 of the Ease Curve and adjust the key in a way similar to the way you adjusted the key in the previous exercises.

If you decide that you don't want to use the Ease Curve settings you've created, you can delete an Ease Curve by selecting the Ease Curve listing in the left panel and clicking the Delete Ease/Multiplier Curve tool.

Next, let's see how to adjust the camera motion to avoid going through the roof of the Villa as the camera approaches the courtyard. To do this, you'll need to use the Position listing of the Track View dialog box.

Adjusting the Camera Trajectory Using the Track View

Now let's take a look at another way that the Track View can help you *fine-tune* the camera motion.

1. Move the Track view dialog box up so that you can get a clear view of the Left viewport.

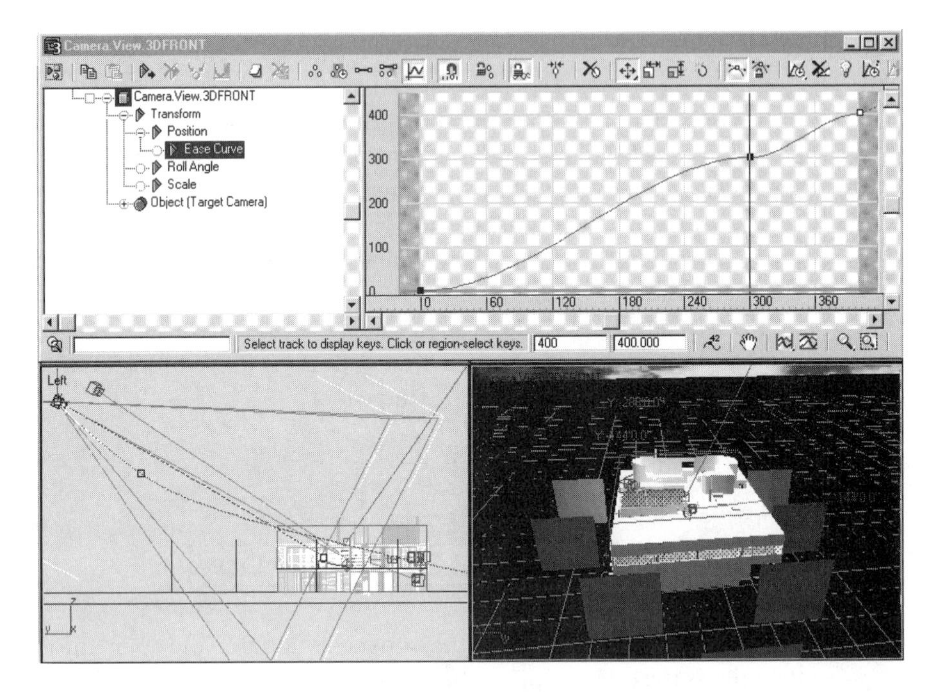

2. Click the Position listing in the left panel of the Track View. You see the graph in the left panel change to show three curves. (See Figure 11.13.)

The graph you see in the right panel appears when the Function Curve tool is selected on the Track View toolbar, and the Position Transform listing is selected as shown in Figure 11.13.

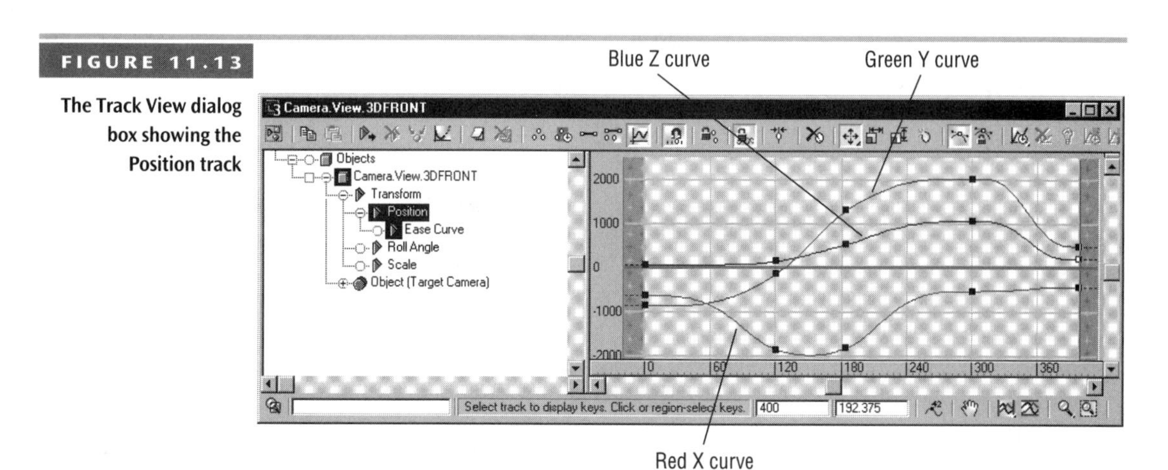

FIGURE 11.13

The Track View dialog box showing the Position track

The Position Function curve is a graphic representation of the camera motion. Unlike the camera trajectory, the Position Function curve displays the changes in the X, Y, and Z coordinates as separate lines. Each line represents a different axis in the coordinate system: The Red is X, the Green is Y, and the Blue is Z. One way to remember this relationship is that the red, green, and blue colors are usually abbreviated as RGB, so you can correlate RGB with XYZ. Don't worry if the graph doesn't make any sense to you right now. You'll see in the next exercise how you can make practical use of it.

If you created a preview of the animation so far, you'd see that the camera passes through the roof of the Villa before landing in the courtyard. To avoid this, you can use the Position Function curve to adjust the shape of the camera trajectory so that it avoids the roof. Try the following exercise to see how this works.

1. Use the Zoom and Pan tools to adjust the Left viewport to look like Figure 11.14.

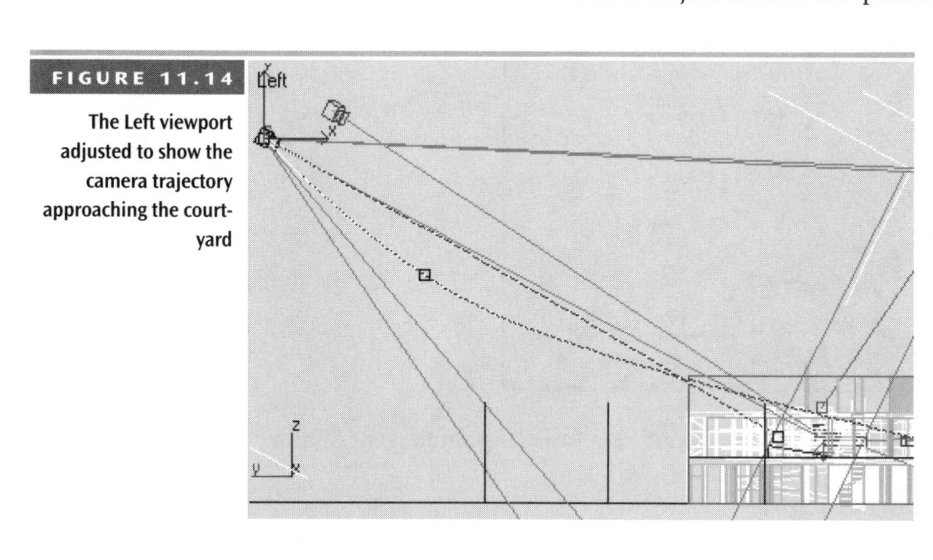

FIGURE 11.14

The Left viewport adjusted to show the camera trajectory approaching the courtyard

2. On the right Position Function curve, click the key at the far right end of the blue curve, as shown in Figure 11.15.

FIGURE 11.15

Click the key at the far right end of the blue curve, as shown here.

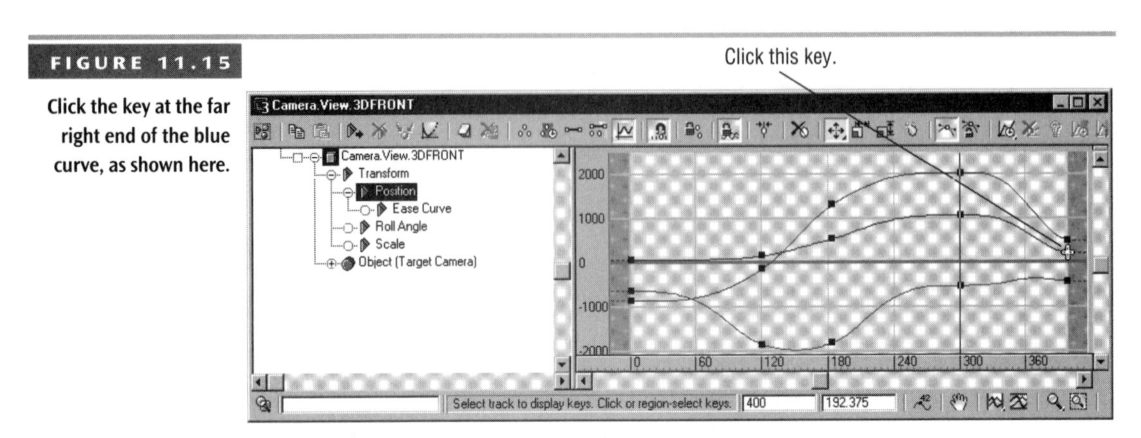

Remember that the blue curve represents the Z axis for the transforms applied to the camera.

3. Right-click the same key. The Camera.View.3DFRONT/Position dialog box displays.

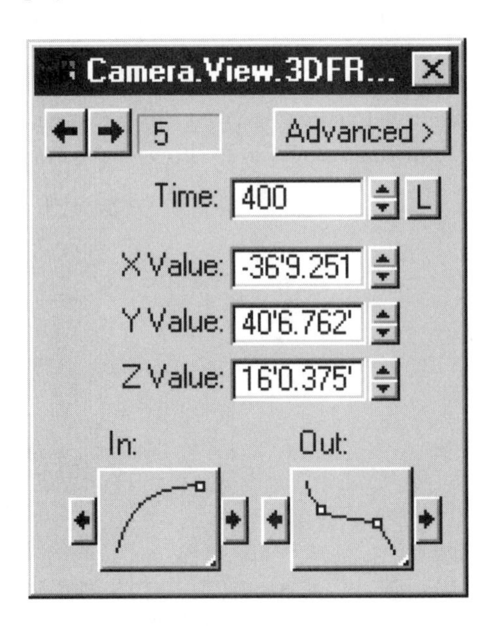

4. In the In parameters rollout, select the Custom tangent option.

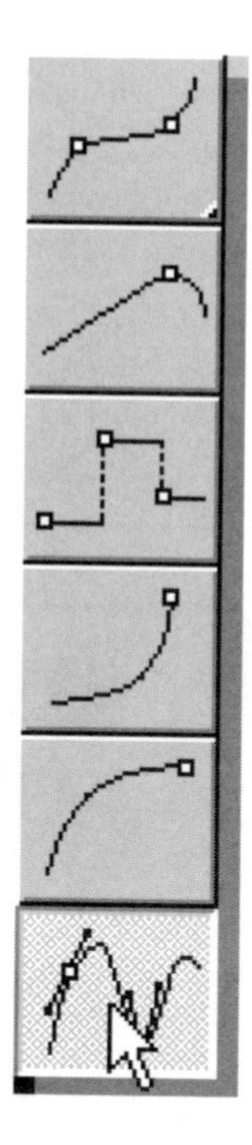

NOTE **The Position dialog box is actually a duplicate of the Key Info (Basic) rollout in the Motion tab for the selected keyframe. Selecting the Custom Tangent option here also selects the Custom Tangent option for keyframe 5 in the Motion tab of the Command Panel.**

You'll see a Bézier handle appear at the selected key in the Position Function curve.

5. Close the Position dialog box. Then, with the Move Keys tool from the Track View toolbar selected, move the Bézier handle upward so it looks similar to Figure 11.16.

FIGURE 11.16

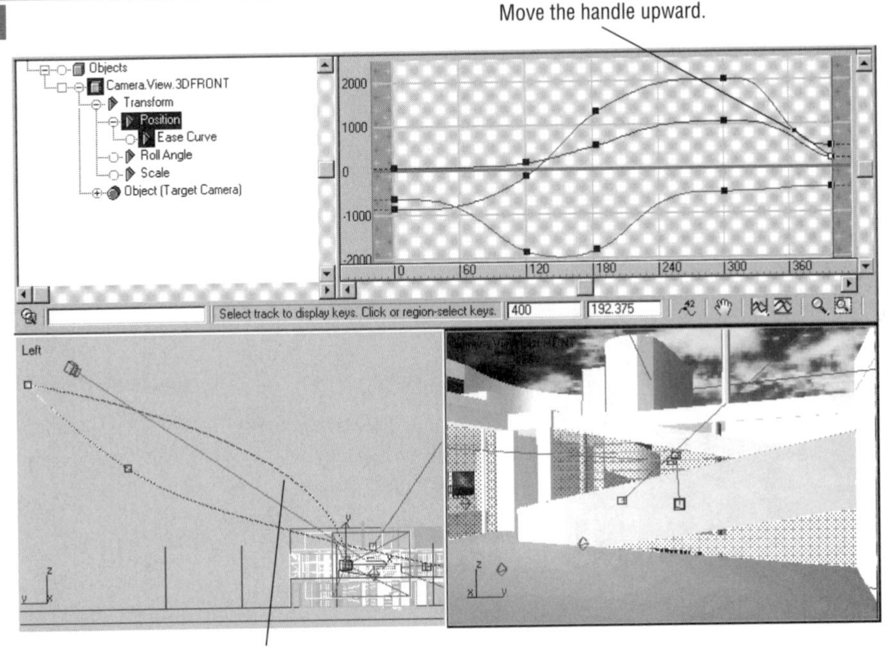

The Function curve with the Bézier handle pointing upward and a view of the resulting camera trajectory

Notice what happens to the camera trajectory in the Left viewport. It now curves upward. This helps move the trajectory away from the roof.

By altering the Z curve of the Position Function curve, you altered the trajectory. If you take time to study the blue curve, you see that it is really a graph that represents the Z coordinate of the camera over the 400 frames. The same is true for the X and Y red and green curves. You can manipulate the keys using a combination of the Custom tangent option for the In and Out key parameters and the Position Function curve.

As you can see from this and the previous section, you have a great deal of control over the motion of an object through time and space. Next, you'll look at ways of adjusting the time so that you can add motion to the beginning of your animation.

I'd like to point out that the Custom tangent option and the resulting curve in the Position Track View and the trajectory are affected by the prior tangent setting that the Custom tangenttion replaces. Had the prior In tangent setting for Keyframe 5 been the Smooth tangent option, instead of the Slow tangent option, the resulting curve in the trajectory and the Z-axis curve of the Track View would be different. Instead of the curved trajectory shown in Figure 11.16, you would see a curve that resembles the one in Figure 11.17.

FIGURE 11.17

The Track View curve and trajectory after changing the In tangent option from Smooth to Custom

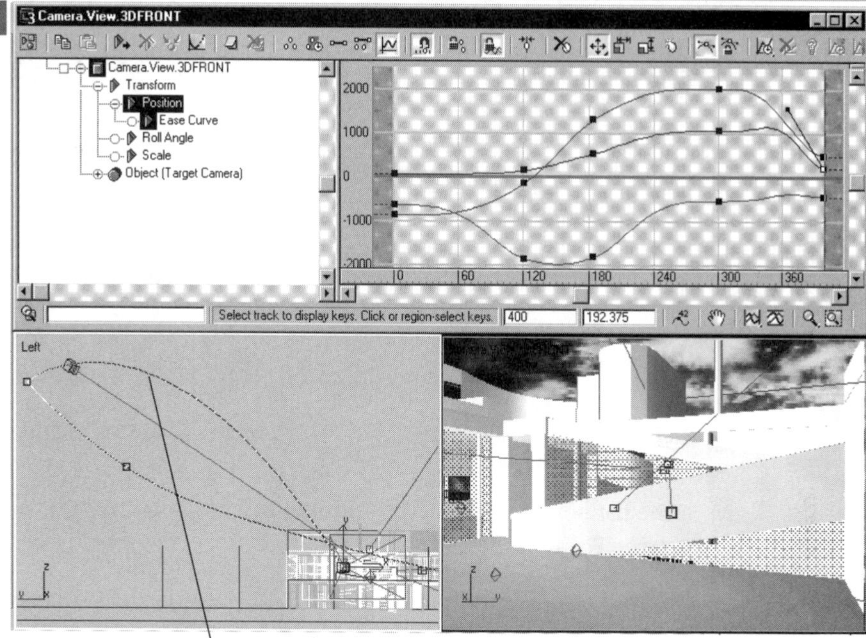

The curve in Figure 11.17 is biased toward keyframe 4 at the upper left corner of the Left viewport. This is quite different from the Left viewport view in Figure 11.16, where the trajectory curve is biased toward keyframe 5. This is a subtle feature and one that often goes unnoticed until you become confused by the seemingly random way the Custom Tangent option affects a curve.

TIP You can adjust the camera trajectory while watching a playback of the animation in the Camera viewport. Make the Camera viewport active; then click the play button in the Time controls. As you watch the playback of the animation in the camera viewport, adjust the curve in the Track View dialog box.

Using the TCB method for adjusting Keyframe Transitions

If you find that the track View is too complex, you can also use the Tension Continuity Bias (TCB) controller for your keyframe transitions. If you've used the older DOS version of 3D Studio, the TCB controller should be familiar to you. Instead of offering a set of tangent options for the In and Out keyframe parameters, you use three settings—Tension, Continuity, and Bias—to control a keyframe transition.

The default keyframe controller is called a Bézier controller. You can change to a TCB controller by doing the following.

1. Select a keyframe key. Then, in the Motion tab of the Command Panel, open the Assign Controller rollout.
2. In the list box of the Assign Controller rollout, open the Transform listing and click the Position listing to select it.

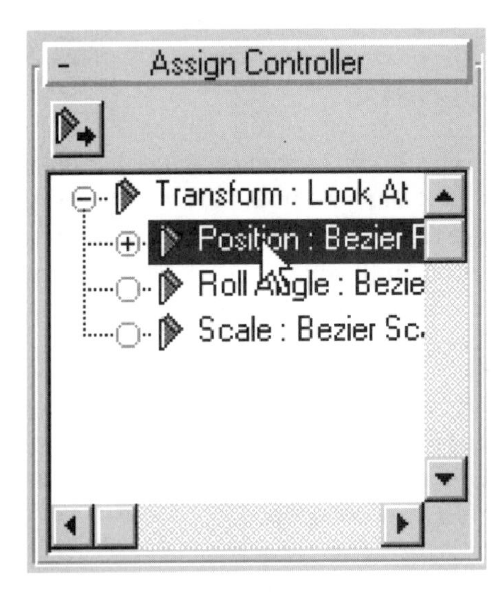

3. Next, click the Assign Controller tool in the upper left corner of the rollout.

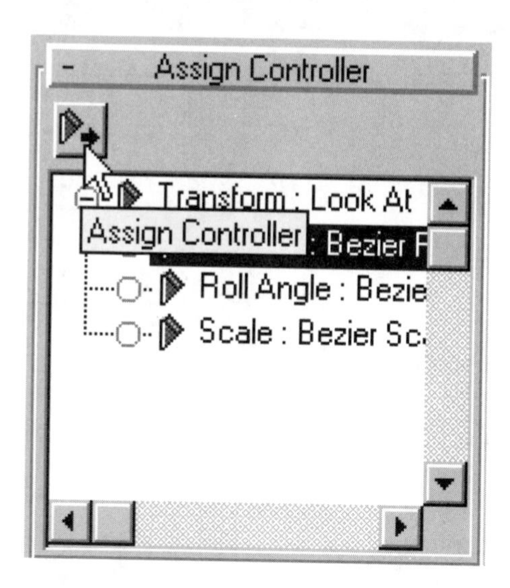

The Assign Position Controller dialog box displays.

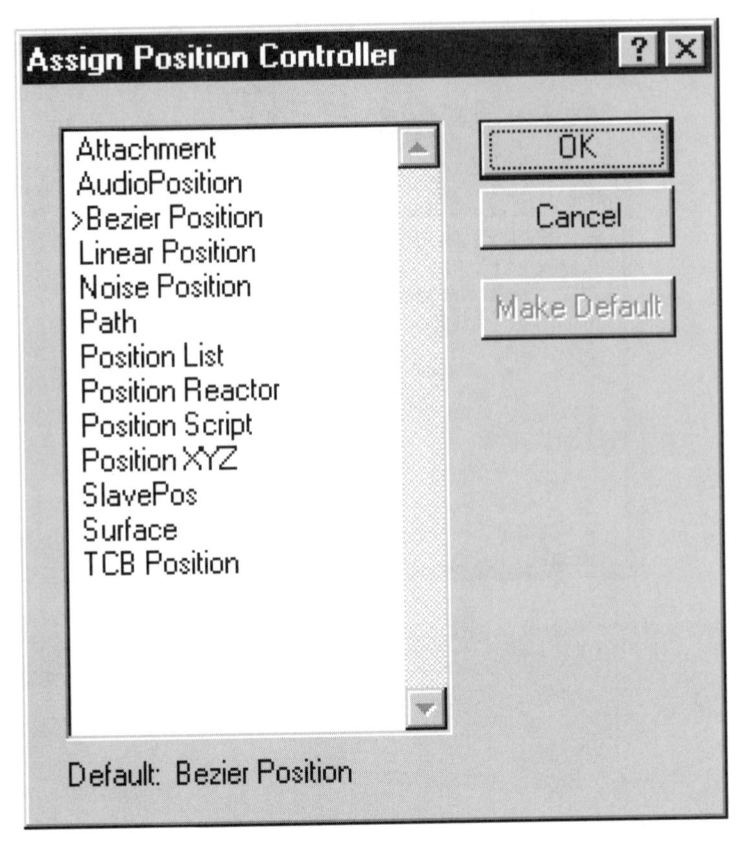

4. Select TCB Position and click OK. The Key Info rollout of the Motion tab will change to show parameters for a TCB controller.

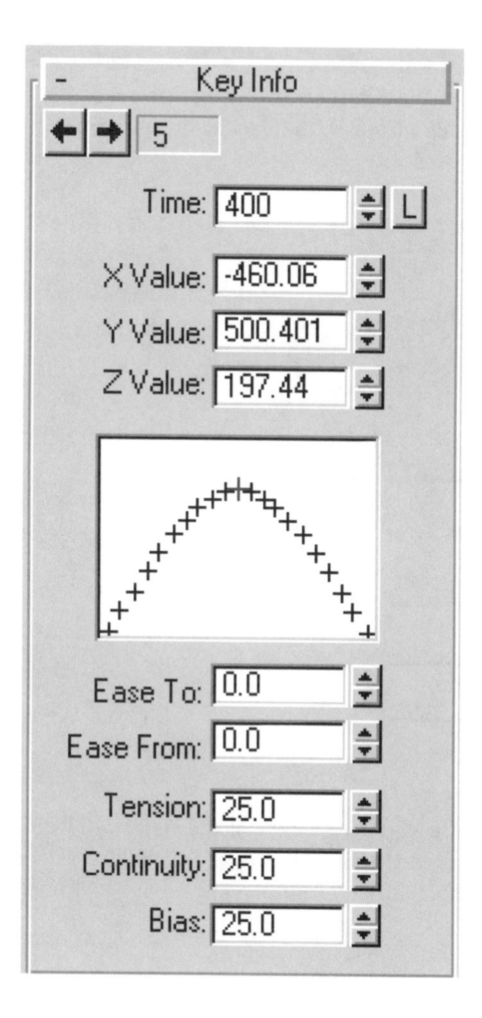

You see the familiar Time and X, Y, and Z Value spinners, but you also see a graphic and five new settings named Ease To, Ease From, Tension, Continuity, and Bias. The graphic shows you an example of how the frames approach and recede from the current keyframe. The default setting shows the keys as black crosses transitioning through a bell-shaped arc. At the top of the arc is a red cross representing the actual keyframe.

You can adjust the Ease To and Ease From settings to compress the frames around the keyframe in a manner similar to the Slow tangent option you used in an earlier exercise. Using negative numbers expands the frames around the keyframe.

Continued on the next page

The Tension option alters the duration of the frames around the keyframe. A value greater than the default 25 increases the density of the frames around the keyframe, while a 0 spreads the frames out.

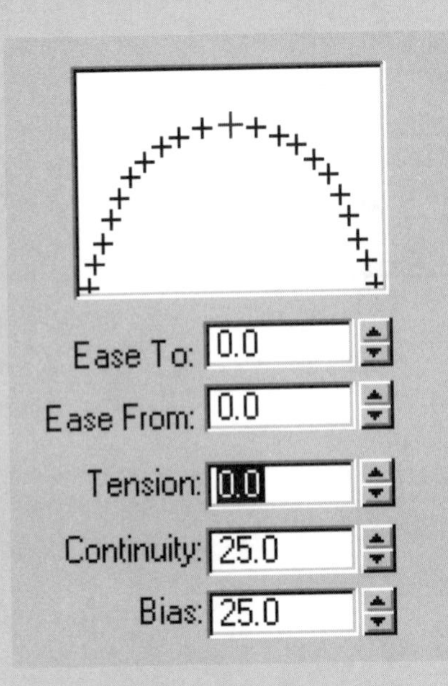

The Continuity setting affects the curvature of the trajectory through the keyframe. A value greater than 25 pushes the trajectory outward, while a value of 0 causes the trajectory to form a straight line to and from the keyframe.

Continued on the next page

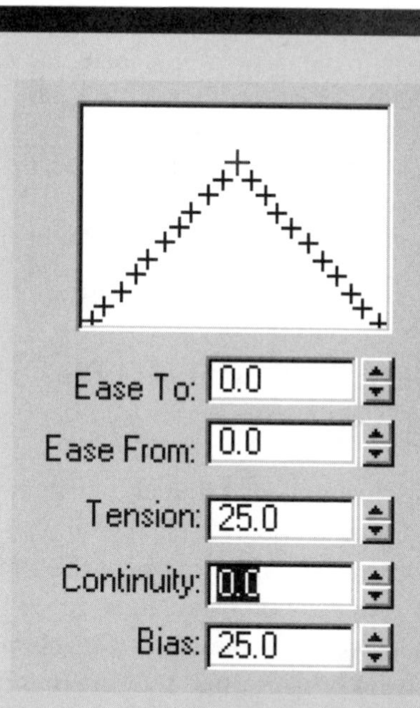

Finally, Bias pushes the trajectory curve to one side of the keyframe or the other, literally biasing the curve. A number less than 25 adds bias to the left side of the graphic, and a number greater than 25 biases the curve to the right side.

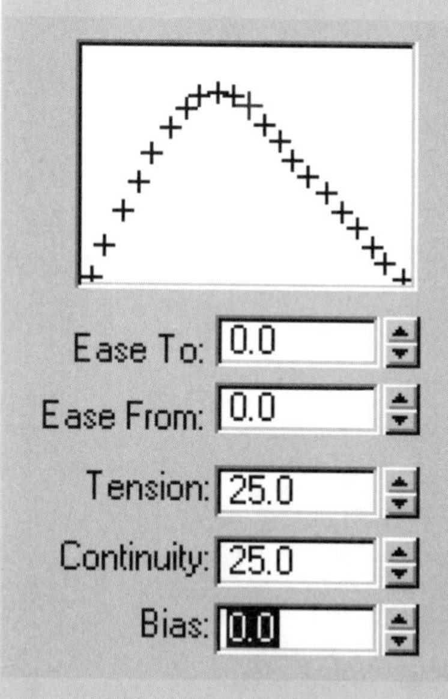

Continued on the next page

You can use the TCB controller to perform the same tasks as the Bézier controllers. For example, in place of the Slow tangent option in the In or Out key parameter, you can use the Ease To or Ease From settings to slow the camera as it approaches the keyframe. The TCB controller offers finer control from a single rollout than does the default Bézier controller. Also, you still have access to many of the same Track View functions you've used in previous exercises. You cannot, however, make changes to the individual X, Y, and Z Position Function curves.

Increasing the Number of Frames Between a Selected Set of Frames

You saw earlier how you can increase the number of frames to increase the overall time and slow down the animation. You can also increase the number of frames within a specific range of frames through the combined use of the Time Configuration dialog box and an object's Key Info parameters. To see how this works, try increasing the number of frames between keyframe 4 and keyframe 5. Right now there are 100 frames between these two keyframes, and they are numbered from 300 to 400.

The first step is to create some additional frames to work with.

1. Click the Time Configuration tool to open the Time Configuration dialog box.

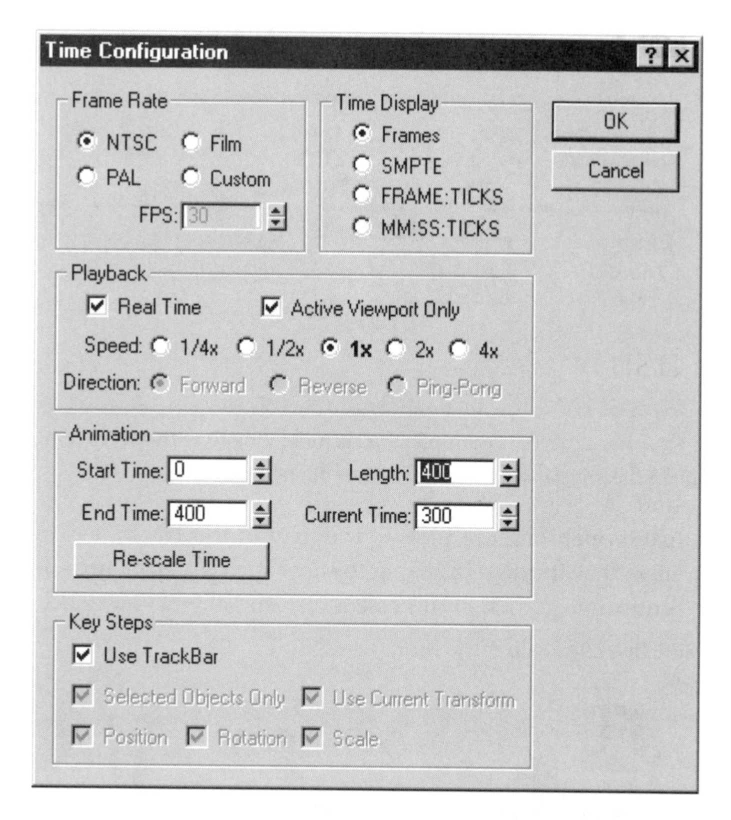

2. In the Animation group, change the Length input box to read **500**; then close the dialog box.

You've just added 100 frames to the animation, though you haven't actually changed the camera motion in any way. If you look at the Time slider, you can see that the keyframes are still in the same location relative to the frame numbers. The next step is to expand the time between keyframes 4 and 5. You do this through the Track View.

1. Open the Track View dialog box.
2. Select the Position listing under the Camera.View.3DFRONT Transform listing.

3. On the Track View toolbar, click the Edit Time tool.

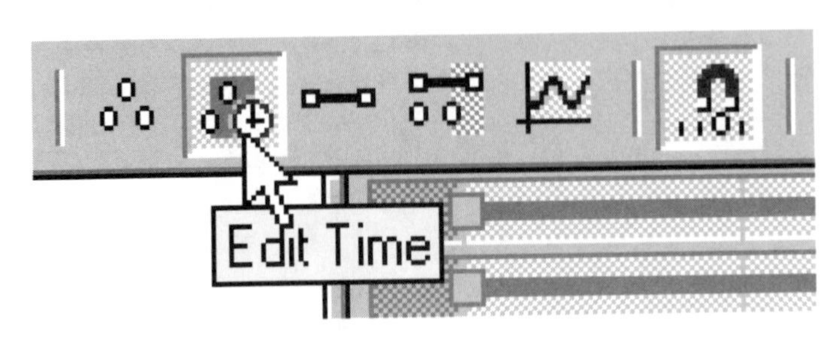

TIP **You can select multiple objects for scaling time by Ctrl-clicking on their Position listing in the left panel of the Track View dialog box.**

This opens a set of tools to the right of the Track View toolbar. It also changes the view in the right panel to show the keys and range bars for objects that are animated, which in this case is just the camera you've been working with.

4. Click the Scale Time tool.

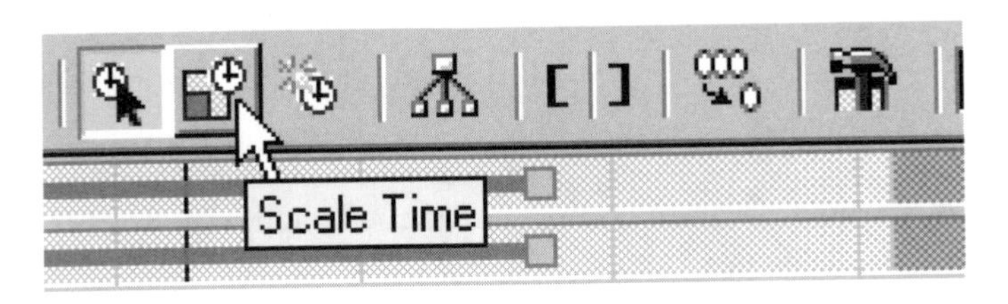

5. Now click and drag the cursor from the Position key at frame 300 to the key at frame 400. You'll see the range of frames displayed in the Key Time and Key Value boxes at the bottom of the window (see Figure 11.18).

FIGURE 11.18

Selecting the range of frames to scale and the Key Time and Key Value boxes

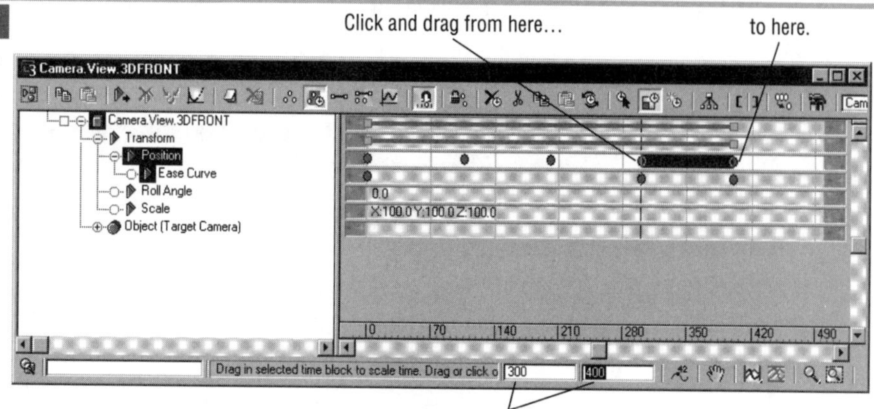

6. Click the Key Time display box at the bottom of the Track View dialog box and enter **300**. This step is to ensure that the range you select starts at frame 300 exactly.
7. Press the Tab key to go to the Key Value box, then enter **400** ↵. Again, this is to ensure that the range of frames includes frame 400 exactly. If the exact frame number is not important, you can skip steps 6 and 7 and just *eyeball* the range in step 5.
8. Click and drag the Position key at frame 400 to the right and watch the Key Value box. Keep moving the key to the right until the Key Value box reads 500; then release the mouse.

You've just scaled the time between frames 300 and 400 to include an additional 100 frames. The keyframe that was at frame 400 is now at frame 500. You aren't quite finished yet, though. You may have noticed that the trajectory of the camera between frames 300 and 500 has changed. You need to adjust the Z curve of the Position Function curve so that the trajectory returns to its former shape.

1. If you haven't done so already, move the Track View dialog box so that you have a clear view of the Left viewport.
2. Click the Function Curve tool on the Track View toolbar.
3. Click the Position listing in the left panel.
4. With the Move Keys tool selected, adjust the Z-axis curve Bézier handle for *downward*. As you do, watch the trajectory in the Left viewport.

5. Adjust the curve so the trajectory looks similar to Figure 11.19.

FIGURE 11.19

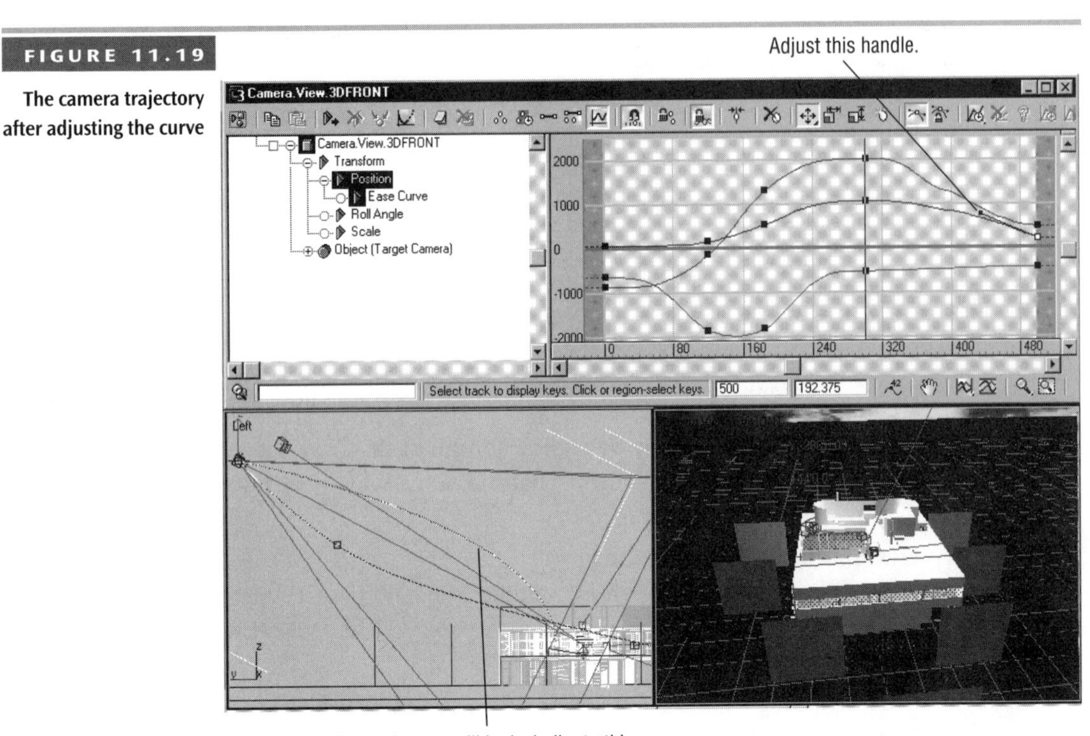

The camera trajectory after adjusting the curve

If you look closely at the trajectory curve in the Left viewport, you'll notice that the dots are clumped together about one-third of the way from keyframe 4 to keyframe 5. This is because, although you scaled the time between the two keyframes, the Ease Curve settings remained the same as before. You need to adjust the Ease Curve keys to conform to the new keyframe locations.

1. Click the Ease Curve listing in the left panel of the Track View.
2. Select the key to the far right of the curve at frame 400. The key should appear white and you should see the 400 in the Key Time box at the bottom of the window.
3. Click the Key Time box and change its value to **500**.
4. Press Tab to go to the Key Value box and enter **500** ↵. Now the dots in the camera trajectory are as they were before.

This last exercise is crucial to ensure that the smoothness of the animation is maintained.

TIP If you find that, after scaling a range of time, an object's motion does not complete its full range of motion, check the Ease Curve settings in the Track View. Frequently, if the Ease Curve data are not adjusted correctly, portions of an animated object's trajectory will appear to be missing.

Scaling Time between Keyframes

You've been shown a general way to scale a range of time. The Track View allows you to scale any range of time, regardless of where that range falls in the animation. It happens that, in the example, you edited a range of time that fell between two keyframes. If you are specifically scaling time between keyframes, you can use the parameters in the Motion tab to simplify the process. Here are the steps you can take:

1. With the Animate button active and the animated object selected, go to the keyframe you wish to move in the Key Info (Basic) rollout of the Motion tab.

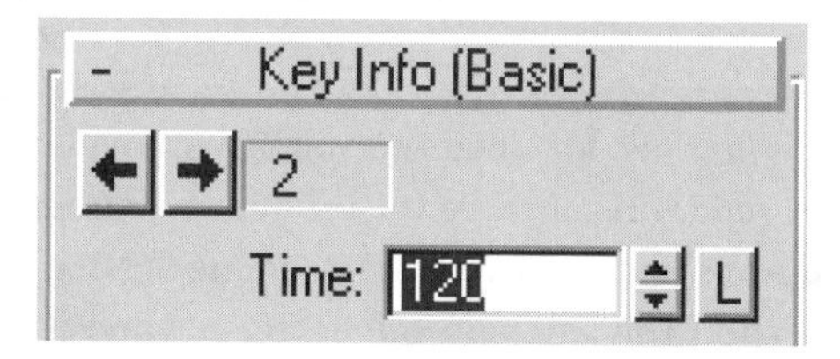

2. In the Key Info (Basic) rollout, change the Time value to the new frame number.

This is much simpler than using the Track View, but you can use this method only to scale time between keyframes of a single object. The Track View allows you to scale any time range regardless of the location of keyframes, and you can scale time for multiple objects as well.

Speeding Up the Preview Rendering Time

Let's take another look at a preview of the animation. Since you've increased the number of frames, you may want to adjust the preview so it doesn't take quite so long to process.

1. Choose Rendering ➢ Make Preview.
2. In the Make Preview dialog box, change the Every Nth Frame value in the Frame Rate group to **2**. This causes the preview to render every other frame, reducing by half the overall time it takes to create the preview.

3. Change the Playback FPS setting to **15**. Since you've got half the number of frames being created, you will also want to cut the frame rate in half to maintain the correct speed for the animation.
4. Click the Active Time Segment radio button in the Preview Range group to make sure that the entire animation is rendered. This is important, because you added some frames to the end of the animation.
5. Make sure that the Camera viewport is selected in the Render viewport drop-down list at the bottom of the dialog box, then click Create.

The preview animation won't be as smooth as before, but you'll get a fairly good idea of the camera motion.

If you really want to have VIZ render all of the frames in the preview, but you also want to speed up the rendering time, you can reduce the detail of the preview in a number of ways. For example, you can select a rendering level in the Rendering Level drop-down list that is less demanding on the system. The default is Smooth + Highlights, which takes the most time to process. You might choose Wireframe or Facets from the list to help shorten the rendering time. Another option is to change the image size to something smaller than 320 x 240. The Image Size group offers an input box that lets you control the image size as a percentage of the finished output.

TIP If your rendering is destined for video and you plan to render to fields, it is a good idea to create a preview rendering at twice the number of frames of the final output. (*Fields* are the interlaced scans that make up a single frame in NTSC video. To learn more about Fields, see Chapter 13.) This will help you detect any object collisions that might occur between fields. For example, a camera may momentarily collide with an object in the design, temporarily causing a blank field. This collision may occur only in a single field of your animation, and would go undetected when turning off field rendering. Such a collision would cause an annoying flash in the final animation when you use field rendering but would not be detected if you created a standard preview of each frame.

Adding Frames to the Beginning of a Segment

You've seen how to add time to the end of a time segment. Now let's look at how you add time to the beginning. You've already been exposed to some of the tools to do this. As before, you'll use the Time Configuration dialog box to add more time to the overall animation. Then you'll use the Track View dialog box to shift the animation sequence forward in the time track.

1. Click the Time Configuration tool to open the Time Configuration dialog box.
2. In the Animation group, change the Length setting to **550**, then click OK.
3. Open the Track View dialog box if it isn't already open.
4. Click the Position listing in the left panel.
5. Click the Edit Ranges tool on the Track View toolbar.

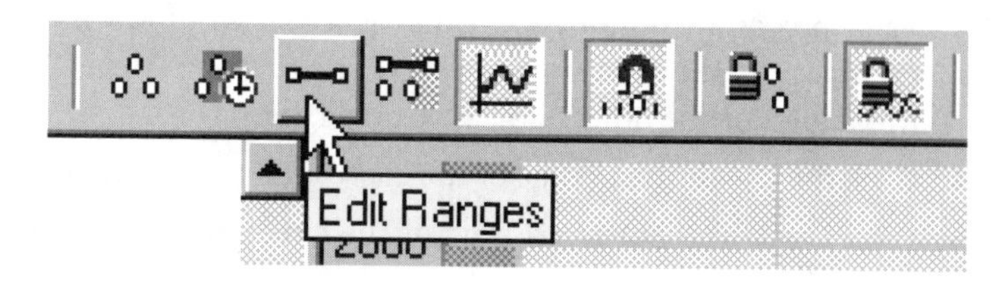

The right panel will change to show a set of range bars instead of the function curves.

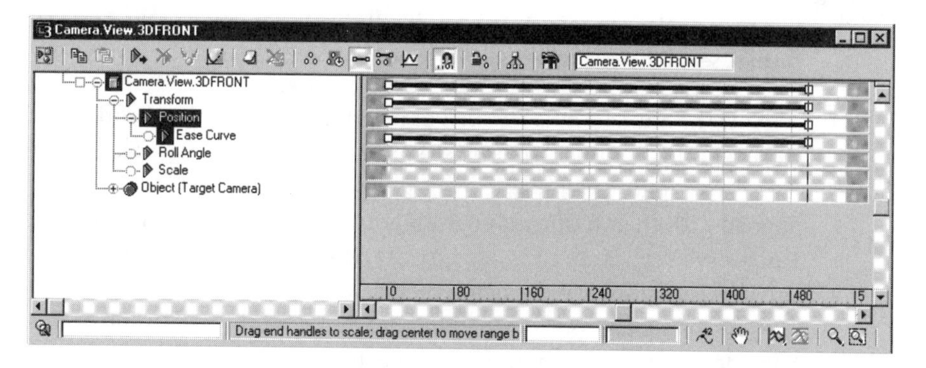

6. Click and drag the Camera.View.3DFRONT bar to the right. As you do, watch the Key Time box at the bottom of the Track View dialog box and adjust the range bars so that the Key Time shows 550. Notice that all of the bars move in unison.

You've moved all of the keys 50 frames forward in time so that now the first key is at frame 50 and the last key is at frame 550. But if you move the Time slider and watch the Camera viewport, you'll notice that the last 50 frames are missing. This is because the Ease Curve settings for the last 50 frames have been truncated. You'll need to make some adjustments to the Ease Curve values to set things right.

1. Click the Ease Curve listing in the left panel of the Track View dialog box.
2. Click the Function Curves tool on the Track View toolbar.

3. With the last key on the far right end of the Ease Curve selected, click in the Key Value box at the bottom of the dialog box. It will show its old value of 500.000. Change it to **550**. You'll see the curve rise to the 550 level. You'll need to change the values for the other two Ease Curve keys.
4. Click the key in the middle of the curve and change its Key Value to **350**.
5. Click the key at the beginning of the curve and change its Key Value to **50**.

TIP **You can also select all the keys at once, then move them simultaneously in a vertical direction to their correct location. To select multiple keys, you can Ctrl-click each key or use a selection region. To constrain the vertical motion of the Track View Move Keys tool, select the vertical arrows from the Move Keys flyout.**

Now the animation is restored to its prior state with the addition of 50 frames at the beginning. In this last exercise you saw the importance of keeping track of the Ease Curve settings. Things can get confusing if the Ease Curve key values are not aligned with their frame numbers. If you're an advanced user, you can play with the Ease Curve key values to create special effects. For now, you'll want to make sure that the Ease Curve key values match their associated times.

Now that you've got some additional frames at the beginning of the animation, let's add some camera motion at the beginning.

1. Move the Time slider to the far left, to frame 0.
2. Adjust the Top viewport so that you can see the camera at frame 0. You can use the Pan tool to adjust your Top viewport to look similar to Figure 11.20.

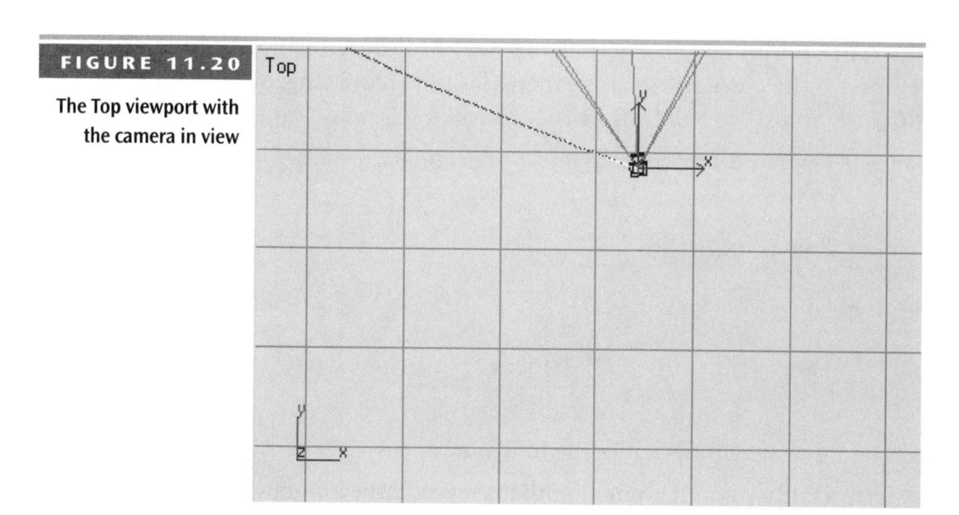
Top

FIGURE 11.20

The Top viewport with the camera in view

3. With the Animate button still active, click the Select and Move tool and move the camera downward to the position shown in Figure 11.21.

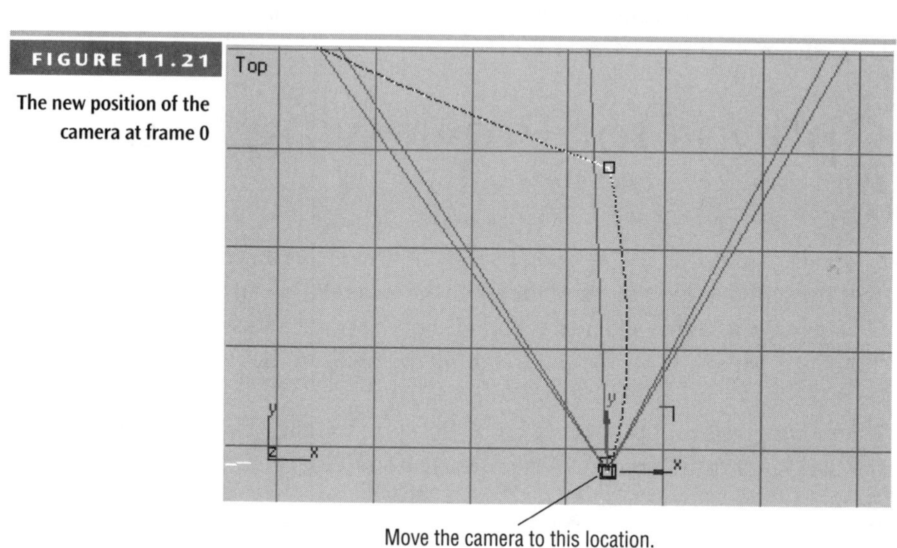
Top
Move the camera to this location.

FIGURE 11.21

The new position of the camera at frame 0

The keyframe you just added is now the new keyframe 1. All of the other keyframes have advanced to the next higher keyframe number.

Now you need to adjust the In and Out settings for the keyframes that are affected by the new camera position.

1. In the Motion tab, make sure that the Key Info (Basic) rollout shows that keyframe 1 is the current keyframe, then select the Slow tangent option in the Out flyout. You'll see the trajectory between keyframes 1 and 2 straighten.
2. Advance to keyframe 2 by clicking the key selection arrow.

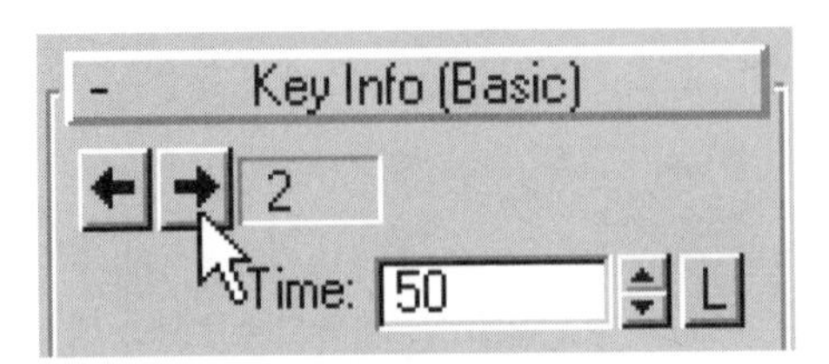

3. Select the Slow tangent option in the In flyout.

You now have a fairly smooth animation that shows off the building from several vantage points. At this point, you may want to explore some different ways to study the results of your work.

Throughout this chapter, you've created preview animations or used the Frame slider to check your camera motion. The next section will show you some additional ways to preview the motion in your model.

Other Options for Previewing Your Motion

In Chapter 6 and earlier in this chapter, you learned how to create a preview animation that gives you a pretty good sense of the speed and overall time of your animation. You can also use the Frame slider to get an idea of the camera motion by manually sliding the bar at a slow rate and watching the result in the Perspective view.

A third way to study the motion in your animation is to use the Time Controls located at the bottom of the Command Panel (see Figure 11.22).

FIGURE 11.22

The time controls

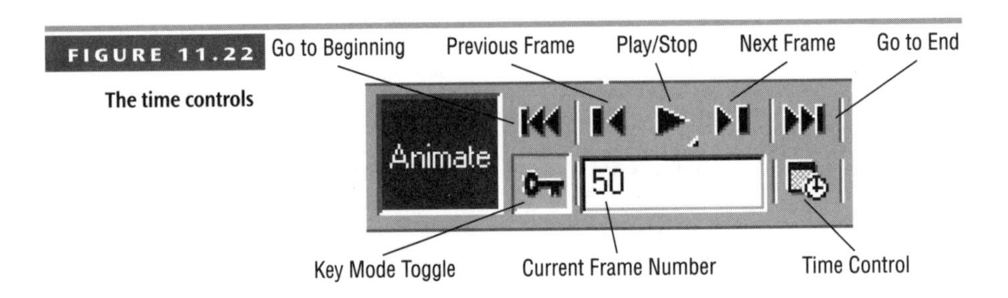

These tools work in a way similar to buttons on a VCR, with some additions. The Go to Start button moves you to the first frame of the active segment. The Go to End button moves you to the last frame. The Next Frame and Previous Frame buttons move you one frame at a time either forward or backward. If you make the Key Mode toggle active by clicking on it, the Next Frame and Previous Frame buttons will advance the Time slider to the next keyframe. The Play Animation button plays the active segment in a continuous loop. The Play Animation button is also a flyout, offering an option to play the animation for a single selected object.

The playback is useful for getting a quick idea of how your animation is working. Try it out on what you've got so far.

1. Click the Perspective view to make it active.
2. Click the Playback button below the icon panel and watch the playback for a few seconds.
3. Click the Stop button to stop the playback. The Playback button turns into a Stop button when the animation is playing.

The animation is played back as a wirefame view. VIZ attempts to play back the animation at the full 30 frames per second and will use what is called *Adaptive Degradation* to achieve a full-frame rate. Adaptive Degradation degrades the image to allow VIZ to display each frame quickly. You can alter the way your view is displayed to help improve the playback speed. For example, by default, VIZ degrades the image to a wireframe for the playback. You can force VIZ to limit the degradation to a shaded view with facets.

1. Choose View ➢ Configure… The Viewport Configuration dialog box displays.
2. Click the Adaptive Degradation tab, then click Facets in the Active Degradation group.

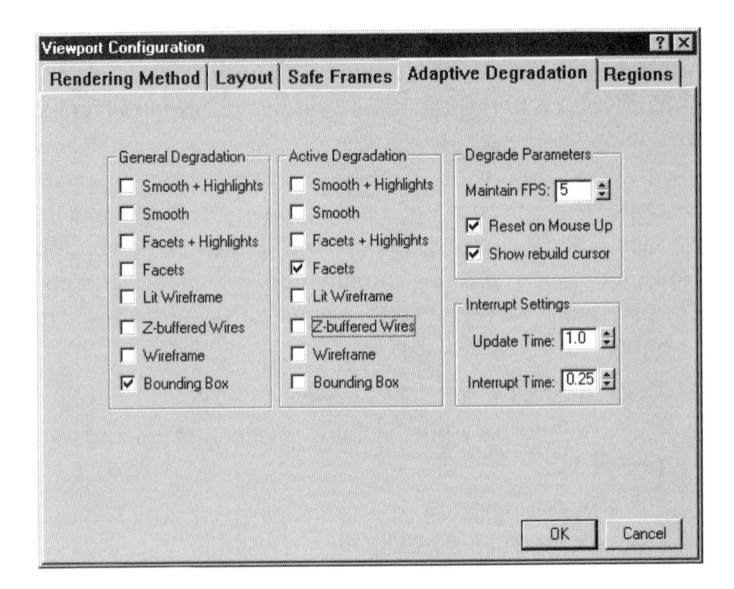

3. Click Z-buffered Wires to turn off this setting.
4. Click OK, then click the Playback button. Now the playback maintains a shaded view, but the animation is a bit rough, skipping frames to maintain the desired frame rate.

NOTE **You may have noticed that the Viewport Configuration dialog box shows two groups with the same settings. The General Degradation group affects inactive viewports while the Active Degradation group affects active viewports.**

If you want a smoother playback at the expense of detail, you can use the Bounding Box setting as the degradation setting.

1. Choose View ➢ Configure… The Viewport Configuration dialog box displays.
2. Click the Adaptive Degradation tab, then click Bounding Box in the Active Degradation group. Since the options are check boxes instead of radio buttons, the Facet option remains checked and active.
3. Click OK, then click the Playback button. Now the playback degrades the display of objects to bounding boxes, but the animation is much smoother.

Even though the Facet option is still selected, VIZ *drops down* to the next available setting—Bounding Box—in order to maintain the smoothness of the playback.

As you've just seen, these different options offer a variety of ways of previewing your animation. These tools will let you get a sense of the motion in the animation at each change you make. They are an aid to refining your animation, so make liberal use of them.

Moving the Camera Target through Time

So far in this chapter, you've touched on all the major editing activities you might run into while creating a camera path. You can also make changes to the camera target. The target can be manipulated independently of the camera it is attached to. A camera target's trajectory can be completely independent of the camera itself, though you'll want to carefully choreograph the motion of both the camera and the target.

Try the following exercise to see the effects of camera target motion.

1. In the upper Top viewport, adjust the view so that you can see the Villa courtyard as shown in Figure 11.23.

FIGURE 11.23

Adjust the Top viewport to show this view.

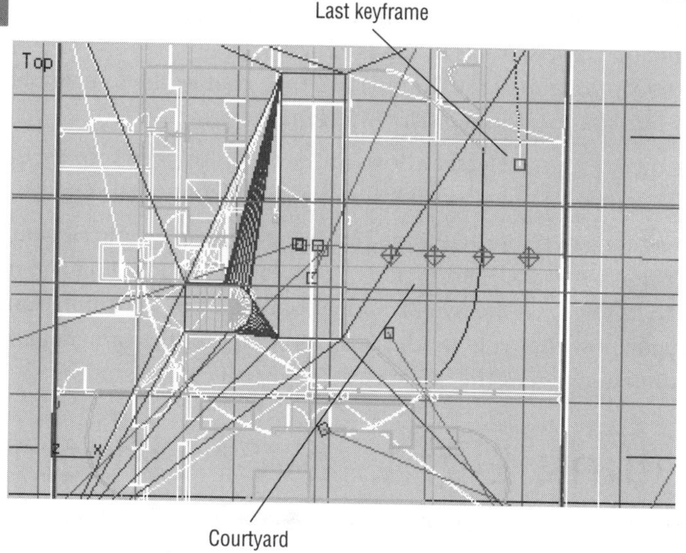

2. Move the Time slider to the last frame so you can see the camera in the Top viewport.
3. Click Select by Name to open the Select Objects dialog box.
4. Locate and select Camera.View.3DFRONT.Target from the list, then click Select.
5. Use the Select and Move tool to move the camera target to the location shown in Figure 11.24.

FIGURE 11.24

Move the camera target to this location.

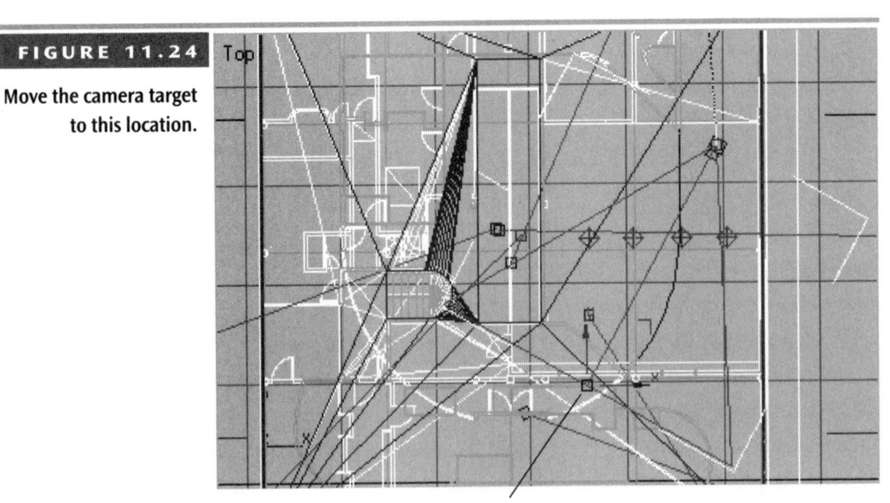

Now you've created a motion for your target. The target has just two keyframes. Just as with the camera path, you can adjust the keyframe's In and Out settings, as well as function curve settings in the Track View.

1. In the Motion tab of the Command Panel, change the In parameter flyout of the Key Info (Basic) rollout to Slow Tangent.
2. Use the keyframe selector arrows at the top of the Key Info (Basic) rollout to go to keyframe 1, then select the Slow tangent flyout in the Out parameter.

The target trajectory is often forgotten as the cause of erratic camera motion. Remember that when you start to add camera target motion, you will need to pay attention to its effect on the overall animation. If part of the animation seems too *jerky* and you know that you've adjusted everything for the camera path to create a smooth animation, check the target path for abrupt changes.

Controlling Lights over Time

This chapter has been devoted to showing you ways of controlling the motion of objects. In this section, you'll learn that you can adjust a light over time. You'll also learn how properties of a light, such as intensity, can be made to change over time.

Now let's suppose you want to fade the sunlight while simultaneously brightening the interior lights. In addition, let's suppose you want this done at the end of the animation, viewing the courtyard while the camera is no longer moving. To accomplish this in the following example, you'll use several of the tools you already learned in this chapter.

1. First, add some time to the end of the animation. Click the Time Configuration tool to open the Time Configuration dialog box.
2. Enter **600** in the Length input box, then close the Time Configuration dialog box.
3. Open the Track View dialog box, then click the Select by Name tool to open the Select Object dialog box.
4. Select SUN from the Select Object list and click Select.

SUN displays in the Track View dialog box in the left panel.

5. Click the Plus sign next to the SUN listing, then click the Plus sign next to the Object (Target Directional Light) listing that displays. Notice that the parameters for the SUN directional light appear under the Object (Target Directional Light) listing (See Figure 11.25).

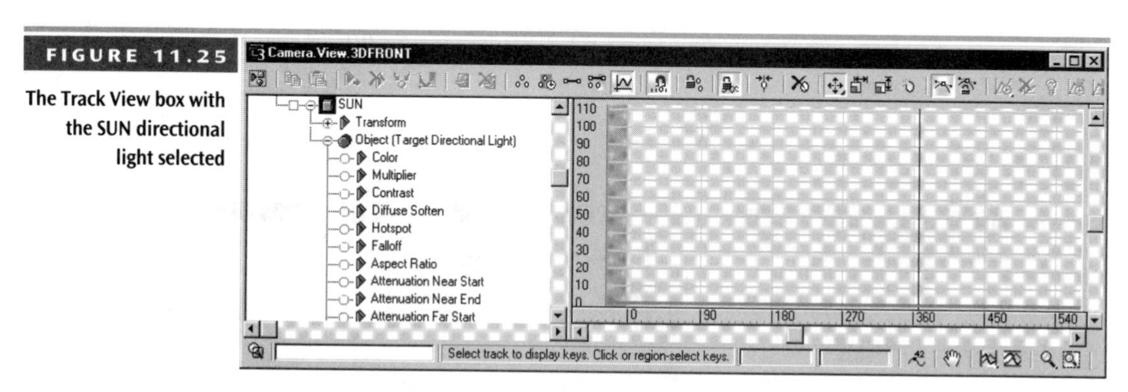

FIGURE 11.25

The Track View box with the SUN directional light selected

The SUN directional light is not currently animated. In the following exercise, you'll add keyframes to the SUN through the Track View dialog box.

1. Click the Edit Keys tool in the Track View dialog box.

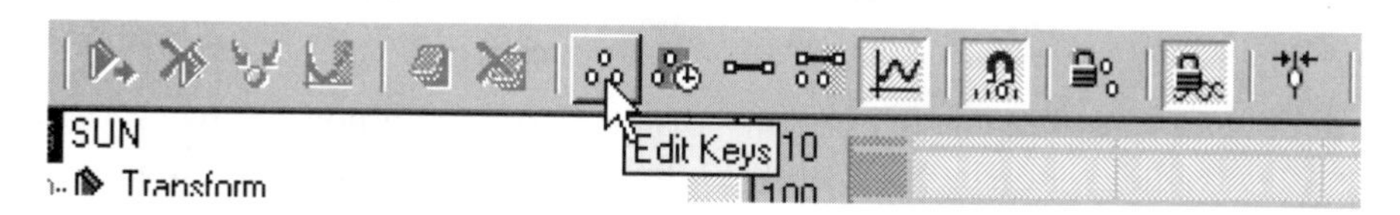

A different set of tools appears to the right of the toolbar.

2. Select the Add Keys tool on the Track View toolbar.

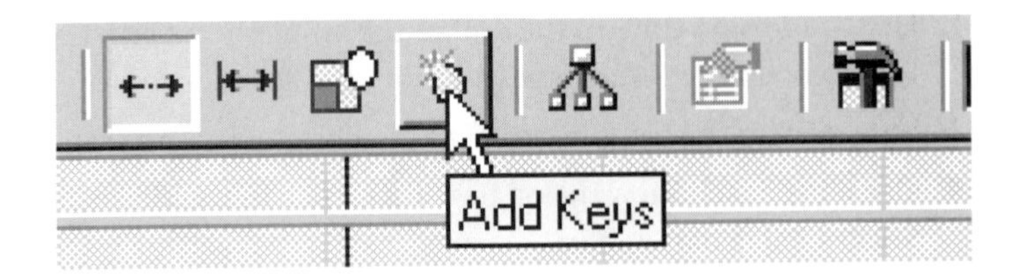

3. Click the Multiplier listing in the left panel.
4. In the right panel, click the Multiplier track at a location that is close to frame 550, as shown in Figure 11.26.
5. Click the Key Time box and enter **550** ↵ to set the new key to frame 550.
6. Click the Multiplier track at a location that is close to frame 600, as shown in Figure 11.26.
7. Click the Key Time box again and this time enter **600** ↵ to set the new key to frame 600.

FIGURE 11.26

Place keyframes at frames 550 and 600.

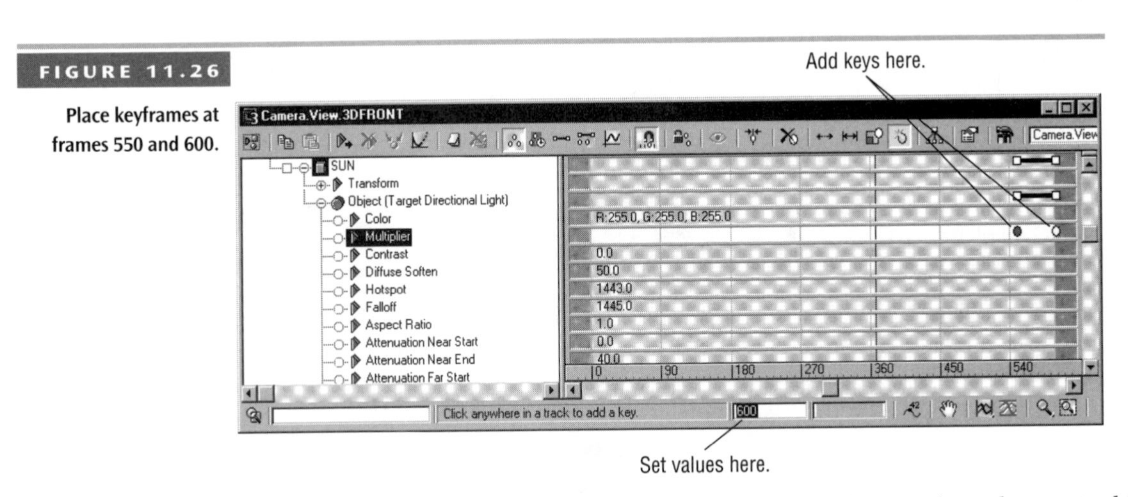

The Multiplier track of the SUN directional light now has two keys that control its value over time. The final step is to adjust the Multiplier value at frame 600.

1. Right-click the key at frame 600. The Sun Multiplier dialog box displays.

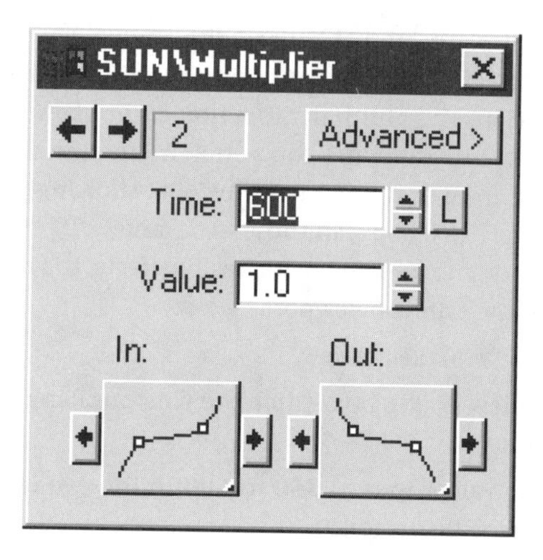

2. Click the Value input box and enter **0** ↵, then close the dialog box.

   You've just set up the SUN directional light to dim from full intensity to zero intensity between frames 550 and 600.

3. With the Multiplier listing selected, click the Function Curves tool on the Track View toolbar.

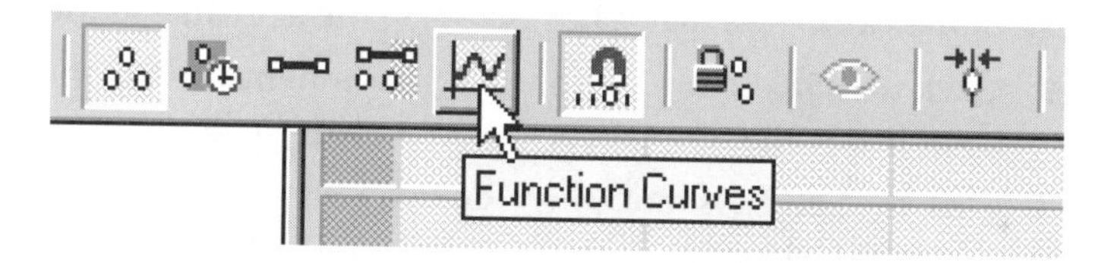

In the right panel, you see the curve for the Multiplier value over time.

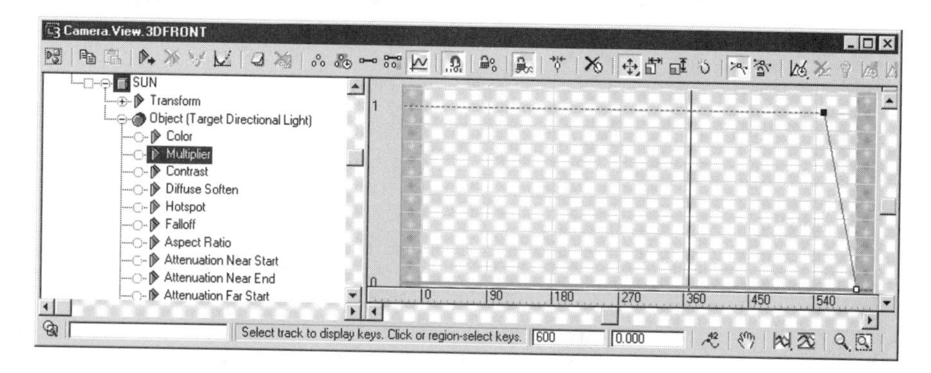

In this last exercise, you added two keys to the Multiplier track. You could have added just the last key at frame 600 and set the Multiplier value to 0 at that key. This would have caused the SUN directional light to dim gradually over the entire length of the animation. The key at frame 550 ensures that the Multiplier value stays constant at 1.0 until frame 550. The Multiplier function curve gives you a graphic representation of how this works by showing you a straight line from frame 0 to frame 550. The line then drops from frame 550 to frame 600, showing you the change in the Multiplier value from 1 to 0 between those two frames.

To see whether the modification you made really affects the model, you can create a preview animation of the Camera viewport.

1. Choose Rendering ➢ Make Preview.
2. In the Make Preview dialog box, Click the Custom Range radio button in the Preview Range group.
3. Change the range values to read **550** to **600** in the two input boxes just below the Custom Range radio button.
4. In the Render Viewport drop-down list at the bottom of the dialog box, select Camera.View.3DFRONT, then click Create. After building the preview, you'll see a short animation showing you roughly how the lights dim over time.

Notice that in the last frame of the sample animation, the design is still lit. To really darken the design, you'll need to change the ambient lighting over time in the same way that you changed the SUN directional light object.

1. In the Track View dialog box, scroll up the left panel to the Environment listing.
2. Click the Plus sign next to the Environment listing, then click the Ambient Light listing that displays below Environment.
3. Click the Edit Keys tool. Then add two keys at frame 550 and at frame 600 in the Ambient Light track, just as you did for the Multiplier track of the SUN directional light.
4. Right-click the key at frame 600. The Ambient Light dialog box displays.

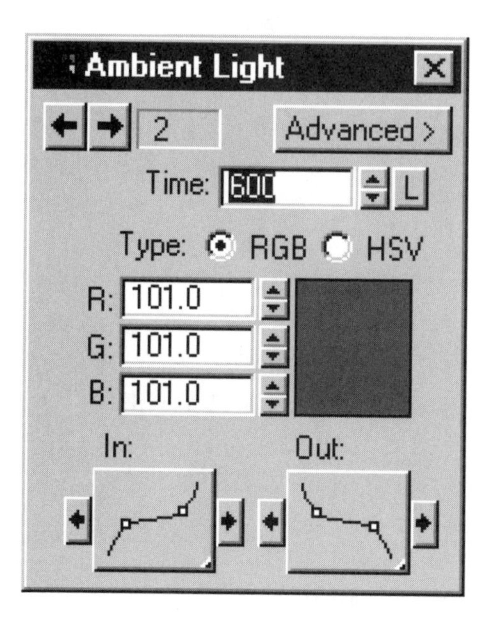

5. Right-click the spinners for the R, G, and B input boxes to set their values to 0. You can also click the color swatch to open the Color Selector, then adjust the Value setting to 0.
6. Close the dialog box, then re-render a preview animation. This time the design darkens to a greater extent.
7. Save the file as **Myfirstanimation.max**.

You still have the Omni-court lights illuminating the courtyard and the Omni-interior lights lighting the interior of the Villa. You can perform the same steps you used to change the SUN directional light to change the Omni lights multiplier over time.

Summary

You've had an opportunity to try out most of the tools you'll need to create walk-through or flyby animations. As you've seen, there are many ways that you can control the motion of a camera, or of any object, for that matter. You've focused your efforts on a camera, but you can apply the same methods to any object in VIZ.

In the next chapter, you'll continue your exploration of VIZ's animation tools. You'll learn how objects in the environment affect the look of your animation and how you can work with objects to produce study and final animations.

You'll also learn about the different options for animation file output and how you can use the animation tools to automate the rendering of multiple still images.

chapter 12

Understanding Animation Files

FEATURING

- *Render File Output Options*
- *Working with Backgrounds and Props*
- *Automating Multiple Still Image Output*
- *Using the Walkthrough Assistant*
- *The Animation File Output Options*

Understanding Animation Files

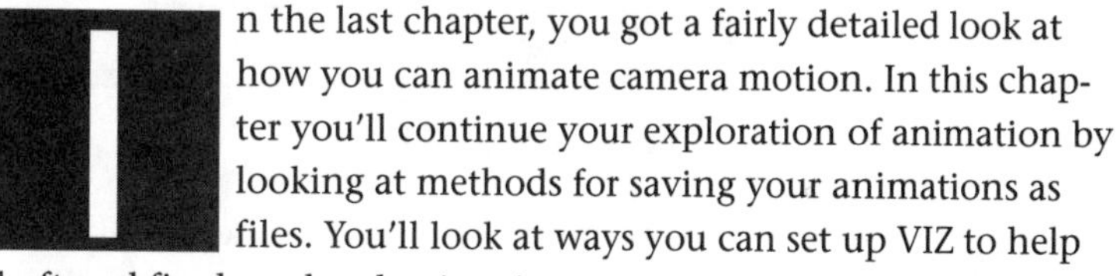

In the last chapter, you got a fairly detailed look at how you can animate camera motion. In this chapter you'll continue your exploration of animation by looking at methods for saving your animations as files. You'll look at ways you can set up VIZ to help you produce both draft and final rendered animations.

You'll also look at how animations differ from still images in the way you put a VIZ design file together. The arrangement of objects and methods you use to create a still image has different requirements from those of an animation. You'll examine some of those differences and their effect on your work.

Render File Output Options

Now let's take a look at the options you have for animation output. This is really a big subject, so you'll start with the basics of study animations versus finished animations.

Before you've gotten to a point where you think you're ready for a final animation, you'll want to generate a study animation to make sure all of the elements are working together. You'll want to do this because of the time it takes to generate a full, finished animation. For a very elaborate design, a 20-second animation can take days to render, so before you commit your computer to 48 hours of nonstop rendering, you'll want to be completely sure that everything is perfect.

You can create a study animation by turning off some key features that may not be crucial for studying the motion of objects in your animation. You can also reduce the resolution of the animation to help speed things up.

Creating a Study Animation

In the following exercise, you'll create an animation file to be viewed in VIZ. It won't be a finished product by any means. The advantage of using the Renderer output is that you will be better able to see the lighting change over time, and you'll also see how the shadows affect the animation.

The first animation you'll do will focus on the last few frames of the animation, to ascertain that the spotlight is indeed dimming at the end.

1. Open the file you saved in the last chapter. You may also use `Mysavoye12.max` from the companion CD.
2. Click the Camera.View.3DFRONT viewport to make it active.
3. Click the Render Design tool on the Standard Toolbar.

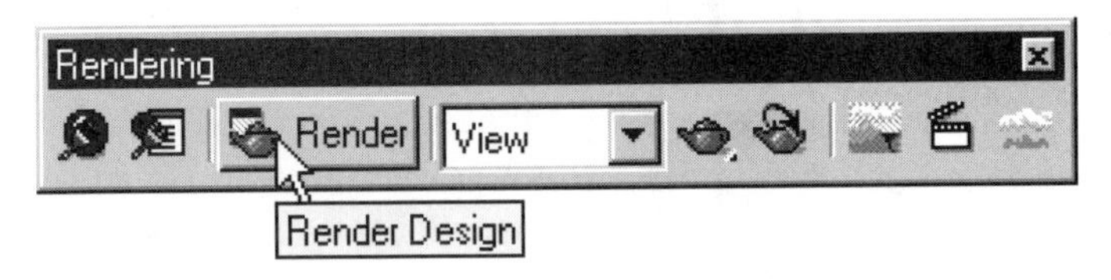

4. At the bottom of the Render Design dialog box, click the Draft radio button.

VIZ lets you maintain two separate sets of rendering settings, Production and Draft. You've been using the Production settings so far. The options for the Draft settings are the same, but they are saved separately. You might think of the two types of settings as two separate but identical dialogs that are maintained by VIZ. Changes in one dialog do not affect the other.

1. In the Time Output group, click the Range radio button, then enter a range from **550** to **600** in the range input boxes.

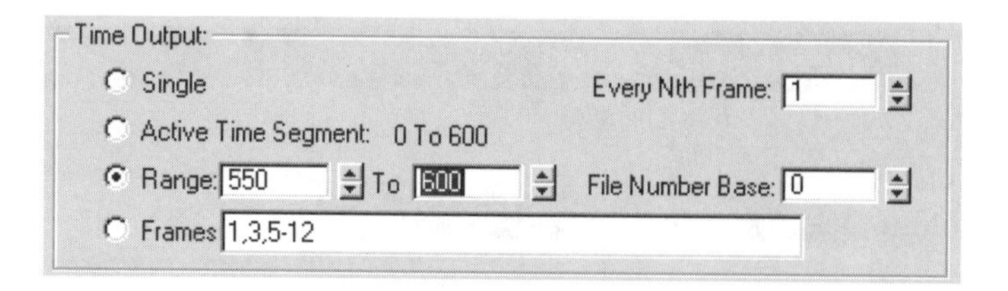

2. Click the 256 × 243 button in the Output Size group to reduce the size of the output.
3. To remove the check, scroll down the dialog box to the VIZ Default Scanline A-Buffer rollout and click the Anti-Aliasing check box in the Anti-Aliasing group. This will greatly improve the speed of the rendering, but it will create a rendering that shows jagged edges on objects.

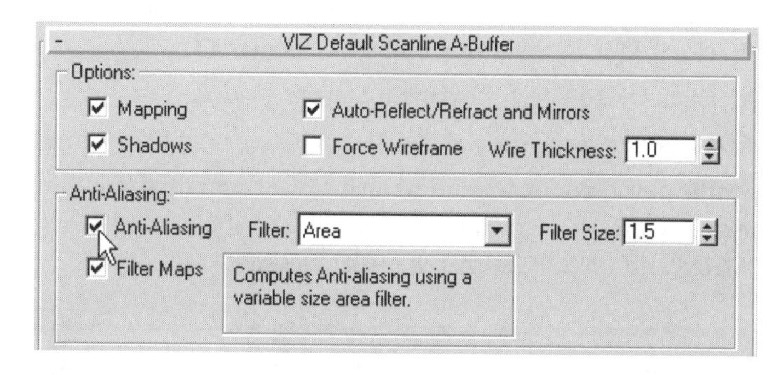

4. You've set up the Draft Render settings for a *quick* rendering. To see that you really do have two sets of rendering settings, click the Production radio button at the bottom of the dialog box. You'll see the old settings appear in the dialog box as if you hadn't changed anything.

Now go ahead and create the partial animation of the villa.

1. Click the Draft radio button at the bottom of the Render Design dialog box to return to the draft settings you made in the last set of steps.
2. Click the Files button in the Render Output group of the Common Parameters rollout; then in the Render Output file dialog box, select the AVI File (*.avi) option from the Save as Type drop-down list and enter **Myfirstanimation** as the file name.
3. Click Save. You'll see the Video Compression dialog box for AVI files.

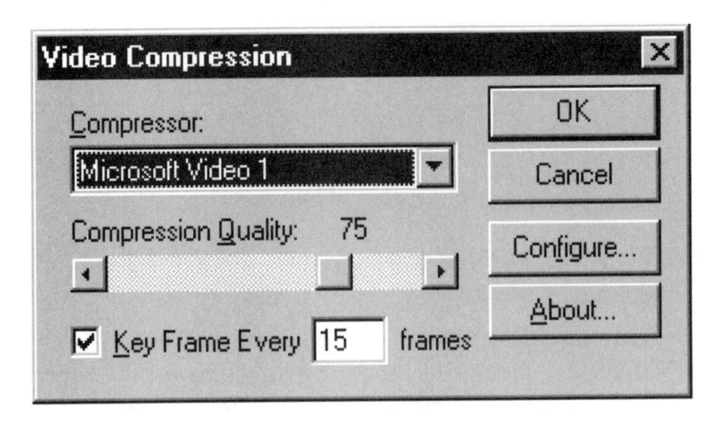

This dialog box lets you control the quality of your AVI animation file. You can also select the method of compression used on your animation. You'll get a closer look at these issues later in Chapter 13.

4. Click OK to select the default values.
5. Click Render in the Render Design dialog box. VIZ begins the rendering process.

At this point, you may want to take a break and do something else. Even with the time-saving measures, the animation will take about 15 minutes to fully render on a 500MHz Pentium II PC with 128 megabytes of RAM.

TIP **If you prefer not to wait, click Cancel in the Rendering dialog box. You can use the sample `Myfirstrendering12.avi` file for the next exercise.**

Once the animation is created, you can view the rendered animation from within VIZ using the Display Image command or by locating the .avi file using the Windows Explorer and double-clicking it.

1. Choose Tools ➢ Display Image... The View File dialog box displays.
2. Locate and select `Myfirstanimation.avi`, then click Open. The Windows Media Player opens and plays back the animation. If you have another application set to playback .avi files, then that application will open and play the .avi file.

As you can see, the animation is still pretty crude, but at least we can tell whether the lights are doing what we want them to.

Creating a Quick Overall Study Animation

Now suppose you want to get a quick view of the overall animation to make sure everything is working as planned. In the next exercise, you'll adjust some of the frame output settings to limit the number of frames that are animated. This will help reduce the total animation time so you'll see the results more quickly. You'll use a different file format that offers a bit more control at file creation.

1. Make sure the Draft radio button is selected in the Render Design dialog box, then click the Active Time Segment radio button in the Time Output group.
2. In the Every Nth Frame input box, enter **2**. This will cause the renderer to create an animation that skips every other frame.
3. Click the Files button in the Render Output group, then in the Render Output files dialog box enter **Mysecondanimation** for the File name.
4. Select MOV Quick Time File (*.mov) in the Save as type drop-down list and click Save. As you'll see in a moment, the QuickTime file format lets you set the playback frame rate.
5. Click the Setup… button in the Render Output file dialog box. The Compressing Settings for the QuickTime file display.

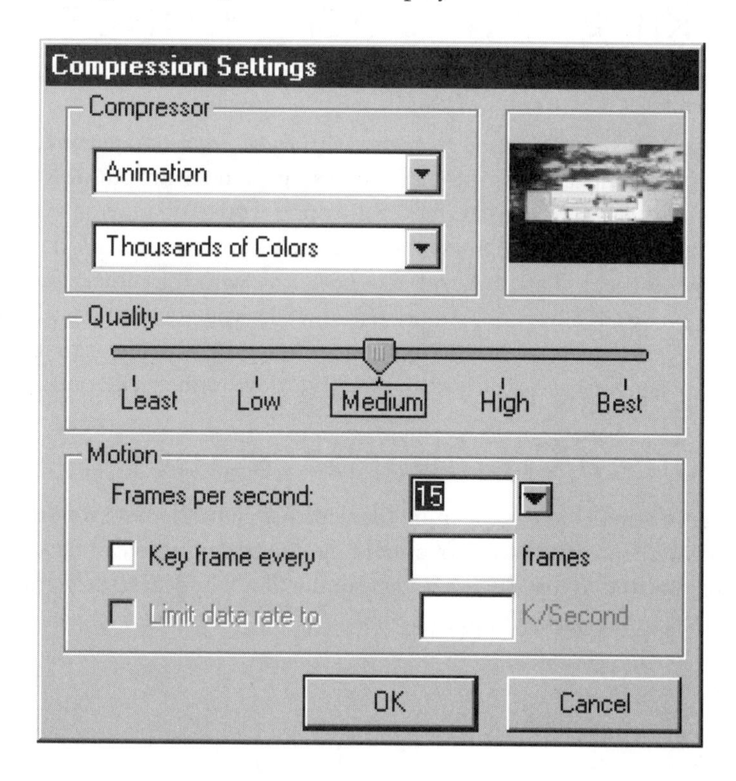

6. Change the Frames per second setting to **15**. Note that you can set the Quality slider and also select the color depth for the .mov file. Click OK after setting the Frame rate.
7. Click the Render button. This time the rendering will take a bit more time.
8. Use the View file dialog box (Tools ➢ Display Image...) to play back the animation when it is finished rendering. If you prefer, you can cancel the rendering and use the `Mysecondanimation.mov` file from the companion CD for the next exercise.

This animation is still crude, and you may detect that it is not quite as smooth in the playback as the prior animation, but it gives you a far better idea of how the final rendering will look than did the preview animations you used in the last chapter. It also shows us some problems that need fixing. The next section addresses those problems and offers some solutions.

Working with Backgrounds and Props

Perhaps the most obvious problems with the animation are the trees. You created the trees to optimize rendering speed for a single rendering, but now that you're creating a flyby animation, the flat trees really don't work. You may have also noticed that the background sky stayed the same while the rest of the animation moved by. This shows us that the background does not move with the camera, adversely affecting our illusion. It remains the same no matter where you are in the model. This section will show you some ways of dealing with backgrounds and props that will give your rendering a greater sense of realism. You'll start with the background.

Creating a Credible Background

In animations such as the .mov file you created in the last section, where you are showing an outdoor flyby of a building, the background can be a simple gradient from bottom to top. Such a background will not appear to be static since there are no objects in the background to define a point of reference as the camera moves.

1. Choose Rendering ➢ Environment. The Environment dialog box displays.

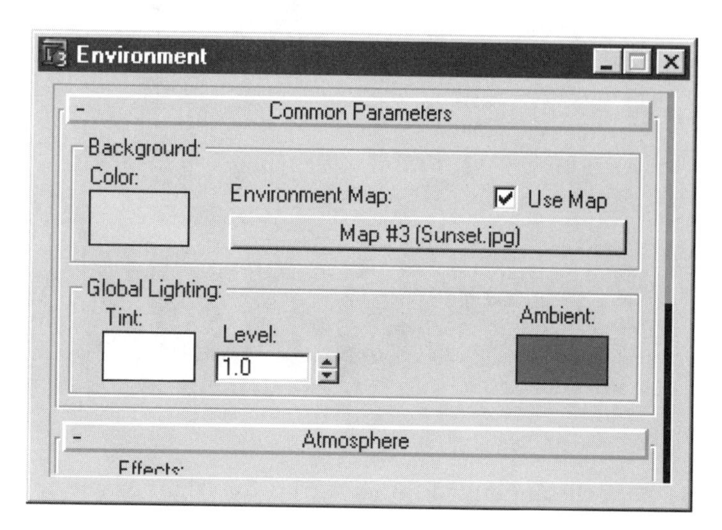

2. Click the Map #3 (Sunset.jpg) button. The Material/Map browser appears.
3. Select Gradient from the list and notice the sample in the upper left of the dialog box. It shows a grayscale gradient from black at the top to white at the bottom.
4. Click OK to select the gradient map.

You've switched to a gradient map for the background, but you will want to add some colors of the gradient.

1. Click the Material Editor tool on the Standard toolbar to open the Material Editor.
2. Use the slide bar on the right to view the third row of sample slots just below the ones visible in the dialog box.

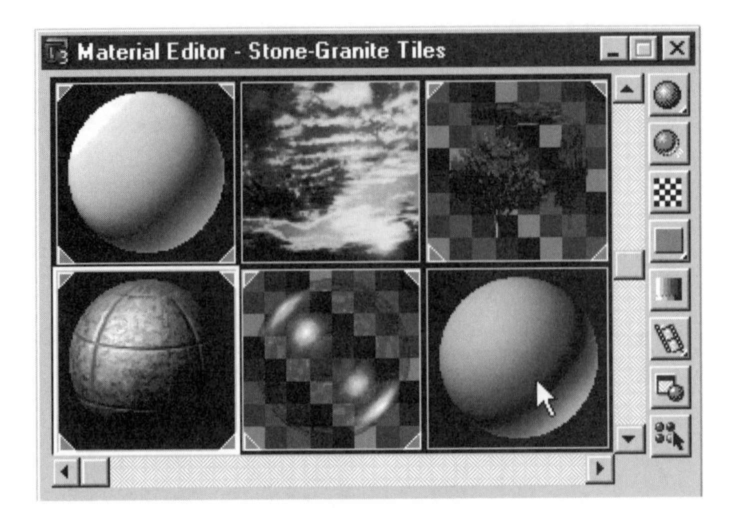

3. Click the undefined slot at the bottom right to select it, then click the Get Material tool.

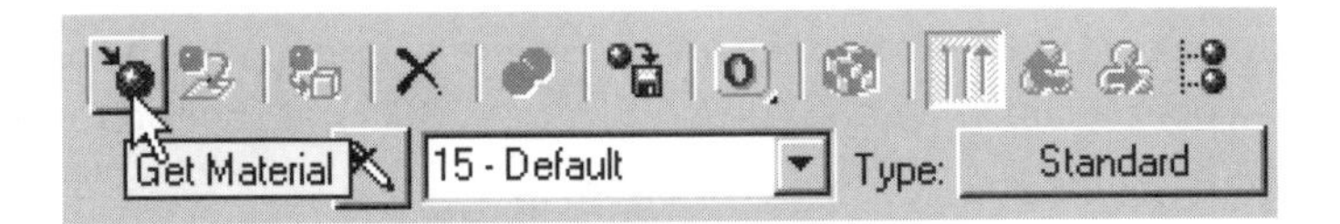

4. In the Material Map dialog box, click the Design radio button in the Browse From group, then double-click the Map listing that shows (Gradient)[Environment] in the name. The slot now shows the gradient.

Once you've got the gradient in the sample slot, you can begin to play with its parameters.

1. Scroll down Material Editor to the Gradient Parameters rollout, then click the color swatch labeled Color #1.

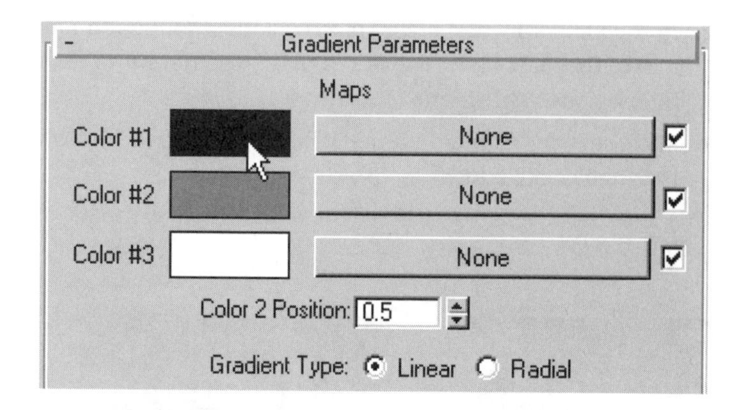

2. In the Color Selector dialog box, set the Hue setting to **155**, the Saturation (Sat) setting to **220**, and the Value setting to **100**.
3. Click Close. In Gradient Parameters, click the color swatch for Color #2.
4. At the Color selector, set the Hue setting to **155**, the Saturation to **125**, and the Value to **255**.
5. Click Close when you're done, then close all of the other dialog boxes. Now you see a color gradient background in the Camera viewport.

Now let's take a look at what the new rendering will look like.

1. Make sure the time slider is on frame 1, then click the Render tool on the Render toolbar.

2. In the Render Design dialog box, click the Production radio button at the bottom of the dialog box. For this exercise, you'll want to use the settings you used for previous single frame renderings.
3. Make sure the Camera.View.3DFRONT is selected in the Viewport drop-down list, then click Render.

After a few moments, you will see the rendered view display on your screen (see Figure 12.1).

FIGURE 12.1

A rendered view of the model with a new gradient background

The new background looks like a typical clear sky with a gray horizon. It won't matter that the background remains the same throughout the animation since the gradient colors won't give away the fact that they are not moving with the camera. Of course, you can use the gradient background for still images as well.

TIP You can create an animated background by using an .avi file for background image. Likewise, you can create an animated texture by using an .avi file for a texture map.

Using a Texture Map and Hemisphere for the Sky

The gradient background offers the illusion of a clear sky, but what if you want to add some clouds? You can simulate a cloudy sky by adding a flattened dome over your model, then assigning to the dome a texture map that uses a bitmap of a cloudy sky. Here's how it's done.

First you'll add the hemisphere object.

1. Right-click the Top viewport, then click the Zoom Extents tool.
2. In the Create Tab of the Command Panel, click the Geometry button and select Sphere.
3. In the Top viewport, click and drag a sphere from the center of the building as shown in Figure 12.2. Make the sphere extend to the corner of the Ground plane with a radius of about 1060 feet.

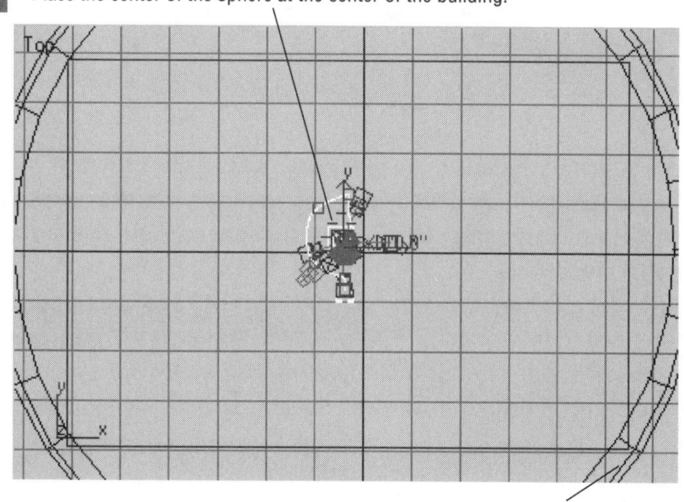
Place the center of the sphere at the center of the building.
The sphere edge

FIGURE 12.2

Create a sphere with a radius of 1060 feet.

4. Right-click the Front viewport, then click the Zoom Extents tool.
5. In the Command Panel, change the Hemisphere parameter for the sphere to **0.7**. Most of the sphere will disappear leaving the top-most portion. Change the name of the sphere from Sphere01 to **Skydome** so you can keep track of its function.
6. Move the Hemisphere so that its base is just below the ground plane as shown in Figure 12.3.

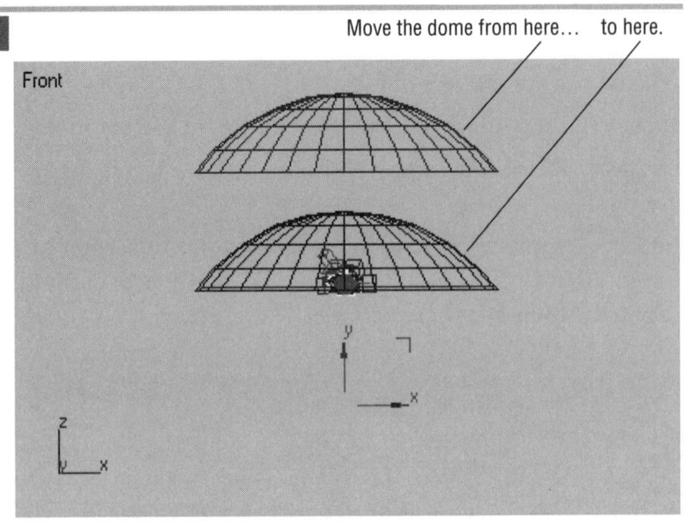

FIGURE 12.3

Move the hemisphere downward in the Z axis so that its base is just below the ground plane.

When you adjust the Hemisphere parameter, VIZ flattens the bottom of the sphere and places a surface on the flattened area. You need to place the bottom of the flattened sphere below the ground plane so that the sphere's flattened surface doesn't appear in your camera view.

Now you've got a dome over your model, which will become the sky. Spheres are normally intended to be viewed from the outside, so when VIZ creates a sphere, the normals are pointing outward. In this situation, you want your sphere to be viewable from the inside, so you need to invert the direction of the skydome's normals.

1. With the skydome hemisphere selected, click the Modify Tab.
2. Click the Edit Stack button in the Modifier Stack rollout, then select Editable Mesh. You won't need to make changes to the skydome's parameters, so this operation will help conserve memory and simplify the object.
3. Click the Element button in the Selection rollout to enter the element sub-object level.
4. Click the skydome to select it at the element sub-object level.
5. Scroll down to the Surface Properties rollout, then click the Flip button in the Normals group. You'll notice that the Camera view will change so that you no longer see the background gradient. Instead you see the inside of the skydome, showing you that the normals really are flipped.
6. Scroll back up to Modifier Stack and click the Sub-Object button to return to the Object level.

The skydome is just about ready. You now need to create a material to apply to the skydome to simulate the clouds. The material will also require a UVW Map.

1. Open Material Editor, then scroll down the Sample slots and click an unused slot.
2. Rename the selected slot's material name as **Skydome,** then open the Map rollout at the bottom of the dialog box.
3. Click the Diffuse Color Map button, then in the Material/Map browser, double-click Bitmap.
4. In the Select Bitmap image file dialog box, open the `\3dsVIZ3\Maps\Skies` folder, then locate and select `Ksc-sky3.jpg`. This is a fairly generic sky with a few clouds.
5. Click Open. Return to Material Editor and you see the sky bitmap in the sample slot.
6. With the skydome object selected, go ahead and click the Assign Material to Selection button on the Material Editor toolbar.

The sky will turn white. This is because the skydome material requires a UVW Map which doesn't exist yet.

You're just about finished creating the sky. The last item you need to take care of is the UVW Map. For this situation, the best map will be the Planar map. You want as much of the material map as possible to fit on the skydome, and the Planar map is the only one that will do this. You'll get the most natural-looking sky by mapping the skydome material as a flat plane against the skydome object.

1. Close the Material Editor dialog box. In the Modify tab, click the UVW Map modifier button. The Planar map is the default, so you don't really need to do much else. VIZ automatically aligns the map to the skydome object and adjusts the UVW Map to fit the skydome.
2. Right-click the Top viewport and click the Zoom Extents tool to get a better view of the UVW Map Gizmo.
3. Right-click the Camera viewport, then click the Quick Render tool to see the results. The sky appears, but it is too dark.

Since there are no lights directed toward the skydome, it appears as a dark background. You can add an omni light, whose only purpose is to light the skydome.

1. Close the Virtual Frame Buffer window and right-click the Top viewport.
2. Go to the Create Tab in the Command Panel, select the Lights button, and then click the Omni button.
3. Click the center of the dome to place an omni light there.
4. In the Command Panel, change the name of the new omni light to **skydomelight** and turn off its Cast Shadows parameters in the General Parameters rollout. Also make sure that the multiplier parameter is set to 1.

Now you've got a light for the skydome. You'll want to make sure that it illuminates only the sky.

1. In the General Parameters, click the Exclude button.
2. In the Exclude/Include dialog box, click the Include radio button in the upper right corner.
3. Select Skydome from the list box to the left, then click the right-pointing arrow to move the selection to the list box on the right.
4. Click OK to close the dialog box.
5. Right-click the Camera viewport, then click the Quick Render tool again. This time the sky appears brighter.

Now you have a sky that will stay in one place as the animation moves through the scene. Since the sky bitmap is now assigned to an object in the model, it will remain fixed in relation to the rest of the model. The net effect will be that the sky will appropriately follow the rest of the objects in the scene as the camera moves along its path.

TIP You can also create an interesting effect by combining the gradient background with the skydome sky. If you adjust the Opacity setting for the skydome material to a value less than 70, the gradient background will begin to show through the skydome object.

Making the Trees Appear 3D in the Animation

As I mentioned earlier, the trees look fine as long as you render a view that shows them facing forward. When you see them from the side, however, as in frame 170, the fact that they are just flat planes becomes more apparent. For the final animation, you'll want some trees with more depth so that they appear as real trees, though you may want to stick with the flat trees for your trial animations.

In Chapter 10, you learned how you can use VIZ's Xref commands to include other designs in a model. In this section, you'll look at how you can use Xrefs to substitute simplified geometry for quick study animations and then include more complex geometry for the final rendered output. In this particular case, you'll use two versions of the trees.

First, let's temporarily turn off the sky to work with the trees.

1. Click the Display tab in the Command Panel.
2. Make sure the skydome object is selected, then click the Selected Off button.
3. In the Top viewport, zoom into the building so that you can see the building and trees easily, as in Figure 12.4.

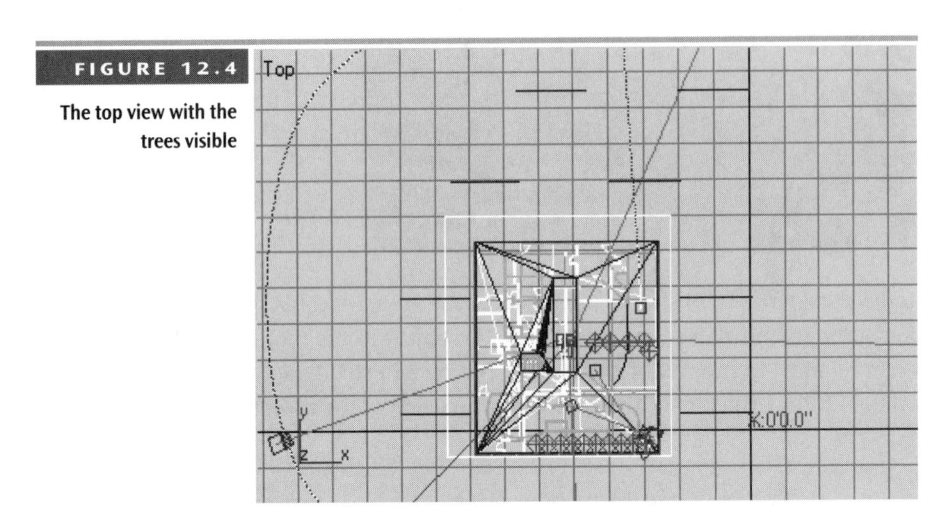

FIGURE 12.4 The top view with the trees visible

4. Click the Select by Name tool on the standard toolbar, then select Tree01 through Tree08 from the list box.
5. Click Select to complete your selection, then choose File ➢ Save Selected. The Save File dialog box appears.
6. Enter **Treesimple** for the file name, then click Save.
7. Now delete the trees from the design by pressing the Delete key.

You've just saved the trees from your model as a separate file. You can easily restore them as Xrefs by doing the following:

1. Choose Insert ➢ Xref Designs.
2. In the Xref Designs dialog box, click Add.
3. In the Open File dialog box, locate and open the `Treesimple.max` file.
4. Close the Xref Designs dialog box. You see the trees restored to your design.

You've exported your trees, then brought them back into the villa as an Xref design. As you'll see, this will let you switch easily between your original trees and a set of more complex trees.

The next step is to create a file that contains the new, 3D trees. You'll use the trees that are available in AEC Tools.

1. Save the villa file, then open the `Treesimple.max` file.
2. Click the Create tab in the Command Panel, then click the Geometry button.
3. Open the drop-down list in the Create tab, then select AEC Extended. You'll see a set of new options in the Create tab.
4. Click the Foliage button in the Object Type rollout. You see a list box appear in the Create tab showing you some sample images of foliage. This is the Favorite Plants palette.
5. Scroll the Create tab panel up so you can get a better look at the palette, then use the scroll bar to the right to view the sample images.

You can see that there are quite a few options for decorative plants and trees. VIZ offers a few more plants than those presented in the list box.

1. Click the Plant Library... button just below the palette. The Configure Palette dialog box displays. You see that there are some additional trees listed that do not appear in the list box in the Create Tab.

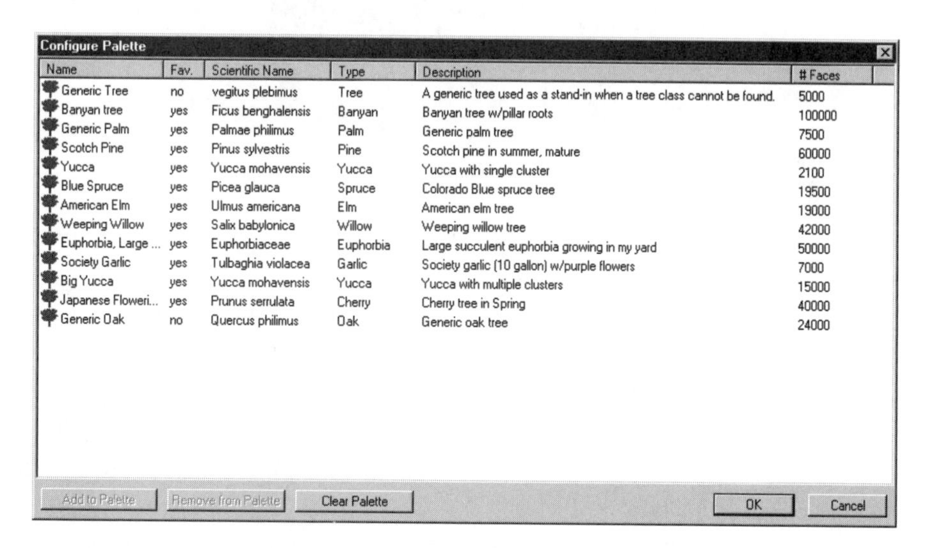

2. Click the Generic Oak listing and click Add to Palette.
3. Click OK, then scroll down the panel. The Generic Oak appears in the list box of the Favorite Plants rollout.

Here you see that you can include a few additional trees in the list box for your model. The Configure Palette dialog box also lets you remove a specific plant from the palette or clear the entire palette at once, using the three buttons at the bottom of the dialog box.

You've seen how you can add a plant to the palette. Next, you'll use the American Elm to replace the flat trees in the design.

1. Click the American Elm in the palette, then click the location shown in Figure 12.5 to place the tree in the same location as an existing tree. The tree appears in the viewports.

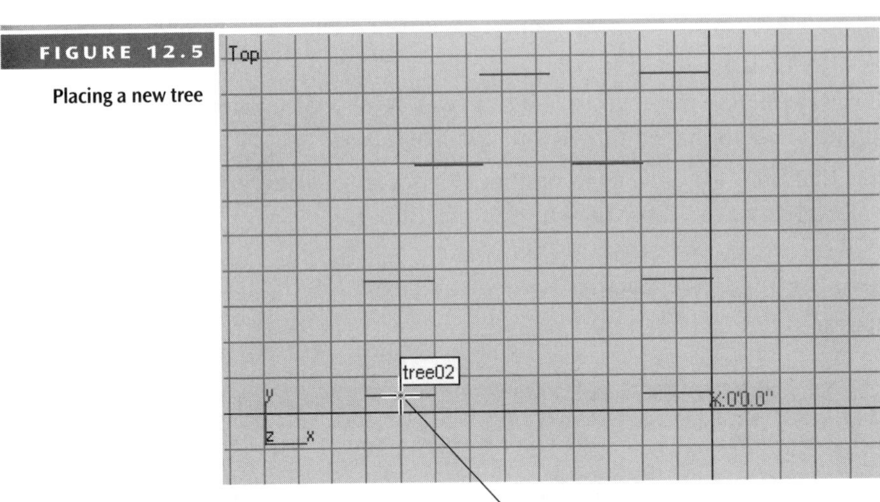

FIGURE 12.5

Placing a new tree

2. Open the parameters rollout just below the foliage palette in the Command Panel, then change the height to 22 feet.
3. Go ahead and click each of the flat tree locations in the design to place a new American Maple where each of the old trees is. Each time you place a tree, change the height parameter to **22′**.

Once you've gotten the trees placed, you can remove the original flat trees.

1. Click the Select by Name tool on the standard toolbar to open the Select Objects dialog box.
2. Select Tree01 through Tree08 from the list box and click Select.
3. Press the Delete key to Delete the old trees.
4. Now save the file as **Treesfull**. Choose File Save as; then in the Save File As dialog box, enter **Treesfull** in the File name input box and click Save.

For the final step, you'll go back to the villa design file and exchange the simple flat trees for the new set of American Maples.

1. Open the villa design you saved earlier.
2. Choose Insert ➢ Xref Designs...
3. In the Xref Designs dialog box, click the `Treesimple.max` listing and click the Enabled check box in the Xref File group. The trees disappear from the viewports.
4. Click the Add button in the upper right corner of the dialog box.
5. In the Open File dialog box, locate and open the `Treesfull.max` file. The American Elm trees appear in the design.
6. Close the Xref Designs dialog box.

Now let's take a look at the results.

1. Move the time slider to frame 170.
2. Click the Display tab of the Command Panel, then click All On to turn on the skydome.
3. Click the Quick Render tool. Notice that this time the rendering takes a lot more time.

The trees will render as full trees in the animation, but you can imagine how long it will take to render the animation if one frame takes too long. This is why you really want to make sure that everything in your animation is correct before you commit to creating the full, finished animation.

TIP You can get a rough estimate of the full render time of an animation by multiplying the time for a typical frame by the number of frames in the animation. Note, however, that some frames may take a considerably longer or shorter time, depending on the camera's relationship to complex geometry in the design. VIZ will take longer to render scenes where the camera is close to complex geometry.

You may have noticed that you didn't remove the `Treesimple.max` Xrefs from the villa design. Instead, you disabled them, then imported the `Treesfull.max` file. This way you can keep track of the two files associated with the trees. When you want to switch back to the flat trees, you can do so easily.

1. Click Insert ➢ Xref Designs…
2. In the Xref Designs dialog box, highlight the `Treesfull.max` listing, then uncheck the Enable check box.
3. Click the `Treesimple.max` listing and click the Enable check box to restore these trees.
4. Click the Close button.

Now you're back to the original, flat trees. These flat trees can serve as stand-ins for the American Elms while you work on your animation.

Speeding Animation Rendering with Shadow Maps

You can greatly shorten the rendering time of your animation by changing the shadow parameters for the SUN directional light from Ray Traced to Shadow Map. Since the trees are made up of individual leaves, their shadows will be more accurate with the Shadow Map shadow than were the shadows of the flat trees. You'll want to increase the shadow map size to ensure that your rendering shows enough detail in the shadows of the building. You can also narrow the falloff parameter of the SUN directional light to encompass just enough of the building so that it is lit in the animation. This will reduce the area that the shadow map must cover and increase the resolution of the shadow map in relation to the building. See Chapter 8 for a detailed discussion comparing shadow maps with Ray Traced shadows.

Adding a Moving Car

Your animation work so far has involved moving a camera around the villa. Of course, you can animate other props in your model. Let's add a car to the villa animation to see how to control the behavior of objects other than cameras. By animating a car, you'll explore how you can rotate an object through time. You'll use a simple box to represent a car to see how you can make an object move smoothly in an animation.

First create the box that will represent the car.

1. Click the Top viewport, then click the Min/Max Viewport toggle to enlarge the view.
2. Click the Skydome object, then in the Display tab click Selected Off.
3. Click the Create tab in the Command Panel, then click the Geometry button. Select Standard Primitives from the Create tab drop-down list and click Box.
4. Click and drag the box shown in Figure 12.6, then click again to fix the height of the box.
5. In the Parameters rollout, set the Length to be **15'**, the Width to be **5' 6"**, and the height to be **40"**.
6. Change the name of the box to **Car01**.

FIGURE 12.6

Adding the box representing the car

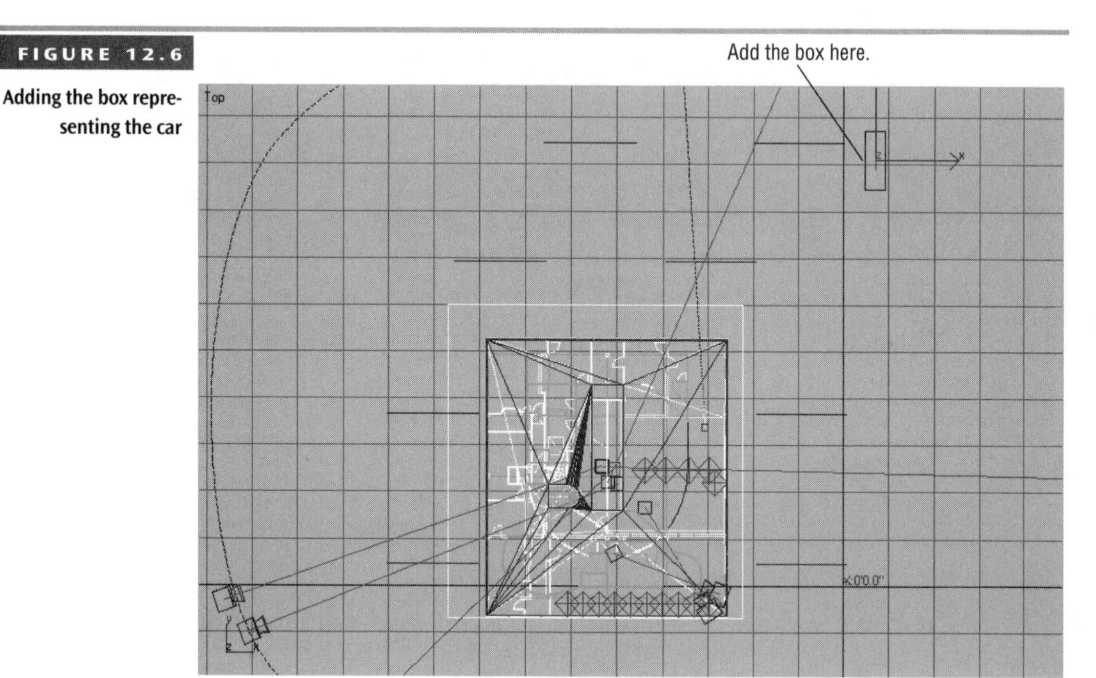

Now that you have a box representing a car, it's time to animate it. Just as with the camera, you'll need to enter the Animate mode, select a time in the time slider, and then move the car.

1. Click the Animate button on the Time Controls toolbar.
2. Move the time slider to frame 200.

3. Click the Select and Move tool, then move the car to the position shown in Figure 12.7.

FIGURE 12.7

Move the car to the new location at frame 200.

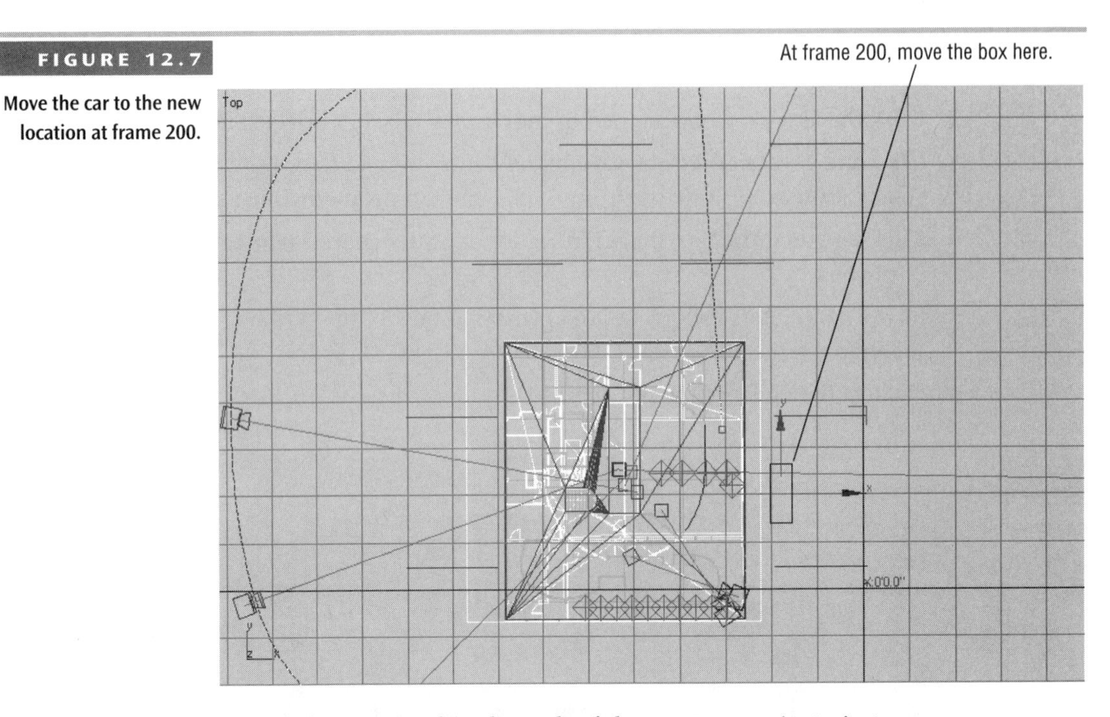
At frame 200, move the box here.
Top

To help you visualize the path of the car, turn on its trajectory.

1. Right-click the car, then select Properties.
2. In the Display Properties of the Object Properties dialog box, click By Layer to change the display property of the car to By Object.
3. Click the Trajectory check box, then click OK.

Now you've got a visible trajectory. Let's adjust the beginning and ending keyframes so the car starts and stops smoothly on its path.

1. Click the Motion tab in the Command Panel.
2. In the Key Info (Basic) rollout, click and drag the In flyout parameter and select Slow.

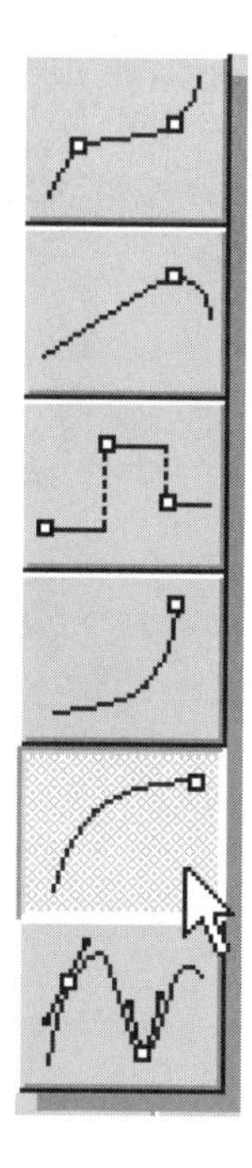

3. Click the Key number arrow in the upper left corner of the Key Info (Basic) fly-out to go to keyframe 1.
4. Select the Slow tangent option for the Out parameter.
5. Move the time slider from frame 0 to frame 200 and watch what the car does.

You can see that the car moves in a straight line between the two keyframes. The orientation of the car has not changed, so the car looks like it is moving slightly sideways. Finally, the car is driving through a tree.

Next, you'll modify the trajectory of the car so that it avoids the tree. You'll also add some rotation to the car so that it looks like it's turning into the building.

1. Move the time slider to frame 120. This is where you'll add another keyframe in order to move the trajectory away from the tree.
2. With the Select and Move tool still active, move the car to the location shown in Figure 12.8.
3. Click the Select and Rotate tool, then rotate the car clockwise so that it is aligned with the trajectory at this keyframe (see Figure 12.8). By rotating the car at this point you are adding a rotation key.

FIGURE 12.8

Move the car to this location at frame 120.

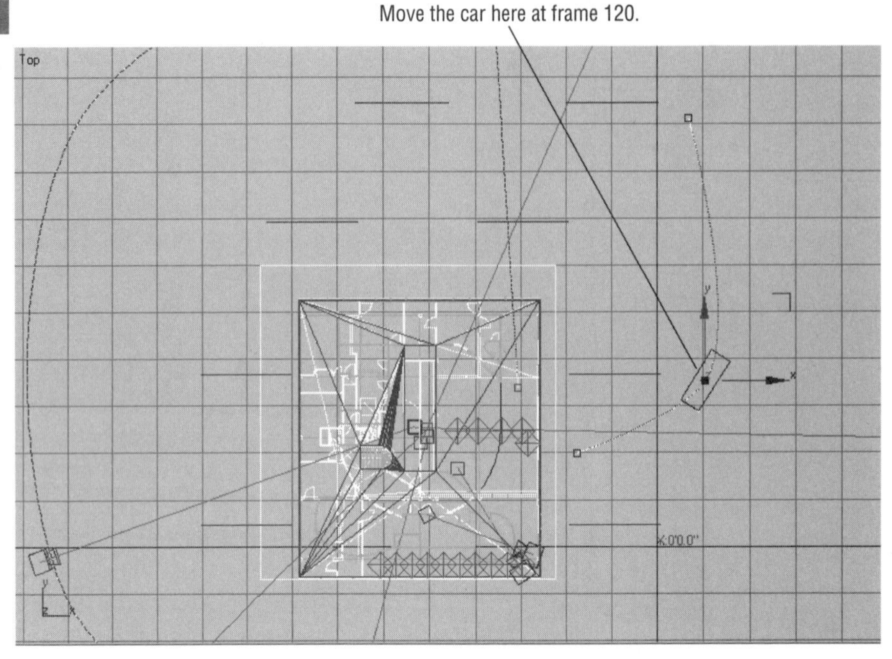
Move the car here at frame 120.
Top

4. Now click and drag the time slider between frames 0 and 200 to see the motion of the car.

The car moves around the tree and turns, though the turning is not well coordinated with the trajectory. The car also does not complete its turn at frame 200 where it comes to rest. You need to add a few more rotation keys to make the car's motion fit its trajectory.

1. Go to frame 200 to keyframe 3 of the trajectory.
2. With the Select and Rotate tool still selected, rotate the car so that it is aligned with the trajectory as shown in Figure 12.9.

FIGURE 12.9

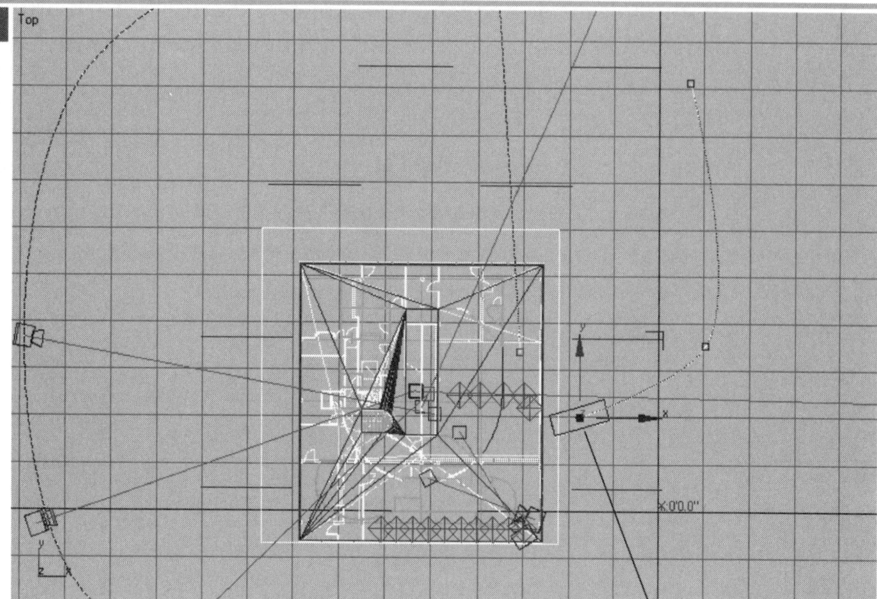

Align the car with the trajectory at keyframe 3.

3. Go to keyframe 1 and align the car with the trajectory.
4. Now check the animation again by moving the time slider between frames 0 and 200.

The car now turns, but it is still somehow out of sync with the trajectory. To fine-tune the car's motion, you'll need to add some additional key locations for the rotation.

1. Set the time slider to frame 93, then use the Select and Rotate tool to align the car to the trajectory.

   This location was chosen because it is about where the car begins to increase its turning rate.
2. Move the time slider to frame 135 and again align the car to the trajectory. This frame was selected because, at this point, the car is coming out of the turn.
3. Now test the animation again by sliding the time slider from 0 to 200 and back.

The car now follows the trajectory in a more natural carlike fashion.

You've added several rotation keys in this exercise. Unlike the position keyframes, rotation keys do not appear on the trajectory. They do, however, appear below the time slider as additional key dots while the car box is selected. The rotation keys also have parameters that can be adjusted in the Motion panel and in the Track View.

1. With the car selected, click the Rotation button at the bottom of the PRS Parameters rollout (not the Rotation button in the Create Key group). The Rotation key parameters appear in the Key Info rollout.

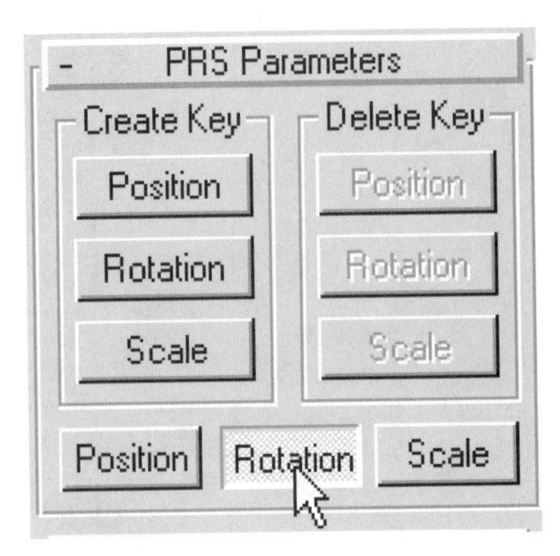

2. Scroll down the Command Panel to the Key Info rollout. You now see the Key Info panel for the rotation parameters.

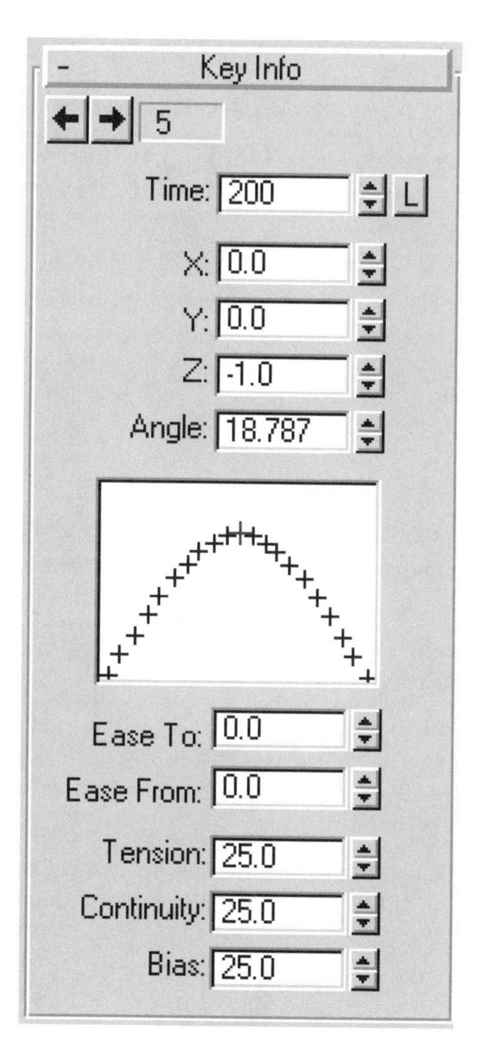

Notice that it is a TCB controller instead of the Bézier controller you worked with in the camera animation. (see Chapter 11 for more on the TCB controller.) You can fine-tune the rotation of the car using the TCB parameters at each key, though the current settings may be just fine for this project.

You've seen how you can use the Rotate transform tool over time to make the car move through its trajectory as a car normally would. You have the same types of control over the rotation of the car as you do with the position. You can also use Track View to fine-tune the car's motion.

Using a Spline for an Animation Path

The animated car example is a fairly complex way to get a car to turn a corner. This example was used to show you some of the issues you'll face when rotating an object through time. To animate the car, you can use another method that is much quicker than the one shown in the exercise, though it offers a bit less control over the animation.

The Animation ➢ Follow Path option allows you to assign a motion to an object using a spline object for the path. The advantage of using this option is that the object's motion will follow the spline, and its orientation will also be aligned with the direction of the spline, so you won't have to deal with adjusting the object's orientation at the keyframe locations.

To use this feature, do the following.

1. Use the Line Shape tool to draw a spline curve that indicates the path of your object.
2. Use the Time Configuration dialog to set a time range for the object's motion.
3. Select the objects you want to animate.
4. Choose Animation ➢ Follow Path.
5. Select the path you drew in step 1.

The selected object moves to the start of the spline. The spline and the objects are linked so that if you move the spline or change its shape, the animation of the object will follow. Note that the selected objects will align with the path with their X axes pointing along the direction of the spline.

When you are using the Animation ➢ Follow Path option, VIZ will display the Path Parameters rollout in the Motion tab when you select the animated objects. You won't see the Key Info rollouts. The Path Parameters rollout lets you adjust banking and smoothness of the path. It also lets you select a different path for the object's motion.

Automating Multiple Still Image Output

Animations are great tools for presenting designs, and they can be quite helpful in understanding what a design will ultimately feel like to inhabit. But the tools you use for animation can also be used to help you automate the creation of still images. In particular, they can be great time-saving tools for creating the more traditional elevation views of a building or the top, front, and side views of objects for technical illustrations.

In this section, you'll see how you can automate the creation of elevation views of the villa by animating another camera in the design.

Setting Up a Camera for Elevations

The first step in this automation project is to set up a camera to display an Orthographic Projection instead of a perspective view.

1. Go to the Top viewport and, if it isn't already enlarged, enlarge it using the Min/Max Viewport toggle.
2. Adjust the viewport so it looks similar to Figure 12.10.
3. Click the Create tab in the Command Panel, then click the Camera button.
4. Click Target in the Object Type rollout, then click and drag the point indicated in Figure 12.10 directly to the right of the villa.

FIGURE 12.10

The Top viewport and new camera

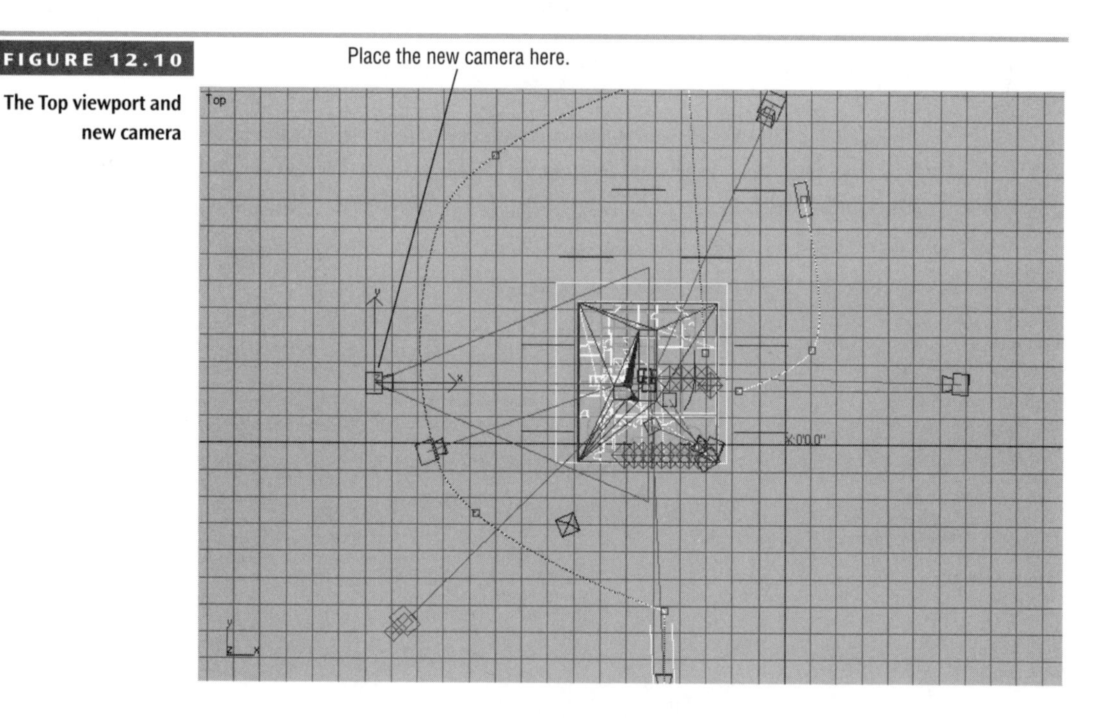
Place the new camera here.
Top

5. Drag the cursor to the center of the villa plan and release the mouse.
6. Rename this new camera **Elevation01**.

The camera parameters need to be altered so that it will display a typical elevation view, which is a type of Orthographic Projection view.

1. First, click the Min/Max viewport toggle to view all of the viewports.
2. Right-click the Camera.View.3DFRONT viewport label in the upper left corner of the Camera viewport, and then select View ➢ Elevation01. This will allow you to see the changes you make to the Elevation01 camera settings.
3. With the Elevation01 camera selected, click the Modify tab of the Command Panel, then in the Parameters rollout, click the Orthographic Projection check box.

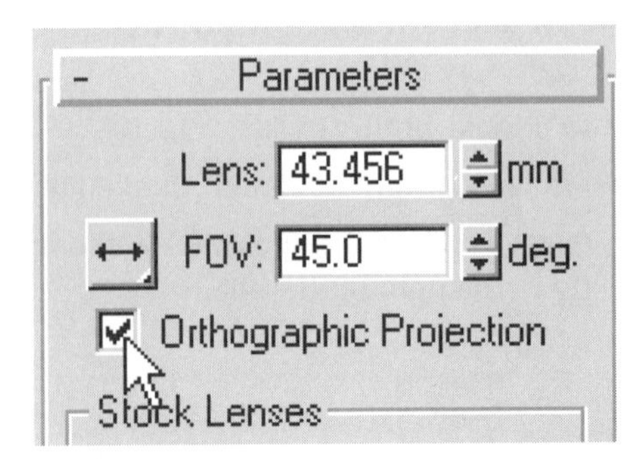

Notice that the Elevation01 viewport changes to show a side view of the building.

4. Adjust the FOV spinner so that the Elevation01 viewport looks similar to Figure 12.11.

FIGURE 12.11

The Elevation01 viewport, showing the orthographic projection of the villa

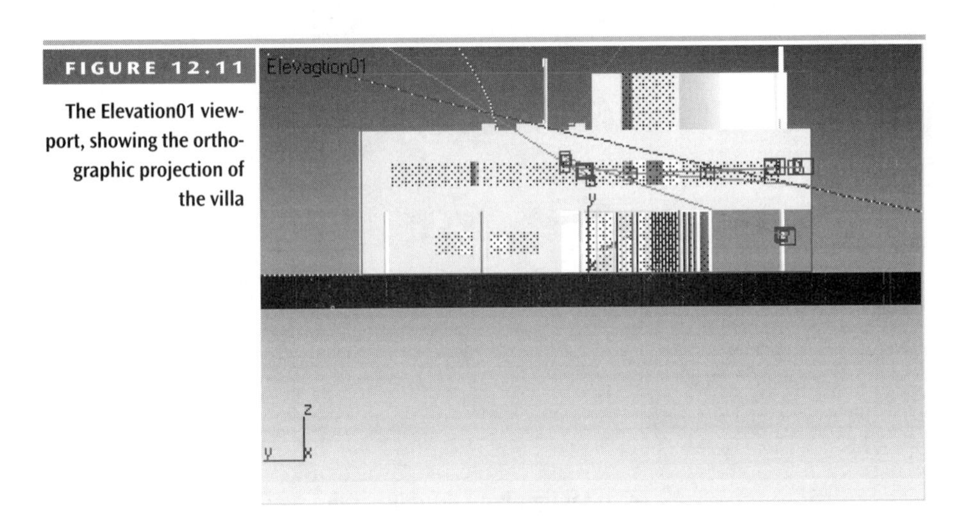

You'll need to make one more adjustment to the camera. The view in the Elevation01 viewport is a bit too high. You'll need to raise the camera location to center the view.

1. Adjust the Front view so that it looks similar to Figure 12.12.
2. Click the Select by Name tool, then in the Select Objects dialog box, shift-click Elevation01 and Elevation01.Target from the list box and click Select.
3. Click the Select and Move tool, then in the Front Viewport, move the Elevation01 camera and target vertically so that the camera's centerline is slightly above the center of the building as shown in Figure 12.12.

FIGURE 12.12

Move the camera vertically so that it is in the position shown here.

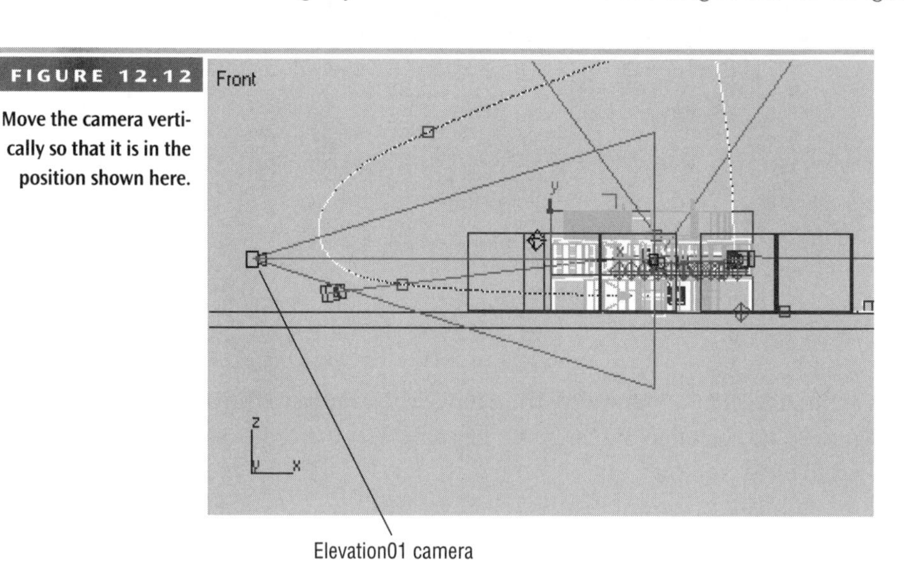

You can use the Elevation01 viewport to see the results of your move. You may continue to make adjustments until you like the view in the Elevation01 viewport.

Setting up the Four Elevations

With the Elevation01 camera created and its parameters set, the final step is to set up the four views using the animation features of VIZ. You'll turn on the Animate mode, and then, at three different frames, you'll set up three camera positions, one for each of the other three elevations.

1. Click the Animate button on the Time Controls toolbar.
2. Move the time slider to 10. The selection of frame 10 is really just an arbitrary decision. It can be any number you choose: 10 is easy to remember.
3. In the Top viewport, move the Elevation01 camera to the location shown in Figure 12.13. Make sure that you move only the camera and *not* the camera *and* the target.

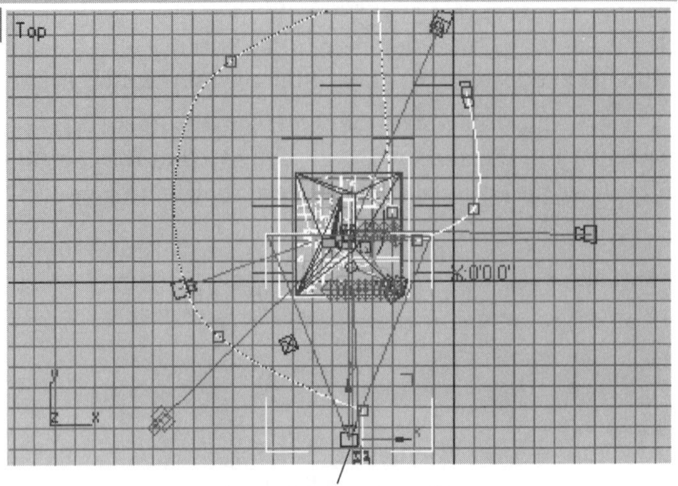

FIGURE 12.13

Move the camera to this location for the second elevation.

Camera location at frame 10.

You can use the Elevation01 camera viewport to help align the camera.

4. Move the time slider to frame 20, then move the camera to the position shown in Figure 12.14. Again, make sure that the camera is perpendicular to the surface of the building. You may also use the Elevation01 viewport to make sure that the camera includes the entire building in its view.

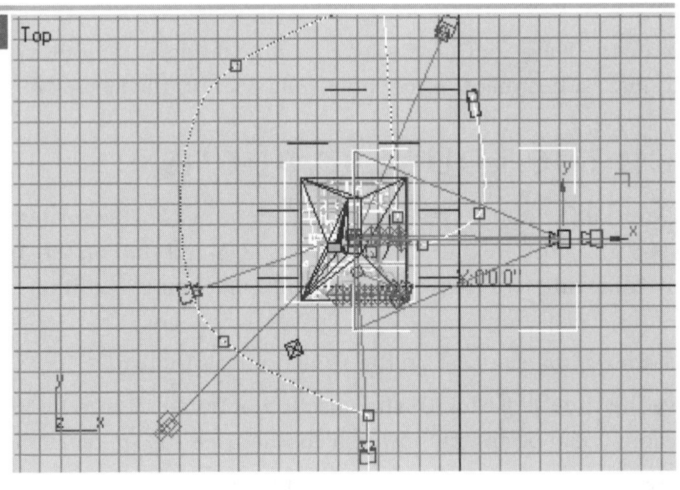

FIGURE 12.14

Move the camera to this location for the third elevation.

5. Move the time slider to frame 30, and then move the camera to the last elevation position shown in Figure 12.15.

FIGURE 12.15

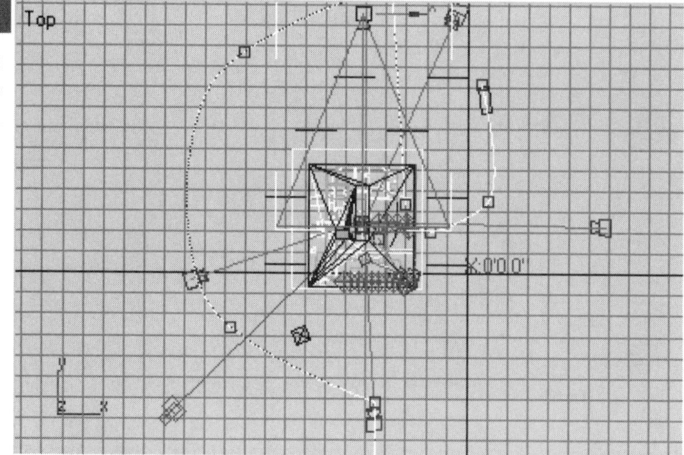

Move the camera to this location for the last elevation.

TIP If you prefer to have no intermediate frames between the four elevation camera positions, you can use the Step flyout In/Out option in the Key Info (Basic) rollout for each of the elevation keyframes.

You now have four frames that show the villa's four elevations. As a final step, you'll need to create a copy of the SUN directional light that follows the camera. Typically, rendered elevation views use a light source from the upper left corner of the view, so you'll need to create a copy of the sun to simulate that orientation.

1. Move the time slider to frame 0.
2. Shift-click and drag the SUN directional light to the location shown in Figure 12.16.

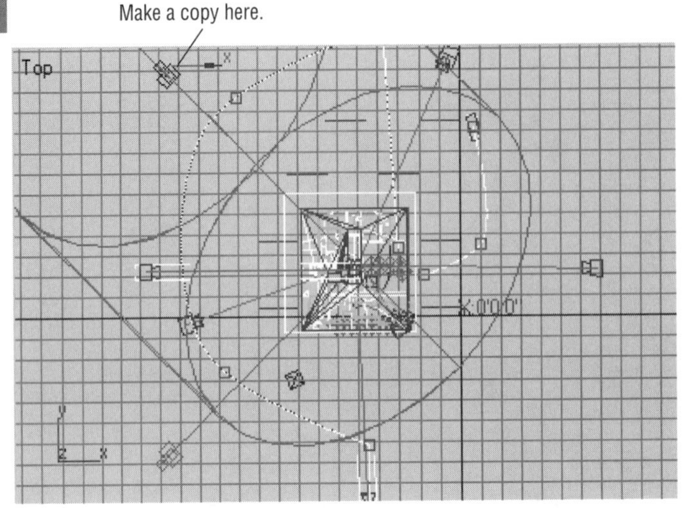

FIGURE 12.16

Make a copy of the SUN directional light at this location.

3. In the Clone dialog box, give the new directional light the name **SUNelevation01**.
4. Click the Copy radio button, then click OK.
5. Move the time slider to Frame 10, then move the new Sunelevation01 direct light to the location shown in Figure 12.17.
6. Repeat step 5 for frames 20 and 30. Use Figure 12.17 to guide you in the location of the Sunelevation01 directional light.

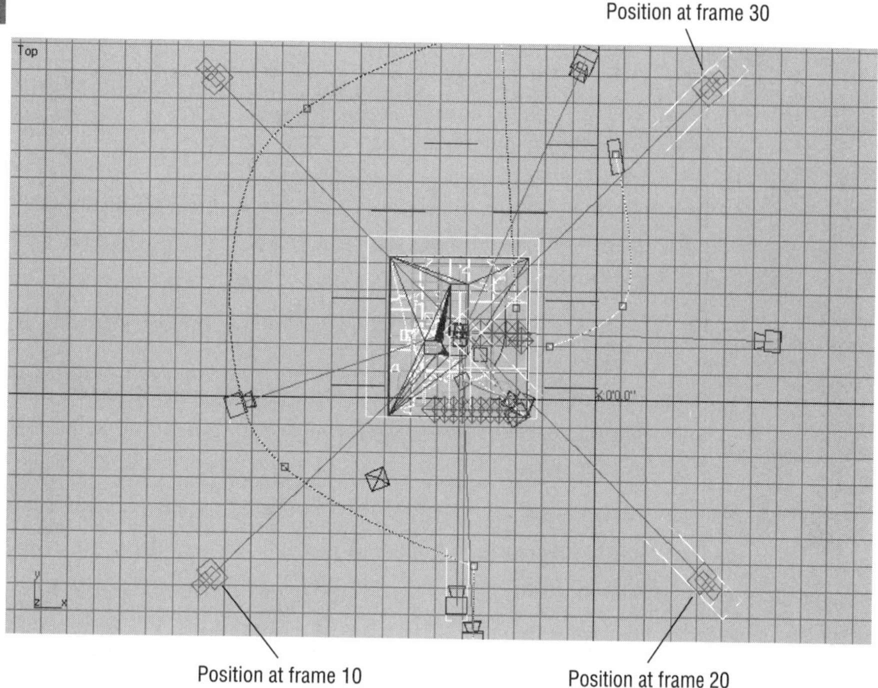

FIGURE 12.17

Positioning the sun for each elevation

You're just about ready to render your elevations. You need to make a few adjustments to the design.

1. Select the original SUN directional light, then in the Modify Tab of the Command Panel, click the On check box in the General Parameters to turn off this light.
2. Choose Insert ➢ Xref Designs... In the Xref Designs dialog box, select `Treesimple.max` and uncheck the Enabled check box to hide the trees. If you don't do this, they will obscure the view of the building. Go ahead and close the dialog box.

Now that you've got the design set up with a camera for the elevations, the rendering part is simple. VIZ gives you the option to render selected frames of an animation instead of the entire sequence of frames. You'll use this feature to create your elevations.

1. Click the Render tool on the Render toolbar to open the Render Design dialog box.

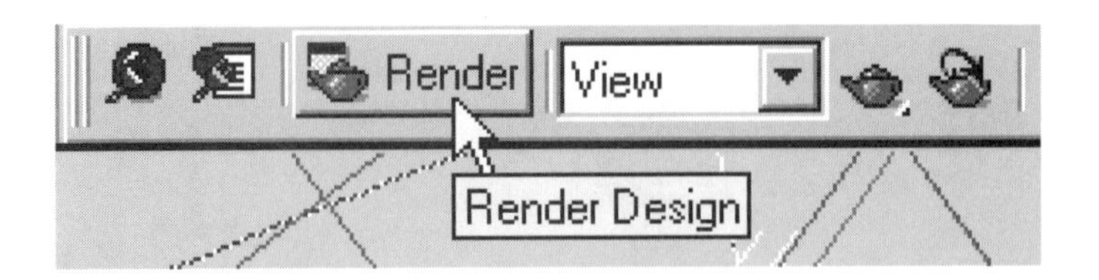

2. In the Render Design dialog box, make sure the Production radio button at the bottom of the dialog box is selected and then click the Frames radio button in the Time Output group.
3. In the Frames input box, enter **0,10,20,30**. This tells VIZ to only Render frames 0, 10, 20 and 30.
4. Click the Files button in the Render Output group, then in the Render Output File dialog box, enter **Myelevations** for the name, and select TIF in the Save as type drop-down list.
5. Click Save. In the TIF Image Control dialog box, click Color and then OK.
6. Make sure Elevation01 is selected in the Viewport drop-down list at the bottom of the dialog box, then click Render. VIZ proceeds to render the four elevation views.

VIZ will create four files, each with `Myelevations` as the first part of the name. A number is appended to the name to indicate which frame of the animation the rendering represents.

Of course, you can use VIZ's animation tools to automate the rendering of a set of perspective or isometric views. You can now walk away and take care of other things while VIZ renders your views unattended. If your views take a long time to render, you may want to set things up to render overnight.

The elevations you render will look a bit stark. You can add trees and people to add some life to the images. The addition of landscaping, people, and cars to liven up a rendering is referred to as *entourage*. You can add entourage to your still images later in an image-editing program, or you can include trees and people in the model to be rendered with the building. Trees such as the flat magnolia trees already in the model can be used even in front of the building by making them slightly transparent. You can also use trees that show no foliage, such as the Generic Tree from the Foliage palette of the AEC Extended objects.

Rendering a Sun Shadow Study

Another great non-animation use of VIZ's animation tools is the creation of sun shadow studies. In some situations, a project may require a shadow study of a building to make sure its shadows do not adversely impact a landscape feature or another building nearby. You may also be called upon to create a sun shadow study to help analyze a building's heat gain and energy usage. The Sunlight system tool in conjunction with the Animation tools can make quick work of such a task.

In the following exercise, you'll use the villa to create some shadow studies using the Top viewport. In the following section, you'll learn how you can use the Animation features to create both stills and animations of the building's shadows over time.

The first step is to accurately place the sun in the design.

1. Adjust the Top view so it looks similar to Figure 12.18.

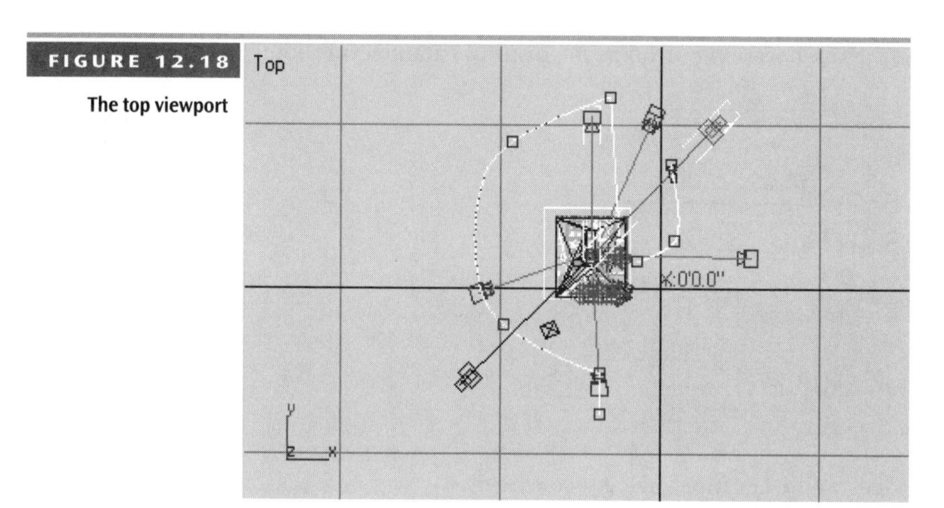

FIGURE 12.18 The top viewport

2. Turn off the Animate button and click the Create Tab; then click the Systems button.

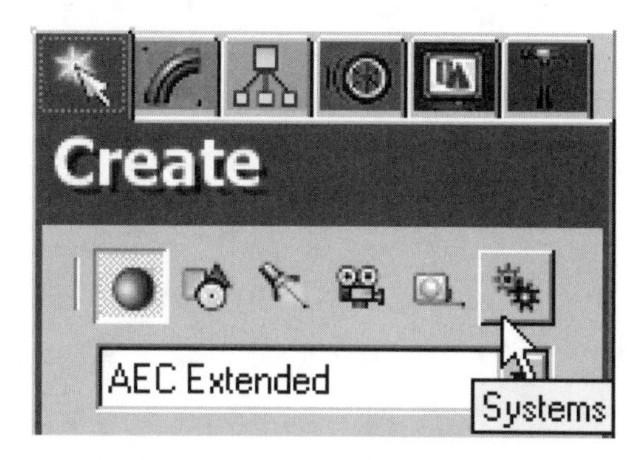

3. Click the Sunlight button in the Object Type rollout.

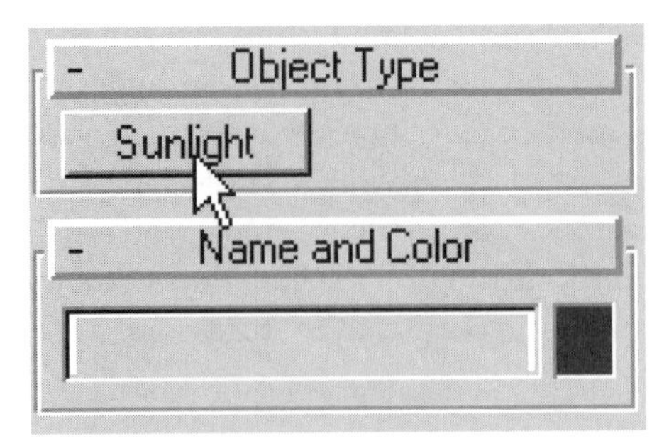

4. Click the Get Location button in the Control Parameters rollout.

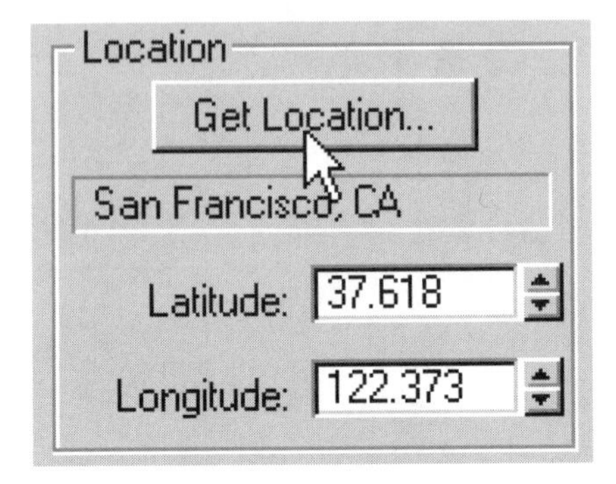

The Geographic Location dialog box appears.

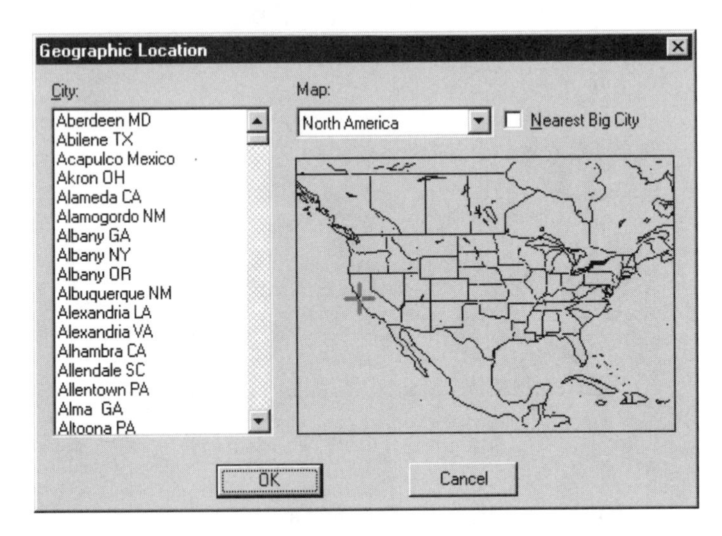

5. Select Europe from the Map drop-down list. You'll see a general map of Europe appear in the dialog box.

6. In the list to the left, locate and select Paris, France. A cross displays on the map at the location you select.
7. Click OK.

The Villa Savoye is located in a town called Poissy, whose nearest major city is Paris. For the purposes of this exercise, Paris will be close enough, but if you wanted to be absolutely precise, you could use the Latitude and Longitude settings in the Location group of the Control Parameters rollout to enter the exact location of Poissy.

Now you are ready to place the sun in the plan.

1. In the Top viewport, click and hold at the center of the building. As you drag the mouse, you'll see a compass rose appear, changing in size as you drag the mouse.
2. Adjust the compass rose so that it is about the size shown in Figure 12.19, then release the mouse.

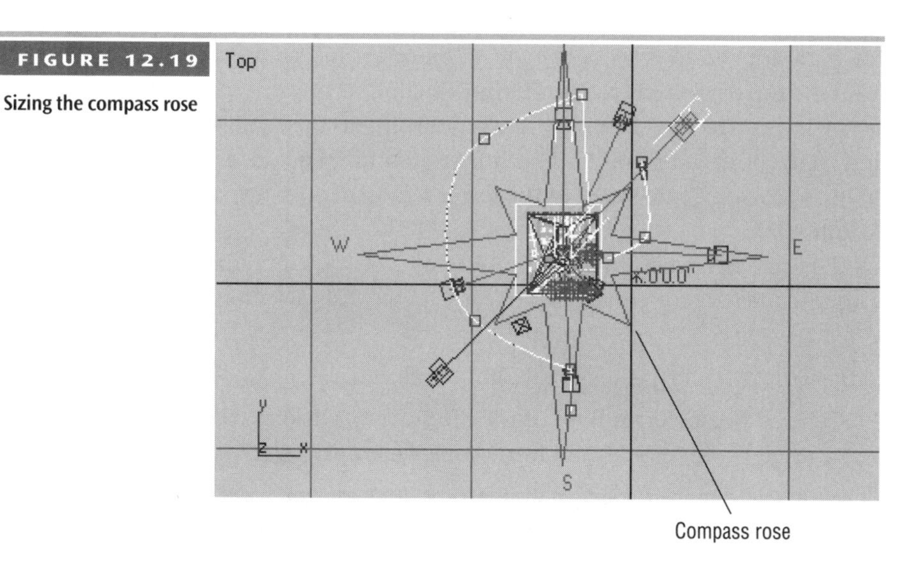

FIGURE 12.19
Sizing the compass rose

Now as you drag the mouse, a directional light appears and moves across the viewports. This is the SUN system's Sunlight object.

3. Adjust the Sunlight so that it is close to the edge of the viewport, then click the mouse to fix its location.

You now have a sun that you can control over time. Try the following to see the effects of the time settings. The default location of the Sunlight directional light is the time and date set on your computer's clock. Next, you'll change the sunlight location for 2 o'clock in the afternoon on March 21, 2000.

1. In the Control Parameters rollout, set the time to 14 hours, 0 minutes, and 0 seconds. The settings are in 24-hour time, so 2 o'clock is 1400 hours.
2. Set the date for March 21, 2000, and make sure that the daylight savings time check box is not checked. Notice that the sunlight changes location as you adjust the date and time.
3. You may need to increase the spread of the sunlight, so click the Modify tab, open the Directional Parameters rollout, and increase the Falloff parameter to **150′**.

You also need to orient the sun correctly in relation to the building. For the villa, north is actually in the lower left corner of the Top viewport. You can change the orientation of the compass rose and thereby change the true north direction.

1. Click the Motion tab in the Command Panel and scroll down to the Site group of the Control Parameters rollout.
2. Change the North Direction setting to **225**. You'll see the compass rose and Sunlight directional light change position to reflect the new north direction.

In the Top view, true north is actually about 135 degrees in a counter-clockwise direction from the top of the screen. The North Direction setting interprets values as degrees in a clockwise direction, so to point north directly to the right in a positive X axis direction, you would enter **90**. The North Direction input box does not accept negative values, so to point true north to the lower left corner of the top viewport, you need to enter **225**.

Finally, you'll want to turn off the other suns you have in your model. The SUN directional light is already off, so you need to turn off the SUNelevation01 directional light.

1. Click the Sunelevation01 directional light to select it.
2. In the General Parameters rollout of the Modify tab, click the On check box to remove the check mark and turn off the Sunelevation01 light.

Now let's set up some times for the shadow study. Suppose you want to see the shadows at three-hour intervals, starting at 6 o'clock. You'll want to set the first hour a bit before the 6 o'clock time in case you want to create an animated study of the sunlight.

1. Select the Sunlight directional light, then click the Motion tab of the Command Panel.
2. Set the Hours parameter in the Time group of the Control Parameters rollout to **3**.
3. Move the time slider to frame 0, then click the Animate button to turn on the Animate mode.

4. Move the time slider to frame 70, then change the Hours setting to **21**.

You now have a range of time that you can use to generate single images or a two-second animation showing the movement of shadows across the ground on March 21, 2000. To create a set of individual renderings for the times you set, do the following:

1. In the Top viewport, adjust the view to look like Figure 12.20.

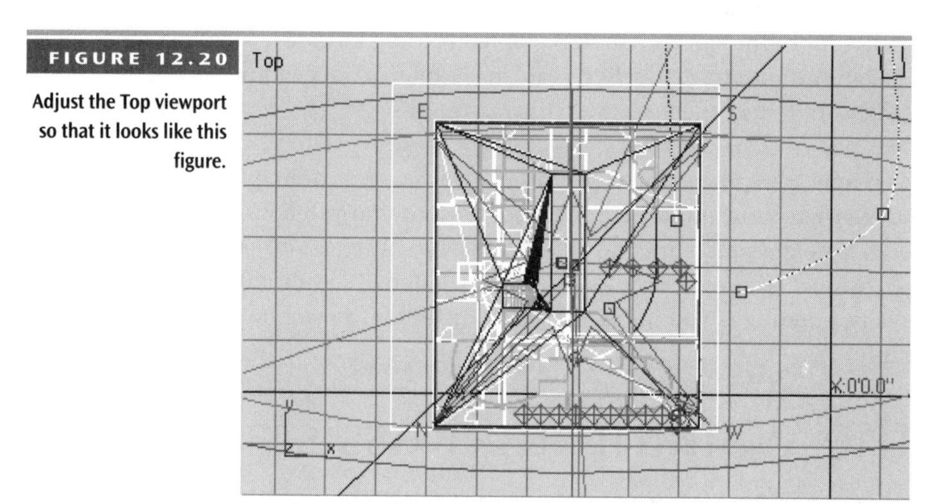

FIGURE 12.20

Adjust the Top viewport so that it looks like this figure.

2. Open the Render Design dialog box and make sure the Production radio button at the bottom of the dialog box is selected.
3. Click the Frames radio button in the Time Output group.
4. Enter the frame numbers that correlate with the times of the day that you want to render, separated by commas. For five single views at three-hour increments, enter **10,20,30,40,50** without spaces.
5. Use the File... button to enter the name **Sunstudy** for your file output and then click Save.
5. Make sure Top is selected in the Viewport drop-down list at the bottom of the dialog box, then click Render.

VIZ will render five views of the Top viewport, each showing the shadows of the building on the ground at the times indicated for each frame.

To create a short, animated shadow study, do the following:

1. Set up the Top viewport as described in the last set of steps.
2. Open the Render Design dialog box and click the Draft radio button at the bottom of the Render Design dialog box.
3. Click the Range radio button and enter a range from frame 0 to frame 60.

4. Click File and enter **Shadowstudy** for the file name and **.AVI** for the Save as type drop-down list.
5. Click Render to create the shadow study animation.

You may want to include the trees from the `Treefull.max` design in the shadow studies to see their effect on the shadows. Both the still images and the animation can be helpful tools in your work, and as you've seen from these exercises, they don't really take that much time to generate.

As you've seen from the exercises in this chapter, you can have several animations in a single design. You just have to select a camera to animate, depending on which animation you want to use, then select the time range or set of frames for your final output.

You've seen how you can create a wide variety of animations from flybys to shadow studies. There's one more method for animations that you'll want to know about. You can generate a more intimate look at a design, using a tool called the *Walkthrough Assistant*. The Walkthrough Assistant is designed specifically for simulating the view of a building as you walk through it. The following section will show you how it works.

Using the Walkthrough Assistant

Walkthroughs can give you a sense of what a space is really like. They can play a major role in selling a project to a client. They can also show you what is good or bad about a design in ways that still images cannot. The Walkthrough Assistant simplifies the creation of a walkthrough animation so you can concentrate on what you want to show in the walkthrough and not get too bogged down in the technical side of In and Out tangents and keyframes (though it certainly helps to know about such things).

Before you can use the Walkthrough Assistant, you'll need a spline indicating the walkthrough path.

Start by creating a path for your walkthrough, using a line shape.

1. Turn off the Animate button.
2. Use the Min/Max Viewport toggle to enlarge the Top viewport.
3. Click the Create tab in the Command Panel, click the Shapes button, and then click Line.
4. You'll want a curved path, so click and drag the start of the line at the point indicated in Figure 12.21.
5. Click and drag two more points to form the curved spline shown in Figure 12.21.

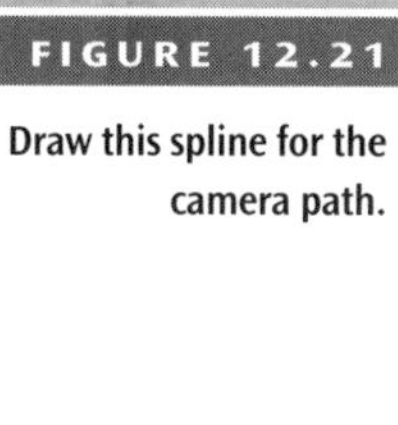

FIGURE 12.21

Draw this spline for the camera path.

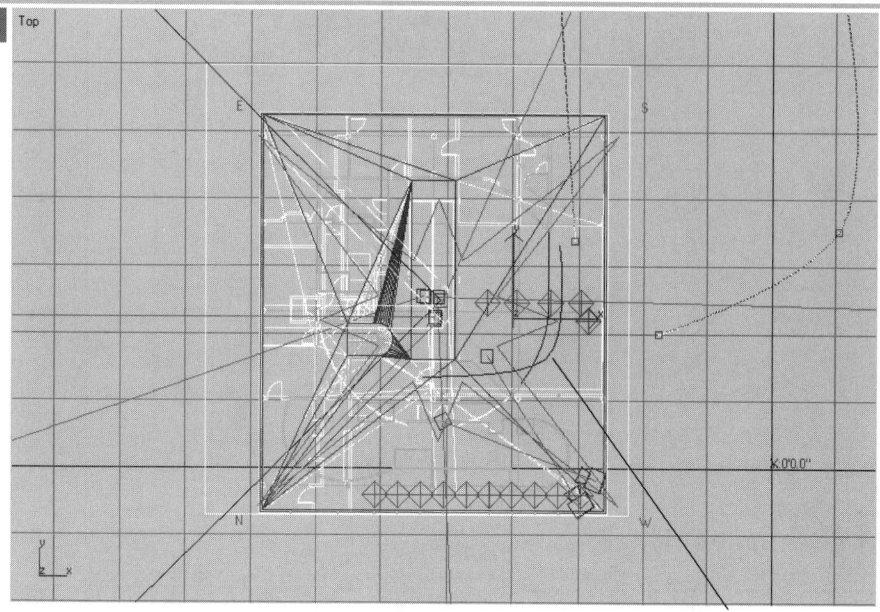

You've just created the path for the walkthrough. Remember that you can edit the curve using the Vertex option at the Sub-object level in the Modify tab. You also don't have to worry if your path isn't perfect. You can edit the spline to fine-tune the walk-through animation path even after you've created the animation.

Creating a Walkthrough Camera

Now you're ready to use the Walkthrough Assistant.

1. Choose Animation ➢ Walkthrough Assistant. The Walkthrough Assistant dialog box appears.

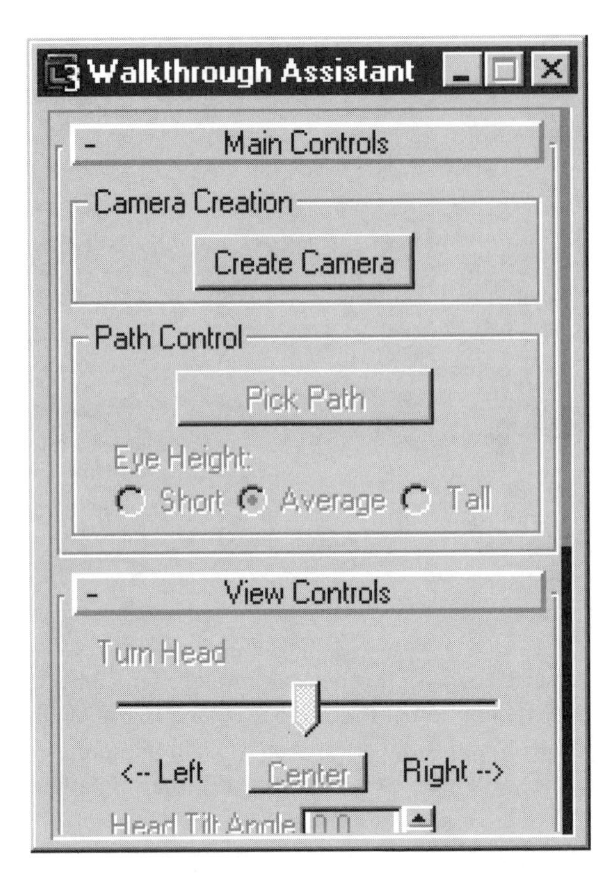

2. Click Create Camera. You see a camera appear near the origin of the design. This camera has a fixed name of Walkthrough_Cam. Don't change its name; otherwise VIZ will lose track of it the next time you open the file.
3. Click the Pick Path button in the Walkthrough Assistant dialog box, then click the path you just created. The camera moves to the beginning of the path (see Figure 12.22).

FIGURE 12.22

The camera at the beginning of the path

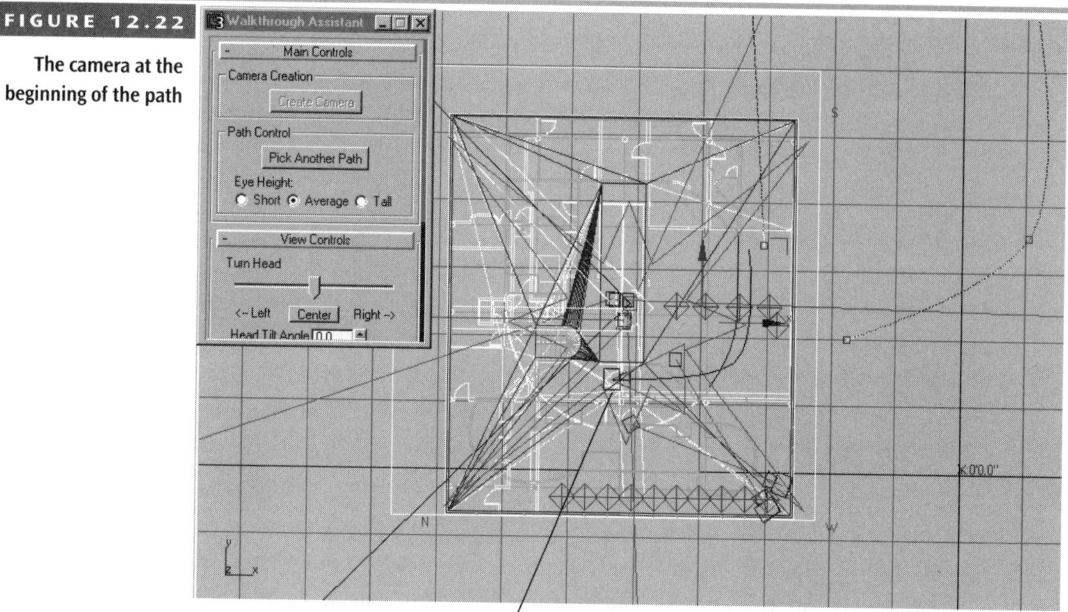

Since the last camera you created (the Elevation01 camera) had the Orthographic projection setting turned on, the new Walkthrough_Cam camera will also have this setting turned on. You'll need to turn it off for the walkthrough.

1. Open the Select Object dialog box.
2. Select Walkthrough_Cam from the list and click Select.
3. Click the Modify tab in the Command Panel. In the Parameters rollout, make sure Orthographic Projection is not checked.

Setting the Walkthrough_Cam Height

When the Walkthrough Assistant associates a camera with a path, it automatically places the camera and path at a height of 5 feet 5 inches above the XY plane of the world coordinate. Since this is a walkthrough of the courtyard level, you need to raise the camera and path to a level appropriate for a person standing in the courtyard.

1. First click the Min/Max Viewport toggle to view all of the viewports. If you look carefully at the Left or Front viewport, you'll see that the camera is at ground level, as shown in Figure 12.23.

FIGURE 12.23

The camera at ground level

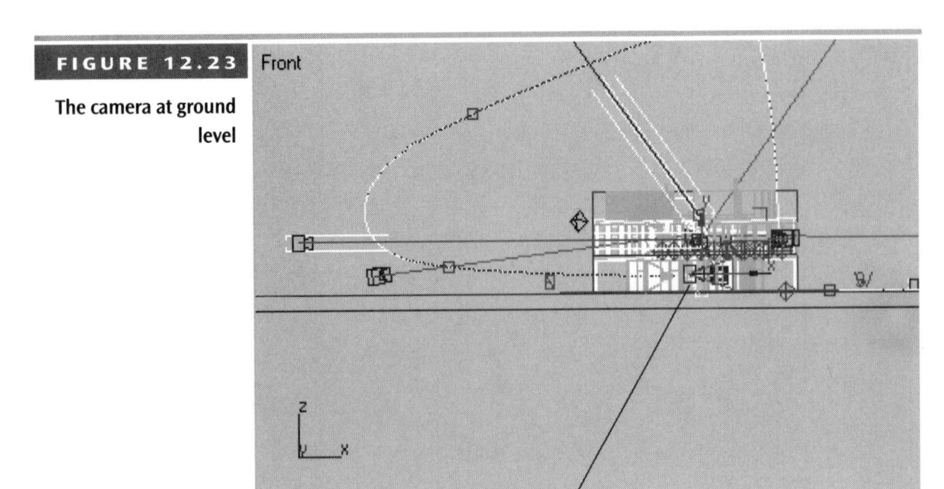

2. Right-click the Elevation01 camera viewport label, then select View ➢ Walkthrough_Cam. You see the view from the Walkthrough_Cam camera in the viewport.
3. Toward the bottom of the Walkthrough Assistant dialog box, open the Advanced Controls rollout.
4. In the Camera Controls group, change the Camera Height to **192** for 192 inches or 16 feet.
5. Now move the time slider from left to right. Notice that in the Top viewport, the camera moves along the path for the entire length of time (you may need to move the Walkthrough dialog box out of the way). You can also watch the walkthrough in the Walkthrough_Cam viewport.
6. Place the time slider at frame 0 and click the Click to Render Preview button in the Walkthrough Assistant. After several seconds, you see the current view from the Walkthrough camera.

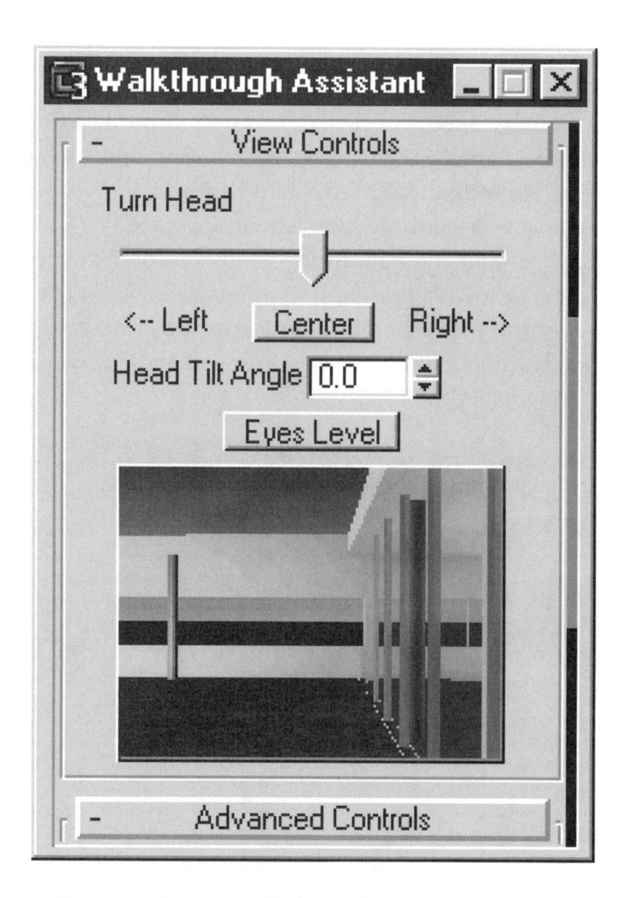

You now have a walkthrough set up. You could leave it as it is for a walkthrough that simply follows the path you drew. You can also control the direction that the camera points as it moves along the walkthrough trajectory.

1. Click the Animate button to turn it on.
2. Move the time slider to frame 280, then move the Turn Head slider in the Walkthrough Assistant dialog box to the left. Watch the camera in the Top viewport as you do this. The camera turns to the left. You'll also see the view in the Walkthrough_Cam viewport change as you turn the camera.
3. Move the time slider from frame 0 to frame 600 to see the camera motion now. You see that the camera swivels as it moves along the trajectory. Once past frame 280, the camera remains at its sideways orientation relative to the path.

As you can see from this brief demonstration, you can quickly generate a walkthrough of a design with this tool. With the Walkthrough_Cam floater open, you can easily see and control your animation. With the Animate button on, you can adjust the orientation of the camera through the animation. If you need to make a change in the path, you can do so by editing the spline you selected for the walk-through path.

The Walkthrough_Cam is a special camera that is only controlled through the Walkthrough Assistant dialog box. For 90 percent of walkthrough applications, this shouldn't be a problem. The Walkthrough Assistant dialog box offers nearly all of the settings you'll need to create a walkthrough of a building space. As you've seen already, you can select a path for the walkthrough and control the direction of view with the Turn Head slider in the Walkthrough Assistant dialog box. The Head Tilt Angle option lets you control the vertical orientation of the camera.

The Advanced Controls rollout also lets you adjust camera settings such as field of view, camera height, and target distance.

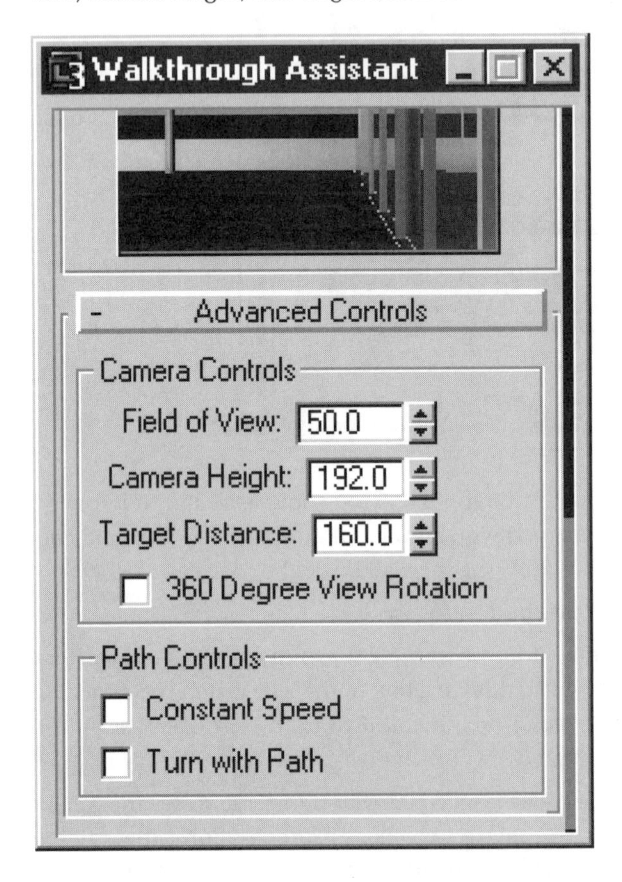

The Path Controls group lets you control the camera speed along the path and direction the camera follows on the path. Generally speaking, you don't need to use the Constant Speed option. The Turn with Path option lets you control whether the camera points in the direction of the path or maintains a constant direction regardless of the path. When you first create a camera and select a path, the camera automatically follows the direction of the path, even though the Turn with Path setting is off. You can then change the Turn with Path setting by turning it on temporarily, then turning it off.

As with other animated objects, you can use the Track View dialog box to make adjustments to the Walkthrough_Cam camera motion. For example, you can edit the Ease Curve for camera rotation to smooth the transition of the rotation.

The Animation File Output Options

Before we end this chapter, you'll want to know about the animation file formats. Most of these formats are the same as those for single still images, with a few twists.

You have several format options for animation file output, each with its advantages and disadvantages. The following describes each option along with its advantages and disadvantages.

Autodesk Flic Image File (*.flc, *.fli, *.cel) This is Autodesk's own animation file format. It is limited to 256 colors. You need the Autodesk animation player to view files in this format; however, it has become such a commonly used format that many desktop video player applications, such as the Windows Media Player, will play it.

The playback rate will vary depending on the power of the computer and the speed of your hard drive. The smaller image size of 320 × 200 will play back faster, and for test animation this can be more than adequate.

AVI File (*.avi) AVI stands for Audio-Video Interleaved and it is perhaps the most common type of animation file on the Windows platform. You can use .avi files for both animated materials and animated backgrounds.

These .avi files can use any number of compression schemes, known as codecs (*codec* is short for compressor/decompressor). When you use this file format, a dialog box appears, allowing you to select a codec. The usual choices are Cinepak, Intel Indeo 3.2, Microsoft Video 1, and Autodesk RLE. You may also install other codecs onto your system such as MPEG-1, or Motion JPEG codecs for specialized video output devices. (A complete discussion on codecs is beyond the scope of this section.) You may want to experiment with the codecs you have available to see which one gives you the best results.

Other .avi file settings include compression quality and Keyframe Every N Frames. The compression quality slider offers a tradeoff between image quality and file size: the better the image quality, the larger the .avi file will be. The Keyframe Every N Frames lets you control .avi keyframes that are not the same as the keyframes you've encountered in VIZ animations; .avi keyframes have more to do with the way animation files are compressed.

Targa (*.tga) This is perhaps the most universally accepted format for high quality video animation. Like the GIF file format, it produces a single file for each frame. Since a typical Targa file is close to 1 megabyte in size, you will use up disk space in a hurry using this format. Still, it is the format of choice when you want the best quality video output. It offers a wide variety of resolutions, and color depth up to 32-bit color (24-bit plus alpha channels). You can use Targa files for still images, and it is a good format for transferring to Apple Macintosh systems, because it usually requires little if any translation for the Mac platform.

Color and Mono Tiff (*.tif) These file formats offer high-quality color or monochrome output. They are similar to the Targa format for quality, though Tiff files are used primarily for still images and pre-press. This format also produces one file per frame of animation. If your images are destined for print, this file format is the best choice, but be aware that there are both a PC and a Mac version of this file format. If you're sending your file to a Mac, make sure you've translated it to a Mac Tiff file. This can be done easily with Photoshop or with another high-end image-editing program.

BMP RGB and 256 (*.bmp) The BMP format is the native Windows image format. It is not as universally used as the Targa format for video animation; still, most Windows graphics programs can read BMP files. RGB refers to 24-bit color, or color depth of 16 million.

JPEG (*.jpg, *.jpeg) This format is a highly compressed, true color file format. JPEG is frequently used for color images on the Internet. The advantage of JPEG is that it is a true color format offering very good quality images at a reduced file size. One drawback of JPEG is that it does introduce distortions into the image. The greater the compression used, the more distortion is introduced.

Gif (*.gif) While GIF files are not supported by VIZ as an output file format, it is an important file format that should be mentioned here. This is a highly compressed image file format that is limited to 256 colors. This file format is popular because it is easily sent over the Internet and is frequently used for graphics on Web pages. GIF files can also contain very small animations. You can convert a series of animated GIF frames into an animation by using a number of software tools, including Adobe's Image Ready, which is a product that ships with Adobe Photoshop 5.5. There are also free and shareware products that can turn a series of animation frames into animated GIF files.

PNG (*.png) The PNG file format is similar to GIF and JPEG in that it is primarily used for Web graphics. It has a variety of settings, mostly for controlling color depth.

EPS (*.eps, *.ps) EPS, or Encapsulated PostScript, is a file format devised by Adobe for describing page layouts in the graphic arts industry. If you intend to send your renderings to a pre-press house, EPS and TIFF are both popular formats in the industry.

Kodak Cineon (*.cin) The Kodak Cineon file format (CIN) is intended for the film industry. It is a standard format for converting motion picture negative film into a digital format. Many special effects houses use this format and other software to help create the special effects you see in movies. Frames rendered to this format are recorded as individual files.

MOV (*.mov) QuickTime is Apple's standard format for animation and video files. Its use is not limited to the Macintosh, however. It is somewhat equivalent to the AVI file format native to the PC, but MOV animations are of generally better quality.

While not directly related to animations, MOV files can also be QuickTime VR files. QuickTime VR is a kind of virtual reality that uses images stitched together to simulate a sense of actually being in a location and being able to look around. QuickTime VR is frequently used on the Internet on real estate sites to show the interiors and exteriors of homes. It is also popular at auto sales sites that show a 360-degree view of the interiors of new cars. Photo-stitching applications are available to construct QuickTime VR files from a set of images.

SGI's Image File Format (*.rgb) and the RLA Format SGI has a following in the film and video industries, and they have developed a format designed to work with their own animation software and hardware. The RGB format offers 16-bit color and alpha channels. The RLA format offers a greater set of options, including additional channels for special effects.

RPF Image Files (*.rpf) The RPF file format is a new 3D Studio VIZ file format that supports arbitrary image channels for special effects and other types of post-processing of images. It is similar to the SGI RLA format.

Several of these file formats create a single animation file, like the AVI and FLC file formats. Other file formats are intended as single files per frame such as the Targa and CIN formats. The single-frame formats require an application such as Adobe Premiere 5.1 to turn them into viewable animations. Their chief advantage is that you can maintain a high level of quality in your animation files, then use the files as a source to produce other formats for different applications. Targa files, for example, can be rendered for the highest level of resolution and picture quality. The Targa files can then be processed through Adobe Premier to generate AVI or MPEG-1 files for the Internet, or Motion JPEG for video output.

TIP If you are using 3D Studio MAX, you can use the Video Post feature to do some preliminary video editing.

True Color Versus 256 Colors

Three of the formats we have discussed, Flic, GIF, and BMP, offer 256-color output. You can get some very impressive still images from 256 colors, but when you start to use animation, the color limitation starts to create problems. One major problem is called color *banding*. This occurs when an image has a gradient color. Instead of a smooth transition of colors over a surface, you see bands as shown in Figure 12.24. The effect is similar to that of the Posterize option in many paint programs.

FIGURE 12.24

Two images rendered in VIZ. The one on the left shows what the image should look like under good conditions. The one on the right shows color banding caused by a limited color palette.

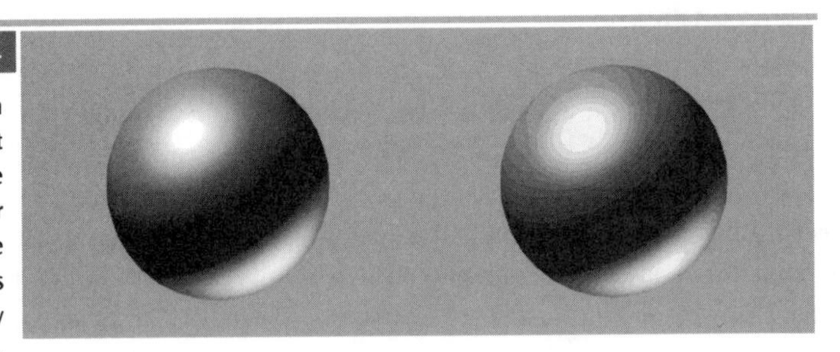

This color banding may be fine for limited applications such as previewing animations, but you will want to use true color output for your finished product. True color images such as those offered by Targa, Tiff, and JPEG files do not suffer from banding. They also offer smoother edges on models with lots of straight edges. If you don't need the absolute best quality, you might consider the JPEG output option. It provides high resolution and true color in a small file size. You can render a 10-second animation with JPEG files and in some cases use less than 40 megabytes of disk space. Most of today's desktop graphics and video-editing software can read JPEG files.

File Naming in Animations

When you choose any of the file formats other than Flic, AVI, or MOV, VIZ generates a file for each frame of your animation. The name of each frame is given a number so their sequence can be easily determined by other programs.

VIZ will only use the first four characters of the name you provide in the Animation File Name dialog box. For the rest of the name, VIZ will add a number. For example, if you enter the name **Savoye** for the animation file output using the Targa file format, VIZ will create a set of files with the names `Savo0000.TGA`, `Savo0001.TGA`, `Savo0002.TGA`, and so on.

This is true even if you are rendering only one frame of your animation. For single frames, VIZ will truncate the name to the first four characters, then attach the frame number to the name. For example, if you render frame 100 from the Savoye7 file, you will get a file named `Savo0100.TGA`.

Choosing an Image Size

Still image sizes will vary depending on the medium of presentation. A minimum resolution for 8 × 10 inch prints, for example, is 1024 × 768. Larger poster-size prints will require much larger resolutions. Video animations, however, will not usually exceed 752 × 480. The resolution will be determined by the type of device you are using to record to videotape. For example, using the old step-frame recording method that records a single frame at a time directly to videotape, you would typically render to an image size of 512 × 486. Other real-time video playback devices can use seemingly odd sizes such as 320 × 486 or 352 × 240. The horizontal resolution is stretched to fit the size of the screen so the higher the horizontal resolution you use, the more detail appears in the final output. The aspect ratio of the animation does not change.

Animating for film requires much higher resolutions, simply because the typical theater screen is so large.

If you intend to have your animation played back on computers only, you can keep the resolution down to the levels used for video. I'll discuss video resolution in more detail in Chapter 13.

Other File Options

Besides the formats I've described here, there are also digital video formats such as the Windows AVI formats, MPEG-1 and MPEG-2, and Motion JPEG, to name a few. In addition, there are some proprietary formats from non-linear video-editing products. These file options, while not directly supported by VIZ, are usually supported through *plug-ins*. Plug-ins are external programs that attach themselves to VIZ to add functionality. Such file output plug-ins are provided by hardware manufacturers who support these formats for their computer video-editing hardware. I'll discuss these digital video formats in more detail in Chapters 14 and 15.

Summary

This concludes our animation tutorials for VIZ. There are many issues I didn't touch on in this book. These include network rendering to help speed rendering, character animation, and the use of Video Post, a feature of 3D Studio MAX, to aid in the editing of animations. My intent has been to show you the basic tools you'll need to get up and running with VIZ. The tutorials and references that come with VIZ are excellent sources for delving deeper into this great program, and there are many other excellent books that cover VIZ in more detail.

In Chapter 13, I'll discuss what you can to do with your animations. There, you'll learn about the ins and outs of video and video editing.

chapter 13

Transferring Your Animations to Video

FEATURING

- ***Introduction to TV Video***
- ***Translating Computer Images into Video***
- ***Video Formats***
- ***Video Quality Testing***
- ***Using Computer Video***
- ***Squeezing Video onto a Hard Drive***
- ***Video and VIZ***
- ***Setting Your Monitor to SMPTE Standards***

Transferring Your Animations to Video

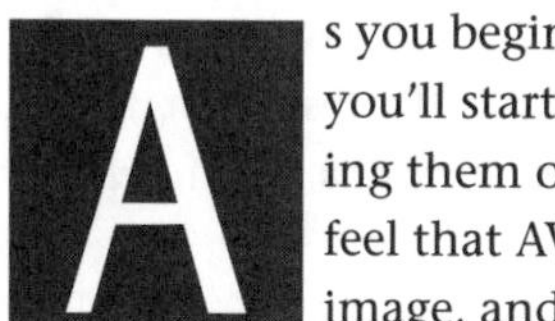

s you begin to explore VIZ's animation capabilities, you'll start by creating AVI files from VIZ and viewing them on your computer monitor. But you may feel that AVI files do not produce the greatest quality image, and you'll eventually want to see your work in the best possible light. This means you'll want to translate your animations into full-color television video. But moving your VIZ animations from computer to television is no simple task. Computer video is quite different from television video. Before you create your first demo video reel, you'll need to know some basic facts about television video.

This chapter is intended to help you bridge the gap between computers and television. I'll first explain how television gets its picture. You need to know how TV video generates images in order to maximize the quality of your VIZ output. I'll also discuss some of the hardware available to translate your computer animation to video tape. Along the way, you'll learn some of the terms used in the video industry, and their significance to your work as an animator.

This chapter doesn't contain much in the way of tutorials, so you can read it at any point in your work. We'll begin with the basics of how TV video works.

Introduction to TV Video

Television was originally devised as a means of transmitting live visual information over the airwaves in a way similar to radio. The inventors devised a way to convert visual information into a modulated signal that could be transmitted through the air just like radio signals. The receiver of this signal, a television set, then converted the signal into a series of pictures, which in turn appeared as a black and white moving image.

Today, the method remains virtually the same as when it was first devised, except that now color and stereo sound have been added. A standard was set up so that television manufacturers could design their sets to receive the same broadcast signal regardless of where it was used. That standard is known as the NTSC standard in North America and Japan. Europe and parts of Asia have two of their own sets of standards known as *PAL* and *SECAM*.

The NTSC standard was established in the early 1950s. It defines how visual information is encoded into broadcast signals, and how those signals are in turn converted back into visual information. NTSC stands for the National Television System Committee, though many in the broadcast industry jokingly refer to it as the "Never The Same Color" standard. For our discussion, we'll focus on the NTSC standard.

NOTE **A new standard called the ATSC (Advanced Television Systems Committee) standard for high-definition TV lays out the requirements for HDTV (high-definition television). While the US is moving toward HDTV, that is not the mainstream format as of this writing, so we'll concentrate on the NTSC standard in this discussion.**

How Television Gets Its Picture

You're probably aware that motion pictures are actually still images that are flashed on a screen so rapidly that they appear to be in motion. For film, these images are shown to us at a rate of 24 pictures per second. In NTSC video, that rate is 29.98 pictures per second (25 per second in Europe), but we call them *frames* in video instead of pictures. If you've gone through the VIZ tutorial in Chapter 11, then you are already familiar with the idea of frames.

Understanding a Video Frame

Although motion pictures and video both use sequential frames to create the sense of motion, the way each medium displays a frame is quite unique. In motion pictures, each frame is like a photograph and the entire frame is displayed at once. In video, each frame is actually drawn onto a screen over a very short period of time—1/29.98th of a second, to be exact.

The frame on a TV monitor is the result of electron beams that scan across the face of the television screen (see Figure 13.1). In 1/29.98th of a second, these electron beams zigzag across the screen 525 times to produce a single picture. As the beams strike the screen, they excite the electrons in the special coating of the screen to produce light. The intensity of the beams controls the intensity of that light. So to produce a picture, the beams vary in intensity as they scan across the screen. Higher intensities produce bright spots on the screen, while lower intensities produce darker spots. The net result is a visual image.

FIGURE 13.1

Scan lines on a television screen

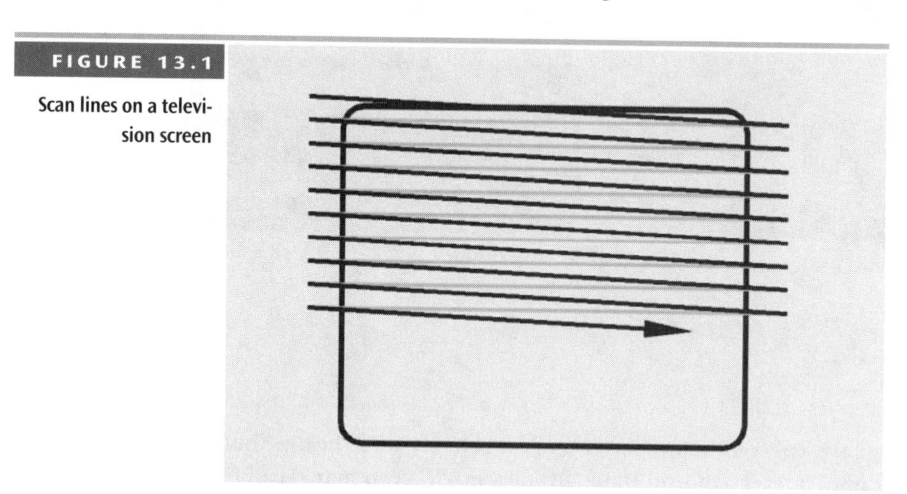

These scan lines are most apparent in old black-and-white televisions. If you would place your nose up to one of these old sets, you'd actually see the scan lines. Furthermore, you'd see that the line varies in shades of gray across the screen (see Figure 13.2).

FIGURE 13.2

A magnified view of an old black-and-white television screen

In today's typical color television, there are actually three beams that scan across the screen, one for each color in the RGB color model. You may recall from the last chapter that the RGB color model is an additive one. By combining varying intensities of red, green, and blue, you can produce an infinite number of colors. So the beams in a TV monitor vary in intensity as they scan across the screen to produce full-color, full-motion video images (see Figure 13.3).

FIGURE 13.3

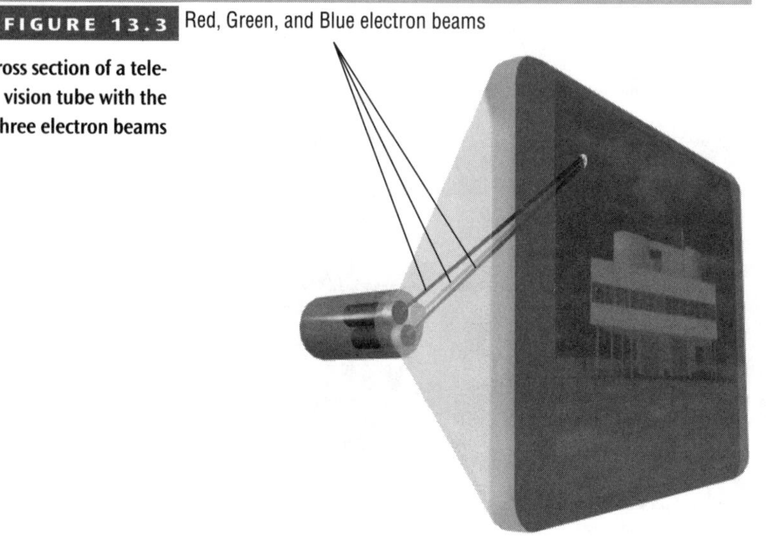

A cross section of a television tube with the three electron beams

How Television Resolution is Determined

The number of scan lines on a television screen is fixed at 525 horizontal scan lines. You might think of these lines as being analogous to the vertical resolution of a computer monitor. However, not all of these lines are used for visual information. The actual number of scan lines devoted to the picture is 486. The remaining scan lines are used to convey nonvisual electronic information to your TV screen.

If you've ever seen the picture on your TV slowly scroll vertically while you're trying to tune in to a weak station, you've see these non-visual scan lines. They look like blank bars across the screen. These scan lines carry the *equalizing pulse* and the *sync pulse*, though other information can also be carried, such as closed-caption data or teletext information. The equalizing pulse and sync pulse can actually be seen if you look at this blank area carefully (see Figure 13.4).

FIGURE 13.4

A graphic representation of a TV monitor showing the equalizing and sync pulses. The equalizing pulse is called a *hammerhead* because of its shape.

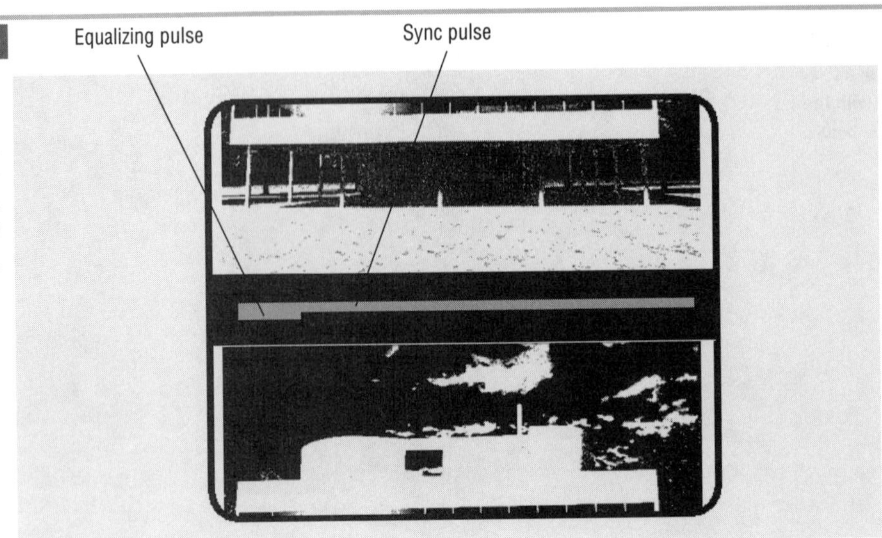

The purpose of these pulses is significant, and if you really get involved with your video quality you'll want to know more about them. But for our discussion here, just know that they are there to help stabilize your TV image. They are like the sprocket holes in a filmstrip, helping to maintain a steady rate of film feed through a projector. In the case of the video frame, they tell your television where a frame begins and ends, among other things.

Horizontal Television Resolution

While the vertical resolution of a computer screen is similar to the horizontal scan lines of a TV, we can't really use this same comparison when describing horizontal resolution in TV monitors.

In a computer, your screen is divided into picture elements, or *pixels,* as they are more commonly called. Each pixel is assigned a color that is a combination of the red, green, and blue color components. When all the pixels are viewed at once, you see an image, a text page, or a program icon (see Figure 13.5). Programs in your computer control the colors that are assigned to each pixel.

FIGURE 13.5

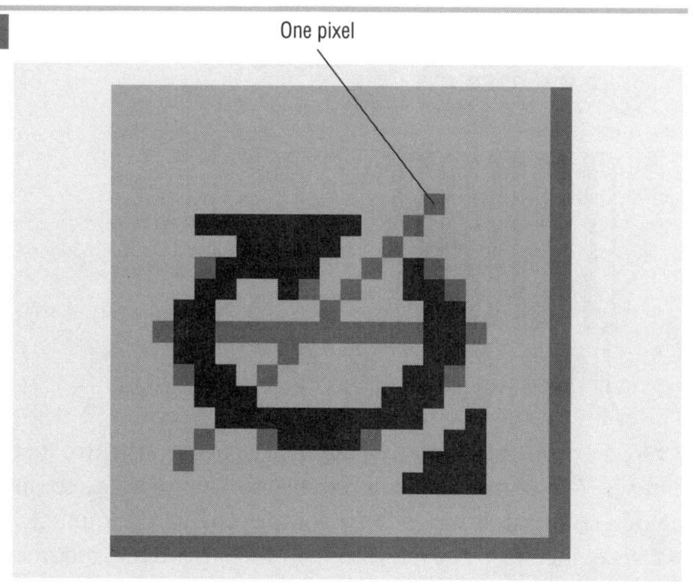

An enlarged view of an icon from Windows 98 showing the pixels making up the icon

Computers are designed to portray static images with a limited amount of movement. Televisions, on the other hand, are designed from the ground up to display moving images. Instead of methodically defining each individual pixel of an array of pixels, as in a computer, television produces a constant stream of ever-changing light intensity that repaints the entire screen every 1/29.98th of a second.

In a television, the scan lines race across the screen to trace out an image. The scan lines vary in intensity in order to produce the various colors on the screen. This variation of intensity is perhaps the closest thing to the horizontal resolution of a computer monitor, but, since the variation is not fixed to any particular amount per scan line, it is difficult to give a specific number like the horizontal resolution of a computer display.

To better understand horizontal resolution in video, we'll look at an image that is often used to test a TV's ability to reproduce an image clearly. Figure 13.6 shows a comparison of how a series of black and white vertical stripes might be generated on a computer monitor versus how it would be generated on a television.

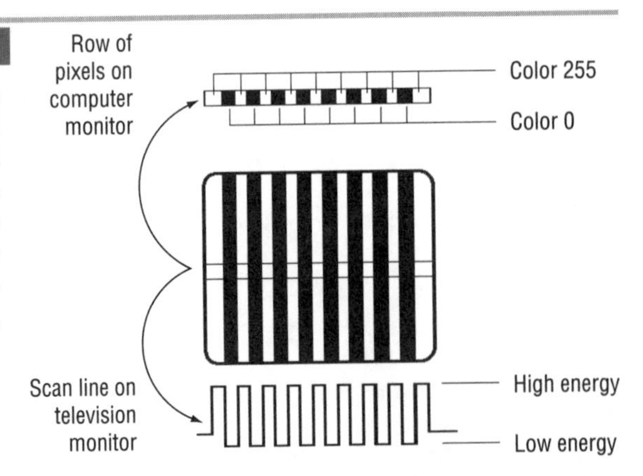

FIGURE 13.6

The top panel shows how the black and white pattern of vertical lines is drawn on a computer monitor. The lower panel shows how it is drawn on a television monitor.

Figure 13.6 points out an interesting difference between the two methods of displaying an image. The change in color from black to white in the computer is a matter of changing a color value, which boils down to changing a numerical value in the computer's display memory. The television, on the other hand, requires the scan line intensity to change quite rapidly as it scans across the screen. The rate at which the television is able to change this intensity over time determines the horizontal resolution of the television.

For example, suppose we make the spacing between the vertical bars very small. For the television, the change in intensity of the scan line has to increase in frequency as the spacing becomes smaller. Remember that the scan line traverses the width of the screen in a fixed amount of time: 0.00013th of a second, to be precise. The computer, on the other hand, needs only to rearrange the value of the pixels in its display system.

So the horizontal resolution of a television is really determined by its capacity to modulate the scan line over a fixed interval of time. This is actually more like the ability of a stereo system to reproduce high-frequency sounds. The higher the frequency a stereo system is able to reproduce accurately, the higher we rate the system. The greater the frequency a scan line is able to produce, the more horizontal *resolution* we get from the video image.

Translating Computer Images into Video

The previous discussion might lead you to believe that it's nearly impossible to convert a computer image into a video image. Fortunately, there are many products available that are capable of making the conversion fairly painless for computer 3D animators. In this section, you'll be introduced to some of the general concepts behind computer-to-video conversions of animations. Later in this chapter, I'll discuss some of the common devices in use today for converting computer files into video clips. The first and most basic device you'll look at is the video frame buffer.

Translating Images from Computer to Video

A video frame buffer is a computer add-in device, usually in the form of a card that fits into an internal slot, that sends an image out as a video signal that a TV or VCR can understand. It reads a computer image file, then translates it into a video signal that can be sent to a recorder or video monitor.

Frame buffers can translate a computer file into a single video image, but your animation consists of several hundred files, one for every frame of your animation. A frame buffer alone will not turn your files into a video. You need a way to convert each individual file into a stream of images.

In the past, video animators used a method called *step frame recording* to transcribe computer-generated frames onto videotape. In this method, each frame of an animation is *laid down* on video tape one at a time. As an analogy, you might imagine a filmstrip with its individual pictures strung out along its length. Step frame recording essentially places the animation frames in sequence on videotape, in a similar fashion.

Besides the frame buffer, two other devices are needed to accomplish step frame animation. The first of these devices is a computer accessory called a VTR controller. As the name implies, a VTR controller controls a VTR deck through the computer. By giving the VTR controller special instructions, which you can enter through your computer, you can have it locate specific frames on a videotape.

The second device is a professional frame-accurate VTR deck that is capable of being controlled by the VTR controller. Most professional-level VTRs will work with a VTR controller, but they must include a time code generator as part of their circuitry. A time code generator enables a VTR to locate specific frames on the tape. It places a special time code on the tape that serves as a sort of indexing system. The time code can be read by the VTR to locate specific frames.

This time code is presented in a standardized way showing hours, minutes, seconds, and frames in the following format:

```
01:30:45:29
```

This example shows a frame location on videotape as being at 1 hour, 30 minutes, 45 seconds, and 29 frames from the beginning of the time code. This is the SMPTE (pronounced *simptie*) standard for representing the frame *address* on videotape. (SMPTE stands for the Society of Motion Picture and Television Engineers.)

Step frame recording is not as prevalent as it once was, but the basic idea of converting an animated frame into a video frame still persists. As you become more involved in the production of your video animation, you'll find that you're using the SMPTE time code more often in your work.

Ancient History: Step Frame Recording

Before the days of digital video, you needed two pieces of equipment to convert the frames of a VIZ animation to a videotape. The two devices, the VTR controller and the professional VTR, worked in conjunction with a video frame buffer to place each frame onto videotape. First you entered the *inpoint*. This was the exact location on the tape, in SMPTE time code, where the animation was to start. Once you'd done this, you could begin the recording, which took the following steps:

1. The frame buffer read a computer image file, then sent the image to the VTR.
2. The VTR controller backed the tape up to a point roughly 10 seconds *before* the location of the actual frame. This is called a pre-roll. The VTR Controller then started the tape in motion. The 10 seconds of tape before the actual frame location were used to accelerate the tape up to full speed.
3. As the tape reached the point where the frame was to be inserted, the VTR controller told the VTR to record the image being sent to the VTR by the frame buffer.
4. The tape continued to roll for a second or two, then stopped.
5. The frame buffer read the next image file in the sequence and the process was repeated for every frame of the animation.

The VTR controller took care of the recording. You usually didn't have to do anything but wait. As you might imagine, the recording process took several hours but depending on the type of VTR and frame buffer, you got a very high quality video from such an arrangement. The video quality also was, and still is, dependent on the condition of the VTR, the recording format used, and the quality of the video signal coming from the frame buffer.

Video Formats

When discussing video formats, the recording medium and the format are considered one and the same, so when I mention formats here, I'm really referring to a physical tape and a recording system as well. In the home consumer market, we are familiar with basically three formats: VHS, Video-8, and Hi-8. In the high-end home market, you also see digital-8 and Mini-DV formats. But in the world of professional video, there are many more formats available, each with its own set of advantages and disadvantages. This section provides a summary of tape formats that you, as an animator, will want to know about. Let's start with a brief look at how color was introduced to television.

Color and Video

In the mid-1930s the FCC determined the range where video signals could be placed in the airwaves. Originally, since television resolution was limited and there was no color, the amount of the allotted bandwidth (or space on the airwaves) used in early television was quite small. Few people believed the entire bandwidth would ever be used or even needed. This is similar to the idea in the early 80s that 64K was more than adequate for personal computers. As video resolution increased, more of the bandwidth was used. When color was added, a separate portion of the bandwidth was used to carry color information, further crowding the video bandwidth.

NOTE **Color information is actually encoded into the *luminance* information of a video signal, but a detailed discussion of how this is done goes beyond the scope of this book. For a more in-depth discussion of this topic, along with a discussion on video signal testing methods, refer to *NTSC Video Measurements: The Basics*, available from Tektronix, Inc., Measurement Business Division. You can also check out their Web site at** `www.tek.com/Measurement/App_Notes/NTSC_Video_Msmt/`.

This leads us to our current situation, where the video bandwidth is saturated. Much research and effort have been invested to squeeze more information into the current limited bandwidth, but video bandwidth remains pretty much as it was in the early 50s, when color was first introduced. Today the color portion of the video signal is called the *chrominance component*. The other component, called *luminance*, carries the brightness information and is similar to the original black-and-white signal of pre-color television.

The NTSC standard mentioned at the beginning of this chapter defines how chrominance is encoded with luminance to form a compact signal. Unfortunately, a byproduct of the chrominance-luminance encoding is a type of interference called *chromacrawl*. Chromacrawl is most obvious in the reds and blues and can be characterized as a *bleeding* of colors from their true location in a video image.

Chrominance, Luminance, and Formats

One way to reduce the effects of chromacrawl is to keep the chrominance and luminance signals separate. You may have seen the term Y/C in reference to S-video connectors found in S-VHS or HI-8 video decks and on computer-to-video translators.

Video engineers use Y to symbolize luminance and C to symbolize color, hence the term Y/C. When you see an S-video connector on a video deck, it generally means that the luminance signal is carried over a separate channel from the color signal. In contrast, a typical composite signal jumbles all the video signals into one carrier signal, which in turn *muddies* the video image. This composite signal is the lowest common denominator in the NTSC video world. This is the type of signal carried between your consumer VHS deck and your TV monitor, usually in the form of a cable terminating in an RCA jack.

Y/C separation in mid-level consumer video hardware such as S-VHS and HI-8 offers a step up in quality from the typical video product. When you get into the high-end consumer and professional formats, you will find that the signal is further separated into red, green, and blue color channels. Devices that are capable of distributing the video signal in separate RGB channels are called *component* systems. You typically find component video in DVD players and digital video recorders. In fact, the Y/C separation provided by the S-video connector is actually considered a pseudo-component system because, while it doesn't fully separate the video signal into its RGB color components, it does separate luminance and chrominance.

NOTE **A format called *D2* is a digital composite format. While its ability to maintain good quality after many copies is superior, D2's composite signal reduces its ability to offer sharp color rendition.**

By keeping these video signals separate, you get a sharper video image with less chromacrawl. If you compare a video image produced on a component-based format with one from a composite-based format, you see a distinct blurring of reds in the composite format.

So we find video formats falling into three categories, loosely based on whether they offer component, pseudo-component, or composite channels for input and output. Now let's look at the specific formats and how they differ.

Finding the Best Format

If you talk to 10 different videographers, you'll probably get 10 different opinions on what is the best video format. But there are really two parts to video production: acquisition and editing. A format good for one may not be well suited to the other. Acquisition requires portability and convenience. Editing requires robustness and generational stability, or the ability to hold a good image through several copies. You need the right tool for the job, and the job may require different tools at different times. Table 13.1 lists the more common formats, along with a brief description of each.

Table 13.1: Video Formats and Their Use

Format	Description
D1 and D9	Digital, component, high-resolution video used primarily for video editing. D9 has a more portable form factor than D1.
D2	Digital, composite, high-resolution video used for editing.
Betacam SP and Digital Betacam	Analog or digital, component, high-resolution video used for acquisition and editing.
M-II	Analog, component, high-resolution video used for acquisition and editing. Equal to Betacam SP but less popular.
DV, DVCAM	Digital, component, FireWire, medium-resolution video used for acquisition and editing. Edit decks for this format are usually capable of playing Mini-DV tapes.
Mini-DV	Digital, component or Y/C, medium-resolution video used for acquisition.
Hi-8	Analog, Y/C, medium-resolution video used for acquisition and editing.
S-VHS	Analog, Y/C, medium-resolution video used for editing.
3/4 Umatic SP	Analog, component, medium-resolution video used for editing and acquisition.
8mm	Analog, composite, low-resolution video for the home market. VHS Analog, composite, low-resolution video used for the home market.

I've listed the formats from the highest level of quality at the top to the lowest at the bottom. These formats can be divided roughly into four categories: broadcast, industrial, prosumer, and consumer, with some overlap. For example, D1 through 3/4 Umatic SP could all be considered broadcast-level formats, the highest level in quality. Umatic SP is frequently used at the industrial level, as are Hi-8 and S-VHS. But Hi-8 and S-VHS are available in consumer-level products such as home VCRs and video cameras. Another way to look at these formats is by their use.

Formats for Acquisition

Acquisition simply means taking video with a portable camera. In a very short time, video cameras have captured a major share of the consumer market. And the quality level of some of the consumer products is quite good. You even hear of journalists taking them to far-off places, using them for a brief time, then throwing them away, not unlike the early Nikons in the 50s. Here's a brief rundown on formats used most frequently for acquisition.

The lowest common denominator is the VHS format. It is a format that JVC invented and propagated through heavy advertising and support. It is not considered to be a very good system, but we're stuck with it. Early on, when the consumer video market was young, Sony introduced the Beta format, which was superior to VHS. But JVC just did a better job of marketing and supporting VHS, and the rest is history. Some of the first consumer-level video cameras were VHS. Later, Video-8 consumer-level cameras offered a more compact and convenient size.

NOTE If you plan to use a Hi-8 deck to record your animations, make sure you use good-quality, short-length tape. The shorter tapes are more robust because a thicker base is used. Also avoid using the first and last several minutes of the tape, as these areas are where the tape is most likely to stretch.

Mid-level formats in use for acquisition are 3/4-inch Umatic SP, DV, Hi-8 and S-VHS. Hi-8 and the newer DV are perhaps the most popular with videographers and journalists because they can produce a good quality image and are extremely portable. They also hold color better than their competing format, S-VHS. Also, while Hi-8 is said to produce *drop-outs,* actually, tape quality plays an big role in HI-8 video performance. S-VHS and 3/4-inch Umatic SP seem to lag behind HI-8 in popularity for acquisition. S-VHS is bulkier, as is 3/4-inch Umatic SP.

S-VHS Versus Hi-8 Versus Mini-DV

At a glance, output from both S-VHS and Hi-8 look pretty good, and they are comparable in price. But one video engineer I spoke with didn't even think S-VHS was a viable medium. He regarded Hi-8 as a reasonable medium because it is highly portable. It also produces a good video signal, which is important when working in conjunction with other video formats.

In fact, a Hi-8 video signal matches the quality of the digital D2 format in most respects except one: signal-to-noise ratio. Here is where Hi-8 really shows the limitations of its small format. A poor signal-to-noise ratio shows up as a kind of flickering. This flickering can best be seen on a blue screen. To see the effects of poor signal-to-noise, try recording a blue screen on a VHS deck, then play it back. Instead of a uniform, smooth blue, you will see the color *dance* and flicker.

The Mini-DV format is similar in size to the Hi-8 tape, but offers good image quality and less noise. Other types of video problems occur, however, due to data compression. Mini-DV editing decks are also more expensive than Hi-8 editing decks. Mini-DV decks frequently use a FireWire connector to transfer data to computers, and there are many video capture cards on the market that support FireWire. The advantage here is that your animations remain in a digital format from your computer to tape. FireWire, otherwise known as the IEEE 1394 High Performance Serial Bus, is a type of high-speed port that resembles a USB port. Invented by Apple Computer in the early 90s, it didn't catch on until Sony started using it in its consumer video equipment. It is capable of data transfer rates of up to 400 Mbps, which makes it an excellent medium for the transport of digital video.

Continued on the next page

At the high end, Betacam SP is the standard broadcast-level acquisition medium. The cameras, while not exactly small, are manageable, and they produce the best image available without going to a high-end digital format. While there is a debate raging now regarding the superiority of Betacam SP over the newer DV formats, Betacam SP is still regarded by most as the industry standard for broadcast quality.

Tapes for Editing

Betacam SP is also the favored editing format. Video material holds up well over many generations of edits, making it an excellent medium for editing. With Betacam SP's all-around good performance, it's no wonder it is the industry standard.

D1 is strictly an editing format. It has the best generational stability and it is a component system. It is also a digital format, meaning that visual information is stored as binary numbers. In an ideal situation, a videographer will use Betacam or even Hi-8 in the field, then dub those tapes to D1 for editing. By the way, most of the non-news programs you see on TV are shot on 35mm or even 16mm film, then dubbed to D1. (Film does a much better job of capturing subtle color differences.) A format called D9 is similar to D1, but it uses a cartridge that looks very much like a standard VHS tape (not surprising, since D9 was developed by JVC, the creators of VHS).

D2, also a digital format, suffers from being a composite format. In some instances D2 does not look as good as Betacam SP. But both D1 and D2 offer superior digital registration, making these two formats the best for overlaying video images. Overlaying is a process whereby different video sources are merged on top of each other to produce a video montage or other video special effect.

The Best Format for Animation

While the issues of acquisition versus editing are important to videographers, they aren't quite so important to computer animators. Most of us will want to stick to the best format for editing.

NOTE Services that convert computer animation files to D1 format usually offer computer to Betacam SP conversion or computer to Digital Betacam conversion.

The ideal is to record directly to D1 or D9, and provided you have the right equipment, you can have a service bureau do this for you. The process for converting your single-frame animation files to D1 goes as follows: you first generate your animation frames in TGA or TIFF format, then back them up on a tape or other high-capacity removable media. The type of media used depends on the service bureau that you are going to use to make the conversion from the backup. Once you have the D1 tape, you need to rent studio time to edit and transcribe your animation to a more portable format such as Betacam SP.

The next option is to use Betacam SP. Most of us may not even be able to detect the differences between material from a D1 tape and a Betacam SP tape. And chances are you won't be editing down so many generations that you'll notice any image degradation. Also, it's cheaper to rent facilities for editing in Betacam SP than for D1.You can rent a Betacam SP deck with a time code generator for around $350 per day. If you're using a real-time playback system on your computer, you can also use a stripped-down Betacam SP deck, which is less costly to rent or own. By the way, Betacam is said to be capable of reproducing around 720 vertical lines of resolution.

If you're on a budget, but you'd like to own your own equipment, Hi-8 and S-VHS are not bad alternatives for industrial-level work. Note that these formats support an equivalent of about 400 vertical lines of resolution. Mini-DV decks are more expensive than S-VHS and Hi-8 but offer about 500 vertical lines of resolution. There are also dubbing decks that have both Mini-DV and S-VHS tape transports.

Video Quality Testing

I've discussed various issues regarding video quality as it relates to the hardware used to present and record it. But there is one topic that touches on all aspects of video quality, and that is video testing.

Video quality might seem at first glance to be a fairly subjective thing. It either looks good on the monitor or it doesn't. But video equipment is really quite forgiving when it receives a poor video signal. Today's modern consumer video equipment will do its best to give you a clear picture. Also, variations from television to television can greatly affect the way a video looks. If your animation video is producing a marginal video signal, it can still look pretty good on your monitor. But it may not look so good on another system, or its image may degrade rapidly after only one copy. The only way to be really sure your video is at its best is to check the signal from your source material—your original videotape.

You may have heard the term *broadcast quality*. Some believe that broadcast quality is synonymous with the Betacam SP format. This may be true to some degree, but having a video recorded on Betacam SP doesn't guarantee that your video will be of broadcast quality. The true meaning of this term is that your video produces a signal that conforms to the NTSC standard, period. The reason this is important is that conformance guarantees that your video will look the way you intended it to look on the widest possible range of video equipment. It also means that your video will be accepted by a television station or production facility when it comes time to broadcast your animation to the world. NTSC conformance is the first test of any video destined for broadcast.

Why should a production facility care about conformance to a standard? When video is edited, it must go through a myriad of electronic circuits and equipment, each adding a bit of distortion to the original signal. The equipment itself expects the signal to behave a certain way otherwise distortions may be magnified. When a video source conforms to the NTSC standard, people editing your work can be confident that the final product will be as close to the original work as possible. But if the source material does not conform, then it's anybody's guess as to where the image will be once it's edited. So quality assurance in the video industry starts with a tape that produces a broadcast-quality signal.

Conforming to the NTSC standard means testing a video signal on two very common pieces of professional video equipment. They are called a *vectorscope* and a *waveform monitor.* These two devices test, among other things, the chrominance and luminance signals we discussed earlier. The vectorscope is used to examine the chrominance portion of a signal, and the waveform monitor is used to look at the signal in general. Both of these devices can detect problems in a video signal that may not surface immediately on a video monitor.

I won't go into any detail on how these devices are used, but don't feel intimidated by their names. You can learn how to use these devices in an afternoon. The point is, the vectorscope and waveform monitor are your key to producing broadcast-quality video. If you intend to produce animations for the professional video market, you will want to at least be familiar with these devices and perhaps even own them at some point. Remember that in the world of professional video, quality *can* and *will* be measured. No matter how good your video may look on your monitor, its quality and acceptability depend on whether it is up to the NTSC standard.

Using Computer Video

So far you've learned about video in general. Next, you'll look at how you can assemble and view your animations directly through your computer. Computer video, or desktop video as it is often called, is growing by leaps and bounds. It can be used to aid in the production of traditional broadcast video as well as for multimedia production and presentations. There are also an increasing number of applications that are aimed at generating animations for the Internet.

Real-Time Recording Systems

In recent years, products called *video capture boards* have appeared on the market. They enable you to convert your home or professional video into a digital format on your computer. Once it is on your computer, you can then edit your video without the expense of multiple VTRs and other video-editing equipment. Many of these products also allow you to convert your animation frames into a video that can be played back from your computer's hard disk instead of from videotape. The quality of the image these devices generate varies greatly, as do their prices, but lately quality has gone up while prices have fallen.

VIZ users can take full advantage of this revolution in desktop video. It's far easier and faster to convert a series of animated frames to a video using a video capture device than it is to use the traditional step-frame method described earlier. In most cases, you can take a set of rendered frames or an AVI file and import it into a video-editing program such as Adobe Premiere 5.1, then *print* the animation to videotape through the video capture device. The price of such devices is also with the reach of anyone with a PC. You can produce good-quality video output to videotape with products costing as little as $150.

You can also do a lot of post-processing and editing of your animation using the video editing software supplied with desktop video systems. But to understand how video on a computer can help with editing, it will help to know a bit about how video editing works in the first place.

A-B Roll Editing

The traditional method of editing video tape requires an editor to plan a video sequence down to the frame. He or she then joins video segments end to end, adding transitions, voiceovers, sound effects, and more. The segments may come from different parts of a videotape, or even from different tapes.

NOTE **If you are part of a team producing a video that contains your animations, you may be asked to produce two copies. This is because the editor will want two originals to perform A-B roll edits.**

A common editing method called A-B roll editing uses two VTRs to access the segments of video from the source material. Two sources are needed in order to create smooth transitions between segments. Both sources are synchronized, then played simultaneously. The editor adds the transition from one source to the other at the appropriate moment in the video. The output from the two source VTRs, including the transitions, is recorded onto a third VTR.

If all the source material is on one tape, then the editor must make a copy of the original to be able to play back different segments together to add transitions or re-arrange the sequencing of the segments. Unfortunately, copying video causes degradation of the video quality.

A-B roll editing is a laborious process that requires the editor to make several copies of original video footage. Since the copies are then used to create a third edited copy, the final product is often a 5th- or 6th-generation copy, which means that its quality has diminished.

But the real problem occurs when the editor needs to insert or replace a segment within the video. The editor cannot simply splice in the new segment as you might do with film. The editor must either re-edit the entire video or reduce the quality of the video by using the final edited version as one of the source tapes to produce a new final tape.

The Digital Video Advantage

Videotape is a linear format. In order to get to a location on the tape, you must *roll* through the tape until you get to the desired point. Digital video eliminates the linear nature of video and gives you direct access to the portion of the video you want, when you want it. You can access frames and segments in a more direct manner instead of having to fast-forward or reverse over a tape. Digital video also allows you to perform cut-and-paste operations in a way similar to the clipboard used with word processors. This reduces the need to make multiple copies of source material.

Even when you do need to copy video material, the copies do not degrade the original video image. You can copy whole video segments or parts of a segment fairly easily and in less time. And finally, you can insert segments into the middle of a finished video without having to re-edit the entire video or lose quality. This is a direct benefit of the nonlinear quality of digitial video.

Online Versus Offline Editing

There are many advantages to computer video editing, but there is one major drawback. Encoding video into a computer format causes quality loss (see "Squeezing Video onto a Hard Drive," later in this chapter). But through a method called *offline editing,* you can take advantage of computer video editing without giving up quality.

The traditional A-B roll editing described earlier is a form of what is called *online editing.* You edit the video material directly. Another method, called offline editing, allows you to use a computer to edit a facsimile of your original video. The facsimile contains all the information of the original video, including its SMPTE time code from the source videotape. When you complete your edits on your computer, you create what is called an edit decision list or EDL. This EDL is a text file that contains all the information about the location, sequence, and special effects transitions used to create your final computer-edited facsimile. You can then take this EDL to a postproduction service where the final video is assembled using the source video tape.

Offline editing lets you quickly edit your video without having to worry about losing quality to video compression. Using this method, your original video is never really transferred to the computer. But computer video is rapidly improving in quality, and for animators it can be an acceptable medium for a good percentage of your work. The next section offers an introduction to computer video to help you better understand what it has to offer.

Squeezing Video onto a Hard Drive

The key to computer video is file compression. Without some means of reducing the size of video image files, computers could not be used to produce video. Let's take a closer look at why compression is so important.

When you start to render animations in full video resolution, you find that a single frame takes quite a bit of hard disk space. A typical, uncompressed 512 × 486 resolution image takes about 800K of disk space. A higher resolution, say 752 × 480, requires one megabyte. You can imagine how quickly your animations will fill up your hard drive at one megabyte per frame. At that rate, ten seconds of animation, or 300 frames, requires 300 megabytes of disk space.

But aside from the sheer size of these video frames, the ability of the computer to actually open and display these frames as video would require a data rate of around 30 megabytes per second. Even by today's standards, this data rate is impossible to achieve on a desktop computer.

This is where compression comes in. If you can get the file size for each frame down, you can store more video and reduce the rate of data the computer needs to pump out.

Lossy Compression Means Loss of Quality

In Chapter 12, I mentioned one file format that offers full color at high resolution and with a relatively small file size. JPEG (Joint Photographics Experts Group) is a standardized method for compressing image files, and it has become quite common. If you've used the World Wide Web, chances are you've seen at least a few JPEG images.

JPEG compresses files by throwing away redundant information. Unfortunately, the moment you throw away any image information you start to lose image quality. JPEG does allow you to control the amount of compression. The lower the compression, the better the image quality.

There are image compression schemes specifically designed for video. One called Motion JPEG has become a popular format for the higher-quality video capture boards. Motion JPEG applies compression to each frame of an animation, which also results in a loss of quality. But since we only see each image for an instant, the loss of information is not as apparent as it might be if we viewed each frame individually.

Video purists tend to shy away from video capture devices because of this loss in quality. To the untrained eye, however, a good-quality video capture device produces output that looks every bit as good as video from a VTR.

InterFrame Compression Versus Intraframe Compression

Another popular video compression scheme is called *MPEG* (Moving Pictures Experts Group). MPEG offers a much higher compression rate than Motion JPEG and has a growing following among digital video enthusiasts. In fact, MPEG is being used commercially in the satellite distribution of video to homes, for DVD movies, and on the Web.

MPEG offers as much as a 200 to 1 compression ratio. File sizes are so small that full-length VHS-quality videos can be distributed on ordinary CD-ROMs. The smaller size also means that the data rate required to play back MPEG video is fairly low—low enough, in fact, to play back easily on most desktop computers.

MPEG achieves its high compression rate because it performs what is called *interframe compression.* Unlike Motion JPEG, which compresses each individual frame *(intraframe compression),* MPEG looks at a series of frames to see what information is redundant, not only within each frame, but over several frames as well. It then attempts to throw out this redundant material that occurs over a set of frames. MPEG is not the only compression scheme that does this, but it manages to do it without an unbearable loss in quality. MPEG does introduce some distortions, commonly known as artifacts, especially in scenes where there is lots of motion.

NOTE If you've ever watched a football game transmitted over a satellite system, chances are you've seen the image start to scintillate. The MPEG artifacts are causing that scintillation.

There are advantages to both inter-frame and intraframe compression schemes: you choose the compression scheme depending on what you want to do. Interframe compression schemes like MPEG generally do not allow editing, simply because a frame is not an independent item in this scheme. There are some systems that offer MPEG editing by converting MPEG files into a format that is editable with video editing software. But with such systems, there is some image quality degradation due to the translation from one compression scheme to another. Motion JPEG doesn't suffer as much from this problem because each individual frame is accessible. Though some image degradation is unavoidable with compression schemes, the problem is reduced with Motion JPEG.

The AVI Codecs

There are many other video compression methods available, all of which degrade the video quality to some degree. Some of the methods are geared toward presenting video only on a computer.

If your animation is destined for computer presentation, chances are you'll use the AVI file format. AVI, which stands for Audio Video Interleave, is the standard Windows file format for digital video. AVI allows you to select from a variety of compression/decompression methods, commonly known as *codecs*. You've already been introduced to these codecs in Chapter 12, but as a reminder, here's a rundown of the most common codecs and their uses.

Cinepak Is designed for high-quality video playback from a computer. This codec is considered to produce the best quality.

Intel Indeo Is designed for high-compression ratios and is best suited for multimedia.

Intel Indeo RAW Applies no compression to video. Use this to maintain the highest level of image quality while transporting your file to other digital video programs like Adobe Premier.

Microsoft RLE Is designed to keep file size down by reducing the color depth. It is primarily designed for 8-bit animations.

Microsoft Video Is similar to RLE in that it reduces the color depth of the file. It is designed for 8- and 16-bit animations and videos.

None Applies no compression at all to your file. Like the Intel Indeo RAW format, you would use this to store image files at their best level of quality, sacrificing disk storage space.

MPEG1 and MPEG2

There are actually several different versions of MPEG. The most common formats for video are MPEG-1 and MPEG-2. MPEG-1, layer 3, more commonly known as MP3, is also popular on the Internet, though its primary use is as an audio file. MPEG-4 is emerging as a standard for interactive video. It offers very high compression, with some virtual reality characteristics that allow viewers to interact with the content. MPEG-4 offers a means of combining sound, video, and still images into one package. For this discussion, I'll concentrate on MPEG-1 and MPEG-2.

Continued on the next page

The main difference between MPEG-1 and MPEG-2 is resolution: MPEG-1 displays a 352 × 240–pixel NTSC image (358 × 288 for PAL), while MPEG-2 displays 720 × 480 NTSC (720 × 576 for PAL). Also, since MPEG-2 contains enough information for a full 486 scan lines, it can reproduce video fields.

Real-time MPEG-2 compression for live video usually requires expensive hardware, but you can find fairly inexpensive real-time capture solutions for MPEG-1. As for your VIZ animations, software-only options are available for both MPEG-1 and MPEG-2. For about $300, you can find software only-compression utilities that will convert AVI files into MPEG-1 or MPEG-2. Bitcasting, Ligos Technologies, and Xing Technologies are three companies that offer software-only MPEG compression utilities. A company called Darim also offers a product called DVMPEG that, when installed, becomes a codec option from any application that produces AVI files, including VIZ and Adobe Premier.

MPEG output is fairly straightforward. The latest versions of the Windows Media Player will play back MPEG-1 files on your computer monitor. If you want to send your MPEG-1 animations to a VCR, you'll need hardware, usually in the form of a PCI card that installs inside your computer, or a USB or parallel port video capture device. If you have a CD-ROM recorder, you can also copy your MPEG-1 files onto a CD-ROM for easy distribution.

If you want to play back MPEG-2 files, you'll need to spend a bit more on an MPEG-2 output device. Again, Darim offers a low-cost MPEG-2 output device in the form of a PCI card. Darim's card, called the DVMPEG Plus, is designed with the PC animator in mind. It offers the ability to create MPEG-2 files directly from VIZ while allowing you to play back the MPEG-2 files, either to the computer screen or out to a VTR, through S-video, or composite RCA connections. There are other, more expensive options for MPEG-2 output from Darim and other manufacturers that offer component output, if you need it (component output offers better color saturation).

If you're willing to spend a little more to keep your MPEG-2 files in their digital format, you can find DVD recorders that will allow you to record your MPEG-2 animations onto DVD disks, which can then be played back on any DVD player. As of this writing, Pioneer offers a DVD-ROM recorder for around $5000. This is a little more expensive than a basic, stripped-down Betacam SP VTR.

Video Capture Options

The output quality of computer video is constantly improving. In fact, there is something of a revolution occurring in the video industry as professional level equipment moves into digital formats and personal computers become more powerful. There are high-end versions of video capture boards that are designed for professional broadcasters, but there are also inexpensive consumer-level products, some of which produce suprisingly good output.

Most VIZ users won't need the professional-level equipment, unless you plan to have your work appear on TV on a regular basis. If you do fall into this category, you may want to consider the products offered by DPS, such as their dpsReality product. For those of us who will produce an occasional animation meant for limited distribution, the Darim Vision Corps DVMPEG and DVMPEG Plus can produce MPEG-2 files directly from VIZ. If you intend to do some light editing of your animations, Pinnacle Systems offers several products that allow you to combine live video footage with animated sequences. Their $150 Studio DC10 Plus is a great way to jump into animation inexpensively. The Studio DC10 Plus offers Motion JPEG compression and Y/C output to videotape at a resolution of 640 × 480 and 60 fields per second. Keep in mind that the MPEG-2 format will offer a much higher compression rate than Motion JPEG.

You can learn more about digital video by looking at some of the offerings available on the market. Here's a listing of the companies I've mentioned that are known for their digital video products that are geared toward the PC animator.

Darim Vision Corp.

43218 Christy St.,

Fremont, CA 94538, U.S.A.

www.darvision.com

(510)-770-5005

Digital Processing Systems, Inc.

11 Spiral Drive, Suite 10

Florence, KY 41042

www.dsp.com

(800)-775-3314

Pinnacle Systems (including Targa products)

280 N. Bernard Avenue

Mountain View, CA 94043

www.miro.com

(888)-484-3366 (sales)

Video and VIZ

A lot of this chapter has covered video in a general way, and having a deeper understanding of video can only enhance your 3D work. But there are some specific issues we can discuss as they relate to VIZ animations. In this section, you'll look at two options in VIZ that are closely tied to the video medium. These options are *field rendering* and *gamma correction.*

Field Versus Frame Rendering

You know that there are only 525 scan lines in a television monitor. Those 525 lines are actually divided into two sets of 262.5 lines each. In the NTSC standard, these two sets of scan lines are called *fields*. But how do you get half a scan line in a field? Figure 13.7 shows how these two fields are drawn onto a screen.

FIGURE 13.7

Two fields are drawn to make a complete frame.

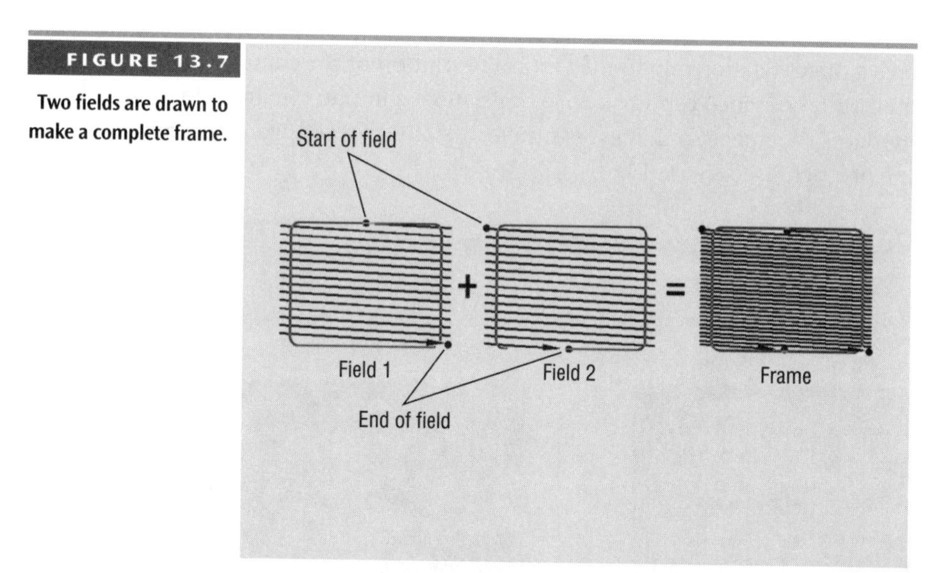

A frame is created by drawing first one field in 1/59.94th of a second, then the another field at 1/59.94th of a second. The lines of one field are drawn between the lines of the other. This intertwining of two fields is called *interlacing*.

We normally think of video as 29.98 frames per second at 525 scan lines per frame. But you could also think of NTSC video as 59.94 fields per second at 262.5 scan lines per field. For all intents and purposes, a field contains a complete picture. You could say the NTSC is actually 60 low-resolution pictures per second.

In professional VTRs, you can see the effect of the two fields, especially when you freeze the frame of an action scene. The screen seems to vibrate back and forth. The two interlaced fields showing two slightly different pictures cause this jittery effect. Modern VCRs provide a feature that eliminates one field from a freeze frame so you can see the image more clearly without the jittery effect.

To a videographer, fields are really just a technical side note. But as an animator, they are a major consideration when you are creating your masterpiece. It is important because you can take advantage of fields when you render your animations. I'll get into fields as they relate to your animation work a bit later in this chapter. Now lets look at ways of converting computer animation frames into video.

NOTE **A typical computer uses what is called *progressive scanning,* which draws the entire screen in one pass. Interlacing tends to produce a slight flickering, while progressive scanning computer monitors produce a steady picture. The US is gradually moving toward the HDTV standard that includes both interlaced and progressive scan modes and higher resolutions of up to 1920 × 1080.**

Fields have a direct relationship to the vertical resolution of the computer image. When a frame buffer or video capture device translates a computer image into a TV signal, it interlaces the image so that every other horizontal row of pixels becomes one scan line of a field (see Figure 13.8).

FIGURE 13.8

Converting rows of pixels into scan lines in a field

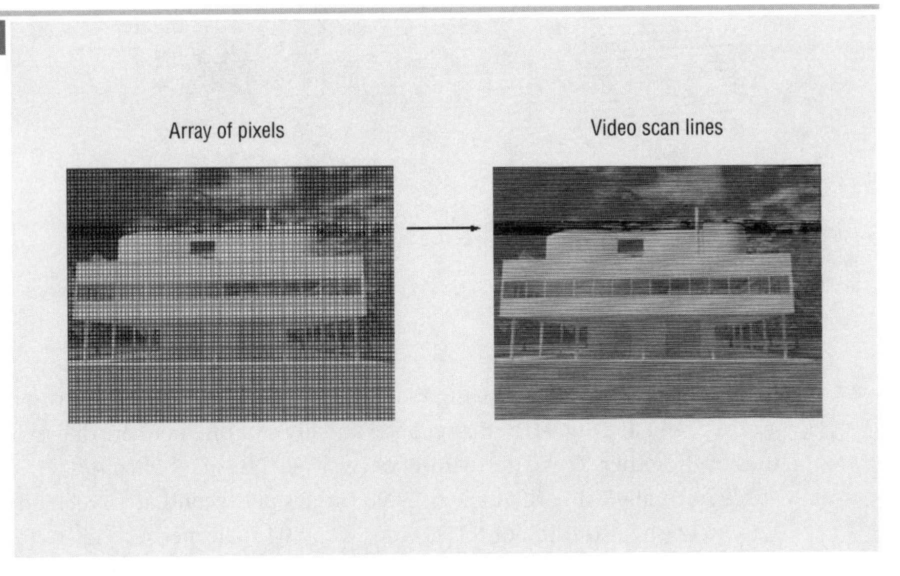

In our discussions of VIZ in Chapter 12, we always give examples of rendering each frame. But you also have the option to have VIZ render fields separately. You may recall that fields are really like low-resolution frames because each contains a complete picture. In fact, two fields of the same frame can be slightly different in their content due to the motion that occurs in the 1/59.94th of a second between fields. So if you have an animation that contains a lot of motion, you will want to render fields instead of frames. By rendering fields, you will produce animation that will be smoother. On the other hand, if your animation is a fairly slow one without any quick action or motion, you can save some rendering time if you render frames.

TIP Saving rendering time can be important for time-critical projects. The time difference between rendering fields and rendering frames can be significant.

Setting up VIZ to Render Fields

Setting up VIZ to render fields is fairly easy. When you open the Render Design dialog box, just make sure that the Render to Fields option is checked in the Options group of the Common Parameters rollout. As the frames render, you will see messages in the Rendering dialog box telling you that each field is being rendered.

As VIZ renders fields, you will notice that each field is rendered individually, as if it were a frame. Once both fields of a frame are rendered, then the frame is saved as a file. Since VIZ must transform the model for each field, the time to render a frame is longer. Transform means making adjustments to each moving part of the animation for the field or frame.

Field rendering is only suitable for video. It will distort the appearance of animations such as AVI files or single frame TGA files destined for computer viewing.

Understanding Gamma Correction

In very simple terms, *gamma* means brightness. VIZ offers the Gamma Correction dialog box to help correct differences in the brightness between various video systems.

Gamma correction is basically a way of standardizing the brightness between your computer and TV video monitors. Even two different computer monitors are not likely to display the same image in quite the same way. There are so many variables that can affect the brightness of a monitor, such as the brightness and contrast settings, the software drivers used for VIZ, and even the ambient light in your room. Not only are there differences from one computer monitor to the next, there are also even greater differences between computer monitors and TV Video monitors. Gamma correction is a way to ensure that what you see on your computer screen will be as close as possible to what you see in your final video output.

Gamma also compensates for the differences between the way VIZ generates color *brightness* in an image and the way display devices actually reproduce brightness. VIZ and most other animation programs produce brightness in a linear fashion. Figure 13.9 shows a graph depicting the way VIZ produces color brightness.

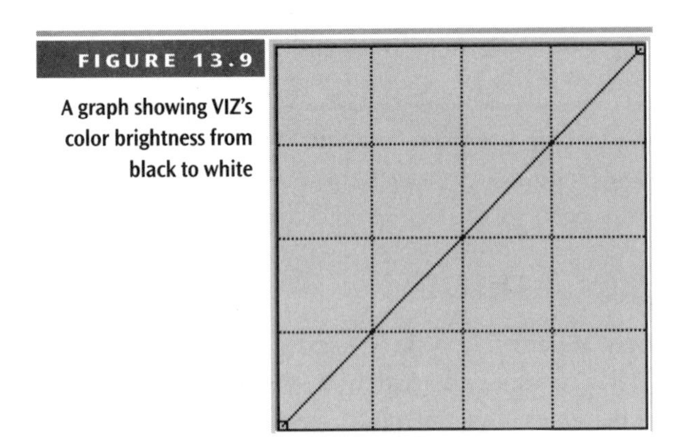

FIGURE 13.9

A graph showing VIZ's color brightness from black to white

Black is at the origin of the graph at 0,0, while white is at the top at 255,255. But if you look at a graph showing the way most display devices reproduce the same levels of brightness, you will see a curve with a dip in the middle, as in Figure 13.10.

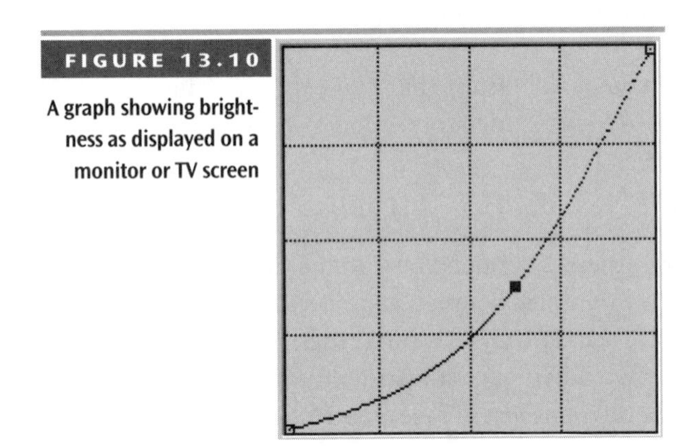

FIGURE 13.10

A graph showing brightness as displayed on a monitor or TV screen

Since a monitor shows lower levels in the mid portion of the brightness curve, you need to increase the brightness intensity at these mid-range levels. Gamma correction gives you a way to compensate for this dip in the display device's curve.

Turning on and Adjusting Gamma Correction

There are several ways to set gamma correction, depending on your hardware. Frequently, a frame buffer or video capture device will provide some means for correcting gamma settings. You can also set gamma in VIZ.

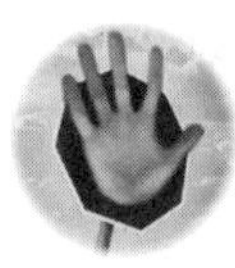

WARNING **Keep in mind that you should set gamma in either your frame buffer or VIZ, but not both.**

The first step is to make sure to compensate for the monitor on which you are using VIZ.

1. In VIZ, choose Tools ➢ Options.
2. In the Options dialog box, click the Gamma tab. You see the Gamma Options.

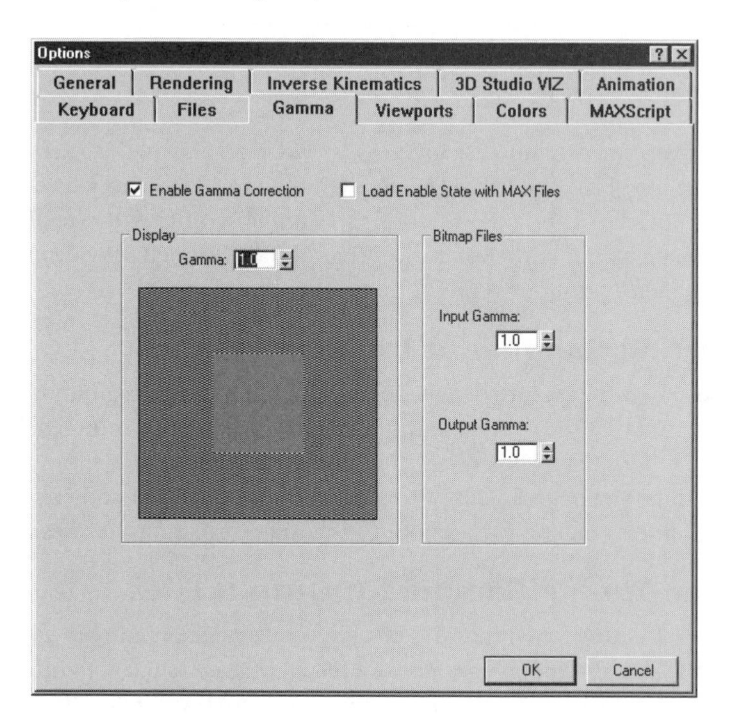

3. Make sure the Enable Gamma Correction check box is checked.

4. Use the spinner in the Display group to adjust the concentric square image so that the inner square has the same brightness as the outer square. It helps to squint your eyes a bit or move as far from the square as possible to make this adjustment. Another thing to do is to use averted vision. Instead of looking directly at the square, look to one side at about 30 degrees away from the square as you adjust the gamma setting. By using averted vision, you engage the receptors of your eye that are more sensitive to brightness.
5. Next, you need to make sure that the output file's gamma setting is corrected for TV video. Change the Output Gamma setting in the Bitmap Files group to **2.2**. This is the recognized value for TV video gamma.
6. Click Close to exit the gamma setup.

This set of steps will ensure that the image you see on your computer monitor is adjusted for the brightness that VIZ is generating in the image files it produces. It is a good idea to adjust the Display Gamma, whether you are using TV Video or not.

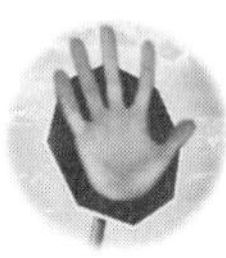

WARNING **Make sure that the Output Gamma is set to 1 if you are using VIZ only for printed renderings.**

If your work frequently involves TV video and printed matter, you may want to make use of the Load Enable State with the MAX Files check box in the Gamma tab. With this box checked, VIZ stores the gamma settings with the file. Using this option can help maintain the gamma settings of files destined for video separately from files that are for print only.

Setting Gamma for Imported Files

If you're using imported video footage for animated backgrounds or materials, you may find that the gamma settings are not correct for your design. The Gamma tab of the Options dialog box offers the Input Gamma setting to allow you to *un-gamma correct* imported images. This setting will require some trial-and-error testing on your part unless you know the amount of gamma correction that was applied to the image.

Fine-Tuning Gamma for Output Files

The 2.2 setting for Output Gamma is a good starting point, but gamma correction can be a trial-and-error process of rendering an image, then comparing its TV video output to the image rendered on your computer screen. If you're really concerned about image accuracy in your video output, this is really the only way you can check gamma correction. You'll want to check and compare the gamma settings periodically, since the brightness of both computer monitors and TV monitors will diminish over time.

Also remember to readjust the gamma settings when you replace your computer or video monitor since, as we mentioned earlier, no two devices will display the same image with the same degree of brightness. Remember to calibrate your video monitor to a color bar before you visually adjust the VIZ gamma settings (see "Setting Your Monitor to SMPTE Standards" later in this chapter). You may also want to check the gamma settings more frequently with new equipment as the brightness of video monitors falls off more rapidly when they are new.

Video-Legal Colors

In an earlier discussion, I mentioned a problem called chromacrawl that is a result, in part, of the crowded NTSC bandwidth. This problem can be a very serious one, especially if you have intense, highly saturated colors in your animation. In general, you will want to keep color intensity from getting too *hot* by using *video-legal* colors. There isn't any particular setting or chart I can point to that will describe what these video-legal colors are, but VIZ can help you locate them in a rendering using the Video Color Check option in the Rendering Design dialog box and in the Materials dialog box. Here's an example of how you can use the Materials dialog box to check for illegal video colors.

1. Open the Material Editor in VIZ.
2. Select a sample slot for the material you suspect might produce illegal video colors.
3. Click the Video Color Check button.

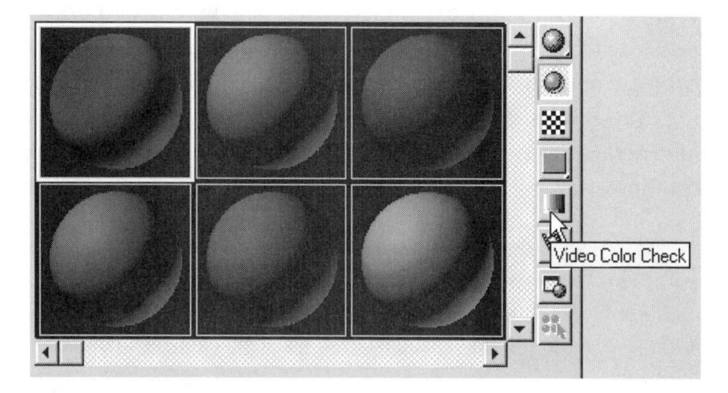

The illegal colors, if any, will appear as black in the sample slot image.

You can try this on a made-up material that uses pure-bright red for its diffuse color.

You can also check a rendered image for video legal colors using the Render Design dialog box.

1. While in a file you intend to render to videotape, click to open the Render Design dialog box.
2. In the Options group, click Video Color Check.
3. Click Render. The Virtual Frame Buffer window will display your rendering with any illegal colors displayed as black. Figure 13.11 shows an example of an image that contains illegal colors.

FIGURE 13.11

Image with illegal colors shown in black

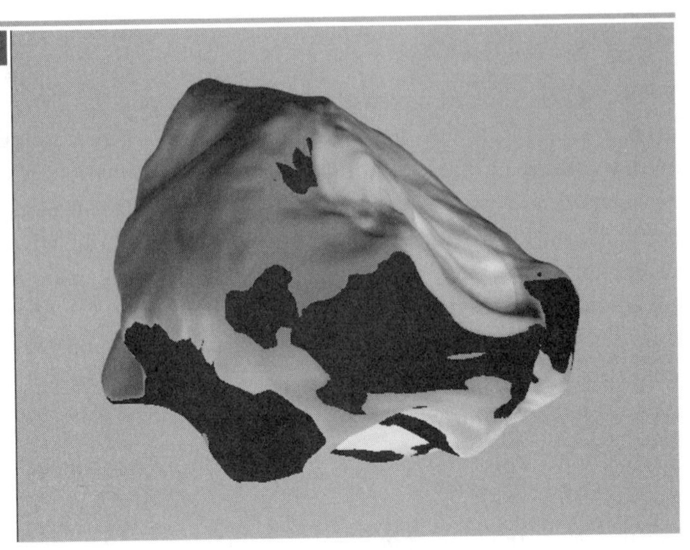

You may want to create two image files, one with Video Color check turned on and the other with it turned off. That way you will be able to compare the two images to see which colors are the problem colors. Once you find them, you can make adjustments to your materials to compensate for the illegal colors.

In general, highly saturated reds and blues will cause problems, so try to keep these colors toned down.

TIP Another way to check these colors is to import the bright frame into Photoshop, then apply the Filter ➢ Video ➢ NTSC Colors option to the image. This option will *tone down* any colors that are too saturated for NTSC video, and you will see the difference in the image.

Finally, you can adjust the way VIZ treats illegal video colors by making changes to settings in the Options dialog box. If you open the Rendering tab of the Options dialog box, you'll see a group labeled Video Color Check.

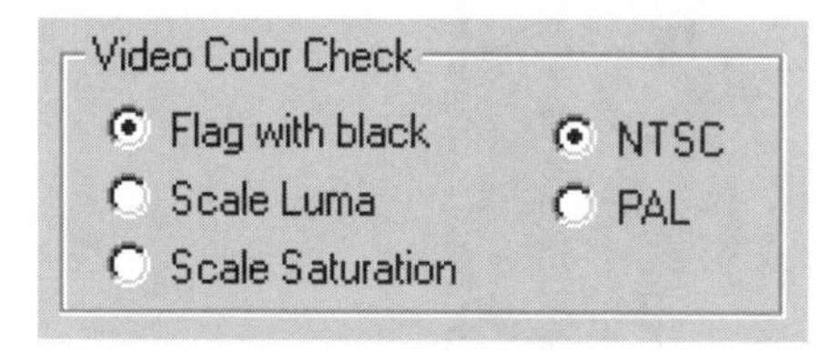

This group offers options that relate to the way the Video Color Check options in the Render Design and Material Editor work. Table 13.2 provides a description of these options.

Table 13.2: The Video Color Check Options in the Rendering Tab of the Options Dialog Box

Option	Function
Flag with Black	Causes illegal colors to appear as black.
Scale Luma	VIZ automatically darkens illegal colors to conform to video standards.
Scale Saturation	VIZ automatically adjusts chroma of illegal colors to conform to video standards.
NTSC/PAL	Sets Video Color Check to check for NTSC or PAL colors.

Setting Your Monitor to SMPTE Standards

I've mentioned that before you actually set gamma correction for your video monitor, you will first want to calibrate it. This means you will want to do a visual adjustment of your monitor's chroma, hue, and brightness. The purpose of this is, once again, to ensure that you are working within video standards, so that your animation won't look completely different on someone else's video system.

These steps assume you are using a professional video monitor and not a consumer-level television screen. Consumer televisions do not offer the controls required to perform the calibration accurately.

To calibrate your monitor, you use the SMPTE color bar shown in Figure 13.12. (Unfortunately, we can't show this picture in color.) You can obtain these color bars from any number of sites on the Internet. Just do a search for SMPTE color.

FIGURE 13.12

The SMPTE color bars. The labels and outlines of the colors are provided for clarity and do not appear in the actual color bars.

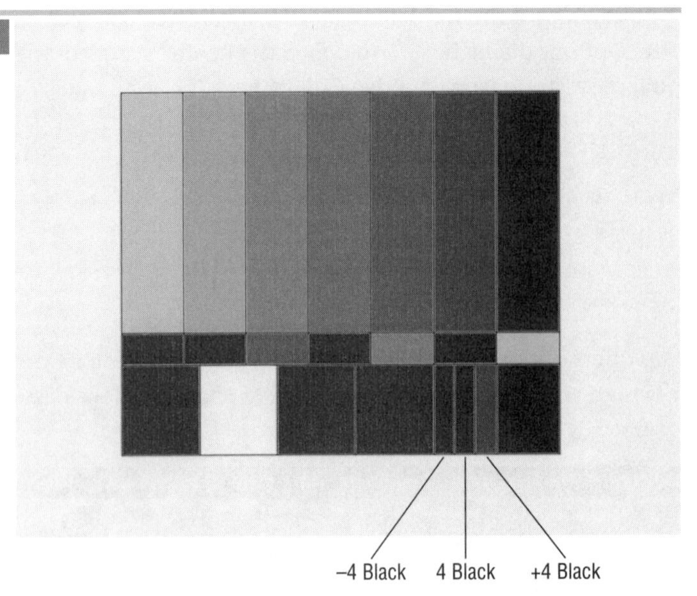

Once you've got the SMPTE colors displayed on your video monitor through the frame buffer, do the following steps:

1. Turn off the red and green colors on your monitor. Most professional monitors will have switches that will do this; some even have a single switch that turns off the red and green colors at one time.
2. Use the chroma control to match either of the outer blue chroma set bars to the main color bar above it. (see Figure 13.13)

FIGURE 13.13

Match these blue chroma set bars, using the chroma control.

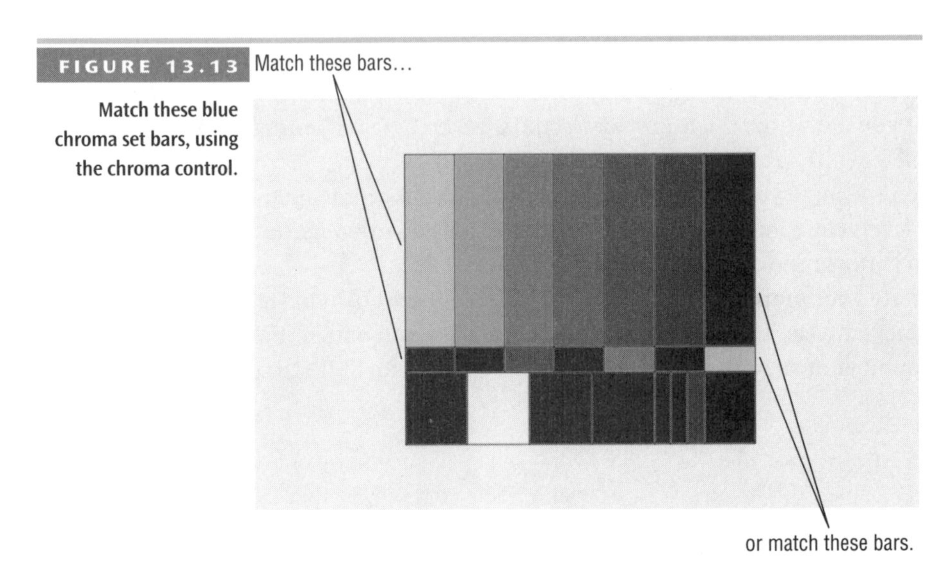

3. Use the hue control to match either of the middle blue chroma set bars to the main blue bar above it (see Figure 13.14).

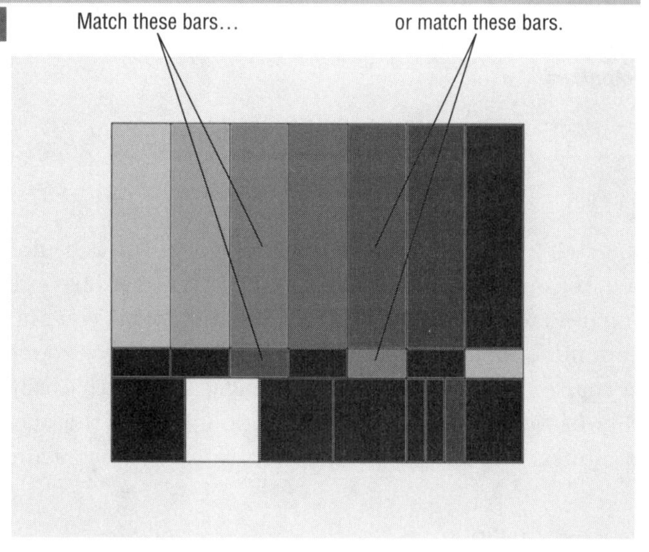
Match these bars…
or match these bars.

FIGURE 13.14

Match these blue chroma set bars, using the hue control.

4. Turn the red and green colors back on; then adjust the brightness so the +4 black bar is just visible and the –4 black bar is not visible (see Figure 13.15).

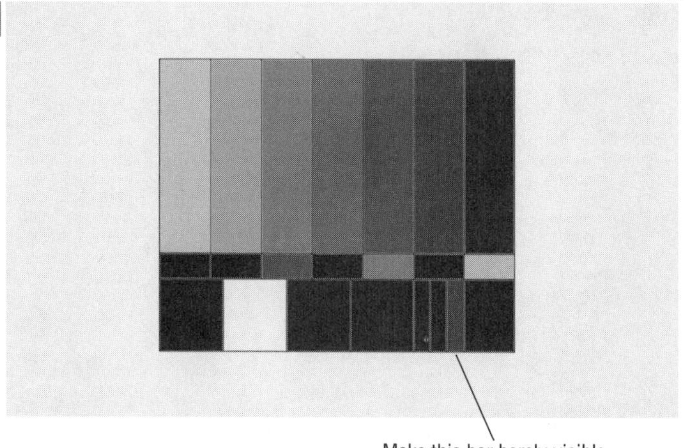
Make this bar barely visible.

FIGURE 13.15

Adjust the brightness so that the +4 black bar is just visible and the –4 black bar is invisible.

I've suggested using color bars found on the Internet, but many of the frame buffers come with their own color bars. By calibrating your monitor in either way, you can ensure that what you see will be close to what others will see on their monitors.

TIP **If you are limited to using a consumer-level television for your video production, you can use a consumer video-testing product to calibrate your TV. The *Avia Guide to Home Theater,* by Ovation Software, and *Video Essentials,* by Joe Kane Productions are two DVD video products that walk you through a complete set of video calibrations, including the SMPTE color bars.**

Summary

This concludes our introduction to the world of video. This is by no means a comprehensive survey of the video industry. I hope, however, that I have given you the information you need to produce the best possible animations you can with VIZ. If you want to learn more about the art and science of video, check your local community college for courses. You can also contact The Bay Area Video Coalition in San Francisco, California for other sources of information. BAVC is the largest member-supported, nonprofit center for video in the country. Here is their address and phone number:

Bay Area Video Coalition
2727 Mariposa, 2nd Floor
San Francisco, California 94110
(415) 861-3282
Web site: `www.bavc.org`
e-mail: `bavc@bavc.org`

chapter 14

Using Photoshop with VIZ

FEATURING

- *Creating a Tree Map in Photoshop*
- *Creating the Opacity Map*
- *Using Photoshop to Create a Montage*
- *Creating Bump Maps for Elaborate Textures*
- *Modeling with Displacement Maps*
- *Using the Material Editor to Create Displaced Geometry*

Using Photoshop with VIZ

You've probably got a number of other programs that you use on a daily basis. Most people have a word processor and a spreadsheet program along with utilities for virus and internet security. Business users will have a personal information manager and database. Frequently, computer users will use one program to create data that ends up in a different program from its source. For example, you might create a spreadsheet, then move the spreadsheet data to a word processing document, or you might insert text from a word processing document into an AutoCAD drawing.

As a VIZ user, you'll have the same needs as others to create data in one program and move it to another. You may find that your designs begin in a CAD program before they are brought to VIZ. There are also custom material maps that you will want to create and edit, which require software other than VIZ. On the other hand, your rendered image from VIZ may be part of a presentation that is being produced in Adobe Photoshop or in another image-editing program. VIZ images may also be destined for a page on the Internet, which may require the use of a Web page–design program.

In this chapter, you'll explore ways that you might use an image-editing program with VIZ. You'll explore Photoshop as a tool to help create a texture map, specifically the tree image and opacity map you used in Chapter 8. You'll also learn how you can use Photoshop to embellish an existing rendering or even to edit geometry in VIZ.

To start your exploration of Photoshop, you'll begin by looking at how the tree bitmaps in Chapter 10 were created.

Creating a Tree Map in Photoshop

An image-editing program is a must if you're working with VIZ. There are many very good image-editing programs available; unfortunately, I can't cover them all. So for this section, you'll concentrate on Adobe Photoshop 5.5. Figure 14.1 shows a typical view of the Photoshop 5.5 Window.

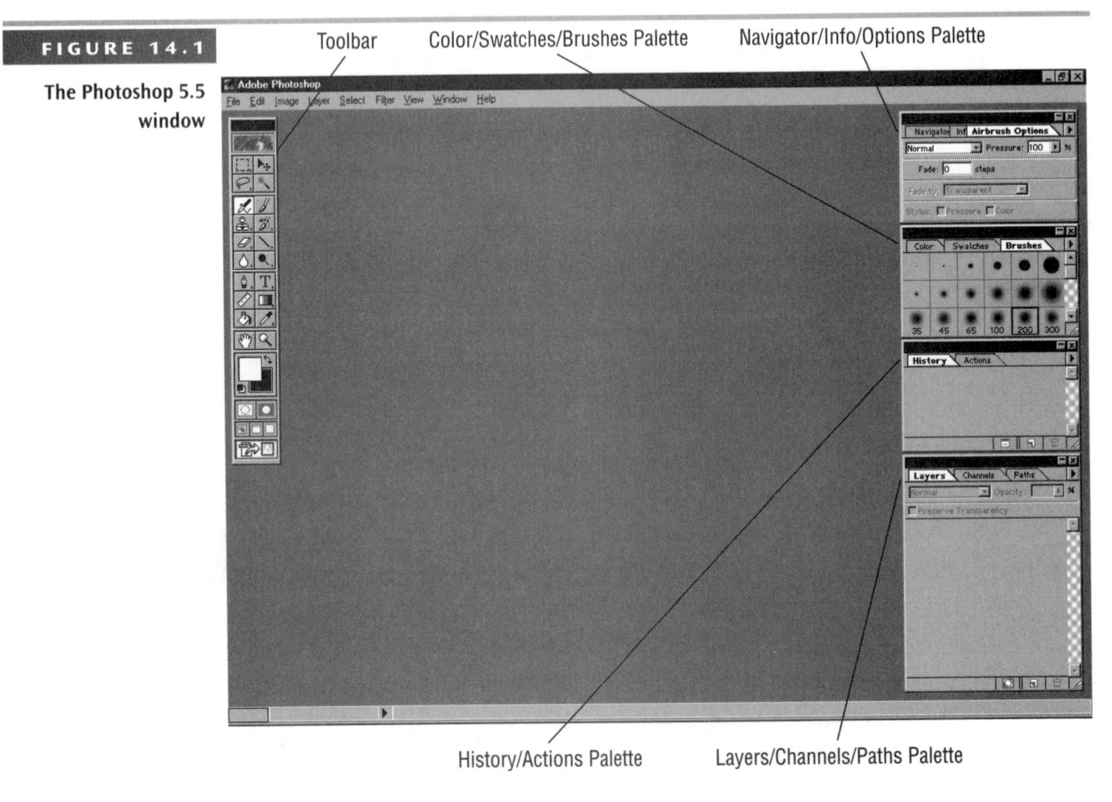

FIGURE 14.1

The Photoshop 5.5 window

To the left you see the main toolbar, and to the right there are several tool palettes arranged vertically. The toolbar contains tools for specific tasks such as painting, line drawing, masking, and color selection, to name a few. Figure 14.2 shows you the name of each function on the toolbar.

FIGURE 14.2

The Photoshop toolbar

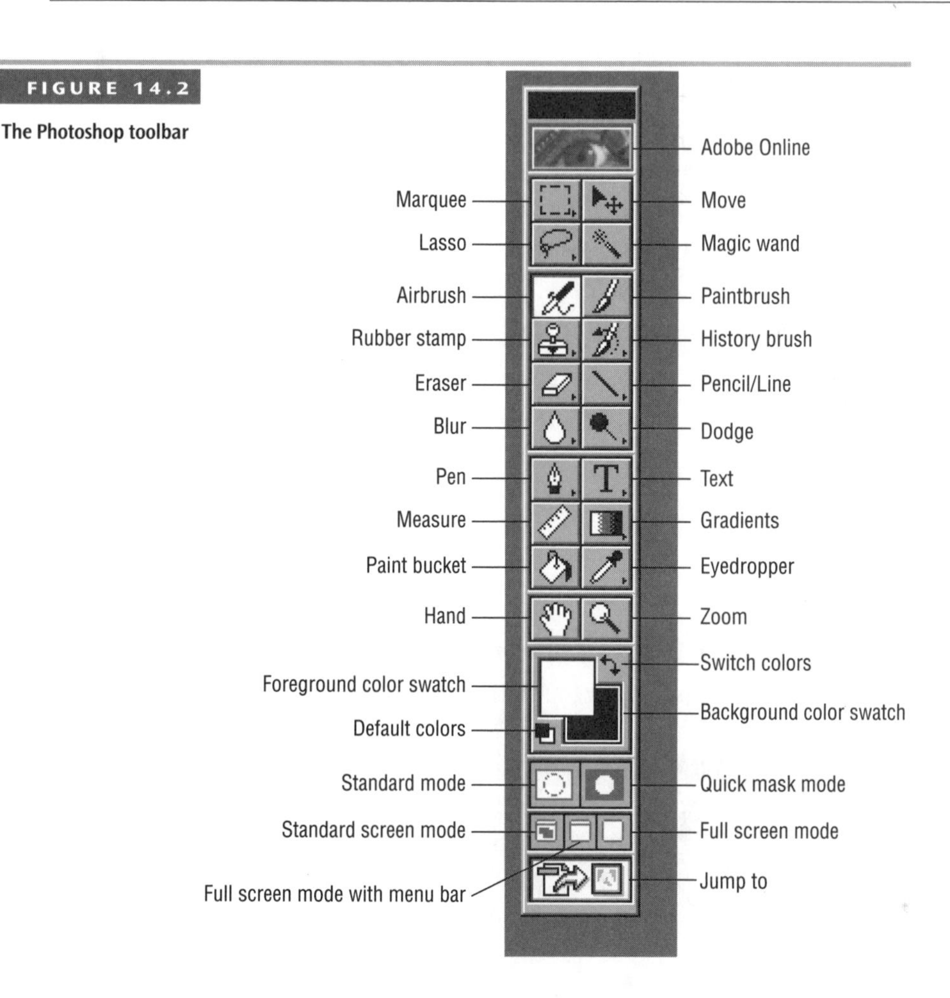

The palettes on the right give you control over tool and image settings and display functions. Each palette serves multiple functions that can be accessed through the tabs at the top of the palette. For example, the palette at the top offers Navigator, Info, and Options tabs. The Navigator tab gives you control over the view of your image. The Info tab displays color information as you drag the cursor over your image, and the Options tab offers options for the currently selected tool on the toolbar. You'll get a chance to use a few of these palettes and tabs as you work through the Photoshop exercises.

Selecting Areas in an Image

Now that you've gotten a brief introduction to Photoshop, let's jump in and use it to create a tree map for VIZ. The first thing you'll do is to remove the extraneous parts of the image around the photograph of the tree.

1. Start Photoshop, then use File ➢ Open to open the `Magnolia.tif` file from the companion CD.
2. Select the Magic Wand tool from the toolbar.

The Magic Wand selects areas of similar colors when you click a color in the image.

3. Click the Options tab to open the Options palette.

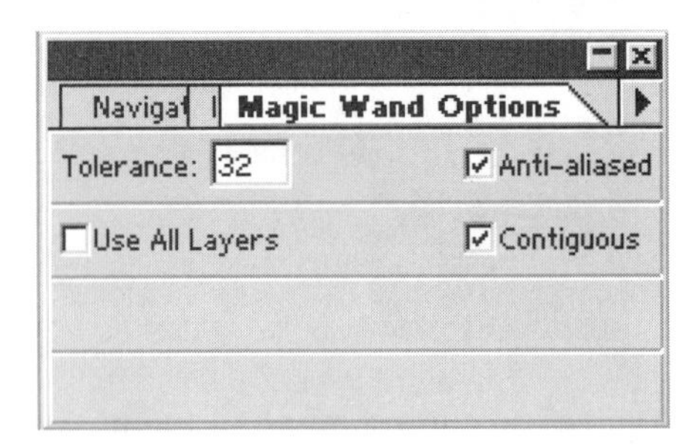

4. Make sure the Tolerance is set to 32 and that Anti-Aliased is not checked. The Tolerance setting determines how much variance from the selected color Photoshop will accept into the selection. A high number means a higher acceptance of different colors.
5. Click the image in the area shown in Figure 14.3.

FIGURE 14.3

Click here to start selecting areas to be deleted.

6. Hold down the Shift key and continue to click in the areas around the outside of the tree to select them as shown in Figure 14.4.

FIGURE 14.4

Selecting additional areas around the tree

The Shift key in conjunction with any selection tool will allow you to add additional areas to the selection. If you happen to select a portion of the tree by accident, choose Edit ➢ Undo to undo the last Magic Wand selection.

Don't worry if you haven't selected all of the areas of the image outside the tree. You'll need to use some additional tools to outline some of the areas that cannot be selected with the Magic Wand tool.

You've got a lot of the areas selected for deletion. Before you actually delete those areas, let's change the default background color to something closer to the tree leaf color.

1. Click the Dropper tool on the toolbar.

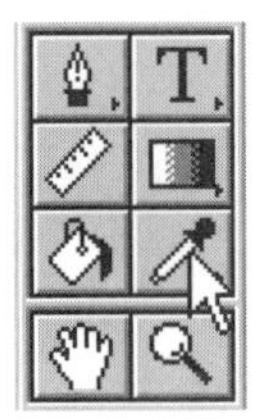

2. Click an area of the tree as shown in Figure 14.5.

FIGURE 14.5

Click an area of the tree with the dropper.

The dropper copies the color you click into the foreground color swatch on the toolbar.

3. If the color swatch appears too yellow, try clicking on another part of the tree until the color swatch appears a light green color. You can click and drag the dropper over the image to see the color swatch change in real time as you move the dropper over the image.

4. Click the Switch Color icon just above and to the right of the toolbar color swatches. The foreground and background color swatches switch places.

5. Now press the Delete key. The background color displays in the selected area.

The steps you've just taken ensure that the background color matches a neutral color from the tree. This is done in case the opacity map that you create later doesn't completely align with the image.

Selecting Areas with the Lasso

Many of the areas in the image still need to be removed. You've accomplished just about as much as you can by using the Magic Wand tool. Now you'll have to use the Lasso tool to manually outline other areas. First, enlarge an area to work on.

1. Click the Zoom tool on the toolbar.

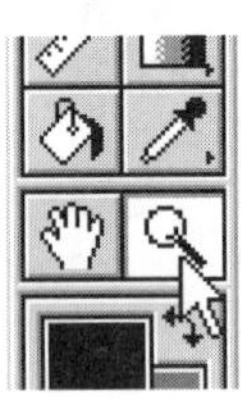

2. Click the lower left corner of the image so your view looks similar to Figure 14.6.
3. Click the Lasso tool.

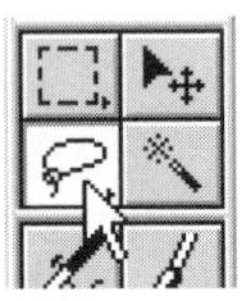

4. Make sure the Anti-Aliased option is not checked on the Lasso Options palette, then click and drag the Lasso tool around the edge of the tree to trace its outline as shown in Figure 14.6. Try to be as accurate as you can around the trunk of the tree. You needn't be too fussy about the leaves.

FIGURE 14.6

Select the area outlined in this figure.

5. When you're done outlining, release the mouse button. If you're not happy with the outline, just start over again.
6. Press the Delete key when you're satisfied with your outline.

This exercise shows the limitations of the mouse. If you plan to use Photoshop a lot, it's a good idea to get a small table with a stylus.

Now continue with the other areas around the tree.

1. Use the Hand tool or the scroll bars in the image window to pan the view over to the right as shown in Figure 14.7.
2. Use the Lasso tool again to outline the area to the right and the areas where the tree trunk begins to branch out as shown in Figure 14.7.

FIGURE 14.7

Select the areas outlined in this figure.

3. As you finish outlining one area, hold down the Shift key and outline the next. The Shift key lets you create multiple selections.
4. When you're done, press the Delete key.
5. Continue to pan to the next area of the image and use the Lasso tool to delete the unwanted areas around the tree.

6. When you're done, select the Zoom tool, then right click the image and select Fit on Screen from the right-click menu. You're image should look similar to Figure 14.8.

FIGURE 14.8

The image after removing most of the area around the tree

Selecting Specific Colors

There are still some areas within the tree that need to be removed. You could use the Lasso tool to remove them, but that would be a bit tedious and time-consuming. The Color Range command can help expedite the selection of areas that are of a particular color:

1. Choose Select ➢ Color Range… The Color Range dialog box displays.

2. Click and drag a location in the image that shows some of the blue sky background through the top of the tree as shown in Figure 14.9.

FIGURE 14.9

Click this area.

3. As you drag the mouse, watch the color swatch on the toolbar. When the swatch becomes a light blue color, release the mouse. The Color Range dialog box show a graphic depicting the areas that match the color swatch.

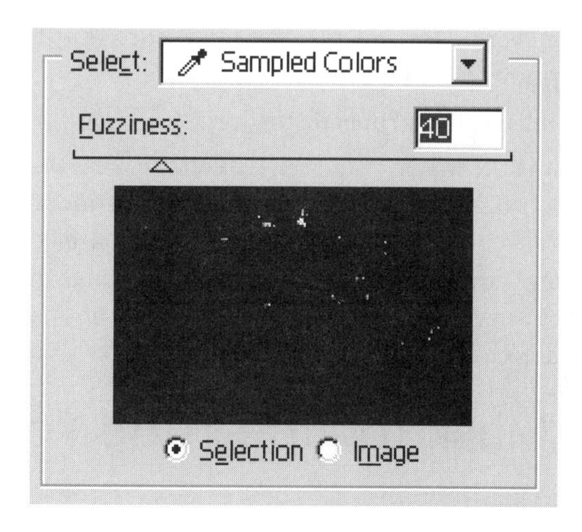

4. In the Color Range dialog box, move the Fuzziness slider to the right until the Fuzziness input box shows 60. As you do this, notice that the white areas in the sample image increase in size.
5. Click OK. You see the selections appear in the image.
6. Click the Delete key to delete the selected area.
7. You've finished editing the image. Go ahead and save it as **MagnoliaIM.tif**.

The IM in the name tells you that it is the image, as opposed to the opacity map. You'll create the opacity map next.

Creating the Opacity Map

You may recall that the opacity map is the map that tells VIZ which part of the image is to be transparent and which is to be opaque. The next set of exercises will guide you through the process of creating an opacity map directly from an image map of the tree.

The first step is to select the area defining the transparent part of the bitmap.

1. Click the Magic Wand tool on the toolbar.

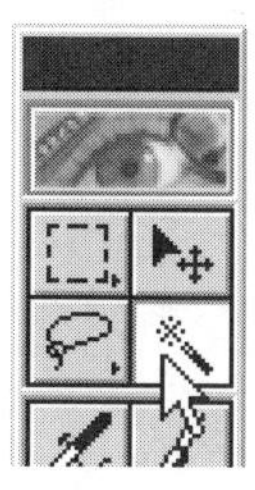

2. On the Magic Wand Options palette, make sure that the Anti-Aliased and Contiguous options are both turned off.
3. Click the green background outside the tree.

Notice that this time the Magic Wand selected all the areas that match the color of the background. This is the result of turning off the Contiguous option on the Magic Wand Options palette. While the Magic Wand with the Contiguous option turned off seems to offer the same functionality as the Select Color Range dialog box, remember that the Select Color Range dialog box additionally offers the Fuzziness slider to control the acceptable range of colors for the selection.

Using Quick Mask to Fine-Tune Your Selection

If you look carefully at the Magic Wand selection, you'll see that there are a few spots in the tree that really shouldn't be part of the background. You can use the Quick Mask mode to fine-tune your selection. Here's how the Quick Mask works.

1. Click the Edit Quick Mask tool on the toolbar. The image changes to show a red mask around the tree. The red indicates the areas that are *not* selected.

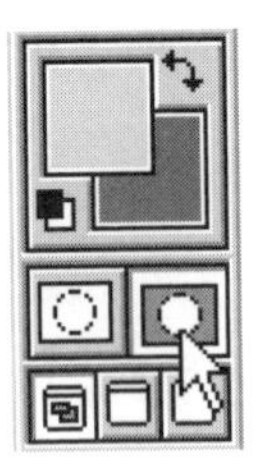

2. Zoom into an area that needs some additional editing. In our example, an area near the top of the tree needs some work, as shown in Figure 14.10.
3. Click the Paintbrush tool, then paint in the areas where the Magic Wand selected parts of the tree. The areas you paint are covered with the red mask color (see Figure 14.10).

FIGURE 14.10

The top of the tree showing some spots that were selected by the Magic Wand tool that you do not want selected

4. You can adjust the size of the Paintbrush tool by clicking the Brushes tab on the palette to the right and selecting a brush size from the palette.

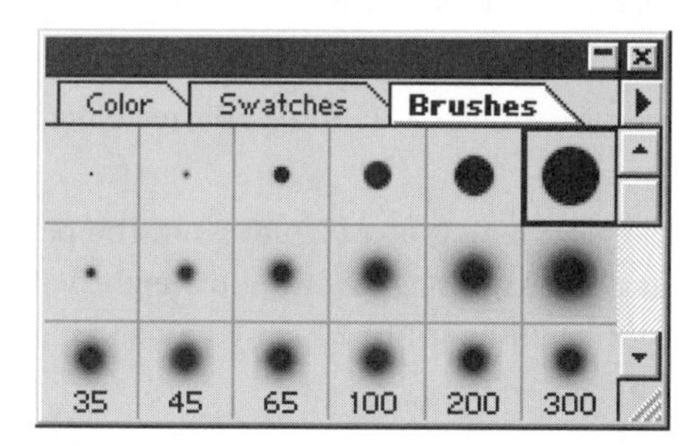

5. Pan around the image and paint over any areas that you want to exclude from the selection. As you work, you can temporarily switch back to a normal view of the image to check the selection, as it is easier to see the marching ants selection outline.
6. Click the Zoom tool, then right-click the image and select Fit on Screen to view the entire image.
7. Click the Edit in Standard Mode button. The image returns to normal without the red mask.

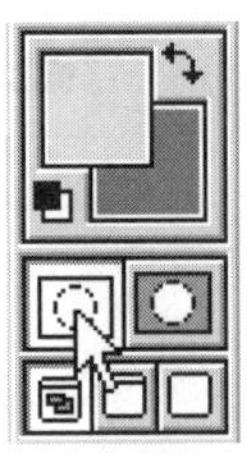

Photoshop uses red as a mask color because that is the color of a material called rubylith that is used by graphic artists to mask unwanted portions of an image when preparing art for printing. When you enter the Edit Quick Mask mode, you see the image just as a graphic artist using rubylith would see it.

While you can use the Paintbrush tool to paint in masked areas that were missed by the Magic Wand tool, you can also use the Erase tool to erase portions of a mask to create additions to the selection.

Transferring a Selection to a New File

Now that you've got the selection you need for the opacity map, the next step is to transfer the selection to a new file.

1. Choose Edit ➢ Copy or press Ctrl+C to copy the selection to the Windows Clipboard.
2. Click File ➢ New. The New dialog box displays and the parameters for the new file appear. Note that the Image Size Width and Height values are based on the contents of the Windows Clipboard to which you just copied the selection from the `Magnolia.tif` image.

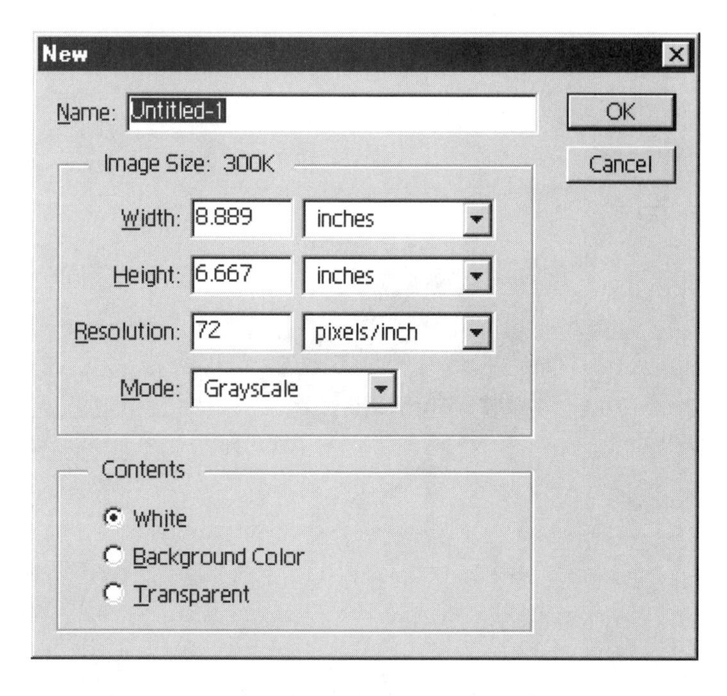

3. Click OK. A blank window displays and becomes the active window.
4. Choose Edit ➢ Paste or press Ctrl+V to insert the contents of the clipboard.

Changing a Color to Black

You've just about got the opacity map created. Remember that black is supposed to represent the transparent area of a map, so you'll need to change the green to black. Here's how it's done.

1. Choose Image ➢ Adjust ➢ Replace Color… The Replace Color dialog box displays.

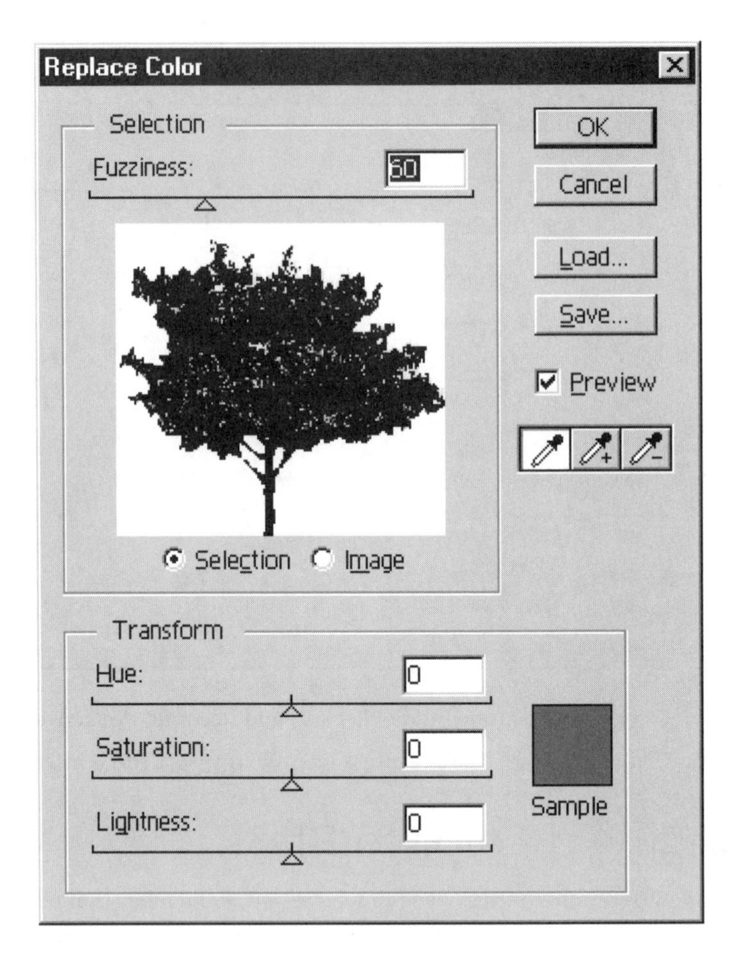

2. Use the dropper to select the green background.
3. In the Replace Color dialog box, move the Lightness and Saturation slider all the way to the left. This will change the selected color to black.
4. Close the Replace Color dialog box.

At this point, if you detect any stray areas you want to remove from the image, you can use the Paintbrush tool to paint them out.

Softening the Edges with the Airbrush Tool

In addition, if some of the edges of the tree seem too regular or smooth, the tree may take on an unnatural look in VIZ. You can *roughen* the edges of the opacity map to introduce some irregularity to the edges and create a more natural appearance.

Let's go ahead and try this using the Airbrush tool.

1. Click the Airbrush tool on the toolbar.

2. Click the Options tab to the right on the top palette and select Dissolve from the Pressure drop-down list. This will give the airbrush a spattered texture. The default normal option gives the airbrush a smooth gradient appearance, which is not what you want in this situation.

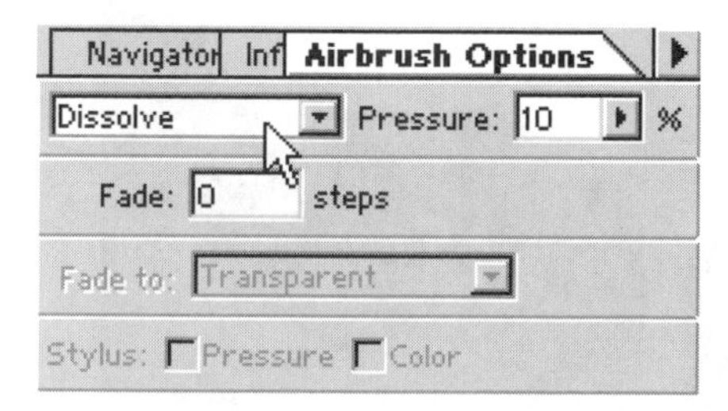

4. Set the Pressure value to 10. This keeps the airbrush flow to a manageable level, allowing you to gradually build up coverage.
5. Go to the Brushes palette and select the brush option from the far right of the top row.

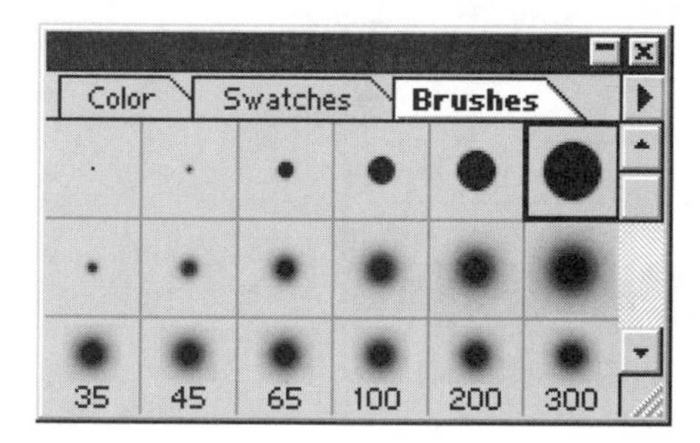

6. Click and drag the airbrush near the left side of the tree at the location shown in Figure 14.11. Starting in the black area, carefully and gradually move the airbrush into the white area to introduce some irregularity to the edge as shown in Figure 14.11.

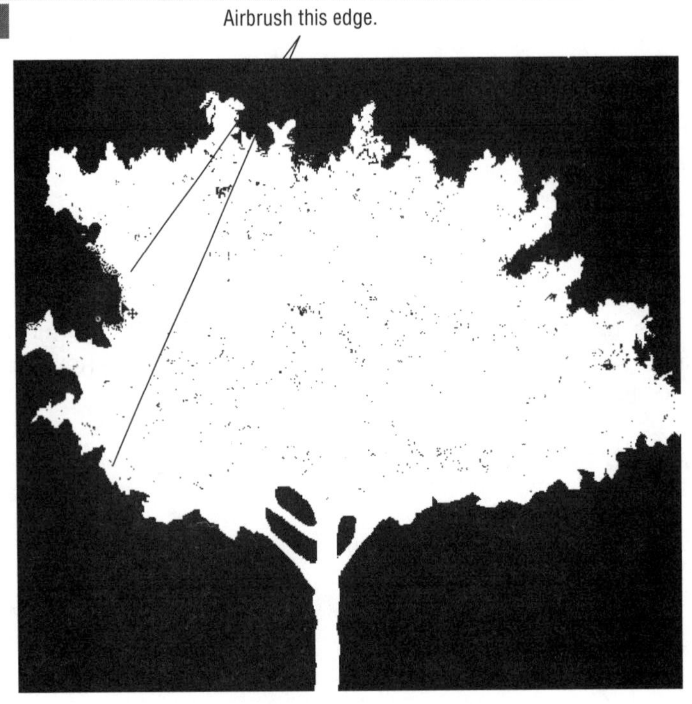

FIGURE 14.11

Airbrushing the edge of the tree to introduce some irregularity to the tree edge

7. If you get carried away, you can use Edit ➢ Undo. You can also use the trashcan on the History palette. In fact, you can undo several steps back by selecting the step from the History panel and clicking the trash can.

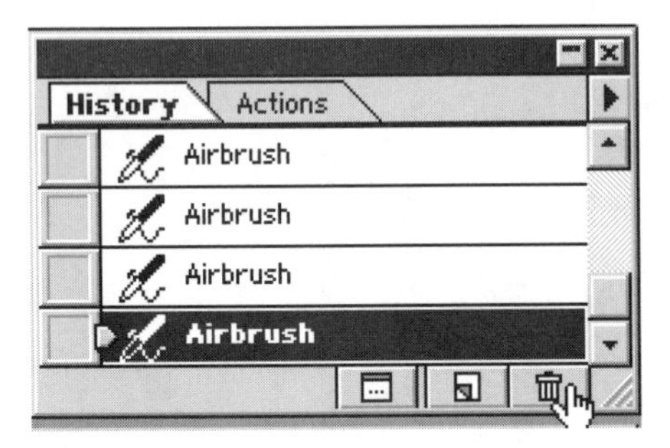

The opacity map is ready to be saved. This final step is not as obvious as it may seem.

1. Choose File ➢ Save a Copy.
2. In the Save a Copy dialog box, locate the directory where you've stored the sample files from the companion CD.

3. In the Save As drop-down list, select TIFF. Actually, you can select any file format that VIZ will recognize, including JPEG or GIF. Using one of these formats can save some file space.
4. In the File Name input box, enter the name **MagnoliaOP** to distinguish this file as the opacity map for the magnolia tree.
5. Click Save. You've got your tree maps ready to go.

You may wonder why you didn't use the standard File ➢ Save As option to save your opacity map image. When you pasted the image into the new window, Photoshop automatically created a new layer. Layers in Photoshop are similar to layers in VIZ and AutoCAD. They act as tools to help you organize parts of an image. You can see the layer on the Layers palette in the bottom right corner of the Photoshop window.

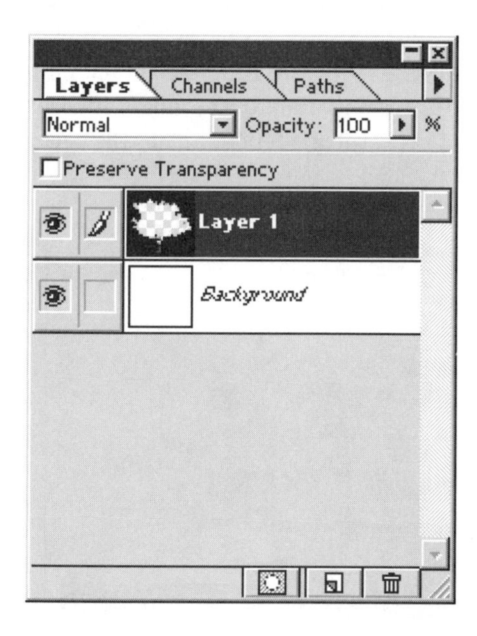

If you try to use File ➢ Save As to save the image, Photoshop will only allow you to save it as a .psd file, which is Photoshop's native file format. This is because .psd is the only file format that is capable of storing the layer information.

If you think you'll be further editing an image file, it's a good idea to use the .psd file format since it does store types of data that other formats do not. In fact, it would in any case be a good idea to save your opacity map as a .psd file in case you find that it isn't quite right when you view it in VIZ.

Now that you've got your image and opacity maps, you can use Material Editor in VIZ to combine the two image files into a material as you did in Chapter 8.

Although you've seen how you can create a tree in these exercises, you can apply the same process for creating people and other props in your VIZ design. As long as you're not creating an animated walk through, props such as the flat tree in the villa design can be great time-savers, and if carefully done, they can add a high degree of realism to your renderings.

Using Photoshop to Create a Montage

You've seen one example of using Photoshop as a tool to create a material to be used with VIZ's Material Editor. You can also use Photoshop to enhance finished, rendered images from VIZ. For example, you can insert different backgrounds into a VIZ rendering, or you can add people and trees to an elevation created in VIZ.

In this section, you'll learn how you can combine graphics into a rendering in a montage. You'll use the northeast elevation of the villa, which was rendered during an exercise in Chapter 13. This particular rendering has the background turned off so you can more easily add a sky.

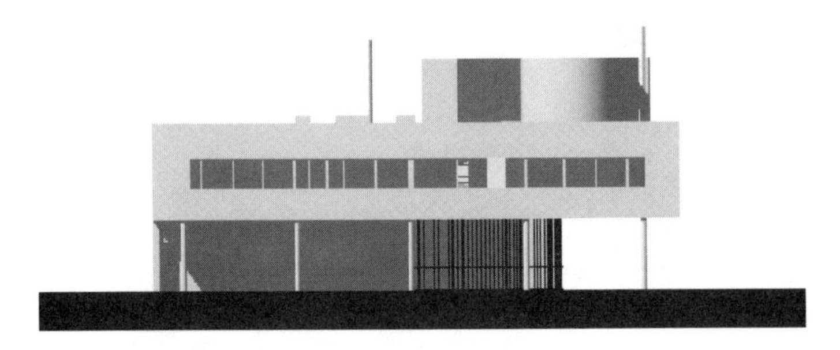

Start by adding a sky to the background. The main trick in performing this task is to limit the area in which the sky is to appear.

1. In Photoshop, open the file called `Sample_elevation.tif` from the Companion CD.
2. Click the Magic Wand tool on the toolbar, then click the Contiguous option on the Magic Wand Options palette to make it active.

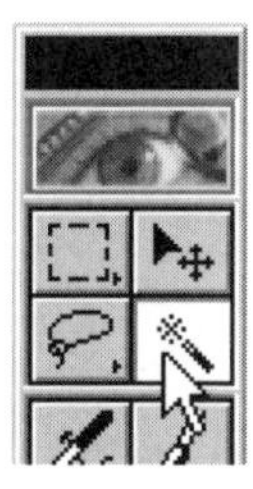

3. Click the blank area where you want to place the sky, as shown in Figure 14.12.
4. Shift-click in the isolated area below the second floor that should also show sky (see Figure 14.12).

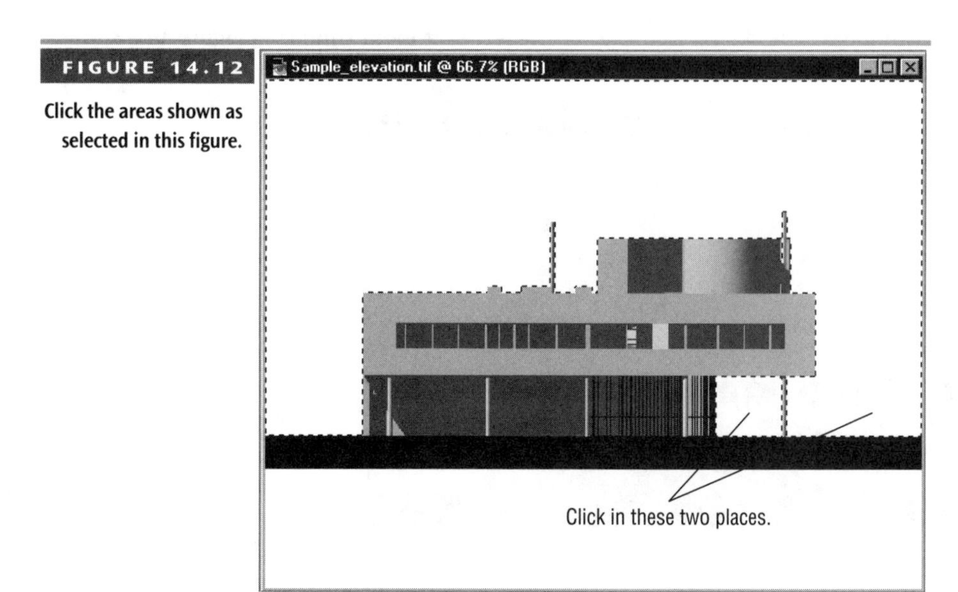

FIGURE 14.12

Click the areas shown as selected in this figure.

In other situations, you may find that there are additional areas that need to be selected for the sky. You can continue to shift-click those areas using the Magic Wand tool.

The next step is to open the file you'll use as the sky background and paste it into the elevation.

1. Locate and open `Ksc-sky1a.jpg` from the companion CD.
2. With the `Ksc-sky1a.jpg` file open, press Ctrl+A to select the entire image, then press Ctrl+C to copy the image to the clipboard.
3. Click the Sample_elevation window to make it active, then choose Edit ➢ Paste Into. The sky displays in the Sample_elevation window, only in the selected area.

The size of the Sample_elevation file and the sky file are different so when the sky is inserted, it doesn't quite fit in the elevation. You can adjust the size and location of the sky using the Move tool and the Transform options.

1. Click the Move tool on the toolbar.

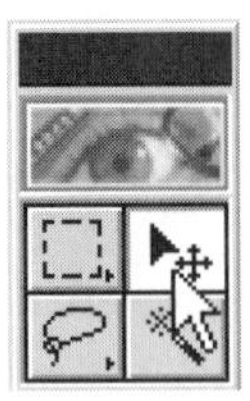

2. Click and drag the sky background to the left so it looks similar to Figure 14.13.

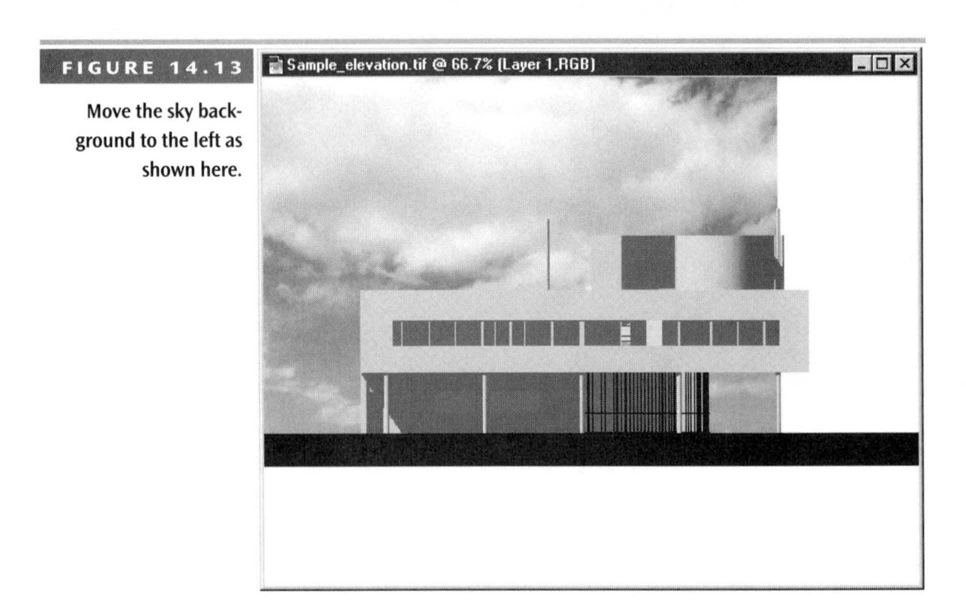

FIGURE 14.13

Move the sky background to the left as shown here.

3. To adjust the size of the background, choose Edit ➢ Free Transform. You see a transform border and handles appear on the background image as shown in Figure 14.14.
4. Click and drag the handle in the lower right corner of the background to the right so that the background fills the entire image.
5. When you've finished adjusting the size of the background, press ↵.

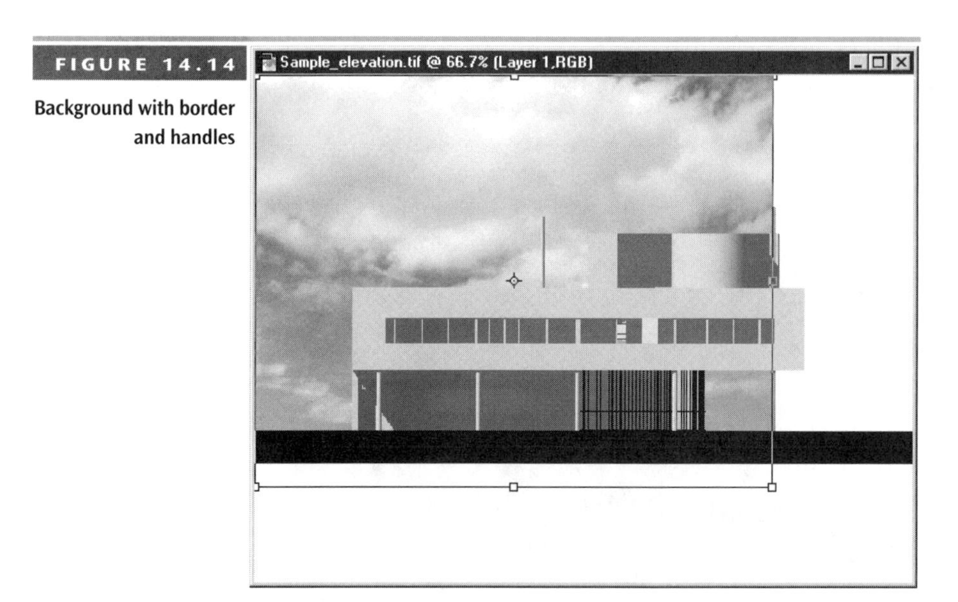

FIGURE 14.14

Background with border and handles

The background is now in place. Notice that you now have a new layer called Layer 1. If you need to use the Free Transform option again at a later date to change the background, you can select Layer 1 and choose Edit ➢ Free Transform with Layer 1 active.

Adding a Tree in the Foreground

Adding a background to the VIZ image is tricky only because you need to know how to paste an image into selected areas. For pasting images into the foreground, the trick is to make sure that you select only the portion of the pasted image that you want.

Next, try adding a tree to the image in front of the villa elevation. In this exercise you'll select a tree in a way that will make the tree somewhat transparent. This is done so the tree doesn't hide too much of the building.

1. Open the file called `CamphorAM.tif` from the companion CD. This is an image used for a tree map that you saw in the aquatic center rendering.
2. Choose Select ➢ Color Range.
3. Use the dropper to click the green area outside the tree.
4. Set the Fuzziness setting to **60**, then click OK. The green area around the tree is selected.
5. Choose Select ➢ Inverse. This inverts the selection so that the tree—but not the background—is selected.
6. Press Ctrl+C to copy the tree to the clipboard.

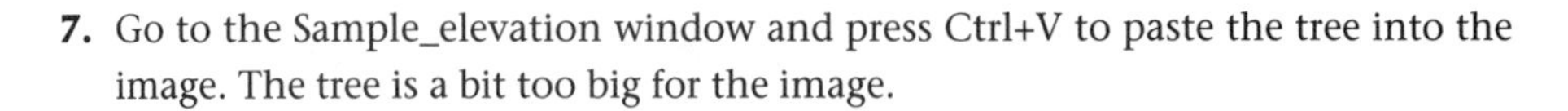

7. Go to the Sample_elevation window and press Ctrl+V to paste the tree into the image. The tree is a bit too big for the image.

Once again you'll want to employ the Free Transform option to adjust the size of the addition to the elevation.

1. Choose Edit ➢ Free Transform.
2. Click and drag the Transform handle in the lower right corner upward and to the left while holding the Shift key. By holding the Shift key, you maintain the width and height proportion of the tree (this proportion is called the aspect ratio).
3. Adjust the tree using the Transform handle so that it is roughly the size shown in Figure 14.15.
4. Move the tree so that its base is on the ground. Press ↵ when you're done.

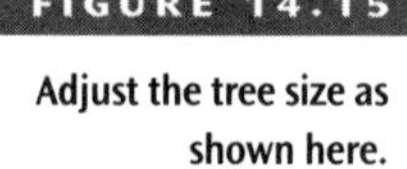
FIGURE 14.15

Adjust the tree size as shown here.

The tree has a somewhat transparent look. This is because you were directed to set the Fuzziness value to 60 in the Color Range dialog box. With the Fuzziness value at 60, Photoshop selected a range of colors a bit beyond the green background, including parts of the tree. By making the tree slightly transparent, you can place it in front of the building without obscuring the building too much. As long as you don't get carried away, the transparency of the tree lets you add landscaping to the image without obscuring the view of the building. You may also want to apply a blur filter to the tree layer to subordinate the tree image.

TIP **You can also reduce the Opacity setting on the Layer Palette to give the tree some transparency.**

You may want to add other images such as people and cars to the elevation. These can be added using the same steps you used to add the tree.

FIGURE 14.16

The elevation with the addition of people

Creating Bump Maps for Elaborate Textures

You've seen how you can mix a diffuse map and an opacity map to create the illusion of a tree, similar to a prop in theater set. But diffuse and opacity maps are not the only combinations of maps that are useful in VIZ. For example, you can combine bump maps with diffuse maps to very quickly create complex forms. For example, suppose you want to create a wall made of stone or splitface block. You would drive yourself crazy creating such a detailed item by trying to model the object block-by-block or stone-by-stone. By combining diffuse and bump maps, you can make quick work of such a project.

Try the following tutorial that combines Photoshop, AutoCAD, and VIZ to help create an elaborate block wall.

Using AutoCAD for the Outline

First, start by using AutoCAD to create the basic outline of the block wall. If you're using a different program, try to follow along to create the 96-inch by 48-inch block wall described here.

1. Open AutoCAD, then click the Rectangle tool on the Draw toolbar on the left side of the AutoCAD window.

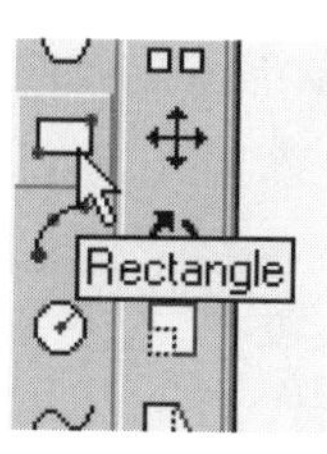

2. Type **0,0**↵ to start the rectangle at the origin of the drawing.
3. Type **96,48**↵ to place the other corner of the rectangle. This creates a rectangle that is 96 inches wide by 48 inches high. These dimensions will accommodate six verticle courses of block.
4. Click the Zoom Realtime tool.

5. Now right-click and click Zoom Extents to view the entire rectangle. Click and drag downward with the Zoom Realtime tool to get a better view.

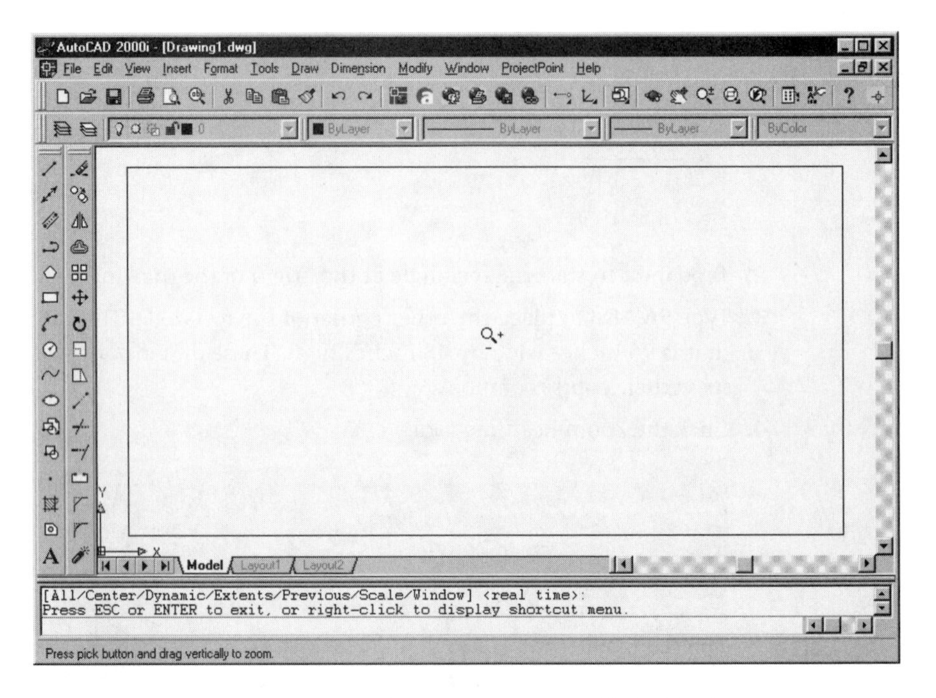

You've got the basic outline. The next step is to add the block pattern.

1. Click the Hatch tool on the Draw toolbar.

2. In the Boundary Hatch dialog box, click the sample swatch.

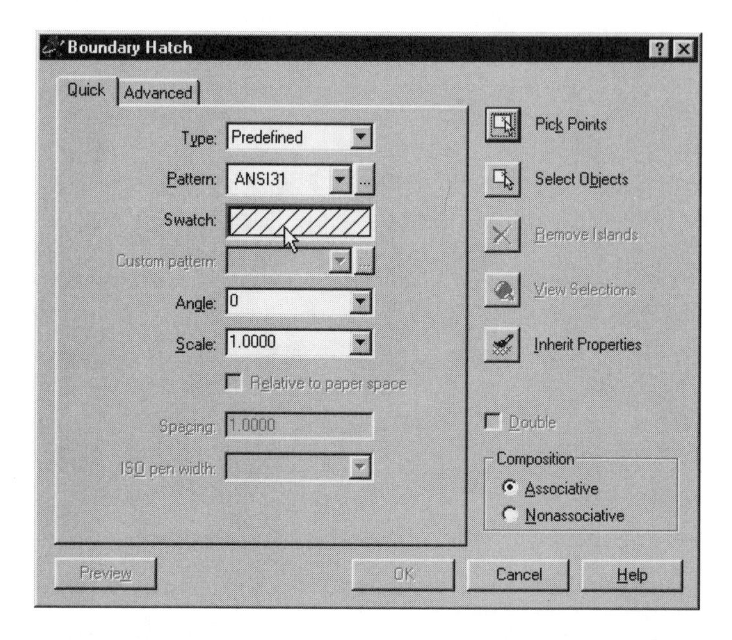

3. On the Hatch Pattern Palette, click the Other Predefined tab.
4. Click the ARB816C pattern shown in the dialog box, then click OK.

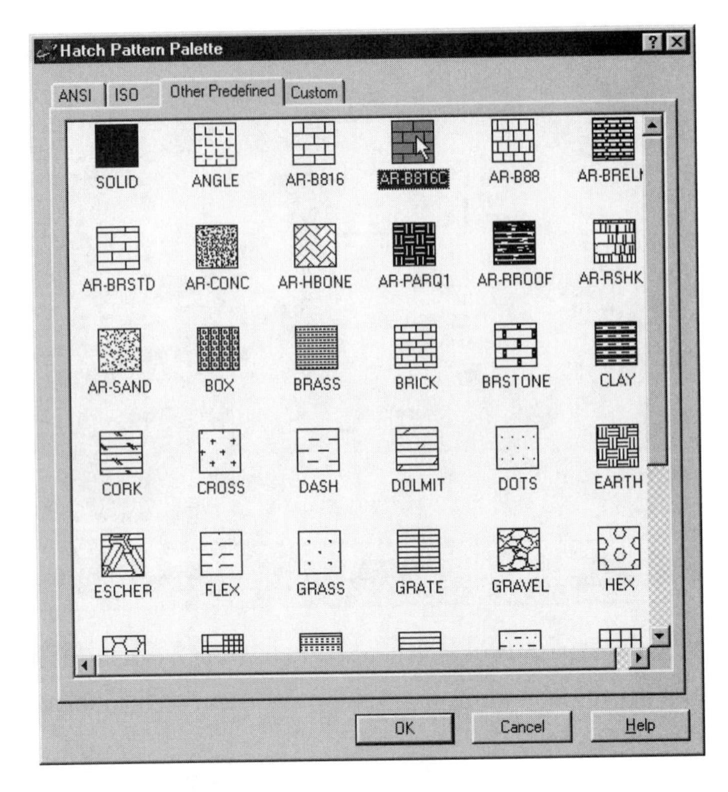

5. Back in the Boundary Hatch dialog box, click Select Object. The dialog box temporarily disappears to allow you to select an object.
6. Use the Square cursor to select the rectangle, then press ↵. You return to the Boundary Hatch dialog box.
7. Click OK. The hatch pattern appears in the drawing.

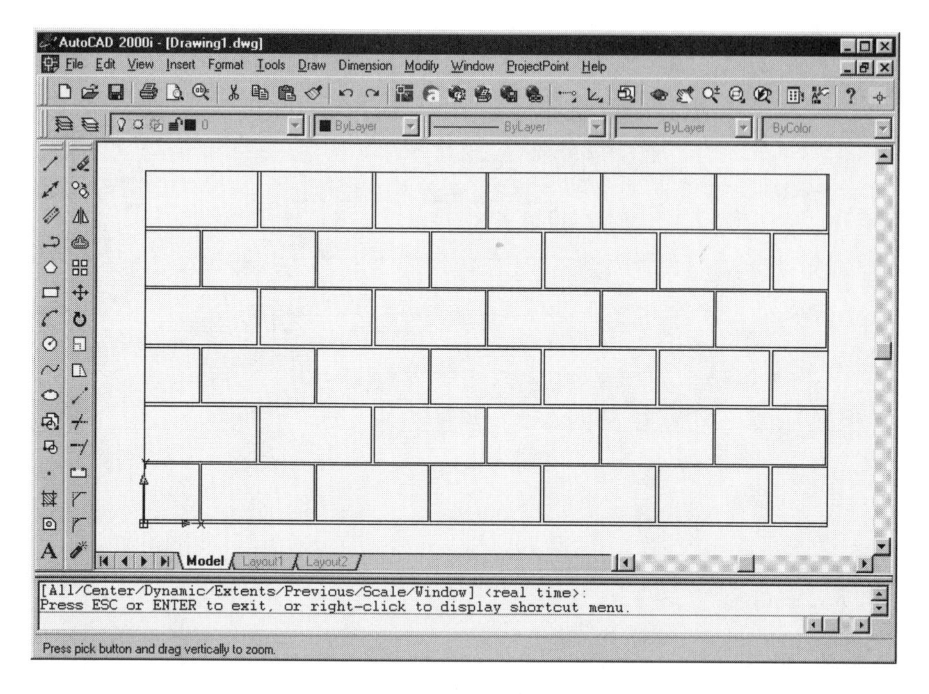

You now have the basic block pattern over which you can build an image map for a splitface block wall. AutoCAD is perfect for this particular task. It would take quite a bit longer to create this pattern accurately in a non-CAD graphics program.

Next, you need to get the AutoCAD image to Photoshop. There are several ways to do this. AutoCAD can be set up to print a bitmap file capable of being read by Photoshop; however, you'll use a simpler method for the block wall.

1. If you see the UCS icon in the lower left corner of the screen, type **ucsicon** ↵ **Off** ↵ to turn it off. You don't want the UCS Icon to appear in the image that is copied to the clipboard.
2. With the AutoCAD window in full view and the cursor out of the block area, Press the Alt+Print Screen keys. This copies the entire content of your screen to the clipboard.
3. Return to Photoshop, then click File ➢ New. Remember that a new file in Photoshop will be sized according to the content of the clipboard, so you'll see the New dialog box showing the size of your display for the new file size.

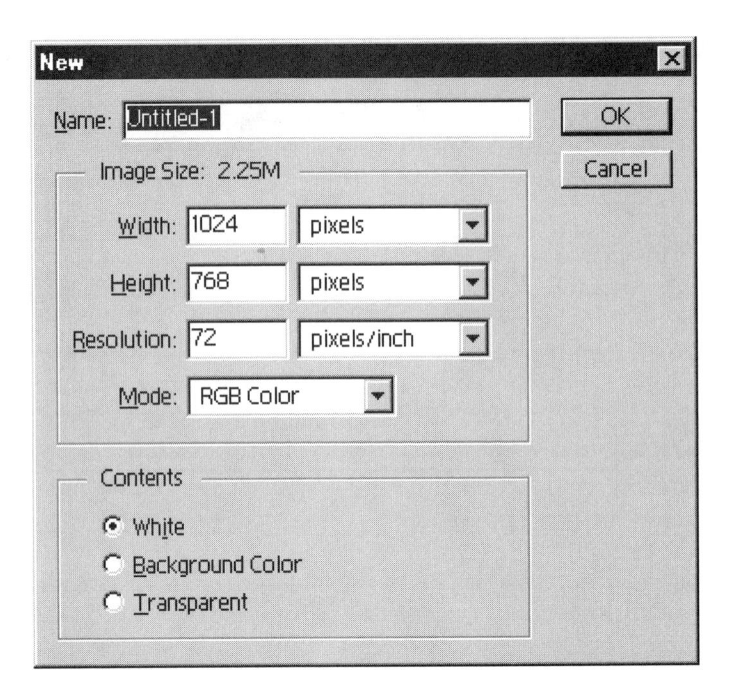

4. Click OK. When the Untitled window displays, choose Edit ➢ Paste or press Ctrl+V. The image of your screen displays in the window.

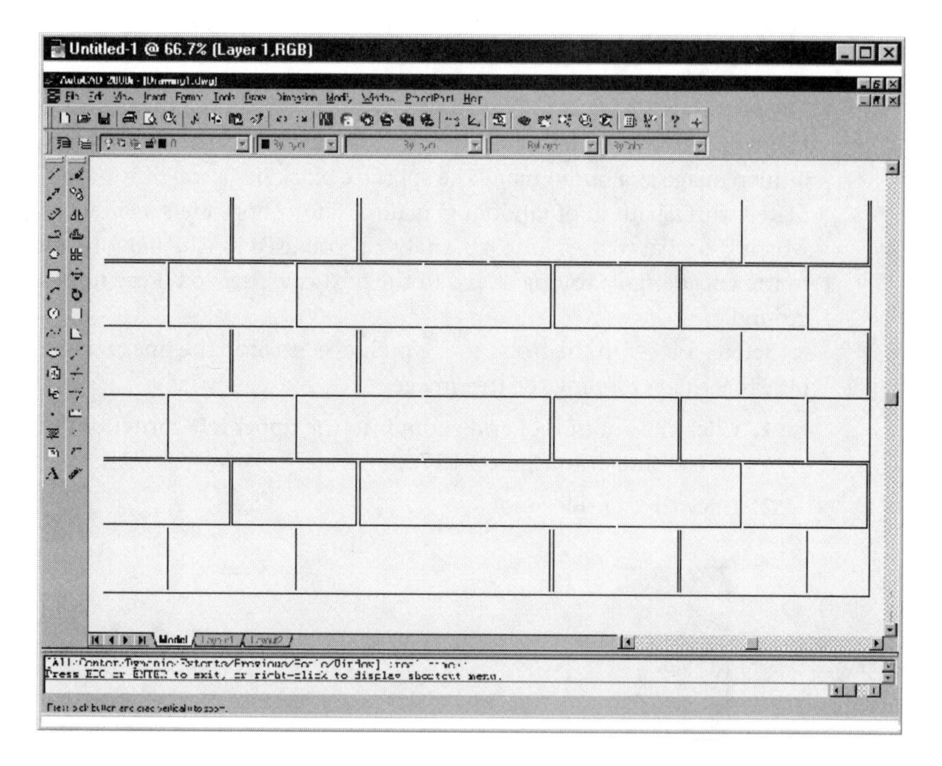

5. Once you've successfully copied the AutoCAD screen to Photoshop, go ahead and close AutoCAD. You don't need to save the block drawing.

Transferring the AutoCAD image through the clipboard is adequate for what you're doing here. You don't need a super-accurate AutoCAD image to create the block pattern.

Building Textures in Photoshop

The next step is to start to build a pattern that VIZ can use to create a texture. Remember that VIZ uses shades of gray to create a sense of bumpiness when using a bitmap image as a bump map. The splitface block has a rough surface that can be simulated with a pattern of random gray dots. Photoshop offers a Filter called Noise which is similar to the Noise material map you used in Chapter 8 to give the ground in the villa design a rolling effect. In the next exercise, you'll use noise as a background.

Before you get to the Noise tool, you'll need to crop the image down. This will be a bit easier than cropping the tree image.

1. Click the Zoom tool and zoom into the upper left corner of the image so your view is similar to Figure 14.17.
2. Click the Marquee tool.

3. Click and drag the mouse at the location shown in Figure 14.17, but don't let go of the mouse quite yet.

FIGURE 14.17

Enlarged view of the image

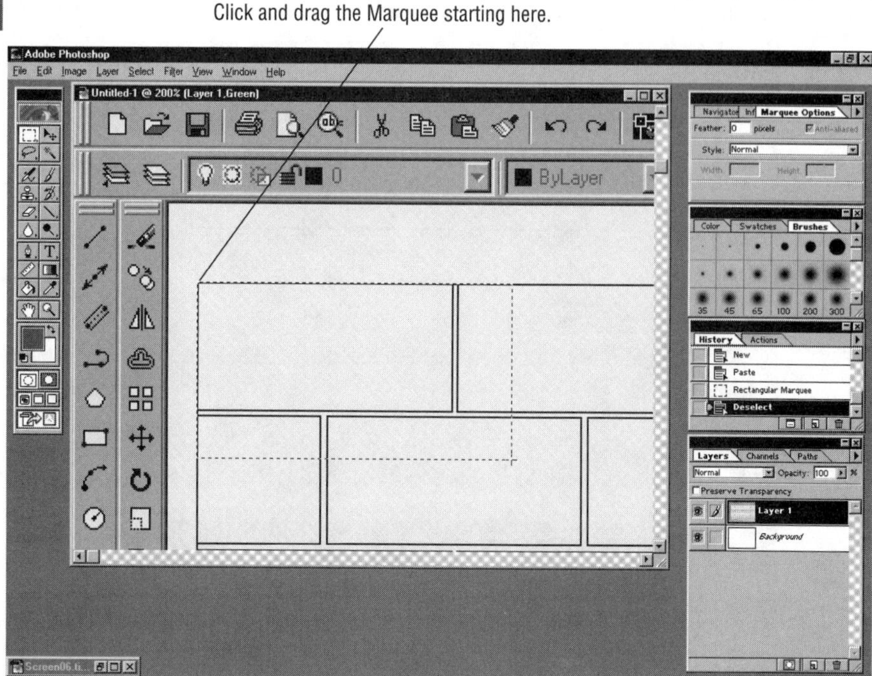

4. Drag the mouse downward and to the right. The display will automatically pan to the lower right corner of the image.
5. When your image looks similar to Figure 14.18, release the mouse. You should see the marching ant marquee indicating your selection.

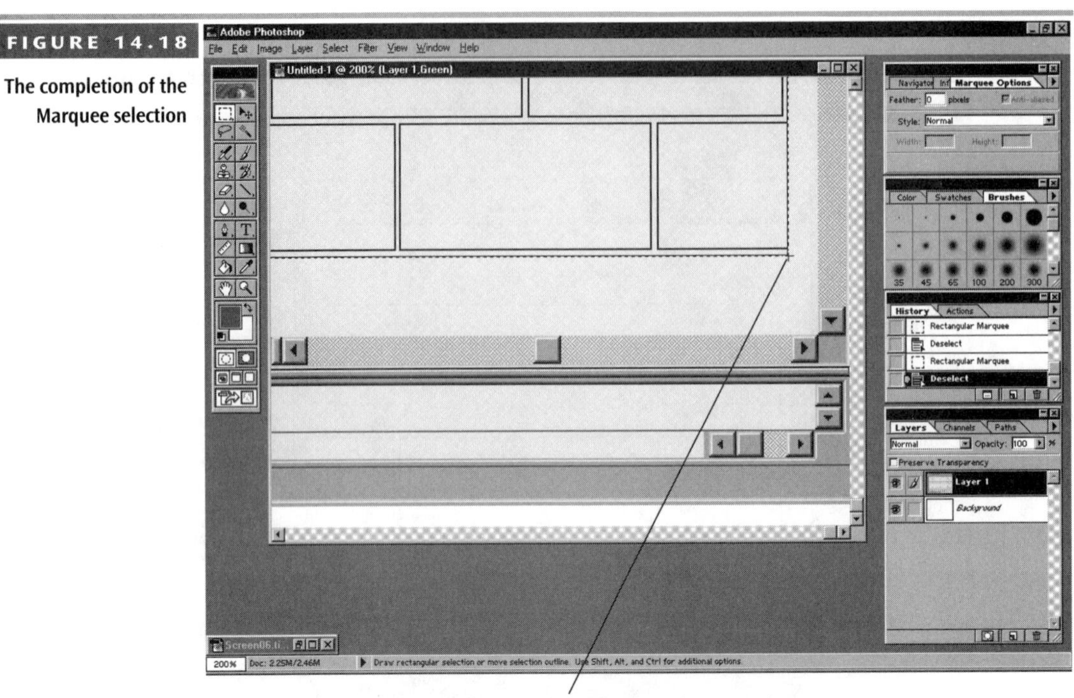

FIGURE 14.18

The completion of the Marquee selection

You could have placed the Marquee selection while viewing the entire image, but it would have been difficult to select a point close to the corners of the block wall outline. Using the Zoom tool lets you get close enough to make an accurate selection and the Marquee tool lets you automatically pan to other parts of the image by moving the cursor to the edge of the image.

Now that you've made the selection, you need to crop it.

1. First, get an overall view of the image: click the Zoom tool, then right-click within the image and select Fit on Screen.
2. Choose Image ➢ Crop. The image is reduced to the block pattern.

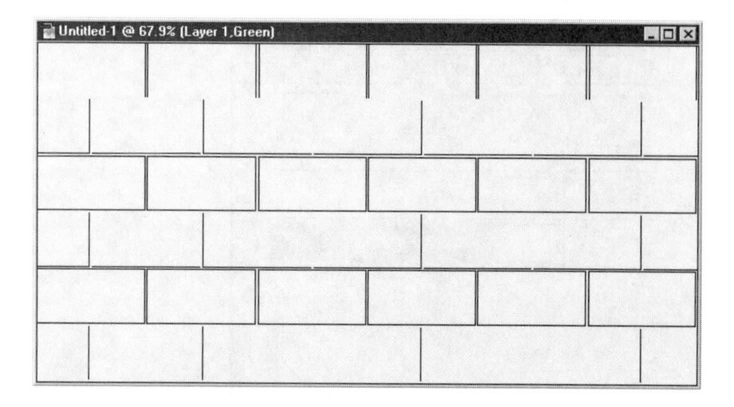

Now you're ready to add some noise. First, take a look at the Layer palette in the bottom right portion of the Photoshop window.

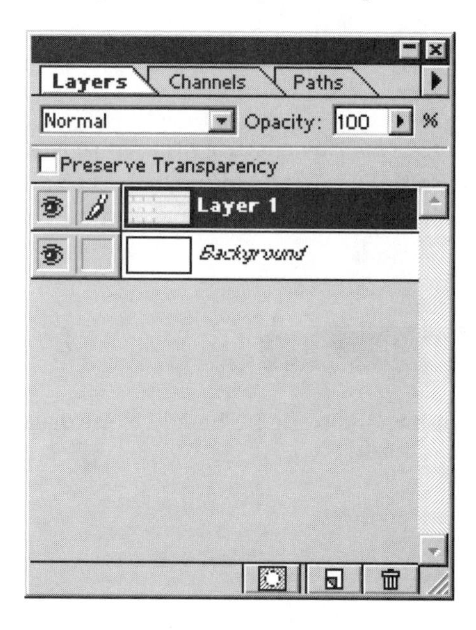

You'll see two layers listed: the background and Layer 1. The background is the content of the image before you pasted the AutoCAD screen into the image. Layer 1 contains the pasted image. Photoshop automatically creates a new layer when something is pasted into a new RGB file.

In the next exercise, you'll add noise to the background; the noise will be used by VIZ to create the rough texture of a splitface block.

1. In the layer Palette, click the Background label to make it the current active layer. It turns black to show that it is active.

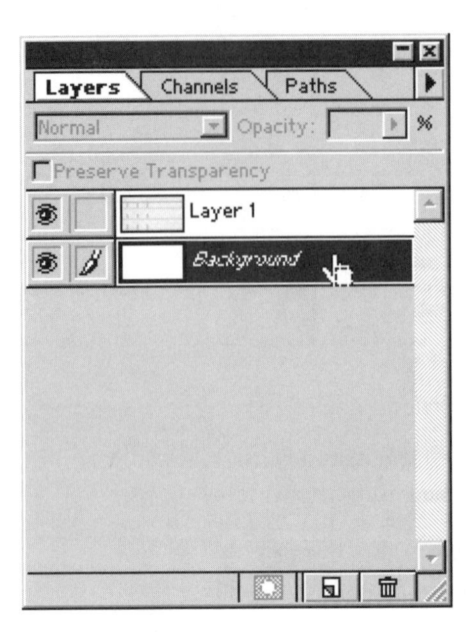

2. Temporarily turn off Layer 1 by clicking on the Eye icon to the far left of the Layer 1 listing on the Layer Palette. This is the Layer Visibility button. The eye disappears and the block pattern also disappears in the Untitled image window.

3. Choose Filter ➢ Noise ➢ Add Noise… The Add Noise dialog box displays.

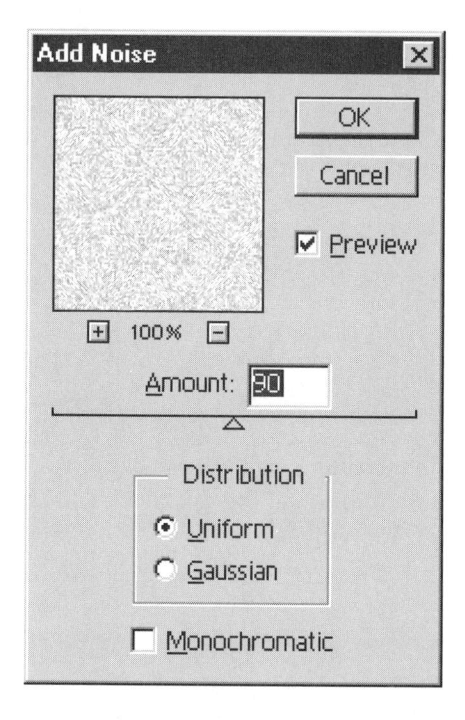

4. Click the Monochromatic check box, then adjust the Amount slider to around 400. Notice that the sample image in the dialog box and the Untitled image window both change as you do this.
5. Click OK to accept the Add Noise setting.
6. On the layer Palette, click the Layer Visibility box for Layer 1 to turn it back on. The Noise disappears in the image window because Layer 1 completely covers it.

You've added the noise to the background, but you need to make some adjustments to Layer 1 to allow the noise to appear in the image. You also need to fill in the mortar joint in the Layer 1 image. Start with the mortar joints.

1. Click the Zoom tool, then zoom into the block pattern so you can see the mortar joint clearly as in Figure 14.19.

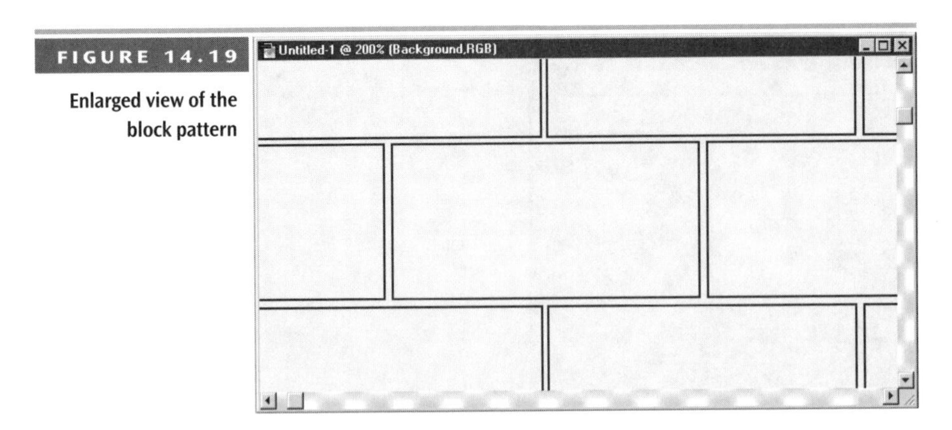

FIGURE 14.19

Enlarged view of the block pattern

2. Make sure the foreground color swatch shows black. To reset the foreground to black and the background to white, you can click the Default Colors icon below and to the left of the color swatches.

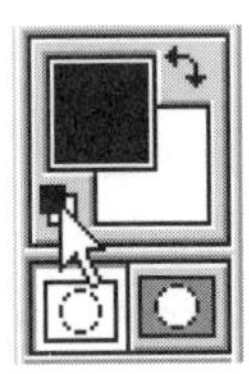

3. Click the Paint bucket tool.

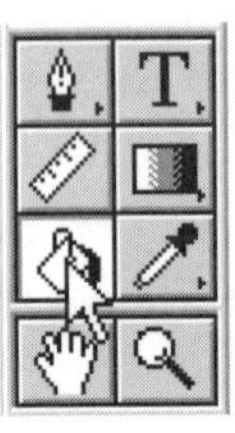

4. In the Layer palette, click the Layer 1 label to make Layer 1 the active layer.
5. Click the tip of the dripping paint icon on the white area of the mortar joint in the image window. The white area is filled with black.
6. Click the Zoom tool, then right-click within the image and select Fit on Screen to get the overall view of your image.

Now you need to remove the white area so that the background can show through.

1. Click the Magic Wand tool.
2. In the Magic Wand Options palette, make sure that the Anti-Aliased and Contiguous options are both turned off.
3. Click the Magic Wand tool in any white area of the image.
4. Choose Edit ➢ Clear or press the Delete key to remove the white areas from Layer 1. The background now shows through between the mortar joints.

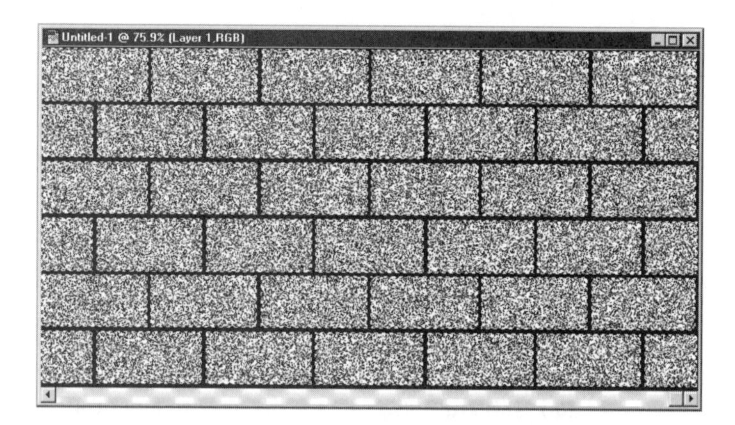

Creating a Chain Link Fence with AutoCAD

In Chapter 9, You may have noticed a chain-link fence in the background of the aquatic center. That fence was created using the same techniques described in this chapter. Here's how the fence was created.

In AutoCAD, a simple crosshatch was created using the AutoCAD Boundary Hatch tool.

The view of the hatch pattern was adjusted so that it filled the display as much as possible. Once this was done, the Print Screen key was pressed. This copies the contents of the entire screen into the Windows clipboard. Photoshop was then opened and File ➢ New was selected to create a new file. Remember that File ➢ New uses the contents of the clipboard to determine the size of the new file. The Paste option was then used to paste the captured screen into the Photoshop window.

The Marquee tool was used next to single out the area displaying the crosshatch. Image ➢ Crop was then used to crop the image down to the selected area. The image was saved as a TIFF file, which was then used in VIZ as an opacity map.

Testing the Image in VIZ

You've got a start on a splitface block map. Let's take a look at the results so far. First, save the image in a file type that can be read by VIZ.

1. Choose File ➢ Save a Copy.
2. In the Save a Copy dialog box, locate the `\3DVIZ3\Maps` folder in the Save In drop-down list.
3. In the Save As drop-down list, select TIFF.
4. Enter **Splitface_bump** in the File Name input box.

Remember that as soon as you start to add layers to a Photoshop image, the Save or Save As file option only allows you to save the file as a native Photoshop file. This is because only the native Photoshop file format can store layer information. You need to use the Save a Copy option to create an image file that VIZ can read.

Now let's take a look at the results in VIZ.

1. Open VIZ, then open the sample file, called `Splitface.max`, from the companion CD. This is a file containing a simple box that is 192 inches wide by 48 inches high by 8 inches deep. The file also contains a light source, and the background and ambient lighting have been set to a neutral color.
2. Open Material Editor and make sure the first sample slot in the upper left corner is selected.
3. Scroll down to the Map rollout and open it, then click the Bump map button labeled None.
4. In the Material Map browser, double-click Bitmap.
5. In the Select Bitmap Image File dialog box, locate and select `Splitface_bump.tif`. The sample slot now shows the bump texture on the sphere.

TIP You can also use the Noise map in VIZ to create a bumpy surface, but by using Photoshop to create a bitmap bump map, you have more control over where the bumpiness occurs.

The bump map you created in Photoshop is now part of a material definition, but you need to make a few adjustments. The color is not quite right, and it's too shiny. Let's make these adjustments and add the material to the sample wall.

1. In Material Editor, click the Go to Parent tool.

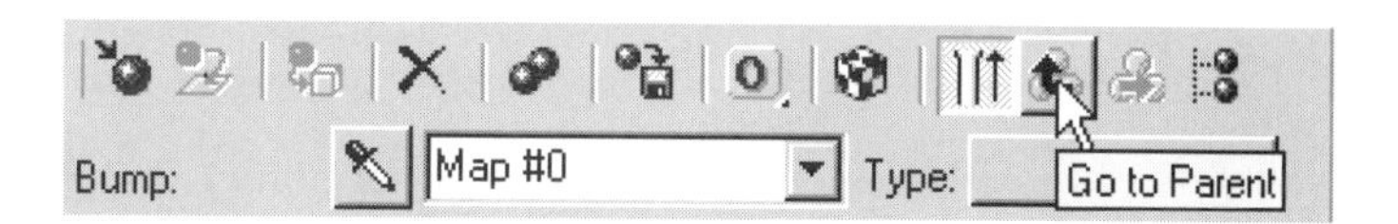

2. In the Maps rollout, change the Bump map Amount value to **200**.
3. Scroll up the panel to the Specular Highlights group of the Phong Basic Parameters and right-click the Specular Level and Glossiness spinners to set both of these options to **0**.
4. Click the Diffuse color swatch and, in the Color Selector dialog box, set the Saturation to **0**.
5. Back in the Material Editor dialog box, click the Ambient color swatch and set its Saturation setting to **0**, then click Close in the Color Selector dialog box.
6. The material from slot 1 has already been applied to the wall, so to get an idea of how the material looks, click the Quick Render tool in the standard toolbar. You see the wall rendered with the new splitface block pattern (see Figure 14.20).

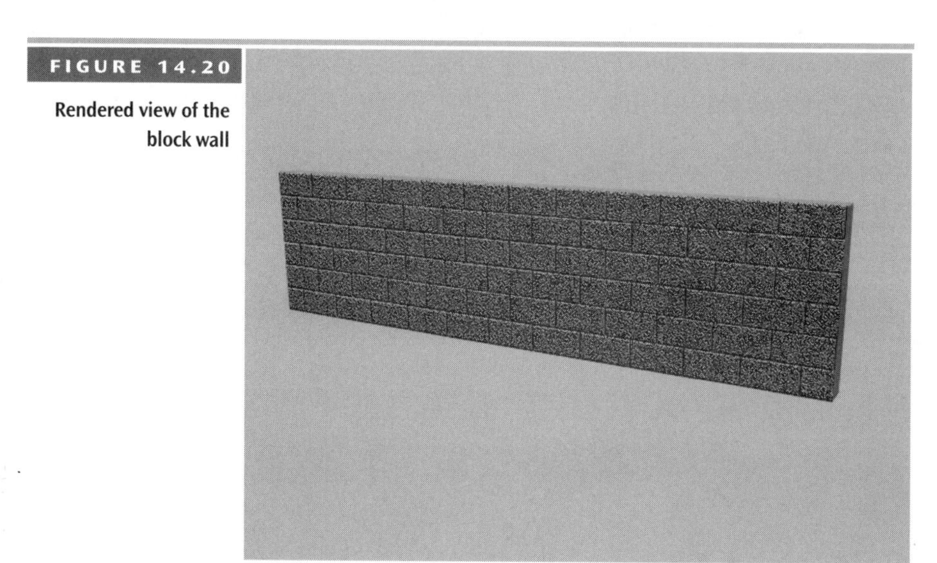

FIGURE 14.20
Rendered view of the block wall

Everything that defines the wall as a block wall is there, but it looks too uniform and colorless. You'll need to add some variation to the bump map to give it a more natural appearance. You'll also want to start bringing in some color. In the next section, you'll learn how you can start to build your Photoshop image to include these features.

Adding Irregularity and Color to the Material

You've got a start on the bump map for the splitface block wall. In this section, you'll start to play with the bump map image in Photoshop while keeping VIZ open so you can see your changes as you go along. That way, you'll get a better sense of how your Photoshop edits affect the material in VIZ.

WARNING **If you are using Windows 98 or have less than 128 megabytes of RAM, you may want to close VIZ while you're working in Photoshop. If you have a system running Windows NT 4.0 or 2000 and at least 128 megabytes of RAM, you will have no problem having both Photoshop and VIZ open at the same time.**

To add some irregularity to the block surface, you'll want to include some wide patches of dark and light tones to the image while maintaining the rough appearance of the surface. You can do this by adding some dark tones with the airbrush tool. You'll want to keep your airbrush work on a separate layer in case it doesn't come out exactly the way you want. By airbrushing on a different layer, you won't affect the other layers in an irreversible way.

1. Go back to Photoshop, then click the right-pointing arrow at the top of the Layers palette.

   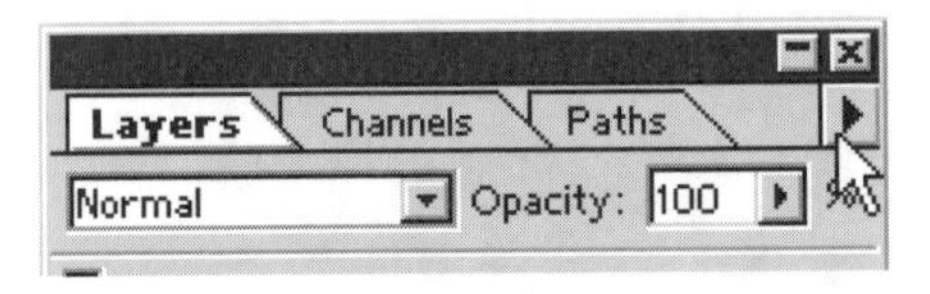

   This opens the layer menu.

2. Click New Layer... The New Layer dialog box displays.

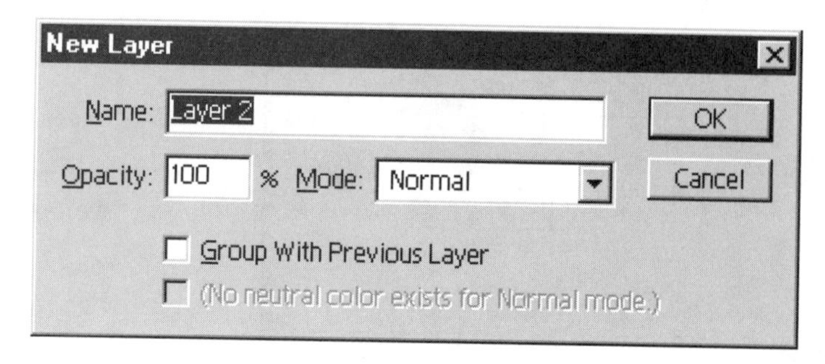

3. Enter **Airbrush** for the name, then click OK.

You now have a new, blank layer called Airbrush, and by default, the new layer is the currently active one. A new layer is transparent, so you don't see any changes to the image.

TIP You can change the name of an existing layer by opening the layer menu with the arrow button and selecting Layer Options. A dialog box opens, allowing you to set the layer name.

Now go ahead and add some irregularity to the pattern using the airbrush tool.

1. Click the Airbrush tool on the toolbar.

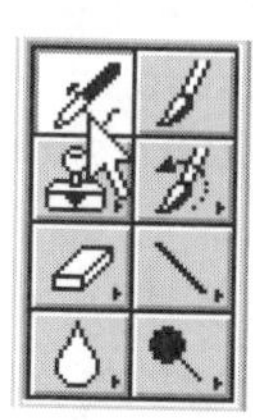

2. In the Airbrush Options palette in the top right corner of the Photoshop window, select Dissolve from the drop-down list.
3. Set the percent Pressure value to **10**.

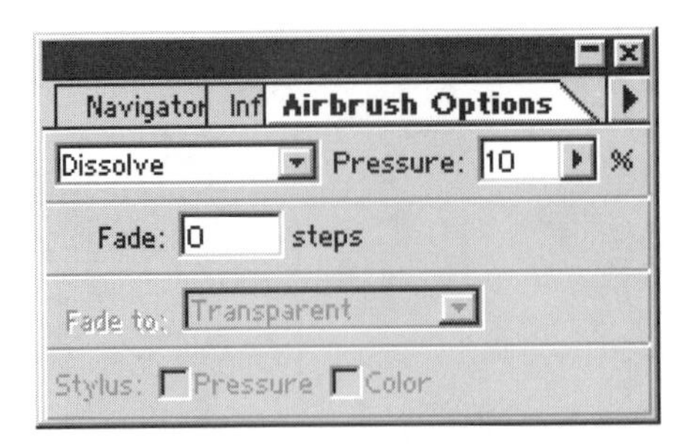

4. In the Brushes palette, select the slot labeled 35.

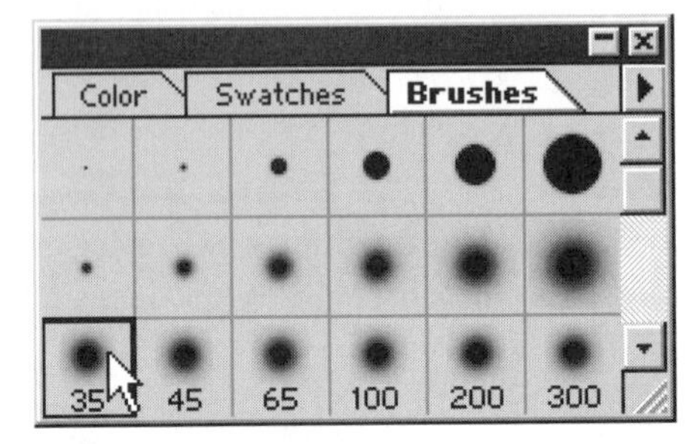

5. Set the color swatch on the toolbar to black.
6. Now go ahead and start to brush in some areas over the image. With the value of 10 percent in the pressure setting, you'll be able to gradually build up areas of darkness. Brush in areas of each block in a pattern similar to that shown in Figure 14.21.

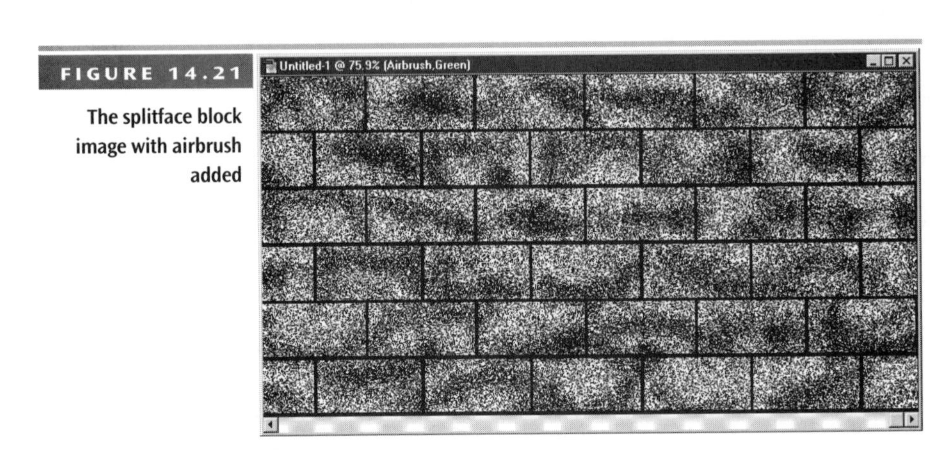

FIGURE 14.21

The splitface block image with airbrush added

If you get carried away and blacken an area too much, use the Switch Colors icon on the toolbar to switch the foreground from black to white, and airbrush over the black areas.

After applying the airbrush, you'll begin to get a sense of depth variation, even in the flat Photoshop image. Once you're satisfied with the airbrush, take a look at its effect in VIZ.

1. In Photoshop, choose File ➢ Save a Copy, then save the file again under the same name as before: `Splitface_bump.tif`.
2. Go to VIZ and return to Material Editor.
3. Scroll down to the Maps rollout and click the `Splitface_bump.tif` button.
4. In the Bitmap Parameters rollout, click Reload.
5. Click the Quick Render tool on the Render toolbar. The block wall now begins to look a bit more realistic with some variation in the surface.

The surface of the block wall now takes on a rough appearance created by the random airbrush areas added to the `Splitface_bump.tif` image.

Adding Color through Photoshop

Frequently, splitface block is used as a decorative element with color. You can add color through VIZ by adjusting the Ambient, Diffuse, and Specular color swatches in Material Editor. Again, this would result in a somewhat bland-looking surface. As you learned early on, you can apply a diffuse map to a material to add a pattern or color to a material. In this section you'll add some color by creating another bitmap file that contains color information.

Start by creating a new layer in Photoshop that will hold the color image.

1. Go back to Photoshop. In the Layers palette, click the arrow in the upper right corner and select New layer.
2. Enter the name **Color Pattern** for the layer name and click OK. Remember that new layers are transparent, so the image won't change.

Now create a color for the blocks.

1. Click the Foreground color swatch.

2. Set the Hue (H), Saturation (S), and Brightness (B) settings as shown in Figure 14.22. This will create a tan color.

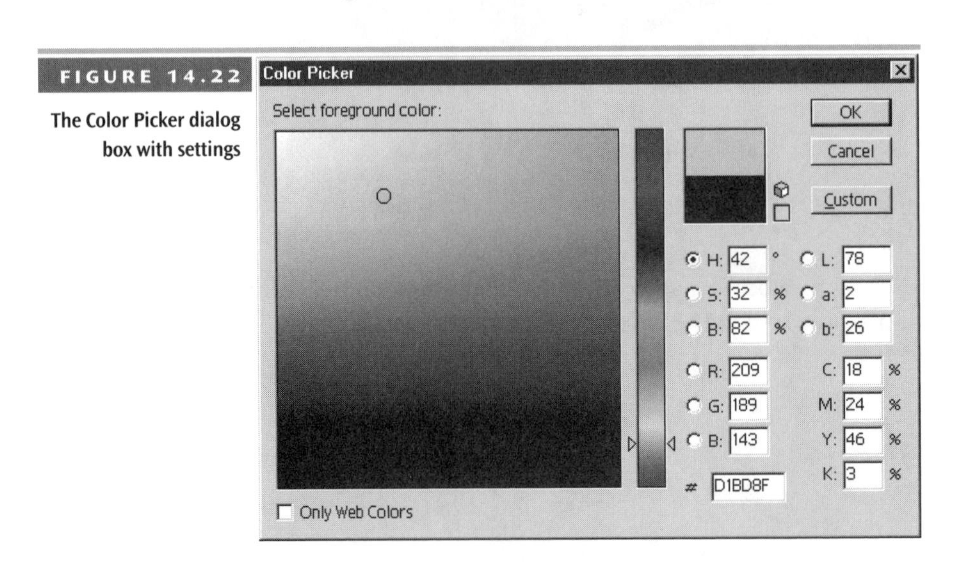

FIGURE 14.22

The Color Picker dialog box with settings

3. Click the Paint Bucket tool. Then, with the Color Pattern layer selected, click within the image. The color will fill the entire image.

Now add some noise to the color to give it a sense of texture.

1. Click Filter ➢ Noise ➢ Add Noise...
2. In the Add Noise dialog box, set the slider to 90.
3. Click Uniform for the Distribution group and make sure Monochromatic is not checked. Close the dialog box.

There's one more feature you need to add to the image. The mortar joint should be a darker color to set it off from the rest of the pattern.

1. Click Layer 1 in the Layer palette to make it active, then click the Layer Visibility button for the Color Pattern layer to temporarily turn it off.
2. Press Ctrl+A or choose Select ➢ All to select the entire layer.
3. Press Ctrl+C, then press Ctrl+V. This copies the layer to the clipboard, then pastes it back into the image. You now have a new layer called Layer 2, and it is the active layer.
4. In the layer Palette, click the Color Pattern Layer Visibility button to turn it back on. You see the tan color return to the image window.
5. In the layer palette, click and drag the Layer 2 label upward so that it is above the Color Pattern layer listing as shown in Figure 14.23.

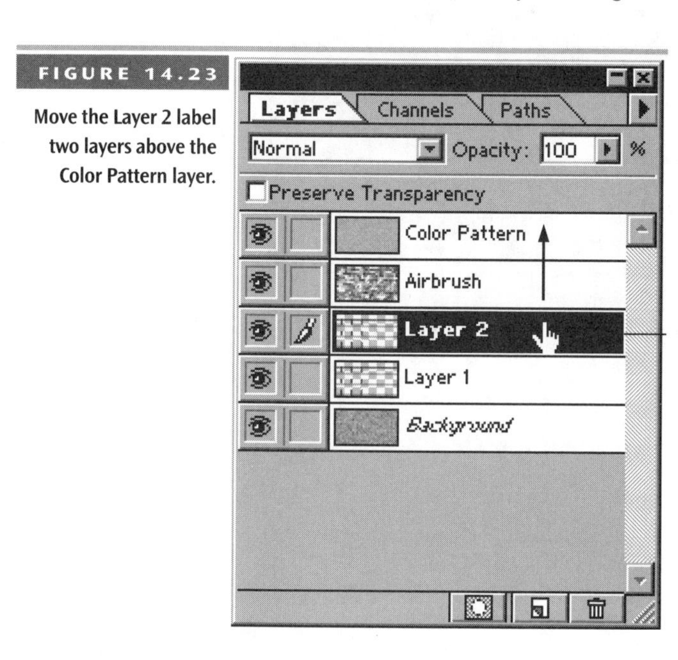

FIGURE 14.23

Move the Layer 2 label two layers above the Color Pattern layer.

When you see the dark bar appear above the Color Pattern listing, release the mouse button. The mortar joints appear in the image.

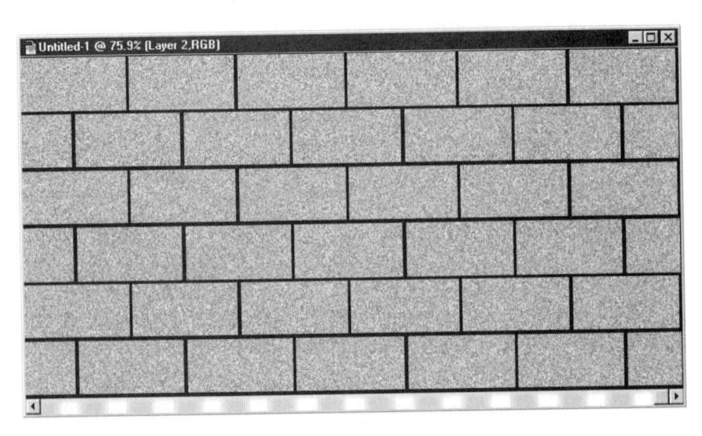

Last of all, let's give the mortar joint a dark brown color.

1. With Layer 2 selected in the Layer palette, click the Magic Wand tool.
2. Click the mortar joint in the image. The *crawling ant* selection displays around all of the mortar joints.

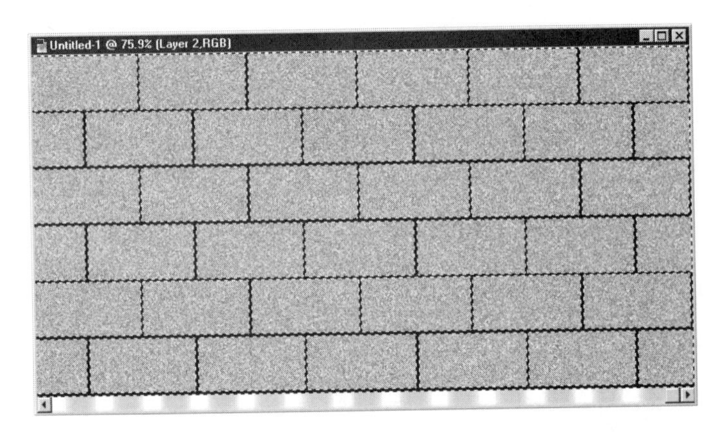

3. Click the Foreground color swatch on the toolbar. In the Color Picker dialog box, set the H, S, and B settings as shown in Figure 14.24.

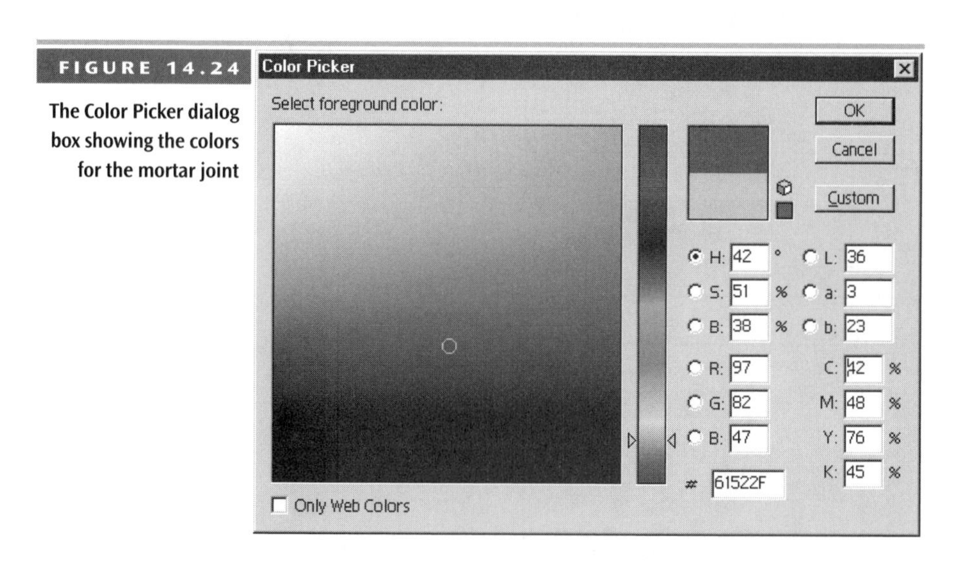

FIGURE 14.24

The Color Picker dialog box showing the colors for the mortar joint

4. Click OK to close the Color Picker dialog box, Zoom into an area showing the mortar joint, select the Paint bucket tool, then click the mortar joint. The new color fills the joint lines.
5. Zoom back out to the overall view of the image.
6. Click the Marquee tool, then click the image to remove the selection.

You've got the mortar joints and the block color ready for your diffuse map. As an added twist, let's change one row of blocks so that they do not display any color. This will create a block wall with one course of gray block.

1. First, make sure that Color Pattern layer is selected in the Layer Palette.

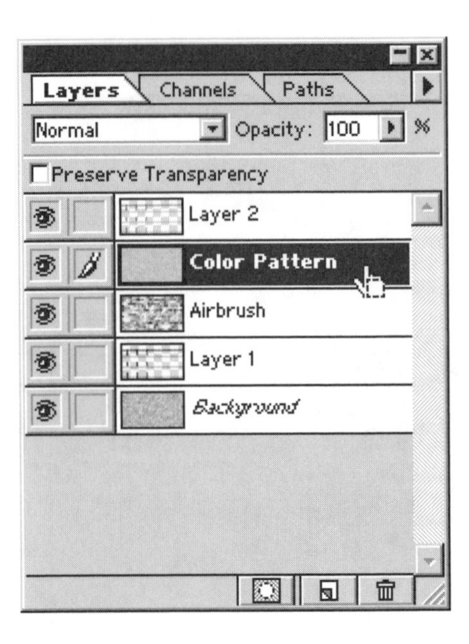

2. Click the Marquee tool.

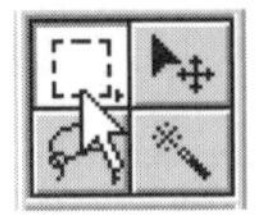

3. Click and drag a rectangular selection as shown in Figure 14.25.

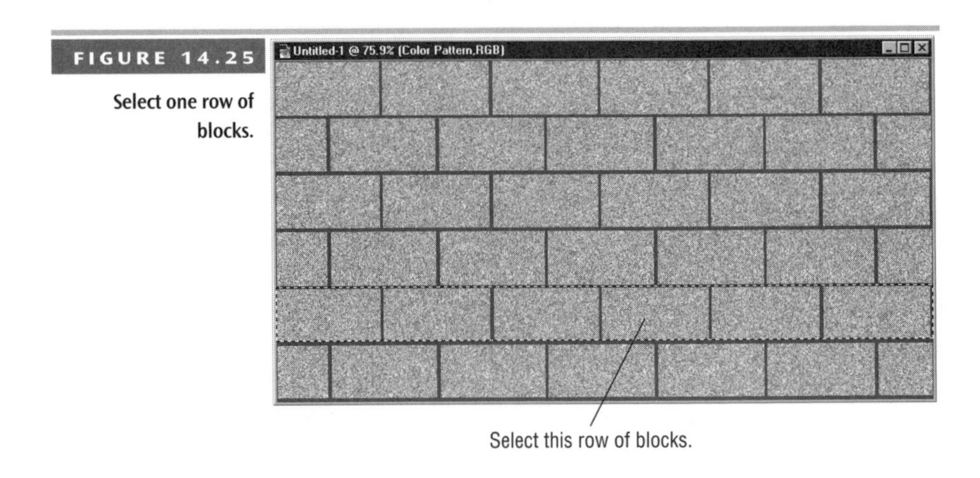

FIGURE 14.25

Select one row of blocks.

4. Press the Delete key to remove the selected area.
5. The layer underneath the Color Pattern Layer shows through, so you'll need to turn the lower layers off. Click the Layer visibility buttons for the Airbrush, Layer 1, and Background layers.

The final step is to save the image as a file for VIZ.

1. Choose File Save a Copy.
2. Save the file as a TIFF file with the name **Splitface_Dif**.

You're now ready to add the `Splitface_dif.tif` file to the material in VIZ. Before you do that, take a moment to review what you've got in Photoshop.

The file in Photoshop contains several layers that make up the components for both the bump and diffuse maps. You can selectively turn layers on and off to obtain the appropriate mix of layers for each type of map. You can save the file as a Photoshop .psd file for later editing in case you decide to make further changes to the `Splitface_Bump` and `Splitface_dif` files.

Now let's see how the addition of a Diffuse map will affect the block wall in VIZ.

1. Go to VIZ and click the Go To Parent button in Material Editor to go to the Maps rollout.
2. Click the Diffuse Color Map button, then in the Material/Map Browser, double-click Bitmap.
3. In the Select Bitmap Image file dialog box, locate and open the `Splitface_dif.tif` file.
4. Click the Quick Render tool on the Render toolbar. The image is rendered with some additional color.

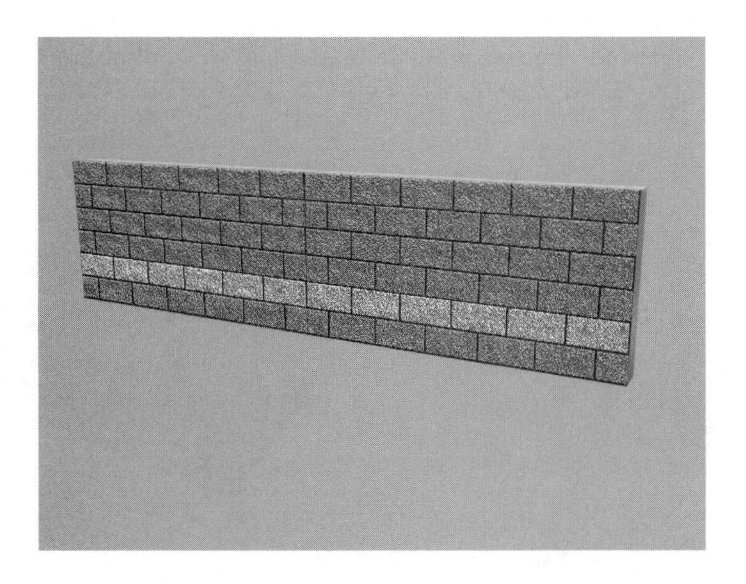

Now you can clearly see the mortar joints. In addition, you also see the band of gray block at the second row from the bottom. The color of the gray band can be controlled by adjusting the Ambient, Diffuse, and Specular color settings for the material, without affecting the rest of the block wall.

You can go on to make other changes to the `Splitface_dif.tif` image in Photoshop. You can add another color to the block course you deleted earlier, or you can modify the colors of all of the blocks. By keeping and editing bitmap information in Photoshop, you can keep parts of materials such as the blocks and mortar in the splitface block example aligned. You needn't limit the materials to bump and diffuse maps. Some fairly elaborate decorative architectural elements can be generated using Specular and reflection maps that are carefully aligned.

While you were shown how Photoshop can be used to create textures and colors for VIZ materials, you've also seen that the Windows environment lets you use the two programs simultaneously in an almost seamless way. By switching from Photoshop to VIZ and back, you can fine-tune a material's appearance in a VIZ rendering.

Modeling with Displacement Maps

You've seen how you can use a bump map to simulate a rough surface like the splitface block in the previous exercises or a rolling surface like the ground in the villa design. Another map option, called a displacement map, performs a function similar to that of bump maps, but instead of applying a texture, actually deforms geometry into new shapes. The effect is akin to a vacuum mold in which a flat surface is stretched over a form to create an object. In this case, the form is a bitmap where dark areas represent lower levels of a surface and light areas represent higher levels, in a way similar to bump maps. Figure 14.26 shows how a displacement map correlates with a grayscale image file.

FIGURE 14.26

A sample displacement mesh and the image from which it was created

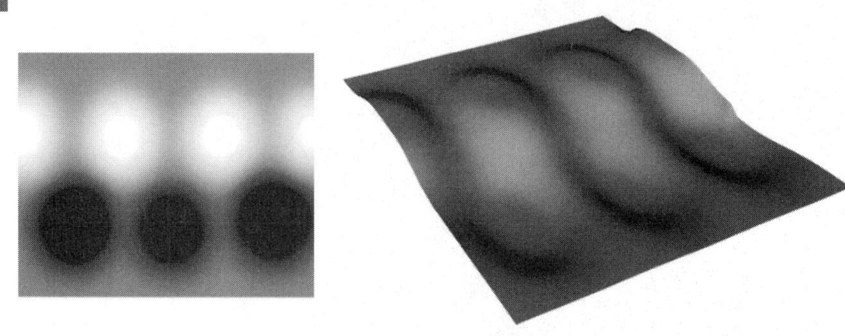

The image, called `Disp_dots.jpg`, was created in Photoshop by using the airbrush tool to create the dots. The background was first filled in with a gray tone, then the black and white dots were sprayed in using the airbrush tool. As you compare the image with the mesh, you can see that the black dots correspond to the dips in the mesh and the white dots correspond to the bumps. Since the dots are airbrushed with soft edges, they create a smooth transition from high to low in the resulting mesh.

There are two ways that you can create mesh forms with displacement maps. You can go through the Material Editor and create a material containing a displacement map, or you can use the Displace modifier to apply a bitmap directly to an object to deform it into a new shape.

Using the Displace Modifier

The Displace modifier is probably the easiest way to convert a bitmap into a deformed surface. In the following exercise, you'll use the Displace modifier to get a feel for how the process works. You'll create the object in Figure 14.26 by using the sample `Disp_dots.jpg` image file from the companion CD.

1. In VIZ, choose File ➢ Reset. At the warning message, go ahead and click No. You don't really need to keep the changes to the wall. Then at the second warning, click Yes to continue with the reset.
2. In the Create tab of the Command Panel, click Plane, then click and drag a plane that is roughly 125 by 100 as shown in Figure 14.27.

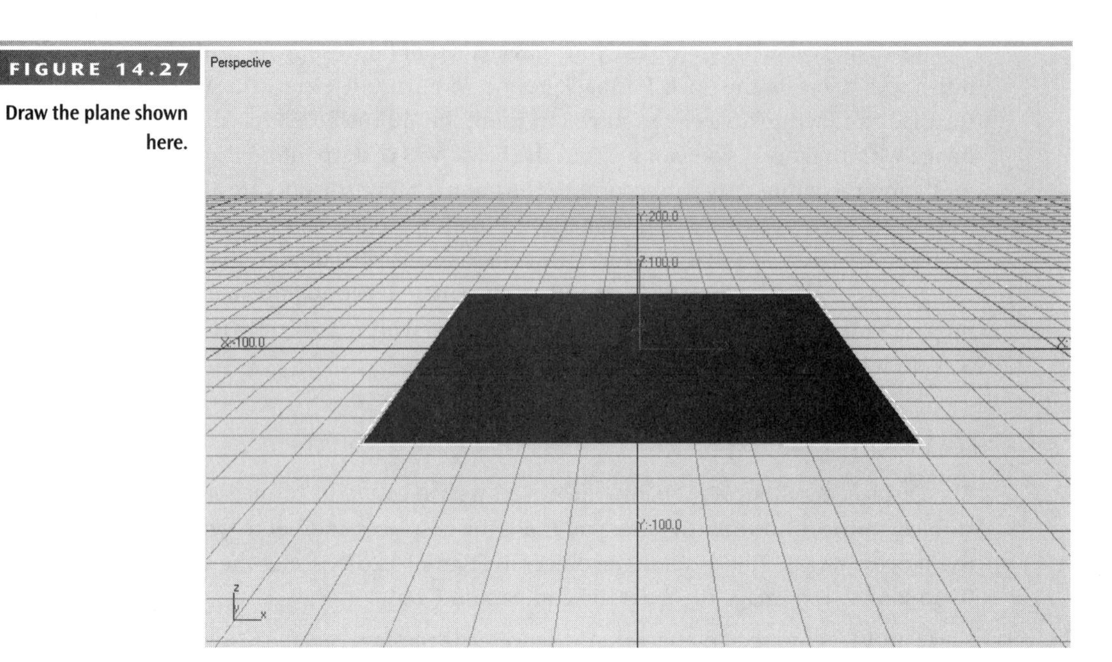

FIGURE 14.27

Draw the plane shown here.

3. Adjust the Length parameter to 125 and the Width parameter to 100. For now, leave the Length Segs and Width Segs at the default 4 value. You'll adjust these settings later.
4. Open Material Editor and assign the default material in the upperleft slot to the plane object. This is done to allow you to see the surface features of the plane a bit more clearly.

The Plane is perhaps the best type of geometry to use to demonstrate the effects of the Displace modifier, though you can use the Displace modifier on any NURBS surface, patch, or editable mesh.

Now let's go ahead and apply the bitmap from Photoshop.

1. Click the Modify tab, then select More… from the Modifiers rollout.
2. Select Displace from the Modifiers dialog box, then click OK.
3. Back in the Modify tab, click the Bitmap button labeled None in the Image group of the Parameters rollout.

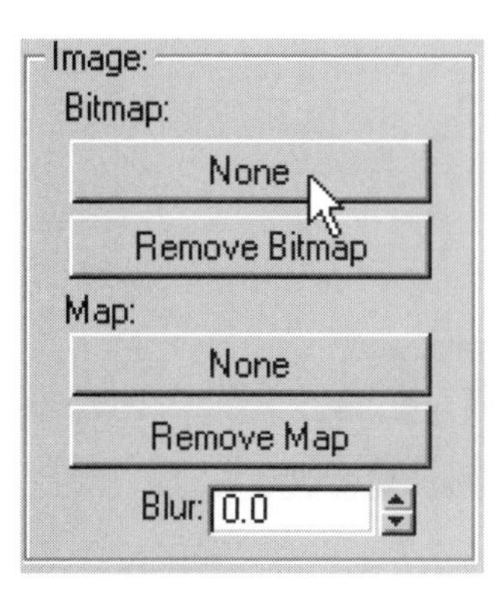

4. Locate and open the file called `Disp_dot.jpg` from the installed samples of the companion CD.
5. Go to the Displacement group and change the Strength setting to **12**. You'll notice that the plane starts to distort, though it doesn't look anything like the one in Figure 14.26.

You've applied the `Disp_dot.jpg` bitmap but have yet to get the results you might expect. The reason is that the mesh contains only a 4 by 4 array of segments. You'll need to increase the number of segments in the Plane before you begin to see the form of the bitmap.

1. To get a better idea of what's going on with the mesh, right-click the Perspective label in the upperleft corner of the viewport and select Wireframe.
2. Scroll up to the Modifier Stack rollout and select Plane from the drop-down list.

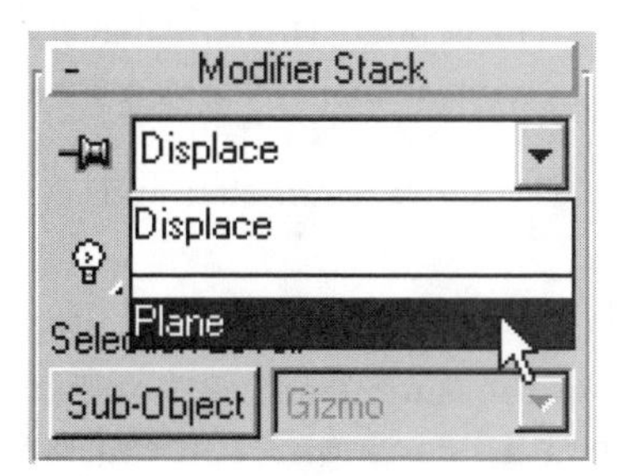

3. In the Parameters rollout, change the Length and Width Segs values to **40**. Now you can see the form more clearly.
4. Click the Quick Render tool to see the mesh as a rendered surface.

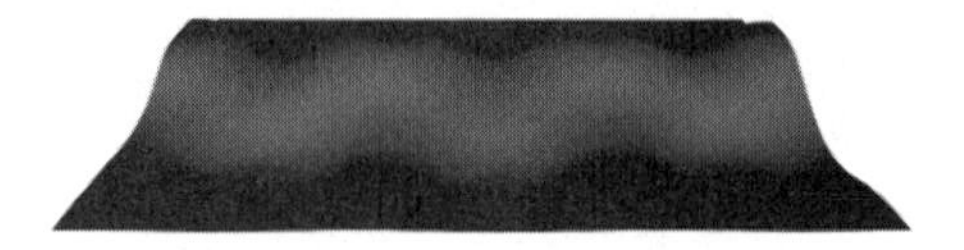

Now you can see that you can use a bitmap image to deform a surface. You don't have a lot of control over the details of the form, but you can create some interesting geometry using this method. For example, you can use a bitmap to create a free-form terrain.

NOTE **You may have noticed that the Image group of the Displace parameters offered two sets of options: Bitmap and Map. Although you used the Bitmap option, you could also have used the Map option to apply a bitmap. The Map option lets you use other types of maps such as the procedural maps offered in the Material/Map Browser. You can use both Bitmap and Map options to combine maps to displace a mesh.**

Now let's go back to the Displace Modifier parameters and see what some of the other options do.

1. In the Modifier Stack rollout, select Displace from the drop-down list.
2. In the displacement group of the Parameters, click and drag the Strength spinner upward to 30. The Strength value indicates the distance from the black to the white portions of the bitmap.
3. Click the Luminance Center check box and change the Center value to **.5**. The mesh drops down. The Luminance Center lets you control which shade of gray in the bitmap determines the center of the displacement.
4. Scroll down to the Map group and change the length value to **95** and the Width value to **75**. Now the surface really looks like a vacuum-formed plastic object with a flange.

5. Use the U Tile spinner to increase the U Tile value, and then do the same for the V Tile value. As you increase these values, the number of bumps across the width of the plane increases.

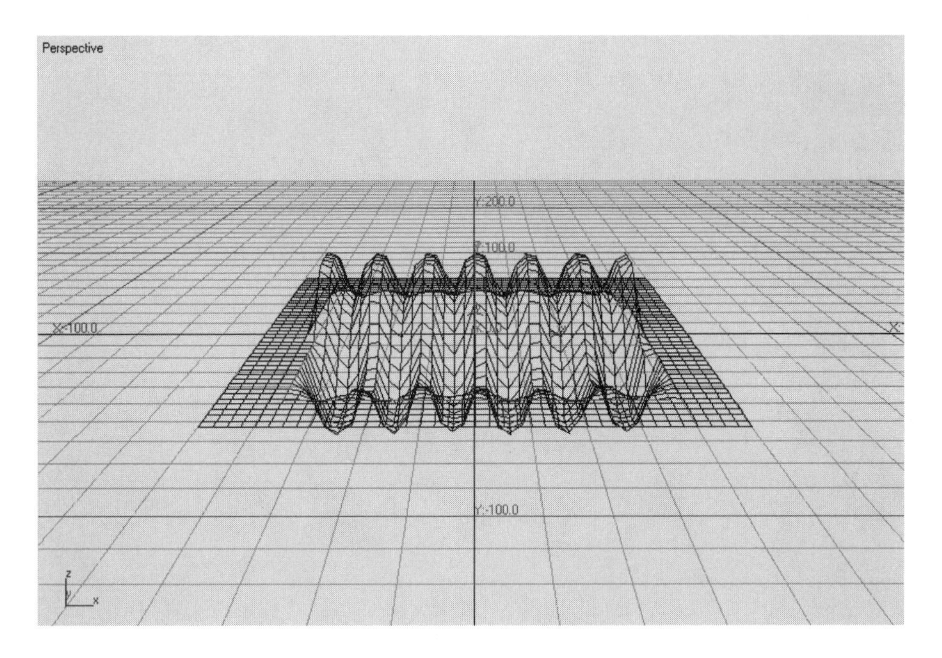

Notice that the Map group shows the Planar radio button selected. This is the default map gizmo setting. In fact, since the Displace modifier works with maps, the Map group mimics the Map settings for the UVW Map modifier.

You used the Displace modifier on a plane geometry object, though you can use it on any NURBS surface, patch, or editable mesh. Once you've finished working with the object, you can collapse its stack using the Edit Stack button in the Modifier stack. By doing so, you will help conserve memory and help improve VIZ's performance. You can then start to edit the mesh by going to the sub-object level.

Using Material Editor to Create Displaced Geometry

If you want to apply a displacement map to an object other than a NURBS surface, patch, or editable mesh, you can use the Displace Map option in Material Editor. This option works in conjunction with the Displacement Approximation modifier to perform the same function as the Displace modifier, but on a wider range of objects. For example,you can form a decorative feature on a building or create signage using the combination of Displace, Opacity, and Diffuse maps in Material Editor and apply the resulting material to a cylinder or other geometry.

In this section, you'll create a fictitious concrete landscaping bench using an image file to create the details of the geometry (see Figure 14.28).

FIGURE 14.28

A concrete bench

The image file was created entirely in Photoshop using the line tool for the top and bottom bars and the Text tool to create the word *Brilliant*. This could really be anything from a scanned photograph to an imported AutoCAD line drawing. The point is that it is a bitmap image in which the dark areas represent low surfaces and light areas represent high surfaces.

Let's get started with the bench by creating the basic geometry.

1. Choose File ➢ Reset to reset VIZ.
2. Make sure the Geometry button is selected in the Create tab of the Command Panel, then click Cylinder.
3. Click and drag from the origin of the Perspective view and give the cylinder a radius of 30 inches. Make the height 24 inches.
4. Click the Modify Tab in the Command Panel and click the UVW Map Modifier button.
5. Scroll down the Parameters rollout and click the Cylindrical Mapping radio button.
6. If the Map Gizmo does not conform to the shape of the cylinder, click the Fit button in the Alignment group.

With the UVW Map modifier added and set to Cylindrical, any material maps applied to the cylinder will appear around the perimeter. The next step is to create a material that uses a displacement map.

1. Open the Material Editor dialog box.
2. With the default slot selected, scroll down and click the Maps rollout to open it.
3. Click the Displacement Map button labeled *None*.
4. In the Material/Map Browser, double-click the Bitmap listing.
5. In the Select Bitmap Image File dialog box, locate and open the file named `Displace_sample.jpg` from the companion CD. You'll see the sample slot image distort into something unrecognizable. Don't worry about it right now. You'll see the results of the displacement map more clearly a bit later.
6. Click the Assign Material to Selection button to assign the material to the cylinder.
7. Go ahead and do a quick rendering to see the results.

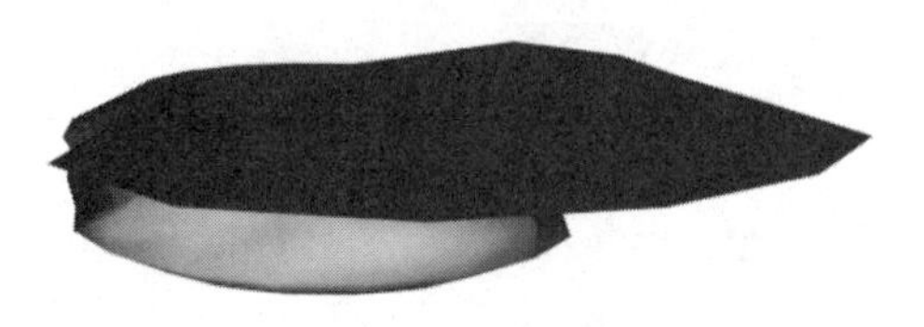

Your rendering doesn't really look anything at all like the `Displace_sample.jpg` image. You need to add to the cylinder a modifier that gives you some control over the way the displacement map affects the cylinder.

1. Scroll up to the Modifier rollout in the Command Panel, then click the More button.
2. In the Modifiers dialog box, select Displacement Approx., then click OK.
3. Render the image again. This time you begin to see more clearly the effects of the displacement map.

The Displacement Approx. modifier is needed to apply the displacement map correctly to the object. There are still a few changes that need to be made, however. The amount of displacement is too great, and a single version of the map wraps completely around the cylinder. You want to reduce the strength of the displacement and have the map repeat four times around the perimeter so it is readable.

The following steps will increase the number of times the displacement map displays around the cylinder.

1. Choose UVW Mapping in the Modifier Stack drop-down list.

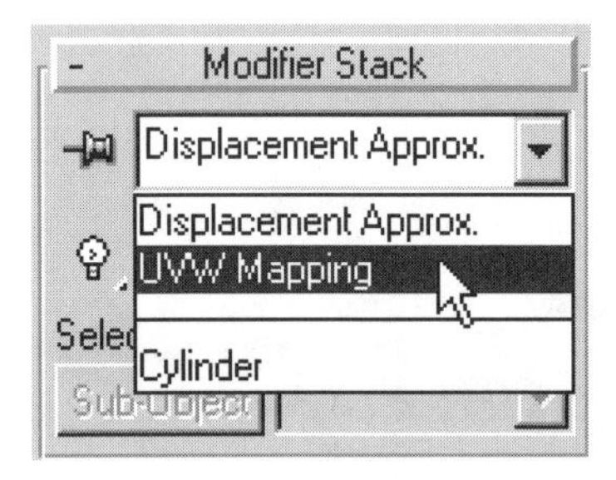

This brings up the UVW Mapping parameters.

2. Scroll down to the U Tile setting in the Mapping group of the Parameters and change the U Tile setting to **4**. Remember the U setting is similar to the X coordinate. By setting U Tile to 4 you cause the map to repeat 4 times around the perimeter of the cylinder.
3. Render the design again. The rendering regresses to an unrecognizable form.

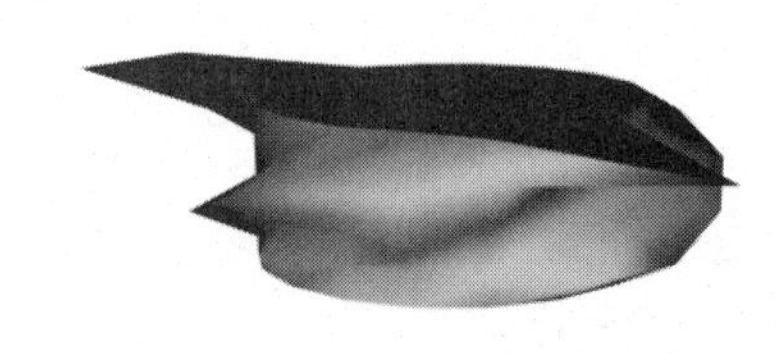

By increasing the number of times the map is repeated over the surface, you have increased the complexity of the displacement map in relation to the cylinder surface. You may recall that, in an earlier exercise for the Displace modifier, you needed to increase the number of segments in the mesh surface in order to have the displacement map take effect. You need to do the same in this situation. You need to increase the number of segments on the cylinder wall to give the displacement map enough segments to work with.

You can go back to the Cylinder object level to increase the number of segments for the side of the cylinder.

1. First right-click the Perspective label in the upper left corner of the viewport and select Wireframe. This will allow you to see the cylinder segments more clearly.
2. In the Modifier Stack drop-down list, choose Cylinder.

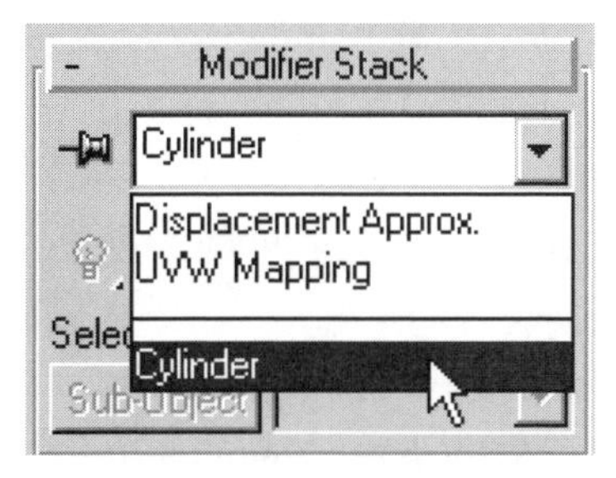

3. In the Parameters rollout, change the Height Segments value to **12** and the Sides value to **72**. The sides of the cylinder will show segments that are close to being square.

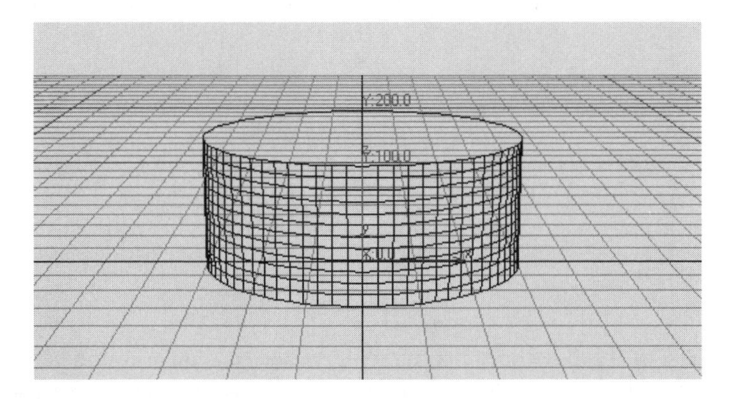

4. Click the Quick Render tool again. Now you can see the map clearly.

The depth of the displace map shows you that it isn't just a bump map. When the cylinder is rendered, VIZ converts the flat cylinder wall into a displaced mesh that will cast shadows and stand up to close-up views, even though the cylinder remains a plain cylinder in the Design viewports.

Now let's see how to reduce the depth of the displacement to something a bit more reasonable. You'll also add some noise to the Bump map setting to give the object a granite look.

1. Open Material Editor; then go to the Maps rollout.
2. In the Maps rollout, change the Amount setting for the Displacement map to **20**.
3. Click the Bump Map button labeled *None*.
4. In the Material Map Browser, select Noise and click OK.
5. Back in Material Editor, change the Size parameter in the Noise Parameter rollout to **0.1** and change the Blur setting in the Coordinate group to **0.01**.
6. Click the Go to Parent button on the Material Editor toolbar, then adjust the Bump map setting to **100**.
7. Go ahead and create another quick rendering of the object.

You now have a pretty convincing model of a fairly complex form, and you created it without having to do a lot of editing. The displacement map does take a toll on rendering time, but in some situations it can save you time in building your model.

Converting a Displacement Map into an Editable Mesh

You may find yourself in a situation where you need to edit an object that you've formed using a displacement map like the one in the previous section. Unfortunately, displacement maps only take effect when you render the image. Meanwhile, the object to which the displacement map is applied remains in its basic form in the VIZ viewport. In the case of your exercise example, the cylinder remains a cylinder and does not become a displaced mesh.

There are two tools that you can apply to gain access to the mesh that is created using a displacement map. The first is a global modifier that displays the mesh in the viewports so you don't have to wait until the design is rendered to see the result of the displacement map. Try the following to see the effects of the Displace Mesh global modifier:

1. Make sure the cylinder is selected, and then in the modify tab of the Command Panel, click the More... button.
2. In the Modifiers dialog box, select *Displace Mesh option, then click OK. You'll have to wait a moment while VIZ converts the viewport display of the cylinder to show the actual mesh of the displacement map. When VIZ is done, you'll see the cylinder with the displacement map in mesh form. Figure 14.29 shows a close-up view of the cylinder with the *Displace Mesh modifier active.

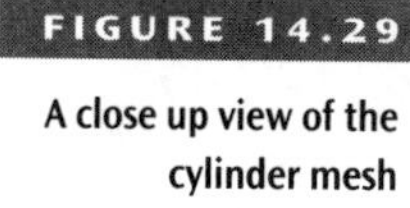
FIGURE 14.29

A close up view of the cylinder mesh

You can now see why the last rendering took a bit more time. With the displacement map added, the mesh is quite dense and complex. You can reduce the complexity of the mesh by reducing the number of segments in the cylinder. You can also select the Low settings for the Subdivision Presets under the Displacement Approx. modifier.

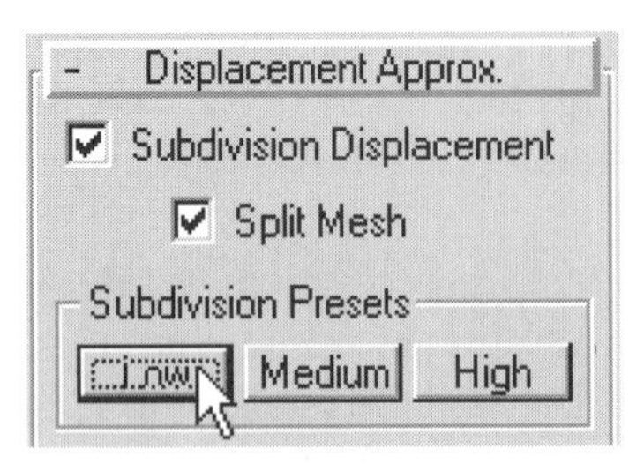

Using a low setting will reduce the smoothness of the mesh and give it a rough appearance, so you may want to use the Low setting for meshes that will only be viewed from a distance.

Text in VIZ

In this example, text was used to show off the capabilities of the Displacement map feature, but in most cases you'll want to create text using the Text Shape object found in the set of Spline Shape options of the Create tab. A text shape acts just like any other shape in that it can be extruded to form 3D objects. You can also apply modifiers to text shapes. One modifier that is especially useful with text shapes is the Bevel modifier (see Bevel in Appendix B).

You can apply any font that is available in the Windows font library to Text Shapes. Text can also be edited and its parameters changed, as long as it is not collapsed into editable meshes or editable spline. For example, you can create a text shape that spells out *Brilliant,* extrude it, apply a material to it, then later change the text to read *absolutely brilliant.* Through the Text Shape's parameters, you also have control over fonts, justification, size, kerning, leading, underlining, and Italics.

Creating an Editable Mesh from a Displacement Map

The *Displace Mesh modifier allows you to see the displacement map so that you can use the Transform tools to adjust the size and orientation of the object within the design. It doesn't let you edit the object's surface, however. If you need to make changes on a sub-object level, you can create a special type of clone of the object that is a full mesh representation of the object with the displacement map. You can then use the clone to make further changes and hide or delete the original object.

To create this copy, use the Snapshot dialog box as demonstrated in the following exercise.

1. Choose Modify ➢ Snapshot.
2. In the Snapshot dialog box, make sure the Single radio button is selected in the Snapshot group and the Mesh Clone Method is selected, then click OK.

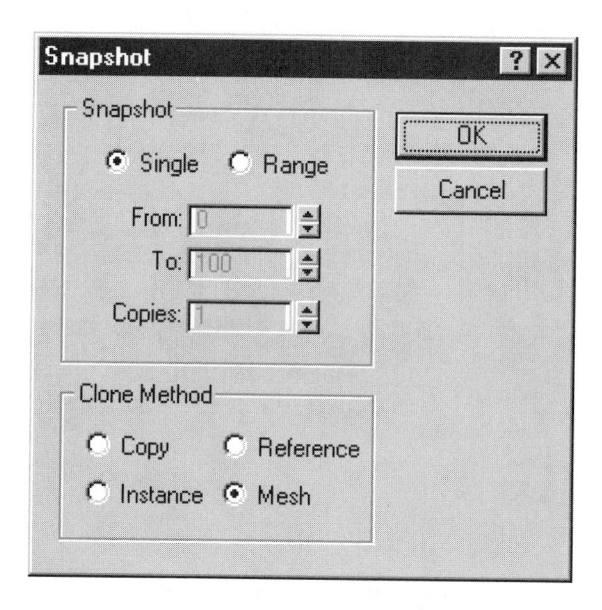

3. Use the Select and Move tool to move the cylinder to the left so you can get a clear view of the new displacement mesh. You'll experience some lag time between the time you move the cylinder and when the cylinder actually moves on the screen.
4. Remove the *Displace Mesh modifier from the cylinder's modifier stack by selecting Displace Mesh from the Modifier Stack and clicking the trash can button. You may have noticed that the *Displace Mesh modifier slows VIZ's reaction to your input, so deleting it will help save some time. When the *Displace Mesh modifier is removed, you see the original cylinder revert to its former shape.

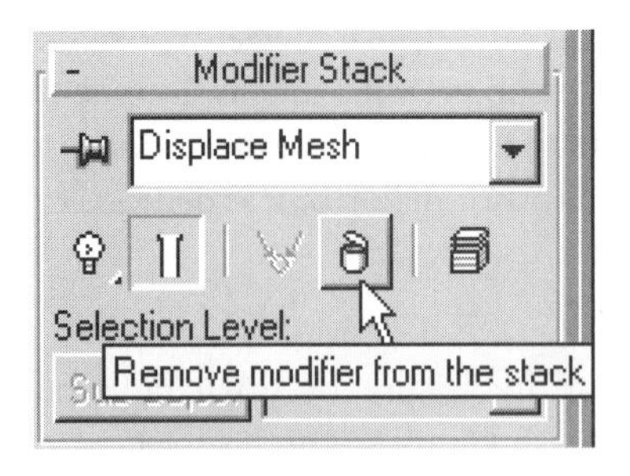

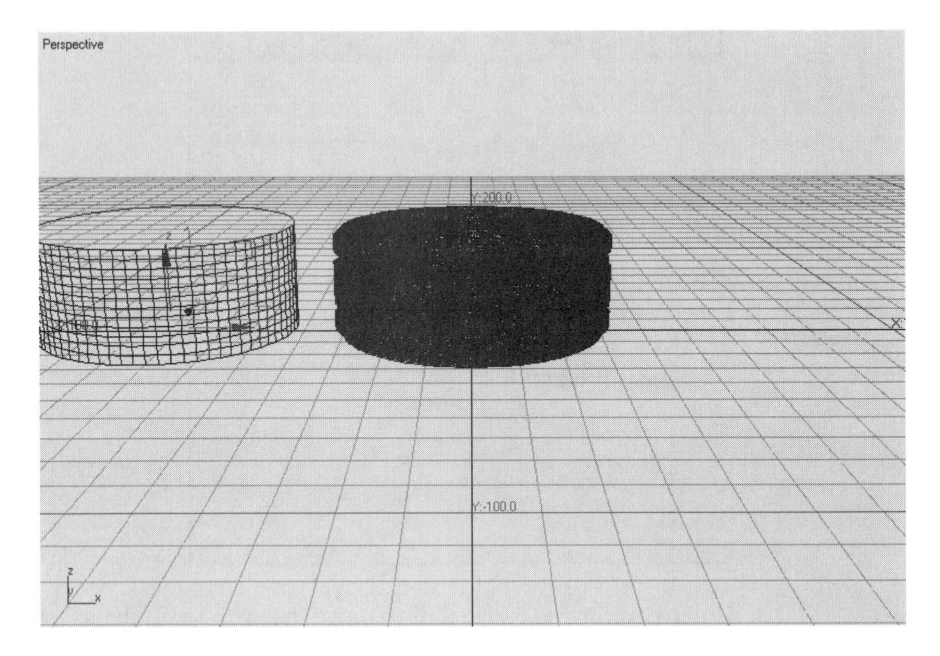

5. Render the view of the cloned cylinder. You see that it is an exact copy of the original cylinder, but that the copy is an editable mesh rather than a cylinder with several modifiers attached.

TIP **You can think of the Snapshot dialog box as a tool to *collapse* a displacement map object into an editable mesh.**

As you've seen in these exercises, the displacement modifiers require the surface to have at least enough segments to accommodate the form. This means that with complex forms, you'll have to create a mesh with lots of segments, which also means that you can quickly expand your file size using the Displacement modifier. For this reason, you may want to restrict the use of this modifier to those types of geometry that can take the best advantage of its features.

Cloning with Snapshot

The Snapshot dialog box is mainly intended to clone an animated object at a particular point in time. For example, suppose you have an animation of an object deforming over time and you want to create a clone of the object at a specific point in the deformation. Snapshot is designed to perform this function. As its name indicates, Snapshot takes a *snapshot* of an object at a particular moment in time. The clone created by Snapshot does not inherit the animated motion or deformation of the source object.

In architectural applications, you may rarely, if ever, use Snapshot to clone an animated object, but you may use it more often as a tool to convert a displacement map into an editable mesh as shown in these examples.

Summary

This chapter offered a glimpse into some of the ways bitmap images can be used to enhance your VIZ designs. You started out by exploring the more traditional functions of Photoshop for editing images. Then in the latter part of the chapter, you saw how images created in Photoshop can be used to actually form mesh objects.

Image-editing programs such as Photoshop add so much functionality to VIZ that, as you begin to use VIZ in earnest, you feel somewhat crippled if you don't have access to such a program. The importance of having an image-editing program cannot be overstressed.

You may want to take some time to explore some of the ways that you can use an image-editing program for your own work. Perhaps you can make use of the Displace modifier to create an otherwise difficult architectural detail, or there may be a part of an object that is particularly troublesome to model. that the displacement map tools can help create. If you prefer using a program other than Photoshop, you may want to examine ways to use your favorite image-editing program to create bump and displacement maps. A judicious use of these tools can go a long way toward simplifying your design creation in VIZ.

chapter 15

COMBINING PHOTOGRAPHS WITH VIZ DESIGNS

FEATURING

- *Mesh Editing with a Photograph*
- *Adding Detail with Photographs*
- *Matching your Design to a Background Image*

Combining Photographs with VIZ Designs

Photography plays a big role in the design process, so it shouldn't be a big surprise that photographs are also an important part of your work with VIZ. Architects use photographs to study proposed building sites and to record the progress of a construction project. Photographs are also used to record design details that need to be reproduced or restored.

In Chapter 14, you explored the relationship between image editing programs and VIZ. You saw how image editing programs can be an integral part of your model creation. In this chapter, you'll continue that exploration by looking at how photographs play a role in your work with VIZ.

In the first part of this chapter, you'll learn how you can simulate detail in a model of a car by using modified photographs. You'll use a combination of mesh modeling and a series of photographs of a car to create a car that you can use as an entourage element in your designs. This will give you a chance to try out some new mesh modeling tools and will also allow you to see how photos can help simplify the creation of certain types of objects.

In the second part of the chapter, you'll learn how to match a building to a background photograph of the building site. This process gives you a chance to see what a building will look like when it is completed in its proposed location. Matching a VIZ design to a photographic background is also an essential presentation tool that is often required as a part of a design review submission.

Mesh Editing with a Photograph

In most of your work with VIZ, you'll be using the geometry and shape tools you learned about in the first four chapters of this book, but there will be the occasional odd form that will require some new and different modeling methods. In this section, you'll take a tour of mesh modeling by creating a car in VIZ. The car won't be perfect, but it will give you a chance to explore a few methods that you haven't yet learned about in VIZ. You can use the car as part of your entourage for outdoor renderings, and hopefully, with the skills you learn here, you'll be able to create other cars and design elements as well.

Establishing the Basic Form

In Chapter 4 you used a scanned image of a floor plan sketch as the basis of a 3D model. In this section, you'll create a car using a photograph as an aid. You'll start with a Left viewport side view of the car, which you'll use as a template to help mold a mesh into the shape of a car.

1. Reset VIZ, then click the Min/Max Viewport toggle to get a view of all four viewports.
2. In the Create tab of the Command Panel, click the Box tool. Then in the Top viewport, create a box that is 160 inches in length by 67 inches wide by 28 inches high. You can roughly place the box in the Top viewport, then adjust the Length, Width, and Height parameters in the Command Panel.
3. Set the Length Segs parameter to **16**, the Width Segs to **3** and the Height Segs to **5**.
4. Click the Zoom Extents All tool to fill the viewports with the box.
5. Right-click the Left viewport, then click the Min/Max toggle tool to enlarge it.

Now you're ready to bring the image into the file. You'll place the image of the car in the Left viewport as an aid to help mold the car's profile. The image won't appear to be the proper size at first, so you'll have to do some adjusting once the image is brought in.

1. Click View ➢ Viewport Image ➢ Select...
2. In the top of the Viewport Image dialog box, click Files.

3. In the Select Background Image dialog box, locate and open the `Mazdaside.tif` file. This is a file from the companion CD.
4. In the Aspect Ratio group of the Viewport Image dialog box, click Match Bitmap; then click OK. The car appears in the viewport.

NOTE All of the photographs in this chapter were taken with a Kodak 120 digital camera. Compared to what is available now, the Kodak 120 is a bit outdated, yet it is capable of taking some good snapshots. Scanned photographs also work just as well, though a digital camera makes quick work of capturing images and bringing them to your computer.

The next step is to adjust the view magnification so that the box is the same width as the image of the car.

1. Use the Zoom and Pan tools to adjust the view so that the length of the box matches the length of the car in the viewport, as shown in Figure 15.1. You don't want to change the size of the box since it's already at the appropriate size for the car, so you adjust the view to fit the background.

FIGURE 15.1

Adjust the view so that the box displays at the same length as the car.

2. Once you've got the length matched up with the image, choose View ➢ Viewport Image ➢ Select…

3. In the Viewport Image dialog box, click the Lock Zoom/Pan option, then click OK.

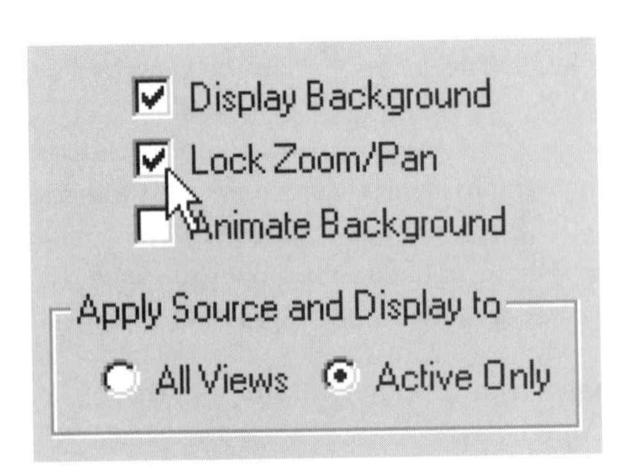

The image will shift out of view.

4. Use the Pan tool to move the image back into the center of the viewport.
5. Use the Move tool to move the box back over the car, as shown in Figure 15.1.

The Mazda has a slight taper from back to front, so you'll add a taper to the box before you start to form the box to the profile.

1. Click the Modify tab, then click the More button in the Modifiers rollout.
2. Select Taper, then click OK.
3. In the Taper Axis group, click Y for the Primary setting and click Z for the Effect setting.
4. Adjust the Amount parameter in the Taper group to **24**.
5. Select Box from the Modifier Stack drop-down list to gain access to the Box parameters.
6. Adjust the Height parameter down to about **0.24**. The box should look similar to Figure 15.2, with the bottom aligned with the image and the top just a bit below the side windows.

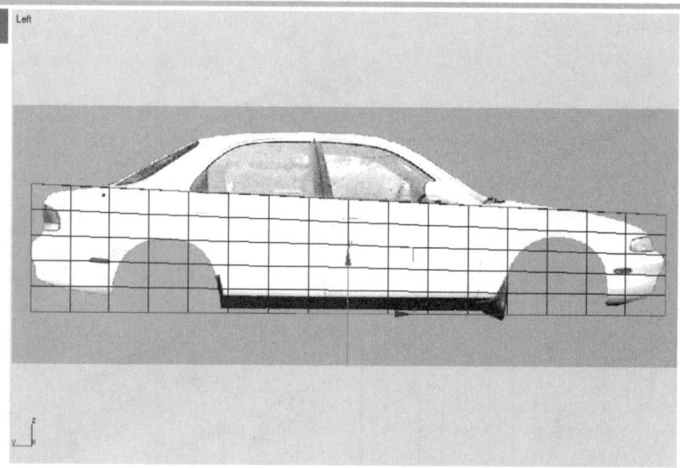

FIGURE 15.2

The box with the Taper modifier and the background so far

You were asked to set the vertical segments to **5** so you would have enough vertices to work with in order to mold the form of the car. The next step is to collapse the stack to a mesh so that you can begin to edit the mesh to shape the box to the form of the car.

1. Click the Edit Stack tool in the Modifier Stack.
2. In the Edit Modifier Stack dialog box, click Collapse All, then click OK at the Warning message.
3. Click OK to close the Edit Modifier Stack dialog box.

With the stack collapsed, you no longer have access to the box parameters, but you can still edit the box on the sub-object level.

WARNING Remember that collapsing a stack is an irreversible process. If you want to experiment, you can use the Temporary Buffer to save the state of your design before applying the Collapse All option in step 2. You may also use the Undo option to *Un-collapse* the stack as long as you haven't applied too many changes to the design since Collapse All was applied.

Moving Vertices

You can now begin to edit the vertices of the box. As you adjust the shape of the box in the following exercise, you'll be selecting and moving vertices. You'll be selecting vertices in the Left viewport using a rectangular selection region. This selection region allows you to select several vertices at once across the width of the box, as shown in Figure 15.3

FIGURE 15.3

Selecting a set of four vertices in the Left viewport actually selects eight vertices across the width of the box.

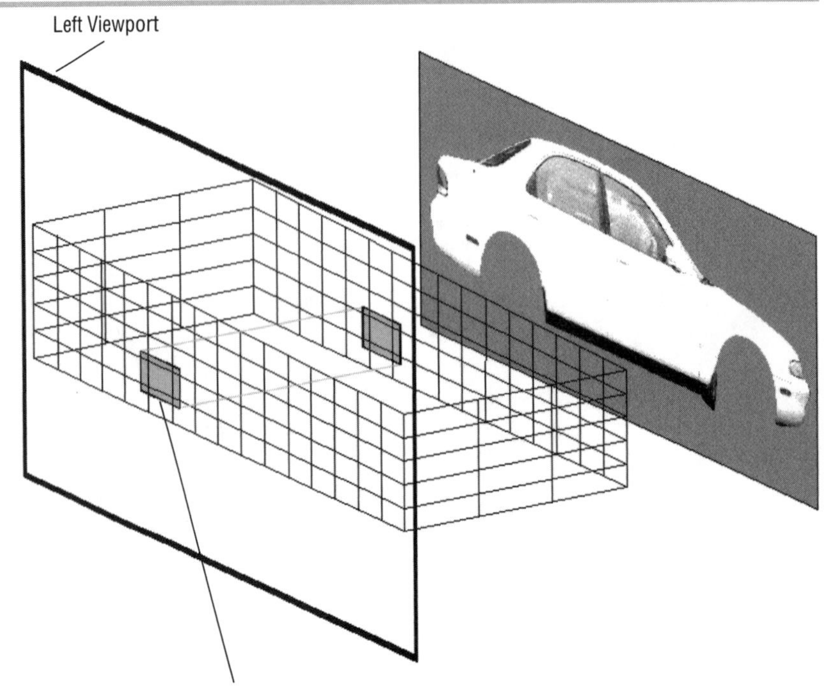

1. Click the Vertex button in the Selection rollout of the Command Panel and make sure that the Ignore Backfacing option is not on.

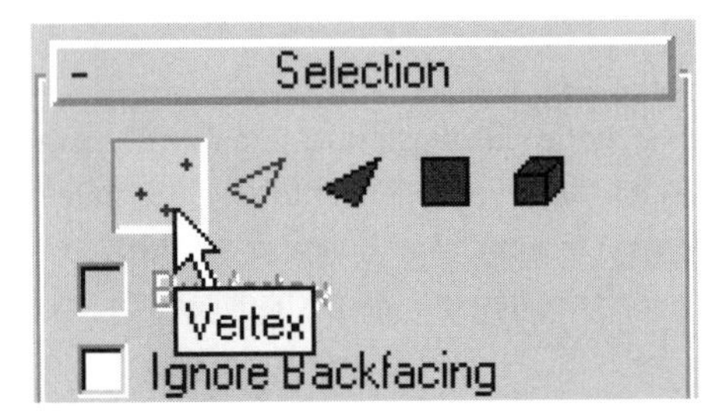

2. Make sure the Rectangular Selection Region is selected on the standard toolbar.

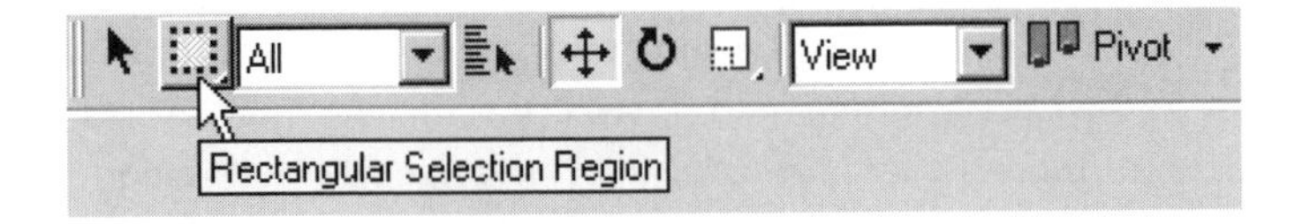

3. Click the Select and Move tool and place a selection region around the area shown in Figure 15.4.

FIGURE 15.4

Select this region.

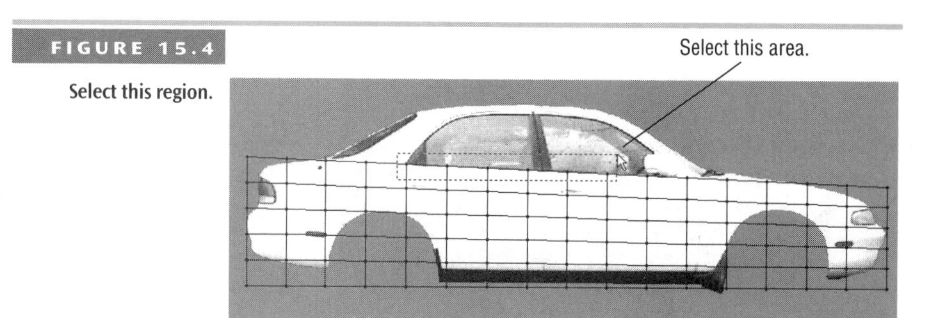

4. Click and drag the selected vertices upward so that your view looks similar to Figure 15.5.

FIGURE 15.5

Move the vertices upward.

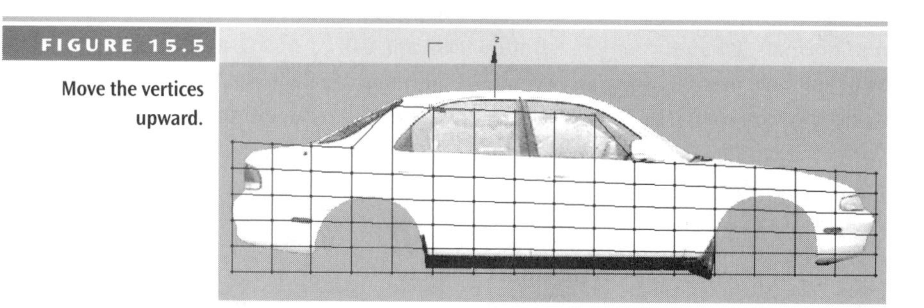

5. Now adjust the top row of vertices individually so that the top of the box follows the profile of the car as shown in Figure 15.6. You want to hold the vertices slightly below the very edge of the profile of the car since the car bulges outward toward its center.

FIGURE 15.6

Adjust the top vertices as shown here.

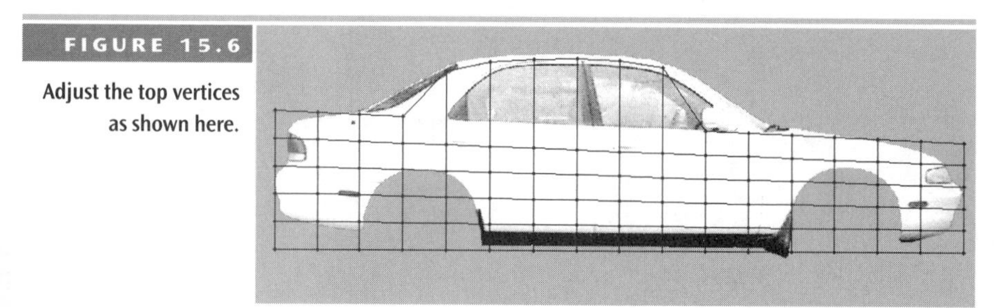

6. Continue to adjust the profile around the front, back, and bottom of the car. Also adjust the vertices on the side of the car near the front and back. Use Figure 15.7 as a guide in adjusting these areas.

FIGURE 15.7

Adjust the vertices to follow the outline of the front, back, and bottom of the car.

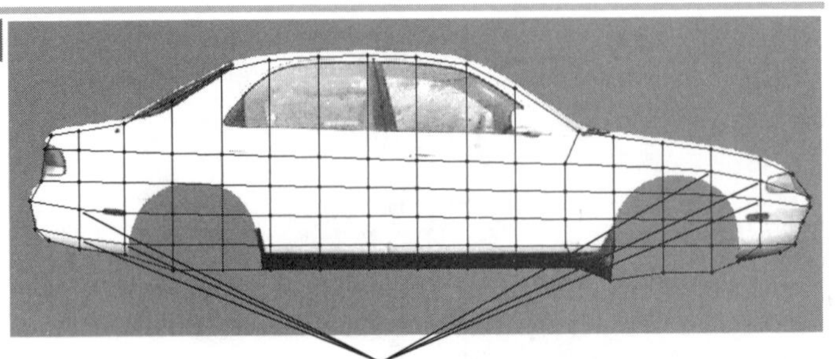

Adjust these vertices on the side of the car along with the profile.

TIP In step 1, you were directed to make sure that the Ignore Backfacing option was turned off. This option, which is off by default, controls sub-object selections based on the direction of normals. When turned on, Ignore Backfacing will cause VIZ to ignore sub-objects whose surface normals point away from the view and are invisible. When off, VIZ selects everything. You want it on in these exercises to affect both sides of the box.

Adding Curvature

The next step is to adjust the vertices through the middle of the car to create a slight bulge. Although the bulge you create is really made up of flat polygons, you'll use VIZ's smoothing tools to simulate a smooth, curved surface.

1. Press **T** to switch to the Top viewport. By pressing **T**, you can bypass using the Min/Max toggle to jump to a different, enlarged viewport view.
2. Select the vertices in the middle of the box, avoiding the vertices at the very top and bottom of the box, as shown in Figure 15.8.

FIGURE 15.8

Select the vertices shown here.

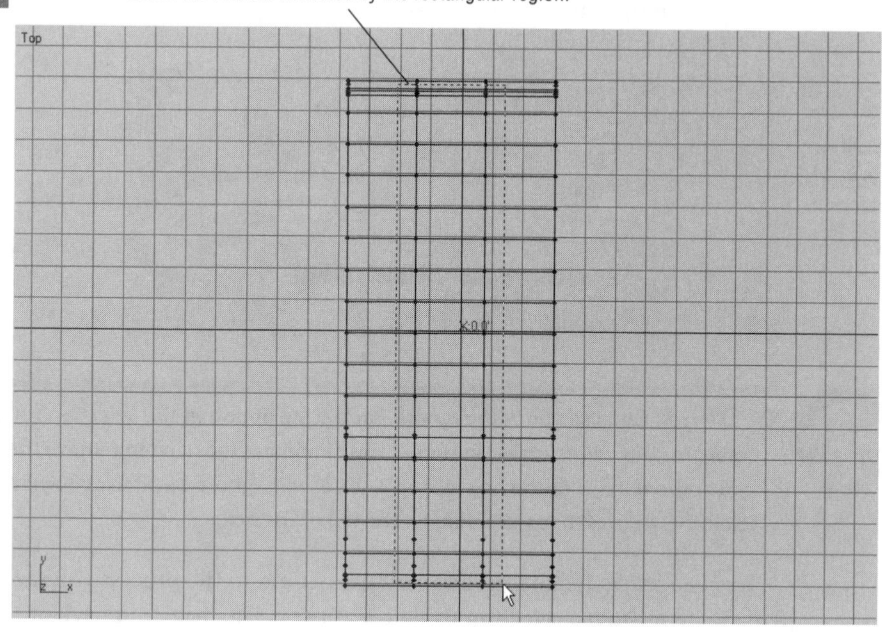
Select the vertices indicated by the rectangular region.
Top

3. Click **L** to return to the Left viewport.
4. Hold down the Alt key and select a region shown at the bottom of the Box as shown in Figure 15.9.

FIGURE 15.9

Select this region while holding down the Alt key.

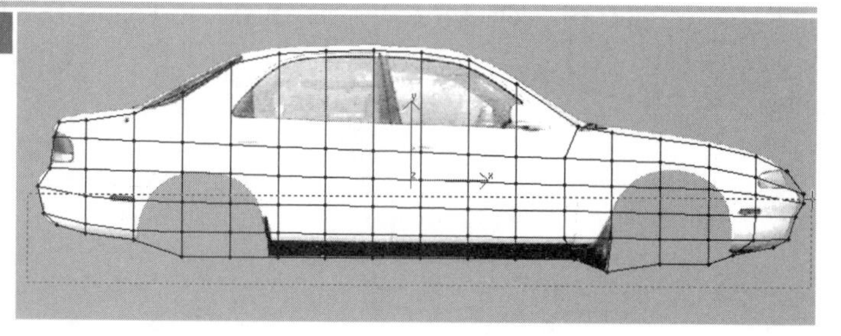

Notice that while you hold down the Alt key, the cursor shows a minus sign. This tells you that you are removing items from a selection. In this case, you are removing the vertices at the bottom of the box from the selection. Since you originally selected the vertices from the Top viewport, your selection included a set of vertices from both the bottom and the top of the box. You only want to edit the top vertices.

5. Now go ahead and move the vertices upward to match the profile of the car, as shown in Figure 15.10.

FIGURE 15.10

Move the middle vertices upward to match the profile of the car.

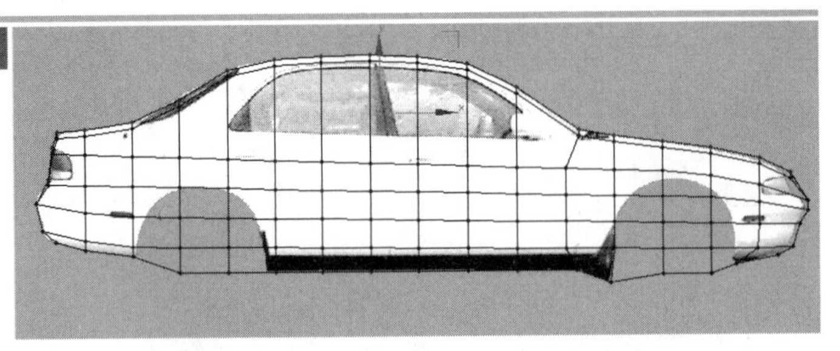

TIP You can also check the Ignore Backfacing option in the Selection rollout in step 1 before making the selection in step 2. This eliminates the need to remove the vertex selection at the bottom of the box in step 4 since, with Ignore Backfacing turned on, VIZ only select the vertices that are visible on the top of the box.

You've added a bulge to the top of the car, and in the process you saw how you can remove items from a selection using the Alt key. The front and back of the car also bulge outward. Do the following to add a bulge to the front first.

1. Press **T** again to go to the Top viewport.
2. Use the Region Zoom tool to enlarge the front of the box as shown in Figure 15.11.
3. Using a region selection, select the vertices shown in Figure 15.11; then move them downward.

FIGURE 15.11

Move these vertices downward.

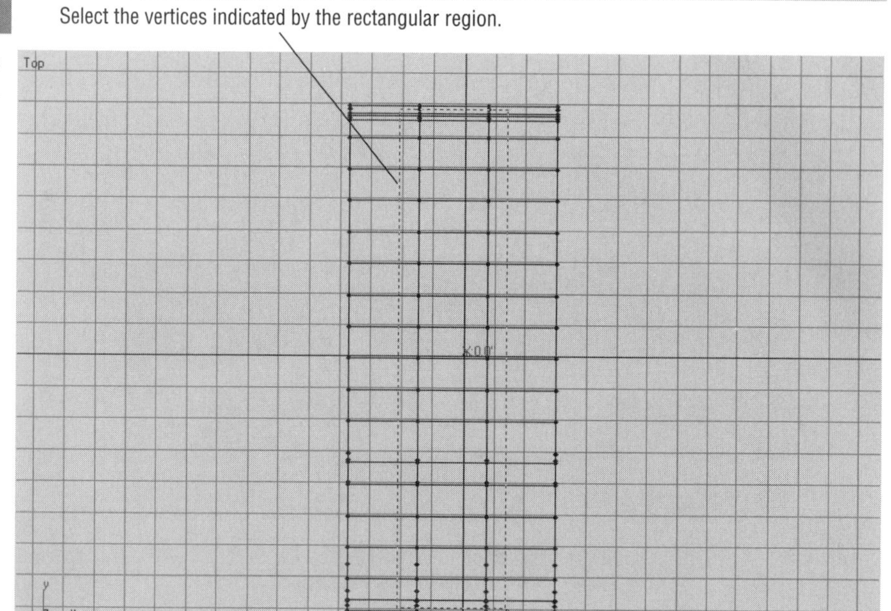
Select the vertices indicated by the rectangular region.
Top

4. Pan to the other end of the box and move upward the vertices shown in Figure 15.12.

FIGURE 15.12

Move these vertices upward.

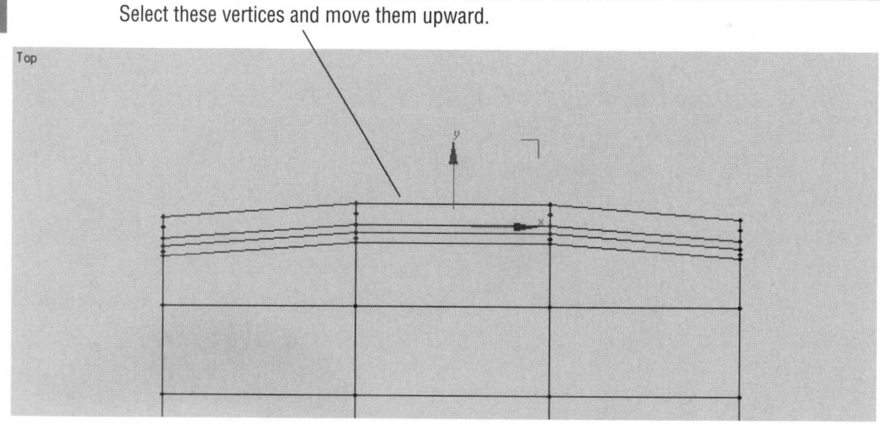
Select these vertices and move them upward.
Top

By now the front and back of the box have been stretched beyond the profile of the car. The next step is to move the entire front and back into place.

1. Type **L** to go back to the Left viewport, then select the vertices shown in Figure 15.13.
2. Move back the vertices that are in the front of the box so that they are again roughly aligned with the car's image.
3. Do the same for the back of the car. Your view should look similar to Figure 15.13.

FIGURE 15.13

The car so far

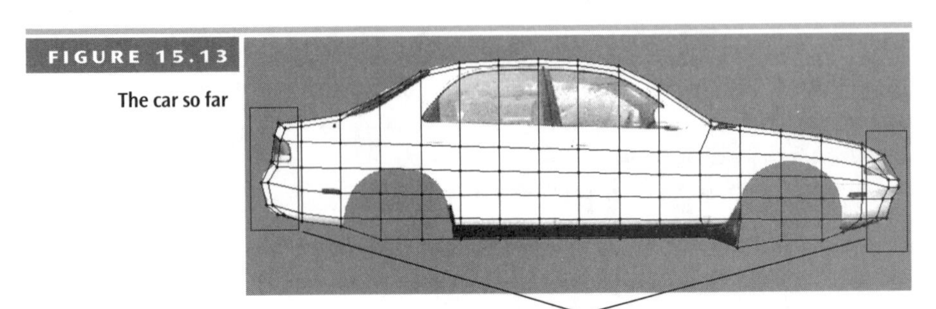

Select these regions and move them back into alignment with the background image.

4. Type **P** to view the Perspective viewport. Use the Zoom, Pan, and Arc Rotate tool on the Viewport toolbar to adjust the view so it looks similar to Figure 15.14.

FIGURE 15.14

A perspective view of the car so far

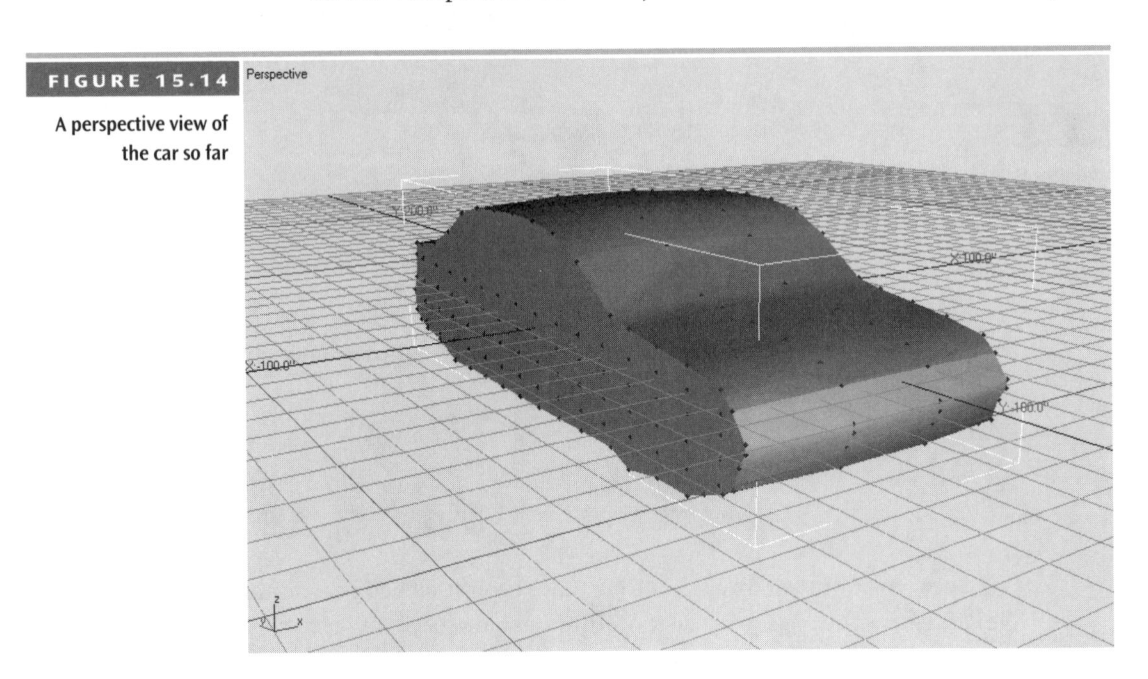

The car has really taken shape now, and you could almost use it as is. There are just a few more details that need to be taken car of before the car is ready for use.

Right now, the car has vertical, flat sides. You'll want to add some slope to the sides of the car and also add a slight bulge to the side to give the impression of curvature.

Start by bending the sides inward toward the top.

1. Type **F** to go to the Front viewport.
2. Click the Zoom Extents tool to enlarge the car.
3. Click the Select and Rotate tool, then use the Rectangular Selection Region to select the vertices shown in Figure 15.15.

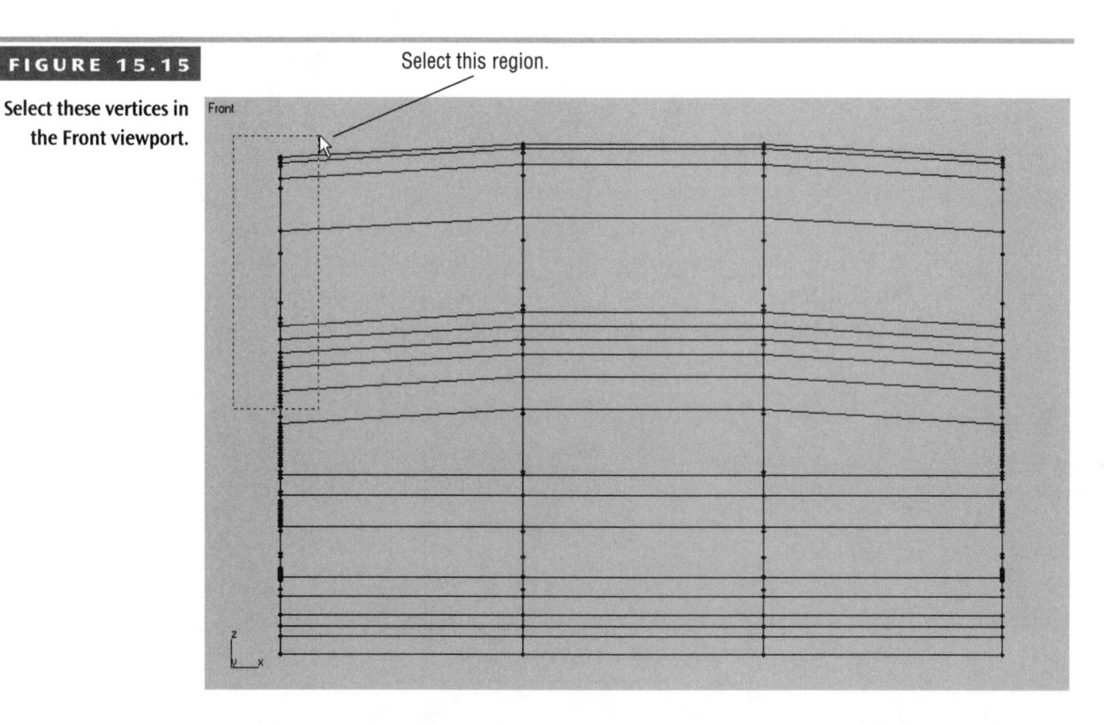
Select this region.
Front

FIGURE 15.15

Select these vertices in the Front viewport.

4. Click and drag the blue Z axis upward to rotate the vertices. As you do this, watch the readout at the bottom of the VIZ window. When the readout shows –12 degrees, release the mouse.

5. Click the Select and Move tool, then click and drag the X axis arrow to the right until the vertices at the bottom of the selected group of vertices are aligned with the rest of the side of the car, as shown in Figure 15.16.

FIGURE 15.16

Move the vertices so that the bottom of the selection is aligned with the rest of the side.

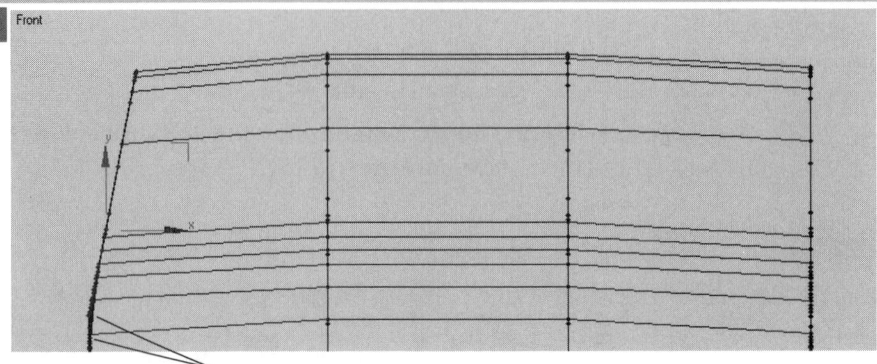
Front
Align these vertices vertically.

6. Repeat the process described in steps 3 through 5 for the other side of the car, but this time make sure you rotate the vertices in the opposite direction from that of step 4. The result should look like Figure 15.17.

FIGURE 15.17

The car after editing the vertices on the right side

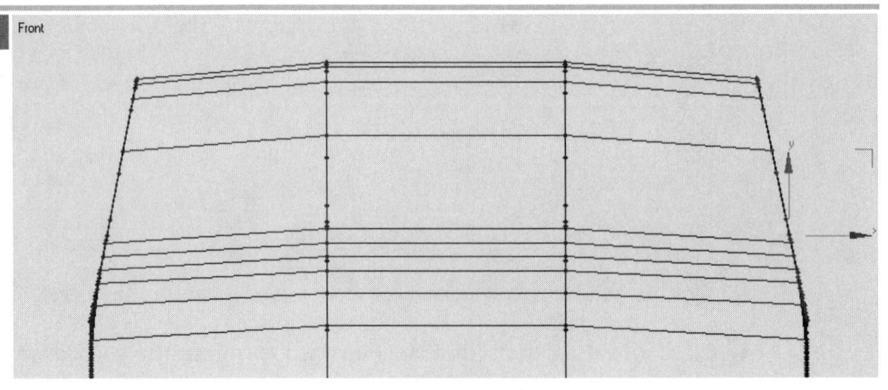
Front

Now add the bulge in the sides.

1. Type **L** to go to the Left viewport.
2. Click and drag the Rectangular Selection Region tool on the standard toolbar to open the flyout; then select the Fence Selection Region tool.

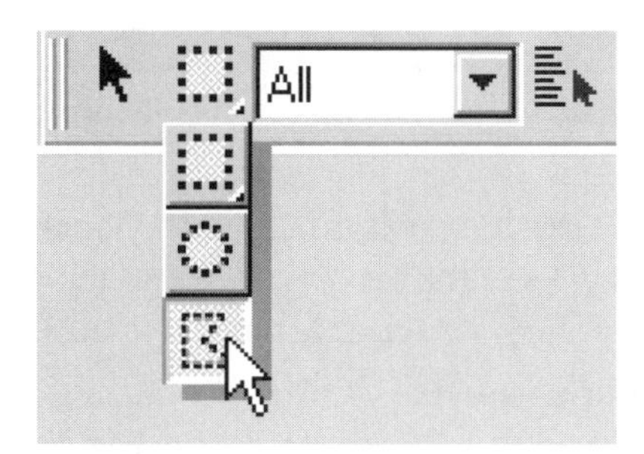
All

3. Click the Select and Move tool, then click and drag within the area shown in Figure 15.18 to start the fence selection.
4. Continue to select points so that the vertices shown in Figure 15.18 are selected. To close the fence selection, place the cursor over the beginning of the selection fence and when you see the cursor turn into a cross, click the mouse.

FIGURE 15.18

Selecting the fence selection area

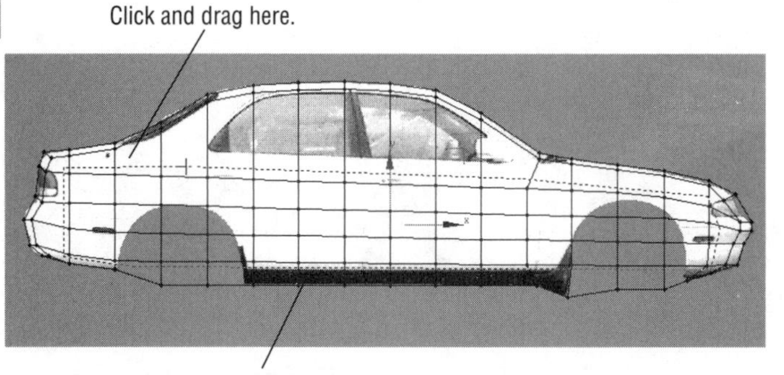
Click and drag here.
Enclose this area with a fence selection region.

5. Save this selection set by first right-clicking a blank area of the standard toolbar and selecting Selection. The Selection toolbar opens.
6. In the Selection toolbar input box, enter **sidebulge**. You'll want to be able to return to this selection set a bit later.

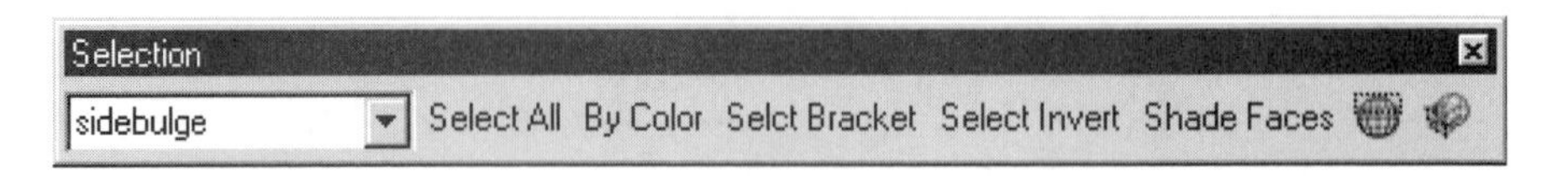

Remember that since you're selecting points in an orthogonal view, you are actually selecting vertices on both sides of the car. You need to remove the vertices from one side of the car so you only affect a single side when you move the vertices.

1. Type **F** to go to the Front viewport.
2. Hold down the Alt key, then click and drag the location shown in Figure 15.19. Continue to hold the Alt key while selecting points to enclose the vertices shown in Figure 15.19.

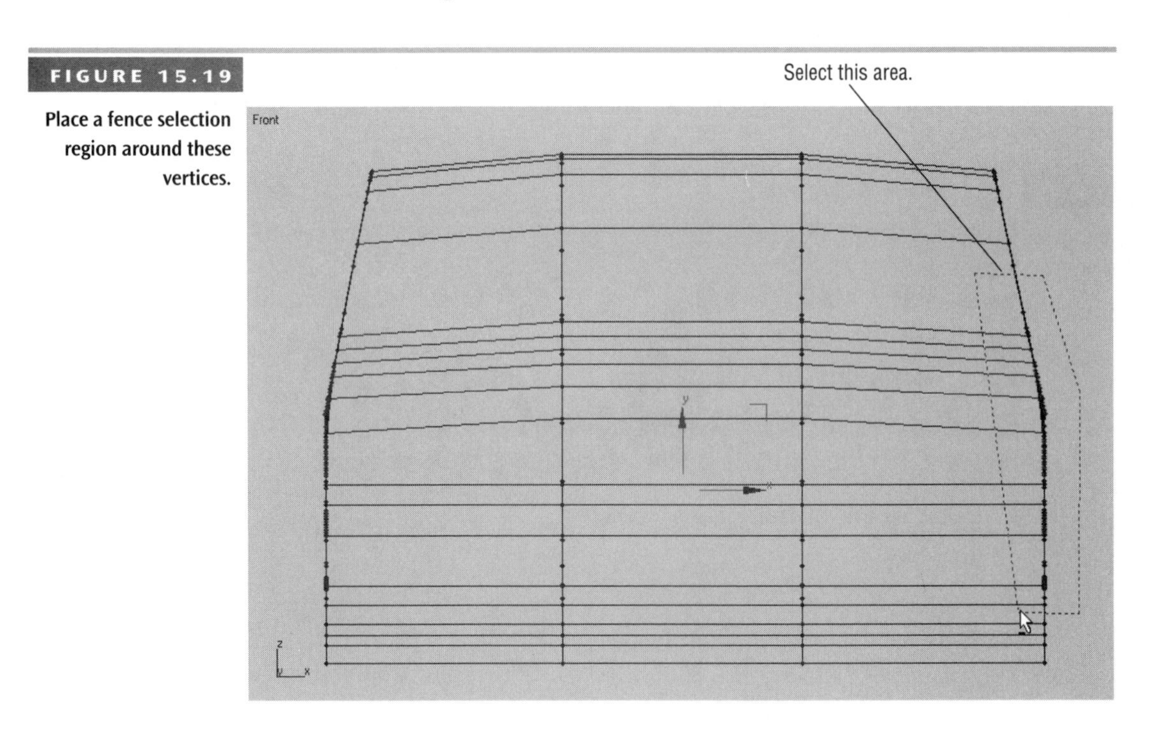

FIGURE 15.19

Place a fence selection region around these vertices.

3. When you've completed the selection by closing the fence selection region, the vertices on the right side of the car will be removed from the selection set.

4. Click and drag the red X axis arrow to the left, as shown in Figure 15.20, to add a slight bulge to the side of the car.

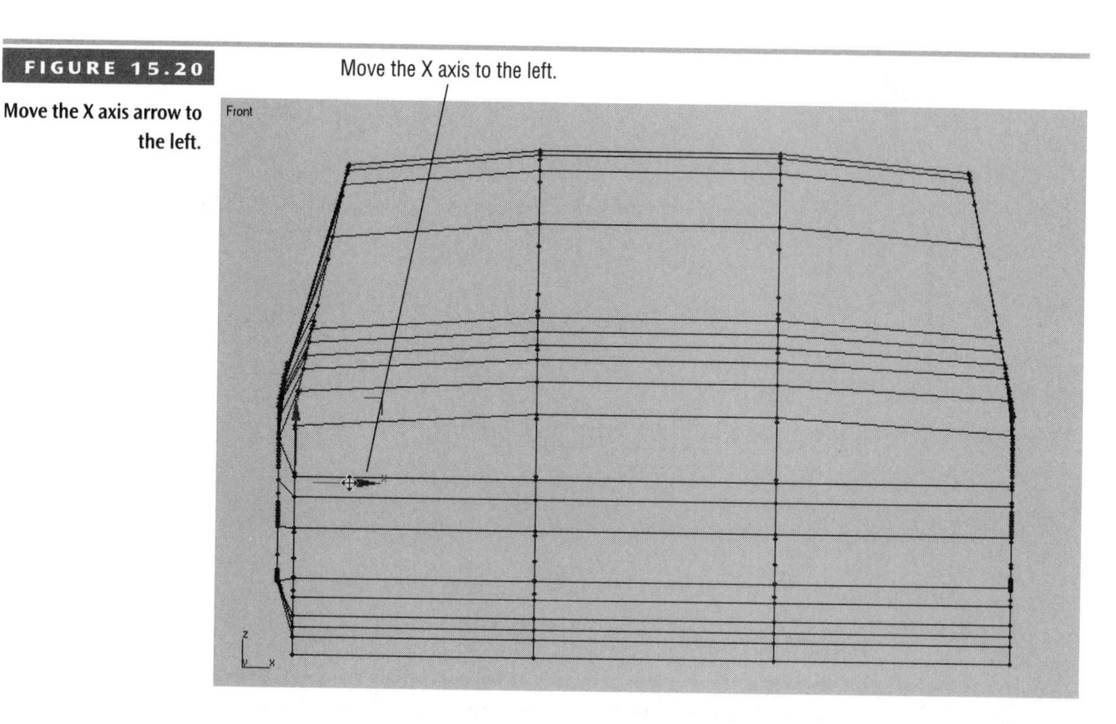
Move the X axis to the left.
Front

FIGURE 15.20

Move the X axis arrow to the left.

You've got one side done. Now go ahead and add the bulge to the other side.

1. On the Selection toolbar, select Sidebulge from the drop-down list. This restores the vertex selection you had before you removed the vertices from the right side of the box.
2. Hold down the Alt key, and this time select the vertices on the left side of the car.
3. Move the vertices to the right to add the bulge to that side of the car. Your view should look similar to Figure 15.21.

FIGURE 15.21

Add the bulge to the right side of the car.

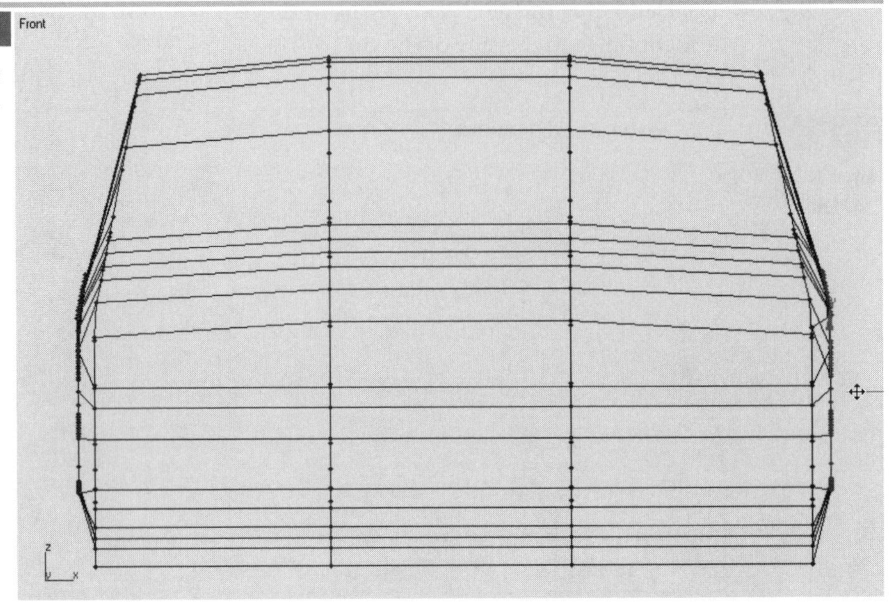

You've completed the vertex editing for the car. The next step is to apply smoothing to the mesh to remove some of the sharp edges.

TIP So far, you've used a single box to represent the entire car. Since a car is symmetrical, you can also model half of the car, then mirror-clone that half and attach and weld the two halves together. Either way is acceptable, and each offers advantages over the other. The method you choose is a matter of preference.

Smoothing the Surface

In the first part of this book, you saw how spheres and other types of rounded geometry appear smooth, even though the surfaces are really made up of faceted polygons. This smooth appearance is created by smoothing groups that are applied to the faces of an object.

A smoothing group is an integer from 1 to 32 that identifies whether two adjacent faces are to be smoothed or not. If two adjacent faces are assigned the same smoothing group, 30 for example, then they will appear to blend together in a smooth surface instead of showing a sharp edge between the two faces.

You can apply smoothing to geometry by using the Smooth Modifier. For editable meshes, you can apply smoothing through the face, polygon, or element sub-object level. Try the following exercise to add smoothing to the car mesh.

1. First choose File ➢ Save As and save the file as **Carmesh01**. You'll come back later to the car that you save at this stage to look at some other mesh smoothing options.
2. Type **P** to view the car in the Perspective viewport.
3. In the Command Panel, click the Element button in the Selection rollout.

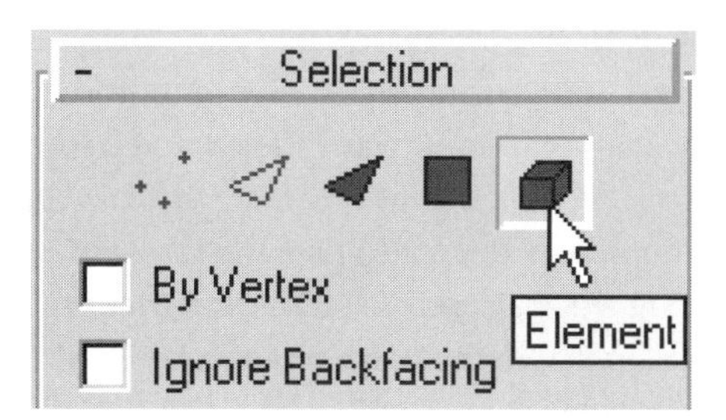

4. Click the car to select it as an element.
5. Scroll down the Command Panel to the Surface Properties rollout.
6. In the Smoothing Groups, set the Auto Smooth value to **90**, then click the Auto Smooth button. The car's surface changes to a smoother appearance.

The Auto Smooth option doesn't actually smooth out the geometry of the car. It is a setting that causes VIZ to smooth over the edges of surfaces in rendered views.

Here you used the Auto Smooth option to smooth the mesh. You can be very specific about which face you want to smooth by selecting the face and applying a smoothing group to that face. Remember that adjacent faces must have similar smoothing groups before they are smoothed.

You've completed the mesh editing portion of the car. Right now, it still looks like an amorphous blob, vaguely resembling a car. The next step is to apply a map to create the illusion of the car's surface details.

Adding Detail with Photographs

The goal of the car exercise is to create a reasonably convincing car without creating a huge file. After all, the car will serve only as part of your entourage and is not the main focus of your design. Still, you don't want the car to be too cartoon-like.

In the next set of exercises, you'll add a material to the car. The material will include a photograph of the side of the car to give the impression of the details we're used to seeing in a car. Along the way, you'll learn some tricks in preparing the bitmap for the car as well as methods for preparing the UVW Mapping modifier to align the map to the car's surface.

Creating a Material for the Car Side

Start by creating the material that will be mapped to the car's side:

1. Open the Material Editor.
2. With the upper left sample slot selected, scroll down and open the Maps rollout.
3. Click the Diffuse Map button. Then, in the Material/map Browser, click Bitmap and click OK
4. In the Select Bitmap Image file dialog box, select and open `Mazdaside dif.tif`. This file from the companion CD is an edited bitmap image of the side of the car.

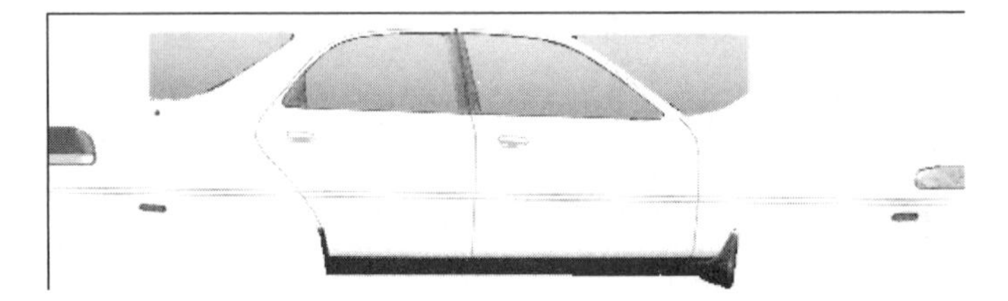

The `Mazdaside dif.tif` image isn't exactly what the car looks like. The front and back windshield have been stretched, and so have the headlights and taillights. Also, the outline of the car has been eliminated. These changes were made to facilitate the way the image will be mapped on the car mesh. You'll see the effects of this map on the mesh a bit later.

Next, you'll want to add an opacity map for the wheel wells of the car.

1. In the Material Editor, click the Go to Parent tool on the Material Editor toolbar.

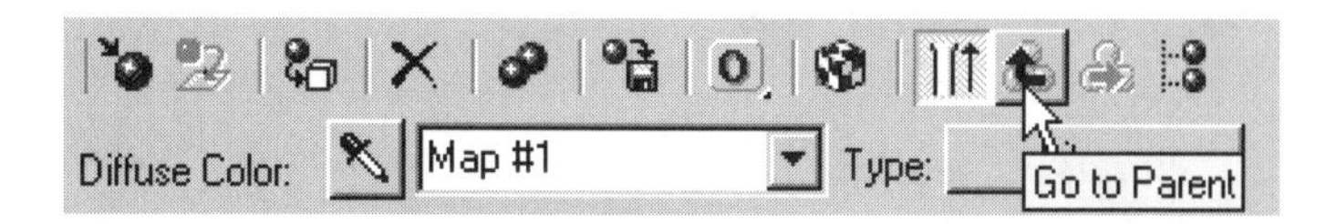

2. Click the Opacity Map button.
3. Click Bitmap in the Material/Map browser and click OK.
4. Select and open the `Mazdaside OP.tif` file. This is an image that outlines the wheel wells of the car.

5. In the Modify tab of the Command Panel, click the Sub-Object button to turn off the sub-object level.
6. Back in the Material Editor, click the Assign Material to Selection button, then close the Material Editor.

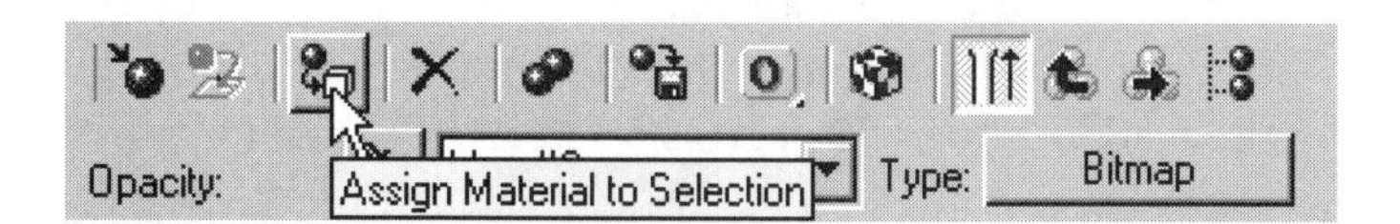

Adding the UVW Map

Next, you'll need to apply a UVW Mapping modifier to the car mesh to align the material maps to the side of the car. In this situation, a planar map will work best.

1. In the Modify tab of the Command Panel, click the UVW Map button.
2. Scroll down the Command Panel to the Alignment group and click the X radio button.

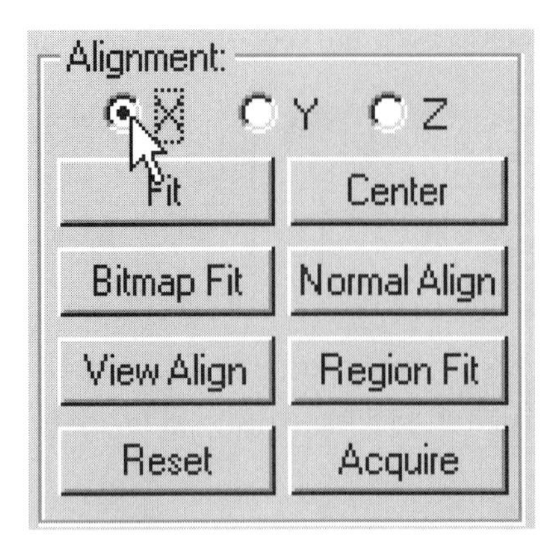

By default, VIZ assigns a planar map to the object, but the map is aligned with the Z axis of the mesh. The Map needs to be aligned with the X axis to align the map images to the side of the car.

The map is now aligned with the appropriate axis, but it is oriented in the wrong direction. You need to rotate the map 90 degrees so that the point of the map gizmo points upward, and the green side of the gizmo points to the front of the car, as shown in Figure 15.22:

1. Scroll back to the top of the Command Panel and click the Sub-Object button to gain access to the UVW Map gizmo.
2. Click the Select and Rotate tool on the standard toolbar, then click and drag the red X axis of the Map gizmo downward. As you do this, watch the numeric readout at the bottom of the VIZ window. Adjust the gizmo rotation so that the readout shows 90 degrees, then release the mouse button.
3. Scroll down to the bottom of the Command Panel, then click the Fit button in the Alignment group. The gizmo now fits the car mesh as shown in Figure 15.22.

FIGURE 15.22

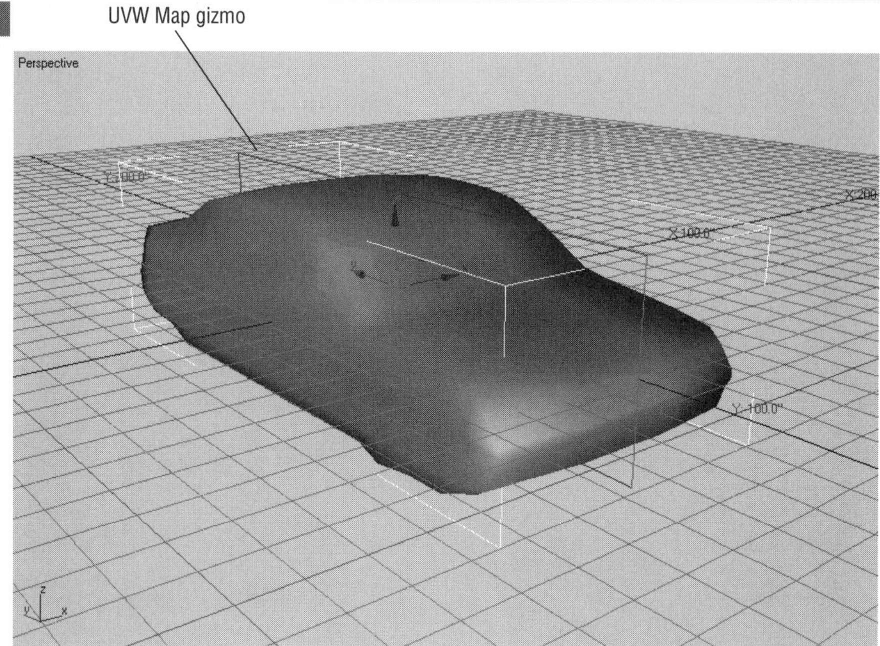

The UVW Map gizmo in its proper location and proportion

4. Click the Quick Render tool to see how the car looks with the Material map (see Figure 15.23).

FIGURE 15.23

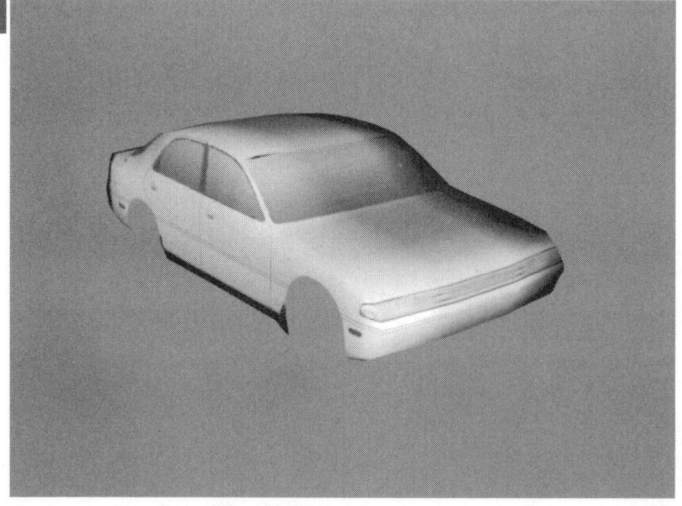

The car rendered

It's not a great looking car, but it will pass when placed at a distance from the camera. There are a few adjustments you may need to make. For example, the front windshield posts may be distorted, as in Figure 15.24. This is caused by the bitmap being stretched over a broad area of the windshield. If this happens in your model, you can move the vertices of the mesh so that the windshield pillars fall on a flat portion of the mesh.

FIGURE 15.24

The windshield pillar is out of alignment.

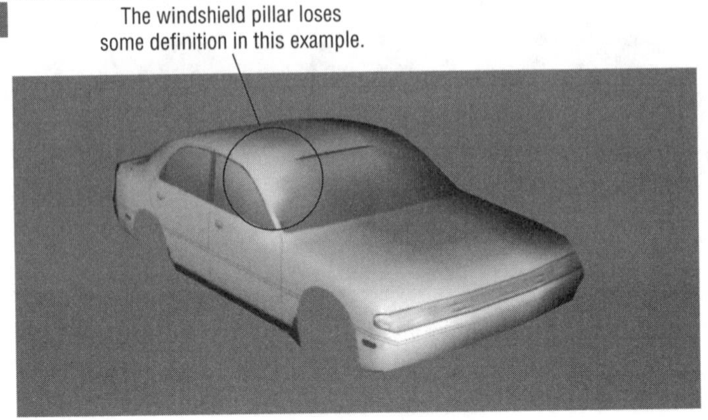
The windshield pillar loses
some definition in this example.

1. Minimize the Virtual Frame Buffer window, then type **L** to go to the Left viewport.
2. In the Command Panel, click the Sub-Object button to return to the object level, then select Editable Mesh from the Modifier Stack drop-down list.
3. Click the Vertex button in the Selection rollout, then use the Select and Move tool to move the Vertices around the windshield toward the right, as shown in Figure 15.25.

FIGURE 15.25

Adjusting the windshield forward

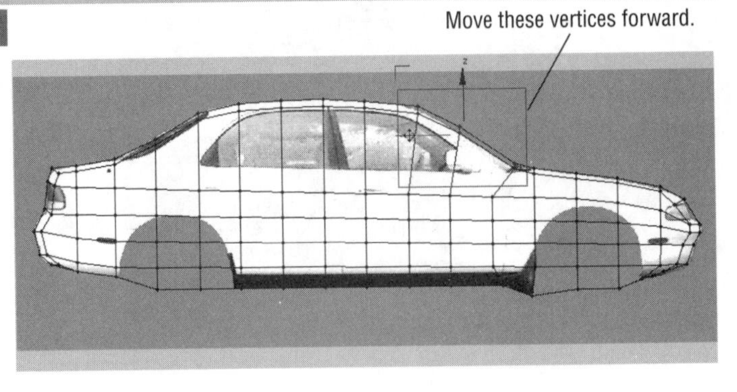
Move these vertices forward.

4. Click the Sub-Object button to go back to the object level, then select UVW Mapping from the Modifier Stack drop-down list to return to the top of the Modifier Stack.
5. Type **P** to return to the Perspective view, then click the Quick Render tool. The windshield pillar is better defined this time.

If you look at the `Mazdaside dif.tif` bitmap image, you see that the front and back windshields have been distorted to extend way beyond the boundaries of the car. This is done just so you can make the type of adjustments you made in the last exercise. You can move parts of the mesh and still maintain the appearance of the windshield. The same holds true for the headlights and taillights.

Adding the Front to the Car

Using a single bitmap for the side of the car works fine for side views and perhaps even for the rear views of the car, but the front of the car needs a bit more detail to make it more convincing. In Chapter 14, you learned that you can add multiple bitmaps to a single object. In this section, you'll learn first-hand how to add a second map to a separate set of mesh faces to add headlights and a grille to the car.

First, create a multi/sub-object material.

1. Open the Material Editor dialog box; then, if you aren't already at the Parent material level, click the Go to Parent button on the Material Editor toolbar.
2. Click the Type button labeled Standard on the Material Editor toolbar.

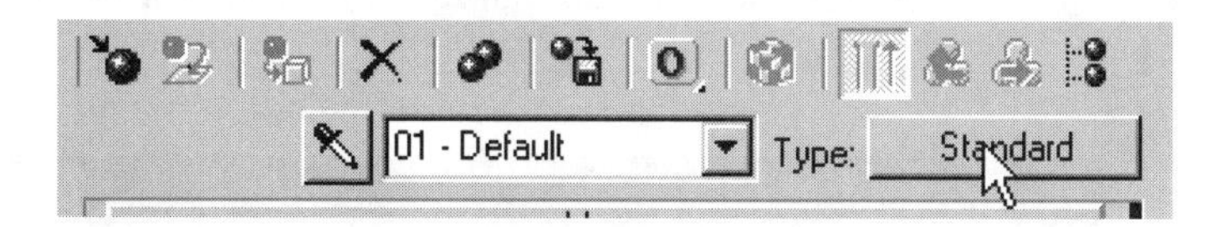

3. In the Material/Map Browser, click the Multi/Sub-Object listing and then click OK.
4. In the Replace Material dialog box, click Keep old material as sub-material, and then click OK.

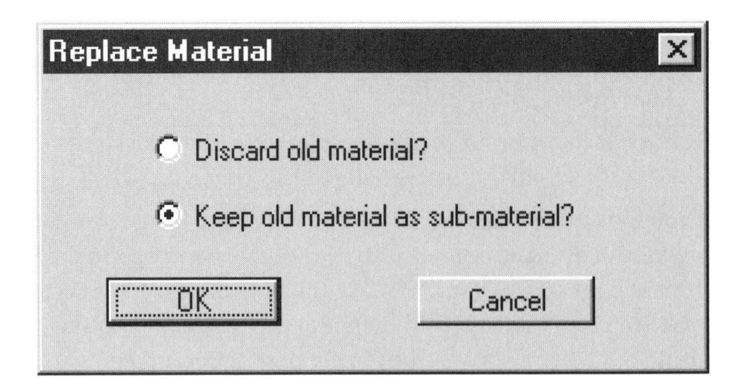

5. In the Material Editor dialog box, click the Set Number button in the Multi-/Sub-Object Basic Parameters rollout.

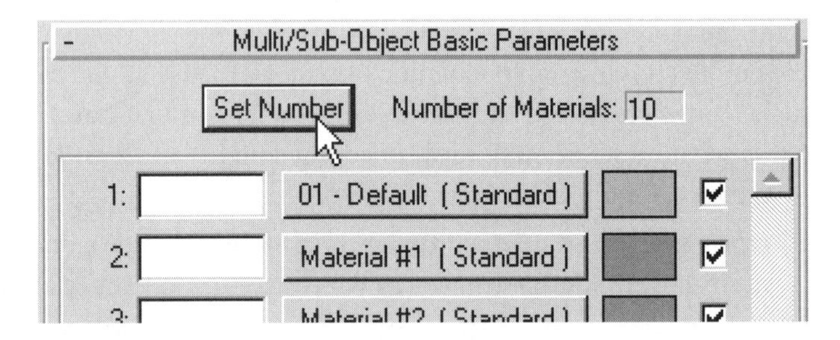

6. In the Set Number of Materials dialog box, enter **2** for two materials; then click OK.

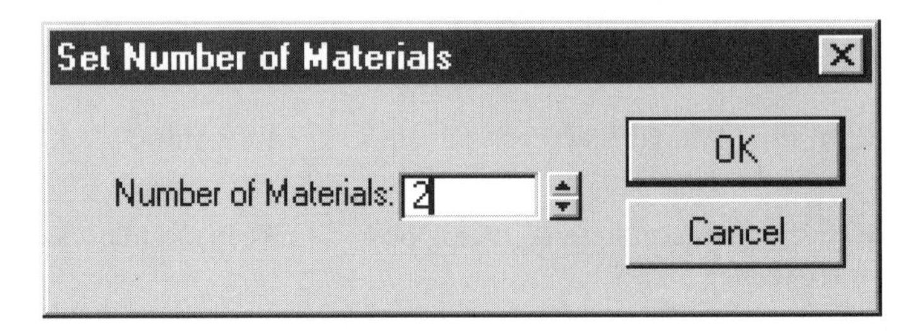

Next, add a material to the multi/Sub-Object material.

1. Click the Material button in row 2 of the Multi/Sub-Object Basic Parameters rollout.

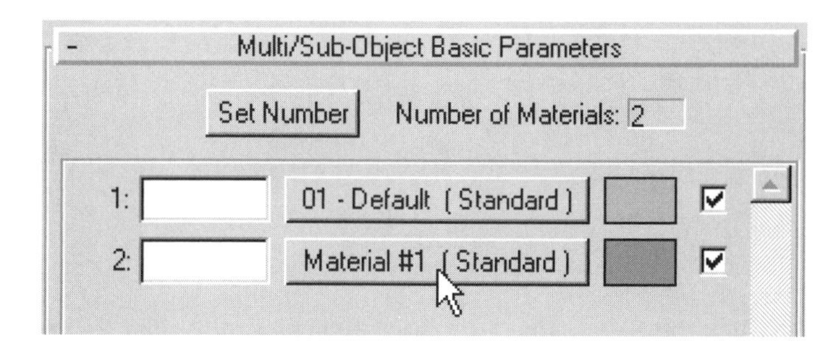

2. Scroll down to the Maps rollout and open it.
3. Click the Diffuse Color Map button.
4. In the Material/Map Browser, click Bitmap and then click OK.
5. Locate and open the `Mazdafront.tif` file.
6. Back in the Material Editor, change the Map Channel value in the Coordinates rollout to **2**.

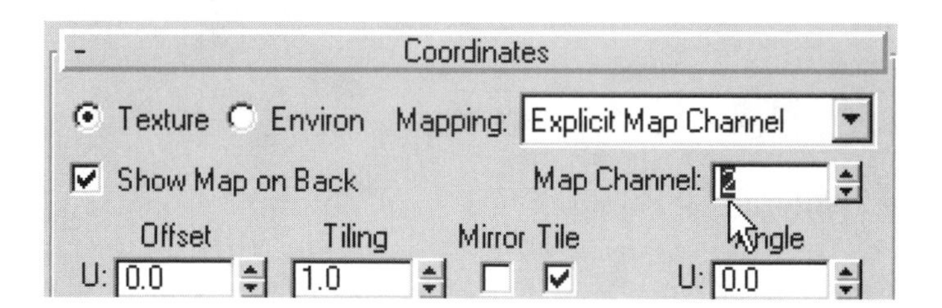

7. Click the Go to Parent tool to return to the parent level of the material.

By setting the Map Channel value to **2**, you will be able to assign a UVW Mapping modifier to the `Mazdafront.tif` bitmap.

Now let's focus on the mesh to see how to apply the `Mazdafront.tif` map to the front of the mesh. Start by isolating the polygons that you'll use for the map of the front of the car.

1. Close the Material Editor dialog box and, if it isn't already on the screen, type **L** to display the Left viewport.
2. Change the Selection region to the Fence Selection region on the standard toolbar.
3. Make sure the car mesh is selected; then in the Modify tab of the Command Panel, select Editable Mesh from the Modifier Stack drop-down list.

4. Click the Polygon button in the Selection rollout.

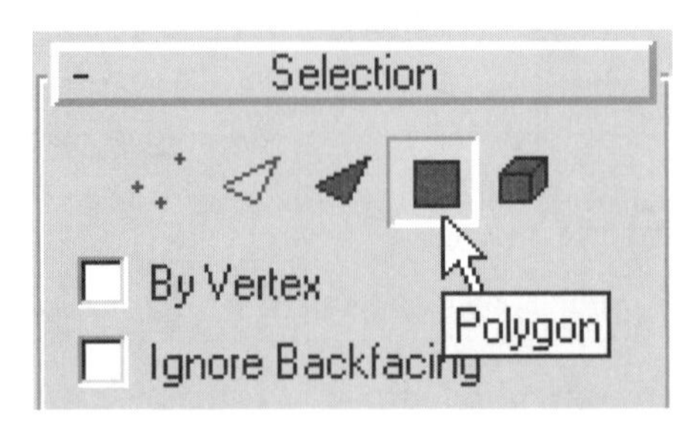

5. Click the Select Object tool on the standard toolbar and place a fence selection region around the area shown in Figure 15.26.

FIGURE 15.26

Select these polygons with the Select Object tool.

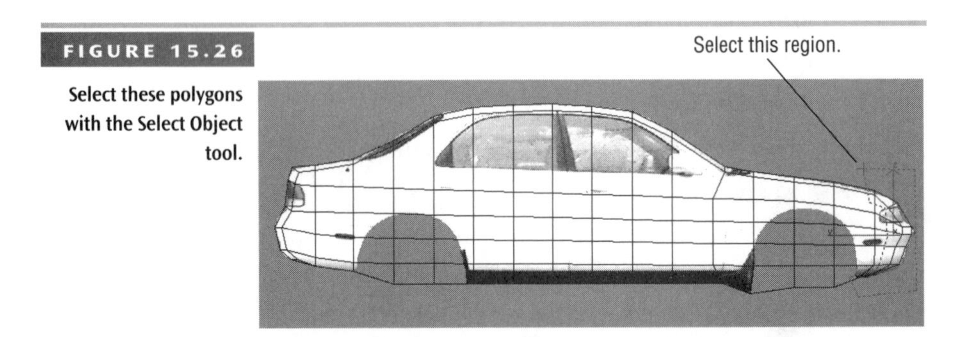

6. With the polygons selected, scroll down the Command Panel to the Material group of the Surface Properties rollout. Then change the ID setting to **2** to match the polygons with the material 2 of the Multi/Sub-Object material.

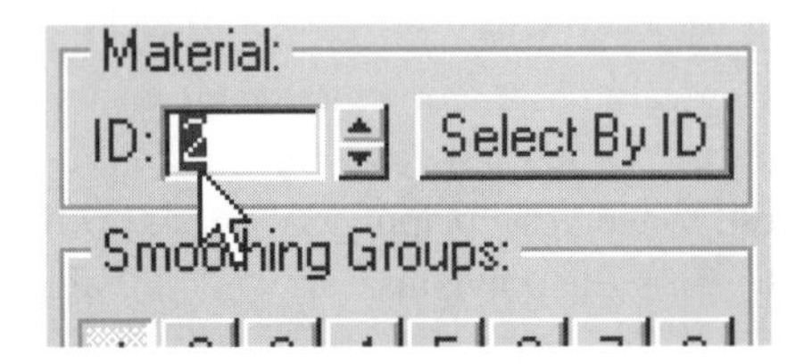

Next, you'll need to apply a UVW Map modifier for the polygons that you just assigned to the second material. You'll also need to adjust the orientation of the map to face the polygons.

1. While still in the sub-object level of the mesh, click the UVW Map button in the Modifier rollout. While it may not be obvious at first, you'll see the UVW Map gizmo appear at the front of the mesh near the selected polygons.

2. Type **P** to view the Perspective viewport, then right-click the Perspective label in the upper left corner of the viewport. Select Wireframe. This will allow you to more clearly see the UVW Map gizmo.
4. Scroll down the Command Panel and click the Y radio button from the Alignment group.
5. Click the Fit button, also in the Alignment group.
6. In the Channel group, change the Map Channel value to **2**.

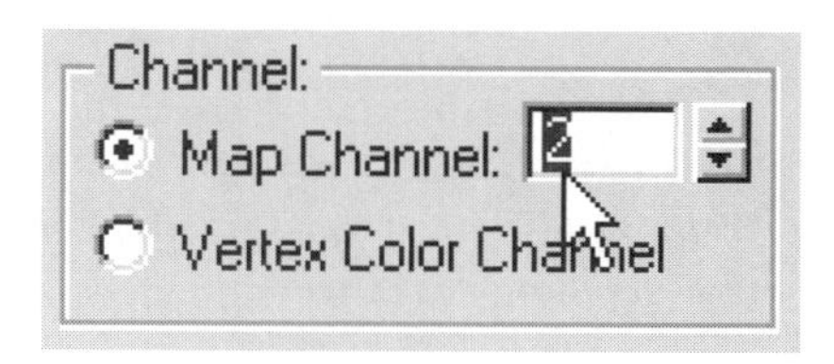

By remaining in the Polygon sub-object level in step 1, the UVW Map modifier automatically aligns the Map gizmo to the selected polygons. This also makes it easier to use the Fit option in step 5.

You're just about ready to render your model to see the results, but first you need to do a little *house cleaning*.

1. Select Editable Mesh from the Modifier Stack drop-down list.
2. Click the Sub-Object button to exit the sub-object level.
3. Select the top UVW Mapping listing in the Modifier Stack drop-down list.
4. Click the Quick Render button to see the results of the UVW Mapping addition.

Now the front of the car appears as part of the model. If you look at the front corner of the car, you see that the side and front are not quite aligned. You can adjust the UVW Map gizmo to align the two maps.

1. In the Modifier Stack rollout, select the UVW Map listing that corresponds to the front of the car. This should be the middle modifier in the stack.

2. In the Mapping group of the UVW Map parameters rollout, adjust the Width parameter to **75**. This stretches the UVW Map horizontally.
3. Render the perspective view again.

This time, the headlights from the sides start to merge with the headlights from the front. You can move the gizmo vertically to get the maps to align vertically.

1. Click the Sub-Object button. This gives you access to the Map gizmo.
2. Click Select and Move to, then click and drag the map downward in the Z axis to align it with the map on the side.
3. Render the Perspective view again.

You may need to adjust the front Map gizmo a few times while rendering the view to get the location just right. You may also need to adjust the Length setting of the Mapping parameters to align the headlights with the side view.

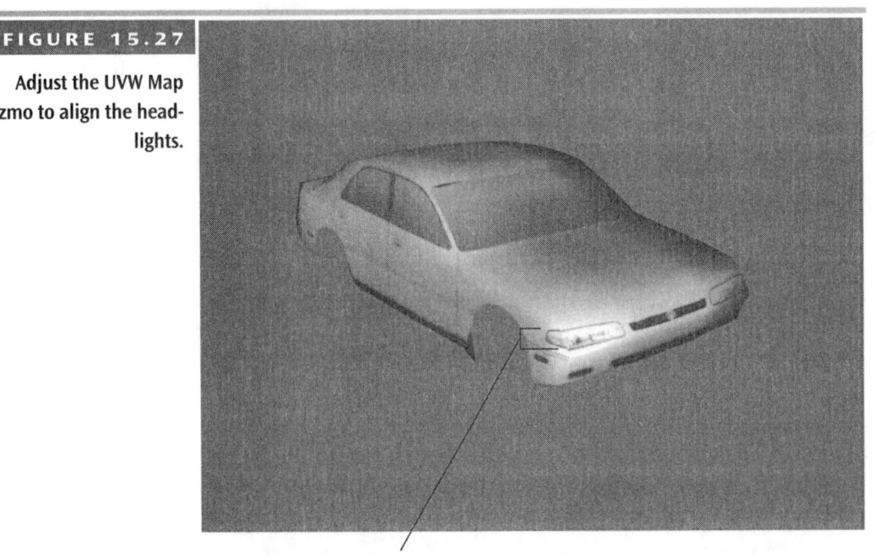

FIGURE 15.27

Adjust the UVW Map gizmo to align the headlights.

For the final touch, you'll need to add wheels. To save some time, you can import a set of wheels that were created for this model.

1. Choose File ➢ Merge.
2. In the Merge File dialog box, locate and open the `Carwheels.max` file.
3. In the Merge dialog box, click All, then click OK. The wheels display in the design.
3. Use the Top and Side views to move the wheels into their proper locations, then render the Perspective view again.

4. Save the car as **Carmesh02.max**.

The car isn't perfect, but at a distance it's fine, and it won't take up a lot of memory. Now that you've got a basic car, you can start to make copies of it, adding different color schemes and modifying the shape a bit for each copy to create a set of cars for your entourage. You can use the methods described here to create other vehicles as well.

TIP Once you've finished the car, you may want to use the Group command to collect the parts of the car into a single group.

Smoothing the Mesh

The car you created still has some rough edges that are especially noticeable in close-up views. VIZ offers the MeshSmooth modifier. It will smooth out sharp corners of a mesh by adding additional faces or polygons. This increases the amount of memory the mesh occupies, but for some situations, it may be worth it.

In the following exercise, you'll try out the MeshSmooth modifier on an earlier version of the car mesh. You may recall that in an earlier exercise in this chapter, you saved the car mesh as `Carmesh01.max`. You'll use that design file to experiment with the MeshSmooth modifier.

1. Open the `Carmesh01.max` file.
2. If you see only a single viewport, click the Min/Max viewport button to view all four viewports.
2. Select the mesh representing the car body. If the Modify tab of the command panel shows that the mesh is in a sub-object level, click the Sub-Object button.
3. Click the Modify tab in the Command Panel, then click the More button in the Modifier rollout.

4. Select MeshSmooth from the Modifier dialog box and click OK. The mesh becomes smoother with additional polygons.

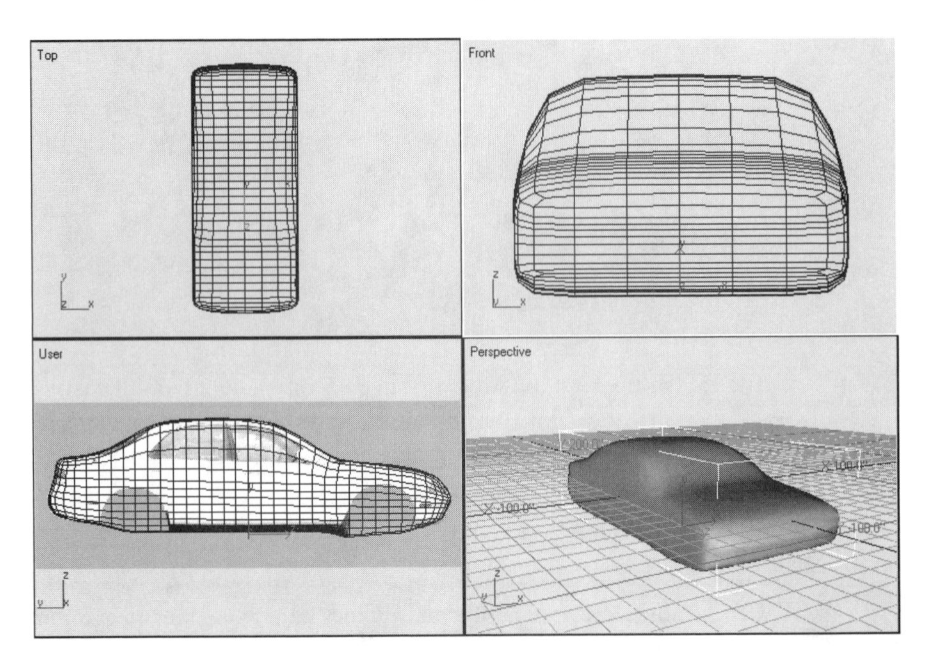

From here, you can add the materials just as you did before, but this time the results will be a bit more realistic because of the smoother surface of the car body.

The MeshSmooth modifier actually generates a second mesh, using the original mesh's vertices as control points. The vertices of the original mesh exert a *pull* on this second MeshSmooth mesh, and you can control the amount of pull exerted by the vertices. The following exercise shows you how you can control the MeshSmooth mesh by adjusting the Display/Weighting parameters of the MeshSmooth modifier.

1. Scroll down the Command Panel to the Display /Weighting group, then click the Display Control Mesh check box.

   Now you see the edges used to control the MeshSmooth mesh. They are most easily seen in the Perspective view with the Smooth+Highlights option turned on.

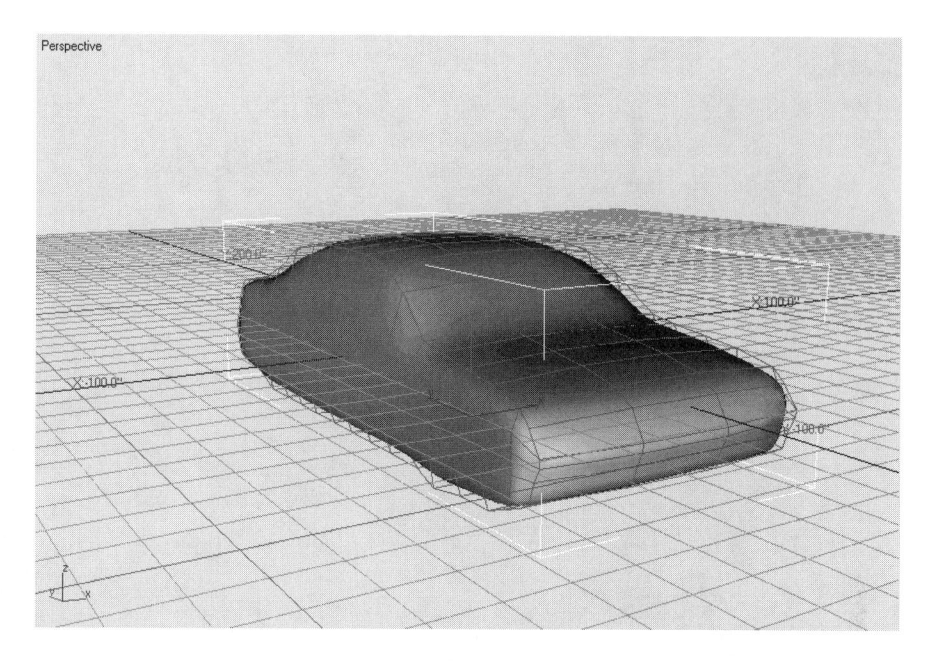

2. Enlarge the Front viewport.
3. In the Modify tab, click the Sub-Object button and make sure that Vertex is selected in the Select Level drop-down list.
4. Use the Select Object tool with the Fence Selection Region to select the vertices shown in Figure 15.28. Remember that you can select one set of vertices, then use the Ctrl key with the Select Object tool to select the second set.

FIGURE 15.28

Select these two sets of vertices.

Select these sets of vertices.

Front

5. In the Command Panel, scroll down to the Display/Weighting group and change the Weight value to **4.0**. Notice how the sides are pulled tighter toward the selected vertices. The profile of the car is now a bit more *sedan-like* than before.

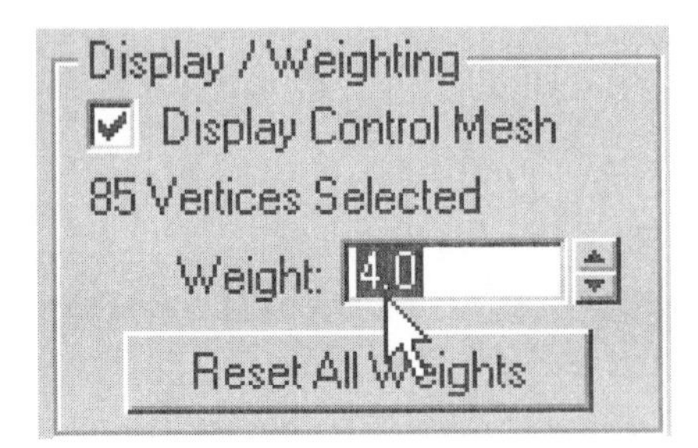

You can continue to fine-tune the shape of the car by selecting vertices and adjusting their weight. For example, you can round out the corners of the car by selecting the corner vertices and reducing their weight. Once you've arrived at a shape you like, you can collapse the stack to reduce the object to an editable mesh to conserve memory. Figure 15.29 shows the car with the MeshSmooth modifier applied and with a few adjustments to the weight of the vertices in selected places.

FIGURE 15.29

A rendering of a car that uses a MeshSmooth modifier

One of the more common questions architects seem to ask about 3D software is whether it will allow them to do the type of free-form shaping of objects that you've seen in this chapter. While the focus in these exercises has been on the creation of a car as a prop in your designs, you can certainly apply these methods to architectural elements, and perhaps even to the main form of your design.

Matching your Design to a Background Image

One of the more interesting uses of VIZ is to combine a photograph with a design to create a view of a building as it will appear in its intended location. This is an excellent way to help your client understand the look and scale of your design. It can also play a crucial role in the planning phase of a project, where this type of image may be required as part of a design review submission.

In this section, you'll use VIZ's Camera Match tools to place a model of an apartment building in a background photograph of the apartment's intended site. The apartment is located in San Francisco, California, so the model has a Sunlight system light source set up for San Francisco at 1:30 in the afternoon on July 4, 2000. This is the same time that the background image was taken (see Figure 15.30).

TIP It's a good idea to make note of all of the camera settings used to take the background photograph. Information such as the focal length of the camera lens and the position and height of the camera can help you determine whether you are on the right track when aligning a model to the background. You will also want to keep track of the date, time of day, and the direction of true north. This information will help you accurately match the sun in your design to the location of the sun in the background.

FIGURE 15.30

The background image of the site for the apartment building and a sample rendering of the apartment building

Setting Up the Model and the Image

Before you can align a design with a background image, you need to find at least five locations in the image that you can correlate with locations in the design. In the design, you can create an object, such as a rectangular base, that can be easily located in the photograph. The photographic image for the apartment site already has an outline of the base of the apartment drawn in for you (see Figure 15.31).

This base is 5 feet, 8 inches high and matches the building's footprint. The height of 5 feet, 8 inches was used because it is a known height in the image. The sides of the base were established by locating the building's corner location in the image. While it hasn't been done for this photograph, frequently poles of known heights are placed at the corner points of the building before the photograph is taken so that known points can be more easily established.

The vanishing points of the photograph were located so that the outline of the box could be established. AutoCAD was used to help locate the vanishing points. The photograph was brought into AutoCAD using the Image command. Then the vanishing points were established by drawing lines over the photograph.

FIGURE 15.31

The AutoCAD image with vanishing points drawn in

The locations of the vanishing-point lines were carefully noted and then drawn in over the image in Photoshop. Photoshop could also have been used to find the vanishing points, but because AutoCAD offers some specialized tools for drawing vector graphics, it was much easier to find the vanishing points in AutoCAD.

A box was added to the VIZ design of the apartment that corresponds to the 5 foot, 8 inch tall base that was drawn over the photograph. The box will be used to align the model to the image, as you'll see in the following exercise.

Adding the Background Image

You now know that you'll need to do a little background preparation before you can match a design to a photograph. The next step is to do the actual matching in VIZ.

Start by assigning the background to the VIZ design file.

1. Open the file called `Noriega.max` from the companion CD. This is file containing the 3D model of the apartment building.
2. Add the background image to the viewport by first choosing View ➢ Viewport Image ➢ Select...
3. In the top of the Viewport Image dialog box, click Files...
4. In the Select Background Image dialog box, locate and open the `Noriegaview.tif` image file from the companion CD. This is the image file that contains the additional outline of the apartment base.
5. Back in the Viewport Image dialog box, make sure that the Match Bitmap radio button is selected in the Aspect Ratio group.
6. Also make sure that the Lock Zoom/Pan check box is not checked, then click OK. After a moment, the image will appear in the viewport.

You've got the image in the viewport, but you also need to tell VIZ that you want an image to be included as the background for renderings.

1. Choose Rendering ➢ Environment...
2. In the Environment dialog box, click the Environment Map button, which is currently labeled None.
3. In the Material/Map Browser, click Bitmap, then click OK.
4. In the Select Bitmap Image File dialog box, locate and open the `Noriegaview_render.tif` file from the companion CD. This is an exact duplicate of the `Noriegaview.tif` file without the outline of the base. You can also select `Noriegaview.tif`, but if you do your final rendering will contain a few stray layout lines.
5. Go ahead and close the Environment dialog box to move it out of the way.

Now you're ready to start using the Camera Match tools.

Adding the Camera Match Points

The Camera Match tools are in two sets. The first set lets you place helper objects in the model. These helper objects, called *CamPoints,* will then be used with the second set of tools to match locations in the design with locations in the background image.

The model contains a box named Alignobject whose sole purpose is to facilitate the alignment of the design with the background photograph. You'll use the Alignobject box to accurately place the CamPoints in the design at their appropriate locations.

Start by setting up VIZ to select endpoint snaps and by hiding all of the geometry except the Alignobject box.

1. Right-click the Snap button at the bottom of the VIZ window.

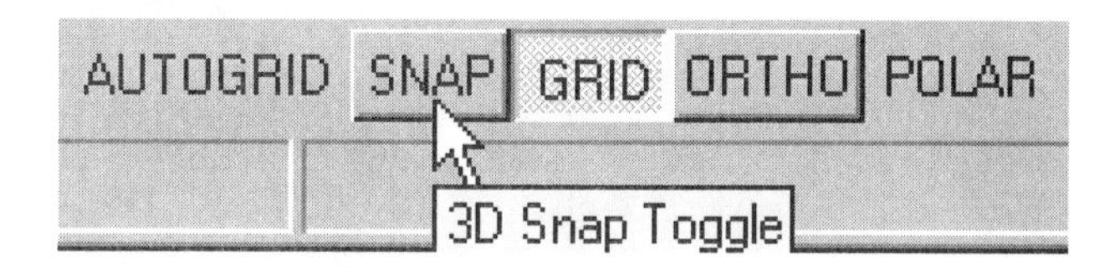

2. In the Grid and Snap Settings dialog box, place a check by the Endpoint option, then close the dialog box.
3. Use the Select Object tool to select the green base object named Alignobject, as shown in Figure 15.32.

FIGURE 15.32

Select the Alignobject object in the design.

4. Click the Display tab in the Command Panel, then click the Unselected Off button in the On/Off rollout.

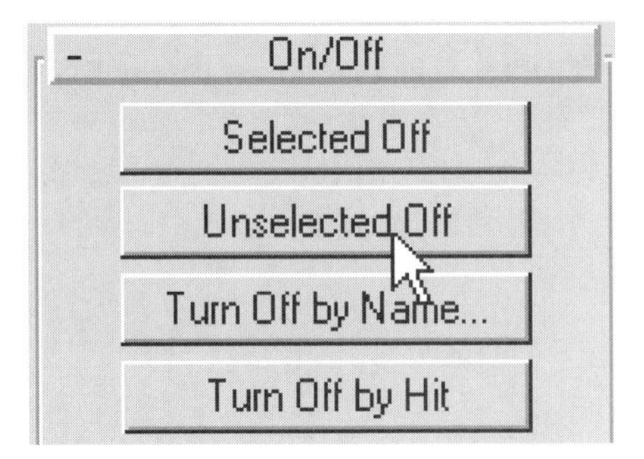

You now have just the Alignobject box showing. This will make it easier to place the CamPoint helpers.

The next step is to place the CamPoint helpers in the model.

1. Click the Create tab in the Command Panel, then click the Helpers button.

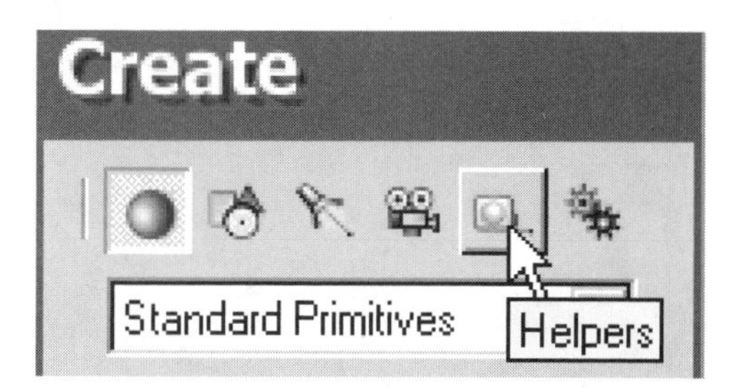

2. Select Camera Match from the Helpers drop-down list.

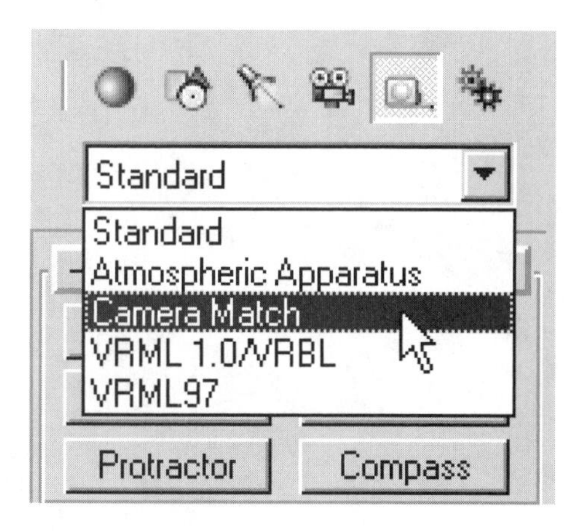

3. In the Object Type rollout, click CamPoint.
4. Make sure that the Snap mode is active, then click the bottom front corner of the Alignobject box, as shown in Figure 15.33.
5. Back in the Command Panel, change the CamPoint01 name in the Name and Color rollout to **Front Bottom**. This will make it easier to identify the CamPoint you just created.

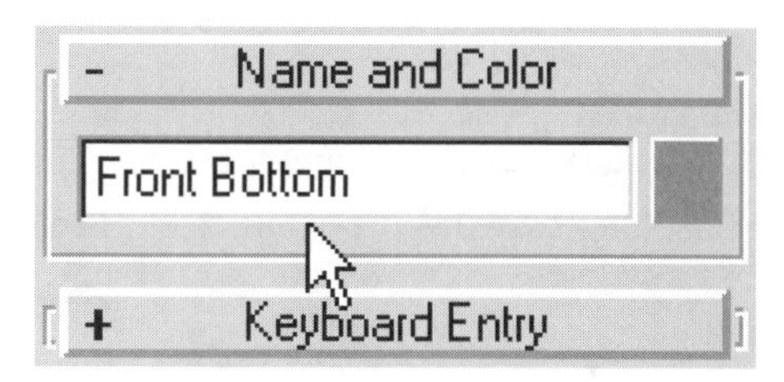

6. Next click the top front corner of the Alignobject box, as shown in Figure 15.33.
7. Change the name in the Name and Color rollout to **Front Top**.
8. Place the rest of the CamPoints, Left Top, Left Bottom, and Right Top, shown in Figure 15.33, as you did for the Front Top CamPoint. Click the location in the design, then change the newly added CamPoint's name to reflect its location.

FIGURE 15.33

With the endpoint snap active, click the corners of the Alignobject box.

You've now got 5 CamPoints in place. That is the minimum number that VIZ needs to align a design with a background image. You've seen how the Alignobject box helps make quick work of placing the CamPoints in the design. You can also place the CamPoints in your design by entering their coordinates, using the Camera Match Keyboard Entry rollout. But using geometry like the Alignobject box is a bit more straightforward.

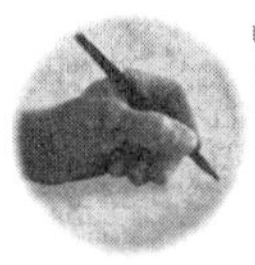

NOTE The Alignobject box was created specifically for the Camera Match operation and isn't really part of the building, so remember to turn it off when rendering the model.

Aligning the Camera Match Points to the Background Image

The next set of steps will require some care. You'll locate the places in the background image that correspond to the CamPoints you've just created.

1. Click the Utilities tab in the upper right corner of the Command Panel.
2. Click the Camera Match button. You'll see the CamPoint Info rollout appear with a list of the CamPoints you just created.
3. Click the Front Bottom listing in the CamPoint Info rollout, then click the Assign Position button.

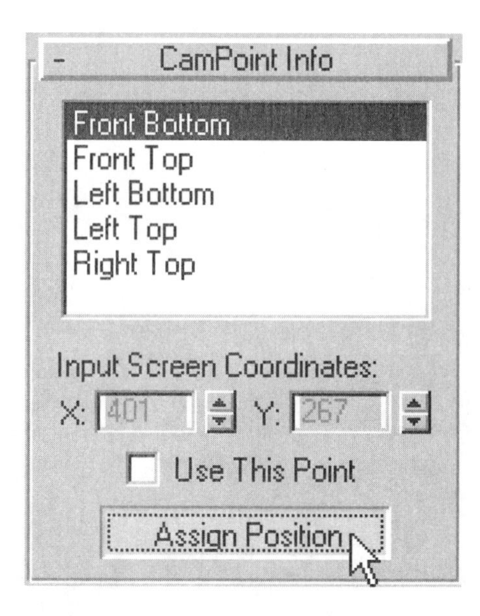

4. Click the location (shown in the background image) that corresponds to the Front Bottom CamPoint in the design (see Figure 15.34). A small cross appears at the point you click. Try to be as precise as you can in placing the cross. If you don't like the location, you can continue to click points until you have the cross placed in a location you're satisfied with.

5. Since this is the first point you are aligning, you'll see a Camera Match Warning message. Click Yes at the warning message.

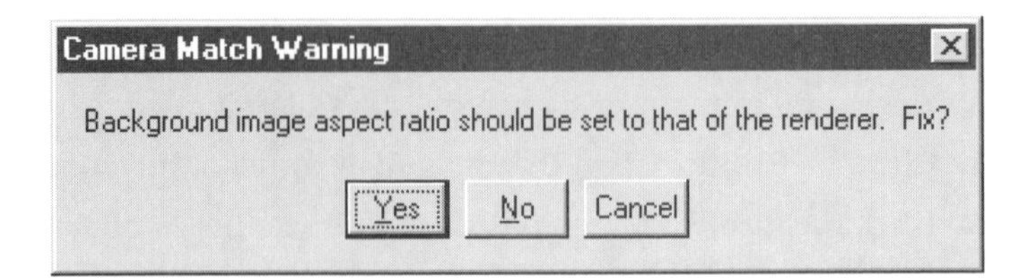

6. Select Front Top from the list in the CamPoint Info rollout, then click the top corner location in the background image as shown in Figure 15.34.
7. Repeat step 6 for each of the remaining three CamPoints.

FIGURE 15.34

Click the CamPoint name in the CamPoint Info rollout; then with the Assign Position button active, click the points shown in the figure.

VIZ now has enough information to create a camera that matches the design geometry to the background image.

1. Scroll down the Command Panel so that you can see the Camera Match rollout clearly.
2. Click the Create Camera button.

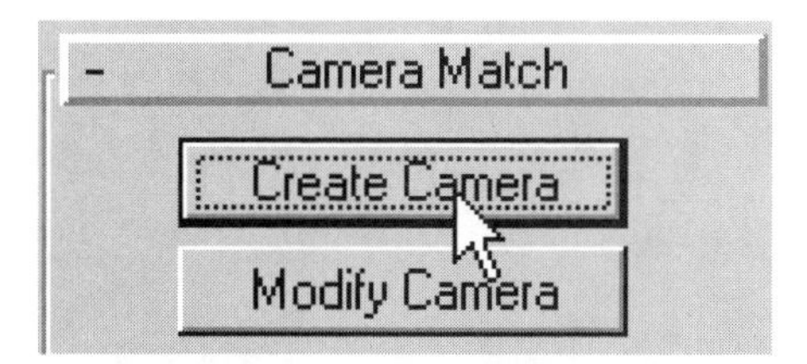

Nothing seems to have changed, but you'll see a value appear in the Current Camera Error message in the Camera Match rollout. When you click the Create Camera button, VIZ creates a camera that matches the view of the design with the background image.

TIP **A good value for the Camera Error is any value from 0 to 1.5.**

3. To see how the camera matching worked, right-click the Perspective viewport label in the upper left corner of the viewport and select Views ➢ Camera01. This is the camera that the Create Camera button created. The box will move into position over the image.
4. Click the Display tab in the Command Panel, then click All On in the On/Off rollout. The rest of the building appears in the viewport, as shown in Figure 15.35.

FIGURE 15.35

The apartment building in position

5. Select the Alignobject box and click Selected Off in the On/Off rollout. You don't want the Alignobject box to appear in the rendered view.
6. Click the Quick Render tool on the Render toolbar. The apartment is rendered with the background as shown in Figure 15.36.

FIGURE 15.36

The rendered apartment building with the background

Once you have a rendering matched to a background, your work is not completely finished. As you see in Figure 15.36, the building obscures some of the objects that are in the foreground. You can use Photoshop to bring those parts of the image back into the foreground, using the techniques you learned in Chapter 14.

1. Save the rendered image as a file called **`Apartment.tif`**.
2. In Photoshop or another image editing program, open both the `Apartment.tif` file and the original background image, `Noriegaview_render.tif`.
3. Resize the `Noriega_render.tif` image to the size of the rendered image. To do this in Photoshop, choose Image ➢ Image Size… Then in the Image Size dialog box, change the Width and Height settings in the Pixel Dimension group to values that match the VIZ rendering.

WARNING Make sure that the Constrain Proportions and Resample Image check boxes are checked when you do this.

4. Use the Lasso tool to carefully trace around the tops of the cars in the `Noriega_render.tif` image.

5. Type Ctrl+C to copy the selection to the clipboard. Then go to the rendered image of the apartment building.
6. Type Ctrl+V to paste the cars into the rendered view.
7. Use the Move tool to move the pasted cars into their proper locations.
8. Repeat the process for other items in the foreground such as the mailbox and stop sign. Figure 15.37 shows the results of the changes to the image rendered in Photoshop.

FIGURE 15.37

Editing the rendering in Photoshop.

Matching the Design Image Quality to the Background

You may find that the building doesn't quite match up with the background image in ways other than orientation and size. For example, the contrast in the building may be too low compared with the contrast in the background, or there may be a grain in the background that is not present in the rendered building. These differences can cause the design to stand out from the background, making it obvious that it is a computer rendering superimposed onto a photograph.

You can make adjustments to the lighting and materials in the design to compensate for contrast and lighting differences, but noise in the background image has to be handled differently. You can deal with both noise and contrast by taking a slightly different approach to final rendering of the design.

Now that you've got the design aligned with the background image, you can go ahead and render the image without the background. You can then use Photoshop or another image-editing program to merge the rendered design into the background image. By doing this, you have control over the rendered image of the building apart from the background. You can add noise or adjust the contrast of the rendered design in Photoshop to match the background before the two images are merged. Figure 15.38 shows the rendering redone using this method, comparing it with the rendering and background combined in the VIZ output.

FIGURE 15.38

The rendered apartment

TIP To set up VIZ to render a view without the background, choose Render ➢ Environment and turn off the Use Map option in the Background group. You can always turn the background back on by reversing this procedure.

Summary

In these last two chapters, you've seen how important an image-editing program can be in your work with VIZ. In some situations, an image-editing program can mean the difference between finishing a project on time or struggling for hours over some annoying detail in your design. It takes some experience working with VIZ to know when to use a bitmap image instead of creating an object. The information in these chapters should give you a head start in working with image files and photographs.

You also got a glimpse of how AutoCAD can be used in conjunction with VIZ as an image-editing tool. In this chapter, you saw how a photograph can be analyzed to establish vanishing points and locations, using AutoCAD. In Chapter 14, you also learned how AutoCAD and other CAD programs can be used directly to generate bitmap images of geometric shapes. In the next chapter, you'll learn how you can use AutoCAD files directly as a basis for geometry in VIZ.

chapter 16

Using AutoCAD with VIZ

FEATURING

- *Creating Topography with Splines*
- *Setting up an AutoCAD Plan for VIZ*
- *Importing AutoCAD Plans into VIZ*
- *Exploring the File Link Manager*
- *Adding Stairs*
- *Importing a Truss*

Using AutoCAD with VIZ

In Chapter 14, you had some exposure to the ways that you can use Photoshop interactively with VIZ. Another product that is very useful with VIZ is AutoCAD. You can use AutoCAD as an aid in creating material maps and to help you analyze photos for VIZ backgrounds. In this section, you'll look at ways that AutoCAD can be used more directly with VIZ to create geometry.

AutoCAD is an excellent tool for creating 2D geometry. Much of your work as a designer will require accurate renditions of your designs in the traditional plan and elevation views. Frequently, designs begin as 2D plans anyway, so having the ability to import an AutoCAD drawing is a natural extension of VIZ.

In Chapter 7, you learned how to import an AutoCAD 3D model into VIZ. In this section, you'll explore the ways that you can import AutoCAD line drawings as a starting point in the creation of VIZ geometry.

Creating Topography with Splines

In Chapter 14, you learned to create geometry by using a displacement map. A displacement map, which is similar to a bump map, creates a deformed surface based on the light and dark areas of a bitmap image. You could use a displacement map to create terrain by drawing light and dark areas in an image and then using that image as a displacement map, as shown in Figure 16.1.

FIGURE 16.1

A bitmap image and the terrain created

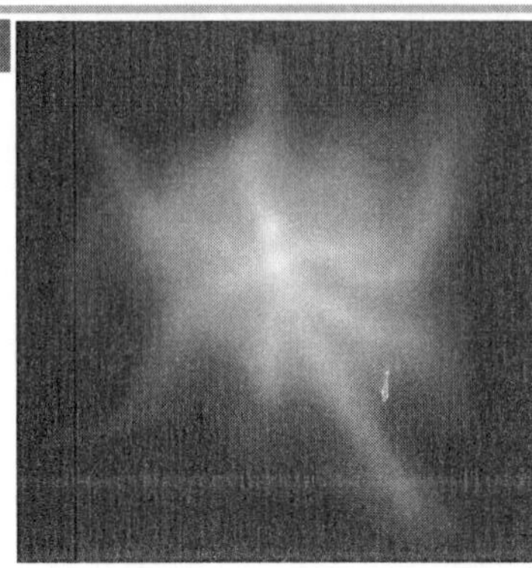

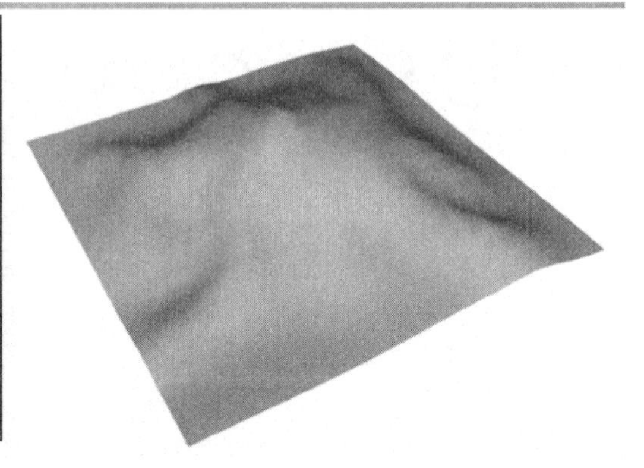

This type of terrain modeling is fine for free-form shapes, but if you want to have an accurate model of terrain based on survey data, you need to use other tools to create your terrain model. In this section, you'll learn how you can quickly create a terrain model from contour lines generated in AutoCAD. You'll also get a look at ways of linking files from AutoCAD to allow you to maintain one data source for both AutoCAD and VIZ.

1. Start VIZ; Choose Insert ➢ Linked DWG…
2. In the Open dialog box, locate and open the `Contour.dwg` file. This is an AutoCAD file that contains a series of contour lines, as shown in Figure 16.2. The contour lines are AutoCAD Splines.

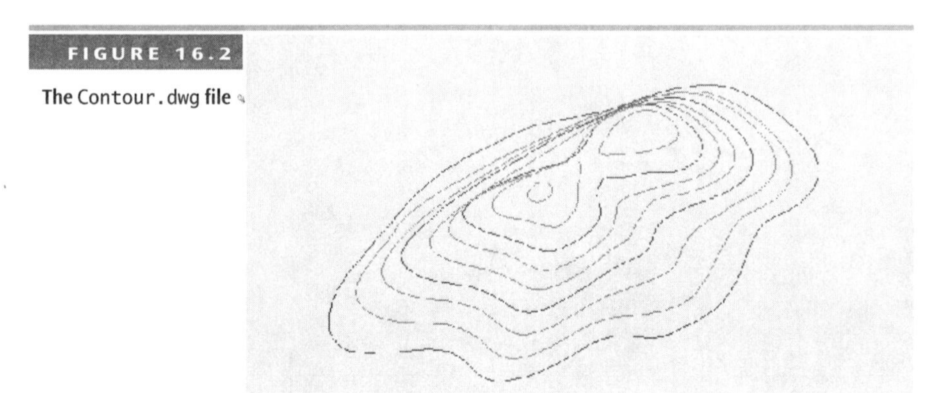

FIGURE 16.2

The Contour.dwg file

3. In the File Link Settings dialog box, click OK.

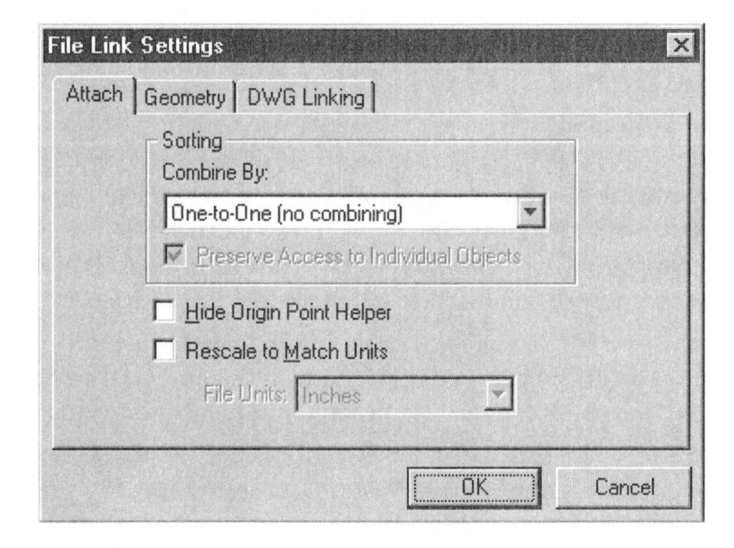

The contours appear in the VIZ Perspective viewport.

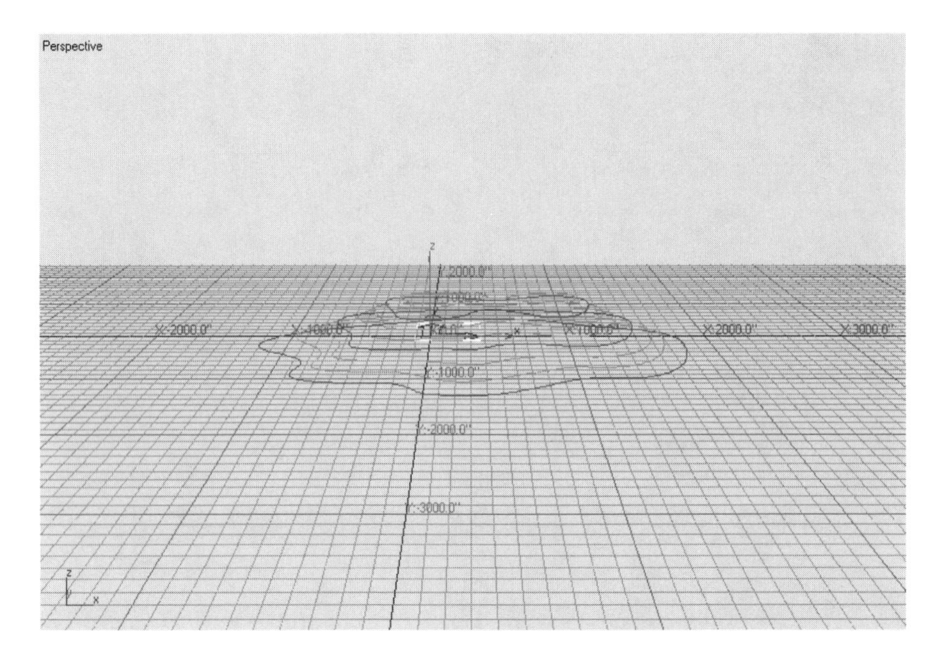

By importing an AutoCAD file as a linked file, you keep the imported geometry linked to the original AutoCAD file. As you'll see a bit later, this link will enable you to update the VIZ design whenever changes occur to the AutoCAD file.

Now let's see how the contours can be turned into a surface model:

1. Click Select by Name to open the Select Object dialog box. Select all of the objects except `contour.dwg.01`. This is the AutoCAD contour object. VIZ names the objects by their AutoCAD Color numbers. `Contour.dwg.01` is an additional object that VIZ creates to identify the origin of the imported drawing.
2. Make sure that the Geometry button is selected in the Create Tab of the Command Panel, then choose AEC Extended from the Create tab drop-down list.

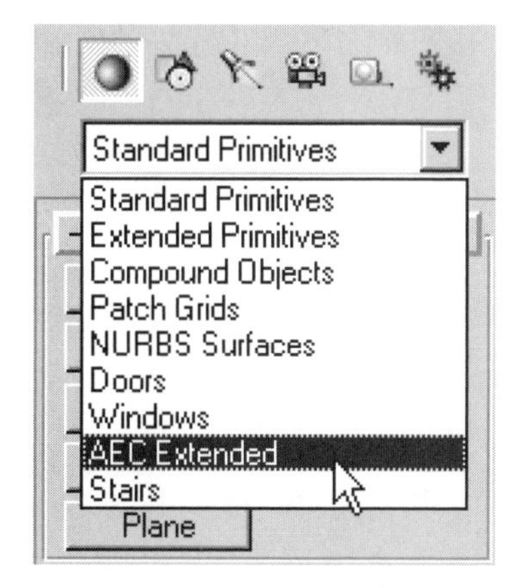

3. Click Terrain from the Object Type rollout.

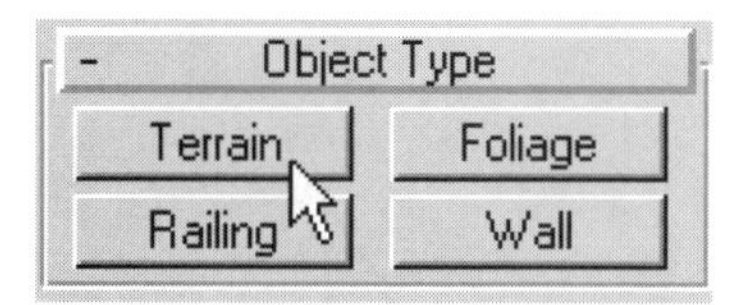

A surface appears over the contour lines.

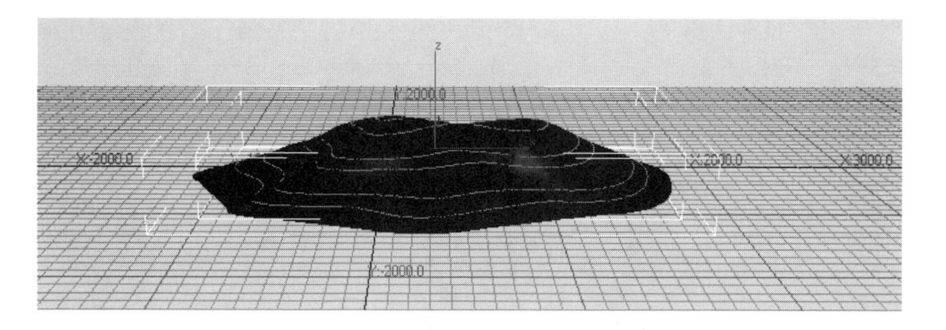

TIP As an alternative to steps 2 and 3, you can click the Terrain Compound Object tool in the Create AEC tab of the tab panel.

VIZ creates a terrain object based on the contour lines. You can improve the visibility of the terrain's shape by using the Color by Elevation option.

1. Scroll down to the Color by Elevation rollout and open it.
2. Click the Create Defaults button in the Zones by Base Elevation group.

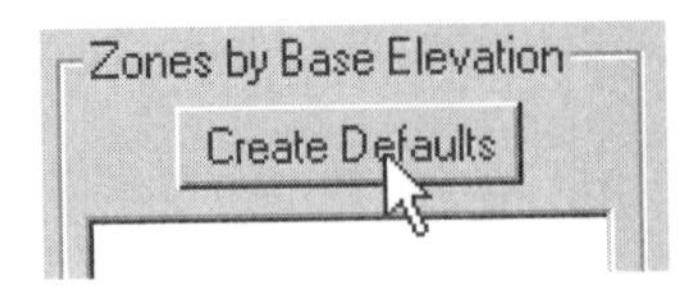

The Terrain object changes to show a series of colored bands.

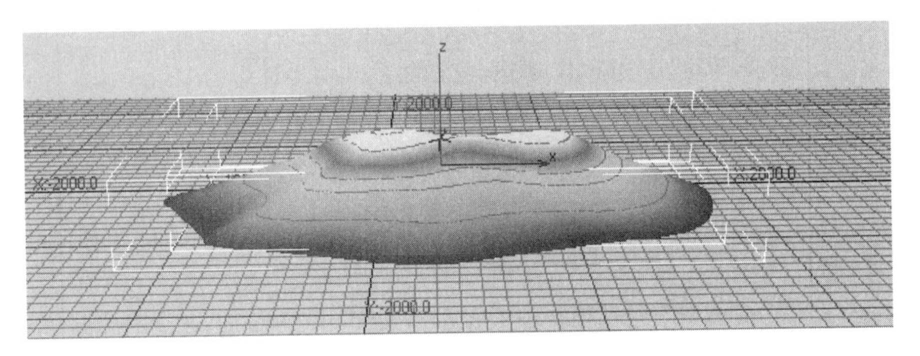

The values in the Zone by Base Elevation group list box tell you the base elevation for each of the colors. You can change the color and the base elevation.

1. Select the item at the top of the list in the list box of the Zones by Base Elevations group.
2. In the Color Zones group, click the Base Color swatch.

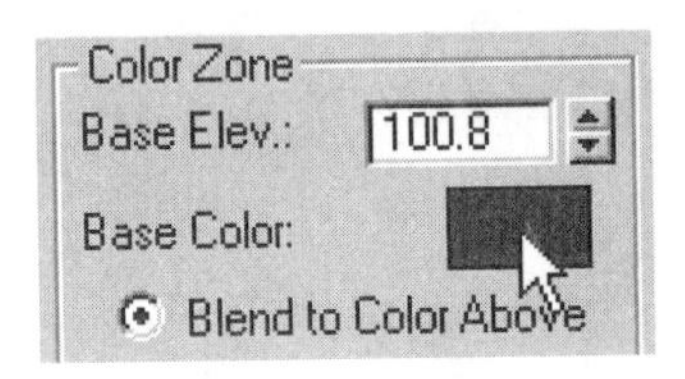

3. In the Color Selector dialog box, click the cyan (blue) color in the Hue/Blackness color selector.

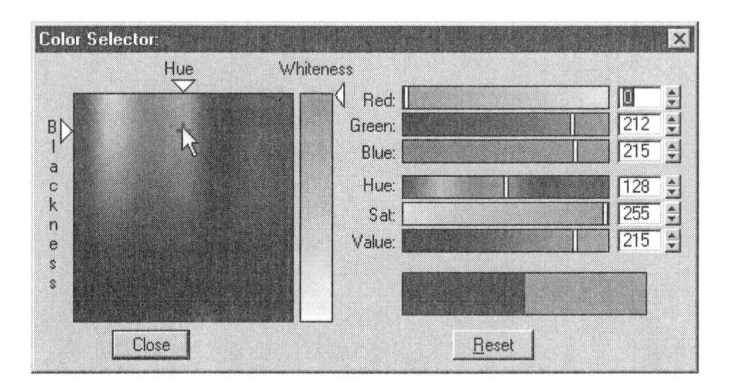

4. Click the Modify Zone button in the Color Zone group. The base of the Terrain object changes to the blue color you selected.

You can also change the vertical location for a color by changing the Base Elev value in the Color Zone group. This doesn't have any effect on the shape of the terrain object. It only changes the location of the color.

Updating Changes from an AutoCAD File

You imported the AutoCAD contour map using the Insert ➢ Linked DWG option. By using this option, you link your VIZ design to the `Contour.dwg` file in a way that is similar to Xref files in both VIZ and AutoCAD. Changes in the `Contour.dwg` file will affect any VIZ file to which it is linked.

Let's suppose that you have some corrections to make to the AutoCAD contour drawing that will affect the terrain object you've just created. You can change the AutoCAD drawing file, then update the VIZ design to reflect those changes.

1. If you have AutoCAD 14 or greater or AutoCAD LT 98 or greater, open the `Contour.dwg` file in AutoCAD and make the changes shown in Figure 16.3.

FIGURE 16.3

Stretch these points outward.

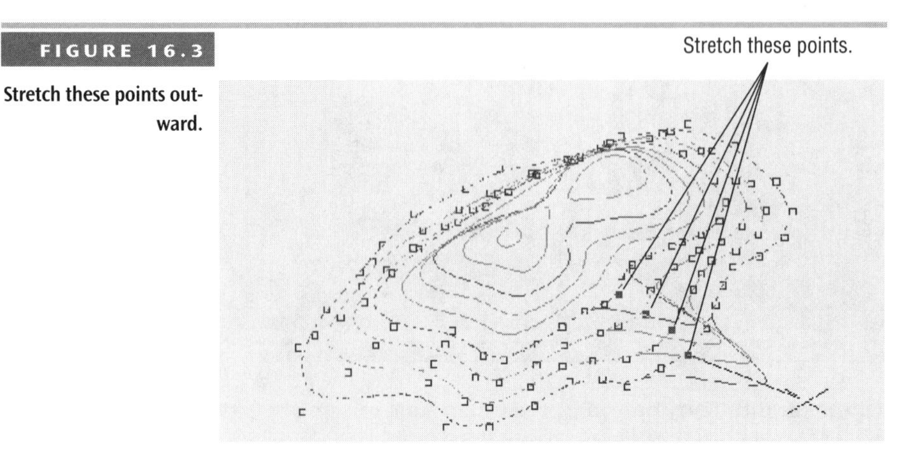

2. If you don't have AutoCAD, use the Windows Explorer to delete the `Contour.dwg` file, then make a copy of the `Contour modified.dwg` file and rename it **`Contour.dwg`** to replace the file you deleted. The `Contour modified.dwg` file contains the changes shown in Figure 16.3.
3. In VIZ, choose Insert ➢ File Link Manager...
4. In the File Link Manager dialog box, click the `Contour.dwg` listing in the Linked Files list box at the top of the dialog box.
5. Click the Reload... button.

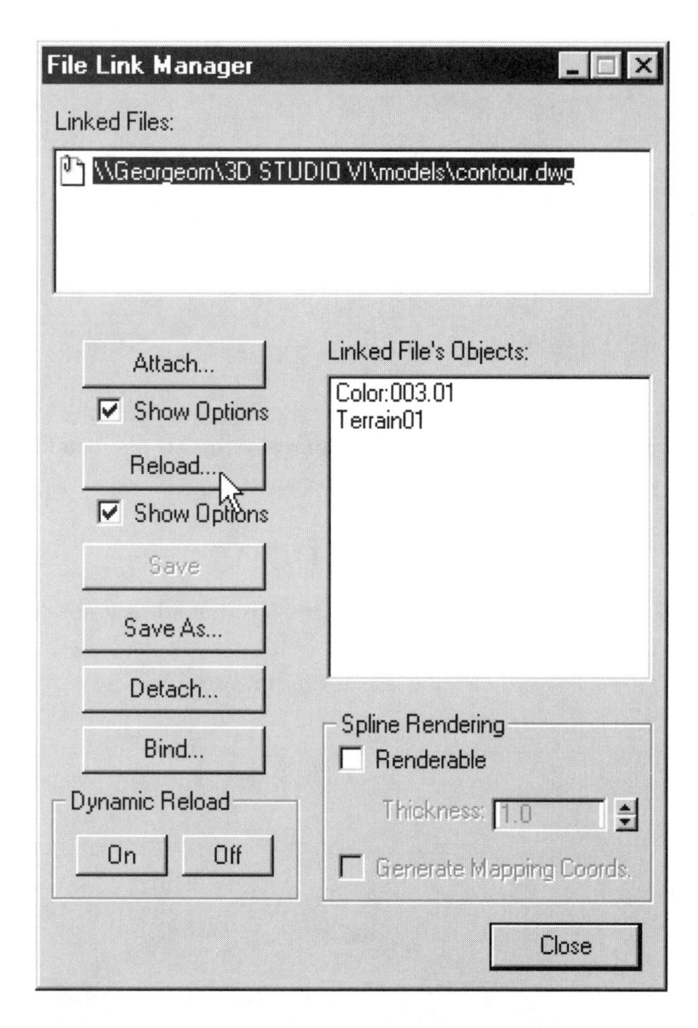

6. In the File Link Settings dialog box, click OK. The file will be reloaded and the changes will be imported into the current VIZ file.
7. Close the File Link Manager dialog box. The changes are now visible in the Terrain object.

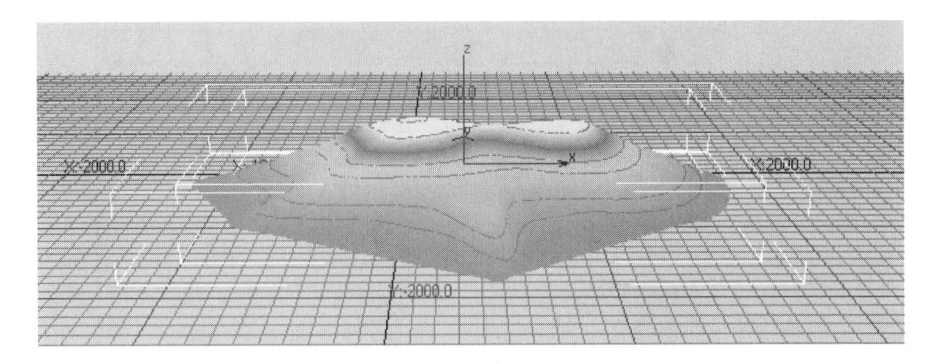

Like Xref files, VIZ designs that are linked to AutoCAD files can be updated to reflect changes that are made to the source AutoCAD file. You'll get a chance to take a closer look at this feature later in this chapter.

Exploring Terrain Options

The Terrain object has quite a few parameters that allow you to make adjustments to the terrain. For example, if you prefer, you can have the terrain appear as a terraced form instead of a smooth one, as shown in Figure 16.4.

FIGURE 16.4

The Terrain object with the Layered Solid option

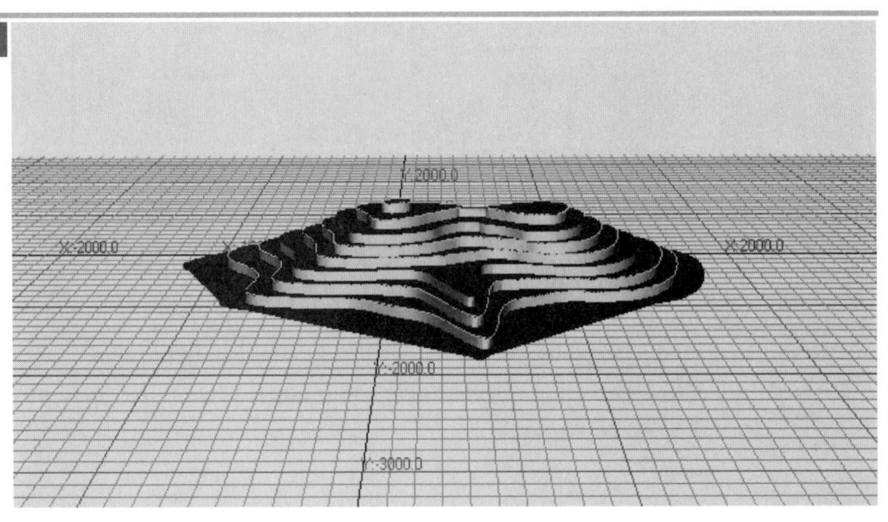

NOTE The Layered Solid option of the Terrain object creates a surface that resembles a traditional site plan model made of foamcore.

You've already seen how a few of the Color by Elevation rollout options work. Here's a rundown of the rest of the Terrain object parameters.

Pick Operand Rollout

These options allow you to add other splines to an existing Terrain object.

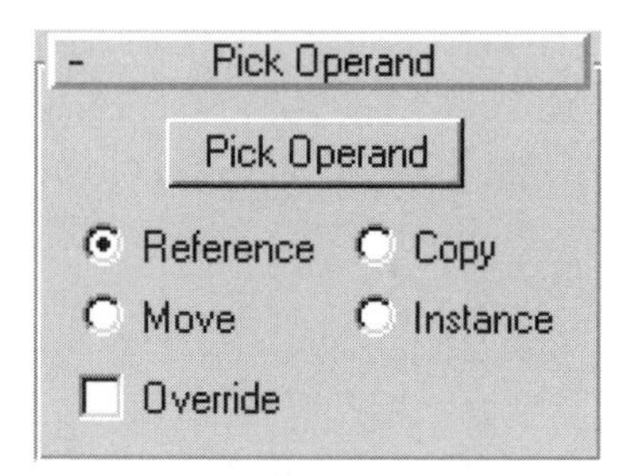

The splines used for the Terrain object are referred to as the operands of the Terrain object. When a Terrain object is created, a reference clone of the selected splines is added as part of the Terrain object. This is the default option in the Pick Operand rollout. When adding additional splines, you can choose the type of clone you wish to use instead of the Reference clone. The Override option lets you replace one operand with another.

Parameters Rollout

The Parameters rollout offers settings that control the overall form of the Terrain object. The Operands group lets you selectively delete operands from the terrain.

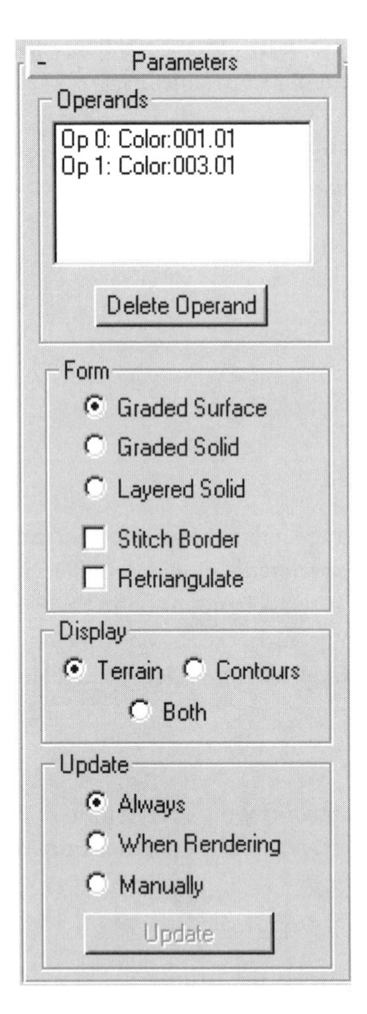

The Form group gives you control over the way the contour data is formed into a terrain. Graded Surface creates the type of terrain you've seen in previous exercises. Graded Solid creates a solid form that encloses the entire terrain, including the underside. Layered Solid creates a terraced form. The Stitched Border option improves the formation of terrain where open splines or polylines are used in the contour. Retriangulate helps to generate a terrain that follows the contours more closely.

The Display group allows you to view the terrain as either a surface terrain, contour lines, or both. The Update group lets you control the way that the Terrain object is updated when the operands are edited. Always updates the Terrain object as soon as a contour is modified. When Rendering updates when you render the design. You can also use the Update button with this option. Manually updates the terrain only when you click the Update button.

Simplification Rollout

VIZ uses the vertices of the original contour polylines to generate the Terrain object. The Simplification Rollout options give you control over the number of vertices used to generate the terrain.

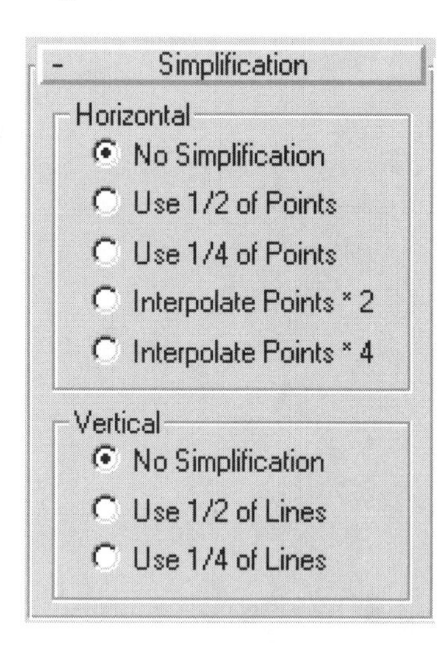

In the Horizontal group, the Use 1/2 of Points and Use 1/4 of Points options both reduce the number of points used from the contour line. These procedures reduce the accuracy of the terrain, but they also reduce the complexity of the geometry, thereby making the terrain's memory requirements smaller. The Interpolate Points options increase the number of points used. Interpolate Points * 2, for example, doubles the number of vertices used by interpolating new points between the existing points in the contour.

The Vertical group determines whether all of the selected contour lines are used. You can reduce the terrain's complexity by using either the Use 1/2 of Lines or the Use 1/4 of Lines option.

Color by Elevation Rollout

VIZ lets you color the Terrain object by elevation. This lets you visualize the terrain more clearly and helps you identify elevations by color coding them.

The Maximum Elev. and Minimum Elev. options display the maximum and minimum extents of the terrain, based on the contour data. The Reference Elev. option lets you establish a reference elevation that is used for assigning colors to the terrain. If this value is equal to or less than the lowest contour, VIZ generates five color zones for the terrain, as you saw in an earlier exercise. If the Reference Elev. is greater than the lowest contour, VIZ then treats the lower elevations as water, using the Reference Elev. value as the water level. Water is given a blue color by default.

The Zones by Base Elevation group gives you control over the individual colors for each color zone. As you've seen from the exercise, the Create Defaults button applies the colors to the terrain object based on the current settings of the rollout. You can also change the color of each zone by selecting the zone elevation from the list box and using the Base Color swatch to select a color.

The Blend to Color Above and Solid to Top of Zone radio buttons let you choose to blend colors between zones or to have each zone one solid color. By default, colors are blended. You can change from blended to solid by selecting the zone elevation from the Zones by Base Elevation list, selecting Solid to Top of Zone, then clicking the Modify Zones button. The Add Zone and Delete Zone options add and delete zones.

Setting up an AutoCAD Plan for VIZ

If you're an experienced AutoCAD user, you may find it easier to create at least some of your 3D model in AutoCAD and then import the model to VIZ to refine it. You can also import 2D plans and elevations into VIZ and build your 3D model in VIZ. In this section, you'll explore the ways you can set up an AutoCAD 2D drawing to take advantage of VIZ's modeling tools.

One of the drawbacks to importing fully developed 3D models from AutoCAD is that frequently the surface normals of the AutoCAD model are not all oriented in the same direction. You can use VIZ to adjust the normals to point in the same direction, but that takes time. It's usually more efficient in this situation to apply two-sided materials to the offending objects and leave it at that. The use of two-sided materials increases rendering time somewhat, but this disadvantage is often offset by the enormous amount of time it would have taken to adjust misaligned normals.

You can avoid the normals problem altogether by taking a few additional steps while creating your model in AutoCAD. In the next set of exercises, you'll use AutoCAD to prepare a plan for export to VIZ. If you don't have AutoCAD, you can skip to the section entitled, "Importing AutoCAD Plans into VIZ."

1. Open AutoCAD 14 or later, then open the `Savoye-ground.dwg` file. This is the ground floor plan of the Villa Savoye that you worked with earlier in this book.

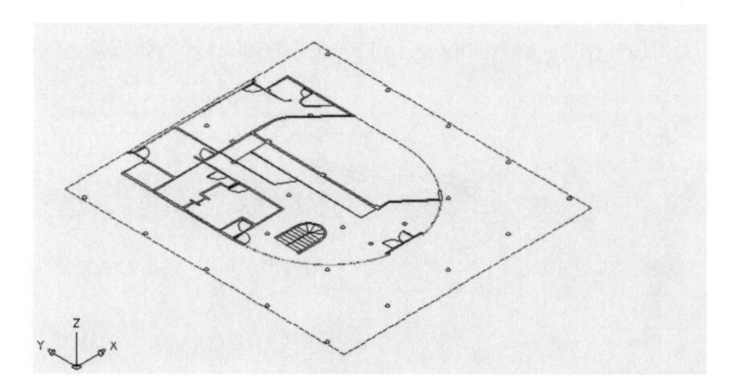

2. Select Wall-viz-EXT from the Layer drop-down list on the standard toolbar.

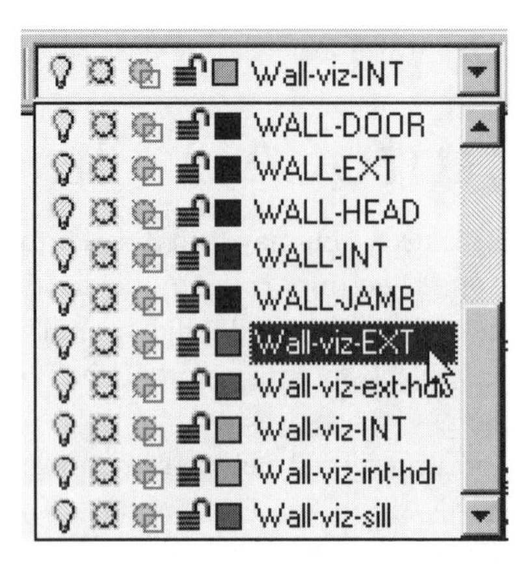

3. Use the Zoom Region tool to enlarge your view so it looks similar to Figure 16.5.
4. Choose Draw ➢ Boundary…
5. In the Boundary Creation dialog box, click Pick Points. The dialog box will temporarily disappear to allow you to select points on the screen.

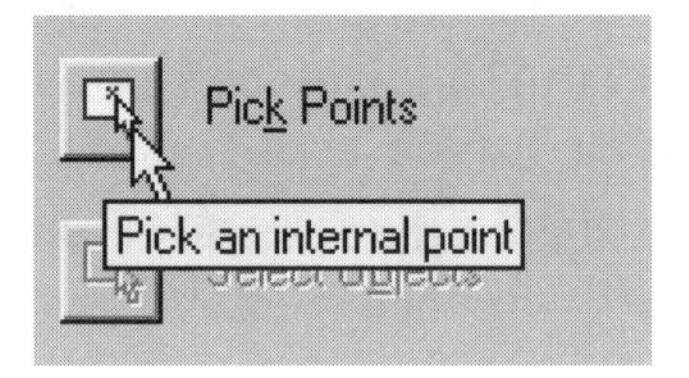

6. Click the points shown in Figure 16.5 and press ↵ when you're finished.

FIGURE 16.5

Selecting points inside the exterior walls

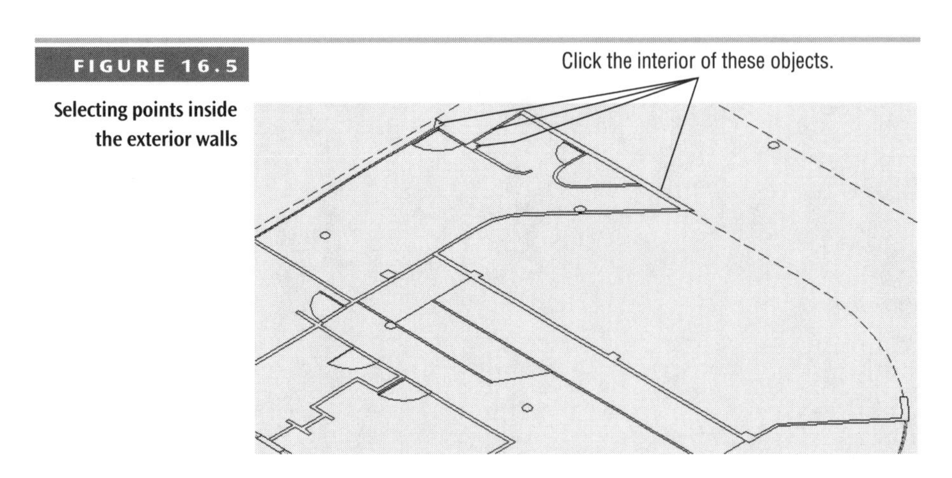

A magenta outline of the wall appears, outlining the areas you select.

The magenta outline is a continuos polyline, which will become a spline in VIZ. Since Wall-viz-EXT is the current layer, the outline is placed on the Wall-viz-EXT layer. The layer's color is magenta, so the wall acquires the layer's color of magenta.

Next, continue to add the outlines of the exterior walls using the Boundary Creation dialog box.

1. Use the Pan tool to adjust your view to look similar to Figure 16.6.
2. Open the Boundary Creation dialog box again and click the Pick Points button.
3. Select the points indicated in Figure 16.6.

FIGURE 16.6

Selecting other points for the exterior wall

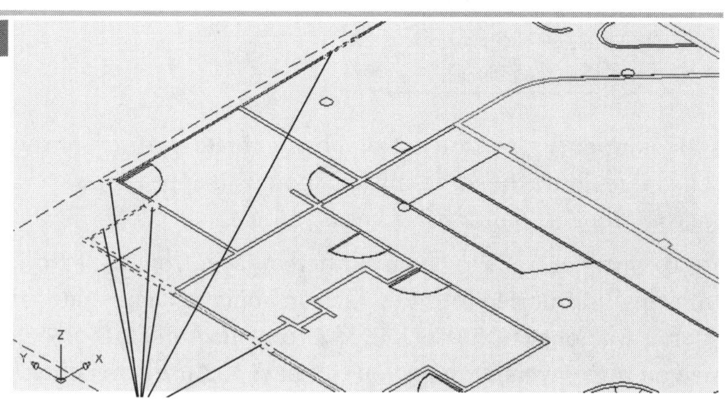

4. Press ↵ when you've selected all of the points.
5. Adjust your view as shown in Figure 16.7.
6. Use the Boundary Creation dialog box again to select the areas indicated in Figure 16.7. Press ↵ when you're done.

FIGURE 16.7

Select points in the walls near the curved glass.

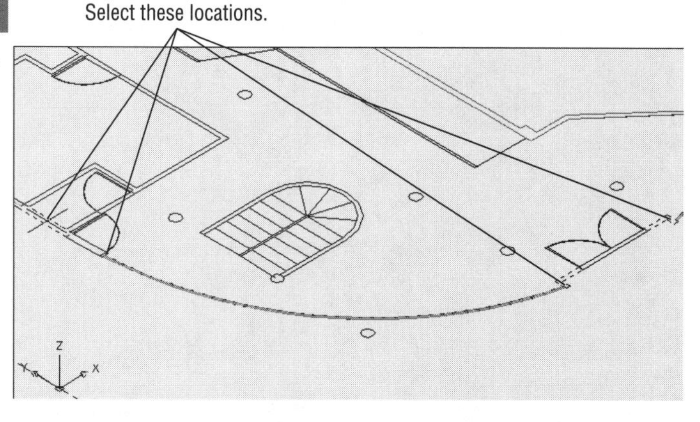
Select these locations.

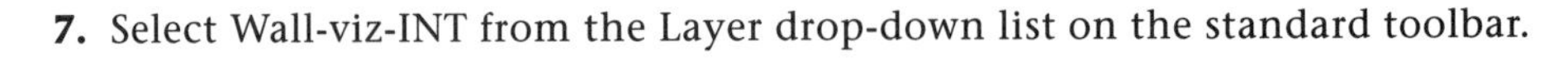

7. Select Wall-viz-INT from the Layer drop-down list on the standard toolbar.

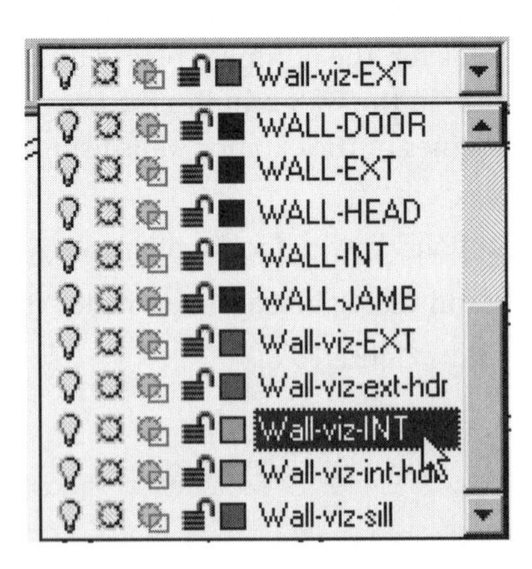

8. Use the Boundary Creation dialog box to create outlines of the interior walls. When you're done, the interior walls should all appear in the cyan color, which is the color for the Wall-viz-INT layer.

You want the interior walls to be on a different layer from the exterior walls so that when the drawing is imported into VIZ you can apply separate materials to the interior and exterior wall objects. By default, VIZ converts AutoCAD objects into VIZ objects based on their layers, though you can have VIZ use other criteria for converting objects if you choose.

Go ahead and use the Boundary Creation dialog box to outline the other portions of the drawing.

1. Choose the Wall-viz-int-hdr layer from the Layer drop-down list, then use the Boundary Creation dialog box to outline all of the door headers as indicated in Figure 16.8.

FIGURE 16.8

Outline the door headers of the interior walls.

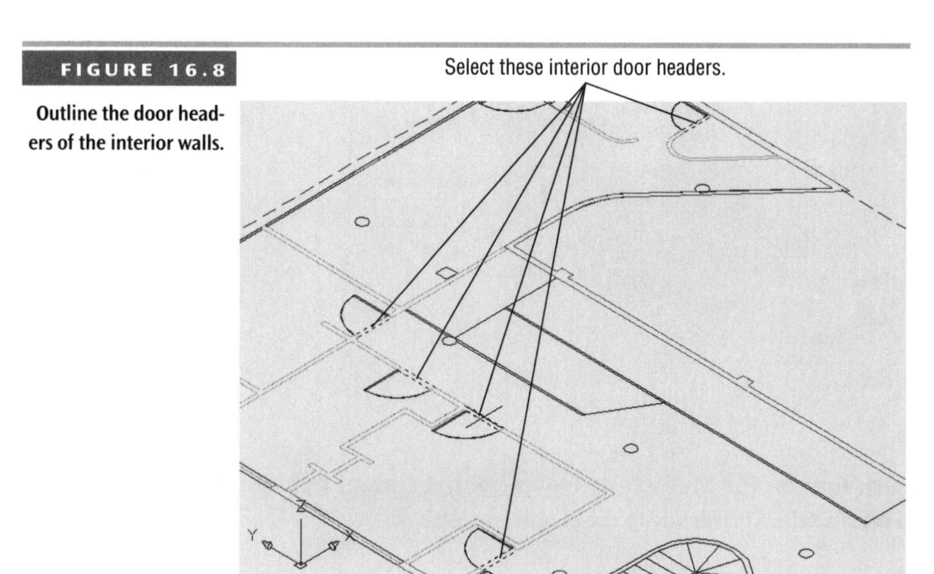
Select these interior door headers.

2. Choose the Wall-viz-ext-hdr layer, then use the Boundary Creation dialog box to outline the door headers over the exterior doors.
3. Turn off the Glass layer, then make the Wall-viz-sill layer current.
4. Use the Boundary Creation dialog box to outline the areas where the windows are indicated in the plan, as shown in Figure 16.9.

FIGURE 16.9

Outline the window areas.

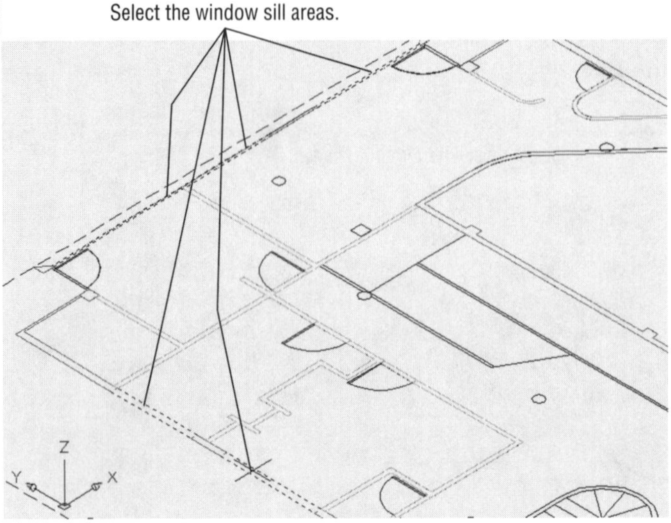

Select the window sill areas.

5. Finally, turn off the Mullion-vert layer, set the current layer to Mullion-horiz, and outline the areas indicated in Figure 16.10.

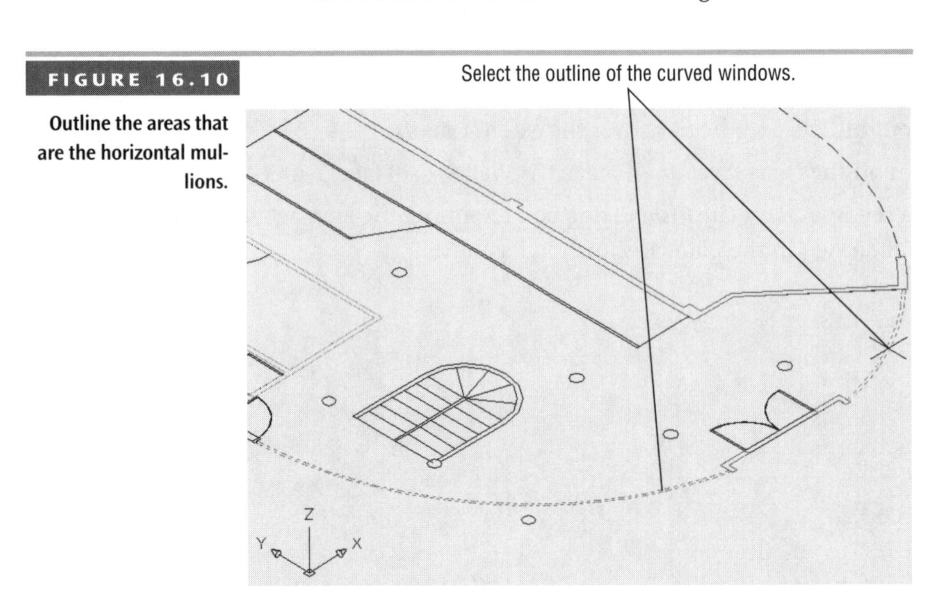
Select the outline of the curved windows.
Z
Y
X

FIGURE 16.10

Outline the areas that are the horizontal mullions.

6. Make sure all of the layers are turned back on, then choose File ➢ Save as and save the file as **MySavoye-ground-viz**.

The main point of these exercises is that you want to segregate the different parts of the drawing so that later, in VIZ, you can control the extruded heights of the separate layers individually. You ensure that you can by using layers in AutoCAD to organize the closed polylines that are to be extruded in VIZ.

You use the Boundary Creation dialog box to ensure that the polyline outlines are continuous and closed. You can also just use the Polyline tool on the Draw toolbar to trace over the wall outlines if you prefer. The Boundary Creation dialog box makes the work a lot easier.

NOTE At times you will encounter an error message while selecting areas with the Boundary Creation dialog box. This is usually caused by one of two things: either the area you select is not completely closed, or a single line intrudes into the space you're trying to outline. Also, the entire boundary has to be visible on the screen when you attempt to create a new spline. Check for these problems and try Boundary Creation again.

Importing AutoCAD Plans into VIZ

Now that you've got the plan set up, you can import it into VIZ and make fairly quick work of the conversion to 3D. You've done all of the organizing in AutoCAD, so all that is left is to extrude the building parts to their appropriate heights.

1. Open VIZ and choose File ➢ Reset. You don't need to save your changes, so click No at the Do you want to save your changes? warning and click Yes at the Do you really want to reset? warning.
2. Choose Insert ➢ AutoCAD DWG…
3. In the Select File to Import dialog box, locate and open the `MySavoye-ground-viz.dwg` file. If you haven't done the previous AutoCAD exercises, you can open the `Savoye-ground-viz.dwg` file from the companion CD.
4. In the DWG Import dialog box, click Merge Object with Current Design, then click OK.
5. In the Import AutoCAD DWG File dialog box, make sure the settings are the same as those shown in Figure 16.11.

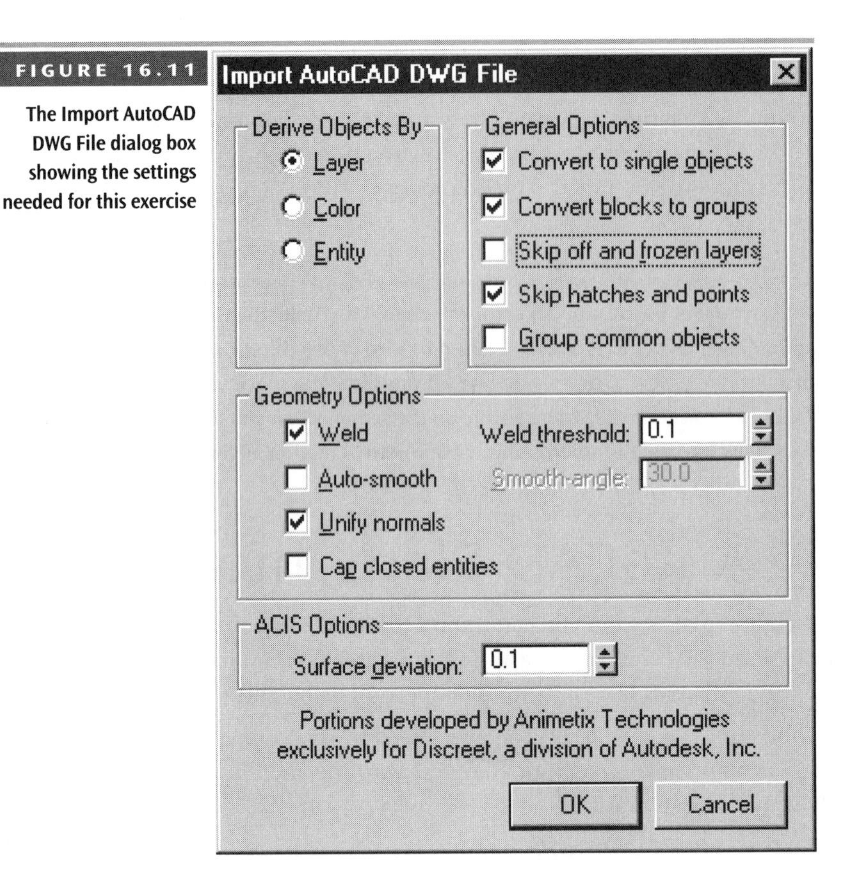

FIGURE 16.11

The Import AutoCAD DWG File dialog box showing the settings needed for this exercise

6. Be sure that the Unify Normals check box is checked. This is an important setting because it tells VIZ to align all of the normals so that they are pointing outward.
7. Click OK to import the AutoCAD file. The plan appears in the viewport.

The next step is to set up a comfortable view of the model so that you can easily maneuver within it.

Finally, to make your work a little easier, do the following:

1. Right-click the Perspective label in the upper left corner of the viewport, then select Views ➢ User, or type **U**. Your view changes to an orthographic projection instead of a perspective view.
2. Choose View ➢ Views ➢ SW to view the design as an isometric view from the southwest corner.

3. Click the Zoom Extents tool to view the plan, then use the Zoom tool to enlarge it further so it looks similar to Figure 16.12.
4. Finally, click the Grid button at the bottom of the VIZ window to turn off the grid.

FIGURE 16.12

The view so far

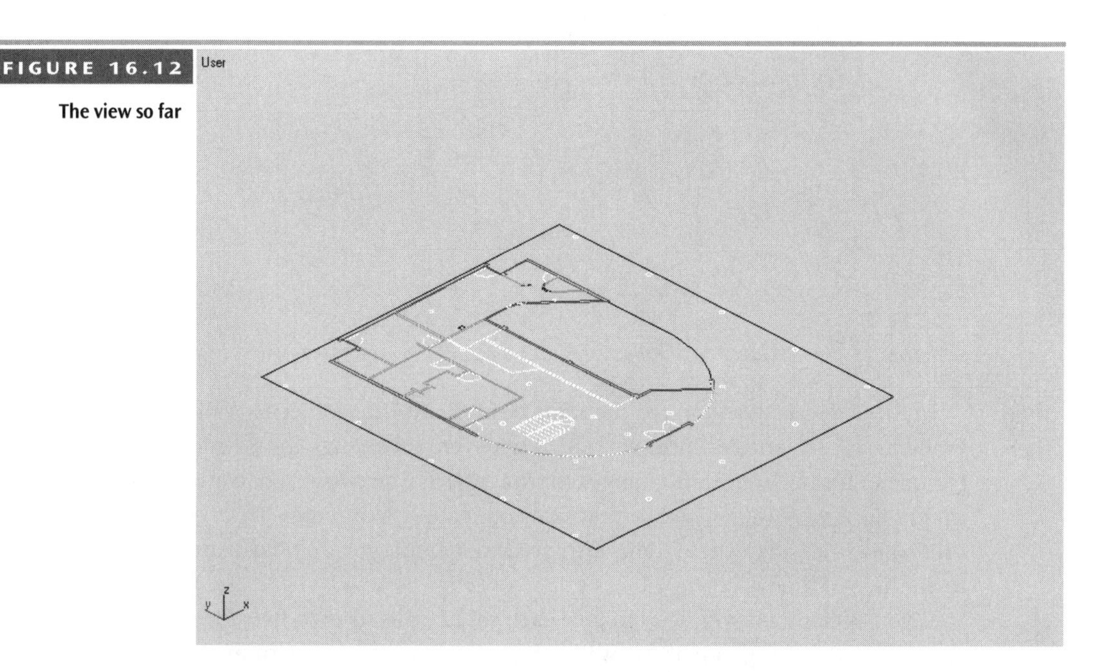

The next step is to start extruding the walls. The polyline outlines that you created in AutoCAD are converted to closed splines in VIZ, so you need only to select the splines and apply the Extrude modifier.

1. Click the Select by Name tool on the standard toolbar to open the Select Objects dialog box.
2. Select Wall-viz-INT.01, Wall-viz-EXT.01, and Mullion-vert.01 from the list, then click Select. Remember that you can select multiple, nonconsecutive items from a list by holding the Ctrl key while you click.
3. Select the Modify tab in the Command Panel and click Extrude.
4. In the Parameters rollout, set the Amount input box to **9′6″**. The walls display in the viewport.

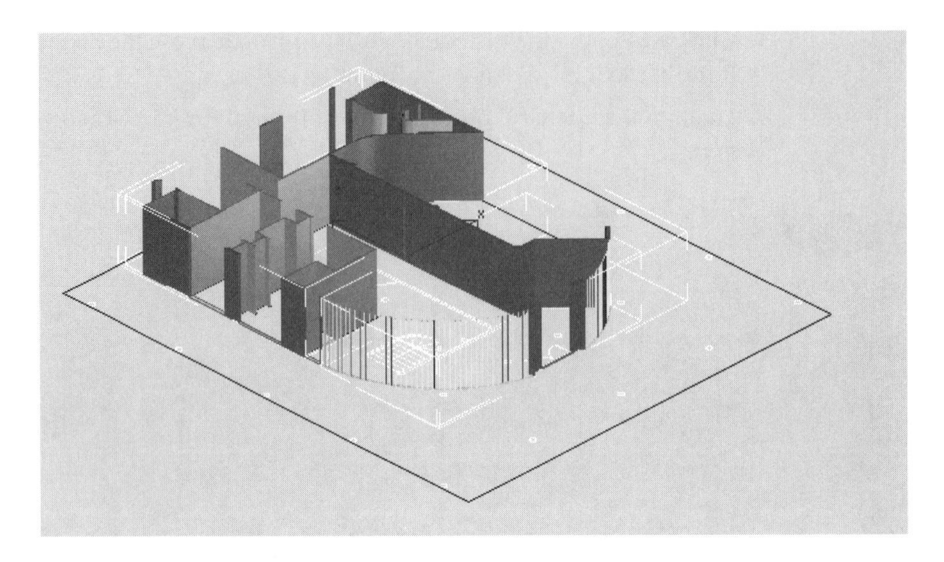

In this exercise, you applied the same modifier to three objects: Wall-viz-INT.01, Wall-viz-EXT.01, and Mullion-vert.01. Whenever you change the Extrude Amount parameter for one object, it changes for the others. The two sets of walls and the vertical mullions were segregated so that you could apply a different material to each of them, but since all of these items are the same height, you applied a single modifier to all three of them.

If you decide that you need to give each set of walls its own Extrude modifier, you can do so by clicking one of the walls, then clicking the Make Unique button in the Modifier Stack rollout.

Now let's continue with the door headers and the walls around the windows:

1. Open the Select Objects dialog box again. Then select Wall-viz-ext-hdr, Wall-viz-int-hdr, and Wall-viz-sill.01.
2. Click the Extrude button in the Modify tab, then change the Amount value in the Parameters to **1'6"**.
3. Click the Select and Move tool, then Right-click the Select and Move tool.
4. In the Move Transform type-in dialog box, change the Z value in the Offset:World group to **96**. The door headers all move to their positions above the doors.
5. Close the dialog box to get a better view of your design.

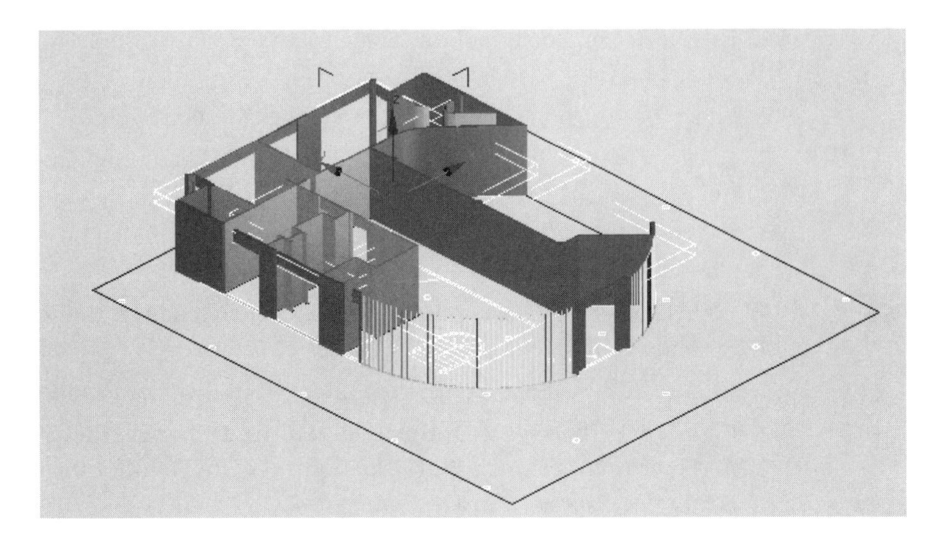

You may have noticed that in step 4 only the Offset:World group showed values. This is because you have more than one object selected. The Absolute:World values have no significance for multiple selection because several objects can have different locations in the design.

Also, just as with the walls, you use a single modifier to effect changes to two objects.

Now take a closer look at the windows. You have the window headers in place but they also need a portion of wall to fill in below the windows. You'll need to copy the window headers and change their Extrude amount.

1. Select the Wall-viz-sill.01 object. You can use the Select Object dialog box to do this, or you can just click one of the window headers toward the back of the building.
2. With the Select and Move tool selected, shift-click the blue z-axis arrow of the selected header downward to make a clone of the window header object, roughly placing the copy at ground level.
3. In the Clone Options dialog box, make sure the Copy radio button is selected. You can keep the Wall-viz-sill.02 name. Click OK to accept the clone settings.
4. Right-click the Select and Move tool on the standard toolbar, then change the Z value in the Absolute:World group to **0**.
5. Change the Amount value in the Parameters rollout of the Modify tab to **32**.

You now have the walls in place. Since you did some prep work in AutoCAD, the work in VIZ went fairly quickly. Even so, there are still a few items that need to be taken care of. The horizontal mullions for the curved window need to be created.

1. Use the Region Zoom tool to enlarge your view of the plan near the entrance to the right, as shown in Figure 16.13.
2. Select the horizontal mullion outline named Mullion-horiz.01.
3. Click the Extrude button in the Modify tab, then change the Amount parameter to **2**.
4. Choose Edit ➢ Clone, then in the Clone Options dialog box, click OK. The clone is now the selected object.
5. Right-click the Select and Move tool; then change the Z value in the Absolute:World group to **32**.
6. Choose Edit ➢ Clone again; then click OK in the Clone Options dialog box.
7. Right-click the Select and Move tool and change the Z value in the Absolute:World group to **9'4"**. The horizontal mullions for the curved window are now in place as shown in Figure 16.13.

FIGURE 16.13

A close-up view of the entrance and curved window

To finish off the ground floor of the Villa, you need to add the glass.

1. Open the Select Object dialog box and select Glass.01.
2. Click the Extrude button in the Modify tab, then change the Amount parameter to **9'6"**.

The glass appears in only one area. This is because the Glass object is a single spline and not an outline. You may recall from Chapter 3 that the normals of a surface will render the surface visible in only one direction. To compensate for this limitation, you can turn the Glass.01 spline into an outline.

1. In the Command Panel, select Editable Spline from the Modifier Stack rollout.

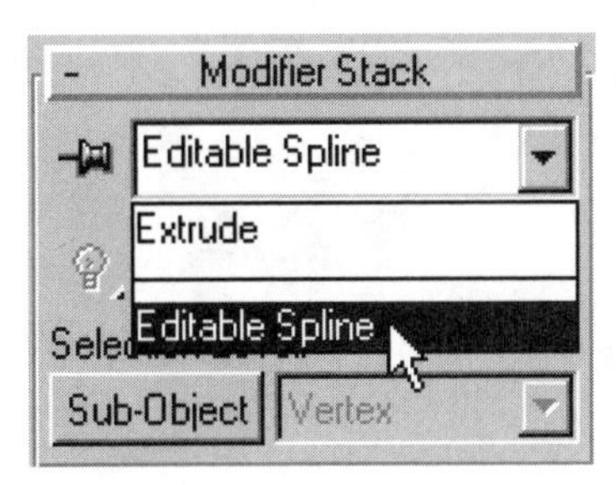

2. Click the Spline button in the Selection rollout.

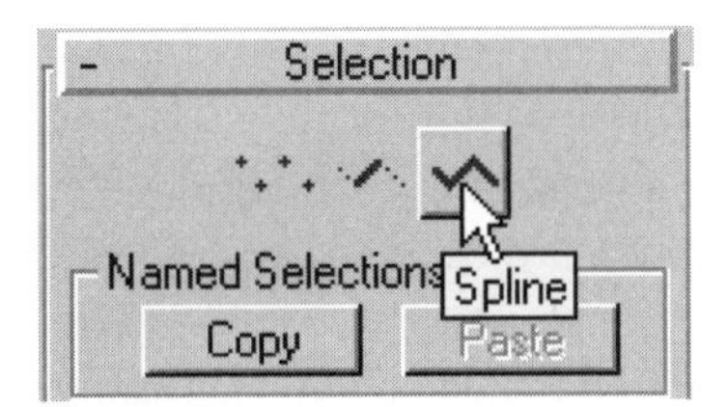

3. Click the Zoom Extent tool to view the entire design.
4. Click the Select Object tool on the standard toolbar, then place a selection region around the entire building to select the entire Glass.01 spline.
5. Scroll down to the Outline button in the Geometry rollout and enter **0.2↵** for the Outline value. You won't see any changes at this viewing distance, but the glass is now an outline instead of a single line.
6. Scroll back up to the top of the Command Panel, then click the Sub-Object button to exit the Sub-Object level.
7. Select Extrude from the Modifier Stack rollout. The glass now appears in all of the appropriate places.

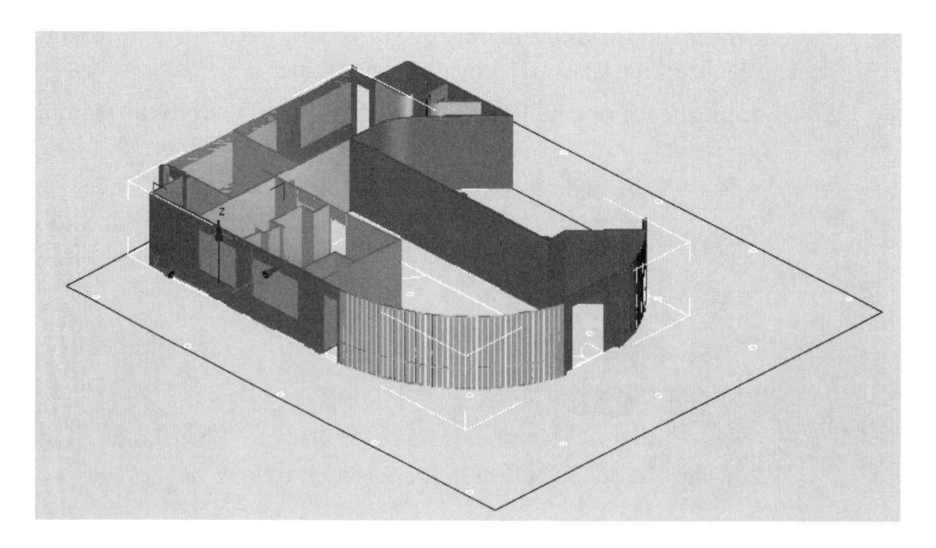

8. Save this file as **Savoye-ground.viz**.

You could have left the glass as a single line. Although this makes it difficult to see in a shaded viewport, you can apply a two-sided material to the glass so that it will appear in a finished rendering. Although a two-sided glass material takes a bit longer to render, the single-line glass material is a less complex geometry. This makes the file a bit smaller. For this reason, if your model contains lots of curved glass, it may make sense to leave the glass as a single line. Otherwise you may want to convert all of the glass in your model to outlines. As you've seen here, that's fairly easy to do in VIZ. It takes a bit more work to accomplish the same results in AutoCAD.

You may have noticed also that in the last exercise you gave the glass a full height of 9 feet 6 inches, even though in many cases the glass only filled a height of 64 inches or less. You can do this because VIZ takes care of the small details of object intersections. In those places where the glass occurs within a wall, VIZ hides most of the glass, and it is displayed only where it appears in an opening, as shown in Figure 16.14. VIZ also takes care of the intersection of the vertical and horizontal mullions.

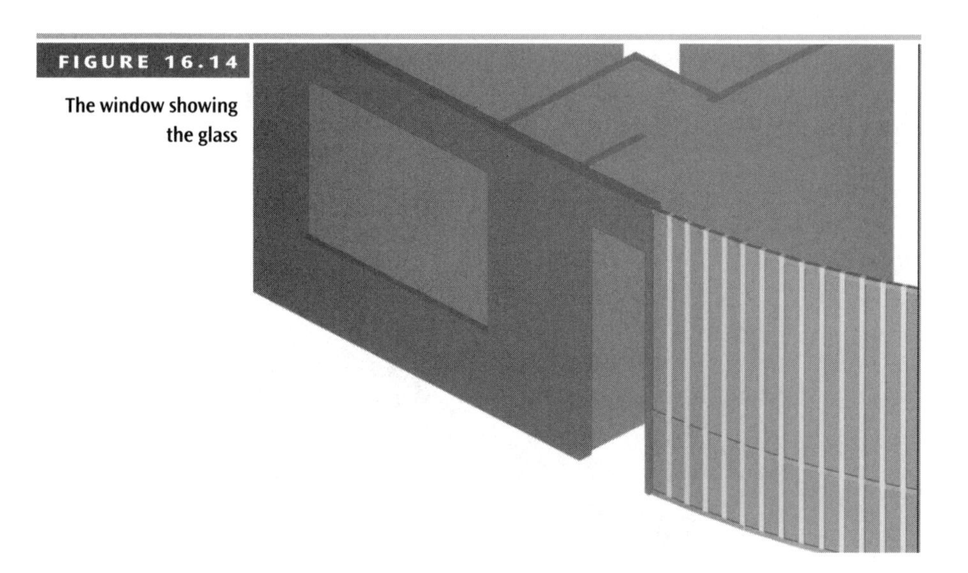

FIGURE 16.14

The window showing the glass

Creating a Floor with Openings

You've seen how the ground floor of the Villa can be set up in AutoCAD to make quick work of the extrusions in VIZ. The second floor and rooftop can be done in the same way, but the floors between the different levels require a slightly different approach.

Both the second floor and roof surface have openings that need some special attention when setting up for export to VIZ.

1. Go back to AutoCAD and open the `Savoye-second.dwg` file.
2. Create a layer named **VIZ-floor** and make it the current layer.
3. Use a Polyline to outline the second floor as shown in Figure 16.15.

FIGURE 16.15

Outline the second floor.

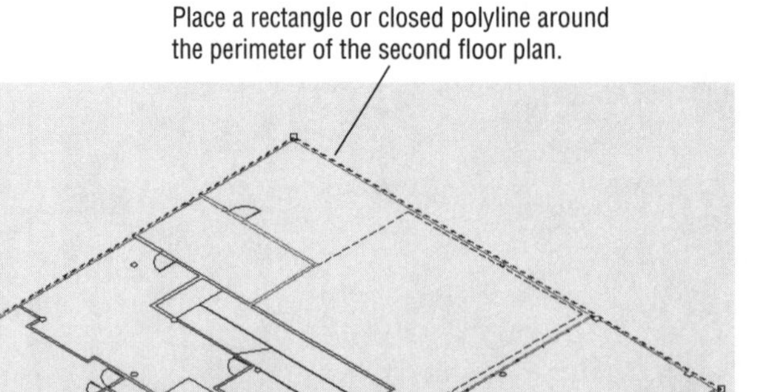
Place a rectangle or closed polyline around the perimeter of the second floor plan.
Z
Y
X

4. Turn off all of the layers except VIZ-floor, Stair, and Ramp, then zoom into the stair as shown in Figure 16.16.
5. Enlarge the view of the stair. Then outline the stair with a closed polyline as shown in Figure 16.16. (In this operation, you're drawing the outline of the stair opening in the floor.)

FIGURE 16.16

Outline the stair.

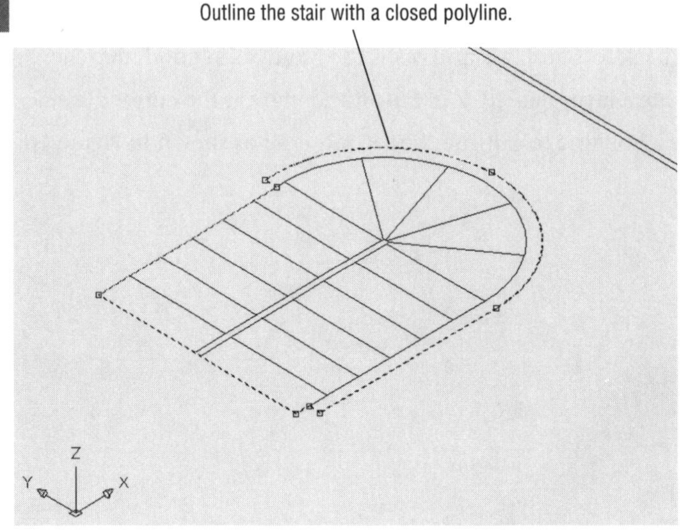
Outline the stair with a closed polyline.
Z
Y
X

6. Pan over to the ramp. Then draw an outline of the ramp with a closed polyline, as shown in Figure 16.17.

FIGURE 16.17

The outline of the ramp floor opening

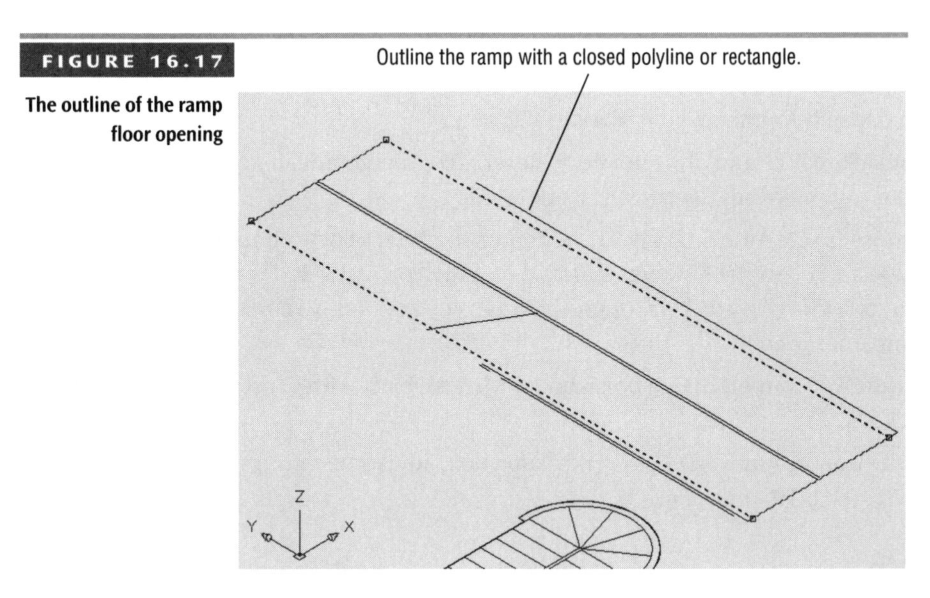
Outline the ramp with a closed polyline or rectangle.
Z
Y
X

You've got all of the additional line work you need to export the floor of the second story to VIZ. A few more steps are needed to complete the setup for VIZ.

1. Turn off all of the layers except the VIZ-floor layer.
2. Use the Zoom Extent tool to view your work so far. You now have the outline of the second floor and the two openings through the floor.

FIGURE 16.18

The outline of the second floor

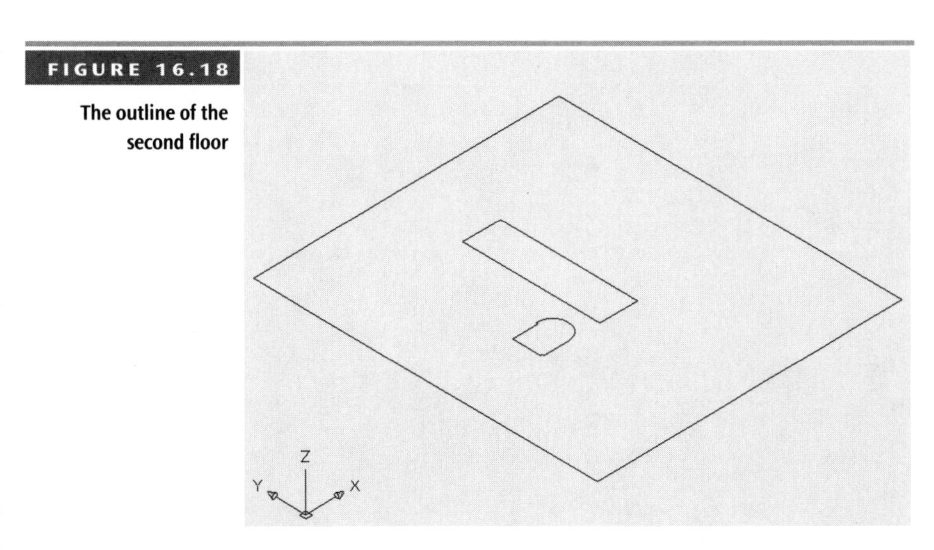
Z
Y
X

3. Choose File ➢ Save to save your changes.

Basically, you've outlined the second floor and its openings with closed polylines. In addition, you've turned off all of the layers except for the floor outline and openings. This last step limits the objects that VIZ imports to just those items you added to the AutoCAD file.

The next step is to import your work to VIZ.

1. Go back to VIZ and choose File ➢ Reset. You can go ahead and reset the file since you've already saved your work.
2. Choose Insert AutoCAD DWG… Then in the Select File to Import dialog box, locate and open the `Savoye-second.dwg` file you just saved from AutoCAD. If you don't have AutoCAD, open the `Savoye-second-viz.dwg` file from the companion CD.
3. In the DWG Import dialog box, choose Merge Object with Current Design, then click OK.
4. In the Import AutoCAD DWG File dialog box, adjust the settings to match those of Figure 16.19, then click OK.

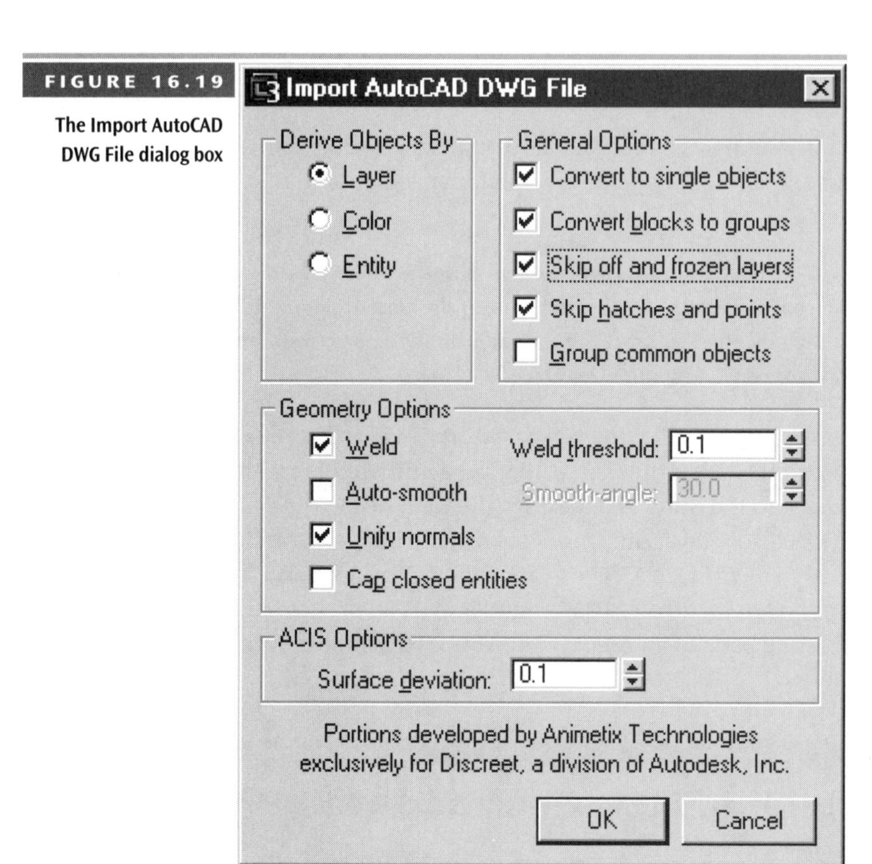

FIGURE 16.19

The Import AutoCAD DWG File dialog box

You see the outline of the second floor that you created in AutoCAD.

The final step is fairly easy. You only need to extrude the spline, and the openings will appear automatically.

1. Click the Select object tool; then click the floor outline.
2. Select the Modify tab in the Command Panel; then click the Extrude button.
3. Set the Amount parameter to **18**. You now have the second story floor, complete with openings.

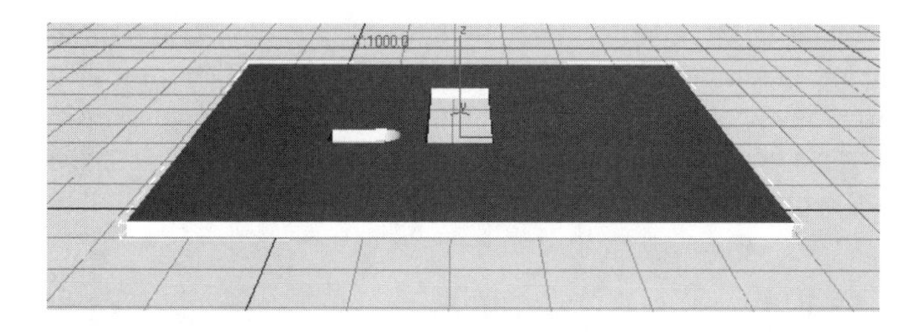

4. If you like, go ahead and save this file as `Savoye-secondfloor.max` for future reference.

VIZ automatically subtracts closed splines that are enclosed by other splines. On the second floor, ramp and stair openings are automatically subtracted from the second floor perimeter.

TIP As an alternative in AutoCAD, you can convert the closed splines of the stair, ramp, and floor into regions, then subtract the stair and ramp regions from the floor outline. AutoCAD regions are converted into VIZ surfaces.

You were asked to turn off all of the layers in AutoCAD except for the Viz-floor layer. This allowed you to limit the objects that were imported from AutoCAD into VIZ. You can go back to the AutoCAD file, turn the wall, header, and other layers back on, then turn the VIZ-floor layer off. Once you've done that, you can import the other second story elements into a VIZ file, then merge the floor and the walls. Of course, you can also turn on all of the layers and import all of the AutoCAD drawing at once. But importing parts of an AutoCAD file can help simplify your work and keep it manageable.

Using Building Elevations and Wall Profiles from AutoCAD

In the last section, you learned how to convert outlines of a building plan into a floor with openings. You can employ the same procedures for converting building elevations from AutoCAD to VIZ 3D designs. For example, in AutoCAD you can outline an elevation of the Villa, using concentric rectangles for the second floor outline and the windows. You would then import the outlines to VIZ and extrude them, just as you did with the floor. That would give you the exterior walls of the building that you could rotate into a vertical position.

Using this method, you can even include other detail such as the window mullions. Once you've done this for all four exterior walls, you can join the walls to form the second floor exterior walls, complete with window openings and even window detail.

Another great tool for forming building exteriors and interiors is the Loft tool. Sometimes a simple vertical extrusion won't be enough for walls. You may be working with a design that makes use of strong horizontal elements, such as a wide cornice or exaggerated rustication. You can make quick work of such detail by using VIZ's Loft tool. Draw the profile of the wall and the building footprint in AutoCAD. Make sure each of

Continued on the next page

these items is on a separate layer and is made of polylines. You can then import the AutoCAD file into VIZ and use the Loft Compound object tool to loft the wall profile along the building footprint in a way similar to the Ronchamp roof exercise in Chapter 5. This is especially helpful if the building footprint contains lots of curves and corners that would otherwise be difficult to model.

Exploring the File Link Manager

Earlier in this chapter, you were introduced to the File Link Manager when you imported topographic contour lines from AutoCAD. In that example, the File Link Manager allowed you to update the VIZ terrain model when a change was made to the AutoCAD .dwg file. You can also use the File Link Manager with floor plans to help maintain design continuity between AutoCAD and VIZ.

Try using the File Link Manager with the second floor of the Villa in the following exercises:

1. Choose File ➢ Reset to reset the file.
2. Choose Insert ➢ File Link Manager…
3. In the File Link Manager dialog box, click Attach…
4. Locate and open the `Savoye-second.dwg` file you edited in AutoCAD. If you don't have AutoCAD, use `Savoye-second-viz.dwg` from the companion CD.
5. In the File Link Settings dialog box, click the DWG Linking tab and make sure that the Convert Drawing Layers to Design Layers option is *not* checked.

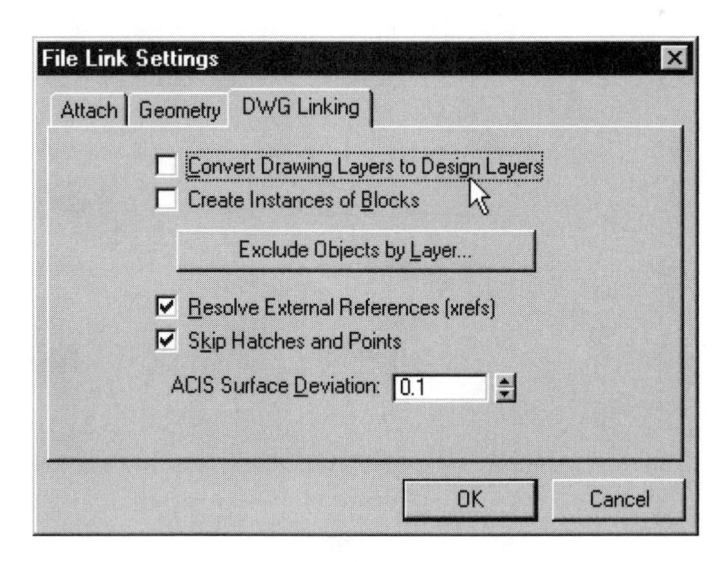

6. Click the Attach tab, then make sure the Layer option is selected in the Combine By: drop-down list in the Sorting group.

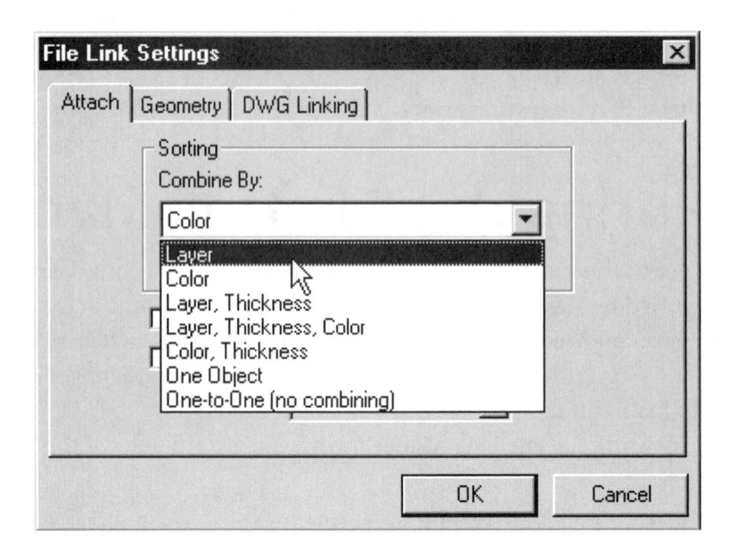

7. Click OK and close the File Link Manager dialog box. The plan displays in the Viewport.

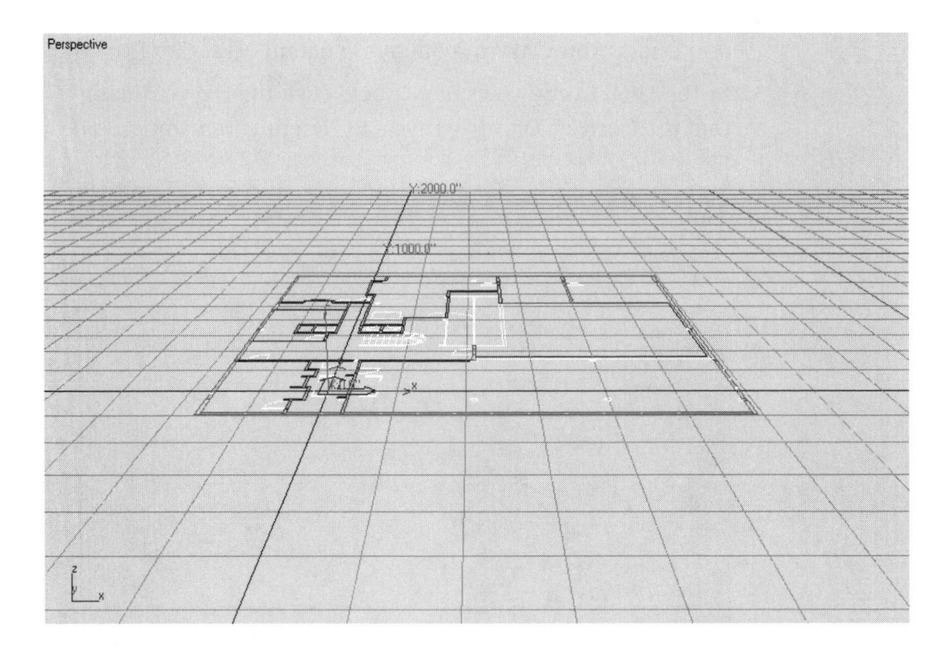

TIP When you turned off the Convert Drawing Layers to Design Layers option in step 5, the Layer option was enabled in step 6. Had you turned on the Convert Drawing Layers to Design Layers option, Layers would not have appeared as an option in the Combine By drop-down list in step 6.

You can now select and extrude objects as you did for the `Savoye-ground.dwg` file you imported earlier.

1. Open the Select Objects dialog box; then select the Layer:Wall-viz-INT.01 and Layer:Wall-viz-EXT.01 objects.
2. Click the Modify tab in the Command Panel, then click the Extrude button.
3. Set the Amount parameter to **9'6"**. The interior and exterior walls display in the model.

As you can see, the method for extruding the walls is exactly the same for the linked AutoCAD file. This is due in part to the options you chose earlier when importing the file. You were directed to set up the linked file so that layers were converted to objects. This mimics the standard way that VIZ imports non-linked AutoCAD files.

You can also choose to import AutoCAD layers as VIZ layers. You can then control layers as you would in AutoCAD, using the AutoCAD layer names preserved in VIZ. The drawback to this method is that the imported objects are given names based on their AutoCAD colors, which can be a bit confusing in VIZ.

Editing Linked AutoCAD Files

Now let's take a look at one of the key advantages of using the File Link Manager instead of the simpler DWG file import.

1. Go back to AutoCAD and open the `Savoye-second.dwg` file.
2. Turn on all of the layers and use the Stretch command to stretch the walls as shown in Figure 16.20.

FIGURE 16.20

Stretch these walls as shown here.

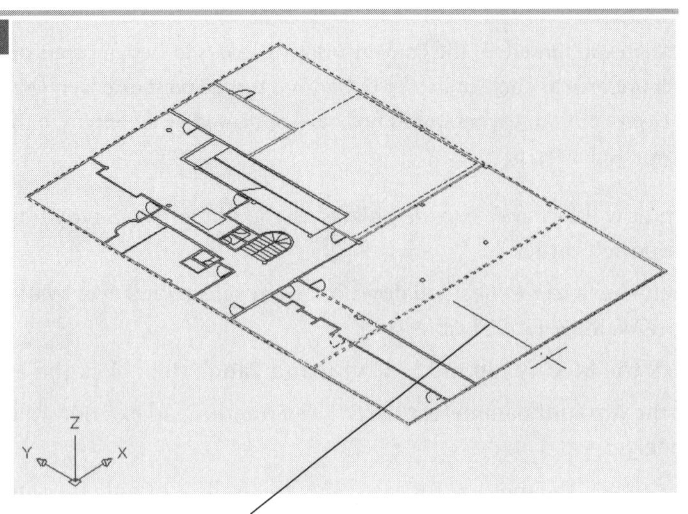

3. Choose File ➢ Save to save the changes.

NOTE **If you don't have AutoCAD, use the Windows Explorer to make a copy of the** `Savoye-second-viz.mod.dwg` **file from the Companion CD as** **`Savoye-second.dwg`**. `Savoye-viz-mod.dwg` **contains the modifications described in the previous exercise.**

4. Go back to VIZ, then click Insert ➢ File Link Manager.
5. In the File Link Manager dialog box, select the `Savoye-second.dwg` listed in the Linked Files list box, then click the Reload button.
6. In the File Link Settings dialog box, click OK. Then close the File Link Manager dialog box.

The VIZ design is updated according to the changes made in the AutoCAD file.

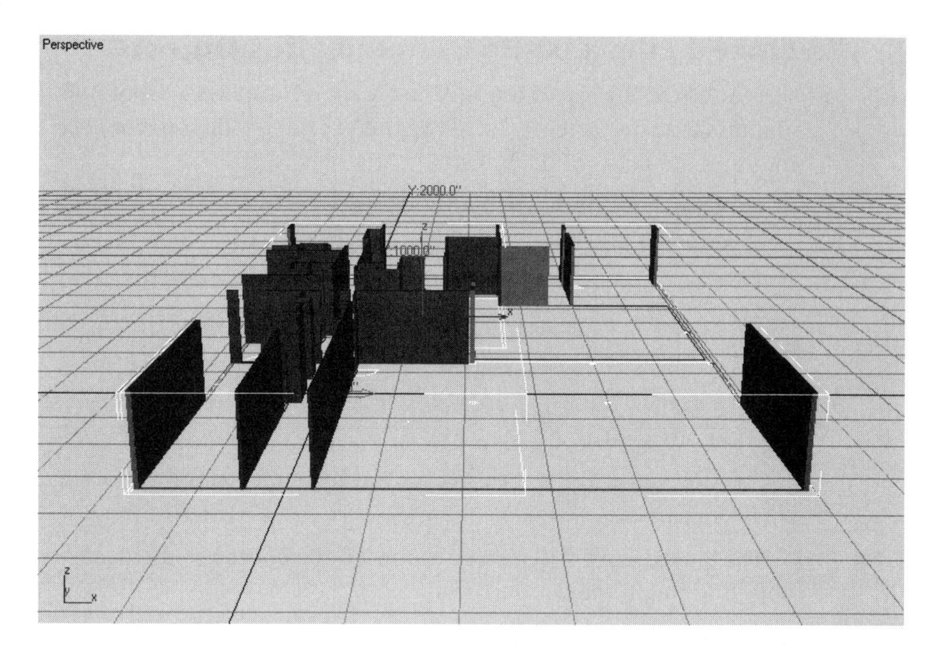

You've seen how you can update VIZ designs when changes occur in a linked AutoCAD object. If you add objects in AutoCAD, those objects are also added to the VIZ design. If the new object is added to a layer that already exists, and the objects associated with that layer are attached to a modifier, then the new object is also controlled by the modifier. For example, if you add a rectangle to the AutoCAD drawing on the Wall-viz-EXT layer, the new rectangle will be extruded to the 9'6" height, just like all of the other objects on the Wall-viz-EXT layer. New objects that have a thickness or that are extruded within AutoCAD will be ignored by VIZ unless they are placed on a newly created layer.

Understanding the File Link Manager Options

In the previous exercise, you were able to try out a few of the File Link Manager options. The File Link Manager, like so many other VIZ features, offers numerous options to tailor your work to the particular needs of your project. In the limited space of this book, you won't be shown an example of every option available, but you can get started with this feature after reviewing the exercises. Here's a summary of the File Link Manager's options.

Linked Files List Box/Linked Files Objects

The list box at the top of the File Link Manager displays a list of AutoCAD .dwg and .dxf files that are currently linked to the VIZ design file. An icon next to the filename indicates the status of the linked file:

- A paper clip indicates that the source file has not changed and that there are no errors in the link.
- A question mark indicates that a file cannot be found.
- A red flag indicates that the file has changed since import and that it must be reloaded using the Reload button.
- A grayed-out page indicates that a different file has been selected through another path.
- A curved arrow indicates that the Dynamic Reload option has been turned on for this file.

The Linked File's Object list box toward the bottom of the dialog box lists the objects found in the selected file.

Attach…

The Attach… button lets you attach an AutoCAD .dwg or .dxf file to the current VIZ design. Files can be attached from versions 12 through 2000 of AutoCAD. If you are using a CAD program other than AutoCAD, you can use the .dxf file format instead of the .dwg format, although many CAD programs today support the .dwg file format directly.

With the Show Options check box selected, you will see the File Link Settings dialog box shown in previous exercises after you've made a file selection with the Attach… option. See the description of the File Link Settings dialog box later in this section.

Reload

As you've seen in previous exercises, this option lets you manually reload a linked AutoCAD file. An abbreviated form of the File Link Settings dialog box appears when you click this button, if you have the Show Options check box checked.

Save/Save As

If you make changes such as object transforms to the linked design in VIZ, you can save those changes to the source AutoCAD file. The application of modifiers will not affect changes to the source file.

Detach

Detach removes a linked file from the current VIZ design. Use this option with caution, as it deletes all of the linked objects in the design.

Bind

The Bind option detaches any links to the source AutoCAD file while maintaining the objects in the current VIZ design. The VIZ design then becomes an independent design file and can no longer be affected by the source AutoCAD file.

Dynamic Reload Group

Selecting the On option in the Dynamic Reload group causes VIZ to automatically reload the source AutoCAD file whenever that file is updated. The default Off option tells VIZ to reload the source AutoCAD file only when the Reload button is selected.

Spline Rendering Group

You can set up VIZ to render linked splines as tubes by activating the Renderable option in the Spline Rendering group. With this option checked, you can set the thickness for the rendered splines in the Thickness input box. You can also have mapping coordinates applied to the rendered tubes by turning on the Generate Mapping Coord. option.

Understanding File Link Settings

When you import a linked AutoCAD file, you have the option to control the way that file is imported through the File Link Settings dialog box. This dialog box appears by default when you've selected a file for linking, but you can set up VIZ to avoid this dialog box by turning off the Show Options check box in the File Link Manager dialog box.

As you saw in previous exercises, the options selected in the File Link Settings dialog box can make a huge difference in the way the resulting VIZ file is organized. Since AutoCAD and VIZ use entirely different ways to organize data, this dialog box is necessary to make some sense of the way AutoCAD .dwg files are converted to VIZ files. To help in the translation process, VIZ uses a type of compound object called a *VIZblock*. All linked AutoCAD objects are converted to VIZblocks, which are typically a collection of AutoCAD objects based on their layer or color assignment.

For example, objects in an AutoCAD file that reside on layer 0 are collected into a single VIZblock. The name of the VIZblock will depend on the settings you choose in the File Link Settings dialog box. In the previous exercise, you chose the Layer option in the File Link Settings dialog box Sorting group. You can further refine the way VIZ combines objects through a combination of layer, thickness, and color, or you can have VIZ import each AutoCAD object as a single object in VIZ.

Organizing Objects by Color

In the first part of this chapter, you imported a contour drawing using the default settings in the File Link Settings dialog box. The default method groups AutoCAD objects by their color. In addition, the AutoCAD layers are imported into the VIZ file. In this way, imported objects maintain their layer assignments just as they exist in the source AutoCAD file. The objects are converted into VIZblocks and given names based on their color. For example, objects assigned the red color, which is color number 1 in the AutoCAD color naming convention, are given a name beginning with Color:001.01.

If the Preserve Access to Individual Objects option in the Attach tab of the File Link Settings dialog box is turned on, you have access to individual objects in the VIZblock compound object. You can select individual objects by going to the Sub-Object level of the VIZblock and selecting the object name from a list box.

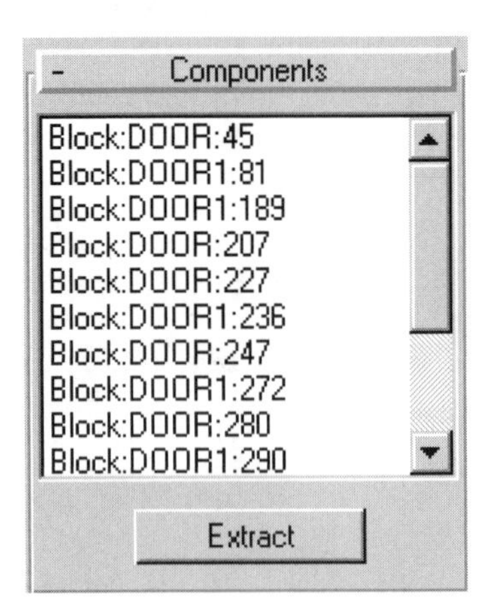

If the Preserve Access to Individual Objects option is turned off, you cannot edit the imported object on a sub-object level.

Organizing Objects By Layer

In a recent exercise, you chose a slightly different method for importing the AutoCAD linked file. You were directed to import the `Savoye-second.dwg` file objects *by layer.* This caused VIZ to collect the AutoCAD Objects into VIZblocks according to their layer. The VIZblock names matched the layer names to which the objects were assigned in AutoCAD. The actual layers from the AutoCAD file were not imported. As mentioned in the exercise, this method matches the standard way that VIZ imports AutoCAD files using the Import ➢ AutoCAD DWG option. In order to do this, you had to turn off the Convert Drawing Layers to Design Layers option in the DWG Linking tab of the File Link Settings dialog box.

The Attach Tab Options

Let's take a look at the options in the File Link Settings dialog box, starting with the Attach tab.

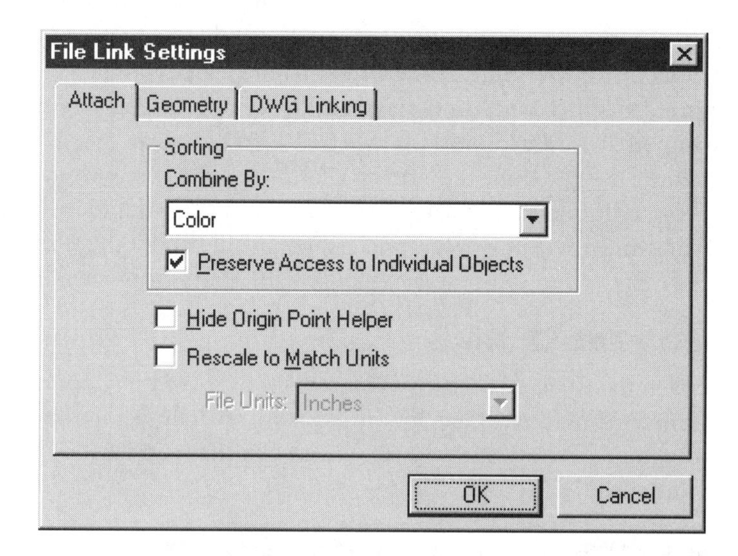

The Sorting group lets you select the method VIZ uses to create the VIZblock objects. The Combine By list box gives you the following options:

Layer Combines objects according to their layer assignment in AutoCAD.

Color Combines objects according to their color assignment in AutoCAD. Note that since blocks can contain objects with multiple color assignments, only the color of the block itself is used when converting AutoCAD blocks.

Layer, Thickness Combines objects in a nested fashion. First objects are converted into VIZblocks according to their layer assignment. Then, within each VIZblock, objects are combined as a sub-group by their thickness.

Layer, Thickness, Color Combines objects in a way similar to the Layer, Thickness option, with the addition of a color sub-group.

Color, Thickness Combines objects in a nested fashion by first combining objects of the same color into VIZblocks, then creating sub-groups based on the objects' thickness.

One Object Converts all of the objects of an imported file into a single VIZblock. If the Preserve Access to Individual Objects option is turned on, the VIZblock will allow access to the individual objects on a sub-object level. If the

Preserve Access to Individual Objects option is turned off, the entire imported file is a single VIZblock.

One-to-One Converts every AutoCAD object into a linked object in VIZ.

Two other settings in the Attach tab offer control over the orientation and units of the imported file. When VIZ imports a linked file, it creates a User Coordinate System helper. This is an object that marks the origin of the imported file. This helper is also selected immediately upon importing the file. You can hide the User Coordinate System helper by turning on the Hide Origin Point Helper option.

The Rescale to Match Units option, when turned on, lets you determine how units from the imported file are interpreted by VIZ. When Rescale to Match Units is turned on, you can use the File Units drop-down list to select the base unit to which the imported base unit is to be translated. For example, if you want to make sure that an AutoCAD drawing's base unit is centimeters, you would check the Rescale to Match Units option, then select Centimeters from the File Units drop-down list.

Geometry Tab Options

The options in the Geometry tab give you control over the way imported objects are converted into VIZ objects. These options are similar to those found in the Geometry group of the Import AutoCAD DWG File dialog box that you see when you use the Import ➢ AutoCAD DWG option.

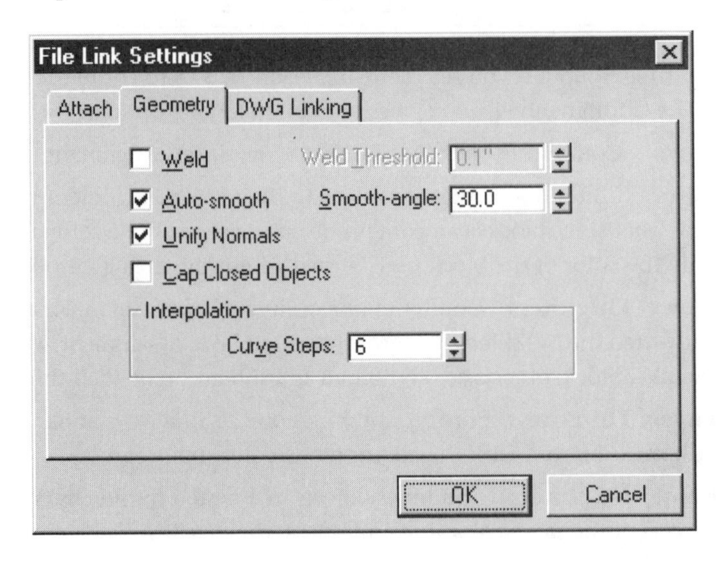

Weld Determines whether coincident vertices of imported objects are joined, or *welded*, together to form a contiguous object. When Weld is turned on, the Weld Threshold setting is used to determine how close together objects need to be before they are welded.

Auto-smooth Determines whether to apply smoothing to contiguous surfaces in imported objects. When Auto-smooth is turned on, the Smooth-angle setting is used to determine the minimum angle to which smoothing should be applied.

Unify Normals Attempts to align all of the normals of an object so that they point outward from the center of the object.

Cap Closed Objects Causes VIZ to apply an Extrude modifier to closed objects such as closed polylines or rectangles. In addition, the Cap Start and Cap End extrude modifier options are applied.

The Curve Steps option of the Interpolation group gives you control over the way curves are converted. A low Curve Steps value causes curves to appear as straight segments, while higher values generate a more accurate curve.

DWG Linking Tab Options

The options in the DWG Linking tab give you control over the way layers, blocks, AutoCAD Xrefs, hatches, points and 3D Solids (ACIS Surfaces) are converted.

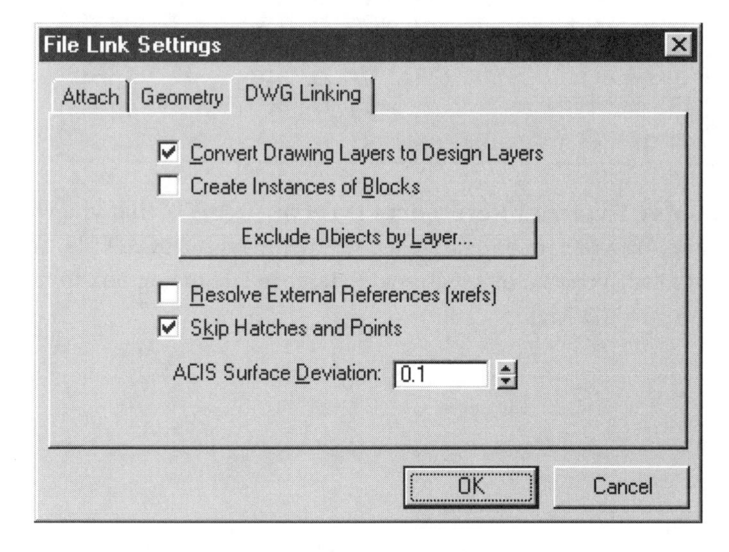

Convert Drawing Layers to Design Layers Does just what it says. With this option turned on, AutoCAD layers are converted into layers in the VIZ design. Objects are then given names based on the settings in the Attach tab of the File Link Settings dialog box. When this option is turned on, the layer-related options are not available in the Sorting group of the Attach tab. With this option turned off, you can have name objects based on their layer assignments in AutoCAD.

Create Instances of Blocks Converts multiple copies of AutoCAD blocks into Instance clones in VIZ. The way these clones are organized depends on the option you select in the Sorting group of the Attach tab. By turning this option on, you cause blocks in VIZ to behave in a way similar to blocks in AutoCAD.

Exclude Objects by Layer Opens the Select Layer dialog box, which allows you to select layers to be excluded from the link.

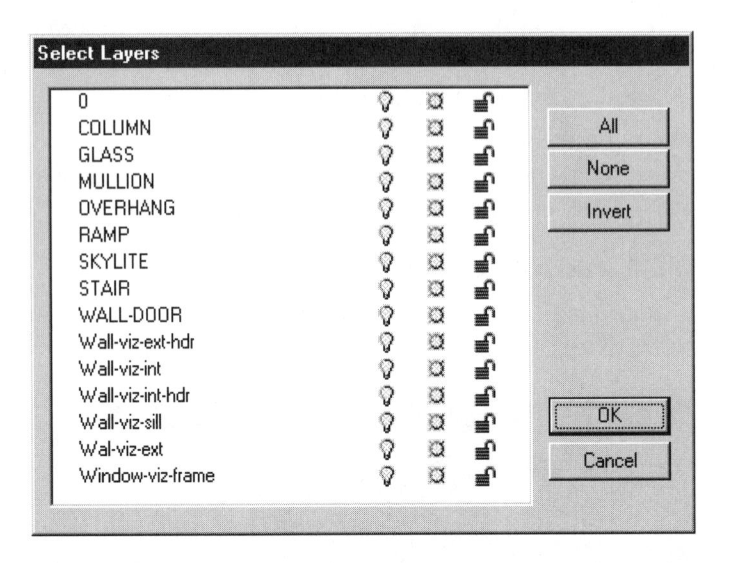

Resolve External References (xrefs) Tells VIZ that you want to import AutoCAD Xrefs that are attached to the linked AutoCAD file. You are presented with the Resolve External Reference File dialog box to help you locate the AutoCAD Xref.

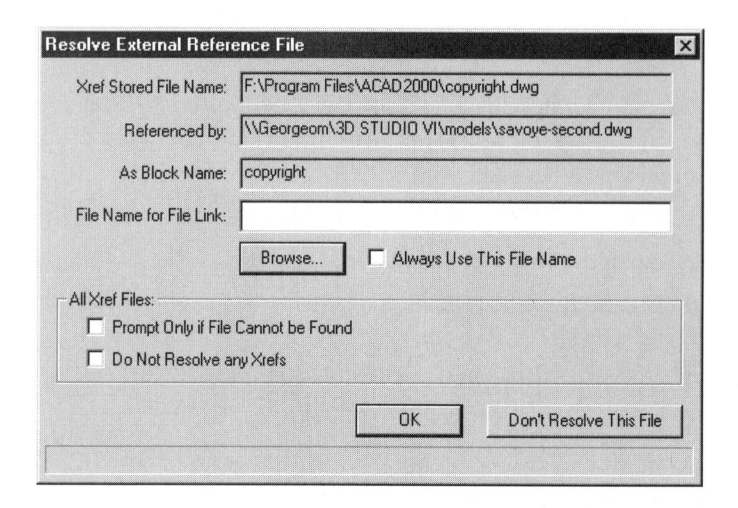

You can turn on the Prompt Only if File Cannot be Found option in the Resolve External Reference File dialog box if you want this dialog to appear only when VIZ cannot find an Xref. The Imported Xref becomes a single block that is a component of a VIZblock.

Skip Hatches and Points Does just what it says. With this option turned on, AutoCAD Hatch and Point objects are ignored by VIZ.

ACIS Surface Deviation Gives you control over the way VIZ translates AutoCAD 3D solids into VIZ objects. Smaller values produce more accurate translations, but increase file size.

The File Link Manager offers many options, which makes it a good alternative to simply directly importing an AutoCAD file using the Insert ➢ AutoCAD DWG… or AutoCAD DXF… options. You can always use the Bind option to sever the link and make the imported data a *stand-alone* VIZ file.

Adding Stairs

VIZ offers a number of AEC tools that can make quick work of the more common building design functions. You've already seen how walls, doors, foliage, and terrain work. In this last section, you'll use a few of the AEC stair tools to build one flight of stairs in the Villa design. In general, the stair tools are pretty straightforward.

Tracing over Imported Lines

To practice adding stairs, you'll use the ground floor file that you created earlier in this chapter. The imported stair plan in the `Savoye-ground.viz` file will provide the framework for your stair.

1. Open the `Savoye-Ground.viz` file you created earlier in this chapter.
2. Open the Select Object dialog box and click All.
3. Ctrl-click the Stair.01 item in the list to remove it from the selection, then click Select.
4. Click the Display tab in the Command Panel and click Selected Off.
5. Click the Zoom Extents tool to view the stair.
6. Right-click the Snap button at the bottom of the VIZ window and make sure Endpoint is selected in the Grind and Snap Settings dialog box. Go ahead and close the dialog box.
7. Click the Snap button to turn on the Snap mode.

You'll create the stair in three sections: the two straight runs and the circular portion. Since the straight runs are identical, you will create one and copy it to the other side.

To create the first stair run, do the following:

1. Click the Create tab in the Command Panel.
2. With the Geometry button selected, select Stairs from the drop-down list.

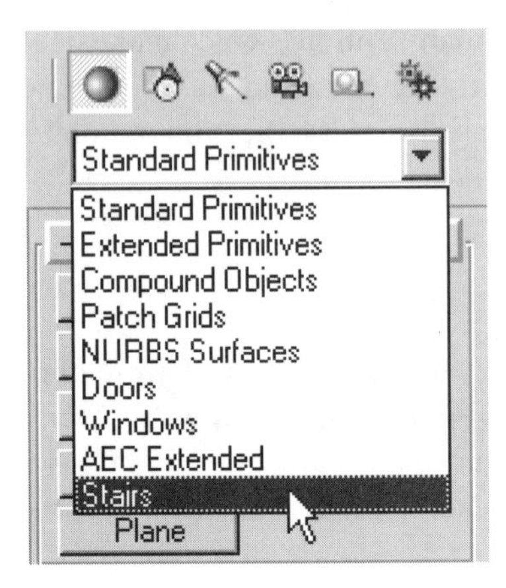

3. Click Stairs from the Object Type rollout.
4. With the Snap mode turned on, click and drag from the corner shown in Figure 16.21.

5. Drag the cursor to the second location shown in Figure 16.21, then let go of the mouse button.
6. Click the third location shown in Figure 16.21.

FIGURE 16.21

Click and drag from the corner, as shown here.

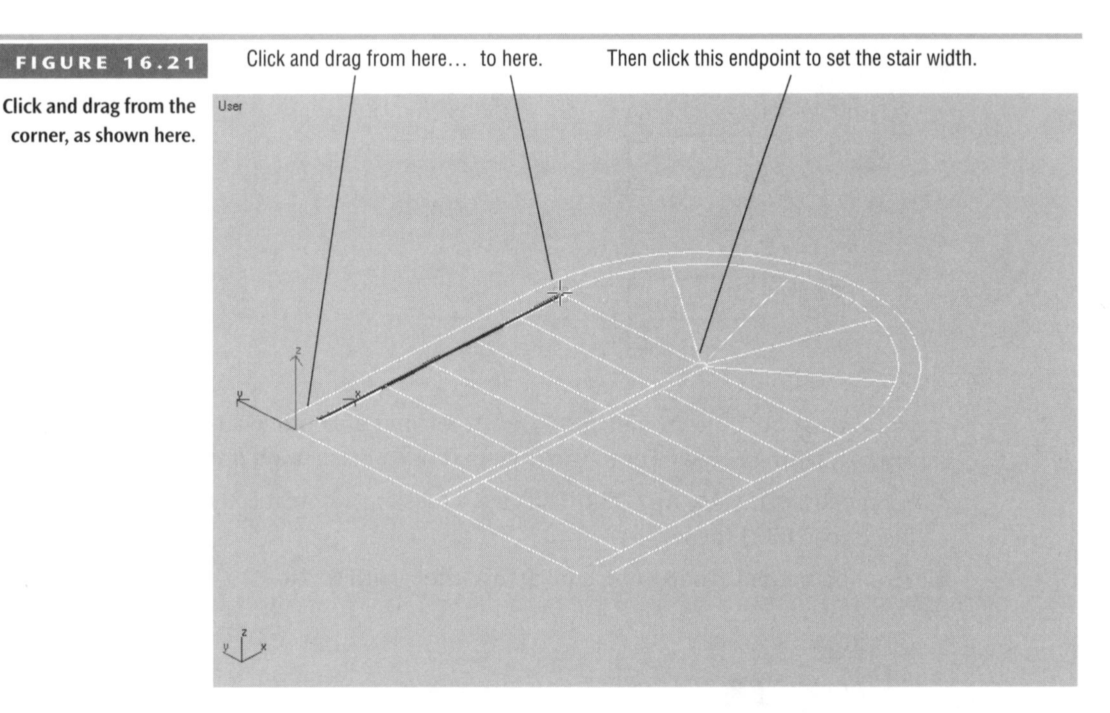
Click and drag from here...
to here.
Then click this endpoint to set the stair width.
User

7. Move the mouse upward to set the height, then click OK. You will set the exact height in the next exercise, so you don't have to worry about the look of the stair for now.

You've got the stair established in the design. Now you can make some adjustments to its parameters so that the stair dimensions are appropriate to the Villa dimensions.

Adjusting Stair Parameters

The total distance from the ground floor to the second floor is 11 feet, or 114 inches. This makes each of the 18 steps 7.333 inches high. There is a bit of a trick to setting stair heights with the Stair tools. You want to first tell VIZ the number of steps, then work on the overall height and the height of the risers.

1. In the Create tab of the Command Panel, scroll down to the Rise group of the Parameters rollout.
2. Set the Riser Ct setting to **7**, then click the Pin Riser Count button to the left of the setting. This locks the riser setting to 7.

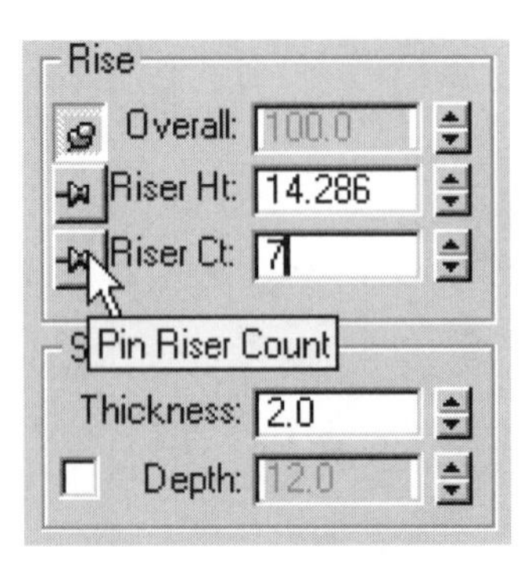

Notice that now the Overall and Riser Ht settings are both available, while the Riser Ct setting is grayed out. Also note that one pin is always down.

3. Set the Riser Ht value to **7.333**. The Overall setting automatically adjusts to the height of 51.331 inches.
4. Scroll up to the Layout group and change the length to **76**.

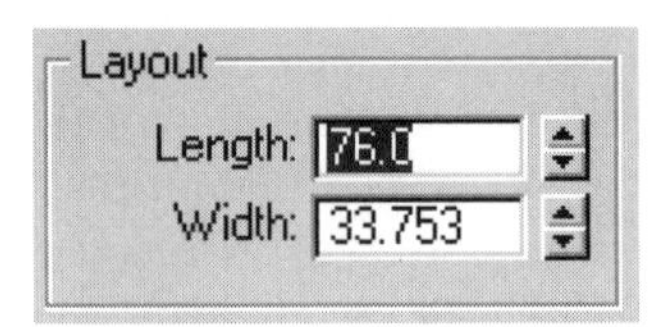

5. Scroll up to the Type group and click the Closed radio button.

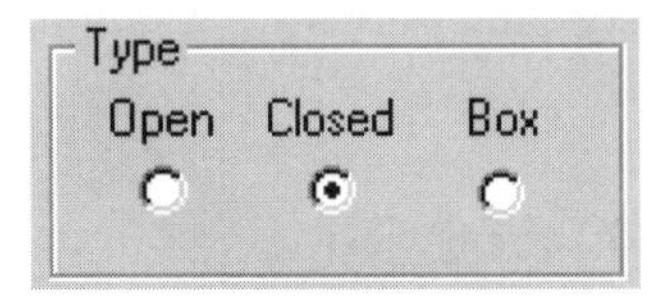

VIZ will draw a set of stairs with one less riser than indicated in the Riser Ct parameter. VIZ leaves off the top riser of the stair because the stair length parameter measures the stair from the nosing of the first stair tread to the nosing of the top stair tread. This means that the top stair tread is left out of the length calculation.

When setting up the stair height, it's easiest to start by first setting the number of stair risers. The trick is to use the Pin Riser Count button to lock the riser number. You can then easily adjust the height by adjusting either the overall or riser height.

TIP **Here's another method that works: Pin the riser count, then set the overall height. Next, pin the overall height and then set either the riser count or riser height.**

Creating a Circular Stair

You now have the first part of the stair ready. The circular portion is next.

1. Click the Min/Max toggle to view all four viewports.
2. Click the Zoom Extents All tool to enlarge the view of the stairs in all of the viewports.
3. In the Top viewport, move the straight stair to the left to give yourself some room to create the circular portion of the stair, as shown in Figure 16.22.

Now you are ready to use the Spiral Stair tool.

1. Turn off the Snap mode.
2. Scroll to the top of the Command Panel and click the Spiral Stair option.
3. In the Top viewport, click and drag the center of the circular portion of the stair plan as shown in Figure 16.22.
4. Drag the mouse to set the radius of the stair to the width of the stair and release the mouse, as shown in Figure 16.22.

FIGURE 16.22

Selecting points to place the circular portion of the stair

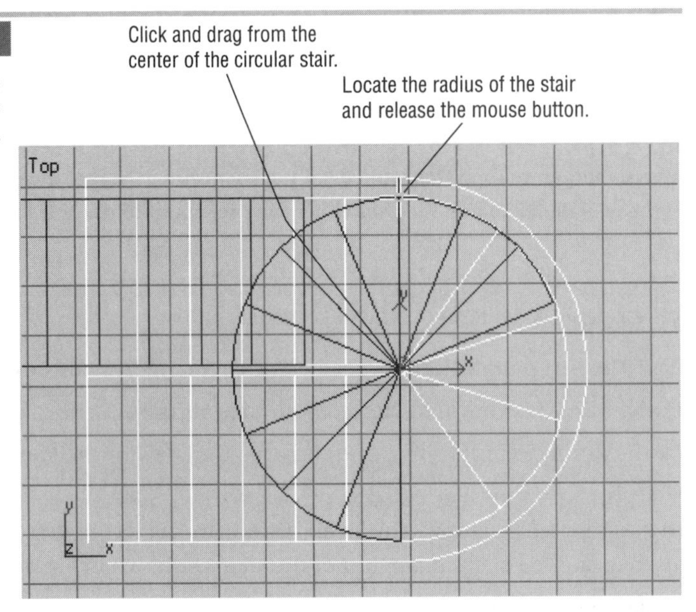
Click and drag from the center of the circular stair.
Locate the radius of the stair and release the mouse button.
Top

5. Move the mouse upward and click to set the height of the stair. Once again you can click any height, since you'll adjust the height accurately in the Command Panel.

There are a few problems with the circular portion. It's turning the wrong way and it extends beyond the 180° arc of the stair in plan. The following steps will quickly take care of these problems.

1. Click Closed in the Type group to match the straight portion of the stairs.
2. Scroll down to the Layout group and click the CW (clockwise) radio button.
3. In the Rise group, change the Riser Ct value to **6**, then click the Pin Riser Count button.
4. Set the Riser Ht value to **7.333**.
5. In the Layout group, set the Revs value to **0.602**.
6. Use the Select and Rotate tool to rotate the circular stair in the Top viewport so that it is oriented correctly in the plan.
7. Use the Select and Move tool to move the circular stair vertically in the Left viewport so that it is aligned with the top of the straight stairs.

At this point, you only need to align the circular stair in the vertical axis. You'll move the stair components into position once you have them all constructed and in the proper orientation.

Finishing the Stair

Now make the clone of the straight stair and move the clone into position.

1. Click the Zoom Extents All tool to get a clear view of the work so far.
2. Click the straight stair in the Left viewport, then shift-click and drag the y-axis upward so that the bottom of the straight stair aligns with the top of the circular stair, as shown in Figure 16.23.

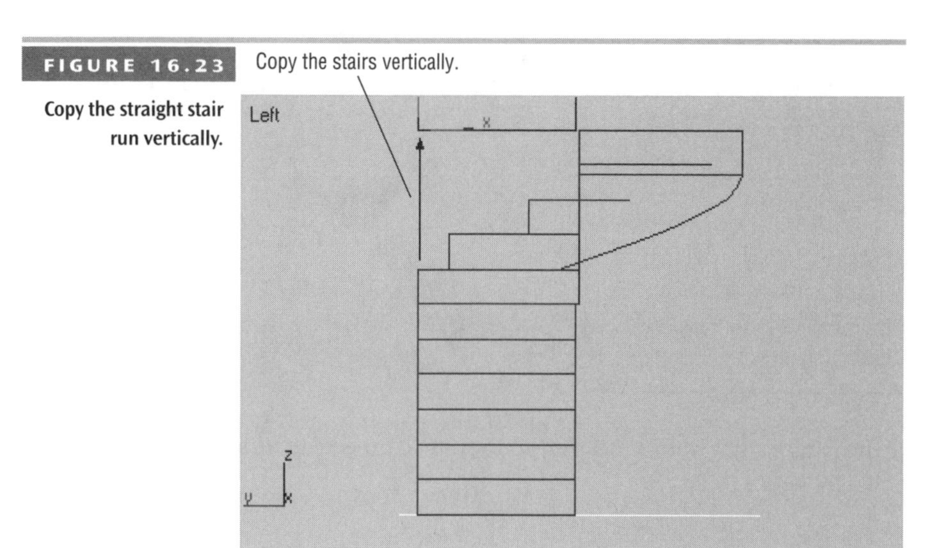

FIGURE 16.23 Copy the straight stair run vertically.

3. In the Clone Options dialog box, click OK.
4. Right-click the Top viewport, then click the Select and Rotate tool.
5. Select the Center pivot option from the Pivot flyout on the standard toolbar.

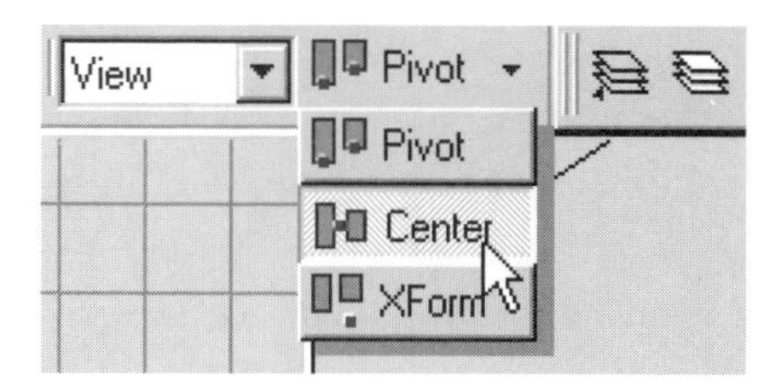

6. Click and drag the z-axis of the cloned stair upward in the Top viewport to rotate the stair 180 degrees.
7. Move the cloned stair downward to align with the circular stair, as shown in Figure 16.24.

FIGURE 16.24

Move the clone into position.

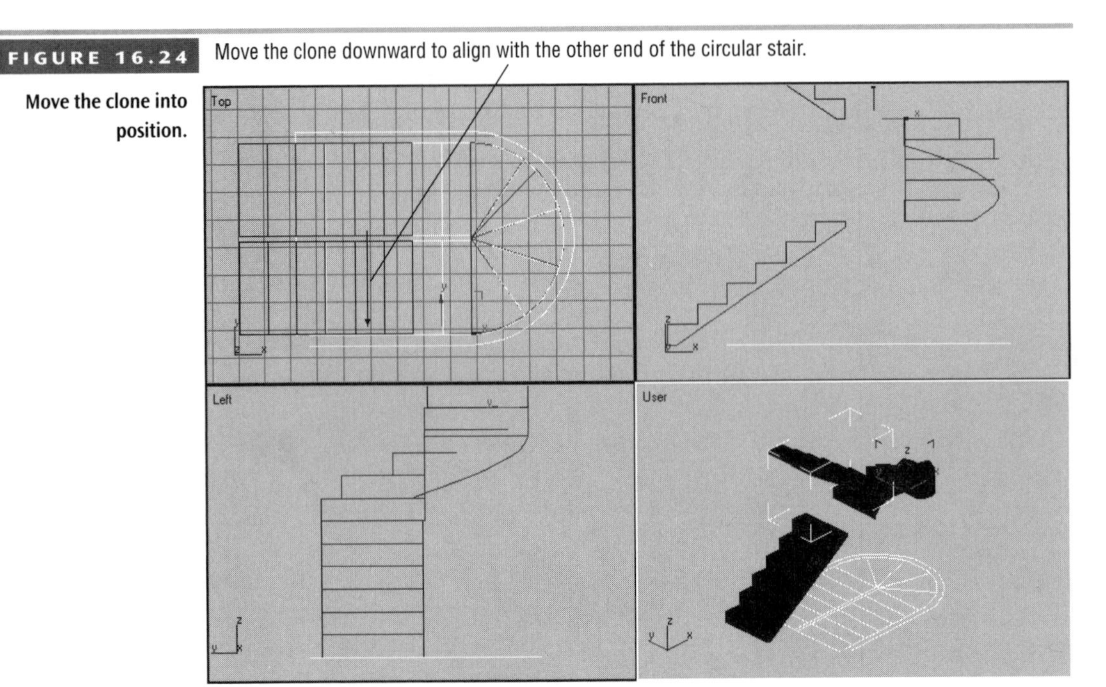
Move the clone downward to align with the other end of the circular stair.
Top
Front
Left
User

8. Move the two straight stairs to the left so they are connected to the circular stair, as shown in Figure 16.25.

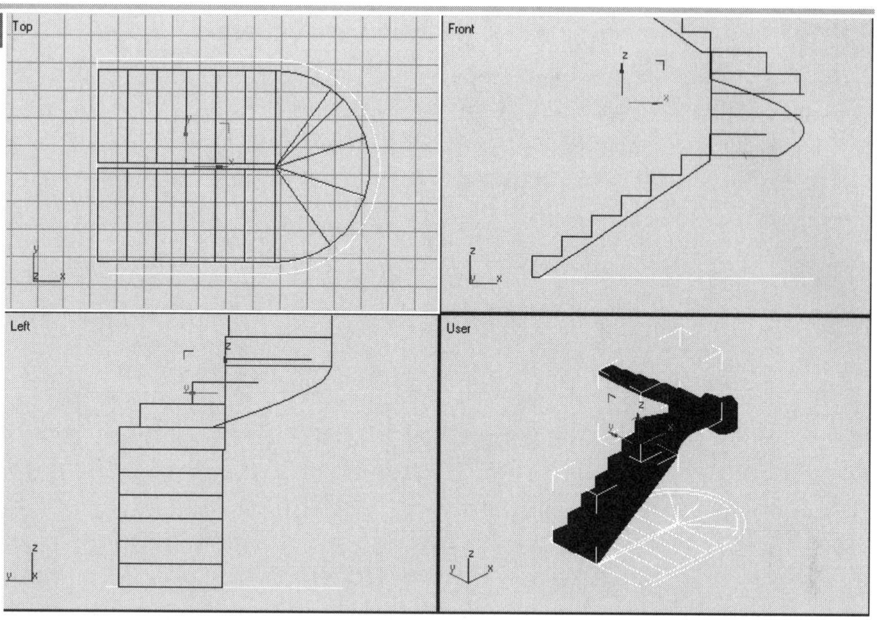

FIGURE 16.25

The straight stairs moved into position next to the circular stair

You don't have to worry about being absolutely accurate when placing the stair components together. When you consider construction methods, an eighth inch tolerance for locating building components is about as accurate as you can expect, and for most rendering and modeling purposes, positioning objects visually is usually good enough.

Adding the Stair Walls

You've now got some stairs from the ground floor to the second floor. You still need the walls that surround the stairs. Start by drawing a line that forms the inside edge of the wall.

1. Right-click the Perspective viewport, then click the Min/Max viewport toggle to enlarge it.
2. Right-click the User label in the upper-left corner of the viewport and select Wireframe. This allows you to easily select points on the stair.
3. Use the Arc Rotate tool to rotate the view so it looks similar to Figure 16.26.
4. Click the Create tab, then click the Shapes button and select Line.
5. Turn the Snap mode back on, then click the points indicated in Figure 16.26. Remember that you can press the backspace key if you select a point by accident.

FIGURE 16.26

Drawing the inside edge of the wall

Select the points indicated by the Xs starting at the bottom of the stairs.

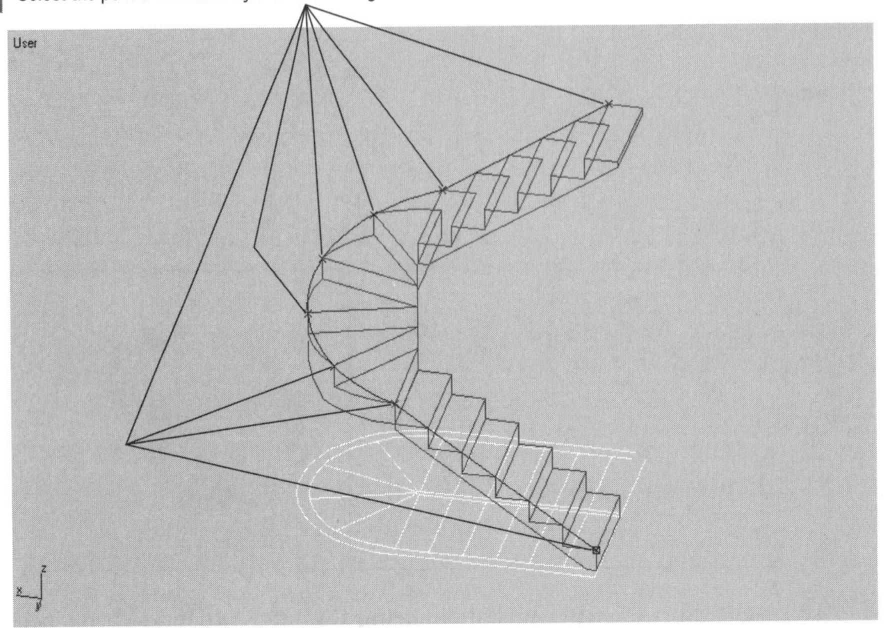

You've got a path set up, but the curved portion of the path needs to be smoothed out to form a curve. You'll employ a method you learned in Chapters 4 and 5 to change the vertices at the curved portion of the path.

1. Click the Modify tab, then click the Vertex option in the Selection rollout.
2. Turn off the Snap mode because it may interfere with the following steps.
3. Use the Select Object tool to right-click one of the vertices in the curved portion of the stairs as shown in Figure 16.27.
4. Select Smooth from the right-click menu.
5. Repeat steps 2 and 3 for each of the vertices in the curved part of the stair, as indicated in Figure 16.27.

FIGURE 16.27

Change these vertices into smooth vertices.

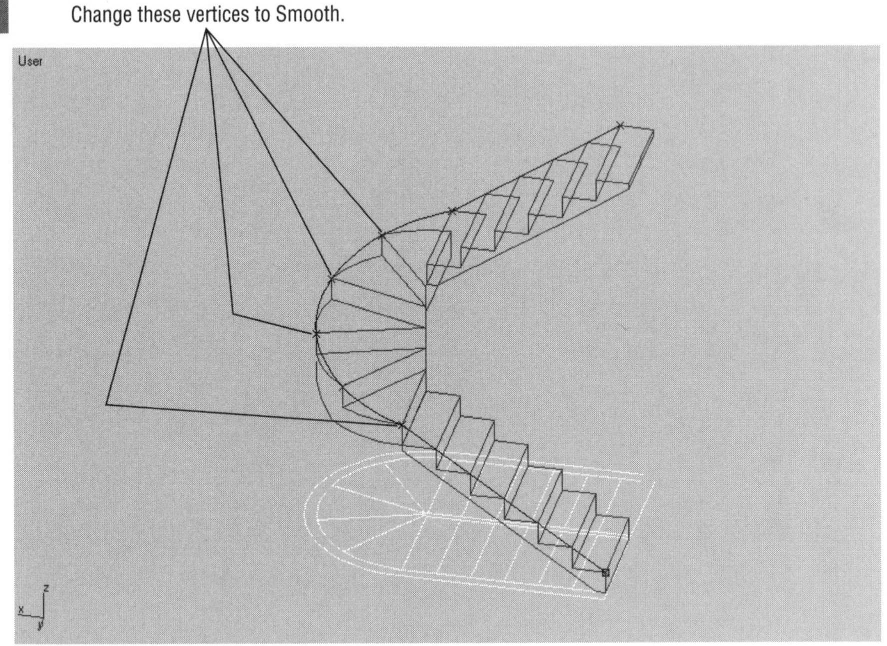
Change these vertices to Smooth.
User

1. Click the Spline button in the Selection rollout.
2. Click the spline you just created.
3. Scroll down to the Outline parameter and set the Outline value to **6**. You see the line turn into an outline.
4. Scroll up to the Modifier rollout, then click Extrude.
5. Change the Amount parameter to **50**.
6. Move the wall downward in the z-axis about 7 inches so the bottom of the wall aligns with the bottom of the stair.
7. Click the Zoom Extent tool to get a complete view of the stair, as shown in Figure 16.28.

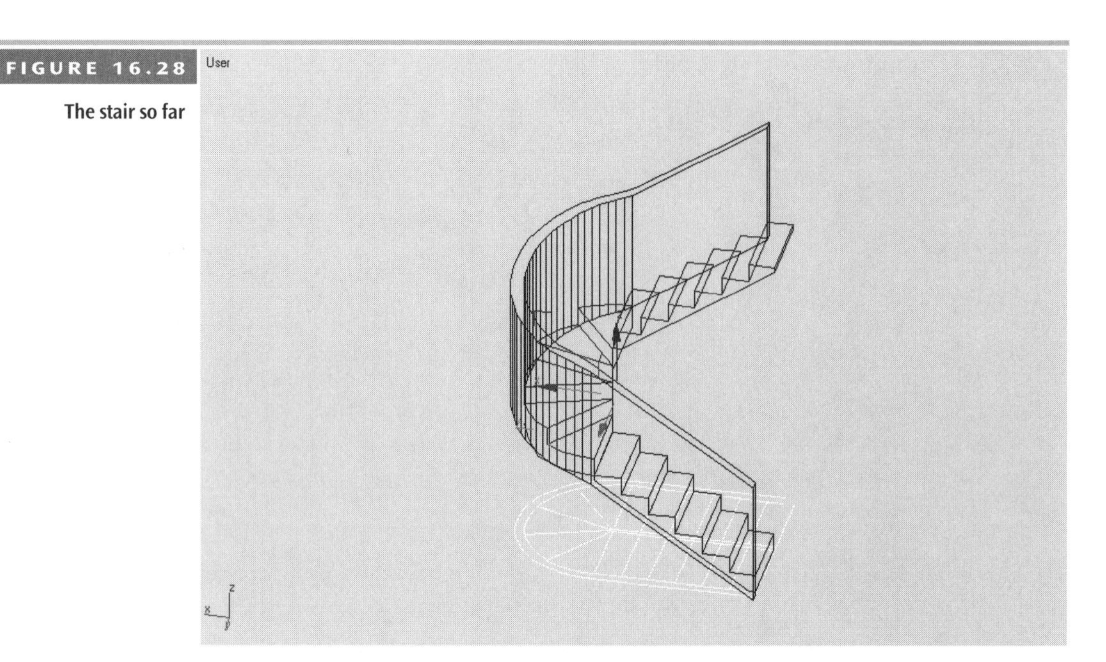

FIGURE 16.28

The stair so far

The wall needs to be extended by one stair step at the top of the stairs. You can go back to the spline vertex sub-object level to make this modification.

1. Zoom into the top stair so your view looks similar to that of Figure 16.29.
2. Choose Line from the Modifier Stack drop-down list.
3. Click the Vertex button in the Selection rollout.
4. Click the Select and Move tool and place a rectangular selection region around the two end vertices indicated in Figure 16.28.

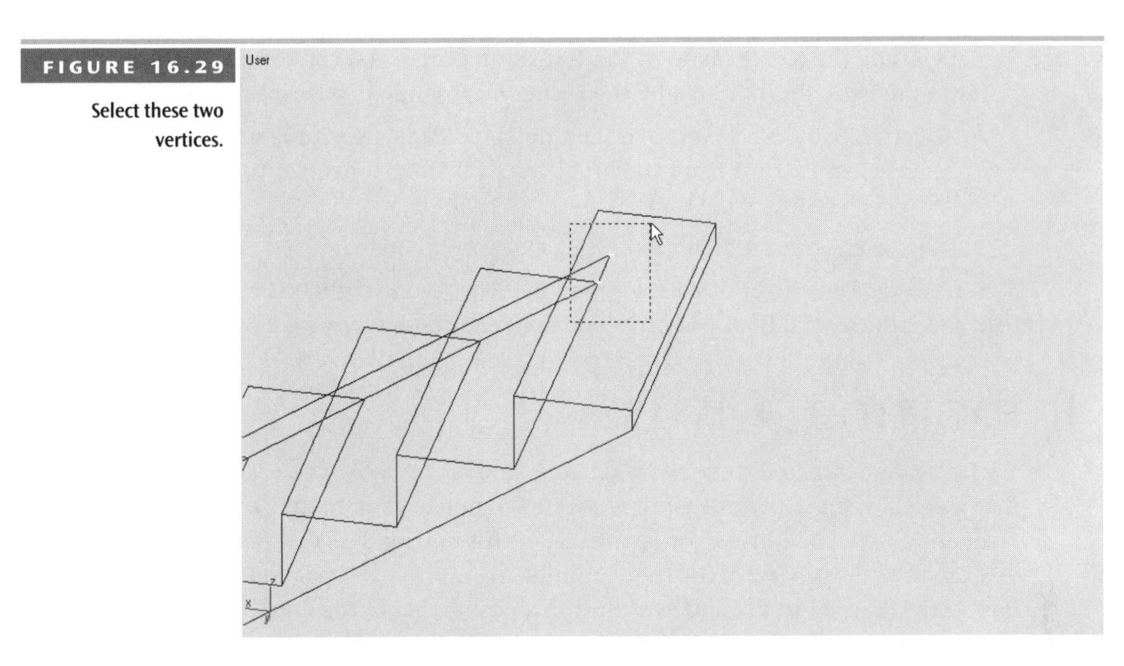
User

FIGURE 16.29

Select these two vertices.

5. Click and drag the blue axis corner mark of the Transform gizmo to move the vertices into the position shown in Figure 16.30.

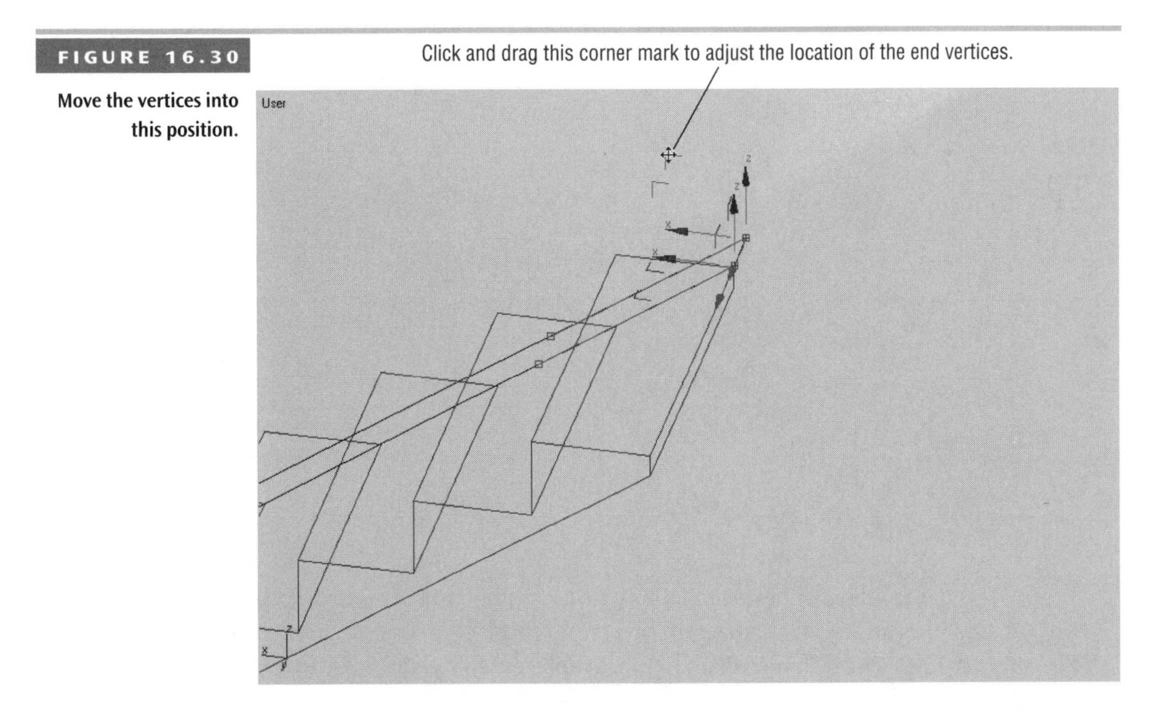
Click and drag this corner mark to adjust the location of the end vertices.
User

FIGURE 16.30

Move the vertices into this position.

By using the corner marks of the Transform gizmo, you can restrict the motion to the two axes indicated by the corner mark while in a Perspective viewport.

6. Click the Sub-Object button in the Command Panel to exit the sub-object level, then select Extrude from the Modifier Stack drop-down list to return to the extruded version of the wall.
7. Click the Zoom Extent button to get a view of the stairs.

You've made one flight of stairs for the Villa. The second flight is the same as the first, so for the second floor you can clone the stairs you just created.

Importing a Truss

You've nearly reached the end of this chapter and of the book. There is one last item that you will want to become familiar with to complete your mastery over VIZ. Frequently, you'll be called upon to include a truss in your design. If it's a flat truss, you can draw a side view of the truss in AutoCAD using closed polylines, then import the drawing to VIZ and extrude it in a way similar to the floor of the earlier `Savoye-second.dwg` example. If the truss line drawing is imported as a single object, VIZ will automatically subtract the truss web from the outline of the truss, as shown in Figure 16.31.

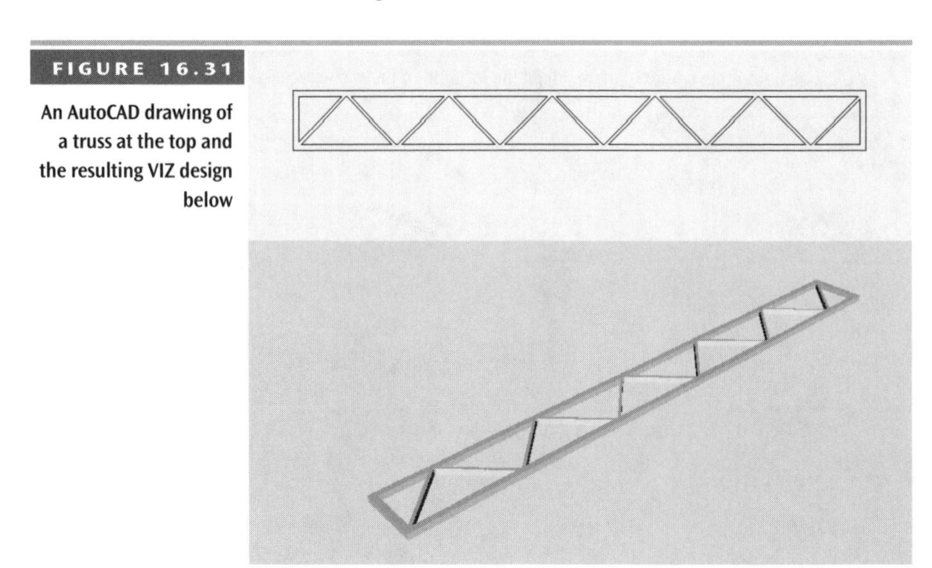

FIGURE 16.31

An AutoCAD drawing of a truss at the top and the resulting VIZ design below

Tubular trusses can be created easily from engineering 3D line diagrams. Figure 16.32 shows an AutoCAD diagram of a truss whose components are to be made of tubular steel. The different diameters are represented by different layers in this model.

FIGURE 16.32

A 3D line diagram of a truss in AutoCAD

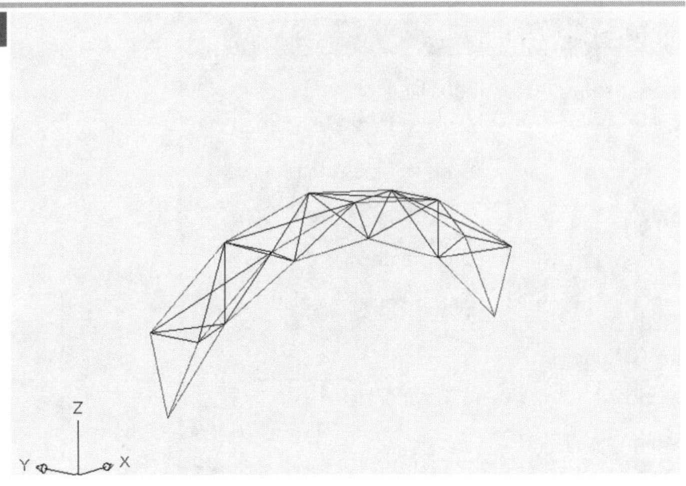

The following exercise will show you how the model can be turned into a renderable truss in VIZ:

1. Choose File ➢ Reset to reset VIZ.
2. Choose Insert ➢ AutoCAD DWG..., then select and open the `Truss.dwg` file from the companion CD.
3. In the DWG Import dialog box, click OK.
4. Make sure the Import AutoCAD DWG File dialog box settings are the same as those shown in Figure 16.33, then click OK.

FIGURE 16.33

The Import AutoCAD DWG File settings

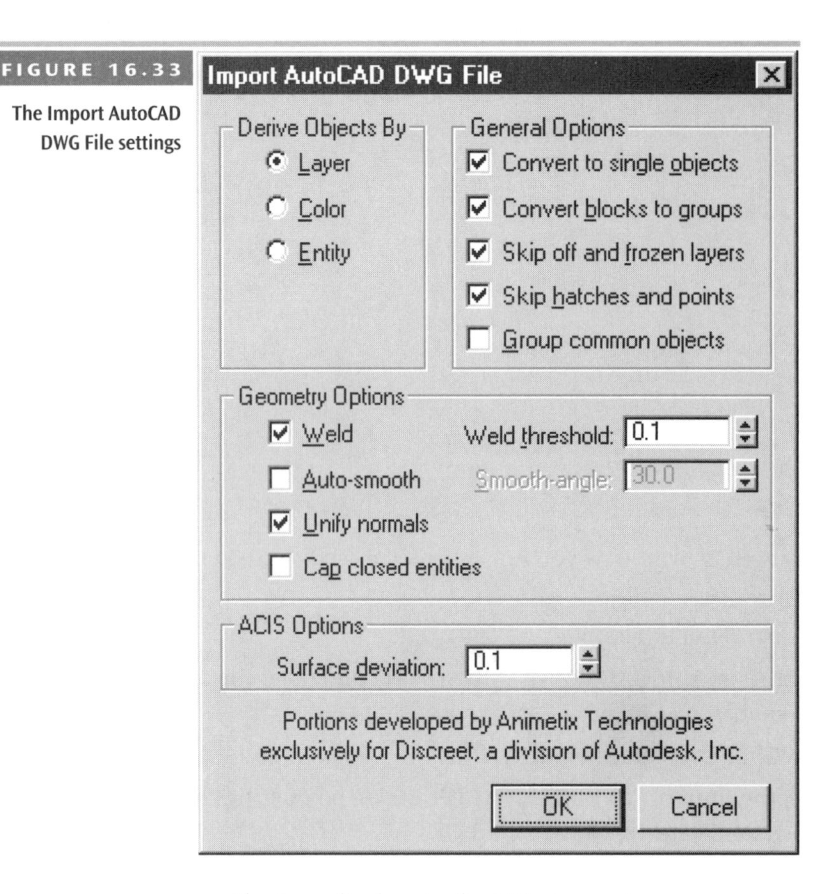

The truss displays in the VIZ viewport.

With the truss imported into VIZ, you only need to change a parameter to alter the way VIZ renders the lines.

1. Select one of the blue struts of the truss.
2. Click the Modify tab of the Command Panel.
3. Open the General rollout, turn on the Renderable option in the Rendering group, and change the Thickness to **4**.
4. Select one of the magenta lines in the Perspective viewport.
5. In the Command Panel, click on the Renderable option and change the Thickness value to **6**.
6. Do a quick rendering of the truss. You see that the rendered view converts the line work into tubes. Figure 16.34 shows a rendering of the truss from a different angle.

FIGURE 16.34

The rendered truss

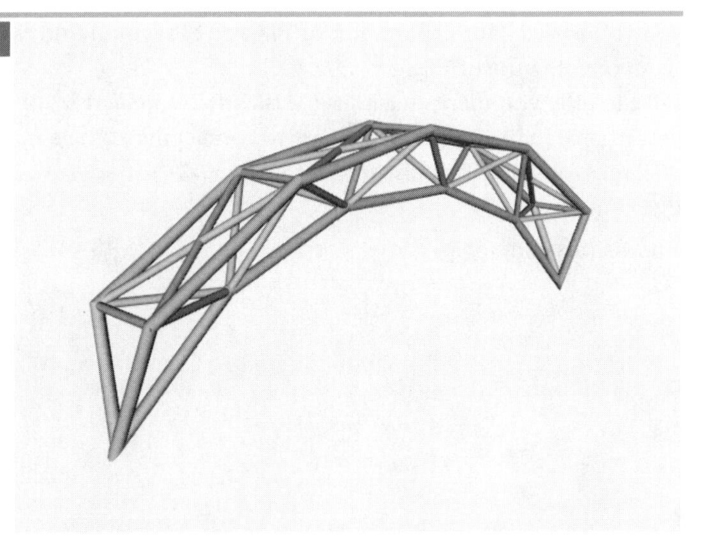

TIP **You can use the File Link Manager to import linked AutoCAD drawings and still use the General rollout parameters to create the truss shown in the previous exercise.**

You've seen this before in Chapter 4, where you were quickly introduced to the Rendering group of the General rollout. Here you see a practical use for this set of options. Without much work in VIZ, you can create a reasonable-looking truss. You just need to remember to place the different-diameter truss members on different layers.

You can also make quick work of window mullions using this method. Typically, mullions are square, but if they are to be viewed from a distance, you can use single lines for mullions and set up the General parameters to have them render as tubes. From a distance, you won't really be able to tell that they are tubes. Another obvious use of this method is to create guardrails.

Summary

CAD programs are the workhorses of the design industry. They offer a way to accurately represent designs and to communicate designs ideas to others. By allowing you to use your existing CAD data, VIZ enables you to quickly provide the all-important third dimension to your design visualizations.

This brings you to the end of *Mastering 3D Studio VIZ*. You weren't shown every available feature in VIZ, but you were introduced to the main tools you'll need to produce professional-level work.

I hope you've enjoyed your exploration of VIZ and that you'll find this book a useful tool in your ongoing use of VIZ.

If you'd like to offer comments regarding *Mastering 3D Studio VIZ,* or if you have any questions regarding the program, feel free to contact me at the e-mail address listed here. Thanks for choosing *Mastering 3D Studio VIZ.*

George Omura

Gomura@sirius.com

Appendix A

Installation Notes

Installation Notes

To use the tutorials in this book, you'll want to be sure you've installed most of the components that are available on the 3D Studio VIZ installation CD. This means that you'll need at least 560 megabytes of free disk space for the VIZ files alone. In addition, you will want to install the sample files from the Mastering 3D Studio VIZ companion CD. This will require another 500 megabytes of space.

Installing VIZ

Installing 3D Studio VIZ is fairly straightforward. Upon inserting the 3D Studio VIZ disk in your CD-ROM drive, the Windows Autostart feature will automatically start the installation program on the VIZ CD. If Autostart is disabled, open the Windows Explorer and double-click the Startup application on the VIZ CD. You are presented with a choice of installing VIZ, Internet Explorer, or Quicktime.

After selecting the VIZ installation option, you are presented with the licensing agreement. After clicking the I Agree button, the Do you want to view the Readme file now? dialog box appears. You can always look at the Readme file later. After the Readme message comes the dialog to enter your serial number and CD key.

The next window is important in relation to this book. You'll want to do a full installation so you can take advantage of all of the files available on the VIZ CD. When you get to the Setup Type dialog, choose the Custom option, then click Next.

You'll then see the Select Components dialog box. Make sure that all of the options in the Left list box are checked except for the MAX SDK option and the DGN I/O option. As indicated at the bottom of the dialog box, you'll need 550,470K of disk space for this installation.

Once you've selected the appropriate options, you can proceed with the rest of the installation. If you've already installed VIZ and found that some of the items mentioned in this book are not present in your version, you can run the VIZ installation again as described here, but remove the Program Files and HWL (Hardware Lock) Drivers from the list of components to be installed in the Select Component dialog box.

If this is the first time you've installed VIZ, then you'll be asked to supply an authorization code when you start VIZ. You can choose to postpone the entry of your authorization code to a later date, but if you do so, you have a 30-day limit until VIZ refuses to start without the code. You can obtain the code by phone, fax, or e-mail as instructed by the VIZ opening screen.

VIZ and Windows 98

If you are running VIZ on Windows 98, it is very important that you download the `core.dll` patch from the Autodesk VIZ Web site. This is an update of the `core.dll` VIZ program file that is located in your 3D Studio VIZ folder. It allows VIZ to run smoothly on Windows 98 and helps to reduce memory requirements in NT.

To locate this patch and other VIZ software updates, follow these steps:

1. Go to the Autodesk Web site at `www.autodesk.com`.
2. Select Product + Support. You want to locate the software updates for 3D Studio VIZ.
3. On the Product + Support page, select 3D Studio VIZ under 3D Visual Effects.
4. On the 3D Studio VIZ page, click Support and Training.
5. On the Support and Training page, click Updates, Drivers, Utilities.
6. On the Update, Drivers, Utilities page, click 3D Studio VIZ R3.
7. You'll see a list of downloadable files. Locate the file named `core.exe` and click it. The download process then begins. Follow the on-screen instructions for download. Make note of the location to which the file is downloaded.

WARNING Since Web sites change frequently, use these steps as a guideline to obtain the `core.exe` update. Of course, you may download any of the other options you think you may need from the Updates, Drivers, Utilities page.

The `core.exe` file is a self-extracting, compressed version of the `core.dll` file. Once the file is downloaded, you'll need to replace the old `core.dll` file with the one you just downloaded.

1. Use Windows Explorer to locate `core.dll` in your existing VIZ installation. The `core.dll` file can found in the `\3DSVIZ3` folder.
2. Locate and rename the existing `core.dll` file to `core.old`. To do this, right-click the `core.dll` file and choose Rename, then type in **core.old**. This step is taken to ensure that you can restore the old `core.dll` later if you need it.
2. Use Windows Explorer to locate the downloaded `core.exe` file, then double-click it.
4. You'll see a message explaining the steps to install the patch. Click OK.
5. In the WinZip Self-Extractor dialog box, click Unzip. If you have installed VIZ on a drive other than C, make sure you change the location of your 3D Studio VIZ 3 folder shown in the Unzip To Folder input box.

Installing the Companion CD

Before you start the tutorials in this book, you'll want to install the sample files from the companion CD you got with this book. The CD contains many other programs and sample files that you may find useful in your work with VIZ.

To install the software from the companion CD, place the CD in your computer's CD-ROM drive and follow these steps:

1. You'll see a message telling you that you need Quicktime 4 to play sample movies included on the CD. Click the type of operating system you have or click Continue to skip the QuickTime installation.
2. Next you'll see the software license agreement. Click Accept.
3. The next screen is a menu that lists the different programs and files on the CD. To install the sample files, click Book Files.
4. In the WinZip Self-Extractor dialog box, click Unzip. If you want to install the files in a location other than the one shown in the Unzip to Folder input box, you can enter a different directory before you click Unzip. You may also click Browse to find the location for the sample files.
5. Once the Unzip operation is complete, you can exit all of the dialog boxes.

After step 4, you can continue to install other options or exit the installation. You can always return to the installation menu later.

TIP If for some reason the installation process does not start automatically when you insert the CD in step 1, use the Windows Explorer to view the contents of the CD. Locate the `clickme.exe` file and double-click it.

Appendix B

Modifiers and Materials

Modifiers and Materials

VIZ offers a multitude of modifier and material options—so many in fact, that to do a tutorial on all of them would require a multivolume book. After reading the first few chapters of this book, however, you will have a good understanding of how VIZ works, and you'll be able to use most, if not all of the modifiers and materials with a little experimentation and some help from this appendix.

This appendix is intended to give you general information about the modifiers and materials and to show you what types of features are available. If you need more detailed information about the modifiers and materials, the VIZ Online Reference offers full descriptions of the options and parameters for all of the items discussed in this appendix. Choose Help ➢ Online Reference. Click the Search tab in the panel to the left, enter the name of the item in the Type in the Word(s) to Search for input box, then click List Topics. If you see only a single panel in the Online Reference, click the Show button in the Online Reference toolbar.

Modifiers

The tutorials in this book cover the more commonly used modifiers in VIZ. Every now and then, you'll find a need to use one of the other modifiers that are not discussed at any length in the Online Reference. For those situations, you can find a description of all of the modifiers in this section and, hopefully, it will be enough to get you started. Even if you don't need them now, you may want to review the functions of these modifiers so that you know what is available.

Modifiers on the Modifier Rollout

The modifiers are located in two places—at the top of the Modify tab in the Command Panel and in the Modify dialog box, which is opened by clicking the More... button in the Modifier rollout of the Modify tab.

The modifiers in the modifier rollout can be edited to suit your needs. By clicking Configure Button Sets in the Modifier rollout you can open the Configure Button Sets dialog box.

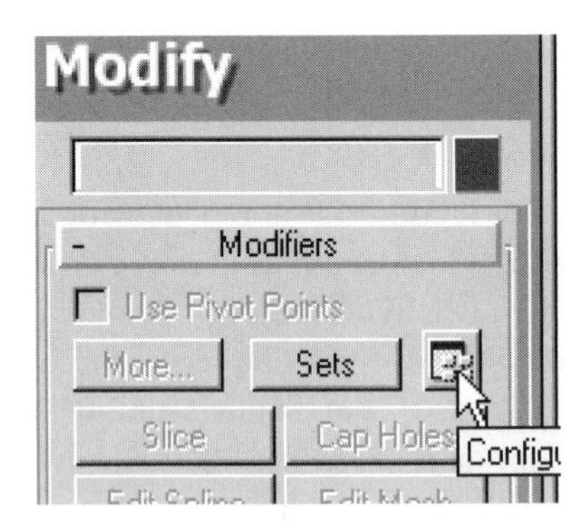

This dialog box lets you edit the set of modifiers shown in the Modifier rollout. You can also create other sets to help you organize modifiers. The following describes the default set of modifiers found in the Modifier rollout.

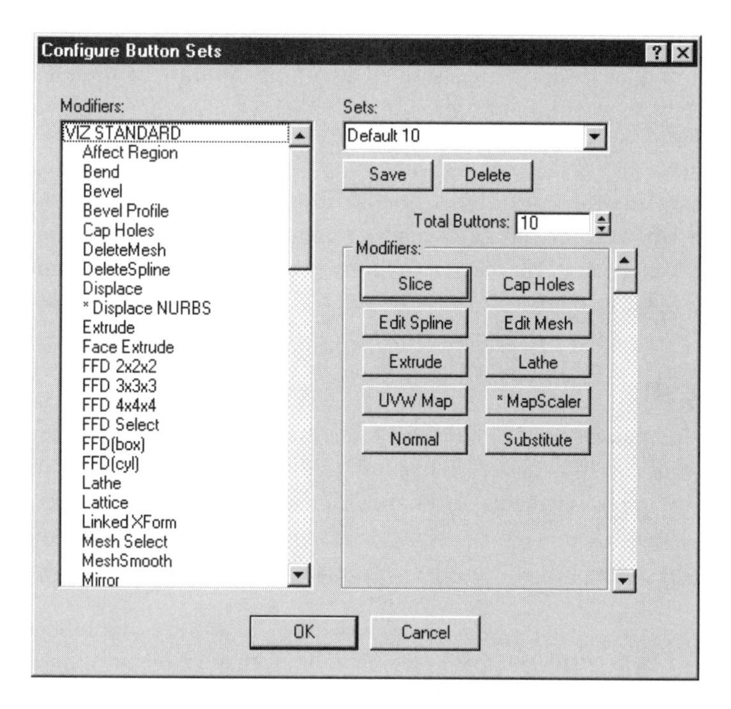

Slice

Slice allows you to define a plane through which objects can be cut. There are two ways that Slice can affect an object. The most obvious is to split an object into two objects. Slice gives you the option to keep both parts of the split object, or you may hide one part. Slice also lets you refine an object along the intersection of the slice plane with the object.

Cap Holes

Some editing procedures will leave openings in a mesh. You may, for example, use the Slice modifier to slice a cylinder into two halves. Each half will have an opening at the slice plane. The Cap Holes modifier can be used to close the openings.
In VIZ, a hole is a closed loop of edges with a single face. Cap Holes works best on planar holes, but it also works on nonplanar holes.

Edit Spline

The Edit Spline modifier may seem redundant since it duplicates the parameters for spline objects, with a few limitations. Edit Spline offers flexibility in editing splines by allowing you to position edits in the modifier stack. For example, you can use Edit Spline to test out spline edits. Since it is a modifier, you can easily discard changes made using Edit Spline by deleting it from the modifier stack—something you cannot do using the basic parameters for a spline. It is also useful for applying changes to several shapes at once by applying a single Edit Spline modifier to a set of objects. You may also want to maintain other modifiers which would otherwise be affected by changes to the basic parameters of the shape.

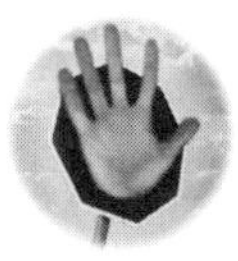

WARNING The Edit Spline modifier uses much more memory than does a simple editable Spline object. For this reason, try to avoid using this modifier unless you really need the flexibility it offers.

Edit Mesh

Like the Edit Spline modifier, Edit Mesh seems a bit redundant, as it duplicates the parameters for editable meshes. Edit Mesh offers great flexibility in editing meshes by allowing you to position edits in the modifier stack. You can experiment with changes in a mesh, maintain other modifiers and parameters that would otherwise be altered by mesh edits, or edit multiple mesh objects.

WARNING The Edit Mesh modifier uses much more memory than does a simple editable Mesh object. For this reason, try to avoid using this modifier unless you really need the flexibility it offers.

Extrude

Extrude is used to extend 2D shapes into the third dimension in a linear fashion. Both VIZ shapes and shapes imported from other CAD programs can be extruded. The Extrude modifier offers the option to cap ends, which closes the openings formed by the top and bottom of an extruded shape. You can also select the type of mesh that is created with Extrude.

Lathe

Lathe is used to revolve 2D shapes into the third dimension in a circular fashion. Both VIZ shapes and shapes imported from other CAD programs can be extruded. The Lathe modifier offers the option to cap ends, which closes the openings formed by the beginning and end of an extruded shape. You can also select the type of mesh that is created with Lathe.

UVW Map

This modifier lets you control the orientation of maps on the surface of an object. It also lets you control the size and aspect ratio of a map in relation to the object to which it is mapped. UVW Map offers a set of mapping types that allow you to tailor the map to the shape of an object. For example, if you are applying a material to a cylindrical shape, you can use the Cylindrical mapping parameter that projects the map in a cylindrical form. A UVW Map gizmo gives you a visual reference for the location and orientation of the mapping parameters. You can use the transform tools to adjust the Map gizmo.

Map Scaler

When you scale an object that has a map applied to it, the map is scaled with the object. In many situations, you want the material map to maintain its original scale, regardless of the scale of the object to which it is mapped. The Map Scaler modifier allows you to *lock* a map's scale so that changes to the object do not affect the associated map.

Normal Modifier

When you create geometry in VIZ, the normals of the geometry are pointing outward and you do not have control over their orientation. You can gain control of the normals of VIZ geometry by collapsing the stack and reducing the geometry to an editable mesh. Unfortunately, once you do that, the geometry looses its parametric functions. The Normal modifier lets you control the normals of VIZ geometry without forcing you to give up parametric functions.

Substitute

The Substitute modifier lets you substitute one object for another. This feature is useful if you have a very complex design and want to simplify part of it to help speed up editing or rendering. You can substitute a complex object for a simplified one while editing. Then, at render time, you can have VIZ restore the original complex object. You may also do the reverse for quicker rendering of sample views. The substitute object can come from the current design or from an external file. Substitute objects are removed by deleting the Substitute modifier from the stack.

The Substitute modifier is view-dependent, so when you apply it, you must choose the object you want to substitute and the viewport that is to be affected. You can select an object from an external file using the Select Xref Object option in the Substitute parameters.

World-Space Modifiers

World-Space modifiers (WSM) are modifiers that use the world space as their point of reference, as opposed to the object space of the object to which they are attached. The Map Scaler modifier is a good example of a World-Space modifier since it associates the map of an object with the world space and is not affected by the object space of the object to which it is attached. An object using the Map Scaler can be scaled to any size or shape, and any maps attached to the object will not be scaled.

The World-Space modifiers are at the top of the list of the Modifier dialog box, so they are also listed first here.

Camera Map

At times, you may need an object to be invisible, yet still maintain a presence in a design. For example, suppose you have a fairly detailed background image that shows a garage, and you want to create the illusion of a car entering the garage. You can create a simple box with an opening similar in shape to the background garage opening, then use the Camera Map modifier to blend the box into the background. Once this is done, you can animate the car to drive into the box. The net effect is that the car appears to drive into the garage in the background image in your final animation. This allows you to keep the geometry simple, yet still have a fairly detailed-looking animation.

The Camera Map modifier applies a planar UVW map to an object, and it aligns that map so that it is perpendicular to a specified camera. The map is typically the same as the background, giving the illusion of an invisible object. Since the object can cast and receive shadows, you can create different effects. For example, if you are using the Camera Match tool to match a building design to a photo of a building site, you can use the Camera Map modifier to include shadows on buildings in the background.

There are two versions of the Camera Map modifier. The WSM version can be used when a camera is in motion, as it updates the map at each frame. Object-Space version works best when there is no camera motion (see also Matte/Shadow maps).

Displace Mesh

If you assign a displacement map to an object, you usually won't be able to see the effects of the map until it is rendered. Displace Mesh modifier allows you to see the effects of a displacement map while you're editing. The Displace Mesh can also let you convert a displacement map into an editable mesh as described in Chapter 15.

Displace NURBS

The Displace NURBS modifier performs the same function as the Displace Mesh modifier, but it is applied to NURBS objects.

Patch Deform

This modifier allows you to deform an object based on the form of a Patch object. A Patch object is an object that can be formed into a smooth, curved surface by editing its vertices. You can, for example, create a plane, then convert the plane into an editable patch. The vertices of the editable patch can then be edited to shape the plane into a smooth, curved surface of any shape you want. Such a surface can be used to deform other objects, using the Patch Deform modifier.

There is a World-Space modifier version and an Object-Space modifier version of the Patch Deform modifier. You would use the World-Space version if you wanted the object to move to the location of the patch. You would use the Object-Space version if you wanted the object to remain in its current location while being deformed.

Path Deform

The Path Deform modifier works in a way similar to the Patch Deform modifier, but uses a spline or NURBS curve instead of a patch object. For example, you can use this modifier to deform an object along the path of the spline. An example of this would be the curving of text to conform to the shape of a round column or sphere. Like the Patch Deform modifier, Path Deform comes in a World-Space version and an Object-Space version. The World-Space version causes the object to move to the path used for the deformation while the Object-Space version does not move the object.

Surface Mapper

The UVW Map modifier has a fixed set of seven mapping options that allow you to apply a map to most forms. But what happens when none of those options will work for your design? If you have an organic form that requires custom mapping, you can use the Surface Mapper modifier.

The Surface Mapper requires that you create a NURBS surface that you edit to the form of the required map. You form the NURBS surface around the object to which you are applying the map and assign the same material to both the NURBS surface and the object. Once this is done, you apply the Surface Mapper modifier to the object or objects. The map is projected onto the modified object, based on the direction of the normals on the NURBS surface.

SurfDeform

The SurfDeform modifier works in a way similar to the Patch Deform modifier, but uses a NURBS surface instead of a patch object. You can use this modifier to deform an object, based on the shape of a NURBS surface, similarly to the way in which a patch surface would be used.

Object-Space Modifiers

The Object-Space modifiers follow the World-Space modifiers in the Modifier dialog box. As mentioned at the beginning of the World-Space modifiers section, Object-Space modifiers use object space as a point of reference. Most of the time, you'll be using the modifiers in this section. You'll also notice that a few of the Object-Space modifiers are duplicated in the World-Space modifier set. This gives you the option to use those modifiers with either world or object space.

Affect Region

The Affect Region modifier lets you apply a bump to a surface. The bump is controlled by two points. One point sets the base of the bump, while the other locates the tip of the bump. Each point can be adjusted independently of the other. You can control the bump's shape through Falloff, Pinch, and Bubble parameters.

Bend

You can bend an object on any axis by using the Bend modifier. You can control the degree of the bend, where it occurs, and the axis about which it occurs. This modifier is demonstrated in Chapter 2.

Bevel

Bevel allows you to extrude a 2D shape and add a beveled edge. The Bevel Values rollout for this modifier allows you to set the height of the extrusion. You can use three levels of beveling. Each level has its own height and outline settings, so you can control beveling by adjusting the height and changing the outline value, expanding or contracting the shape of the outline at the selected level. The Surface parameters let you control the segments of the extrusion and whether the sides are curved or straight. Typically, Bevel is used to bevel text, but it can be used for other 2D shapes (See Figure B.1).

FIGURE B.1

A sample of the Bevel modifier used on text

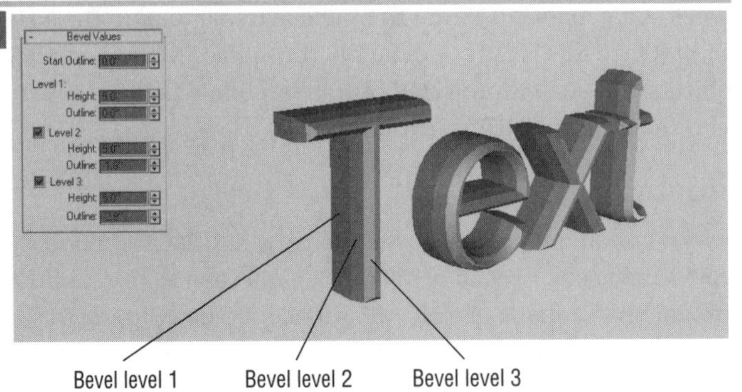

Bevel Profile

Bevel Profile is like a simplified Loft tool. You can use it to extrude a shape along a path. This modifier is an excellent tool for creating extruded forms such as elaborate picture frames or curved stairs. To use it, you draw an outline of the object, using a spline. Draw another open spline indicating the profile of the object. Select the outline, then apply the Bevel Profile modifier. In the Parameters rollout of the Bevel Profile modifier, click the Pick Profile button and select the spline you want to use as the profile. The outline is extruded to the shape of the profile (see Figure B.2).

FIGURE B.2

An example of the Bevel Profile modifier

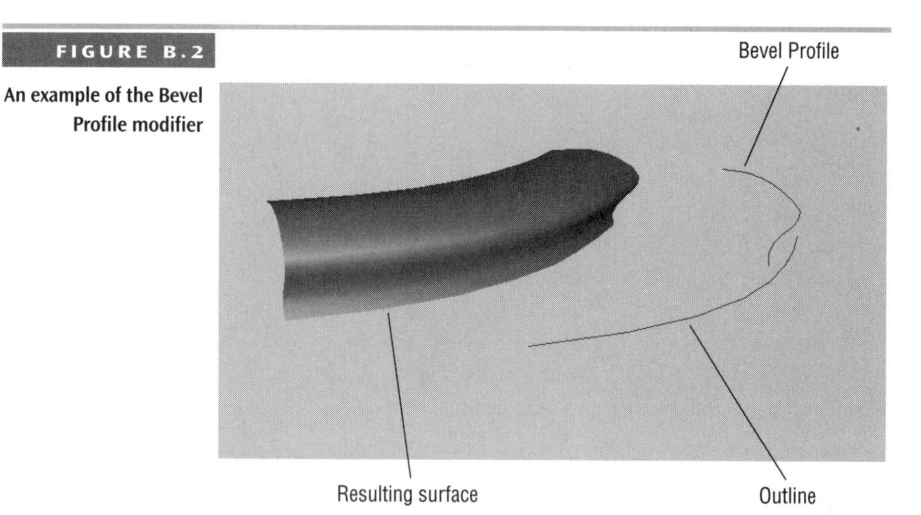

Once a shape has been extruded using the Bevel Profile modifier, you can modify the shape by adjusting either the profile spline or the original extruded shape.

Camera Map

See Camera Map under World-Space Modifiers.

CrossSection

The CrossSection modifier is a powerful tool that lets you connect splines to form surfaces. (If you're an AutoCAD user, you can think of CrossSection as a super Rulesurf or Edgesurf command.) It's called the CrossSection modifier because with it you can draw cross sections of an object, then join the cross sections together to form a surface.

When used in conjunction with the Surface modifier, CrossSection lets you form elaborate Patch surfaces by defining the surface edge with two or more 3D splines. First you draw the splines, then attach them together into a single object, using the Attach option in the Modify tab. You then apply the CrossSection modifier, which connects the vertices of the separate splines. Finally, you can *skin* over the splines with the Surface modifier (See Figure B.3).

FIGURE B.3

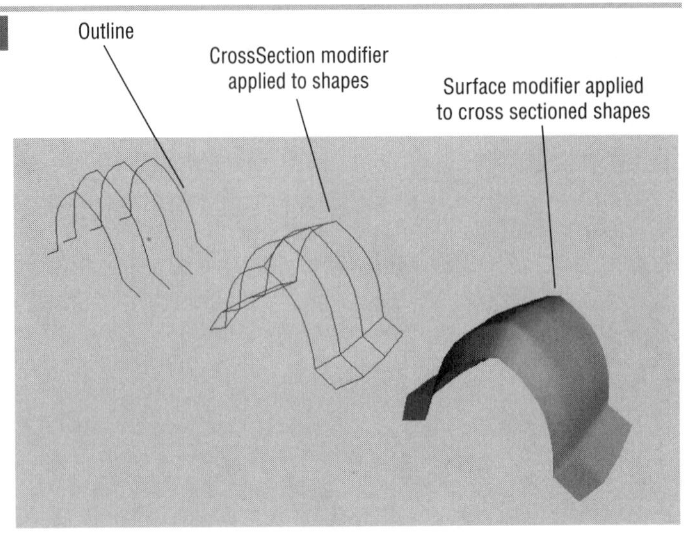

Creating a surface using the CrossSection modifier and the Surface modifier

The order in which the splines are created is as important as the location of the starting vertex of the splines. You want to be sure that the splines *point* in the same direction, with the beginning vertex of each spline placed in the same orientation relative to the rest of the spline. Figure B.4 shows how the splines are all oriented with their starting points to the left of the figure.

FIGURE B.4

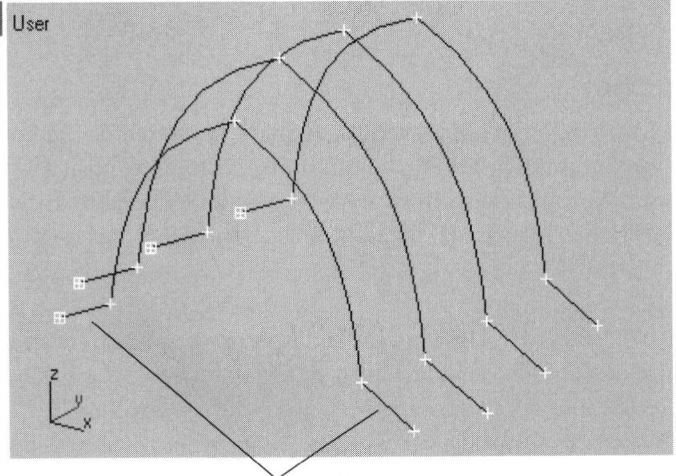

Aligning the spine vertices

If you collapse the stack of a surface created using the CrossSection and Surface modifiers, you have a patch surface that can be edited in the same way as any other patch surface.

DeleteMesh

You can think of the DeleteMesh modifier as a tool that lets you try out deletions in a mesh. Since it is a modifier, it can be placed anywhere in the modifier stack. Here's how it works: go to the sub-object level of an object and make a selection of the items you want to remove. If it is a surface patch or NURBS surface, you can isolate mesh surfaces for deletion by using the Mesh Select modifier. Once you've made your selection, apply the DeleteMesh modifier. The selection will be deleted. Since DeleteMesh is a modifier, you can restore the deleted items by removing DeleteMesh from the stack.

Delete Spline

Delete Spline is similar to DeleteMesh except that it works on splines rather than on meshes. Sub-object selections are limited to vertices, segments, and splines.

Disp Approx

The Disp Approx modifier allows you to apply a displacement map to an object. A tutorial for this modifier can be found in Chapter 14.

Displace

Displace lets you form a surface using a bitmap image. It is similar to applying a bump map material to an object, but instead of simply creating the illusion of a bumpy surface by changing the surface normals, Displace actually changes the geometry to a bumpy surface. See Chapter 14 for a detailed description of the Displace modifier.

Edit Patch

The Edit Patch modifier lets you edit an object as if it were an editable patch object (see Appendix C for more on editable patch objects).The Edit Patch modifier uses a good deal of RAM, as it must make a copy of the selected geometry in RAM to perform its functions. Nevertheless, Edit Patch is offered for those occasions when you want to try out options, or when prior modifiers or parametric options must be left in place.

Face Extrude

The Face Extrude modifier allows you to extrude selected faces of a mesh. You must first make a selection of faces on the sub-object level of an object. You can then apply the Face Extrude modifier to affect the selected faces. While you can use the Extrude option at the sub-object level of a mesh, the Face Extrude modifier offers a few additional options such as Scale and Extrude from Center. You can achieve a beveled effect with these options.

FFD (Free Form Deformation)

The Free Form Deformation modifier lets you deform objects in a general way by offering lattice control points to pull and stretch objects (See "Understanding NURBS" for a description of CVs.) When you apply the Free Form Deformation modifier, a lattice box appears around the selected object. You can use the control points on the box to push or pull the object's form (See Figure B.5). The lattice box is a type of gizmo and does not represent actual geometry.

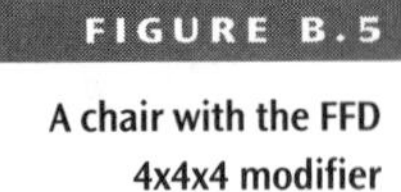

FIGURE B.5

A chair with the FFD 4x4x4 modifier

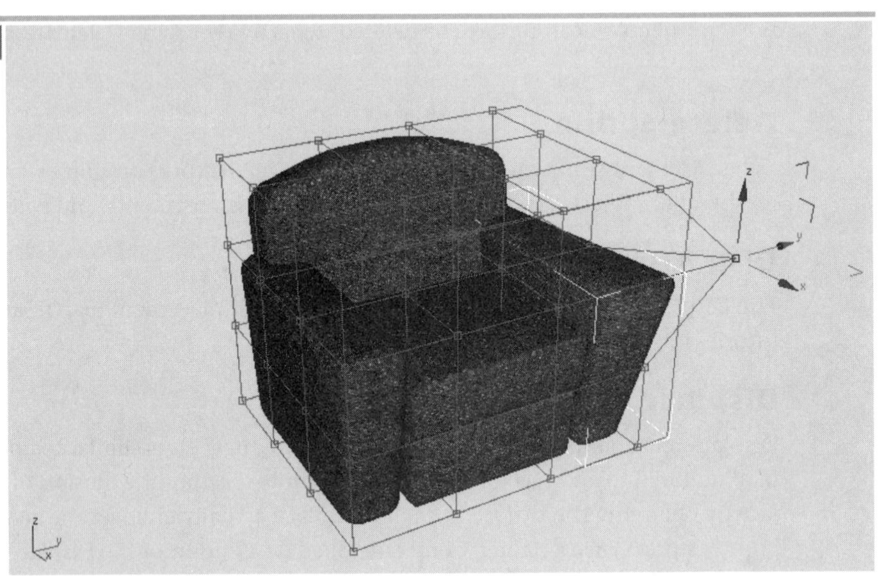

The FFD modifier is offered in three types: 2×2×2, 3×3×3, and 4×4×4. Each type places a different box around the object. The FFD 2×2×2 modifier, for example, places a box with control points at each corner.

FFD (Box)

The FFD (Box) modifier is similar in function to the FFD modifier but adds the capability to control the number of control points. With FFD (Box), you are not limited to the 2x2x2 through 4x4x4 lattice of the FFD modifier, as shown in Figure B.6.

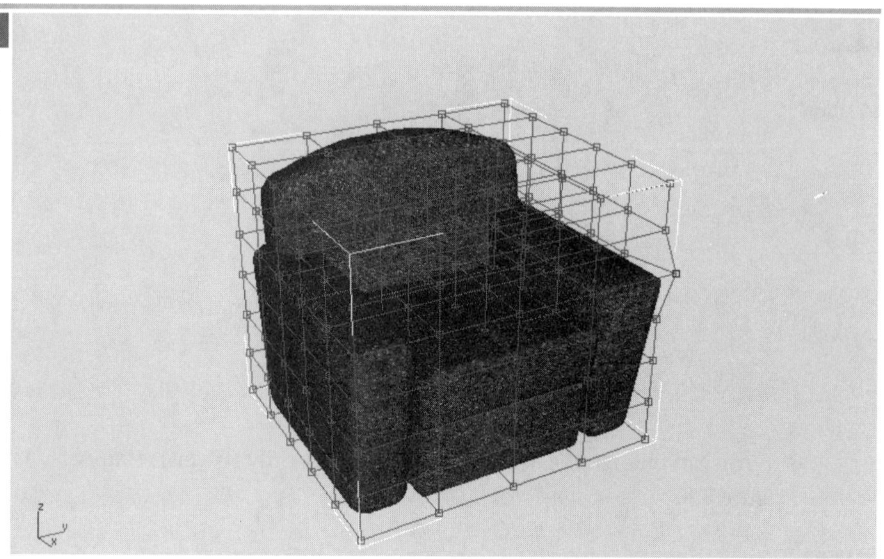

FIGURE B.6

An FFD (Box) modifier applied to a chair using a 5×6×7 lattice

FFD (Cyl)

Like the FFD (Box) modifier, FFD (Cyl) allows you to set the number of control points in the control lattice, but instead of a box, FFD (Cyl) places a cylindrical lattice around the object.

Fillet/Chamfer

The Fillet/Chamfer modifier lets you convert a spline vertex into a filleted corner (rounded) or a chamfered corner. It only works on vertices that connect straight segments, and it will not join two disconnected segments. To use it, select a shape, then apply the Fillet/Chamfer modifier. The Vertex Sub-Object level is automatically opened, allowing you to select a vertex for editing. You can either select a vertex and enter a fillet or chamfer value in the Edit Vertex rollout, or you can set a fillet or chamfer value first, then select a vertex and click the Apply button.

Lattice

The Lattice modifier lets you convert the segments of a shape or the edges of an object into joints and struts. The effect is similar to that of converting a mesh object into a wireframe, but expressing the wireframe as renderable geometry (See Figure B.7). A geodesic dome is a good architectural example of using a latticed geosphere.

FIGURE B.7

A tapered cylinder converted into a lattice

You can change the selected object so that only its vertices appear, as shown in Figure B.8.

FIGURE B.8

A tapered cylinder with its vertices converted into octahedrons

In addition, Lattice allows you to display both vertices and struts to form some unusual objects. You have control over the number of sides of the struts or the type of geometry used at the vertices. You can also change the scale of the joints and struts.

Linked Xform

The Linked Xform modifier lets you apply the transforms (Move, Scale, Rotate) of one object to another object or set of objects.

Material

When you apply a Multi/Sub-Object material to an object, you need to assign a material ID to selected faces of the object in order to correlate a sub-material with the selected faces (see Chapter 15 for a detailed look at Multi/Sub-Object materials). The Material modifier lets you do just that.

The Material modifier is not needed for editable meshes. It is intended for other types of objects that do not offer access to mesh-level editing. For those objects, you need to apply the Mesh Select modifier first in order to select mesh faces. You can then apply the Material modifier to assign a material ID.

MaterialByElement

The MaterialByElement modifier applies the different materials of a Multi/Sub-Object material to the different elements of an object. This is done randomly.

Mesh Select

The Mesh Select modifier allows you to gain access to the sub-object level of an object to select part of the object. You can then apply another modifier to affect only what you selected with Mesh Select. For example, you could use Mesh Select to select part of an object and then you could apply Bend to only the selected parts. You can use Mesh Select to pass selections up the stack to other modifiers or to gain access to mesh sub-object selection for Patch and NURBS surfaces.

MeshSmooth

MeshSmooth does just what the name implies: it smooths a mesh so that sharp corners are rounded. It does this by increasing the complexity of the mesh. The smoothed form can be edited by using control vectors in a way similar to NURBS CVs (See Appendix C for more on NURBS CVs.) See Chapter 15 for a detailed description of this modifier.

Mirror

Mirror performs the same function as the Mirror tool on the VIZ Modify toolbar to the left of the VIZ window. Since it is a modifier, you can control the mirror effect as part of the object's modifier stack.

Ncurve Sel/Nsurf Sel

Ncurve Sel and Nsurf Sel allow you to place sub-object selections anywhere in the stack of a NURBS object. This is similar to the Mesh Select modifier but is only used for NURBS.

Noise

The Noise modifier randomly repositions the vertices of an object to simulate an uneven surface. You can adjust the strength of the noise to create a relatively smooth surface or a mountainous terrain. The effectiveness of Noise is dependent on the amount of segmentation of the object.

Normalize Spline

The Normalize Spline modifier places additional control points along a spline. The control points are spaced at regular intervals. This can be useful when using splines for motion paths where a constant speed is required.

Optimize

The Optimize modifier simplifies the geometry of an object while maintaining an acceptable level of detail. This offers the benefits of faster rendering time and less RAM usage.

PatchDeform

See Patch Deform in the "World-Space Modifiers" section of this appendix.

PathDeform

See Path Deform in the "World-Space Modifiers" section of this appendix.

Preserve

The Preserve modifier lets you *clean up* a mesh that has been edited on a vertex sub-object level. Often when a mesh is edited by moving vertices, the resulting form takes on a rough appearance. The Preserve modifier will help smooth out that rough appearance.

To use the Preserve modifier, you must first make a copy of the object you wish to modify. Make your changes to the copy's vertices, and then, with the Vertex sub-object level still active, apply the Preserve modifier. Use the Pick Original button of the Preserve modifier to select the original object from which you made the copy. You can then use the other Preserve modifier controls to adjust the mesh.

Push

If you need to create a bulging shrunken appearance, you can use Push. The Push modifier has a single parameter that pushes or pulls the vertices of an object from its center.

Relax

Relax is similar to Push, but instead of pushing vertices out from the object's center, Relax softens the corner edges of an object or generally *relaxes* an object's shape to something smoother, with less pronounced surface change.

Ripple

Ripple modifies an object's surface to produce a concentric rippled effect. You can control amplitude, wavelength, phase, and decay of the ripple.

Skew

The Skew modifier skews an object as shown in Figure B.9. You can control the direction and strength of the skew. You can also limit the skew to a section of the object.

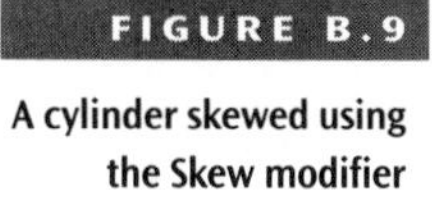

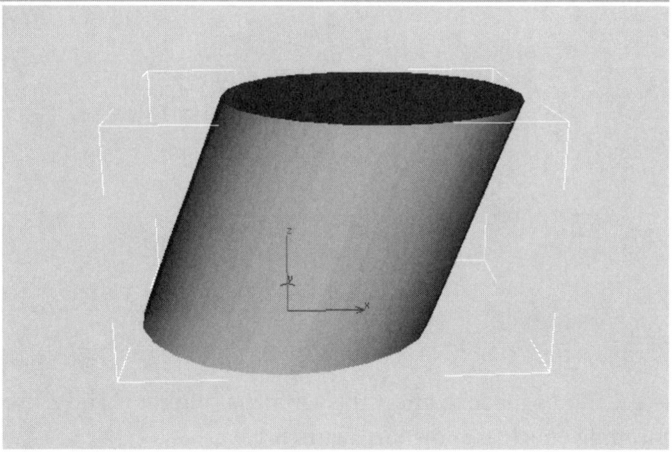

FIGURE B.9

A cylinder skewed using the Skew modifier

Smooth

The Smooth modifier applies auto-smoothing to the surface of an object. While you can usually apply smoothing to an editable mesh at the sub-object level, Smooth allows you to control the smoothing as a item in the mesh's modifier stack.

Spherify

The Spherify modifier lets you distort an object into a spherical shape. It offers a single parameter that lets you control the amount of distortion you can apply to the object.

Spline Select

The Spline Select modifier lets you affect sub-object selections of splines. This is useful for making sub-object selections for modifiers that are far removed from the source object in the modifier stack.

Squeeze

Squeeze lets you move the vertices of an object along the Z axis. The vertices closest to the object's pivot point are moved the farthest. If you apply Squeeze to a box, for example, the vertices at the center of the top surface are pushed or pulled farther than the ones toward the edge, creating a bulging effect or a cupping effect as shown in Figure B.10.

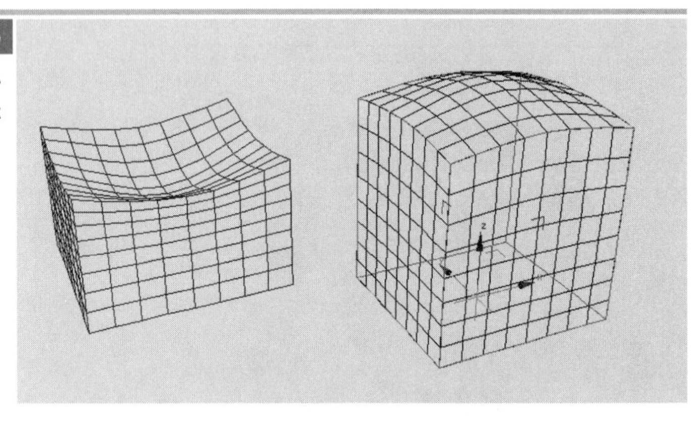

FIGURE B.10

Using the Squeeze modifier on a box

Squeeze can also be made to affect the vertices along the Y and Z axes to create a flare or a crimping effect, as shown in Figure B.11.

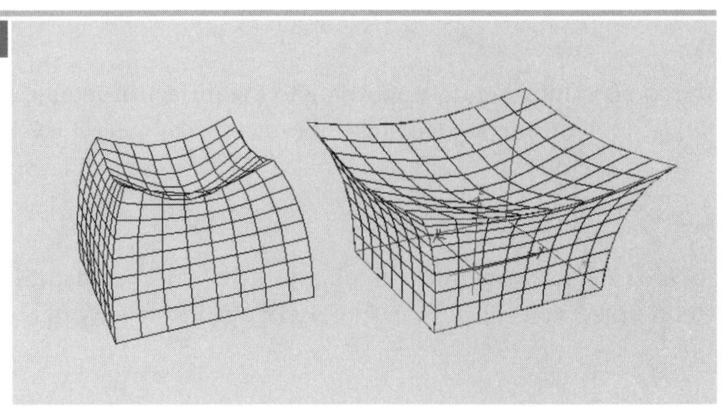

FIGURE B.11

Flaring and crimping a box

STL-Check

If you plan to export your VIZ model for use with stereolithography equipment, you can use the STL-Check modifier to check your design for correct export.

Stretch

If you just want to squash or stretch an object along a single axis, you can do so using the Stretch modifier. By applying a positive stretch value to this modifier, the object elongates along the selected axis while contracting along the other two axes, as shown in Figure B.12. Applying a negative Stretch value causes the object to shrink along the selected axis while bulging out in the plane of the other two axes as shown in Figure B.12.

FIGURE B.12

Sample boxes that are stretched and squashed using the Stretch modifier

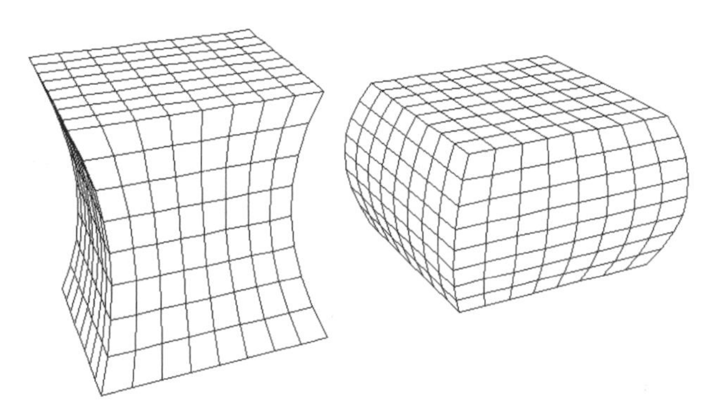

Surface

The Surface modifier applies a patch surface over a set of interconnected spline segments. The segments must all be of one object and must be joined at their vertices. The Surface modifier applies patch surfaces to three- and four-sided polygon formations of the interconnected segments. See "CrossSection" earlier in this section and "Understanding Patches" in Appendix C.

SurfDeform

See SurfDeform in the "World-Space Modifiers" section of this appendix.

Taper

The Taper modifier allows you to taper an object along a specified axis. See Chapters 2 and 4 for a more detailed look at the Taper modifier.

Tessellate

The Tessellate modifier divides the faces of a surface into multiple, smaller faces. It can have the effect of smoothing a surface. You can also use it increase the number of faces in a region of a surface for further editing. If Tessellate is applied to an object, all of the faces of the object are tessellated. You may also enter the Face sub-object level to select a specific set of faces for tessellation.

FIGURE B.13

A surface before and after tessellation

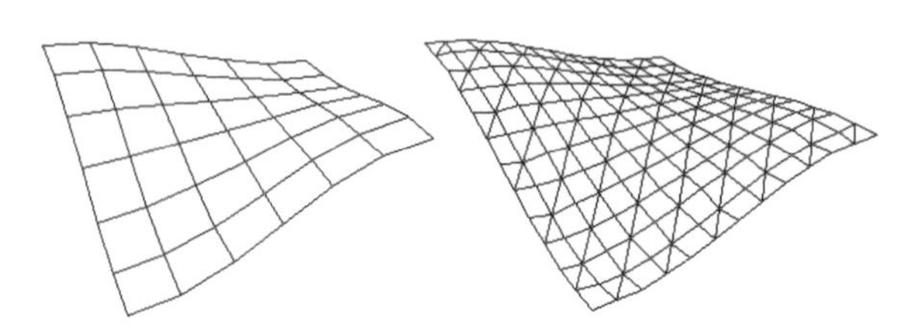

Tesselate is also an option in the Face, Polygon, and Element sub-object levels of editable meshes.

Trim/Extend

The Trim/Extend modifier works just like the Trim/Extend options in the sub-object level of shape objects. You can trim open spline segments to other existing, overlapping segments within a single object, or you can extend open segments to other segments within the same object that lie in the direction of the segment end. The Trim/Extend modifier is offered for those situations where it is preferable to include Trim/Extend operations within the modifier stack.

Twist

The Twist modifier deforms an object by twisting it along a selected axis. Figure B.14 shows a box that has a Twist modifier.

FIGURE B.14

A twisted box.

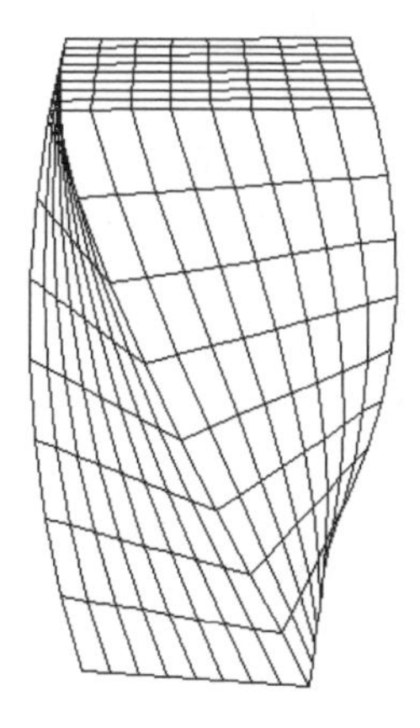

UVW Xform

You can use the UVW Map modifier to control the way a material map is applied to an object. Many VIZ objects offer built-in mapping, such as the general coordinates for standard primitives and lofted objects. Unfortunately, those built-in mapping coordinates do not offer the tiling and offset options found in the UVW Mapping modifier. The UVW Xform modifier is offered to allow tiling and offset control over mapping in objects that have built-in mapping.

Vol. Select

The Vol. Select modifier lets you make sub-object selections based on a volume. You have the choice of three volume types—Box, Sphere, and Cylinder. A selection gizmo in the shape of the volume type you select appears in the design. You can then select the sub-object level of the Vol. Select modifier to move the volume gizmo into place to make the selection.

Wave

The Wave modifier produces a wave effect on the selected geometry. The smoothness of the wave is determined by the number of segments in the object. More segments produce a smoother wave.

Xform

The Xform modifier is intended to allow transforms within specific locations in the modifier stack. This makes it useful for trial purposes since you can easily delete the Xform modifier from the stack, something you cannot do with the standard Xform tools on the standard toolbar.

Materials and Maps

The main part of *Mastering 3D Studio VIZ* focuses on a few of the materials available in VIZ, and for 80 percent of your projects, your needs won't go beyond the material types shown in the tutorials of this book. For the remaining 20 percent, you'll find the range of materials offered by VIZ indispensable. This section provides a description of all of the materials available in the VIZ Material/Map Browser. Just as with the preceding Modifier section, you may want to read about these material options for future reference.

Materials (Blue Sphere)

When you select both the Materials and Maps options in the Show group of the Material/Map Browser, you'll see a list of options that show either a blue sphere or a green parallelogram. The items at the top of the list with the blue spheres are materials; the green parallelograms show the maps. The main difference between the two is that the materials in the list represent types of materials available, whereas the maps are components of Materials.

None

This option allows you to remove a material or map specification.

Blend

You can mix two materials into a single material by using the Blend material. Blend offers the ability to control the strength of each material.

Composite

Composite materials allow you to superimpose up to ten materials. You can apply additive or subtractive opacity to each material or control the strength of the individual materials.

Double Sided

You can assign a different material to the front and back of an object with a single surface by using the Double Sided material. When you select this material type, you can use the Double Sided basic parameters to select a material for the Facing material and the Back material.

Matte/Shadow

A Matte/Shadow object has the effect of making itself and anything behind it invisible. It is most frequently used in conjunction with environment maps where a design is to be blended into a photograph. For example, suppose you have a fairly detailed background image of a photograph that shows a garage, and you want to create the illusion of a car entering the garage. You can create a simple box with an opening similar in shape to the background garage opening, then apply the Matte/Shadow material to the box. Once this is done, you can animate the car to drive into the box. The net effect is that the car appears to drive into the garage in the background.

Matte/Shadow objects can also be used to add shadows to objects in a background image. For example, suppose you are using the camera match tools to match a car design to a background image of the building's site. In the real world, your design would cast shadows on the ground, but in your VIZ design, you would leave out the ground so that the ground in the background image can come through in the rendering. Unfortunately, when you do this, the design does not cast a shadow on the ground. This unnatural absence of a shadow creates an odd, floating appearance. You can add a ground plane to your design and assign the Matte/Shadow material to this ground plane. The ground plane will be invisible when it is rendered, yet it will receive a shadow, creating the illusion that the car is casting a shadow on the ground of the background image.

Figure B.15 shows a rendering of the car from Chapter 15, using the background from the camera match exercise of Chapter 15. Notice the shadow of the car in the image. To obtain that shadow, a surface was placed under the car, and a Matte/Shadow material was applied to the surface. The Receive Shadow option was also turned on for the Matte/Shadow material.

FIGURE B.15

A 3D car model is rendered onto a background image.

Matte/Shadow materials behave in a way similar to the effect of the Camera Map modifier. The main difference here is that the Camera Map modifier is view dependent, while the Matte/Shadow material affects all views.

Multi/Sub-Object

The Multi/Sub-Object material is like a collection of separate materials under a single material name. Multi/Sub-Object materials are useful in situations where you want to assign multiple materials to a single object. See Chapter 15 for more on the use of Multi/Sub-Object materials.

Raytrace

Ray Traced materials reflect and refract light in a way that simulates one of the ways light actually works. The term *Raytrace* comes from the way the program traces the path of light from a pixel in the rendered image back to the light source. Ray Traced materials are best used for transparent or shiny materials, such as glass or water, that reflect or refract light. Figure B.16 shows a rendering of a sample file from VIZ. The vase in the figure uses a Ray Traced material.

FIGURE B.16

A goblet using a Ray Traced material

Shellac

A Shellac material lets you create a shellac effect by combining two materials. One, called the Base material, is used for the underlying base. The second, Shellac material, is applied over the base with some transparency. You can control the transparency and blending of the shellac material.

Standard

The Standard material is the default material in the Material Editor. It is covered in some depth through the tutorials in this book. It offers a wide variety of shaders, and you can include several different types of maps (described in the next section). With the available combination of shaders and maps, you can create nearly any effect you need for materials.

Bottom/Top

The Bottom/Top material lets you assign a different material to the top and bottom of an object. An example of this might be a two-tone car body. You can control the position and blending of the two materials.

Maps (Green Parallelogram)

The Standard Materials discussed in this book allow you to apply maps in several different ways. Maps can be used to control reflection, opacity, bumpiness, and transparency, etc. This book focuses on the use of bitmaps for most of the material map applications, but there are several other map types that you'll want to know about. Here is a listing describing the different map types and how they might be used.

None

This option is used to remove a map assignment from a material.

Bitmap

The Bitmap option is described thoroughly in this book. It allows you to use any bitmap image as a material map. It is perhaps the most flexible option, since thousands of bitmaps can be acquired from a wide variety of sources. You can create fairly credible materials through the use of bitmaps.

Bricks

The Bricks Map is a procedural map that allows you to parametrically control the map's appearance. You can control the type of brick joint as well as the color and texture of the brick pattern through this map. The Bricks map differs from the Brick material seen in the standard material library in that it offers more control over the appearance of the brick, through parameters.

Cellular

The Cellular map is a procedural map that creates a variety of cellular or granular material effects. With this map you can create materials ranging from terrazzo to polystyrene foam. The VIZ Online Reference also mentions using the Cellular material for the ocean surface. Cellular map is fairly complex, so you may want to experiment with it on your own to see what types of results it produces.

Checker

The Checker map is a procedural map that creates a checkerboard pattern. You can assign a color or another map to the squares of the checkerboard. You can also add noise to create a more natural appearance.

Composite

A Composite map is a map formed from the combination of other maps. Alpha channels are used to control blending of the composite maps.

Dent

Dent is a procedural 3D map that produces a random, dented surface. You can control the depth and size of dents through the map's parameters. You can also apply other maps to the Dent map to create a multicolored surface.

Falloff

The Falloff map is primarily used as an opacity map. When applied to a sphere as an opacity map in its default mode, the sphere appears most transparent at its center and least transparent around its edges, like a clear balloon or glass ball. This is the same effect as the Falloff setting in the Extended Parameters rollout of the Standard Material, with some added control.

Flat Mirror

The Flat Mirror map is used primarily as a reflection map. It produces a mirrorlike finish on a flat surface, reflecting the environment and objects nearby. To use this material, you must apply it directly to coplanar faces of an object on a sub-object level. This can be done by including Flat Mirror in the reflection channel in a sub-material of a Multi/Sub-Object material.

Gradient

The Gradient map lets you create a color gradient using two or three colors. You can perturb the gradient by applying a noise parameter.

Gradient Ramp

The Gradient Ramp map is similar to the Gradient map, but it allows for a greater range of colors.

Marble

The Marble map simulates the appearance of marble. You can control the color of the marble veins and the background. You can also adjust the size of the veins.

Mask

The Mask map uses two maps. One map is used as a base map, while the second map is a mask. The mask controls the visibility of the base map.

Mix

The Mix map allows you to combine two colors, two maps, or a color and a map.

Noise

The Noise map creates random noise in the form of a gray scale pattern. It looks a bit like the static from an older TV set. Noise can be used to create a bump pattern or a granite surface. Parameters let you adjust the scale and intensity of the noise.

Output

Bitmap maps offer control over the bitmap image through the Output rollout. Such controls are not available for many of the other procedural maps. The Output map is like a modifier for procedural maps that gives you the same Output rollout options as Bitmap maps. See Chapter 7 for a detailed look at the Output rollout for Bitmap maps.

Paint

Paint is a highly specialized map that allows you to use the Discreet Logic Paint program to paint a map directly onto a 3D object.

Perlin Marble

Perlin Marble creates a marble pattern using what is called the Perlin Turbulence algorithm. The Perlin pattern has a more swirled appearance.

Planet

The Planet map is designed to simulate the surface of a planet, complete with oceans and continents. It is primarily designed to be used as a diffuse map.

Raytrace

Like the Ray Traced material, the Raytrace map provides Ray Traced reflection and refraction for objects it is assigned to. It is most suitable for highly reflective surfaces or transparent materials. See "Raytrace" (materials) for more information.

Reflect/Refract

The Reflect/Refract map simulates reflection and refraction of backgrounds in the environment of the design. It does this by mapping the environment onto a cube surrounding the mapped object, then using that cube as a reflection map.

RGB Multiply

The RGB Multiply map combines the effects of two maps. This map is commonly used for bump maps.

RGB Tint

The RGB Tint map lets you apply a color tint to another map. You first insert the RGB Tint map, then through its parameters you attach a second map. You can then use the R, G, or B color swatch in the RGB Tint parameters to tint the second map.

Smoke

The Smoke map creates a smokelike pattern. It is more commonly used as an opacity map for simulating smoke.

Speckle

The Speckle map creates a speckled appearance using two colors, two maps, or a color and a map. You can use it for diffuse or bump maps to create a speckled-egg look.

Splat

Splat produces a splattered paint look. Its controls are similar to those for Speckle. You can use two colors, two maps, or a color and a map to produce the splat effect.

Stucco

The Stucco map is designed to create a stucco surface and is commonly used as a bump map.

Swirl

Swirl creates a swirl pattern from two colors or maps.

Thin Wall Refraction

The Thin Wall Refraction map creates the illusion of refracting glass. When applied to a thin box representing a glass panel, it offsets the view behind the glass panel, simulating a refracted appearance. This map requires less time to render than the Reflect/Refract map or the Raytrace map. Therefore, in well-lit, close-up views, it offers a good alternative to those maps.

Vertex Color

You can apply regions of color to an editable mesh by assigning color to vertices in the mesh. These vertex color assignments become visible when you apply the Vertex Color map to the mesh. To apply a color to a vertex, select the mesh, then click the Modify tab. Click the Vertex option in the Modify Tabs Selection rollout, select a vertex or set of vertices, scroll down to the Vertex Color group, and edit the colors. After assigning a color to a vertex, create a material that uses the Vertex Color map as a diffuse map, then apply the material to the object.

Water

The Water map simulates the surface of water. It can be used as a diffuse and bump map at the same time to create a rippling, waterlike surface. You can control the amplitude and size of ripples.

Wood

The Wood map simulates the qualities of wood grain. It is a 3D procedural map, which means that the wood grain effect is carried through the volume of the object to which it is applied. If you cut a notch out of the object, for example, you'll see the grain accurately reproduced in the notch as in a real piece of wood. You have the option of controlling two colors for the wood grain, the grain thickness, and the amount of noise or *straightness* in the grain.

Appendix C

Patches and NURBS Surfaces

PATCHES AND NURBS SURFACES

There are two VIZ objects that have not been covered in the main body of this book, though they certainly play a major role in VIZ designs. Patches and NURBS Surfaces are objects that allow you to quickly form curved surfaces by deforming their geometry. If you want to be able to *sculpt* a shape, then you'll want to know about these objects. Patches and NURBS are often used in character animation and other design disciplines in which forming curved shapes are a major part of the design tool set.

Understanding Patches

A patch object is a collection of Bézier patches that consist of vertices, edges, and surfaces similar to mesh objects. The main difference between mesh objects and patches is that the patch vertices can be controlled using Bézier handles. These handles can be moved to apply a curve to the edges of the patch. The segments connecting patch vertices are splines that can be curved. Meshes always have straight-line segments connecting their vertices. In a sense, patches are like splines that have surface.

Perhaps the best way to understand Patches is to see how one can be created and edited. Most of the standard primitives can be converted into editable patches. Let's take a look at how a Plane standard primitive can be converted into an editable patch and then edited.

Converting a Plane into an Editable Patch

First create a plane using the Standard Primitives option of the Geometry tool in the Create tab of the Command Panel. The Length Segs and Width Segs parameters will influence the number of vertices of the patch. Once you've created the plane, use the Edit Stack tool in the Modify tab to convert the surface to an editable patch. The plane will appear to be subdivided into smaller segments.

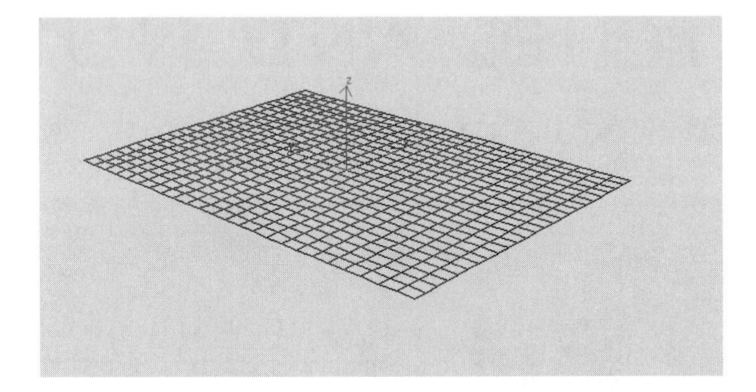

These subdivisions are a visual aid. The resulting editable patch contains vertices at the locations of the segment corners of the original plane. You can see the vertices clearly if you select the Vertex sub-object level from the Selection rollout of the editable patch.

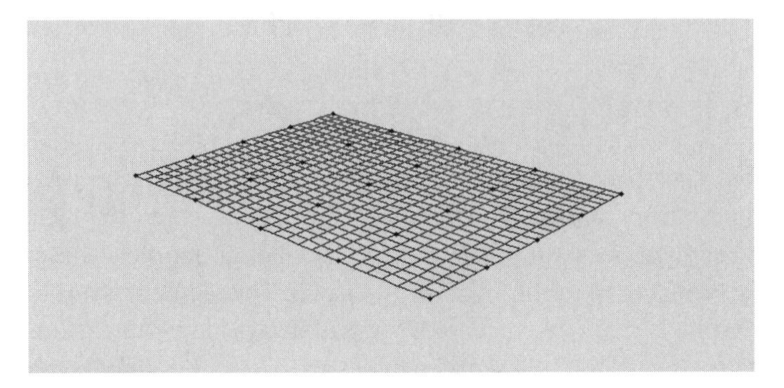

Notice that the rows and columns of vertices are in the same location as the segments of the original plane standard primitive. If you increase the number of segments in the plane, then the resulting editable patch will contain more vertices.

At the vertex sub-object level of the editable patch, you can move the vertices to *sculpt* the surface. The subdivisions on the plane, called view steps, let you see the deformation of the surface as you move the vertices, as shown in Figure C.1

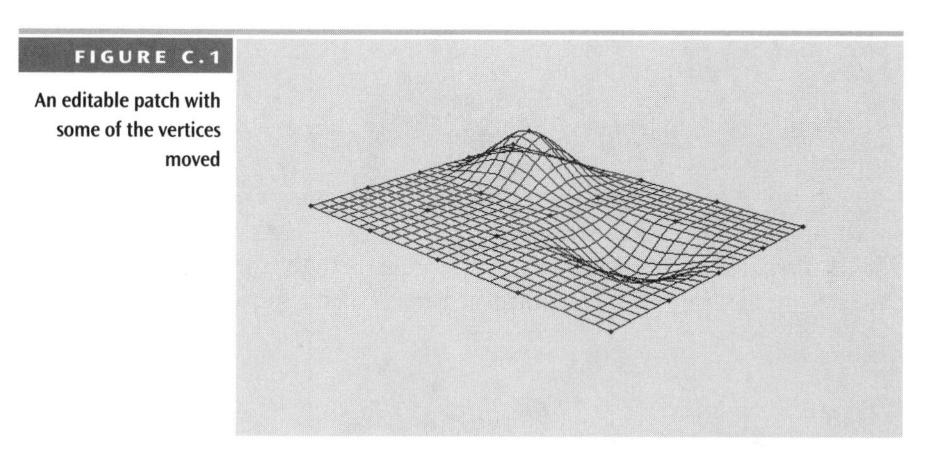

FIGURE C.1

An editable patch with some of the vertices moved

The Surface group of the editable patch Geometry rollout lets you control the number of view steps within each patch.

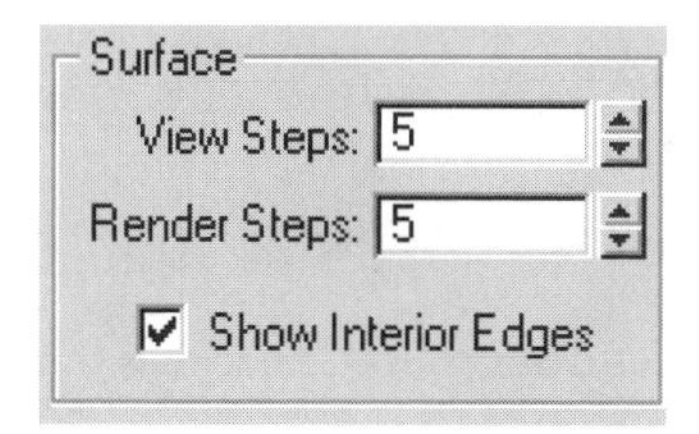

You may also use the Edge or Patch sub-object level to *sculpt* the surface of an editable patch.

Converting Other Standard Primitives to Editable Patches

You can convert any standard primitive into a editable patch object. The resulting patch depends on the type of object you use for the conversion. A sphere, for example, becomes an editable patch whose surface facets are arranged like those of a geosphere.

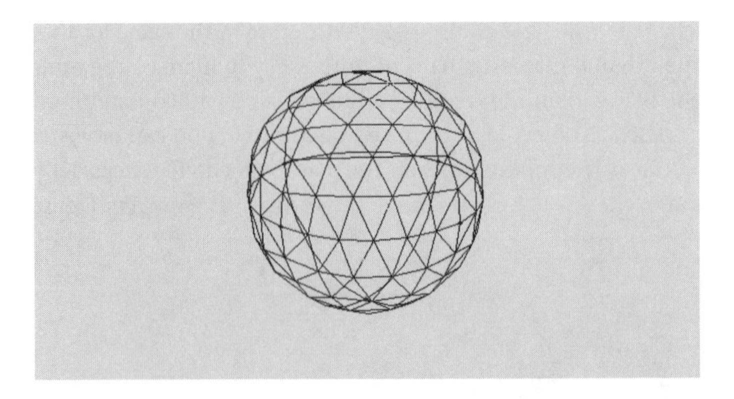

The density of vertices is dependent upon the number of segments of the original sphere from which the editable patch is derived.

When a box is converted to an editable patch, the corners of the box become the vertices of the editable patch. There are no intermediate vertices on the surface of the box.

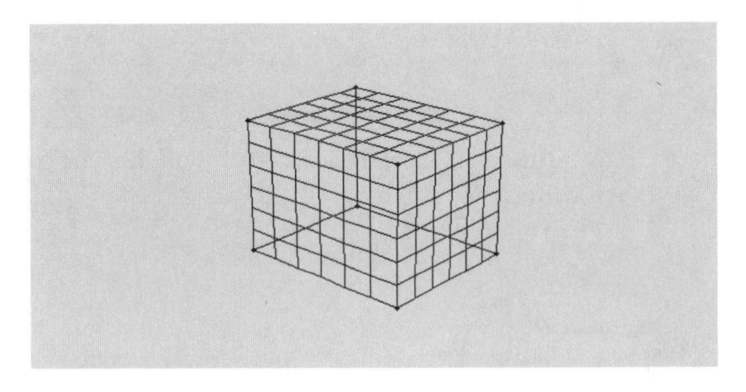

At the sub-object level, the corner vertices display Bézier handles that can be moved to deform the box.

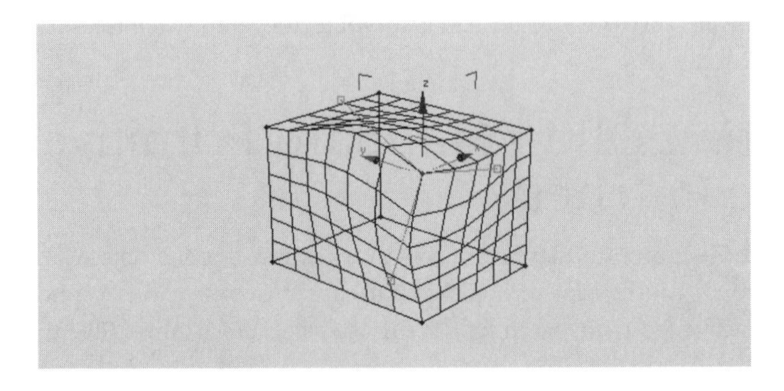

This may seem like a limitation, however you can deform the surface of any box by using the Patch Deform modifier. This modifier allows you to deform the surface of an object, based on the deformation of an editable patch. For example, you can apply the deformation of the patch shown in Figure C.1 to the top of a box to achieve the shape shown in Figure C.2.

FIGURE C.2

An editable mesh box with its top deformed by using the Patch Deform modifier and the Editable Patch shown in Figure C.1

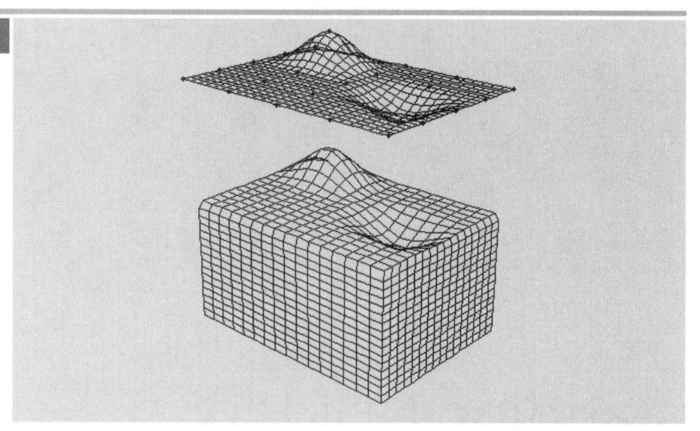

You first select the object or sub-object level you want to deform, then add the PatchDeform modifier. The modifier then offers a button that lets you select the Patch surface that you want to use to describe the deformation. You can then *sculpt* the object by editing the Patch surface.

Cylinders, Cones, Tubes, and Pyramids will all convert to editable patches with their vertices limited to the edges of the planar surfaces. For example, a cylinder will convert to an editable patch with vertices at the top and bottom surfaces in the four quadrants of the cylinder, as shown in Figure C.3

FIGURE C.3

A cylinder showing the vertices of the editable patch

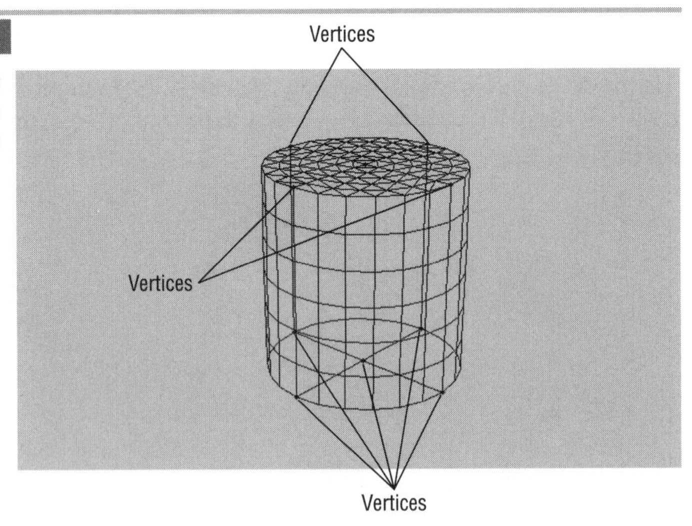

Understanding NURBS

NURBS stands for Non-Uniform Rational B-Splines. I won't try to explain what all of that means. Just be aware that NURBS have their basis in a mathematical structure that plays an invisible role in their formation. Don't let this scare you away from using them. You can use NURBS surfaces and curves in a very practical way without delving too deeply into their structural underpinnings. However, it will help to understand their behavior on a practical level.

Looking at NURBS Curves

Lets start by looking at a NURBS curve and how it behaves. If you click the Shape tool in the Create tab, then select NURBS Curves from the Shapes drop-down list, you are presented with two options: Point Curve and CV Curve. The Point Curve option lets you draw a curve by indicating points through which the curve passes as shown in Figure C.4.

FIGURE C.4

A NURBS Curve using the Point Curve option

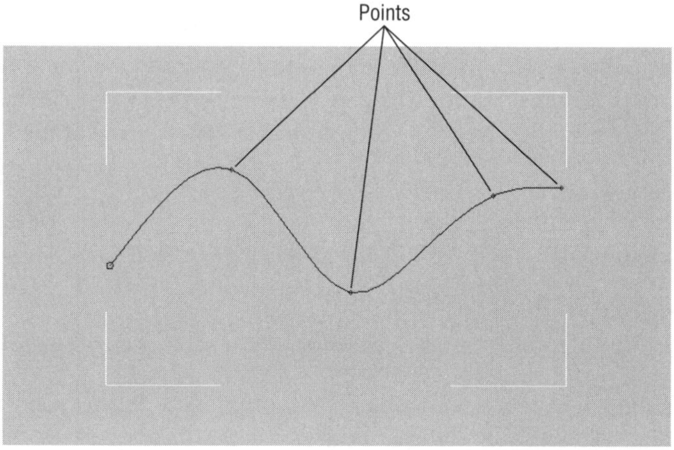

The CV Curve option lets you draw a curve by indicating the location of *Control Vertices*. A single Control Vertex is referred to as a CV. Instead of passing through a CV, the curve is *pulled* in the direction of the CV, as shown in Figure C.5.

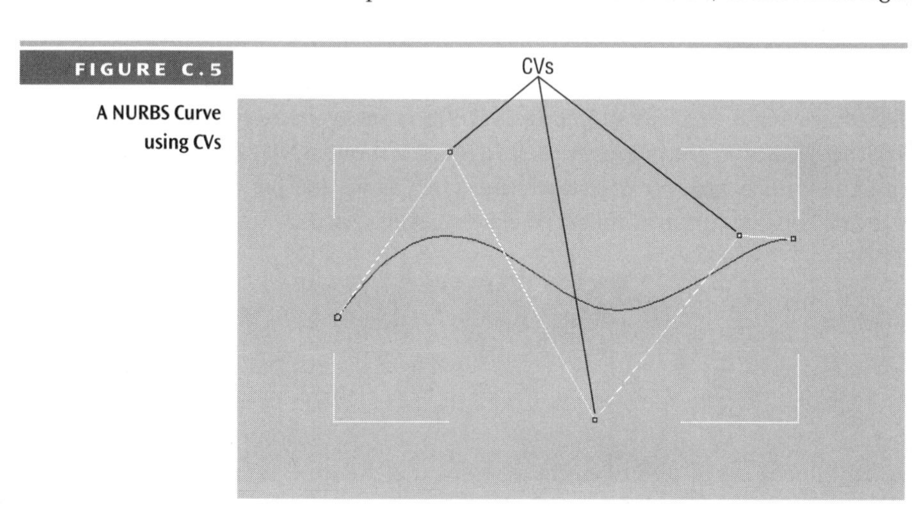

FIGURE C.5

A NURBS Curve using CVs

VIZ offers parameters that allow you to control the weight or *pull* of a CV to sharpen or soften the curve at the CV location. Multiple CVs can be combined to increase the pull at a given location. For example, you can combine three CVs at one point to form a corner as shown In Figure C.6. You can also increase the pull of a single CV. CVs can be added using the options in the Refine group of the CV parameters.

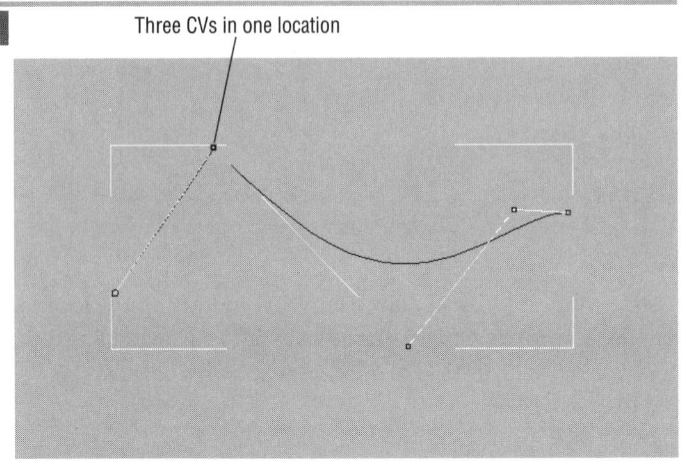

FIGURE C.6

A curve shown with three CVs combined in one location.

A NURBS surface works in a way similar to a NURBS curve. Vertices of a NURBS surface can be either points on the curve, or CVs. Figure C.7 shows a NURBS surface with point curves. The surface makes contact with the vertex. Note that the segments of the surface are not related to the number of vertices in the surface.

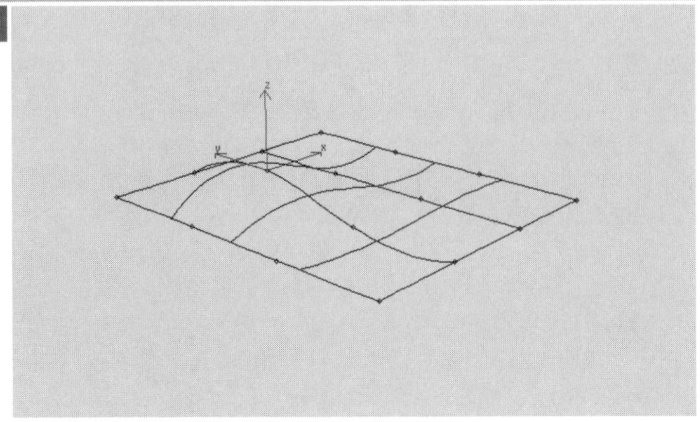

FIGURE C.7

A NURBS surface using point curves

CVs in a NURBS surface exert a pull on the surface, but are not necessarily on the surface itself, just as CVs on a curve are not on the curve itself. See Figure C.8.

FIGURE C.8

A NURBS surface using CVs

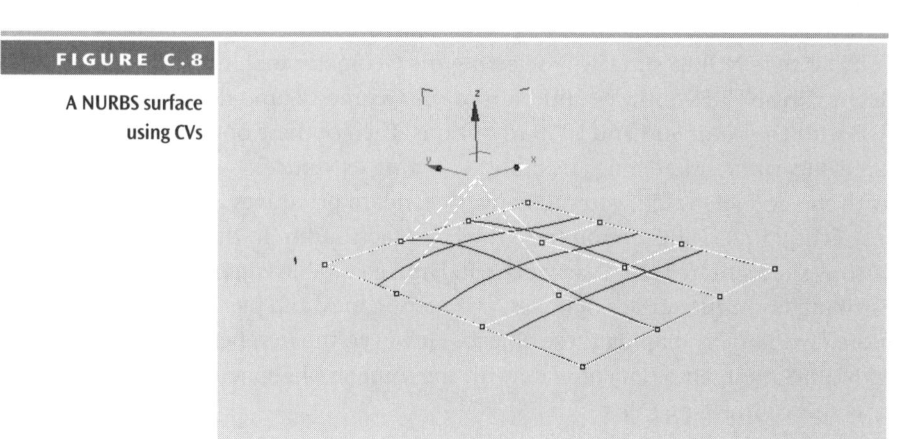

Just as with NURBS splines, you can increase or decrease the pull of a CV by adjusting its weight parameter. You gain access to the weight parameter of a CV by entering the Surface CV sub-object level of the NURBS object. You can then select a vertex and adjust its Weight parameter in the CV rollout.

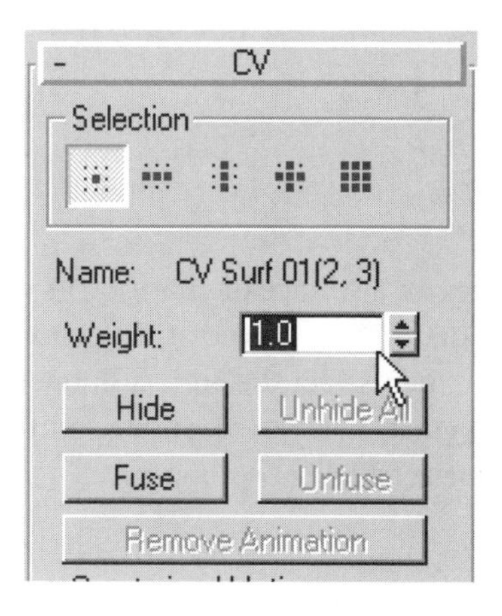

Creating NURBS Surfaces from Standard Primitives

You can create a single NURBS surface by selecting the Geometry tool in the Create tab and selecting the NURBS Surfaces option from the Geometry drop-down list. You are presented with the Point Surf and CV Surf options. Each of these options lets you create a flat NURBS surface that you can edit by adjusting its vertices.

Just as with the Editable Patch, you can convert standard primitives into NURBS surfaces by selecting the NURBS option from the Edit Stack button in the Modifier Stack. Such converted surfaces use CVs by default. Unlike Editable Patches, the vertices are distributed over the surface of boxes, cylinders, cones, and pyramids, giving you a bit more flexibility in shaping these objects. However, the number of vertices of a converted NURBS mesh does not correlate with the number of segments of the original object, as shown in Figure C.9.

FIGURE C.9

The box to the left is the original box, and the one to the right is the converted NURBS box.

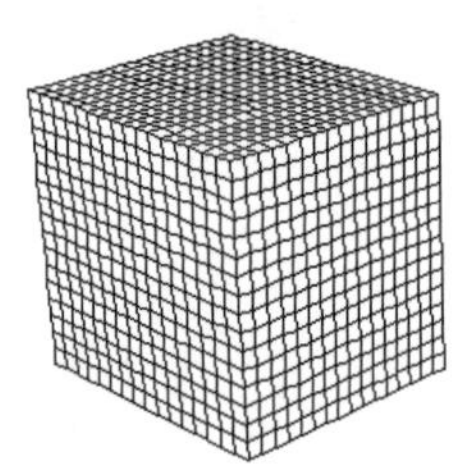

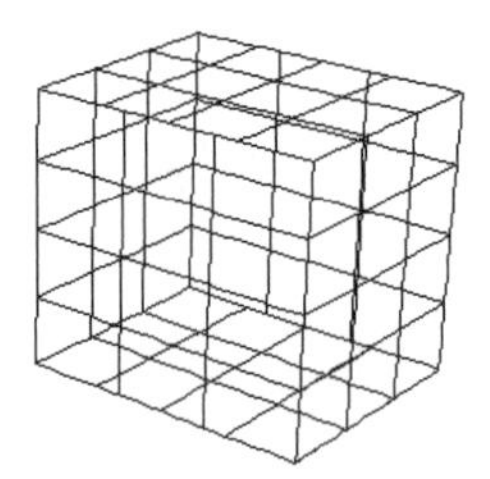

You can increase the number of vertices on a surface or change CVs to points on the surface by using the Convert Surface dialog box. To access the Convert Surface dialog box, first select the NURBS surface, then select the Surface Sub-Object level. Select the surfaces you want to edit, then click the Convert Surface button in the Surface Common rollout. The Convert Surface dialog box appears.

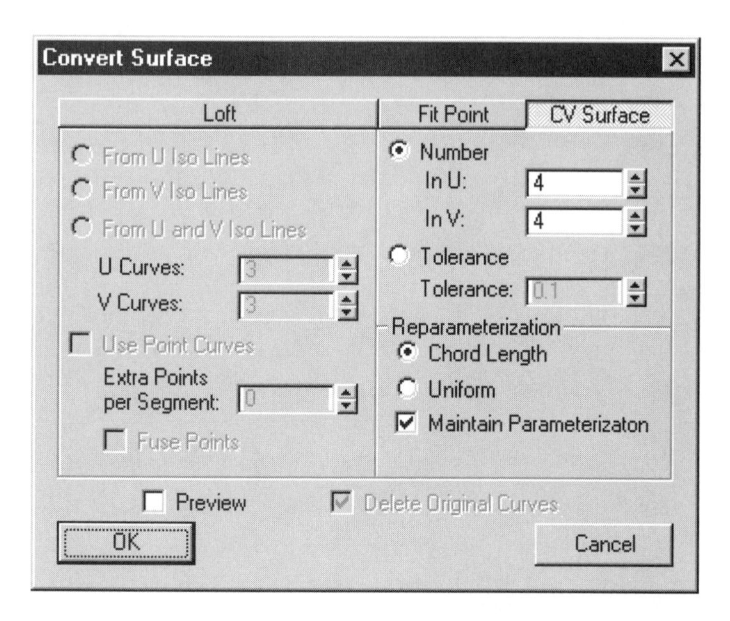

The Fit Point will change the vertices defining the surface from CVs to points on the surface. Click the Number radio button and adjust the In U and In V options to change the number of vertices on the surface.

Applying a NURBS Deformation to an Object

You can use the SurfDeform modifier to apply the deformation of a NURBS surface to the surface of another object. This works in a way similar to the Patch Deform modifier described in the earlier section discussing Editable Patches. You first select the object you want to deform, then add the SurfDeform modifier. The Surf Deform modifier then offers a button that lets you select the NURBS surface that you want to use to describe the deformation. If you need to, you can then turn the NURBS surface off to hide it from view.

You can use the SurfDeform modifier in conjunction with a NURBS surface to add the trough in the roof of the Ronchamp tutorial in Chapter 5. Instead of using the Soft Selection parameters to move the vertices of the roof, you can create the trough shape using a NURBS surface, then apply the NURBS surface deformation to the roof. You would do this after the Boolean operation to remove the smaller towers from the roof.

Appendix D

Helpers and Effects

Helpers and Effects

Mastering 3D Studio VIZ 3.0 focuses on the tools you'll need to create presentations of your designs. There are a few tools that you'll want to know about that weren't discussed in the main part of the book.

Helpers are nonrendering objects that can assist you in creating your model. Some helpers are designed specifically for animation while others help you take measurements in your design. Another set of helpers gives you control over the effects tools.

Effects are tools you can use to add a dramatic touch to your final renderings. For example, you can add film grain if your rendering is to be matched to a grainy background, or you can add a lens flare. You can also add atmospheric effects such as fog or combustion.

This appendix is intended to give you general information about the helpers and effects and to show you what types of features are available. If you need more detailed information about the helpers and effects, the VIZ Online Reference offers full descriptions of the options and parameters for all of the items discussed in this appendix. Choose Help ➢ Online Reference, click the Search tab in the panel to the left, enter the name of the item in the Type in the Word(s) to Search for input box, then click List Topics. If you see only a single panel in the Online Reference, click the Show button on the Online Reference toolbar.

Helpers

Chapter 15 shows you how to use the Camera Match helper to align a design to a background image. There are also a number of other types of helpers. The Standard helpers are general purpose helpers that aid in measuring and linking objects. Atmospheric Apparati are gizmos that help you control atmospheric effects. The Camera Match helpers assist you in matching a design to a background image. The VRML helpers assist you in creating VRML (Virtual Reality Modeling Language) worlds.

Standard Helpers

Standard helpers can assist you as you build your design models. You can use them to mark location, measure distances, and create a local grid system.

Dummy

A Dummy helper is simply a box with a center location. It is used primarily as a linkage point for hierarchical linkages. At first glance, dummy objects seem fairly useless, but they can be a powerful aid in editing your models and are especially useful for animations.

Here's an example of a dummy used for editing. You may find that when using the Transform tools, you need a pivot point that is not available from the standard set of pivot centers on the standard toolbar. You can link an object to a dummy, then use the dummy's center point for transformations. The dummy can be located anywhere in the design. Depending on how the link is set up, you can apply transforms to the dummy instead of to the linked object, and the object will use the dummy's center for the transforms. The following steps describe how you can set this up.

First create the dummy:

1. Click the Helper button in the Create tab and select Standard from the Helpers drop-down list.
2. Click Dummy, then click and drag within a viewport to place and size the dummy object. Remember that the dummy does not render, so you can make it a size that is convenient for editing.
3. Move the dummy to the desired pivot point.

Next, link the dummy to an object:

1. Right-click the border of any toolbar, then select VIZ tools from the right-click menu. The VIZ Tools toolbar appears.

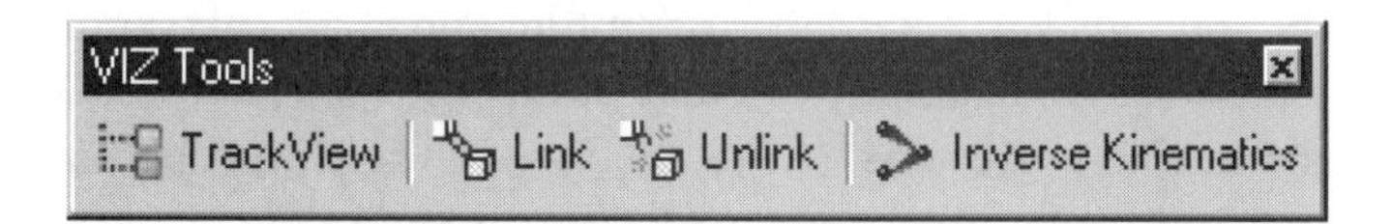

2. Click the Select and Link tool on the VIZ Tools toolbar.

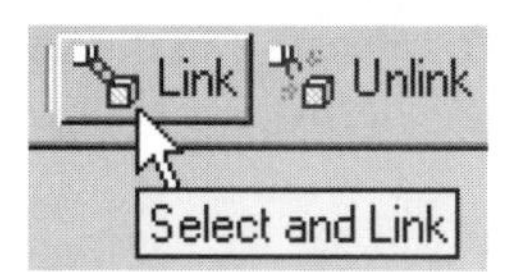

3. Click and drag the object that you want to link to the dummy. A dashed line appears from the selected object.
4. Continue to drag the mouse to the dummy. When you see the link cursor appear, release the mouse. This makes the dummy the parent in the linkage.

Next, use the rotate tool to test the link. By rotating the dummy you also rotate the object that is linked to it.

1. Click the Select and Rotate tool.
2. Select the dummy object and rotate it. Notice that the linked object rotates with the dummy about the dummy's center.

Links are hierarchical, which means that one object in the link has dominance over the other. This is usually described as a parent-to-child relationship. In the example described here, the dummy is the parent of the object. Wherever the dummy goes, the child object goes. On the other hand, the child can go anywhere. You can move the object to change the relationship between the dummy and the object, but if you move the dummy, the child object must follow.

Multiple objects can be linked to a single dummy. You can also have objects linked to other objects in a chain. Remember that when linking an object using the Select and Link tool, the first object you select becomes the child object.

You can also link objects to a dummy, then animate the dummy. For example, you can link a camera and camera target to a dummy to move both the camera and target in unison. In fact the target is the camera's child.

Grid

Most of the time you will use the World-space coordinates while creating and editing objects. You can also create a user or custom grid as a local coordinate system in which to work. For example, you may have a need to create a set of objects that are oriented at a 45-degree angle from the plane of the World-space grid. You can create a user grid and rotate it on any axis. Once this user grid is created, you can add objects whose orientation is based on the user grid instead of on the World-space grid. The following steps demonstrate how user grids work.

1. Click the Helpers button in the Create tab and make sure that the Standard option is selected in the Helpers drop-down list.

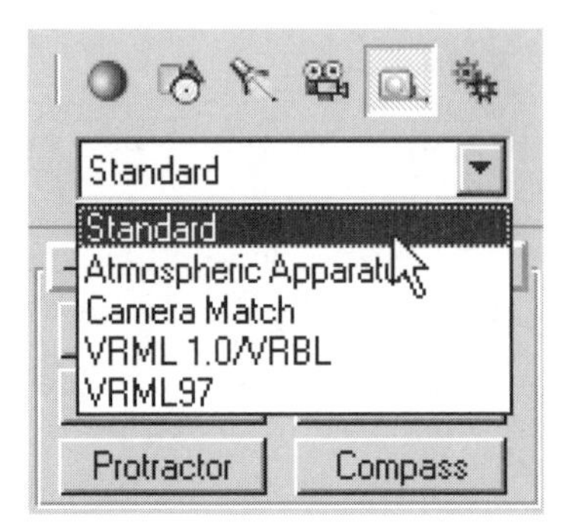

2. Click and drag within the Perspective viewport to place the user grid.
3. Click the Select and Rotate tool on the standard toolbar, then click and drag the red X axis of the grid to rotate the grid approximately 45 degrees in the X axis.

You've just created a user grid and rotated it.

4. Click the Geometry button in the Create tab, then create a box. Notice how the box is aligned with the grid. When you create a user grid, it automatically becomes the active grid on which objects are built.
5. Try creating other objects. Try moving objects to see how they react.

The objects are aligned to the user grid and use the user grid for transformations.

To return to the World-space grid, do the following:

1. Click the Select Object tool and click a blank area in the viewport to clear any selections.
2. Right-click within the viewport.
3. Select Active Grid ➢ Home Grid. The viewport displays the home grid, which is the grid for the World-space coordinates.

You can use the Active Grid option in the viewport right-click menu to gain access to other user grids you may have created. User grids have parameters to set grid size and spacing, and you can name them for easy reference.

NOTE Along with the user grid, you'll want to know about the Autogrid feature. Autogrid creates a temporary user grid that is aligned to the surface of an object. To use Autogrid, click the Autogrid button at the bottom of the VIZ window. Select an object to create from the Create tab of the Command Panel, then place the cursor on the desired surface of an object. A center gizmo will appear and align itself to the surface on which the cursor rests. You can then click and drag to create the new object on the surface. Click the Autogrid button again to turn it off.

Point

If you need to mark a location in your model for future reference, you can use the Point helper. A Point helper is just a Point to which you can snap using the Pivot snap option. Points can be named for easy reference. They appear as small X marks along with coordinate arrows.

Tape

You can find the distance between two objects using the Tape helper.

1. Choose the Tape button in the Standard Helpers Object Type rollout.
2. Click and drag the first point you want to measure.
3. Drag the cursor to the second point and release the mouse. The tape helper appears as a box at the first point you click and as a vector at the second point. The distance measured by the Tape helper is displayed as the grayed out Length parameter in the Tape Helpers Parameter rollout.

Once placed, the tape helper (or its target) can be moved to measure other distances—or you can just delete it.

Protractor

You can find the angle between two objects by using the Protractor helper.

1. Choose the Protractor button in the Standard Helpers Object Type rollout.
2. Click and drag the protractor to the location for the pivot point of the angle between the objects.
3. Click the Pick Object 1 button in the Protractor's parameter rollout, then select the first object.
4. Click the Pick Object 2 button and click the second object. The angle between the two objects is displayed in the parameter rollout just below the two Pick Object buttons.

Once placed, the Object 1 and Object 2 target locations can be changed by repeating either step 3 or step 4.

Compass

The Compass helper displays a compass rose in your design. It is typically inserted as part of the Sunlight System tool for placing the sun accurately in your model, but you can also insert the compass helper independently of the Sunlight System tool.

Atmospheric Apparatus

VIZ offers atmospheric effects to simulate fog, glowing lights (volume light), and combustion from fires. The fog and combustion effects can be confined to a specific volume through the use of Atmospheric Apparatus helpers.

The Atmospheric Apparatus helpers are three gizmos that define the space to which the atmospheric effects are confined. These gizmos have the effect of giving form and location to the fog and combustion effects. (Volume light does not need an atmospheric apparatus because it is given a location by association with a light source.)

The three Atmospheric Apparatus gizmos offered are BoxGizmo, CylGizmo, and SphereGizmo. Their names tell you the shape that they apply to the effect you assign them to. (See the "Effects" section to learn how to assign an apparatus to an effect.) You can place an atmospheric apparatus in a design by selecting the apparatus from the Atmospheric Apparatus Helpers Object Type rollout and clicking and dragging on a location in the design. You can then adjust the dimension of the apparatus gizmo through its parameters.

Camera Match

The Camera Match CamPoints are used to locate points in your design that are matched to points on a background image. You place at least five CamPoints in your design that you can associate with the background image by using the Camera Match option in the Utilities tab of the Command Panel. Chapter 15 provides a detailed tutorial on how to use these helpers.

VRML 1.0/VRBL and VRML97

Virtual Reality (VR) is the name given to any computer-generated environment in which you can place yourself and freely move around in real time. Some of the first applications of VR were in flight simulators designed to help train pilots. As interest in VR grew, it was viewed as a potential tool for the design industry to help architects visualize and experience spaces.

In its early days, VR was a high-tech tool accessible to only a few big companies that could afford it. But as personal computers became more powerful, its use caught on in the home computer game world. Now, a technology that was once thought of as exotic seems fairly commonplace, especially to computer game users. In the mid 90s, VR became a prominent part of the Internet and the World Wide Web. Through the Virtual Reality Modeling Language (VRML, pronounced *vermal*), VR became cheap and easily accessible to the general public.

VRML was created through the efforts of a handful of people closely involved with the development of virtual reality and the World Wide Web. They sought a means of conveying 3D worlds through the internet and found what they were looking for in a system developed by Silicon Graphics, Inc. (SGI). That system, called *Open Inventor,* was a programming library used to help create 3D applications. A subset of Open Inventor was developed and placed in the public domain through the good graces of SGI. That subset was at the root of a software specification called VRML 1.0. VRML 1.0 has evolved into later releases such as VRML97. Autodesk created its own flavor of VRML called VRBL, which is based on VRML 1.0.

While VRML created a stir when it first became available, architects have been slow to embrace it. It remains more a curiosity than a well-used tool.

When SGI, a major proponent of VRML, dropped their well regarded VRML viewer named Cosmo in 1998, most VR users feared that VRML was all but dead. But VR is far from dead on the Internet. VR is now experiencing a rebirth in a form called Web3D. Since there are no big companies like SGI promoting Web3D, there are many competing companies with their own ideas about what VR can be. Many of the Web3D software offerings are actually better than VRML97. See the following links for more information as of this writing:

www.web3d.com
www.metastream.com
www.superscape.com
www.cult3d.com
www.shout3d.com
www.pulse3d.com

Despite the decline of VRML, the VRML file format remains a viable medium for VR. There are still many programs that can import and export VRML files. If you're the least bit interested in VR, you may want to become familiar with VIZ's VRML options. With them, you can create VR environments from your designs and gradually move to the Web3D format as it evolves.

NOTE You can find the last version of the Cosmo VRML viewer on the Companion CD. Cosmo is a Web browser plug-in that allows you to explore VRML worlds.

VIZ offers a set of VRML helpers that let you set up VRML views, actions, and hyperlinks. The following describes the VRML 1.0/VRBL helpers. The VRML97 helpers are described in the next section.

Inline

The Inline helper places a gizmo in the design that can be linked to a URL. Through the VRML Inline parameters, you can enter a specific URL or select from a list of bookmarks.

VRML/VRBL

The VRML/VRBL helpers let you specify a location in your design which, when approached, triggers an action such as a jump to a hyperlink (Hyperlink Jump), a camera jump (Set Camera), or an animation (Animate). The options in the Parameter rollout for this helper let you assign the action or link to the helper. They also allow you to set the proximity to the helper within which the action is triggered.

LOD

LOD stands for Level of Detail. With this helper, you can set up your VRML file to adjust the level of detail of objects depending on the distance between the object and the viewer. This helper requires the creation of two copies of the object that you want to control with LOD. Each copy must have a different level of detail (see the VIZ Online Reference for a detailed description on how to use this helper).

VRML97

VRML97 is the newest standard for VRML worlds, and it includes several enhancements not found in the earlier versions of VRML. VIZ offers a set of helpers that can aid you in taking advantage of the extended features of VRML97.

Anchor

The Anchor helper lets you assign a trigger action to an object. The action can be a hyperlink or a camera jump.

AudioClip

The AudioClip helper lets you include sound files in your VRML file. It is used in conjunction with the Sound helper.

Background

The Background button gives you control over the background of your VRML file. You can select colors or images.

Billboard

You can set up an object to always point in the direction of the viewer by using the Billboard helper. Place the Billboard helper in the design and use the Select and Link tool on the VIZ Tools toolbar to link an object to the Billboard helper.

Fog

The Fog button opens a rollout that lets you add fog to your VRML environment.

Inline

You can include other VRML97 files in the current design. Such files are like Xrefs for VRML files. The Inline helper acts as a proxy object to which you can assign a URL pointing to the inline VRML file.

LOD

See "LOD" for VRML 1.0/VRBL.

NavInfo

The NavInfo button lets you determine the characteristics of the viewer within your VRML97 world. It places a NavigationInfo node in your design that tells the browser how to move about in your world. You can specify the type of movement, such as walk, examine, or fly. You can also specify the height of the viewer's eye level (Avatar Size). You can even include headlights and set visibility limits.

ProxSensor

You can have sounds or animations play whenever the viewer of your VRML world enters a region of your world. The ProxSensor button lets you place a ProximitySensor node in your design that is associated with an action object in your design. Whenever the viewer crosses into the node, the associated action object will be activated.

Sound

Sound lets you add spatial or ambient sounds to your design. You can control the direction and intensity of the sound. To use Sound, you must use the AudioClip option to specify a sound file for your design. Once this is done, you can use the Pick Audio Clip option in the Sound rollout to assign a sound to the Sound helper.

TimeSensor

An animation in your VRML world can be split into different time segments using the TimeSensor options. You can set a trigger object to play different segments of an animation.

TouchSensor

You can have an object act as a trigger for playing animations using the TouchSensor options.

Effects

There may be times when you need to apply an effect to your design to simulate certain conditions. For example, you can create a foggy environment by using the Fog atmospheric effect, or you can simulate a shallow depth of field by using the Depth of Field rendering effect. You can gain access to these effects and others like them in the Environment and Render Effects dialog box.

Atmosphere Effects

You can open the Environment dialog box by choosing Rendering ➢ Environment. Once open, you can scroll down the Environment dialog box to the Atmosphere rollout.

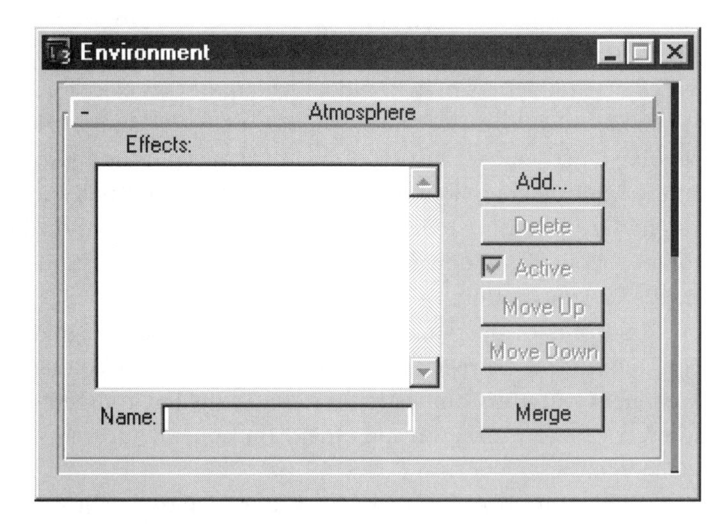

This is where you'll find the Atmospheric Effects. If you click the Add button in the Atmosphere rollout, you see the Add Atmospheric Effect dialog box.

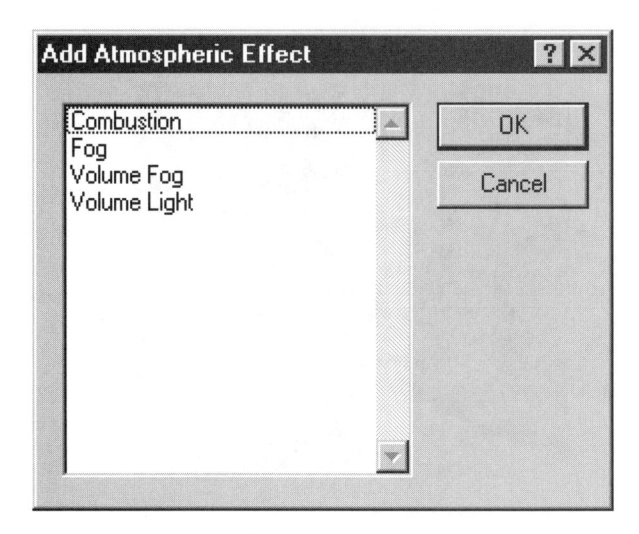

When you select one of these options, the option is placed in the Effects list box of the Atmosphere rollout. You can then click the listed item to open its parameter rollout and begin to use the effect. The following sections describe the atmospheric effects and how to use them.

Combustion

The Combustion effect creates the appearance of smoke and light from a fire or explosion. You can choose either a Fireball effect or a Tendril effect to simulate the fire from a fireplace. Flame characteristics and motion can also be set.

To place a combustion effect in your model, you must first place an Atmospheric Apparatus gizmo in the design (See "Atmospheric Apparatus" in the "Helpers" section of this appendix.) Once you've placed the gizmo and given it the appropriate size, click Add in the Atmosphere rollout of the Environment dialog box and select Combustion. In the Environment dialog box, select Combustion in the Effects list of the Atmosphere rollout. Scroll down the dialog box to the Combustion parameters and click the Pick Gizmo button.

Select the Atmospheric Apparatus gizmo you placed in your design. Once this is done, you can render your perspective or camera view to see the combustion effect. You can experiment with the Combustion settings in the Environment dialog box to achieve the effect you want. You can add other Atmospheric Apparatus gizmos to add more complexity to the effect.

You can also add multiple Atmospheric Apparatus gizmos to adjust the shape of the combustion effect. Figure D.1 shows a candle flame that uses three SphereGizmos and a Cylgizmo to shape the flame.

FIGURE D.1 Several Atmospheric Apparatus gizmos are used to create the flame on the candle.

Fog

You can create fog in your design by using the Fog Atmosphere effect. There are two types of fog effects, Standard and Layered. To use the Standard type, take the following steps:

1. If you don't already have a camera for your rendered view, create one before you add fog.
2. Select the camera you are using for your rendered view, then go to the Environment Ranges group of the camera's parameters.
3. Turn on the Show option, then set the Far Range value to a distance just beyond the objects in your design.
4. Adjust the Near Range value to a location just in front of the objects nearest the camera. These Environment Range settings affect the range in which the fog will take affect.
5. Open the Environment dialog box and add the Fog effect.
6. Select Fog from the Effects list box of the Atmosphere rollout, then scroll down the Environment dialog box to the Fog parameters and select the Standard radio button.
7. Set the Far% value in the Standard group to 50 as a starting point for the fog.

Once you've taken these steps, you can render the camera view and see the results. See Figure D.2.

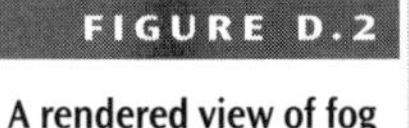
FIGURE D.2

A rendered view of fog

You can make adjustments to the fog by changing the Far and Near range settings for the camera. You can also adjust the intensity of the fog by adjusting the settings in the Standard group of the Fog Parameters.

The Layered fog option creates the effect of a blanket of fog or a mist rising from a water surface. For example, you can simulate ground fog by doing the following:

1. After adding Fog to the list of Effects in the Environment dialog box, choose the Layered radio button in the Fog group of the Fog parameters.
2. In the Layered group of the Fog parameters, set the Top value to the height of the fog, 10 inches for example, and set the Bottom value to 0 (assuming that the ground level is a 0 in World-space coordinates). Set the fog Density to 30 or 40 percent.
3. Turn on the Horizon Noise and click the Top Falloff radio button.
4. Render the view to see the results. See Figure D.3.

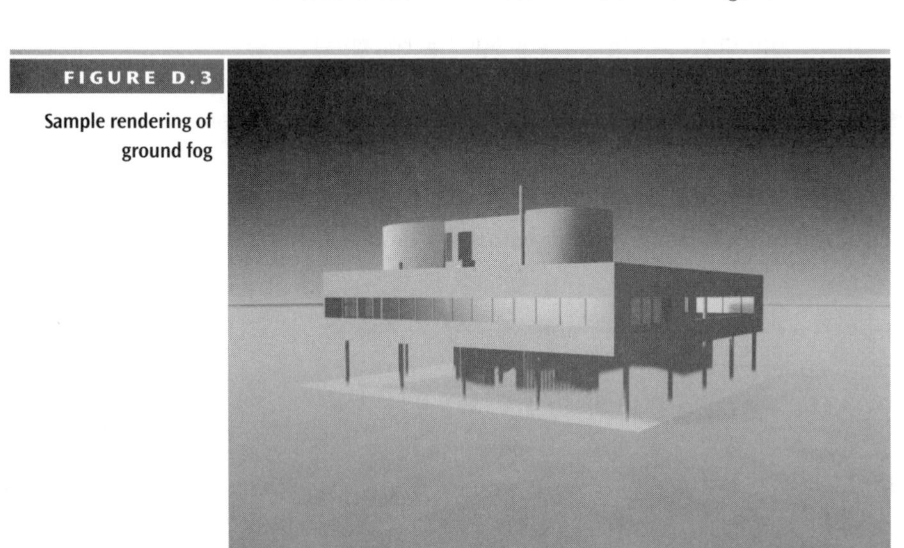

FIGURE D.3

Sample rendering of ground fog

Volume Fog

Volume fog creates a more cloudlike fog effect with varying densities. It can be used to create a puffy cloud effect. You can apply volume fog to an entire design by adding it to the Effects list in the Atmosphere rollout of the Environment dialog box. If you want to confine the Volume fog to an area, you can add an Atmospheric Apparatus helper to the design and assign the helper to the Volume fog. You can do this by clicking the Pick Gizmo button from the Gizmo group of the Volume Fog Parameters rollout and selecting the Atmospheric Apparatus helper. The shape and size of the Atmospheric Apparatus determines the area in which the Volume fog appears.

Volume Light

One of the more popular effects for night scenes is the glowing light fixture. Unfortunately, you can't just add a light source in a VIZ design and expect it to look like it's glowing. To create a glowing effect around an Omni light, for example, you need to use the Volume Light effect. Here are the steps to set it up:

1. Choose Rendering ➢ Environment, then use the Add button in the Atmosphere rollout to add the Volume Light effect to the Effects list.
2. With the Volume Light options selected in the Effects list, scroll down the Environment dialog box to the Volume Light Parameters rollout, click the Pick Light button, and select the Omni light that you want to appear to glow.

You can render your design at this point and see the effects of the Volume Light. You may find that the glow is too large. To adjust the size of the glow, you need to make some changes to the lights parameters.

1. Use the Select Object tool to select the Omni light you selected in step 2 of the previous list.
2. Click the Modify tab of the Command Panel, then scroll down and open the Attenuation parameters rollout.
3. Turn on the Show option in the Far Attenuation group. This turns on the gizmo that shows you the limits of the far attenuation for the selected light.
4. Adjust the Far Attenuation end value so that the Far Attenuation gizmo is the size of the desired glow.
5. Render your view again to see the results.

You can use the Volume Light effect on spotlights and directed lights to create a glow around their light paths. A spotlight's or directed light's cone will glow when it is added to the list of lights under the Volume Light effect.

Rendering Effects

In addition to the Environment effects, you can apply other visual effects to the final rendering of your design using the Rendering Effects dialog box. You can open the Rendering Effects dialog box by choosing Rendering ➢ Effects…

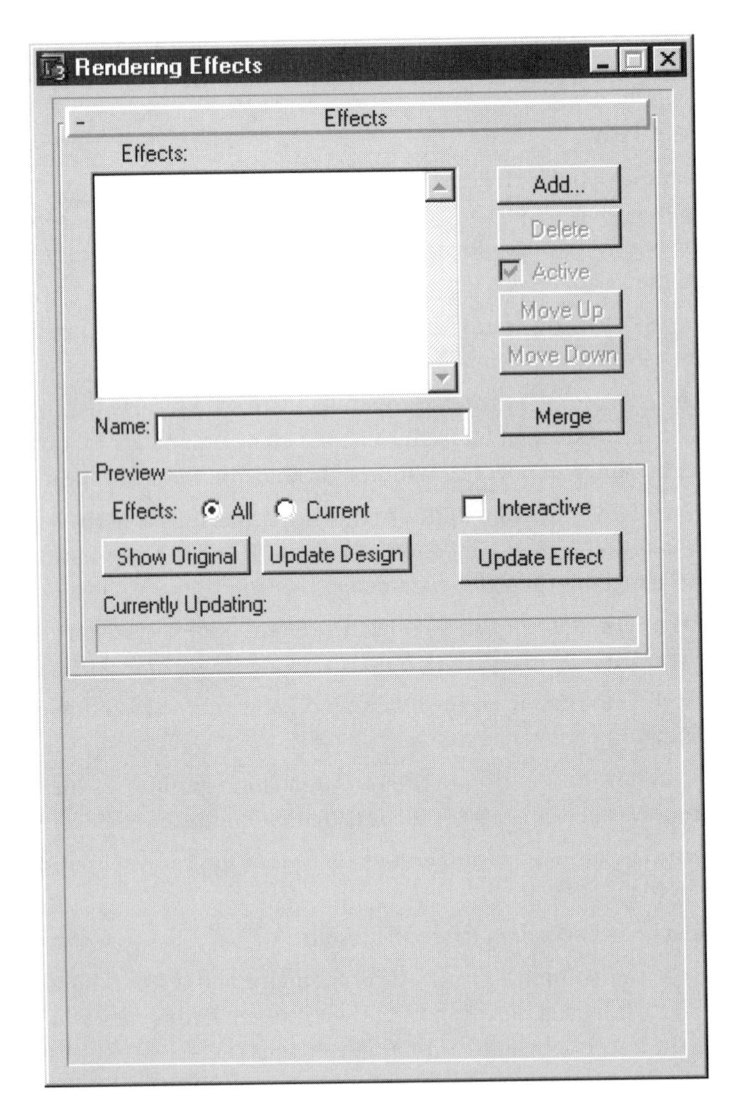

Just as with the Atmosphere rollout in the Environment dialog box, you add effects by clicking the Add button in the dialog box and selecting an effect from the Add Effects list. Once you've added an effect, it appears in the Effects list box of the Rendering Effects dialog box. You can then render your design to see how the effect changes the rendering.

Once you've rendered the design with an effect, you can experiment with the effect settings, then use the Update Effect button in the Preview group to see the results of your changes. You don't have to rerender the design. This saves time when you need to fine-tune the rendering effects settings.

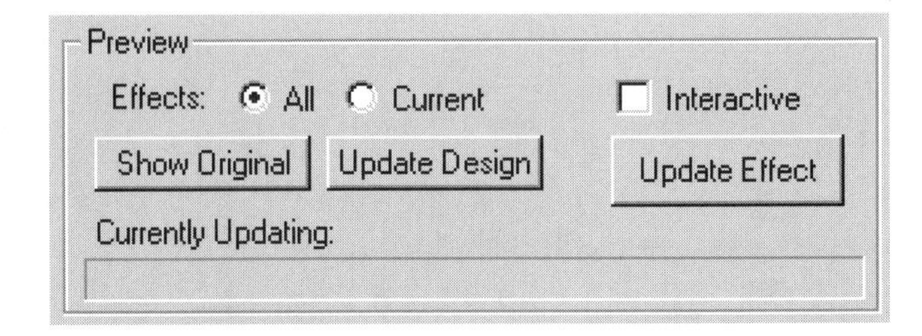

To adjust the parameters of an effect, select it from the Effects list box. Then scroll down the dialog box to set the parameters for the selected effect.

The following describes the standard list of effects available in VIZ. Note that to gain access to all of the effects listed here, you must install all of the extra features from the VIZ Installation CD. See Appendix A for information on installing VIZ.

Lens Effects

The Lens effects are a set of effects that simulate the way camera lenses refract light. To use these effects, you need a light source somewhere in front of the camera. When you add the Lens effects to the Effects list in the Rendering Effects dialog box, you gain access to the Lens Effects Parameters rollout.

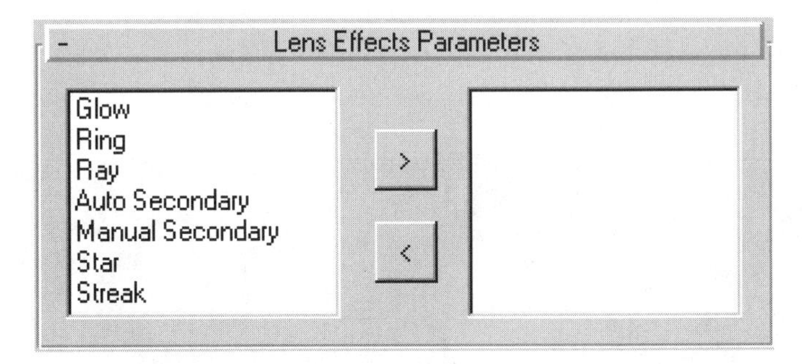

In the Lens Effects Parameters rollout, you can select an effect to add to the design. You select the desired effect from the list on the left, then click the right-pointing arrow to add the effect to the right-hand list.

Once you've added an effect to the right-hand column, you can assign it to a light source. To do this, scroll down the Rendering Effects dialog box to the Lens Effects Globals rollout.

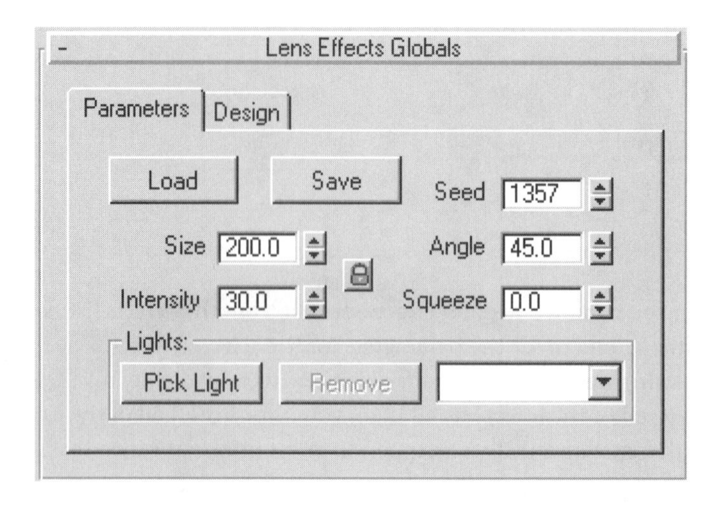

Select the Parameters tab and click the Pick Light button in the Lights group. Select the light source in any viewport. You can then render your design to see the results. VIZ first renders the view without the effect, then applies the effect to the finished rendering. It may take a second or two before the effect is applied. Once you've viewed the rendering, you can adjust settings for the effect in the Lens Effects Globals parameters. You can use multiple lens effects as your needs require them. The following list describes each effect.

Glow Places a glow around a light source, simulating atmospheric diffraction.

Ring Places a ring around a light source.

Ray Produces an array of single pixel lines radiating from a light source, emulating scratches on a lens.

Auto Secondary Produces multiple lens flares simulating refraction from lens elements.

Manual Secondary Produces a single lens flare simulating lens refraction.

Star Creates a starlike pattern of highlights with up to 30 points.

Streak Creates a light streak similar to a pair of rays from a star pattern.

Blur

The Blur effect blurs the final rendered image. You can blur the whole image or blur selectively based on non-background or luminance settings. Figure D.4 shows an image that uses the Blur effect with the Luminance option in the Pixel Selection tab turned on. Notice that the candle and table top show sharp edges, while areas around bright areas are blurred.

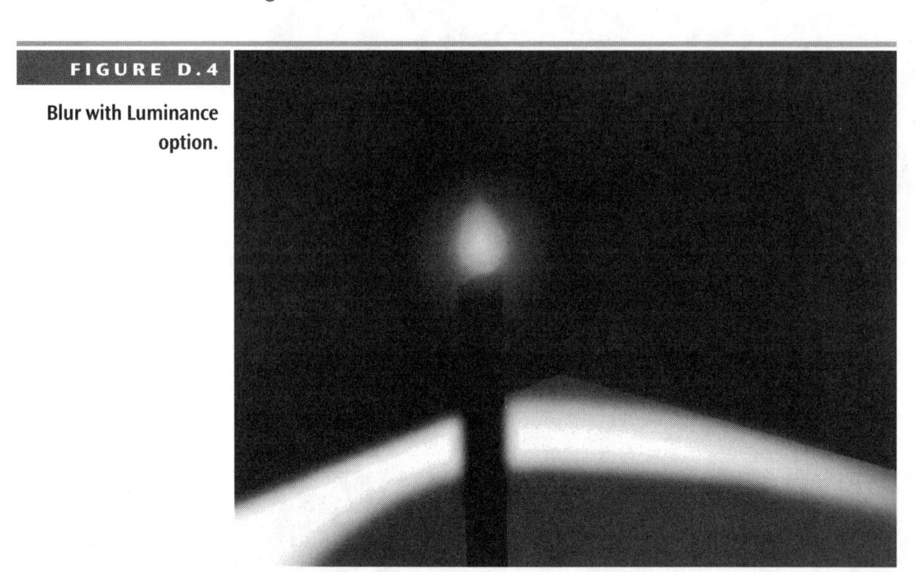

FIGURE D.4

Blur with Luminance option.

The Map Mask option lets you mask specific areas for blurring.

Brightness and Contrast

The Brightness and Contrast effect is useful for matching the brightness and contrast of a design to a background. You can set this effect to act only on the objects in the design and not affect the background. The Update Effect option is especially useful with this effect.

Color Balance

The Color Balance effect lets you adjust the red, green, and blue color balance of your rendering. The Update Effect option is especially useful with this effect since you can alternately adjust color balance, then click Update Effect to see the results.

File Output

The File Output effect lets you save the results of a rendering before certain other effects are applied. For example, you can add the File Output effect after a Lens effect, but before a Blur effect, to save a snapshot of the rendering before the Blur effect takes place. You control where the snapshot takes place by the location of the File Output effect in the Effects list. You can also select a channel rather than a whole image to save.

To place the File Output effect in a particular location in the Effects list, first add it to the list using the Add... button. Then use the Move Up or Move Down button to move the File Output effect up and down the list.

Film Grain

You can add a film grain to a design by using the Film Grain effect. This is useful if you are matching your design to a grainy background image. You have the choice to add grain to the background or to leave the background untouched. The Update Effect button is useful with this effect as it lets you fine-tune the graininess of your rendering to match a background.

Depth of Field

The Depth of Field effect creates the effect of a shallow depth of field by blurring objects that are a certain distance from the camera. This is useful for blending a design into a blurred background.

To use this effect, use the Pick Cam button to select the camera that will use the effect. You also need to select an object on which to focus by using the Focal Node button.

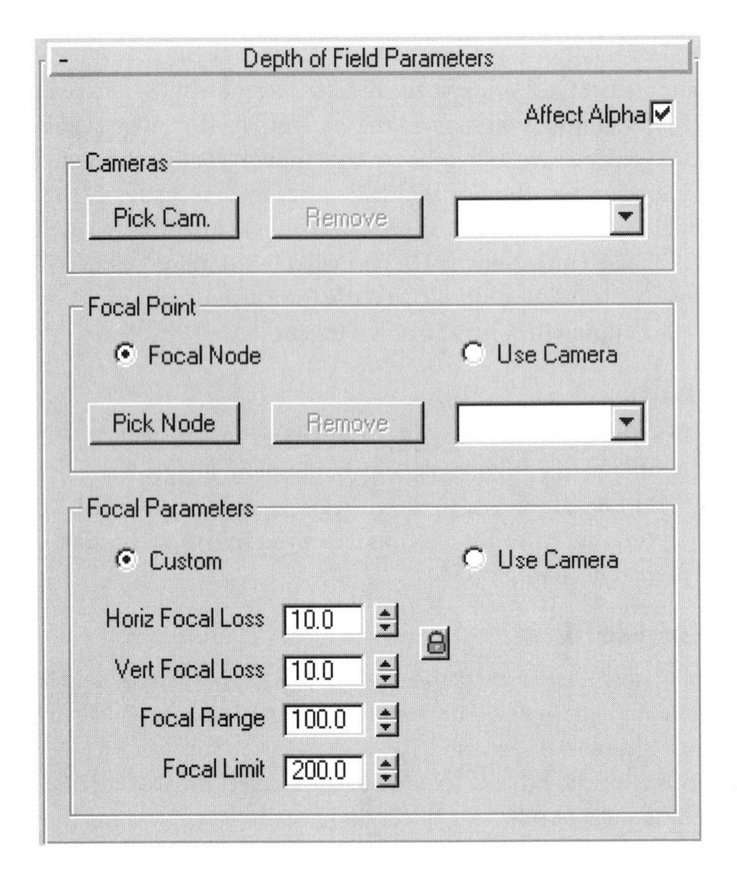

Other options let you set the degree of blurring.

INDEX

Note to the Reader: Page numbers in **bold** indicate the principal discussion of a topic or the definition of a term. Page numbers in *italic* indicate illustrations.

A

B

C

D

E

F

P

S

U

V

W

X

Y

Z